DECISION-MAKING IN URBAN PLANNING

Decision in Urban

AN INTRODUCTION TO

Beverly Hills / London

-Making Planning

NEW METHODOLOGIES

Edited and with Introductory Notes by

IRA M. ROBINSON

University of Southern California

For information address:

SAGE PUBLICATIONS, INC.
275 South Beverly Drive
Beverly Hills, California 90212

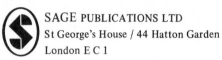

SAGE PUBLICATIONS LTD
St George's House / 44 Hatton Garden
London E C 1

Printed in the United States of America

International Standard Book Number 0-8039-0089-9

Library of Congress Catalog Card No. 77-127994

FIRST PRINTING

For Irene and the Boys

ACKNOWLEDGMENTS

The author would like to thank his USC colleague, Alan Kreditor, for his advice and comments on the Introductory Essay and the various introductory notes which he reviewed in draft form. The author is also indebted to his publishers, for their encouragement and cooperation throughout the course of the work. He is, of course, grateful to the original publishers of these selections for making them available for use in his book, and most importantly, his greatest debt is to his collaborators—the authors of the various individual chapters, without whose cooperation it is literally true that this book would not have been possible.

FOREWORD

Britton Harris

Over the past two decades there have been considerable changes in the conception and practice of city planning. Some of these changes aim directly at a redefinition of roles, while others, in my estimation, aim at a redefinition of roles through a redefinition of methods. This volume attempts to bring together a systematic portrayal of these new methods from the works of many individuals who have participated in this process of change.

The systematic presentation of this book follows in a formal way a well established paradigm of the planning process. It deals with the setting of goals, the formulation of alternatives, the prediction of outcomes, and the evaluation of the alternatives in relation to the goals and the outcomes. I have discussed this paradigm in some detail in "The Limits of Science and Humanism in Planning,"* and in general I feel that it is important and useful despite the fact that each step may be subject to severe criticism. Goals, for example, are frequently only established in the process of plan making. Alternatives as presently generated are not exhaustive and perhaps show inadequate imagination. The prediction of results is frequently naive and depends on an inadequate social science. Despite all of these criticisms, however, the paradigm has an internal consistency and a genuine correspondence with the real world.

There is however a much deeper criticism of the views which are brought together here. A careful reading of at least some of the articles will suggest that despite a general orientation toward the development of systematic methods, there are fundamental social and philosophical divisions within the planning profession. One of these might be termed the division between the bureaucratic and the innovative approaches. Another might be termed the division between immediate social action and long-run utopias. Still another might be called the division between environmental preservation and operational efficiency. Finally, there might be said to be a division between humanistic and engineering measures of performance and definitions of welfare. There is not space in this preface to discuss these latent conflicts or differences in any detail; rather than attempt this, I shall essay a vignette of the current crisis in urban planning which may serve as helpful additional orientation to the reader above and beyond the excellent guideposts which are to be found in the essays themselves.

It might be maintained that urban planning is in crisis because cities are in crisis because society is in crisis. It would be presumptuous to put forward any

*Journal of the American Institute of Planners, Vol. 33 (Sept. 1967), pp. 324-335.

very strong view as to how these crises can be overcome, but perhaps not presumptuous to suggest how they have arisen and how they have affected the practice of planning.

The modern crisis is principally one of growth, and perhaps its motto should be "nothing fails like success." In one sense, all of our troubles are as old as the spoken history of man–greed, violence, intolerance, and xenophobia. Yet they are made novel in a revised context where the experience of mankind is richer, and his cynicism greater; where his numbers are greatly multiplied, and his technical means of doing both good and evil are likewise vastly multiplied; where his mastery over the environment and his power to destroy it are enormously increased.

The largest city of antiquity–Rome–had about 1,000,000 inhabitants, and there was only one of her. Until about 1825, Bombay, Calcutta, and Madras were administrative and trading posts of not over 25,000 population, and at that same time, Chicago was a frontier stockade surrounded by semi-hostile tribes. The great successes of the industrial revolution have changed this situation beyond recall. On the average, these successes have raised the condition of man around the world. They have improved his nutrition and his health, lengthened his life, and increased his effective fertility. They have consequently increased the population of every part of the world. Simultaneously, the changes of the last century or two have also proportionately increased the literacy, knowledge, and effectiveness of the population. The impact of this growth upon cities has been much more than proportionate: cities have grown because the industrial and post-industrial revolutions have both required and facilitated growth, and at least as much because the industrial revolution in agriculture has meant that the countryside did not require growth in population. These two forces may still be seen working in different ways in the advanced and developing nations.

These changes did not take place without pain and maladjustments, but I think that these have been exaggerated. The celebrated and often denigrated anomie of urban life is in one aspect an important form of freedom and social mobility, which does not exist in rural life or in the folk society. More generally, the events of the twentieth century seem to show that the social evils of today do not reside solely in the cities nor in the developed urban societies. Furthermore, gross though those evils may have been, they are but a fraction of the potential for ill which has now been accumulated–a potential for mass starvation, for ecological collapse, or for world atomic warfare. These threats and their forerunners are not creations of the city nor indigenous to it. They arise out of a matrix of past growth and present social organization, and bear upon the city as upon the whole world.

Planning is anticipatory decision-making, and if things were not apt to go without it, it would not be needed. Planning is primarily a social activity conducted by groups in a social setting. But planning does not have as its object solely social things; these are important both as ends in themselves, and as means to social and individual control over other physical objects. Planning takes place at different levels—a man may plan for himself and his family, a city may plan, a nation or hopefully the world may plan. Planning does not plan for what it cannot control, but it may devise a strategy for dealing with uncertain contingencies. We do not plan clear weather; we plan umbrellas.

Modern urban planning is to an extent a focus of present-day unease over the future of man. The scale is one which bridges the gap between the human content of disaffection suffering, and the technology of engineering together with the technocracy of bureaucratic government. The anticipatory role is forced upon it; we feel the cold breath of disaster behind us. Both in our nations and in our cities, we are quite plainly entering a period when the solution of social problems is becoming more pressing in many arenas than the solution of material and technical problems. This is indeed most probably a period of rapid and basic social change of the type which punctuates longer eras of relative placidity.

Due to the rapid past growth of population and technology, the problems of social change which are here implied are embedded in a very complex system of social and technological relations. Not only is great skill needed to achieve any improvement over current prospects, but if (as may readily be believed) the system is easily destabilized, then the tenacity of the required effort may invite disaster.

It is not very surprising that this array of needs and responsibilities has tended to confound and distress the planning profession. There are seemingly at least four principal reasons for the air of change within the profession. First, the sense of urgency which I have mentioned has been intensified by the U.S. involvement in Viet Nam, by the racial friction in U.S. cities, and by the demonstrated fragility of the natural environment. Second, the operation of municipal governments in the United States is caught in the pincers of the rising relative cost of services and construction on the one hand, and the rising aspirations and demands of urban populations on the other. Third, the traditional architectural training of the planning profession is no longer adequate to meet challenges of the present complexity and diversity. Finally, the profession of urban planning seems to be attracting young students who see this as one of the last places where a bureaucrat may actually "put his hands on" social change—to both feel it and move it. This sentiment results from the independence of the military industrial complex and the remoteness of basic social revolution in the United States, coupled with the demise, the hardening, or the bureaucratization of social reform programs after the early New Deal.

In the course of trying to look a bit more deeply at the impact of these things upon the profession of planning itself, let us identify and explore one added and indirect influence. At least the first three factors above bear directly not only upon the profession of planning but upon cities themselves, and not unnaturally, these entities have sought other means of relief, or other guidance to means of relief, from their problems. Such means have been freely offered by well-meaning advocates, as well as by self-serving careerists. Aside from the politicians themselves—who as the final arbiters of social law must also regard themselves as the final experts—there are two principal sources of expertise supplemental to or substituting for the planning profession. These are the systems engineers on the one hand, and the experts in public administration on the other. Perhaps a third trend may be found in a wide range of social revolutionary attitudes of great variety and indistinct resolution.

The systems engineers bring some expertise and substantial pretensions to the problems of the city. Their principal system expertise seems to be relative to complex organizations which are mission oriented. There is in any case a good deal of difference between the mission of reaching the moon, and the mission of survival and welfare for society and the city. The systems engineer can in general deal best with subsystems and specific tasks, and he therefore suboptimizes. This is a charitable description.

The expert in public administration looks at urban problems from the viewpoint of rational decision-making and effectuation. This may be expressed in terms of the budget-makers' system of PPB (program planning and budgeting), or of the development coordinator's balanced programs. Both of these views are hemmed in by the restrictions of existing standards and political constraints, and considerable inspiration and determination is required to surmount them and to produce a genuinely innovative program.

There is, however, no inherent contradiction between the systems engineering and the public administration approaches.

The social revolutionary approach may in all conscience be justified. It stands outside of the system and either basically attacks it or tries to steer it, through political pressure and manipulation, into entirely new courses of action. What is wished here is essentially a redistribution of power. Seemingly, this collection of forces and interests suffers from certain intrinsic difficulties. The whole spectrum of this group of antagonists to conventional city planning is too diverse and ill-coordinated to be fully effective, except in occasional negative action. There are diverse basic interests which need to be reconciled. There are fundamental divisions regarding the extent of social change which is actually required. And there are different theories as to the effective measures to be taken to solve any particular problem, that is, as to the way things work. Most important in my view is a confusion of levels: the problem of organizing cities will continue to exist under any social system—and the proposals for reorganizing society do not solve these problems either now or in the future.

In this confused and difficult situation, as it has been unfolding over the past quarter-century, the traditional planning profession has been absorbing new ideas and newly trained personnel, and has been searching for a new identity. This process is most obvious in America because the complexity of problems is greatest here, because the growth of competing professions is more rapid, and because the existing profession has no firmly entrenched position. Apparently the most successful direction of search is guided by concepts of systems analysis and computer technology, but there is a sharp dichotomy between this direction and that guided by ideals of social reform.

In my view, it has not yet been resolved whether this division is in principle necessary or even possible. But at this early date we cannot form any very clear picture as to how such differences might be resolved. By the time the process has been played out, institutions, professions, people, and individuals will have changed. No matter how deeply the reader may himself be engaged in these debates and in the use of their results, he should observe with some detachment the process of the evolving discussion. He is here invited to witness some minor skirmishes in the evolution of the sociology of knowledge and of governance.

It goes without saying that I have my own views as to the most important aspects of this skirmish and as to the ways in which they may hopefully evolve. Perhaps some of these ideas, tendentious though they may be, will be useful to the reader in further sorting out his own thoughts.

In the largest framework, the technical problems which are discussed in this volume cannot be solved outside of a social milieu or without the simultaneous solution of a host of social problems. In this area, however, I have two marked prejudices. The first is that there are grave dangers in the single-minded pursuit of immediate solutions to immediate social problems. Without a longer-term perspective, I do not believe that these solutions are apt to prove viable. At the same time, I believe that diverse social groups may be intimately involved in seeking these longer-term solutions and that this requires a much deeper and more knowledgeable involvement in the planning process. My second point, therefore, is that the development of more objective methods of planning will ultimately remove a large part of the planning process from the subjectivism of the professional planner and place it more nearly in the public domain. Concomitantly, large sectors of the public will find that freedom of access to planning information and planning methods is an important instrument of social action.

In my view, an important item on the agenda of the development of planning methods is the domestication of operations research and computer science and, by implication, of the computer itself. This domestication is but a special case of the desperately needed social control of technology. In this case, however, the technology is that of social knowledge and social action, and therefore has a special importance. Unfortunately, the present planning profession has a keen appreciation of the weaknesses of this technology, but a weak appreciation of its strengths, and almost no capability to bring it to heel. The technologists themselves are but very slowly becoming aware of their limitations.

The expansion of social science knowledge is a third interesting arena. With the large-scale problems of our social system as they are currently developing, a holistic and systematic knowledge of society is required. On the one hand conventional social sciences do not reach an adequate level of system understanding, but the fields of systems engineering and general system theory are as yet quite inadequate in their understanding of social mechanisms and in their synthetic capabilities.

I should, finally, emphasize that the search for viable and productive novel plans is a most subtle and difficult problem. The current collection of essays probably underestimates this problem, and it is doubtful whether it will yield in any case to exclusively systematic methods. It is in this arena that one may anticipate a last-ditch stand by designers and intuitionists in their dispute with the new methodologists. From the point of view of cognition and creativity, this is a most fascinating area.

University of Pennsylvania
Philadelphia, Pennsylvania

CONTENTS

Acknowledgments 6

FOREWORD—*Britton Harris* 9

INTRODUCTION—*Ira M. Robinson* 21

PART ONE:

ADAPTATION OF NEW METHODS TO EACH STEP IN THE PLANNING PROCESS

Section 1—GOAL-SETTING

Introductory Note 33

1. *Performance Goals and Achievement Goals* 43
   JOHN FRIEDMANN

2. *Identifying the Public Interest: Values and Goals* 49
   WILLIAM L. C. WHEATON and MARGARET F. WHEATON

3. *Toward a Framework for Defining and Applying Urban Indicators in Plan-Making* 61
   DAVID E. BOYCE

4. *Goals, Priorities, and Dollars* 85
   GERHARD COLM

Section 2—PLAN-FORMULATION

Introductory Note 95

5. *Charting Possible Courses of the System* 103
   J. BRIAN McLOUGHLIN

6. *Quantitative Models of Urban Development: Their Role in Metropolitan Decision-Making* 115
   BRITTON HARRIS

7. *A Land Use Plan Design Model* 139
   KENNETH J. SCHLAGER

8. *Technological Forecasting: Techniques in Perspective* 151
   ERICH JANTSCH

Section 3—PLAN-EVALUATION

Introductory Note 177

9. *A Goals-Achievement Matrix for Evaluating Alternative Plans* 185
   MORRIS HILL

10. *Criteria for Evaluation in Planning State and Local Programs* 209
    HARRY P. HATRY

11. *Systems Evaluation: An Approach Based on Community Structure and Value* 241
    CHARLES G. SCHIMPELER and WILLIAM L. GRECCO

12. *Community Impacts, Trade-Offs, and Priorities* 269
    J. K. FRIEND and W. N. JESSOP

Section 4—PLAN-IMPLEMENTATION

Introductory Note 311

13. *The Planning-Budgeting Process* 319
    AN FORAS FORBARTHA

14. *Urban Improvement Programming Models* 343
    DARWIN G. STUART

15. *Robustness in Sequential Investment Decisions* 377
    SHIV K. GUPTA and JONATHAN ROSENHEAD

Section 5—PLAN-REVIEW AND FEEDBACK

Introductory Note 391

16. *System Guidance, Control and Review* 395
    J. BRIAN McLOUGHLIN

17. *Continuous Master City Planning* 409
    MELVILLE C. BRANCH

PART TWO: SOME SELECTED CASE STUDIES

Introductory Note 423

Section 1—MODEL CITIES PLANNING

18. *Planning Requirements for Model Cities Program* 427
Model Cities Administration
Department of Housing and Urban Development

19. *Chicago Model Cities Program: Five-Year Forecast* 459
Office of the Mayor
Chicago Model Cities Program

Section 2—COMMUNITY RENEWAL PROGRAM

20. *Application of Programming Approach to Development Planning* 485
Philadelphia Community Renewal Program
City Planning Commission

Section 3—LAND USE-TRANSPORTATION PLAN

21. *The Southeastern Wisconsin Land Use-Transportation Plan* 517
Southeast Wisconsin
Regional Planning Commission

Section 4—HOUSING AND RESIDENTIAL RENEWAL

22. *The San Francisco Community Renewal Simulation Model* 555
San Francisco Department of City Planning

SELECTED BIBLIOGRAPHY 597

Index 615

Contributors 625

INTRODUCTION

Since the early 1950s, the field of city (or urban) planning in the United States has been moving through a period of rapid change and evolution, in both theory and practice—some have called it a revolution, so dramatic is the transformation. One of the most striking aspects of this metamorphosis is occurring in the area of planning methodology—the focus of this volume of readings. A body of new methods is emerging to help city planners make better decisions about what is the most desirable and feasible future to seek and what needs to be done to achieve it. These methods have been developing to satisfy the new methodological needs demanded by the American planner's changing roles and functions—these changes being another manifestation of the transformation the field of city planning has been undergoing in the past two decades. The editor's purpose in this Introduction is to discuss these methodological improvements in light of the planners' changing roles and functions, and thereby provide a context for the collection of papers that follow.

The focus of planning is shifting from the preparation of a single product, the master plan—a single document that presents a tidy blueprint for the sometime future—to a process- and-program-oriented activity. (For a detailed discussion of this and other changes mentioned below, see Fagin, 1968.) Planning is now viewed as a continuing process of moving towards provisional goals rather than the delineation of an ideal end-state to be achieved at some future date. While always keeping the city's long-range goals in mind, the planner now emphasizes a variety of middle-range or short-range programs, continuously moving and redefining targets. This has led to the introduction of new types of short- and middle-range plans and programs, including, among others, the community renewal program, the model cities program, and the ten-year improvement plan, to complement the traditional five-year capital improvements budget. At the same time, there has occurred a broadening of concern from the traditional physical base to one that now encompasses economic, social, and environmental problems as well as the considerations in private development that interact with public action.

These changes have been accompanied by, and were largely the result of, the efforts of local decision-makers to enlist the technical expertise of planners as analysts of complex, pressing, and immediate urban problems and as advisors concerning most government activities. In general, as Herbert Gans has noted, cities are asking planners not to hide themselves in planning commissions which exist often as ivory towers erected by civic leaders who consider themselves above politics; instead, they are demanding that the planners become active advisors to city hall, so that they can participate in the day-to-day decision-making process (Erber, 1970).

In short, American city planning today is characterized by a new comprehensiveness in its approach, roles, and functions. The concept of a single planner, producing a single long-range plan focusing only on land use, circulation, and public facilities, and working for one agency, is outmoded. The planner today is doing more things and for a variety of clients: he is concerned with the immediate and middle-range as well as the long-range future, with economic development, health, education and public safety, as well as housing, land use, and urban design.

To conform to this new comprehensiveness in its approach to planning and in its roles and functions, the planning profession in the United States has been searching for a concomitant workable planning methodology to replace its traditional methods derived from such antecedents as architecture, landscape architecture, and geography. In this search, city planners have been turning both to other planning milieus (e.g. transportation, industry, business, and even defense) and to fields and disciplines they had previously ignored (e.g. economics, mathematics, operations research, and systems engineering) for concepts and methods that might be adapted and applied to urban planning. They have also been turning to other countries, especially the United Kingdom, for ideas and techniques that are potentially adaptable to U.S. problems. Some of the methods and techniques from these other milieus and disciplines being adapted by city planners to the various steps in the planning process include systems analysis and its applied management tool for governmental decision-making, the planning-programming-budgeting system (PPBS); mathematical programming; simulation models; gaming; sensitivity analysis; and benefit-cost analysis.

The reaching outward on the profession's part was an inevitable comcomitant of the new comprehensiveness of the field. The expanding subject-matter and content of urban planning (e.g. the increased emphasis on social and economic factors) had the natural effect of freeing the planner to look beyond his own restricted boundaries and his own traditional sister fields, such as architecture, to other fields, for possible methodological adaptations.

In addition, as a logical extension of its new comprehensiveness, some members of the profession have begun to subscribe to the views postulated by Melville Branch, Henry Fagin, Herbert Gans, Paul Davidoff, and Tom Reiner—to mention a few—that planning is basically a methodology, a set of procedures applicable to a variety of activities aimed at achieving selected goals by the systematic application of resources in programmed quantities and time sequences designed to alter the projected trends and redirect them toward established objectives. In short, it has become increasingly recognized that urban planning is but one branch of a family of disciplines and activities which plan and use planning methods, e.g. administration, management, budgeting, engineering, and systems analysis. It is now seen that there is a great similarity between the process that both the business administrator and the government budgeting official go through to reach planning decisions, and that of the urban planner. From this premise, it was natural to look to these applied fields for possible methods that would be applicable to urban planning.

Being a synthetic field, it is nothing new for city planning to borrow concepts and approaches as well as methods from other fields and disciplines. During the 1930s and immediately following World War II, there was a great deal of borrowing from the social and behavioral sciences, reflecting the planners' concern in those years for the sociological, economic, and human-behavior aspects of planning.

During the current stage of the field's development, when attention is being focused on the need to make planning more analytical and quantitative as well as more closely aligned to the policy-making, decision-making, and administrative aspects of government, it is not surprising that the planners turn primarily to the new fields of systems analysis and the policy sciences, the administrative and managerial sciences, and transportation engineering, where advances are being made in just those methods of potential use to urban planning. The profession has been turning to these fields and disciplines for an additional important reason: their manipulative methods, at least potentially, deal with the city on a holistic and synthesizing basis—the implicit credo of all urban planners. By way of contrast, although the traditional disciplines such as economics, sociology, demography, biology, hydrology, and the like have contributed much, and still do, to our understanding of cities, of people's use of cities, and of the interaction of cities with a natural ecosystem, none of them, as Britton Harris notes, deals holistically with people, with metropolitan systems, or with the total environment (Erber, 1970).

Selective borrowing from these fields and disciplines is producing an entirely new set of planning methods to replace those traditionally used in the past. The handicraft tools used until just recently are giving way to man-machine computer systems for processing, analysis, and control. The development of key statistical indicators of change, rooted in improved information and data systems, permits planners to continuously meter and monitor population, economic, financial, physical, and other changes in a city, thus providing a framework for periodic adjustments to plans and programs. Paralleling this shift, scientific methods of explanation, prediction, and evaluation are replacing the traditional methods of description and prescription. Newly developing mathematical models are enabling the planner to simulate what would happen if given policies were adopted, and thus pretest, before decisions are made, the relative effectiveness of alternative courses of action in accomplishing stated ends. Moreover, some of the predictive models are being used in reverse, as it were, to actually generate alternative plans based on preestablished rules and policy assumptions. The evaluation of proposed plans, heretofore based upon the personal experience, private intuition, and reputation of the individual planner (a holdover from the architectural origins of the fields), is changing fundamentally in approach to include systematic assessment of alternatives, utilizing benefit-cost analysis and similar techniques. New approaches and techniques aimed at relating long-range planning with short- and middle-range programming and budgeting functions are emerging as well.

PURPOSES OF THIS READER

These methods, being relatively new, are still not fully integrated into the planner's lexicon or kit of tools. Interest in them is growing, however, and scattered attempts have been made to use them in actual planning situations. Indeed, the terms systems analysis, mathematical models, cost-effectiveness, futuristic planning, and planning-programming-budgeting system are occurring with increasing frequency in planning literature and conferences and in the practice of urban planning. But, despite the growing interest in the potential application of these new methods, city planners vary in their attitudes, from those who condemn them outright to those who heap blind praise, and in between are those who are confused, skeptical, mystified, or afraid.

In discussing the current attitude of the planning profession towards PPBS, one observer has likened it to the attitude of a group of experimental biologists who successfully crossed a talking parrot and a Bengal tiger and produced a strange new animal; although no one knew exactly what it was, whenever it talked, they certainly listened (Downs, 1967). Likewise, there is a great deal of talk about the other new planning methods without any real understanding of what they are, and more to the point, how they relate—or could relate—to urban planning.

Part of the reason for the confusion over use of the new methods stems from the very fact that much of their conceptual and methodological development has occurred outside of urban planning. Different versions and applications of the same basic methods have been advanced in the fields of economics, business administration, public administration, management science, industrial engineering, and military and defense analysis. Although there are interrelationships and overlaps among many of these methods, each field has tended to develop its own particular terminology and frame of reference.

As a consequence, when city planners have tried to adapt these methods in terms of urban problems, issues, and needs, certain inconsistencies or ambiguities have inevitably resulted. Borrowing from these other concepts has, therefore, been selective and partial. Since there has been no clear statement of the possible broad areas of application to the urban planning process as a whole, a number of individual attempts to apply these methods to a particular phase or aspect of urban planning have been tried.

Since many of the attempts to apply the methodological improvements have not been particularly successful, or at least have fallen short of their original expectations, many planners are at best skeptical or dubious, and, at worst, outright critical.

These difficulties in getting many city planners to accept and use the new methods are compounded by the fact that the literature on them is highly dispersed and frequently found in sources not formally or commonly thought of as urban planning, and therefore not readily available, or easily accessible, or frequently consulted by city planners.

This volume of readings is an attempt to clear up some of the confusion, ambiguity, inconsistency, and mystery surrounding the new planning methods. It aims to bring together in a framework which city planners can understand the most relevant and appropriate literature available on these new methods, including examples of the few scattered attempts to actually apply some of them in urban planning.

It is this editor's belief that the methods discussed herein offer an enormous potential for making urban planning more rational and comprehensive, and thus more effective and more relevant. The volume attempts to capture the essence of the emerging new planning methods at a particularly crucial period in the life of our cities and the history of the planning profession. If the methods described in this volume are perfected and become more widely used by urban planners at all levels of government, and especially at the local level, there still might be hope for our cities. However, no claim is made here that urban planning methods alone can save our cities—many other factors are involved, not least in importance is the need for political-institutional improvements; nevertheless, even with such changes, cities will face questions as to what to do and how to do it—which are methodological issues.

Of equal importance perhaps will be the response of the planning profession to the use of these new methods. It is quite possible that unless the planner can keep pace with the intellectual and substantive developments in planning methodology, he will find his traditional role as an integrator and synthesizer largely assumed by some new group of planners (e.g. from the new fields of systems analysis and the policy sciences) who may, in fact, be better equipped to conduct specific studies and analyze specific programs, relegating to the planner the role of specialist in land use, community facilities, and urban design. During the current period of ferment in the planning profession, when planners are attempting to redefine their roles, purposes, and functions, the new planning methods assume special relevance and significance. These new roles and purposes will not materialize unless the planner has the commensurate skills to carry them out; the ability of the planner to achieve his purposes is largely a function of the techniques he uses.

This volume, however, is not meant to be a "how-to-do-it" book—a manual or cookbook on how to put together these new planning methods. Its purpose is to describe and explain the methods, why they are valuable, when they can be used, and something about our experiences in using them. It is this editor's opinion that we are not yet ready to produce a manual on new planning methods, for they are only now at the cutting edge of development. They are not completely adaptable as yet, for they are still being shaped and honed, and thus cannot be fastened down in a manual. After reading and studying this volume, the interested reader should at least be in a better position to go to the book shelves on operations research, systems analysis, PPBS, industrial engineering, business and public administration and so on, and better understand the value to urban planning of the methods developed in these other fields.

The planning profession is maturing in its use of these sophisticated methods. It would seem useful and appropriate at this time to try to capture or mark this maturing process. The profession currently needs this kind of bench mark—a chance to look at itself and see where it is in the area of planning methodology as a basis for determining where to go—which is not allowed by the current dispersed literature describing these methods. This volume aims to serve as such a bench mark.

The idea for this volume, as well as most of the materials included, stems from the editor's experience, extending over a recent three-year period, as the instructor responsible for developing and teaching a new basic core course in planning methods to graduate planning students at the University of Southern California. As most teachers, students, and practitioners in urban planning will readily testify, there are few adequate textbooks or source books to use in the classroom or the planning office. This situation is true of practically all aspects of planning theory and practice, but especially so in the area of planning methodology. And, as far as this editor is aware, there are no books which deal comprehensively with planning methodology, let alone with new planning methods.

While there has been in recent years a substantial increase in planning literature of value to planning educators, most of it focuses on the subject matter or content of urban planning (e.g. housing, transportation, the ghetto) and the urban crisis in general—its primary purpose being either didactic or to increase our knowledge about these urban phenomena. These are worthwhile aims, although it is just as important, if not more so, for the planning student to enlarge his understanding of, and sharpen his skills for, making planning decisions.

If one subscribes to the viewpoint expressed earlier that planning is basically a set of procedures for making decisions about the future in accordance with certain established goals, then what makes urban planning a discipline—and its practice, a profession—is what it does and how it does it, not where or to what it is done. It would follow that if planners are to claim a special capability for planning a city's future, then this claim is justified, not because they are experts on the city, but because they are experts on determining what is the most desirable and feasible future to seek and what needs to be done to achieve it. The planner should be an expert on the methodology by which planning is done. In turn, this expertise would suggest that at a minimum, the planner should be familiar with the more important new methods now developing in other fields which have potential applicability to this purpose. For these reasons, the absence of suitable books on current and evolving planning methodology is a serious shortcoming.

The lack of such books is felt particularly in planning education. In recent years, courses in planning methods and planning theory have become more common in the curriculum of planning schools. (See, for example, the recent survey of the use of theory in the curriculum of planning schools by Henry C. Hightower, 1969). When the pioneering instructor of such a course looks around for suitable textbooks and source books, he generally finds, as this editor did, that there is a paucity of such books dealing with planning methodology—understandably so in view of the comparatively recent interest in the subject. Accordingly, the bibliography for class reading typically comprises a long list of references, scattered among a variety of sources—often not strictly planning sources—from journal articles, to single chapters from books or ephemeral reports, to unpublished papers, but no books which as a whole could be used as texts or source books.

The editor's hope is that this volume in the first instance will fill the gap in the literature on urban planning methodology and thereby be useful to teachers and students as well as practitioners of urban planning as an introduction to this subject. But, in addition, he hopes that politicians, public officials, and the growing number of professionals and experts in related fields who have been recently attracted to the field of urban planning will find it valuable. He trusts that the volume will prove of interest as well to the increasing number of citizens who have become concerned about and involved in issues affecting our environment and our cities. A careful reading of the papers in this book should provide them with insights and understanding about the sophisticated, complex methods being used today by some planners and likely to be used extensively in the future by most planners.

ORGANIZATION OF THIS READER

The volume is organized into two main parts. Part One, the heart of the volume, deals with the new planning methods themselves. To provide the reader with a meaningful and systematic framework for understanding these new methods, the selections are organized around the steps or stages in the now familiar and well-established model of the rational planning process. According to this model, a planner would be acting rationally if he undertook five interelated steps. (These steps represent a slight modification of those commonly accepted as comprising the planning process. See Meyerson and Banfield, 1955: 312-322; Harris, 1963: 23-24; and Harris, 1967: 324-325.) He would:

(1) Identify the problem or problems to be solved, the needs to be met, the opportunities to be seized upon, and the goals of the community to be pursued, and translate the broad goals into measurable operational criteria;

(2) Design alternative solutions or courses of action (plans, policies, programs) to solve the problems and/or fulfill the needs, opportunities, or goals, and predict the consequences and effectiveness of each alternative;
(3) Compare and evaluate the alternatives with each other and with the predicted consequences of unplanned development, and choose, or help the decision-maker or decision-making body to choose, that alternative whose probable consequences would be preferable;
(4) Develop a plan of action for effectuating or implementing the alternative selected, including budgets, project schedules, regulatory measures, and the like;
(5) Maintain the plan on a current and up-to-date basis, based on feedback and review of information to adjust steps 1 through 4 above.

Each of these stages represents a separate section in Part One. While they are treated separately, and in a linear sequence, in actual practice the five steps represent a circular or cyclic process. Evaluation procedures enter into the process at the outset in the identification of problems and goals; they also influence the design of alternative solutions and the form in which predictions are cast for evaluative purposes. Likewise, the problems of implementation and effectuation enter into the design, prediction, and evaluation stages both as constraints and as costs and benefits which must be taken into account.

The various new methods are discussed under one of the five stages of the planning process to which they appear to be particularly applicable. They were selected to emphasize their major contribution to each of the stages. Needless to say, some of the methods are applicable to several stages: urban indicators are discussed under goal-setting, though they are also useful for plan review and feedback. Also, while many of the selections cover several different methods, they are included in those sections for which they are particularly relevant.

To better understand the nature of and rationale for the new methods discussed, each section is preceded by an introductory note written by the editor which (1) summarizes the traditional methods used to deal with each step in the rational planning process, (2) briefly sketches the historical evolution of the methodological improvements over the past two decades, and (3) notes the special contributions of the selections included, as well as of relevant papers not included, to the development of a new planning methodology.

To illustrate the applicability of some of the new methods to a variety of urban planning problems, Part Two includes selections and excerpts from four types of case studies: model cities planning, the community renewal program, land use-transportation planning, and housing and residential renewal. These examples are presented for two purposes: first, for comparative purposes to illustrate the similarities and differences of the case studies with respect to their use of the five-step rational planning process, and second, for examining the extent to which each of the case studies employs any or all of the methods discussed in Part One.

As in Part One, an introductory note precedes the four case studies, the purpose of which is to provide some background regarding each of the examples, as well as to indicate the character of the specific methods used.

BASIS FOR SELECTION OF MATERIALS

This volume is designed, as is the purpose of most readers, to collect materials which are presently not readily available or easily accessible to the many persons interested in the subjects they cover. In compiling this volume, selections have been taken both from well-known authorities in the urban planning field and from those whose work is not so well known, as well as those whose major interest falls outside of urban planning but whose ideas make a contribution to urban planning methodology.

It was inevitable that the process of selection forced the elimination of many valuable writings. Whole areas of concern often classified as planning methods were omitted because they do not meet the editor's definition of planning methodology which includes those steps and procedures involved in the process of deciding what to do and how to do it in order to achieve given goals. Thus, eliminated from discussion are so-called planning techniques, which are the specific tools used in planning, such as graphical (e.g. maps), statistical (e.g. correlation analysis), informational (e.g. information and data systems and computer techniques), and implementation and administrative (e.g. role of citizen participation, zoning, subdivision regulations)–which are used to operationalize each of the methods in the planning process. While the volume deals with methods for determining, formulating, and operationalizing community goals, such as directly tapping the opinions and attitudes of citizens and residents by means of social survey research, attitude testing, and so on, it does not deal with the specific techniques for carrying out such surveys or analyzing their results. Likewise, this volume does not include material on the techniques used for carrying out the substantive studies so basic to plan-making, e.g. population, land use, economic base, housing, and other studies such as F. Stuart Chapin, Jr. covers in his now classic book, *Urban Land Use Planning.*

Similarly, this volume is not directly concerned with explaining such new planning concepts as the community renewal program, the model cities program, or the annual development program, which are sometimes referred to as methods, but in the editor's concept are in reality, planning instruments. However, in Part Two, several of these are included as case studies to illustrate use of the new planning methods in implementing these instruments.

Even within those subject areas which are covered in this volume, many interesting and valuable selections had to be omitted. Because the editor tried to present an overview of overall planning methodology–in short, depth of coverage has been sought–it was inevitable that otherwise valuable selections were eliminated. This breadth, admittedly, has been much more difficult to achieve than if a narrower focus had been attempted; it would be much easier to compile a reader on the use and application of cost-benefit analysis in urban planning, than a reader which gives an overview of the various methods used in urban planning, including cost-benefit techniques.

Sacrifices have been made in the choices of particular selections which do not necessarily represent the best work of each author, nor even the best material on the subject. Sometimes the best may be available in a readily obtainable source or may be in such a lengthy form that it does not lend itself to excerpting or cutting without distorting essential elements of its description or logic. Indeed, despite their length, excerpts from a few long pieces, because of their special contribution, are included; in such cases, the editor, in his introductory note, briefly explains the nature and substance of the material eliminated from the selection. Moreover, in some cases, because of space limitations, the tossing of a coin literally determined the final selection between two or three pieces considered equally suitable to illustrate a particular planning method.

It is undoubtedly certain that many persons will feel that some of the pieces which have been excluded are superior to those which have been chosen. It is the editor's hope, however, that all of the material will be judged to be of high quality, and that in bringing these readings under one cover, he has provided a useful reference for both the beginning student and the most advanced scholar, for the practicing planner, and for the interested public official and citizen. It is also hoped that some amends for these omissions have been made by reference in the editor's various introductory notes to those that are especially noteworthy and by their inclusion in the Selected Bibliography at the end of the volume.

PART ONE

ADAPTATION OF NEW METHODS TO EACH STEP IN THE PLANNING PROCESS

SECTION 1

GOAL-SETTING

INTRODUCTORY NOTE

Since planning–whether it is for the development of a city as a whole, or the programming of one of its components (say, education or housing)–may be defined as the process of determining goals and designing courses of action by which these goals may be achieved, the setting of goals is clearly basic to this process. Without a clear idea of the goals to be sought, it is not possible for the planner either to specify possible courses of action or to evaluate their desirability and feasibility.

Most planning discussions about goals generally fall into two categories. First are those which seek to identify, examine, or promote specific goals, e.g. "shall we have single class or multi-class communities?" The discussions found in *Goals for Americans* (President's Commission on National Goals, 1960) and especially Catherine Bauer Wurster's paper therein on urban development goals, as well as the special 1964 volume of the *Annals* devoted to goals and standards for urban renewal (Mitchell, 1964), are excellent examples of this approach. However, it should be noted that neither these nor similar reports spell out the costs of achieving the desired goals or recommend priorities among the goals.

Second, goals are often discussed in terms of the problems facing a community. We are flooded today with books, magazine articles, special congressional committee reports, and speeches about the urban crisis and the specific problems comprising that crisis, e.g. congestion, dirt, noise, insecurity, obsolete facilities, poverty, inadequate city revenues, and so forth. When goals are discussed at all (or even established) they usually represent the "desire" components of these problems, and although a problem does in fact consist of both a goal, or desire, and the impediment(s) to goal-realization, it is an unfortunate fact that most public and technical attention is usually focused on the impediments rather than on the goals. The nature of public opinion and pressure is such that once problems rise to the level of public awareness and possible political action, the related goals receive little attention. And yet, if a problem can be said to represent a discrepancy between an existing condition state and a desired condition state, then it is hardly possible to ignore the question of goals.

Until recently, however, there has been scant discussion about the nature of goals as they relate to the planning process, or most importantly, about an appropriate methodology for goal-setting. On this point, Stuart Chapin (1963: 225) wrote:

> "At the outset, it might be observed that while goals of planning have been at the forefront of planning thought since the early literature on utopias, only in relatively recent times has the identification of goals been made an integral part of the technical work of planning. This spotlighting of goals bids well to be a characteristic of the sixties, not alone in planning, but pervading many fields."

Chapin's prediction was accurate, for the 1960s was indeed a period in which there was widespread discussion about goals and objectives in the planning profession and among city planning agencies. This discussion has been going on not because planning has always operated without goals and objectives (though there are instances where this would appear to be true), but rather because its goals have been poorly defined, or inconsistent with other public goals, or the goals have been those of the planners rather than of their clients or customers. Four methodological issues or questions are challenging planners today, and will increasingly do so in the future. They face the need (1) to establish a process which relates overall community goals to specific functional goals, (2) to develop procedures for consultation with the public regarding their goal choices which are meaningful, (3) to devise measures which can make the choices by the public relevant and useful, (4) to translate broad goals into specific objectives and operational criteria. The papers in this section address themselves to the first three issues; since the need for specific objectives and operational criteria is primarily related to the evaluation of alternative plans, the fourth issue is discussed in Section three.

PERFORMANCE GOALS VERSUS ACHIEVEMENT GOALS

An important characteristic of both the philosophy of rational planning and the precepts of its practitioners has been to include many (if not all) planning goals within the same plan. In other words, comprehensiveness has been a tenet of city planning—a striving for the total welfare of all residents of the city insofar as conditions are affected by and through the physical environment, rather than a partial or sectoral approach related, say, to education alone, or the urban and regional economy, or to any other aspect of life taken in isolation, or to any special population groups or areas of the city, such as low-income ghetto minorities, or middle-class suburbanites.

In less formal language, the comprehensive ideal of planning and thus its desire for comprehensive goals, is founded on the belief that private decision-makers (households, firms) and the public decision-makers with a particular mission (highway departments, public transportation agencies, housing authorities, hospital agencies) are concerned with the welfare of their own immediate circle–be it one's family or business or governmental function. The planner needs to coordinate, integrate, design, and decide on the basis of the total public welfare, taking into consideration the overall (or most) aspects of the life of the city and a longer time-span perspective.

In recent years, studies of decision-making in politics, business, and public administration have raised serious challenges to the logic of comprehensiveness, and thus to the possibility of comprehensive planning goals. Alan Altshuler (1965) notes, for example, that comprehensive planners claim to guide the work of specialists, to evaluate specialist proposals, and to coordinate the work of specialist agencies in the overall public interest through the vehicle of the master plan. He argues that in order to do this, comprehensive planners must "understand the overall public interest, at least in connection with the subject matter (which may be partial) of their plan . . . [and] possess causal knowledge which enables them to gauge the approximate net effect of proposed actions on the public interest." Drawing upon the findings from a series of case studies, he illuminates the dilemma of a profession committed to a synoptic view. On the one hand, true comprehensiveness could result in a superficial knowledge of the work of specialists that the planner claims to evaluate for its effects on the general welfare; on the other hand, a deeper concern with a partial goal (e.g. economic growth of the central area or downtown) must mean an abandonment of the comprehensive position.

John Friedmann answers Altshuler's arguments in the paper included in Chapter One. He points out that the dilemma posed by Altshuler is real and formidable only so long as we think of the planner as the man whose job it is to tell the other specialists how to do their jobs because he knows so much about them and can coordinate them into a master plan which is based on a superior view of the public interest.

Friedmann resolves this apparent dilemma by, first, clarifying the concept of comprehensiveness, and second, suggesting how the city planner and his overall community goals, should relate to the specialist planner and his specific functional goals. Comprehensiveness in city planning, he says, refers primarily to an awareness that the city is a system of interrelated social and economic variables. To uphold the principle of comprehensiveness, therefore, it is sufficient to insure that (1) functional programs be consonant with the city-wide system of relationships (as well as with all relevant variables) and (2) a process is established that will maximize the specialized contributions of technical experts to the solution of urban problems.

To achieve these objectives, Friedmann suggests that a distinction be drawn between performance goals and achievement goals as these relate to policy planning and program planning, a concept originally suggested by Sidney Sonenblum and Louis Stern (1964) in a paper devoted to a discussion of economic planning at the national and state levels. Performance goals are concerned with the city as a whole, and are the primary focus of policy planning; policy planning aims to maintain the city as a delicately balanced socio-spatial system in a state of dynamic equilibrium. Achievement goals are concerned with maintaining or reaching acceptable levels of achievement in a variety of functional activities or sectors such as health, education, urban renewal, and transportation; program planning is concerned with achievement goals and objectives which relate to individual functional areas. The performance goals for a city, Friedmann suggests, should be incorporated into an urban development framework or *policies* plan and from this plan would be derived specific *program* guidelines to reach the achievement goals in all the subject areas that are of concern to the city for a period of five to ten years.

The distinction Friedmann draws between performance goals and achievement goals is a significant one, and is a subject of increasing interest to planners today. It draws its intellectual insights from the field of systems theory and systems analysis, which has led the planner to think of goals in terms of the expected or desired outcomes/results/performance of his plan. In addition, using the systems approach, the planner now recognizes that a city, like all systems, is hierarchical in nature. Single components of the planner's systems (e.g. a residential neighborhood, a sewage works) will be systems in their own right to the architect, urban designer, and civil engineer respectively who will seek optimum solutions for them. But these specific optima may be sought within broader limits and ranges (e.g. a density of ten to twenty houses per acre or nine to ten million gallons of water per day). If the ranges are adhered to, the planner's system, i.e. the overall city-system goals, may be unaffected by whatever particular design solution is arrived at by the specialist agencies for housing and sewage disposal. As long as the planner defines the units, components, and goals of his system (the city as a whole) in such a way as to maximize the freedom of the public and private decision-makers to optimize their systems within his framework—and as long as both he and the public and private specialists realize the nature of their interrelationships—it is possible to consider comprehensive goals for a city which, in essence, represent performance criteria or requirements for the whole city-system.

PUBLIC INVOLVEMENT IN GOAL-SETTING

Under the traditional model of planning, it is assumed that there is some unified conception of the public interest or general welfare which is the special responsibility of the planning commission (with its professional staff), at least in the field of physical development for cities and urban areas. It is then assumed that the commission is both capable and responsible for establishing long-term development goals which provide a broad perspective and give substance to the community's short-term, specific, day-to-day activities. These long-term goals are expressed in the long-range comprehensive or master plan.

Traditionally, the standard procedure for defining the goals of a plan involved primarily staff responsibility; these goals were identified on the basis of the planner's perception of community goals. His sources for these goals statements were usually a combination of cursory observation and experience in his contacts with the public, with civic groups, and with pressure groups of all kinds and, in part, his own values and intuition as to what the goal content should be.

This traditional approach to goal-setting for planning was brought to the profession by the architect, landscape architect, and civil engineer whose methods are well-suited to a unitary setting, e.g. a single client such as a private corporation, an architect's office, or a single-function government agency, where there is usually basic agreement over the goals of the organization, ability to predict the future with considerable precision, and centralized control over the resources needed to achieve the goals (see Webber, 1965: 291). These features are clearly not characteristic of democratic local governments with their multiple goals and diffuse authority systems.

In recent years, planners have recognized the diverse nature of community goals, and different approaches have evolved to identify them.

While we can find a few isolated efforts in the past to involve wider groups, outside the planning staff, in goal-formulation, application of these techniques was rare; these efforts did not alter the basic reliance upon professional judgment for the identification of community goals. Recent anti-poverty programs, "maximum feasible participation" theories, and the critics of past procedures have changed this approach. Today, much of the planning profession is groping for new methods to directly involve the public in the goal-formulation process.

In accordance with this new philosophy, many cities around the country (e.g. Dallas, Los Angeles, Phoenix) have instituted programs, or are contemplating doing so, designed to establish their planning goals by directly involving a wide variety of business, professional, religious, and other citizen groups (see Southwest Center for Advanced Studies, 1967; Los Angeles Regional Goals Project, 1967). All of these attempts at goal-formulation include some measure of citizen participation involving not only planners but either individual citizens or non-governmental professionals with some responsibility for the citizen interests.

While these programs for achieving public involvement in the goal-formulation stage of planning admittedly represent a marked advance over past procedures, they have been a subject of considerable controversy. In their paper, William and Margaret Wheaton, based on a review of several of these programs, conclude that the evidence suggests that the selection of people to be involved, the selection of subject matter to which their attention was directed, and the methods for achieving consensus, all contributed to final goals statements which are fairly abstract, synthetic, or restricted as compared with known priorities of at least some sections of the population. They are led to ask whether these so-called democratic procedures may not often produce a narrower, more restrictive set of goals, or even one which deliberately ignores the most urgent desires of some fraction of the population who, for one reason or another, are not involved in the consultations. By way of comparisons, the authors point to several recent planning documents (e.g. the Philadelphia Plan and the New York City Community Renewal Program Report) which did not lay so much stress on consultative procedure but which appeared to have done a more satisfactory job of trying to reflect the diverse aspirations of the population of their cities.

In view of these and other problems encountered in trying to directly involve the public in defining goals for the community, the Wheatons suggest use of other techniques—such as gaming, or scaling techniques (Lamanna, 1964), or other measures of the intensity of preference suggested by Tullock (1967) and Coleman (1966)—which systematically try to sample the attitudes, preferences, and desires of the population. In contrast to the traditional polling techniques, which commonly ask such questions as "do you want more parks? " these techniques deal with such "forced" choices as "How many parks would you trade (give up) for how many jobs?"

In this editor's view, a most promising method, noted by the Wheatons, is the use of a semi-projective game situation. Robert Wilson (1966), for example, conducted a game in which respondents from two southern cities were supplied with a limited amount of play money ("chips") and were forced to spend it judiciously among a variety of the component elements of a residential neighborhood. People were forced, through the game, to disclose the relative importance to themselves of various aspects of the neighborhood. They could not declare themselves in favor of everything; they had to weigh the elements carefully in order to demonstrate their preferences.[1]

The hope of these methods, the Wheatons suggest, is that with the information obtained on the attitudes, preferences, and desires of the population, our political leaders (including the executive and legislative branches) might be better able to balance the claims of different sections of the population and different areas of the city, and the different preferences of all of us.

MEASURES FOR DETERMINING GOALS

Even if the planner finds suitable procedures for consulting with the public in a meaningful way regarding their goal choices, he still needs to develop suitable measures and informational tools by which the citizens can make relevant and useful choices. Several of the types of relevant measures still in the formative stage are discussed in the papers in this section.

As Friedmann himself acknowledges, the key to his approach, discussed earlier, is the development of adequate performance goals for the city-system as a whole. This requires a set of social accounts for urban areas that would permit policy planners to measure the current state of the city by a few simple indices. Planners would then be able to say when the city is performing optimally, and when it is not, where the city is going and how rapidly it is getting there.[2] These measures, if presented to citizens in a simple, understandable, and concise manner, would help them to make meaningful choices about goals for their community.

The development of such measures and accounts for urban areas is one of the most formidable and important tasks facing the planning profession today. Fortunately, there has emerged recently a growing interest in what have come to be called "urban indicators" (the counterpart of "social indicators" on the national level). Research is underway aimed at investigating the conceptual, methodological, and operational problems associated with the development of urban indicators (Bauer, 1966; Gross, 1966; Gross and Springer, 1967; Moynihan, 1967; Perle, 1970).

One of the papers in this section by David Boyce (who is on the faculty of the Department of Regional Science at the University of Pennsylvania) deals with the use of urban indicators in the urban/regional plan-making process from both a theoretical and empirical standpoint. Boyce helps to clarify this concept by showing the relationship between indicators on the one hand, and standards, criteria, and forecasts on the other; each of these concepts is viewed as being related to a particular type of performance characteristic. Thus, indicators are placed in a comprehensive system of performance characteristics.

Within this typology, standards and criteria are viewed as normative characteristics, while indicators and forecasts are non-normative. Further, indicators relate to past and present performance, forecasts relate to future performance, and standards and criteria can involve the past, the present, or the future.

The empirical component of the paper involves searching through six major metropolitan transportation and land-use studies in order to isolate statements concerning performance characteristics.

Boyce's concluding remarks regarding the application of urban indicators to urban plan-making are most pertinent.

One of the more significant recent developments in planning methodology for goal-setting has been the recognition that determination of the appropriate goals and priorities for a city can only be made in light of research into their costs, as these relate to the resources available, and their consequences. Every city needs more and better housing, transportation, economic development, community facilities, and other aspects of city life. But, rarely can a city fulfill all of its goals; it either lacks sufficient resources, or it is held back by competing (and often conflicting) goals among different groups within its population. Therefore, before one can select the appropriate goals for a city, it is necessary to determine the advances that could and should be made with respect to the goals tentatively postulated, the costs in either dollars or available resources, the compatibility of the several goals, and the relative priorities and combinations of goals.

Although the paper by Gerhard Colm in Chapter Four of the volume addresses itself to these issues from the standpoint of national goals, it is included because of the potential application of his method to urban planning. His paper is the introduction to a report (Lecht, 1966) which studied the estimated cost of achieving the objectives recommended by the 1960 Presidential Commission on National Goals (referred to earlier) in sixteen areas of our national life, e.g., urban development, social welfare, education.

In addition to employing a set of performance and achievement goals similar in approach to Friedmann's, the Lecht study advanced the latter concept one step further, and introduced the notion of *aspiration* goals. Achievement goals represent a continuation of current conditions and current standards, while aspiration goals are targets which reflect the need to provide for rising standards. These aspiration goals represent what "knowledgeable people" regard as desirable achievement and what could be obtained if the specific goal under consideration were to have high priority. In other words, the estimates of the cost of the aspiration goals do not allow for the fact that advocates of other goals may make claims for the same financial or real resources. Therefore, a further step is needed (which Lecht's study did not take), namely, to estimate feasible priority contributions of goals, which would require a reconciliation of the aspiration goals with the performance goals for the country (or city) as a whole. If the sum of aspiration goals exceeds, for example, the projected total resources (as was the case in Lecht's study), an order of priorities must be established for goal realization.

In the end, in this editor's opinion, what is needed in the goal-setting stage of the planning process is a continuing dialogue and debate between the professionals and both the politicians and citizens. Their ongoing discussions could be enriched by use of urban indicators, social accounts, gaming simulation techniques, and projections of the "costs" of achieving various goal standards. As pointed out by Dr. Colm, goals research can assist the public in making better judgments by clarifying the issues and by providing information about the likely costs and other consequences of possible alternatives.

The discussion would also be aided, this editor believes, by utilizing simulation models (such as those reviewed in Section Two of Part One in this volume) in one form or another, which would permit tracing the more important dynamic interrelationships between different components of the city and especially their sensitivity to different public policies for land development, economic growth, conservation, and the like. With the aid of such models or analogies, the outcomes of different policies and their relationships to varied goals and objectives "packages" can be more readily assessed; with the information thus developed, city planning staffs could better explain to the interested public as well as to the decision-making legislature and participating municipal departments, the implications and consequences of proposals concerning a particular planning objective. In this way, a priority of planning goals and objectives which are both desired and feasible could be determined from the interplay of technical information and political-citizen values and goals. When new goals are taking shape through the political-representative process, it should also be possible to forecast their probable impact and even to design policies and preparatory actions to be adopted in anticipation of the time when these emerging goals become stated desires and specific planning objectives of the body political. This approach might be likened to an analytical "mirror" in which various public and private agents of change and direction for the future can "see" the probable results of contemplated action, and select ahead of time what goals, objectives, and policies they want to pursue (Branch and Robinson, 1968).

NOTES

1. A similar technique is now being developed in a research project at the University of Southern California (for which this editor is principal investigator) under a grant from the U.S. Public Health Service, the primary purpose of which is to determine "users' " preferences for different elements and attributes of the residential environment, as these relate to their health and well-being.

2. These measures would be comparable to the set of national indices for gross national product, employment, and related variables which national planners are able to use in planning the national economy.

Chapter 1

PERFORMANCE GOALS AND ACHIEVEMENT GOALS

John Friedmann

Professor Altshuler's essay is a valuable addition to the small but growing list of studies of American city planning practice.[1] The collective impact of these studies has been to shatter the received image of planning as a profession and as an institution. At the core of this image, Professor Altshuler asserts, lies the ideal of comprehensiveness. And this, he continues, "must refer primarily to a special knowledge of the public interest." The city planner views himself as the stern guardian of the public interest.[2] This particular role conception, however, often interferes with his desire to have a substantial influence over policy and program decisions. Professor Altshuler implies that the traditional self-image of planners constitutes a serious impediment to the effectiveness of planning. Thus he challenges the profession: either revise your image or resign yourselves to continued impotence. The purpose of my remarks is to take up this challenge and suggest an image of planning that is more consonant with the institutional setting within which planning must occur.

I shall define planning as a way of managing the non-routine affairs of the city. This is a broad and loose conception that intentionally extends the scope of city planning activity beyond its present preoccupation with the physical arrangements of objects in space to all the subject concerns for which the city carries a responsibility, including:

(1) Economic expansion, full employment, efficiency of governmental operations
(2) Social welfare, crime, juvenile delinquency, racial integration
(3) Education: programs and facilities

Reprinted from Journal of the American Institute of Planners, Vol. 31, No. 3 (August 1965), pp. 195-197, by permission of the publisher. Note: Original title of the article was "A Response to Altshuler: Comprehensive Planning as a Process."

(4) Housing construction, redevelopment, neighborhood conservation
(5) Public transportation
(6) Sanitation and public health
(7) Cultural and recreational programs and facilities
(8) Control over land uses
(9) Urban design values

Professional fields of competence have grown up around all of these concerns. It is thus no longer possible for any single person to pretend to the universality of his technical abilities, nor is it possible to demonstrate that control over land uses or urban design values–the traditional areas of city planning emphasis–are the critical points of coordination. The technical expert is replacing the comprehensive planner in influencing the decisions that guide a city's development.

Actual planning experience bears out this contention. But in defense of his position, the professional city planner may argue that this fragmentation among technicians of the power to influence decisions sacrifices the view of the whole which has been the traditional claim to the legitimacy of planning.

It seems to me that this assertion in defense of comprehensiveness rests on an incorrect conception of the term. Comprehensiveness in city planning refers primarily to an awareness that the city is a system of interrelated social and economic variables extending over space. To uphold the principle of comprehensiveness, therefore, it is sufficient to say, first, that functional programs must be consonant with the city-wide system of relationships; second, that the costs and benefits of these programs must be calculated on the broadest possible basis; and third, that all "relevant" variables must be considered in the design of individual programs. It follows that comprehensiveness is not a special feature of the planner's mind, a mind trained to a holistic view, but must be achieved by a process that will maximize the specialized contributions of technical experts to the solution of urban problems.

How might such a process be organized within a typical large American city? To answer this question, it is necessary to draw a distinction between policy and program planning. The former is chiefly concerned with the maintenance and achievement of *performance goals* for the city as a whole, the latter with the attainment of *achievement goals* for specific functional activities or sectors.[3] Policy planning looks toward maintaining the city as a delicately balanced socio-spatial system in a state of dynamic equilibrium. Unfortunately, we are still lacking a set of social accounts for urban units that would permit policy planners to measure the current state of the city by a few simple indices.[4] Planners are consequently unable to say when the city is performing optimally and when it is not, something that national planners, reading the indices for gross national product, employment, and related variables, find relatively easy to do for the economy. This failure to evolve a widely accepted system of urban social accounts reflects the absence of a theory of the city. Urban policy planners must therefore resort to partial equilibrium solutions as approximate measures of the total performance of the city.

Although these measures do not constitute a system, it is possible to combine them loosely into an urban development framework or *policies* plan and to derive from this plan specific *program* guidelines in all the subject areas that are of concern to the city for a period of five to ten years. Responsibility for formulating the development policies plan would rest with a Council of Urban Development Advisors attached to the office of the city's chief executive. The intention here is to duplicate at the city-scale a general planning function that is currently being carried out in most countries at the national level and which has its counterpart in the United States in the Council of Economic Advisors. In addition to responsibility for the formulation and revision of the development policies plan, the proposed Council would:

(1) Prepare an annual state of the city report[5]
(2) Engage in policy-oriented research
(3) Coordinate the statistical work of the city
(4) Establish a city-wide information system
(5) Give specific policy advice to the mayor
(6) Coordinate policy by working with task forces and special commissions that may be appointed to deal with special policy areas (the Council here might serve as a general secretariat for any staff work that needed to be done).

The medium-term program guidelines that are derived from the general premises of the development policies plan would serve as a basis for the administrative agencies of the city in designing detailed program statements. To achieve a satisfactory measure of program coordination among sectors and across geographic space, operational programs would have to pulled together in the form of an urban capital budget and, corresponding to this budget, a development map. The effective time horizon of these two documents would be substantially less than for the development policies plan of the city, and most of the energies of the planning staffs would, in fact, be devoted to the task of preparing coordinated program statements for the coming budget year, with two- or three-year projections serving as a basis for program evaluation.

Such a programming function is perhaps best centralized in the city's budget office. It could function effectively, however, only to the extent that trained programming staffs are working in each of the city's departments and specialized agencies. In coordinating sectoral programs, the budget office would be guided by the urban development plan and related policy statements that are evolved by the Council of Development Advisors. It might also attempt to initiate a formal process whereby citizen groups are brought in to advise on the functional and spatial allocations in the budget. Towards this end, a Citizen Budget Advisory Council could be appointed on the nomination by local interest groups.

To complete the structure of planning, two more offices would need to be created at the executive level: *one*, an Office of Urban Design responsible for the physical planning aspects of capital improvement projects and the development of appropriate design criteria for controlling the visual form of the city, and *two,* an Office of Land Use Planning whose function would be administer the city's land use plan in coordination with all other planning offices and with specific responsibility for zoning and subdivision control.

I believe that this system of planning functions—policy, program design, and land use—organized as separate offices at the highest level of city administration would go a long way toward meeting Professor Altshuler's challenge to the planning profession. It would do so by:

(1) Enlarging the scope of what is normally considered city planning to include all matters of interest and concern to the city
(2) Establishing a process of consultation and coordination that would be built directly into the decision-making structure of the city
(3) Separating within this process distinct policy and program planning functions operating on different time scales
(4) Orienting planning functicns to development tasks and partial equilibrium solutions rather than to the formulation of a general equilibrium model in the form of a long-range master plan
(5) Maximizing the potential contributions of technical experts in a variety of subject fields, relying on a process of continuing, structured relationships among them to achieve the comprehensiveness which woul' continue to be one of the major aims of planning.

If this argument is accepted, it follows that the planning profession will need to deepen its interest in the methodology of policy and program planning and to make room in its professional curricula for the development of specialized competences in fields where only rudimentary instruction is currently provided.

NOTES

1. Martin Meyerson and Edward C. Banfield, *Politics, Planning and the Public Interest* (New York: Free Press, 1955); W. H. Brown, Jr. and C. E. Gilbert, *Planning Municipal Investments* (Philadelphia: University of Pennsylvania Press, 1961); Alan Altshuler, *The City Planning Process* (Ithaca: Cornell University Press, probably late 1965); Robert T. Daland and John A. Parker, "Roles of the Planner in Urban Development," in Chapin and Weiss, eds., *Urban Growth Dynamics* (New York: Wiley, 1962); Roscoe C. Martin, ed., *Decisions in Syracuse* (Bloomington: Indiana University Press, 1961); F. F. Rabinowitz, *Politics and Planning.* On the Role of the Expert in Urban Development. Unpublished Ph.D. dissertation, Department of Economics and Political Science, M.I.T., Cambridge, Mass., 1965; and Gary Greeson, *A Location Decision: The Boston Common Parking Garage.* Unpublished Thesis. Department of City and Regional Planning, M.I.T., Cambridge, Mass., 1965.

2. The usefulness of the concept of public interest is itself fiercely disputed. See Carl J. Friedrich, ed., *The Public Interest.* Yearbook of the American Society for Political and Legal Philosophy, Vol. 5 (New York: Atherton Press, 1962).

3. For a discussion of performance and achievement goals, see Sidney Sonenblum and Louis H. Stern, "The Use of Economic Projections in Planning," Journal of the American Institute of Planners, 30, No. 2 (May 1964), p. 111.

4. Current work on urban social accounts is summarized in Werner Z. Hirsch, ed., *Elements of Regional Accounts.* Published for Resources of the Future, Inc. (Baltimore:

Johns Hopkins Press, 1964). Unfortunately the scope of these investigations is almost exclusively confined to economic variables.

5. See, for example, Southwestern Pennsylvania Regional Planning Commission, *State of the Region '64.* (200 Ross Street, Pittsburgh, Pennsylvania.)

Chapter 2

IDENTIFYING THE PUBLIC INTEREST: VALUES AND GOALS

William L. C. Wheaton and Margaret F. Wheaton

Planners have always believed that there is some unified public interest or general welfare which was the special responsibility of the planning profession, at least in the field of environment. The American Institute of Planners constitution states that "its particular sphere of concern shall be the planning of the unified development of urban communities and their environs and of states, regions, and the nation." Dunham notes that planners believe they are best qualified to evaluate land-use proposals because they are experts in the interdependencies of land use; they have a general or comprehensive viewpoint; and they can coordinate specialist plans for the benefit of all.[1] Altshuler adds that "their [the comprehensive planners] claims to comprehensiveness, therefore, if they are to be persuasive, must refer primarily to a special knowledge of the public interest."[2]

But Altshuler goes further when he states that public planners must have "some conception of the public interest. Since plans are proposals of concerted action to achieve goals, [the planner] must express his conception [of the public interest] as a goal or a series of goals for his community . . . [and] the goals must win approval from a democratic political process." Altshuler goes on to say that "the comprehensive [public] planner must assume that his community's various collective goals can somehow be measured at least roughly as to importance and welded into a single hierarchy of community objectives." Often the public assumes that the planner does indeed have a special responsibility for

AUTHOR'S NOTE: Reprinted from *Urban Planning in Transition,* edited by Ernest Erber, pp. 152-164. Published by Grossman Publishers. Copyright © 1970. Reprinted by permission of the authors and The American Institute of Planners.

the public interest in urban affairs. "Many [people] do believe, however, that professional planners can come closer to achieving [comprehensiveness] on numerous vital issues than other participants in the urban decision process."[3] Where planners are called upon to arbitrate public conflicts, the public defers to the professionals' judgment as if it were authoritative and based upon some final principles. Such convictions are part of the ethical and ideological base of all the professions. Perhaps they are necessary to maintain morale. Certainly they are helpful in maintaining ethical standards because the very pursuit of the public interest is one of the base criteria by which society defines professions.

Altshuler's analysis of the planning process deals with the substantive element of the planner's special skills and responsibility for the public interest, and ratification or legitimation of his judgments by the procedural element of guiding and terminating public discussion. Thus we have the two-headed problem in identifying the public interest: the method by which the public interest is defined, and the content of that public interest.

Recent planning thought tends to recognize that all individuals have competing goals. We all want rest; we all want excitement; we all wish to be rich, and in some degree we all wish to be lazy. Society, being made up of individuals, naturally includes groups who have special interests in one field or another. The conservationists place an unlimited value on every redwood tree, while the industrialist sees no reason why society's needs for lumber cannot be served with profitably exploitable trees. All of us as automobile users want better highways, and on direct and level routes, while some of us who will be affected by this goal resist relocation, the destruction of the city, the separation of neighborhoods, or the ruination of the natural landscape. In the end, there is bound to be competition between these interests, there is bound to be conflict between ends and means, and there is bound to be bargaining as a means of reconciling competitive or conflicting goals.

Our society has happily relied upon the market as the main means for bargaining and resource allocation. Indeed, some recent actions by local governments suggest the reintroduction of the market as a distribution mechanism for those public goods which satisfy the market criterion of substitutability. For example, refuse collection can be divided into two services: two cans once a week is good, or one can twice a week is another and competitive good. Price differences in the cost of the service provide a market mechanism whereby consumers can express their utility differences in demand for convenience. It is clear beyond question that the market has proven to be a superior means of adjudication, if only in the sense that it produces a substantially larger pie to be divided. There is some evidence, further, that the "smaller" shares of the larger pie derived from the market system are substantially larger than the proportionally larger shares in smaller pies derived from "more equitable" systems. But these facts, if they are facts, do not relieve us of controversy. Indeed, they exacerbate it, and they certainly do not relieve us of the problem of the allocation of nonmarket goods, a steadily increasing proportion of the total pie in all societies.

The market cannot allocate merit goods: fresh air, safety, education to some level, have no readily ascertainable market price. Some of these goods must be allocated by political means in any society. With growing urbanization and increased interdependency among groups of the population, the proportion of such goods rises steadily.

Planners have shared at secondhand in the philosophical debates about the general welfare. Too often, as we now recognize, planners have merely reflected the narrow class bias and values characteristic of their social origins. They have placed great emphasis on long-range values which they felt to be neglected by others. They have tended to emphasize the preservation of nature over the needs of man. The main body of their work has been concerned with property values rather than human values. Within property values their chief concern has always been with the property of those who were better off in society rather than the property—or, rather, lack of it—of those who were less well-off.

Despite these persistent class biases, every history of the planning movement also stresses the extreme concern of its leaders with problems of greater equity and justice for all; their important role in establishing movements in the fields of housing, health, welfare, recreation, and education, which were concerned with the lot of the underprivileged; and their persistent concern with the development of institutions and professional procedures which would give the needy the support of the profession in public and private decision-making. Indeed, the few systematic histories of the planning movement which we have, including Scott's exhaustive work now about to be published, stress the broader welfare interests of most of the founders and leaders of the movement, and their persistent frustration over the fact that the clients of planning have often been disinterested in the welfare goals of planning and chiefly concerned only with their own goals.

In recent years, we have benefited from an increasing concern with welfare goals within the profession, largely reflecting society's more intense concerns with the problem of equity. In addition, however, the profession has begun to draw more heavily upon the larger body of thought in economics, political science, and sociology which expounds the biases built into our institutions and which explores in theory and in practice the processes of decision-making, the gaps between the rhetoric of the public interest, and the performance of some narrower interest. This literature has contributed considerable depth to our thinking and accelerated the search for better means of defining the public interest in any particular situation. Only in planning reports do we find a continuation of the naive assumption that there is a general public interest and, as we will indicate later, there will be very good reasons why this is so.

Politics as the means for the identification and allocation of the nonmeasurable, nonmarket goods has always been an acute concern of planners. However, the economists have pursued the method of politically defining the public welfare with considerably greater rigor than the planners. Arrow's analysis of the procedure in a democratic society was a classic statement in the field. His contribution was to outline the conditions for voting in a democracy, and to analyze the results of majority rule for terminating the voting.

His conclusion, the "general impossibility theorem," says that there is a paradox in voting with the majority rule, and thus there was no decision rule which was democratic. The solution to the paradox has been suggested by several authors, and essentially involves relaxing one or more of Arrow's five conditions for a democratic decision process: [4] a free triple, or at least three alternatives; the positive association of individual and social values, or the transivity of (adding) individual votes to get a social choice; the irrelevance of independent alternatives, or that other alternatives do not influence the preference among those under consideration; nonimposition, or not unanimity; and nondictatorship.

Rothenburg observed that one solution to the impossibility theorem lay in the social decision process of the family. [5] Family choices are group choices, and continued harmony suggests a minimum consensus on operating decisions. Family choices reflect interpersonal comparisons of utility, delegation of decision-making, authority within functional limits to a working stability, and temporal development of a common value system. Rothenburg's "family" analysis actually attacks several of Arrow's conditions, but two are most important. First, interpersonal comparisons of utility imply differences in the intensity of preferences, a murky area that political economists have tried to avoid, and this relaxes the condition of the irrelevance of independent alternatives. Second, a common value system implies an underlying unanimity of values, which violates the condition of nonimposition.

Tullock exorcises the ghost of the Arrow problem by demonstrating its irrelevance in realistic voting procedures, such as Roberts' Rules or its variants. [6] This involves a theoretical analysis of voting strength on different proposals, given some rule by which all the proposals are available for analysis and discussion before the voting begins—that there is some information about each other's position on each alternative and the relative intensities of preference, and that each alternative is taken up in a certain voting order, i.e., pairwise comparisons of alternatives. This very realistic procedural model relaxes Arrow's condition of a free triple and permits bargaining between alternatives rather than a yes-no vote on each. Further, Tullock's model assumes an underlying single-peaked preference curve, or some common value system in which unanimity occurs.

The most interesting solutions to Arrow's voting paradox seem to relax the condition of the irrelevance of independent alternatives. Both Rothenburg and Tullock use it, in combination with others, to provide their solutions; Rothenburg in the interpersonal comparisons of utility, and Tullock in relative intensities of preference. The irrelevance of independent alternatives assumes an equal intensity of each vote, and the independence of the preference between the available alternatives and some other alternatives. However, other alternatives do influence voting on the available choices, as is seen in Tullock's model where all the choices are proposed before the voting begins. The fact that other alternatives, than the two under consideration at the immediate moment, affect one's voting behavior on these alternatives, implies differences in the intensities of preferences for the different alternatives. This has led Coleman to construct a very interesting vote exchange model, where low-valued votes are traded for high-valued ones.[7] Though Mueller correctly analyzes the logical imperfections of Coleman's model in the abstract, such as the influence of dissembling and Indian-giving in the vote trading, still Coleman's model more closely approximates the real world political process than Mueller's highly idealized vote market model.[8]

The general conclusion from these models is the importance of bargaining in the political process. Different people and groups which have different concepts of the public interest must somehow find a common ground by bargaining. The ends of some groups require the adoption of means which conflict with the ends of other groups. Only in the haggling of the market, the adjudication by the courts, the enactments of legislative bodies, and the administrative acts of legitimate authority, can we discover what that balance between conflicting ends and the means to achieve those ends may be.

In the past, the standard procedure for defining the goals of a plan involved only staff responsibility. While we can find efforts to involve wider groups in goal formulation in the "Action for Cities" plans of the 1930s, in the use of simple polling techniques in the 1940s and 1950s, these efforts have not altered basic reliance upon professional judgment. Poverty programs, "maximum participation" theories, and the critics of past procedures have changed all of that. Today the profession is groping, somewhat ineptly, for new methods.

Three recent efforts at identifying the public interest are interesting because of their very different approaches to public involvement in the goal definition process. The City of Chicago 1964 report, "Basic Policies for the Comprehensive Plan of Chicago," takes one approach.[9] A "series of regional meetings was held" to explain the policy proposals. Oral and written comments and criticisms were received, and subsequently modifications were made in the basic policies. Unfortunately this summary treatment of the process by which the basic policies were made does not provide much illumination into the very intricate decision-making processes which are the meat of the theoretical models. There is no indication of how widely copies of the proposals were circulated, or whether they aroused any general public interest. There is no way of knowing the extent to which comments and criticisms were incorporated in the final report. There is no indication whether the modified policies were accepted by vote or by some less defined form of consensus. Thus only an elementary level of community participation can be presumed. At least the informed and concerned citizens of the city had some opportunity to be "involved" in establishing these goals. The planners or politicians were not alone in this endeavor.

In 1966 and 1967, the city of Los Angeles sought citizen participation in the definition of its planning goals.[10] It convened a number of meetings of representatives from professional societies whose professional responsibilities were concerned with the "environment." Less than twenty such societies are listed, including architecture, landscape architecture, city and regional planning, transportation, interior design, and environment (the local AIP chapter was among them). There is nowhere in the report a tabulation of the number of people involved in this effort. We infer from the report that, in discussing parts of the total goals group, the sub-groups involved reached decisions by some mild form of consensus without voting. An occasional unanimous conclusion is noted. Further, the group of representatives describes itself as an advocacy body rather than a representative one, with an interesting definition of advocacy: that of advocating their goals to the general public in order to gain wider approval. Yet there is a disclaimer that the statement "in no way implies that it represents the official position of any or all of the various professional organizations."

At a later stage in this procedure, the original group of professional societies was expanded to include representatives of art, political and social sciences, public administration, economics, law, geography, real estate, systems technology, management consultancy, and social welfare. This is still a professionally oriented group, not a politically oriented one, therefore the group as a whole is presumed to have some special knowledge of the public interest in order to be qualified for participation.

In 1966 and 1967, the city of Dallas promoted an effort to define goals for Dallas, actually sponsored by two apparently nongovernmental agencies, the American Assembly and the Southwest Center for Advanced Studies.[11] This interesting effort combined several different techniques for evoking expressions of preference. First, thirteen writers drafted essays on problems facing Dallas. Second, a Dallas assembly, consisting of eighty-seven residents of Dallas and near-by areas, "chosen to represent a diversity of citizens–in backgrounds, creeds, races, viewpoints, interest, occupations, and geographical residences"– met to discuss and formulate goals in a first conference. The recommended goals of this meeting were printed, going through two editions and a total of 17,000 copies, and distributed to citizens and local groups. Then neighborhood meetings were held, thirty-three in all, to discuss the twelve sets of goals, and at which "*votes* were taken and recorded on changes or additions recommended." These were in turn returned to the Dallas assembly for a second conference, at which the *Goals for Dallas* were given their final formulation. It is noteworthy that such a diversity of techniques for soliciting public opinions were used. This is a most ambitious effort to elicit wider public participation in formulating social choice, yet it still stops short. There is no indication that these goals have been officially presented to or adopted by the elected politicians for the city; thus, final accountability is absent.

All three attempts at goal formulation by widely separated governmental entities included some measure of citizen participation, which means that other than the planners were involved. Further, the recognition that some kind of "public discussion" was necessary was a basic part of the efforts, whether this meant discussion by citizens or nongovernmental professionals with some responsibility for the citizen interests. Lastly, though the final decision mechanism is unclear, the effort to reach a social consensus is clearly a part of each of the procedures. This is some advance over past goal formulation efforts.

The substance of the public interest may vitiate even the most apparently democratic of processes. What is actually said and done may fall considerably short of our professional pretensions. In these cases both internal and external evidence suggests that the selection of people to be involved, the selection of subject matter to which their attention was directed, and the methods for achieving consensus, all contributed to final goal statements which are fairly abstract, synthetic, or restricted as compared with known priorities of at least some sections of the population.

For comparative purposes, the actual content of goals on two subjects—housing and employment—still the most critical in most modern cities, will be examined in each of the cities. In Chicago, the Comprehensive Plan seems to have a most ambitious and enlightened set of housing goals. The report states that it is the objective of the city of Chicago "to improve . . . the housing quality of all existing residential areas . . . [and] to meet the needs of moderate- and low-income families. . . ." The report does not say that the city *will help* to achieve this end, it says that the city *will act* to achieve it. Yet when the policies for achieving these basic objectives are examined, they are less than bold. The policies are "to undertake programs of code enforcement, spot clearance, . . . to encourage the maintenance of these areas . . . to strengthen or accelerate programs . . . building on projects *already under way or completed.*" There is certainly little new here.

To meet the needs of moderate- and low-income families, the city proposes "to encourage banks and savings and loan associations to make mortgage loans more readily available in older communities . . . [and] to expand [public housing] through purchase and rehabilitation of existing structures, leasing units in private buildings, and construction on scattered sites." But when the actual improvement plan is analyzed, the city plans to expand the public housing units from an existing supply of 35,000 to a possible upper estimate of 70,000 in a fifteen-year effort. This would fall woefully short of the actual needs, which by the report's estimate is "250,000 households with annual incomes under the 'poverty line' of $3,000 in 1959." Furthermore, there is not even any estimate made of the need for expanding the housing units needed by moderate-income families, i.e., those "who are above the limits for [public housing] units yet find the housing supply within their means limited."

The report commits the city firmly to equality of housing opportunity. The city encourages this "fair housing" objective for the whole metropolitan area, yet stops short of positive action recommendations. In another arena, region-wide opportunities for recreation, the city actively proposes that the state of Illinois take the initiative in purchasing open space for metropolitan recreation opportunities for all to use. There is no comparable recommendation that the state purchase land, even "vacant land," for metropolitan public or open housing opportunities. We may be permitted to wonder about a concept of the public interest which implies that it is more important for the state to support equality in exercise than in housing.

In Los Angeles, the actual programs to achieve the goals and objectives are not available to test their real meaning. However, as in Chicago, there is an objective to achieve " 'open housing' . . . throughout all portions of the metropolitan region" though there is no way to check on the way in which this is to be achieved. In contrast to Chicago, the Los Angeles goals do not even mention any intention of providing public housing for those who need it, however need might be determined.

Dallas expresses even less concern for housing its people properly. Its general goal is to assure "its indigent and needy at least minimum requirements for . . . housing—with reasonable access thereto—" and its specific goal is "to strengthen the Community Council of Greater Dallas . . . to assure provision of needed services. . . ." Dallas neither clearly backs "fair housing" nor expresses any real public intent to provide housing for "its indigent." Indeed, following immediately on even this equivocal goal, there is the statement: "Recipients of these services should be required to pay for them in whole or in part as financial circumstances permit." Evidently if you are poor you are not going to get much out of Dallas, and, if you do, you had better be able to pay for it.

In employment, the outlook is even bleaker. In Chicago, the only goal related to employment mentions the necessity of job training and "merit employment." Job training includes "vocational training and adult education courses in public schools, as well as in service training by industries," but merit employment is not elucidated further.

In Los Angeles, one bold goal statement proposes "maximum employment opportunities and choices" and goes on to specify this by an objective to "utilize in full our productive potentials by restoring full employment in a decade . . . [and to] synchronize effective training programs with job creation."

In Dallas, the employment goal says that "human energies and skills . . ." should be intelligently, imaginatively, and boldly employed, an undoubtable consensual statement. Its more specific objective includes "educational and special training programs" to develop human resources, not for the purpose of individual support and dignity, but to assure "adequate manpower." Furthermore, the following objective is "to *change* the undereducated and undermotivated into contributors to the total economic well-being," (our italics) as if the full cause of unemployment lay in the inherent nature of those unemployed!

We might try to rank these efforts at goal definition on these scales: credibility as goals of the population of the city, explicitness of statement of goal, explicitness of means for achieving the goals, and degree of effort to involve the population in goal definition. On the first three scales we would roughly rank the Chicago report first, the Los Angeles report second, and the Dallas report third. That is, the Chicago report's goals are more credible as expressing the desires of its people, more explicit as goal statements, and contain numerous (though wholly inadequate) statements of means for their accomplishment. The Los Angeles report is clearly second on these over-all measures, though it would score better on some details. The Dallas report would be clearly third.

On the other hand, procedurally the Dallas effort appears to score highest; Los Angeles again is in the middle, and Chicago lowest. While this demonstrates nothing, it at least forces us to ask whether a more "democratic" procedure may not often produce a narrower, more restrictive set of goals, or even one which deliberately ignores the most urgent desires of some fraction of the population.

We can go further and assert that some other recent planning documents which did not lay so much stress on consultative procedure appear to have done a more satisfactory job of trying to reflect the diverse aspirations of our people. Both the Philadelphia Plan and the New York City Community Renewal Program Report, for instance, make very explicit statements regarding quantitative needs for housing, by price class, tenure, and location. These plans provide the public with some explicit statements of what must be done to achieve a certain goal, and at what rate. Further, they implicitly weigh the disparate need of some for housing and jobs, against the less intensive desires of a larger number of others for better transportation, more parks, and better schools. But even here, in the very best of our reports, it is impossible for even the best-informed citizen to weigh the choices and register his preferences, as he can in the market place, or as political leadership must do in the haggling over public policy decisions.

Planning faces a dual problem. The first is to devise measures which can make choices relevant and meaningful. The second is to devise procedures for consultation which are meaningful. As Friedmann has noted, the present state of a city or region is measured by a set of social accounts, and these are so poorly developed that it is often difficult to ascertain where we are going, much less how rapidly we are getting there.[12] We face formidable professional tasks in developing these measures, in establishing them as normal parts of the process of planning and administration, in devising measures of the effects of different policies on different sub-sets of the population, or upon different preferences. The present state of the practice is very poor. It is very indifferent in the best cases.

We face similar, and perhaps worse obstacles in developing procedures for consultation. As Altshuler has observed, though the theoretical problem is the legitimation of goals by public discussion, the practical problem is finding the discussants.[13] Too often, too few have either the interest or the knowledge required for effective participation. Advocacy planning may be helpful in politicizing those who are not concerned and raising their voices to the level of audibility.[14] But when universal voices are heard, the higher level of cacophony is unlikely to make the task of political leadership much easier, or political office more attractive to the wise. We must go back to the social sciences and develop far more systematic procedures for sampling the desires of the population; not with simple questions, "Do you want more parks?" but with forced choices: "How many parks would you trade for how many jobs?" We must elaborate the popular use of gaming techniques, of scaling techniques such as those devised by Lamanna,[15] and of other measures of the intensity of preference, suggested by Tullock and Coleman, so that political leadership can better balance the claims of different sections of the population, different areas of the city, and the different preferences of us all.

But there is a further problem. At present it appears clear that much of the time, political leadership does not want an explicit statement of issues, or measures of progress, or wider public involvement. When power and resources to affect improvements are pitiably weak, this reluctance to face issues is understandable, and the propensity to paper them over with motherhood statements and the appearance of consensus is strong. In the long run we must strengthen the ability of political leadership to respond, before we will have warm support for effective efforts to measure preferences or poll people. In the meantime, we must fortify those planning officials who try, by making such procedures a mandatory part of professional standards, and by public criticism of those who fail to adhere to them.

Planners can no longer rely upon either simple goal statements or simple consultation procedures. As a profession, we must devise new ways of measuring choice alternatives and new means for reaching the people.

NOTES

1. Dunham, Alison. "A Legal and Economic Basis for City Planning." Columbia Law Review, 58, May 1958.
2. Altshuler, Alan. "The Goals of Comprehensive Planning," Journal of the American Institute of Planners, 31:3, August 1965.
3. Ibid.
4. Arrow, Kenneth J. *Social Choice and Individual Values,* New York: Wiley, 1951.
5. Rothenberg, Jerome. *The Measurement of Social Welfare,* Englewood Cliffs, New Jersey: Prentice-Hall, 1961.
6. Tullock, Gordon. "The General Irrelevance of the General Impossibility Theorem," Quarterly Journal of Economics, 81:2, May 1967.
7. Coleman, James S. "The Possibility of a Social Welfare Function," American Economic Review, 56:5, December 1966.
8. Mueller, Dennis C. "The Possibility of a Social Welfare Function: Comment," American Economic Review, 57:5, December 1967.
9. Department of Development and Planning, City of Chicago. *The Comprehensive Plan of Chicago.* Chicago: City of Chicago, December 1966.
10. Environmental Goals Committee, Los Angeles Region Goals Project. *Environmental Goals for the Los Angeles Region.* Los Angeles: City of Los Angeles. Spring 1967.

11. *Goals for Dallas.* Southwest Center for Advanced Studies, Dallas, Texas, May 1967.

12. Friedmann, John. "A Response to Altshuler: Comprehensive Planning as a Process," Journal of the American Institute of Planners, 31:3, August 1965.

13. Altshuler, Alan. *The City Planning Process.* Ithaca, N.Y.: Cornell University Press, 1965.

14. Davidoff, Paul. "Advocacy and Pluralism in Planning," Journal of the American Institute of Planners, 31:4, November 1965.

15. Lamanna, Richard A. "Value Consensus among Urban Residents," Journal of the American Institute of Planners, 30:4, November 1964.

Chapter 3

TOWARD A FRAMEWORK FOR DEFINING AND APPLYING URBAN INDICATORS IN PLAN-MAKING

David E. Boyce

Two provocative questions often encountered in discussions of urban indicators and their application to urban planning are (a) what indicators are important or significant, and (b) how can such indicators be applied in preparing and evaluating plans. Widely divergent views are typically expressed on these matters. On the one hand, it is sometimes maintained that there exist very few, if any, indicators relevant for planning. A fairly convincing example of this viewpoint is sometimes cited regarding indicators for a metropolitan land use plan. One set of indicators that quickly comes to mind for evaluating land use alternatives is their transportation costs and requirements; however, few if any additional land use indicators can be suggested that seem so strikingly pertinent on the regional scale.

On the other hand, some planners have suggested the development of a range of urban indicators analogous to the economic indicators for the national

AUTHOR'S NOTE: The author wishes to thank Chris McDonald for his penetrating criticism and discussion of earlier drafts of this article, and for the inspiration and stimulation derived from his own more rigorous and extensive explorations of performance characteristics and their representation. The author has also benefited from concepts and definitions developed by Andre Farhi, from discussions with Norman D. Day, and from planning report analysis conducted by Luis Bueso; the considerable shortcomings of this preliminary account of research in progress is the responsibility of the author alone. The financial support of the Bureau of Public Roads, Federal Highway Administration, is gratefully acknowledged.

Reprinted from Urban Affairs Quarterly, Vol. 6, No. 2 (December 1970), pp. 145-171 by permission of the author and publisher, Sage Publications, Inc.

economy. One drawback to this approach is the lack of an urban macro-theory with spatial and temporal variables upon which to base such indicators. However, neither of these views has succeeded to date in denying or confirming the viability of the concept of urban indicators and their application to urban planning.

In contrast to past approaches to identifying urban indicators, this paper places indicators in a larger definitional framework which also includes standards, criteria, and forecasts. Once the relationship of indicators to these concepts is tentatively fixed, the way is cleared for an exploratory search for relevant indicators through the examination and analysis of statements of standards and criteria. Since much effort has been devoted by metropolitan planning agencies to the definition of such normative statements, a rich assortment of material is readily available for this analysis.

This paper presents some findings and analyses concerning a general framework relating urban indicators to forecasts, standards, and criteria. The material presented here should be considered preliminary and exploratory. It by no means adequately represents the depth and rigor of analysis conducted by the author and his associates during recent months. A much more careful and extensive formulation of these same concepts is to be contained in Boyce, McDonald, and Farhi (1970).

PERFORMANCE CHARACTERISTICS–CONCEPTS AND STRUCTURE

In this section the term *performance characteristic* is defined, and its meaning is elaborated and related to definitions of *standard, criterion, indicator,* and *forecast.* The concept of performance characteristics itself may be associated with the notion of problem-solving or design to meet a predetermined set of specifications (or standards, in the usual sense of the term) as is typical of many engineering and architectural problems. In those professions, designs tend to be executed in response to more or less well-defined problems. Often, the requirements of the design are carefully specified in advance; next, the designer prepares one or alternative solutions to meet these specifications. The design is then evaluated in terms of the cost and feasibility of meeting the specifications.

In engineering and architecture, specifying design standards that are feasible, or can be met, is usually not a difficult task. This is not solely because function or purpose is better defined, but also because the standards tend to be more or less independent of each other, or tend to have very simple interdependence relations. As an example, consider the problem of highway design. Typically, standards for cross-section, alignment, and grade are specified. Designs are developed for a particular problem by applying these standards to the problem. This type of problem-solving or search procedure may be conducted either manually or automatically.

Occasionally, the problem is so complex that more perplexing dependencies arise among the design standards. For example, in extremely rugged terrain it may not be possible to satisfy the standards at all, or only at extremely high cost. In this case it may be necessary to reexamine and modify the specifications themselves, that is, it is necessary to reiterate through the problem-solving process. Moreover, automated search procedures may fail in these cases.

In planning problems, in particular urban land use and transportation problems, similar design procedures apply. However, the variables of these problems tend to have a highly interdependent, complex structure. Accordingly, design standards cannot be specified independently, drawing upon previous design experience as in engineering and architecture. Nor can their interdependencies be easily foreseen and expressed. Instead, tentative standards must be specified and then modified in a cyclic or iterative manner in response to feasibility constraints and decision maker preferences.

Moreover, only a few selected variables are under the control of the public sector, in contrast with the case of engineering design. In a "forward-seeking design process," input variables (control variables together with exogenous variables) are typically the basis for forecasting values of endogenous or output variables, which are then evaluated. In engineering, the principal output variable tends to be cost, given that feasible solutions can be found. In planning, there are many output variables, often but not always including cost. Therefore, in these complex problems it is useful to extend the use of standards to *evaluating* the values of output variables as well as specifying values of input control variables (the values of exogenous variables being determined external to the design process).

In the final analysis, the question of whether a variable is an input or output variable depends in large part on the particular forecasting model chosen. Although in theory one can always conceive of a new model which would treat each variable in its most natural role for the purpose at hand, in practice one is generally faced with the improvised use of existing models. In this practical sense the problem of plan design and plan evaluation combine into a single problem, namely, specifying the composition and values of a set of performance characteristics; this is achieved by the systematic examination of alternative sets of performance characteristics as embodied in alternative plans.

Performance Characteristics

In the most general sense, a performance characteristic is a statement consisting of: (a) a definition which identifies some characteristic of a system as a function of its primitive qualities and attributes; and, (b) a specification of the relationship of this characteristic to a desired, observed, or forecast performance value. More rigorously, let us treat the statement as a mathematical expression, of the form:

$$X \rightarrow X'$$

Suppose also that the system may be defined in terms of variables

$$x_1 \ldots x_n$$

The lefthand side of a performance characteristic statement consists of some function of these variables or of a subset. In the simplest case this function may be specified in a quite nebulous form, such as:

$$f(x), f(x_1,x_2), g(x_1,x_4,x_{18}), \ldots$$

In other performance characteristic statements it may already have achieved a certain degree of definition:

$$x_1/x_2, x_1/2x_3, x_1^a, x_1^2, \ldots$$

Thus, the functional form may be quite simple (a number or ratio) or more complex (a density function containing linear operators, weightings, or powers).

The righthand side of a performance characteristic statement consists of some performance *value* which is to be assigned to, or associated with, the lefthand side. In the simplest case this value consists of some variable or constant, such as:

$$x_n, x_{15}, a, 2, 98.6 \text{ degrees} \ldots$$

In general, these values may be desired (standards and criteria), observed past or present (indicators), or future (forecasts).

In many common performance characteristic statements, however, the value on the righthand side will itself more often consist of another function of variables and constants, such as:

$$f(x_2, x_{11}, x_{12}), x_7/2x_{10}, 98.6 \pm 0.4, \ldots$$

In the latter case,

$$F(X) \rightarrow F'(X')$$

is a more intuitively attractive expression than

$$X \rightarrow X'$$

for the general form of a performance characteristic statement.

Finally, these whole expressions,

$$X \rightarrow X', F(X) \rightarrow X', F(X) \rightarrow F'(X'), \ldots$$

may themselves be interpreted as functional forms, and the arrow which assigns the characteristic (lefthand side) a performance value (righthand side) may be treated a little more formally. That is to say, it may be identified with various types of operators or connectors, such as "equals," "is less than," or "is greater than":

$$F(X) = F'(X'), F(X) < F'(X'), F(X) > F'(X'), \ldots$$

Four types of statements of performance characteristic are now considered. These definitions should only be taken as indicative of those the author and his colleagues are testing in their ongoing research.

Standards

A standard is a performance characteristic that takes on only two values, satisfactory (1) and unsatisfactory (0):

(1) $f(x_1 \ldots x_n) = 1$, for certain values of $x_1 \ldots x_n$;

(2) $f(x_1 \ldots x_n) = 0$, for the remaining values of $x_1 \ldots x_n$.

In other words, the set of possible values of $x_1 \ldots x_n$ can be divided into two disjointed and complementary subsets:

(1) $(x_1' \ldots x_n')$ such that $f(x_1' \ldots x_n') = 1$, called satisfactory states, or states that meet the standard;

(2) $(x_1'' \ldots x_n'')$ such that $f(x_1'' \ldots x_n'') = 0$, called unsatisfactory states, or states that do not meet the standard.

Thus, a standard can be defined as a binary function. Such a function, when it completely specifies the relevant aspects of a situation, implies that decision makers are indifferent about the specific values of $x_1 \ldots x_n$ as long as $f(x_1 \ldots x_n) = 1$. Moreover, suppose that

$$f(x_1) = 0, \text{ if } x_1 < a,$$
$$\text{and} \quad f(x_1) = 1, \text{ if } x_1 \geqslant a.$$

By extension, the threshold value, a, can also be called a standard. Note that this threshold value may be stated as changing with time; in this case both the x's and the value, a, should have time subscripts.

Criteria

Now suppose that the following is the case:

$$f(x_1') > f(x_1''), \text{ if } |x_1' - a| < |x_1'' - a|,$$

where x_1' and x_1'' are two values for x_1. In this event, the value x_1' is preferred over x_1'' because it is closer to a. This type of performance characteristic is called a criterion, and by extension, the value a is called a criterion.

If $a = 0$, then the criterion type of statement is concerned with minimization of the value of x_1, assuming x_1 is restricted to positive values ($x_1 \geqslant 0$). If a is extremely large, $a \to \infty$, then the criterion statement is concerned with maximization. In general, criteria are performance characteristic statement for which the desired performance value of the characteristic is the one which is as close as possible to some specified value.

By these definitions, standards and criteria constitute a partition of the set of all possible normative-type statements of this simple form into two subsets.

(Naturally, this is only one of many conceivable partitions.) A typical extension of these concepts to compound statements is the following:

if $x_1 = \gamma$, then apply the standard: $f_1(x_1 \ldots x_n) = a$;

if $x_1 \neq \gamma$, then, apply the criterion: $f(x_1') > f(x_1'')$, if $|x_1' - a| < |x_1'' - a|$.

Many such compounded and concatenated statements are possible, and their potential application in this context is being explored. The remaining definitions of performance characteristics pertain to nonnormative-type statements.

Indicator

An indicator is a performance characteristic statement of the following type:

$$I_t = f(x_1^t \ldots x_n^t)$$

where $f(x_1^t \ldots x_n^t)$ is the performance value of the characteristic or function for values of $x_1 \ldots x_n$ observed at time t, past or present. When values of the characteristic are observed over a period of time,

$$I_t = f(x_1^t \ldots x_n^t), \quad t = 1,2, \ldots T,$$

they are known as a time series on that indicator.

Forecast

A forecast is a performance characteristic statement of the following type:

$$F_{t'} = f(x_1^{t'} \ldots x_n^{t'})$$

where $f(x_1^{t'} \ldots x_n^{t'})$ is the performance value of the characteristic for values of $x_1 \ldots x_n$ pertaining to some future time t'. Such forecasts are by definition conditional upon the values, $x_1^{t'} \ldots x_n^{t'}$, assigned to $x_1 \ldots x_n$. These values may be: (a) control variables subject to specification by the decision-making authority; (b) exogenous variables determined from outside the system (by acceptance or by assumption of the decision-making authority); or, (c) endogenous variables previously forecast by the authority.

If the performance value—the function on the righthand side of the expression—includes control variables (a), the resulting forecast is thus conditional upon the values specified for them by the decision-making authority. Such control variable values may, and often do, include standards and criteria. If the performance value includes only exogenous variables (b), then the forecast is conditional only upon the values assumed or accepted for these. Such values may be, and often are, specified by other decision-making authorities.

If, however, the performance value, $f(x_1^{t'} \ldots x_n^{t'})$, includes endogenous variables, there exists an interesting situation. Suppose that these endogenous variables are forecast by the decision-making authority using a *model.* Then the functional relationships making up this forecasting model are, in turn, forecast-type performance characteristic statements. Moreover, they are necessarily defined on the values of some set of control, exogenous and endogenous variables, too.

That is to say:

$$F_{t'}(x_1 \ldots x_n) = f(\text{control variables } x_a^{t'} \ldots x_e^{t'}, \text{ exogenous variables } x_f^{t'} \ldots x_i^{t'}, \text{ endogenous variables } x_j^{t'} \ldots x_n^{t'})$$

and,

$$F_{t'}(\text{endogenous variables } x_j^{t'} \ldots x_n^{t'}) = f\ (\text{control variables, exogenous variables, endogenous variables}).$$

Note that, inasmuch as indicators, and time series on indicators, are ultimately employed in lieu of observed values for $x^{t'}$, some assumption of constancy or invariance must always be involved in such a chain of forecast-type statements.

In general, then, "performance characteristics" is a term for a statement associating a function on a set of variables with another set of variables or constants depicting desirability (standards and criteria), observations on the past and present state of the real world (indicators), and conditional predictions of the future state of the real world (forecasts). Note that the desirability or normative-type statements can strictly refer to the past and present as well as the future, as shown in the following diagram.

	past and present	future
normative	standards and criteria	
nonnormative	indicators	forecasts

In this sense, standards and criteria are quite similar to indicators, the principal difference being whether the values of the righthand side of the statement are desired or observed. If defined in this manner, the functional forms of standards and criteria are compatible with those of indicators and forecasts, and the performance values of each can be directly compared to determine progress toward the desired state. If future standards and criteria are compared with present indicators, this corresponds to a comparison between expected demand and existing supply. This is perhaps the most common use of the urban indicator concept.

Given the above relationships, the difficult search for definitions of useful indicators may be substantially solved. If useful definitions for standards and criteria can be identified, then these same definitions can be utilized in defining urban indicators. This approach is explored in some depth in the next section.

SEARCHING FOR RELEVANT URBAN INDICATORS

In order to analyze systematically the structure and content of statements of standards and criteria in urban planning, several major metropolitan land use and transportation planning programs were selected for examination. These included Baltimore, Boston, northeastern Illinois (Chicago), San Francisco Bay Area, southeastern Wisconsin (Milwaukee), and Twin Cities. A bibliography listing the sources of these statements, together with a detailed comparative analysis of the programs, is found in Boyce, Day, and McDonald (1970). The statements themselves are listed in an appendix to Boyce, McDonald, and Farhi (1970). Although it is recognized that all desired statements are not expressed in specific terms, it was still considered valid to study those that were. Statements of goals, objectives, standards, and criteria were therefore extracted from the reports documenting these programs. These statements were edited for a common format and organized into a three-dimensional framework.

The first dimension pertains to the major *subsystems* of the metropolitan system. These subsystems strongly reflect the emphasis of the programs on physical systems. They are as follows:

(1) general
(2) residential
(3) commercial
(4) industrial
(5) open space
(6) transportation
(7) utilities and services
(8) government and institutional

Items 2, 3, and 4 pertain mainly to functions of the private sector, whereas items 5-8 pertain to the public sector. Item 1 includes only the most general or comprehensive statements, i.e., those pertaining to all subsystems. This classification worked reasonably well in the analysis, although it is highly aggregated insofar as public services are concerned.

The second dimension in the framework pertains to the major attributes or *components* of systems and subsystems affected by the statements, as follows:

(1) societal characteristics
(2) activity characteristics
(3) facility characteristics

Item 1 refers to statements about society, i.e., the population or specific subpopulations. For example, statements about age, race, and income of households are classified under this item. Item 2 pertains to the "operating" characteristics of both the private and public systems, for providing goods and services. Item 3 relates to the "hardware" characteristics, by means of which these goods and services are produced. This dimension is only partly successful in that there is considerable overlap in the statements among these three components. A more satisfactory treatment requires a more complex categorization of system components.

The third dimension of the classification framework considers the *scope* of each statement:

(1) elements
(2) relationships

Some statements refer to an element of a subsystem and component. Others pertain to relationships between or among subsystems and components. This dimension seeks to distinguish between these two types. The elemental-type statements are easy to classify in this regard. The relationship-type statements are more difficult since each could be classified under two or more functional areas. In each case an effort was made to classify each relationship-type statement under the more dominant heading.

Number of Statements by Category

The above framework results in a 48-cell, three-way matrix or tableau. At a very simple level, one index of the focus of these land use and transportation programs is given by a count of the number of statements classified by subsystem, component, and scope. Such a statement count may be slightly misleading for three reasons. First, the number of possible statements cannot be expected to be uniform across subsystems, components, and scope. Second, the procedures used to extract statements were by no means exhaustive. In particular, the main emphasis was on verbal statements. Graphic and mathematical statements received only limited attention.

Third, there is the shortcoming of any such statistical approach toward qualitative data—that a straightforward frequency count does not necessarily bear much relation to the meaning of various categories of performance characteristics statements. That is, various statements and types of statement do not have the same significance in facilitating analytic procedures, or the same relevance in evoking useful actions or responses from decision makers. Despite these three limitations, the statement count presented in Table 1 may be helpful in gaining an impression of the variety of statements, without examining the entire list given in Appendix B of Boyce, McDonald, and Farhi (1970).

Table 1 provides some indication of the relative emphasis of several aspects of the programs. First, there has been more emphasis on elements of subsystems than relationships between subsystems; the number of statements about elements is 242, whereas the number about relationships is 140. This is somewhat surprising considering there are 28, or $[n(n - 1)]/2$, pairs of

TABLE 1
STATEMENT COUNT OF OBJECTIVES AND STANDARDS

Subsystems	*Components Emphasizing*						
	Societal Characteristics		*Activity Characteristics*		*Facility Characteristics*		
Statements About	*Element*	*Relation*	*Element*	*Relation*	*Element*	*Relation*	*Total*
1. General	8	2	16	6	8	3	43
2. Residential	6	1	18	7	22	22	76
3. Commercial	1	2	7	12	11	20	53
4. Industrial	0	2	5	1	6	10	24
5. Open space	6	1	25	8	12	7	59
6. Transportation	0	1	8	16	57	9	91
7. Utilities and services	1	0	6	7	4	1	19
8. Government and institutional	0	0	11	2	4	0	17
Subtotal	22	9	96	59	124	72	
Total	31		155		196		382

subsystems about which relational statements could be made, whereas there are but 8, or n, possibilities for elemental statements. Moreover, in a planning program which emphasizes comprehensiveness, relationship-type statements could be expected to have considerable importance.

Second, the emphasis on facility characteristics and activity characteristics and the near exclusion of statements on societal characteristics is about as expected, given the strong physical planning orientation of the programs. Third, the distribution of emphasis with regard to functions highlights some interesting biases. Transportation is by far the most important area, which is not surprising, given the orientation and funding of these programs. The four land use systems—residential, open space, commercial, and industrial—follow in that order. This ranking appears to be consistent with one's a priori impressions of the emphasis given these systems. The "general" category also appears quite strong, whereas the utilities, services, government, and institutional categories receive scant attention.

Analysis of Statement Content

Within the context of this overall set of statements, two functions—transportation and open space—are now analyzed in a preliminary and indicative manner. The purpose of the analysis is to explore whether these statements do indeed have common structural forms which may be interpreted in terms of the above definition of performance characteristics, i.e.,

$$f(x_1 \ldots x_n) \lesseqgtr k, \text{ where k is some constant of variable.}$$

In this context, any function, f(x), may conveniently be thought of as an imperative verb acting on a direct object. For example, the function, x^2, may be translated into (or transformed to) the imperative verb, *square,* defined on the direct object *x*. The mathematical function x^2 may thus be reinterpreted as the sentential function "square x"; or the whole expression $f(x) = x^2$, as "square x and assign the value to f(x)." In the latter case, x^2 acts as the direct object of an "assignment to f(x)" command; and x itself could be considered an indirect object.

In the same fashion, the mathematical forms $<, =, >$ may be interpreted as verbs. In the expression $f(x_1 \ldots x_n) \lesseqgtr k$, they have the constant k as their direct object. In the case of $f(x) = x^2$, the whole function x^2 may be considered the object. To illustrate this point, consider a generalization of the latter example. Let $f(x) = x^a$, where a is a constant. This compound function reads *raise* x *to the power* a, *and assign the value to* f(x). Now consider the statement.

$$x^a < k.$$

This can be interpreted as *raise* x *to the power* a *such that the result is less than* k. Similarly,

$x^a = k$: *raise* x *to the power* a *such that the result equals* k.
$x^a > k$: *raise* x *to the power* a *such that the result is greater than* k.

These very simple examples may appear somewhat contrived, but are plausible verbal transformations of the mathematical statements. The benefits of this formulation become clear when examining the statements extracted from planning programs.

As a first example, examine the analysis of elemental statements for transportation considered as activity characteristics in Table 2. The left side of the table lists several statements extracted from agency reports prepared for the areas indicated. The right side of the table analyzes each statement according to the formulation defined above. For example, statement 1 is a very general goal statement concerning the transportation system and its uses. The verb *improve* may be regarded as a function, f(•), of the direct object variables, *connecting links.* The verb, *to accommodate,* connects this function with a second set of variables or constants, *movement of people, goods, ideas,* which may be considered the direct object of accommodate, and an indirect object of improve. In this case, the direct object may be identified with a means, and the indirect object with an end.

In the case of statement 1, the verb accommodate might be interpreted as a standard-type performance characteristic. In other words, accommodate connotes setting some level of achievement as contrasted with maximizing or minimizing. Statements 2, 3 and 4 are of the same type. Each connotes achieving some level of service for transportation activities.

TABLE 2
ELEMENT STATEMENTS OF ACTIVITY CHARACTERISTICS OF THE TRANSPORTATION SUBSYSTEM

Statement	*Function*	*Variables*	*Connector*	*Variable or Constant*
1. Improve the connecting links that accommodate the movement of people, goods, and ideas within the area and with the rest of the world (NE Illinois)	Improve	connecting links	to accommodate	movement of people, goods, ideas
2. Provide a transportation system that gives mobility to the citizens of the several jurisdictions, visitors to the region, and the goods needed to conduct everyday affairs. The system should offer efficient and convenient service to and from, and within, the region (Baltimore)	Provide	transportation system	(to give)	mobility to citizens, visitors, goods
3. Provide a means of travel for those who cannot drive a car, and offer others an alternative to driving through transit (Twin Cities)	Provide Offer	means of travel alternative means	for for	nondrivers drivers
4. Maintain or increase the proportion of transit ridership to each urban center (SE Wisconsin)	Maintain, increase	transit ridership	(to serve)	each center
5. Encourage more ridership on the rail transit system in particular, and mass transportation in general (NE Illinois)			to encourage	transit ridership
6. Alleviate traffic congestion, reduce travel time, increase safety and minimize cost of the transportation system (NE Illinois)			to alleviate to reduce to increase to minimize	traffic congestion travel time safety cost of transportation system

Statements 5 and 6 may be interpreted as incomplete statements in that there is no function, f(•), specified, but only the purpose, or vice versa. For instance, one could consider each of these statements to have the implied function, *improve (transportation system).* Also, more specific functions could be defined. For example, for statement 5, *decrease (fares), decrease (headways), increase (speed),* and *raise (highway tolls),* would be possible partial statements to precede the partial statement *to encourage transit ridership.* Other interpretations are also conceivable, of course.

Table 3 analyzes a set of statements regarding the relationship of transportation activity characteristics to othe; subsystems or the relationship between transportation modes. In this case, an *s* or *c* is used to suggest whether the connector depicts a standard or criterion-type performance characteristic. In some cases, the verb used could depict either, as designated by (s, c) or (c,s) depending on which seems dominant. Their actual status could be made less ambiguous by contextual information. In general these statements are more complete, perhaps because they describe the relationship of one system to another.

Tables 4 and 5 extend the analysis of the transportation subsystem to statements regarding facility characteristics as contrasted with the activity characteristic statements of Tables 2 and 3. The statements in these tables appear to fit the tentative formulation quite well, perhaps better than in Tables 2 and 3. In part, this is because the extracted statements are somewhat more specific.

In contrast to Tables 2-5, Table 6 presents three sets of detailed standards extracted from agency reports. These standards can also be placed into the form of Tables 2-5, but they are much easier to understand in tabular form. For example, consider the following statement for the first line of Table 5: "Provide local transit service with stops every 660 feet to serve areas with a minimum of 600 passengers/bus/day for high density areas of ¼ mile radius." In this case, *provide* is the function, *local transit service* is the variable, *to serve* indicates a standard-type performance characteristic, and *600 passengers/bus/day for high density areas of ¼ mile radius* is the level of service to be met.

Tables 7 and 8 are further exploratory examples of the analysis of statements, in this case for the activity and facility characteristics of open space. Element and relationship types of statements are combined in these tables. These analyses further suggest the similarity of statement types. Nearly all of the statements in these two tables tend to be of the standard type of performance characteristic. Table 9 provides examples of detailed open space standards comparable to the transportation standards in Table 6.

Analysis of the Types of Connectors in Tables 2-9

Whether a statement is classified as a standard or a criterion in the above tables depends largely on the nature of the verb used as a connector between the function on the left and the variable or constant on the right. In some cases, the

TABLE 3
RELATIONSHIP STATEMENTS OF ACTIVITY CHARACTERISTICS OF THE TRANSPORTATION SUBSYSTEM

Statement	*Function*	*Variables*	*Connector*	*Variable or Constant*
1. Guide growth by providing or denying land access (Baltimore)	Provide, deny	land access	to guide (s,c)	growth
2. Induce the growth of larger centers that will offer greater choice of goods, services, and employment through the use of selective access (Twin Cities)	Use	selective access	to induce (c) thereby offer (c,s)	growth of centers and greater choice
3. Develop an integrated transportation-land use system which will effectively serve the existing regional land use pattern and promote the implementation of the regional land use plan, meeting the anticipated traffic demand generated by the existing and proposed land use (SE Wisconsin)	Develop	integrated system	to serve (s) to promote (c) thereby meet (s)	existing land use, land use plan, and traffic demand
4. Reduce the amount of travel necessary for daily activities through a better arrangement of land uses. The total number of vehicle miles of travel should be minimized by reducing trip length, total number of trips, or both (Baltimore)	Arrange Reduce (c)	land use trip length, number of trips	to reduce (c) to minimize (c)	daily travel vehicle miles of travel
5. Place heavy emphasis on mass transportation to reduce (a) the volume of air pollution produced by automobiles, (b) excessive consumption of land due to low density sprawl (NE Illinois)	Emphasize	mass transportation	to reduce (c)	air pollution land consumption
6. Encourage the development of a new form of rapid transit to expand the areas of work and residence and the number of people for which a choice of transportation mode is available (NE Illinois)	Develop	transit technology	to expand (c) to provide (s)	areas of work and residence, choice of mode
7. Provide modified rapid transit service to reduce peak loadings on highways (SE Wisconsin)	Provide	transit service	to reduce (c)	peak loadings on highways
8. Arrange transit routes to minimize transfers and duplication of service (SE Wisconsin)	Arrange	transit routes	to minimize (c)	transfers, service duplication

TABLE 4

ELEMENT STATEMENTS OF FACILITY CHARACTERISTICS OF THE TRANSPORTATION SUBSYSTEM

Statement	*Function*	*Variables*	*Connector*	*Variable or Constant*
1. Develop an integrated regional transportation system consisting of highways, transit and terminal facilities that will effectively and economically meet the demands of the future as well as the present pattern of regional growth (SE Wisconsin)	Develop	integrated regional transportation system	to meet (s)	present and future demands
2. Combine the best feature of auto, bus, rapid transit and commuter rail facilities into a balanced transportation system to provide for the maximum safety, speed, comfort, and flexibility in the movement of people and goods within the area (NE Illinois)	Combine	auto, bus, rail facilities	to maximize (c)	safety, speed, comfort, flexibility
3. Develop an efficient transportation system that minimizes:	Develop	transportation system	to minimize	
(a) cost, while meeting all other objectives;				(a) cost, subject to other objectives
(b) total vehicle hours of travel, by adequate capacity and high levels of geometric design to increase travel speeds;				(b) vehicle hours of travel
(c) accident exposure, in freeways, expressways, and transit;				(c) accident risk
(d) the use of land for transportation facilities (SE Wisconsin).				(d) land consumption
4. Use the best available technology to manage traffic to prevent unacceptable congestion (Twin Cities)	Use	technology of traffic management	to prevent (s)	unacceptable congestion
5. Provide expressways with a median strip for transit lines (NE Illinois)	Provide	median strip in expressways traffic	to operate (s)	transit service
6. Separate vehicular and pedestrian traffic to reduce conflict in congested areas (NE Illinois)	Separate	traffic	to reduce (c)	conflict

TABLE 5
RELATIONSHIP STATEMENTS OF FACILITY CHARACTERISTICS OF THE TRANSPORTATION SUBSYSTEM

Statement	*Function*	*Variables*	*Connector*	*Variable or Constant*
1. Locate and design transportation facilities so as to:	Locate and design	transportation facilities		
(a) minimize destruction of neighborhoods and community development;			(a) to minimize (c)	disruption of neighborhoods
(b) avoid penetration of residential planning units with through traffic;			(b) to not penetrate (s)	residential units
(c) avoid penetration of environmental corridors of prime natural resource areas except as necessary to provide access to such areas;			(c) to not penetrate (s)	environmental corridors
(d) avoid destruction of visually pleasing buildings, structures, and natural features;			(d) to not destroy (s)	pleasing structures and features
(e) avoid interfering with views of and from such features;			(e) to not interfere (s)	with views
(f) enhance the enjoyment of the natural landscape and the aesthetic quality of the cityscape and areas through which they pass (SE Wisconsin)			(f) to enhance (s,c)	enjoyment and quality of landscape
2. Serve medical, regional shopping and community centers by the rail system and these centers to expressways via arterial streets (NE Illinois)	Provide	transit and highway facilities	to serve (s)	centers
3. Locate access and exit points on highway facilities to meet metropolitan traffic and land development needs (Twin Cities)	Locate	interchanges	to serve (s)	travel demand and land development

TABLE 6
EXAMPLES OF STATEMENTS ON TRANSPORTATION SUBSYSTEMS

Activity Characteristics

1. Provide appropriate service for all transit routes exceeding the following average weekday passenger volumes:

	Minimum	*Area Radius*	*Distance Between Stops*
Local transit	600/day/bus	¼ mile-high density ½ mile-medium density	660 feet
Modified rapid transit:			
All day	600/day/bus	3 miles	No stops
Limited	300/4 hrs./bus	3 miles	No stops
Bus rapid transit	21,000/day per freeway lane	3 miles	2 miles
			(SE Wisconsin)

Facility Characteristics

1. Highway route and interchange standards:

	Freeways and Expressways		*Arterials and Collectors*		*Local Routes*	
	Spacing Route	*Standards Access*	*Spacing Route*	*Standards Access*	*Spacing Route*	*Standards Access*
Near CBD	1-2 miles	1-2 miles	½ mile	¼ mile	¼ mile	Every block
Urban	2-4 miles	1-2 miles	½-1 mile	¼ mile	¼-½ mile	Every block
Suburban	4-6 miles	2-3 miles	1-2 miles	¼ mile	½-1 mile	Every block
Rural	6 or more	3 or more	2-4 miles	¼ mile	1-2 miles	Every block
					(Twin Cities)	

2. Design speed standards:

	Overall Design Speeds in Miles per Hour			
	Downtown	*Intermediate*	*Outlying*	*Rural*
Freeways	35-55	40-55	55-65	60-70
Expressways	25-40	30-45	40-50	50-60
Arterials:				
Divided	15-25	25-35	35-45	45-60
Undivided	15-25	20-35	25-40	40-50
Collectors	10-20	15-30	20-35	40-50
Local	5-10	10-20	15-25	30-40
			(SE Wisconsin)	

TABLE 7
STATEMENTS OF ACTIVITY CHARACTERISTICS OF THE OPEN SPACE SUBSYSTEMS

Statement	*Function*	*Variables*	*Connector*	*Variable or Constant*
1. Satisfy outdoor recreation needs through a harmonious relationship between natural landscape and resources and man's use of land, and through the preservation and conservation of natural environment qualities (Twin Cities)	Satisfy	recreation needs	by providing for (s)	harmonious use, preservation and conservation
2. Insure wise use and conservation of the limited land, air, and water resources and the protection of agricultural areas, mineral deposits, natural vegetation and wildlife from urban encroachment (NE Illinois)	Insure	wise use and conservation of natural resources		
3. Preserve open space to:	Preserve	open space		
(a) enhance the total quality of the regional environment;			(a) to enhance (c,s)	total quality
(b) maximize essential natural resources availability;			(b) to maximize (c)	resource availability
(c) give form and structure to urban development;			(c) to structure (s)	urban development
(d) facilitate the ultimate attainment of a balanced year-round outdoor recreational program providing a complete range of facilities for all age groups (SE Wisconsin)			(d) to attain (s)	outdoor recreational program
4. Establish and maintain a system of parks and parkways for each zone or population center as an open space system of local scale for intensive use (Twin Cities)	Establish and maintain	parks and parkways	for use of (s)	each zone or population center
5. Acquire recreation sites in advance to meet projected requirements, emphasizing the conservation of historic and scenic sites, lake shores, and water courses with public use potential (Twin Cities)	Acquire	recreation sites	to meet (s)	projected requirements
6. Acquire green belts to delimit population centers (Twin Cities)	Acquire	green belts	to delimit (s)	population centers

verb used clearly connotes a criterion: minimize, reduce, expand. In these cases, the more (or less) of the righthand side, the more preferred is the situation.

In other cases a standard is perhaps indicated: meet, prevent, serve. Here achieving a specific level or amount of the variable is the preferred result. Still other verbs are ambiguous in this regard: enhance, offer, guide. Their actual status could, however, be made less ambiguous by introducing qualifiers, or by contextual information. A classification summarizing the tables is given in Table 10.

Relationship of the Analysis to Urban Indicators

Earlier in this paper a definitional relationship was established between urban indicators and urban standards and criteria. Now it is useful to examine this relationship in terms of Tables 2-9.

Tables 6 and 9 provide specific statements of standards and criteria, that is, they define desirable levels or magnitudes of constants and variables in relation to functions of variables. If these functions are computed solely on observations rather than desires, then they are urban indicators. For example, observed levels of transit service, spacing, and speed variables akin to those in Table 6 could also be reported as indicator-type statements. The comparison of such indicators with the corresponding standards would be very useful, particularly if compiled over a period of several years. The same comment applies to the open space standards of Table 9.

The interpretation of Tables 2-5, 7, and 8 as indicators is more difficult in that they are not defined operationally. In this sense they are also of limited immediate use as standards. Nevertheless, sets of specific indicators might be readily defined based on these tables. As an example, consider Table 2. Statement 1 concerns improving connecting links to accommodate movement. Urban indicators for connecting links include zone-to-zone travel, time and cost, and accessibility measures based on time, cost, and location of activities. Operational standards would be defined in the same manner: desired zone-to-zone travel times or speeds; desired zone-to-zone travel costs or unit costs; desired levels of accessibility measures.

Statement 6 is also of interest for these reasons. In this case the statement only concerns the desired level of the variable or constant on the righthand side, e.g., reduce travel time, minimize cost. Here, observed travel time, cost, congestion measures (speeds), and accident rates are the relevant indicators for comparison with desired levels or forecast levels. In a similar fashion, specific indicators can be defined for each statement of a standard or criterion. In the process of doing so, the standard or criterion is also defined more operationally.

USING PERFORMANCE CHARACTERISTICS IN PLAN-MAKING

Although the main emphasis of this paper concerns definitional aspects of urban indicators in the context of urban planning, it is useful to conclude with a

TABLE 8
STATEMENTS OF FACILITY CHARACTERISTICS OF THE OPEN SPACE SUBSYSTEM

Statement	*Function*	*Variables*	*Connector*	*Variable or Constant*
1. Acquire public access to lakes and rivers and expand wildlife management areas in stream valleys, marshes, and flood plains adjacent to built-up areas (Twin Cities)	Acquire Expand	public access wildlife areas	to adjacent to	lakes and rivers built-up areas
2. Establish large areas of permanent open space within the urban region (between the corridors) where they can absorb pollution from the air (NE Illinois)	Establish	large areas of open space	to absorb (c)	air pollution
3. Establish public parks and other open spaces where opportunities for natural resources management are present (NE Illinois)	Establish	open space areas	to manage (s)	natural resources
4. Preserve all prime agricultural lands for agricultural uses, to provide a reserve for future needs and to insure preservation of those rural areas which provide wildlife habitat and which are essential to shape and order urban development (SE Wisconsin)	Preserve	prime agricultural lands	to provide (s) to insure (s) to shape and order (s)	reserve for future needs wildlife habitat urban development
5. Designate areas having unique historic, scientific, cultural, educational, or scenic value, or containing unusual flora or fauna, for public acquisition for open space, or maintain in agricultural use (NE Illinois, SE Wisconsin)	Acquire	areas for open space	having (s)	historic, scientific, cultural, educational or scenic value

TABLE 9
EXAMPLES OF STATEMENTS ON OPEN SPACE SUBSYSTEMS

Reserve open space as follows:

Regional parks and recreational land:	40 acres/1,000 persons
Local park and recreational land:	100 acres/1,000 persons
A minimum regional aggregate of:	5 acres of woodlands/1,000 persons
	(SE Wisconsin)

Regional open space sites of 100 acres or larger should be located within 20 minutes of centers of population and serve 20% of the population at 30 minutes time distance on an average summer Sunday.

(Bay Area)

	Acres per 1,000 Persons		
Standards for Open Spaces	*Regional*	*Local*	*Total*
Public park recreation	15	15	30
Private recreation	3	5	8
Green space, health, welfare, well-being	36	10	46
Subtotal	54	30	84
Add 20% for intensive midsummer use	10	6	16
Total	64	36	100

(Bay Area)

brief, general statement regarding their application to plan-making. This section summarizes several ideas elaborated on in more depth in Boyce, McDonald, and Farhi (1970) and does not attempt to deal with the problem in the more rigorous manner attempted there.

Typically, standards and criteria have been applied in urban planning in preparing alternative plans and evaluating their performance (see also Boyce, Day, and McDonald, 1970). Standards used in preparing plans include densities, lot sizes, open space requirements, parking ratios, and so forth. These provide allocation rules for determining the amount of land and public facilities required to serve a population of a specified size. More often, however, standards have been used in an evaluative sense: cost, speed, average trip length, and so forth. In this case, the question is whether a particular alternative meets the standards established for the plan. In both of the above applications, urban indicators and forecasts provide useful information concerning the discrepancy between the existing situation and the plan.

Several major problems exist with regard to the classical plan-making procedure briefly outlined above. First, how do the standards and criteria, and the more general objectives and goals, originate? Experience indicates very clearly that it is not possible to assume that these are known a priori. Second, what aspects of an alternative plan should be evaluated? Again, it is clear from the experience of planning agencies that benefits and costs are only one dimension of the evaluation process. Furthermore, to argue that all variables can

TABLE 10
A TENTATIVE CLASSIFICATION OF VERBS USED IN STANDARDS AND CRITERIA

Standards		*Criteria*	*Both*
Accommodate	Attain	Induce	Give
Serve	Delimit	Promote	Offer
Meet	Manage	Reduce	Guide
Prevent	Insure	Minimize	Offer
Operate	Shape	Expand	Enhance
Not penetrate	Order	Maximize	
Not destroy	Have	Absorb	
Not interfere	Is, equals		
Provide	Structure		

be converted to benefits and costs ignores the relatively primitive status of operational planning methods. Third, for what geographical scale, for what period of time, and for what activities should plans be prepared and evaluated? Fourth, what is the role of forecasting models in such a process? These questions are addressed below by outlining a revision of the plan-making and decision process.

First, define an adopted plan to mean a list of performance characteristics for the relevant spatial, temporal, and activity categories. Such a list includes a sublist of forecast-type performance characteristic statements, some of which are the consequence of others. It also includes a sublist of standards and criteria with adopted or tentative levels or magnitudes for each spatial unit, for each time period and each activity group considered important by decision makers. Moreover, assume that all these statements are consistent, that is, they do not result in contradictory situations as tested by the forecasting and analysis capability available.

Now, the process of determining the righthand sides, or values, of these performance characteristic statements as well as which types to include, is defined as the plan-making process. And this includes the process of determining the values of standard and criterion-type statements. This process is considered to be a dialogue between planners and decision makers, with planners preparing and evaluating alternatives, and decision makers commenting on them, choosing among them, and directing the search for other alternatives.

The process begins, for example, by the planners postulating tentative alternative values for each performance characteristic, predicting the consequences of the values, and evaluating these consequences. The decision makers consider these alternatives, compare the proposed values of performance characteristics to their current values (urban indicators), and suggest additional values for study. Some of their directions may include requests for information at another scale, for another time period, or pertaining to another activity group that may be of particular interest.

In such a process, how is it determined what standards are used to prepare alternatives and what standards are used for evaluation? The answer to this question rests on what design procedure is used, and operationally may be constrained by the models available to predict the consequences of a given set of input (control and exogenous) variables. Each such model designates certain variables as input and others as output or endogenous. Different models of the same set of activities may imply much different views of the roles of these variables.

For example, one model with average trip length as an exogenous variable and employment density as a control variable may provide a prediction of residential density. Another model with both residential and employment density as control variables may predict average trip length. In each case, both the inputs and outputs are subject to evaluation since their relative position is only a function of the model and, more generally, the plan preparation procedure, and not an inherent property of the decision situation itself.

How then do decision makers proceed in adopting values for performance characteristics? When presented with a set of alternative plans displaying the consequences of alternative tentative values for these standards and criteria, decision makers have the following options:

(1) request that different values of input (control) performance characteristics, or different characteristics, be used in revising one or more alternatives;
(2) determine the final value of an input performance characteristic;
(3) revise the value of an output performance characteristic for evaluating alternatives or add or substitute new or redefined characteristics;
(4) determine the final value of an output performance characteristic;
(5) request that certain interactions of variables now in the forecasting procedure be ignored in future alternatives;
(6) request that certain interactions of variables not in the forecasting procedure be included in future alternatives.

In all of these judgments, decision-makers will refer to current values of each performance characteristic (urban indicators) to appreciate the desirability of change from the past and present situation proposed in each alternative. Moreover, trends in these indicators are very useful in determining the feasibility of plan implementation, that is, whether the desired value is in the direction of the trend or in the opposite direction.

Finally in summary, the above general description should be viewed as an activity that is carried out on a continuing basis over time rather than on a once-and-for-all basis. Tentative values for performance characteristics may be debated and analyzed for several months or years before agreement is reached. They may then be reviewed annually or at such time as changes in assumptions or conditions warrant such review. On the other hand, urban indicators must also be compiled over time to be useful in judging progress toward plan implementation. These past, current, and desired values of performance characteristics, then, become the focus of the continuing planning process.

REFERENCES

Boyce, D. E., N. D. Day and C. McDonald (1970) "Metropolitan Plan Making." Regional Science Research Institute Monograph Series 4. Philadelphia.

Boyce, D. E., C. McDonald, and A. Farhi (1970) "Methodology for Plan Making." Report to the Federal Highway Administration. Philadelphia: Regional Science Dept., University of Pennsylvania.

Chapter 4

GOALS, PRIORITIES, AND DOLLARS

Gerhard Colm

We often hear the rhetorical question: Why should we go to the moon before conquering the common cold? Or we are asked: Why should vacuum cleaners for our homes be essential to our standard of living, but street cleaners an unfortunate expense? This is the way in which "the man (or woman) on the street"—or a Harvard professor—raises questions of national priorities.

The social sciences cannot give the final answer to these and similar questions. The answers emerge from the interplay of value judgments made by millions of people in the market place and through the political process. But research can assist these millions of people in making better judgments by clarifying the issues and by providing information about the likely consequences of the alternative decisions that might be made. It is the task of goals research to clarify such issues and to provide relevant information for people in public and private life who must or wish to take a position on such choices. The present work is a contribution of the National Planning Association to this field. It is the purpose of this essay to place the subject of this book in the broad perspective of goals research.

Thoughtful readers looking at *Goals, Priorities, and Dollars* may wonder how it is possible to deal objectively with national goals. Are not attitudes toward national goals very largely determined by the values and traditions embedded in our culture? And, where a deliberate decision has to be made in a pluralistic society, should not the choice be left primarily to the judgment of individuals in accordance with their interests and their consciences? A few decades ago, I am sure, there would have been general doubt that national goals could or should be a legitimate field for detached research.

Reprinted from *Goals, Priorities, and Dollars: The Next Decade,* by Leonard A. Lecht, pp. 1-16, published by The Free Press. Copyright ©1966. Reprinted by permission of the publisher.

National goals could not become a subject of research before there had arisen a national goals consciousness and a recognition that decision-makers needed help in the clarification of goals and of the consequences of decisions to be made concerning them.

EMERGENCE OF A NATIONAL GOALS CONSCIOUSNESS

In permissible simplification, we may distinguish four phases in the evolution of a national goals consciousness.

1. In the first phase, national goals are not articulated as such. Individuals try to find remunerative jobs; they strive to better their standard of living; they grumble about merchants who raise the price of goods. Businessmen work to make profits, improving their machinery and their methods in order to gain in the competitive struggle. However, people interested in jobs, price stability, and business investments are not aware that they are pursuing national goals of full employment, price stability, and economic growth.

2. The second phase is characterized by a crisis. When the pursuit of individual and corporate interests becomes frustrated on a large scale, it becomes clear that more is involved than individual or corporate failure. Out of the experience of the Great Depression and the Second World War, full employment, price stability, economic growth, and international economic balance emerged as national goals. These were *performance goals* because they were related to the restoration of a desirable economic performance. The adoption of the Employment Act of 1946 can be regarded as the milestone symbolizing that the American people had become performance-goal conscious.

These goals are related to a satisfactory level and to the general character of economic activity; they are not concerned with the substance, the results of that activity.

3. In the third phase, we are concerned not only about whether our economic machinery is in smooth working condition, but also about what it produces. These concerns arose temporarily during the war emergency, when the question "guns or butter?" was asked. It was believed that, after the war, the concern for the type and quality of our production could safely revert to individual preferences expressed through demand in the market place and the conventional process of government policy formation. Again a crisis was necessary to make us aware of what may be called *achievement goals.* It had been taken for granted that, in a democratic society, not only economic performance but also education, research, and technological achievements were superior to achievements in any other type of society. This confidence was shaken by Soviet accomplishments, especially the orbiting of Sputnik spacecraft in 1957. Competitive coexistence in this and other fields provided a challenge which compelled us to look critically at deficiencies in our own achievements. Of course, there has been periodic dissatisfaction with the deficiencies in medical

training and other aspects of education, and with poverty and especially with poor housing. But, for the first time, it was felt necessary to look at the achievement of Western society as a whole and at the allocation of resources as it is accomplished through the market and the political process.

4. In the second and third phases, it was the experience of failure and frustration which resulted in a reexamination of assumptions taken for granted, and in the birth of a new goals consciousness. The fourth phase is one in which, after controversy and debate, some general acceptance of these goals emerges and consensus is approached, at least to the extent of absence of significant opposition to the goals. In this phase, controversy centers more on the speed and the means with which to pursue the goals than on the goals themselves. It is also the phase in which the mutual relationship between performance goals, especially a desirable rate of growth, and achievement goals is recognized. I do not suggest that concern with education or health is something new. But what is characteristic of this phase of development is the recognition that the development of resources (economic growth) is desirable because it promotes achievement of the many goals we are pursuing. Equally characteristic of this phase is the recognition that pursuit of the goals, in such fields as education, research, industrial modernization, urban development, and so on, contributes to economic growth. At this phase it becomes urgent to study the mutual interrelationship between economic performance on the one side of the ledger, and the resources which are mobilized and utilized in pursuit of individual and collective goals on the other side. Various goals have a different impact on economic growth. Therefore, growth depends not only on the intensity of efforts in pursuit of goals but also on the combination of goals which is selected for pursuit through the public and private sectors of the economy.

In this phase, goals research becomes feasible because some consensus is evolving about goals which are desired. Goals research becomes required because choices need to be made about priorities and combinations of goals and the manner in which to pursue them. Here the need for scientific guidance arises. It is the phase which we have now entered.

THE APPROACH TO GOALS RESEARCH

Partly in response to the shock that the Soviet space achievement brought to the American public, President Eisenhower appointed a Commission on National Goals. The report of that Commission, published in 1960, was significant in that a group of outstanding leaders from different walks of life recognized the importance of a critical examination of our national goals, but no attempt was made to evaluate what advances could and should be made with respect to these goals and what the costs would be either in terms of dollars or of resources. Also, the compatibility of the several goals and the relative priorities in pursuit of them were not examined. Nonetheless, the work of the Eisenhower

Commission was very significant because it helped to articulate the rising concern for national goals. Many studies followed, concerned with individual goals, such as education, health, research, and others. The National Planning Association recognized the need for providing information for those concerned with the totality of, and the interrelationships among, the national goals. It established a Center for Priority Analysis in response to that need.

The present first study of the Center for Priority Analysis deals with the economics of national goals. That means, it deals with the resources utilized in the pursuit of the goals. The economics of goals is only one of several aspects of goals research, and even the economics of goals cannot be merely economics. By their nature, goals are related to the basic values of a society and in that respect reach beyond economics. Economics is concerned with the development and use of resources and with the resources needed for accomplishing goals. This is, however, not the same as saying that we are concerned only with the means which serve given ends. For example, one of the resources involved is manpower. Manpower, however, is human beings, and work is a part of human life. Human beings and the quality of life are ends. Therefore, the manner in which human resources are used and the conditions under which managers and laborers work are means in one sense and ends in another.

We are dealing with the distribution of resources among various goals. But the manner by which the use of resources is determined (e.g., the freedom of individuals to choose among existing opportunities) is also a goal. Some functions must be determined and possibly performed by government, and some degree of compulsion and regulation is inevitable. These positive and negative values cannot be measured. When the economist in our culture speaks of the "dollar costs of national goals" he specifically assumes that he is working within the frame of a social system in which human self-determination is one of the major goals and in which some degree of compulsion is inevitable. He cannot measure to what extent the goal of human freedom and dignity is or is not accomplished. He also cannot measure to what extent respect for human freedom and dignity promotes or hinders achievements of other goals. But the fact that it cannot be measured does not mean that the goal of human freedom will be omitted from the economist's analysis. It enters as a restraint in the consideration of means to be selected in the pursuit of goals. In determining, for example, a feasible and desirable rate of growth, the degree of controls which will be needed should be considered.

Goals-consciousness does not mean that all deficiencies in goals will be or should be remedied by direct government action. The largest part of resources is allocated through the market mechanism by individuals—as consumers, as workers, as farmers, as managers of corporations, and so on. The result of the allocation of resources by the market and political processes can be and is observed and should be appraised. Achievements and deficiencies are noted. All over the country, groups of experts and citizens ask themselves such questions as: Does our educational system give us satisfactory results? Do we make necessary advances in physical and mental health? Do we provide the basic and applied research needed for technological progress? Are our homes and cities adequate by modern standards of living and transportation? Are we conquering poverty and eliminating race discrimination in our own country? Are we contributing adequately to the development of allied and friendly countries in other parts of the world? If there are serious deficiencies in achieving goals, how can the market mechanism be improved to remedy the deficiencies? What government action may be needed to remedy deficiencies in the market mechanism and to improve the performance in the public sector? These and similar questions regarding goals are raised and debated by many individuals and organizations throughout the United States. Goals research as conceived here would not provide the answers to these questions, but could contribute information for those seeking an answer.

SOME BASIC CONCEPTS

In the attempt to make goals amenable to research it is useful to introduce some distinguishing concepts. Of all performance goals, the most important is the rate of economic growth. Here we distinguish three interrelated sets of assumptions. First, it is possible to estimate the probable rate of growth that would result from continuation of *present policies* of Government and *present attitudes* of business, labor, and consumers. A present policy rate of growth might give us, for example, a rate of 3% per annum or less for the United States. With continued increase in the labor force and productivity-raising technology (but present hours of work), this rate of growth would result in a rapid rise in the rate of unemployment and heavy cyclical fluctuations. A change in the attitudes of business and labor and in Government policies would certainly follow. To evaluate these changes, it is necessary to construct a second model of growth which would prevent a rise of unemployment, counteract recessions, make it possible to realize desirable objectives, but would not require drastic controls. This construction gives us the *target* rate of growth and a device for considering the change in policies and attitudes consistent with that target. Let us assume that we reach the conclusion that, considering all factors involved, a long-term rate of growth of 4.5% should be the target. Now why is not the sky the limit for a target? Why 4.5% and not 6 or 8%? The highest sustainable rate of growth compatible with other national objectives is believed to be 4.5%. Aiming at a substantially higher rate of continuing growth would be likely to create conflicts between the goals of domestic growth and international balance of payments, or might necessitate Government controls not believed acceptable under peacetime conditions but deemed necessary in order to prevent bottlenecks and price rises. This is where the previously mentioned restraints become important.

The establishment of targets of economic performance is useful for a consideration of policies. The setting of targets, however, is not prediction. In order to make projections which may be needed as realistic benchmarks for the guidance of business decisions and many other purposes, we introduce as a third concept a *judgment* rate of growth. An estimate, in this case, is based on the assumption that policies and attitudes will change in the direction of the changes required by the targets. In reality, attitudes change only after some time has lapsed, and there will be slippages in the process of formulation, legislative adoption, and implementation of policy changes. To continue our numerical illustration we assume that the long-term judgment rate of growth in the United States will be somewhat above 4% which is less than the target rate but substantially more than the present-policy rate of growth.

We make similar distinctions with respect to achievement goals. The base estimate is again that of a continuation of the present condition, in this case the continuation of present standards in education, health, and so on, for determining the costs of goals. We assume, for example, that for each category of schools, costs per pupil remain the same. Corresponding estimates can be made for the other achievement goals. Total costs rise only because of increase in population, changes in the age and occupational distribution of the population, and movement of the population from rural to urban communities. Actually, a large part of the prospective increase in the production of goods and services is "preempted" by the need to provide for a growing and increasingly urbanized population.

Estimates of the *preempted* increase in production are significant because they are based on continuation of present political and individual preferences and take account mainly of the relatively predictable increase in population of various age groups, and of trends in geographic and occupational shifts in the population. The fact that a large part of the expected increase in the economic potential will be absorbed by rising use of resources for existing goals narrows the amount of resources which can be mobilized and utilized by future *discretionary* decisions about new goals or improved standards for existing goals.

The next step, also with respect to achievement goals, is the formulation of targets which reflect the need to provide for rising standards in addition to the rise and shift in population. The combination of the desired improvement in standards with the rise and changing distribution of population gives us the *aspiration goals.* These reflect what knowledgeable people regard as desirable achievement and what could be obtained if the specific goal under consideration were to have high priority. In other words, the estimate of aspiration goals does not allow for the fact that advocates of other goals may make claims for the same financial or real resources. These aspiration goals reflect the subjective judgment of knowledgeable people, but they are not arbitrary. They are regarded as realistic by people who are familiar with one particular field, but who do not consider the place a particular goal may have in the totality of goals.

A further step is needed to estimate *feasible priority combinations of goals.* This requires a reconciliation of the aspiration goals with projections of the judgment rate of growth. If the sum of aspiration goals exceeds the projected production total, priorities must be established. The decision-makers on priorities can best be served if they obtain information on alternative priority combinations which are internally consistent and consistent with the projected economic potential.

We have distinguished conceptually between performance and achievement goals as the two sides of an economic account (comparable to the distinction between sources and uses of funds). In the study we are directly concerned with the achievement goals. To repeat, what combination of achievement goals can be realized depends on the success in economic performance. Actually, there is a close interrelationship between the two kinds of goals. The economy will grow in a satisfactory manner only in the pursuit of national goals. Conversely, little progress in the direction of achieving our goals can be made if the economy fails to grow in a satisfactory manner.

The achievement goals include the goals of individuals and their families, the goals of businesses to modernize and expand their operations, the goals pursued through government programs at Federal, state, and local levels. Thereby it becomes possible to relate the resources in dollars or manpower required for each goal, and for all goals combined, to a total Economic Budget (total gross national product), or to a total manpower budget for the nation as a whole. This makes goals research operational.

QUALITY AND QUANTITY

The quantification of the costs of goals in a manner which makes them comparable with resource availabilities is essential for making goals research applicable. However, we cannot express qualities in quantities without losing something. While some such loss is unavoidable, the goals researcher and those using the findings of goals research must be fully aware of this limitation. I have already referred to the fact that ultimate goals such as human dignity and freedom enter quantitative goals research only as a restraint on policies (e.g., minimizing government regulation and controls). Goals research is not directly concerned with ultimate values but with the proximate values–such as national security, individual well-being, and cultural achievements–on which people can often agree who disagree on ultimate values.

There are goals in our civilization which have become goals only because we have to compensate for "costs" which are not measured in our usual cost accounting. Combating pollution of air and water, restoring scenic beauty, and providing for recreational facilities are activities that belong in this category. These are goals, costly goals in our society, even though of lesser need in less industrialized societies. The importance of these goals affects the comparability of costs of goals between countries of different culture.

Expressing the production of goods and services in terms of GNP also disregards certain qualities. With rising national income, consumers can buy more goods–this is reflected in GNP. But with rising ability to buy, the consumer also obtains a greater freedom of choice in the use of his income, which is a source of additional satisfaction (although sometimes also of a headache). On the other hand, our society compels the individual to spend money on socially prescribed clothing or on commuting, which may be items of not unqualified "enjoyment" and might better be treated as social costs rather than as fulfillment of goals. Nevertheless, in our system of national economic accounts (or national economic budgets), expenditures for these purposes are treated as consumption–and are thereby regarded as contributing to the achievement of goals.

Very important advances in quality of products or services escape statistical measurement. A substantial portion of the benefits of automation, for example, accrues to the consumer in terms not of lower costs, but of higher quality and of speedier service. It has been estimated that the improvement in the quality of goods and services corresponds to something like a 1% hidden increase in the GNP per annum. Thus, when we refer to a 4% per annum long-term increase (judgment model) in the measured supply of goods and services available for meeting our national goals, we may in reality refer to a yearly increase of 5% in the ability to meet goals and in the costing of goals.

THE NATIONAL PLANNING ASSOCIATION'S COSTING OF GOALS

In the present study by Dr. Leonard Lecht for the Center for Priority Analysis, an estimate was prepared of the measurable dollar costs which would be involved in pursuing the aspirations for each of the achievement goals of the American economy. The aspiration goals were based on estimates prepared by experts for the various fields. Again, it should be emphasized that the study is not supposed to show the aspirations of these experts, nor those of the National Planning Association (NPA) advisory committee and staff, but what are, to the best of their judgment, the aspirations of "knowledgeable people" in the respective fields. After elimination of double counting, the costs for all these goals were summed up and compared with the total annual production of goods and services which could be expected to be available at that future time. Thereby, it became possible to compare these aspiration goals with resources expected to be available to meet them.

The result of this comparison supports two broad conclusions. First, substantial advances toward the achievement of these goals appear to be feasible.

Second, not all aspirations for all goals can be met simultaneously within the given period of time.

The sum of all aspiration goals exceeds substantially what can be achieved even if a satisfactory performance of the economy is assumed. It follows that priority decisions need to be made for bringing aspirations and resources into balance. Does that mean that our experts are over-ambitious and should set their sights lower? I would not draw that conclusion at all. I believe that the experts should be ambitious for the fields with which they are concerned. They should set the sights too high rather than too low, but they should recognize that society has to reconcile goals and resources.

Every person with experience in government budget-making knows that devoted and imaginative bureau chiefs will always submit program proposals in excess of those which can be granted. This means, however, that a mechanism must exist for reconciling aspirations and resources. In Government proper, this function is performed by the Chief Executive, with the assistance of the Budget Bureau and the Cabinet, and by the Legislature.

Fifty years ago it became essential for a democracy such as the United States to develop a more meaningful budget system in order to enable the officials in the Executive and the Legislative branches of Government to base budget decisions on the best possible factual information and also to enable interested individuals to judge the wisdom of actions taken by the Government. This process of providing meaningful information for the decision-makers in Government is far advanced but by no means completed. We are today, with respect to decisions on national goals, where we were about fifty years ago in the development of government budgeting.

For national goals, the priority decisions are made by governmental processes and the market system. These actions involve every citizen, either as a decision-maker in public and private life or as a person who accepts these decisions or voices disagreement, thereby attempting to work toward changes in the future.

PERSPECTIVES IN GOALS RESEARCH

The estimates of the dollar costs of aspiration goals should be very useful for those who wish to form an opinion of the advances which can be made within the limits of available resources. We *can* go a good part of the way toward achieving the aspiration goals. However, these estimates also show the limits and the necessity for public and private decision-makers to adopt priorities in the pursuit of the goals. A necessary refinement consists in translating the dollar terms of the cost estimate into manpower requirements. This might show that, for certain goals, restraints from competing claims may become effective sooner than suggested by the dollar estimates. Work on estimating the manpower requirements for the various goals is in progress at the NPA Center for Priority Analysis.

In the present study, the costs of the goals have been added up, with adjustment only for overlapping and consequent double counting. However, the various goals are so related to each other that progress toward one goal facilitates the achievement of some of the others. In other cases, various goals compete for the same kind of manpower or other resources and, therefore, may conflict with each other. For example, up to a certain point, more adequate education and training of scientists or engineers would diminish the number of scientists and engineers immediately available for practical research work, because a longer period of education and training would be required, and a larger proportion of graduates would be absorbed by teaching rather than become available for practical work. Only in the longer run would more adequate education and training increase the quantity and quality of scientists and engineers available for research and development. Alternative combinations should therefore be presented both with a shorter and a longer time horizon. Priority analysis should aim at analyzing such relationships and presenting alternative, internally compatible packages of goals.

Thus, one function of goals research aims at trying out alternative priority combinations of goals that are compatible with each other and with the resources that can be activated in their pursuit. Another function of goals research is the study of the manner in which the forces of society are mobilized in pursuit of these goals. We said before that our society became goals-conscious through failure and frustration. However, a steady, less dramatic process seems to be evolving now in which goals are more rationally formulated and forces of society are mobilized for the realization of the goals. In our democratic society, which are the key positions for determination and realization of goals? What are the motivations of individuals in these key positions? To what extent are their actions based on relevant information, and to what extent on prejudice or obsolete knowledge? What kinds of information resulting from goals research should they have? These are some of the problems on which research has been initiated through other projects of the Center for Priority Analysis.

Considering these and many other questions it is clear that the present study is merely a first—though, I believe, significant—expedition into an uncharted territory. Some other studies have been initiated and will follow. Much more needs to be done. Even this first attempt at estimating the dollar costs of our aspiration goals should be regarded as the beginning of a continuing undertaking which will need to be redone and revised periodically. Our aspirations don't stand still. What is a gleam in the eye of some visionaries today may become a goal recognized by realistic and knowledgeable people tomorrow—and what is regarded as a goal today may become obsolete tomorrow. The establishment of the NPA Center for Priority Analysis and the publication of this book testify to the belief that goals research will have to play an important role in our dynamic democratic society.

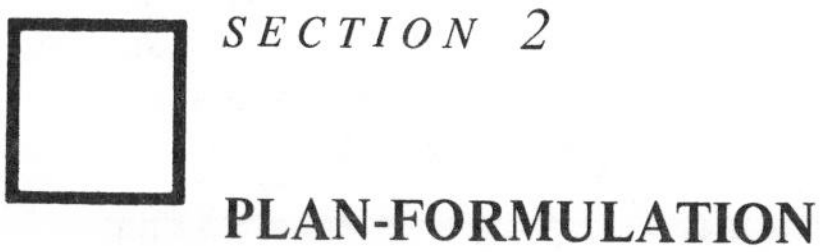

SECTION 2

PLAN-FORMULATION

INTRODUCTORY NOTE

In conformance with the rational model of the plan-making process, the planner, having identified the goals and objectives of his community (city or metropolitan area), next prepares a design (or plan) or several alternative designs or plans, meant to be the means for realizing the community's goals. Until about twenty years ago (and to a much less extent since then), the most common procedure used by the planner to formulate his plan could be characterized as follows: the plan-formulation process begins with a survey of population, employment, land use, and streeet traffic, including forecasts of trends in each of their variables; then these data are translated into forecasts of future needs for land, highways, schools, and other public facilities, based on a set of agreed-upon standards. Based on these forecasts of needs and the approved list of goals, he develops a land use, circulation, and community facilities plan for the next twenty to thirty years; often he also recommends development of one or more public housing projects, recreation areas, and other special projects, such as a civic center. The plan is expressed principally by a map depicting the ultimate pattern of physical development for the area and the public facilities essential to its functioning.

This approach to the nature of the city plan dates back to the 1920s when the legislation and concept behind the master plan were formulated by persons such as the lawyer Edward Bassett (1938), who stated in his book on the master plan that the scope of the plan should be limited to what can be shown on a municipal map: elements like streets, sidewalks, street trees, parks, streams, lakes, public building sites, and the general districts for which private land should be zoned. Most of the plans prepared prior to 1950 epitomized this viewpoint. The entire plan was shown on one sheet of paper—the map on one side and the assumptions, goals, standards, and development principals on the reverse; or, if brevity was among the planner's virtues, along the margin.

This oversimplified view of planning is rapidly becoming extinct. The belief that a single plan or a single mind can or should plan for the future development of an entire community is being replaced by a greater sense of the complexities of city growth and of the planning process. Disappearing, too, is the traditional master map-making approach with its emphasis on streets, buildings, and so forth. (Graphic plans remain, but these are incidental elements and not the primary expression of the master plan.) The planner no longer puts exclusive emphasis on the long-range comprehensive plan, a single document that purportedly harmonizes all aspects of the urban environment. Rather, planning is now viewed as a process- and program-oriented team activity, moving towards provisional goals rather than delineating ideal end-states to be achieved at some future date. Planners now think in terms of both long-range plans (twenty or more years) as well as short and middle-range programs (three-to-ten years' focus). Moreover, the scope of planning and of plans and programs now extends as broadly as the problems to which planning can be addressed—be they physical, social, economic, or political; or functional, such as health, public safety, transportation, social welfare, education, leisure, and housing and urban design.

Reflecting this new concept of the nature of planning, J. Brian McLoughlin, in his paper in Chapter 5, argues that since the city is viewed today as a dynamic, open, interdependent system evolving in response to many influences, it is logical to suggest that plans for it should be cast in similar form. In his paper, McLoughlin describes the implications of this "systems view of plans." He likens the planner to a helmsman steering the city: the plan is the charted course showing where the city should go and how it can get there. The basic form of a plan should be a statement which describes how the city will evolve in a series of steps, say five years at a time, thus focusing the planner's attention on the well-being of the city at all times and not simply at some distant future date.

Also disappearing along with the single-sheet, one-shot view of the master plan is the corresponding concept of the methodology used by the planner to prepare his recommended plan. Since the early 1950s, a new approach to plan-formulation has become fairly common. As discussed by J. Brian McLoughlin in Chapter 5, it has two distinguishing characteristics: (a) it focuses on the formulation of alternative plans or proposals—what McLoughlin refers to as various "trajectories" of the urban system, sequences of the states or courses through which the system might pass in the years ahead; and (b) it uses new mathematical techniques, particularly computerized models, to aid in formulating the alternatives.

There are several reasons why planners turned to the development of alternatives, in contrast to the traditional one-shot plan, perhaps the most important being politicians and public now seeking greater involvement in the plan-making process. The submission of alternative plans (with the attendant evaluations–a subject discussed in Section 3) to elected officials and the citizenry provides an opportunity for public discussion about the key issues facing the community, such as environmental pollution, economic growth, race and poverty.

In a recent review of the plan-making process in thirteen metropolitan planning programs (Boyce et al., 1970), the authors identified two methodological stages in the formulation of alternatives: (a) generating the organizational principles or concepts of each alternative plan; and (b) elaborating and detailing the land use and transportation alternatives, following the identification and selection of the generative concepts. The first stage commonly uses methods such as: (1) identifying a series of "plan forms," each exhibiting a singular organizing principle for the physical structure of the area, e.g. concepts such as "linear city," "satellite towns," "compact city," and "spread city"; (2) varying the assumptions about the development process itself and/or the exercise of planning powers affecting development; (3) specifying alternative sets of development objectives and/or design standards; and (4) identifying alternative responses to key problems and formulating alternative plans for key structuring systems such as sewers, highways, etc. (Note that the second and third methods correspond closely to those suggested by McLoughlin in his paper.)

In the second stage of elaborating the alternatives, the authors found increasing use of computer models of land use and urban growth and development for distributing population and economic activities in space. This is not surprising, as planners have been increasingly interested in the development and use of mathematical models for prediction purposes since the early 1950s. It had become clear by that time that the traditional approach to–and techniques for–predicting the future "trajectories" of urban areas was no longer useful.

Traditionally, the planner considered himself the "architect" of the city, the city-builder; thus, the basis for validating or testing his predictions was his own conventional wisdom, personal experience, judgment, persuasiveness, reputation, or intuitive design capacities. This approach reflects the architectural origins of the profession where the client layman tends to rely on the professional judgment of his architect which he does not question; indeed, in most cases, the client is unable to visualize his building from the architectural drawings. But, clearly, predicting the consequences of a plan for an urban area is of an entirely different order of difficulty than a judgment about how a person's soon-to-be-built house is likely to function and look. An urban area is a very complex functional entity in which people, businesses, and institutions interact vigorously, and in which most development takes place under private initiative, often not completely subject to direct public control, and in response to influences and forces which are not yet fully understood. The use of mathematical models, especially simulation models, held the promise of providing the planner with improved capability for understanding the forces and factors affecting growth and development of his community and thus predicting the various states through which it might pass, given certain assumptions as to policy and external conditions.

As in the case of the other methodological improvements in planning, discussed in this volume, no one person or event was responsible for these changes in the approach to plan-formulation, although several people and events can be singled out for their special contributions.

Much of the impetus for these new methodological developments is attributed to the spate of metropolitan transportation studies initiated by the planning and building of the federal interstate highway system in the late 1950s. These studies focused the attention of many highway planners and engineers on the need for much better methods for urban transportation planning. The Federal Highway Act for the first time required the use of new planning methods in a comprehensive transportation planning process in each metropolitan area as a requisite for federal aid for highway construction.

The approach that began to evolve was founded on the development of several alternative metropolitan land use and transportation plans as the basis for adopting a comprehensive development plan and program for a region. The Boyce et al. review found that the consideration of alternative comprehensive metropolitan land use and transportation plans has become the focus of planning activities of most large metropolitan regions since the mid-1950s.

One of the early path-breaking metropolitan transportation studies was the Penn-Jersey Transportation Study (which came to be known as PJ). Under the intellectual leadership of Britton Harris, who was its director of research (and whose article, "Quantitative Models of Urban Development," is included as Chapter Six of this book), PJ planners began work on a simulation model to test the respective potential impacts over time of alternative staged "packages" of public policies, especially in transportation. They also included urban renewal, housing, open space, public finance, metropolitan organization, and other elements of urban policy. PJ was destined to have the most profound long-range effects on the development of models for urban planning and urban development; although its immediate practical impact on the Philadelphia region may have been limited, it stimulated a whole host of related research in universities and in transportation study agencies around the country.

One of the better examples of the more recent regional transportation studies was undertaken by the Southeastern Wisconsin Regional Planning Commission. Its work is included as a case study in Part Two of this volume.

The development and use of mathematical models for planning had its beginnings in the early 1950s. One of the pioneers was J. Douglas Carroll, Jr., who began to apply, first in Detroit and then in Chicago (the latter with the pioneering Chicago Area Transportation Study known as CATS), large-scale data-handling techniques to the prediction of traffic movement among diverse land users. Alan M. Voorhees (1955) constructed and tested a gravity model to explain urban movement. Gerald A. P. Carrothers, in a 1956 issue of the AIP Journal, presented an historical review of the gravity and potential concepts of human interactions–perhaps the first article to appear in that journal on the potential users of mathematical models in urban planning. And in 1959 a special issue of the AIP Journal, edited by Voorhees, was devoted to a review of the emerging new models.

Based on the foundation laid in the 1950s, the following decade saw an enormous increase in urban modeling activity, with significant advances in the subject matter covered and techniques used. To a great extent, this activity was stimulated and financed by the federally assisted community renewal programs (CRP's). One of the more significant of these efforts was the San Francisco Community Renewal Simulation Model, developed by Arthur D. Little, Inc. (ADL) for the San Francisco Community Renewal Program. The paper in Part Two, by the staff of the San Francisco Department of City Planning, describes what the model was intended to do, records the changes that have been made, notes and evaluates the most recent operations of the model, and makes recommendations regarding its further development and its potential for use in the progress of the department and the city.)

In addition to their use for explanation and prediction purposes, the new mathematical techniques together with the computer are also being experimented with actually to "design" the alternative plans themselves. Under this approach, the plan-designer first selects an objective to be maximized or minimized–for example, to minimize the amount of substandard housing or the total cost of construction, or to maximize employment opportunities or choice of housing. He then formulates a number of conditions which must be met by the plan, such as budgetary restraints, land use restrictions, density limitations, accessibility considerations, and so on. The computer can then find feasible solutions if they exist and can improve upon these solutions until the "best" pattern or "least cost" has been achieved. The plan-designer can experiment with different formulations by varying the objectives or the restraints.

The land use plan design model described by Kenneth J. Schlager in Chapter Seven of this volume (which was developed for the Southeastern Wisconsin Regional Planning Commission referred to above) is one of the outstanding examples of this newer approach to the design process. Using linear programming, the objective in this experimental solution was to minimize total public and private investment costs, subject to a number of design restraints including (a) a set of design standards in terms of restrictions on land use relationships and (b) a set of needs or demands for each type of land use based on a forecast of future urban activities. The problem, as stated, was to "synthesize a land use plan design that satisfies both the land use demands and design standards considering the current state of both natural and man-made land characteristics, at a minimal combination of public and private costs." The output of the program was a complete land use plan.

Because of the tremendous progress that had been made in model development by the mid-1960s, the AIP Journal in 1965 issued a reprise of the earlier Voorhees number, this time edited by Britton Harris. It emerged, in the words of the editor, "with new faces in the chorus and with a somewhat jazzier orchestration . . . [, a] sampler from the second act of model development" (Harris, 1965).

The new approach to plan-formulation, in particular the preparation of alternatives, would have been impossible were it not for the advances in high-speed computer development. Anyone who has experienced or observed the process of comprehensive plan-making for a city or large metropolitan area is aware of the volume of detailed work that rapidly becomes unmanageable, the problem of quality control over a large clerical staff, the interrelationships that are often overlooked, the simplifying assumptions made, and the detailed consistency checks abandoned–all in the interest of getting the job done to meet some deadline. The advantages in using the computer for helping the planner put together his alternative plans are twofold. First, it enables the enormous volume and detail of work involved in the preparation of alternatives to be rapidly handled and the results to be quickly produced. Second, given this flexibility in generating plans, it gives the planner much more opportunity to test a greater number of alternatives–including new policies and programs and different combinations of policies and programs–and to quickly assess the implications of these alternatives.

While many of the mathematical models did not at once become operational, this is perhaps less significant than the fact that there *has* been group progress in planning competence. The judgment of an individual professional, which previously was the sole criterion, is limited by his personal capacity and experience, but the predictive capability initiated by investigations undertaken by metropolitan and transportation studies, by CRP's around the country and by others, is susceptible to considerable improvement just because it is a synergistic activity. Each study builds on the achievements of its forerunners. The current approach to the validation and testing of plans extends the prediction period significantly, and, with the use of modern computers, enables the testing of a substantially greater number of alternatives in much greater detail and more rapidly than is possible by manual methods.

Simulation modeling is still generally in its infancy, and should continue to influence significantly the theory and practice of urban planning. Most importantly, it should make the planner more effective. There remain, however, many unresolved technical problems and issues regarding the utility and accuracy of models for planning purposes. In his paper, Chapter 6, which reviews the nature and characteristics of different types of models, Britton Harris discusses some of these issues and offers suggestions for resolving them.

From another direction, an entirely new approach to formulating plans for the future has arisen. It is called "futures" planning or "futuristic" planning.[1] This is promoted, not so much by urban and regional planners, although some of them participate, but by persons quite diverse in background, including economists, political scientists, sociologists, biologists, psychiatrists, scientists of all kinds, and engineers. It's been said that these "futurists" or "futurologists" constitute a new profession for the study of the future, having made prophecy a serious and highly organized enterprise. While this new approach to planning has been oriented thus far primarily to world and national planning for economic development and population growth, and to corporate, managerial, and defense planning, there has recently been an interest in its application to cities and metropolitan areas.

Futures planning as described and prescribed by futurists is different from planning *for* the future; it is an attempt to manipulate or plan *the* future. A basic characteristic of this orientation is the use of such terms as "designing," "inventing," or even "making" the future. When the future is being planned for, rather than designed, the implication is that the planner is trying to make specific and limited accommodations to the broad and overall characteristics of the future he considers either immutable or too formidable to be fundamentally rearranged or restructured. Futurists argue that traditional or non-futures planning does not challenge the future in its entirety, nor does it conceptualize it in its full range. That is to say, the planner looks at the future as if it were a mystical externality to which his plans would have to respond, conform, or selectively resist. Thus, for instance, planning for growth is not the same as planning growth, which in futures terms would require an explicit decision to make growth the future or an aspect of it. Inventing and designing best describe this orientation.

The crucial activities involved in futures planning are the following: to project alternative futures that are more or less likely to occur in terms of available as well as new forecasting methods, to choose between these alternatives in terms both of feasibility and desirability—based on benefit/cost analysis as well as less quantifiable but more explicit normative criteria, and to construct the time sequence of a matrix showing likely and desirable policies and "chance" events (i.e. perturbations) that would increase the probability of achieving the chosen future among the many possible futures.

Two additional characteristics of futures planning, it is claimed, differentiate it from present practices. One is the almost brutal emphasis on the total system, i.e. that it is the future of the whole rather than the future of the part which needs inventing; the second, perhaps even more significant, is the emphasis on the fact that the "invented" future—being probabilistic and uncertain, both as to its feasibility and desirability—must accommodate, or rather not pre-empt, its own future, unlike end-state plans.

The impact of designing the future as a new approach depends to a great extent on the quality of the tools with which the alternative futures are forecast. The forecasting methodology, or "technological forecasting" as it is sometimes referred to, differs only slightly in intent from projection, prediction, and prophecy.

The method of forecasting varies in the case of different theorists and practitioners. Erich Jantsch, in his paper, Chapter 8, surveys the use and development of forecasting techniques (based on a seven-month survey in 13 countries) and identifies some 100 such techniques. Jantsch also found that in the United States it is mainly the corporate-planning or management consulting-services divisions of consulting firms that offer forecasting services to others; however, between 500 and 600 medium and large-sized American companies had established in-house forecasting function as part of their regular operations. Jantsch notes that the two approaches that seem to be making the heaviest impact on forecasting technology are operations research and systems analysis. Based on his survey Jantsch classifies the many techniques he found into four main groups: (1) exploratory, (2) normative, (3) feedback, and (4) intuitive.

Despite the differences, the method of forecasting exhibits some recognizable patterns and tendencies. As noted by Jantsch, it does not, for instance, discriminate against intuition; neither does it rely exclusively on pure cognitive processes. It consistently emphasizes the interrelatedness and interconnectedness of the many elements of the future being forecast. This clearly is an outgrowth of systems analytic methodology, and hence the future is perceived and analyzed as a dynamic and more or less open system. In this system the many components or subsystems can only be described and then projected in terms of their complex interrelationships with other systems. This mapping activity is often better carried out if the boundaries of the future system being forecast are clearly defined, such as in the case of a particular technology. It is for this reason that futures forecasting is generally associated with technological forecasting since, as noted above, it is in that instance that the results of the method of forecasting, no matter what specific techniques are used, are the most fruitful in terms of confidence and reliability.

NOTE

1. The description of futures planning is based in part on a formulation provided by the editor's USC colleague, Jivan Tabibian.

Chapter 5

CHARTING POSSIBLE COURSES OF THE SYSTEM

J. Brian McLoughlin

"Plan formulation, in essence, is the choice of those projected or simulated future states of the system which yield optimum conditions. These optimum conditions are described by reference to the performance criteria derived from the goals."[1]

When dealing with complex systems it is very difficult to derive at "one shot" the optimum (or near-optimum) condition, although methods which attempt to do this are under development and will be discussed later. It is much easier to build a range of alternatives which might straddle the optimum and to test and evaluate them. A process of successive re-formulation and re-testing will then enable us to discover the best possible solution.

The alternatives referred to are of course various "trajectories" of the urban or regional system–sequences of states through which it might pass. The variation among alternatives may be induced in the simulation in a number of ways. Essentially these derive from variation in two sets of assumptions–those concerning public policies (e.g. about economic growth, housing subsidies, centralized or dispersed forms of development, land conservation, public transport, etc., etc.) and those relating to private (household, corporate and institutional) responses or initiatives. Variations in one or the other or of both in different combinations will yield a number of different trajectories of the system as its evolution is simulated (Figure 1).

The numbers of alternatives produced will depend upon a number of considerations, but the resources of time, money, manpower and data-processing equipment will be the main ones. These factors affect not only the ability to

Reprinted from *Urban and Regional Planning: A Systems Approach,* by J. Brian McLoughlin, pp. 231-235, 252-262. Published by Faber and Faber (London) and Praeger Publishers (New York).

produce the different trajectories, but also to accomplish adequate testing, evaluation and re-design.

More difficult to decide is the question of what *sorts* of alternatives to produce. Should simulation vary the future size of population and employment in the area? Or of policies for land conservation? Or particular types of activity in more detail such as extractive or recreational industries? Or of some, or all of these in combination?

Clearly the opening sentences of the chapter provide the clue. The basis of the variations should derive from the goals and objectives which have been agreed upon as the starting point for the planning program. For example, if the question of maximizing economic growth is so important that it overshadows all other goals, or indeed is the *only* goal, then obviously the basis of developing alternative trajectories will be first, different assumed rates of growth (to enable examination of what rates are feasible), different ways of achieving faster growth

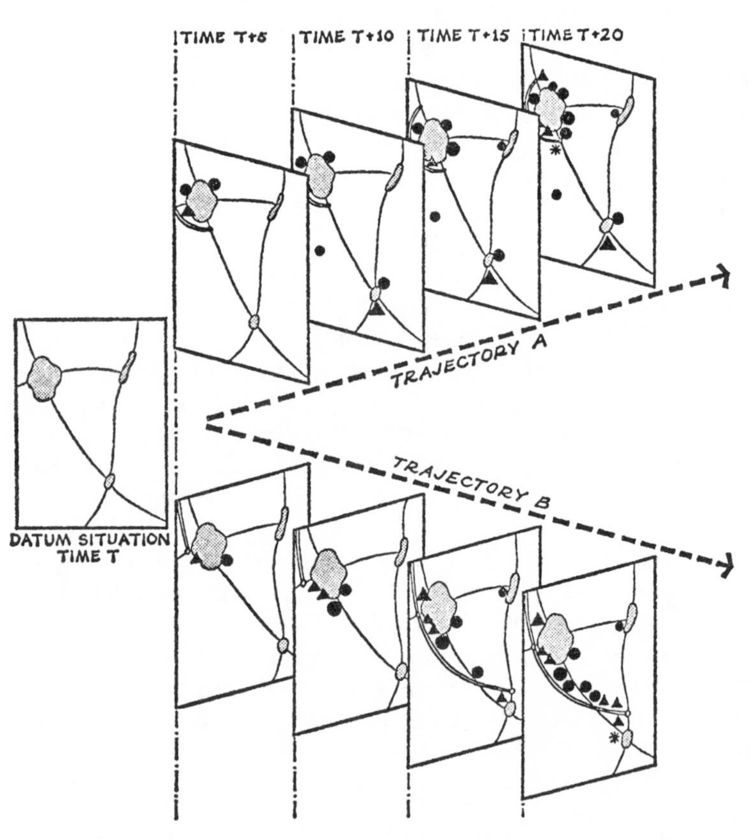

Figure 1: SYSTEM TRAJECTORIES

(e.g. by way of stimulating existing economic activity, introducing new industries, improving infrastructure together with different spatial configurations of employment centers, housing areas and so forth). Or, again, if the main goal is to maximize population growth, the variations should consist of different assumed rates of inward migration combined with diverse ways of settling the population in existing and new residential areas. In both these examples, it is not only a *constant* rate which may be varied, but also the rate at *different periods in the future.*

But if the size of the population and/or economy of the study area is not a matter of public concern and therefore does not appear in the goals statement then the variations must reflect other issues. Since we are talking about physical planning, it is variation in the spatial patterning of growth, the various "anatomies and physiologies" which the city or region could assume in the future which will enable us to derive alternatives. The same principle applies: that the variations induced should be a reflection of important goals and objectives.

If it is clear that the question of the degree of centralization or dispersal (or jobs or people, or both) which a city should have is an urgent issue, then the alternatives must reflect this. If one of the goals is to discover the optimum "mix" of public and private transport facilities these "mixes" must vary between alternatives. Similarly with other issues: conservation of agricultural land or particular areas of scientific or scenic interest, the exploitation of a major new transport facility, the location of a large center of higher education—whatever the question may be, the alternatives must be devised so as to give the best opportunity of seeking the optimum.

If alternatives are not carefully related to goals and objectives there is the real danger that they will either fail to reflect certain important issues which the planning process is being used to study, or worse still, be almost irrelevant. To spend the client's time and money on studying variations on a theme which is of little or no concern is irresponsible and may be worse than a misguided (but honest) attempt at a one-shot solution. Far too many plans have derived from the study of physical-form alternatives—e.g. "satellite towns," "linear growth," "suburban sprawl," "circuit linear," "polynucleated" (National Capitol Planning Commission, 1962).[2] Of course, it is true that in so doing, different dispositions of jobs, population, shopping and recreational areas have been studied, together with different transport systems. But it does not necessarily follow that they will have been studied in the best way since there may be little or no variation in one or more of these as between a number of physical forms. To study different physical forms *as such* is justified only where physical form *as such* is a principal issue embodied in the goal statement (as it may well be in areas of great architectural, historic or scenic attraction). Alternatives must reflect the goals sought; the means must reflect the ends.

Having established the basis on which alternative trajectories are to be generated it is necessary to decide on the form of simulation to be used. This was referred to in the closing section of the previous chapter when dealing with the projection of the system as a whole. The type of simulation chosen will depend on a number of factors: the size of the planning area, the availability of data, the data-processing resources at hand, the skills and size of staff and, of course, the time and money which can be devoted to this part of the task.

The size of the area for which plans are being prepared will influence the kind of simulation chosen. Although larger regions and towns are not *inherently* more complex as systems (complexity being governed by how the system is defined), nevertheless, for a given size-range of component—say an employment concentration of about 1,000 jobs and a residential unit of around 2,000-3,000 persons it is obvious that greater complexity is encountered in larger settlements, if only because the number of possible states of the system increases drastically with the number of its components. Thus, relatively simple simulation methods might suffice for small-to-medium sized planning areas but more sophisticated methods will be needed in those of bigger population unless of course a very coarse-zone approach is being made, perhaps as a prelude to more intensive analysis.

Very often the quality of data will strongly influence the choice of simulation method. For example, if full demographic economic and "land" data are available at a fine-zone level for two or more dates including a datum year, it is possible to choose a sophisticated simulation method which might model the growth patterns of the area in terms of a large number of small zones. However, if consistent data is lacking for such fine zones, being available for say twenty local authority areas only in a large conurbation, then this may limit the choice initially to a twenty-zone simulation model of fairly modest design.

Obviously the choice will be influenced by data-processing resources. If one has only an electric calculating machine and the very occasional use of a small computer it is no good trying to devise and operate a simulation process involving hundreds or thousands of calculations to achieve one step. Equally, the trap of attempting "big" simulations merely because one happens to have access to a large computer should be avoided.

If the planning exercise is working to a strict deadline this will inevitably encourage the use of simple methods of proven effectiveness. Last, and by no means least, the director of the operation will of course, choose a simulation method which he knows can be understood and operated with confidence by his staff, although a certain amount of learning on the job may be admitted as a calculated risk.

Four broad types of simulation process will now be described in outline.*

THE PLAN-MAKING PROCESS IN GENERAL

We have discussed the relationship of possible alternative system trajectories to varied goals and objectives, looked at a number of technical procedures for

*Not included herein.—Ed.

generating these trajectories via simulation, and finally pointed out that on occasions "one-shot" equilibrium states can be studied in appropriate circumstances. We must now attempt a summary description of the sequence of operations by which the recommended land use and transportation plan is designed. This will of necessity include a number of *evaluative and testing* operations which are mentioned for the sake of completeness here, although their detailed treatment is deferred to the next chapter.

No better outline of the plan-making process has been given than that by Mitchell (1959) to a Presidential Committee. He begins by listing the prerequisites: inventories (survey information) of present transportation facilities and services; movements of persons, goods and vehicles; population, employment and land use; the economics and financing of developments in land and transport; the various powers and responsibilities of central and local governments and other public bodies concerned with urban and regional development; the best possible projections of population, employment, income and economic growth for the area as a whole.

Next, and drawing in part from these previous studies, a dynamic metropolitan growth model needs to be constructed, expressing the relationships among the components and influences on the future area distribution of population, jobs and land uses. The model must include variables which describe the "amount, nature and location of transportation facilities and services."

Parallel with this a traffic model is necessary which will generate, distribute and assign (to networks) the movements which will be demanded between sub-areas. This model will have been derived from origin/destination data related to land uses and "other commonly found generative factors."[3] Also, a model or sub-routine is needed to assign the expected movements to the networks and to divide such movements into those which would be made by private and public means.

With these major tools at hand, the goal-and-objectives part of the process must be carried to the stage at which clear principles emerge for the generation of alternative land use and movement problems.

Now, using the metropolitan growth model and holding transportation considerations constant (i.e. assuming past trends to continue and commitments to be binding in road building, public transport and parking policy) a first spatial distribution of population and major employment types is made. On this "land use" basis, alternative transportation (i.e. networks and public transport systems) schemes which vary the emphasis given to public and private means are tried out.

The metropolitan growth model is again used, this time allowing the different access-opportunities embodied in the alternative transportation schemes to influence the spatial distributions of population and employment. At this point therefore we have a set of internally consistent land use and transportation plans.

But the public transport and road networks have not been tested to see in more detail what sizes and levels of service would be required to cope with the expected volumes. The traffic assignment model must now be called upon to produce this information. Study of the results may show that certain of the alternatives are not feasible. For example, one may depend upon a high degree of private vehicle usage and call for very large expenditures on new road construction. Another may demand levels of service in certain parts of the public transport system which are likely to be unattainable within the bounds of reasonable investments.

The remainder should not be subjected to first-level cost/benefit analysis to help determine the most efficient "mix" of public and private transportation.

At this stage a near-optimal land use and transportation plan should have emerged "which is both desired and apparently attainable." Further refinements in land use dispositions and transportation systems should be attempted until the best balance is attained (see also Chapin, 1965: 458).

The remainder of the process of plan-making comprises an assessment of the capital and operating costs involved, the public powers available or desirable for accomplishing the plan, and the "long-range programming of stages of development . . . studies should be made to assure that at obvious stages the transportation system will function effectively." Arrangements should be made for further study and revision as necessary, for the preparation of more detailed development plans'—e.g. for roads, public transport, recreation and schools and "comprehensively for smaller areas within the metropolitan region in the spirit of the general plan."

If this work were to follow strictly the ideal sequence of the planning process set out in Chapter 5 [of the book], description of the form and content of general plans would follow discussion of the evaluation of alternatives. By now it is obvious that such a sequential treatment is not possible down to the last detail. Furthermore, this is a convenient point at which to deal with plan content.

FORM AND CONTENT OF PLANS

In Chapters 7 and 8 [of the book] we discussed the description and the projection and simulation of our system and foreshadowed the manner in which plans may be expressed and the material they should contain. We said then that the essence of describing an urban system is to indicate the locations and sizes of various types of activities and spaces, and the patterns and volumes of communications and channels. Such a description indicates the state of the system at a point in time; a sequence of these will describe a sequence of states, that is, a trajectory. We have now seen how projection and simulation produce such system trajectories; we shall deal in the next chapter with the selection of one of these to be recommended as a plan.

The form of the plan is therefore that of a trajectory of states at suitable time-intervals (say five years). The manner of presentation in general should be designed to be as lucid and informative as possible and at the same time to serve as a satisfactory tool for day-to-day implementation and control. It must be comprehensible to the general public and their elected representatives, and suitable for use by the planner and his fellow-professionals in the public service. Obviously, the principal documents must make the fullest use of all appropriate means of communication—the written word, maps and diagrams, charts and tables. But let us begin in the middle, so to speak, and work outwards.

The central core of the plan's content will be the trajectory of system states produced in the technical office. Each of these will consist of a map or other cartographic device which indicates the amount of each activity type located in a fairly large number of small areas. These areas will be the basic spatial units used in all the technical work or larger groupings of these. For example, if the basic unit has been the 1-kilometer square of the national grid, or the wards and parishes, then a system-state description will be provided by indicating the amount of each activity in all of these "cells" or some aggregation of them. If the activity classification comprised two types of population, a socio-economic "indicator" and four types of economic activity, then seven figures in each cell would describe the *activity* element in the system-state. And if "spaces" were described by, say, area of land in non-agricultural uses, area in agricultural use, area not used, numbers of dwellings, shopping floor space and manufacturing floorspace, then six numbers per cell would describe the *spaces* element in the state of the system.

The *communications* element may be described either by an inter-zonal flow matrix, or by a diagrammatic representation, or both, for each main type of communication being considered (e.g. morning peak, home-work, private cars; 16 hour day commercial vehicle trips). If the technical procedures used have included the assignment of these flows to the networks, then a separate description of these may be unnecessary; if not, a map or maps showing the main *networks* being considered must be produced.

A series of such documents, one for each state or time period in the trajectory could serve as an irreducible minimum for professional planners to understand and operate. But even they would probably feel the need for something more communicative for many purposes. An obvious development is to produce from these core statements a series of simple maps, preferably in color notation, which indicate the general form of the city or region showing its main land uses and transportation networks at each stage of its evolution. Each one could be annotated to show totals of population, employment, areas of land devoted to each major activity, and any other matters of interest and importance (Figure 2). It is a great help if significant areas of change and the preceding state are distinguished and annotated. Certain activities of particular significance could be the subject of a special series of abstracts; for example, "new" land to be used for residential purposes at each stage, and residential area improvements

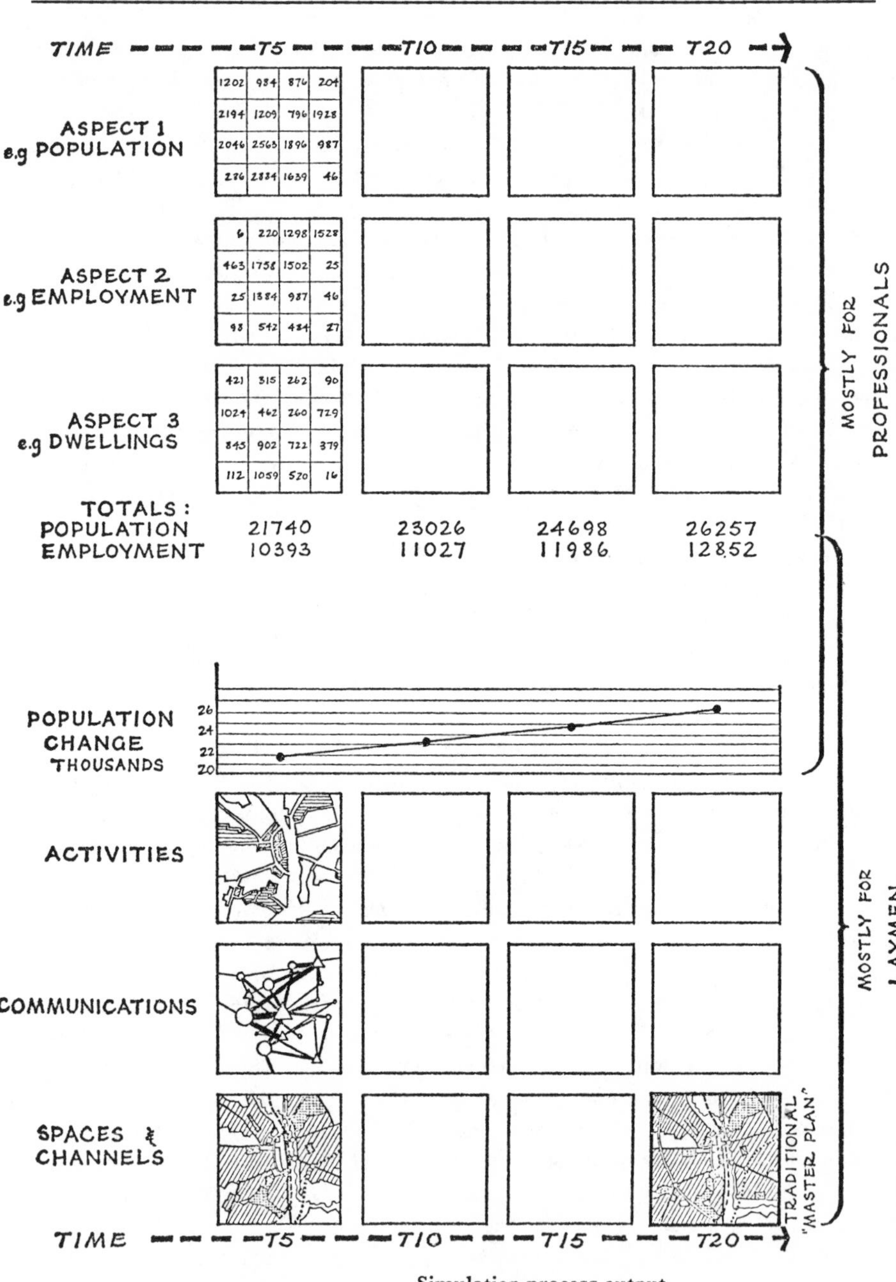

Figure 2: SIMULATION PROCESS OUTPUT

and redevelopments could form such a special series. The road and public transport systems could be given similar treatment. In an area where recreational activities are of prime importance, as at the coast and in certain inland areas, these could be picked out and highlighted by a special series of maps and diagrams (see Figure 2).

But these numerical and cartographic descriptions must be fully explained by an adequate written document. The outline which follows is illustrative only and should not be regarded as a model of form, sequence or emphasis; instead it indicates the necessary content in broad terms.

Obviously the first requirement is to tell the general reader, and especially members of the lay public, what statutory force (if any) the documents have, and where appropriate the opportunities that exist for the making of representations, who has commissioned the plan, by whom it was prepared, whether it is produced for reaction and comment as an interim statement or is presented as a final view. There should be a clear statement of the goals and objectives which the plan seeks to achieve; where necessary and possible "operational" measures can be given—e.g. to accommodate a population of 950,000 by about the year 1990, to raise the average *per capita* income of the area to £X by the same date . . . and so on.

Reference should be made to the processes of discussion and consultation which enabled these objectives to be defined, and the authority with which they are vested (e.g. are they the professional planners' assumptions based on the best available information, or were they adopted by resolution of a public body).

The ways in which these planning objectives are related to those set for larger and smaller administrative areas should be clarified as far as possible. For example, a county will refer to objectives defined at the national and regional levels and also to those of its "second-tier" local government units and other local agencies (e.g. major industrial groups and social welfare bodies).

It will not always be possible to clarify all such issues. Perhaps it has been necessary to fill out the basis of the planning exercise by making various assumptions, for example about government policy regarding the growth of employment or the level of investments in transport and housing. If this be the case, then the assumptions themselves, their logical basis, and their effects on the content of the plan must be clearly stated.

There must be a full discussion of the implications of all the foregoing matters on the major *dimensions* of the plan; that is, the expected changes in population, employment and land development. (Detailed treatments of such things as population projection, densities of development, etc., should be contained in the technical appendices which are referred to later.) As always, these changes should be expressed in programmatic terms—as stages of growth at intervals of future time. The effects of changes in major determinants such as government and local government policies, technological and social developments and in other kinds of assumptions should be estimated and the effects of such changes at different times should be distinguished. For example, if the "dimensions" of the plan in terms of economic growth have been based upon the assumption of a direct continuation of government policy, the scale of the expected effects of significant changes should be indicated, distinguishing for example between the outcome for the area if such changes occurred early as opposed to later in the planning period.

The heart of the matter in such a document is to explain fully how *alternative spatial distributions* of the main elements (population, employment, recreation, shopping and commercial districts, the transportation networks, etc.) were arrived at, and how the recommended plan was isolated. The reasoning behind each alternative must be explained and include an account of the public policy/private aspiration "bundle" relating to each alternative. It must be shown that each one is internally consistent, and how it would affect patterns of land development and of movement. The resulting trajectories–sequences of change in the spatial distribution of main elements–should be described as fully as is necessary; this verbal treatment will be clearly cross-referenced with the statistical, diagrammatic and cartographic statements mentioned earlier in this chapter. Again, detailed explanations of the technical methods by which the trajectories were derived should be given in an appendix.

The criteria by which the alternatives were tested and evaluated should be listed and arguments advanced for each in turn, and for all the criteria collectively. The exclusion of any particular criterion which might seem obvious should be explained. The relationships between the chosen criteria and planning objectives should be indicated. Finally, the "weighting" given to each criterion when combined to produce a final selection should be the subject of reasoned argument, which should include a demonstration of the effects of altering the weighting and a discussion of the implications for choice. For example, the recommended plan may have emerged because of a particular combination of "weights" for, say, total travelling time and amount of land used for new residential development. It may be that slightly different weighting of these criteria would result in another plan alternative being the "winner" (Hill, 1968). Obviously, then, the basis for the choice of these criteria and their degree of emphasis needs full and cogent argument. If the problem of weighting has been approached by attempting to reduce as many measurements as possible to terms of money, then the basis of assumptions about unit costs and the conversion of expenditure to capital sums should be carefully explained.

Finally, a full verbal account of the sequences of change in the patterns of land use and movement should be given. There should be a brief review of the evolution of the area over a period (of say, 50 years) in broad outline, drawing attention to any salient features (e.g. the effects of a technological development in the area's principal industry, the building of an important new road or the discovery of a new mineral resource).

Next, the "state of the system" at the datum year, the year to which most of the factual information relates, should be described, drawing out the principal problems which physical planning is capable of tackling. Then, the narrative should continue with a clear but flowing treatment of the stage-by-stage evolution of the area as recommended in the plan (cross-referenced always with the maps and figures described earlier). Particular mention should be made of the major public works which are proposed, the sequence in which they occur and their approximate timing. Also, the ways in which household, industrial, commercial and other preferences about location, development, movement and the quality of living and working environments will be catered for by the plan must be explained. For example, if restraint is to be placed on an expected demand for housing at certain locations then this should be explained and justified as should the encouragement of, say, commercial growth in other parts of the planning area.

The text should avoid in these sections mere re-statement in words of what has been set out clearly in numerical and map form elsewhere. It should concentrate on those aspects which are mostly suitably explained by the written word; it should not duplicate but rather *complement* the maps and figures.

A series of appendices will be necessary to cover technical details of data sources and methods, survey, analysis, projection, simulation and evaluation. A full account of recommended techniques of implementation, control and review operations will also be necessary (see Chapter 11*). This section might also cover data-management recommendations and suggestions for a "research agenda"—items needing further investigation either by the planning authority itself or by specialized research agencies—to improve data, projection, simulation, control and so forth.

In summary, the form and content of the general land use and communications plan should be designed so as to satisfy the following conditions:

(1) to give a clear indication of the sequence of states which the urban system should take up at specified times;
(2) to enable the layman, the elected representative and the professional planner to understand precisely what is intended;
(3) to make clear the arguments and assumptions on which the plan is based, including an explicit statement of goals and objectives and the degree to which these are achieved;
(4) to provide the operational means for implementing the plan by a continuous process of management of the urban system;
(5) to do all these things with the maximum clarity of communication using the most appropriate media (including cartographic, pictorial, diagrammatic, statistical/numerical and verbal means).

*Not included herein.—Ed.

NOTES

1. I am indebted to Dr. G. F. Chadwick for this form of words.
2. References not included herein.–Ed.
3. It is now becoming possible to build simple traffic models suitable for this stage of the plan-making process which do not derive from special detailed surveys of movement or from "home interviews" of a sample of households, firms etc., but in contrast are derived from "land use" data (e.g. zonal residents, workers, floorspace) and calibrated against simple volumetric traffic data, or even use assumed or "borrowed" parameters. Clearly such models are intended for use in plan-making and could not be used for the detailed design of roads, junctions etc. (Jamieson, MacKay and Latchford, 1967; Farbey and Murchland, 1967).

Chapter 6

QUANTITATIVE MODELS OF URBAN DEVELOPMENT: THEIR ROLE IN METROPOLITAN DECISION-MAKING

Britton Harris

Decision-makers and social scientists have a common interest in understanding the quantitative dimensions of metropolitan development and its functional processes. This identity of interest is expressed by the fact that each, from his own point of view, is interested in conditional predictions regarding function and development. The scientist makes use of conditional prediction as a method of testing theories. The decision-maker or the planner uses conditional predictions in a much more practical and immediate sense. He is interested in evaluating the putative consequences of innovations and changes in policy designed to affect urban processes. These evaluative forecasts are conditional predictions in identically the same sense as those made by the social scientist for the testing of theories. The difference between the approaches in these two different contexts arises not out of the formal content of the methods, but out of the selection of variables and of measurements of consequences, that is, the selection of inputs to and outputs from the predictions, which are made by means of these experiments.

Without further systematic elaboration, I will therefore assume this formal identity of interest throughout the balance of the discussion. I will bear in mind and occasionally illustrate possible divergences of focus between the social scientist and the policy-maker.

THE NATURE OF MODELS

The current vehicle for conditional prediction regarding metropolitan growth and development in this broad context is a computerized mathematical model or group of models. For purposes of this discussion, I wish to restrict the use of the term "model"; thus I find it necessary to define three distinct ways in which the term "model" is used and to focus on one of them.

Generally, a model is a representation of reality, and therefore the act of setting forth a model represents a commitment (however temporary) to a theory. For example, physicists may speak of "the Bohr model of the atom." Note, in this connection, that the model in question is carefully designed to correspond with some conception of reality; this correspondence and the intent of the scientist in identifying it clearly define such a model as a theory.

A second and very different application of the term "model" is to a purely mathematical formulation without regard to content. Some people thus speak of linear programming and dynamic programming models or of a linear regression model, with the main focus on the mathematical structure. These mathematical models are viewed as some sort of general forms with lives and identities of their own. It is perhaps not often enough remembered that these models represent no more than purely formal relationships until we specify variables, constraints, and so on—that is, until we assert that real-world phenomena have a certain mathematical form. The point is subtle but important that a model must be "of" something, and hence that a mathematical model is not a model but a form. The model or theory consists in a statement that real-world phenomena are isomorphic to or can be well represented by a particular form. The really serious difficulty here is that available mathematical forms frequently do not fit real-world phenomena, and that new forms must be invented in order to establish an isomorphism.

In order to distinguish between theories and operating models, I prefer to reserve the term "model" for an operational concept, and to suggest the substitution of the term "theory" for "model" wherever this substitution is needed, as in the case of the Bohr model above. Given this assumption, I can reiterate my earlier definition: "A model is an experimental design based on a theory."[1] This definition is certainly far from perfect, but it tends to emphasize two aspects of models that I consider to be of major importance. First, it stresses the connection between models and theories, while at the same time admitting models to be frequently truncated theories, sacrificing richness and completeness for operational purposes. It may be that a few descriptive models escape this definition because very little can be said about their related theory. Second, the definition emphasizes the experimental content of the theory, by which I mean that a model is an experimental means of putting the theory into contact with the real world. This contact of experimentalism may take a number of different forms.

It may be noted that the term "model" as defined has no mathematical or computer references, and I suppose it is possible to imagine and even to construct a model that is logical rather than mathematical, that is in fact expressed verbally, but that can nonetheless be used for experimental purposes. To continue the definition, therefore, a mathematical model is an experimental design based on a theory, in which relationships are expressed in functional form and interactions are subject to manipulation. In general, the functional relationships assumed for a model are quantitative in the sense that they imply the use of ratio scales, but this is not necessarily true, for the functional forms implied may be defined by the model design, but not by the theory. Thus, the experimental use of models tests not only the congruence of the theory with reality, but also the congruence of the model with the same reality. It is sometimes important to remember that overthrowing the latter does not necessarily overthrow the former.

THE POLICY-MAKING PROCESS

Having laid the groundwork for my discussion of models, I would like to make a few comments on the process of metropolitan policy-making. I view this process from the standpoint of a planner and, to a considerable degree, from a standpoint of a space planner. I first of all take the view that the management of the scarce resource of space is a predominant problem in metropolitan development and that social welfare and economic development problems are strongly colored by spatial considerations. Secondly, I consider that the present tendencies of development in human settlement are far from optimal and, if allowed to continue, will produce unacceptable conditions. In the light of the complexities of spatial organization, a piecemeal and problem-oriented attack on these trends is not likely to be successful. I therefore see the need for planning, which is future-oriented decision-making, and for planning which considers the total urban metropolitan system. Thirdly, since metropolitan areas change slowly, and since human artifacts in the urban environment endure for many decades, I think that our orientation to the future must have a fairly long-range view. Finally, I think that the decision-making process must contain a strong drive toward social optimality. This drive will probably not be wholly successful, but it is clear that we need to produce a much better urban environment, even if it is somewhat short of being the "best possible." To summarize, therefore, I will concentrate hereafter on optimal, long-range, metropolitan planning, with some considerable emphasis on its spatial aspects.

The planning and public decision-making process has three essential phases for purposes of the present discussion. These phases are design (or invention), prediction, and evaluation. Although the phases are encountered in that order in practice, the process is a cyclic one and can be entered at any point. Quite clearly, in particular, the general form of the criteria on which putative decisions will be evaluated must be known in advance, or the process of design may be abortive. Still further, the selection of useful policy measures, or design features, depends on some prior knowledge (however fragmentary) of the effects predicted for them.

It is conceivable that in certain contexts, this three-stage process can be collapsed into a single operation. Thus, for example, we can imagine an optimizing model of warehouse location which essentially creates successive "designs" of patterns of location, predicts their costs, and determines whether this is the best pattern or, if not, how it can be improved. At the conclusion of this process, a design has been generated whose effects are known and which is evaluated as the best achievable.[2] For this process to be readily feasible in this form, a number of conditions must be met. First, the policy design space must be tractable under systematic exploration, and consequently is desirably both continuous and unimodal. Second, the effects must be easily predicted, and either the effects themselves or their evaluation or both should be analytically derivable. Finally, the evaluative criterion must be one-dimensional, well defined, and readily calculable. In addition, it must be arrived at by a transformation which is the same function as is used in the optimum-seeking procedures themselves. These requirements, taken together, are very stringent and not easily satisfied in practice, and for this reason the actual process must usually be divided into at least the three phases discussed above. This ideal process, however, is worthwhile as a goal and as a guide to model-building.[3]

THE DIMENSIONS OF MODELING

The variety and depth of the discussion in this volume make it unnecessary for me to review in detail the history of our knowledge of the urban environment and of our attempts to extend this understanding. While there are many problems related to modeling that might bear careful scrutiny, I have chosen to limit myself to two major aspects of the problem. In the immediately following sections, I shall develop a sequence of dichotomies or antinomies which define some of the major dimensions of the strategy of model-building. In the sections following this discussion, I shall examine in some detail some of the theoretical and practical problems that have arisen in actual model construction in the general framework of land use prediction.

We may usefully define five or six dimensions of difference between various models. The following list suggests the nature of these dimensions:

(1) descriptive versus analytic,
(2) holistic versus partial,
(3) macro versus micro,
(4) static versus dynamic,
(5) deterministic versus probabilistic,
(6) simultaneous versus sequential.

We might also classify models in various ways according to the extent to which they deal explicitly or implicitly with each of the three major phases of the planning process. However, the six dimensions outlined here are centered on, but not exclusively related to, the prediction or simulation phase of planning. This is the phase of the planning process in which the economist should be particularly interested, since it deals with the representation of real-world phenomena, in the context of the behavior of individuals and firms allocating scarce resources. This view can be expanded, partly in an economic context, to consider all of those benefits and utilities that ultimately depend on public decisions.

The dimensions under consideration interact strongly with each other, and cannot usefully be considered in isolation except for purposes of discussion. The interrelations between dimensions are strong enough so that they are not perfectly orthogonal, but I do not believe that the correlation of any pair is so strong that we could usefully eliminate one of them. The variation along dimensions is not usually dichotomous, so that we could in principle generate from these six dimensions a very extensive typology. Considering only the polar extremes, we have a possible sixty-four types of models, of which perhaps only a score of types contain useful examples. Even so, it is more economical to discuss the typology in terms of its dimensions than it is to attempt to present a complete classification and discussion of a large number of models or to attempt to draw the typology itself out of this discussion.

Descriptive versus Analytic Models

The distinction between descriptive and analytic models is of special interest to those who take an economic view of urban metropolitan development. One might reclassify this dimension as expressing the antinomy between induction and deduction. One is forced, of course, to recognize that each of these logical and scientific approaches has its own important role, and to recognize that frequently the strategy of investigation and the development of theory lead to a controlled interaction of the two models of procedure. Clearly, however, the inductive or descriptive approach represents an exploratory investigation into the types of covariation which appear likely to sustain efforts toward theoretical analysis, precise formulation of relationships, and the testing of theories. The analytic or deductive approach can scarcely be undertaken without more or less detailed statements of universal relationships which one hopes will stand up against rigorous comparisons with the real world. Although the spectrum of possible approaches is more or less continuous, it would appear that the analytic approach necessarily has to make statements about cause and effect which are quite specific and which are possibly testable at both the aggregated level and at the level of individual actors in the processes under study.

It is relatively easy to adduce examples both from general economics and from urban locational theory to illustrate these ideas. Much of the earliest writing in general economics was inductive and descriptive in nature, and this tradition has even continued into modern times in some treatments of business cycles and of short-range economic forecasting. Clearly, however, much more rigor has been introduced into this science by the specification of functional and causal relationships. Some of these are aggregative, as in econometric models of the national economy, while in other fields, such as the theory of the firm, the focus is on individual decision-making entities and the causes for their actions.

In coming to grips with the urban functional and developmental system, similar disparate approaches can be recognized. On the one hand, for example, in another paper at this conference, Hoover refers to the negative exponential relationship of density and distance as one of the major observed regularities in metropolitan arrangements. On the other hand, Muth's paper analyzes a large number of more or less behavioral postulates regarding housing supply and demand, and attempts to relate these both to economic theory and to observed data. While there is obviously some connection between these ideas, it is plain that the density law is purely descriptive, since it is not derived from any detailed specification of cause and effect, while the detailed examination of the behavior of aggregates of households has yet to be integrated into a complete analysis of urban function and development. Earlier efforts to carry out this integration by Muth and others seem to me so far to require too strong assumptions,[4] while the theoretical integration by Alonso, Wingo, and others has not yet been adequately tested empirically.[5]

It seems likely that if we examine the continuum from largely descriptive to highly analytical models, we can obtain some clues as to the general requisites for adequate performance and satisfactory content. Insofar as the analysis treats of economic quantities, these should be present in the model and the analysis. For example, it seems somewhat captious to analyze the economic aspects of location and development without specifically dealing with land values, housing values, and rents. These data, however, are often omitted or represented by proxy variables because they are difficult to obtain. On the other hand, some models which contain these price variables when dealing with housing do not really contain any quantity variables. That is, the quantity of housing is taken to be one dwelling unit, regardless of size or condition. In dealing with locational aspects as these influence the space market, we frequently find that no real economic variables regarding transportation costs and times are entered into the model, but that these in turn are proxied by various distance measures.

It is also evident that locational choices are influenced by factors that affect household utilities and business profits in indirect ways difficult to measure. On the household side, these influences may include amenities, health, safety, educational opportunities, and desires for social segregation or integration. For businesses, the influences may include forms of access to the market and to factors of production through interactions which are rarely recorded and difficult of measurement. Not only the measurement, but also the conceptual treatment of variables of this type are rather difficult to approach with existing economic theory and techniques.

Another economic concept worth some exploration is the full extent of the relation between supply and demand. Most theories and models of locational behavior concentrate principally on the demand for land and structures. Supply models have tended to deal mainly with the supply of additions to the stock of structures, something that is not, of course, equivalent to the supply of services, which must be equilibrated with demand. Owing to the existence of large and relatively unconvertible stocks of capital, this supply of services in a metropolitan area is relatively fixed at any point in time, but the modes by which it changes would repay more intensive study than it has yet received. The supply of land in the metropolitan area is largely fixed, but the supply function that helps to determine rates of development is probably very complex, resulting from the interaction of personal, institutional, and business factors, and containing dynamic elements related to speculation, anticipations, and knowledge of the market.

In view of these difficulties and omissions in the practical construction of models and testing of theories, it is not surprising that there tends to be a substantial gap between the most precise economic formulations of locational behavior and the practice of empirical investigation and model construction. It appears that the complete information demands for the construction of adequate models from the analytic point of view are most severe, and that some compromise is inevitable. There is, however, one compromise which seems likely to be counterproductive and which I should recommend be avoided: this is a concentration on comparative studies among cities. Such studies are useful in a limited context to provide a classificatory system for cities which are to be studied in more detail, and to indicate the types and ranges of variation which must be accounted for in any complete theory. Beyond this, however, the available data for any sizable set of urban areas turn out to be so sparse that a very large number of significant economic variables must be represented in the model by proxies. These investigations are thus robbed of much real analytical content.

We can drive this point home by asking a relatively simple question. In any particular metropolitan area, how useful would the results of a comparative analysis be in predicting the future population of center-city neighborhoods and suburban municipalities? Quite clearly, predictability would tend to be rather poor. The converse of this proposition, however, has not been tested, and I believe it very likely that properly designed models, developed and tested for a particular city, would have considerable validity and predictive accuracy when adapted to other cities.

The detailed specific metropolitan model therefore offers three advantages over comparative metropolitan studies of a descriptive nature. First, for single metropolitan areas, detailed data may be more easily acquired, and the model may be made to correspond more precisely with an analytical concept or theory of metropolitan relationships. Second, within the metropolitan area a specific model of this type will probably have greater predictive power. And third, the application of such a model in a new context provides more powerful and satisfactory means of testing theories than do the usual statistical measures of goodness of fit.

Holistic versus Partial Models

The distinction between holistic and partial models, our second dimension, tends to point most sharply to a parallel distinction between policy-making and academic analysis. In establishing urban metropolitan development policy for a long time horizon, the decision-maker is ultimately forced to consider not only the total environment, but the totality of ultimate effects, both direct and indirect, of given policies. He is thus implicitly concerned with a holistic approach to the analysis of the metropolis. The academician, on the other hand, and especially the discipline-oriented academician, can in many instances afford to hold the environment constant and examine its impact on a subsystem of the metropolitan area. This is the approach of partial equilibrium economic analysis.

The obvious economies of partial analysis of metropolitan problems, and its strong support from the discipline orientation and from the practice of past academic research, argue strongly for a partial analysis strategy, and quite correctly so. Holistic models will thus be built up out of partial models, communicating with each other and interacting in a computer, much as the subsystems of the metropolitan area interact in the real world.

There are two or three problems inherent in this approach, which can be overcome by careful planning. First, it seems likely that the actual communication between subsystems is much more complex and diverse than at first appears to be the case. The implication for research is that models of subsystems and of partial equilibrium must contain a larger number of variables or a larger number of functional connections with the "constant" environment; these models must be "richer" than in the past. This injunction raises some statistical problems, since the tendency is to reduce rather than to increase the number of independent variables, and since these variables in the metropolitan sphere are apt to be collinear in consequence of the long-term operation of locational processes. A second difficulty arises from the fact that partial models are apt to use variables not ordinarily predicted by any other partial model. Thus, for example, the analysis of residential location would wisely make use of the variable, rents. In this case, however, a collection of models designed to be holistic and to be used for predictive purposes would have to include a model of the housing market which generates rents, since this is a given of the residential location model. In special cases, through the use of equilibrium concepts, prices and locations can sometimes be generated by the same model. A third and obvious difficulty in the application of partial analysis arises from the need to ensure that the division of the total problem into subproblems is not only exhaustive, but also realistic in the over-all system sense. This realism dictates that the hypothetical interaction between subsystems be minimized insofar as possible. Nonetheless, because of technological or administrative considerations, subsystems with high levels of interaction with other subsystems–transportation, for example–be separately treated.

There is another sense, and a more troublesome one, in which we may view the dichotomy between holistic and partial models. We can imagine a model or a system of models which deals realistically with space utilization, location, and some of their costs and benefits. To what extent should this model be expanded to include aspects of social interaction, education, health, and other important problem areas in metropolitan development? The inclusion of these factors would presumably increase the problems of model construction by an order of magnitude, yet these areas of public policy compete for budgets and provide utilities to the population that are of great and perhaps overriding importance. Still further, should this model be expanded to include aspects of regional economic development, competition with other regions, and feedbacks due to improved or deteriorating local public services? Finally, could the model be expanded to include all or part of the political and planning process, predicting not only the direct effects, but also the political acceptance and implementation effectiveness of various policies?

If we thus proceed stepwise in expanding the number of variables and processes that are endogenous to our model system and reducing the number that are exogenous, we shall wind up with a holistic model that represents the totality of human social development. I am by no means opposed to or disheartened by the prospect of attempting to construct such models, but I think we must recognize a hierarchy of problems and of competencies, and for practical reasons stop this process short of the ultimate goal at this time. I do believe, however, that there is an important need to begin work on integrating the effects of social and educational policies into models dealing with space use and spatial distributions in the metropolitan area.

Macro- versus Micro-Models

There is a widespread latent dispute in the field of locational theory and modeling over the relative fruitfulness of macro- and micro-models. This therefore is our third dimension of variation among models. Similar controversies arise in the field of economics. I shall merely touch on some of the seemingly more important aspects of this difference.

First of all, let us recognize that basically many aspects of the final results we wish to predict are aggregated, or macro-results. We are interested in total population (possibly by groups), total transportation system utilization (by mode and by hour of the day), total community facility utilization (by location and by class of user), and so on. We are even interested in total, over-all benefit versus cost calculations. On the other hand, it is equally clear, first, that the impacts of metropolitan conditions fall on individuals, families, and organizations, and must be evaluated in terms of their welfare, and second, that these same entities make a large number of the decisions which help determine the levels of the aggregate variables in which we are interested. Thus it would appear that the interests of prediction for decision-making might be well served by aggregative models, but that analytical completeness and accuracy would be better served by disaggregated models, possibly based on the simulation of the behavior of individual decision units.

This distinction, however, is clouded. Any theory and model can be more or less analytical. Even highly aggregated models of economic behavior, such as econometric national forecasting models, make use of hypothetical or observed relations derived from the theory of the firm. Here, some considerable sectoral disaggregation has been undertaken and clear distinctions are made between production and moneyflows which respond to different rules of behavior. In metropolitan modeling, similar extensive disaggregation by types of entities and by aspects of their behavior within broad locator classes has frequently been found desirable. This desirability is recognized equally by more sophisticated decision-makers or those concerned with very specific problems, and by academicians interested in theoretical and predictive accuracy. Even those, such as Lowry, who most strongly favor the use of aggregative models [6] recognize the interest, utility, and importance of extensive *areal* disaggregation. In any event, most of the aggregated metropolitan models make more or less use of theories, concepts, introspective, and observation regarding behavior at the micro level.

The central issue regarding the relationship between models of the process of individual decision-making (or behavior) and aggregative models is probably the question of rules of aggregation. This question, however, takes two forms. In the first instance, if the behavior of individual units within an aggregated group may be expected to vary, there may be both mathematical and statistical difficulties in predicting the appropriate average behavior for the group as a whole. Second, important instances may exist in which the behavior or response of a particular aggregate differs from any simple function of the response of its constituent individuals. This might be true of neighborhoods and subcommunities within the metropolitan area. It would seem likely that neither case can be adequately studied without microanalytical research on the behavior of decision units in the metropolis, which may ultimately provide a sound basis for finding and using the appropriate levels of disaggregation.

It is perfectly obvious that the construction of holistic, analytic, and disaggregated systems of models is at the present stage very difficult, because adequate data are not available to sustain the necessary research. Since it seems unlikely that a complete range of necessary data will ever be available for an entire metropolis (or that there would ever be assembled a research staff capable of using it in time), it necessarily follows, I believe, that while piecemeal research on specific topics will proceed at the microanalytical level, most functioning models will be more or less aggregative. Note, however, the discussion which follows regarding deterministic versus probabilistic models. It is also evident that presently available data will not in general sustain very sophisticated micro-analysis. Lowry appears to take the position that macro-models, in any event, may be more satisfactory than micro-models; I take his view to reflect, at least in part, the fact that, given presently available data, the assumptions and finagling which are necessary to achieve greater disaggregation are counter-productive and may indeed be unsound.

I cannot, however, pursue this argument to the point where it may be contended that aggregative models are apt to be intrinsically more accurate than disaggregative models. This may in fact be the case if the measure of accuracy is taken as the fit for an observed situation in the present or recent past. If, however, we take the view that one of the major sources of future change will be changes in mix of the underlying population, then the dangers of overaggregation in relation to prediction become apparent. The process of aggregation itself, especially where the proper rules of aggregation would be nonlinear or discontinuous, effectively debars the model from adjusting properly to future changes in mix. The use of aggregative models therefore inevitably freezes some portions of the present mix of population attributes and behaviors. Disaggregation tends to reduce this mix and its attendant dangers, and microanalytical models might completely eliminate it except insofar as the mixture is inherent in the behavior of decision units themselves.

Static versus Dynamic Models

Urban analysis and decision-making deal implicitly with change and with trends of development, and consequently require the use of models which are in some sense dynamic. On the other hand, questions of optimization are more easily approached through considerations of static equilibrium. This antinomy is the basis for our discussion of the fourth dimension of variation among models.

Urban planning has traditionally been oriented not only toward the future, but also toward the prefigurement of future states. These states take the form not only of architectural and city planning utopias such as the garden city and the *Ville Radieuse,* but of exploratory devices like the sketch planning for the year 2000 in Washington, D.C.,[7] and finally of action-oriented detailed targets such as may be summarized in a comprehensive plan. While these views of the future of the city or the metropolis tend to cut through or ignore most of the problems of implementation and developmental paths, I believe that they have serious significance. I also believe that their implications can fruitfully be explored through the use of economic and quasi-economic equilibrium concepts. These concepts imply, together with equilibrium, an optimum condition which may or may not coincide with the social welfare optimum as defined in the decision process. Indeed, this is one of the main difficulties in the use of economic models for optimizing. The other is the character of the policy space, which is discontinuous, unbounded, and has many local optima.

Analytically, there are other serious difficulties with optimizing and equilibrium concepts. One of these has to do with the fact that in the real world most locators are never in equilibrium, and therefore the observation of their equilibrium tendencies may be more or less difficult. This difficulty is of varying importance as between one class of locators and the next. Retail trade probably reaches an equilibrium of sorts rather rapidly. Residential location is far from being at a general equilibrium, but during any year a very large number of locational decisions could be observed from which strong and valid implications about equilibrium tendencies might be drawn. Large institutions such as hospitals and universities, medium and large-size manufacturing establishments, and collections of establishments with large agglomerative economies, such as a garment center, are generally very far from equilibrium. In these latter cases, the costs of moving are so great that very substantial locational diseconomies would be incurred. Since the entities involved are large and diverse in nature, the frequency of entry of new entities able to make optimal locational decisions is very low, and may not provide an adequate observational basis for the determination of the true equilibrium conditions or tendencies.

A second and converse analytical difficulty may arise in certain cases where a system or subsystem is, in fact, tending to equilibrium. If the equilibrium in some sense represents a balance between two opposing forces (such as density and accessibility), then the variables representing these forces may become increasingly collinear. In this situation, the statistical observation of the equilibrating process becomes very difficult. We must be careful to distinguish this case (which I believe to be real, important, and intractable) from a more elementary, but still troublesome situation. This more primitive case arises when the analyst uses a large number of variables in an experimental framework and creates collinearity by using variables or groups of variables which, in fact, measure the same phenomenon. In this case, the reduction of the variable set is reasonable and legitimate. However, in the case where the collinearity arises out of an approach to equilibrium, the elimination of variables demolishes the representation of the real-world phenomena.

These analytical difficulties merely serve to emphasize the fact that the system of scientific interest is a dynamic one which ought, at least in some aspects, to be the subject of dynamic theories and modeling. At the same time, many of the real decision problems faced in metropolitan areas are related to the dynamic characteristics of the metropolis rather than to static optimal conditions. As a consequence of these joint considerations, a large proportion of all modeling effort is directed towards the construction of models that are in some sense dynamic. In principle, a dynamic model can be formulated as a system of differential equations or difference equations. The latter formulation corresponds formally to the use of lagged variables in the familiar econometric models of economic growth and cyclical fluctuation. It is in general somewhat unusual to find a model explicitly formulated in one of these manners, owing to the analytic complexity of metropolitan relationships. We find, instead, the use of recursive sets of models in which the changes taking place in a given period depend on the state of the system at the beginning of this period, and hence indirectly on the changes of the preceding periods and the states at earlier times.

This formulation is well suited to linked sets of partial models, and corresponds precisely in a fundamental sense with the basic characteristics of a difference equation formulation.

The critical problems in the construction of dynamic metropolitan models have to do with the manner in which the influence of time is entered into the system, and concomitantly with the manner in which dynamic influences are measured and analyzed. Here one must inject a note of caution, pointing out that, for metropolitan areas, the available time series data are very sparse, non-comparable, and incomplete in the areas of interest. For this reason, many standard econometric strategies fail badly, leading to ever more aggregative, generalized, and uninformative analyses and models. For purposes of the theory and experimental modeling of metropolitan dynamics, time is first of all injected by introducing exogenous changes into the model, such as economic growth, population migration, and income change. These important variables are, as a practical matter, frequently analyzed and projected under the same roof as the work of intrametropolitan modeling, but they are conceptually distinct and belong in the realm of interregional and national economic projections. The dynamic behavior of locators and developers, which propertly belongs within an intrametropolitan model, can be analyzed with some difficulty on a sector-by-sector and disaggregated basis. The dynamic and time-dependent behavior of these parts of the metropolis requires careful attention over an adequate time span, together with a design of analysis which attempts to isolate the invariant aspects of behavior and to "partial out" a multitude of environmental influences. For these reasons, the "spectrum" of manufacturing location may cover thirty years or more; of retail trade location, five to ten years; and of residential location, five to fifty years, depending on our view of the processes involved.

Thus, even if we take a generalized view of location, a fixed ten-year intercensal period is a Procrustean bed for analysis. We may usefully attempt to sidestep this issue by assuming that, over a short period of time, we can sample the spectra of a number of different classes of locators; such a sample could be cross-sectional with respect to the populations, but longitudinal with respect to their behaviors. The problem then becomes one of sample size, and is much more satisfactorily resolved with respect to residential locators and "mom-and-pop" stores than it is with respect to shopping centers and large manufacturers.

Reference to economic "models" of the first type, or theories, suggests that any truly dynamic, intrametropolitan, locational model contains implicit in its structure conditions regarding stability and steady-state equilibrium; I have yet to see these matters adequately explored. Such an exploration could be a two-edged sword (or should I say a Wilkinson-Occam's razor?) which would dissect, on the one hand, the inherent characteristics of the model and, on the other hand, policy implications for sustained adequate adjustments within the metropolitan area.

Probabilistic Models

The manifold uncertainties, both real and apparent, surrounding metropolitan development and human behavior give rise in some quarters to a hankering after probabilistic rather than deterministic models of urban metropolitan development. If I correctly understand the thrust of this desire and the characteristics of models of different types, then it would appear that most emphases on probabilistic models are misplaced and counterproductive. There are probably in principle only one or two important and useful applications.

We must clearly recognize that there will always be a probabilistic element in the simulation of metropolitan phenomena, based on the fact that individual behaviors do indeed contain elements of free will and of social and personal history which are inaccessible to us for analysis and prediction. Thus, in a particular defined group of the population, some will buy books and others will buy TV; some will drive to work and others will take the bus. When we assign proportions to these behaviors, we are dealing in probability, and their analysis is subtle and complex. But the construction of models in which these proportions are deterministically calculated does not fall within the class of probabilistic models for this discussion.

There is a large class of uncertain events that impinge to a greater or less extent on any projection model. These include most particularly unpredictable cultural and technological changes of major magnitudes. They also include, perhaps, selected major intrametropolitan decisions such as, say, the relocation of a large factory, hospital, office, or university. In analyzing the implications of these uncertainties, a probabilistic model which internally generates the random events is surely inappropriate. These events and their effects, if important enough to be examined, should be under the control of the investigator, and should be entered as inputs to runs of the model.

There is perhaps an intermediate scale of uncertain decisions whose variational impact on metropolitan development is worth examination through probabilistic models. A class of such decisions might be the decisions by small developers over a relatively short period of time, say five to ten years. The object of this type of experimentation would be to discover the range of variation to be expected from constrained random decisions in the over-all pattern of metropolitan development. The general experience of simulation in situations with fairly large numbers of actors has been that the range of variation resulting from successive runs is relatively small, and that the outcomes are highly peaked to their central tendency. This peakedness increases with the length of the runs and the number of actors. Thus, the area of appropriate investigation is circumscribed to a rather narrow intermediate range.

This range almost certainly does not include individual household decisions and the decisions of small establishments. While it may be entirely appropriate to conduct research on the basis of observations on these entities, there appears to be no compelling necessity for probabilistic simulation with random behavior programmed within the model. The work of Orcutt and others suggests, however, one important expection to this dictum.[8] If it is determined, for example, that the number of significant dimensions of variation between households is very large, then the cross-classification of these dimensions may create an exorbitant number of behaviorally distinct household classes. This is serious enough in a static model, but additionally in a dynamic model the transfer of housholds from one class to another may itself be probabilistic according to very complex rules. In these situations, a probabilistic simulation may be conducted by creating a very large sample of the population of households, and allowing their attribution to classes to arise naturally out of their defined characteristics and their transitions from one state to another. In this case, the probabilistic treatment of households represents a solution method to a very difficult computational problem. It is to be expected, however, that the random distribution of outcomes will be of little or no interest in itself. In fact, the expense and difficulty of running a model of this type is great enough to preclude any deep exploration of such randomness.

Simultaneous versus Sequential Simulation

The final dimension along which we may classify models is on the basis of whether their treatment of different groups of locators is simultaneous or sequential. This distinction is not a very profound or troublesome one, and is included mainly for the sake of completeness and clarity.

It is generally recognized that many metropolitan locational and development decisions are made in a manner which is in principle simultaneous. In practice, most models must deal with mathematically intractable locational relationships which do not lend themselves to analytic solutions, and which are therefore solved by iteration. The fact that iteration has the appearance of a process in the actual operation of a model should not be taken to belie the fact of simultaneity. Simultaneous solutions are inherently required by static models, since variables are not lagged and the history of the system does not determine any aspect of the locational pattern. But simultaneous systems of mutual locational determination have two difficult operating characteristics. First, the fewer the exogenous spatially distributed inputs (such as fixed transportation facilities or fixed unique locators), the more sensitive and less rapidly convergent is the iteration process. In the extreme case, with no fixed facilities and an unbounded plane, the location pattern may be indeterminate and the iterations may not converge. The second and more troublesome difficulty arises from a different kind of indeterminacy. Given non-linear interactions between locators, the iteration process may converge only to a local equilibrium, and there may be many such. In these cases, the final solution depends on the starting values used in the iterative process, and this in turn may open up opportunities either for injecting normative decisions or for taking account of the history of the system.

Even in a dynamic model it is possible to achieve simultaneity, if this is desired, by iterative solution of the successive steps in the recursive locational model, or by other specific features of the initial model design. The iterative procedures are so cumbersome, however, that it has become customary to operate sectoral locational models sequentially within each recursive step. In this case, successive recursions are thought of as providing an opportunity, if one is needed, to replace iterations and to take account of the interactions between locators. Alternatively, and more popularly, the succession of locational models is represented as having some relationship to the sequence in which actual development takes place and to the lags which are observed in the real world. Thus, for example, residential location may be regarded as a price-setting activity in the suburban fringe, even leading the rest of the model through speculation. If manufacturing location is then made to depend in part on the price of land, it can usefully follow residential location in the recursive operation of the model. This may in fact, of course, result in a geographical lead on the part of manufacturing, which could be forced further toward the periphery in its search for cheap and sizable tracts of developable land.

Quite clearly, considerations of simultaneity versus sequence present a troublesome and perhaps damaging set of problems when we are dealing with static models. In the case of dynamic models, however, and especially dynamic model systems, an exploration of these questions can be a fruitful source of insight into the true behavior of metropolitan growth patterns.

APPLICATIONS OF THE DIMENSIONS OF MODELING

I have now concluded a basic review of the dimensions along which models may be classified. Perhaps a close reading of what I have said will reveal my own prejudices, but these are better stated directly and with appropriate qualification. I uncompromisingly favor the analytic approach to theorizing and model construction, enlightened by an adequate inductive understanding of the phenomena which we are examining. Analysis must almost certainly proceed on a partial basis, but I believe that we shall be able to construct increasingly satisfactory holistic models by plugging partial models into a total system. Our models must, I feel, deal with aggregates of the population, of land, of structures, and of public monies. But these aggregates must be defined in a realistic sense, and the rules of aggregation of decision units must be well explored and clearly undstood. This implies many studies and much theory at the micro level, well related to the construction of macro-models. I see different roles for static and dynamic models, and I suggest that the related equilibrium aspects of each are an important unexplored area for theoretical and empirical research. In the construction of dynamic models, I recommend especially scrupulous attention to the definition and measurement of the dynamic elements (state changes and decisions) by which the operation of time is introduced into the model. I foresee that the most efficient and economical models will be deterministic in nature, although they may assign probabilities to various categories of decision-makers. The success of this approach, however, will depend on whether we can efficiently classify decision-makers into a very limited number of groups, failing which stochastic models must be used as a solution method. I favor systematic rather than random exploration of the uncertainties of our projection procedures. My choice between simultaneous and sequential models is largely one of convenience.

In the following portion of the discussion,* I present critiques of a number of models of metropolitan development which are of current interest and applicability. These critiques will be fairly general, covering, insofar as possible within the confines of this paper, the general conceptual form of the model with its advantages and disadvantages, data requirements, tests of reliability, and usefulness in the planning process.

I approach the job of a critical evaluation of models work in a somewhat ambivalent frame of mind. On the one hand, I may perhaps urge the pursuit of some forms of conceptual precision with what amounts to moral fervor. On the other hand, I am quite aware that both in my own work and in many other practical efforts, this type of precision must frequently be sacrificed to operating exigencies, including data availability and the allocation of time and funds. In what follows, therefore, I hope that I may view the work of others with the same charitable indulgence which I grant myself when faced with practical problems. In principle, I wish to give them full credit for the efforts they have exerted and the useful ideas they have brought forward. At the same time, it is clearly necessary for the progress of the modeling field that some conclusions be drawn from these efforts as to the difficulties and pitfalls which the user might expect to encounter and, even more important, as to the shortcomings that might be considered and possibly overcome in the design of other locational models. It goes without saying that my own conclusions in this regard are debatable, and I hope that such a debate will ensue to the general benefit of the field.

A brief digression on the subject of statistical objectives in relation to models is also in order. It seems to me that, in explaining aggregated areal phenomena at about the level of the traffic zone or census tract, it should in principle be possible to achieve coefficients of determination in the vicinity of .95 to .99. These levels imply roughly that the relative error of estimate may exceed 20% or 10% in more than one-third of the cases. Coefficients of determination at this high level are apt to appear unreasonable to the statistician or the experienced worker in model formulation, but the errors associated even with estimates of this precision are apt to seem unreasonable to the average planning director who critically examines the results of a modeling experiment. In certain cases, the source of the error may be identified as a point at which the model identifies unrealized trends and thus in a sense predicts better than the real world. This can be a useful feature. In other cases, however, one must look for a reduction in error either through improved or more relevant data, or through a more realistic specification of the model.

*Not included herein.–Ed.

Where the objective of the model is to derive parameters from micro data pertaining to individuals or households, coefficients of determination of .20 may be very good, and coefficients as high as .50 are rarely if ever achieved in practice. Here, in my opinion, the coefficient of determination is not a guide to the accuracy or reliability of the model. Such microanalyses are, however, frequently used as a basis for aggregated projections, and applied to some base period an estimate of reliability can be obtained.

Still another contrast in this area must be mentioned. There is a general impression that adding variables or functional forms makes it almost certain that R^2's in the vicinity of one can be readily obtained. This is in fact not the case, and many phenomena, even on an aggregated basis, are extremely resistant to full "explanation." In general, therefore, I do not automatically decry a failure to obtain the high levels of explanation that I believe to be desirable. The obverse situation may also obtain: very high levels of the coefficient of determination do not necessarily imply that a projection model will be wholly successful. Here the situation is somewhat more difficult to analyze, since, as noted above, we have no easy way to apply the model to a base that is very different from the data to which it was fitted. In order to determine the projection implications of a particular model, we must therefore scrupulously examine not merely the statistical measures applied to its calibration, but the structure of the model itself and any possible inconsistencies and contradictions which it may contain. It is even conceivable that, by reformulating a model, we may lower the R^2 for the period of calibration, yet on theoretical grounds increase our confidence in its predictive accuracy.

MAJOR ISSUES IN MODELING

We may now pose, on the basis of the salient characteristics of models and our sketch of current practice, a number of related questions regarding the utility and accuracy of models for both scientific and decision-making purposes.

One of the central issues revolves around the so-called validation and testing of models and theories. Owing to the great lack of time-series data, we must customarily find that dynamic models are validated by the goodness of fit to the data from which they have been originally developed. An important class of exceptions may be noted in the case of the Lowry model and the Lakshmanan-Hansen model of retail trade, where locational patterns depend on trip-making behavior and where, therefore, the reproduction of phenomena is in part independent of the fitting of parameters. Similar conditions will apply to a developed form of the Herbert-Stevens model, when and if it is completed.

Even these cases of indirect validation are not strong enough for my taste, and I should like to see stronger tests devised for the predictive capability of models. It is out of the question to wait ten or twenty years for new data to be generated for such tests. Very rarely, it might be possible to test a model for a given city on the decade 1940-1950, having fitted it to the decade 1950-1960. Tests on the decade 1960-1970 will be possible within about five years. Meanwhile, I would seriously suggest that a far more potent and generally available test would be to apply models and parameters developed for, say, Chicago, to, say, Minneapolis-St. Paul. The mere contemplation of such a test imposes on the theorist and the model-builder the responsibility for a general analytic framework which is transferable to very different situations, and for the derivation of relatively invariant parameters. But when projection models are designed for use in cities which will have, within the period of projection, twice the population and twice the income per capita, I do not think that it is unreasonable to seek such a level of generality.

Another route for exploring the performance of models used for projections is to examine in detail, as suggested above, some of their inherent dynamic and equilibrium properties. This line of investigation is properly used in the model design stage. It is probably even more difficult and subtle than I imagine, and I repeatedly call attention to it partly because it has almost totally been neglected.

Dynamic and static equilibrium also probably have strong implications for optimization, and hence for welfare. They are thus related directly or indirectly to the evaluation stage of the planning process. In a general sense, we may suggest that a static equilibrium may be implicitly defined in an analytic model by the achievement of optimal conditions (given competition and the environment) by each of a large number of groups of locators. In a dynamic model, movement and change are activated by a striving toward a similar optimal status. It is, of course, possible that the second-order conditions for equilibrium or a nelglect of externalities influencing behavior may lead to a situation, like the Prisoners' Dilemma, in which individual optimum-seeking does not lead to optimum arrangements, and may not lead to equilibrium. In models that are more nearly descriptive, such as Lowry's or Hill's, the welfare implications of these tendencies towards equilibrium are difficult to define, but in other cases the states achieved might be related to the performance of the plan in producing desired satisfactions.

This line of development is, I believe, particularly important because the present generation of models produces outputs which are very difficult to relate to the decision-making process. These outputs may, in fact, in many cases be incomplete, in that they do not define many of the consequences that are of interest to decision-makers. In other cases, even given a complete set of outputs, these may be so many and so diverse and our knowledge of the transformation function into an index of performance so fragmentary that the models have not produced much digestible useful guidance. What is here suggested is, therefore, that the process of constructing useful models for prediction may be made to depend on built-in evaluations by locating groups within the models, in such a way that a measure of performance is automatically generated by aggregating the evaluations.

In pursuing this line of investigation, two related cautionary notes must be struck. First, it is perfectly clear that the optimization function which defines the utilitarian satisfaction of individual groups in the locational marketplace and which is necessary to motivate the locating activities in a model may correctly and of necessity disregard externalities and other social costs or benefits which will influence the planning decision-makers' choices. These considerations properly belong in a complete evaluative model. But similar concepts might well be applicable within the process of optimizing from the behavioral standpoint. Their absence suggests a market mechanism which is imperfect from the social point of view. Such a discovery at the interface between predictive modeling and evaluation then reflects back into the policy design process. It suggests the possibility of basic changes (such as user charges) in the plan to be tested, which may in turn induce changes in the models themselves.

The second caution deals with the somewhat limited scope of locational models that deal with spatial allocation to the neglect of complete and specific consideration of important social problems. It is true that even a pure locational model can touch upon important aspects of the concentration and segregation of ethnic and lower-income strata of the population, their deprivation of adequate housing and community facilities, and their failure to secure adequate access to suitable employment opportunities. These aspects of the spatial distribution of social problems are far from unimportant in metropolitan decision-making. It is, however, likely that important aspects of education and mobility are going to move increasingly into the center of decision-making, and that these aspects are almost totally absent from locational models. Since these problems press for consideration in budgets and in policy-making, they cannot indefinitely be deferred from systematic and scientific examination in the total metropolitan context. I believe, however, that our current capability for analyzing these problems theoretically and for quantifying relationships through the use of models is very meager. I would anticipate that in the immediate future the developments in these fields will have to be parallel to but not integrated with locational modeling, but that in as little as five years' time, these two strains of analysis and decision-making can be merged.

A GLOBAL PERSPECTIVE

Up to this point, I have conducted the discussion largely on the basis of an inside view of model-building in relation to decision-making. I now wish to step outside of this framework and draw out two major implications from my experience. These implications respectively support the importance of models, and suggest the desirability of cautious limitations in the claims that can be made for them.

The positive claim that can assuredly be made for the models of the foreseeable future is that they will make possible much more accurate and informative projections of the effects of alternative policies. This greater accuracy will rest in part on the analytic studies necessary to implement parts of the model-building process. But more important, the increases in accuracy and insight will result from an increased capacity to deal in detail, and especially in area detail, with large and complex metropolitan systems. This capability will be achieved through the intelligent exploitation of the immense bookkeeping and computational capabilities of the computer.

Insofar as designers and decision-makers can find means by which to relate to the process of computer simulation and projection, there will be immense gains in the fruitfulness and cogency of their own work and thinking. Indeed, it is not too extreme to suggest that the gains that can be achieved by these relations are to some considerable extent independent of the accuracy of the models and of their operational capabilities. The mere exercise of trying to make design and decision considerations sufficiently clear and explicit that they may influence model-building has a remarkably disciplining and clarifying effect. This observation, indeed, suggests that the major focus referred to above on *operational* models is partly in error. Such a concentration may tend to separate the designer and the decision-maker from simulation because it is not couched in their terms and thus becomes an inscrutable mystery. At the same time, the simplistic premises of operational modeling tend to fly in the face of the deepest and most strongly felt experiences of many of those outside the modeling process. This gives rise to a dispute which is in many ways homologous with the dispute between science and humanism.

If, indeed, projection experiments with the metropolitan system can be useful in the senses I have discussed, this success will be a substantial breakthrough in systems modeling. In spite of the extensive present discussion of the success of systems analysis with respect to space engineering, transportation planning, and the like, it still remains true that no successful complete model of a complex biological or social entity has yet been made operational. Thus, for example, there is no successful model of the complete function of a cell, let alone of an organism; nor of a school, let alone of a metropolitan area. The difficulty in modeling such complex systems may be discussed in the same context as certain very deep epistemological problems which arise in relation to planning design and decision-making.

The device which is being used to simulate metropolitan function and which in addition it is hoped can be useful in relieving the planner of some design and decision-making problems, is the digital computer. This computer is sequential and one-dimensional in its operation, very much like the sequential nature of causation in the physical sciences, and the historical development in science and technology as a whole. We may usefully question the extent to which this sequential concept of cognition, causation, and operation can be made to coincide with the complex systems organization at the biological and social level, of which man's mental processes are a part.

This is not to suggest that the cognitive processes involved in design and decision (or the operation of systems to which they apply) are devoid of logic. It implies, rather, that the applicable logic may be more complex than has previously animated our science and technology and our social science predictions. If this suggestion is to any degree correct, it follows that, for some time to come, the most efficient performance of the most complex aspects of the planning process will best be performed by "human computers"–or planners–rather than by electronic digital computers. In my own mind, there is fairly clear separation between the parts of the planning process appropriate for assignment to these different treatments. The boundary between these parts of the process will move in various ways as we gain experience, and depending on circumstances. Considering, moreover, that planning is a social process, there is a strong implication that the human computers who engage in design and decision-making in what we are pleased to call an intuitive fashion, should make their methods ever more widely available and widely understood. Thus, at the same time that we set limits on our immediate ambitions for scientizing the planning process, we must also mark out the path by which personal, intuitive, and subjective processes become the object of some degree of scientific understanding and replication.

It thus appears that an appropriate consideration of this problem may lead in the direction both of more genuine democracy, but narrowing the differences between the elites and general public, and towards a greater unification of human endeavor by creating a broader common ground between the so-called sciences and humanities.

NOTES

1. Britton Harris, "The Uses of Theory in the Simulation of Urban Phenomena," *Journal of the American Institute of Planners,* Vol. 32, No. 5 (September 1966) and *Highway Research Record No. 126: Land Use Forecasting Concepts* (Highway Research Board, National Council-National Academy of Sciences, 1966).

2. An example of this procedure is the solution to the generalized Weber problem (Alfred Weber, *Theory of the Location of Industry,* translated by C. Friedrich [University of Chicago Press, 1929]) and the warehouse location problem which are discussed in some detail by Leon Cooper, "Solutions of Generalized Locational Equilibrium Models," *Journal of Regional Science,* Vol. 7, No. 1 (Summer 1967).

3. For a more detailed discussion of this problem, see my paper, "The City of the Future: The Problem of Optimal Design," *Papers and Proceedings of the Regional Science Association, 1966* (in press).

4. Richard F. Muth, "The Spatial Structure of the Housing Market," *Papers and Proceedings of the Regional Science Association,* Vol. 7 (1961); and David R. Seidman, "An Operational Model of the Residential Land Market," paper presented at Seminar on Models of Land Use Development, Institute for Environmental Studies, University of Pennsylvania, October 1964 (mimeo).

5. William Alonso, *Location and Land Use–Toward a General Theory of Land Rent* (Harvard University Press, 1964); and Lowdon Wingo, Jr., *Transportation and Urban Land* (Resources for the Future, 1961). See also the first steps towards an empirical investigation

of these matters in John Herbert and Benjamin H. Stevens, *A Model for the Distribution of Residential Activities in Urban Areas,* PJ Paper No. 2 (Penn-Jersey Transportation Study, Pennsylvania State Department of Highways), abridged in *Journal of Regional Science,* Vol. 2, No. 2 (1960); and my unpublished paper, "Basic Assumptions for a Simulation of the Urban Residential Housing and Land Market," Institute for Environmental Studies, University of Pennsylvania, July 1966.

6 Ira S. Lowry, "A Short Course in Model Design," *Journal of the American Institute of Planners,* Vol. 31, No. 2 (May 1965).

7. U.S., National Capital Regional Planning Council, *Year 2000 Policies Plan,* 1963.

8. Guy Orcutt, John Korbel, Alice M. Rivlin, and Martin Greenberger, *A Microanalysis of Socio-Economic Systems: A Simulation Study* (Harper, 1961).

REFERENCES

Alonso, William. *Location and Land Use–Toward a General Theory of Land Rent.* Cambridge: Harvard University Press, 1964.

Berry, Brian J. L. Department of Geography Research Paper No. 85. *Commercial Structure and Commercial Blight.* Chicago: University of Chicago, 1963.

Chapin, F. Stuart, Thomas G. Donnelly, and Shirley F. Weiss. *A Probabilistic Model for Residential Growth.* Chapel Hill: University of North Carolina, Institute for Research in Social Science, in co-operation with U.S. Department of Commerce, Bureau of Public Roads, May 1964.

Chapin, F. Stuart and Shirley F. Weiss. *Factors Influencing Land Development.* Chapel Hill: University of North Carolina, Institute for Research in Social Science, in co-operation with U.S. Department of Commerce, Bureau of Public Roads, August 1962.

---. *Some Input Refinements for a Residential Model.* Chapel Hill: University of North Carolina, Institute for Research in Social Science, in co-operation with U.S. Department of Commerce, Bureau of Public Roads, July 1965.

Harris, Britton. "The Uses of Theory in the Simulation of Urban Phenomena," Journal of the American Institute of Planners, Vol. 32, September 1966.

---. *Highway Research Record No. 26: Land Use Forecasting Concepts.* Washington: National Academy of Sciences–National Research Council, Highway Research Board, 1966.

---."Some Problems in the Theory of Intra-Urban Location," Operations Research, Vol. 9, September-October 1961.

---. "A Model of Locational Equilibrium for Retail Trade." Paper presented at a Seminar on Models of Land Use Development, Institute for Urban Studies, University of Pennsylvania, October 1964. Mimeo.

---. "Inventing the Future Metropolis." Paper prepared for the Catherine Bauer Wurster Memorial Public Lecture Series, sponsored by the Harvard Graduate School of Design and Massachusetts Institute of Technology. May 1966. Mimeo.

---. "The City of the Future: The Problem of Optimal Design." Paper presented at 13th Annual Meeting, Regional Science Association, St. Louis, Mo., November 1966. Mimeo.

Herbert, John, and Benjamin H. Stevens. "A Model for the Distribution of Residential Activities in Urban Areas," Journal of Regional Science, Vol. II, No. 2, 1960.

Journal of the American Institute of Planners. Special issues: "Urban Development Models: New Tools for Planning," Vol. 31, May 1965; "Land Use and Traffic Models," Vol. 25, May 1959.

Lowry, Ira S. *A Model of Metropolis.* Memorandum RM-4035-RC. Santa Monica: The RAND Corporation, August 1964.

---. *Seven Models of Urban Development: A Structural Comparison.* P3673. Santa Monica: The RAND Corp., September 1967.

Muth, Richard F. "The Spatial Structure of the Housing Market," *Papers and Proceedings of the Regional Science Association,* Vol. 7, 1961.

Orcutt, Guy, John Korbel, Alice M. Rivlin, and Martin Greenberger. *A Microanalysis of Socio-Economic Systems: A Simulation Study.* New York: Harper, 1961.

Seidman, David R. *A Linear Interaction Model for Manufacturing Location,* Penn-Jersey Transportation Study. Philadelphia: Delaware Valley Regional Planning Commission, 1964.

Wingo, Lowdon, Jr. *Transportation and Urban Land.* Washington: Resources for the Future, Inc., 1961.

Chapter 7

A LAND USE PLAN DESIGN MODEL

Kenneth J. Schlager

Postwar advances in applied mathematics and electronic computation have stimulated great interest in the application of mathematical models and data processing systems to urban and regional planning. Significant progress has been made in the application of these techniques to urban transportation planning, and more recently a number of research projects aimed at the development of land use models have been initiated. There seems little question that the long-range potential impact of these methods will be revolutionary, but some critics have questioned the relevance of current planning models to the real problems of planners. The obvious question is: what problems are current models able to solve?

Even a brief review of current land use planning models will reveal a strong emphasis on explaining and predicting human behavior. Quite correctly, many of these models include the word *forecasting* somewhere in their title description.[1] Such an approach conceives of the urban complex as a phenomenon to be explained scientifically and as a changing configuration that can be predicted in the same way that the solar system can be predicted from the theories of physics. Indeed, such an approach is well designated as applied social physics. The philosophy underlying this approach is the natural result of the direct transfer of the methodology of the physical sciences.

PLAN DESIGN: THE CENTRAL PROBLEM

A contrasting viewpoint conceives of the urban complex as a subject for design. In this approach, the plan is a conscious synthesis of urban form to meet

Reprinted from the Journal of the American Institute of Planners, Vol. 31, No. 2 (May 1965), pp. 103-111, by permission of the publisher.

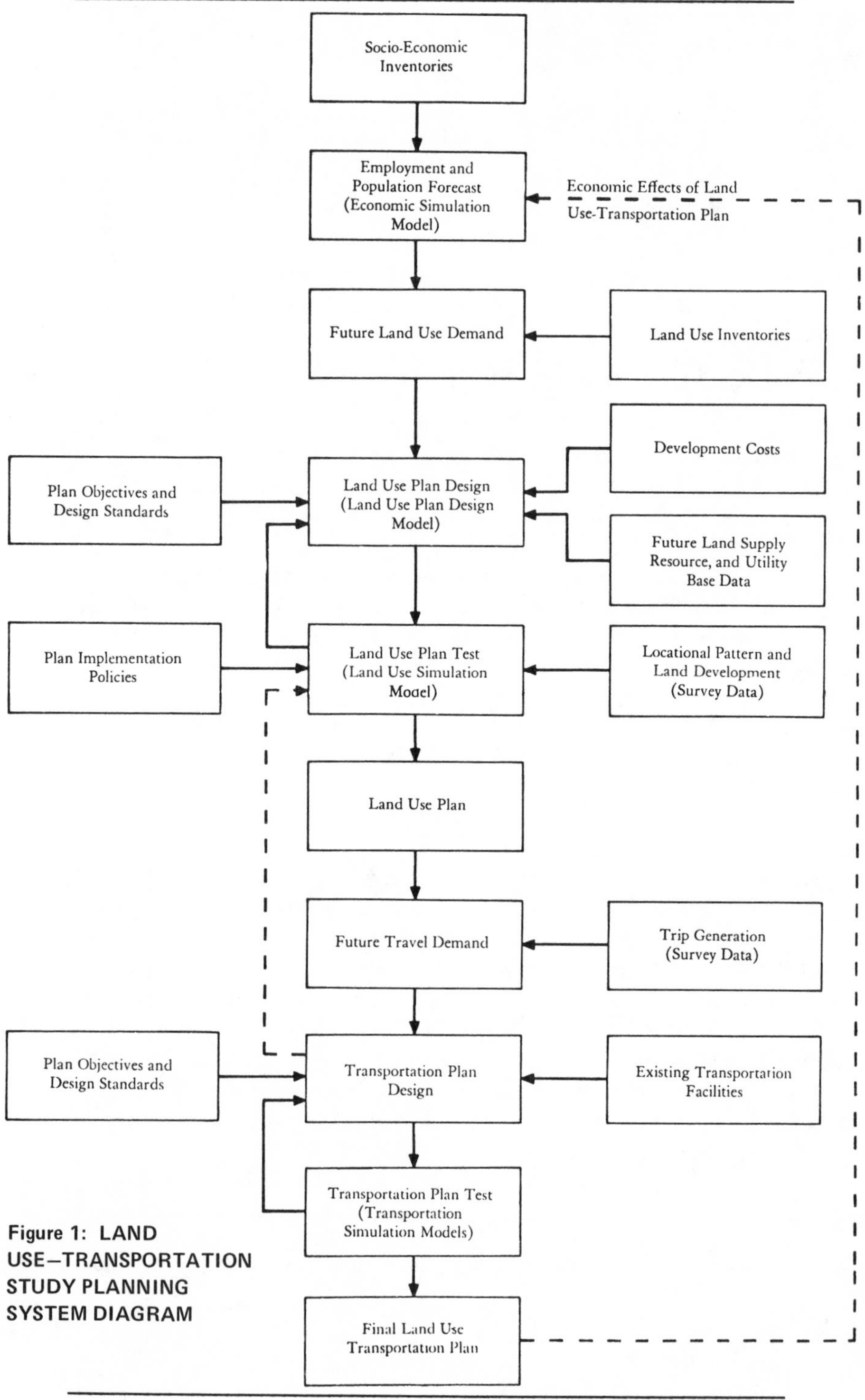

Figure 1: LAND USE–TRANSPORTATION STUDY PLANNING SYSTEM DIAGRAM

human needs. Rather than serving as a negative restraint on undesirable aspects of human behavior, the plan serves as a positive force for the directed development of the community.

This design viewpoint is not new. It has provided the basis for architectural and engineering achievement for centuries. What is new, or at least overlooked in recent years, is the possibility of using recent advances in applied mathematics and electronic computation for plan design. Design, and not explanation and prediction, becomes the primary problem for solution.

The subject of this paper is land use plan design and a land use plan design model now under development. Design, however, is but one of a sequence of functions in the planning process. For this reason, the introduction of the design model will be preceded by a discussion of the role of mathematical models in a specific land use-transportation planning sequence.

A system diagram illustrating the functional relationships in the planning process is shown in Figure 1. Although this diagram specifically represents the planning sequence related to the formulation of a regional land use-transportation plan, it is typical of other planning sequences.

The first function in the planning sequence is that of forecasting population and employment, as a basis for determining future land use requirements. In the current Land Use-Transportation Study of the Southeastern Wisconsin Regional Planning Commission, new methods of socio-economic forecasting are being investigated in an attempt to provide more accurate and comprehensive employment and population forecasts. These new techniques, which center around the Regional Economic Simulation Model, are the subject of another paper[2] and will not be discussed in detail here. Whatever the method used, population and employment forecasts must be provided as the output of the first step of the planning sequence.

In the second function, aggregate land use demand requirements are determined by applying a conversion coefficient, usually designated as a design standard, to each employment and population category. Such a multiplication and summation will result in a detailed classified set of aggregate demands for residential, industrial, commercial, and other land uses. These aggregate demands provide one of the primary inputs to the third function: plan design.

Plan design lies at the heart of the planning process. The land use plan design function consists essentially of the allocation of a scarce resource, land, between competing and often conflicting land use activities. This allocation must be accomplished so as to satisfy the aggregate needs for each land use and comply with all the design standards (derived from the plan objectives) at a reasonable cost.

The plan selected in the design stage of the planning process must be implemented in the real world. Private decisions of land developers, builders, and households may run contrary to the land pattern prescribed in the plan. This problem of plan implementation is the function of the third stage of the planning process illustrated in Figure 1, land use plan implementation test.

Land use plan implementation is simulated in the Land Use Simulation Model by detailed representation of the decision processes of households and business firms influential in land development. Public land use control policies and public works programs are exogenous inputs to the model. In practice, a number of experimental simulation runs must be performed with different land use control policies and public works programs until a set of policies and programs are determined that result in the implementation of the target land use plan. The feedback on the diagram between land use development and land use plan design accounts for the changes that will probably be needed in the plan design to make it realizable. The output of the third stage of the process is a land use plan capable of practical implementation.

The remaining stages of the planning sequence depicted in Figure 1 relate to the development of a transportation plan. The primary inputs to a transportation system are the trips generated as a function of land use. For this reason, the land use plan is shown in the diagram as an input to the transportation plan design. No models are indicated in the transportation plan design function: none exist, to my knowledge. Trip distribution and traffic assignment models may be used to test the plan intuitively designed by the transportation planner. As a result of model simulation, the transportation plan network is revised until a satisfactory system is developed.

Although each function in the planning process is important to the final realization of a creative and practical plan, the vital role is played by plan design since it is the focal point of all preceding and succeeding planning activity.

THE LAND USE PLAN DESIGN PROCESS

To appreciate the need and requirements for a land use plan design model, it is necessary to examine closely the design process in general and the land use plan design process in particular. Analytical discussion of the design process is rare. Most of the literature on design is based on intuitive and artistic concepts or styles that have predominated in certain periods of history.

An exception to this general scarcity of literature is a recent work by Alexander which defines the design problem in terms of a "fit" between the problem statement and its solution:

> "It is based on the idea that every design problem begins with an effort to achieve fitness between two entities: the form in question and its context. The form is the solution to the problem; the context defines the problem. In other words, when we speak of design, the real object of discussion is not the form alone, but the ensemble comprising the form and its context."[3]

Achieving this fit between the form and its context is not a simple task, for the many requirements that make up the context of the design problem often interact in a complex manner. Attempts to satisfy one design requirement often lead to a violation of another. Faced with such complexity, the designer may be tempted to ignore the real design problem and substitute a traditional design. Although such an approach may be acceptable in a political sense, the original problem remains unsolved.

Difficulties in the design process derive primarily from the inability of the human designer to manipulate simultaneously a large number of interacting design relationships. Mathematics, particularly in its newer forms such as modern algebra, provides a powerful tool for the manipulation of these relationships for the more effective solution of design problems.

To be useful in design synthesis, mathematical formulations must comply with two conditions related to Alexander's definition of a "selection problem": *one,* "It must be possible to generate a wide enough range of possible alternative solutions symbolically"; *two,* "It must be possible to express all criteria for solution in terms of the same symbolism."[4] While Alexander does not pursue the direct solution of selection problems by means of mathematical techniques, his definition provides useful criteria for the systematic formulation of such problem.

Land use plan design, despite its admitted complexity, possesses certain inherent characteristics that meet Alexander's requirements of a selection problem. The first requirement, involving the generation of a wide range of alternative solutions symbolically, is naturally achieved in land use plan design by reason of the common measure of all land use plans: the land itself. All land use plans for areas ranging from the smallest subdivision to multi-state regions may be expressed symbolically by three sets of variables:

(1) The type of land use (quality variables)
(2) The density of land use (quantity variables)
(3) The geographic location (location variables)

Typically, the land area concerned will be subdivided into a grid of "zones" of equal area. The location variable is determined by the geographic coordinates of the zone in question. For each zone, the types and densities of land uses may be expressed as a measure of the activities in that zonal area. The amount of detail provided will depend on the coarseness of the grid. For small areas, a zone may be as small as individual residential lot parcels. In large regions, they may be counties or even states. The key point to be observed is that all land use plans may be expressed by these three classes of variables.

The grid nature of the coordinate system does not limit the results to rectangular plans. On the contrary, the most complex and irregular plan may be expressed with the designated variables if an appropriate grid size is selected.

The second condition, relating to the symbolic relationship between alternative forms and design requirements, is also complied with in the land use plan design problem. All design requirements or "standards" restrict in some way the set of acceptable land use plans. For a design model, these requirements may be divided into two primary classes:

1. Requirements that restrict the minimum or maximum numerical value of a land use or a relationship between land uses *within a grid zone* (intra-zonal

standard). Examples of these requirements are the exclusion of flood plain areas from development in a given grid zone (maximum value standard) or prevention of the simultaneous development of both industrial and residential land in the same grid zone (relationship standard).

2. Requirements that restrict a relationship between land uses *between grid zones* (inter-zonal standard); for example, the need to provide an elementary school within a specified distance (or time) of all residential units.

In either class, the design requirement can be expressed symbolically as an algebraic equality, or more often an inequality, using the three classes of variables noted above. Again, compliance with this condition, like the first, is possible because land use planning is concerned with a single measurable resource, land. That these claims of symbolic design alternative generation and requirements-alternatives comparison are authentic will become more apparent as the design model methodology is explained further.

It is useful at this point to provide a specific, succinct statement of the land use plan design problem, indicating the nature of both the design requirements and the design alternatives. To an experienced urban planner the problem will certainly not be new, since it is the same basic problem that he has been concerned with intuitively during his past design experiences. The problem, as stated below, may seem excessively quantitative, and the emphasis on minimal costs may appear unnecessary, but fundamentally it is the same problem of urban form design that has challenged man since cities were found useful. In brief, the problem of the designer of urban form is:

1. Given design requirements expressed as:

a. A set of design standards in terms of restrictions on land use relationships that may exist in the plan

b. A set of needs or demands for each type of land use based on forecasts of future urban activity

2. Synthesize a land use plan design that satisfies both the land use demands and design standards considering the current state of both natural and manmade land characteristics, at a minimal combination of public and private costs.

The conceptual basis for minimal costs, it must be emphasized, is not to provide a cheap plan but to avoid unnecessary expenditures of precious resources as long as the design standards and land demands are complied with in the plan design.

Intra-zonal design standards may take the form of limitations on density or restrictions of the types of land use that may coexist within a zone. An example of an inter-zonal design standard would be the provision of a regional shopping center within a certain travel time of every residential area. Land use demand requirements would restrict the set of acceptable plans to those that provided the aggregate total of each land use need over the entire design area. The current state of the land, whether developed or in a natural state, is a primary consideration in plan synthesis because of the relationship of the land to both the design standards and the costs associated with new or renewed development.

THE DESIGN MODEL

Two related mathematical techniques will now be discussed as possible frameworks for a land use plan design model. The first technique, linear programming, has a record of successful accomplishment in other fields and has efficient, highly developed computational procedures. Dynamic programming, the second and newer technique, while not as productive in previous applications or standardized computational procedures, is less restricted in its assumptions and, potentially at least, is a more flexible framework for a land use plan design model.

Both linear and dynamic programming are sometimes classified as subsidiary fields under the general title of mathematical programming. Such a general classification is desirable, inasmuch as both fields have as their objective the solution of problems involving the optimization (maximization or minimization) or some objective, such as cost, within the restrictions of certain constraints such as design standards. The techniques involved differ considerably, however, with linear programming imposing rather severe restrictions on the nature of both the objective and constraints while dynamic programming is almost unrestricted in its formulations of both the objective and constraint functions. Linear programming models, on the other hand, can usually be solved by the use of standardized computational procedures, while dynamic programming usually provides at least a serious challenge and often insurmountable obstacles to an efficient computational solution. With either technique, the sheer size of many land use plan design problems bring with them what has been called the "curse of dimensionality," which militates against any simple "brute force" approach to solution.

The linear programming formulation of the land use plan design model problem is straightforward. The objective function relates to the cost of developing land for a given land use:

$$c_t = c_1 x_1 + c_2 x_2 + \dots c_n x_n$$

where the variables (x) may represent residential, industrial or other land uses in given areas and the constants (c) the costs of developing this land. Land use categories may be subdivided into subsidiary classes such as single family residential, multi-family residential, and the costs may be related to the topography and soil characteristics of the area. With each subdivision, of course, the number of variables grows larger, and the computation time for a model solution is increased. In practice, a compromise must be made between the desire for detail and reasonable solution times. With the rapid developments in computer technology, however, this problem will be of decreased significance in the coming years.

The equality and inequality constraints in the linear programming formulation of land use plan design include the following:

1. The total demand requirement for each land use category (equality constraint):

$$d_1x_1 + d_2x_2 + \ldots d_nx_n = E_k$$

where E = regional land use demand requirement for each land use; and d = service ratio coefficients which provide for supporting service land requirements, such as streets, which are necessary for primary land use development.

2. Maximal (minimal) limits on land uses within a zone

$$x_1 + x_2 + \ldots x_n \leqslant F_m$$

where F_m = upper limit on land use n in zone m.

3. Interzonal or intrazonal land use relationship constraints

$$x_n \leqslant G\, x_m$$

where G = ratio of land use n allowed relative to land use m with land uses m and n in the same or different zones.

The land use demand equality constraint (1) follows a standardized format with one equation for each primary land use category. Since some land uses such as single family residential are usually subdivided further according to lot sizes, the number of demand equations in a typical design model may exceed 20 relationships. It is important to emphasize that only primary land uses such as residential, industrial, agricultural, and recreational land are directly determined. Service ratios incorporated in the d parameters account for secondary land uses such as local streets and parks.

The second and third categories of constraints reflect the design standards and may take a wide variety of forms. The maximal constraint will usually reflect a density standard, but it also may provide for the exclusion of an unsuited soil type area for a given type of land use. Land use relationship constraints will result from design standard restrictions on coexistent land uses within a zone or in adjacent zones. Accessibility standards for employment and shopping areas will also be reflected in this type of constraint.

The above constraint relationships reflect the types encountered so far in experimental plan design model runs in test areas. Other constraint forms may be needed when a complete regional plan design is attempted, but they may be easily included as long as they are linear, continuous constraints. Nonlinear discontinuous constraints are not possible with linear programming and account for the primary disadvantages of the method.

For a region subdivided into about 30 zones, the size of a typical linear program for a land use plan design is about 60 equality and inequality constraints and 400 variables. Computer time on an IBM 1620 computer is about three hours. On larger systems, such as the IBM 7090, it would take less than 30 minutes.

MODEL APPLICATION

Some initial experience with applications of the model will now be detailed in order to provide the reader with an idea of the input data requirements and computational characteristics of the model.

Four primary sets of input data are required for model operation:

1. The costs of unimproved land and land development for each primary land use activity for each type of soil.

2. The aggregate demand for each primary land use activity.

3. Design standards which reflect the plan objectives and restrict the set of acceptable plans by limiting interzonal and intrazonal land use relationships.

4. The current land inventory, which will include both land use activities by area and soil characteristics.

Land development cost data may be obtained either by engineering estimates or by statistical analysis of recent land development in the area. The former approach has been used in the initial tests of the model in the Waukesha city pilot area. Collection of land development cost data is always expensive and in many cases difficult or even impossible to obtain. Land developers are usually extremely reluctant to reveal their costs, and the cost data obtained are of uneven quality since many developers do not maintain complete records. For all these reasons, engineering cost estimates are usually preferable if competent professional experience is available.

In the Waukesha area, separate land development cost estimates were made for five sizes of residential lots with their associated service land uses, such as streets, neighborhood shopping, schools, and parks. Additional cost estimates were made for industrial, regional shopping, and regional park land uses. These were not gross estimates but detailed analyses of the costs of each improvement related to both the land use and the type of soil involved. All estimates were subdivided into their component parts, each with its individual cost.

Separate cost estimates were prepared for each of three classes of soil. Soil data were obtained from a comprehensive soil survey made in southeastern Wisconsin as part of the Land Use-Transportation Study. Unimproved land costs presented a special problem since they could not be obtained from engineering estimates. Assessed and equalized land value data were obtained from each of the communities and were adjusted on the basis of prices realized in recent land transactions in the area.

Initial tests of the model used historical aggregate land use demands for 1950-1962 to provide comparisons between actual and "optimal" land development in the area. Typically, however, a design application of the model will require forecasts of future land use demands, which may be obtained by applying design standards to forecasts of population and employment in the region of interest.

The various forms of design standards usually provided were described in the previous section. In current tests of the model, design standards were limited to the exclusion of development from areas such as flood plains, along with the provision of service ratios for the amounts of secondary land (streets, parks) required to suppor the primary land uses. Design standards for the regional land use plan are still in preparation and will be used in model tests as soon as they become available.

An inventory of both current land use activities and soil characteristics is critical for model application. In current tests, developed areas were eliminated from consideration for future land development. It is possible, however, to consider redevelopment in the form of urban renewal as a set of alternatives in the design. For this approach, redevelopment costs would be required. Through the use of the soil inventory, it was possible to assign a development cost to each subarea in the test area.

Proper presentation of the Land Use Plan Design Model output is an important consideration in achieving acceptance of its design by planners and governmental officials. Initial model outputs were in tabular form and were meaningful only to someone familiar with the operation of the model. Improved presentation was later achieved by tabular designation of the intensity of each land use activity in each zone. Printed output was supplemented by colored land use maps manually prepared from the tabular print-out.

AVAILABLE MATHEMATICAL MODELS

Although linear programming provides a reasonably satisfactory framework for a land use plan design model, it possesses certain inherent disadvantages that restrict its usefulness in design. The primary limitation is the need for continuous rather than discrete values for the land use variables. Land use design choices are by nature usually discrete rather than continuous. The basic element of residential land use is the subdivision rather than the lot. Industrial land use units tend to be industrial parks rather than individual factory sites, much less land acreage. While it is possible to round off the linear programming solution to satisfy these natural discrete levels, such a solution does not usually correspond with the associated discrete optimal combination.

A second limitation of linear programming is the need for both a linear objective function and linear constraints. The linear objective function is not a severe limitation, because the inaccuracies introduced by a linear approximation of costs are usually less than the errors of cost estimation. In the few instances where known nonlinear cost functions occur, such as in the plant capacities of areawide facilities for water supply or sewage treatment, the cost break may usually be satisfactorily approximated by a multivariable series of linear cost variables.

Nonlinear constraint relationships present a more serious problem. Certain design standards are inherently nonlinear, and a linear approximation sometimes provides an unsatisfactory substitute. When a design model is not able to provide satisfactorily for a design standard, it loses most of its usefulness.

Dynamic programming, another member of the mathematical programming family, has the potential for removing the two primary restrictions inherent in linear programming. Although dynamic programming may be used to solve the same land use plan design problem, it is based on a different class of mathematical procedures, which are capable of handling discrete and nonlinear objective functions and constraint relationships.

Richard Bellman of the Rand Corporation was the originator of dynamic programming and has developed the theory and application of this multi-stage approach to decision making to a high degree in the last decade. A large number of classes of dynamic programming processes have been formulated for problems in production scheduling, rocket trajectories, and feedback control systems, but the class of process of primary interest in design is the allocation process.[5] In a dynamic programming model, the basic cost and design relationship are similar to those defined for the linear programming model, but the method of computation differs and permits the use of more complex and discrete relationships.

THE DESIGN VIEWPOINT IN URBAN PLANNING

The ultimate contribution of this paper will depend on its success, or the lack of it, in accomplishing at least a partial reorientation of land use model development toward design. Although the importance of forecasting land use development was indicated by the role of the Land Use Simulation Model briefly described earlier in this paper and detailed in another recent paper,[6] the dangers and limitations of non-design-oriented models that are only remotely related to the synthesis of better urban and regional plans should be apparent.

The need for design model in urban planning is fortunately accompanied by greater possibilities for their success. Industrial applications of mathematical models in normative functions such as production scheduling and optimal product design have been conspicuously more successful than attempts to simulate human behavioral patterns in a market. Quite simply, it is much easier to use a model to tell people what they *should do* than to explain *what they are doing.* Given the fantastic complexity of the modern metropolis, would it not be well to emphasize model development in areas that promise both a significant contribution and a high probability of success?

The image of design in urban planning as a remnant of a bygone age of the "city beautiful" must be replaced by a new design concept based on the creative synthesis of complex plans using all the tools provided by modern technology.

NOTES

1. Traffic Research Corporation, *Review of Existing Land Use Forecasting Techniques,* presented to the Boston Regional Planning Project (Toronto, 1963).

2. Kenneth J. Schlager, "Simulation Models in Urban and Regional Planning," *Technical Record,* Southeastern Wisconsin Regional Planning Commission, Waukesha, Wisconsin, II, No. 1 (1964).

3. Christopher Alexander, *Notes on the Synthesis of Form* (Cambridge: Harvard University Press, 1964), pp. 15-16.

4. Ibid., pp. 74-75.

5. Richard E. Bellman and Stuart E. Dreyfus, *Applied Dynamic Programming* (Princeton: Princeton University Press, 1962).

6. Schlager, op. cit.

Chapter 8

TECHNOLOGICAL FORECASTING: TECHNIQUES IN PERSPECTIVE

Erich Jantsch

"The key to progress in forecasting is not yet the use of a particular tool. It is, as in other fields of intellectual inquiry, the maintenance of a proper viewpoint–a viewpoint expressed in Whitehead's succinct injunction to seek simplicity and also to distrust it."

–Irving H. Siegel

INCENTIVES AND OPPORTUNITIES

Siegel's words, written in 1953, still characterize the situation today and will be valid for some time to come. It may even be generally stated that techniques at present are not developed to replace the "viewpoint" emphasized by Siegel but to enforce and improve the selection of proper "viewpoints." Even with techniques, technological forecasting today is much more an art than a science. Virtually all users of special techniques in technological forecasting stress an aspect of their experience which they invariably consider to be the most valuable: that the use of techniques greatly enhances the recognition of relevant factors, their relationships with the problem in question, and their inter-relationships.

The bulk of technological forecasting today is done without the explicit use of special techniques. However, it would be difficult to draw a clear dividing line between use and non-use. The adoption of a "viewpoint," or a general attitude

Reprinted from *Technological Forecasting in Perspective* by Erich Jantsch, Chapter II.1, pp. 109-132. Published by and for the Organization for Economic Co-operation and Development, Paris, France, 1967. Reprinted by permission of the author.

towards the forecasting problem, structures thinking and "informed judgement" in a characteristic way and may imply qualitative or even quantitative relationships between factors. If these elements are stated explicitly, they may add up to a simple formal model which can be used for the simulation of the partial processes involved. Almost every practical intuitive forecast uses implicitly one or more iterative steps between exploratory and normative thinking, with cross-checking against an "environmental matrix."

The need for formal techniques was not felt until a few years ago. While the beginning of systematic technological forecasting can be situated at around 1950, with forerunners since 1945, the existence of a more widespread interest in special techniques first made itself felt about a decade later, in 1960, with forerunners already experimenting in the late 1950s. Now, in the mid-1960s, a noticeable interest is developing in more elaborate multi-level programming. The first tentative ideas for an integration of technological forecasting models into future systems of information technology are being sketched in informal papers.

Just as, during the past few decades, and even in past centuries, there has been occasional technological forecasting, in similar fashion, a few very simple techniques–corresponding to basic attitudes rather than to simulation–have long found occasional use: trend extrapolation on a phenomenological basis, brainstorming, and possibly some early versions of "scenario-writing." An elaborate multi-level technique formulated in 1942–Zwicky's "morphological approach"–did not receive wide diffusion and has continued to suffer an unfortunate fate ever since, although it is complementary to other more recently developed elaborate techniques and fill a "gap" that can be recognized today.

Technological forecasting is one of the latest additions to a family of systematic forecasting activities. If the very old art of weather forecasting is omitted from consideration, a number of "precursive" activities are encountered as part of this family such as economic and business forecasting, while forecasting in the political and social areas is more or less developing parallel to technological forecasting. From the techniques point of view, there is considerable "cross-fertilization," but perhaps less than one might expect or than would appear feasible. Economic analysis on the basis of discounted cash flow methods is a valuable addition to technological forecasting, as is the use of certain matrix techniques. More elaborate econometric and business models can be adapted to problems of technological forecasting only within certain limits; in general, the economic and business areas have developed sophisticated techniques only for short-range forecasts, whereas the main interest for technology is in long-range forecasts. However, there are numerous refinements which have arisen from the concentrated effort on the economic and business forecasting techniques that may be adapted, such as risk evaluation and various forms of probabilistic forecasting.

On the other hand, forecasting techniques developed in the political, social, and technological fields–especially those centering on "social technology"–can to a considerable degree mutually benefit from each other. Military forecasting in the non-technological areas may also produce some "spin-off" in the form of techniques.

The two basic approaches that are making the deepest impact on technological forecasting techniques—*operations research* and *systems analysis*—were first explored and developed in response to military incentives. Operations research dates back to World War II developments in the United Kingdom and the United States, and systems analysis has been pioneered by the RAND Corporation in the United States since 1948. Critical path and PERT methods (the latter developed for the Polaris missile program) also sprang from military planning requirements.

These developments would seem to constitute a vast source of technological forecasting techniques which has so far been exploited only to a small degree. While the possibilities of reasonably sized tasks for operations research and systems analysis are nearly exhausted in the military field—there are almost no problems left in U.S. defense that can be solved with linear programming—technological forecasting is only starting to explore them for its own purposes.

Another very important area of "precursive" activity is *computer development* and the vast evolving field of *information technology*. Technological forecasting has not yet acquired sufficient "status" to inspire developments in these areas, but in a few years it will find a ready-made framework for decision-making in business, military, political, and possibly social environments, and will be accommodated without difficulty.

The *mode of diffusion* of ideas and concepts in the area of technological forecasting techniques is comparable to modes that can be observed in early research phases in many fields. A glance at the bibliography at the end of this report, in particular at its sections dealing with techniques, will confirm the impression that a relatively large number of significant ideas are first communicated by internal reports, informal papers, unsolicited proposals, conference papers, preprints of tentative versions of manuscripts, and other forms outside the realm of "open literature." Generally, this has nothing to do with the possibility of these ideas being of a confidential nature. Rather, the tentative and exploratory nature of many of the ideas prompts their authors to communicate through informal "progress reports" material which will later be written up in generally accessible publications.

A company such as Honeywell (U.S.), with justifiable pride in its PATTERN scheme (see section II.4.5* [of the book]) after two years of testing and the first year of successful full-scale operation, adopted a policy of encouraging publication and conference contributions. As the inclusion of a technological forecasting function is regarded, by a number of companies with a modern public relations concept, as a positive "image"-creating factor, the use of special techniques is also bound to be so regarded. The open attitude encountered in this connection played a decisive role in the collection of information on forecasting techniques for this report.

*Not included herein.—Ed.

Among periodical publications, the "IEEE Transactions on Engineering Management" (Institute of Electrical and Electronics Engineers, New York—until 1962 published by the Institute of Radio Engineers as IRE Transactions on Engineering Management) have become the "home" of papers on ranking procedures for research and development projects, based on economic analysis, operations research, and decision theory approaches. More recently, the Battelle Memorial Institute, which follows a policy of open publication of techniques in this area, has chosen the Design Engineering Conferences of the ASME (American Society of Mechanical Engineers, New York) as a vehicle for discussion, with previous publication in the series of ASME Papers, and subsequent inclusion in ASME periodicals. Occasionally, techniques are discussed in the Harvard Business Review and in scattered operations research journals.

The course of Professor James R. Bright at the Graduate School of Business of the Harvard University in Boston, Massachusetts, contains the first attempt systematically to teach technological forecasting techniques to management students.

Two American institute in the general area of management sciences are now including discussions of technological forecasting techniques in their courses on long-range corporate planning:

The American Management Association (AMA) in New York, in long-range planning courses held in December 1965 and April 1966, included sessions on technological forecasting, with background papers contributed mainly by the Battelle Memorial Institute. AMA is also active in Europe and could become instrumental in spreading techniques there;

The Institute of Management Sciences in Pleasantville, New York, within the framework of its "College on Planning," seems to take technological forecasting techniques into account.

Special conferences and conference sessions, attempting to survey the advancing frontier in the state of the art of techniques for technological forecasting, bear testimony to the rapidly growing interest in this area:

The French periodical *Réalités,* on the occasion of its 20th anniversary, sponsored a "Colloque de l'Avenir" ("Symposium on the Future") on 29th and 30th March 1966, in Paris, purporting to be devoted entirely to the methodology of long-range forecasting and anticipation. Forty of the best-known experts in this field attended the conference, which apparently concentrated on methods suitable to "social technology"; unfortunately, the published account in *Réalités* is very poor and has obviously suffered from the process of filtering down to a journalistic level.

The US Air Force sponsored a Symposium on Long Range Forecasting and Planning, with emphasis on techniques, on 16-17 August, 1966, at the Air Force Academy in Colorado Springs, Colorado, with attendance mainly from the armed forces; the proceedings are unclassified and are available from the US Government Printing Office in Washington, D.C.

Prof. James R. Bright is organizing a conference on "Technological Forecasting for Industry" to be held on 22-25 May, 1967, at the Industrial Management Center, Lake Placid, New York. The results of this conference will be made available in book form (Prof. Bright, 1964, 1961, has formerly published two books which partly grew out of symposia in closely related areas.)

The National Security Industrial Association (NSIA), in Washington, D.C., is planning for autumn 1967 a classified symposium on research and development in the 1970s which is expected to include a "brilliant" session on technological forecasting, with particular emphasis on techniques.

TYPES OF TECHNIQUES AND THE STATE OF THE ART

The following three points are to some extent dependent on each other and are characteristic of all existing techniques for technological forecasting. They

have been developed for a "man-technique dialogue" and are very sensitive to man's knowledge and his capacity for imaginative thinking, technical and value judgment, and synthesis. Essentially, human forecasting is not replaced, but structured and enhanced, by these techniques; in particular, the human forecasting potential is extended where large input and complex relationships are involved.

are partial techniques which cover only a fraction of a complete technological forecasting process; their combination may result in more highly, but not yet fully integrated techniques (on the basis of today's state of the art).

are auxiliary aids to decision-making, which normally has to be based on broader information than can be provided by these techniques.

Roughly 100 distinguishable techniques or elements of techniques are briefly reviewed and, as far as possible, outlined in the following chapters* [of the book]. Not all of them can be called "technological forecasting techniques" or were intended for this purpose; however, they are all related either to the entire complex of technological forecasting or to some of its aspects.

No fundamental distinction is made in this report between *qualitative* and *quantitative* techniques because there is no clear boundary line in many cases, and the same technique can take either approach. Qualitative assessment, in many respects–mergers of technologies, impact of complex systems, scenarios and anticipations of the future, qualitative goals and objectives–has attained equal importance with quantitative assessment.

The many approaches–whose large number characterizes the present experimental phase in this area–can be classified by different criteria. In line with the findings of Part I* of this report, a fundamental distinction is made between exploratory and normative technological forecasting. In the technology transfer scheme, which has been introduced in Part I for the representation of the direction and levels of technological forecasting, exploratory forecasting techniques simulate movement in the direction of technology transfer, and normative forecasting techniques screen technology transfer by running against its movement. A fully integrated forecasting process is a feedback process, employing both directions. One class of techniques defies classification by this

*Not included herein.–Ed.

scheme: direct applied intuitive thinking, which in some way represents "a view from outside."

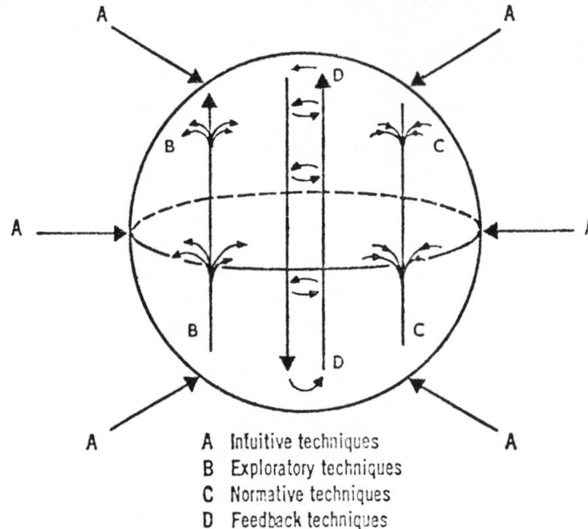

The main transform directions of these four types of techniques can then be illustrated by the use of the "technology transfer sphere," explained in Part I. A sphere characteristic of a closed society is chosen here because normative and feedback techniques find their full use only in such closed spaces. The other techniques, on the other hand, can be fully used also in tulip-shaped spaces, characteristic of an open society (normative and feedback techniques could be used in such spaces only at the lower levels).

In the technology transfer space, the lowest and the highest levels, i.e. the "starting levels" for exploratory and normative forecasts respectively, can be

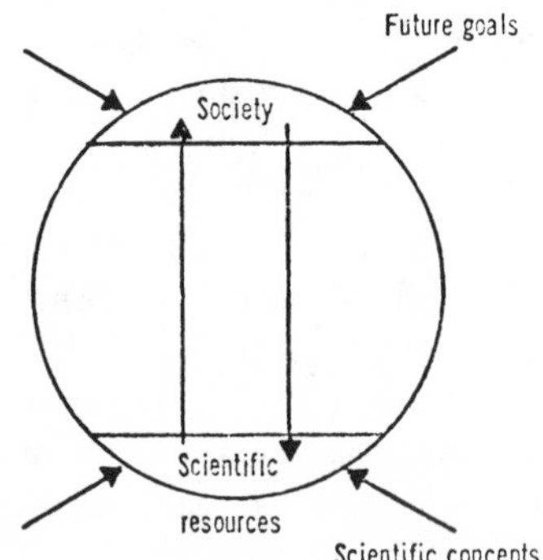

imagined to receive continuous streams of "spiritual energy" flowing in from the irrational surrounding space. These streams become visible in the form of scientific discovery and of social goals and their ethical background. (This is a very simplified picture, of course, serving only to illustrate a specific point here.) No fully integrated forecasting is possible if these inflows cannot be assessed. There is no formal technique for dealing with scientific discovery through systematic exploratory forecasting in sight; normative forecasting, however, can stimulate scientific discovery and guide fundamental research. The forecasting of broad social goals and ethical patterns of the future is not a completely hopeless undertaking; as a matter of fact, schemes to improve intuitive thinking to this end, for example, the "Delphi" technique (see section II.2.3*), and to stimulate systematic anticipation and evaluation of future goals for the sake of present as well as future action (see section II.5.1*), are being actively developed and tested.

In the past, technological forecasting techniques have aimed primarily at forecasting, in the exploratory direction, technology transfer up to the level of

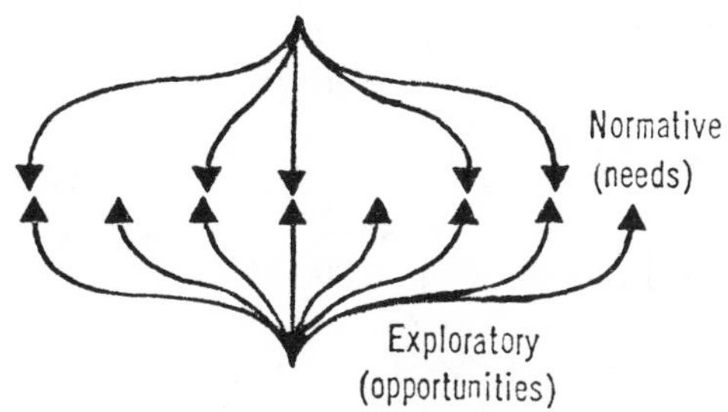

"Elementary Technology" (still below the "equator" of the sphere) and only in the two-dimensional vertical cross-section representing the technological process itself. For the purposes of industrial product planning, a number of short-stretch techniques, bridging the "equator" in the exploratory, and later in the normative, direction have been added. The extension to the higher levels, the recognition of the full potential of normative techniques, and the extension to the non-technological dimension, have been accomplished only in the past few years, and are still in a very early, experimental phase. Feedback techniques are not yet operational.

A complete technological forecast today has to match normative forecasting (needs, desires) against exploratory forecasting (opportunities).

Intuitive techniques have only recently found a first critical approach in the "Delphi" technique. Such techniques permit, in principle, "random access" to all levels. In particular, they represent at present the only hope of finding sets of valid starting points for normative techniques at the highest levels ("social goals"). The alternative—reaching up to these levels by exploratory techniques (scenarios, etc.)—would yield some sets by laborious iteration and alternative approaches, but is not sufficiently comprehensive to be considered satisfactory.

Exploratory techniques can be sub-divided into two classes which indicate their potential application:

*Not included herein.—Ed.

Techniques *generating new technological information,* comprising the following groups: extrapolation of technical parameter and functional capability trends, "learning curves," extrapolation of contextual mapping, morphological research, possibly also scenario-writing (not yet demonstrated);

Techniques *structuring and processing given technological information,* comprising the following groups: historical analogy, scenario-writing and iteration through synopsis, probabilistic transform methods, economic analysis, operational models, techniques dealing with the aggregated level.

This distinction is more important, since any complete technological forecasting process has to include one or more techniques for generating new technological information–in other words, for specifying the nature and/or some of the essential characteristics of future technologies. Although this aspect constitutes the oldest concern of technological forecasting, its state is not at all satisfactory, and may even be said to be underdeveloped in relation to other forecasting aspects. The art of trend extrapolation, which a number of enthusiastic forecasters have accepted as a challenge, deals only with a small part of the desired new technological information. Technical parameters and functional capabilities are not sufficient for forecasting impact in economic and social environments; they are more useful for military purposes for which trend extrapolation is a very valuable tool today. In the future, the art of trend extrapolation will be severely affected by feedback effects from better technological forecasting and planning. The "historical inertia" inherent in any trend forecast may be influenced significantly by this feedback; after all, such a feedback effect constitutes the very incentive for undertaking technological forecasting. On the other hand, the feedback from planning that has already accelerated progress in the military field may not be maintained at the same rate, and the trend towards more horizontal technology transfer in the civilian sector may act as a decelerating factor. We have not yet measured the dimensions of technology transfer, and to attempt to forecast the vertical component as if it were isolated constitutes a doubtful approach.

The most systematic approach to the generation of new technological information is "morphological research," a technique for obtaining a comprehensive and unbiased spectrum of functional technological systems, sub-systems, etc. The feasibility evaluation which imparts operational value to this approach can be aided by trend extrapolation and other information-generating techniques.

If normative forecasting, which is rapidly growing in importance, is adequately to realize the promise inherent in it, it will have to be supplemented by techniques which provide as complete a spectrum as possible of technological opportunities. "Morphological research," aided by trend extrapolation, is the best available possibility (but is not yet widely applied): trend extrapolation used alone is the second best (and is already being applied systematically in connection with Honeywell's PATTERN scheme for normative forecasting). Outside the realm of techniques, intuitive thinking is the reliable and still "natural" alternative as well as the indispensable cement for all insufficient and not fully integrated techniques.

The other class of exploratory techniques, those structuring and processing given technological information, are relatively abundant. Their importance will increase with the extension of exploratory forecasting to the upper (the impact) half of the "technology transfer sphere," and with the use of large-scale forecasting to evaluate large amount of input data and programmed relationships. One has only to look at the difficulties which the correct assessment of the influence of the time factor on economic benefits presents without discounted cash flow methods, to appreciate the role of this class of techniques. They will be essential for future feedback systems. Nevertheless, they will attain their full importance only when the modest start made at present with computer models has led to the inclusion of technological forecasting in future systems of information technology.

The application of *normative techniques* depends on a greater abundance of opportunities, primarily in the technological areas, than can be handled under given budgeting or other constraints. This is the typical situation today; however, it cannot be assumed automatically for an indefinite future as, up to now, it could not be assumed throughout man's history. Also, normative techniques are meaningful only in a sufficiently closed society, or for those levels of technology transfer which can be assumed sufficiently closed. This prerequisite is fulfilled today for reasonably well-defined technological programs, such as, for example, those in the defense and space fields, and is beginning to be met for burning social or national issues in countries that are future-oriented by inclination or necessity (leaving aside the question of dictatorships in this context): the United States, France, Sweden, followed at a distance by Italy, the Netherlands, Canada, and a few others. The majority of Western industrialized countries have not matured to this stage (and, it will be emphasized in this report, such maturity is most necessary if dirigism is to be avoided).

In the United States, Vice-President Hubert Humphrey, then a Senator, introduced a resolution in the Senate on 10 September 1964, calling for the establishment of a Presidential Advisory Staff on Scientific Information Management. On that occasion he stated: "There is an urgent need in industry and government alike for new techniques and systems for management information in assisting officials responsible for crucial policies and decisions of our society. Upon the discovery and use of such new techniques and systems depends not only the solution of many current problems, but our continuing status as a world leader. . . . [It has become] abundantly clear that many of the current and impending problems of our society will remain insolvable until we discover and adopt information management and decision-aiding techniques which are commensurate with the changes which have occurred and will occur in our national and international environment." This statement was made in the light of the favorable impression created by the successful operation of the newly-born PATTERN scheme, the most elaborate of the normative technological forecasting techniques. The "Delphi" panel on "Automation" forecast the widespread use of computerized techniques aiding decision-making in the 1970s.

Normative techniques benefit from the present emphasis on the development of operations research, decision theory, and systems analysis.[1] A general appraisal of the value of decision theory for engineering management has been made by Combs (see Sweezy, 1965). Brandenburg (1964) and Baker and Pound (1964) have summarized and critically discussed a number of simple two-level (in terms of technology transfer levels) normative techniques, which are often referred to as "ranking procedures for research and development projects" (by which term the exploratory economic analysis approaches are usually also covered).

The best and most flexible principle available for normative forecasting today is the relevance tree, which is the basis for PATTERN and a number of other techniques. It is also the most "transparent" principle, providing a wealth of additional insight. A certain limitation to the number of levels and branching points is imposed by the preparatory and updating effort, which quickly increases; the calculation work, which can be easily programmed for a computer, does not constitute a bottleneck. A particular advantage of relevance tree concepts, which may differ in the evaluation schemes and refinements applied to the lower levels, lies in the fact that they could use common "head-ends" prepared centrally. This may become important in areas where the government has an interest in bringing its policies to bear among widely dispersed contractors, for example in the defense or space areas.

Network techniques are promising for special aspects of normative forecasting, particularly for the evaluation of different systems concepts. The use of operational models seems to be of less significance in normative than in exploratory forecasting; it will probably be applied mainly to the problem of selection from among complex alternative developments.

The potential of systems analysis has so far remained almost untapped for the purposes of technological forecasting. Systems analysis is applied by the pioneers in the field–RAND Corporation, System Development Corporation, General Electric's TEMPO Center, all in California–whose tasks frequently include, or are related to, problems of technological forecasting. Systems analysis is a general approach that has to be adapted to each new job–there is no rigorously set routine which can be easily transferred to other users.

Feedback techniques may ultimately be constructed out of the elements of exploratory and normative forecasting, or will be based on newly developed elements. In principle, it would not seem feasible on the basis of today's techniques to combine them to form a fully-integrated feedback system covering all levels and directions of technology transfer. What do seem feasible today, however, are multi-level feedback systems on the basis of a "man-technique dialogue," and partial feedback systems covering only two or three levels or certain directions of technology transfer.

Feedback systems are a natural consequence of the same conditions that have brought normative forecasting to the forefront. It may be assumed that considerable effort will be devoted to their development and perfection once decision-making techniques have been adopted in areas of broad national and social concern.

"By-pass" techniques, with the exception of intuitive thinking, have not generally been explored up to the present time (although a few qualitative techniques, such as historical analogy, seek to establish direct forecasting relationships between non-adjacent levels). Their feasibility must still be regarded as uncertain. The basic aim of "by-pass" techniques is to make it possible to start from one technology transfer level and obtain "random access"

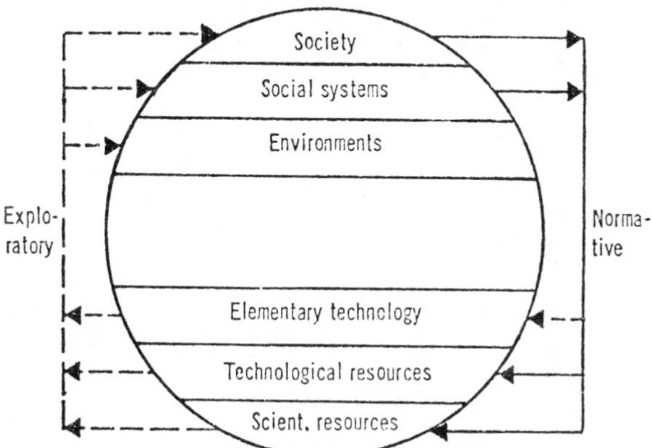

to any other level. An urgent need for such techniques seems to exist primarily in the normative direction. In integrated normative forecasts that range from the highest to the lowest levels of technology transfer, there is an inevitable–and apparently substantial–loss of information. (This would be a problem amenable to exploration by information theory.) In addition, certain significant aspects and values seem to escape ordering by hierarchic principles.

It would be of the greatest significance if reliable techniques could be developed that permitted, for example, the derivation of the necessary tasks for fundamental research and fundamental technological development directly from social goals, national objectives, high-level missions, etc. (In a way, this is implicitly attempted on an intuitive basis by the COSPUP reports–see Chapter I.4.) Such "by-pass" procedures would be even of much greater importance if alternative sets of anticipated goals–not only the goals valid at present–were taken into account in future schemes (see section II.5.5*). Intuitive thinking on the basis of the "Delphi" technique (see section II.2.2*) already seems to be yielding a few preliminary results in this direction by formulating future desirata in the form of functional technological capability.

*Not included herein.–Ed.

A *table of the individual techniques* and elements of techniques which are reviewed in the following chapters is provided below and may give a broad idea of their applicability and their principal orientation. The graphic indications are necessarily imprecise and are open to discussion. Techniques extending over many levels seem to be relatively rare. Exploratory techniques are crowded into the lower (technological) levels, while normative techniques are firmly anchored in the upper (impact) levels but penetrate courageously into the technological levels.

It will be recalled that the significance of the eight levels of technology transfer was given in Chapter I.1* of this report:

I = Scientific resources
II = Technological resources
III = Elementary technology
IV = Functional technological systems
V = Applications
VI = Environments
VII = Social systems
VIII = Society

The following graphic signs are used in the table which follows.

★ (★)	Level of (isolated) application (with brackets : doubtful or less formal)
■	Substantial combination with horizontal factors
---+——+——►	Direction and penetration of transform method (vertical marks : individual evaluation for that level possible; dotted line : uncertain)
◄—·—- - ——- -+	Strong stimulation for (human) feedback

TECHNIQUE (with section number showing where it is discussed in this report)	LEVELS OF TECHNOLOGY TRANSFER							
	I	II	III	IV	V	VI	VII	VIII
II.2. *INTUITIVE THINKING*								
II.2.2. *Brainstorming*								
Straight brainstorming		(★)	★	★	★	★	(★)	(★)
"Buzz group" technique			★	(★)				
"Oper. creativity"		★	★					
II.2.3. *"Delphi" technique*				(★)			★	★
II.2.4. *Utopia and science fiction*								★
II.3. *EXPLORAT. FORECAST.*								
II.3.2. *Extrapolation of time-series, anal. models*								
Adams			★					
Isenson		■	■					

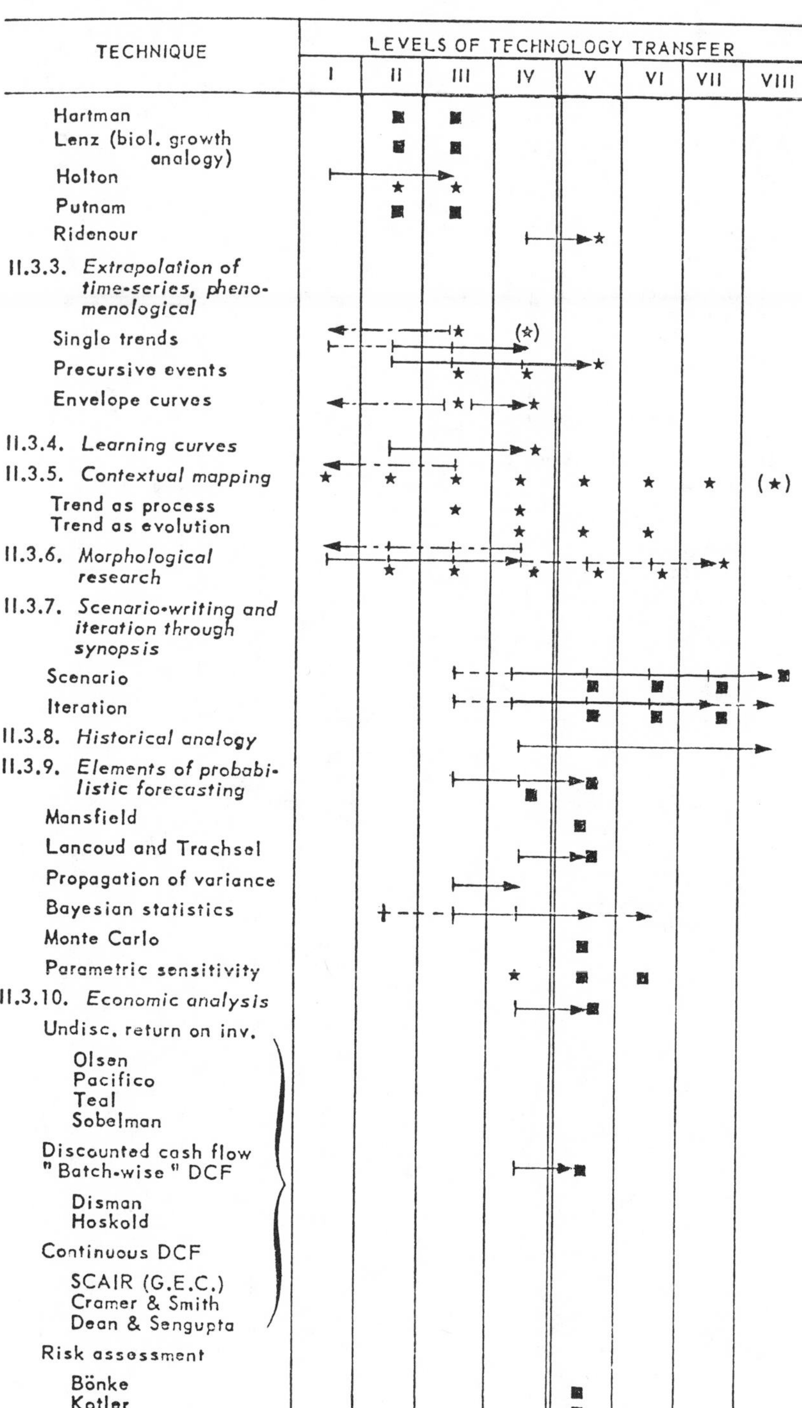
TECHNIQUE
LEVELS OF TECHNOLOGY TRANSFER
I
II
III
IV
V
VI
VII
VIII
Hartman
Lenz (biol. growth analogy)
Holton
Putnam
Ridenour
II.3.3. Extrapolation of time-series, phenomenological
Single trends
Precursive events
Envelope curves
II.3.4. Learning curves
II.3.5. Contextual mapping
Trend as process
Trend as evolution
II.3.6. Morphological research
II.3.7. Scenario-writing and iteration through synopsis
Scenario
Iteration
II.3.8. Historical analogy
II.3.9. Elements of probabilistic forecasting
Mansfield
Lancoud and Trachsel
Propagation of variance
Bayesian statistics
Monte Carlo
Parametric sensitivity
II.3.10. Economic analysis
Undisc. return on inv.
Olsen
Pacifico
Teal
Sobelman
Discounted cash flow
"Batch-wise" DCF
Disman
Hoskold
Continuous DCF
SCAIR (G.E.C.)
Cramer & Smith
Dean & Sengupta
Risk assessment
Bönke
Kotler

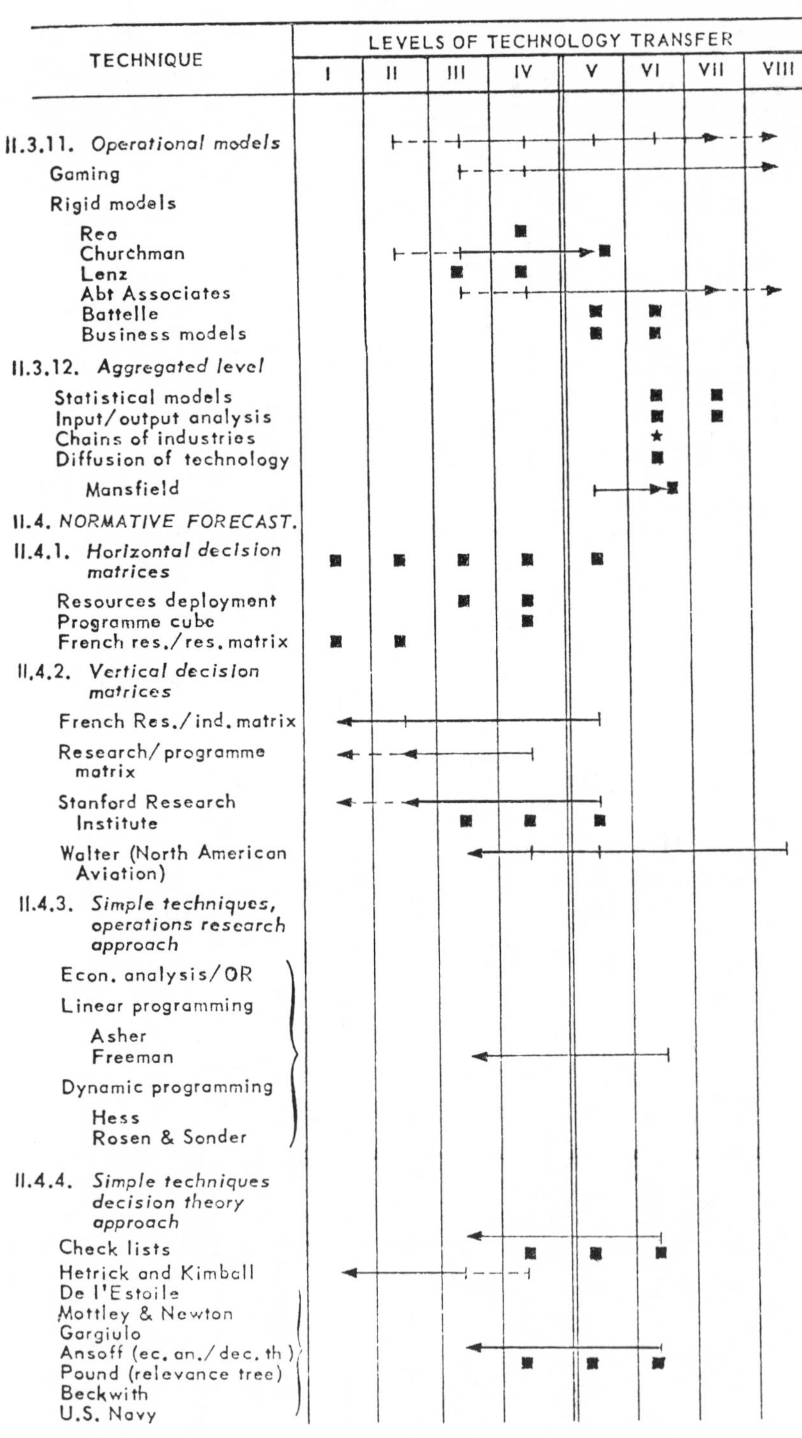
TECHNIQUE
LEVELS OF TECHNOLOGY TRANSFER
I
II
III
IV
V
VI
VII
VIII
II.3.11. Operational models
Gaming
Rigid models
Rea
Churchman
Lenz
Abt Associates
Battelle
Business models
II.3.12. Aggregated level
Statistical models
Input/output analysis
Chains of industries
Diffusion of technology
Mansfield
II.4. NORMATIVE FORECAST.
II.4.1. Horizontal decision matrices
Resources deployment
Programme cube
French res./res. matrix
II.4.2. Vertical decision matrices
French Res./ind. matrix
Research/programme matrix
Stanford Research Institute
Walter (North American Aviation)
II.4.3. Simple techniques, operations research approach
Econ. analysis/OR
Linear programming
Asher
Freeman
Dynamic programming
Hess
Rosen & Sonder
II.4.4. Simple techniques decision theory approach
Check lists
Hetrick and Kimball
De l'Estoile
Mottley & Newton
Gargiulo
Ansoff (ec. an./dec. th)
Pound (relevance tree)
Beckwith
U.S. Navy

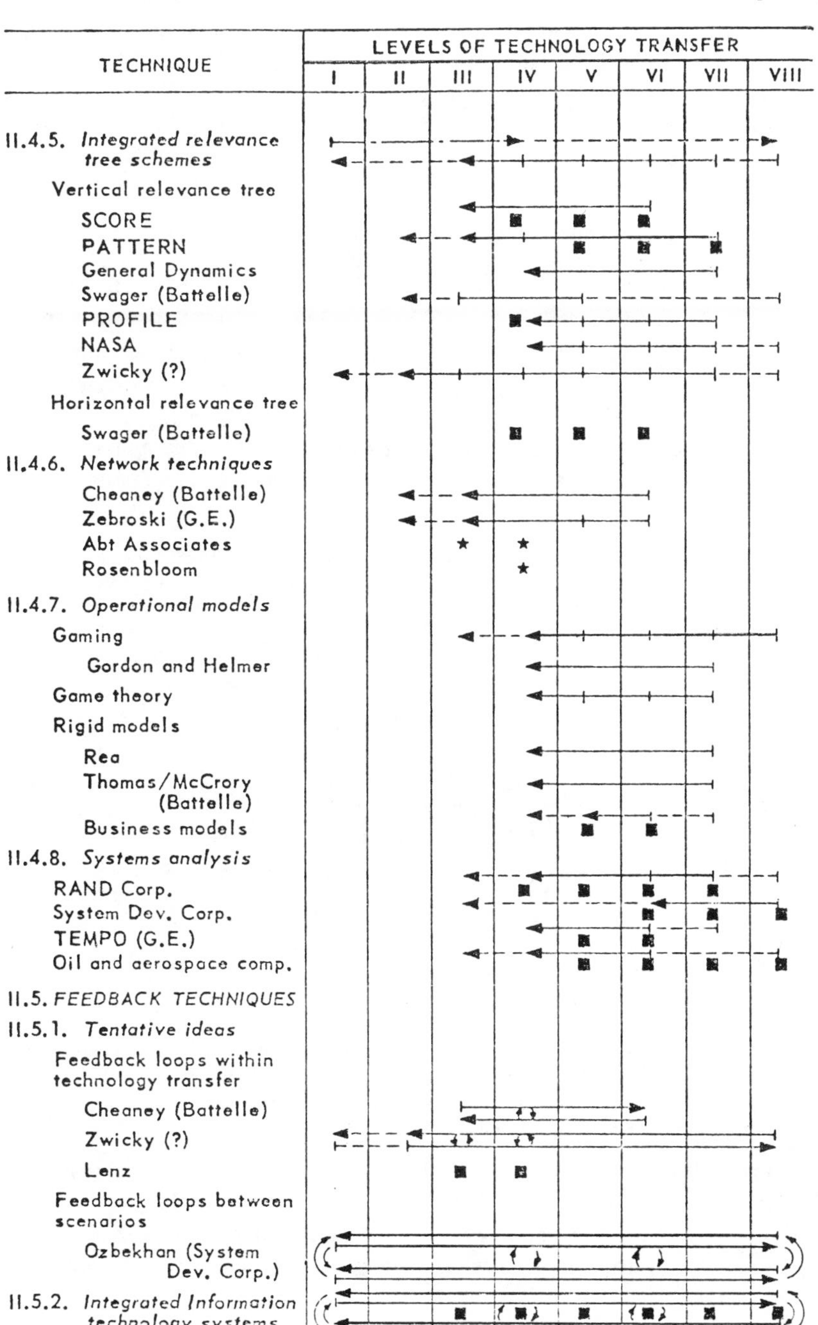
TECHNIQUE
LEVELS OF TECHNOLOGY TRANSFER
I
II
III
IV
V
VI
VII
VIII
II.4.5. Integrated relevance tree schemes
Vertical relevance tree
SCORE
PATTERN
General Dynamics
Swager (Battelle)
PROFILE
NASA
Zwicky (?)
Horizontal relevance tree
Swager (Battelle)
II.4.6. Network techniques
Cheaney (Battelle)
Zebroski (G.E.)
Abt Associates
Rosenbloom
II.4.7. Operational models
Gaming
Gordon and Helmer
Game theory
Rigid models
Rea
Thomas/McCrory (Battelle)
Business models
II.4.8. Systems analysis
RAND Corp.
System Dev. Corp.
TEMPO (G.E.)
Oil and aerospace comp.
II.5. FEEDBACK TECHNIQUES
II.5.1. Tentative ideas
Feedback loops within technology transfer
Cheaney (Battelle)
Zwicky (?)
Lenz
Feedback loops between scenarios
Ozbekhan (System Dev. Corp.)
II.5.2. Integrated Information technology systems

This surprisingly large number of techniques, or even of groups of techniques using the same approach, should not cause too much confusion. There are relatively few which really constitute "breakthroughs" in their area. Apart from the older art of trend extrapolation and its more recent refinements through S-curve and envelope curve extrapolation, there have been only three really important developments:

the "Delphi" for the improvement of intuitive thinking;
the "morphological approach" to exploratory forecasting;
the relevance tree principle as a basis for a number of normative forecasting techniques.

Future "breakthroughs" may be achieved in the areas of gaming and operational computer models, systems analysis, and feedback systems; important ideas have already been conceived in these fields.

An *optimum* complete large scale *forecasting scheme* would employ, on the basis of techniques in an operational state in 1966, a combination of the following techniques:

1. The "Delphi" technique for the unbiased selection of social and other high-level goals, possibly aided by scenario-writing or operational models in the economic, political, military and social areas.

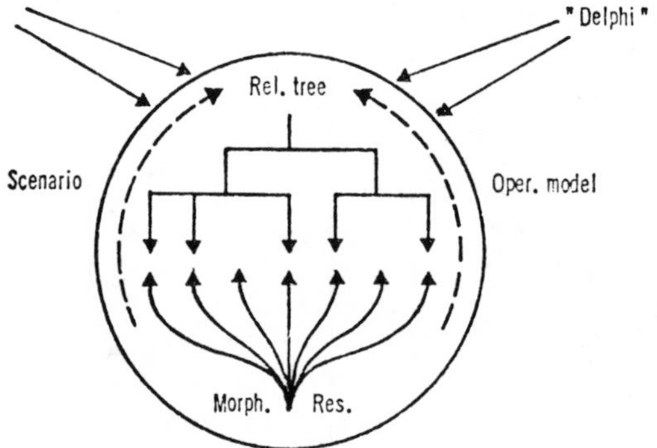

2. "Morphological research," aided by trend extrapolation, for an unbiased exploration of possible and feasible technological opportunities.
3. A relevance tree scheme, such as PATTERN, for the clearly structured introduction of the normative basis to make the proper selection.

Honeywell's actual forecasting scheme centered around PATTERN looks similar, but employs only trend extrapolation and scenario-writing.

In an optimum forecasting scheme embracing a limited number of alternatives (for example on the higher levels) total systems analysis would replace the relevance tree.

Different purposes will, of course, favor different optimum concepts of such a combination. Whereas, in the example above, exploratory and normative transforms meet near the "equator" and are matched there without penetrating deeply into each other's hemispheres, one may desire deeper inter-linking of the two opposite transforms. The problem in that case would become over-determined, which may not be undesirable in highly uncertain problem areas. Feedback may also be facilitated by such deeper inter-linking.

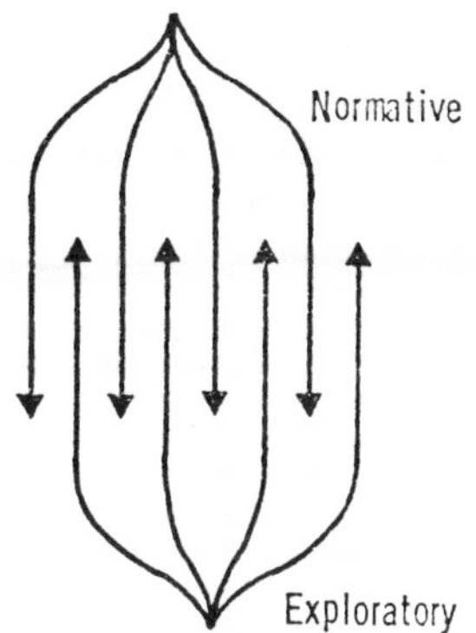

Attention may also be drawn to the importance of *"bonding" between levels,* or between different techniques in the same combination. Economic analysis provides an excellent means for performing certain "bonding" tasks, for example between the systems and the use level, and may assume even greater importance if economic (monetary) units can be introduced for the quantification of forecasting problems in a wider context. The first attempts to quantify social goals in terms of dollars may pave the way to a more universal "language" for the formulation of forecasting problems, which, moreover, would seem to be a prerequisite for integrated computer techniques and for their future inclusion in large information technology systems.

Probabilistic forecasting–the evaluation of input information (data and relationships) which is introduced in the form of probability distributions so as to produce probability distributions as the output information–is being attempted, but is in a very experimental stage. The development of probabilistic forecasting is clearly one of the crucial problems faced in the development of forecasting techniques.

Cross support on different levels, for example the usefulness of a specific material for various components, of a component or sub-system for various primary systems, etc., has so far remained in a rather unsatisfactory state. A few techniques take it into account in an additive way or by a modification of the score, and PATTERN has kept a place open in its system for future refined evaluation. The present emphasis on "communalities" in the U.S. defense research and production program may be expected to encourage developments along this line.

Although feedback models are not yet operational, a few techniques are particularly *stimulating for feedback.* This is the case, confirmed by reported experience, of trend extrapolation, contextual mapping and "morphological research," all of them leading to a situation in which fundamental research and exploratory development are asked to provide answers to urgent questions that may trigger basic thinking or even research programs. Problems of the greatest importance have been recognized and solved in this sequence, which came into being with technological forecasting. This function of technological forecasting would seem to merit particular attention in future developments.

If the technological forecasting problem is structured by *typical questions* asked, the following pattern of applicable techniques emerges on the basis of today's state of the art:

Question	*Applicable Technique*	*State of the Art*
1. Scientific breakthroughs	?	
2. Technological breakthroughs	Trend (envelope curve) extrapolation?	Uncertain
	Morphological research	Useful, partly proved
	Relevance tree	Feasible
3. Areas of fundamental research and exploratory development to be favored	Trend (envelope curve) evaluation	Proven, but limited
	Contextual mapping	Feasible
	Morphological research	Very useful, partly proved
	Economic analysis Horizontal decision matrix Vertical decision matrix Simple operations research Simple decision theory	Useful within limits
	Relevance tree	Very useful, proved
	Normative operational models	Uncertain
	Systems analysis	Potentially very useful, proved
4. Nature of technological innovation	Brainstorming	Doubtful
	"Delphi" technique	Useful within limits
	Morphological research	Very useful, proved
5. Technological performance (technical parameters, functional capability, etc.)	Trend extrapolation (analytical)	Unsatisfactory
	Trend extrapolation (phenomenological)	Useful, proved
	Contextual mapping	Feasible
	Morphological research	Useful in combination with trend extrapolation, etc.
	Systems analysis	Feasible?
6. Development time	"Delphi" technique	Tested, some doubts
	Trend extrapolation (analytical)	Unsatisfactory
	Trend extrapolation (phenomenological)	Useful, proved
	Learning curves	Tested, needs much further evidence
	Network techniques	Feasible
7. Development costs	Learning curves	Unproved
	Network techniques	Feasible?
8. Return on investment	Economic analysis	Very useful, especially discounted cash flow

Question	*Applicable Technique*	*State of the Art*
9. Production costs	Learning curves	Tested, needs much further evidence
10. Maintenance costs	?	
11. Horizontal impact (especially market impact)	Economic analysis	Useful in combination with other techniques
	Operational models (gaming)	Promising, unproved
	Operational models (rigid models)	Useful, proved for established business areas, unproved for general technological acceptance
	Systems analysis	Useful, proved
12. Vertical impact	Scenario-writing	Promising, being tested
	Iteration through synopsis	Useful, partly tested
	Historical analogy	Uncertain, partly tested
	Operational models (gaming)	Very promising, being tested
	Operational models (rigid models)	Promising, unproved
	Systems analysis	Useful, proved
13. Lower level goals (tasks, missions, etc.)	Brainstorming	Doubtful
	"Delphi" technique	Useful within limits
	Scenario-writing	Feasible
	Horizontal decision matrix	Useful, partly proved
	Vertical decision matrix	Useful, being tested
	Relevance tree	Very useful, proved
	Systems analysis	Potentially very useful, partly proved
14. High level goals (national, social, etc.)	Brainstorming	Very doubtful
	"Delphi" technique	Very promising, partly tested
	Utopia, science fiction	Potentially partly useful, unproved
	Scenario-writing	Useful, proved
	Operational models (gaming)	Potentially useful
	Operational models (rigid models)	Potentially useful in auxiliary function

This is an impressive list, especially since it reflects systematic development over little more than five or six years. Some of the best operations research and systems analysis experts may feel tempted to contribute new and more sophisticated techniques for coping more adequately with the questions which technological forecasting seeks to answer.

UTILIZATION OF TECHNIQUES

The use of techniques is by no means a measure for determining the quality of technological forecasting. Two of the three big American institutes offering technological forecasts—the Stanford Research Institute and Arthur D. Little, both producing continuous series of technological forecast reports—generally do not employ elaborate techniques; the third, the Battelle Memorial Institute, joined the pioneers in the development of technological forecasting techniques only fairly recently.

The users of forecasting techniques are virtually unanimous in agreeing that at the present stage the primary gain from this exercise is the greatly improved insight into the nature and inter-relationships of influencing factors and into the sensitivity of solutions to their variation. The possibility, within a consistent pattern, of evaluation discrete alternative solutions probably ranks as the second most valued gain.

A well-organized company may, paradoxically, find less incentive to using techniques if it has attained a degree of insight which it cannot itself substantially improve. A sophisticated American electronics company abandoned the use of a number of quantitative (simple) techniques[2] when, by virtue of a thorough, fully-integrated organization of the planning side, it really "got on top" of the technological innovation process. "Projections distracted from planning."

The "insight" argument is also a factor in a certain hesitation by top management people to approve the use of more elaborate techniques. In modern future-oriented companies—represented by the better-than-average American industrial company in an innovating branch—management attitude seems to favor the moderate use of techniques but to limit them to simple and transparent types. The widespread use of simple two- and three-dimensional matrix techniques reflects this attitude. Sometimes, simple and elaborate techniques are used side by side, not so much to supplement each other, but to suit different inclinations at different management levels. Honeywell (US), the company which generated and applies the most elaborate relevance tree technique, PATTERN, also uses simple matrices that are reportedly found "more convincing" by top management people, while middle-level management places a great deal of confidence in PATTERN—which attains the maximum degree of transparency to be expected of an elaborate model.

Another important factor which is assessed quite differently in different companies, is the economic value of more elaborate forecasting techniques or, more precisely, the "return on investment." Elaborate techniques cause expenses that are not negligible even for big companies. In section II.4.5 an estimate is given for PATTERN, which cost approximately $250,000 to set up at the outset for use in Honeywell's military and space activities, and which may involve somewhere between $50,000 and $100,000 per year in updating and operation expenses. An even more stringent requirement is the use of high-quality technical and operations research people whom a company may hesitate to assign to an experiment the outcome of which is uncertain. Moreover, considerable time—possibly several years—may be needed to adapt a complex technique to the characteristics of a company. Continuous confidence, perhaps even enthusiasm, are required if the company is successfully to weather such a period of adjustment. Technological forecasting, at least in its more sophisticated forms, is comparable with the problem area of scientific and technical information in this respect: in both cases, it is difficult to assess future benefits in quantitative terms, or to prove past benefits. Nevertheless, confidence in techniques is generally growing wherever they are applied, and results are considered encouraging.

A factor which constitutes a more delicate problem may be found in a management attitude that tends to regard the simulation of one's own decision-making as superfluous. This argument is also raised by Ayres (1965) with respect to U.S. military administrations.

Finally, some of the proposed methods seem to be insufficiently close to reality, or to constitute ad-hoc procedures suitable to a narrow sector or a particular company only. Brandenburg (1964) and Baker and Pound (see Baker and Pound, 1964) in their critical review of a number of simple "ranking procedures" based on economic analysis, operations research and decision theory approaches, point out a number of short-comings of this type. Multi-dimensional considerations such as "project success" are often introduced as single indices equal in weight to a number of other factors.

Baker and Pound also tried to assess the number of U.S. companies and government laboratories, out of a total of roughly 50, in which these "ranking procedures" were known, tested or applied. The result, for 1964, indicates very low utilization. Ranking procedures based on an operations research or decision theory approach were generally tested or applied only in the originating companies or laboratories, and testing—though reportedly successful—sometimes did not lead to practical application. Most companies were not aware of procedures developed elsewhere. One may conclude that it is too early to expect a broader diffusion of experimental approaches which generally do not merit wider recognition. In 1964 the enthusiastic "pioneer" and the "self-made man" who solves urgent problems through his own efforts in a simple manner were the rule. The year 1966, with interest in technological forecasting growing rapidly in many companies and laboratories in the United States, and with successes such as PATTERN becoming widely known, may already mark a transitional period leading to the beginning of "cross-fertilization."

Kiefer (1964), in a review of the U.S. chemical industry in 1963, names five companies using check lists (plus one company which was considering them and one that had abandoned their use), 11 companies using discounted cash flow methods to assess the expected "return on investment" for research and development projects in an advanced stage (four of these companies employed formulas which also included other factors, such as probability of success, etc.), one company (Monsanto) which used economic analysis in combination with other more refined techniques, and one company (Hercules Powder) that ran business models on an analog computer for each project.

On the basis of the present investigation, which concentrated on industrial branches of an innovating character (primarily the electrotechnical, chemical and petrochemical, petroleum, pharmaceutical, and aerospace industries) and on military technological planning, the following general picture emerges as of 1966 (unless otherwise indicated, reference is to the U.S. scene):

Type of Technique	*Utilization*
	A. Technological Development Environments
Brainstorming	More or less out of date in the U.S., still found useful in a few European companies and in NATO in a version which includes systematic preparation.
"Delphi" technique	Tests planned by TRW Systems (U.S.).
Trend extrapolation on phenomenological basis	Extensive use, including refined S-curve and envelope curve extrapolation, in military environments in both the U.S. and Europe, in industry mainly in the U.S.; most systematic use is for the preparation of input information to PATTERN scheme (Honeywell), necessitating hundreds and thousands of individual evaluations.
Contextual mapping	Limited application in a few places, growing importance.
Morphological research	According to its author, 30 industrial applications already, the most thorough application being to jet propulsion systems at Aerojet; also applied to basic astronomy.
Scenario-writing	Applications only where higher-level goals are to be explored, for example at Honeywell for the preparation of their PATTERN scheme, and at the big oil companies, in Europe as well as in the U.S.
Iteration through synopsis	Systematic application by Unilever (Brech) in the United Kingdom. Less systematic applications apparently numerous, including the big oil companies in Europe.
Economic analysis	Practically all companies with large research and development programs. Discounted cash flow methods are used by approximately 20 to 25 per cent of the companies visited and are generally applied to well-defined projects in the advanced development stage. The Swedish Wallenberg group (ASEA, Ericsson, etc.) applies it rigorously for project selection. Ranking procedures based on refinements of DCF are used in several places, for example SCAIR in GEC (United Kingdom).
Exploratory operational models–gaming	Possibly occasional application of business games; under consideration by Canadian Paper and Pulp Research Institute, growing general interest.
Exploratory operational models–rigid computer models	Integrated business models are also used for forecasting (Xerox Corp., U.S.) but are very rare; ad-hoc models are used occasionally; applications in the military technological area (?).

Type of Technique	Utilization
Horizontal decision matrices	Wide use, especially research/resources matrices; some rigorous application for decision-making (Boeing).
Vertical decision matrices	Some applications, especially of the research development programme type; ambitious three-dimensional matrix to link space developments to social end-uses applied by North American Aviation.
Simple decision techniques based on an operations research approach	In spite of the interest of professional operations research people, only few applications so far; generally combined with economic analysis (maximization of total expected net value); possible a "growth field."
Simple decision techniques based on a decision theory approach	Numerous applications of check lists with and without rating, but apparently decreasing in number; some numerical formulae in military environments for ranking (France) or partial problems (U.S. Navy), few in industry.
Integrated multi-level relevance tree schemes	Six known applications of PATTERN, (Honeywell, military/space and medical, NASA, U.S. Air Force); at least three applications of other techniques (including NASA); under development at the Battelle Memorial Institute; under consideration by U.S. Navy; arousing great interest–enthusiasm as well as scepticism–and the wish to design similar techniques in a simpler way so as to reduce the substantial effort involving setting them up; operations of a "pioneering" character possibly giving rise to applications in wider technological and governmental decision-making areas.
Network techniques	Application, for example, by General Electric Atomic Power Dept., under consideration at the Battelle Memorial Institute.
Normative operational models–rigid computer models	A few applications for new consumer products (BBDO's "Demon" and the 3M Company's "New Products" models in the U.S.); a model in preparation for use by the U.S. Air Force; the Battelle Memorial Institute is considering applications.
Systems analysis	Pioneered and applied to tasks involving technological forecasting by the RAND Corp., System Development Corp., and General Electric's TEMPO; also in industrial environments such as General Electric Atomic Power Dept. or North American Aviation; can probably be applied usefully only where sophisticated management environments exist.
	B. The Aggregated Level
"Delphi" technique	Application to population forecast tested (doubtful).
Exploratory aggregated level techniques	Applications of statistical models (Battelle Memorial Institute, CECA) input/output analysis (Quantum Science Corporation, RAND/U.S. Air Force, attempted for U.S. economy by Harvard Economic Project), chains of industries (France's BIPE), horizontal diffusion models on empirical basis; forecasts of energy consumption, number of telephone subscribers and telephone traffic are beginning to incorporate technological change in the models used.

Type of Technique	Utilization
Horizontal decision matrices	French national research/resources matrix, in experimental stage.
Vertical decision matrices	French national research/industry matrix, being tested.
	C. Environments of "Social Technology"
"Delphi" technique	First tests have been made (RAND Corporation), others in progress (U.S. Air Force), great interest aroused.
Contextual mapping	Being considered for application.
Morphological research	According to its author, applications are being considered for city planning and education.
Scenario-writing	Pioneered by the RAND Corporation, System Development Corporation, and particularly the Hudson Institute (Kahn, Brennan); applied to the "Year 2000 Program" of the American Academy of Arts and Sciences and other broad programmes with a socio-economico-political context.
Historical analogy	Systematic testing by the American Academy of Arts and Sciences ("The Railroad and the Space Program"); large-scale use doubtful.
Exploratory operational models–gaming	Considered as an important tool by all leaders in "social technology," but apparently not yet applied to problems involving technological forecasting.
Exploratory operational models–rigid computer models	Proposed by Abt Associates to OECD, considered important by leaders in the field, but apparently not yet applied.
Normative operational models–gaming	Gordon and Helmer's "Game of the Future," being tested in 1966.
Systems analysis	Applications by the RAND Corp. (cities and vehicles of the future, etc.), System Development Corp. (education, etc.), General Electric's TEMPO (cities of the future).
Feedback models	Development phase, pioneered by System Development Corporation (U.S.).

OUTLOOK FOR THE NEAR FUTURE

A few modest "forecasts on forecasting" may be ventured with respect to the further development of techniques. In a true normative spirit, they are all based on clearly recognizable requirements:

In the immediate future, interest will focus on the improved integration of techniques over many levels of technology transfer, either by the combination of available elements and partial techniques or by the designing of new techniques;

Better "bonding" of vertical forecasts with horizontal forecasts will be attempted on various levels (not only on the impact level), for both exploratory and normative techniques; particular attention may be directed to the horizontal integration of normative sets of goals, missions, etc.–in other words, non-technological goals and missions will influence technological forecasting on a more systematic and comprehensive basis; consistent sets of social goals may include variables for different countries, etc.;

Techniques will use dynamic formulations (not "snapshots"); this will be the case, *inter alia,* for assessing impact and stipulating goals and missions (which up to now have largely represented views of the present);
Techniques will increasingly adopt a total systems approach;
Feedback techniques will become the predominant problem a few years hence;
Feedback control techniques, i.e. techniques for regulating feedback by adaptations of the entire forecasting function, will follow;
Computer uses will increase, first in military and government technological environments, then in industry as well;
Cross support will receive much more attention in relation to future forecasting techniques, with developments pointing in the direction of "module thinking";
The use of intuitive thinking will become respectable and will be greatly improved, especially in the area of social goals; techniques for improving and evaluating consensus will be generally developed further;
Exploratory techniques minimizing prejudice and bias will be cultivated;
Better understanding of historical inertia and other factors influencing technological progress will give rise to techniques for improved time-dependent estimation and extrapolation;
Efficient normative "by-pass" techniques may be developed that would make it possible to determine some of the worthwhile tasks for fundamental research directly on the basis of higher-level criteria;
Technological forecasting will become an integrated function in future comprehensive information technology systems (see a discussion of this point in section II.5.2*).

As to the evolution of technique utilization, one might attempt an analysis over time of the "precursive events" to be found in sophisticated management techniques and in computer uses for management tasks in the public domain as well as in industry. The trend shown by such a study would certainly be characterized by a rapid rise.

Technological forecasting today is a child of less than ten years old. Only a small fraction of the total number of potential users has so far had an opportunity, or felt an incentive, to decide on the level of sophistication on which to tackle it. The coming years will constitute the decisive period of adolescence that will form the character of the future mature adult.

NOTES

1. We are not concerned here with the varying definitions assigned to these terms. Sometimes "operations research" is taken as the heading for all three areas.
2. A few numerical techniques are still in use as strictly auxiliary means.

REFERENCES

Ayres, Robert U. *On Technological Forecasting,* Report HI-484-DP, Feb. 10, 1965, revised version HI-484-DP(Rev.) Jan 17, 1966. Hudson Institute, Harmon-on-Hudson, N.Y. (Restricted).

Baker M. R. and W. H. Pound. "R and D Project Selection: Where We Stand," IEEE Transactions on Engineering Management, Vol. EM-11, No. 4, Dec. 1964, p. 124-134.

Brandenburg, Richard G. "Quantitative Techniques in R & D Planning" (A survey of the State of the Art), unpublished paper, Pittsburgh, Pa.: Carnegie Institute of Technology, July 1964.

Bright, James R. (ed.) *Research, Development, and Technological Innovation,* Homewood, Ill.: Richard D. Irwin, 1964.

--- (ed.) *Technological Planning on the Corporate Level,* Division of Research, Harvard Business School, Boston, Mass., 1961.

Kiefer, David M. "Winds of Change in Industrial Chemical Research," Chemical and Engineering News, Vol. 42, March 23, 1964, pp. 88-109.

Siegel, Irving H. "Technological Change and Long-Run Forecasting," Journal of Business of the University of Chicago, Vol. XXVI, No. 3, July 1953, pp. 141-156.

Sweezy, Eldon E. "Technological Forecasting–Principles and Techniques," paper presented at the Fourth Symposium of the Engineering Economy Division, American Society for Engineering Education, Chicago, Ill., June 19, 1965.

SECTION 3

PLAN-EVALUATION

INTRODUCTORY NOTE

Planners today are being challenged to compare and evaluate the alternative plans they produce in a more rigorous fashion than formerly appeared necessary.

Previously, the planner's stated criteria for his proposed plan, and for justifying the specific quantities and qualities of land use, transportation, and public facilities he recommended, were usually couched in terms such as "balanced," "orderly," "economical," "efficient," and "coordinated," without specifying the criteria underlying these broad objectives. Frequently, he also justified his proposals by using such statements as "this will achieve a maximum of X (e.g. tax revenues) consistent with a minimum of Y (e.g. disruption of neighborhood values)"–which to many of his listeners seemed either naive or unconscious double talk.

The need to more precisely state criteria for plan-evaluation became increasingly apparent after around 1956, when urban planners in a major way began to get involved with two nationwide building programs: the national highways system and urban renewal. These programs propelled the planners into the arena of public controversy. Issues such as relocation, the splitting up of urban neighborhoods by a proposed freeway, or the making or breaking of local shopping districts demanded more than just platitudes from the planner. Moreover, planners were being asked for more specific and detailed information about the effects of their alternatives. Sharp questions were posed, such as: What will be the potential flow of people and goods on the proposed highways at different hours in the day? What is likely to be the impact of renewal and freeway proposals on the citywide housing market, on racial patterns, on municipal services and taxes, on the attraction or discouragement of new industry, on the amenities of in-lying areas? Under this sort of probing, planners were forced to identify social costs (though they did not call it this) of freeway and renewal projects that disrupted neighborhoods, uprooted families and long-tenured local businesses, or destroyed highly valued views of favorite (often historical) buildings, hills, and water bodies. They began to be as concerned in their recommendations with the so-called intangible values gained or lost as with those costs and benefits more easily convertible into dollar amounts.

Most recently, planners have been seeking operationally useful criteria that can be used to evaluate performance against their planning objectives, and methods for weighing the criteria. In particular, serious efforts are underway to find evaluation criteria which do not unduly weight decisions in favor of those considerations that are inherently quantifiable or can easily be made so. In addition, an intensive search is proceeding to develop criteria and operational indices which place less stress on measuring *things* and more stress on measuring the potential impacts on *people.*

The planner now recognizes that only very rarely if ever will any plan, policy, or program he recommends have uniform application across an entire urban area. Almost inevitably, the impacts, consequences, costs, and benefits of his recommendations will fall upon particular segments or sections of the city. For example, urban renewal programs are aimed at older central city neighborhoods, while OEO poverty program serve low-income families. Moreover, these neighborhoods and families form only a certain proportion of the city's developed area and population. Thus, in comparing their alternative plans, policies, and programs, city planners are now faced with such questions as: How many people will have to travel how far and at what cost to enjoy the various kinds of recreation facilities and open spaces proposed? What is the "price" of preserving open spaces to the community, to the social and economic patterns of urban growth, or to our productive capacity? How many and which people will have their taxes increased, and by how much, as a result of a proposed urban renewal project? Which businesses will be benefited and which ones disadvantaged by the contemplated changes in the land use patterns? How will the proposed industrial development affect the population's income, and which people will be affected more and which less, and by how much? Which neighborhoods of the city will receive the greatest benefit from the proposed capital budget?

Not only does the planner need to identify the impact of his proposals on different groups in the community and the scale of the impact, but in order to decide which plan to recommend, he requires some technique to help him determine which of the impacts are more significant, so to speak, than others. Thus, planners are asking such questions as: How important is one incidence group compared to others? How important are those groups (or subareas or socio-economic classes) which have been left out, upon whom various recommendations have no effect? Should large-scale redevelopment of inner-city neighborhoods be given preference over large-scale rehabilitation of neighborhoods on the outskirts, or should the city concentrate instead on strengthening strategically located industrial districts?

Moreover, as a reflection of the planner's evolving role as advisor to the mayor which is involving him more and more with the operating (as well as capital) budgets of separate government departments and agencies, he is being called upon to review and evaluate their program proposals. Accordingly, he is faced with such questions as: What are the relative "payoffs" for the community from pursuing one "bundle" of policies versus another? Which of the alternative housing programs and alternative public-works projects would be more effective and least costly? Would programs aimed at improving housing be more effective and less costly than programs designed to increase job opportunities in order to improve the quality of life of ghetto residents?

Attempts to answer the sorts of questions enumerated in the previous paragraphs confront the planners with analytical requirements substantially more demanding than traditional cost-benefit analysis that has proved valuable, for example, in planning water resources projects. Two persons who recognized early the need for planners to develop more rigorous plan-evaluation techniques were Nathaniel Lichfield, a British town planner-land economist, and William L. C. Wheaton, co-author of one of the papers in Section 1.

Extending the concepts and principles underlying cost-benefit analysis, Lichfield has proposed the use of a "balance sheet of development" which compares all the good and all the bad consequences of a proposed course of action, the evaluation being concerned not only with the single goal of economic efficiency (the goal of traditional cost-benefit analysis) but with all benefits and all costs with respect to all community goals (Lichfield, 1956; 1960; 1962; 1964; 1965; Lichfield and Margolis, 1963). Lichfield has also applied his method to various planning situations (1962; 1965; 1966; 1969; Lichfield and Chapman, 1968).

William Wheaton, in a 1963 paper, reviewed the reports on the metropolitan plans for Denver and Washington, D.C., which presented, discussed, and "evaluated" several alternatives for each city. Wheaton acknowledged that in many respects they were among the best of metropolitan plans (at the time of his article) and recognized that they had received considerable acclaim in the city planning profession. For this reason they reflected adequately the 1963 existing state of practice in the field and the philosophical and scientific foundations of that practice. But, Wheaton found them wanting; they failed to provide specific criteria for choice between the alternatives presented; they depended instead upon the traditional planning intuitions and concepts regarding the desirable physical forms of the city. Developments in operations research, Wheaton felt at the time, should make it possible to establish some measurable criteria (he suggested some crude examples) and to provide government officials and citizens with at least limited indications of the costs and benefits of alternatives and the means necessary for their implementation.

The new methods discussed in this section represent a logical extension to, and development of, those proposed by Lichfield and Wheaton.

In his paper in Chapter Nine, Morris Hill proposes a method for plan-evaluation which, on the one hand, is a superior substitute for traditional cost-benefit analysis and, on the other hand, carries forward some of the basic ideas underlying Lichfield's balance sheet of development technique. He notes that benefit-cost analysis was developed as a technique for examining plans with respect to their fulfillment of economic objectives—usually economic efficiency. Although lip service is given to so-called "intangibles," they do not really enter directly into the analysis of most transportation and development plans. Urban objectives generally have several dimensions: cultural, political, ethical and aesthetic, as well as economic. To presume only one dimension would lead to a suboptimal solution.

Hill refers to his method as the "Goals-Achievement Matrix," which meets his two requirements for a useful plan-evaluation technique. The first requirement is that objectives (or specific attainable goals) should be put into operational form as far as possible; that is, they should be expressed in such a way that progress towards them or retrogression from them, is measurable on some appropriate scale. Second, he introduces the requirement that numerical weightings should be assigned to express the relative importance of each objective for each section of the community. To determine the weights to be assigned to the various goals, Hill suggests consideration of one or more of the following sources or techniques: community decision-makers, the general public by means of a referendum, a selective sampling of the affected groups, public hearings, and the study of the pattern of previous allocations of public investment. The second feature requires also that the various sections of the community, or the various "publics" who comprise the population of the area, be identified. This can be done by reference to income group, occupation, location, or any other preferred criteria. The costs and benefits of actions directed toward each particular objective or goal, as borne by the several sections of the community, are weighted to reflect the importance of each goal in the eyes of each group.

In Hill's scheme, all costs are represented as negative contributions to objectives, so that each quantifiable objective would have a cost-benefit account in terms of some measurable index. His matrix, then, consists of the following: goals, with relative weights determined by a study of the community's aspirations and problems; relative weights assigned to different groups in the population, reflecting their feelings about each goal; and the costs and benefits of a proposed plan (or action) expressed in monetary, physical, or quantitative terms. Where all the costs and benefits can be expressed in the same quantitative terms, summation can be performed; in the rare cases where this is possible, use of monetary units seems the most likely.

In approaching the question of comparing tangibles with intangibles, Hill points out the importance of developing valid scales of measurement and stresses the need to correctly identify and use different scales (nominal, ordinal, interval, and ratio in ascending order of complexity); he also gives useful examples of the sorts of planning objectives which are appropriate to the different types of scales.

Finally, Hill discusses the ways in which the results of his proposed method can be presented to decision-makers so that they can be useful.

The paper in Chapter 10 by Harry P. Hatry (former deputy director of the State-Local Finances Project sponsored by the George Washington University and now with the Urban Institute in Washington, D.C.) is directed mainly at the problem of defining criteria as part of planning-programming-budgeting systems; however, the ideas and concepts expressed are equally applicable to city planning. As Hatry points out, government planners find that they need evaluation criteria (or "measures of effectiveness") because funds and physical resources are scarce—there are not enough available to satisfy all needs and proposals; and that to perform this evaluation, it is necessary to identify specific criteria that can be used to evaluate expected performances against the governmental objectives. As noted above and more fully in the introductory note to Section One, this is the same problem faced by city planners. For this reason, Hatry's comments about the nature, scope, and characteristics of the criteria that are needed and his suggested list of specific criteria that are likely to be pertinent for illustrative government programs should prove of value to planners engaged in evaluating city plans.

Schimpeler and Grecco, in their paper, propose a procedure for evaluating alternative transportation system design concepts, based on a comprehensive, weighted hierarchy of community decision criteria, or community goals and objectives. Heretofore, the authors point out, criteria utilized in plan-evaluation have generally been easily quantified economic considerations. Their approach, which was developed for use by the Louisville (Kentucky) Metropolitan Comprehensive Transportation and Development Program, utilizes a broader, more comprehensive class of criteria, including social values, along with traditional economic factors. Also, their approach assumes involvement of community decision-makers in structuring the community decision criteria, with the professional planners using the criteria, weighted by the decision-makers, in the evaluation of planning proposals.

A task force from the Mayor's Citizens Advisory Committee (representing a cross-section of highly respected, influential citizens of metropolitan Louisville) was used as the representive community decision-making group for criteria-evaluation. (It was hoped that a more diversified evaluation group, including elected officials and influential businessmen, could eventually be formed.) Though it was assumed that this group would be involved in structuring the list of specific community objectives or decision criteria, the list of some 35 objectives actually evaluated was initially put together by local planners.

Each member of the Mayor's Committee was asked to individually weigh each objective, using both a raw ranking and a rating scale technique. In the first technique, the general idea is to rank order all objectives from 1 to 35, then determine overall rankings by summing those of individual members. The second technique utilizes a 0–10 rating scale, and asks individual members to rate each objective as to relative importance along this scale. Overall ratings are again the sum of those of individuals. The normalized results of the two methods are then combined to get an average ranking or utility value.

Based on the hierarchy of community planning goals and objectives that have been established, including a numerical utility measure or criterion weight assigned to each objective statement, the authors then develop a decision model to use in evaluating three alternative transportation plans under consideration.

The basic approach they propose for this purpose is an effectiveness matrix technique, which consists of multiplying the utility scores associated with each objective by the predicted effectiveness values established by a group of professional planners who indicated the probability of each of the three plans achieving that objective. Then, for each alternative these products are summed to arrive at a total utility score. The alternative with the highest total utility score is to be preferred.

A scoring model which extends the effectiveness matrix technique was also utilized, by using a panel of judges or community decision-makers.

The paper by J. K. Friend and W. N. Jessop (British operational researchers) is taken from their book, *Local Government and Strategic Choice: An Operational Research Approach to the Processes of Public Planning,* which is concerned with developing a "technology for strategic choice" in local policy-making and planning. Based on their four-year program of research in the City of Coventry, during which time they observed the ways in which decisions were made and plans formulated (described in the first part of their book), the authors, then, through a series of linked hypothetical but realistic case examples in local and regional planning, offer a range of suggestions regarding the possibilities of developing more effective aids to guide choice in complex strategic situations. Their paper, which deals with one of these case examples, is concerned primarily with the problem of priorities.

To deal with this problem, the authors discuss various methods, including several aimed at identifying, measuring, and weighing the range of possible effects of alternative solutions (e.g. plans, policies, programs) on different groups within the community, both in the immediate and more long-term future; the scale of each type of effect; and the relative values attached to the various effects. The specific unit of measurement they use to estimate the effects of alternative solutions on various groups in the population in their hypothetical "city," they call an "effect unit" (eu, for short).

Using this unit of measurement, they show how to estimate the direct effects of particular decision options for six different groups of people, i.e. local taxpayers, national taxpayers, existing municipal tenants, prospective municipal tenants, schoolchildren, and shoppers. With this basic data, they demonstrate which of the range of alternative solutions would be most desirable if, first, the objective of the policy-makers was to impose the minimum tax burden on the local taxpayer; second, the policy-makers wanted to balance this objective with another consideration—e.g. improving shopping facilities—by use of "trade-off rates." They also demonstrate how the list of "best" solutions varies with different trade-off rates; and fourth, how different decision options are combined to control the joint effects.

The authors point out the importance of the range of effect measures selected for analysis. While they assumed only six effect measures, for purposes of illustration, their proposed method permits extension of this range further by consideration of the costs and benefits incurred by various other sectors of the community. For example, if there was a high level of unemployment in the city, the planners and/or decision-makers might wish to evaluate alternative solutions according to the extra employment they could be expected to provide for the workers in the local construction trades. Also, they might wish to make an explicit evaluation of the traffic or environmental effects in a certain area of the city which could be expected to result indirectly from the early completion of, say, a new shopping center, or the potential loss of trade which might be reflected on existing shop owners.

Similarly, the planners might wish to extend the range of effect measures not only by the inclusion of certain effects impinging on other sectors of the community, but also by a further division of some of the original six sectors into sub-groups to whose interests they might wish to give differential treatment. For instance, they might wish to consider separately the interests of those existing public housing tenants with particularly low incomes, or those would-be tenants now living in particularly overcrowded conditions, or those schoolchildren with particularly difficult commuting problems.

In the view of this editor, use of the techniques discussed in this section should improve enormously the art of plan-evaluation methodology. It is also clear to him that application of these new techniques is made much easier today with the availability of computers. The positive effects that the computer has had on the generation and testing of plans, referred to earlier, have similar consequences for the plan-evaluation procedure (Harris, 1965). So long as the generation and testing of plans remained an arduous and slow process, opportunities to compare alternative plans were extremely limited. Under the circumstances, plan-evaluation was largely a subjective process which, in turn, led to many difficulties in achieving a consensus. Now, with the feasibility of generating and testing larger numbers of different plans at relatively low cost, a new stride forward has been taken toward assuring that comparisons and evaluations of these plans may be made much more objectively on the basis of more complete information.

Chapter 9

A GOALS-ACHIEVEMENT MATRIX FOR EVALUATING ALTERNATIVE PLANS

Morris Hill

Alternative plans for public investment, designed to serve a similar set of purposes, have been prepared. Which plan better serves the set of purposes? Can this be determined in a systematic manner? In a free enterprise economy, the market mechanism is generally accepted as the primary means for the allocation of resources. The public sector, by its very nature, is not able to rely primarily on the economic market mechanism for its investment decisions, and alternative means have to be employed to serve this purposes.

The evaluation of alternative plans for public investment is one step in the planning process in the public sector. It is assumed that the planning process should be rational. Rational planning is defined as a process for determining appropriate future action by utilizing scarce resources in such a way as to maximize the expected attainment of a set of given ends.[1] Cost-benefit analysis as a means of plan evaluation will be studied in the light of this criterion.

TRADITIONAL COST-BENEFIT ANALYSIS

Cost-benefit analysis was developed as a technique to serve this very purpose, with particular emphasis on the evaluation of plans for a single sector. It was originally conceived during the 1930s and 1940s for the evaluation of alternative courses of action in the design of water resource projects and served the single

AUTHOR'S NOTE: This paper has been supported by the Regional Science Research Institute of Health (Grant No. EF-00700) for research into Comprehensive Programming of Public Facilities. I would like to thank Gerald A. P. Carrothers, Robert E. Coughlin, Maynard M. Hufschmidt, and Benjamin H. Stevens for their helpful suggestions and thoughtful criticism.

Reprinted from Journal of the American Institute of Planners, Vol. 34 No. 1 (January 1968), pp. 19-29, by permission of the author and the publisher.

goal of economic efficiency.[2] The goal was defined as the maximization of the net project contribution of the national income.

The cost-benefit model was conceptually derived from the theory of the firm and the endeavor of the firm to maximize its profits. Faced with the need to choose among a number of projects, the profit-maximizing entrepreneur compares the profitability of alternative projects by determining the profits (considered over an extended period of time) of each project, calculated on the basis of the monetary revenues and costs predicted to accrue, and relates these to the capital invested. He then chooses the most profitable projects. In the face of limited resources, the entrepreneur allocates his resources by developing the projects chosen to the point where marginal revenues equal marginal costs. According to welfare economic theory,[3] such private profit maximization by individual firms in an economy of pure competition leads to optimal community welfare.[4]

In an analogous manner, cost-benefit analysis can be conceived as a process whereby a public agency in pursuit of economic efficiency allocates its resources (land, labor, and capital) in such a way that the most "profitable"[5] projects are executed and developed to the point where marginal benefits equal marginal costs. Thus the last dollar invested in a project brings a marginal economic return at least as high as that possible were the funds spent in some other way. However, so direct an extension of the private allocation model to allocation in the public sector raises a number of problems. The private and public models are analogous only if (1) no barriers exist to the flow of funds and resources, (2) benefits and costs can be determined at competitive market prices, (3) there are no external economies or diseconomies, and (4) no other external effects exist.

These conditions are rarely evident in the public sector (and seldom in the private sector). As was explained, the existence of a public sector in a free enterprise economy is justified, in part, by the absence of some of these very factors. Public resources are limited, and barriers to the flow of funds and resources do exist in the public sector. The value of benefits and costs cannot all be expressed in market prices; some cannot even be quantified. External effects and indivisibilities are particularly evident in investments in the public sector.

Hence cost-benefit analysis of alternative investments in the public sector should record social costs and benefits as well as private costs and benefits.[6] It should be abe to guide public action when market prices do not accurately reflect the consequences for society of a public investment, or when, by virtue of the indivisible nature of collective goods, no market exists from which to observe directly objective evidence of the community's valuation of the social marginal product. The analysis should also be designed to register the value of other products or inputs that are subject to externalities and interdependencies.

When costs and benefits are not available in market prices, the cost-benefit model imputes them as if they were subject to market transactions. In order to take into consideration social costs and benefits, the analysts are required to "compensate for the rigidities and defects of the market which prevent market prices from being reliable."[7] When imputing market prices, the analyst should distinguish between those items that are ordinarily evaluated in the market because they are often produced privately, those that are never evaluated in the market but are subject to monetary valuation, and those that are outside the scope of the market and cannot be priced in monetary terms. The last class of goods and services are intangibles.

Although lip service is generally paid to the consideration of the intangibles, they do not really enter into the analysis. The net result of this is that the effects of investments that can be measured in monetary terms (whether imputed or derived from the market) are treated implicitly as being the most important effects. In fact, the intangible costs and benefits may indeed be the most significant.

Furthermore, the conversion of some consequences into monetary terms and the restriction of the evaluation process to an economic analysis may lead to an erroneous decision resulting from the confusion of the original purpose of a course of action with its secondary consequences. For instance, if the major purposes of a metropolitan park are, first, to provide recreation services of a particular quality to the metropolitan population and, second, to structure the development of the city, how likely is a recommendation based solely or primarily on changes in adjacent land values, tourist expenditures, and so forth, to lead to a realization of the primary objective? [8]

The cost-benefit method was designed not only to choose the course of action that maximized "economic efficiency," but it was also assumed that in the process of doing so economic welfare was maximized. In order that the cost-benefit criterion maximize economic welfare, the following conditions must be met: [9]

(1) Opportunity costs are borne by beneficiaries in such a way as to retain the initial income distribution.
(2) The initial income distribution is in some sense "best."
(3) If the marginal social rates of transformation between any two commodities are everywhere equal to their corresponding rates of substitution except for the area(s) justifying the intervention in question, then welfare can be improved by such intervention. To the extent that the objective is pursued to the point where the social marginal rates of transformation between commodities in this sector and other sectors are similarly equal to the rates of substitution for other paired commodities, welfare is optimized.

How likely is it that these conditions will be met in the allocation of public resources? The first condition is only partially feasible for most of the cases dealt with by cost-benefit analysis. The second condition is, at best, questionable; and in the real world, the third condition is improbable. Thus, whereas cost-benefit analysis identifies the most efficient course of action (efficiency being defined as above), it is questionable whether this course of action also maximizes economic welfare. The achievement of maximum economic efficiency is most likely to approximate the achievement of maximum economic welfare for those public activities that most closely approximate private economic activity and have well-defined products subject to market transaction.

Cost-benefit analysis, as it has been described, is more suitable for ranking or comparing courses of action designed to attain roughly the same ends rather than for testing the absolute desirability of a project. This is partly so because all estimates of benefits and costs are subject to errors of forecasting. An even greater limitation is the difficulty of getting a measure of desirability. Thus, economic cost-benefit analysis cannot provide guidance in the allocation of investments among the various public sectors, such as transportation, education, or housing. Given two diverse projects–a school *vs.* a road, for example–each costing the same amount, and a budget sufficient to build only one of them, cost-benefit analysis can give no guidance in the choice. In our current state of knowledge there exists no common scale for comparing the benefits of a new school and a new road.

THE BALANCE SHEET OF DEVELOPMENT

Thus far we have described the application of cost-benefit analysis to the evaluation of alternative courses of action as applied to a single goal, economic efficiency. This goal has been interpreted as being equivalent to the maximization of national or regional product and, under certain very restrictive conditions, the maximization of economic welfare. Cost-benefit analysis has also been used for the comparison of all the "good" and all the "bad" consequences of a proposed course of action in one "balance sheet of development." This technique, proposed and applied by Nathaniel Lichfield, differs significantly from cost-benefit analysis as described above. This formulation not only is concerned with the single goal of economic efficiency but considers all benefits and all costs with respect to all community goals in one enumeration. This balance sheet of costs and benefits is intended to enable the choice of a course of action that will in some way maximize the achievement of community goals. Perhaps more than anyone else, Lichfield has applied cost-benefit analysis as described above to urban development planning.[10] Lichfield describes the method for the evaluation of development plans as follows:

> "The program for a plan is regarded as a series of development projects, interrelated in time and space, which must be implemented if the plan is to be realized. The program is visualized as completed and for each project or group of projects are enumerated the parties who will be concerned with producing and operating them (both private and public) and, also the parties who will consume the services provided, whether they buy them in the market or collectively through rates and taxes. For each party is then forecast the costs and benefits that will accrue. Each such item is measured in money or physical terms as far as possible or otherwise noted as an intangible. If alternative plans are being compared, the analysis aims at the difference in costs and benefits that will arise under each alternative. It is possible by this approach to produce systematically, in descriptive and tabular form, a complete set of social accounts which show all the significant costs and benefits which would result from the implementation of the plan, or from alternative plans and their incidence. These accounts can then be "reduced" by eliminating double counting, transfer payments, common items, etc. This is the 'planning balance sheet' which provides a summary of the planning advantages and disadvantages to the public at large."[11]

TABLE 1
THE BALANCE SHEET OF DEVELOPMENT

	Producers							
	Plan A				*Plan B*			
	Benefits		*Costs*		*Benefits*		*Costs*	
	Cap.	*Ann.*	*Cap.*	*Ann.*	*Cap.*	*Ann.*	*Cap.*	*Ann.*
X	\$a	\$b	–	\$d	–	–	\$b	\$c
Y	i_1	i_2	–	–	i_3	i_4	–	–
Z	M_1	–	M_2	–	M_3	–	M_4	–
	Consumers							
X^1	–	\$e	–	\$f	–	\$g	–	\$h
Y^1	i_5	i_6	–	–	i_7	i_8	–	–
Z^1	M_1	–	M_3	–	M_2	–	M_4	–

In the conceptual table illustrating the "balance sheet of development" (Table 1), the various sectors that are affected by the plans are considered both as producers (expressed as X, Y, and Z) and as consumers (expressed as X^1, Y^1, and Z^1). The costs and the benefits that would accrue to the various sectors, if either of the plans under consideration (Plan A and Plan B) were effectuated, are indicated. The costs and the benefits are recorded as capital (once for all) items or annual (continuing) items.

Let us now consider the various types of entries that are recorded in the cells of the table. If a \$ symbol precedes a letter, then that cost or benefit is expressed in monetary terms. If M followed by a numerical subscript is recorded in the cell, then the cost or benefit is expressed in quantitative but nonmonetary terms. An *i* represents an intangible item, the subscripts indicating the nature of the intangible. A dash (–) in a cell indicates that no cost or benefit of that type would accrue to that sector if that plan were executed. Once the "balance sheet of development" has been prepared, the costs and the benefits that would accrue to each sector are reduced, aggregated, and compared for each plan under consideration.

Lichfield has shown how this "balance sheet of development" may be applied to the evaluation of plans in a number of instances.[12] He claims that by providing this framework within which all the relevant consequences of a planning proposal can be considered, the analyst is laying the basis for a more rational decision. In this context, the measurement of costs and benefits, though desirable, is not strictly necessary. A precise description of the costs and benefits enables the decision-maker to balance the monetary costs and benefits with the intangible costs and benefits. By indicating the incidence of costs and benefits, the analyst identifies the sections of the community that will bear the costs and the sections of the community that will receive the benefits. The balance sheet will also enable the decision-makers to appraise those elements in the design that are high in cost or low in benefit. All this, in Lichfield's estimation, will lead to more "educated," responsible, and rational policy decisions.

How valid is the balance sheet for its proposed purpose? How useful is it for the evaluation of alternative courses of action? The costs and benefits that are enumerated refer to different objectives and are not all relevant for a single objective. For instance, in the analysis of the costs and benefits of the retention of the San Francisco Mint, the historic value of the Old Mint to San Francisco and the nation, the economic contribution to the San Francisco economy of visitors to the Mint, and the value of the office space to the Federal Government are not relevant for any single objective, unless that objective is the catch-all and consequently meaningless one of "enhancing community welfare." Thus a major criticism of the "development balance sheet" is that it does not appear to recognize that benefits and costs have only instrumental value. Benefits and costs have meaning only in relation to a well-defined objective. A criterion of maximizing net benefits in the abstract is therefore meaningless. Whereas benefits can be computed referring to different planning objectives, the benefits and costs are not necessarily additive or comparable. It is meaningful to add or compare benefits and costs only if they refer to a common objective. Furthermore, since benefits and costs can legitimately be compared only in terms of an objective, if the objective is of little or no value both for an entire community and for any sections within it, then the benefits and costs referring to the objective are irrelevant for the community in question. For instance, if a community as a whole and all interests within it set no value on the retention of historic buildings, it is not legitimate for an analyst to consider the elimination of a building of historic value as a cost even though he personally believes it to be so.[13]

Not only does the "balance sheet of development" omit the explicit identification of some of the objectives[14] served by the proposed course of action, but there is no means of knowing whether the costs and benefits listed are relevant for inclusion in the balance sheet of development.

We have now identified two conceptions of cost-benefit analysis and pointed out their deficiencies.

First, we have described how benefits and costs are determined in order to measure the preferability of alternative courses of action with respect to the objective of maximization of economic efficiency. A major danger inherent in this approach is that if the primary emphasis is on efficiency, other objectives may get "short shrift" because of the manner in which the problem is structured. Efficiency can perhaps be measured more precisely and reliably than other objectives, but this does not entitle it to an honored status.[15]

Second, we have described "the balance sheet of development," a technique whereby benefits and costs measure all the "good" and "bad" consequences of alternative courses of action relating to a range of objectives. Although this method thus has a broader perspective than traditional cost-benefit analysis, it fails to recognize that costs and benefits can be compared only if they can be related to a common objective.

THE GOALS-ACHIEVEMENT MATRIX

Since single-objective cost-benefit analysis and the development balance sheet are not satisfactory for the evaluation of alternative courses of action, what procedure might better serve this purpose? A method of plan evaluation which we shall call the goals-achievement matrix is here proposed. In this discussion we shall use *goal* as the generic term and define it as "an end to which a planned course of action is directed." Goals may involve getting something the actor does not have or giving up something the actor does have. The goals of planned action may be categorized on the basis of specificity as ideals, objectives, and policies. These may be considered as directions, regions, and points in value space, respectively.

An *ideal* is like a horizon allowing for indefinite progression in its direction but always receding, such as equality, freedom, or justice. An *objective* denotes an attainable goal that has instrumental value in that it is believed to lead to another valued goal rather than having intrinsic value in itself. Objectives are defined operationally so that either the existence or nonexistence of a desired state or the degree of achievement of this state can be established. A *qualitatively-defined objective* is one that, following the execution of a course of action, is either obtained or not in terms of intuitive observation. A *quantitatively-defined objective* is one that is obtained in varying degree. The extent to which such an outcome is obtained can be measured. A *policy* is the specification in concrete details of ways and means for the attainment of planned objectives.

For the purposes of the goals-achievement matrix, goals should, as far as possible, be defined operationally, that is, they should be expressed as objectives. In this way the degree of achievement of the various objectives can be measured directly from the costs and benefits that have been identified. Thus, the ideal of increased economic welfare can be defined in terms of objectives relating to the rate of increase or the absolute increase of the gross national product or the gross regional product. Similarly, the ideal of a healthy environment can be expressed in terms of objectives such as reduction in air pollution, reduction in water pollution, reduction in the rate of accidents, and so forth.

Requisites are a category of values that are not specific goals of plans but enable the planner and decisionmaker to set guidelines. Requisites set limits to objectives and the policies by which objectives may be realized. They enter into consideration primarily at the time that the alternate plans are generated and developed, that is, before the lans are evaluated in terms of the desired goals. Requisites indicate the necessary conditions that must be satisfied in order that the plans will not be rejected. However, they do not provide a sufficient basis for the acceptance of plans. The satisfaction of both a set of objectives and a set of requisites is necessary and sufficient for a plan to be acceptable. Typical requisites are feasibility, immediacy, and interdependence. By *feasibility* we mean, can existing fiscal, legal, political, and social conditions facilitate the execution of the plan? *Immediacy* refers to the priority to be assigned to the execution of the planned facility, given the existing political and social conditions. *Interdependence* refers to significant interaction between the sector under consideration and any other sector. For instance, when planning transportation facilities, the interaction between these facilities and the nature, magnitude, intensity, and location of the activities served by the transportation route or system is a primary consideration.

Constraints are a particular type of requisite. The achievement of specified levels of particular objectives may serve as constraints on the acceptability of alternative plans irrespective of the weight of these objectives in the total array of objectives.[16] Thus, the maintenance of air pollution below specified levels may serve as a constraint on the choice of alternative transportation plans even though the reduction of air pollution, expressed as an open-ended objective, may not be highly valued by the community.

Certain additional terms are used in the method with definitions somewhat different from those elsewhere in the literature. A consequence is a change in a given situation caused by a policy. Consequences that are positively valued in terms of a given end are *benefits;* when negatively valued in terms of a given end, they are *costs.* If costs and benefits are quantifiable, they are *tangible;* if they are not quantifiable,[17] they are termed *intangible. Direct* costs and benefits refer to consequences within the sector of the proposed investment accruing to the users and the suppliers of the goods or services provided. *Indirect* costs and benefits refer to consequences in sectors other than the sector of the proposed investment.[18]

Procedure

The evaluation of the alternative courses of action requires the determination for each alternative of whether or not the benefits outweigh the costs, measured in terms of the total array of ends. For each goal, a cost-benefit account is prepared. Depending on the definition of the objective, the costs and benefits are expressed as:

(1) Tangible costs and benefits expressed in monetary terms.
(2) Tangible costs and benefits which cannot be expressed in monetary terms but can be expressed quantitatively,[19] usually in terms derived from the definition of the goal.
(3) Intangible costs and benefits.

For each objective and for each alternative course of action, costs and benefits are compared, aggregated where possible, and reported separately. The decision-maker is then in a position to weigh the alternative courses of action against each other.

The weighting that is introduced into the analysis is that which reflects the community's valuation of each of the various objectives and its valuation of appropriate *incidence* of benefits and costs. It is therefore necessary to identify those sections of the public, considered by income group, occupation, location, or any other preferred criterion, who are affected by the consequences of a course of action since inevitably the consequences are unlikely to affect all sections of the public served uniformly. The incidence of the favorable and unfavorable consequences accruing to sections of the public should, of course, be taken into consideration by the decisionmakers. This information is extremely important if charges and compensation payments are employed in order to implement a planning proposal. It is also useful to have this information available in order to predict the reaction of the existing institutional power structure to the planning proposals. The weights applied to the incidence of objectives can be interpreted as the community's desired distribution of the benefits relating to particular objectives. Thus the aggregated set of incidence weights applying to all the objectives can be considered as representing the community's conception of "equity."

Any rational determination requires the evaluation of anticipated consequences while allowing for the possibility of unanticipated consequences. The validity of the evaluation is, of course, strengthened by the increase of knowledge of anticipated consequences and the minimization of unanticipated consequences. *Uncertainty* concerning anticipated consequences is best treated by probability formulation. In general, a range of possible outcomes is preferable to the prediction of a unique outcome. To simplify the computation the following procedure may be used. If an outcome would be substantially affected by a particular contingency, for example, technological innovation, a supplementary comparison of alternative courses of action can be made in terms of this modification. In general, allowance for uncertainty should be made indirectly by use of conservative estimates, requirement of safety margins, continual feedback and adjustment, and a risk component in the discount rate. Estimates made at low discount rates are highly sensitive to variations in the estimate of future events. Higher discount rates lead to less sensitivity to variations in the estimates of future events.

There may be differential sensitivity to uncertainty in the various public sectors. Thus the costs and benefits of water supply improvements may be more predictable (as well as identifiable) than the costs and benefits of a new school. There are also differential sensitivities in the predictability of incidence.

The *time dimension* of costs and benefits deserves mention at this point. Costs and benefits occurring in different time periods are not of equal weight. One cannot fully describe the costs and benefits of alternative courses of action without saying when they are to be incurred. This aspect has received considerable attention in the literature [20] and will not be discussed in detail in this study.

Costs and Benefits in the Goals-Achievement Matrix

In this analysis, costs and benefits are always defined in terms of goal achievement. Thus benefits represent progress toward the desired objectives while costs represent retrogression from desired objectives. Where the goal can be and is defined in terms of quantitative units, the costs and benefits are defined in terms of the same units. Where no quantitative units are applicable, benefits indicate progress toward the qualitative states that the objective describes, while costs indicate retrogression from these objectives. For the same objective, costs and benefits are always defined in terms of the same units if the objective can be expressed in quantitative terms. Thus, if a benefit of x units accrues, it can be nullified by a cost of x units, provided both costs and benefits apply to the same objective. This interpretation of costs and benefits differs markedly from the traditional conception of costs and benefits. In general, costs have traditionally been defined as the value of goods and services used for the establishment, maintenance, and operation of the project, while benefits are the value of immediate products, or services, resulting from the courses of action for which the costs were incurred. Thus in the proposed formulation, costs may or may not be resources of land, labor, or capital (as project costs are usually thought of); this is dependent on the definition of the goal. The same applies to benefits.

The following, then, is the final product for every plan. The set of goals is known and the relative value to be attached to each goal is established. The objectives are defined operationally rather than in abstract terms. The consequences of each alternative course of action are determined for each objective. The incidence of the benefits and costs of each course of action measured in terms of the achievement of the goal is established for each goal. The relative weight to be attached to each group is also established. The product of the analysis is conceptualized in Table 2.

In the table, a, β, γ, . . . are the descriptions of the goals. Each goal has a weight 1, 2, 3, . . . as has been previously determined. Various groups of people or establishments *a, b, c, d, e,* . . . are identified as affected by the course of action. These groups may be combined in any meaninful manner in order to indicate the differential incidence of costs and benefits. A relative weight is determined for each group, either for each goal individually or all goals together. The letters A, B, . . . are the costs and benefits that may be defined in monetary or nonmonetary units or in terms of qualitative states.

Costs and benefits are recorded for each objective according to the parties that are affected. A dash (–) in a cell implies that no cost or benefit that is related to that objective would accrue to that party if that plan were effectuated. A particular party may suffer both costs and benefits with respect to a particular objective. Thus, the reduction of noise may be a relevant

TABLE 2
THE GOALS-ACHIEVEMENT MATRIX

Goal Description:		*α*			*β*	
Relative Weight:		*2*			*3*	
Incidence	*Relative Weight*	*Costs*	*Benefits*	*Relative Weight*	*Costs*	*Benefits*
Group a	1	A	D	5	E	–
Group b	3	H }	J	4	–	R
Group c	1	L }		3	–	S
Group d	2	– }		2 }	T	–
Group e	1	–	K	1 }		U
		Σ	Σ			
Goal Description:		*γ*			*δ*	
Relative Weight:		*5*			*4*	
Group a	1 }		N	1	Q	R
Group b	2 }		–	2	S	T
Group c	3 }	M	–	1	V	W
Group d	4 }		–	2	–	–
Group e	5 }		P	1	–	–
		Σ	Σ			

objective of a plan for improved transportation facilities. A particular location may simultaneously experience a decrease of noise from one source, perhaps as a result of the proposed diversion of heavy automobile traffic from that location and an increase of noise from another source, such as from a new transit route that is proposed for that area.

For certain of the goals Σ indicates that summation of the costs and benefits is meaningful and useful. The total costs and benefits with respect to that goal can then be compared. This will be the case when all the costs and benefits are expressed in quantitative units. It is obviously not the case for the intangible costs and benefits of all the goals can be expressed in the same units. In the rare case where they can be—which may occur when only one or two goals are valued by the community—it may be possible to arrive at a grand cost-benefits summation. However, this is most unlikely.

For each course of action, the product of the analysis is similar to Table 2. As was mentioned, in the face of uncertainty, a range of costs and benefits is preferable to the prediction of a unique outcome. Thus the letters A, B, . . . should be considered not as a single value but rather as a range of values.

Comparison of Quantitative and Qualitative Objectives

A question that inevitably arises is how are the objectives that are expressed in qualitative terms to be compared with objectives expressed in quantitative terms?

It can be argued that, to some extent, the distinction between quantitatively defined objectives and qualitatively defined objectives is artificial.[21] Any property that can be quantified can also be expressed in qualitative terms. Similarly a qualitative description may involve implicit quantification. For instance, the specification of the color of an object implies no more than the specification of the wave length of the light reflected from it. As time passes, man's capacity to express qualitative phenomena in quantitative terms will inevitably increase since one of the purposes of scientific endeavor is to define phenomena as precisely as possible. However, it is also quite evident that advances in quantification require qualitative judgments relating to the development of valid scales of measurement, since the usefulness of a scale is dependent on judgments of the relevance of what is measured and the adequacy of the definition of the property that is measured.

There is a hierarchy of classes of scales of measurement that can be employed for the measurement of quantities.[22] These scales enable the interpretation of the quantities assigned in measurement and require increasingly restrictive conditions to be satisfied as the hierarchy is ascended. Listed by ascending order of complexity, restriction of initial premises and range of applicable measurement, the major classes of measurement scales and their basic empirical operations are:

(1) *The nominal scale,* which classifies and numbers entities.
(2) *The ordinal scale,* which ranks entities.
(3) *The interval scale,* which provides equal intervals between entities and indicates the differences or distances of entities from some arbitrary origin.
(4) *The ratio scale,* which provides equal intervals between entities and indicates the differences or distances of entities from some nonarbitrary origin.

In general, it is desirable to measure the characteristics of a phenomenon on the highest order scale that can validly be employed. Conversely, it is most important to recognize the scale of measurement that has been employed and not to treat the measures obtained as if they pertained to a higher order scale of measurement.

In postulating objectives and proposing measures for their achievement, it is assumed that the measures of achievement of the objectives can be classified according to a scale of measurement, and such classification will be suggested in each case. It should be explicitly stated that the proposal of a measure implies that the focus of interest is restricted to that characteristic of a phenomenon that is measured. Abraham Kaplan[23] states that "every measurement involves some degree of abstraction: certain things are omitted in the numerical description for this is always based on a determinate set of properties and relations to the exclusion of others." The measures that are employed for describing a phenomenon can thus be successful in varying degree. It is obvious that the achievement of quantitatively defined objectives can be more easily measured than the achievement of qualitatively defined objectives. However, at least the simplest two measurement scales in the hierarchy, the nominal scale and the ordinal scale, can be employed for the measurement of the achievement of qualitatively defined objectives. It might further be possible to employ suitable surrogates that adequately reflect the extent of achievement of qualitatively defined objectives and can be measured on higher order measurement scales. In the final analysis "the validity of a measure depends on the extent to which it measures what it purports to measure."[24] The measures of goal-achievement that are proposed should thus be judged by this criterion and, where deficient, should be improved so that they might better satisfy this criterion.

The following outline is a possible set of objectives that would be affected by the plan for a new transportation route and a set of measures of these objectives. The objectives might be those of the entire community affected, of sections of the community affected or of the users of the transportation system and are classified accordingly.

I. OBJECTIVES MEASURABLE ON A RATIO SCALE

User Objectives

(1) Increase of accessibility: measured in average travel time and, when valid, in monetary terms.

(2) Accident reduction: measured in terms of numbers of fatalities and injuries. Injury costs and property damage measured in monetary terms.

Community Objectives

(1) Economic efficiency: measured in monetary terms.

(2) Regional economic growth: measured in monetary terms.

(3) Income distribution: measured in monetary terms.

(4) Fiscal efficiency (defined as net returns to the fisc): measured in monetary terms.

(5) Reduction of air pollution: measured in terms of the amount of pollutants per unit volume of air.

II. OBJECTIVES MEASURABLE ON INTERVAL SCALE

User and Community Objectives

Noise reduction: measured in decibels or sones.

III. OBJECTIVES MEASURABLE ON ORDINAL SCALE

(A) *Objectives that can be measured on ratio or interval scales if suitable surrogates are employed.*

User Objectives

(1) Comfort of travel (defined as the absence of physical and mental strain): Surrogate measures are (i) Probability of standing in transit vehicles; (ii) probability of traveling on congested route.

(2) Convenience of travel (defined as ease of performance): Surrogate measures are: (i) Number of changes of mode of travel between origin and destination; (ii) aggregate amount of waiting time in changing mode of travel; (iii) Agregate amount of walking required, measured in time or distance in getting from origins to destinations; (iv) reliability of transit service, measured in probability of service being provided as scheduled.

Community Objectives

(1) Reduction of community disruption: Surrogate measures are: (i) Displacement of buildings and activities measured in numbers of buildings and

people displaced and the monetary costs, direct and indirect, of relocation; (ii) extent of interference with existing market areas and service areas of community services and businesses measured by number of intersections of trip origin and destination lines.

(2) Preservation of open space: Surrogate measures are: (i) Open space threatened as percentage of total community open space; (ii) Acessibility to alternative open space serving similar purposes.

(B) *Objectives that can be measured only on ordinal scales even if surrogates are employed.*

User and Community Objective

Visual Enhancement: A set of criteria can be postulated that can enable the evaluation of a transportation route from from both the user's point of view and the point of view of adjoining communities. Such criteria can be employed with respect t o the features of the roadscape, the traveler's perception of space and motion, the travler's sense of orientation and location, the integration of the facility into the surrounding area, the screening of traffic, and so forth. The explicit and systematic use of such criteria as proposed by analysts such as Appleyard, Lynch, and Meyer[25] or Tunnard and Pushkarev[26] enables the measurement of the visual effects of transportation improvements on an ordinal scale.

Community Objectives

Preservation of Historic Sites and Buildings: A set of criteria for the comparative evaluation of historic sites and buildings along the lines suggested by Tunnard and Pushkarev[27] could be employed when such sites or buildings are threatened by transportation improvements.

The Comparison of Goals Achievement

Let us assume that the effect of a plan on the achievement of a set of objectives and the weights of the objectives and their incidence have been established. How is the effectiveness of this plan in achieving the set of objectives to be compared with the effectivness of an alternative plan, if the objectives have been measured in various types of units on different scales of measurement? Various strategies might be employed:

Goals-Achievement Account. The simplest strategy is to present the decision-maker with the entire goals-achievement account without attempting to synthesize the extent of goals-achievement. This approach is obviously least demanding of the planner and most demanding of the decision-maker. In this case the decision-maker would have before him a statement of the extent of achievement of the various objectives that includes an indication of the extent of achievement of the objectives with respect to diverse locations and/or groups within the community. This is compared with the weights of the objectives for the entire community as well as the differential weights of the objectives for the various locations and/or groups within the community. The onus would then be on the decision-makers to trade off the extent of achievement of the set of objectives with the weights of these objectives. For instance, Plan A increases regional economic growth by $x and increases aggregate accessibility by y hours, regional economic growth being considered a more important objective than the increase of accessibility. However, Plan A is less desirable than Plan B with respect to its visual effects, being valued equally with the increase of accessibility in the community. Plan B increases regional economic growth less than Plan A and increases accessibility more than Plan A. The decision-maker must then compare the weights ascribed to the objectives with the differential achievement of the objectives by Plans A and B and choose the more desirable plan by weighing all the information. This approach would leave the rigor of the planner's analysis less open to criticism than the subsequent approaches but places a greater onus on the decision-maker.

The Weighted Index of Goals-Achievement. According to this approach, the combined weight of the objectives and their incidence is assigned to the measures of achievement of the objectives. The weighted indices of goals-achievement are then summed and the preferred plan among the alternatives compared is that with the largest index. This approach requires several arbitrary assumptions concerning the interrelationship of the measures of achievement of the individual objectives and is subject to some of the criticism that has been made of the balance sheet of development with respect to the aggregation of benefits and costs referring to different objectives. It is also subject to a criticism that has frequently been made of the use of indices, that the index cannot be understood in terms of a single unit of measurement and is thus difficult to interpret. However, it does provide an easily determined summary of the effects of plans on the achievement of objectives by the community. Since the index is determined in a similar manner for all alternative plans under consideration, it does enable a comparison to be made.

The simplest approach, and one that is subject to least criticism, is to treat all objectives as if they have been measured on the least demanding of measurement scales, an ordinal scale. The plan would then be evaluated with respect to each objective to determine whether it increases, decreases, or leaves goals-achievement at about the same level for the community as a whole and for groups within it. Similar, but arbitrary, values would then be assigned, say +1 if goals-achievement is enhanced, −1 if goals-achievement is decreased, and 0 if there is no effect on goals-achievement. Then the weights of the individual objectives and their incidence would be introduced and an index of goals-achievement would be determined for the entire plan. Let us assume that Plans A and B are being compared with respect to their effectiveness in increasing accessibility while minimizing community disruption. Let us assume the relative weights of these objectives and their incidence for Groups a and b to be as stated in Table 3. Let us assume that Plan A increases accessibility for Group a while decreasing it for Group b, while Plan B decreases accessibility for Group a while increasing it for Group b. Plan A disrupts the neighborhood of Group a considerably but has no effect in this respect on Group b. Plan B by contrast does not disrupt Group a's neighborhood but does disrupt Group b's neighborhood. The outcome is recorded in Table 3.

TABLE 3
GOALS-ACHIEVEMENT BY MEASUREMENT ON ORDINAL SCALE–SUMMARY

	Weighted Accessibility			Weighted Community Disruption		
		(community wt. = 2)			(community wt. = 1)	
	Weight	*Plan A*	*Plan B*	*Weight*	*Plan A*	*Plan B*
Group a	3	+6	−6	3	−3	0
Group b	1	−2	+2	2	0	−2
Total		+4	−4		−3	−2

Result: Weighted index of goals-achievement Plan A = 1
Plan B = −6

Plan A is thus preferable to Plan B

By measuring the achievement of all objectives on an ordinal scale, the analysis does not use all the information that it has available on the extent of achievement of objectives. Accessibility can be measured on a ratio scale, and community disruption can be measured on an ordinal scale. If a surrogate measure is employed, community disruption can also be measured on a ratio scale. Thus, information that can be fairly precisely measured concerning the extent to which the plans influence goals-achievement is omitted.

An alternative approach that is subject to much more criticism along the lines mentioned but does take the extent of achievement of objectives into account can be employed. Each of the measures of achievement of objectives on interval scales or on ratio scales can be weighted and summed. Thus, if accessibility has been increased by 3 units (and has a weight of 2) and if economic growth increases by 2 units (and has a weight of 3), then the index that reflects the extent of achievement of these objectives and their weights would be 12. An obvious deficiency of this approach is that the units employed for measuring the objectives are arbitrary. Thus the increase of accessibility could be expressed in minutes instead of hours and the extent of increase of accessibility would then be 180 units, not 3 units. This would create an index of 366, with accessibility having an overwhelming weight in the index. The only defense for the use of such an index is that it is being applied in a similar manner for all the plans under consideration. However, it should be employed only if the units of measurement of goals-achievement can be so manipulated that they are approximately of the same order. It should be noted that if objectives can be measured only on an ordinal scale, then they cannot be incorporated into the index. Thus Plan A may have an index of goals-achievement of 12, while Plan B may have an index of 14. However Plan A may have more desirable visual effects than Plan B. Visual effects, being measurable only on an ordinal scale, cannot be included in the index. The planner or decision-maker will then have to trade off the visual impact of Plans A and B with their effectiveness in achieving other objectives.

Goals-Achievement Transformation Functions

Ackoff[28] has proposed a method for relating outcomes measured in different units to avoid some problems confronted when aggregating measures using different units of measurement. The approach is difficult to put into operation but is promising conceptually. Outcomes measured on one scale are transformed into units in which outcomes on another scale are measured. A distinction is made between the treatment of objectives measured on qualitative scales and those measured on quantitative scales.

With respect to quantitative objectives, such as those measurable on interval or ratio scales, quantities on one scale are equated with quantities on another scale and then the relative values on the first scale are determined on the second scale. In transforming the scales, it becomes evident that the relative importance of units on one scale may not be equivalent to the relative importance of units on the other scale. Thus if the achievement of an objective such as the reduction of air pollution (measured in amount of pollutants per unit volume) is transformed to a scale on which the increase of accessibility is measured, the second unit of air pollution reduction may not be as important relative to the increase of accessibility as the first unit of air pollution reduction since the danger of air pollution to a community may not increase linearly with the increase in the amount of air pollutants per unit volume. The transformation functions are thus unlikely to be linear in form.

The problem is considerably complicated if there are more than two quantitative objectives, all measured in different units of measurement. It is then desirable to develop transformation functions that can enable the transformation of all the outcomes to a single scale. A monetary scale is probably most useful for this purpose. While the units of measurement would be the same as those used in traditional cost-benefit analysis, there is a most important difference in the method of analysis. Outcomes are not translated into monetary units a priori and considered only in terms of the economic efficiency objective. Instead, the accounting system reflects the weighted set of community objectives that are explicitly stated. The measures of achievement of objectives are explicitly translated into monetary units in such a manner that the relative weights of the objectives and their incidence are reflected in the transformation.

Ackoff suggests that transformation functions can be employed to trade off the achievement of qualitative objectives, that is, those measured on ordinal or nominal scales with the achievement of quantitative objectives. Thus visual enhancement, say, would be explicitly traded off on a monetary scale with regional economic growth. This assumption deserves more exploration but is much more tenuous than the use of transformation functions for comparing the achievement of quantitative objectives.

Relative Weights in the Goals-Achievement Matrix

The key to plan evaluation by means of goals-achievement analysis is the weighting of objectives, activities, locations, groups, or sectors in urban areas. How might these weights be determined?

In general, the problem of setting objectives and the relative valuation of objectives by the community ought to be approached from a particular theory of government. In a constitutional democratic state, for instance, there is general agreement that elected representatives should have ultimate responsibility. However, even if elected officials wish to act rationally in their evaluation and choice of alternative courses of action with respect to the objectives that they wish to pursue, they might be loathe to express their relative valuation of these objectives, a priori. In practice, goals and their relative weights may thus have to be determined iteratively as a result of a complex process of interaction among elected officials, administrators, planners, and various formal and informal groups reacting to explicitly stated objectives and the alternative courses of action proposed to meet these objectives.

The determination of community objectives and their relative valuation by the community is thus no easy task and requires considerable research. There is no single approach to the problem that is universally applicable; the methods that are employed will differ from one community to the next, from one sector to the next, or from one governmental context to the next. The planner's intuitive knowledge of a community, based on experience and professional expertise, is very important in the development of the initial hypotheses concerning community objectives. Among the direct approaches that might be adopted in the formulation of objectives and their respective weights are consultations with elected officials, consultations with members of the community power structure,[29] consultations with community interest groups, sampling of various "publics" in the community,[30] and public hearings.[31] Alternatively, indirect approaches might be employed. The patterns of behavior of groups within the community might be analyzed in order to establish their underlying objectives and the relative importance of these objectives to the community and groups within it. Another indirect approach is the analysis of the pattern of previous allocations of public investments in order to determine the goal priorities implicit in previous decisions on the allocation of resources.[32] The resources available to a planning agency—particularly budget, time, and professional expertise—impose important constraints on the methods that may be employed in the goal formulation process. In any event, it is desirable to approach the determination and valuation of community objectives from different points of view, simultaneously.

Even if the relative valuation of objectives has not been determined empirically, the effect of changes in weights on the relative desirability of alternative plans may be usefully explored.[33] Different sets of weights might be assumed, and the effect of particular weights on the choice of the preferred plan can be determined. The effect of incremental changes in relative weights can also be examined.

Limits on the Application of the Goals-Achievement Matrix As a Tool for Plan Evaluation

At this stage it should be expressly asked what the goals-achievement matrix is intended to do and what it is not intended to do. Like cost-benefit analysis and the balance sheet of development, the goals-achievement matrix cannot determine whether a project should be executed or not. In all cases, the need for the project that is proposed is treated as a "given." All of these methods of evaluation are designed primarily for the comparison and ranking of alternative projects rather than for testing their absolute desirability.

Further, the goals-achievement matrix has been devised for the evaluation of plans for development in a single functional sector. Both the goals-achievement matrix and cost-benefit analysis differ in this respect from the balance sheet of development that has been applied to the evaluation both of development plans for single functional sectors and for multiple sector development plans. However, Coughlin and Stevens[34] have recently proposed a method for the evaluation of multifunctional planning packages such as a city's capital improvements programs. The goals-achievement matrix and the Coughlin-Stevens method of evaluation are in essence complementary; and the former can, in some respects, be considered as an elaboration of certain aspects of the latter.

A Preliminary Appraisal of the Goals-Achievement Matrix

This, then, is the overall framework that is proposed. While this method calls for an extremely complex, time-consuming, and expensive task, the conceptual framework is recommended as a basis for rational decision-making.[35] It may be contended that the product of the goals-achievement matrix is exceedingly complex and thus difficult for the decision-maker to digest. While this approach does not lend itself to a single number outcome, as is the case with the single efficiency goal conception, it is more expressive of the complexity of the consequences of urban development. Knowledge of the effects of alternative courses of action with regard to all valued objectives, and knowledge of the incidence of these effects with respect to various aggregates of people should enable the decision-maker to arrive at more rational decisions.

By determining how various objectives will be affected by proposed plans, the goals-achievement matrix can determine the extent to which certain specified standards are being met. Is the transportation plan likely to meet minimum accessibility requirements and minimum standards of comfort and convenience? Are levels of air pollution and noise likely to exceed specified standards? Is the fatal accident rate within prescribed acceptable limits? These are the types of questions that the goals-achievement matrix is designed to answer. It can also determine the costs of meeting specified standards in terms of the degree of achievement of other "open-ended" objectives that would have to be forfeited. Different plans have different trade-offs between the achievement of objectives and standards, and these can also be compared.

The key to decision-making by means of the goals-achievement matrix is the weighting of objectives, activities, locations, groups, or sectors in urban areas. By the application of relative weights, it is possible to arrive at a unique conclusion. The goals-achievement matrix is not very useful if weights cannot be objectively determined or assumed. The development of methods for the determination of weights is thus of first priority for the successful application of the goals-achievement matrix.

A major disadvantage of the goals-achievement matrix method of evaluation is that interaction and interdependence between objectives is not registered. Until interaction between objectives is accounted for in the analysis, the goals-achievement matrix is recommended only for the evaluation of plans in a single sector. It is therefore of limited application in the evaluation of capital programs that include recommendations for projects that serve more than one sector. Extensive research into the treatment of goal interdependence in the evaluation of plans is thus strongly recommended.

It is true that the sheer complexity of problems involved in the analysis will severely test our capacity to solve them. As Milliman points out:

> "The complexity of public decision-making tends to increase with such factors as the number and interdependence of the variables involved, the length of time horizon, the degree of uncertainty and the number of intangible considerations."[36]

In practice it will be seen that only a relatively small number of goals are relevant or significant. Furthermore, functional, institutional, legal, financial, and jurisdictional requisites tend to limit the amount of work required for the evaluation of alternatives. Thus, particular substantive areas served by the plan, as well as environmental conditions, will tend to reveal relevant goals, time horizon, and other factors.

Although the task remains complex, its complexity is no excuse for abandoning the attempt. The comparison of alternative courses of action with respect to the goals in view and the identification and measurement of the costs and benefits of these courses of action with regard to the achievement of the goals is proposed as the "rational" way to approach the problem. Methods should be judged on the basis of whether or not they lead to proper conclusions if it can be assumed that the numbers and descriptions used in the analysis are the right ones. Obtaining the right numbers and the descriptions of the intangible effects, though a fundamental problem, is separate and distinct from the problem of developing methods of evaluation.

NOTES

1. This definition and the model of the rational planning process outlined below is consistent with the definitions of the planning process to be found in Paul Davidoff and

Thomas A. Reiner, "A Choice Theory of Planning," Journal of the American Institute of Planners, 28 (May 1962), pp. 103-6, and in Martin Meyerson and E. C. Banfield, *Politics, Planning and the Public Interest* (New York: Free Press, 1955), pp. 303-29.

The conception of rationality herein implied is consistent with that proposed by Herbert Simon, *Administrative Behavior* (New York: Macmillan, 1947), p. 47, and by Talcott Parsons, *The Structure of Social Action* (2d ed.; New York: Free Press, 1949), p. 58. According to Parsons: "Action is rational insofar as it pursues ends possible within the conditions of the situation and by means which among those available to the actor, are intrinsically best adapted to the end for reasons understandable and verifiable by positive empirical science."

2. Roland N. McKean, *Efficiency in Government Through Systems Analysis* (New York: John Wiley & Sons, 1958), p. 19.

3. William J. Baumol, *Economic Theory and Operations Analysis* (Englewood Cliffs, N.J.: Prentice Hall, Inc., 1961), Chap. 13, pp. 246-75.

4. This is so for a given income distribution and provided there are no external economies and diseconomies.

5. Profit is here defined as the difference between total benefits (returns) and total costs.

6. "Private" is used in the sense of direct out-of-pocket costs and benefits to suppliers and consumers. "Social" refers to the direct costs and benefits as well as all others stemming from or induced by the public investment.

7. U.S. Federal Interagency Committee on Water Resources, Subcommittee on Evaluation Standards, *Proposed Practices for Economic Analysis of River Basin Projects* (Washington, D.C.: Government Printing Office, 1958), p. 7.

8. In this respect, John Kenneth Galbraith has said in a lecture at New York University in November 1965, as reported in Architectural Forum, 125, No. 5 (December 1965), 61-2: "Economists and politicians still measure accomplishment by indices relevant to the popular concerns of 30 years ago.... If the gross national product grows adequately and unemployment declines, this, pro tanto, means success. If our cities, at the same time, become unlivable in part as a product of this growth and the smoke, sewage, trash and traffic that it spawns, that is unfortunate but not highly relevant."

9. According to John V. Krutilla, "Welfare Aspects of Benefit-Cost Analysis," Journal of Political Economy, 69, No. 3 (1961), 226-55.

10. Nathaniel Lichfield has expounded and applied his ideas in the following articles and books: *Economics of Planned Development* (London: Estates Gazette, Ltd., 1956), pp. 253-80; "Cost Benefit Analysis in City Planning," Journal of the American Institute of Planners, 26 (November 1960); Cost Benefit Analysis in Urban Redevelopment (University of California, Institute of Business and Economic Research, Real Estate Research Report No. 20, 1962); Nathaniel Lichfield and Julius Margolis, "Benefit-Cost Analysis as a Tool in Urban Government Decision-Making," in Howard G. Schaller (ed.), *Public Expenditure Decisions in the Urban Community* (Washington: Resources for the Future, 1963), pp. 118-46; "Cost-Benefit Analysis in Plan Evaluation," The Town Planning Reviews, 35 (July 1964), 159-69; "Spatial Externalities in Urban Public Expenditures," in Julius Margolis (ed.) *The Public Economy of Urban Communities* (Washington: Resources for the Future, 1965), pp. 207-50; "Cost Benefit Analysis in Urban Redevelopment. A Cast Study–Swanley," Urban Studies, III (November 1966), 215-49.

11. Nathaniel Lichfield, "Cost-Benefit Analysis in Plan Evaluation," The Town Planning Reviews, 35 (July 1964), 165.

12. Lichfield has applied cost-benefit analysis to various redevelopment plans in the San Francisco area in *Cost-Benefit Analysis in Urban Redevelopment;* to the comparison of two alternative city plans for Cambridge, England, in *Spatial Externalities in Urban Public Expenditures: A Case Study,* and to the comparison of plans for Swanley in *Cost Benefit Analysis in Urban Redevelopment. A Case Study–Swanley.*

13. An analyst might call a community's attention to certain costs and benefits that had not been recognized. However, it is questionable whether the analyst should attach values to these costs and benefits that are contrary to the values of the community.

14. In his recent work in Swanley and Cambridge, Lichfield has identified effects on some community objectives. However, the community's relative valuation of the objectives is not considered.

15. A major contribution to cost-benefit analysis techniques whereby income redistribution effects are considered simultaneously with effects on economic efficiency has resulted from research conducted under the auspices of The Harvard Water Program. See Arthur Maass, Maynard Hufschmidt, et al., *Design of Water-Resource Systems* (Cambridge: Harvard University Press, 1962).

16. However it can be shown that the expression of objectives as constraints is equivalent to placing a relative weight on the objective. See Maass, Hufschmidt, et al., ibid., pp. 67-87.

17. A quantity of a magnitude is defined as anything capable of being greater or smaller than some other thing. Thus the consequences of a course of action can be related to a scale requiring: (a) classification of the consequences and (b) ranking of the consequences. Measurability requires the additional criteria (a) that it is possible to define a unit and (b) that it is possible to define addition operationally.

18. The same costs and benefits may be direct or indirect according to the perspective of the analysis, that is, according to the sectoral definition by jurisdiction to be direct but its consequences on mass transit facilities within the same geographic area, indirect. However, for the transportation planner or the city planner, the effects of the highway on transit facilities are direct.

19. Typical costs and benefits in this category may be the number of traffic fatalities that can be expected on a highway of a particular quality, or the noise level, measured in decibels, of a particular facility.

20. For an excellent survey of the literature devoted to the treatment of time preference uncertainty and other aspects of public investment theory, see A. R. Prest and R. Turvey, "Cost-Benefit Analysis: A Survey," in *Surveys of Economic Theory: Resource Analysis* (New York: St. Martin's Press, 1966), pp. 155-207.

21. Abraham Kaplan states in *The Conduct of Inquiry* (San Francisco: Chandler Publishing Co., 1964), p. 176, that "No problem is a purely qualitative one in its own nature; we may always approach it in quantitative terms." He further suggests (p. 207) that "whether something is identified as a quality or a quantity depends on how we choose to represent it in our symbolism." This position is supported by Russell L. Ackoff, who in *Scientific Method: Optimizing Applied Research Decisions* (New York: John WIley & Sons, 1962), p. 20, suggests that "any qualified property is potentially capable of being expressed quantitatively in terms of a range along a scale."

22. For a general review of the usefulness of measurement scales for planning purposes see Gerald Hodge, "Use and Misuse of Measurement Scales in City Planning," Journal of the American Institute of Planners, 29 (May 1963), 112-21.

23. Abraham Kaplan, p. 207.

24. M. Jahoda and others, *Research Methods in Social Relations* (New York: Dryden Press, 1954), p. 109.

25. Donald Appleyard, Kevin Lynch, and J. R. Meyer, *The View from the Road* (Cambridge: M.I.T. Press, 1960).

26. Christopher Tunnard and Boris Pushkarev, *Man-Made America: Chaos or Control* (New Haven: Yale University Press, 1963).

27., Ibid., p. 414.

28. Russell L. Ackoff, pp. 32-44.

29. This approach has been adopted, in part, in the preparation of plans for the Minneapolis-St. Paul metropolitan area and in other urban areas.

30. Richard A. Lamanna, "Value Consensus Among Urban Residents," Journal of the American Institute of Planners, 30, No. 4 (1964), 317-22.

31. *Problems, Goals and Choices* (Chicago: Northeastern Illinois Planning Commission, 1965).

32. Burton A. Weisbrod, "Income Redistribution Consequences of Government Expenditure Programs," paper presented at Second Conference on Government Expenditures, Brookings Institution, Washington, D.C., 1966.

33. Morris Hill, "A Method for Evaluating Alternative Plans: The Goals Achievement Matrix Applied to Transportation Plans" (Ph.D. dissertation, University of Pennsylvania, 1966).

34. Robert E. Coughlin and Benjamin H. Stevens, "Public Facility Programming and the Achievement of Development Goals," Papersrepared for the Seminar on Land Use Models, Institute for Urban Studies, University of Pennsylvania, Philadelphia, October 1964.

35. For an example of goals-achievement analysis to a planning problem, note the comparison of alternative plans for Cambridge, England, in Morris Hill, Chap. 8, pp. 215-99.

36. J. W. Milliman, "Decision Criteria for Capital Improvements in Urban Areas with Special Reference to the Theory and Practice in Philadelphia" (unpublished first draft of paper sponsored by Resources for the Future, Washington, D.C., July 1963), p. 22.

Chapter 10

CRITERIA FOR EVALUATION IN PLANNING STATE AND LOCAL PROGRAMS

Harry P. Hatry

This paper aims at clarifying and developing some of the fundamental concepts of the approach to governmental program planning commonly included under the term "planning-programming-budgeting (PPB)" system. This paper represents a first attempt at identifying specific criteria (i.e., measures of effectiveness) for use in evaluating alternative proposals for programs for carrying out major State and local governmental functions.

To date there has been little written that attempts to identify specific criteria useful for government program analysis. This paper discusses the criteria problem and makes the rash attempt to identify meaningful criteria in the hope that it will stimulate further efforts both within individual governments and by professionals outside governments who are experienced in analytical techniques. The list of criteria provided here is far from being either exhaustive or definitive.

It is to be emphasized that for individual program analyses, considerable effort will still need to be applied to the determination of evaluation criteria appropriate to the specific problem. The list of criteria contained in . . . this paper can be used as a starting point.

AUTHOR'S NOTE: The author wishes to express his appreciation to the following persons for their time spent in reviewing early drafts of this paper and for their most helpful suggestions: Alan J. Goldman, of the National Bureau of Standards; Prof. Jesse Burkhead, of Syracuse University; Joel Posner, of the International City Managers Association; Nestor Terleckyj, of the U.S. Bureau of the Budget; and John F. Cotton, of the State-Local Finances Project. Reprinted from a study submitted by the Subcommittee on Intergovernmental Relations (Pursuant to S. Res. 55, 90th Congress) to the Committee on Government Operations, United States Senate (Washington, D.C.: U.S. Government Printing Office, 1967), pp. 1-29.

The emphasis in this paper is on nonmonetary criteria where the author feels the greatest effort is needed in State and local government program analyses.

In order to place the material in this report in clearer perspective the nature of planning-programming-budgeting systems is summarized. [1]

BASIC PURPOSE OF PLANNING-PROGRAMMING-BUDGETING (PPB) SYSTEMS

PPB systems are aimed at helping management make better decisions on the allocation of resources among alternative ways to attain government objectives. Its essence is the development and presentation of relevant information as to the full implications—the costs and benefits—of the major alternative courses of action.

PPB systems do not examine many aspects of government management. Such problems as budget implementation, the assessment and improvement of the work-efficiency of operation units, manpower selection, and the cost control of current operations are outside PPB. Cost accounting and non-fiscal performance reporting systems are very important in providing basic data required for PPB analyses (as well as for fiscal accounting and management control purposes); however, such systems are usually considered to be complementary to PPB rather than being directly part of it.

PPB systems hope to minimize the amount of piecemeal, fragmented, and last minute program evaluation which tends to occur under present planning and budgeting practices.

There is actually little new in the individual concepts of PPB. The concepts of program and performance budgeting with their orientation toward workload data and toward program rather than object classification (such as personnel, equipment, and so forth) have been applied by a number of governments since at least 1949, when the Hoover Commission strongly recommended their use. The analytical methods, such as marginal analysis and cost-benefit analysis, are familiar tools of economic analysis. What is new is the combination of a number of concepts into a package and the systematic application of the package in total to government planning.

MAJOR CHARACTERISTICS

The primary distinctive characteristics of PPB are:

(1) It calls for an identification of the fundamental objectives of the government.

(2) It requires explicit consideration of future year implications.

(3) It calls for systematic analysis of alternative ways of meeting the governmental objectives. This characteristic is the crux of PPB. The selection of the appropriate criteria for the evaluation of each alternative against relevant objectives is the subject of the main body of this report.

Note that the terms "PPB" and "program budgeting" as traditionally used are not equivalent. Typically the term "program budgeting" has been limited to budgeting systems emphasizing categorizations by programs without explicit provision for the systematic analysis and multiyear perspective of PPB.

MAJOR COMPONENTS OF A PPB SYSTEM

A PPB system typically has the following components:

1. An across-the-board governmental program structure. One of the first steps performed in instituting PPB is the identification, at least tentatively, of the government's basic objectives. Based upon these, the government's activities are grouped into categories, which aim at grouping together activities (regardless of organizational placement) that contribute toward the same objectives. An abbreviated example of a PPB program structure is shown in the appendix.*

2. A multiyear program and financial plan. At any given point in time there should exist an approved multiyear plan which uses the program structure categories discussed above. The plan is in two major parts. The first part is the "financial plan." All pertinent costs are considered–including capital costs as well as noncapital costs, and associated support costs (such as employee benefits, associated vehicle and building maintenance costs) as well as direct costs. Major associated external revenues should be identified where appropriate and the expected net cost to the jurisdiction indicated. The program, or output part of the plan, should contain the major measures which indicate to the users of the plan the scope and magnitude of the approved programs. Five years in addition to the current fiscal year has typically been selected for presentation in these multiyear plans.

3. Program analyses. The systematic identification and analysis of alternative ways to achieve government objectives is the cornerstone of PPB.

The analysis of a program issue should result in the identification and documentation of–

(1) The fundamental governmental objectives involved;
(2) The major feasible alternatives;
(3) For each alternative the best available estimates of the total program costs for each year considered;
(4) For each alternative the best available estimates of the benefits (and/or "penalties") relevant to the objectives for each year considered;
(5) The major assumptions and uncertainties associated with the alternatives; and
(6) The impact of proposed programs on other programs, other agencies, other levels of government, and on private organizations.

The presentation and discussion of alternatives and of the costs and benefits of each goes considerably beyond the scope of typical budget justification material which describes specific budget funding requests and goes beyond the scope of material generally included in physical planning studies.

*Not included herein.–Ed.

To be most useful, the analysis should indicate preferred program mixes at different funding levels since specific funding levels should seldom be chosen without explicit consideration of the change in costs and benefits (i.e., the "marginal" costs and benefits) in going from one level to another.

The analysis process should not ignore the political and legislative constraints that are relevant. The analysis should seek to optimize resource allocation within these contraints. However, analysis also should be used to indicate the potential penalties arising from them. This will provide information to government decision-makers suggesting how worthwhile it might be to try to overcome these constraints. In the short run these may indeed be firm constraints; for the long run, however, changes may be possible.

This type of analysis places emphasis on the preparation of quantitative information, but when this information is not available, qualitative materials should be included to place the issues in proper perspective.

In PPB, analysis can take many different forms and can be done at many levels of refinement. However, it is useful to distinguish two levels—a less-refined, less-rigorous analysis, and "in-depth" analysis. Each is briefly described below.

Less-rigorous analysis. This level of analysis is very likely, at least initially, to be the most prevalent. Where in-depth studies are not attempted or prove of slight use, a considerably improved understanding of program alternatives can be achieved through less-rigorous, less-refined analysis. A great deal can be achieved for resource allocation problems through the identification and examination of the six elements listed above.

Although these elements are also essential for in-depth studies, their investigation even without the more rigorous analytical tools can provide considerable illumination.

Much of the real gain from existing PPB systems has probably been derived from the "dialog"—the questioning and response—among the decision-makers, the proposal makers, and the program analysts. Much of the relevant analytical work done thus far in government PPB systems has resulted not from very sophisticated, technical analyses, but from penetrating questioning and the improved perspective obtained on the issues by applying this less-rigorous level of analysis.

"In-depth" analysis. A fully implemented PPB system should provide for the preparation of in-depth studies, often referred to as cost-benefit studies—also sometimes called cost-effectiveness or cost-utility analyses. These studies draw heavily upon the analytical tools of the professional disciplines, including mathematics, economics, operations research, engineering, and the computer sciences. They also seek the six elements listed above, but with a much closer examination. The studies attempt to identify, quantitatively to the extent possible, the cost and benefit implications of the range of feasible alternatives.

Cost-benefit analyses can seldom provide complete answers. They are intended primarily to provide information to decision-makers concerning the major trade-offs and implications existing among the alternatives considered. This information would then be available for use by decision-makers, along with any other information available– e.g., that pertaining to political, psychological, and other factors which may not have been included in the cost-benefit study.

Program analysis, at either level, is not easy. It is still true that program analysis (or whatever it may be called) is still as much an art as a science. Probably the most important limitations on the undertaking of meaningful analyses are:

(1) Problems in defining the real objectives;
(2) The presence of multiple, incommensurable benefits;
(3) Inadequacies of data relevant to the analysis, including information as to what effect each alternative course of action will have on the objectives as well as information describing where we are today; and
(4) Difficulties in considering a time stream of costs and benefits and not simply the evaluation of costs and benefits for a single point in time.

4. Program updating procedure. PPB requires explicit provision for the revision and updating of resource decisions. The system must be responsive to changing needs and changing information. The latest multiyear program and financial plan can form the "base" from which proposals for program changes can be made.

CONCLUSION

PPB potentially can help State and local governments deal with public problems ahead of time, in a comprehensive manner, and can place in much improved perspective the principal issues on resource allocation. The visibility of relevant information (on costs and benefits of pertinent alternatives) provided by PPB is the key element.

There are considerable difficulties and potential misuses that can occur. Certainly, too much should not be expected of the system. It should never be expected that PPB will be able to give definitive answers, but rather considerably improved information pertinent to resource allocation and program selection decisions.

An integrated PPB system is designed to provide information that is so vital to decision-making in our complex governmental structure. It is primarily a tool for high level decision-making, it will not be worth while unless the high level management understands it, wants it, and uses it.

THE CRITERIA PROBLEM

A major part of a program planning process is the attempt to estimate the contribution that each alternative program, or mix of programs, makes toward meeting fundamental governmental objectives. For the purpose of this paper, the terms "goals," "aims," "purposes," "missions," or "functions" may be substituted for "objectives." The need for evaluation criteria arises because funds and physical resources are scarce; there are not enough available to satisfy all needs and proposals. (The term "measures of effectiveness" is sometimes used by analysts instead of "criteria.") Thus the problem of choice arises, and evaluation of proposals is needed to make the best use of available resources. To perform this evaluation, it is necessary to identify specific criteria that can be used to evaluate performance against the governmental objectives.[2] For example, if a governmental objective such as "to reduce crime" was identified, then it would be appropriate to use crime rates as the major criterion (but not necessarily the only criterion) for evaluating activities aiming at these objectives. That is, in comparisons between various proposals, each proposal's effect upon the anticipated future crime rates would need to be estimated.

As the example indicates, the selection of criteria depends upon the objectives that are formulated. Also the process of selecting the criteria will often suggest the need for revision of the objectives. Thus, the establishing of objectives and criteria are interacting processes. In this paper, the emphasis is on criteria; objectives are discussed and presented only briefly. Ideally, a thorough discussion of State and local government objectives would be undertaken first.

An important characteristic of both "objectives" and "criteria" as used in this paper is that they are intended to be "end" oriented rather than "means" oriented. That is, they are intended to reflect what is ultimately desired to be accomplished and for whom, not ways to accomplish such objectives. For example, the phrase, "to disperse cultural facilities rather than concentrating them in a single locality" is a means "to provide adequate cultural opportunities to all." Use of the former phrase as the statement of objective rather than the latter would lead to somewhat different criteria, such as "the number of cultural facilities." Program analysis would better compare dispersal programs with centralized programs as alternative means to providing adequate cultural opportunities.

Also, the concept of objectives as used in this paper avoids inclusion of specific numerical magnitudes. For example, a statement of objectives such as "to reduce crime rates 10 percent" should be avoided. For program analysis it is seldom appropriate to prespecify magnitudes. The specific amount of improvement that should be sought should generally not be determined until after the alternatives have been evaluated as to the costs and benefits of each and after these trade-offs are understood.

The criteria for program analyses ideally should have the following general properties:

(1) Each criterion should be relevant and important to the specific problem for which it is to be used. (This will depend upon the fundamental objectives to be satisfied.)

(2) Together the criteria used for a specific problem should consider all major effects relative to the objectives. Enough criteria should be evaluated to

cover all major effects. The use of insufficient criteria can be very misleading. For example, programs to improve housing conditions should in general consider not only the number of acres of slums removed but also the effects upon the persons removed (perhaps by including a second criterion: the number of persons still living in substandard dwelling units).

Although it would make the evaluation considerably easier to have only one criterion, or at least very few criteria, the important thing is to avoid excluding major considerations from an analysis.

As indicated in the previous example, probably any single objective, if emphasized too much without considering other needs, could lead to excesses and result in even worse conditions. Other examples are: sole consideration of safety in moving traffic could result in excessive trip delay times; in the law enforcement area, sole concentration on crime rates might lead to programs that result in excess control of individual movement.

With all the criteria expressed in terms of one unit (such as the dollar) or two units (such as the dollar and some nonmonetary unit), neat, analytically optimizable solutions would usually be possible. However, forcing the analysis into oversimplified forms may hide many major considerations. Use of multiple evaluation criteria seems, in general, to be unavoidable.

(3) Each of the criteria ideally should be capable of meaningful quantification. This involves two major problems. The first is the measurement of the current and historical magnitudes of each of the criteria. This measurement is needed to give a clear picture of the magnitude of the problem, to determine how well the jurisdiction is actually doing toward meeting its objectives, and to provide a basis for making projections into the future. For the housing example used above we would want to be able to measure how many acres of slums and how many people living in substandard dwelling units there currently are, and how many were living in such units previously.

The second problem is the estimation of the future magnitudes for these criteria for each of the alternative programs being considered. Projecting into the future is always hazardous. One of the most, if not the most, difficult problems in program analysis is the estimation of the effects on the criteria of the various courses of action. Historical data are important both for measuring progress and for making inferences as to what has caused any changes that have occurred. This latter information is very important for preparing estimates of the effects of future courses of action.

In practice, it is very difficult, and probably impossible, to meet perfectly all three of these ideal properties of criteria. The list of criteria on pages 230 to 236 . . . is a first attempt to identify the major criteria that are likely to be pertinent for governmental programs. An explicit attempt has been made to make the list conform with the first two properties (that is, relevancy and coverage) given above for ideal criteria. However, the list is certainly far from definitive in either depth or coverage. It is also somewhat idealistic; the analysts' ability to estimate meaningfully the effects of alternative programs upon the criteria (the third property given above) will undoubtedly be limited in many instances–particularly with current information systems.

On occasion, it may be necessary to utilize purely qualitative measures such as, "In reducing crime, alternative A is more effective than alternative B but less effective than C." This ranking procedure might be partially quantified by having experts apply their judgments to some type of ranking scale. This would produce such a result as, "In reducing crime, alternative A has a value of 80 on the specially prepared ranking scale, B has a value of 65 and C a value of 85."

Thus in practice, even though criteria are not completely capable of being satisfactorily quantified, criteria that have the other two properties may still be useful.

The list of criteria . . . is hoped to be a reasonable starting point from which individual governments would develop a sound set of criteria appropriate to their own specific problems and governmental objectives. Many of these criteria are already in use. For an individual problem, the analysts will need to determine the specific criteria appropriate to that problem. The list . . . may help to suggest the appropriate ones. Each interested reader is encouraged to think through and work out what he feels to be an improved list.

With few exceptions, only nonmonetary criteria are listed in this paper. It is assumed that, in general, all problems will need to consider the actual monetary effects of each alternative course of action proposed. That is, one objective in all problems will be to keep monetary costs as low as possible for any level of program effectiveness aimed for. However, it is a premise of this paper that in the past too much emphasis has been placed upon attempting to translate all program effects into dollar terms. It is true that if this could be done meaningfully, the evaluation of alternative and final program selection would be eased considerably since the quantitative evaluations would all be expressed in the same unit–the dollar.

Realistically most governmental problems involve major objectives of a nondollar nature. Not only is it very difficult for analysts to assign dollar "values" to such nondollar objectives, but it is also questionable whether it would be desirable even if it could be done. Thus, questions of the value of such effects as reducing death rates, reducing illness incidences and severities, improving housing conditions, and increasing recreational opportunities should not become simply a problem of estimating the dollar values of these things.

The analysts should rather concentrate upon the estimation and presentation, for each alternative, of full information as to the actual dollar effects and the effects upon the nonmonetary criteria. This is the primary function of program analysis–and of "cost-effectiveness," "cost-benefit," "cost-utility," or "systems analysis," terms which for the purpose of this paper are all assumed to be equivalent. Attempts to force the criteria into commensurability are in most cases not worth much effort. It should be left to the decision-makers to provide the value judgments needed to make the final program decisions. [3]

DISCUSSION AND QUALIFICATIONS

The aforementioned illustrative criteria which follow are subject to a number of substantial qualifications and warnings; these are discussed below.

Criteria Must Relate to Governmental Objectives

As has been already indicated, the problem of selecting the appropriate criteria is dependent upon the problem of specifying objectives correctly. Thus, for a traffic-control problem, if the problem had originally been stated solely in terms of "reducing the number of traffic accidents," and if the analysts had limited themselves solely to this objective, the only criterion would have been the number of traffic accidents. Alternatives which, for example, restricted traffic flow such as by slowing down traffic considerably, would still tend to be the most "cost effective" since the rapidity of traffic movement was not implied in the statement of objectives and therefore was not included in the criteria.

For each major program area identified in the list, a brief statement is first given which summarizes the assumed objectives of the major program area. The criteria listed for the major program area should ideally provide a specific basis on which to evaluate the contribution that each alternative course of action makes to these objectives. If the reader prefers different statements of objectives, he is also likely to be led to somewhat different criteria.[4]

The specific objectives of a jurisdiction also depend upon the jurisdiction's own concept of the extent of the government's role in each program area. In many instances, there are likely to be considerable differences of opinion as to the proper role of the government. However, in general, such functions as law enforcement, fire protection, and water supply are usually assumed to be primarily governmental functions. Such other functions, however, as health, intellectual development, job opportunities, and leisure-time opportunities may rely heavily upon private sectors. Nevertheless, governments do have some role in most of these, usually at least having a part in helping the "needy" to reach certain minimum standards.

A related problem is that of the many and periodically changing ways in which government's role is divided among the various levels of government such as among city, county, State, and National, and, of increasing importance, special regional organizations.

The specific role played by the government in each individual jurisdiction must be considered in selection of the appropriate criteria.

In this paper no consideration is given to the question of "national objectives" such as national prestige and national security. It would seem that for State and local governments such issues, though of considerable interest, are peripheral to these governments' functions.

State and local governments, however, must, of course, be concerned with the notions of individual liberty, privacy, freedom of choice, and democratic processes. The degree to which each program option may impinge upon these individual rights and processes should, of course, be considered in a complete evaluation.

There are Different "Levels" of Criteria

One of the major difficulties in specifying criteria is that there are many different levels of criteria. The specific criteria that are appropriate will depend upon the specific problem at hand.

At the highest level we might say that all government programs aim at contributing "to the maintenance and improvement of the well-being of humanity." This overall objective is too general; it is very difficult to measure, is vague, and is not very useful for analysis. The objectives and related criteria presented in the list are at a lower level. However, they are intended to provide the major criteria that should preferably be used in governmental program analyses. These criteria may still be at too high a level for many problems.

Thus, for example, if we are concerned with examining the desirable size and nature of public health nursing services, it is likely to be very difficult to relate some of these services directly to mortality rates, morbidity rates, or days of restricted activity. Preferably, estimates would be made of the effect of alternative levels and mixes of public health nursing services and other types of health service alternatives on each of these criteria. However, because of the difficulty in linking the nursing service programs to these criteria, it may be necessary to use some "indirect," "proxy," or "substitute" criteria. One expedient might be simply to estimate the caseload that can be handled by each public health nursing service program proposed.

Another example: For the objective, "to prevent (deter) crime," judging accused persons can be considered one of the pertinent types of activity. "Judging" itself can be said to have the following subobjectives:

(a) To be fair.
(b) To be swift.
(c) For the guilty, to provide appropriate sentence (neither excessive nor overly lenient).

Alternative programs for "judging" could each be compared through criteria that reflected these subobjectives. Nevertheless, the crucial question would remain as to what extent meeting these criteria to various degrees would deter crime.

Such subcriteria as are indicated in these two examples are not included in the criteria list, but may often be necessary for individual analyses.

Unfortunately, "program size" indicators such as discussed in the public health nursing example (i.e., caseload) tell little about the important effects, e.g., the effects upon community health that the program achieves. Presentation of only this information to the decision-makers leaves it completely to the decision-makers to make subjective judgments as to the effects of the service.

Presentation of the costs and the program size indicator for each alternative is better than nothing, but leaves much to be desired.

It should be recognized that, in most cases, at least some information can be obtained relating programs to the major criteria. For example, it may well be possible to examine current and past records of the jurisdiction and other jurisdictions and to relate to some extent the more fundamental health criteria to program size; inferences would then be made as to the probable future effects of the newly proposed programs. A second approach is to conduct experiments (controlled as much as is practical) in which characteristics other than those investigated are similar from one group to another. Pertinent information would be kept about these groups, and inferences subsequently would be drawn as to the effects of the program characteristics.

Such information gathering does, of course, cost money. Also, the experimental approach may take a long time before useful results become available—possibly too long for the immediate problem but still useful if similar problems are expected to be of concern when the results do become available. In the absence of analytical techniques that identify the best approach to given objectives, the jurisdiction probably can afford to (and indeed may have to) experiment to some extent.

The point is that the program analyst should not be quick to accept lower level criteria such as program size indicators as the only criteria on which he can obtain information.

Criteria are Grouped Under Seven Major Program Areas

The criteria presented are grouped under each of seven "major program areas":

(a) Personal safety.
(b) Health.
(c) Intellectual development and personal enrichment.
(d) Satisfactory home and community environment.
(e) Economic satisfaction and satisfactory work opportunities.
(f) Satisfactory leisure-time opportunities.
(g) Transportation-communication-location.

Together, these major program areas are intended to encompass the great majority of the activities of a governmental jurisdiction. Though many such classifications could be made, these appear to be a reasonable set for discussion of criteria for evaluation of governmental programs. . . .

Many, if not most, analyses will at least initially concentrate upon but one part of these major program areas. In some of these analyses it may be necessary to utilize lower level criteria. For example, for an issue raised on manpower training programs the criterion "percent of enrollees satisfactorily completing the training program" might be appropriate. However, as already noted above unqualified use of such a lower level criterion for program selection could be misleading. The more fundamental problem of government relevant to manpower training is to get unemployed (or underemployed) persons satisfactorily employed and self-sufficient. The mere fact of graduation from a training program does not mean reduced unemployment. Employment and earning criteria, even if not feasible to use directly as criteria, should be recognized as being more truly the objectives of manpower training.

Most program-oriented categorizations of governmental programs (called program structures in PPB systems) will also contain a major category for general government activities. This will include such activities as the government's financial, legal, and legislative activities. No criteria are included in the list for these activities. The viewpoint of this paper is that these general government activities are primarily supporting services to the other, primary, government functions. That is, these activities are not themselves aimed at achieving fundamental governmental purposes. [5]

More Than One Criterion will Frequently be Needed for Individual Problems

For each of the seven major program areas, several criteria are listed. In some cases there is some overlap and redundancy. However, for the most part, each of the criteria contains some potentially important aspect not contained in the other criteria. As has been already noted, the evaluation of program alternatives would be eased considerably if all criteria were commensurable, i.e., expressed in some common unit such as "dollars." However, practically speaking, few major program issues can be meaningfully evaluated solely in terms of a single criterion. [6] The analysts should concentrate upon providing as full and accurate information as possible as to the effects of each program alternative on each of the criteria, leaving it to the decision-makers to weight the criteria. [7]

Interactions Occur Among Program Areas and Among Criteria

Though the list of criteria is divided into major program areas, this is not meant to imply that all program analysis problems will necessarily fall into one major program area, and only one. On the contrary, major governmental problems will frequently spill over into more than one program area. For example, mass transit system proposals could have significant impact on many if not all of the listed major program areas: Traffic safety is directly affected by the substitution of a mass-transit system for individual automobiles; an inexpensive mass-transit system might permit low-income workers to consider job opportunities further away than they can currently afford; families who wished to live further out in the country might be able to do so with a convenient, rapid, inexpensive transit system; recreational opportunities previously too far away and too expensive to reach might be opened to certain segments of the public; individual health and intellectual development might be furthered (indirectly) by the combination of the preceding effects; certain penalties could also occur, such as the transit system having an adverse effect on the physical attractiveness and living conditions of the areas where it is constructed; air pollution and noise effects would also occur.

Another example is that of education programs that in addition to contributing to individual intellectual development also lead to improved employability and reduction in unemployment.

Thus, specific programs may simultaneously have many complex and interacting effects on many program areas and many criteria.

It is important in program analyses to attempt to consider and evaluate all such effects to the extent that they might be important to the decision-making process.

It will be Necessary to Distinguish "Target Groups"

An important aspect of program evaluation is the identification of the specific population groups that receive benefits (or penalties) from each program proposed. Though not specifically included in the list, it will often be appropriate to break down further certain of the criteria into subcriteria in order to distinguish specific clientele, or "target groups." For many issues a government will be interested in distinguishing the effects of alternative programs on specific population groups identified by such characteristics as age, sex, race, income, family size, education, occupation, geographical location, special handicaps, etc. For example: For many health issues, distinctions by age, income level, family size, etc., may be required to evaluate the effects of various health programs on each category within such groups. Another example: It will probably be necessary for many law-enforcement issues to distinguish crimes committed by adults from those by juveniles.

Though neither the objectives nor the illustrative criteria . . . explicitly single out "equal opportunity" objectives the use of target groups in the criteria will provide information on such objectives.

Criteria Need to be Thoroughly Defined

No attempt is made in this paper to define the listed criteria. However, when utilizing criteria it is important to have clear, thorough definitions. In almost all cases, misinterpretations (often subtle ones) can occur if complete definitions are not provided. For example, for major types of crimes it is necessary to define each type of crime, e.g., does "larceny" include thefts of automobiles and bicycles; does it include thefts of any magnitude or only those beyond a specific dollar value? Another example: What is meant by "restricted activity" when the number of days of restricted activity for health reasons per person per year is to be estimated? Again, how is "poverty" defined when the number of persons and families in the jurisdiction's "poverty population" is estimated? Or, what is meant by "substandard" when dwelling units are evaluated?

Definitions should generally specify such things as who is involved, how, what time period is to be covered by the criteria, what geographical location is included, etc. For example, for measuring restricted activity due to health reasons, it is necessary to know—

(a) What specifically is meant by "restricted activity"?

(b) Whether the whole population of the jurisdiction is involved or some specific segment such as "all males between the age of 16 and 21 living in the North Smithtown" section of the city.

(c) Whether the magnitudes are to be on a "per person per year" basis or on some other.

Some attention should also be given to the influence of time which may affect the definitions. For example, wherever a dollar figure is involved in defining a criterion, price-level changes over time may alter the meaning. For example, if "larceny" is defined to include only thefts over $50 at current price levels, price-level rises will automatically bring more thefts into the category even though there is no change in the total number of thefts of each type. Explicit provision will be needed for adjustments of the criterion, based upon price-level changes. Another type of change over time that may occur is change in the jurisdiction's boundaries, possibly requiring adjustments to make compatible the magnitudes assigned to the criteria for different years.

Criteria can be Expressed in Different Forms

Given that a certain factor is considered sufficiently important to be included as an evaluation criterion, there frequently will be a variety of forms in which the criteria can be expressed. Five such choices are noted below:

(a) Both "absolute" numbers and rates are called for by the criteria included in the list. Absolute numbers by themselves can present a misrepresentation of the situation. For example, the total number of various crimes or of traffic accidents, though, of course, of interest in themselves, do not reflect the associated levels of activity. Crime rates and traffic accident rates (the latter related to the volume of traffic) will give improved perspectives as to what is happening in those areas. Both forms are probably needed by the decision-makers.

(b) Some of the criteria listed below call for "averages"; for example, "average waiting time for the use of certain recreational facilities." In such cases, the analysts will frequently also need to consider the distribution of waiting times as well as the average. There is danger that if only the average is considered, important information may be ignored. For example, the average waiting time throughout the week on a city's golf courses may be 15 minutes, which, if it were applicable at all times, would probably be quite acceptable to the city's golfers. However, the distribution of waiting times for specific times of the week might show prolonged, perhaps several-hour, waits during certain hours of the weekends, probably causing considerable annoyance among golfers and suggesting the need for corrective action. Use of only the overall average would hide the pertinent information.

In the criteria list the dangers of the use of averages for waiting times of recreational facilities have been reduced considerably by requiring the calculation of the averages for specific key periods.

Wherever "averages" are considered for use in criteria, consideration should be given to the possibly important information that such criteria hide.

(c) In many instances it will be desirable to compare the magnitudes for the criteria with the magnitudes existing in other, similar jurisdictions, both the current magnitudes and those estimated for the future. For example, local crime rates may be compared with those of other parts of the country (perhaps by using the FBI's uniform crime reports).

The relative conditions, such as displayed by the ratios of the jurisdiction's own crime rates to those of the Nation, or some segment of it, could be used as criteria. It may also be of interest to compare health, education, recreation, unemployment, and housing conditions to conditions elsewhere.

Care should be taken to ascertain that the figures are really comparable since definitions and reporting systems can differ substantially. For example, the crime reports referred to above have been criticized for lack of uniformity.

Too much concentration on "what the other fellow is doing" is not desirable; the absolute forms of the criteria (for example, the total amount of crime in the government's own jurisdiction) should not be neglected.[8]

The list of criteria . . . does not specifically include comparisons with other jurisdictions. As appropriate, the criteria could readily be modified to reflect such comparisons.

(d) Certain criteria can be displayed either as the "total number" of something or as a "reduction (or increase) in the number" of this thing. For example, "total number of accidents from cause X" could also be shown as "reduction of the total number of accidents from cause X." The use of the term "reduction" implies that there is a base from which the alternatives are measured. When alternative courses of action are being compared, the "reduction" is simply the difference between the base and the number resulting from the alternative.

The "reduction" form is the more direct way of showing effects but does not indicate the level still existing. In the list of criteria below both forms are sometimes shown.

(e) Certain of the individual criteria might be combined in various ways to form a new, single criterion. For example, for health programs the "number of sick days" might be multiplied by the severity index (if there is one) to give a "severity-sick-days index." This procedure is sometimes followed in order to reduce the number of criteria for analytical simplification. The list of criteria . . . does not include examples of these combined criteria.

Estimates of the Criteria Magnitudes are Needed for Each Year of the Plan

Another aspect of the criteria problem arises from the necessity in program analysis to consider program impacts on each year for several years in the future.

Though various pressures usually act to emphasize current and near future needs, good governmental planning obviously requires consideration of the longer range needs. In preparing its plan of action, a government needs to assure that the plan would provide desired goods and services in each year of the plan.

Different alternative courses of action will affect different years in different ways. One mix of programs may, for example, result in greater benefits for the near future, while another mix of programs might emphasize current investments that are expected to produce superior benefits in later years. Therefore, in deciding among courses of actions the magnitude of each criterion for each year is an important consideration.

The weighting of the importance of each particular year of the plan will probably be the province of the decision-makers rather than the analysts. The main job of the analysts will be to provide as complete and accurate information as possible as to the nature and phasing of the program impacts, leaving it to the decision-makers' judgments for the final weightings of one year versus another.

A Monetary Criterion is Always Needed

The one common criterion in all problems of choosing among alternative programs is the monetary (i.e., dollar) effects of each alternative. This criterion is not repeated for each major program area in the list of criteria given below, but should be assumed to be pertinent in each case. Primarily nonmonetary criteria are included in the list. In a few cases a monetary criterion seemed to be necessary as a proxy to reflect important social factors, and these are included in the list.

The term "monetary criterion" as used here refers to the actual dollar changes that would occur (for each alternative program mix as compared to some base)–but not including dollar values imputed to nonmonetary things. These dollar changes, whether affecting the government's own financial picture or that of other sectors of the economy, should be considered in the evaluation. Effects on the various sectors, as well as on the various clientele groups, should be identified separately so that the decision-makers have a clear perspective of the impacts.

Theoretically, all of the nonmonetary criteria listed below could be translated into dollar values by estimating, in some manner, the dollar "worth" to the government (or to some other specified group) of changes in the magnitudes of each of the criteria. For example, it might be estimated that the population of the jurisdiction would be willing to pay x dollars to reduce the number of criminal homicides per year from Y to Z. It is, however, a premise of this paper that such translations present some almost insurmountable obstacles (at least with the current state of the art of program analysis) and at best will represent the judgment of one limited group of persons at one point in time. Therefore, it is always desirable to display the values for the specific nondollar criteria, such as those listed so that the actual decision-makers have full information with which to make their own judgments. Information that attempts to estimate the dollar "value" to specified target groups for changes in the nondollar criteria can also be presented to the decision-makers if the analysts believe such information to be useful. For those who insist upon translating all units into dollar terms, the list of criteria might at least be a guide to the major factors to which dollar values have to be attached.[9]

The Monetary Criteria can be Very Complex

Before we leave the subject of the monetary criteria as applied to program evaluation, the complexity of these criteria should be noted. The monetary effects of a program alternative can be of many types. These effects include the following elements (note that the term "cost" refers only to dollar costs):

Program Costs. These are the governmental costs that are incurred in undertaking the activities called for by the program. These costs include the various administrative and other support-type costs as well as those directly incurred.

Program Monetary Effects Within the Government. As a result of the activities called for by the program, certain government costs may be increased or decreased. For example, a slum-clearance program might in future years result in reductions in fire and crime protection services for the cleared area; on the other hand it might lead to increased demand for park and recreation services. A slum-clearance program would also have some effect upon the tax base of the jurisdiction.

Program Monetary Effects Outside the Government. Many of the monetary effects of governmental programs will occur outside the jurisdiction, perhaps affecting the private sector of the economy or other jurisdictions. Changes in transportation systems or in housing, for example, will have considerable effect on many types of businesses in the area. Such effects may be important in many kinds of studies. Governments are generally interested, for example, in monetary measures of gross business and income in relation to persons and businesses within their jurisdictions. Specific examples of such economic measures include: manufacturing value added, retail and wholesale sales, amount of bank deposits, and industrial capital expenditures. (However, it should also be recognized that too much emphasis can be placed upon such measures. For example, attracting businesses into the area though increasing total sales and total earnings, could also adversely affect the overall physical attractiveness of the community.) Another example of effects upon the private sector is the effect upon insurance rates of illness, fire, and crime prevention programs.

It is not desirable to add all of these dollar effects [i.e., (a) plus (b) plus (c)] to yield one overall monetary impact. The impact on each sector should be presented to avoid obscuring pertinent considerations.

It will not always be clear whether an item is a "program cost" or a "program monetary effect." (Other terms that have been used to distinguish these are "direct versus indirect" and "primary versus secondary.") However, the important thing is not the classification but the identification and consideration of these monetary effects if significant to the program at hand.[10]

Another major problem in handling monetary changes is the time pattern associated with the cash flow. As discussed above, the time pattern is of importance to a government. The use of a "discount" (i.e., interest) rate to translate actual net dollar flow (after consideration of both in-flows or outflows into a single "present value" is frequently recommended. This discounting procedure has the advantage of–

(a) Reducing the complexity of evaluation by replacing the several dollar figures (i.e., one for each year of the time period) by one number, the present value.

(b) Reflecting the time value of money in the sense that, in general, money this year is worth more than the same amount of money next year since potentially it can be put to work now and grow into a larger sum by next year.[11]

Unfortunately, however, despite the well-grounded economic basis for discounting (as the procedure is commonly called), there are some difficulties and drawbacks such as the following:

(a) First, there is considerable disagreement over the appropriate discount rate to be used. The range usually debated appears to be 4 to 10%. The rate chosen can have a significant effect upon the results, if, for example, the competing programs have major differences in their expenditure patterns. Nevertheless, uncertainty as to the appropriate rate is not sufficient reason to avoid discounting.

(b) A more important concern to governments is found in the practical constraints in their annual funding capabilities. Major fluctuations in revenue needs from one year to the next may present insurmountable difficulties. It seems, therefore, that whether or not discounting is deemed appropriate, the actual (i.e., unadjusted by the discount rate) time-phased dollar flows should be shown to the decision-makers. In addition, the discounted present values of the alternatives can be provided (perhaps for more than one discount rate). This suggested procedure applies to monetary flows both inside and outside the government.

In most cases, the use of discounting will probably be of secondary concern relative to the many other problems of program analysis.

Nevertheless, as a practical matter, governmental decision-makers are likely to have strong time preferences as to funding requirements of their jurisdictions and need to be shown the time-phased monetary implications of the alternative courses of actions.

As has already been noted, the purpose of this discussion has been to indicate the scope and complexity potentially involved with the monetary criterion. Most of the remainder of this paper is directed at nonmonetary criteria.

The Criteria are Not Intended for Use in Organizational Evaluations

The criteria discussed in this paper are not intended for the purpose of measuring the efficiency of the administrative organizations of a government (such as the police or fire department). The measurement of day-to-day operational performance, though important, is not the subject of this paper.[12] The criteria in this paper are intended for the purpose of evaluating proposed program alternatives, not of evaluating staffs' or departments' current operating efficiency.

Measurements of Program Size are Also Needed but Not as Evaluation Criteria

Governments that install a formal planning-programming-budgeting system, in addition to undertaking individual program analyses, will probably also prepare a multiyear program and financial plan. One of the main parts of this plan is an "output plan," a presentation that indicates the estimated outputs obtainable from the program plan for each year covered by the plan. At first glance, it might appear that the outputs contained in these output plans should be the evaluation criteria, the measures of effectiveness, utilized in the program analyses–such as those discussed and presented in this paper. In practice, however, the "outputs" contained in the formal multiyear plan will probably have to be somewhat different. They are more likely to be measurements that indicate the magnitude or size of the program rather than its effectiveness. "Effectiveness" is too intricate a subject to present simply as a string of numbers not accompanied by evaluative comments. However, certain common and fairly clearly understood effectiveness measures such as crime and accident rates would probably be appropriate and desirable for inclusion in the formal output plan. In any case, measurements indicating the magnitude of each program (for example, the number of persons treated in public hospitals, the number of miles of highway, the number of acres of playgrounds, etc.) will be information useful to readers of the government's formal multiyear program and financial plan.

This paper does not attempt to list the program-size measure that might be appropriate for use in a multiyear program and financial plan.

Criteria for Government-Citizen Relations May be Desirable

For many of the services which a government provides to its citizens, the pleasantness, courtesy, quietness (e.g., in the case of waste collection), etc., involved in the provision of the service are factors in the overall quality of the service. To some extent these factors are more a problem of operational performance than of program planning. Nevertheless, to the extent to which program planning is involved (for example, a proposal to provide training of policemen on police-citizen relations would be a program-planning problem), these factors need to be considered. Generally, however, they will be secondary to the fundamental purposes of the service. While measures for these factors are not presented in the illustrative criteria below, it may be appropriate for a particular jurisdiction to include such criteria for certain of its analyses.

Uncertainties and Political Considerations are Additional Evaluation Factors

In addition to such nonmonetary criteria as are presented, and the various monetary benefits and costs, other considerations enter into final program decisions. Such factors as the amounts of uncertainty and risks involved (which should be indicated and quantified in the analysis to the extent practicable) and various political considerations may also play important parts in the final decisions. These factors can also be considered evaluation criteria and should not be ignored. Wherever possible they should be discussed, and quantified to the extent practicable, in the analysis.[13]

Criteria Frequently will be Difficult to Measure

As has already been indicated, it will undoubtedly be extremely difficult to get good historical information on many of these criteria and to make good estimates of the future magnitudes of the criteria for the various program alternatives.[14] In some of these cases, information systems can be feasibly developed to provide improved information in the future. In cases where this appears impossible, it will still be desirable to make crude estimates—based upon judgment if nothing else.

As already noted, at the very least, alternatives can be ranked on each criterion or, a more complex technique, experts can be asked to assign a value to each criterion for each alternative based upon an arbitrary scale (for example, 1 to 10). Public opinion polls, using appropriate sampling techniques, can be used to obtain information on various "intangible" criteria (though there are many difficulties in such polls). Even this information will often be helpful. If even qualitative estimates cannot reasonably be made, substitute criteria will be necessary.

It is to be emphasized that even though an important evaluation criterion resists quantification, this does not mean it should be ignored in the analysis. Relevant qualitative information should be provided; or at the very least the inability to say anything meaningful about the criterion should be clearly pointed out along with its possible implications. The decision-makers will then at least be alerted to the problem.

Intangibles will Always be With us

The decision-maker will inevitably be faced with major intangibles. In addition to the difficulties discussed above certain important aspects of governmental (and perhaps personal) objectives are bound to be omitted from the criteria that are quantified or discussed qualitatively. Since even the type of criteria presented here falls short of indicating ultimate "value" or "utility," and even if all the listed criteria could be satisfactorily quantified, intangibles would still remain. For example, though the number of families living in "substandard" dwelling units is a tangible figure, the "value" of reducing this number by various amounts is primarily intangible.

Most often the governmental executives will have to make these judgments themselves. There also will be times when such intangible issues should be put before the legislative branch or directly before the voters.

Program analysis, with the use of such criteria as are contained here, can only aim at improving the relevant information on the issue at hand. It does not need to, nor can it, provide the definitive answers on program selections.

ILLUSTRATIVE LIST OF CRITERIA FOR THE EVALUATION OF PROPOSED PROGRAMS [15]

I. PERSONAL SAFETY [16]

Objective: To reduce the amount and effects of external harm to individuals and in general to maintain an atmosphere of personal security from external events.

A. Law Enforcement

Objective: To reduce the amount and effects of crime and in general to maintain an atmosphere of personal security from criminal behavior. (To some persons the punishment of criminals may be an important objective in itself as well a means to deter further crimes.)

1. Annual number of offenses for each major class of crime (or reduction from the base in the number of crimes).
2. Crime rates, as for example, the number per 1,000 inhabitants per year, for each major class of crime.
3. Crime rate index that includes all offenses of a particular type (e.g., "crimes of violence" or "crimes against property"), perhaps weighted as to seriousness of each class of offense.
4. Number and percent of populace committing "criminal" acts during the year. (This is a less common way to express the magnitude of the crime problem; it is criminal oriented rather than "crime oriented.")
5. Annual value of property lost (adjusted for price-level changes). This value might also be expressed as a percent of the total property value in the community.
6. An index of overall community "feeling of security" from crime, perhaps based on public opinion polls and/or opinions of experts.
7. Percent of reported crimes cleared by arrest and "assignment of guilt" by a court.
8. Average time between occurrence of a crime and the apprehension of the criminal. [17]
9. Number of apparently justified complaints of police excesses by private citizens, perhaps as adjudged by the police review board.
10. Number of persons subsequently found to be innocent who were punished and/or simply arrested.

Notes

(a) Criteria 1 through 6 are criteria for the evaluation of crime-prevention programs. Criteria 7 and 8 are aimed at evaluating crime control after crimes have occurred (i.e., when crime prevention has failed). Criteria 9 and 10 and to some extent 6 aim at the avoidance of law-enforcement practices that themselves have an adverse effect upon personal safety. Criterion 6 and to some extent 8 aim at indicating the presence of a fearful, insecure atmosphere in the locality.

(b) Some argue that the primary function of criminal apprehension and punishment is to prevent future crimes; and, therefore, that criteria 7 and 8 would not be sufficiently "end" oriented, but rather "means" oriented, and would not be included in the list.

(c) For many analyses it would probably be appropriate to distinguish crime activity by the type of criminal, including such characteristics as age, sex, family income, etc. (juvenile delinquency is an obvious subcategory).

B. Fire Prevention and Firefighting

Objective: To reduce the number of fires and loss due to fires.

1. Annual number of fires of various magnitudes (to be defined).
2. Fire rates, for example, number per 10,000 inhabitants per year.
3. Annual dollar value of property loss due to fire (adjusted for price level changes).
4. Annual dollar value of property lost due to fire per $1 million of total property value in the locality.
5. Annual number of persons killed or injured to various degrees of seriousness due to fires.
6. Reduction in number of fires, in injuries, in lives lost, and in dollars of property loss from the base. (These are primarily different forms of criteria 1, 3, and 5 and can be substituted for them.) This reduction might in part be obtained by, for example, drawing inferences from the number of fire code violations (by type) found.[18]
7. Average time required to put out fires from the time they were first observed, for various classes of fires.

Notes

(a) Criteria 1 through 6 are intended for evaluation of fire prevention programs. Criteria 7 and to some extent 3, 4, and 5 can reflect the results of programs which aim at the control of fires after they have started. Criterion 7 also is a proxy for the anxiety related to duration of fires.

(b) It may be appropriate to distinguish among geographic areas within the jurisdiction.

II. HEALTH

Objective: To provide for the physical and mental health of the citizenry, including reduction of the number, length, and severity of illnesses and disabilities.

1. Incidence of illness and prevalence (number and rates).[19] (Armed Forces rates of rejection for health reasons of persons from the jurisdiction could be used as a partial criterion.)

2. Annual mortality rates by major cause and for total population.[20]

3. Life expectancy by age groups.

4. Average number of days of restricted activity, bed confinement, and medically attended days per person per year. (Such terms as "restricted activity" need to be clearly and thoroughly defined. Also, probably more than one level of severity of illness should be identified.)

5. Average number of workdays per person lost due to illness per year.

6. Total and per capita number of school days lost owing to illness per year.

7. Number of illnesses prevented, deaths averted, and restricted-activity days averted per year as compared with the base. This is primarily a different form of such criteria as 1 through 6.

8. Average number of days of restricted activity, of bed confinement and of medically attended days per illness per year.

9. Number and percent of patients "cured" (of specific types of illnesses and various degrees of cure).

10. Some measure of the average degree of pain and suffering per illness. (Though there seems to be no such measure currently in use, some rough index of pain and suffering could probably be developed.)

11. Some measure, perhaps from a sampling of experts and of patients, as to the average amount of unpleasantness (including consideration of the environment in the care area) associated with the care and cure of illnesses.

12. Number or percent of persons with after-effects, of different degrees, after "cure."

13. Number or percent of persons needing but unable to afford "appropriate health care"—both before receiving public assistance and after including any public assistance received.

14. Number or percent of persons needing but unable to receive "appropriate health care" because of insufficient facilities or services.

15. Some measure of the overall "vigor," the positive health, of the populace, rather than simply the absence of illness—such as "the average per capita energy capacity." Meaningful measures are needed.

Notes

(a) A number of subobjectives can be identified for this major program area. Those subobjectives and the criteria that attempt to measure each are as follows:

(1) Prevention of illness—criteria 1 through 7.
(2) "Cure" of patient when illness occurs including reduction of its duration—criteria 1 through 9.
(3) Reduction of unpleasantness, suffering, anxiety, etc., associated with illness—criteria 10 and 11.

(4) Reduction of after-effects–criterion 12.
(5) Making necessary health care available to the "needy"–criteria 13 and 14.

Note, however, that during consideration of the overall problem of health, these subobjectives will often compete with each other. For example, with limited funds, they might be applied to programs aimed primarily at preventing an illness or at reducing its severity (or at some mix of these programs). Also note that criteria 1 through 7 are affected by programs that are directed at curing illnesses as well as those directed at preventing them.

(b) The criteria can be defined to distinguish among specific types of illnesses as well as to consider the aggregate effect on individuals of all possible illnesses. For certain problems the incidence of a specific disease may be of concern, whereas for other problems the incidence of illness per person per year, regardless of specific disease, might be the appropriate criterion. One such breakdown which is very likely to be desirable distinguishes mental health from physical health, though even here there will be interactions.

(c) Note that such common measures as "hospital-bed capacity" or "utilization rates of available medical facilities" are not included above since these are not fundamental indicators of the effectiveness of health programs.

(d) As with most of the major program areas, program analyses will need to consider the contributions of other sectors, including private institutions and activities undertaken by other jurisdictions.

(e) The role of governmental jurisdictions may emphasize health services for certain specific target groups such as the needy, and the very young. Therefore, it will frequently be appropriate to distinguish target groups by such characteristics as family income, race, family size, and age group.

(f) To further focus on the positive side of health, in addition to the use of criterion 15, such criteria as 4 might be replaced by such criteria as "average number of healthy days (appropriately defined) per person per year."

III. INTELLECTUAL DEVELOPMENT

Objective: To provide satisfactory opportunities for intellectual development to the citizenry. See also notes (b) and (c) below.

1. Annual number and percent of persons satisfactorily completing various numbers of years of schooling.
2. Annual number and percent of dropouts at various educational levels.
3. Annual number and percent of each age group enrolled in educational institutions.
4. "Intellectual development attainment" measures, such as performance on various standardized achievement tests at different ages and educational levels.[21] Major educational areas, for example, reading skills, reasoning skills, and general knowledge, might be measured.

5. Performance on the achievement tests indicated in criterion 4 as related to intelligence tests (to indicate attainment relative to capacity).

6. Annual number and percent of students continuing their education at post-high-school educational institutions.

7. Participation in selected cultural and civic activities (and perhaps the number of persons who read newspapers, or at least certain parts of them).

Notes

(a) Criteria 1, 2, and 3 emphasize quantity of formal education received. Criteria 4, 5, 6, and 7 attempt to indicate the quality of education received. Since formal education is not the only means to intellectual development, criteria such as 4, 5, and 7, when various age groups are considered, should be applied to persons regardless of whether they are in school or not or how much formal education they have had. Criterion 6 also provides some information as to the success of education to stimulate intellectual curiosity. None of the criteria provides much help in measuring the development of individual creativity, if it can indeed be developed.

(b) Education not only affects intellectual development but also social development. The above criteria (with the minor exception of 7) fail to measure such things as "social adjustment," "responsible citizenship," and increased "personal pleasure." Such criteria as crime rates, juvenile delinquency rates, including school vandalism, etc., such as are used for major program area I, "personal safety," might be used to draw inferences on certain aspects of social adjustment.

(c) "Education" clearly may be a means to other ends (for example, to lower crime rates) as well as an end in itself. In fact some persons may consider education to be primarily a means to increase future dollar earnings and therefore would consider the above criteria solely as proxy measures for getting at earnings. If so, education programs would better be considered under major program area V, "economic satisfaction and satisfactory work opportunity for the individual." The perspective here is that education and, more broadly, intellectual development, has more than economic value to individuals and society, and is, therefore, an important end in itself. The objectives: to increase earnings, to increase job opportunities and job satisfaction, and to supply needed scarce skills are, in the categorization used in this paper, considered under major program area V. Education programs are some of the means to these ends and in this role would need to be considered in performing such program analyses.

(d) To estimate quality of formal education, frequently such "proxy" indicators are used as "annual expenditures per student," "professional-student ratios," "number of professionals with advanced degrees," "teacher salary levels," etc. These are less direct, lower level criteria than those given above, but nevertheless may be of some use if qualified sufficiently.

(e) The role of government in intellectual development varies considerably among jurisdictions.

(f) It will frequently be appropriate to distinguish target groups by such characteristics as: race, family income level, family size, and sex.

IV. SATISFACTORY HOME AND COMMUNITY ENVIRONMENT [22]

Objective: To provide opportunity for satisfactory living conditions.

A. Satisfactory Homes

Objective: To provide opportunities for satisfactory homes for the citizenry, including provision of a choice, at prices they can afford, of decent, safe, and sanitary dwellings in pleasant surroundings.

1. Number and percent of "substandard" dwelling units. More information would be provided by identifying more levels than just two. In any case, "substandard" should be fully defined; the definition should include consideration of crowding, physical deterioration, unsatisfactory sanitation, etc.

2. Number and percent of substandard units eliminated or prevented from becoming substandard. (This is essentially another form of 1.)

3. Acres of blighted areas eliminated and other areas prevented from becoming blighted areas.

4. Total number and percent of persons and families living in substandard dwelling units.

5. Number and percent of persons and families upgraded from one level of housing (for example, "substandard") to a higher level (for example, "standard") or prevented from degrading to a lower level. This is essentially another form of 4.

6. Measure of neighborhood physical attractiveness. Perhaps (a) as indicated by the number of negative conditions estimated by neighborhood inspectors, including adverse physical appearance, excessive noise, lack of cleanliness, offensive odors, excessive traffic, etc.; or (b) an index based upon a public-opinion poll of persons passing through the neighborhood and/or experts.

7. Measure of neighborhood psychological attractiveness. Perhaps an index based upon a public-opinion survey of persons living in the neighborhood and/or experts.

8. Average, and distribution of, property values adjusted for price level changes. Expected changes, from year to year, in property values might also be used as a criterion.

9. Number of fires, other accidents, deaths, and injuries resulting from housing deficiencies.

Notes

(a) Important secondary effects (such as change in crime and juvenile delinquency rates, in health conditions, in fire problems, and in job opportunities) are likely to result from changes in housing conditions and urban redevelopment. Criteria relating to these effects are included under the other major program areas.

(b) It will frequently be appropriate to distinguish target groups by such characteristics as family income, race, family size, and location.

(c) Criteria 1 through 5 aim at provision of housing, with 4 and 5 probably the most important, since they directly evaluate effects on people rather than things. Criteria 3 and 6 and probably 7 evaluate the physical attractiveness of the neighborhood. Criteria 7 and 8 are attempts at evaluating the overall quality of the housing and living conditions. Criterion 8 is included here rather than under major program area V, economic satisfaction, as a measure of the overall quality of the neighborhood; that is, property values are used as a proxy for the many features contributing to the attractiveness of the property. Criterion 9 measures the safeness of housing.

B. Maintenance of a Satisfactory Water Supply

Objective: To provide sufficient water in adequate quality where and when needed.

1. Water-supply capability relative to average and to peak demand.
2. Number of days per year during which water shortages of various degrees occur. (Downtime for repairs should be included.)
3. Measure of "quality of water (e.g., biological oxygen demand and percent of solid waste removed) supplied to homes or businesses. (If waste water is not recycled, the quality of the effluent fed back into streambeds, etc., could be used as a criterion.)
4. Measures of taste, appearance, and odor of water–perhaps based upon such factors as amount of chlorination or upon opinion samplings of water users.
5. Measures of hardness and temperature of water.
6. Annual number of illnesses and other incidents due to low quality water.
7. Annual number of complaints of water odors due to low quality water.

Notes

(a) Criteria 1 and 2 are measures of the sufficiency of the quantity of water supplied. Criteria 3 through 7 are measures of the quality.

(b) Each of the quantity measures is also dependent upon the minimum quality level established. That is, more water can generally be supplied if the quality requirements are reduced. Program analysis will need to consider such trade-offs.

(c) The seasonal and diurnal effects of water supply and demand has to be considered in the analysis.

(d) It may be appropriate to distinguish individual user needs such as water for home consumption, for industrial use, for recreational needs, for irrigation, etc., each of which will have its own quantity and quality characteristics.

NOTES

1. This summary is drawn from Harry P. Hatry and John F. Cotton, "Program Planning for State, County, and City." State Local Finances Project. George Washington University, January, 1967.

2. The term "output measure" is also occasionally used instead of "criteria." However, when "output measure" is used, it often is used to encompass not only program evaluation criteria (the subject of this paper) but also indicators of the size of programs such as the number of cases handled, the number of fire stations, policemen, teachers, hospital beds, etc., which though of considerable interest are not major evaluation criteria in the sense used in this paper.

3. However, if the analysts can uncover some clues as to the worth that the jurisdiction's public does assign to such nonmonetary criteria, this information should also be provided to the decision-makers (but not substituted for the basic information on the nonmonetary effects) to assist them in making their judgments. For example, various surveys of the public might give some information as to the degree to which persons currently might be willing to exchange money for changes in the nonmonetary criteria magnitudes. Highway tolls, for example, do indicate that the persons still using the highway are willing to pay at least the price of the toll for the advantages provided by the highway over alternate routes.

4. Persons with different perspectives, different cultures, would probably develop a different set of objectives–thereby implying somewhat different criteria. For example, the caveman would probably insist upon a major program area entitled "Food Supply," and one labeled "Mate Procurement." (The latter would be a tough one for State and local governments.)

5. The point, however, can be made that these activities do contribute to the fundamental function of providing "democracy."

6. However, frequently it may be reasonable to concentrate the analysis on one key, nonmonetary criterion, and treat the other criteria as study constraints or as relatively minor considerations. Even in these instances, however, two criteria, one monetary and the other nonmonetary, will need to be explicitly evaluated. As has been indicated, forcing a dollar value on a nonmonetary criterion does not in general seem a good practice.

7. A technique occasionally used with multiple criteria is to have experts in the specific field estimate the relative weights of each criterion. By applying the prechosen weights, the multiple criteria can be combined into one index thus permitting a ranking on the same scale of all the alternatives. As with attempts to translate all nonmonetary criteria into monetary units, such a practice can too easily be misleading. It is the author's belief that if the analysts believe that the resulting information is meaningful, it may be provided to the decision-maker, but the basic information as to each program alternative's effect upon each of the individual criteria before any weights are applied should always be provided so that meaningful information is not obscured.

8. It is also to be noted that the mere fact that the projected magnitudes for a criterion indicate a retrogressing situation (either relative to other jurisdictions or even relative to earlier years within the jurisdiction) does not in itself necessarily indicate that the jurisdiction's programs are poor. External conditions outside the control of the jurisdiction (such as a significant shift in the characteristics of the population due to immigration or the entry of a new disease virus from outside) can cause the retrogression. Selection of program alternatives should be made as to which alternative is best relative to the others; i.e., which minimizes the adverse situation, even though none of the alternatives is estimated to cause an absolute improvement in the conditions.

9. Occasionally, the criterion "added future earnings" is used to estimate the value of increasing life expectancy and the value of reducing illness. If this criterion is used alone or predominantly, the evaluation can be misleading. For example, elderly persons or others out of the labor market are at a significant disadvantage, as are housewives (depending upon the amount imputed as their "earnings"). The use of future earnings seems to imply that such factors as growth in "GNP" are the fundamental objectives whereas the value of merely increasing GNP (without, for example, considering per capita GNP and the standard of living) would not seem to be the critical issue in our current society. A very pertinent question is: How does the loss of the individual affect the individual and the remaining population? We know how it affects the individual–and the significant effect is not a monetary one. How it affects the remaining population is a very complex question. Individual population groups, such as those close to the decedents, the taxpayers, the insurance-paying public, the businessmen who lose the decedents' spending power, etc., are each affected in different ways. For a more extensive discussion of these points see the Schelling reference listed in the bibliography. [Not included herein.–Ed.]

10. Arguments as to whether such cost reductions should be considered as an offset to total costs or as an addition to "benefits" is important if cost-benefit ratios are being used as the primary evaluation criterion: however, reliance on such ratios is not good practice. The question as to whether to consider such cost reductions as belonging on the cost or benefit side should not affect a decision.

11. Discounting is partly a substitute for the explicit consideration of all effects; that is, if the before-and-after sides of all facets of the economy were explicitly included, this procedure would directly show the time value of the money, and advantage (b) would not apply.

12. Though some of the criteria discussed in this paper probably could be used in the measurement of organizational performance, they would seldom by themselves be adequate for that purpose. The criteria in this paper are probably too aggregative: seldom will one government department or agency have full control over these criteria. More specific and more directly related criteria (for example, the average time that it takes to get the firetrucks away from the station after an alarm is received, the number of public assistance cases handled per caseworker per month, etc.) are needed to measure organizational efficiency. Such measures are useful in program analysis as planning factors from which estimates of overall program costs and effectiveness are built up, but are not the fundamental criteria sought for program evaluation purposes.

13. Note that good analysis in general will not make a decision-maker's job easier. In fact to the extent that it provides him with additional considerations that previously were hidden, good analysis can actually make his job harder. Good analysis should, however, provide him with considerably improved information on which to base his decisions.

14. For some criteria, it may be that "reported" data are known to be incomplete. In such cases, estimates of the unreported cases should also be made if this is at all possible. If not, the analysis or the definition of the criteria should at least make clear the omission. Examples of such unreported data are the incidences of various illnesses and of unreported crimes.

15. This is only a partial outline of programs analyzed by Mr. Hatry. See the original study paper cited earlier for criteria regarding employment, recreation, and transportation programs.–Ed.

16. Criteria for personal safety are here presented for two subcategories: "Law Enforcement" and "Fire Prevention and Firefighting." Other subcategories could be identified such as "Traffic Safety" (in this paper relevant criteria for traffic issues are included under major program area VII) and "Protection From Natural and Manmade Disasters." The appendix illustrates the particular subcategories that might be included under this, as well as the other, major program areas. [Not included herein.–Ed.]

17. A major purpose of criterion 8 as used in this list is to reflect the psychological reduction in anxiety due to the length of this time period. Note that it is not the purpose of this or any of these criteria to evaluate the efficiency of the police organization.

18. From current data on the violations found, estimates could be prepared of the number of additional violations that would be found and corrected if more fire-code inspectors were added. However, the more important (that is, the higher level) criterion is not the number of violations found and corrected by the reduction in the number of fires and in the loss of lives and property. To get to this higher level criterion, estimates would have to be made of the consequences of not finding and correcting such violations. This footnote is included to indicate the kinds of inferences that are likely to be needed in program analyses. Similar situations can be identified for many of the other criteria presented in this list.

19. Here and in the following material the term "illness" is also intended to cover disability and impairments.

20. Suicide rates should be included; these are likely to provide some indication of the overall mental health of the community. Note that reducing mortality from certain causes would presumably increase mortality from other causes. Life expectancy criterion 3, is thus a more important overall criterion.

21. Armed Forces rejection rates–for intelligence reasons–of persons from the jurisdiction could be used to provide a partial measure.

22. Two subcategories have been singled out for illustration: "Satisfactory homes" and "maintenance of a satisfactory water supply." Others such as "maintenance of satisfactory air environment," "noise abatement," and "sanitation," can also be identified as subcategories and require selection of appropriate criteria that also help to evaluate home and living conditions.

Chapter 11

SYSTEMS EVALUATION: AN APPROACH BASED ON COMMUNITY STRUCTURE AND VALUE

Charles G. Schimpeler and William L. Grecco

Although a great deal of sophistication has been reached in the urban transportation planning process, this same level of sophistication has not been reached in plan evaluation. With regard to this general field of research, certain focal points within the problem area have been isolated. They are (a) criteria for evaluating alternatives, (b) techniques for identifying objectives, and (c) use of models in the design process.

This paper presents a technique for utilizing a weighted hierarchy of community decision criteria, or community goals and objectives, in a systematic evaluation of alternative transportation system design concepts. Heretofore, criteria utilized in plan evaluation have generally been easily quantified economic considerations. An alternative to that approach is considered here which utilizes a broader, more comprehensive class of criteria, including social values along with traditional economic considerations. Applied decision theory is used to establish orderly methods of making comparisons between the various alternative design concepts or philosophies.

A group of professional land-use and transportation planners establish effectiveness values for the design concepts relative to each item in a comprehensive statement of community decision criteria. The decision model utilizes these effectiveness values along with utility values associated with each element in the criteria set and proposes for adoption that plan possessing the

AUTHORS' NOTE: This paper was sponsored by the Committee on Transportation System Evaluation and presented at the 47th Annual Meeting. Reprinted from The Highway Research Record No. 238, 1968, pp. 123-124, 130-138, 141-149, by permission of the publisher.

highest aggregate "plan effectiveness" as defined herein. Various interesting techniques relating to this approach have been published previously and are summarized here.* Several proposals for mathematical programming procedures for use in systems design are discussed that may prove useful in eventually structuring a truly optimal approach to system design and evaluation.

The central problem considered in this research is the evaluation of alternative system design concepts by a group of professional planners and engineers on the basis of the probability associated with goal achievement, assuming the adoption of each of the three alternative proposals. Effectiveness values for each alternative with respect to each of the criteria are presented and the rationale associated with the development of these values is given. Detailed presentations relative to community decision structure, statement of community decision criteria, weighting of the elements in a comprehensive hierarchy of community decision criteria, and the statistical analysis of scaling or weighting techniques are beyond the scope of this research; however, results obtained in these areas are summarized insofar as they relate to this paper.

Direct application of these procedures in land-use form analysis, land-use plan evaluation, detailed transportation plan evaluation, and transportation corridor analysis is discussed.* Interesting extensions of these procedures in the areas of mathematical programming and more detailed and explicit definition of "yardsticks" for measuring plan effectiveness are presented.*

ESTABLISHING A WEIGHTED HIERARCHY OF COMMUNITY DECISION CRITERIA

This section is presented to indicate how a set of community goals and objectives could be formulated and weighted. The weighted community decision criteria are essential to the proposed method of plan evaluation emphasized in this paper. The method proposed assumes involvement of community decision-makers in structuring a list of specific community decision criteria. Professional planners would use the decision criteria, weighted by the decision-makers, in the evaluation of planning proposals. The central problem in this research is the development of analytical methods for plan evaluation, having as input to this evaluation a set of weighted community goals and objectives.

Since the plans to be evaluated were for metropolitan Louisville, a task force from the Louisville Mayor's Citizens Advisory Committee was used as the criteria evaluation or community decision-making group. The task force represented a cross section of highly respected, influential citizens of metropolitan Louisville (the area used as the experimental laboratory). This group is interested in and familiar with the area's community goals and objectives.

Although it was convenient and entirely satisfactory in this research to utilize

*Not included herein.–Ed.

the committee for criteria weighting, a more general criterion for the selection of such a committee may be stated as follows:

> "The committee should consist of direct and indirect influentials including popular public officials and representatives of commerce and industry who are influential in controlling development decisions, and those indirect influentials who, by reason of their personal stature and demonstrated interest, are effective in shaping policy on important community issues."

An alternative presentation of this criterion is the following block diagram:

COMPOSITION OF CRITERIA FORMULATION COMMITTEE

	Influentials	
	Possible Direct	*Actual Indirect*
Representors	A	C
Implementors	B	D

where the letters are defined as

A = popularly elected officials;

B = other heads of public and semi-public bodies, executives of commercial and industrial firms;

C = unbiased, interested citizens;

D = other indirect influentials including groups A and B acting outside the area of their direct control.

Procedures used in the establishment of a weighted set of community decision criteria (i.e., specific statements of community goals and objectives) are as follows:

(1) Professional planners established a tentative set of community goals and objectives, explicitly and concisely stated.

(2) The criteria evaluation group met for general discussion and modification of each item in the statements of community goals and objectives. The end product was a complete statement of community goals and objectives, modified in view of the comments and opinions of the decision-makers or criteria evaluation group. The resulting statements of community goals and objectives are shown in Appendix A.

(3) Each member of the criteria evaluation group was asked to individually weight the various sets of criteria by the ranking and rating methods of Appendix B.

(4) The decision-makers or criteria evaluation group met and were asked to re-evaluate their initial weighting of the elements of the criteria statements. No committee members changed their initial values.

The aggregated weightings thus obtained, as given in Appendix C, were used in the plan evaluation decision model.

For the two techniques used, the following statistical results were obtained:

(1) A high level of agreement among judges using the scaling techniques was observed.
(2) Criteria weights obtained by the methods applied were highly correlated in both rank order and interval-level measure. Criteria weights obtained by any given method were highly correlated with criteria weights obtained by averaging all methods.
(3) Each judge demonstrated transitivity of preference throughout all methods used.

PLAN EVALUATION: THE DECISION MODEL

Two similar approaches to the development of a decision model used in alternative plan evaluation are the effectiveness matrix approach and a scoring mode. This section will develop the mathematics associated with these techniques and will present an actual application of the effectiveness matrix approach. The scoring model extends the effectiveness matrix technique by treating a stratification of judges by background and interest groupings.

The Effectiveness Matrix Technique

At this point, it is assumed that a hierarchy of community planning goals and objectives has been established and that a numerical utility measure or criterion weight has been assigned to each objective statement. Three alternative community plans are under consideration. Outlined in this section is a procedure for evaluating the three alternative proposals.

Definition of Terms. Consider here the set of community planning objectives G_j where $j = 1, 2, \ldots, n$, n being the total number of decision criteria under consideration. Second, three plans are proposed for evaluation. The set of plans under consideration is designated by P_i, where $i = 1, 2, 3$. Associated with each community planning objective G_j is a numerical utility value u_j $(j = 1, 2, \ldots, n)$ which was determined by the procedures of Appendix B. Regardless of the system of decision criteria under consideration, the following equality must hold:

$$\sum_{j=1}^{n} u_j = 1$$

The purpose of this discussion is to describe a procedure for objectively utilizing weighted community decision criteria in the evaluation of physical development plans; therefore, "effectiveness" (e_{ij}) and "plan utility" U_i are defined. Effectiveness (e_{ij}) is a measure of the probability that objective j can be achieved if plan i is adopted. U_i is a measure of the total utility of plan i based on the evaluation of plan i relative to all objectives.

The Effectiveness Matrix. The effectiveness matrix was developed by a committee of planners representing the professional disciplines associated with the comprehensive planning process. The effectiveness value (e_{ij}) is assigned on the basis that an e_{ij} of 1.0 implies that achievement of objective j is assured under plan i, and an e_{ij} of 0.0 implies that achievement of goal j under plan i is practically impossible. If all plans i have no effect on the achievement or prevention of objective j then all e_{ij} associated with that objective are undefined and the unrelated criterion will be dropped from the effectiveness matrix. Values of e_{ij} will be estimated to the nearest tenth by each evaluator, using the previously defined guidelines. Elements of the final effectiveness matrix (e_{ij}) will be documented later in this section with a statement of reason for the numerical value given. In general terms, the effectiveness matrix will have the following form:

EFFECTIVENESS MATRIX

	Criterion				
Alternative Plan	G_1	G_2	G_3 ...	G_j ...	G_n
P_1	e_{11}	e_{12}	e_{13} ...	e_{1j} ...	e_{1n}
P_2	e_{21}	e_{22}	e_{23} ...	e_{2j} ...	e_{2n}
P_3	e_{31}	e_{32}	e_{33} ...	e_{3j} ...	e_{3n}
.	.	.	.	.	.
.	.	.	.	.	.
.	.	.	.	.	.
P_i	e_{i1}	e_{i2}	e_{i3} ...	e_{ij} ...	e_{in}
.	.	.	.	.	.
.	.	.	.	.	.
.	.	.	.	.	.
P_m	e_{m1}	e_{m2}	e_{m3}	e_{mj}	e_{mn}

In generalized vector notation, the effectiveness matrix may be represented by E.

The Decision Model. A decision model that determines a total effectiveness for each of the plans P_i (i = 1, 2, 3) with respect to the given decision criteria structure G_j (j = 1, 2, 3, 4, 5) follows. For each plan (i), the total utility is the sum of the products of the individual numerical utility of the plan with respect to objective j (e_{ij}). The model is mathematically stated as follows:

$$U_i = \sum_{j=1}^{n} e_{ij}\, u_j \quad (i = 1, 2, \ldots, m)$$

where U_i = total utility associated with plan i; e_{ij} = probability that objective j can be achieved if plan i is adopted, and u_j = numerical measurement of utility associated with community planning objective j.

In the generalized vector notation, the decision model may be stated as follows:

$$\begin{bmatrix} e_{11} & e_{12} & e_{13} & \cdots & e_{1j} & \cdots & e_{1n} \\ e_{21} & e_{22} & e_{23} & \cdots & e_{2j} & \cdots & e_{2n} \\ e_{31} & e_{32} & e_{33} & \cdots & e_{3j} & \cdots & e_{3n} \\ \cdot & \cdot & \cdot & & \cdot & & \cdot \\ \cdot & \cdot & \cdot & & \cdot & & \cdot \\ \cdot & \cdot & \cdot & & \cdot & & \cdot \\ e_{i1} & e_{i2} & e_{i3} & \cdots & e_{ij} & \cdots & e_{in} \\ \cdot & \cdot & \cdot & & \cdot & & \cdot \\ \cdot & \cdot & \cdot & & \cdot & & \cdot \\ \cdot & \cdot & \cdot & & \cdot & & \cdot \\ e_{m1} & e_{m2} & e_{m3} & & e_{mj} & & e_{mn} \end{bmatrix} \begin{bmatrix} u_1 \\ u_2 \\ u_3 \\ \cdot \\ \cdot \\ \cdot \\ u_j \\ \cdot \\ \cdot \\ \cdot \\ u_n \end{bmatrix} = \begin{bmatrix} U_1 \\ U_2 \\ U_3 \\ \cdot \\ \cdot \\ \cdot \\ U_i \\ \cdot \\ \cdot \\ \cdot \\ U_m \end{bmatrix}$$

Or, this can be stated as:

$$U = Eu$$

where $u = (u_1, u_2, u_3, \ldots, u_j, \ldots, u_n)^T$ is a column vector whose components represent the utility values associated with each of the n community decision criteria, and $U = (U_1, U_2, \ldots, U_m)^T$ is a column vector whose components represent the plan utility associated with each of the m alternative development plans, and E is the m x n matrix defined earlier.

The plan possessing the highest total utility would be the alternative plan recommended to the community decision-makers for formal adoption.

A Scoring Model

Work in the area of development of scoring and profitability models for evaluating engineering projects within an industrial firm presents results that may be applicable in alternative plan evaluation (see Dean and Nishry, 1965). A suggested application is presented here.

Previous definitions of G_j, u_j, e_{ij}, and U_i apply here. At this point the scoring concept is exactly the same as the effective matrix technique described earlier. Consider a panel of judges or community decision-makers, individually representative of different and definable socioeconomic sectors of the community. Vogt (1967) and others have indicated that community decisions should reflect the makeup of the community relative to socioeconomic group stratification. The model presented previously could be modified as follows:

$$U_i = U_i^1 + U_i^2 + \ldots + U_i^k + \ldots U_i^p$$

$$U_i^k = a_k \sum_{j=1}^{n} u_j^k e_{ij}^k$$

where

U_i = total score for alternative plan i;

U_i^k = score for alternative plan i as determined by the kth socioeconomic group (k = 1, 2, . . . , p);

u_j^k = criterion weight for objective j as determined by the kth socioeconomic group;

e_{ij}^k = value of plan i relative to the criterion j as determined by the kth socioeconomic group; and

a_k = fraction of the area population represented by the kth socioeconomic group.

As a minor but logical modification of this scoring model, one may consider the development of utility values by different socioeconomic groups of citizens while considering only one set of effectiveness values established by one group of professional planners. This problem may be formulated as the following matrix multiplication:

$$\begin{bmatrix} e_{11} & e_{12} & e_{13} \cdots & e_{1j} \cdots & e_{1n} \\ e_{21} & e_{22} & e_{23} \cdots & e_{2j} \cdots & e_{2n} \\ e_{31} & e_{32} & e_{33} \cdots & e_{3j} \cdots & e_{3n} \\ \cdot & \cdot & \cdot & \cdot & \cdot \\ \cdot & \cdot & \cdot & \cdot & \cdot \\ \cdot & \cdot & \cdot & \cdot & \cdot \\ e_{i1} & e_{i2} & e_{i3} \cdots & e_{ij} \cdots & e_{in} \\ \cdot & \cdot & \cdot & \cdot & \cdot \\ \cdot & \cdot & \cdot & \cdot & \cdot \\ \cdot & \cdot & \cdot & \cdot & \cdot \\ e_{m1} & e_{m2} & e_{m3} \cdots & e_{mj} \cdots & e_{mn} \end{bmatrix} \begin{bmatrix} a_1u_1^1 & a_2u_1^2 & a_3u_1^3 \\ a_1u_2^1 & a_2u_2^2 & a_3u_2^3 \\ \cdot & \cdot & \cdot \\ \cdot & \cdot & \cdot \\ \cdot & \cdot & \cdot \\ a_1u_j^1 & a_2u_j^2 & a_3u_j^3 \\ \cdot & \cdot & \cdot \\ \cdot & \cdot & \cdot \\ \cdot & \cdot & \cdot \\ a_1u_n^1 & a_2u_n^2 & a_3u_n^3 \end{bmatrix} =$$

$$\begin{bmatrix} U_1^1 & U_1^2 & U_1^3 \\ U_2^1 & U_2^2 & U_2^3 \\ \cdot & \cdot & \cdot \\ \cdot & \cdot & \cdot \\ \cdot & \cdot & \cdot \\ U_i^1 & U_i^2 & U_i^3 \\ \cdot & \cdot & \cdot \\ \cdot & \cdot & \cdot \\ \cdot & \cdot & \cdot \\ U_m^1 & U_m^2 & U_m^3 \end{bmatrix}$$

Or,

$$Eu = U$$

where

$E = (e_{ij})$ is a $m \times n$ matrix. The typical element represents the probability that goal j will be achieved if alternative plan i is adopted;

$u = a_k u_j^k$ is a $n \times 3$ matrix. The typical element represents the utility value (criterion weight) for criterion j as determined by socioeconomic group k. In this example 3 socioeconomic groups are considered; a_k is the fraction of the area population represented by socioeconomic group k.

$U = (U_i^k)$ is a $m \times k$ matrix. The typical element represents the aggregate utility (score) assigned to alternative plan i by socioeconomic group k.

By summing U_{ik} value for each row (i) of the U matrix, a utility value (score) for each alternative plan (i) may be obtained. The values will be weighted in a manner consistent with the socioeconomic group composition of the community.

Model Application and Presentation of Results

The effectiveness matrix technique for plan evaluation has been applied and the results are presented here. The model is described in vector notation U = Eu. The transposed effectiveness matrix E^T is given in Appendix D. The columns represent the 3 alternative plans evaluated and the rows of the matrix represent the 35 criterion statements or community planning objectives. Two professional planners from The Falls of the Ohio Metropolitan Council of Governments (the regional planning authority for the Louisville metropolitan area) and three professional transportation planners from the Louisville Metropolitan Comprehensive Transportation and Development Program participated in the plan evaluation process. The e_{ij} values of Appendix D represent the consensus of this group of professionals.

The components of the column vector u are the utility values associated with the 35 decision criteria or community objectives. This vector is given in Appendix C in the column headed Average Values, u_j. As stated earlier, the Task Force 5 values were used in the plan evaluation model because this group formulated the statements of goals and specific objectives and was, therefore, more familiar with the criteria as well as the community involved. Note that the vector u is a 35-component column vector.

The 3 X 35 matrix E was multiplied by the 35 X 1 column vector u to produce a 3 X 1 vector U. That vector is stated as follows:

$$U = (U_1, U_2, U_3)T$$

or

$$U = (0.38, 0.52, 0.60)T$$

where each of the values U_i represent the aggregate planned utility associated with each of the three alternative development plans.

Because these plans are transportation system design concepts only, they have not been developed in sufficient detail to provide cost estimates. This precluded the possibility of doing a complete cost-effectiveness analysis.

The aggregate results indicate that the least preferred alternative is plan 1 (Appendix E*). That plan is based on extensive improvements of existing at-grade arterial facilities. The second proposed alternative design concept, plan 2 (Appendix F*) is based on extensive construction of freeway facilities with no rail mass transit. Plan 2 possesses an aggregate utility approximately 37% higher than that possessed by alternative design concept 1. Finally, the most preferred alternative is plan 3 (Appendix G*), based on a balance of new freeway construction and rail mass transit. The rail mass transit-oriented alternative possesses an aggregate plan utility 58% higher than that of the first design alternative and 15% higher than the freeway-oriented design concept.

In the remainder of this section the reasoning involved in the determination of various e_{ij} values is discussed and "yardsticks" for use in determining the respective effectiveness values are identified. The objective statements are shown as quotations and appropriate comments follow.

"Insure safe public facilities." The transit-oriented system was judged most effective in assuring safety, with the freeway alternative second. A yardstick for the measure of effectiveness here may be a study of accident records on various types of transportation facilities, particularly the study of such accident records on facilities in the metropolitan area.

"Provide for adequate public safety regulations and their enforcement." The

*Not included herein.–Ed.

high effectiveness for plan 2 indicated that the experts felt enforcement of freeways was by far the easiest type of enforcement. Numerous accident or friction points exist in plan 1, while significant policing problems in transit vehicles and stations exist with plan 3.

"Provide for the removal of contaminants (solid, liquid, and gaseous)." The transit-oriented alternative was most preferred here because of the fact that it removes many vehicle miles of travel from the surface street system, thereby reducing air pollution caused by vehicular exhaust. A yardstick to be used in a measurement of effectiveness here may be aggregate vehicle miles of travel. This statistic is highest on a surface street-oriented alternative (plan 1) and, therefore, that alternative is the least desirable.

"Minimize maintenance costs of public facilities." Wide rights-of-way make the freeway alternative less desirable than the surface street alternative; however, maintenance would be most expensive in a transit-oriented system. A yardstick in determining this effectiveness could be the development of maintenance cost records by type of facility.

"Insure maximum effectiveness of public utilities (including transportation facilities) by design and locational considerations." The freeway-oriented alternative was most desirable in this case, furnishing good access to many major public facilities. The inflexibility of mass transit is reflected in the lower effectiveness value of plan 3. Aggregate hours of travel could be a yardstick relative to this objective as well as the accessibility index produced as a part of the standard trip analysis procedures.

"Develop a balanced, effective, and integrated transportation system which provides for the accessibility requirements of each land use." Balance is implied by transit orientation in transportation system development and this implication is reflected in the high effectiveness value of plan 3. The surface street concept is the least effective of these three plans. Yardsticks may be developed in this area, such as analysis of travel by various modes, measurements of delays and frequency of service, and determination of aggregate travel time and aggregate travel costs.

"Develop public improvement programs within available financial resources." Here, plan 1 and the freeway-oriented plan have the highest effectiveness values. The low effectiveness value associated with the mass transit concept reflects the customary subsidy associated with that type of program. The existence of a financing system, such as the highway trust fund based on road user taxes, reflects a system development within available financing.

"Maintain highest equitable property values." Studies have indicated a skyrocketing of property values in freeway and mass transit corridors; however, accessibility by any means seems to enhance property values. The effectiveness values reflect this greater activity in transit corridors.

"Insure effective utilization of mineral, vegetation, air, and water resources." In the opinion of the professionals developing the effectiveness matrix, this objective is not related to or affected by transportation system design concepts.

"Establish a strong economic base through commerce that will bring money into the community." The effectiveness values indicate that a transit-oriented system is stronger relative to inducing a new industry into a community. A freeway-oriented system providing access to suburban areas for industrial park and new plant development was the second preferred, while the alternative based on improvement of existing facilities received a low value for this objective.

"Establish trade development that provides maximum convenience to consumers." The effectiveness values indicate an edge for a transit-oriented alternative over a freeway-oriented alternative with the improvement of existing street concept receiving a somewhat lower value. Although improvement of existing streets provides for more convenience to neighborhood shopping centers, possibly it impedes access to regional and central business district type facilities.

"Insure the optimal utilization of all land." Again, the transit-oriented alternative received an edge reflecting that this system, a transit-freeway system, provides the best access to land in an urban area. The freeway-only alternative was second and the improvement of existing street facilities was the least preferred or the least effective alternative.

"Achieve increased disposable income for all people." Due to the greater accessibility to work locations for all of the population, the mass transit alternative possessed the highest effectiveness value. Again, for reasons of overall accessibility, the freeway-oriented alternative was second. The planners felt that a street system would not provide access to job centers, particularly for that element of the population that could not afford to maintain an automobile.

"Preserve historic sites and areas of natural beauty." Although plan 1 requires less new right-of-way, it was felt that it was the least desirable alternative because it would result in overloaded conditions or street facilities serving historic sites and sites of natural beauty. Proper alignment of a mass transit line could provide mass access to these facilities, thereby resulting in that alternative's receiving the highest effectiveness value.

"Promote adequate public libraries, museums, and cultural activities." Again, the greater overall accessibility provided by a transit-oriented system resulted in that system's receiving the highest effectiveness value.

"Protect meaningful local tradition and encourage civic pride." The greater accessibility of the freeway-only and transit-freeway alternatives results in the high effectiveness for these two plans. The professional planners felt that civic pride is encouraged by a good transportation system, another reason for the high effectiveness values of plans 2 and 3.

"Establish the mechanism for adequate preventive and remedial health programs and facilities." This objective is not related to or affected by transportation system design concepts.

"Develop educational facilities and opportunities for citizens at every level." Again, the high accessibility provided by a mass transit system resulted in that system's receiving the highest effectiveness value. The second highest value is possessed by the freeway-oriented system, with a very low effectiveness value assigned to plan 1, which would not provide good access to high school and higher education activities and facilities.

"Eliminate injustice based on discrimination." In this case, the more accessible systems, plans 3 and 2 respectively, receive the lowest effectiveness values. The planners reasoned that this type development encouraged the development of ghettos for impoverished minority groups.

"Develop needed public welfare programs." The planners indicated that this objective was unrelated to transportation system development.

"Encourage development of religious opportunities." Again, the high accessibility systems as depicted in plans 3 and 2 respectively received the highest effectiveness values.

"Develop an aesthetically pleasing environment." Although this objective is mostly sensitive to urban design concepts, the panel felt that by placing mass transit systems in subways in congested areas, aesthetics could be realized more readily. Also, heavy travel on surface streets was judged not to be consistent with pleasing aesthetic values.

"Establish open-space programs." Concentration of traffic on rail or on limited-access freeways was judged to be most consistent with the establishment of open-space programs.

"Provide adequate recreational facilities utilizing parks, rivers, and lakes." A surface system was judged to provide the greater accessibility to the type of recreation described in this objective. The inflexibility of the mass transit system resulted in its receiving a low effectiveness value.

"Improve the framework (channels, systematic use) for citizen participation in governmental functions." This objective is unrelated to transportation system development.

"Establish equitable taxation policies (bases, mixes, rates)." This objective should be applied in transportation system analysis to assure that equitable cost-sharing is established between users and nonusers and to assure that transportation facility development costs are equitably distributed between participating agencies charged with the responsibility for developing these facilities. The low effectiveness value for the mass transit system indicated that the subsidy normally associated with this type system development is a taxation inequity.

"Achieve efficient governmental administration, representative of all citizens." This objective is not related to transportation system development.

"Develop adequate government staffs and personnel programs (high job standards, reasonable salary ranges, effective delegation of authority)." This objective is not related to transportation system development.

"Establish sound governmental fiscal programs." Again, the subsidy normally associated with mass transportation is regarded as not a sound fiscal program.

"Develop an effective, long-range, metropolitan-wide planning process." This objective implies that transportation and development policies must be coordinated and that studies of both lead to the development of a planning process and implementation devices which accomplish the goals for the least expenditure of direct and indirect costs. The development of an integrated system as reflected in plan 3 seems to be most consistent with this objective.

"Establish effective control mechanisms." This objective is unrelated to transportation system development.

"Encourage rehabilitation and conservation neighborhood programs." The low effectiveness of the transit-oriented alternative implies that many neighborhoods cannot be effectively served by an isolated transportation system such as a mass transit system. The development of a street system coordinated with urban redevelopment projects is an obvious technique implied in the implementation of this objective.

"Provide adequate low-cost housing." The transit-oriented alternative received the highest effectiveness value because the planners establishing these values felt that low-cost, high-density housing could be served best by a transit-oriented transportation system.

"Develop neighborhood units." The surface street system providing good transportation access to neighborhoods was judged to be most effective. A yardstick to be used in a measurement of the compliance of various plans with this objective could be the measurement of vehicle-pedestrian conflicts at the neighborhood level and the measurement of through traffic within neighborhoods.

"Promote a wide variety of housing types as required within the community." The high effectiveness for plan 3 reflects the planner's opinion that rail mass transit could serve high-density residential corridors and promote most effectively the wide variety of housing mentioned in this objective.

As will be stated in the next section, the area of developing yardsticks for measuring the extent to which a plan is compatible with the various objectives presents a most challenging area of further research. This section has provided some examples or guidelines for the development of quantitative and effective yardsticks, along with comments concerning the thinking of the professionals in arriving at the effectiveness values.

SUGGESTED FURTHER APPLICATIONS AND EXTENSIONS

It is anticipated that continuing application and refinement of these techniques will be made a regular part of the Work Program of the Louisville Metropolitan Comprehensive Transportation and Development Program. Obvious applications of the techniques to the work in Louisville are (a) for improvement of the existing recommended plan, (b) for use in the evaluation of alternative land-use forms now under consideration by development planning agencies, and (c) for use in the analysis of selected transportation corridors.

Improvement of Selected Plan

The study consultant will recommend a transportation plan to the Transportation and Development Program. It is proposed that the plan evaluating schemes of this research be applied to that selected plan in a diagnostic manner. The recommended plan will be analyzed in detail relative to each of the community objectives in the weighted hierarchy of community goals and objectives given in Appendix C. On the basis of this evaluation, an analysis of the recommended plan can be made. In the areas where the plan is weak with respect to certain goals and objectives, action to remedy such shortcomings in the plan will be considered.

Currently, a study by The Falls of the Ohio Metropolitan Council of Governments is concerned with the development of a more complete set of community goals and objectives. The goals and objectives study will be carried out over the next two years and will result in a more comprehensive statement of goals and objectives than presented here. At that time, the scheme for evaluation will be repeated subsequent to the weighting of the decision criteria. Again, modifications of the transportation plan will be considered on the basis of the results of the study.

Alternative Land-Use Forms

The current transportation planning program in the Louisville metropolitan area has been based on a single land-use form, defined by the Louisville and Jefferson County Planning Commission as "planned sprawl." Other fundamental land-use forms such as satellite cities, radial corridors, and others are being considered by the development agencies of the area. When a comprehensive plan based on an alternative land-use form is available, a more extensive application of these procedures will be possible. At that time, the procedures may be used to evaluate the alternative land-use forms, the alternative transportation plans associated with these forms, and, finally, alternative comprehensive transportation plans associated with these forms, and, finally, alternative comprehensive development plans that encompass both land use and transportation.

Corridor Analysis: Route Planning Studies

In addition to the recommendations relative to new freeway systems and new arterial systems for a metropolitan area, a large effort of the continuing planning process relates to the improvement of existing facilities within that area.

One of the significant tasks associated with this improvement of existing facilities is corridor analysis or route planning studies. It is anticipated that the techniques of this research will be most useful in the development of plans associated with the improvement of existing facilities. Alternative routes may be considered and each of these alternatives may be evaluated in the context of the community goals and objectives structure presented.

An immediate suggestion relative to the application of these techniques in route planning is the development of a pilot study or set of guidelines for the application of these techniques to the planning analysis of an individual corridor instead of a total transportation system.

Defining the Decision Variables: A Work Program Reflecting Specific Objectives

The earlier sections of this research have presented an approach to plan evaluation based on a weighted hierarchy of community decision criteria or goals and objectives. Hopefully, the procedures resulting from this research presented in the earlier sections will provide planners with a straightforward, efficient, and effective methodology for weighting goals and objectives and evaluating alternative plans. It is recognized, however, that the techniques proposed are suboptimal in many respects. Many "givens" are imposed upon the process. Planning is treated as a "second-order" governmental function below the policy-making and financing processes. Possibly, if decisions at the primary level could be guided quantitatively by the weighted hierarchy of community goals and objectives, a truly optimal approach would exist.

Studies of suboptimization (see Hitch, 1953) indicate that "good" decision criteria at any level are consistent with "good" decision criteria at higher levels. Quantitative solutions based on the wrong criteria (in this case "wrong" givens input to the planning process) are tantamount to answering the wrong question, and this may well apply to the community development process. With most metropolitan governments, well-defined criteria do not exist at the higher level, and this results in suboptimal lower level planning decisions.

This section proposes a procedure for top-level community decision-making using cardinal utility values in an optimal allocation of community resources.

One may consider the mapping of a closed, precisely defined set of community values onto a set of community goals; of goals onto objectives; and finally, a set of community objectives onto a set of items constituting a community work program. Expenditures of public revenues on each of the items of the work program may be considered as the decision variables ($x_1, x_2, \ldots, x_j, \ldots x_n$) of a mathematical programming formulation. For example, decision criterion j may relate to the "establishment of open space programs for metropolitan use"; x_j would then represent the expenditure of public revenues in dollars on open space programs. A set of decision variables would be defined along with items of a work program in such a manner that every community objective would be represented by a work program item (or items) insuring the fulfillment of that objective.

Conceptual Formulation of an Allocation Model

The preceding section defined decision variables. In considering a particular decision variable, x_j, it is possible to associate with that variable a "cost coefficient" indicative of the utility associated with the work program item represented by that decision variable.

It may be considered desirable to maximize the aggregate of the dollar expenditures multiplied by the utility value associated with each individual expenditure represented by the decision variables. The allocation of tax revenues must be performed within certain constraints. Such constraining relationships may be the availability of total money, the availability of other resources such as land, restrictions implied by time factors, desirable minimum or maximum levels of expenditure for various programs, or desirable interrelationships among the various work program items represented by the decision variables. Further, it would be logical to disallow any negative allocation of money.

An Extremal Methods Approach

This section suggests several applications of standard mathematical programming techniques.

Linear Programming Formulation. The definition of decision variables was considered earlier. Consider a class of parameters (u_j) associated with the decision variables (x_j); the parameters represent the utility values associated with the various community work program items defined by the decision variables. That is,

x_j = number of dollars allocated to community work program j; and
u_j = utility associated with community work program j per dollar spent on community work program j.

An optimal allocation of available funds to the various work programs is represented by the following objective function:

$$\text{Max} \sum_{j=1}^{n} u_j \, u_j$$

where there are possible work program items to which allocation may be made.

Constraints of the following form may be applicable:

$$x_1 + x_2 + \ldots + x_j + \ldots + x_n \leqslant b_1$$

where b_1 represents maximum available funds;

$$x_k \geqslant b_2$$

where b_2 may represent an absolute minimum expenditure such as required for education, police protection, or fire protection.

Due to constraints placed by time requirements associated with various projects, maxima may exist such as

$$a_{ij}\, x_j \leqslant b_1$$

In general, the problem may lend itself to formulation as the general linear programming problem stated as the maximiization of a linear objective function subject to appropriate linear equality or unequality constraints. One constraint is that all allocations are non-negative.

Research in progress at Purdue University considers an optimal allocation of land uses. The formulation proposed could incorporate the concept of using criteria weights (utility values) as cost coefficients in the formulation of the objective function of a mathematical programming problem.

Parametric Programming Analysis. An interesting examination of the linear programming model by standard methods of parametric programming appears to be feasible. Changes in the cost coefficients or the utility values, as in this particular application, may be investigated, and the sensitivity of an optimal solution to changes in these criterion weights or utility values may be examined. Further, it may be possible by means of parametric programming analysis to determine the solution with a relaxation of the total money constraint or changes in other parametric values. With slight changes in certain "given" values, a much more desirable solution may be obtained.

Nonlinear Formulation of the Problem. An interesting concept of marginal utility is that additional incremental amounts of a given item are not as valuable as previous increments of the same size. For example, the third or fourth serving of a dessert would not be valued as highly as the first. Bernouilli and others have postulated that the utility function is not linear and may be described by an exponential or quadratic relationship. The methods of nonlinear programming may be applied in the situation of optimal allocation of community resources. The quadratic formulation proposed by Wolfe (see Dantzig, 1963) or the more general convex formulation (see Hadley, 1964) may be applicable.

Dynamic or Integer Programming Approach. The powerful tool of dynamic programming has been successfully applied in problems where the decision variable is a 0-1 variable, i.e., in a situation where either an allocation is made or it is not made. Integer solutions may be indicated because of the practical situation where it would not be feasible to build a fractional or non-integer portion of a new school.

Plan Evaluation

Many sophisticated techniques developed in the area of economic analyses of plans, particularly transportation plans, must be incorporated in an objective manner in the evaluation process. Much of the work in benefit cost analysis may be applied. Ultimately, an effective means of developing yardsticks to measure compatibility of plans with community values must be researched.

Plan evaluation must be concerned with the manner in which a plan is consistent with community values at a lower level of synthesis than the level of objectives studied here. That is, objectives are often too general and the resulting evaluation may be purely subjective. For use in evaluation of plans of traffic improvement at a more detailed level of analysis, the pertinent objective statements would be further subdivided to establish more meaningful criteria. This may be accomplished within the framework of the procedures presented here.

SUMMARY AND CONCLUSIONS

This paper has presented an approach to the development of a decision model for evaluating alternative transportation system design concepts in the context of a comprehensive hierarchy of community goals and objectives. Various interesting approaches to plan evaluation were discussed as well as several proposals for utilizing potentially powerful normative procedures in system design. Extensive discussion of problems associated with community decision structure, formulation and weighting of goals and objectives, and the statistical analysis of weighting or scaling procedures is beyond the scope of this paper; however, a summary of findings in the areas mentioned is presented. The structuring of several decision models for the evaluation of alternative plans or alternative system design concepts with respect to a weighted hierarchy of community decision criteria is presented. Several immediate applications appear to be feasible and these applications are enumerated. A number of possible extensions of this research are identified. It is concluded that:

(1) A decision model for use in systems evaluation may be simply structured to relate utility values associated with each element in a comprehensive statement of community decision criteria with the evaluation of effectiveness of given system alternatives with respect to these criteria. Simple extensions of such a model may provide for the stratification, by socioeconomic categories or other desirable categories, of the group of persons determining the utility values associated with the community decision criteria, or, for the stratification of professional planners, the group determining the plan effectiveness values.

(2) In addition to their usefulness in plan evaluation as proposed in this research, weighted community decision criteria or quantified expressions of community values could be useful in system design and capital programming.

(3) The procedures structured herein may be useful in the evaluation of alternative land-use forms, detailed alternative land-use plans, detailed transportation system plans, and alternative transportation corridors in addition to the application in evaluation of alternative system design concepts as presented here.

(4) Although the community decision criteria considered herein were formulated for general overall community development, 80% of these criteria were judged to have a meaningful relationship to a specific problem of transportation system development.

(5) The application of the plan evaluation model resulted in the selection of that system design concept based on some improvements of existing at-grade facilities

with a balance of new freeway construction and rail mass transit. This plan possesses an aggregate plan utility 58% higher than that of the first design alternative (extensive improvement of existing at-grade facilities), and 15% higher than the freeway-oriented design concept.

(6) Extensions of this work are needed in the areas of capital allocation model formulation and the associated definition of decision variables for such a model, and the development of effective yardsticks for determining plan effectiveness based on a weighted hierarchy of community decision criteria.

REFERENCES

Ackoff, Russell L. "Individual Preferences for Various Means of Transportation." Report of the National Cooperative Highway Research Program, March 1965.

Alexander, Christopher. *Notes on the Synthesis of Form.* Harvard University Press, 1966.

Churchman, C. W., and Ackoff, Russell L. An Approximate Measure of Value. Journal of the Operations Research Society of America, Vol. 2, No. 2, 1965.

Dansereau, H. Kirk. "Highway Development: Attitudes and Economic Climate." Highway Research Record 187, p. 21-32, 1967.

Dantzig, George B. *Linear Programming and Extensions.* Princeton University Press, 1963.

Dean, Burton V., and Nishry, Meir J. "Scoring and Profitability Models for Evaluating and Selecting Engineering Projects." Operations Research, Vol. 13, No. 4, 1965.

Eckenrode, Robert T. "Weighting Multiple Criteria." Management Science, Vol. 12, No. 3, Nov. 1965.

Fishburn, Peter C. "A Note on Recent Developments in Additive Utility Theories for Multiple-Factor Situations." Operations Research, Vol. 14, No. 6, Nov.-Dec. 1966.

Fishburn, Peter C. "Methods of Estimating Additive Utilities." Management Science, Vol. 13, No. 7, March 1967.

Hadley, G. *Nonlinear and Dynamic Programming.* Addison-Wesley, Reading, Mass., 1964.

Hay, George A., Morlok, Edward K. and Charnes, Abraham. "Toward Optimal Planning of a Two-Mode Urban Transportation System: A Linear Programming Formulation." Highway Research Record 148, p. 20-48, p. 66.

Hemmens, George C. "Experiments in Urban Form and Structure." Highway Research Record 207, p. 32-41, 1967.

Hill, Morris. "A Method for the Evaluation of Transportation Plans." Highway Research Record 180, p. 21-34, 1967.

Hitch, C. J. "Sub-Optimization Problems." Journal of the Operations Research Society, Vol. 1, No. 2, May 1953.

Irwin, Neal A. "Criteria for Evaluating Alternative Transportation Systems." Highway Research Record 148, p. 9-19, 1966.

Jessiman, William, Brussee, C. Roger, Tumminia, Alfred, and Brand, Daniel. "A Rational Decision-Making Technique for Transportation Planning." Highway Research Record 180, p. 71-80, 1967.

Klein, Burton, and Meckling, William. "Applications of Operations Research to Development Decisions." Operations Research, Vol. 6, No. 3, 1958.

Lesourne, Jacques. "The Application of Operational Research to Comparing City Plans." Metra, Vol. 2, No. 4, 1963.

"Optimal Design of a Surface Transit System." New York State Office of Transportation, 1965.

Pessemier, Edgar A. "Measuring of Project Benefits in a Dollar Metric." Unpublished manuscript, Purdue University, August 1966.

"Policies, Standards, and Procedures in the Formulation, Evaluation, and Review for Plans Sources." President's Water Resources Council, U.S. Government Printing Office, 1962.

Ridley, T. M. "An Investment Policy to Reduce the Travel Time in a Transportation Network." Operations Research Center, College of Engineering, University of California, Berkeley, 1966.

"Forecasts and Alternative Plans, 1990." Southeastern Wisconsin Regional Planning Commission, Planning Report No. 7, June, 1966.

Thomas, Edwin N., and Schofer, Joseph L. "Criteria for Evaluating Alternative Transportation Plans." NCHRP Quarterly Progress Report, Transportation Center, Northwestern University, 1965.

Vogt, Robert S. (Vogt-Ivers and Associates). "An Intermediate Report for Project No. 32–Community Goals and Objectives." Louisville Metropolitan Comprehensive Transportation and Development Program, April 1967.

Worrall, R. D. "The Urban Panel as a Longitudinal Data Source." Highway Research Record 194, p. 62-77, 1967.

APPENDIXES

A. STATEMENTS OF COMMUNITY GOALS AND OBJECTIVES

[General community goals (numerals) are subdivided into specific objective statements]

(1) Public Safety Program Development
- (a) Insure safe public facilities.
- (b) Provide for adequate public safety regulations and their enforcement.
- (c) Provide for the removal of contaminants (solid, liquid, and gaseous).

(2) Public Utility and Transportation Development
- (a) Minimize maintenance costs of public facilities.
- (b) Insure maximum effectiveness of public utilities, by design and locational considerations.
- (c) Develop a balanced, effective, and integrated transportation system which provides for the accessibility requirements of each land use.

(3) Economic Development Programs
- (a) Develop public improvement programs within available financial resources.
- (b) Maintain highest equitable property values.
- (c) Insure effective utilization of mineral, vegetation, air, and water resources.
- (d) Establish a strong economic base through commerce that will bring money into the community.
- (e) Establish trade development that provides maximum convenience to consumers.
- (f) Insure the optimal utilization of all land.
- (g) Achieve increased disposable income for all people.

(4) Cultural Development
- (a) Preserve historic sites and areas of natural beauty.
- (b) Promote adequate public libraries, museums, and cultural activities.
- (c) Protect meaningful local tradition and encourage civic pride.

(5) Health Program Development

Establish the mechanism for adequate preventive and remedial health programs and facilities.

(6) Education Program Development

Develop educational facilities and opportunities for citizens at every level.

(7) Welfare Program Development
- (a) Eliminate injustice based on discrimination.
- (b) Develop needed public welfare programs.
- (c) Encourage development of religious opportunities.
- (d) Develop an aesthetically pleasing environment.

(8) Recreation Program Development
  (a) Establish open-space programs.
  (b) Provide adequate recreational facilities utilizing parks, rivers, and lakes.

(9) Political Framework
  (a) Improve the framework (channels, systematic use) for citizen participation in governmental functions.
  (b) Establish equitable taxation policies (bases, mixes, rates).
  (c) Achieve efficient governmental administration, representative of all citizens.
  (d) Develop adequate government staffs and personnel programs (high job standards, reasonable salary ranges, effective delegation of authority).
  (e) Establish sound governmental fiscal programs.
  (f) Develop an effective, long-range, metropolitan-wide planning process.
  (g) Establish effective control mechanisms.

(10) Housing Development
  (a) Encourage rehabilitation and conservation neighborhood programs.
  (b) Provide adequate low-cost housing.
  (c) Develop neighborhood units.
  (d) Promote a wide variety of housing types as required within the community.

B. CRITERIA WEIGHTING TECHNIQUES

This Appendix presents a summary of techniques used in obtaining a weighted hierarchy of community goals and objectives. Fishburn (1966, 1967) lists and classifies 24 methods of estimating utility values. Recent research (see Eckenrode, 1965) has evaluated various methods of collecting the judgments of experts relative to the reliability and efficiency of these methods.

Ranking, rating and two variations of the method of successive comparisons are summarized here.

Ranking Technique

Each member of the various judging panels was asked to place a raw rank by each criterion in the given lists of criteria. The most important criterion was assigned a raw rank of 1, the second most important, a raw rank of 2, etc. Criteria weights, or utility values, are developed as follows.

In general, there will be n criteria in a list of community goals or objectives. A converted rank of n–1 will be assigned to the criterion receiving a raw rank of 1, a converted rank of n–2 to the criterion receiving a raw rank of 2, . . . , and a converted rank of 0 to the criterion receiving a raw rank of n. The composite rank (R_j) for a given objective (j) will be determined by summing the converted ranks of all of the m judges; that is,

$$R_j = \sum_{i=1}^{m} R_{ij}, j = 1, 2, \ldots, n$$

In this expression,

R_j = composite rank of criterion j,
R_{ij} = converted rank of criterion j established by judge i,
n = number of criteria, and
m = number of decision-makers on the panel of judges.

The composite ranks thus determined are then normalized in the following manner:

$$u_j = \frac{R_j}{\sum_{j=1}^{n} R_j}, j = 1, 2, \ldots, n$$

where j = composite weight or utility value associated with community decision criterion j.

Rating Technique

The rating scale technique is the most popular of all procedures used for collecting the judgments of individuals. The numerical type rating scale is used but descriptors are not associated with the integer points on the numerical scale. Appropriate descriptors that would not bias the judges could not be determined.

The lists of criteria to be weighted (i.e., the lists of community goals and objectives) are placed in a column adjacent to a scale marked in units continuously from ten to zero (top to bottom). A rating of zero indicates that there is no value associated with a given criterion and a rating of ten is the highest that may be assigned. Any value along the unbroken continuum may be assigned to any criterion. Even though an approximation will be made of non-integer ratings, the judge was permitted to associate with each criterion an integer or non-integer position on the rating scale. The rating assigned to criterion j by judge i is represented by V_{ij}. Utility values (u_j) or criteria weights for each criterion are determined in the following manner:

$$V_j = \sum_{i=1}^{m} V_{ij} \; j = 1, 2, \ldots, n$$

$$u_j = \frac{V_j}{\sum_{j=1}^{n} V_j} \; j = 1, 2, \ldots, n$$

Method of Successive Comparisons

The following procedures (SC–1) are based on the method of successive comparisons (see Churchman and Ackoff, 1954). The modification of the procedures is as follows:

Step 1 is carried out by placing the criteria in rank order by the utility value determined from the average results of the ranking and rating methods. Step 2 is completed by simply associating with each criterion that average value. The judges then were asked to check the rank order of the criteria as determined by consensus. If the judge agrees, the procedures move to Step 3. If he disagrees, he subjectively reassigns utility values.

Step 1. Rank the criteria according to preference:

$$G_1 \geqslant G_2 \geqslant G_3 \geqslant \ldots \geqslant G_{n-1} \geqslant G_n$$

where $G_1 > G_n$.

Step 2. Tentatively assign the value $u'_1 = 1.00$ to G_1 Then assign preliminary utility measurements u'_j to the remaining criteria in such a manner that u'_j seems to reflect the magnitude of preference for G_j.

Step 3. Compare G_1 vs $G_2 \bigwedge G_3 \bigwedge \ldots \bigwedge G_n$ or G_1 vs $\bigwedge_{j=1}^{n} G_j$

(a) If $G_1 > \bigwedge_{j=2}^{n} G_j$ then, if necessary, adjust u'_1 so that $u'_1 > \sum_{j=2}^{n} u'_j$ and after making this adjustment go to step 4.

(b) If $G_1 - \bigwedge_{j=2}^{n} G_j$ then, if necessary, adjust u'_1 so that $u'_1 = \sum_{j=2}^{n} u'_j$ and after making this adjustment go to step 4.

(c) If $G_1 > \bigwedge_{j=2}^{n} G_j$ then, if necessary, adjust u'_1 so that $u'_1 < \sum_{j=2}^{n} u'_j$. Then repeat step 3 and compare G_1 vs $\bigwedge_{j=2}^{n-1} G_j$; that is, drop the criterion G_n.

Continue dropping the least preferred criterion and comparing until situation 3(a) or 3(b) is encountered. This process must terminate since $G_1 \geqslant G_2$ from step 1.

Step 4. Drop G_1 from consideration and repeat the entire procedure (steps 1 to 3) for G_2. Continue with G_3 and so on until the comparison of G_{n-2} vs

$G_{n-1} \wedge G_n$ is completed. Care should be taken to insure retention of the invariance in u'_1, u'_2, etc. That is, in adjusting values such as u'_2 the relationship $u'_2 > u'_1$ must not be accepted in violation of step 1.

Step 5. The values of u'_j obtained in steps 1 through 4 must now be normalized as follows:

$$u_j = \frac{u'_j}{\sum_{j=1}^{n} u'_j}$$

It is to be noted that the numerical values for u_j are relative, hence the deletion or addition of a criterion G_k, where $u_k \neq 0$, would affect the values calculated.

Successive Comparisons Method: An Alternative Approach

An alternative procedure is proposed by Churchman and Ackoff (1954) when a large number of criteria (7 or more) are to be considered. This alternative procedure may be useful in the specific application of weighting planning criteria. Churchman and Ackoff suggest the following alternative procedures:

Step 1. Rank the entire set of decision criteria on the basis of the average weights obtained by the ranking and rating techniques.

Step 2. Select the highest ranked criterion from the entire set. Let G_s represent this standard criterion. By random assignment, subdivide the criteria that remain into approximately equal-sized goups of no more than 5 criteria per group. Each criterion, other than the standard G_s, should be included in one and only one group.

Step 3. Insert G_s into each group and assign a criteria weight of 1.00 to G_s (i.e., $u'_s = 1.00$).

Step 4. With modifications made above, follow the procedure of steps 1 through 4 of the preceding section to obtain unstandardized criteria weights (utility values) for the objectives in each of the groups formed in step 3 above. (Note: in adjusting the u'_j values, do not change the value of u'_s.)

Step 5. Compare the ranking obtained for all criteria with the ranking of step 1. If the rank orders differ, reconsider the ranking and, if necessary, repeat step 4 of this alternative procedure.

Step 6. When consistent results are obtained, normalize the criteria weights by dividing the value assigned to each criterion by the sum of the values assigned to all criteria. That is,

$$u_j = \frac{u'_j}{\sum_{j=1}^{n} u_j} \quad j = 1, 2, \ldots, n$$

C. WEIGHTED HIERARCHY AND OBJECTIVES

Criteria (see Appendix A for objective statements)	Weighting Techniques							
	Ranking		Rating		Average Values		Range	
	u_j	Rank Order	u_j	Rank Order	u_j	Rank Order	u_j	Rank Order
1a	0.0142	26	0.0270	15	0.0206	17	0.0128	11
1b	0.0505	6	0.0326	11	0.0415	6	0.0179	5
1c	0.0648	3	0.0335	7	0.0496	5	0.0313	4
2a	0.0000	35	0.0280	14	0.0140	31	0.0280	21
2b	0.0611	4	0.0393	4	0.0502	4	0.0218	0
2c	0.0611	5	0.0449	3	0.0530	3	0.0162	2
3a	0.0217	16	0.0192	20	0.0204	19	0.0025	4
3b	0.0031	34	0.0144	31	0.0087	35	0.0113	3
3c	0.0311	9	0.0168	24	0.0239	12	0.0143	15
3d	0.0248	12	0.0192	21	0.0220	16	0.0056	9
3e	0.0155	21	0.0156	26	0.0155	26	0.0001	5
3f	0.0279	10	0.0180	23	0.0229	14	0.0099	13
3g	0.0279	11	0.0168	25	0.0223	15	0.0111	14
4a	0.0089	31	0.0295	12	0.0192	21	0.0206	19
4b	0.0248	13	0.0348	5	0.0298	9	0.0100	8
4c	0.0069	32	0.0250	16	0.0159	25	0.0181	16
5	0.0925	2	0.1050	2	0.0587	2	0.0125	0
6	0.1555	1	0.1272	1	0.1413	1	0.0283	0
7a	0.0173	20	0.0223	17	0.0198	20	0.0050	3
7b	0.0124	27	0.0186	22	0.0155	27	0.0062	5
7c	0.0035	33	0.0141	32	0.0088	34	0.0106	1
7d	0.0111	29	0.0193	18	0.0152	28	0.0082	11
8a	0.0148	24	0.0340	6	0.0244	10	0.0192	18
8b	0.0148	25	0.0327	10	0.0237	13	0.0179	15
9a	0.0206	17	0.0116	35	0.0161	24	0.0090	18
9b	0.0149	22	0.0145	28	0.0147	29	0.0004	6
9c	0.0218	14	0.0145	29	0.0181	22	0.0073	15
9d	0.0103	30	0.0135	33	0.0119	32	0.0032	3
9e	0.0149	23	0.0145	30	0.0147	30	0.0004	7
9f	0.0206	18	0.0154	27	0.0180	23	0.0052	9
9g	0.0114	28	0.0125	34	0.0119	33	0.0011	6
10a	0.0321	8	0.0330	8	0.0325	8	0.0009	0
10b	0.0195	19	0.0285	13	0.0240	11	0.0090	6
10c	0.0218	15	0.0193	19	0.0205	18	0.0025	4
10d	0.0413	7	0.0330	9	0.0371	7	0.0083	2

D. EFFECTIVENESS VALUES

No.	Criterion (objective) Statement	Effectiveness Value		
		Plan 1	Plan 2	Plan 3
1a	Insure safe public facilities.	0.24	0.56	0.82
1b	Provide for adequate public safety regulations and their enforcement	0.32	0.76	0.64
1c	Provide for the removal of contaminants (solid, liquid, gaseous)	0.30	0.44	0.62
2a	Minimize maintenance costs of public facilities	0.44	0.60	0.62
2b	Insure maximum effectiveness of public utilities, by design and locational considerations	0.66	0.70	0.62
2c	Develop a balanced, effective, and integrated transportation system which provides for the accessibility requirements of each land use	0.40	0.62	0.84
3a	Develop public improvement programs within available financial resources	0.72	0.74	0.54
3b	Maintain highest equitable property values	0.58	0.60	0.78
3c	Insure effective utilization of mineral, vegetation, air, and water resources	–	–	–
3d	Establish a strong economic base through commerce that will bring money into the community	0.44	0.76	0.94
3e	Establish trade development that provides maximum convenience to consumers	0.62	0.70	0.72
3f	Insure the optimal utilization of all land	0.62	0.68	0.76
3g	Achieve increased disposable income for all people	0.45	0.80	0.95
4a	Preserve historic sites and areas of natural beauty	0.52	0.60	0.72
4b	Promote adequate public libraries, museums, and cultural activities	0.66	0.66	0.70
4c	Protect meaningful local tradition and encourage civic pride	0.55	0.70	0.85
5	Establish the mechanism for adequate preventive and remedial health programs and facilities	–	–	–
6	Develop educational facilities and opportunities for citizens at every level	0.30	0.70	1.00
7a	Eliminate injustice based on discrimination	0.67	0.53	0.43
7b	Develop needed public welfare programs	–	–	–
7c	Encourage development of religious opportunities	0.30	0.70	1.00
7d	Develop an aesthetically pleasing environment	0.45	0.52	0.68
8a	Establish open-space programs.	0.45	0.65	0.75
8b	Provide adequate recreational facilities utilizing parks, rivers, and lakes	0.70	0.66	0.54

D. Effectiveness Values (continued)

9a	Improve the framework (channels, systematic use) for citizen participation in governmental functions	–	–	–
9b	Establish equitable taxation policies (bases, mixes, rates)	0.68	0.62	0.32
9c	Achieve efficient governmental administration, representative of all citizens	–	–	–
9d	Develop adequate government staffs and personnel programs (high job standards, reasonable salary ranges, effective delegation of authority)	–	–	–
9e	Establish sound governmental fiscal programs	0.67	0.67	0.40
9f	Develop an effective, long-range, metropolitan-wide planning process	0.60	0.68	0.72
9g	Establish effective control mechanisms	–	–	–
10a	Encourage rehabilitation and conservation neighborhood programs	0.70	0.62	0.58
10b	Provide adequate low-cost housing	0.40	0.53	0.80
10c	Develop neighborhood units.	0.64	0.58	0.54
10d	Promote a wide variety of housing types as required within the community	0.42	0.62	0.82

Chapter 12

COMMUNITY IMPACTS, TRADE-OFFS, AND PRIORITIES

J. K. Friend and W. N. Jessop

SECTOR Z AND ITS PROBLEMS

In Chapter 9 [of the book] we focused on the problem of area A, an inner area of our fictitious town which we supposed to be ripe for comprehensive redevelopment. We now turn our attention to sector Z, which we suppose to be a larger and much more heterogeneous area on the opposite side of the same town, extending outwards from the central area to the rural fringe, and posing immediate problems of improvement and new development rather than of total renewal. We will at this point give the town a name–Fluxton–which is intended to be suggestive of any urban community in a state of continuing physical and social change. As in the previous chapter, we will maintain a distinction between "the local planners" (who formulate proposals) and "the policy-makers" (who are publicly accountable for planning decisions), although there is a possibility that these may not represent exactly the same groups of people as for area A, since we are now dealing with a different part of town and perhaps therefore with a different set of problems and of planning perspectives.

The relationship of area A and sector Z to the map of Fluxton we will suppose to be as shown in Map 1.

We will suppose that the local planners are able to divide sector Z into a number of smaller areas, each of which has its own particular characteristics and its own particular problems, as shown in Map 2.

To review the various problems within sector Z, we will start with the older and more central areas and work outwards.

Reprinted from *Local Government and Strategic Choice: An Operational Research Approach to the Processes of Public Planning,* by J. K. Friend and W. N. Jessop, pp. 162-202, 205-206. Published by Tavistock Institute of Human Relations (London) and Sage Publications, Inc.

In area P1, the housing is old and well below current standards, but is still considered to have some useful life before redevelopment. It is becoming increasingly overcrowded, since it serves as a reception area for new immigrants brought to Fluxton by the search for work opportunities. These immigrants may find it difficult to find accommodation in other parts of town, through a combination of several factors–the existing ownership and rent structures, the method of assessing priorities for municipal housing, and possibly a certain amount of discrimination by landlords or others against particular social or ethnic groups. There may be the seeds of many long-term problems in this area, but we will assume that the planners are particularly aware of two particular problems in the shorter term: first, how to provide better play facilities for the

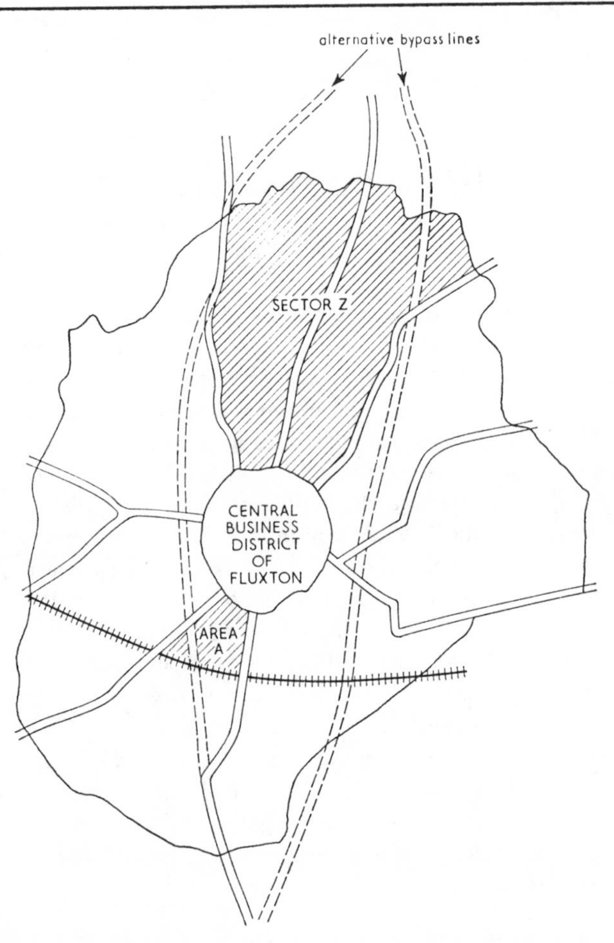

Map 1: OUTLINE MAP OF FLUXTON

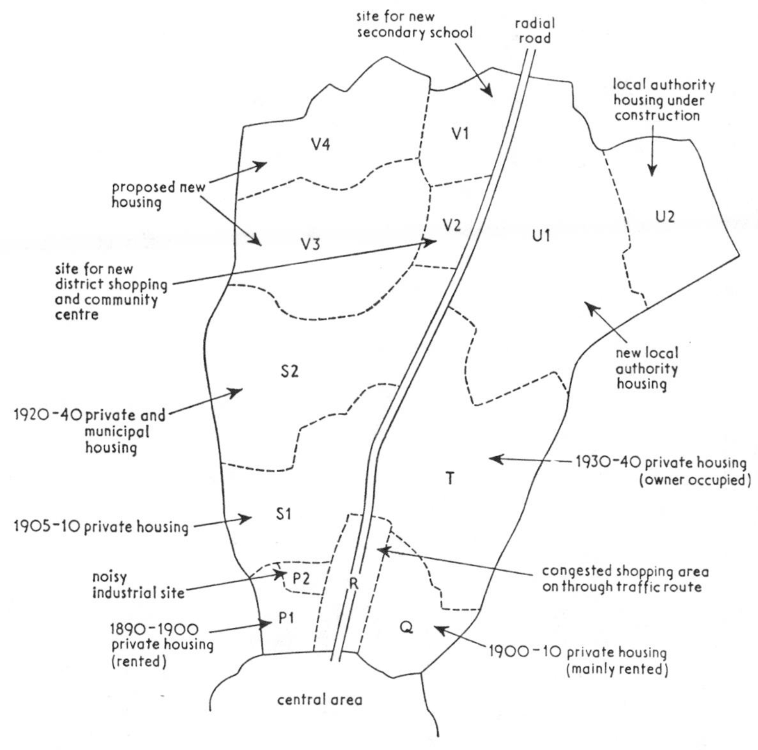

Map 2: FLUXTON: SECTOR Z

residents' children, and, second, whether or not to spend public money on the provision of grants for improvements in standard housing amenities, in the face of uncertainty about how soon the area will be scheduled for comprehensive redevelopment.

Meanwhile, the noisy industrial site at P2 creates a nuisance for the residents of both P1 and S1, and the planners are exerting pressure on the owners to move out to a new industrial estate (whose location is, however, uncertain until a firm line is agreed for the proposed bypass road). Assuming that the site at P2 can be made available for another use in advance of the comprehensive redevelopment of P1, it could provide either a playground for the children of P1 (which is considered by the planners to be socially desirable) or a set of lock-up garages for the residents of S1 (which would be commercially attractive to private developers). There is some possibility that, as a compromise, the site might be divided between these two uses.

The housing in area Q is again sub-standard, though it is not thought to justify wholesale redevelopment within the foreseeable future. The problem here is seen as one of selecting particular sub-areas whose life might be prolonged by

TABLE 1

	Nature of Principal Design Choices	Timing Options, by Year of Program Measured From Current Year as Year 0											
		0	*1*	*2*	*3*	*4*	*5*	*6*	*7*	*8*	*9*	*10*	*Later*
Public development projects in sector Z													
Z1 Housing in U2	None at this stage	•	x	x	x	x	x	x	x	x	x	x	x
Z2 Main drainage for V	Engineering	x	x	•	•	•	•	x	x	x	x	x	x
Z3 Secondary school in V1	Architectural	x	x	x	•	•	•	•	x	x	x	x	x
Z4 Community center in V2	Architectural	x	x	x	x	•	•	•	•	•	x	x	x
Z5 Playground in P2	Land allocation Z5/Z11	x	x	x	x	x	x	•	•	•	•	•	x
Z6 Parking/service area in R	Layout	x	x	x	•	•	•	•	•	x	x	x	x
Z7 Redevelopment of P1	Layout, density, etc.*	x	x	x	x	x	x	x	x	•	•	•	•
Development projects in Z with public/private options													
Z8 Housing in V3	Type, density, layout*	x	x	:	:	:	:	:	x	x	x	x	x
Z9 Housing in V4	Type, density, layout*	x	x	x	x	x	:	:	:	:	x	x	x
Z10 Shopping center in V2	Floor space, layout	x	x	x	x	:	:	:	:	x	x	x	x
Z11 Garages in P2	Land allocation, layout	x	x	x	x	x	x	:	:	:	:	x	x
Other intended actions in sector Z													
Z12 Waiting restrictions in R	Legal*	x	x	x	x	•	•	•	•	•	x	x	x
Z13 Works relocation from P2	Contractual	x	x	x	x	x	•	•	•	•	•	x	x
Z14 Improvements in P1	Areas for allocation of standard improvement grants*												
Z15 Improvements in Q	Areas for discretionary grants and environmental improvement*												
Related actions beyond sector Z: developmental													
Y1 Various housing projects	Type and density*	x	x	•	•	•	•	•	•	•	•	•	•
Y2 Other secondary schools	Location, catchments*	x	x	x	•	•	•	•	•	•	x	x	x
Y3 Industrial estate project	Location*	x	x	x	x	•	•	•	•	•	•	x	x
Y4 Bypass road	Route*	x	x	x	x	•	•	•	•	•	x	x	x
Related actions beyond sector Z: nondevelopmental													
Y5 Housing allocation system	Priority rules for allocation of municipal tenancies*												
Y6 Housing rent structure	General rent levels and system of differentiation*												
Y7 Resource procurement–money	Level of local taxation for next financial year*												
Y8 Resource procurement–staff	Reinforcement of engineering design resources by recruitment or contracting out*												

Key: x = not conceivable that implementation by local authority could start during year shown.
• = implementation could under certain circumstances start during year shown.
: = implementation could start during year shown *if* public development option is chosen.
* = highly significant design options.

the application of more comprehensive improvement policies, both in relation to the houses themselves and also in relation to their immediate environment.

The shopping area at R has a serious environmental problem: it straddles a main through traffic route and there is constant interference between through traffic, local traffic, stationary vehicles, and pedestrians. Present regulations permit loading and short-term waiting in the main road, and it will not be easy to justify any more restrictive policies in the immediate future. One way of relieving traffic congestion would be for the local authority to promote, at its own expense, a scheme for rear servicing and off-street parking facilities, but even this would involve difficult land-acquisition problems. In the long term, hopes are centered on the elimination of through traffic when the bypass is built, together with the creation of a second shopping center for sector Z at V2, farther out from the town center.

We will suppose that there are few immediate problems in areas S and T, apart from the difficulty we have already referred to of finding garage space for the car owners of S1. The only difficulty in area U is the remoteness of the existing shopping facilities at R and of the nearest secondary school. It is planned that these deficiencies will be met through the building of a new local authority secondary school at V1, and of the new district shopping center at V2, with an adjoining community center including library, youth, clinic, and old peoples' facilities. It is considered that the shopping center might be developed either by the local authority itself or through a private agency, although the latter option might carry with it a less immediate prospect of implementation and hence an unnecessary prolongation of the current congestion problem in area R.

Areas V3 and V4 we suppose to be earmarked for housing development, although it is still uncertain whether the housing should be municipal or private. There are no serious problems of land acquisition, but there is a problem of inadequate main drainage capacity for the residential development of this area. The ability to proceed with a main drainage extension scheme in the immediate future is, however, dependent on the ability of the local authority engineer's department to marshal sufficient resources of skilled survey and design staff: this is limited both by difficulty in recruiting engineers of the necessary caliber and by the many competing claims on the services of private design consultants.

The case of sector Z differs from that of area A in that there are at this point of time few unresolved choices of land allocation, the principal exception relating to area P2. There may, however, be many options of priority and of design for specific development projects. We will now consider the more important of these options, and the relationships between them, in a rather more systematic way.

THE OPTIONS OF TIMING AND DESIGN

As a first basis for the more systematic study of the problems of sector Z, Table 1 itemizes the various possibilities for future development within the sector, each with a separate project reference number. The table then goes on to discuss other possible fields of action in sector Z which are not directly concerned with development of land, and concludes with a listing of certain activities beyond the sector boundary which are seen to have a close bearing on decisions within the sector itself.

Under the existing system of local government in Great Britain, it may be noted that responsibility for the various public development projects listed in this table might in practice be divided between different tiers of the local government system, depending on whether or not the population of Fluxton is sufficiently large for the town to have been designated as a County Borough. For the purposes of this case example, we will suppose that, even if a two-tier structure of local government applies in Fluxton, there is a sufficient degree of co-ordination between tiers for our identification of a single group of "local planners" and a corresponding group of "policy-makers" to be as meaningful as in the earlier case example.

For each possible action listed in Table 1–whether it concerns physical development, or the procurement of additional resources, or the application of certain inducements or constraints to the actions of others–we have attempted to specify the nature of the principal design choices which face the local planners. Here we use the word "design" in the broad sense to include only the design of buildings and engineering works but also, for instance, the design of coherent systems of local waiting restrictions or rules for allocation of municipal tenancies. Those design choices which are at this point in time considered particularly crucial for the future of sector Z are marked with an asterisk.

For those actions, developmental and other, where important questions of timing arise, Table 1 also indicates the range of alternative years in which implementation might reasonably be programmed to start, subject perhaps to certain qualifying conditions in each case (we will consider these later). For instance, the entry for project Z3, relating to the building of a secondary school in V1, indicates a belief that its physical implementation must be programmed to start in some year between year 3 and year 6; any year earlier than year 3 is excluded because it is considered that it would be technically impossible to complete the preliminary site acquisition, design, and tendering procedures in less than three years under any conceivable conditions, and any year later than year 6 is excluded because it is considered politically inconceivable–in view of the social pressures for more secondary school places–that the project could in any circumstances be deferred beyond that date. The implementation of project Z1, on the other hand, is due to begin at any time and no option needs to be considered other than year 0, because the project is so far advanced that it is impossible to imagine that a start on construction work might under any conditions be deferred beyond the current financial year.

We have not attempted in Table 1 to suggest what *specific* design options might be available, even for the more significant design problems marked with an asterisk. Clearly, in some of these cases a good deal of preliminary work might be necessary before a sufficient range of feasible alternatives can be formulated.

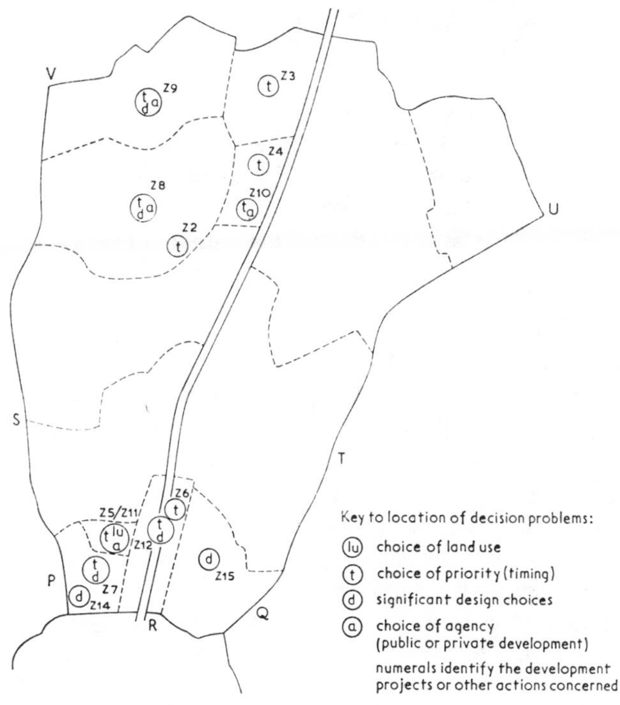

Map 3: SECTOR Z: LOCATION OF DECISION PROBLEMS

In Map 3, we use an outline map of sector Z to pick out the approximate locations where some kind of localized discretion is now seen to arise. Different types of symbol are used to indicate projects and other intended actions for which significant choices of priority and of design have been identified, accompanied in some case by choices of agency and of land use. As is typical in urban planning situations, there is a marked clustering of problems in the inner "twilight" zones, on the one hand, and in the peripheral areas of new development, on the other.

A CLOSER LOOK AT THE CHOICES IN AREA V

Even assuming that a sufficient range of design options can at this stage be formulated for each scheme in Table 1, it is not likely to be easy to enumerate all the relationships between the various different choices of priority and design over sector Z as a whole. The planners might therefore decide to focus initially on those choices which particularly concern area V, which is the part of sector Z where most of the early development will take place and where most of the more immediate timing options arise. Later in this chapter, we shall return to take another look at the problems of area V within the wider perspective of sector Z as a whole, with particular reference to the longer-term problem of the future of the "twilight" areas P, Q, and R.

In looking at area V, we will suppose that the planners decide not to spend any time exploring different design options for the two housing projects (they may have a strong conviction that one particular type of layout should be adopted), nor do they wish to consider development of these estates through a private agency, except in certain exceptional circumstances (because there is a strong unfulfilled demand for municipal housing). For the time being, they may consider that their most crucial choices concern the relative *priorities* of the various development projects which are being considered within area V.

Map 3 shows that there are in all six projects within area V where choices of priority are seen to arise: these are the mains drainage project (Z2), the secondary school project (Z3), the community center project (Z4), the two housing projects (Z8 and Z9), and the shopping center project (Z10). We will suppose that the drainage project (which is a necessary preliminary to housing development in area V) happens to be a very expensive one because of the nature of the terrain, and that its timing is believed to be critically dependent on a reinforcement of the Council's resources of skilled engineering design staff. Also, we will suppose that the accounting structure of municipal housing is such that any public investment in new housing development must be supported mainly through income from the rents of existing tenants. Accordingly, in considering the six choices of project priority within area V, it is believed essential at the same time to consider the range of choices available in the two related fields of housing rent structure and design staff procurement (identified in Table 1 as Y6 and Y8 respectively).

We have therefore now identified a total of eight decision areas relating directly or indirectly to the problem of priorities within area V, and we can proceed to explore the relationships between them in rather more detail. The task of drawing up a complete option graph will be more difficult than in the earlier case study of area A, in that there are more options to consider in each decision area and potentially many more "option bars" between them. As a first step, we will draw up an outline option graph in which the various decision areas and options are all specified in full, but the relationships between decision areas are only shown in outline form: the parts of the graph where such relationships are believed to exist are indicated by the drawing of dotted lines or *links* between particular pairs of decision areas. Each link implies a belief that certain particular combinations of options from the decision areas concerned may either be incompatible or have certain joint effects over and above the effects of either option considered independently.

The outline option graph for the eight decision areas we have now picked out is shown in Figure 1.

The reference number inside each decision area relates to the corresponding reference in Table 3, with the suffixes t and d standing for choices of timing and

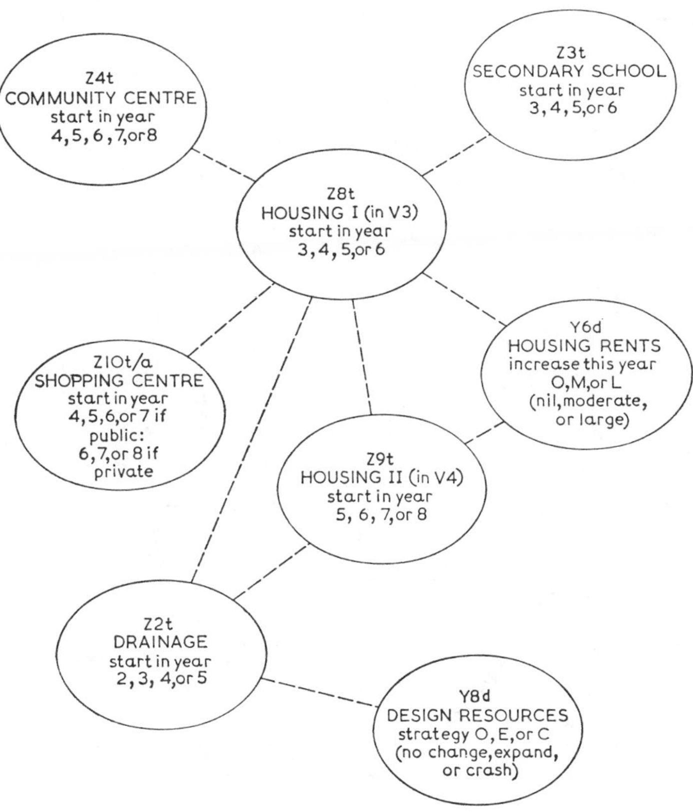

Figure 1.

design respectively. Decision area Z10t/a embraces a joint choice of timing and of development agency for the shopping center, since both public and private development are being considered and it is believed that the range of possible starting years will differ in each case; the development is not likely to be attractive commercially for at least five years, although the local authority might possibly be prepared to develop it early and let it initially at subsidized rentals in order to achieve the social benefit of relieving congestion in the existing shopping area at R.

Within each of the six decision areas which relate to a specific project, Figure 1 indicates the range of possible years in which physical work might reasonably be programmed to start. In the decision area relating to housing rents, it is supposed that only three options are currently under consideration: no increase at all in rents in the current year, a moderate increase, and a large increase. These options may correspond simply to alternative flat-rate increases in the general level of rents, say 0%, 20%, and 40%. Alternatively, their specification might be more complex; for instance, the larger increase might be accompanied by special measures to provide relief for tenants in lower income groups. For the procurement of extra design resources, the planners might again be able to identify three alternatives which we call the nil, expansion, and crash strategies respectively. The expansion strategy might consist of a new recruiting drive for engineers within the local authority itself, while the crash strategy might require extensive contracting out of design work to outside consultants.

THE MEANING OF THE LINKS

In order to translate the outline option graph into a full option graph, it is necessary to look more closely into the practical significance of each of the nine links shown in Figure 1. We will suppose that a close scrutiny of the problem brings out the following specific interpretations:

Secondary School/Housing I. The secondary school project cannot be started more than a year before housing project I is started (because the national education authority is giving priority to "roofs over heads" and is not expected to include the school in its school building programme without some evidence that new housing is on the way).

Housing I/Housing II. Housing project II cannot be started earlier than two years after the start of housing project I (because there are physical reasons for developing in V3 before V4, and because a local shortage of certain resources for construction demands at least a two-year phasing between them).

Housing I/Drainage. The drainage scheme for V must be started at least a year before housing project I (because the houses cannot be occupied until the main drainage is complete).

Housing II/Drainage. The drainage scheme for V must be started at least a year before housing project II (for the same reason as with housing project I).

Shopping Center/Housing I. Private developers could not be expected to start on a shopping scheme in V2 unless housing scheme I had been started at least a year earlier (because they would not expect it to give an adequate return on investment).

Community Center Housing I. There is a free choice of year for the community center, but the benefit it brings initially will depend to some degree on how many houses have been built under housing project I.

Housing Rents/Housing I. Housing scheme I cannot be started before year 7 unless there is at least a moderate rent increase now (for the same reason as with housing project I).

Design Resources/Drainage. The drainage scheme for V cannot be started earlier than year 5 without at least an "expansion" strategy for reinforcing existing resouces of engineering design staff; it cannot start earlier than year 3 without a "crash" strategy.

A SEQUENTIAL NETWORK CHART FOR AREA V

Now that we have considered the significance of the various links, we can see that many (though not all) of them represent relationships of sequence between

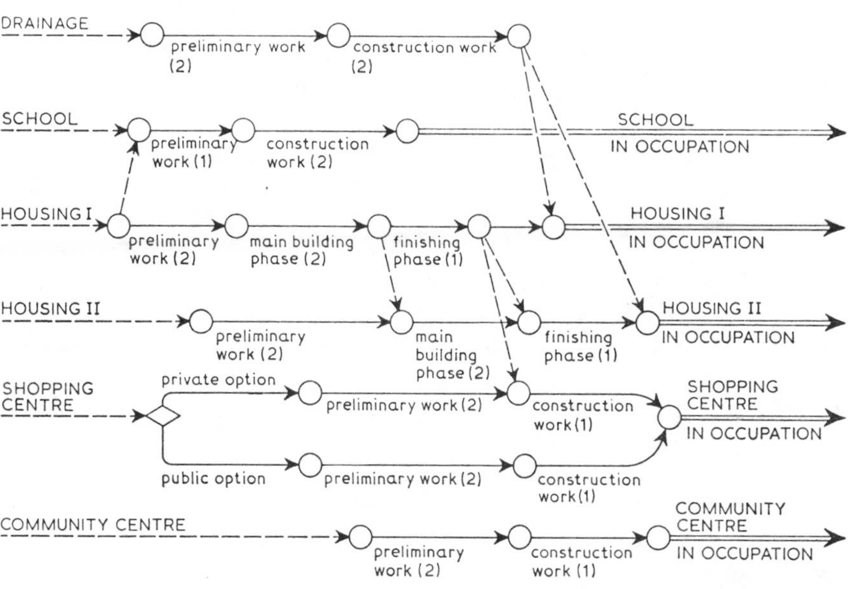

Figure 2.

different projects. We can obtain an idea of their overall effect by drawing up a sequential network diagram for area V, of the type now often used for critical path analysis of individual projects[1]. Without going into too much detail on the individual projects in this case, the necessary sequence of activities might be seen broadly as shown in Figure 2.

In this diagram, the figures in brackets for each main activity represent expected (and very approximate) activity times measured in years. The initial "activity" marked by a broken horizontal line for each project represents a possible delay before a decision to proceed with preliminary work is taken.

Figure 2, while drawn according to the conventions of critical path analysis, indicates that the problem is not one which can be tackled through the search for a single "critical path" to represent the fastest possible way of achieving the program as a whole. Each project (except the drainage scheme for the new housing developments) can function independently as soon as it is completed, and can bring corresponding social benefits from that point on; there is no single end-point in the program to which it is clear that all effort should be directed. The picture presented by the sequential network diagram is also limited by the fact that it does not show the influence on the program of the external choices concerned with housing rents and design resources. Despite these limitations, it gives a useful view of the pattern of sequential relationships linking one project to another in this particular area.

THE COMPATIBILITY OF OPTIONS

The planners have by now carried out sufficient investigation of the relationships within area V to allow many of the links between decision areas to be defined more specifically in terms of "option bars," such as were used in our earlier case example to represent incompatibilities between particular pairs of options. For instance, the proviso that a physical start on the school project cannot be realistically programmed more than one year ahead of a start on the first housing project can be represented as in Figure 3.

It is possible in the same way to replace every other dotted line in the outline option graph of Figure 1 by a set of specific option bars, so that eventually a complete option graph can be built up. However, we will find it more convenient in this example to express the various option bars not by lines on a graph (there would be too many) but by a series of separate "option bar tables" for particular pairs of decision areas as shown in Table 2.

Each block of Table 2 corresponds directly to a particular link in Figure 1, and the first block in fact conveys exactly the same information about compatibility and incompatibility of options as does Figure 3. There is, however, one of the nine blocks—that concerning the linkage between the community center and the first housing project—which includes no incompatibilities at all; it is only included here because of the earlier supposition that the degree of benefit obtained from the community center will be dependent on the relationship between its timing and the timing of the first housing project. This is a case where the linkage between decision areas stands for a relationship of value rather than of incompatibility: and we will return to consider how it may be dealt with at a later stage of the analysis.

A logical analysis of certain of the option bar tables might show that some of the information in them is in fact redundant: for instance, the single incompatibility shown in table (d) (housing II/drainage) is already implicit in tables (b) and (c) (housing I/dranage and housing I/housing II) considered together: if the drainage is deferred to year 5, the first housing scheme must

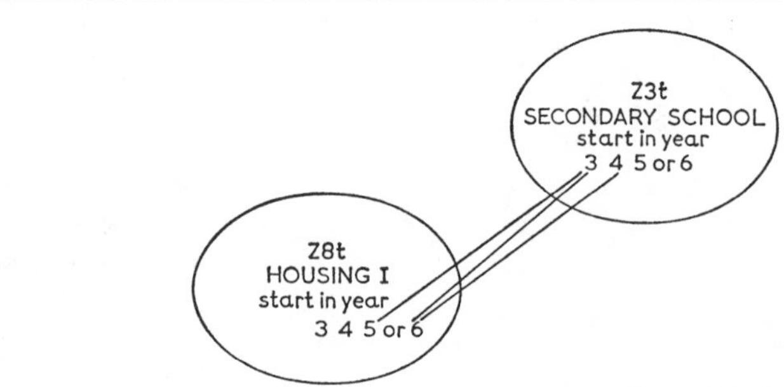

Figure 3.

then be deferred to year 6, which means that the second housing scheme cannot be started until year 8 whatever happens.

It is interesting to detect this kind of redundancy in the option bar tables, but not essential so far as the analysis is concerned. What is more important is to detect whether the combined effect of all the option bars is in fact so restrictive as to leave so feasible solutions to the problem as a whole, necessitating a

TABLE 2

Housing I Year	*Secondary School* Year 3	4	5	6
3	•	•	•	•
4	•	•	•	•
5	x	•	•	•
6	x	x	•	•

Housing I Year	*Housing II* Year 5	6	7	8
3	•	•	•	•
4	x	•	•	•
5	x	x	•	•
6	x	x	x	•

(c)

Housing I Year	*Drainage* Year 2	3	4	5
3	•	x	x	x
4	•	•	x	x
5	•	•	•	x
6	•	•	•	•

(d)

Housing II Year	*Drainage* Year 2	3	4	5
5	•	•	•	x
6	•	•	•	•
7	•	•	•	•
8	•	•	•	•

(e)

	Shopping Center Year						
	Public				*Private*		
Housing I Year	4	5	6	7	6'	7'	8'
3	•	•	•	•	•	•	•
4	•	•	•	•	•	•	•
5	•	•	•	•	x	•	•
6	•	•	•	•	x	x	•

(f)

Housing I Year	*Community Center* Year 4	5	6	7	8
3	•	•	•	•	•
4	•	•	•	•	•
5	•	•	•	•	•

(g)

Housing rents Increase	*Housing I* Year 3	4	5	6
O	x	x	x	•
M	x	•	•	•
L	•	•	•	•

(h)

Housing rents Increase	*Housing II* Year 5	6	7	8
O	x	x	•	•
M	•	•	•	•
L	•	•	•	•

(i)

Design resources Strategy	*Drainage* Year 2	3	4	5
O	x	x	x	•
E	x	•	•	•
C	•	•	•	•

Key: x = option bar
• = feasible combination
O = nil (no change)
M = moderate
L = large
E = expansion
C = crash

reformulation of the original brief. But, as we shall see, the number of feasible solutions in fact turns out to be very large, even when all the constraints have been taken into account, and the problem in this case example lies not so much in the paucity of choice as in its variety.

SOLUTIONS TO THE PROBLEM OF AREA V

If there had been no restrictions to the freedom to combine options from different decision areas, then we could have worked out the number of possible solutions to the problem of area V by multiplying together the number of options in each decision area, as shown in Table 3.

Of these 80,640 possible solutions, only 6,080 in fact remain when the various option bars shown in Table 2 are taken into account. The derivation of this latter figure requires logic and tenacity rather than any acquired mathematical skill: one way of obtaining it is to start with any one of the decision areas in Figure 1—preferably Z8t, relating to the timing of Housing I, because it has more connecting links than any of the others—and to fix for the time being the initial option of year 3. Then, by working methodically through the various links of the diagram, it is possible to eliminate certain options in other decision areas as being ruled out by the option bars of Table 2, and to arrive at a total of 560 solutions involving the particular option of year 3 for the first housing project. The solutions permitted by this initial option are as set out in Figure 4.

In the same way, it is possible to show that the particular options of years 4, 5, and 6 for the first housing project allow 2,520, 1,800, and 1,200 solutions repectively, giving a total of 6,080 solutions altogether.

Because we have assumed that there are no incompatibilities between any option for the timing of the community center (Z4t) and any option in any of the other decision areas, we can simplify the problem to some extent by dividing the total of 6,080 solutions into five sets of 1,216 each, each set being identical apart from its association with one particular option in Z4t. In other words, the

TABLE 3

	Decision Area	*Number of Options*
Z2t	Drainage priority	4
Z3t	Secondary school priority	x4
Z4t	Community center priority	x5
Z8t	Housing I priority	x4
Z9t	Housing II priority	x4
Z10t/a	Shopping center priority/agency	x7
Y6d	Housing rent increase	x3
Y8d	Design resources strategy	x3
		= 80,640 solutions

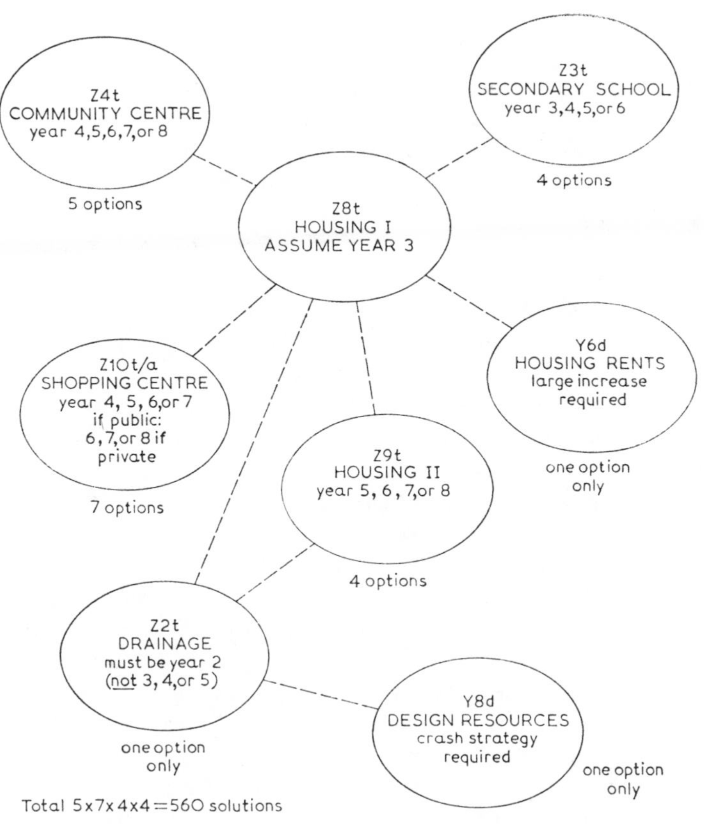

Figure 4.

list of "basic" solutions can be cut down to 1,216 by excluding consideration of the community center problem at all for the time being.

In the case example of the previous chapter, it was found that the number of feasible solutions at no time exceeded seven, so that it was not difficult to proceed on the basis of statements of preference or indifference between them. However, in the present case example, the number of feasible solutions is clearly a good deal too large for the planners to handle in this way, and they will have to look for some means of reducing the problem to more tractable proportions. Perhaps the most obvious way of sifting out the more promising of the 1,216 possible solutions is through a more explicit *measurement* of what the various consequences of each solution are expected to be, and so the question now arises: what yardsticks should the planners choose as a means of selecting the more promising solutions for closer scrutiny and discussion with the policy-makers?

THE MEASUREMENT OF EFFECTS

The effects of any particular choice of solution for the problem of area V will be felt by many different kinds of people—by local residents, by school children, by families now on the waiting-list for municipal housing, by tenants in all parts of town whose rents may be increased, and by payers of local or national taxes. Initially, the planners may decide to estimate only certain direct effects associated with the particular decision areas being considered; for instance, the direct effect of alternative priorities for the secondary school project on schoolchildren and on local taxpayers, and the direct effect of alternative levels of rent increase on the existing tenants of existing municipal dwellings. Later, we will introduce the possibility that the planners might also wish to estimate certain joint effects associated with particular combinations of decision areas; for instance, they might feel that the benefit to be derived from early completion of the shopping center would depend on how much progress had by then been made on the adjacent housing developments.

At this stage, however, our first step will be to draw up a table of expected effects (beneficial or otherwise) associated with choice of particular options within individual decision areas. This we do in Table 4.

Table 4 sets out, in separate columns, a set of estimates of the direct effects of selecting particular options for six different classes of people: local taxpayers (known as ratepayers in the United Kingdom), national taxpayers, existing municipal tenants, prospective tenants of new houses, local schoolchildren, and local shoppers. Each column in Table 4 therefore requires its own specific unit of measurement, whose definition must be given careful consideration.

For each of these units, what matters is not so much the ability to estimate future effects in any absolute sense, as the ability to estimate the relative effects of choosing different options within the same decision area. In order to be consistent, we have in Table 4 adopted the same convention for each of the six scales of measurement: the most beneficial option in each relevant decision area is taken as a reference point and given the value zero, so that any non-zero entry represents a measure of the *penalty,* if any, of choosing some other option in the particular decision area concerned. In other words, the larger the numbers appearing in any column for a given option, the less beneficial that option will be from the point of view of that sector of the community. The specific units of measurement used in each of the six columns we will define as follows:

(1) Effect on local taxpayers (ratepayers). One ratepayer effect unit (eu_r for short) represents the total effect on local taxpayers of applying a unit increment to the existing rate of local taxation for the duration of one year. For instance, under the rating system which at present applies in Great Britain, this unit increment might be taken as the equivalent of one-tenth of a "penny rate." In practical terms, such an increment would mean that the occupier of a house of rateable value £50 would pay an extra 5d. a year, while the occupier of a house of rateable value £100 would pay an extra 10d. a year.

In this exercise we assume that, as is normal practice in British local government, the financing of each public development project is effected

TABLE 4

		Sector of Community Affected					
		Local Taxpayers	National Taxpayers	Existing Tenants	Prospective Tenants	School-children	Local Shoppers
		Unit (explained in text)					
		eu_r	eu_n	eu_t	eu_p	eu_c	eu_s
Decision Area	*Options*	*Estimated Effect (direct)*					
Priority of drainage scheme (Z2t)							
(to serve area V)	2	300	0	0	0	0	0
Year of start on	3	200	0	0	0	0	0
construction	4	100	0	0	0	0	0
	5	0	0	0	0	0	0
Priority of new secondary school (Z3t)							
(for 600 children)	3	90	0	0	0	0	0
Year of start on	4	60	0	0	0	600	0
construction	5	30	0	0	0	1,200	0
	6	0	0	0	0	1,800	0
Priority of housing scheme I (Z8t)							
(for 500 families)	3	0	75	0	0	0	0
Year of start on	4	0	50	0	500	0	0
construction	5	0	25	0	1,000	0	0
	6	0	0	0	1,500	0	0
Priority of housing scheme II (Z9t)							
(for 300 families)	5	0	45	0	0	0	0
Year of start on	6	0	30	0	300	0	0
construction	7	0	15	0	600	0	0
	8	0	0	0	900	0	0
Priority and agency of shopping development (Z10t/a)							
(to serve 2,000 families)	4 (public)	90	0	0	0	0	0
Year of start on	5 (public)	75	0	0	0	0	2,000
construction	6 (public)	60	0	0	0	0	4,000
	7 (public)	45	0	0	0	0	6,000
	6′ (private)	0	0	0	0	0	4,000
	7′ (private)	0	0	0	0	0	6,000
	8′ (private)	0	0	0	0	0	8,000
Housing rents (Y6d)							
(for 3,000 existing	O (nil)	0	0	0	0	0	0
tenants) Size of	M (moderate)	0	0	3,000	0	0	0
increase this year	L (large)	0	0	6,000	0	0	0
Design resources (Y8d)	O (no change)	0	0	0	0	0	0
Strategy for expanding	E (expansion)	40	0	0	0	0	0
engineering design resources:	C (crash)	120	0	0	0	0	0

through a capital loan over some period which is fixed by statute, so that each year by which a project is brought forward in the program penalizes the local taxpayers by a number of ratepayer effect units equivalent to the annual servicing cost of this loan, together perhaps with certain associated running costs for the development concerned. Not all of these costs would begin to come into operation in the same year, but it is a reasonable assumption that the bringing forward of a project by a whole year would make a marginal impact on the local taxpayer equivalent to the loan and running costs over a complete year after the development becomes operative. The corresponding reduction of the burden on future local taxpayers after the completion of the loan period is likely to be given much less weight by the planners and policy-makers, and we will ignore it at this stage of the analysis.

In Table 4, we have supposed the annual loan and running costs to be equivalent to 100 eu_r a year in the case of the drainage scheme, and 30 eu_r a year in the case of the school scheme; this means that, on our earlier assumption that one eu_r corresponds to an annual rate charge of one-tenth of a penny per pound, the ratepayers with the house of rateable value £50 would in effect be paying an extra £2 approximately for every year the drainage scheme is brought forward in relation to its latest possible starting-time (assumed to be year 5), and an extra 12s. 6d. for every year the school project is brought forward in relation to year 6. Also, Table 4 shows that he is affected in some degree by the choice of strategy for engineering design resources, and the choice of year for the shopping project if it is to be developed publicly. He is not affected directly by the choice of year for either housing project, on the assumption that the allocation from the rate fund to the housing account is fixed at an agreed annual sum irrespective of the state of either account.

(2) *Effect on national taxpayers.* One national taxpayer effect unit (eu_n for short) represents the effect of applying some national increment to the existing level of national taxation for the duration of one year. We suppose in Table 4 that the only choices which carry direct implications for the national taxpayer are those concerned with the two housing projects, since each of them carries a direct subsidy from the national housing budget at a fixed annual rate per house built. We have supposed in Table 4 that the two projects include 500 and 300 houses respectively, each house attracting an annual subsidy of .05 eu_n. Whatever the "national taxpayer effect unit" represents in money terms, its effect on any individual taxpayer in the country at large will clearly be extremely marginal, although the cumulative impact of all local authority housing schemes may be quite large.

(3) *Effect on existing municipal tenants in Fluxton.* One existing tenant effect unit (eu_t for short) represents a given percentage increment (say 20 per cent) in the rents of municipal housing, assumed to apply to all existing local authority tenants as from the beginning of the next financial year, and to remain in force for some agreed period of years under a cyclic review procedure. In Table 4, we have supposed that there are 3,000 such tenants in Fluxton, that the "moderate" increase represents a 20% rise and the "large" increment a 40% one, and that all tenants are affected equally. Of course, at some stage the local council might wish to consider a scheme which involved discrimination between tenants according to income; it might then be necessary to adopt two or more different units to differentiate between one category of tenant and another. We will not however consider this complication for the time being.

(4) *Effect on prospective municipal tenants in Fluxton.* One prospective tenant effect unit (eu_p for short) represents a delay of one year in providing a new home for one family at present on the waiting-list for municipal housing: the assumption is, of course, that the new house will be in some way more beneficial to the family than their present accommodation, what ever this may be. It is important to note that this measure makes the simplifying assumption that the benefit of moving to a new home is of equal magnitude for each family likely to be affected, whatever their present circumstances.

(5) *Effect on schoolchildren in sector Z.* One schoolchildren's effect unit (eu_c for short) represents a delay of one year in improving the school environment of one child of secondary school age residing within the proposed catchment area of the new school, which might cover most of the outer zones of sector Z. For every

year by which the new school is delayed, it is assumed that these children will then have to continue for one more year to attend an existing school which is less beneficial in some way; perhaps because it is more distant, or because it is overcrowded, or because it has inferior facilities.

(6) *Effect on shoppers in sector Z.* One shoppers' effect unit (eu_s for short) represents a delay of one year in improving the shopping opportunities of one family residing within reasonable reach of the proposed new shopping center in area V2, i.e. anywhere in the outer zones of sector Z. In Table 4, it is assumed that there are 2000 such families; at this stage of the analysis we will ignore the complication that the number of such families will grow as the two new housing estates in area V become occupied.

Each of these measures has required careful definition, since the choices to be considered in area V affect a large number of different people in their many different roles as local and national taxpayers, actual and would-be tenants, schoolchildren (and their parents), and shoppers. The underlying problem is not simply to estimate total costs or to count up total numbers of houses or school places, but rather to develop working measures to represent, however crudely, a reality compounded of large numbers of different types of disburbance to the affairs of particular people who interact within a complex social system. The estimates given in Table 4 represent only a first step in this direction, but they will suffice for the time being.

MINIMUM TAX SOLUTIONS FOR THE PROBLEM OF AREA V

For each option in each of the seven decision areas which the planners are at present considering, they now have an estimate of impact on each of six different (but overlapping) sectors of the community. They have also discovered that the options concerned can be combined in various different ways to give a choice between 1,216 feasible solutions to the problem of priorities in area V as a whole.

The next step is to explore how the range of alternative solutions might be narrowed down by reference to the six effect measures established so far. An obvious starting-point might be to look at those solutions which impose as small a burden as possible on the local taxpayer. This would involve some tedious calculations if done by hand; given access to an electronic computer, however, it is not difficult to obtain a list of the first ten, or fifty, or hundred solutions selected according to the single criterion of minimizing the local tax burden. Such a list would start as shown in Table 5.

In this list, the computer has worked out the total value of each effect measure for each of the top twelve solutions by simply adding together the corresponding measures for each option included within that solution. For instance, the entry in the eu_p column (effect on prospective tenants) depends on the pair of options selected for the priority of the two housing schemes. Solution 1 involves a three year deferment from the earliest possible year both for scheme I, involving 500 prospective tenants, and for scheme II, involving 300

TABLE 5

	Decision Areas							Sectors of Community Affected					
	Drainage	*School*	*Housing I*	*Housing II*	*Shopping*	*Rents*	*Designers*	*Local Taxpayers*	*National Taxpayers*	*Existing Tenants*	*Prospective Tenants*	*School-children*	*Local Shoppers*
Solution No.	*Options**							*Effect Measures†* eu_r	eu_n	eu_t	eu_p	eu_c	eu_s
1	5	6	6	8	8′	O	O	0	0	0	2,400	1,800	8,000
2	5	6	6	8	8′	M	O	0	0	3,000	2,400	1,800	8,000
3	5	6	6	8	8′	L	O	0	0	6,000	2,400	1,800	8,000
4	5	5	6	8	8′	O	O	30	0	0	2,400	1,200	8,000
5	5	5	6	8	8′	M	O	30	0	3,000	2,400	1,200	8,000
6	5	5	6	8	8′	L	O	30	0	6,000	2,400	1,200	8,000
7	5	6	6	8	8′	O	E	40	0	0	2,400	1,800	8,000
8	5	6	6	8	8′	M	E	40	0	3,000	2,400	1,800	8,000
9	5	6	6	8	8′	L	E	40	0	6,000	2,400	1,800	8,000
10	5	6	6	8	7	O	O	45	0	0	2,400	1,800	6,000
11	5	6	6	8	7	M	O	45	0	3,000	2,400	1,800	6,000
12	5	6	6	8	7	L	O	45	0	6,000	2,400	1,800	6,000
–	–	–	–	–	–	–	–	–	–	–	–	–	–
–	–	–	–	–	–	–	–	–	–	–	–	–	–

*as defined in Table 4.
†units defined in the text, above.

further prospective tenants, giving a total penalty of 3 x 500 + 3 x 300 = 2400 eu_p. The entry in the eu_r column (effect on local taxpayers) may be affected, as Table 4 shows, by the options selected for four different decision areas, concerning the priorities of the drainage, school, and shopping schemes and the strategy for design resources. It will be noticed that each of the first three solutions in the list has a zero entry in the column for eu_r, because each selects the most favorable set of options in the four decision areas which directly concern the local taxpayer. Of course, this does not mean the local taxpayer will pay nothing at all towards the drainage and school projects or towards the cost of engineering design work: it simply means the burden on local taxpayers is at a minimum level within the range of options allowed in the initial formulation of the problem.

THE IDENTIFICATION OF LEADING SOLUTIONS

Looking down the "local taxpayer" column of Table 5, it will be noticed that the solutions tend to fall into groups of three in ascending order of their effect on the local taxpayers. It will also be seen that each successive group of three solutions is in fact identical apart from its association with a different option for the level of the rent increase (nil, moderate, or large), a choice which has been assumed to have no direct impact other than on the 3,000 existing municipal tenants within the town. It appears that, at any rate among these first few solutions in the full list of 1,216, the choice of a rent level for existing tenants in the town as a whole is not relevant to the problem of priorities in area V. For our present purposes, we need therefore to make comparisons only between certain "clusters" of related solutions such as (1, 2, 3), (4, 5, 6) and (7, 8, 9); and in order to do this, we will represent each such group of solutions by a *leading solution* which is at first sight preferable to the others because it imposes a minimum burden on existing tenants. The leading solutions in the first three groups mentioned above can be seen to be solutions 1, 4, and 7 respectively. It is important to note that the remaining solutions in each group will not necessarily be ruled out in the final analysis; it is simply that, if a case is to be made out for the rent increases which they imply, it will have to rest on other considerations which are external to our present limited problem of priorities within area V.

The picking-out of leading solutions enables the full list of solutions to be set out in a rather more compact form. This is shown in Table 6, where the list of all solutions with an effect on local taypayers of 150 eu_r or below (numbering 74 in all) has been compressed into a list of 26 leading solutions, with associated non-leading solutions in parenthesis.

It will be noticed that the solutions do not continue to group themselves in threes indefinitely; there are four groups of solutions from 58 onwards where the possibility of a nil rent increase does not arise, the computer having detected that it would violate one of the option bars set out in Table 2. Another point which emerges from Table 6 is that those leading solutions which include an E or a C in the final option column require an allocation of local tax revenue to the extension of existing design resources, without any corresponding benefit in speeding up the development of area V, at any rate until solution 58 is reached. Again, there is no reason to select such a solution unless it is justified by considerations outside area V, so the list of leading solutions with a local tax penalty of 150 eu_r or below can be compressed still further from 26 to 14, as shown in Table 7.

For the leading solutions which now remain, it will be seen that each increase in the impact on local taxpayers carries with it real benefits for one or more sectors of the community, as indicated by reducing figures in one or more of the last four effect columns. For instance, leading solution 4 brings the school project forward from 6 to year 5 and reduces the schoolchildren's effect measure from 1,800 to 1,200 eu_c, representing the benefit of one year's improved schooling for each of the 600 schoolchildren affected: on the other hand, leading solutions to 10, 13, 22, and 31 progressively reduce the shopping effect measure from 8,000 eu_s to zero, representing up to four years' bringing forward of access to improved shopping facilities for the 2,000 families affected. Other solutions can be seen to produce various degrees of benefit to schoolchildren,

TABLE 6

	Decision Areas							*Sectors of Community Affected*					
	Drainage	*School*	*Housing I*	*Housing II*	*Shopping*	*Rents*	*Designers*	*Local Taxpayers*	*National Taxpayers*	*Existing Tenants*	*Prospective Tenants*	*School-children*	*Local Shoppers*
Leading Solution	*Options**							*Effect Measures†* eu_r	eu_n	eu_t	eu_p	eu_c	eu_s
1(2,3)	5	6	6	8	8′	O	O	0	0	0	2,400	1,800	8,000
4(5,6)	5	5	6	8	8′	O	O	30	0	0	2,400	1,200	8,000
7(8,9)	5	6	6	8	8′	O	E	40	0	0	2,400	1,800	8,000
10(11,12)	5	6	6	8	7	O	O	45	0	0	2,400	1,800	6,000
13(14,15)	5	6	6	8	6	O	O	60	0	0	2,400	1,800	4,000
16(17,18)	5	5	6	8	8′	O	E	70	0	0	2,400	1,200	8,000
19(20,21)	5	5	6	8	7	O	O	75	0	0	2,400	1,200	6,000
22(23,24)	5	6	6	8	5	O	O	75	0	0	2,400	1,800	2,000
25(26,27)	5	6	6	8	7	O	E	85	0	0	2,400	1,800	6,000
28(29,30)	5	5	6	8	6	O	O	90	0	0	2,400	1,200	4,000
31(32,33)	5	6	6	8	4	O	O	90	0	0	2,400	1,800	0
34(35,36)	5	6	6	8	6	O	E	100	0	0	2,400	1,800	4,000
37(38,39)	5	5	6	8	5	O	O	105	0	0	2,400	1,200	2,000
40(41,42)	5	5	6	8	7	O	E	115	0	0	2,400	1,200	6,000
43(44,45)	5	6	6	8	5	O	E	115	0	0	2,400	1,800	2,000
46(47,48)	5	5	6	8	4	O	O	120	0	0	2,400	1,200	0
49(50,51)	5	6	6	8	8′	O	C	120	0	0	2,400	1,800	8,000
52(53,54)	5	5	6	8	6	O	E	130	0	0	2,400	1,200	4,000
55(56,57)	5	6	6	8	4	O	E	130	0	0	2,400	1,800	0
58(59)	4	6	5	7	7′	M	E	140	40	3,000	1,600	1,800	6,000
60(61)	4	6	5	7	8′	M	E	140	40	3,000	1,600	1,800	8,000
62(63)	4	6	5	8	7′	M	E	140	25	3,000	1,900	1,800	6,000
64(65)	4	6	5	8	8′	M	E	140	25	3,000	1,900	1,800	8,000
66(67,68)	4	6	6	8	8′	O	E	140	0	0	2,400	1,800	8,000
69(70,71)	5	5	6	8	5	O	E	145	0	0	2,400	1,200	2,000
72(73,74)	5	5	6	8	8′	O	C	150	0	0	2,400	1,200	8,000
–	–	–	–	–	–	–	–	–	–	–	–	–	–
–	–	–	–	–	–	–	–	–	–	–	–	–	–

*as defined in Table 4.
†units defined in the text, above.

shoppers, and prospective municipal tenants in a number of different combinations.

THE BALANCING OF COSTS AND BENEFITS

Unless the local policy-makers are dedicated to a policy of minimizing the local tax burden at any cost, their preferred solution to the problem of priorities in area V will not necessarily be that appearing on the first line of Table 7. For

TABLE 7

	Decision Areas							*Sectors of Community Affected*					
	Drainage	*School*	*Housing I*	*Housing II*	*Shopping*	*Rents*	*Designers*	*Local Taxpayers*	*National Taxpayers*	*Existing Tenants*	*Prospective Tenants*	*School-children*	*Local Shoppers*
Leading Solution			*Options**					*Effect Measures†* eu_r	eu_n	eu_t	eu_p	eu_c	eu_s
1	5	6	6	8	8′	O	O	0	0	0	2,400	1,800	8,000
4	5	5	6	8	8′	O	O	30	0	0	2,400	1,200	8,000
10	5	6	6	8	7	O	O	45	0	0	2,400	1,800	6,000
13	5	6	6	8	6	O	O	60	0	0	2,400	1,800	4,000
19	5	5	6	8	7	O	O	75	0	0	2,400	1,200	6,000
22	5	6	6	8	5	O	O	75	0	0	2,400	1,800	2,000
28	5	5	6	8	6	O	O	90	0	0	2,400	1,200	4,000
31	5	6	6	8	4	O	O	90	0	0	2,400	1,800	0
37	5	5	6	8	5	O	O	105	0	0	2,400	1,200	2,000
46	5	5	6	8	4	O	O	120	0	0	2,400	1,200	0
58	4	6	5	7	7′	M	E	140	40	3,000	1,600	1,800	6,000
60	4	6	5	7	8′	M	E	140	40	3,000	1,600	1,800	8,000
62	4	6	5	8	7′	M	E	140	25	3,000	1,900	1,800	6,000
64	4	6	5	8	8′	M	E	140	25	3,000	1,900	1,800	8,000
–	–	–	–	–	–	–	–	–	–	–	–	–	–
–	–	–	–	–	–	–	–	–	–	–	–	–	–

*as defined in Table 4.
†units defined in the text, above.

an extra expenditure of 30 eu_r (in practical terms, say, an extra 3d. on the local rate levy for one year), they might note that it would be possible–subject, perhaps to central government approval–to obtain an extra year of use of the new secondary school, to the direct benefit of the 600 children who would expect to be transferred to it. On the other hand, it would involve a sacrifice of 45 eu_r to "buy" an extra year of improved access to shopping facilities for 2,000 families; while for 75 eu_r they would have a choice of one year's benefit for the 600 schoolchildren and also for the 2,000 shoppers, or no benefit for the former and three years' benefit for the latter. They might be surprised to see that no benefit to those on the waiting-list for new homes could be obtained without at least a sacrifice of 140 eu_r (in this case required to pay not for the building of the houses themselves, but for the construction of the necessary drainage system and the mobilization of sufficient resources to allow design work to begin).

If we pick out from Table 7 only those solutions which provide progressive increases in benefit to local shoppers, then we have a list as shown in Table 8.

It will be noticed that, while the impact on local shoppers reduces from 8,000 eu_s to zero in a series of equal steps, the impact on local taxpayers rises first by an increment of 45 eu_r and then by a series of smaller steps of 15 eu_r each. This

TABLE 8

Solution	*Options*							*Effect on Local Taxpayers in* eu_r	*Effect on Shoppers in* eu_s
1	5	6	6	8	8′	O	O	0	8,000
10	5	6	6	8	7	O	O	45	6,000
13	5	6	6	8	6	O	O	60	4,000
22	5	6	6	8	5	O	O	75	2,000
31	5	6	6	8	4	O	O	90	0

stems from the initial assumption that the shopping scheme can only be started before the housing development is under way provided it is undertaken publicly rather than privately. The policy-makers will have to consider whether they are prepared to spend money from the local taxation account in order to advance the shopping development before year 8, and their assessment will inevitably reflect the conflicting pressures to which they may be exposed as elected representatives.

We will suppose in this case that a certain amount of information can be obtained, in one way or another, as to the "appropriate" balance between the conflicting objectives of improving shopping facilities and minimizing the level of local taxes. One form in which this might be expressed is that of a "trade-off rate" between local taxpayer effect units (eu_r) and local shoppers' effect units (eu_s). We will suppose that in this case the appropriate rate is agreed to be 100 eu_s:1 eu_r, which implies that the policy-makers would be prepared to sacrifice 1 eu_r (in practical terms, we suggested that this might translate as an increase of one-tenth of a penny on the local rates for one year) if by so doing they could advance by one year the provision of improved shopping facilities for 100 families at present served by the overcrowded shopping center in area R. By application of this trade-off rate to the figures of Table 8, it is possible to convert the effect of each solution on local shoppers from units of eu_s to units of eu_r, and combine it with the figures in the previous column to give an equivalent measure of the combined effect of each solution on these two sectors of the community, providing a basis for the expression of preferences between

TABLE 9

	Combined Effect Measure (in units of eu_r*) for Alternative Assumptions of Trade-Off Rate Between* eu_s *and* eu_r		
Solution	*(a)* *80* eu_s*: 1* eu_r	*(b)* *100* eu_s*: 1* eu_r	*(c)* *120* eu_s*: 1* eu_r
1	100	80	67
10	120	105	95
13	110	100	93
22	100	95	100
31	90	90	90

solutions. The order of preference between solutions may however be quite sensitive to the choice of trade-off rate, as we illustrate in Table 9 by showing the combined effect measure under alternative trade-off rates of 80:1, 100:1 and 120:1 respectively.

In this table, we have underlined the solution which gives the minimum (or most beneficial) combined effect measure according to each of the three alternative trade-off rates. Solution 1, which is marginally to be preferred at a trade-off rate of 100:1, has a much clearer advantage at a trade-off rate of 120:1 but is inferior to solution 31 at a trade-off rate of 80:1.

Trade-off rates of this kind represent assumptions of value which can in practice be arrived at by a number of different methods. One possibility is that assumptions can be made by the local planners themselves on the basis of their past experience of the value judgements of the policy-makers; another is that the policy-makers can be asked to state explicitly how much they would be prepared to ask the local taxpayers to pay for any given gain in shopping opportunities in area V. Yet again, the policy-makers can be presented with selected lists of alternative solutions and asked to place them in order of preference, so that the relative values they give to different effects can be inferred by the planners. For instance, faced with a choice between the five solutions in Table 9, the policy-makers might express a strong preference for solution 1 and little preference over the remaining solutions (a pattern according approximately with the results of a 120:1 trade-off was shown in Table 9); on the other hand, they might show indecision between solutions 1 and 31 (suggesting, by interpolation in Table 9, a trade-off rate of the order of 90:1). Another type of exercise might require them to express a preference between solutions which incur the same local tax penalty but provide benefits to different sectors of the community. For instance, knowledge of the policy-makers' preference between solutions 19 and 22 in Table 7 would allow the planners to make some further inferences as to the relative values which they attach to educational and shopping improvements respectively.

Whatever the procedure by which trade-off rates are estimated, they can of course represent no more than very rough indicators of the values which should be given to certain broad classes of social effect. The effect measures themselves can do no more than present a highly simplified picture of a complex social reality; and when assessing rates of trade-off between them, it may be necessary to give a good deal of consideration to the particular local circumstances of those affected—in what ways the present opportunities of these particular shoppers or this particular group of schoolchildren may be deficient, and whether in each case certain particular sub-groups may stand to gain or lose more than others.

Having stated these qualifications, we will suppose that an initial set of trade-off rates has been arrived at, by direct or indirect methods, linking all sex effect measures through the common "currency" of the unit eu_r used to measure the effect on local taxpayers. This is shown in Table 10.

TABLE 10

Effect on existing tenants	40 eu_t: 1 eu_r	i.e., 1 eu_t: 0.025 eu_r
Effect on prospective tenants	10 eu_p: 1 eu_r	i.e., 1 eu_p: 0.1 eu_r
Effect on school children in sector Z	15 eu_c : 1 eu_r	i.e., 1 eu_c : 0.0667 eu_r
Effect on shoppers in sector Z	100 eu_s : 1 eu_r	i.e., 1 eu_s : 0.01 eu_r
Effect on national taxpayers	To be ignored	i.e., 1 eu_n : 0 eu_r

Embodied in this table are a variety of important assumptions about social and political values: for instance, the fact that the eu_p unit has been given ten times the value of the eu_s unit implies an assessment that the policy-makers are prepared to pay ten times as much to provide a home one year earlier for a family on the housing waiting-list, as they are prepared to pay to bring forward by one year the provision of improved shopping facilities for one family which already has a home in this area.

By giving no weight at all to the effect on national taxpayers, Table 10 reflects the viewpoint that a local authority cannot be held responsible for protecting the interests of the national taxpayer. From the local authority's point of view, the national taxpayer can be regarded as fair game provided the central government has provided the mechanisms for the provision of grants or subsidies at his expense. It is up to central government to construct a framework which will ensure that money provided from the central exchequer will be used in effective pursuit of the policies which the government of the day wishes to promote.

THE RANKING OF SOLUTIONS USING ASSUMED TRADE-OFF RATES

Now that a set of initial assumptions has been made as to the relative values of the various effect measures, it is possible to attach a *combined effect measure* to each of the 1,216 possible solutions for the problem which has been defined for area V. Because each of the trade-off rates in Table 10 is linked to the "common currency" of eu_r (the local taxpayers effect unit), this particular unit provides perhaps the most convenient base for expression of the combined effect. However, it is important to avoid confusion between quantities which represent combinations of effects and those which express effects on local taxpayers alone, and so for the former purpose we will define a new *aggregate effect unit* eu(A) at the "exchange rate" of 1 eu_r = 1 eu(A). Using the trade-off rates assumed in Table 10, the combined effect measure for any solution can then be expressed in units of eu(A) as shown in Table 11.

Because we adopted the convention of defining each of the original effect measures in a negative sense—to express the degree of penalty or disadvantage associated with deviations from the most favorable set of options for the sector of the community concerned—the combined effect measure will also now have a negative interpretation; the higher the combined effect measure for a given

TABLE 11

Contributions to Combined Effect Measure	*Illustration for Solution 1 of Table 7*	
Effect on local taxpayers, measured in eu_r, 1 eu_r = 1 eu(A)	0 eu_r =	0 eu(A)
Effect on existing tenants, measured in eu_t, x0/025	0 x 0.025 =	0 eu(A)
Effect on prospective tenants, measured in eu_p, x0.1	2,400 x 0.1 =	240 eu(A)
Effect on local schoolchildren, measured in eu_c, x0.667	1,800 x 0.667 =	120 eu(A)
Effect on local shoppers, measured in eu_s, x0.01	8,000 x 0.01 =	80 eu(A)
Combined effect measure		440 eu(A)

solution, the less beneficial will it be from the point of view of "the public interest" as defined by the assumed set of trade-off rates. As we shall see later, this first set of assumptions about trade-off rates must be regarded as open to question at all stages of the analysis; and it is especially important that the "combined effect measure" should not come to be regarded as a final criterion for the expression of preferences between solutions. Rather, it should be used solely as a means to the end of creating a more meaningful dialogue between planners and policy-makers in the context of a continuing planning process.

Just as a computer can be programmed to sort the 1,216 possible solutions according to the criterion of minimizing impact on local taxpayers, so it can be made to re-sort them according to a new criterion of minimum "combined effect measure," adopting the assumed conversion rates given in Table 11. This time, the solutions may appear in a very different order, as shown in Table 12, which lists the first twelve solutions in order of minimum (i.e. most favorable) combined effect measure. The numbers in parentheses refer to the corresponding positions of these same solutions in the earlier order of preference based on impact on local taxpayers alone (see Table 5 and 6).

A REVISION OF TRADE-OFF RATES

Presented with a list of solutions in the order of preference given by Table 12, the policy-makers might note that the first dozen solutions give some choice of schooling or shopping benefits, but none of them hold out any benefits to prospective housing tenants through acceleration of the two housing projects; the first solution which produces some benefit to this sector of the community in fact turns out to come twenty-fifth in the new listing, and to carry a combined effects measure of 525 eu(A).

Faced with this evidence, the policy-makers might perhaps begin to wonder whether, in the original estimates of trade-off rates, sufficient weight had been attached to the social urgency, as they see it, of rehousing families at present on the waiting-list: their new awareness of the difficulty of overcoming the drainage problem may lead them to a more extensive discussion of the social and political aspects of the housing shortage, in the course of which a clearer picture of

TABLE 12

Solution Rank	Drainage	School	Housing I	Housing II	Shopping	Rents	Designers	Local Taxpayers	National Taxpayers	Existing Tenants	Prospective Tenants	School-children	Local Shoppers	Combined Effect Measure‡ eu(A)
	Decision Areas							*Sectors of Community Affected*						
	*Options**							*Effect Measures†* eu_r	eu_n	eu_t	eu_p	eu_c	eu_s	
1(4)	5	5	6	8	8′	O	O	30	0	0	2,400	1,200	8,000	430
2(46)	5	5	6	8	4	O	O	120	0	0	2,400	1,200	0	440
3(1)	5	6	6	8	8′	O	O	0	0	0	2,400	1,800	8,000	440
4(37)	5	5	6	8	5	O	O	105	0	0	2,400	1,200	4,000	445
5(28)	5	5	6	8	6	O	O	90	0	0	2,400	1,200	4,000	450
6(31)	5	6	6	8	4	O	O	90	0	0	2,400	1,800	0	450
7(19)	5	5	6	8	7	O	O	75	0	0	2,400	1,200	6,000	455
8(22)	5	6	6	8	5	O	O	75	0	0	2,400	1,800	0	455
9(13)	5	6	6	8	6	O	O	60	0	0	2,400	1,800	4,000	460
10(10)	5	6	6	8	7	O	O	45	0	0	2,400	1,800	6,000	465
11(16)	5	5	6	8	8′	O	E	70	0	0	2,400	1,200	8,000	470
12(75)	5	5	6	8	4	O	E	150	0	0	2,400	1,200	0	480
–	–	–	–	–	–	–	–	–	–	–	–	–	–	–
–	–	–	–	–	–	–	–	–	–	–	–	–	–	–

*as defined in Table 4.
†units defined in the text, above.
‡defined in Table 11.

relative values may begin to emerge. Perhaps they may also feel that the order of preference given by Table 12 does not adequately reflect the importance they attach to early completion of the secondary school, and that it tends to overstress the social benefits arising from the early completion of the shopping center. The policy-makers might therefore decide that the original set of trade-off rates should be modified to give a closer approximation to their own system of value judgments, as follows:

Effect on prospective tenants	:	value to be increased by 50%
Effect on local schoolchildren	:	value to be increased by 50%
Effect on local shoppers	:	value to be decreased by 40%

The definition of the combined effect measure, as originally given in Table 11, would now be modified as shown in Table 13.

The unit for this modified version of the combined effect measure is now referred to as eu(A′), to distinguish it from the aggregate effect unit eu(A) originally defined in Table 11. With this modification, the computer can be made to repeat the calculations and come up with a revised order of preference. The first twelve solutions in the new order of preference are shown in Table 14.

TABLE 13

Contributions to Combined Effect Measure (modified)	*Illustration for Solution 1 of Table 7*
Effect on local taxpayers, measured in eu_r (1 eu_r = 1 eu(A′))	0 eu_r = 0 eu(A′)
Effect on existing tenants, measured in eu_t, x 0.025	0 x 0.025 = 0 eu(A′)
Effect on prospective tenants, measured in eu_p, x 0.15	2,400 x 0.15 = 360 eu(A′)
Effect on local schoolchildren, measured in eu_c, x 0.1	1,800 x 0.10 = 180 eu(A′)
Effect on local shoppers, measured in eu_s, x 0.006	8,000 x 0.006 = 48 eu(A′)
Combined effect measure (modified)	588 eu(A′)

The solutions which are now thrown to the top of the list include some which have not appeared in any of our previous tables: in particular, six of the first twelve involve an impact on local taxpayers of 300 eu_r or more, making use of the extra local revenue to bring the drainage and housing programs forward by up to two years. Nevertheless, some of the earlier low tax solutions still appear near the top of the list; for instance, the sixth solution in the new list corresponds to the original minimum tax solution and to the third solution in

TABLE 14

	Decision Areas							*Sectors of Community Affected*						
Solution Rank	*Drainage*	*School*	*Housing I*	*Housing II*	*Shopping*	*Rents*	*Designers*	*Local Taxpayers*	*National Taxpayers*	*Existing Tenants*	*Prospective Tenants*	*School-children*	*Local Shoppers*	*Combined Effect Measure‡ eu(A′)*
	*Options**							*Effect Measures†* eu_r	eu_n	eu_t	eu_p	eu_c	eu_s	
1	3	3	4	6	6′	M	E	330	80	3,000	800	0	4,000	549
2	5	5	6	8	8′	O	O	30	0	0	2,400	1,200	8,000	558
3	3	3	4	6	7′	M	E	330	80	3,000	800	0	6,000	561
4	3	3	4	6	8′	M	E	330	80	3,000	800	0	8,000	573
5	3	4	4	6	6′	M	E	330	80	3,000	800	600	4,000	579
6	5	6	6	8	8′	O	O	0	0	0	2,400	1,800	8,000	588
7	5	5	6	8	7	O	O	75	0	0	2,400	1,200	6,000	591
8	3	4	4	6	7′	M	E	300	80	3,000	800	600	6,000	591
9	5	5	6	8	6	O	O	90	0	0	2,400	1,200	4,000	594
10	3	3	4	7	6′	M	E	330	65	3,000	1,100	0	4,000	594
11	5	5	6	8	5	O	O	105	0	0	2,400	1,200	2,000	597
12	5	5	6	8	8′	O	O	70	0	0	2,400	1,200	8,000	598
–	–	–	–	–	–	–	–	–	–	–	–	–	–	–
–	–	–	–	–	–	–	–	–	–	–	–	–	–	–

*as defined in Table 4.
†units defined in the text, above.
‡defined in Table 13.

the ranking of Table 12. If the trade-off rates are now correctly adjusted to reflect the relative values of the policy-makers, then one would expect them to agree that the revised listing gave a reasonable indication of their true order of preference. This could be tested by picking pairs of solutions with the same or similar combined effect measures (e.g. 7 and 8, 9 and 10, 11 and 12) and asking the policy-makers whether they still felt any strong preference between them; if so, then some further adjustments to assumed rates of trade-off could be made.

CHOICE OF ACTION IN THE FACE OF UNCERTAINTY

Assuming for the time being that the policy-makers are satisfied that the new list accords reasonably well with their political preferences, then at last an acceptable basis for choice exists in relation to the problem of priorities in area V.

If they were to ignore the existence of uncertainties in the estimation of combined effects, then there would be no reason why the policy-makers should not select solution 1 in Table 14, whose overall penalty is lower than that of the "second-best" solution by a differential of 9 eu(A′). However, it is extremely unlikely in practice that the various assumptions required for the estimation of a combined effects measure (including the value assumptions implicit in the selected trade-off rates) would be sufficiently clear cut for a differential of 9 eu(A′)–or even perhaps a differential of 50 or 100 eu(A′)–to be regarded as a clear-cut index of preference between alternatives. In fact, as a result of the way the problem was initially defined, one important source of uncertainty is clearly exposed in the first few solutions of Table 14: solutions 1, 3, and 4 will be seen to differ only in the choice of year 6, 7, or 8 for the priority of the shopping development, assuming in each case that this is to be achieved through a private agency. However, the planners may have only a very limited amount of control over the choice of years in which private developers might start; the difference between these three solutions might not therefore be a question of planners' choice so much as of uncertainty (of category UE) in this aspect of their environment. If the conscious choice of solution 1 is likely to result in achievement of solution 3 or 4 in practice, then a case may exist for selecting solution 2 in preference to it, even though its combined effects appear to be slightly less beneficial.

As in our earlier case example, the presence of uncertainties suggests that it might be advisable for the policy-makers at this stage to become committed not to any particular full solution but only to a more restricted "action set" in which a clear choice is made in respect of some of the more urgent decision areas, while as many options as possible are left open within the remaining ones. We will suppose that in this case the most urgent decision areas are thought to be those covered by the second, sixth, and seventh of the option columns in Table 14. The reasons for urgency might be as follows:

Secondary school (Z3t). Decision on whether or not to start in year 3 is considered urgent because, if so, then an application must be submitted shortly to the department of central government responsible for the national school building program.

Housing rents (Y6d). Decision between nil, moderate, and large rent increase (O, M, or L) must be made shortly in respect of the coming financial year.

Design resources (Y8d). Decision between no change, expansion, and crash strategy (O, E, or C) for reinforcement of existing engineering design resources must be decided shortly to allow staff recruitment or consultant contract arrangements to be made.

There are therefore eighteen distinct action sets from which a choice might be made, as shown in Table 15. Here, the first symbol in each group of three refers to the option selected for secondary school priority, the second to the option selected for housing rents, and the third to the option selected for engineering design resources. We have used the symbol X to represent the action of not submitting an immediate application for the school to be built in year 3: in other words, inclusion of X as an element within the action set leaves open the future options of starting work on the school in any of years 4, 5, or 6.

Taking the first twelve solutions as shown in Table 14, the corresponding action sets can be picked out from the second, sixth, and seventh option columns as shown in Table 16.

Of the twelve solutions, we can see that four require the action set (3,M,E) while two require the action set (X,M,E), with X in this case standing for the option of year 4 for the school building project. The other six solutions all involve the action set (X,0,0), with X representing either year 5 or year 6.

THE ROBUSTNESS OF ALTERNATIVE ACTION SETS

If the pattern of occurrence of the various action sets is followed further down the list, the frequencies gradually change and further action sets begin to make an appearance as shown in Table 17 overleaf.

Although we have here worked considerably further down the order of preference than in any of the earlier tables, the 138 solutions which are shown as

TABLE 15

	Start School in Year 3 Rent Increase			*Start School Later (year X = 4, 5, or 6) Rent Increase*		
	O	*M*	*L*	*O*	*M*	*L*
Design resources						
O	(3,O,O)	(3,M,O)	(3,L,O)	(X,O,O)	(X,M,O)	(X,L,O)
E	(3,O,E)	(3,M,E)	(3,L,E)	(X,O,E)	(X,M,E)	(X,L,E)
C	(3,O,C)	(3,M,C)	(3,L,C)	(X,O,C)	(X,M,C)	(X,L,C)

TABLE 16

Solution Rank	*Options*							*Action Set*	*Combined Effect Measure*
1	3	3	4	6	6′	M	E	(3,M,E)	549
2	5	5	6	8	8′	O	O	(X,O,O)	558
3	3	3	4	6	7′	M	E	(3,M,E)	561
4	3	3	4	6	8′	M	E	(3,M,E)	573
5	3	4	4	6	6′	M	E	(X,M,E)	579
6	5	6	6	8	8′	O	O	(X,O,O)	588
7	5	5	6	8	7	O	O	(X,O,O)	591
8	3	4	4	6	7′	M	E	(X,M,E)	591
9	5	5	6	8	6	O	O	(X,O,O)	594
10	3	3	4	7	6′	M	E	(3,M,E)	594
11	5	5	6	8	5	O	O	(X,O,O)	597
12	5	5	6	8	8′	O	O	(X,O,O)	598
–	–	–	–	–	–	–	–	–	–
–	–	–	–	–	–	–	–	–	–

having a combined effect measure of 700 units or less can still all be regarded as reasonably "good" solutions, in that they comprise the top 12% or so of the complete list of 1,216 feasible solutions. One point that emerges strongly from this table is the high frequency with which the action set (X,M,E) appears: although choice of this particular action set only permits one solution with a combined effect measure of 580 units or less, it does leave open a future choice from a large variety of alternative solutions whose combined effect measure is at present estimated to lie somewhere in the region between 580 and 700 units. Action set (X,M,E) is therefore particularly "robust" in the sense in which we used the word in our previous case example; and again the problem arises of whether it is worth while to "buy" this degree of robustness (or flexibility in future choice) at the expense of ruling out those few solutions which at present appear at the very top of the order of preference. In our first case example, we regarded this kind of question as largely a matter for the judgment of the policy-makers; however, in the present case example, we have built up a good deal of quantitative information on the considerations which determine the order of preference, and so a certain amount of further analysis is possible before the final judgment is made.

A CLOSER APPRAISAL OF SOME ALTERNATIVE ACTION SETS

Of the action sets appearing in Table 17, it is only the first three—(3,M,E),(X,O,O) and X,M,E)—which seem at first sight to provide clear advantages either of low overall penalty or of robustness. The planners might therefore decide to take a closer look at the particular implications of these three alternatives, without yet dismissing any of the remaining action sets out of hand.

The attraction of (3,M,E)–a compromise policy on rents and on design resources, combined with an early priority for the school project–is in that it permits the best solution of all according to the combined effect measure (solution 1 at 549 units), while also scoring reasonably well on "robustness," if this is measured by the frequency with which this action set appears in any selected row in the lower part of Table 17. The attraction of (X,O,O)–a laissez-faire policy, with no increase in rents or design resources, and a lower priority for the school project–is that it permits a next-best solution (solution 2 at 558 units), while being slightly more robust than (3,M,E) at one limited stage in the build-up of Table 17. The attraction of (X,M,E)–a lower priority for school building combined with a compromise policy on rents and design resources–is that it also permits a few reasonably high-ranking solutions, such as solutions 5 and 8 at 579 and 591 units respectively, while preserving an exceptionally high degree of robustness in any of the lower rows of Table 17.

It would, however, be a wise precaution for the planners to examine the relative robustness of these three action sets not simply according to the number of reasonably good alternative solutions which each leaves open for future choice, but also according to whether the options which remain available do in fact extend the policy-makers' freedom of choice in directions which may be of some real value to them.

For instance, it is revealing to discover, from a more detailed analysis of those ten solutions of Table 17 which are permitted by action set (X,O,O), that they leave open no future options on the drainage or housing schemes, which must each be deferred until their latest possible starting times. The only choices which do remain open under choice of this action set in fact turn out to relate to the school project–a choice of year 5 or 6–and the shopping project–a choice of year 4, 5, 6, or 7 (public) or year 8 (private). Under the choice of action set (3,M,E), the options remaining open turn out to relate only to the year of the second housing project and to the year and agency for the shopping project. However, in this case, the available options for shopping shopping all relate to the year in which it might be undertaken as a private venture, and therefore do very little to extend the freedom of choice of the local authority. As already suggested, any inducements to develop in a particular year would in all probability be strictly limited, and so the planners might be reduced to making predictions as to which solutions stood the best chances of achievement, instead of attempting to make a deliberate choice between them.

The third action set in our short-list, (X,M,E), occurs with exceptionally high frequency–54 times in the first 138 solutions–and it is not surprising that, on further analysis, it turns out to leave a substantial range of options open on most of the remaining variables. As in the case of (3,M,E), the more detailed analysis–which we do not reproduce here–shows that some of the flexibility apparently allowed by this action set relates to the choice of year for private development of the shopping center, so does not signify real extension to the freedom of action of the local authority. Also, several of the solutions remaining

TABLE 17

Combined Effect Measure (eu(A′))	Cumulative Number of Solutions With Aggregate Effect At or Below Given Level of eu(A′)									
		Breakdown of Total by Action Set								
	Total	*(3,M,E)*	*(X,O,O)*	*(X,M,E)*	*(X,O,E)*	*(3,L,E)*	*(3,M,C)*	*(X,M,O)*	*(X,L,E)*	*Other*
560	2	1	1	–	–	–	–	–	–	–
580	5	3	1	1	–	–	–	–	–	–
600	13	4	6	2	1	–	–	–	–	–
620	22	10	6	5	1	–	–	–	–	–
640	44	11	10	13	6	2	1	1	–	–
660	64	16	10	23	6	3	3	1	1	1
680	93	17	10	36	10	4	4	6	3	3
700	138	19	10	54	11	10	10	8	8	8
•	•	•	•	•	•	•	•	•	•	•
•	•	•	•	•	•	•	•	•	•	•
•	•	•	•	•	•	•	•	•	•	•
•	•	•	•	•	•	•	•	•	•	•

open can be grouped under "leading solutions" as in Tables 6 and 7, in that they incur additional penalties that could never be justified in terms of the limited problem of area V alone. Nevertheless, a detailed analysis of the solutions permitted by action set (X,M,E) does indicate that, even after all these factors have been taken into account, there still remains a genuine freedom of action for the local authority which is superior to that allowed by any other action set.

As a result of this kind of analysis, extended over all alternative action sets, a much clearer case can be established for restricting the final choice of action set to either (3,M,E) or (X,M,E). Neither (X,O,O) nor any other alternative turns out to carry any specific advantages in terms of leaving open particular choices which would otherwise be closed. The choice between (3,M,E), which permits the best solution of all according to current estimates, and (X,M,E), which leaves a somewhat wider margin of flexibility, might perhaps be clarified further through a statistical analysis of the degree of confidence attached to each element of information used in estimating the combined effect measure. However, the application of statistical method is by no means straightforward, because of the subjectivity and interdependence of the estimates concerned.

Another consideration which may affect the final choice is that action set (3,M,E) will not necessarily be successful, because there may be a possibility that the application to start building the school in year 3 will be turned down by the national education authority. This consideration might well influence the local policymakers towards a strategy of acting first on the basis of (3,M,E)–in other words raising the rents, recruiting further design staff, and going ahead with the school building application–with the assurance that, if this application failed, the resultant transformation of (3,M,E) into (X,M,E) would still leave them set on a course of action which conformed both with their current assessments of relative value and with their desire to retain flexibility of future choice.

Although pressures of time might at this stage preclude any further analysis in depth, the planners might be well advised to carry out some quick checks to test whether the policy-makers' emerging preference for a course of action based on (3,M,E)–with the option of (X,M,E) if this fails–might in fact be sensitive to variations in any of the many simplifying assumptions they have made in their analysis of the limited problem of area V. In the remainder of this chapter, we will take a second look at some of these simplifying assumptions, relating them to the three basic categories of uncertainty which we introduced in Chapter 4;* uncertainties in knowledge of the environment (UE), uncertainties as to future intention in related fields of choice (UR), and uncertainties as to appropriate value judgments (UV).

THE QUESTIONING OF ASSUMPTIONS ON OPTIONS AND EFFECTS

Some of the most basic assumptions which underlie the analysis so far relate to the range of alternative options defined within each decision area (first set out

*Not included herein.–Ed.

in Figure 1), and the set of option bars which define the compatibility of pairs of options from different decision areas (as first set down in Table 2). The planners might, however, have doubts whether some of the options included would be feasible in practice, or whether perhaps certain new options could be added; they might also have some doubts in assessing the compatibility or incompatibility of particular option pairs. For instance, it might be just possible (though technically very difficult) to start the two housing projects simultaneously, or it might be quite feasible (though socially very undesirable) to consider deferring the school project until beyond year 6.

If the planners feel particularly doubtful about the validity of some of their initial assumptions in defining options and their interrelationships, and if computer facilities are freely available to them, then they will have little difficulty in repeating their evaluation of solutions under alternative sets of assumptions, to test whether these would lead to any modification of the policy-makers' emerging preference for a course of immediate action based on (3,M,E).

Some further basic assumptions were introduced in Table 4, where the effects of each option were estimated according to six different measures, whose significance was explained more fully in the text. It was assumed in each case that the number of people who stood to gain or lose by the choices of the policy-makers could be estimated with some precision: that there were known to be 3,000 existing council tenants, that the two housing projects would accommodate 500 and 300 families respectively, that the school would accommodate 600 pupils, and that the shopping center would create improved facilities for 2,000 families living in the surrounding areas. In the case of this last estimate, no allowance was made for the expected growth in the number of families from 2,000 to 2,800 as the two housing estates came into occupation, the assumption being that this factor could reasonably be ignored. If, however, it is considered that the validity of this particular simplifying assumption should not be left untested, then it becomes necessary to introduce a new type of refinement into the analytical approach: the idea of attaching an effect measure not only to the choice of any particular option within a decision area, but also, where appropriate, to the choice of a particular *combination* of options from different decision areas. This complication raises no insuperable difficulties in the analysis, and we will consider it briefly below with particular reference to the interaction of the shopping center project with the first of the two housing projects.

THE CONSTRUCTION OF A JOINT EFFECT TABLE FOR HOUSING AND SHOPPING

We will suppose that the expected rate of progress on the first housing project is such that the number of new residents on the estate will increase as follows:

Number of new families in area V3:

1 year after start of housing scheme I	100
2 years after start of housing scheme I	300
3 years after start of housing scheme I	500
thereafter	500

The 2,000 existing families that would stand to benefit from the provision of shops in V2 are all assumed to be resident in the surrounding areas which in Map 2 were labelled S, T, and U. The total number of families within the sphere of influence of V2 can therefore be expected to grow as follows, according to the year in which work on housing scheme 1 is started (see Table 18).

Assuming that the shops will be in full occupation during the second year after work on the shopping center is started, then the effect of each solution on local shoppers will now depend not only on the timing of the shopping development but also on the timing of the first housing scheme. The new set of estimates, derived by adding certain sets of neighboring columns in Table 18, are given in Table 19.

As in the earlier analysis, the effect on local shoppers is measured according to a relative scale taking the earliest possible starting year for the shopping project (year 4) as zero. If the start is delayed from year 4 to year 5, the penalty in effect corresponds to the loss of a full year's trading in year 6, so that the second column in Table 19 corresponds directly to the fourth column in Table 18. If the start is delayed a further year to year 6, the penalty corresponds to the loss of two full year's trading in years 6 and 7, so that the third column in Table 19 corresponds to the sum of the fourth and fifth columns in Table 18 and so on. We can now see what difference the new assumptions have made to the original estimates of shopping penalties, which we reproduce for purposes of comparison at the foot of Table 19. For instance, the effect on shoppers associated with deferring a start on the shopping project until year 7 now exceeds the original estimate of 6,000 eu_S by a margin of 400, 900, 1,300, or 1,500 eu_S, depending on whether the housing project is started in year 6, 5, 4, or 3. In order to allow these adjustments to be incorporated in the main analysis,

TABLE 18

Year of Start of Housing Scheme I	*Total No. of Families Resident in Areas S, T, U, and V3 Who Would Benefit from Shopping Center in V2*						
	3	*4*	*5*	*6*	*7*	*8*	*9 and After*
3	2,000	2,100	2,300	2,500	2,500	2,500	2,500
4	2,000	2,000	2,100	2,300	2,500	2,500	2,500
5	2,000	2,000	2,000	2,100	2,300	2,500	2,500
6	2,000	2,000	2,000	2,000	2,100	2,300	2,500

TABLE 19

Year of Start of Housing Scheme I	Shopping Project Started in Year 4	5	6	7	8
	First Year of Occupation 6	7	8	9	10
	Effect on Shoppers Measured in eu_S				
3	0	2,500	5,000	7,500	10,000
4	0	2,300	4,800	7,300	9,800
5	0	2,100	4,400	6,900	9,400
6	0	2,000	4,100	6,400	8,900
Compare with original estimates of shoppers' effect units ignoring residents of housing scheme I:	0	2,000	4,000	6,000	8,000

we will set them out in the form of what we will call a "joint effect table" for the two decision areas, as shown in Table 20.

In this table, the crosses merely reflect those combinations which have already been ruled out by the option bar assumptions of Table 2 (e). In fact, Table 20 differs from this earlier option-bar table in that each spot, representing a pair of compatible options, is replaced by a numerical entry, representing the joint effect of choosing that particular option pair in units of eu_S, over and above any effects these options may have when each is applied independently. Each entry in the new table can if required be converted to an equivalent in terms of the combined effect measure, by applying the appropriate trade-off rate. In this case, the conversion can be carried out by multiplying by a factor of 0.006, as was indicated in Table 13.

THE SIGNIFICANCE OF THE JOINT EFFECT TABLES

The significance of this particular joint effect table can be judged by making the appropriate modifications to the first few solutions in the order of

TABLE 20

Housing I Year	Shopping Center (agency/year) Public 4	5	6	7	Private 6′	7′	8′
3	0	500	1,000	1,500	1,000	1,500	2,000
4	0	300	800	1,300	800	1,300	1,800
5	0	100	400	900	x	900	1,400
6	0	0	100	400	x	x	900

All entries in shoppers' effect units (eu_S).

preference shown in Table 14. For instance, the top solution in Table 14 involves options of year 4 and year 6′ (private) in the two decision areas with which we are now concerned; reading off from Table 20, this combination is seen to incur an additional effect on shoppers of 800 eu_S, which converts to 4.8 units in the aggregate effect measure: the combined effect estimate of this solution therefore rises from 549 eu(A′) to 553.8 eu(A′) when the joint effect of the housing I and shopping choices is taken into account. When similar adjustments are made to other solutions, certain marginal adjustments appear in the order of preference; within the top twelve solutions as shown in Table 14, solution 8 drops by two places and solution 10 by one. The crucial test, however, will be whether any significant variations arise in the frequencies of occurrence of the various action sets within the more extensive tabulation of Table 17. In fact, the variations turn out to be fairly marginal, and so the local planners can feel reassured that they were not introducing any serious distortions in their analysis when they initially made the simplifying assumption of ignoring this particular joint effect. They have in effect used the principle of sensitivity analysis (which we first discussed in Chapter 4) to satisfy themselves that their choice of action set is not very sensitive to the additional benefit which the new shopping center will bring to the new families in area V3. A similar joint effect table could, of course, be constructed to link the shopping project with the second of the two housing schemes in the adjoining area V4.

The device of the joint effect table makes it possible to extend the AIDA method to deal with further types of relationship between options, other than those of total compatibility or incompatibility. In fact, the original spots and crosses in Table 2 can be interpreted as assumptions that the joint effects associated with particular pairs of options can be treated as either infinitely low or infinitely high. The point at which the magnitude of a joint effect becomes so high as to be treated as an absolute prohibition is of necessity a matter for judgement; here again, the planners might be wise to carry out some quick sensitivity analyses, to test whether the replacement of particular incompatibilities by finite penalty measures would make any significant difference to the final choice of action set.

The device of the joint effect table also makes it possible for the planners, if they so desire, to reintroduce into the analysis at this stage the problem of priority for the new community center in area V2. While it was assumed in Figure 1 that the timing of this project would be related in some way to that of the first housing project, it was also assumed (in Table 2(f)) that this relationship could not be expressed in terms of statements of compatibility or incompatibility between particular option pairs. At this later stage, however, the planners might decide to replace Table 2(f) by a numerical table giving the estimated joint effect of particular combinations upon the prospective tenants of the new housing scheme in V3. There is in fact a strong case to be made that the early development of a community center to serve a new housing estate (perhaps even before the first houses are occupied) can create all the difference between disaffection and delinquency on the one hand a stable and secure social environment on the other. Measurement of such an effect may in practice be particularly difficult; but this does not necessarily preclude the making of *assumptions* about its scale and value in order to test the sensitivity to such assumptions of the emerging preference for particular courses of immediate action.

THE RANGE OF EFFECT MEASURES

In introducing this new consideration of the social value of the community center, we have in effect been questioning whether the range of effect measures taken into account in the earlier evaluation was sufficiently wide to form a reasonable basis for choice by the policy makers. Clearly, the range of six effect measures which the planners chose to take into account in the main analysis is by no means exhaustive, and it is conceivable that the policy-makers might wish to extend this range further by consideration of costs and benefits incurred by various other sectors of the community.

For example, if there was a high level of unemployment in the town, the policymakers might wish to evaluate alternative solutions according to the extra employment they could be expected to provide for the workers in the local construction trades. They might also wish perhaps to make an explicit evaluation of the traffic and environmental benefits in area R which could be expected to result indirectly from the early completion of the new shopping center in V2, or the potential loss of trade which might be inflicted on existing traders. Even if these other effects had not originally been considered sufficiently relevant to the problem of area V to have been included in the main analysis, there is no reason why some rough estimates of their magnitude should not be attempted at this later stage, so as to test whether there is in fact any likelihood that they are sufficiently critical to influence the final judgment of the policy-makers.

Another possibility is that the policy-makers might wish to extend the range of effects measures not only by the inclusion of certain effects impinging on other sectors of the community, but also by a further division of some of the six original sectors into sub-groups to whose interests they might wish to give differential treatment. For instance, they might wish to consider separately the interests of those existing council tenants with particularly low incomes, or those would-be tenants now living in particularly overcrowded conditions, or those schoolchildren with particularly difficult travelling problems. They might consider that the benefit of the new shopping center to the new residents of V3 should be rated higher than its benefit to existing residents of areas S and T, because the former are much more remote from existing shopping facilities than the latter. Perhaps, in the definition of a "shoppers' effect unit," it might be considered appropriate to give, say, double weighting to each new family in area V3 or area U as opposed to each existing family in area S or T. Perhaps in the same way the policy-makers might feel that the definition of a "prospective tenants' effect unit" ought to be adjusted so as to attach extra value to certain particularly deserving categories of would-be tenants.

It is by now becoming apparent that the original choice of a fairly limited set of effects measures rested in fact on a whole range of assumptions about the need to give equity of consideration to many different individuals within the community, each with his or her own special needs or circumstances but each treated for convenience of analysis as a member of some wider group. It is only to be expected that the members of the policy-making group, as politicians and as public representatives, may wish to single out certain sub-groups for preferential treatment; and whatever set of effect measures is chosen must incorporate sufficient diversity to allow legitimate discrimination of this kind.

The search for a satisfactory range of effect measures in fact represents an attempt to achieve a reasonable working balance between two opposing considerations: the need to keep the variety of costs and benefits under consideration sufficiently limited for the analysis as a whole to be widely comprehensible, and the need to include within the analysis a sufficient element of "political richness," defined as the capacity to discriminate between different sectors of the community in pursuit of legitimate social objectives. The search for a sufficient set of effect measures for the evaluation of alternative planning solutions may not be an easy one, and must of itself form an important aspect of the continuing dialogue between officers and elected members. . . .

THE ASSUMPTION OF FIXED TRADE-OFF RATES

In the preceding pages, we have come across uncertainties of value judgment in several different contexts—in the problem of evaluating similar effects over different time periods, in the problem of adjusting effects measures in order to give preferential treatment to particular groups of people, and in the earlier problem of choosing a "trade-off rate" for comparison of different types of cost and benefit. The very idea of a trade-off "rate" itself embodies an assumption that the willingness of the policy-makers to provide, for instance, new school places at the cost of additional local tax expenditure does not vary in any way as the tax burden rises and as the demand for school places becomes progressively more fully satisfied. If this assumption is not accepted, then the concept of a trade-off rate must be replaced by the wider concept of a "trade-off curve" for any pair of effects, or a "trade-off function" relating to any number of effects, acknowledging that the appropriate levels of trade-off for any given situation may be dependent on the particular levels of demand—and of satisfaction of demand—which apply at the time. The idea of the trade-off curve is very much akin to the idea of the indifference curve in economic analysis.

To take explicit account of this further complication would be to make the whole analysis very much more cumbersome from a computational point of view. In practice, the idea of a "trade-off rate" is often likely to be a justifiable simplication, provided it is recognized that this rests on an assumption of a fixed value relationship between different effect measures, and provided that steps are taken to adjust these effect measures to reflect any particularly significant differentiation of values between different sectors of the population, or between different periods of future time. . . .

REFERENCE

1. Battersby, A., *Network Analysis for Planning and Scheduling.* London: Macmillan, 1964.

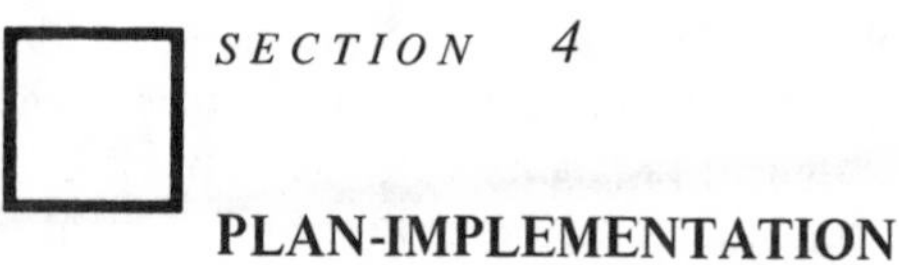

SECTION 4

PLAN-IMPLEMENTATION

INTRODUCTORY NOTE

Historically, American city planners, unlike their European counterparts, have emphasized the making of long-range plans, and considered their job finished after the recommended comprehensive long-range plan has been approved by the Planning Commission and adopted (hopefully) by the legislative body of their city. They considered implementation of the comprehensive plan the task and responsibility of others: the city council, city manager, operating departments, homebuilders, private developers, and businessmen. The city planner assumed the comprehensive long-range plan would serve as a guide to the decisions made on a day-to-day basis by these other parties. This is not to say that the city planner was not concerned at all with implementation—the typical plan usually included a section or chapter describing specific implementation tools, e.g. zoning, subdivision regulations, urban renewal, and indirect measures such as incentives and the like. What was missing, however, was a plan or strategy for implementation, which spells out the specific, detailed courses of action needed to move the city from where it currently is to the desired state as reflected in the long-range plan. The one exception was the capital budget or the capital improvements program which was instituted in several city planning agencies around the late 1940s and early 1950s, as a major tool for effectuating the comprehensive plan.

Martin Meyerson was one of the first planners to recognize that the long-range comprehensive plan was not an adequate guide to action; it is too generalized and remote to seem real. In 1956, in his keynote speech before the American Institute of Planners, he called on the planning profession to take on certain additional "middle-range" functions to bridge ad hoc, project-type planning, and long-range comprehensive planning in order to bring planning, policy and action closer together (Meyerson, 1956). Among his many suggestions was a "detailed development plan" function, the purpose of which would be to phase private and public programs as part of a comprehensive course of action covering not more than ten years.

In the decade and a half since Meyerson laid down his challenge to the planning profession, new short- and middle-range planning instruments, similar to his detailed development plan, have, indeed, emerged. These include the Annual Development Program, the Federal Workable Program, the Community Action Plan, and the Model Cities Program, to mention but a few. In particular, the federally assisted Community Renewal Program (CRP) produced around the country innovative short- and middle-range plans going by various names, the most common being "Ten-Year Improvements Plan."

This is best exemplified in the 1966 *Comprehensive Plan of Chicago,* prepared by that city's Department of Development and Planning. The comprehensive plan is presented in two parts; first is a "policies plan" of diagrammatic representations and statements of major policies to guide future development in seven categories of services or systems within the city. These include policies for residential areas, recreation, education, safety and health, industry, business, and transportation. The second part, the "improvement plan," sets forth specific targets for these seven planning systems in terms of specific quantitative elements for which cost estimates have been prepared. The Improvement Plan was specifically meant to be a middle-range plan, representing the strategy for Chicago's development through achievement of specific improvement targets set for the next fifteen years, and was to be implemented through the annual capital budgets and capital improvement programs. It was to be revised every four to six years, based on a long-range fiscal feasibility analysis.

The CRP experience led one planner (Robinson, 1964) to suggest that the next logical step in city planning should be what he called "Community Development Programming," the key elements of which are:

(1) A set of timed-objectives and operating targets to guide the city's developmental and renewal investments for the following six years—the objectives and targets to encompass economic and social, as well as the physical aspects of city life;
(2) An itemized list of the specific public and private actions that will contribute to the objectives;
(3) A timed-phased and costed set of public programs to be carried out by various departments and agencies over the future six-year period, including a statement of each program's objectives, the agency responsible for its execution, the foreseeable performance targets of each program, the method of evaluating performance, and costs of the program by year over the six years;
(4) An adopted budget and action plan for the first year of the six-year program.

To a degree, Community Development Programming has already begun to happen. A few planners have become general advisers to key politicians—especially mayors—concerning nearly all government activities; and from all evidence, this trend is bound to continue. This means that planners will become more and more tied up with the whole budgetary process. They are already heavily involved in capital budgeting and capital improvement programming; they should become equally concerned with the operating budgets and programs of all departments in the government. When this happens, city planners will be called upon to give advice on programs and program alternatives, to determine the relative effectiveness of specific programs, both before such programs are approved and after they have been executed. As implied earlier, they will review, analyze, and compare the programs of the various departments of local government, and recommend which ones are likely to result in the highest "pay-offs," in terms of achieving the community's goals.

In short, the city planner is currently being called upon (and will be increasingly so in the future) to use his skills—or where they are lacking, to develop them—to advise on the programming and budgeting of municipal programs and projects. This reflects an understanding of the close relationship between plan and action. As Ross (1967) has observed, "Without this relationship, planning is hollow, programming is a farce, and budgeting (or zoning) rules the world."

It is of interest to note that while planners have been recognizing the need for tying together long-range goals and short-range actions, a parallel and complementary movement has been taking place in the halls of the federal and state governments, especially in the offices of the budget and fiscal officers. There is a growing recognition today of the need to relate the budgeting and programming functions to planning, including the importance of identifying the goals and objectives ("missions") of the agencies. There is also more concern with long-range planning and with the substantive or program content of public expenditures, and with the interrelationships between the public and private sectors of the community. Influenced to a degree by practice abroad, especially in the undeveloped regions, the financial planners are now looking comprehensively at the whole evolving community, in seeking to strengthen the economic base of their areas.

This new outlook among government decision-makers and finance and fiscal planners has culminated in the introduction of the planning-programming-budgeting system (PPBS)—witness the priority given to "planning" as the first word in that term.

PPBS emerged as a management tool designed to alleviate the difficulties of current budgeting practices: the failure to define objectives (instead of objects of expense), to use the budgeting process to improve operational effectiveness, and to achieve a rational balance in the allocation of scarce resources among competing functional fields (Millward, 1968: 89). Now, with PPBS, setting goals, defining objectives, and developing planned programs for achieving these objectives are to be integral aspects of preparing and justifying a budget submission. Thus, PPBS merges the planning process and the budgeting process into what Robert Herman (1962) has called "separated togetherness."

The need to relate planning to budgeting and programming is not a completely new idea to some city planners. Rudiments of this idea, and indeed of PPBS, can be found in some of the basic early tests in city planning, such as those written by Ladislas Segoe (1941), and Robert A. Walker (1941). Planners have always sought to make the budget a servant of plans via programs, but they have been rarely successful at the municipal level, except in the case of capital budgeting. Thus, when President Johnson's edict in August, 1965 made PPBS the gospel for the entire federal bureaucracy, old-line fiscal officers were confounded and in many cases resistant to the idea, but city planners were receptive and generally elated. Planners welcomed the introduction of this new management tool for it represented what they considered to be a long-overdue recognition of the importance of planning to the budgeting and programming functions of government.

This new action-orientation of the city planners is posing methodological problems not encountered before, and with which their traditional methods are not capable of dealing. Some of the more important ones are these: How to relate the budgeting and programming process to the long-range plan and planning needs in general? How to determine the optimal timing, sequences, and priorities of programs and projects–both capital and operating? How to identify which programs and program alternatives are likely to have the greatest pay-offs in terms of the community goals? How to estimate which is the best plan of action to recommend if the objective is to minimize costs and the budget spent, or the best plan if the objective is to recommend that plan which is likely to have the greatest impact on achieving goals, regardless of the costs? How to determine which immediate actions to recommend which will not jeopardize certain future long-range options?

New methods and techniques are emerging to deal with these sorts of questions, some of which are described in the papers in this section. As in the case of the other new planning methods discussed elsewhere in this volume, most of them are based on techniques that have their origin in fields and disciplines such as mathematical programming, systems engineering, and economics.

The paper in Chapter 13, which is taken from a manual prepared by An Foras Forbartha (the National Institute for Physical Planning and Construction Research of Ireland), assisted by the United Nations Special Fund, for use by local planning authorities in their planning work in Ireland, aims to show how to relate planning and budgeting. Here the concern is with the planning of amenities and tourism–a subject area, incidently, that is becoming increasingly significant as planners become more and more involved with issues affecting the overall quality of the environment. In contrast to traditional practice in this area, in which emotion-laden and qualitative judgments tend to provide the basis for most plans and proposals, the manual attempts to provide more directly quantitative or economic grounds for desired policies. The methodology proposed by the Irish planners is worth considerable attention.

The sections of the paper from the manual included in the volume cover two of the five steps in what the Irish planners refer to as the form and sequence of a "thought process" required in planning amenities and tourism. Focusing on one of the counties in Ireland, the three sections missing from the paper deal with (1) an analysis of the resources relevant to amenities and tourism (e.g. scenic areas, historic monuments, and the like); (2) an analysis of the client groups (e.g. local people, night visitors and day visitors, and so on) who now use the resources of the county–where they go, what they do, what they need, and how much they spend; (3) comparison of these two basic sets of survey data, by measuring the capacity of the main type of amenity and tourist resources in terms of people and of standards of use or service–comparing numbers of people with the assessed capacity of each resource reveals the adequacy, shortfall, or surplus of capacity in each resource.

The measurement of shortfall or surplus in the resources is then used as a guide to the possible type and extent of increase in use of these resources. This possibility is expressed in terms of several options, each based on an estimate of the possible growth in one of the groups of clients and the consequent increase or change in the pressures they place upon the county's resources. Each option is measured against the resources, to judge what extra demand it would place upon them, i.e. what new shortfalls and surpluses would result. This is done for each of the several options for each of the planning areas within the county. The total impact of each type of option upon the county can then be assessed.

These comparisons of people and resources, with the resulting shortfalls and surpluses for each option in each planning area, are then placed into what the Irish planners call an Amenity Budget, which is designed to measure the cost and benefits of each option or set of options in terms of money and resources. Comparisons of the cost and benefits which each option produces then allows judgments to be made, area by area, on the actual program of capital expenditures, use of resources, and other planning actions which the decision-makers might pursue, or persuade other bodies or individuals to pursue.

Finally, the Irish planners recommend a process for relating planning and budgeting at the different levels of government concerned with planning amenities and tourism and at different time periods.

A significant development relating to capital improvement programming has been the introduction of rather sophisticated and detailed procedures best exemplified by the work being done for the Philadelphia capital program (Coughlan, 1960; Coughlan and Pitts, 1960; Brown and Gilbert, 1961). For example, Robert Coughlan (1960), drawing upon his experience working for the Philadelphia City Planning Commission, develops a framework or system for analyzing and formulating a capital improvement program, given the existence of a comprehensive plan. His proposed framework includes examination of a set of consistent decisions at different levels of project generality and for different time periods, leading to the development of a "comprehensive plan allocation profile." The profile aids in determining how much money should be allocated to each functional group of capital improvements in order to complete the comprehensive plan, within a given budget limit.

This early work was later refined to permit community goals (upon which a comprehensive plan is based) to appear in an objective function directly, that is, a combination of goals which the planner may wish to optimize (Coughlan and Stevens, 1964). The authors propose a method for the evaluation of multi-functional planning "packages" such as a city's capital improvements program. In this conceptual model, the need to distinguish between independent and interdependent contributions of programs to goals is emphasized, as well as the need to identify the indirect effects of the achievement of goals upon each other. In some respects, the proposed method represents an elaboration of certain aspects of Hill's goals-achievement matrix, discussed in Section Three.

Philadelphia planners have also developed new procedures for close integration of capital and operating budgets, and have evolved careful criteria for evaluating project requests. Finally, the Philadephia planners, under its 1962 Community Renewal Program, pioneered in the use of PPBS concepts and methods for the purposes of urban renewal and city planning in general. (This effort is one of the case studies described in Part Two of this volume.)

Another recent trend has been the use of mathematical programming techniques for programming and budgeting purposes. The clear-cut advantage of mathematical programming, as noted in the introductory note to Section Two, is that the technique can generate a large number of alternative plans and programs, permitting the planner to consider many more combinations of program and policy variables than could be put together by hand, and end up selecting one combination which is optimal, optimal being defined as that investment alternative which either maximizes the achievement of the stated community goals, at the same time not exceeding the total available budget, or achieves some minimum set of objectives at the lowest overall cost.

Mathematical programming techniques are being experimented with to help determine the optimal timing and sequencing of capital projects (Burns, 1963).

In his paper in Chapter 14, Darwin G. Stuart explores the potential application of mathematical programming techniques, specifically linear programming, in the development and evaluation of urban improvement programs. Using the Model Cities Program as an example, he develops a simple linear programming model, built around the concepts and techniques of PPBS (e.g. specification of objectives, quantifiable indices, and performance standards; identification of alternative programs and policies and the objectives to which they are related, the impact or effectiveness which they will have in achieving each objective, and the costs associated with varying levels of effectiveness; and appropriate program budgets) and other analytic techniques (e.g. sensitivity analysis). The chief concern of the model is with achieving an optimum allocation of dollars among the various program alternatives available. The model allocates dollars among various Model Cities Program alternatives, either minimizing the total cost or budget spent (given specified minimum levels of goal achievement)—the "minimum budget" solution—or maximizing the achievement of specific Model Cities goals and objectives (given a maximum overall budget)—the "maximum impact" solution.

Examples of the linear programming model are programmed for the areas of housing and employment-income-education and run for a hypothetical model neighborhood, using real and assumed data from Chicago. To show how the basic model can be used to test various kinds of alternatives, four revised solutions of the minimum budget problem are also run; in addition, one of the maximum impact solutions is revised.

According to Stuart, the potential value of models, like the one he developed, is in their ability to identify for decision-makers the relative costs, effectiveness, and trade-offs of alternative programs. In addition, they can tell decision-makers where to put the emphasis—e.g. to look for public housing sites containing mostly substandard housing, to concentrate rent supplements upon poorly housed low-income families, and so on. The more precise we can be in defining these desirable directions of emphasis, the more effectively and efficiently our public funds will be spent.

New implementation techniques are also needed because planners today must concern themselves with current problems; to be sure, they must make an impact on these problems. Indeed, the significance of city planning (as with any type of planning activity)—no matter how far into the future it may set out to look—will depend on the guidance that it can give in the selection of appropriate courses of action to deal with current circumstances.

This awareness of the need to confront the present, but to do so in light of the future, raises some perplexing problems for the planner. One of the most difficult is the need to strike a balance between the pressures for early commitment and the desire for flexibility to adapt to unforeseen circumstances, that is, the need for flexibility of future choice. In short, the planner today wants to respond to the immediate problems at hand, but at the same time he does not want to recommend actions that might foreclose on any of the desirable long-range options that may be open.

As demonstrated by Shiv Gupta and Jonathan Rosenhead in their paper in Chapter 15, this problem is not unique to city planning but is commonly encountered in the long-range investment plans, particularly for expansion or decentralization, of industrial organizations. To deal with this problem, the authors, drawing upon their interests and skills in strategic investment decision-making and information theory, describe an approach and technique which has considerable applicability to city planning. The authors note that long-range investment plans often consist of a number of separate but interacting investments spaced over a number of years. Where there is much uncertainty about external conditions in the future, it is possible that a "best" scheme based on the state of current knowledge will prove during the course of the intervening years to be less than "good."

One way to guard against this danger, they argue, is to ensure that the early (and therefore irreversible) steps in the investment sequence keep open as many options to good schemes as possible. To do so, they introduce the concept of "robustness," which represents a measure of flexibility. The robustness of a set of possible actions is measured by the number of good full solutions which are left open, defining "goodness" in relation to some agreed cut-off point in the order of preference; the hypothesis is that, while future conditions may bring some variations in the order of preference, the retention of a larger number of solutions which now appear near the top of the list of possible options increases the likelihood of being able to select a "near-optimum" solution at a later stage.

To illustrate the practical use of this concept, the authors discuss a case study which deals with the location of sites for new factories in an industrial expansion program.

Friend and Jessop, in their book referred to earlier, utilized the concept of robustness in the various fictitious case examples (including the one described in their paper in Chapter 12) they use to show how the planning process can be made more effective. They find the measure of robustness useful in selecting a set of short-term actions which will go some way toward satisfying the more immediate pressures for commitment and yet leave a sufficient range of options open for future choice when conditions may have undergone substantial change. They demonstrate a method for determining which courses of immediate action will likely provide a greater margin of flexibility for future choice than other alternative actions even within the same decision field.

Chapter 13

THE PLANNING-BUDGETING PROCESS

An Foras Forbartha

STATEMENT OF OPTIONS

The fourth main step in the thought process–having surveyed the resources (section A) and the clients (section B) and analyzed the present impact of the one upon the other (section C)–is to state and examine the main alternative policies of development which appear to be open for the future. This is done by expressing a number of options.

Each option is a simplified goal or aim, different from the other options. This does not mean that only one goal or aim can be pursued at the same time, or that one option could not complement or follow the other. It is simply a method of showing the implications of various possible policies in such a way that one can judge their relative merits and see whether they could be usefully applied

(a) together
(b) in sequence, or
(c) as alternatives.

One purpose of this Manual, as stated in the Introduction* is to describe how a county planning authority may state the goals of *development* and *protection* relevant to amenity and tourism for their county. Development and protection–these are the two prime purposes of a study such as this. On the one hand,

*Not included herein.–Ed.

Reprinted from *Specimen Development Plan Manual: Planning for Amenity and Tourism,* An Foras Forbartha (The National Institute for Physical Planning and Construction Research, Dublin), with the assistance of the United Nations Special Fund (August 1966), pp. 62-77.

one wishes to protect the rich and varied heritage of Ireland, on the other to encourage its economic and social progress.

The options to be stated must take *both* purposes into account and combine them. This is done by arguing straight on from the earlier steps in the thought process, with its emphasis on *resources* and *clients.*

Choice of Options

Each option has an element of both resources and clients, by answering two questions:

(a) how might a group, or groups, of *clients* grow or change?
(b) if so, how might their growth or change be disposed to have the best impact on resources?

Each option is based, in fact, upon *either* a notional change in client groups and their effect on resources *or* a notional change in impact on resources and its implications for change in client groups.

The exact options chosen for analysis will vary from one county to the next, depending on the nature of the surplus resources and the types of change in client groups which might reasonably be expected or pursued. Thus:

(a) a county with very low occupancy rates in its hotels and other accommodation might pose as an option the *efficient use of night accommodation.*
(b) a county on the edge of Dublin might pose as an option *doubling the number of weekend visitors from the city.*
(c) a county which contained an air or ocean terminal might pose as an option *attracting half the incoming tourists from the terminal to spend 2 days in the county.*

Each option chosen must be *one* possible answer to the problem of developing the county: it must be relevant and reasonable for the county, based upon appraisal of its resources and of its present or potential clients.

Choice of Options for Donegal

The appraisal of Donegal, much of which has been described in the first half of this Manual, suggested the following choice of options, which are illustrated graphically on Figure D2.*

Option 1. Increase in holiday-makers (Map 1*). Donegal is well-established as a holiday county. This option is based on an estimate of the share which Donegal might hope to attract of the expected growth in foreign and Irish people taking holidays in Ireland during the next 20 years, and of the probable distribution of that increased number within the county *according to the availability of surplus capacity in day resources* as shown in Map C2.

Option 2. Increase in tourists (Map 2*). Donegal has a small but growing number of people passing through the county on tour. This option is based on an estimate of the numbers of tourists, within the projected national growth

*Not included herein.–Ed.

over the next 20 years, who might come to Donegal, and of their probable movement through the county to areas with a surplus capacity of relevant day resources.

Option 3. Increase in day visitors (Map 3*). By its proximity and resources, Donegal attracts a great number of day visitors from Northern Ireland. Option 3 is based on an estimate of the possible increase in these day visitors over the next 20 years; and of their probable distribution to the different parts of the county, as controlled by accessibility and the surplus capacity of relevant day resources.

Option 4. Increase in all these groups of clients. Because of its large (though localized) surplus of day resources, Donegal might aim to attract increased numbers of *all* these groups–holiday-makers, tourists and day visitors–simultaneously. Option 4 combines the estimates of growth in client numbers from Options 1, 2 and 3.

A major option, or set of options, in every county should, of course, be concerned with changes in one major group of clients, the local people. As explained on page 2, the Donegal Study covered only one "vertical slice" of the county development plan. Where, as is desirable, all elements of this plan are pushed forward together, options can be expressed as suitable for a stated *growth* or *decline* or *movement* of population in the county or for changes in the pattern of *seasonal migration* or other adjustments mentioned earlier.*

For lack of information on what changes might be expected or contemplated in the local population, the Donegal options assumed no change in that client group. The figures used were, for the third quarter:

	Clients Present (average per day)		
	Night Visitors *A*	*Day Visitors* *B*	*Local People* *C*
Present position	8,657	21,385	96,075
Options			
1. Increase holiday-makers	12,592	21,385	96,075
2. Increase tourists	9,425	21,385	96,075
3. Increase day visitors	8,657	24,930	96,075
4. Increase all groups	13,576	24,930	96,075

Calculation of Options

The process of reaching these figures must now be described. It is based, substantially, on targets set by Bord Failte for the increase in numbers of, and revenue from, visitors to Ireland following the publication of the Government's Economic Program. This Program set the target of doubling tourist income between 1960 and 1970. Bord Failte appraised the possibilities of increase for each national group of visitors and set targets for growth in each group for the 1960-1970 decade.

*Not included herein.–Ed.

These targets are set out in *The Marketing Plan for Irish Tourism,* which also shows the progress made towards achieving these targets up to 1964. *The Marketing Plan* further sets out, in some detail, the types of tourist product or resource which may be estimated to attract each group of visitors, and the types of accommodation, facility and service which each group will expect.

From this material, it is quite easy to set up a table* showing for a chosen future date (1985 may be convenient) a projection of Bord Failte's target for 1960-1970 growth in each national group of visitors to the Republic. A broad look at the county's surplus "tourist products," i.e. its resources as analyzed in Section A of the Manual, plus thought about its geographical position relative to each group of visitors, will then suggest whether the county could expect to attract a share of each national group equal to, less or more than its present share as shown.*

Projections of Client Groups

The graphs which follow show projections for each main national group of visitors to the Republic, and for Irish holiday-makers within it, and also show the share of these projections which Donegal might hope to attract. The figures for the Republic (thin line on each graph) are taken or projected from *The Marketing Plan for Irish Tourism* in all cases except Irish holiday-makers, for which group figures come from the *Home Holiday-Makers Survey.* The figures for Donegal (thick line on each graph) are based on the reasoning briefly described above, the chief factors being:

(i) the nature of the county's surplus resources
(ii) its geographical position in relation to main points of entry and tourist routes, as shown on Figure C2.*

The reasoning may be summarized thus for visitors from:

(a) Britain: Donegal can hope to attract a higher portion of British visitors than now because it has a high surplus of tourist products which the British visitor seeks (notably scenic motoring, pony trekking, shooting, fishing, and water sports) and is reasonably well-placed for access from Britain through Northern Ireland (Figure C2).
(b) Northern Ireland (night visitors). Donegal can hope to attract a higher portion of this group than now because it is extremely accessible to Northern Ireland and has many resources which the Northern Irish holiday-maker seeks (roughly the same as those for Britain).
(c) United States and Canada. Donegal is unlikely to maintain a proportionate share of this group because of its relative remoteness from Dublin and Shannon (the main points of entry), the comparative shortness of stay of this group, and the county's relative lack of the sophisticated entertainment which the transatlantic visitors seek.
(d) Other Foreign Countries, mostly the Continent and some Commonwealth countries. A very steep rise is expected in the numbers in this multinational group coming to Ireland. Their demands and lengths of stay vary greatly, but on

*Not included herein.–Ed.

balance it seems likely that Donegal's remoteness from their main points of entry will give it a less than present share of this group.

(e) Republic. This group has a fairly high response to the type of natural resource that Donegal offers, and may well be increasingly attracted to the county for the novelty of going there and its relative freedom from summer congestion.

(f) Northern Ireland (day visitors). As car ownership, personal income and leisure grow in Northern Ireland, Donegal will be in easy day-reach for more frequent visits by more Northern Irish people than now, and can expect to take a growing proportion of day visitors coming into the Republic.

These projections are, of course, very tentative. Bord Failte has set no targets beyond 1970 for numbers visiting the Republic: the share which Donegal now welcomes of each group is not completely certain and the future share the county might hope for is even less certain. For these reasons, a "cone of probability" is shown on each graph to indicate the range within which the figures probably fall. As information improves over the years, this "cone" can be narrowed down. Meanwhile the firm line is simply the center of this cone, used as the basis of options.

The projections on the graphs imply the following figures for national groups, and hence for types of visitor to the Republic and county:

	Numbers in Thousands			
	1960 Actual	*1964 Estimated*	*1970 Target*	*1985 Projected*
Night Visitors from				
Britain to Republic	827	966	1,084	1,280
to Donegal		33.6		42
N. Ireland to Republic	432	519	550	722
to Donegal		114.2		162
U.S.A./Canada to Republic	69	120	270	350+
U.S.A./Canada to Donegal		5.7		10
Other Foreign Countries to Republic	45	82	204	320+
to Donegal		4		9.8
Republic in Republic		439		500
to Donegal		18.3		28.5
Day Visitors from				
N. Ireland to Republic		9,810		12,200
to Donegal		4,728		8,400
Total holiday-makers (option 1)		102.5		170.5
Total tourists (option 2)		73.3		81.8
Total day visitors (option 3)		4,728		8,400

The figures in the bottom box are the figures to be used for Options 1, 2 and 3. These are then broken down seasonally on assumptions similar to those described,* and geographically as shown on Map D1.* The seasonal figure is then

*Not included herein.–Ed.

BRITAIN

NORTHERN IRELAND

U.S. AND CANADA

OTHER FOREIGN

REPUBLIC

NORTHERN IRELAND DAY VISITORS

REPUBLIC PROJECTION

COUNTY PROJECTION (With "Cone of Probability")

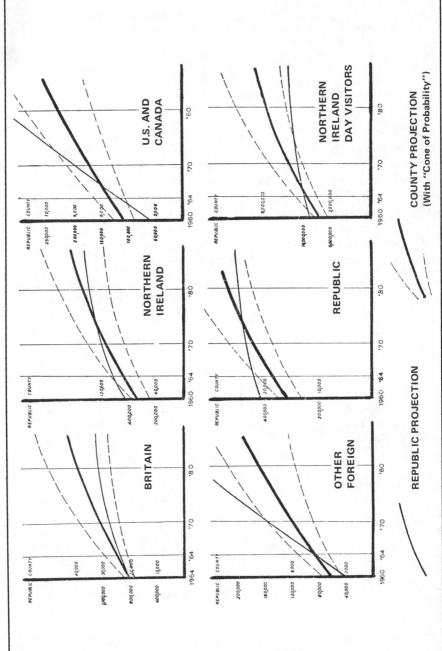

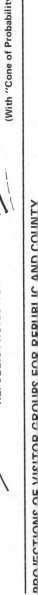

PROJECTIONS OF VISITOR GROUPS FOR REPUBLIC AND COUNTY

divided by 91 (days), as described for day visitors,* to produce the figures for the average number of people present per day for each planning area, of which the table on page 321 is an example.

When a table of this type has been produced for each planning area, the impact of each option upon the resources of that area can be assessed in just the same way as was done for the present situation; and a table can be prepared for each option and area, . . . to show the shortfalls and surplus resources which result.

Capacity Diagram for Options

The material shown in the tables on page 324 can now be expressed graphically in a diagram similar to that shown.* The capacity diagram for options* is a direct extension of that earlier diagram, and contains the following identical elements.

(1) The total number of clients present in 1964, represented by Column D up to the first strong horizontal line
(2) 10 columns, from E to Q, representing the resource base
(3) the present usage of these resources, shown by the strong horizontal line. This now becomes the base line for the options.

The changes from the earlier diagram are all above the strong horizontal line. The following additions or changes have been made:

(4) Column D, representing clients, has been extended upwards to a line which is labelled ultimate.
(5) This new part of Column D has been divided into units, labelled +1, +2, etc. As in Column D below the line, each unit represents say 1,000 people. But the make-up of each 1,000 people may be different above the line. In Donegal, for example, none of the projected options include any local population in their client groups, as so explained on page 321. This means that the client units above the line may have a different impact on resources from those below the line. The make-up, or *client mix,* of each new unit of clients is shown at the base of Column D.
(6) The demand which each new unit of clients places upon each resource is shown by a thin horizontal line. The existing surplus of each resource over and above present usage is shown in the white columns above the line (dotted if the capacity is potential rather than actual). The horizontal lines for each unit thus show how much of the surplus capacity is used by each unit of clients, or how much shortfall is caused by the absence of spare capacity.
(7) The upper line of the diagram, labelled "ultimate," is set by the upper limit of existing (i.e. actual and potential) capacity in Day Resources (Column J) for the reasons described.*

In this way, it can be quickly seen what a given option, with its own mix of future clients, would imply in the use of resources. It should be emphasized that no dates are given beyond the present position, since the speed with which given numbers of clients could be attracted to an area can be varied as a matter of

*Not included herein.–Ed.

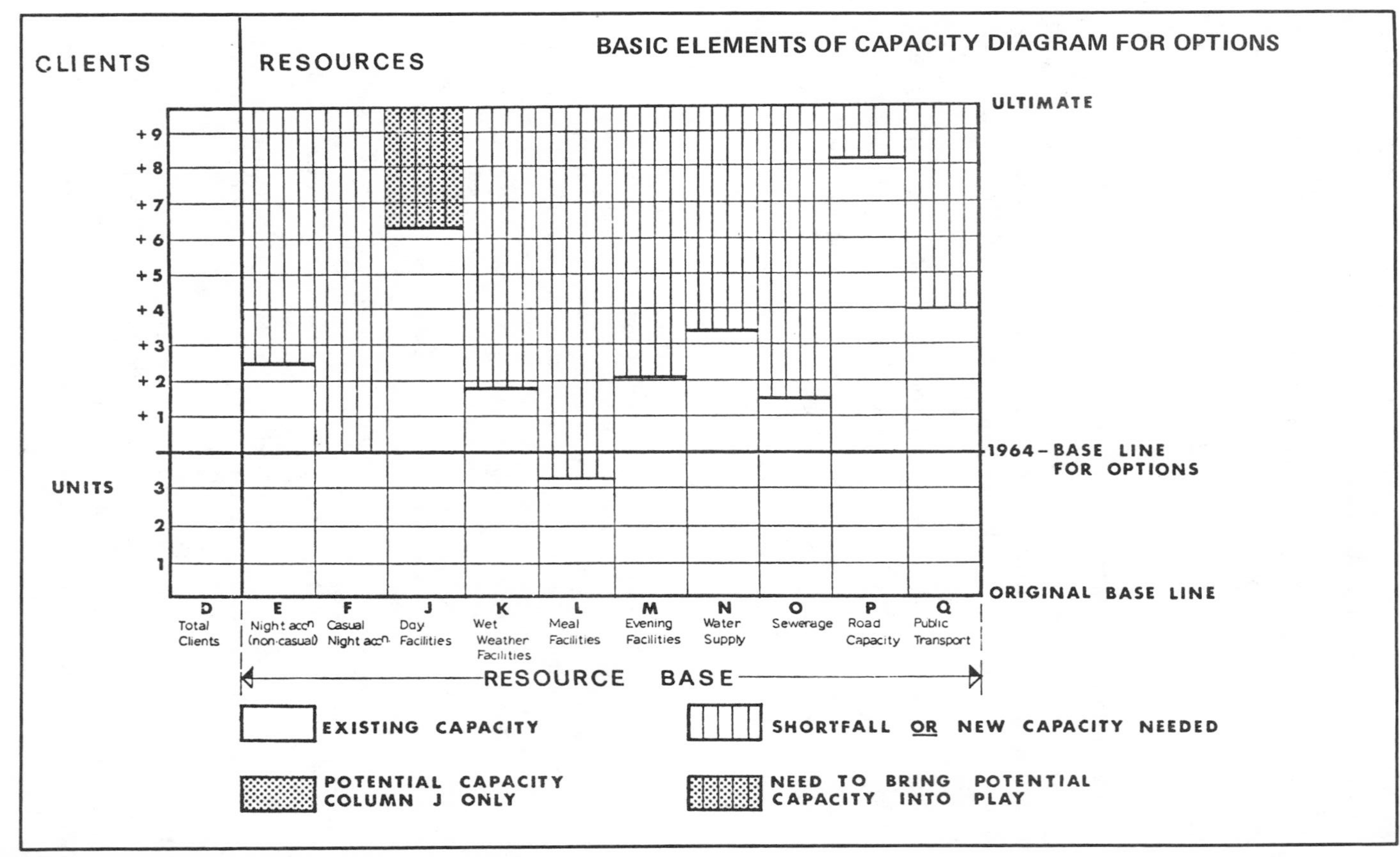
BASIC ELEMENTS OF CAPACITY DIAGRAM FOR OPTIONS
CLIENTS
RESOURCES
ULTIMATE
1964 – BASE LINE FOR OPTIONS
ORIGINAL BASE LINE
UNITS
+9
+8
+7
+6
+5
+4
+3
+2
+1
3
2
1
D Total Clients
E Night accn (non-casual)
F Casual Night accn
J Day Facilities
K Wet Weather Facilities
L Meal Facilities
M Evening Facilities
N Water Supply
O Sewerage
P Road Capacity
Q Public Transport
RESOURCE BASE
EXISTING CAPACITY
SHORTFALL OR NEW CAPACITY NEEDED
POTENTIAL CAPACITY COLUMN J ONLY
NEED TO BRING POTENTIAL CAPACITY INTO PLAY

circumstances or policy. The diagram itself makes no decisions, and has no limit except for the "ultimate" line: it simply illustrates the implications of each option in terms of the use of or demand for resources.

AMENITY BUDGET

The next stage in the thought process is to prepare an Amenity Budget. This is in effect a financial and economic analysis of the preceding material.

An Amenity Budget is a form of Capital Budget. Capital Budgets, wherever they are used, have much the same purpose–to coordinate physical means and physical plans. Basically, their aim is to schedule an *equitable, geographically* balanced and appropriately timed distribution of *limited* capital funds among the many needs which an agency may have. In other words, capital budgeting is a technique for finding out how much things cost and how and when the money should be spent.

The Amenity Budget is designed to do this for planning authorities and other bodies concerned with protection of amenity and development of tourism. These bodies are not concerned only with the financial cost of developing tourism, although this is important to them, but also with the pressure on their amenity resources. Thus the budget is designed to show the impact of given policies upon resources as well as upon costs.

It should be emphasized that a budget does not make decisions. It is neutral. But it does throw light on the many alternatives, or *options,* which lie open to the policy-making bodies. Because these options are numerous, the budget is designed to be flexible.

Budget Diagram

The purpose and content of the Amenity Budget can be outlined best by describing the basic elements of the budget diagram, as shown opposite. This diagram is a further direct extension of the capacity diagram* and of the capacity diagram for options shown on page 326. The budget diagram contains the following elements taken directly from the capacity diagram for options:

1. the total number of clients present in 1964, represented by Column D up to the first strong horizontal line
2. 10 columns, from E to Q, representing the resource base
3. the present usage of these resources, shown by the strong horizontal line, which becomes the base line for the options
4. the upward extension of Column D showing the possible future growth of clients up to the line labelled "ultimate"
5. the division of this new upper part of Column D into units labelled +1, +2, etc.

*Not included herein.–Ed.

The changes and additions to the earlier diagram are as follows:

6. The heading *Resources* at the top has been changed to *Costs,* because we are now concerned not only with the usage of resources as such, but also with the costs which have gone into the creation of existing resources or which are needed to create new resources.

7. For the same reason:

(a) Boxes are provided at the base of the diagram to show the size or amount of resources in each column: and the cost or value of that unit. This is done to permit a direct evaluation of the shortfall or surplus of resources implied by each unit of increase in clients.

(b) Column R is added at the right to show the total costs involved in making up shortfalls of resources at each given unit line.

8. The second major element of the budget diagram, namely *Benefits.* This comprises three columns:

(S) Total Client Expenditure. This is calculated on the basis described in section B of this Manual to represent the estimated annual expenditure represented by each unit of clients in Column D.

(T) Employment. This is an estimate of the number of people directly employed in tourism during the summer as a result of the presence of each unit of clients in Column D. The basis for the estimate is as described.*

(U) Rateable Value. This is an estimate of the total rateable value of properties wholly used for tourism by each unit of clients in Column D. It is based upon average rateable values per seat in evening facilities, as shown in the rating lists held by each county council.

9. In two of the columns, those for total costs and for total client expenditure, the actual amounts involved by each unit of increase in clients are shown. This represents the first step towards a direct cost-benefit analysis.

Preparation of the Budget Diagram

The diagram shown on the previous page can be used either to analyze the present position or to judge the effect of different options for future development: it should not normally be used to show both of these at the same time. Most of the material needed for the diagram comes from earlier sections of the Thought Process, thus:

Present Position

(1) The total of existing clients and the client mix within that total, come from the calculations described.* A suitable size of client unit, say 1,000 people, can readily be chosen.

(2) The demands which each unit of clients places upon the resources (columns E to Q) are calculated from the formulae set out.* This necessary capacity of each resource unit of clients is stated as the unit size in the box at the bottom of the diagram: and the cost of that unit is assessed.

(3) The existing capacity of resources is taken from summary charts, and is drawn on to the Budget diagram at a scale to match the unit size of each resource stated in the bottom box.

*Not included herein.—Ed.

(4) The existing shortfalls or surpluses in resource capacity can then be readily seen, their cost or value assessed, and the total cost of shortfalls inserted in the total cost column.

(5) The benefits resulting from the present total of clients can then be calculated as described in paragraph 8 of page 328, according to the size and composition of each client unit.

Options

(6) The projections of future clients, as shown in the upper part of Column D, are based upon a client mix as stated in one of a series of options (see pages 325 and 327).

(7) The demands which these projected future clients makes upon each resource (columns E to Q) are then calculated as in 2 above and stated in the box at the base of the diagram. The cost or value of each resource unit is assessed and inserted.

(8) The *surplus* existing capacity of each resource (i.e. that capacity which is over and above present demand) is then drawn on to the diagram at the scale of the calculated unit for each resource.

(9) The horizontal unit lines will then reveal the shortfalls which will occur in one or more of the resources at each point below the line labelled "ultimate."

(10) These shortfalls can then be valued according to the stated cost/value of each unit at the base of the diagram. The total cost of making good shortfalls throughout the resource base (columns E to Q inclusive), can then be inserted in the total costs column, and the increase in *Benefits* in the last three columns can then be calculated as described in paragraph 8 of page 328, according to the size and composition of each client unit.

The value of the budget diagram is that it shows:

(a) how much of each resource is needed for each unit of a given mix of clients.
(b) how much it will cost to make good any shortfalls in these necessary resources, i.e. what size of new investment may be needed.
(c) for which type of resource, and hence by whom, this investment must be made.
(d) what will be the increased benefit from making this investment.

The form of the diagram ensures that this information will be directly comparable from option to option. It also is completely flexible in use, having no fixed limits of date or area. The planner and budgeter can assess the consequences of different speeds and types of development by changing from one diagram to another or by moving up and down from one unit line to the next, remembering always that the number of service units must equal the number of client units.

How to Use the Budget

It should be emphasized that the budget is part of the planning process. The budgeting judgment of costs and benefits does not supersede the planning judgment: the two are complementary. Indeed, the impact of clients on resources has to be expressed in physical as well as numerical and financial terms.

BASIC ELEMENTS OF BUDGET DIAGRAM

CLIENTS		COSTS											BENEFITS			
																Ultimate
+9																
+8																
+7																
+6																
+5																
+4																
+3																
+2																
+1																
																1964 Baseline for Options
UNITS 3																
2																
1																
																Original Baseline
	D	E	F	J	K	L	M	N	O	P	Q	R	S	T	U	
CLIENT MIX {A B C		Night Acc[n] (non-casual)	Casual Night Acc[n].	Day Facilities	Wet Weather Facilities	Meal Facilities	Evening Facilities	Water Supply	Sewerage	Road Capacity	Public Transport	Total Costs £	Annual Client Expenditure £	Employment in Tourism	Rateable Value £	
UNIT SIZE	1000															
UNIT COST/VALUE £														—		

The next few pages illustrate how the budget may be used in the planning process. They contain four budget diagrams, all referring to the Cloghaneely planning area and showing the costs and benefits of:

(a) the present position
(b) Option 1
(c) Option 2
(d) Option 3

the options being as expressed on pages 320-321. On the page opposite each diagram are the following items relating to it:

(i) notes on the basis and apparent implications of that diagram.
(ii) an initial cost-benefit comparison, in chart form.
(iii) for the options only, a map of Cloghaneely's amenity and tourism resources, as shown earlier in Figure A 18* showing the possible use of these resources implied by each option. This map forms the basis f~~ the more detailed examination of these resources which will be needed to judge the precise impact and cost of each option.

Cloghaneely–Present Position Budget

This budget is based on the number and mix of clients present in Cloghaneely in the third quarter of the year as shown,* thus:

	Night Visitors	Day Visitors	Local People	All Groups
	A	B	C	D
Total Present	802	1873	4765	7440
Unit Mix	108	252	640	1000

The impact of these present clients upon the resources is as shown.* There are shortfalls in columns E, F and H, so slight that they do not appear in the diagram; and surpluses in all other columns, those in columns J and P being particularly large. In other words, there are ample day resources and much spare road capacity. But any increase in client groups will quickly use up the other spare resources: in particular, any growth in night visitors will demand investment in accommodation.

*Not included herein.–Ed.

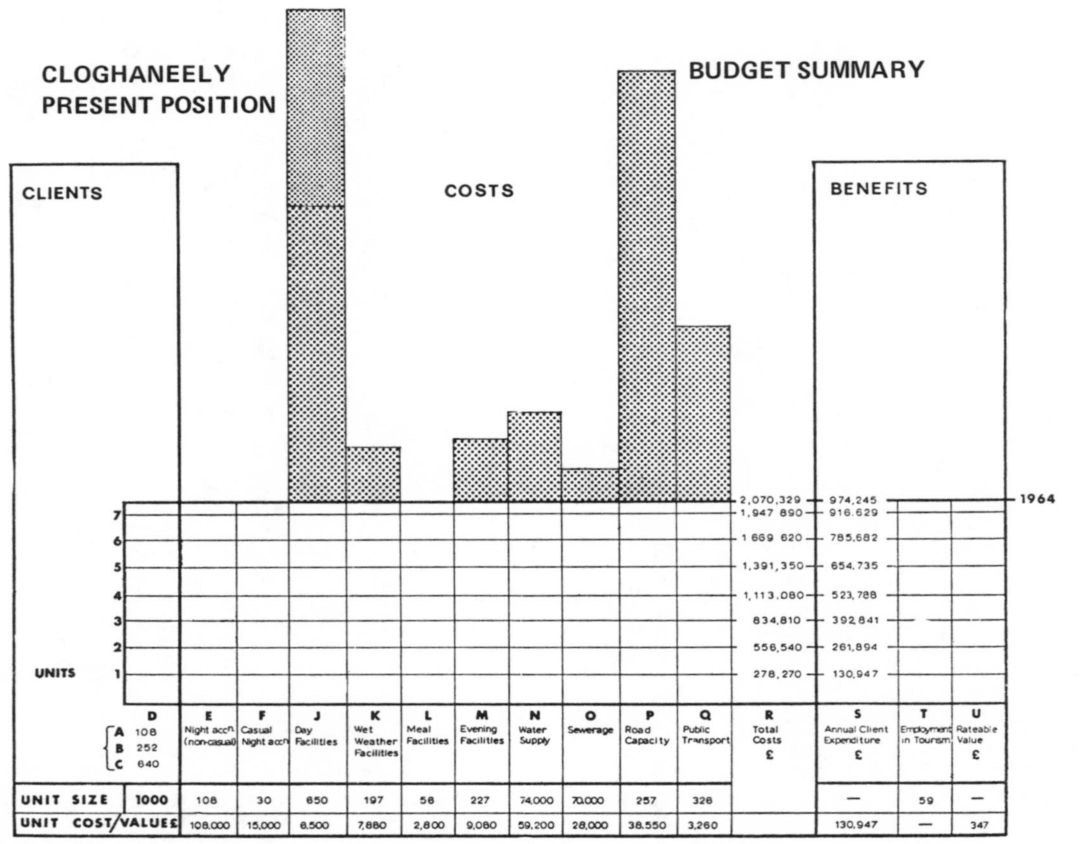
CLOGHANEELY
PRESENT POSITION
BUDGET SUMMARY
CLIENTS
COSTS
BENEFITS
UNITS
7
6
5
4
3
2
1
2,070,329
1,947 890
1 669 620
1,391,350
1,113,080
834,810
556,540
278,270
974,245
916.629
785,682
654,735
523,788
392,841
261,894
130,947
1964
D
A 108
B 252
C 640
E Night accn. (non-casual)
F Casual Night accn.
J Day Facilities
K Wet Weather Facilities
L Meal Facilities
M Evening Facilities
N Water Supply
O Sewerage
P Road Capacity
Q Public Transport
R Total Costs £
S Annual Client Expenditure £
T Employment in Tourism
U Rateable Value £
UNIT SIZE
1000
108
30
650
197
58
227
74,000
70,000
257
328
—
59
—
UNIT COST/VALUE£
108,000
15,000
6,500
7,880
2,800
9,080
59,200
28,000
38,550
3,260
130,947
—
347

The initial cost-benefit comparison below shows the following items:

(i) in column d, the total existing investment in resources in Cloghaneely planning area, represented by the full height of the resource columns (whether plain or stippled) opposite.

(ii) in column a, the part of this total investment that is now used, represented by the white columns below the 1964 line opposite.

(iii) in column b, the part of the total investment that is *not* now used, i.e. the stippled part of the columns opposite. This part of the investment is thus seen to be unproductive.

(iv) in column h, the annual expenditure by client groups in Cloghaneely planning area, made up from expenditures by night visitors (column e), day visitors (column f) and local people (column g).

(v) in the last column below, the "return" which the total annual expenditure represents on the total investment. This is not strictly a measure of direct return from investment, for several reasons–the investment has taken place over centuries; the expenditure is in gross, not net, terms; and the people who made the investment do not necessarily enjoy the income. Nevertheless, this provides the first rough comparison between cost and benefit, ready for further refinement.

Initial Cost-Benefit Comparison £'s 000 Throughout	*Investment*				*Annual Expenditure by Client Groups*					*"Returns"*	
	Existing-Used a	*Existing-Surplus* b	*New (short-fall)* c	*Total* d	*Night Visitors* e	*Day Visitors* f	*Local People* g	*Total* h	*Increase Over Existing* i	*On New Capital (i as % of c)*	*On Total Investment (h as % of d)*
Present position	2,070	1,171	–	3,241	440	426	108	974	–	–	30

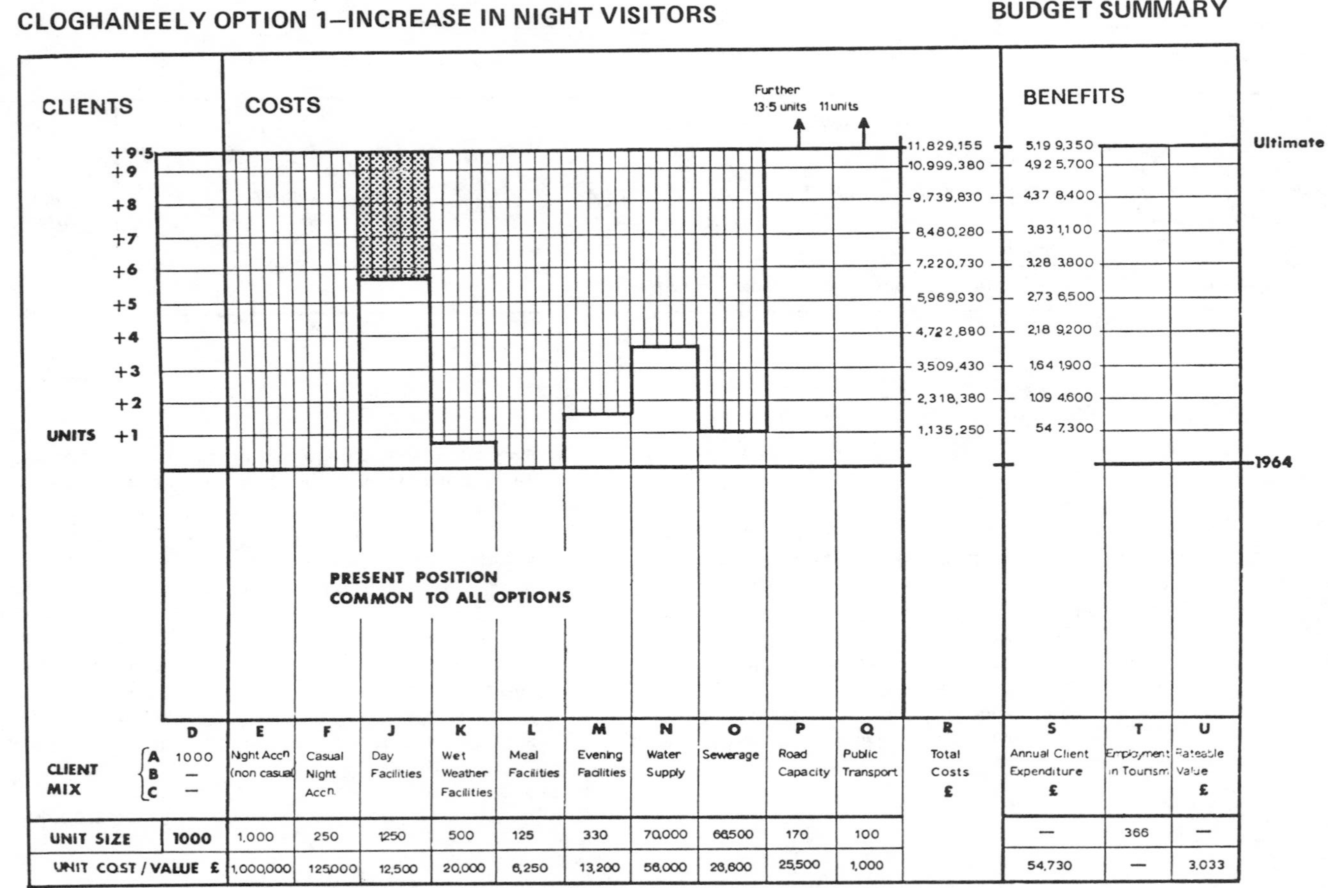

CLOGHANEELY OPTION 1—INCREASE IN NIGHT VISITORS
BUDGET SUMMARY
CLIENTS
COSTS
BENEFITS
Further 13·5 units
11 units
Ultimate
1964
UNITS
+9·5
+9
+8
+7
+6
+5
+4
+3
+2
+1
PRESENT POSITION COMMON TO ALL OPTIONS
11,829,155
10,999,380
9,739,830
8,480,280
7,220,730
5,969,930
4,722,880
3,509,430
2,318,380
1,135,250
5,19 9,350
4,92 5,700
437 8,400
3,83 1,100
3,28 3,800
2,73 6,500
2,18 9,200
1,64 1,900
109 4,600
54 7,300
CLIENT MIX
A 1000
B —
C —
D
E Night Accn (non casual)
F Casual Night Accn
J Day Facilities
K Wet Weather Facilities
L Meal Facilities
M Evening Facilities
N Water Supply
O Sewerage
P Road Capacity
Q Public Transport
R Total Costs £
S Annual Client Expenditure £
T Employment in Tourism
U Rateable Value £
UNIT SIZE
1000
1,000
250
1250
500
125
330
70,000
66,500
170
100
—
366
—
UNIT COST / VALUE £
1,000,000
125,000
12,500
20,000
6,250
13,200
56,000
26,600
25,500
1,000
54,730
—
3,033

Cloghaneely Option 1 Budget

This option is based on an increase of night visitors only. Because night visitors place a heavy demand upon day resources, water supply and sewerage (see formulae*), the surpluses shown on the previous page are rapidly used up: and the "ultimate line" set by the total of capacity comes down to 9.5 units. Heavy costs obviously occur at once in night accommodation: the map shows the definite impact upon this resource. Impact upon other resources is more flexible, though tending to be concentrated in or near the centers suitable for night accommodation.

The cost-benefit comparison below shows the heavy costs involved in this option (column c) and the large increase in client expenditure which results (column i). The "return" on new capital is better than the total "return," but neither is much more striking than the present position.

*Not included herein.–Ed.

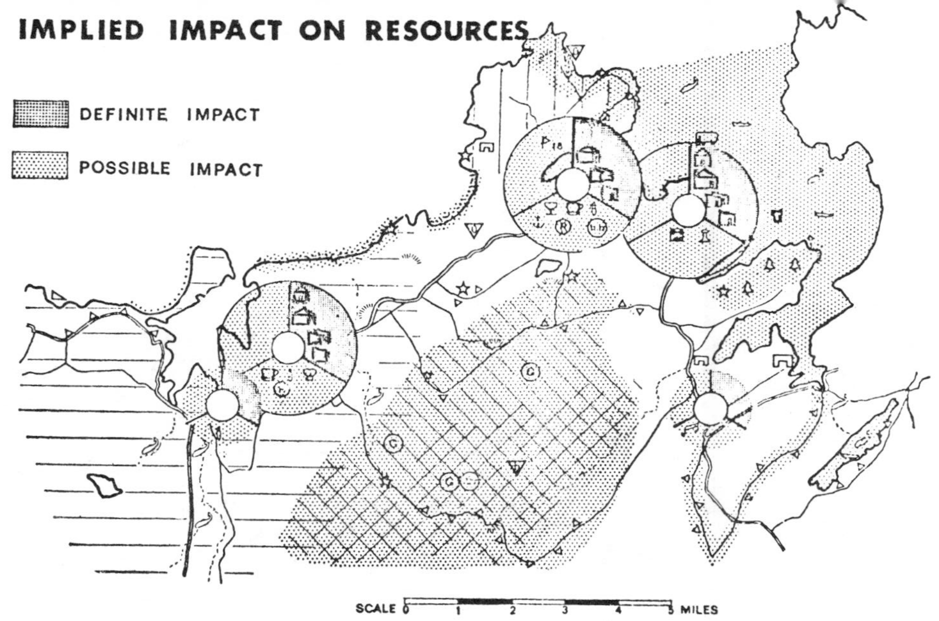

IMPLIED IMPACT ON RESOURCES

DEFINITE IMPACT

POSSIBLE IMPACT

SCALE 0 1 2 3 4 5 MILES

Initial Cost-Benefit Comparison £'s 000 Throughout	Investment				Annual Expenditure by Client Groups					Return	
	Existing-Used a	Existing-Surplus b	New (short-fall) c	Total d	Night Visitors e	Day Visitors f	Local People g	Total h	Increase Over Existing i	On New Capital (i as % of c)	On Total Investment (h as % of d)
Present position	2,070	1,171	–	3,241	440	426	108	974	–	–	30
Option 1											
Increase by 1 unit	2,221	1,020	1,135	4,376	987	426	108	1,521	547	48	35
Ultimate	2,886	355	11,829	15,070	5,639	426	108	6,173	5,199	44	41

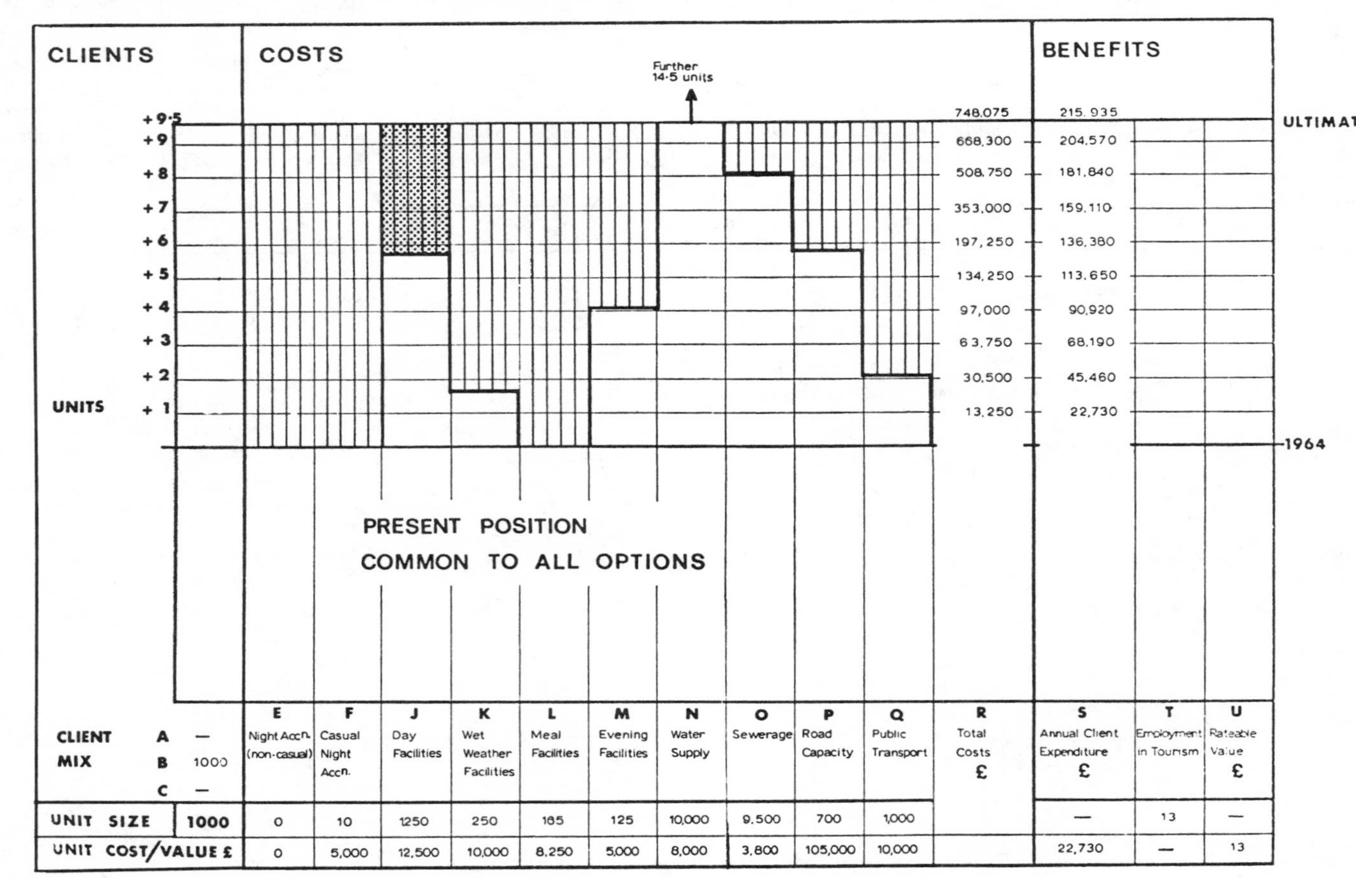
CLOGHANEELY OPTION 2—GROWTH IN DAY VISITORS
BUDGET SUMMARY
CLIENTS
COSTS
BENEFITS
Further 14·5 units
ULTIMATE
1964
UNITS
+9·5
+9
+8
+7
+6
+5
+4
+3
+2
+1
748,075
668,300
508,750
353,000
197,250
134,250
97,000
63,750
30,500
13,250
215,935
204,570
181,840
159,110
136,380
113,650
90,920
68,190
45,460
22,730
PRESENT POSITION
COMMON TO ALL OPTIONS
CLIENT MIX A —
B 1000
C —
E Night Accn. (non-casual)
F Casual Night Accn.
J Day Facilities
K Wet Weather Facilities
L Meal Facilities
M Evening Facilities
N Water Supply
O Sewerage
P Road Capacity
Q Public Transport
R Total Costs £
S Annual Client Expenditure £
T Employment in Tourism
U Rateable Value £
UNIT SIZE 1000
0
10
1250
250
165
125
10,000
9,500
700
1,000
—
13
—
UNIT COST/VALUE £
0
5,000
12,500
10,000
8,250
5,000
8,000
3,800
105,000
10,000
22,730
—
13

Cloghaneely Option 2 Budget

This option is based on an increase of day visitors only. Their usage of resources, except of day resources, has a pattern markedly different from that of night visitors. In particular, they place nil demand on night accommodation (noncasual), and fairly heavy demand on some other resources, notably roads and public transport, in which the surplus capacities are soon exhausted.

The map shows their definite impact upon the service and facilities segments of the activity centres in Cloghaneely, and on certain specific coastal stretches highly suited to day visitors, but flexible impact elsewhere.

The table below shows the very light costs involved in increasing day visitors (at least until the road capacity is exhausted), and the comparatively large increase in expenditure which would result.

IMPLIED IMPACT ON RESOURCES

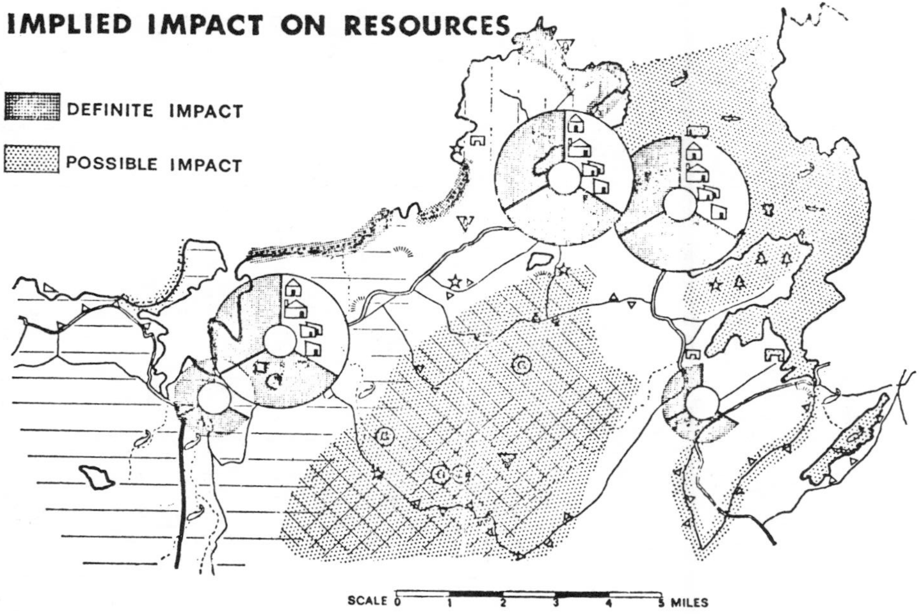

DEFINITE IMPACT
POSSIBLE IMPACT

SCALE 0 1 2 3 4 5 MILES

Initial Cost-Benefit Comparison £'s 000 Throughout	*Investment*				*Annual Expenditure by Client Groups*					*Return*	
	Existing-Used a	*Existing-Surplus b*	*New (short-fall) c*	*Total d*	*Night Visitors e*	*Day Visitors f*	*Local People g*	*Total h*	*Increase Over Existing i*	*On New Capital (i as % of c)*	*On Total Investment (h as % of d)*
Present position	2,070	1,171	–	3,241	440	426	108	974	–	–	30
Option 2											
Increase by 1 unit	2,224	1,017	13	3,254	440	653	108	1,201	227	1,746	37
Ultimate	3,126	116	748	3,990	440	2,585	108	3,133	2,159	289	79

CLOGHANEELY OPTION 3—GROWTH IN NIGHT AND DAY VISITORS

BUDGET SUMMARY

CLIENTS (UNITS)	COSTS: Total Costs £	BENEFITS: Annual Client Expenditure £	
+9·5	4,390 620	3,25 3,660	Ultimate
+9	4,107,030	3,06 2,410	
+8	3,588,850	2,739,920	
+7	3,117,950	239 7,430	
+6	2,649,550	205 4,940	
+5	2,189,900	1,71 2,450	
+4	1,734,000	136 9,960	
+3	1,278,100	1,02 7,470	
+2	841,000	68 4,980	
+1	415,500	34 2,490	
			1964

PRESENT POSITION COMMON TO ALL OPTIONS

	D	E	F	J	K	L	M	N	O	P	Q	R	S	T	U
CLIENT MIX	A 360 B 640 C —	Night Accn. (non-casual)	Casual Night Accn.	Day Facilities	Wet Weather Facilities	Meal Facilities	Evening Facilities	Water Supply	Sewerage	Road Capacity	Public Transport	Total Costs £	Annual Client Expenditure £	Employment in Tourism	Rateable Value £
UNIT SIZE	1000	360	96	1250	340	150	200	31,600	30.000	490	680		—	140	—
UNIT COST/VALUE £		360,000	48,000	12,500	13,600	7,500	8,000	25,280	12,000	73,500	6,800		34,249	—	1,100

Cloghaneely Option 3 Budget

This option is based on an increase in both night and day visitors, in the ratio 360:640. The results are naturally between those of options 1 and 2, with some costs involved in night accommodation and elsewhere. The impact on resources, as shown on the map, becomes definite in all elements of the centers and in certain areas highly accessible to night or day visitors or both: but some flexibility remains in other areas.

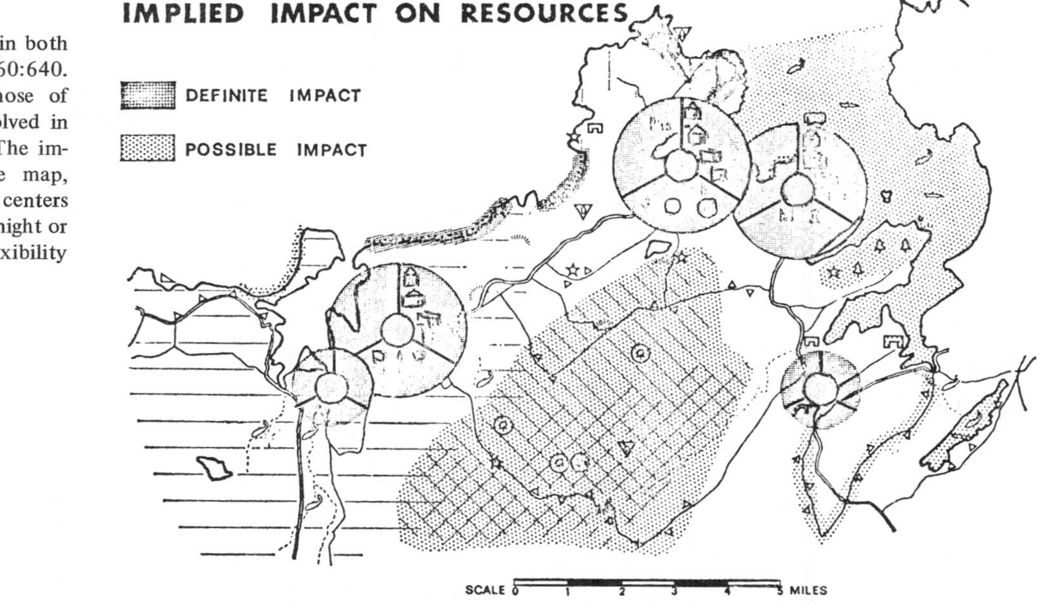

Initial Cost-Benefit Comparison £'s 000 Throughout	Investment				Annual Expenditure by Client Groups					Return	
	Existing-Used *a*	Existing-Surplus *b*	New (short-fall) *c*	Total *d*	Night Visitors *e*	Day Visitors *f*	Local People *g*	Total *h*	Increase Over Existing *i*	On New Capital (*i* as % of *c*)	On Total Investment (*h* as % of *d*)
Present position	2,070	1,171	–	3,241	440	426	108	974	–	–	30
Option 3											
Increase by 1 unit	2,222	1,019	415	3,656	637	571	108	1,316	342	82	36
Ultimate	3,241	0	4,390	7,631	2,314	1,805	108	4,227	3,253	71	55

Plan-Budget Process

The options are stated, and the budget diagram prepared at planning area scale. But the original assessment of resources, clients and options was done at the county scale, as shown earlier in this Manual. Moreover, the policy decisions have to be made at the county level, by bringing together all the material from the planning areas and measuring the total implications in terms of the policies which the county wishes to pursue and the resources it can make available.

It is therefore necessary to state a *plan-budget process.* This process must be suitable not only for the preparation of the initial plan, but also for the regular review of the plan and the preparation of budgets: this will normally happen once a year as part of the county's rate-striking procedure.

A suggested plan-budget process is shown opposite the next page. It can be used either in the preparation of the initial development plan, or each year thereafter. There are three levels in the process—county, planning area, individual resource—and the plan budget process moves from one level to the next during the sequence of thought.

Initial Development Plan

(1) The plan budget process for the initial development plan starts with the full process of survey and analysis stated earlier in this Manual at county scale. The draft options are stated for the county, and a tentative budget is proposed, mainly in the sense of the capital which the county feel that they and other bodies might make available.

(2) These options and draft budget are then examined at planning area scale, and a set of budget diagrams are produced on the lines shown for Cloghaneely on the previous pages.

(3) The plan is then prepared on the lines of the plans shown on the previous pages to show the impact of each option on the specific resources, for example on the beaches, within the planning area. If necessary some more detailed study is done to decide precisely what this impact might be and what consequent costs might occur.

(4) It may be very clear from this study of specific resources that one option would be preferred. The recommendation might therefore come from the level of a specific resource to the planning area.

(5) From the planning area then comes a recommended option and budget to be put together at county level with the recommendations from other planning areas.

(6) At the county level, the sets of material from the planning areas are put together to form recommended options and budget, upon which final decisions are then made.

(7) These final decisions form the basis not only for the county council's own action but also for discussion and agreement with other bodies who may be involved.

(8) When the decisions and agreements have been reached, their implications for each planning area is then expressed.

(9) This is then reflected in the final budgets and design briefs for each resource.

(10) Action then follows at all three levels, not only in the form of building and promotion, but also in on-going study which can provide a continuous checking and refinement of the decisions which have been made.

Annual Review

The plan budget process is repeated each year following the approval of the initial development plan, and follows the same series of steps. Thus each year it is necessary to:

(a) check at county scale the impact of previous decisions, and of any other changes that have occurred upon the resources or the clients and hence on the options which are available, and to state draft options and budget for that year.
(b) check on similar changes at the planning area scale and to prepare draft options and budget.
(c) check any changes in the capacity or usage of specific resources and to decide the implications of the proposed options in terms of cost.
(d) recommend specific changes in resources.
(e) recommend options and budgets for each planning area.
(f) bring these options and budgets together at county scale.
(g) decide the final options and budget for that year, and possibly the draft options and budgets for an on-going period of five years, at the county scale; and make agreements with other bodies accordingly.
(h) express these decisions and agreements for action at planning area scale
(i) put in hand design work on specific resources.
(j) pursue action at all scales, including a start on the planning budget process for the following year.

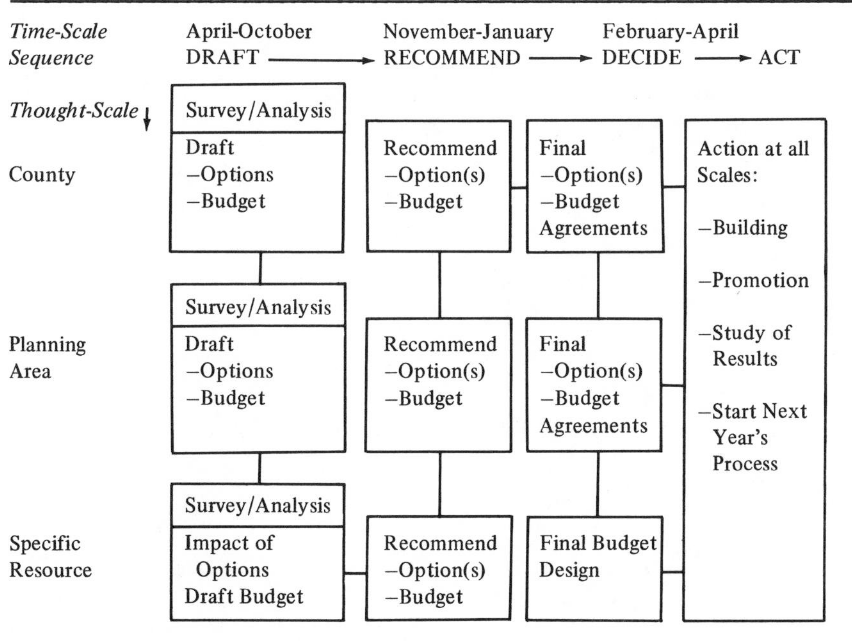

ANNUAL PLAN-BUDGET PROCESS

This chart may look like a merry-go-round, with the end of each year's work being simply the start of the next. This is quite deliberate. Planning is a continuous process, depending upon the constant refinement of information and a constant checking of decisions as the years go by.

Planners are faced with a serious responsibility for the implications of decisions based upon their plans. The seriousness of this responsibility often has an inhibiting effect upon plans. Planners may take years to gather the information that will satisfy their desire for accuracy. But the world will not wait for years, and many a chance may be lost or resource destroyed while the search for fact is being carried out.

The plan-budget process allows for action to start with preliminary information. But it also provides for the checking and improvement of this information which *must* be done if large-scale action is to be safely launched. Annual planning and budgeting with careful back-checking and feed-back will make the budget process a more and more accurate tool for making decisions. Using it in this manner will soon eliminate a large portion of the guess-work in both the public and private development of Amenity and Tourism.

Chapter 14

URBAN IMPROVEMENT PROGRAMMING MODELS

Darwin G. Stuart

INTRODUCTION

One of the most intuitively attractive methods for evaluating alternative urban plans is the use of a programs-objectives matrix. Such a matrix would balance a set of alternative public investment programs (as columns, perhaps) against a group of goals and objectives (as the corresponding rows) which these programs are intended to achieve. Entered in each cell of the matrix would be some measure of how well program x_i contributes to the achievement of goal y_j. This might be nothing more than a zero or one entry, indicating whether or not that particular program is relevant. Alternatively, the number of actual goal-units to be achieved might be shown. Such a matrix enables us to compare how alternative plans or combinations of programs serve to accomplish the overall goals of an urban area. If possible, the summing of the rows will indicate the level of attainment for each goal or objective, while the summing of columns may provide some measure of the investment level required for each program.

Complications are introduced, however, when we use different units of measurement for different objectives and programs. Unless we can establish trade-off rates among these different units, we will not be able to sum every row and every column. We will have to settle for partial, selective comparisons of individual cells and groups of cells, for each of the alternative plans under consideration. As Hill (1968) notes, a complete analysis will require the

AUTHOR'S NOTE: This paper is based upon the author's doctoral dissertation in Civil Engineering at Northwestern University. The advice and encouragement of Professors George L. Peterson, Walter D. Fisher and Arthur P. Hurter are gratefully acknowledged. Reprinted from Socio-Economic Planning Sciences, Vol. 4, No. 2 (June 1970), pp. 217-238, by permission of the publisher.

development of transformation functions which reduce each outcome to a single measurement scale.[1] In his "goals-achievement matrix," three levels of comparison and measurement are distinguished: ordinal (simple rankings), interval (relative scales) and ratio (absolute scales). In his proposed weighted index of goals-achievement, these three types of measurement would be somewhat arbitrarily combined to yield a single evaluation rating.

The concept of a programs-objectives matrix can be more rigorously structured in the form of a mathematical programming problem. Such a mathematical model will require that we do establish a common unit of measurement for goal achievement, because the summing of matrix rows and columns is essential. The key feature of mathematical programming lies in the use of an objective function, a combination of program variables which we wish to optimize. In general, we will want either to minimize overall cost (given some specified minimum level of goal achievement) or to maximize goal achievement (given some maximum overall budget). In addition to an objective function, the basic programs-objectives matrix will usually be augmented by various constraints indicating minimum and maximum limits on certain programs and program combinations.

This paper explores the potential application of mathematical programming in the evaluation of alternative urban plans and improvement programs. After a brief review of past modeling efforts of this type, an examination of the problems likely to be encountered in identifying and measuring specific objectives and programs is presented. The Model Cities Program is used as an example. A simple linear programming model is subsequently developed, built around a matrix of relative effectiveness coefficients, a set of performance standards and appropriate program budgets. Supporting analytic techniques and information systems are also discussed. Finally, potential applications of the model are surveyed, and examples of its use in testing and evaluating basic Model Cities programs and objectives presented.

PAST MODELING EFFORTS

Mathematical programming offers the very powerful advantage of being able to theoretically examine all evaluation contexts. Perhaps the most well-known example is Schlager's the one which minimizes cost or maximizes goal achievement. In effect, the model itself generates alternative plans and programs, in a much more efficient and thorough way than we could ourselves. Because this advantage is such an important one, a number of attempts have been made to apply mathematical programming in urban public investment and plan evaluation contexts. Perhaps the most well known example is Schlager's (1965) Land-Use Plan Design Model, which attempts to minimize total public and private investment costs, subject to various design standards and constraints regarding multiple land-use mix ratios and interrelationships.[2]

Other examples are more directly concerned with multiple urban goals and objectives.[3] In Boston, for instance, a simple model has been developed to evaluate transit link alternatives in relation to four objectives: increased or decreased operating/capital cost ratio, total passenger volume, per cent seated during the peak hour, and peak-hour auto users diverted. Subject to a budget constraint, the model selects that system of links which maximizes the value of a weighted linear sum of the objectives. In another example, a proposal has been made for developing a programming model which would utilize a matrix of effectiveness probabilities. This matrix would define the probability that objective j can be achieved if alternative matropolitan plan component i is adopted. Empirically determined utility values would be assigned to each of 30 objectives. The model would select that overall plan which achieves the highest total utility (sum of individual probabilities time utilities).

Primarily at a conceptual, organizational level, other thinking on the potential of mathematical programming models includes the paper by Coughlin.[4] An analytic framework for formulating a capital improvement program is set forth, anticipating possible treatment as a programming problem. The objective would be to complete as much as possible of the comprehensive plan, within a given budget limit. This early work was subsequently refined to permit community goals (upon which a comprehensive plan would be based) to appear in an objective function directly. In this conceptual model, the need to distinguish between independent and interdependent contributions of programs to goals is recognized, as well as the need to identify the indirect effects of the achievement of goals upon each other. In a third attempt at clarifying the problems of public investment programming models, Peterson distinguishes three basic matrices necessary in balancing a vector of community goals against a vector of public investment opportunities: a programs interdependency matrix, a unit effectiveness or production matrix and a goals interdependency matrix.

The information requirements of this kind of urban-oriented programming model are large—so large in fact, that we are only beginning to scratch the surface of its potential applicability and usefulness in urban and regional planning. In order to develop models detailed enough to yield non-trivial results, we must know a great deal about how different programs affect, in some quantitative way, the achievement of different objectives; how different objectives themselves can be most meaningfully expressed; and how we can best predict the future impacts of programs upon objectives. At present, we are ill-equipped to provide these kinds of inputs for the development of sensitive programming models. Adequate information resources are in short supply, and the development of supporting impact and effectiveness models is itself only just beginning.

This paper attempts only to structure how the continuing development of urban goal-programming models might proceed. Though two operational linear programming models are developed, they are based upon a series of hearty assumptions concerning unavailable or inappropriate data, and hypothetical

TABLE 1

Hypothetical Model Neighborhood: Basic Performance Objectives

Type and Objective Variable	*Socioeconomic Condition*	*Reference Group*	*No. Present*	*% of Reference Group*	*Five-Year Performance Standard*	*% of Reference Group*
Housing						
Y_1	Substandard housing units	Total housing units	6,580	16	2,060	5
Y_2	Other deficient housing units	Total housing units	6,170	15	2,060	5
Y_3	Inadequately housed L-I elderly households	HH 65 and over, income less than $3,000	900	45	300	15
Y_4	Inadequately housed L-I families	Family income less than $5,000	7,840	70	2,240	20
Y_5	Inadequately housed M-I families	Family income $5,000-$8,000	3,200	38	1,010	12
Employment-Income-Education						
Y_6	Unemployed persons	14 and over, civilian labor force	4,030	8	1,510	3
Y_7	Underemployed persons	14 and over, civilian labor force	5,040	10	1,510	3
Y_8	Families with income less than $3,000	Total families	5,600	20	2,240	8
Y_9	ADC cases	Persons under 18	11,130	30	2.600	7
Y_{10}	Annual high school dropouts	Persons age 14-17	1,880	30	1,250	20
Y_{11}	Annual college or jr. college enrollment	Persons age 18-24	1,300	15	2,170	25
Y_{12}	Adults with grade school education or less	Persons 25 and over	29,620	44	20,190	30
Y_{13}	Net new industrial jobs lying within ¾-hr. travel time via public transit	None	–	–	1,000	–
Health-Safety-Environment						
Y_{14}	Annual infant mortality	Live births	180	6	75	2.5
Y_{15}	Annual new tuberculosis cases	Total population	700	0.7	70	0.07
Y_{16}	Annual juvenile arrests	Persons under 18	2,020	5	1,010	2.5
Y_{17}	Annual criminal arrests (excl. minor misdemeanors)	Total population	9,000	9	2,000	2
Y_{18}	Persons unserved by adequate local recreation facilities	Total population	35,000	35	5,000	5
Y_{19}	Persons expressing satisfaction with general environmental living conditions (excl. housing)	5% sample survey	1,000	20	2,500	50
Y_{20}	Persons attending local community planning meetings (annual)	Total population	1,000	1	2,000	2

NOTE: Total population = 100,000; total families = 28,000; total housing units = 41,150.

values are assigned to unknown variables and parameters. These models are not presently intended for actual application. Rather, their purpose is to demonstrate how such models *could* be constructed, given the necessary data and supporting predictive models. It is anticipated that these needed inputs can (and hopefully, will) realistically and eventually be made available. The two models are developed in terms of the goals, objectives and programs of the Model Cities Program, which is aimed at the coordinated improvement of living conditions within the poverty neighborhoods of our central cities.

MODEL CITIES OBJECTIVES

What kinds of specific objectives should be pursued by comprehensive programs designed to alleviate poverty conditions within model neighborhoods? Further, what quantitative indices should be used to measure how each objective is being achieved? Basic goals for the Model Cities Program have been established by Federal legislation, and these can be used in turn to identify more detailed socio-economic conditions and objectives. The basic goals of the program are to rebuild or revitalize large slum and blighted areas, to expand housing opportunities, to expand job and income opportunities, to reduce dependence on welfare payments, to improve educational facilities and programs, to combat disease and ill health, to reduce the incidence of crime and delinquency, to enhance recreational and cultural opportunities, to establish better access between homes and jobs, to improve general living conditions and to foster greater citizen participation in the development of neighborhood improvement programs.[5]

These general, abstract goals carry with them certain implied performance measures or indices—for example, the number or proportion of substandard housing units, the number or proportion of low-income families living under inadequate conditions (deteriorating or dilapidated housing, overcrowding), the number or proportion of families with income under the $3000 poverty level, the annual number or rate of high school dropouts, the annual number or rate of new tuberculosis cases, the number or rate of juvenile arrests, etc. In each case, these kinds of socio-economic conditions enable us to tell whether a basic goal is being achieved. Are the appropriate numbers, proportions and rates increasing or decreasing? A set of basic, measurable objectives for the Model Cities Program (or for other public programs) can be developed simply as a set of desired changes in such numbers, proportions, and rates.

Table 1 illustrates a set of performance objectives for a hypothetical model neighborhood containing 100,000 persons.[6] These objectives fall into three basic groups: housing, employment-income-education, and health-safety-environment. This is not a complete set of objectives, of course, and other important considerations, such as school integration and the relative quality of inner city schools, mental health, air pollution, or residential density might easily enter

TABLE 2
Hypothetical Model Neighborhood: Basic Improvement Programs

Type and Public Improvement Program	*Output Unit*	*Cost/Unit ($) (000)*	*Output Units/$1,000 Expenditure*	*Assumptions*
Housing				
Clearance, existing housing	H.U.	5.0	0.20	
Private redevelopment, new housing (clearance subsidy)	H.U.	4.0	0.25	
Public housing, elderly	H.U.	3.5	0.29	Includes clearance of existing housing
Public housing, family	H.U.	4.5	0.22	Includes clearance of existing housing
Housing rehabilitation, substandard units	H.U.	1.8	0.55	
Housing rehabilitation, other deficient units	H.U.	1.2	0.80	
Moderate-income housing	H.U.	0.1	10.00	
Receivership rehabilitation, substandard units	H.U.	1.3	0.75	
Receivership rehabilitation, other deficient units	H.U.	0.8	1.25	
Rent supplements (5-year)	H.U.	3.5	0.29	
Code enforcement, substandard units	H.U.	0.4	2.50	
Code enforcement, other deficient units	H.U.	0.2	5.00	
Employment-Income-Education				
Community action job training, unemployed	Persons	4.2	0.24	$500/referral; 1/3 of referrals are placed; 1/3 of placements keep jobs
Community action job training, underemployed	Persons	3.4	0.29	Somewhat better performance
Manpower development and training, unemployed	Persons	5.2	0.19	$1,300/referral; ½ of referrals are placed; ½ of placements keep jobs
Manpower development and training, underemployed	Persons	4.0	0.25	Somewhat better performance
ADC job training, unemployed	Persons	3.0	0.33	Similar to community action job training;
ADC job training, underemployed	Persons	2.4	0.42	somewhat lower referral costs
Day care centers, reduce unemployment and underemployment	Persons	0.2	5.00	Partially self-supporting
Industrial redevelopment, new jobs nearby	Persons	1.5	0.67	$90,000/acre; 60 jobs/acre
Industrial redevelopment, reduce unemployment and underemployment	Persons	15.0	0.07	10% of new jobs for unemployed; 10% for underemployed
Industrial promotion, private development, new jobs nearby	Persons	0.1	10.00	Highly variable, but costs/job would be low
Industrial promotion, private development, reduce unemployment and underemployment	Persons	1.2	0.83	10% of new jobs for unemployed; 10% for underemployed
Basic adult education, unemployed	Persons	13.8	0.07	$275/person; 2% gain employment who otherwise would not

TABLE 2 (continued)

Basic adult education, underemployed	Persons	11.2	0.09	Somewhat better performance
Basic adult education, grade school level	Persons	1.6	0.61	$275/person; 1/6 receive grade school diplomas
Neighborhood youth corps, unemployed	Persons	3.0	0.33	$750/referral; ½ of referrals are placed; ½ of placements keep jobs
Neighborhood youth corps, stay in school	Persons	1.2	0.83	$600/referral; ½ stay in school who otherwise would drop out
Vocational education, unemployed	Persons	1.8	0.56	$450/student; ½ students are placed; ½ of placements keep jobs
Vocational education, stay in school	Persons	0.9	1.11	$450/student; ½ stay in school who otherwise would drop out
Upward bound, stay in school	Persons	2.8	0.36	$275/member; 10% stay in school who otherwise would drop out
Upward bound, college enrollment	Persons	0.7	1.43	$275/member; 40% go on to college who otherwise would not
Elementary school construction, stay in school	Persons	36.0	0.06	$1,800/pupil; 5% stay in high school who otherwise would drop out
High school construction, stay in school	Persons	35.0	0.03	$3,500/pupil; 10% stay in school who otherwise would drop out
High school construction, college enrollment	Persons	70.0	0.01	$3,500/pupil; 5% go on to college who otherwise would not
Jr. college construction, college enrollment	Persons	70.0	0.01	$3,500/pupil; 5% of high school students go on to college who otherwise would not
Health-Safety-Environment				
Health center construction	Persons	a,b	–	
Parks and recreation facilities, adequate local recreation	Persons	0.8	1.2	$80,000/acre, each acre serving 10 persons adequately
Parks and recreation facilities, juvenile delinquency	Persons	b	–	
Parks and recreational facilities, environmental improvement	Persons	c	–	
Rodent-vermin control, environmental improvement	Persons	b,c	–	
Police community relations, juvenile delinquency and criminal arrests	Persons	b	–	
Business renewal, environmental improvement	Persons	c	–	
Urban beautification, environmental improvement	Persons	c	–	
Community organization activities, publications	Persons	c	–	

a. Investment in this program does not clearly vary with output units (TB cases, infant mortality) but is determined mainly by feasible facility size.

b. Outputs related to this program are closely dependent upon other programs (above) aimed at improving housing and family income conditions. Estimates of cost parameters are thereby very difficult.

c. Very little data is presently available to relate these programs to appropriate output units (citizens satisfied with environmental conditions, citizen participation).

such a table. The only requirement for additional objectives is that they be quantifiable, expressed in terms of some neighborhood-wide reference group. In this case, they should also be related to one or more of the broad Model Cities goals mentioned above.

Also appearing in Table 1 is a five-year performance standard for each of the 20 basic objectives. Identifying these standards is one of the important clarifying steps in the potential use of both programs-objectives matrices and mathematical programming models. Such standards commonly reflect a desire to bring the appropriate rates and proportions in line with the rates and proportions exhibited by the rest of the city or metropolitan area.[7] In other cases more arbitrary achievement levels may be set, based upon experience and/or judgment. Both kinds of standards are represented in Table 1.

MODEL CITIES PROGRAMS

What kinds of public improvement programs are available for achieving Model Cities objectives? What quantitative measures of investment or intensity for each program should be used? Most important, how can we go about analyzing and predicting the level of impact each program will have upon the objectives to which it is related? Table 2 provides a start in cataloguing the improvement programs which might be made part of a coordinated Model Cities effort. Most of them represent existing city-wide programs administered by various agencies—urban renewal departments, community action agencies, building departments, public housing authorities, boards of education, welfare agencies, state employment services, public health agencies, park and recreation districts, planning and development departments. In addition to coordinating existing programs, the Model Cities agency itself is free to design new, innovative programs to fill gaps and provide additional facilities and services. The programs in Table 2 are also divided into the three basic groups used in Table 1.

Though it may sometimes be desirable to express program inputs or investments in terms of different units (number of building inspectors, acres developed, or job training referrals), the need for a single, common input unit almost inevitably forces us to use a monetary one. In terms of mathematical programming, our chief concern is then with achieving an optimal allocation of dollars among the various program alternatives available. The programs in Table 2 are consequently described in dollar terms, in general relating the cost required to achieve or generate one unit of output, with outputs expressed in terms of the objective units in Table 1 (persons, families, or housing units). These cost figures would usually be determined on a city-wide basis, though some might be peculiar to the particular model neighborhood under study. Most programs are distinguished by the basic objectives or groups of objectives which they affect. Because objectives are expressed in terms of measurable socio-economic conditions, this amounts to the identification of different target areas or populations for each program.

The key to the development of useful urban improvement programming models lies in our ability to make reasonable estimates of these cost per-unit-output figures. Such figures can subsequently be converted to reciprocal output units per $1000 expenditure, a more useful parameter for further use in actually constructing a programming model. The assumptions listed in Table 2 give some indication of the difficulty involved in developing effectiveness parameters of this type. Improvement programs generally have a number of important characteristics or features whose variability can affect program performance. Some knowledge of these features must be gained, and reasonable values assigned or assumed for them. One particularly crucial assumption is that costs are linearly related to output, for each of the programs listed. Another is that the programs operate with relative independence, and that one program does not depend upon an investment elsewhere in order to be effective.

The programs and cost parameters in Table 2 are consequently quite simple in nature. Most of the cost figures are rough approximations, others are purely hypothetical. Complex programs are described as if they could easily be reduced to a single dimension, which, of course, is usually not the case. A great deal of data collection and analysis, carefully structured to yield results expressed in a consistent, usable form, using the input and output units called for by such a matrix approach, will be required in order to generate an expanded, realistic table of this type. A difficult question will lie in deciding how much detail should be (or can be) included. For example, should the various housing programs be further stratified by the age, density and neighborhood location of the housing units involved? Will cost parameters vary significantly with these factors? Similarly, should the various job training programs be distinguished according to the age, experience, education, or background of the individuals referred?

DEVELOPING PROGRAMMING MODELS

The basic tool of mathematical programming involves the bringing together of Tables 1 and 2 to develop a programs-objectives matrix. The relative effectiveness coefficients entered in this matrix (see Table 3) indicate how the different Model City Program alternatives in Table 2 will affect the particular objectives of the hypothetical model neighborhood described in Table 1. The coefficients will vary with different model neighborhoods, and depend upon the magnitudes of specific quantitative objectives. Each coefficient simply tells how much (what percentage) of objective Y_j can be achieved by investing one input unit ($1000) in program X_i.

This percentage of goal achievement constitutes the basic common unit of measurement or transformation for the matrix. An essential kind of program stratification occurs when it is seen that certain programs contribute to more than one objective, and it becomes necessary, where feasible, to distinguish separate program alternatives accordingly. This amounts to a more detailed extension of the identification of target areas and populations mentioned earlier. For instance, in applying the code enforcement of substandard housing units (programs X_{24}-X_{27}) to the four objectives to which such a program is relevant, we may focus upon substandard units which house (a) moderate-income families, (b) below-income families, (c) low-income elderly households, or (d) none of these. Such a distinction clarifies just what this program is capable of accomplishing, and forces us to more rigorously analyze the potential impacts of each program upon each objective.

Not all programs can be fully stratified in this way, however. As a simple example, in the public rehabilitation of other deficient housing units (programs X_{10}, X_{12} and X_{14}) it is not possible to separate the achievement of objective Y_2 from Y_3, Y_4, or Y_5. A reduction in the number of other deficient housing units (Y_2) will simultaneously result in a reduction in the number of inadequately housed low-income elderly households (Y_3), low-income families (Y_4), or moderate-income families (Y_5). The needs and possibilities for this kind of objective-oriented stratification of programs will be an important factor in introducing additional objectives into such an effectiveness matrix.

PREDICTING RELATIVE IMPACTS

The programs-objectives effectiveness matrix, together with the cost parameters upon which it depends, form the central elements in developing programming models for urban improvement. What techniques could be used to develop the impact and effectiveness predictions of Table 2, upon which the success or failure of this approach to plan design and evaluation so closely hinges? The first requirement, of course, and one so basic that its importance is often overlooked, is the development of an adequate information system. Normal administrative records for the various programs in Table 2 may need restructuring so that data in terms of appropriate output units will be generated. In other cases special interview sample surveys within a model neighborhood may be necessary. In general, it will be necessary to disaggregate city-wide information files and administrative records, including the products of the U.S. Census, to at least the model neigborhood level. Ideally, all spatially distributed data should be referenced to a common block-face address coding guide, such as that being instituted for the 1970 Census, to permit maximum flexibility in subsequent analyses.

The simplest kinds of analyses needed to make effectiveness predictions would involve basic cost-accounting statements and records keeping, preferably on a monthly basis. A number of programs, particularly those in the housing area, are generally straightforward in terms of relating inputs (dollars expended) to outputs (demolished, new, or rehabilitated housing units). By simply recording the net public costs required to clear, build, manage, rehabilitate, inspect, or take legal action against segments of a city's housing supply, on a unit-by-unit, month-by-month basis, an information resource can be built from which appropriate average cost parameters can be drawn. However, in order to make relatively accurate predictions, we may wish to perform additional statistical analyses (such as multiple regressions or factor analyses) which relate average costs to basic intermediate factors, such as construction methods and costs, building types, or housing markets. Our cost parameter predictions would then be based upon prior predictions for these factors (assuming we can predict them more confidently, rather than dealing directly with average costs), or we might make other appropriate adjustments to account for them.

Effectiveness predictions in the employment-income-education (EIE) and health-safety-environment (HSE) areas are likely to cause considerably more trouble, and require a good deal more analytic effort. In general, intermediate factors will demand much more attention, since inputs (dollars expended) for various social service and capital improvement programs will not be clearly related to outputs (persons finding employment, staying in school, enjoying better health, avoiding criminal activity, or more satisfied with their environment). These inputs and outputs will interact within complex socio-economic contexts, and some account must be taken of the many intervening variables which might influence results (such as economic health and growth of an area, housing segregation, civil rights movements, neighborhood and family factors and even national or regional trends and issues).

In addition to basic univariate and multivariate statistical analyses (supplemented by appropriate cost-accounting procedures), impact and effectiveness predictions in these areas are likely to call for the development of more elaborate socio-economic simulation models. One of the basic features of such models, which may be built around microcosmic decision-making sequences or around stochastic sampling procedures, lies in describing socio-economic interrelationships so that input or program variables can act as levers. By varying the level of investment in these variables, we are able to simulate how other variables in the system modeled, including appropriate output variables, will be affected. Simulation models might be designed to describe employment markets (perhaps by industrial sector), educational services, medical services, housing markets, the use of community facilities, neighborhood or intra-metropolitan migrations, or other socio-economic systems and activities.[8]

LINEARITIES AND INTERDEPENDENCIES

Developing these kinds of supporting analytic techniques and information systems is a vital, first-phase assignment, preceding any operational use of urban improvement programming models. However, two potentially limiting characteristics of a mathematical programming framework must also be dealt with—linearity assumptions and goal/program interdependencies.

In general, those programs which are found to display nonlinear input/output curves can be approximated by a series of linear segments, or can be handled by assigning appropriate program minimums and maximums. In either case, such programs can be manipulated to fit within a linear framework. For example, consider a program which exhibits steadily increasing costs per unit of output. Simply break this curve into several appropriate linear segments, assign a special sub-variable to represent each segment, determine the maximum input permitted over each segment, and let this set of sub-variables represent the program in the programming solution. These sub-variables will compete with each other and with the other variables in the problem, with, in general, the lower-cost variables entering the solution in ascending order.

A program with steadily decreasing costs per unit of output could be represented similarly, except that minimums would be assigned to each segment to represent the cumulative input preceding it, and only one sub-variable would be permitted in solution. Linear cost coefficients for each segment would be adjusted to include the output generated by its preceding minimum program. For a program with high initial start up costs, and/or high costs to achieve full implementation, but with an essentially linear curve in between, a single program variable can continue to be used. Program minimums and maximums would be set to exclude both tails of the input/output curve from solution, while the linear cost coefficient would again be adjusted to account for the fixed, required minimum preceding it.

The potential problem represented by program interdependencies is, in contrast, a particularly thorny one. The problems and difficulties involved in trying to distinguish dependent and independent (or controlled and uncontrolled) statistical and simulation variables, and in stratifying the effects and interrelationships of one from another, are of considerable magnitude. Attempts to identify an explicit programs interdependency matrix may well prove fruitless. The cost will be high, the period of analysis lengthy, and the temporal stability of such an interdependency matrix unlikely. However, without the formal use of such a matrix, the known dependence of one program upon another can be roughly approximated by specifying appropriate minimums and maximums for the second or required program. It will be necessary, however, to ensure that all program or solution variables operating within a programming model are independent, as reflected in their respective effectiveness coefficients. Overlapping impacts cannot be permitted, because the overall sum of program impacts upon each objective must be matched against a performance standard.

Goal interdependencies, on the other hand, are not particularly crucial, especially if no attempt is made to define a strictly independent set of objectives. Independence among objectives is not really required. Effectiveness coefficients relate objectives to programs only, and not to other objectives. The only independence requirement is that the coefficients for each objective (each row) are individually and consistently determined. The summing of rows will consequently have meaning, while the summing of columns will not. Adding or deleting objectives will not unduly bias a solution, nor will the fact that one objective might mean practically the same as another. It makes no real difference, for example, whether the desire to reduce unemployment overlaps with the desire to raise family incomes, or whether the achievement of one is likely to result in achieving the other.

LINEAR PROGRAMMING EXAMPLES

Using the data presented in Tables 1 and 2, together with information about appropriate program budget constraints, it is possible to construct simple, hypothetical mathematical programming models for both the housing and EIE areas. Both models use a basic effectiveness matrix, such as that shown for housing in Table 3. Both are set forth as standard linear programming problems, capable of utilizing the canned solution algorithms available for most computers (such as the IBM 1130, used here). Other mathematical programming techniques might also be applicable in an urban improvement planning context, but are not developed here. The Boston model mentioned earlier, as an example, used an integer programming formulation, while Schlager's work has been built around dynamic programming variations. Other eventual possibilities include parametric programming, stochastic programming and nonlinear programming.[9]

Both linear programming models may be stated as follows:

$$\text{Minimize} \sum_i x_i \qquad \text{or} \qquad \text{Maximize} \sum_i \sum_j d_j\, a_{ij}\, x_i$$

$$\text{Subject to} \sum_i a_{ij}\, x_i \geqslant y_j \qquad\qquad \text{Subject to} \sum_i a_{ij}\, x_i \geqslant y_j$$

$$\sum_i x_i \leqslant m_j \qquad\qquad \sum_i x_i \leqslant b$$

$$\sum_i x_i \geqslant n_j \qquad\qquad \sum_i x_i \leqslant m_j$$

$$\sum_i x_i \geqslant n_j$$

where x_i = Model City program alternatives, in dollars; y_j = performance standards for each objectives; a_{ij} = relative effectiveness coefficients; d_j = relative weights for each objective (optional); b = total budget avialable; m_j = maximum program budgets; and n_j = minimum program budgets.

TABLE 3

Programs–Objectives Effectiveness Matrix: Housing

Type and Housing Programs Description	Program Variable	Housing Objectives Y_1	Y_2	Y_3	Y_4	Y_5	Total Impact
Redevelopment							
Clearance for M-I housing	X_1	0.30	–	–	–	0.62	0.92
	X_2	–	0.32	–	–	0.62	0.94
Clearance for other land-uses	X_3	0.30	–	–	–	–	0.30
	X_4	–	0.32	–	–	–	0.32
Public Housing							
New construction, elderly	X_5	0.44	–	3.22	–	–	3.66
	X_6	–	0.47	3.32	–	–	3.69
New construction, family	X_7	0.33	–	–	0.28	–	0.61
	X_8	–	0.36	–	0.28	–	0.64
Rehabilitation							
Public housing, elderly	X_9	0.84	–	6.11	–	–	6.95
	X_{10}	–	1.30	8.89	–	–	10.19
Public housing, family	X_{11}	0.84	–	–	0.70	–	1.54
	X_{12}	–	1.30	–	1.02	–	2.32
Moderate-income housing	X_{13}	0.84	–	–	–	1.72	2.56
	X_{14}	–	1.30	–	–	2.50	3.80
M-I Housing							
Public non-profit corp.	X_{15}	–	–	–	–	31.25	31.25
Receivership							
Substandard units, L-I and M-I housing	X_{16}	1.14	–	8.33	–	–	9.47
	X_{17}	1.14	–	–	0.96	–	2.10
	X_{18}	1.14	–	–	–	2.34	3.48
Other deficient units, L-I and M-I housing	X_{19}	–	2.02	13.89	–	–	15.91
	X_{20}	–	2.02	–	1.59	–	3.61
	X_{21}	–	2.02	–	–	3.91	5.93
Rent Supplements							
Low-income families	X_{22}	–	–	3.22	–	–	3.22
	X_{23}	–	–	–	0.37	–	0.37
Code Enforcement							
Substandard units, L-I and M-I housing	X_{24}	3.80	–	–	–	–	3.80
	X_{25}	3.80	–	27.78	–	–	31.58
	X_{26}	3.80	–	–	3.19	–	6.99
	X_{27}	3.80	–	–	–	7.81	11.61
Other deficient units, L-I and M-I housing	X_{28}	–	8.10	–	–	–	8.10
	X_{29}	–	8.10	55.55	–	–	63.56
	X_{30}	–	8.10	–	6.38	–	14.48
	X_{31}	–	8.10	–	–	15.62	23.72

NOTE: Each entry represents the fractional reduction/increase (multiplied by 10^4) in the number of objective units present (substandard housing units, other deficient housing units, etc.) which can be achieved by investing $1,000 in a particular program. For example, in applying clearance of existing housing as a means to reduce the number of substandard housing units, the relative effectiveness coefficient is obtained by dividing the output per $1,000 (Table 2) by the number of substandard units present (Table 1): 0.20/6580 = 0.00003 x 10^4 = 0.30.

In translating this formal mathematical structure into a practical, operational problem (see Tables 4 and 5), a number of clarifications are necessary. First, it should be observed that the budgetary constraints m_j and n_j are actually represented as a series of program budgets, either recombining program variables stratified according to potential target objectives, or combining different programs into functional bundles (such as job training programs). In some cases individual minimums and maximums are also set for specific program (column) variables. The performance standard minimums represent the per cent reduction desired in the appropriate socio-economic condition shown in Table 1 (multiplied by 10^4). If objective function A (maximization) is chosen, an overall budget limit b should be assigned to the total budget row, and maximum performance standards (say within 2 or 3 per cent of the minimums) should be set.[10] Minimum standards may be reduced or eliminated altogether. If objective function B (minimization) is chosen, the total impact row may be ignored, while both minimum and maximum standards are set for each objective.

POTENTIAL APPLICATIONS

The results of running both models are shown in Tables 6 and 7.[11] In both cases, a sensitivity analysis of all variables and parameters is conducted for the "minimize budget" solution. A "maximize impact" solution, with relaxed performance standards and a smaller permitted total budget than the one achieved in the minimum cost solution, is also given. To show how the basic model can be used to test various kinds of alternatives, four revised solutions of the minimum budget problems are also shown: the introduction of a new program, the revision of program budget constraints, the revision of performance standards and the improvement of existing programs. In addition, one of the maximum impact solutions is revised to account for a relative weighting among the objectives. In general, because the exercise of a total budget constraint, carrying across established program and agency lines and funding procedures, is a somewhat unrealistic feature of the maximum impact problem, emphasis is given here to the alternative minimum budget formulation.

OPTIMAL SOLUTIONS

Perhaps the most unsettling aspect of the various linear programming solutions presented lies in the fact that, as the models are presently constructed, no single optimal solution exists. Rather, each solution is one of a family of optimal allocations, each with the same minimum budget or maximum impact value. The differences in these solutions lie in shifts among potential programs where even-cost trade-offs may be made. In general, these shifts will be between programs whose corresponding cost/unit increase and decrease figures are zero.

TABLE 4
Basic Linear Programming Model: Housing

	Redevelopment				Public Housing								M-I Housing		
	X_1	X_2	X_3	X_4	X_5	X_6	X_7	X_8	X_9	X_{10}	X_{11}	X_{12}	X_{13}	X_{14}	X_{15}
Objective Function A															
Impact	0.92	0.94	0.30	0.32	3.66	3.69	0.61	0.64	6.95	10.19	1.54	2.32	2.56	3.80	31.25
Objective Function B															
Budget	1.0	1.0	1.0	1.0	1.0	1.0	1.0	1.0	1.0	1.0	1.0	1.0	1.0	1.0	1.0
Performance Standards															
Y_1	0.30	–	0.30	–	0.44	–	0.33	–	0.84	–	0.84	–	0.84	–	–
Y_2	–	0.32	–	0.32	–	0.47	–	0.36	–	1.30	–	1.30	–	1.30	–
Y_3	–	–	–	–	3.22	3.22	–	–	6.11	8.89	–	–	–	–	–
Y_4	–	–	–	–	–	–	0.28	0.28	–	–	0.70	1.02	–	–	–
Y_5	0.62	0.62	–	–	–	–	–	–	–	–	–	–	1.72	2.50	31.25
Program Budgets															
REDEV	1.0	1.0	1.0	1.0	–	–	–	–	–	–	–	–	–	–	–
PUB H	–	–	–	–	1.0	1.0	1.0	1.0	1.0	1.0	1.0	1.0	–	–	–
PUB ELD	–	–	–	–	1.0	1.0	–	–	–	–	–	–	–	–	–
PUB FAM	–	–	–	–	–	–	1.0	1.0							
REHAB	–	–	–	–	–	–	–	–	1.0	1.0	1.0	1.0	1.0	1.0	–
RECEIV	–	–	–	–	–	–	–	–	–	–	–	–	–	–	–
RENT SUP	–	–	–	–	–	–	–	–	–	–	–	–	–	–	–
CODE ENF	–	–	–	–	–	–	–	–	–	–	–	–	–	–	–
	≥ 375.0	≥ 275.0	≥ 425.0	≥ 375.0											≥ 50.0

TABLE 4 (continued)

	Receivership						Rent Supplements		Code Enforcement								
	X_{16}	X_{17}	X_{18}	X_{19}	X_{20}	X_{21}	X_{22}	X_{23}	X_{24}	X_{25}	X_{26}	X_{27}	X_{28}	X_{29}	X_{30}	X_{31}	
Objective Function A																	
Impact	9.47	2.10	3.48	15.91	3.61	5.93	3.22	0.37	3.80	31.58	6.99	11.61	8.10	63.65	14.48	23.72	Max.
Objective Function B																	
Budget	1.0	1.0	1.0	1.0	1.0	1.0	1.0	1.0	1.0	1.0	1.0	1.0	1.0	1.0	1.0	1.0	Min.
Performance Standards																	
Y_1	1.14	1.14	1.14	–	–	–	–	–	3.80	3.80	3.80	3.80	–	–	–	–	≥6,869.4 ≤7,000.0
Y_2	–	–	–	2.02	2.02	2.02	–	–	–	–	–	–	8.10	8.10	8.10	8.10	≥6,661.3 ≤7,000.0
Y_3	8.33	–	–	13.89	–	–	3.22	–	–	27.78	–	–	–	55.55	–	–	≥6,666.7 ≤7,000.0
Y_4	–	0.96	–	–	1.59	–	–	0.37	–	–	3.19	–	–	–	6.38	–	≥7,142.8 ≤7,300.0
Y_5	–	–	2.34	–	–	3.91	–	–	–	–	–	7.81	–	–	–	15.62	≥6,843.7 ≤7,000.0
Program Budgets																	
REDEV	–	–	–	–	–	–	–	–	–	–	–	–	–	–	–	–	≤3,050.0
PUB H	–	–	–	–	–	–	–	–	–	–	–	–	–	–	–	–	≤4,200.0
PUB ELD	–	–	–	–	–	–	–	–	–	–	–	–	–	–	–	–	≥525.0
PUB FAM	–	–	–	–	–	–	–	–	–	–	–	–	–	–	–	–	≥1,800.0
REHAB	–	–	–	–	–	–	–	–	–	–	–	–	–	–	–	–	≥2,175.0
RECEIV	1.0	1.0	1.0	1.0	1.0	1.0	–	–	–	–	–	–	–	–	–	–	≤6,400.0
RENT SUP	–	–	–	–	–	–	1.0	1.0	–	–	–	–	–	–	–	–	≤1,400.0 ≥84.0
CODE ENF	–	–	–	–	–	–	–	–	1.0	1.0	1.0	1.0	1.0	1.0	1.0	1.0	≤280.0 ≤750.0

TABLE 5
Basic Linear Programming Model: Employment-Income-Education

	Community Action Job Training							*Manpower Development and Training*						
	X_{32}	X_{33}	X_{34}	X_{35}	X_{36}	X_{37}	X_{38}	X_{39}	X_{40}	X_{41}	X_{42}	X_{43}	X_{44}	X_{45}
Objective Function A														
Impact	0.60	1.03	1.68	0.58	1.10	1.88	1.36	0.47	0.81	1.32	0.50	0.95	1.62	1.17
Objective Function B														
Budget	1.0	1.0	1.0	1.0	1.0	1.0	1.0	1.0	1.0	1.0	1.0	1.0	1.0	1.0
Performance Standards														
Y_6	0.60	0.60	0.60	–	–	–	–	0.47	0.47	0.47	–	–	–	–
Y_7	–	–	–	0.58	0.58	0.58	0.58	–	–	–	0.50	0.50	0.50	0.50
Y_8	–	0.43	0.43	–	0.52	0.52	–	–	0.34	0.34	–	0.45	0.45	–
Y_9	–	–	0.65	–	–	0.78	0.78	–	–	0.51	–	–	0.67	0.67
Y_{10}	–	–	–	–	–	–	–	–	–	–	–	–	–	–
Y_{11}	–	–	–	–	–	–	–	–	–	–	–	–	–	–
Y_{12}	–	–	–	–	–	–	–	–	–	–	–	–	–	–
Y_{13}	–	–	–	–	–	–	–	–	–	–	–	–	–	–
Program Budgets														
CA JOB	1.0	1.0	1.0	1.0	1.0	1.0	1.0	–	–	–	–	–	–	–
MDT JOB	–	–	–	–	–	–	–	1.0	1.0	1.0	1.0	1.0	1.0	1.0
ADC JOB	–	–	–	–	–	–	–	–	–	–	–	–	–	–
JOB TRAIN	1.0	1.0	1.0	1.0	1.0	1.0	1.0	1.0	1.0	1.0	1.0	1.0	1.0	1.0
DAY CARE	–	–	–	–	–	–	–	–	–	–	–	–	–	–
INDRED	–	–	–	–	–	–	–	–	–	–	–	–	–	–
INDPROM	–	–	–	–	–	–	–	–	–	–	–	–	–	–
NY CORPS	–	–	–	–	–	–	–	–	–	–	–	–	–	–

NOTE: The relative effectiveness coefficients for objectives Y_{10} and Y_{11} are adjusted to account for the actual number of students attending high school over five years–roughly, double the number attending in any one year, as each class is carried through its own annual sequence. The coefficients for objective Y_9 assumes that 3.0 children will be taken off ADC for every job provided to an ADC parent.

	ADC Job Training			Day Care Centers						
	X_{46}	X_{47}	X_{48}	X_{49}	X_{50}	X_{51}	X_{52}	X_{53}	X_{54}	X_{55}
Objective Function A										
Impact	2.30	2.71	1.96	12.41	21.34	34.82	9.92	18.85	32.33	23.40
Objective Function B										
Budget	1.0	1.0	1.0	1.0	1.0	1.0	1.0	1.0	1.0	1.0
Performance Standards										
Y_6	0.82	–	–	12.41	12.41	12.41	–	–	–	–
Y_7	–	0.83	0.83	–	–	–	9.92	9.92	9.92	9.92
Y_8	0.59	0.75	–	–	8.93	8.93	–	8.93	8.93	–
Y_9	0.89	1.13	1.13	–	–	13.48	–	–	13.48	13.48
Y_{10}	–	–	–	–	–	–	–	–	–	–
Y_{11}	–	–	–	–	–	–	–	–	–	–
Y_{12}	–	–	–	–	–	–	–	–	–	–
Y_{13}	–	–	–	–	–	–	–	–	–	–
Program Budgets										
CAJOB	–	–	–	–	–	–	–	–	–	–
MDT JOB	–	–	–	–	–	–	–	–	–	–
ADC JOB	1.0	1.0	1.0	–	–	–	–	–	–	–
JOB TRAIN	1.0	1.0	1.0	–	–	–	–	–	–	–
DAY CARE	–	–	–	1.0	1.0	1.0	1.0	1.0	1.0	1.0
INDRED	–	–	–	–	–	–	–	–	–	–
INDPROM	–	–	–	–	–	–	–	–	–	–
NY CORPS	–	–	–	–	–	–	–	–	–	–

TABLE 5 (continued)

	Industrial Redevelopment							*Industrial Promotion*						
	X_{56}	X_{57}	X_{58}	X_{59}	X_{60}	X_{61}	X_{62}	X_{63}	X_{64}	X_{65}	X_{66}	X_{67}	X_{68}	X_{69}
Objective Function A														
Impact	6.87	6.99	7.18	6.84	6.96	7.15	7.03	102.06	103.54	105.78	101.65	103.13	105.37	103.89
Objective Function B														
Budget	1.0	1.0	1.0	1.0	1.0	1.0	1.0	1.0	1.0	1.0	1.0	1.0	1.0	1.0
Performance Standards														
Y_6	0.17	0.17	0.17	–	–	–	–	2.06	2.06	2.06	–	–	–	–
Y_7	–	–	–	0.14	0.14	0.14	0.14	–	–	–	1.65	1.65	1.65	1.65
Y_8	–	0.12	0.12	–	0.12	0.12	–	–	1.48	1.48	–	1.48	1.48	–
Y_9	–	–	0.19	–	–	0.19	0.19	–	–	2.24	–	–	2.24	2.24
Y_{10}	–	–	–	–	–	–	–	–	–	–	–	–	–	–
Y_{11}	–	–	–	–	–	–	–	–	–	–	–	–	–	–
Y_{12}	–	–	–	–	–	–	–	–	–	–	–	–	–	–
Y_{13}	6.70	6.70	6.70	6.70	6.70	6.70	6.70	100.0	100.0	100.0	100.0	100.0	100.0	100.0
Program Budgets														
CA JOB	–	–	–	–	–	–	–	–	–	–	–	–	–	–
MDT JOB	–	–	–	–	–	–	–	–	–	–	–	–	–	–
ADC JOB	–	–	–	–	–	–	–	–	–	–	–	–	–	–
JOB TRAIN	–	–	–	–	–	–	–	–	–	–	–	–	–	–
DAY CARE	–	–	–	–	–	–	–	–	–	–	–	–	–	–
INDRED	1.0	1.0	1.0	1.0	1.0	1.0	1.0	–	–	–	–	–	–	–
INDPROM	–	–	–	–	–	–	–	1.0	1.0	1.0	1.0	1.0	1.0	1.0
NY CORPS	–	–	–	–	–	–	–	–	–	–	–	–	–	–

NOTE: The relative effectiveness coefficients for objectives Y_{10} and Y_{11} are adjusted to account for the actual number of students attending high school over five years–roughly, double the number attending in any one year, as each class is carried through its own annual sequence. The coefficients for objective Y_9 assumes that 3.0 children will be taken off ADC for every job provided to an ADC parent.

	Adult Education							N.Y.C.		Vocational Education		Up. Bd.	E.S. Con.	H.S. Con.	J.C. Con.	
	X_{70}	X_{71}	X_{72}	X_{73}	X_{74}	X_{75}	X_{76}	X_{77}	X_{78}	X_{79}	X_{80}	X_{81}	X_{82}	X_{83}	X_{84}	
Objective Function A																
Impact	0.38	0.50	0.69	0.39	0.51	0.70	0.58	0.82	2.21	1.39	2.95	6.46	0.08	0.12	0.04	Max.
Objective Function B																
Budget	1.0	1.0	1.0	1.0	1.0	1.0	1.0	1.0	1.0	1.0	1.0	1.0	1.0	1.0	1.0	Min.
Performance Standards																
Y_6	0.17	0.17	0.17	–	–	–	–	0.82	–	1.39	–	–	–	–	–	≥6,253.1 ≤6,500.0
Y_7	–	–	–	0.18	0.18	0.18	0.18	–	–	–	–	–	–	–	–	≥7,004.0 ≤7,200.0
Y_8	–	0.12	0.12	–	0.12	0.12	–	–	–	–	–	–	–	–	–	≥6,000.0 ≤6,200.0
Y_9	–	–	0.19	–	–	0.19	0.19	–	–	–	–	–	–	–	–	≥7,664.0 ≤7,800.0
Y_{10}	–	–	–	–	–	–	–	–	2.21	–	2.95	0.96	0.08	0.08	–	≥3,351.0 ≤3,500.0
Y_{11}	–	–	–	–	–	–	–	–	–	–	–	5.50	–	0.04	0.04	≥6,692.3 ≤7,000.0
Y_{12}	0.21	0.21	0.21	0.21	0.21	0.21	0.21	–	–	–	–	–	–	–	–	≥3,183.6 ≤3,300.0
Y_{13}	–	–	–	–	–	–	–	–	–	–	–	–	–	–	–	≥10,000.0 ≤10,200.0
Program Budgets																
CA JOB	–	–	–	–	–	–	–	–	–	–	–	–	–	–	–	≥2,300.0
MDT JOB	–	–	–	–	–	–	–	–	–	–	–	–	–	–	–	≥1,700.0
ADC JOB	–	–	–	–	–	–	–	–	–	–	–	–	–	–	–	≥750.0 ≤1,250.0
JOB TRAIN	–	–	–	–	–	–	–	–	–	–	–	–	–	–	–	≤6,400.0
DAY CARE	–	–	–	–	–	–	–	–	–	–	–	–	–	–	–	≤100.0
INDRED	–	–	–	–	–	–	–	–	–	–	–	–	–	–	–	≥600.0 ≤900.0
INDPROM	–	–	–	–	–	–	–	–	–	–	–	–	–	–	–	≤55.0
NY CORPS	–	–	–	–	–	–	–	1.0	1.0	–	–	–	–	–	–	≥750.0
										≤ 206.2	≥ 82.5	≥ 7,200.0	≥ 14,000.0	≥ 7,000.0		

TABLE 6
Alternative Housing Model Solutions

		Sensitivity Analysis							
	Minimize Budget	*Cost/Unit Increase*	*Cost/Unit Decrease*	*Increase Limit*	*Decrease Limit*	*Maximize Impact*	*Introduce New Program*	*Revise Program Budgets*	*Weighting of Objectives*
Objective Function A									
Impact	34,682.3	–	–	–	–	32,940.3	34,830.7	34,689.2	39,650.1
Objective Function B									
Budget	11,373.2	–	–	–	–	9,600.0	11,373.2	9,166.4	9,600.0
Performance Standards									
Y_1	6,869.4	1.19	−1.19	6,886.68	6,810.37	5,230.8	6,869.4	6,869.4	5,230.8
Y_2	6,661.3	0.67	−0.67	6,672.75	6,622.20	7,000.0	6,661.3	6,661.3	7,000.0
Y_3	7,000.0	0.00	0.00	7,384.32	6,016.03	7,000.0	7,000.0	7,000.0	7,000.0
Y_4	7,186.9	−0.00	−0.00	7,188.50	7,184.89	6,709.5	7,300.0	7,158.5	6,709.6
Y_5	6,964.6	0.00	−0.00	7,073.07	6,686.71	7,000.0	7,000.0	7,000.0	7,000.0
Program Budgets									
REDEV	1,450.0	0.64	–	1,646.75	1,450.00	1,450.0	1,450.0	895.0	1,450.0
PUB H	4,200.0	−0.00	0.00	4,270.27	4,179.42	2,939.0	4,200.0	4,200.0	2,939.0
PUB ELD	525.0	0.48	−0.48	568.20	377.44	525.0	525.0	95.0	525.0
PUB FAM	1,800.0	0.61	−0.61	1,833.89	1,684.26	1,800.0	1,800.0	310.0	1,800.0
REHAB	5,264.2	0.26	0.91	5,284.74	5,241.53	3,541.0	5,264.2	3,932.4	3,541.0
RECEIV	1,400.0	−0.36	0.36	1,451.78	1,384.84	1,400.0	1,400.0	3,100.0	1,400.0
RENT SUP	84.0	1.00	−1.00	389.43	0.00	84.0	84.0	84.0	84.0
COD ENF	750.0	−4.44	4.44	754.83	748.59	750.0	750.0	750.0	750.0
PUB NEW	–	–	–	–	–	–	100.0	–	–
Programs in Solution									
X_1	375.0	0.64	−0.64	1,975.00	−1,075.00	375.0	375.0	55.0	375.0
X_2	275.0	0.78	−0.78	602.37	179.15	275.0	275.0	40.0	275.0
X_3	425.0	0.64	−0.64	621.75	367.39	425.0	425.0	425.0	425.0
X_4	375.0	0.78	−0.78	497.18	339.23	375.0	375.0	375.0	375.0
X_5	525.0	0.48	0.21	568.20	306.02	525.0	525.0	95.0	525.0
X_7	1,800.0	0.61	0.15	1,833.89	1,523.51	1,800.0	1,800.0	310.0	1,800.0

TABLE 6 (continued)

X_9	0.0	−0.00	0.00	868.98	−5,949.75	0.0	0.0	0.0	62.1
X_{11}	1,875.0	–	−0.00	1,875.00	1,006.01	614.0	1,775.0	3,795.0	551.9
X_{13}	3,389.2	0.00	0.14	3,409.74	3,319.65	2,927.0	3,489.2	137.4	2,927.0
X_{15}	0.0	1.00	−1.00	1.13	−3.87	50.0	0.0	0.0	50.0
X_{16}	0.0	−0.00	0.00	637.39	−4,364.10	0.0	604.9	0.0	0.0
X_{17}	1,212.7	0.20	−0.00	1,246.56	575.33	1,045.0	353.2	10.2	1,045.0
X_{18}	0.0	0.00	−0.00	15.12	−51.65	0.0	254.5	2,865.3	0.0
X_{19}	0.0	−0.00	0.00	30.91	−9.05	355.0	0.0	224.5	355.0
X_{20}	0.0	−0.00	0.00	30.91	−9.05	0.0	187.3	0.0	0.0
X_{21}	187.3	0.23	−0.00	195.50	156.37	0.0	0.0	0.0	0.0
X_{22}	0.0	0.00	0.00	84.00	−11,289.75	0.0	84.0	0.0	0.0
X_{23}	84.0	1.00	0.00	280.00	−1,564.91	84.0	0.0	84.0	84.0
X_{28}	0.0	0.00	0.00	6.92	−17.71	0.0	4.0	0.0	0.0
X_{29}	95.6	–	−0.00	95.58	87.85	6.8	0.0	64.4	0.0
X_{30}	654.4	−0.00	0.00	662.15	647.50	743.2	746.0	685.6	750.0
X_{33}	–	–	–	–	–	–	100.0	–	–
Programs Not in Solution									
X_6		0.21	−0.21	218.98	−64.12				
X_8		0.15	−0.15	276.49	−80.95				
X_{10}		0.13	−0.13	52.58	−15.40				
X_{12}		0.13	−0.13	52.58	−15.40				
X_{14}		0.13	−0.13	79.59	−23.30				
X_{24}		0.92	−0.92	2.05	−7.00				
X_{25}		0.92	−0.92	2.05	−7.00				
X_{26}		0.92	−0.92	2.05	−7.00				
X_{27}		0.92	−0.92	1.41	−4.82				
X_{51}		0.00	−0.00	2.26	−7.74				
X_{32}		–	–	–	–				

TABLE 7
Alternative EIE Model Solutions

		Sensitivity Analysis						
	Minimize Budget	*Cost/Unit Increase*	*Cost/Unit Decrease*	*Increase Limit*	*Decrease Limit*	*Maximize Impact*	*Revise Performance Standards*	*Improve Existing Programs*
Objective Function A								
Impact	5,043.3	–	–	–	–	4,640.3	4,337.6	5,043.3
Objective Function B								
Budget	172,502.4	–	–	–	–	55,000.0	169,547.7	171,789.8
Performance Standards								
Y_6	6,253.1	0.72	–0.72	–	1,085.91	6,500.0	5,000.0	6,253.0
Y_7	7,004.0	0.90	–0.90	7,289.86	6,297.86	7,200.0	5,000.0	7,004.0
Y_8	6,000.0	0.92	–0.92	6,633.09	5,772.69	6,200.0	5,000.0	6,000.0
Y_9	7,800.0	0.00	0.00	8,777.21	5,896.81	7,800.0	5,000.0	7,800.0
Y_{10}	3,500.0	0.00	–0.00	11,330.35	1,893.95	3,500.0	3,500.0	3,500.0
Y_{11}	6,692.3	25.00	–25.00	–	2,777.12	1,974.1	6,692.3	6,692.3
Y_{12}	3,183.6	3.46	–3.46	3,581.38	1,882.93	3,028.7	3,183.6	3,183.6
Y_{13}	10,000.0	0.11	–0.11	11,530.00	9,520.00	10,200.0	10,000.0	10,000.0
Program Budgets								
CA JOB	2,737.1	0.30	0.16	3,458.28	0.00	3,285.1	2,300.0	2,300.0
MDT JOB	1,700.0	0.14	–0.14	2,205.12	0.00	1,700.0	1,700.0	1,700.0
ADC JOB	1,250.0	–0.44	0.44	1,553.07	0.00	1,250.0	750.0	1,050.1
JOB TRAIN	5,687.1	–	–	–	–	6,235.1	4,750.0	5,050.1
DAY CARE	100.0	–16.14	16.14	125.45	29.10	100.0	100.0	100.0
IND RED	671.6	0.76	–	701.49	671.64	701.5	671.6	671.6
IND PROM	55.0	–13.24	13.24	59.80	39.70	55.0	55.0	55.0
NY CORPS	750.0	0.41	–0.41	7,051.45	–0.00	750.0	750.0	750.0
Programs in Solution								
X_{34}	0.0	0.17	–0.17	596.02	–1,472.30	0.0	922.9	0.0
X_{37}	2,737.1	0.30	0.00	3,458.27	1,484.28	3,285.1	1,377.1	2,300.0
X_{42}	0.0	0.41	–0.41	1,406.87	–505.12	0.0	455.6	0.0

TABLE 7 (continued)

X_{44}	1,700.0	0.14	0.00	2,205.12	241.46	1,700.0	1,244.4	1,700.0
X_{47}	1,250.0	–	0.30	1,250.00	811.25	1,250.0	750.0	1,050.1
X_{50}	28.8	–0.02	0.00	37.96	–112.37	28.1	0.0	0.0
X_{51}	0.0	0.00	0.00	28.82	–72.49	0.0	100.0	46.4
X_{54}	71.2	0.26	–0.02	80.66	62.04	71.9	0.0	53.6
X_{57}	0.0	0.00	–0.00	671.64	–5,043.86	0.0	671.6	0.0
X_{60}	0.0	0.00	–0.00	671.64	–10,016.74	0.0	0.0	671.6
X_{61}	671.7	0.76	0.00	900.00	–4,471.62	701.5	0.0	0.0
X_{65}	55.0	–	–0.00	55.00	–372.96	55.0	55.0	0.0
X_{68}	0.0	–0.00	0.00	55.00	–173.25	0.0	0.0	55.0
X_{74}	5,143.3	0.00	–0.00	5,859.05	4,494.22	6,733.5	14,246.6	6,634.8
X_{75}	10,016.7	–0.00	0.00	10,665.78	9,300.95	7,688.9	0.0	8,525.2
X_{76}	0.0	0.11	–0.11	5,275.76	–1,894.19	0.0	913.4	0.0
X_{77}	0.0	0.59	–0.59	726.72	–3,543.14	726.7	0.0	0.0
X_{78}	750.0	0.41	–0.59	7,051.45	23.28	23.3	750.0	750.0
X_{80}	3,717.4	1.00	–1.00	3,780.45	3,717.24	4,329.8	1,700.8	3,641.8
X_{81}	206.2	–136.50	136.50	986.12	–	206.2	206.2	206.2
X_{82}	7,200.0	1.00	–1.00	27,275.60	–90,679.40	7,200.0	7,200.0	7,200.0
X_{83}	34,075.6	11.38	–0.00	–	32,213.10	14,000.0	34,075.6	34,075.6
X_{84}	104,879.4	–0.00	–	106,741.90	104,879.40	7,000.0	104,879.4	104,879.4
Selected Program Not in Solution								
X_{32}		0.57	–0.57	8,611.98	–437.12			
X_{36}		0.00	–0.00	1,252.84	–2,439.98			
X_{39}		0.52	–0.52	1,700.00	–502.12			
X_{40}		0.21	–0.21	757.63	–1,871.52			
X_{51}		0.00	0.00	28.82	–72.49			
X_{52}		8.21	–8.21	35.52	–25.45			
X_{58}		0.00	–0.00	671.64	–5,043.86			
X_{63}		1.36	–1.36	55.00	–153.58			
X_{73}		0.11	–0.11	5,692.88	–1,894.19			

For example, compare X_{60} and X_{61} in the "minimize budget" and "improve existing programs" solutions (Table 7). The sensitivity analysis for the minimum budget problem reveals that X_{60} could be increased up to 671.6, while X_{61} could be decreased up to 4471.6, both with no added total budget costs. In the second solution, a full shift is, in fact, made between the two, and any combination totaling 671.6 would also be permissible. There are actually an infinite number of optimal solutions, for these problems and for each of the others.

This is disturbing, however, only if an optimal solution is the chief objective of analysis. At least two reasons can be suggested for de-emphasizing the usual role of an optimal solution, whether a single one is achieved or not. First, the very real limitations of input data and parameters should be recognized. Within this complex plan evaluation context, it should be acknowledged that not all important objectives and decision criteria are represented. Some objectives may not be amenable to quantitative measurement, while others may be only partially represented by the performance indices chosen. The uncertainty or probable forecasting error associated with the coefficients in a programs-objectives matrix should also be recognized. No matter what supporting information systems and analytic techniques are developed, these coefficients, and especially the cost-effectiveness parameters (Table 2) upon which they are based, can be regarded only as qualified estimates. Their temporal stability is really unknown. In short, while we may be willing to make limited comparisons among groups of programs and objectives, we are not likely to achieve the level of knowledge implied by a comprehensive optimal solution.

Second, the role of this type of analysis in subsequent decision-making should be properly understood. Political decision-makers are more likely to be interested in what is "good" or "bad" about particular programs and projects, and in how much it will cost to achieve particular objectives. Because some decision factors will almost inevitably rely upon their judgment and intuition, they are less likely to be interested in multiple-program, multiple-objective recommendations which ignore these subjective factors. In particular, because of these limitations and the uncertainties mentioned above, the notion of an "optimal" solution to difficult public investment problems will seem premature and even presumptuous. Perhaps the finality of an optimal solution is crucial here—this kind of final allocation among investment alternatives is what decision-makers themselves wish to accomplish.

This line of thinking suggests that the principal value of mathematical programming lies with the identification of marginal differences or trade-offs among alternative program variables. These trade-offs would be cast in terms of relative deviations from an optimal solution, but the solution itself would stay in the background. It would represent an essentially simple-minded, hypothetical ideal, useful mainly for facilitating relative program, objective and budget comparisons. These comparisons and trade-offs would be made using the sensitivity analysis of the mathematical programming problem. Since the optimal solution actually identified is not only likely to be an arbitrary one, but also subject to serious limitations and uncertainties, primary attention would be focused upon the results of such sensitivity analyses. They are discussed in the following section.

An optimal solution will, however, illustrate the importance of identifying program variables in relation to their specific target populations. For example, the Table 6 housing model solution states that, in order to achieve at least the minimum desired level of improvement for each of the five objectives, an expenditure of some $11.3 million will be required. In this particular solution, the redevelopment and public housing (new construction) programs (X_1–X_5, X_7) are achieved at their minimum levels, with both of the latter (elderly and family public housing) replacing existing substandard units. The sum of $1.9 million should be spent in rehabilitating substandard units for family public housing (program X_{11}), while $3.4 million should be spent to rehabilitate substandard units for moderate-income housing (program X_{13}). In addition, receivership programs should be allocated $1.2 million for the upgrading of substandard units for family public housing, and $0.2 million for the improvement of other deficient units for moderate income families. The sum of $0.08 million in rent supplements should be used to gain better housing for low-income families. Finally, $0.1 million in code enforcement activity should be aimed at other deficient units housing low-income elderly households, with $0.6 million aimed at other deficient units housing low-income families.

In practice, of course, whether this or other solutions are actually selected, it would not be possible to make such allocations to the letter. For example, clearance of poor existing housing for the construction of new public housing is likely to involve both substandard and other deficient units, and not just one or the other, as required by the solution, while it may be necessary to find rent supplement money for a few elderly households, in addition to low-income families. In general, programs can rarely be devoted exclusively to a single target population or group, though programming models tend to result in such all-or-nothing allocations. However, a potential asset of such models lies in their ability to tell us, for each program, *where to put the emphasis*—to look for public housing sites containing mostly substandard housing, to concentrate rent supplements upon poorly housed low-income families. The further we can go in these directions of emphasis, the more effectively and efficiently our public funds will be spent.

SENSITIVITY ANALYSES

A basic method for testing the relative weight or importance of each variable or parameter in a mathematical programming problem (in a sense, testing its "pull" toward or away from an optimal solution) lies in the use of a sensitivity analysis, as shown in Tables 6 and 7.[12] The "cost" in the cost/unit figures is expressed in terms of the units used in the objective function–dollars, or, more specifically, 1000's of dollars. The "units," of course, represent the appropriate performance standard, program budget, or program variable units. (In a sensitivity analysis of the "maximize impact" solution, costs would be expressed in terms of percentage points of goal-achievement.) These cost/unit figures simply say that the value of the objective function will be raised or lowered, for every unit of increase or decrease in the element at hand, by the amount shown. This raising or lowering will take place over the range shown by the increase and decrease limits. The marginal sensitivity of all variables (programs) or parameters (standards, budgets) can be tested in this way.

This kind of analysis for the performance standards of the housing model (Table 6) indicates, for example, that Y_1 is the most costly or difficult to achieve, followed by Y_2, with the cost/unit figures to raise or lower these standards varying over a relatively short range. The zeros shown for Y_3, Y_4 and Y_5 do not mean that it costs nothing to achieve them (absolutely), but rather that, because they are tied to Y_1 and Y_2, and for this particular optimal solution, it would cost nothing to increase or decrease them over the ranges shown. They are achieved, in a sense, simultaneously with the achievement of Y_1 and Y_2. (In general, standards and other row parameters could be extended beyond the ranges shown, but the cost/unit figures and the values for selected other variables and parameters would change.)

An examination of performance standards in this way can reveal which constraints are particularly binding or difficult to meet (for instance, Y_{11} in Table 7), so that we will know in turn which standards can best be reduced in order to reduce total expenditures. We can also determine how much the budget will have to be increased in order to achieve a higher level for some objective, though the permitted increase level may not be very large. For example, to increase Y_8 from 60 per cent to 66 per cent would require an added expenditure of $0.6 million. We do not know which program will absorb this expenditure, however, or what it would cost to go up to 70 per cent. Revising the problem and running it again would, in general, permit us to obtain this additional information.

In a similar way, program budgets can be reviewed to find those which are more or less costly. In the cost/unit increase column, a plus sign indicates a budget minimum which, if reduced, would permit an improved optimal solution (such as REDEV, PUBELD and PUBFAM in Table 6), while a minus sign indicates a maximum constraint which should be increased in order to improve the solution (ADCJOB, DAYCARE and INDPROM in Table 7, with DAYCARE the most promising choice).

The sensitivity of program or solution variables can be interpreted in much the same way. In Tables 6 and 7 alternative programs have been distinguished according to whether they appeared in at least one of the solutions tested. Plus or minus signs in the cost/unit increase column again indicate variables which could be profitably increased or reduced. For example, X_3 (clearance of substandard housing) could be increased up to \$0.6 million, but the cost (increased total budget) for each \$1000-unit of increase will be \$640. This cost/unit figure (or net cost) reflects shifts in the values of other variables which would also take place. If X_3 were decreased, however, the total budget could also be decreased, at a rate of \$640/unit of reduction. Where the objective is to minimize the total budget, solution variables with a minus cost/unit figure should consequently be sought.

A program variable not currently accepted by either model could also be entered into solution at the cost/unit increase figures shown. X_{12} (rehabilitation of other deficient housing units for low-income family public housing) could enter the housing solution at a net cost of \$130 per unit of investment, while X_{40} (Manpower Development and Training for unemployed, low-income family persons) could enter the EIE solution at a net cost of \$210 per unit of investment. In some cases, within similar program groups or programs aimed at the same objective, we can also directly identify equal-cost (or zero net-cost) trade-offs among variables. For instance, X_9 can enter the housing solution (up to a value of \$869,000), as long as X_{11} is correspondingly reduced (up to a value of \$1,006,000), and as long as compensating shifts among other variables take place. These additional shifts can be identified by fixing X_9 or X_{11} at a desired level and running the model again.

REVISED SOLUTIONS

What if an overall budget limit has been specified, and we wish to maximize the effectiveness or impact of all funds expended? Tables 6 and 7 show the results of such a "maximize impact" solution, with a maximum housing budget set at \$9.6 million and a maximum EIE budget at \$55.0 million. Minimum performance standards are not set, so that, in effect, money will be spent upon the most easily realized objectives, until the budget constraint is reached. Y_1 and Y_{11}, for example, become the least well-achieved objectives, and are correspondingly the hardest to achieve.

Comparisons with the original minimum budget solution reveal a number of significant shifts in allocation and the introduction of new variables into solution. In the housing model, X_{11} (rehabilitation of substandard housing for low-income family public housing), and X_{12} are both substantially reduced; X_{15} (moderate-income housing, with a high impact coefficient of 31.25) and X_{19} (receivership proceedings against other deficient housing for low-income elderly households) are new variables; and X_{21} is deleted. In the EIE model similar reallocations take place. In general, these shifts in allocation are to variables with higher total impact coefficients, so that, for example, in the housing model total impact is kept at nearly the same level, while the total budget is reduced by some 15 per cent.

Similar allocation shifts are likely to occur when basic changes in column vectors or constraint parameters are made. Such shifts will generally be toward a more optimal solution, either in terms of minimum budget or maximum impact. The remaining portions of Tables 6 and 7 give examples of the shifts generated by introducing alternative programs, standards and program budgets into the original model solutions. Multiple optimal solutions also exist for each of these examples, and sensitivity analyses should also be performed. In general, sensitivity analyses will show which reallocations are simply equal-cost trade-offs and which are an actual improvement on the previous solution.

The effects of a new housing program—the construction of prefabricated public housing units, mainly on scattered vacant lots—are tested (shown as X_{32} and X_{33} in the housing model), as well as the effects of improved services and delivery for two existing programs—Community Action job training and the promotion of new industry providing jobs for the unemployed and under-employed—in the EIE model. In general, the housing alternative is found to be sufficiently attractive (in terms of its relative effectiveness coefficients) to draw investment away from other programs, while the EIE alternatives (X_{34}, X_{37}, X_{65} and X_{68}) fall short.

"Revised Performance Standards" in Table 7 shows the effects of reducing the performance standards for the four employment-income objectives (Y_6, Y_7, Y_8, Y_9) to a fixed level of 50 per cent. Significant shifts include the entry of Community Action job training programs (X_{34} and X_{35}) into the solution, a change in emphasis among Neighborhood Youth Corps programs (X_{77} and X_{78}) from staying in school to unemployment, and a substantial increase in vocational education programs (X_{80}).

Alternative program budgets in the housing model are also evaluated, with the clearance programs (X_1, X_2, X_3, X_4) set at lower minimums, public housing construction (PUBELD, PUBFAM) set at lower minimums, and the budget for potential receivership programs substantially increased. The results show, in addition to the expected decreases in X_1–X_7, major increases in X_{11} (rehabilitation of substandard dwelling units as public housing for low-income families) and X_{18} (receivership action against substandard housing for moderate-income families) and a major decrease in X_{13} (public rehabilitation of substandard housing for moderate-income families).

Finally, the significance of assigning weights to the objectives in the housing model, for the maximize impact solution, is also considered. Table 6 shows the results of assigning a weight of 2.0 to Y_4, while remaining objectives receive a weighting of 1.0. In effect, this amounts to doubling the effectiveness coefficients for the Y_4 row when computing the row of total impact coefficients (objective function A). The effectiveness coefficients in the performance standard remain the same. In this example, shifts among the allocations resulting from the weighting are not significant.

CONCLUSIONS

These potential applications of mathematical programming in a plan/program design and evaluation context illustrate its versatility as a plan evaluation tool. These results should not, of course, be considered as actual recommendations for the various Model Cities Programs concerned—the data base is far too sketchy for that. However, they are representative of the *kinds* of insights and findings which mathematical programming models could produce, once given appropriate data and supporting analysis inputs. It is hoped that a simple framework for continuing research and development in these supporting areas has been outlined. Whether mathematical programming is explicitly used or not, the information systems and analytic studies called for here are the types most likely to be useful in constructing basic programs-objectives matrices. Parallel research should continue to explore how such matrices might best be recast as urban improvement and public investment programming models.

In short, much work remains to be done before viable urban improvement programming models can actually be developed. This exploratory study indicates that several basic guidelines for continuing research efforts can be drawn.

1. Identifying objectives. Though the need for quantitative measures of goal achievement is clear, options are still open regarding the choice of specific objectives and measurable indices. If these indices are consistently designed to reflect community-wide socio-economic conditions and characteristics (in terms of persons, families, housing units, acres or other basic units), then objectives can be expressed in terms of desired changes in the numbers, rates and proportions associated with these socio-economic conditions. This will permit the establishment of performance standards for each index, and the development of consistent methods for matching programs against objectives.

2. Identifying programs. Alternative programs and policies must be expressed in terms of three essential characteristics—the objectives to which they are related, the impact or effectiveness which they will have in achieving each objective, and the costs associated with varying levels of effectiveness. This will permit the development of cost-effectiveness accounts for each objective, comparing the costs encountered by different programs in achieving a given level of effectiveness (or performance standards), or comparing the different impact levels which can be achieved for a given budget, if assigned to each of the program alternatives. For maximum flexibility, costs should be measured in terms of dollars.

3. Measuring effectiveness. In order to permit comparisons and trade-offs among different programs and groups of programs, a common measure is also essential for the development of mathematical programming models. If objectives are represented as changes in various measurable socio-economic conditions, and programs are expressed in dollars, then basic cost-per-unit-output parameters can be developed, using appropriate person, family, housing, or other units of output or impact. These cost-per-unit-output parameters can then be utilized to develop a matrix of relative effectiveness coefficients. One way to define the common measure of goal achievement needed in such a matrix is to let each coefficient represent the percentage of objective j which can be achieved by each dollar invested in program i.

4. Predicting effectiveness. Programs-objectives effectiveness matrices of this type will require a prodigious amount of supporting research and analysis. Basic cost-effectiveness parameters cannot be estimated without considerable research into the impacts of alternative programs and policies upon their target populations. Unanticipated consequences must also be investigated. These supporting activities will rely upon major progress in the coordinated development of data resources and information systems. Predicting program effectiveness will involve improved cost-accounting and records-keeping procedures, the continuing application of various univariate and multivariate statistical analyses and, in some cases, the development of more elaborate socio-economic simulation models. Identifying and dealing with program interdependencies will present particularly crucial problems for analysis.

5. Sensitivity analyses. Because the level of knowledge implied by an optimal solution is likely to be unrealistic, and because political decision-makers are likely to be unreceptive to such an overall allocation, the primary value of mathematical programming may well lie with the identification of marginal differences among alternative variables and parameters. The sensitivity analysis of all elements—standards, budgets, or programs—within a programming problem can provide a good deal of information on relative costs, effectiveness and trade-offs. Comparison of these marginal sensitivities will, in general, tell us how important each variable or parameter will be in attempting to achieve our overall objective (minimum cost or maximum impact). Revised solutions for a programming problem can also test the relative effects of specific standard, budget, or program alternatives.

NOTES

1. Morris Hill, A Goals-Achievement Matrix for Evaluating Alternative Plans, Journal of the American Institute of Planners 34, 19-29 (January 1968). See also Morris Hill, "A Method for the Evaluation of Transportation Plans," Highway Research Record 180, 21-34, Highway Research Board, Washington (1967). A matrix method for plan evaluation is also proposed in Edward L. Falk, "Measurement of Community Values: The Spokane Experiment." Highway Research Record 229, 53-64, Highway Research Board, Washington (1968).

2. Kenneth J. Schlager, A Land-Use Plan Design Model, Journal of the American Institute of Planners 31, 103-117 (May 1965). Other attempts at applying mathematical programming in a metropolitan planning context have focused upon the aggregate behavior of residential developers and consumers, rather than upon achieving a set of community-wide objectives. See Kenneth J. Schlager, "A Recursive Programming Theory of the Residential Land Development Process," Highway Research Record 126, 24-32, Highway Research Board, Washington (1966) and John Herbert and Benjamin J. Stevens, "A Model

for the Distribution of Residential Activities in Urban Areas," Journal of Regional Science 2, 21-36 (Fall 1960).

3. For accounts of the two models mentioned here, see William Jessiman, Daniel Brand, Alfred Tumminia and C. Roger Brussee, "A Rational Decision-Making Technique for Transportation Planning," Highway Research Record 180, 71-80; Highway Research Board, Washington (1967) and Charles G. Schimpeler and W. L. Grecco, "Systems Evaluation: An Approach Based Upon Community Structure and Values," Highway Research Record 238, 123-152, Highway Research Board, Washington (1968). Mathematical programming models have also been proposed for evaluating low-cost housing alternatives in A. L. Silvers and A. K. Sloan, "A Model Framework for Comprehensive Planning in New York City," Journal of the American Institute of Planners 31, 246-251 (August 1965), and for evaluating urban renewal alternatives in Wilbur A. Steger, "The Pittsburgh Urban Renewal Simulation Model," Journal of the American Institute of Planners 31, 144-149 (May 1965).

4. The more abstract interpretations described here may be found in Robert F. Coughlin, "The Capital Programming Problem," Journal of the American Institute of Planners 26, 39-48 (February 1960). Robert E. Coughlin and Benjamin H. Stevens, "Public Facility Programming and the Achievement of Development Goals," paper prepared for the Seminar on Land-Use Models, University of Pennsylvania, Philadelphia (October 1964); and George L. Peterson, "Complete Value Analysis: Highway Beautification and Environmental Quality," Highway Research Record 182, 9-17, Highway Research Board, Washington (1967).

5. U.S. Department of Housing and Urban Development, "Improving the Quality of Urban Life: A Program Guide to Model Neighborhoods in Demonstration Cities." U.S. Government Printing Office, Washington (1966).

6. The hypothetical figures shown in both Tables 1 and 2 are, for the most part, generalized from actual data, and are intended to be reasonably realistic. They are based upon the 1960 U.S. Census and various municipal agency annual reports and plans, principally from Chicago, Illinois.

7. This use of performance standards is discussed in U.S. Department of Housing and Urban Development, "Measures of Living Quality in Model Neighborhoods." Technical Assistance Bulletin No. 2 (U.S. Department of Housing and Urban Development, Model Cities Administration, Washington, July 1968); and U.S. Department of Housing and Urban Development, Comprehensive Program Submission Requirements, CDA Letter No. 4, Model Cities Administration (July 1968).

8. For reviews of the problems and procedures of urban model-building and analysis in general, see Willard B. Hansen, "Quantitative Methods in Urban Planning," in William I. Goodman and Eric C. Freund (Eds.), *Principles and Practice of Urban Planning,* 277-294; International City Managers' Association, Washington (1968), Ira S. Lowry, "A Short Course in Model Design," Journal of the American Institute of Planners 31, 158-166 (May 1965), and Wilbur A. Steger, "Review of Analytic Techniques for the CRP," Journal of the American Institute of Planners 31, 166-172 (May 1965). Examples of specific simulation models are described in Ira M. Robinson, Harry B. Wolfe and Robert L. Barringer, "A Simulation Model for Renewal Programming," Journal of the American Institute of Planners 31, 126-134 (May 1965), and F. Stuart Chapin, Jr., "A Model for Simulating Residential Development," Journal of the American Institute of Planners 31, 120-125 (May 1965).

9. For a brief discussion of these programming techniques see, for example, John D. C. Little, "Mathematical Techniques: Mathematical Programming," in Philip M. Morse and Laura W. Bacon, *Operations Research for Public Systems,* 199-206. The MIT Press, Cambridge (1967).

10. These maximums are necessary to ensure that objectives are not achieved beyond practical limits. The maximum allowable limit for each y_j is 10,000.0 (or 100 per cent of goal achievement), but, in general realistic levels of percentage goal achievement must be set at a lower figure.

11. In developing these simple operational examples, a number of liberties with data and with complex improvement program interrelationships were taken. Some of the problems and assumptions regarding data and supporting analysis have already been reviewed in preceding sections. A series of additional major simplifications and assumptions were also made. These dealt in part with the stratification of program variables to correspond with individual objectives, the undiscriminating use of average cost figures for each basic program variable, the relative investment life or time span of effectiveness for different programs (here assumed to be equal at five years), the treatment of those community objectives not represented directly in the model (some can be indirectly acknowledged by setting minimums on certain programs) and the setting of program budget constraints. Further discussion of these simplifications, together with additional details on the methodology of model construction, is presented in Darwin G. Stuart, Strategy Analysis in Urban Planning: Evaluation Model Cities Alternatives, unpublished Ph.D. dissertation, Northwestern University (1969).

12. Sensitivity analysis makes use of the dual problems associated with each of these linear programming examples. For a discussion of the basic primal-dual relationships involved, see Stuart, op. cit. (footnote p. 229).

Chapter 15

ROBUSTNESS IN SEQUENTIAL INVESTMENT DECISIONS

Shiv K. Gupta and Jonathan Rosenhead

When an industrial organization wishes to have the advantage of a coherent long-range investment plan, it is recognizing that investment decisions are not independent. A decision to buy a certain type of equipment this year will limit the types of equipment which can be bought subsequently, unless costs are incurred to make different processes compatible. A decision this year on the location of a factory will affect the suitability of other sites for subsequent factories—suitability for meeting unsatisfied consumer demand, or for avoiding vulnerability to political pressure. And, of course, there are both short-term and long-term interactions. It is not just the details of the subsequent decisions which are changed; the potential efficiency of the eventual system may well be limited by the first one or two investment decisions.

Most studies of the long-range planning of investments have dealt, explicitly or implicitly, with the case of a single investment added at one point in time to the existing capital stock. The "long-range" aspect has been limited to the examination of the effects in the future of alternative investments at that decision point. Usually discounted cash flow or net present value techniques are used to allow for the organization's time preference for profits.

The uncertainty of future external conditions is acknowledged as a major reason why planning is necessary (McEachron, 1958). The simplest approach to this problem is to use a single best estimate (or certainty equivalent, see Christenson, 1964) as representing the total of available information about each of these uncertain variables, and then proceed as if this best estimate were a certain outcome. At most, risk and uncertainty are taken into account by exploring the sensitivity of the investment decision to small deviations of the external conditions from these certainty equivalents.

Reprinted from Management Science, Vol. 15, No. 2 (October 1968), pp. B18-B29, by permission of the publisher.

A more sophisticated approach is that of risk analysis (Hertz, 1964). Probability distributions of the uncertain state variables are subjectively estimated, and future conditions are simulated repeatedly by sampling randomly from these distributions. For each simulation the net present value or rate of return of the investment alternative is computed, so that a probability distribution of its value can be built up. Investment alternatives can be compared via these distributions. One investment may have stochastic dominance over another if for all possible levels of return, that investment's probability of achieving that level is the greater; in the absence of dominance, the organization's risk preferences or utility functions must determine the choice between investments with different profit probability distributions.

Where successive investment decisions have been considered as part of one investment plan, the approach has been similar. The net present value or rate of return of different paths through the network of sequential decisions has been computed, and the most profitable sequence chosen by means of dynamic programming; the sensitivity of the result to changes in interest rates, demand levels, etc. is investigated, as in Culhane, Ronaldson and Zimmerman (1966). Alternatively, subjective probability distributions of the uncertain variables are estimated, and repeated simulation and dynamic programming are used to find "optimal" investment sequence (Hespos and Strassman, 1965).

These approaches to sequential investment under uncertainty are valuable extensions of the techniques developed for once-for-all investment decisions. But because the investment is to be carried out in stages—to avoid dislocating production, or to match an expanding market—other possibilities open up. At any point of time during the implementation of the investment plan it is possible to revise or alter those stages of the plan not irrevocably committed. (This is the difference between a plan and a decision: a plan becomes a decision only when it is irrevocable. See Drucker, 1959.) If in the formation of a plan this opportunity for second and third thoughts is not taken into account, then the "optimum" plan may turn out to be sub-optimal after all.

The extent of flexibility for altering later stages in an investment scheme once the first stages have been implemented will depend on three main factors. The first is the physical or practical limitations of the situation.

A physical limitation might occur at an integrated steel works when an oxygen plant of a certain capacity has already been constructed—this will limit the number of furnaces which can be constructed in subsequent stages, and hence restrict steel output. A practical limitation might occur when a national newspaper is planning to decentralize its printing facilities. If it is management policy that the newspaper shall have the same number of pages in all parts of the country, then the size of press installed at the first printing center limits the maximum size of newspaper that can be printed, and therefore limits the size of presses which it is worth installing at subsequent printing centers.

In principle these limitations are not absolute constraints. The implemented stages of the plan can be adapted or even erased, at a certain cost. A policy restriction on future stages of a plan can be removed–at least conceptually there must be some cost equivalent of breaking management's "rules of the game." In practice, however, the cost of removing these physical or policy limitations is usually prohibitive.

The second factor which may restrict the feasibility of an investment plan to meet changed circumstances during its implementation is the plan itself. The structure of the planned investment may be unnecessarily inflexible, so that the initial decision imposes an effective straight-jacket even on stages of the investment plan which will not be implemented for many years. This may happen, for example, when it is decided to expand production facilities by creating one or two large integrated units instead of a larger number of smaller production units.

Alternatively, it may not be the structure of the plan which is at fault, but rather the details of the "good" end state and of the sequence by which it is to be achieved. For example, in an industrial expansion plan, when the number of plants to be built has been chosen, it still remains to decide their locations and the sequence in which they will be built. This is the third factor which can limit adaptability. The sequence which minimizes cost during the interim until the plan is complete may unduly restrict the possibilities of adapting the plan, during implementation, to changes in the environment. This factor should be incorporated, formally or informally, in any plan which theoretically permits the taking of sequential investment decision. It is discussed further in the following section.

ROBUSTNESS OF A PLAN

A major problem in assessing the flexibility to changed circumstances of a planned sequence of investment decisions is the identification of just what circumstances are likely to change and by how much. Estimates of this variability are often and necessarily made, but rarely without a large element of subjectivity and therefore controversiality. In this section a measure of flexibility, called "robustness," is developed which does not depend directly on such estimates.

As a first step a fixed planning horizon may be assumed. This will normally lie in the range five to fifteen years; the lower limit is imposed by the time scale involved in implementing decisions, and the upper limit by the increasing unreliability of predictions of conditions far into the future, together with the foreshortening effect of the time discounting of future benefits. (These limits will vary in different investment circumstances–an extreme case is the planting of fir trees as raw material for paper making, where the lead-time till availability may approach a hundred years.) In many cases the exact planning horizon is fixed arbitrarily at some multiple of five years ahead, or at some date, say, 1975 or 1980, which is divisible by five. While the planning horizon must lie within the time limits imposed by the implementation of decisions and the reliability of information, the precise choice of a planning horizon is not usually critical. Observation suggests a high measure of continuity in human affairs, and human institutions (of which the modern business is one) have been selected, in the evolutionary sense, for their insensitivity to minor perturbations in their environments. Where, however, small differences in the horizon do imply changes in the desirable action for the immediate future, this is an indication that the horizon has not been placed sufficiently far ahead.

The classical approach to dealing with the uncertainty about the values which external conditions will take when the current planning horizon is reached is: either, ignore it; or estimate probability distributions of the possible variations from their expected values of significant external variables; or examine whether small deviations from those expected values result in any change in optimal policy. The first of these alternatives is almost always implausible, and the third alternative is in sensitive cases equivalent to the second, since the likelihood or the occurrence of deviations of the critical size must still be estimated explicitly or implicitly.

There is an alternative approach which avoids the invidious and often controversial allocation of subjective probabilities to uncertain events far in the future. This approach no longer identifies a single desirable end-state for the investment plan; instead *for the expected values of external variables only,* both the apparently best end-state and all those end-states only slightly less advantageous are examined. (March and Simon's [1958] decision-making through "satisficing" is a clearly related approach. Bosman and Mol [n.d.] have considered near optimal solutions in the context of linear programming.) Under reasonable conditions of continuity of the response function, these end-states are the most likely to be among the best end-states for the external conditions which do eventually arise when the planning horizon is reached. Rather than try to identify the favorite among these contenders, we can instead ensure that our early investment decisions permit the achievement of as many of these end-states as possible, that is, that valuable flexibility is maintained. Subsequent stages of the investment plan are left to be determined at later dates, when more recent information is available and the uncertainty consequently reduced. (Comes and Bellon [1966] give a case study in which a similar approach to sequential decisions is used.) There is of course an apparent opportunity cost in achieving robustness–the possible abandonment of the return expected from the "best" end-state. But the cost is more apparent than real when the "best" end-state is based on uncertain information. Stigler (1939) has discussed the cost of building adaptability into plant.

It is clear that this approach does not entirely remove the need to estimate the effects of possible future variations in external conditions. The assumption that good end-states for the expected external conditions are the most likely to be among the best end-states for the eventually realized external conditions is equivalent to an assumption of only limited variation in external conditions, and in the sensitivity of the system to them. The cut-off value for "good" end-states is equivalent to a safety allowance to guard against the variability of the environment, and its size (that is, the number of less than optimal end-states considered) is implicitly related to estimates of the sensitivity of the system to likely variations in external conditions. This sensitivity of the system can of course be measured by repeated simulation. However, in our results the choice of cut-off point for "good" end-states has not affected the choice of robust initial investment decisions.

In the context of our discussion, "robustness" (or flexibility) of a decision or decisions must be measured in terms of the numbers of the "good" end-states for expected external conditions which remain as open options. If a formal definition is required, then the robustness of a decision can be defined simply as the ratio of that number to the number of good end-states considered. One provision which spoils this simplicity is that investment possibilities stated as discrete alternatives may in reality be at points on a geographical or conceptual continuum. If the alternatives are selected at irregular intervals, the robustness of some will appear to be diluted by the existence of nearby alternatives which are approximate substitutes. This point is discussed further in the next section. Further we have found (in the case study discussed in the next section) that there is a strong tendency among management and researchers alike to give greater weight to those end-states with value nearest to the "best" end-state for expected external conditions.

This unequal weighting of end-states (according to their value under expected conditions) could be incorporated in a formal definition of robustness, but only by venturing further into the quagmire of subjective probabilities we have been skirting. Our solution is to use the simple measure (ratio of good end-states), but as a robustness index which must be qualified by other considerations. This impure measure of the flexibility left by early decisions will certainly (if our experience proves typical) be adequate to management, who are quite capable of making their own subjective transformations.

The advantages of robustness over more conventional investment criteria are in the reduction of the need for subjective estimation—only a range of likely variation in outcome, rather than a set of subjective probability distributions; and in the formal abandonment of the search for an unknowable future optimality in favor of the more modest and practical goal of future flexibility.

A practical example of the use of the concept of robustness in a sequential investment problem is given in the next section.

PLANT LOCATION—A CASE STUDY

The ideas developed in the previous section were stimulated by an industrial project—the selection of locations for new factories for a producer of consumer goods selling throughout the United States. We present here a case study in which the use of the concept of robustness is demonstrated.

The Company is a large and growing producer of consumer goods, operating a number of plants in the United States. A standard size for each new plant of 500,000 units capacity per annum had been adopted on engineering grounds. The objective of our study was stated to be to find how many new plants of this size would be needed in 1976, and where they should be located.

The Company believed that it would need to start laying down the first of the plants in the very near future. Our approach (confirmed by a pilot study of a region of 8 states) was to obtain forecasts of demand by area, consider a range of possible locations, and use linear programming (transportation model) to determine the transport cost of supplying the demand from the existing plants plus combinations of the new locations.

The first step was to obtain forecasts of demand for both 1971 and 1976 for each of the 250 market areas into which the Company divides the country. In the available time only a projection based on data of the Company's past sales could be attempted. The national sales were projected by four methods–linear regression and 2nd order exponential smoothing on both the sales and the log sales. Based on these results two forecasts roughly spanning the range were made for both 1971 and 1976; the higher forecast was called optimistic, the lower conservative. State and market area forecasts were obtained from each of these national forecasts by projecting the state's share of the national sales, and the market area's share of the state's sales.

The breakdown into market areas was shown to be necessary by the pilot study. The transportation cost associated with a given system of plants was found to increase by widely varying amounts when sales forecasts were aggregated from market areas into states–the increases ranged from 4% for one system to 31% for another system of plants. This variation was more than enough to render aggregated results useless; the explanation is that geographical distribution of demand *within* a state can have a significant effect on the choice between plant locations, particularly within that state. Another lesson learned from the pilot study was the old one, that of the dangers of sub-optimization. Despite care in the choice of limits for the pilot region, the eventual national results gave considerably different results for the plant locations–in other words, the effect of supply and demand beyond the region's boundaries could not be ignored.

The annual capacity of plants in existence or under construction is 9 million units. Current (1966) sales for the company are 6.4 million units, but have been increasing rapidly, especially in recent years. The conservative and optimistic demand forecasts for 1971 are 7.7 million and 8.5 million units; the conservative and optimistic demand forecasts for 1976 are 9.4 million and 11.2 million.

Our first conclusion from this was that no additional capacity would be needed by 1971, for either conservative or optimistic demand projections. This conclusion was a surprise, and a not altogether acceptable one, to the management of the Company. Under the influence of recent good trading results and of their "feel" for the market, management expected sales to go ahead at a rate faster even than our optimistic forecast. To explore this eventuality, we examined possible factory systems to meet a demand as high as 9.8 million units in 1971 (which implied a demand between 13 and 15 million units in 1976), all the while maintaining that such progress was most unlikely. Fortunately, the indicated locations for the first new factories were the same for these "upper" sales projections as they were for the "conservative" and "optimistic" estimates—though the dates by which they would be required would have to be advanced. In general, the effect of changes in the predicted rate of sales increase was to expand or contract the planning horizon, but to leave the sequence of decisions unaltered.

The second conclusion was that in 1976 between 1 (conservative) and 5 (optimistic) new factories would need to be in operation. (The projected growth in sales, and the changes in capacity which are necessitated, are shown in Figures 1 and 2.) These were to be chosen from among 21 possible new locations (here called A, B, C, . . . U) scattered across the United States, and two possible extensions to existing factories (here called Y, Z). Two new factory units could be erected (to give a factory of 1 million units capacity) at any of the locations except the latter two. The cost of transporting one unit of production from each factory location to each of the 250 market areas was computed, using mileage and a constant cost per mile. (This was preferable to using existing freight rates—the volume of traffic involved is so large that special rates would certainly be negotiated.) These costs, the forecasts of market area demands, the known capacity of existing factories and the fixed (half-million or one million units) capacities of new factories at trial locations were the input to the linear program transportation model. (The nature and availability of raw materials, as well as

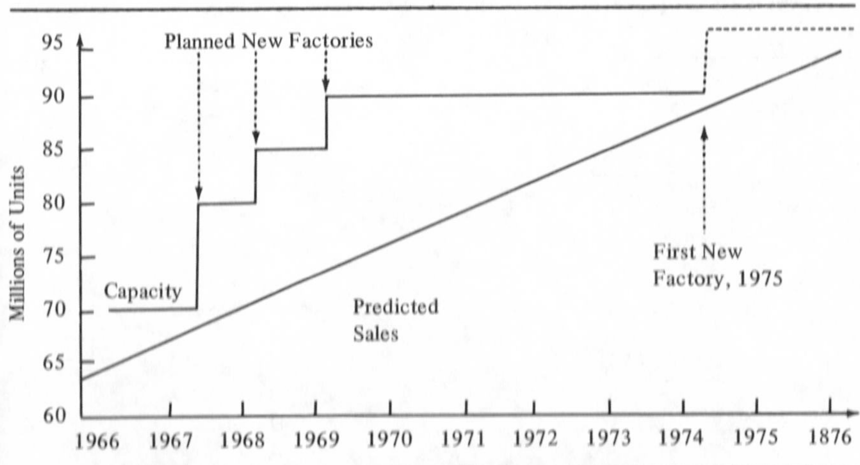

Figure 1: SALES, CAPACITY, FACTORIES—CONSERVATIVE ESTIMATES

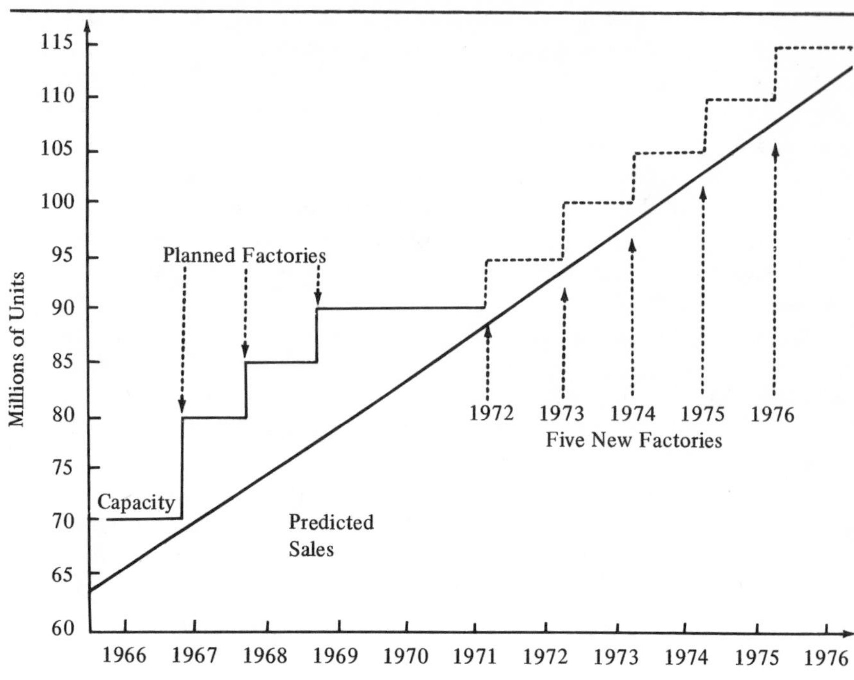

Figure 2: SALES, CAPACITY, FACTORIES–OPTIMISTIC ESTIMATES

TABLE 1
Annual Transportation Cost ($m) of Systems of Factories for the 1976 Conservative Sales Estimates

New Factory Locations	*Transport Cost*
L	9.83
S	10.08
T	10.10
Z	10.33
M	10.58
F	10.72
E	10.73
N	10.81
H	10.95
A	11.29
J	11.33
G	11.36
B	11.55
D	11.56

the weight of packaging of the finished product made the cost of transport to the factories small by comparison with the cost of transporting the goods from the factories to the market areas. Capital and operating costs were effectively the same at the different locations, and so did not affect the results.)

For the 1976 "conservative" case of only one new factory, there were only 23 possible end-states corresponding to each of the 23 locations. The results with the least transportation cost are shown in Table 1.

If this was the only case to be considered there would be a simple conclusion to draw: build the first factory at L, and save upwards of $250,000 per year in transport costs. But other possible sales levels have to be considered.

The 1976 "optimistic" case, involving five new factories, was far more difficult to compute and to analyze. This is where the sequential investment decision problem discussed earlier in this paper became important. Including the possibility of one million unit factories, there are over 70,000 ways of selecting five factory-unit locations from among the 23. Even with the cost of one computer run as low as $2, the total cost of enumerating all alternatives would have been unacceptable. So we were forced to use trial-and-error methods of finding the best factory systems. The search for good systems was ended after 297 runs, by which time no improved results were being found, nor were any new results substantially altering our conclusions. (However our method of analysis is not dependent on finding the absolutely "best" end-state of five new factory locations.)

The annual cost of the factory system with lowest transport cost for the 1976 optimistic sales estimates is found to be $8.88 million. Thirty-one systems with transport costs below $9.30 millions were found, and these are shown in Table 2. The potential savings even from a simple exercise of this kind are great. Many factory systems which intuitively seemed well-located to keep transport costs low proved to have annual transport costs as high as $10.5 million. This is 18% higher than the cheapest system.

System 1 has a cost only $40,000 per year less than System 2, and $400,000 per year more than System 31. Variations in transport rates or in geographical distribution of demand could well produce systematic effects of comparable magnitude. (The safety margin between the cheapest system and the systems not considered as possible alternatives is here $0.52m. To ensure that the margin was large enough to allow for future variability, the analysis was repeated for the 78 systems covered by a margin of $0.82m. The results are substantially the same.) So the argument is strong for taking now only those decisions which cannot wait, and for taking them in a way which preserves flexibility for future decisions.

How many locations *must* be decided now? After fixing on a location it takes close to four years before the factory can be operational. According to the optimistic demand forecasts the first new factory will be needed in 1972, so the apparent answer is "none." However the management does not regard sales of 9.8 million units (necessitating two new factories) as out of the question for

TABLE 2
Annual Transportation Costs ($m) of Systems of Factories for the 1976 Optimistic Sales Estimates

System Rank	*New Factories*	*Transport Cost*	*System Rank*	*New Factories*	*Transport Cost*
1	A,B,M,N,S	8.88	16	B,H,M,N,S	9.13
2	B,G,M,N,S	8.92	17	B,D,J,L,N	9.14
3	A,B,M,N,T	8.96	18	B,M,N,R,Z	9.16
4	B,G,M,N,T	8.98	19	B,J,L,N,R	9.16
5	A,B,M,N,Z	8.99	20	B,H,M,N,T	9.18
6	B,D,M,N,S	8.99	21	A,B,I,L,N	9.20
7	A,B,L,N,R	9.01	22	B,G,L,M,N	9.21
8	B,G,M,N,Z	9.02	23	B,G,I,L,N	9.21
9	B,M,N,R,S	9.03	24	B,H,M,N,Z	9.22
10	A,B,D,L,N	9.05	25	A,G,L,M,N	9.22
11	B,G,L,N,R	9.07	26	B,M,N,S,U	9.23
12	B,D,G,L,N	9.09	27	B,H,L,N,R	9.24
13	B,D,M,N,Z	9.09	28	B,D,H,L,N	9.26
14	B,D,M,N,T	9.11	29	D,M,N,S,U	9.27
15	B,M,N,R,T	9.12	30	A,B,N,R,Z	9.27
			31	A,B,H,M,S	9.28

TABLE 3
Robustness of Locations

Location	*Number of Occurrences*	*Robustness Score (%)*
B	30	97
N	30	97
M	20	65
L	12	39
A	9	29
D	8	26
R	8	26
S	8	26
G	7	23
H	6	19
Z	6	19
T	5	16
I	2	06
J	2	06
U	2	06
		500

1971. Further, they would rather have idle capacity than starve a rising demand and risk the momentum of their sales drive. So it was clear that a decision on one or perhaps two locations would be made very shortly. Therefore we looked for "robust" first and second locations.

The simplest definition of robustness, as the ratio of the number of occurrences of a given location (among the good systems) to the number of good systems, gives the results shown in Table 3.

These robustness-scores must be modified to ensure that a cluster of approximately equivalent locations in one region will not lead to an apparent reduction of robustness. For example, if three possible locations are in different suburbs of one city, every system with one of these locations included can be matched by two equivalent systems. So even if a factory in that city is always necessary to a good system, each of the three individual locations will have a robustness of only 33%. Locations L, S, T and Z (which all fall in one compact region) suffer from this condition in a diluted form–one from among them features in all 31 good factory systems, yet none has a robustness higher than 39%. But jointly, as a location in the particular region, they have a robustness of 100%; that is, all good solutions include a location in that region.

This extension of the robustness idea from locations to nearly autonomous regions must be permitted to counter any biased scatter of potential locations. Analogous extensions may be found in other sequential investment problems.

The (L, S, T, Z) group of locations was the only one with the property which could be identified. So the robust initial locations can be limited to B, N, (L, S, T, Z) and possibly M. As the first three of these alternatives all have very high robustness, the choice between them as locations for initial factories can incorporate other factors.

The most important of these other factors may be called "stability." "Stable" initial decisions are those which create a system which, even in its incomplete state, will perform well. If the optimistic sales forecasts are justified by events a new factory will be built approximately every year, so that the level of cost of operating the incomplete system will be transient. If however there is any doubt that the forecasts will be fulfilled, then there is a possibility that the system consisting of the present factories plus the first one or two new ones, designed as only a temporary phase, might have to operate for a number of years. In either case stable initial choices, giving low cost operations in the (possibly) transient phase, are clearly desirable.

To discover which initial locations are stable, the cost of meeting a demand of 9.3 million units was explored. This rate of demand (expected by late 1972 on the optimistic forecasts) would need one additional factory; the transport costs associated with different locations for this factory are shown in Table 4. (These costs differ from those in Table 1 largely due to the geographical shift in demand.)

The same exercise was carried out for a demand of 9.8 million units, which

TABLE 4
Annual Transport Cost ($m) for a Demand of 9.3 Million Units

New Factory Location	*Transport Cost*
L	9.28
S	9.48
T	9.62
N	9.66
Z	9.69
M	9.73
B	10.30

would necessitate two new factories; the transport costs of the best systems are shown in Table 5.

The results of Tables 4 and 5 show that L is always more stable than its neighbors S, T and Z; as it is also more robust it is clearly to be preferred among the four. This leaves the alternatives as B, N, L and M. M can be excluded from consideration because of its lower robustness and its very low stability—the best system incorporating M as a location incurs cost some $500,000 per year greater than the cheapest system for either 9.3 or 9.8 million units demand. Similarly B, despite its robustness, incurs extra costs of $500,000 to $1,000,000 per year during the interim, and so has very low stability. (These results are confirmed by a similar analysis of the three-new-factory systems.)

Therefore the robust and stable initial decisions are either L or N. If two locations must be decided now, these are they. If only one location is required, it could be either L or N. L will give savings in the short-term, while N (through its greater robustness) offers a higher expectation of long-term savings. The choice between them is one for management.

TABLE 5
Annual Transport Cost ($m) for a Demand of 9.8 Million Units

New Factory Locations	*Transport Cost*
L,N	8.73
H,L	8.75
N,S	9.01
H,S	9.04
A,L	9.06
N,T	9.08
G,L	9.08
H,T	9.11
N,Z	9.15
H,Z	9.17
B,L	9.27
M,N	9.28

The choices of L and N as initial locations for new factories are tactically robust. There is also a way in which the investment plan can be made more structurally robust. The time which must elapse from deciding on a location till the factory is in operation can be reduced by over a year if the Company already owns the site and has completed the basic engineering design work. This will be possible if

(1) an effectively standard plant unit is to be used for each factory, so that only some adaptation to a particular site will be needed; and
(2) suitable sites are purchased ahead of time in enough likely locations–which in our case might be A, B, L, M and N–to ensure that the site procurement delay can be avoided whatever decision is taken next.

Neither of these steps will be disadvantageous to the Company–design and capital costs will be reduced, and property is not unprofitable to hold for a few years. But the main advantage will be in delaying the need for firmly committed decisions, and so increasing the instantaneous flexibility (or robustness) of the plan.

CONCLUSIONS

Two topics of current professional interest are the study of strategic investment decisions and of the value of information. These two areas come together in the consideration of investment decisions which are essentially sequential in nature, so that later decisions in the sequence can be postponed until more up-to-date information is available. Where future variation in uncontrollable factors may significantly affect the outcome of an investment plan, it is inappropriate to aim the plan at the achievement of what appears, on the basis of current information, to be the best end-state for the system. In so doing one may by the initial implemented decisions unreasonably restrict the possibilities remaining for the subsequent decisions, so that little use can be made of the more recent information then available.

The alternative approach described in this paper is, where there are a number of end-states whose outcomes (on the basis of current information) are not much inferior to that of the "best" end-state, to make initial decisions which permit the achievement of as many as possible of these end-states. We have called such initial decisions "robust." Where there are several robust decisions, an appropriate discriminatory factor is "stability"–that is, the ability of the system (as amended by the initial decision or decisions) to perform well should the subsequent stages of the investment plan be delayed or cancelled.

This approach can clearly give initial decisions different from those which arise from simply choosing the best end-state, and then optimizing the path of decisions to reach it. Such a difference arises in the example given–that of choosing factory locations so as to minimize the cost of transport. The end-state with lowest cost consists of new factories at A, B, M, N and S. The path for reaching it would start with S, and continue through N. (See Tables 4 and 5.) The robustness-stability approach leads to L and N as initial decision. The choice of L precludes us from achieving what on current information seems the best end-state. However, interim systems incorporating L perform better than those with S; and L features in more of the good end-states than does S.

The passage of time will show which decision, that based on optimality or on robustness, was the "best" for this case study. However the argument for the criterion of robustness does not depend on reaching a best end-state in a particular problem, but on the advantage in the long-run of the insurance policy of flexibility. In this case-study a small and uncertain future advantage is abandoned, but a larger and sooner (therefore more certain) interim gain is substituted, and valuable flexibility is maintained for future decisions. Whether this is a profitable exchange will depend in any particular case on the certainty of one's knowledge about uncontrollable events on the planning horizon. In many industrial situations, particularly competitive ones, this uncertainty is considerable. In such cases the maintenance of flexibility, as embodied in the concepts of robustness and stability, should have precedence over the pursuit of possibly illusory future advantages.

REFERENCES

Bosman, A., and Mol, J., "Near optimality analysis: an application to crop rotation planning," unpublished paper.

Christenson, C., "Capital Budgeting and Long-Range Planning," in D. B. Hertz and R. T. Eddison (eds.), *Progress in Operational Research Vol. II,* Wiley, New York, 1964, pp. 159-189.

Comes, G., and Bellon, J.-L., "Etude d'une Politique Sequentielle d'Investissements pour la Restructuration d'un Reseau d'Usines," Proceedings of the Fourth IFORS Conference, Boston, 1966.

Culhane, J. H., Ronaldson, A. M., and Zimmerman, R. M., "A Dynamic Approach to Capital Investment–A Case Study," Proceedings of the Fourth IFORS Conference, Boston, 1966.

Drucker, P. F., "Long Range Planning," Management Science Vol. 5, No. 3 (April 1959), pp. 238-249.

Hertz, D. B., "Risk Analysis in Capital Investment," Harvard Business Review, January-February 1964.

Hespos, R. F., and Strassmann, P. A., "Stochastic Decision Trees for the Analysis of Investment Decisions," Management Science, Vol. 11, No. 10 (August 1965), pp. 244-259.

March, J. G., and Simon, H. A., *Organizations,* Wiley, New York, 1958.

McEachron, W. D., "Prediction and Feedback in Business Planning," Operations Research, Vol. 6, No. 4, (July-August 1958), pp. 560-572.

Stigler, G., "Production and Distribution in the Short Run," Journal of Political Economy, Vol. 47 (June 1939), pp. 305-27.

INTRODUCTORY NOTE

In the past, the planner usually considered his job completed when his plan and recommendations were accepted. Rarely did he analyze the effect(s) of his planning measures or programs of action, systematically scrutinize the real results of yesterday's decision, or objectively assess achievement and performance in order to profit from past experience. The planner had no means for taking account of changing community objectives, or unforeseen events, or forecasts that went awry—any or all of which could (and often did) upset, disturb, or make the best plan obsolete. The planner had no mechanism for comparing the actual state of conditions in the year to which his plan was tied and the "planned state," as reflected in the plan, and making any necessary adjustment(s) in light of this comparison. There was no systematic way to determine whether a proposed development (e.g. from a private developer or a public agency), that may not have been designated in the master plan, should be accepted or not—except for some vague statement that such a proposal should "conform to the master plan," nor, if accepted by the planner, what effect this would have on the plan, and how to take this into account in revising the plan. In short, until the early 1950s, the planner had no system for feedback and review, no mechanism for maintaining the plan as current and up-to-date.

Martin Meyerson was among the first planners to recognize the need to develop procedures and mechanisms for feedback and review and for maintaining a current and up-to-date plan. In his now classic speech (Meyerson, 1956), previously discussed in the Introductory Note to Section 4, Meyerson called on the planning profession to maintain a constant feedback of information on both the intended and the unintended consequences of action programs, so that it might better guide future actions.

In the same vein, Robert Mitchell, some five years later, called for the establishment of a continuous planning process which will:

> "incorporate a feedback of information on community change and on the results of planned and programmed action. In this way, as progress is measured, the planning process can adjust to guide development, such as the course of a missile is guided by a feedback of information on its deviation from a projected course" [Mitchell, 1961: 171].

In the subsequent years, paralleling the shift that took place in the focus of planning from the preparation of a single product, the plan, to a process- and program-oriented activity, the concept of feedback and evaluation has become an accepted facet of this approach among most planning agencies. Planners currently favor planning processes which provide for continuous feedback and adjustment in the light of experience and strategies that enable periodic modification of plans; they are more interested today in the "streams of change over time, in sequences of events and situations, and in the periodically shifting patterns, rather than in the snap shots of end-states, or in so-called plans of ultimate development" (Fagin, 1967).

The development of elaborate and complex information systems and data banks in many cities around the country is a reflection of this new approach. In addition, development of specific measurements and informational tools for the purposes of feedback and review is moving in several directions.

Drawing upon the concepts, approaches, and techniques of PPBS, attention is currently being directed to the development of objective yardsticks of achievement for public policies and of quantified information about the effectiveness of the different kinds of policy interventions. Most of the existing so-called "hard" data about public programs are expenditure statistics because these statistics measure what goes into programs rather than what comes out, that is, their outcomes. Lacking are measures of results, of achievements, and of misjudgments.

Two kinds of measurable performance standards are commonly distinguished: "program" performance and "systems" performance. The former measures the degree to which a program might accomplish its given specific objectives or targets. The latter would measure the results of a program in terms of the broad social goals the program was initially designed to achieve. So, for example, the effects of expenditures in the area of health might be evaluated in terms of the increase in the number of hospital beds or para-medical personnel, or by "program performance." However, the effects of expenditures on health may be measured as well in terms of their impact on the general health in the area, through changes in rates of morbidity, life expectancy, infant mortality, or absenteeism from school or work. Such measures would indicate whether our health system was achieving its mission, i.e. they would measure its "systems performance."

Program performance measures are necessary for a systematic approach to internal decision-making for management purposes; quantitative data are now being developed for this purpose in the federal government.

For the planner, however, quantitative evaluation of achievements of programmatic aims is insufficient. What really interests the planner is the total performance of the system and the evaluation of programs in terms of their contribution towards the social aims that initially inspired them. The development of "urban indicators" (discussed earlier) which are similar in concept to systems performance measures should go a long way towards meeting this objective. These would attempt to record social changes at regular intervals in terms of specific social goals. They would provide a framework for evaluating our social policies and programs in terms of their effectiveness in achieving these goals.

The use of urban indicators and the concept of feedback and review are part of a larger, more basic question of "control" of the urban system. In recognition of this, some planners have been directing their attention to this problem of control, not in the traditional, narrow, negative sense of the type of controls needed to implement the plan (e.g. zoning, or subdivision regulations), but as understood in systems engineering and in the biolgoical sciences—in the fullest sense which includes positive stimulus and intervention. J. Brian McLoughlin in Chapter 16 sees a new and exciting prospect for dealing with this problem of control—in the potential application of cybernetics (the science of communication and control in very complex systems) to the guidance of cities and regions, which would greatly increase the sensitivity of the community's control over its environment. One of the present dangers planners face is that, in acquiring great skill in "tinkering" with parts of our cities and environment in general, they have often ignored the repercussions on the system as a whole. The application of cybernetic principles, McLoughlin argues, may lead them in the right direction; in his paper, he demonstrates possible applications.

Some researchers have turned their attention to the specific types of mechanisms that might be employed which take advantage of the improved information available, and are based on the concepts of control explicit in the science of cybernetics. Melvin Webber has recommended the establishment of "intelligence centers" which would serve the multiplicity of groups in urban areas, supplying improved inventories and forecasts (Webber, 1965). They would describe and explain what is happening, report on stocks and flows, and identify cause-and-effect relations. A center would not serve any single client, but rather it would seek to supply information on current conditions and predictions of future conditions to many interested parties, in addition to the city council that pays its bills. To test the accuracy of its predictions and adequacy of the theory underlying the predictions, the center would set up monitoring stations at key junctions throughout the urban system with the signals continuously fed back to the center. An underlying premise of this approach is that control need not be centralized at any specific decision point or that consistent courses of action will be pursued by anybody. Rather, according to Webber's proposal, each of the multiplicity of groups would be aided in searching out its own objectives and its own best current actions, based on the information that is made available.

A related concept is proposed by Melville Branch in Chapter 17. He describes the kind of mechanism he considers necessary to achieve "continuous master city planning" and to insure that city planning will be at least significantly up-to-date to be relevant. The mechanism is a flexible and versatile "planning center" for analysis, display, and decision-making similar to the planning room of many large corporations and on a larger scale to the NASA Space Flight Center. In essence, it is midway between the present brochure-report type of plan, and the computer-assisted, cathode-display simulation which will become practical some time in the future. Implicit in the mechanism he portrays is more careful, vigorous, and meaningful city planning analysis. His emphasis on aerial photography taken at least every year as the background for certain information, and of highly flexible types of display throughout, reflects his conviction that unless city planning is conducted analytically so it can keep "ahead of the game," it does little more than formalize what has already been done, decided, or committed.

Underlying Branch's proposal is a deep awareness, based on his nine years of practical experience on the Los Angeles City Planning Commission and seven years before that as a corporate staff planner for a large private enterprise, of the difficulties faced by decision-makers in trying to improve decision-making in city planning, particularly in view of the conceptual gap between them and staff specialists. This gap has always existed but is accentuated by the current surge of knowledge. As technical information and analytical techniques advance rapidly in many of the substantive areas of concern in city planning, the decision-maker finds it more difficult to follow and comprehend an expanding spectrum of special knowledge. Since keeping up with all of it is intellectually impossible, assimilation of specialized material becomes increasingly marginal for the decision-maker unless a deliberate effort is made to bridge the conceptual gap. Branch hopes that his proposed mechanism will help to build that bridge.

Chapter 16

SYSTEM GUIDANCE, CONTROL AND REVIEW

J. Brian McLoughlin

In this chapter we complete the cycle of the planning process outlined in Chapter 5* by dealing with the implementation of plans. As we saw in Chapter 4* this is essentially *a control activity* where "control" is interpreted in the widest sense, implying not merely the use of the veto but including positive intervention. There, too, we learned how control is "that . . . which provides direction in conformance with the plan, or in other words, the maintenance of variations from system objectives within allowable limits" and that this is of universal application (Johnson, Kast and Rosenzweig, 1963).[1]

The same chapter outlined the control of cities and regions by comparing the actual state with the intended state at regular intervals and carrying out regulative actions on the basis of any divergence revealed. We can now expand that outline by virtue of what we have learned in succeeding chapters and go into more details of the everyday working of the plan.

We have seen in Chapters 8* and 9 that the essence of plans for urban and regional systems is a trajectory of intended states. Also the general form of the trajectory will be a set of matrices or tableaux—one for each future time. These will specify the intended activities and spaces and their associated communications and channels. The activities and spaces will be related to an array of geographical sub-areas (of the total planning area)—e.g. enumeration districts, wards, parishes, zones, kilometer grid cells, etc. The communications and channels will be similarly referenced and will also be mapped in conventional manner to show the intended networks and the volumes they should be carrying at the various times. So much for the intended states of the system.

*Not included herein.—Ed.

Reprinted from *Urban and Regional Planning: A Systems Approach,* by J. Brian McLoughlin, pp. 279-296. Published by Faber and Faber (London) and Praeger Publishers (New York).

The actual states at most times can be known in part only. Information to match up one-for-one with that in the plan may be derived from a variety of sources: the censuses of population, distribution, production, road traffic, as they are taken and published; the statistics of the Ministry of Labour on the locations, sizes and types of employment; development and other public and private agencies' records of operation. To the extent that these are not adequate, the planning authority must attempt to remedy this by carrying out or commissioning its own surveys of the situation.

At the time of writing, information for the control function in planning is not satisfactory for all the reasons mentioned in Chapter 8. But there is good reason to hope that the national censuses will in future be taken at five-yearly intervals (1971, 1976 . . .); also the results should be available much more quickly than in the past and that their content and specification will be far more suited to the operations of many public welfare agencies, including planning authorities. For example, we may hope for more stable definitions of such essential units as "households," for stability of geographical units of analysis (multiples of the 100-meter square cell) and for much better information on employment, economic activity, car ownership and possibly incomes. Improvement in the quality of these important information sources is bound to go ahead more slowly than most planners would like. In the meantime they must try for the best compromise between the expense of extra surveys and more broadly-stated plans–tailored to suit the data which *can* easily be obtained.

Let us assume that as a starting point, the planning authority has succeeded in framing the operational documents in such a way that all the necessary information about *actual* states can be obtained within one year. In other words the plan's intended state for mid-1971 can be compared with the information about the *actual* state (from the 1971 census, etc.) by the middle of 1972; and by the middle of 1977 the actual and intended states for 1976 can be compared; and so on. Let us suppose that 1966 was the datum year for this plan–that is, the time at which all the basic information about the area was carefully established, mapped and tabulated and which served as a take-off point for the main projections of population, employment, dwellings, car ownership, etc.

Now we will imagine ourselves in the planning office during the period 1966 to 1971 and try to understand how the plan is implemented. Our system grows and changes by the alteration of its component parts (activities in spaces) and their connections (communications in channels). The essence of control then is to regulate those disturbances so that the system's actual trajectory matches the intention as closely as possible. Each disturbance–that is each development application, whether for new construction, demolition, change of use or whatever–must be examined for the total effect it is likely to have on the system and whether or not this would result in moving the system in the right direction.

The examination of applications is likely to follow a checklist consisting of a series of questions. Obviously these will fall into four main groups:

(1) Activity

is the *type* of activity proposed consistent with the intentions of the plan? (e.g. residential, economic activity specified by class, recreational, etc.)
is the *size* of activity proposed consistent with the intentions of the plan? (e.g. number of persons, numbers of jobs, volume of production, etc.)
are the other characteristics of the proposal consistent? (e.g. seasonal fluctuation, shift working, etc.)

(2) Space

is the *amount* of space proposed consistent with the plan? (e.g. number of dwellings or towns, floor area, parking spaces, total area of land used, etc.)
is the *location* of space consistent with the plan? (e.g. is the proposal likely to cause difficulty with later development?)
is the *intensity* of space-use proposed consistent with the plan? (e.g. density in persons per acre, workers per acre, etc.)

(3) Communications

is the *amount* of communication proposed consistent with the plan? (e.g. the numbers of trips which are likely to be "attracted" by a workplace or "produced" by a residential proposal; are the rates of trip production and attraction likely to differ significantly from those assumed in the plan?)
are the *types and modes* of communication consistent? (e.g. private vehicles, public transport, air passenger or freight movements, goods vehicle movements, etc.)
are the *frequencies* of communication consistent? (e.g. time of day, peak, off-peak, weekly or seasonal variations)
are the *sensory qualities* of the proposal consistent with the plan? (e.g. massing and general arrangement of buildings, prominent structures, landscape treatment, noise levels, pollution of air and water, aspect, prospect, etc.)

(4) Channels

is this *type* of channel consistent with the plan? (e.g. 400 Kv overhead cables, dual two-lane limited-access road, 36-ins. diameter gas pipeline)
is the *location* (or routing) consistent?
are the *connections,* access points, and junctions consistent?
are the *sensory qualities* consistent? (e.g. design and spacing of towns, design of bridges and cuttings, form of embankments, landscape design, etc.)

Obviously this listing is illustrative only; in practice, only some of these questions may be asked and others would be raised in addition. But essentially they would relate to these four broad groups.

Let us now consider in more detail the problem of comparing intention and actuality when confronted by a specific proposal. Suppose that in a particular part of the area the plan indicated a 1966 population of 1,200 rising to 2,000 by mid-1971. The 1966 census data showed that the actual population was 1,350 persons; in other words, the system had gone slightly off course. In late 1967 the planning authority is presented with a proposal to build 170 private houses on 30 acres of land in this area. Should permission be granted?

First the activity element is examined. The proposal is, of course, expressed in terms of houses and so some estimate must be made of the number of persons likely to live there. The planning officer considers the type of houses, their location and layout and decides to use a conversion factor of 3.4, resulting in an estimate of about 580 additional persons by the time the development is completed. This would raise the population of the area at, say, 1969 to around 1,930 persons–consistent with the plan.

Turning next to the space element the addition of 170 dwellings would raise the total in 1969 to 590 from its 1966 figure of 420. This is found to be well within the plan's intended 700 dwellings by 1971. However, the total land in use in this area would rise to meet the plan's intention of 85 acres–and about two years before time. Further study and discussion with the applicant (a speculative builder) reveals that the intention is to build houses for the upper-income groups in a relatively spacious layout; this is the principal reason for the shortfall on persons and dwellings and the consumption of all the land estimated to be needed. The planning officer checks the information used in the preparation of the plan, paying particular attention to the density assumptions used to relate population and dwellings to land areas; this confirms his previous supposition. Also, he finds that the socio-economic composition of the area would be rather more "white collar" than the plan's intention if the proposal were allowed. This could have implications for car ownership and spending power. But the visual aesthetic character of the area would not be noticeably different from that intended in the plan if the application were approved.

In considering the communications element of the proposal he notes that the increased car ownership might affect the volume of private car trips originating in the area. In its turn, the greater volume of traffic might cause problems from the "channels" point of view, although the access point to the secondary road system shown in the proposal is consistent with the plan's intentions.

Looked at in the round, a proposal of this kind must be considered at two main levels. First, does it conform with the *strategic* intentions of the plan for the town as a whole in terms of population distribution, employment location, the pattern and volume of journeys on the primary and secondary networks and the physical fabric of the area? Secondly, is the proposal consistent with the intentions of the plan at the more *detailed* local level where physical questions predominate: road alignments, access, the location of local schools, shops, parks and playing fields, and the visual and other sensory qualities of the immediate environment?

Each proposal must be examined at both levels. At the strategic or "urban structure plan" level the elements of activity and communication will tend to weigh more heavily than questions of space and channels which will predominate when the proposal is compared with more detailed plans for parts of the planning area.

In the example used, the planning officer has satisfied himself that on most counts the proposal conforms to the plan's intentions. He notes however that his assumptions about density, socio-economic composition, and therefore spending power and car ownership will be to some extent invalidated if he grants permission. He therefore decides to do some fairly rapid checks to see how far these divergences would affect the urban structure policy as a whole.

To do this he returns to the context of the models used in the process of plan design and evaluation. The changed spending power given for the sub-area is estimated and the model which was used to test the sales in major shopping centers is re-run. This shows a rise of about 1% or less in the sales for the nearest suburban area; the effects on all the other centers in the city are imperceptible. This result is well within the range of ± 1.8% error which, he is advised, is inherent in the model's design (largely because of imperfections in data on incomes, expenditures and journeys to shopping centers). The effect on traffic flow estimates of the higher level of car ownership is similarly trivial when the traffic model is brought back into use.

The planning officer thus concludes that if he were to recommend approval of the application he would not be departing from his urban structure plan. It follows that the decision will be based primarily on the consideration of the proposal as it affects the immediate locality. Questions of physical detail, appearance, design of houses, the treatment of landscape, access and relationships with existing development will be the main criteria. If the area is not one for which detailed designs have been prepared—such as in the "action areas" proposed in the recent British legislation—then these issues will be examined in the light of the planning officer's knowledge, experience and judgment.

In his recommendation to the elected members of the planning authority, he is able to distinguish between the quantifiable, and non-quantifiable effects and the implications of the proposals for the functioning of the area as a whole and for the immediate locality.

Similar principles apply in the special cases of control in areas where detailed physical plans have been prepared to coordinate developments in the period up to ten years ahead. In these cases it is relatively simple to see whether or not a proposal fits in with the plan's intentions for physical form—that is, from the points of view of spaces and channels. Checks will be made on building form, floor areas, parking space, access, landscape treatment and so on. But equally the activities and communications elements will be checked. Are the house and flat designs likely to accommodate the numbers and kinds of persons intended in the plan? Are the industrial buildings intended for those types of manufacturer or distribution which were envisaged? How many private car and commercial vehicle trips are likely to be "produced" by and attracted to the development? Notwithstanding the agreement of proposals with a detailed physical plan from the physical-form points of view, there may be divergences from the intended types of activity and communication. Once again, the models used in plan preparation can be brought into service to test the effects of these differences on the workings of the planning area as a whole.

So far, we have been discussing the regulation or control of our system by blocking or releasing private proposals for change. But the same principles apply to capital projects in the public sector—housing, hospitals, schools, swimming pools, roads, generating stations, transport termini, shopping centers and so on. These kinds of developments will usually be smaller in number but of greater unit size than most of the private developments, and differ from them in one particularly important respect. That is, their future occurrence will nearly always have been made known to the planning authority through consultations with the developing departments—central and local government, the nationalized industries and other public bodies. They will have been embodied into the plan and account taken of their nature and location. They too will have been interpreted as activities occupying space, causing communications through channels (or indeed if they are road or railway proposals being themselves channels facilitating communications). While the statutory planning control processes in Britain are different in many cases where public developments are concerned, in general *the same degree of control should apply as if the proposal came from the private sector.* There are two main reasons why this should be so. First, the development intention may have been made known to the planning authority several years in advance, before details are available. The planning authority will have had to use the best information possible at that time when preparing its plan. But when the time comes, the proposal as presented may differ considerably: a two-lane motorway may turn out to be three-lane; a power station when finally designed may be of twice the capacity and four times the bulk; a housing development may occupy the acreage originally indicated but be designed to house twice the number of persons. Secondly, planning legislation and administration in the past has allowed a great deal of public developments to occur without planning control, especially if these were on "operational land" e.g. certain land owned by the nationalized railways, the coal industry, port authorities, etc. As a result, a great deal of mischief has occasionally been done. While innocuous enough from the *physical* point of view (in that the "space" and "channel" elements were already owned and occupied by the public authority) no account could be taken of the activity and communication effects of these changes throughout the urban system.

Let us consider another example; this time we will imagine a proposal for a medium-sized factory which arrives on the planning officer's desk at the beginning of 1969. The firm makes light alloy components for motorcycles and wishes to build workshop floorspace totalling 100,000 square feet and a similar amount of storage and office space. A site area of six acres includes access roads, loading bays, a car park for 200 cars and some small areas of grass and trees along the main road frontage. It is expected that 230 workers will be employed at the factory on completion (June 1970 if all goes well), and that the full complement of 300 would be there by 1971.

The Planning Officer has satisfied himself that the application lies within one of the main industrial areas in the plan, that the amount of land to be used is consistent with the plan's assumptions about worker densities, and that the communications which will arise are also consistent with the plan for traffic movements. His main problems concerns the size of the activity which is measured by the total numbers of jobs in manufacturing.

The models used in plan preparation were modifications of the type used by Lowry (1964) in Pittsburgh. That is, the distribution of population throughout the planning area is assumed to be strongly related to the location and size of certain types of employment, notably certain manufacturing and "central business district" types of jobs. But the response in population distribution—and hence in the demands for housing land, schools, shopping, recreation, and travel—lags about five years behind the distribution of employment. Therefore the successful control of many important aspects in the period 1971-76 will depend to a great extent on the control of the growth and distribution of employment between 1966 and 1971.

The total employment in this part of the town in 1966 was 5,000 and the plan's intention was that this should grow to 6,700 by 1971. Clearly, for such a vital control element, five years is too long an interval between accurate measurements and the planning officer had therefore to devise some means of getting an *annual* estimate of the employment situation throughout his planning area. He had reviewed the various ways in which this might be done. First, he would obtain an annual statement of the planning permissions issued for all developments associated with employment: factories, warehouses, shops, offices, educational establishments and so on. But the grant of planning permission is no guarantee that the development will occur. Next, he considered using reports from the building inspectorate which have the advantage of recording actual occurrence of building, the area in square feet and other useful details. This information is better than counts of planning permissions but is still not satisfactory because it fails to measure *employment,* which is the variable on which so much in the plan depends. The conclusion is obvious: a reasonably accurate annual figure showing the location of all employment classified as necessary must be made available. Statistics can be obtained either from the most appropriate Ministry of Labour source or collected directly by the planning authority's own staff.

The point raised here is of great importance and, while touched on several times before, worth re-statement. It is a general one too and does not apply only to control of the plan with respect to employment, but equally to all the other major variables in which a plan might be expressed: population (totals), number of persons of working age, of school age or of pensionable age; number of motor vehicles in various categories, output of manufacturing activities, turnover and floorspace of retail trades, amount of land developed for different uses, flows of communications through the several networks. It is this:

> The variables used in control must be compatible with those in the plan and all the key variables used in the plan must be measurable by those controlling it.

A thermostat carries out its function by comparing temperature with temperature, and a safety valve works by comparing pressures. Plans for towns and regions expressed in terms of (say) people, jobs and traffic flows can be implemented only if measures of the actual distributions of people, jobs and traffic flows are available to be compared with the plan's intentions. The planning process is unitary, comprising facets which can be considered separately for convenience only. And one of the prime elements which unifies planning is *information* since the planning is in essence a management operation characterized by positive control and guidance. Of all the criteria which govern the design of the information or data system to be used in planning, those related to control are of overriding importance. The most finely-devised plan, based on the best analysis of public objectives and aspirations, drawing on a full and rigorous analysis of the area's past, present and prospective future, and having received the fullest backing of the community is a thing of nought if it cannot be implemented. Writing on control of systems in general, Johnson, Kast and Rosenzweig (1963: 63) say that "there should be a direct correlation between the controlled item and the operation of the system. . . . To meet this requirement, the controlled item should be stated in the language used in the feedback loop. That is why it is important to understand what is to be transmitted before any information is transmitted."

At this point we must deal with some fundamental problems of control, using the word as usual in its cybernetic sense. All highly complex systems achieve *homeostasis* or internal stability in two ways: first, by organization of the internal relations between parts interacting through their connections; secondly, by the capacity to *anticipate and absorb* the disturbances which arise from the system's environment in such a way as to keep the system viable, to enable it to grow and develop in desirable ways. In order to perform this latter function the system must possess some *control device* through which it can sense threatened disturbances, estimate and anticipate their effects and deal appropriately with them. In so doing it must *learn* and thereby improve its predictive characteristics to achieve effective control.

The nature of disturbances which may impinge upon a system are astonishingly diverse. An animal may be threatened with many different kinds of physical attacks from enemies of various kinds; by starvation arising from complex sources, its internal workings as a system may be impaired by physical and neurophysiological damage—so much so that it may go "out of control" and die. The same is true of economic and social systems. The internal ordering and therefore viability of these is threatened by technological changes, war, famine and disease, the actions of competing nations or sections of society.

In order to militate against undesirable outcomes (e.g. riot, civil war, slump in extreme cases) the "controls" of the system must take action which tries to make the resultant outcomes of the disturbances lie within acceptable limits, so that the system can go on surviving and developing. It must be capable of sufficiently flexible and adaptive response to match up to the variety in the disturbances which occur. This seemingly commonsense observation is exemplified in games where opposing players (as in chess) or in teams (as in football) have similar capacity of adaptive behavior to their opponents, and thus an even chance of keeping the outcomes within desirable limits (not being in check, not allowing the opposite side to score a goal). It is seen in much more complex situations such as ecosystems wherein stable or "climax" ecologies tend to arise because the variety in the behavior of predators is matched by that of their various prey—evolution has seen to that.

Perhaps because eco-systems have evolved over such long periods we have failed to realize that a fundamental principle of cybernetic regulation and control underlies them. It is called the Law of Requisite Variety, and in simple terms it states that for effective regulation in any system, *the variety in the control device must be at least equal to that of the disturbances.* It is not necessary for us to give a rigorous proof of the law here since it is available elsewhere (Ashby, 1956: ch. 11); moreover, we are concerned here with the practical implications for control of cities and regions.

Let us begin by considering a typical planning office.[2] In order to cope with the control of an area, some massive reduction of the very high variety of the human environment must be attempted and this is done by means of a development plan. We must think here in a comprehensive way, where "plan" includes all the policy statements, committee resolutions, etc., or additions to the formal plan and its legal amendments. Even though plans have been criticized for becoming too complicated (Planning Advisory Group, 1965) they obviously represent a huge reduction in variety by comparison with the real world. But as we know British planning control is based on "accord with the plan"; so here we have a situation in which the attempt is made to control a very high-variety world using the low-variety tool of the development plan.

How does it work, why is there not absolute chaos (merely relative chaos)? There are two reasons: first, and most important of all, cities and regions are very largely self-regulating. The human-dominated system of the planet's ecology has been managing fairly well for two hundred thousand years or so without the benefit of statutory planning because of the enormous amount of built-in control variety or homeostasis; second, the controllers do not rely only on the low-variety development plan—as Beer explains, they obtain the necessary variety by using ad hoc control. In the planner's domain, this involves the use of an item-by-item study of all kinds of events and an attempt thereby to guide day-to-day actions. When we remember that the basic development plan is a picture showing the area as it might be some ten to twenty years ahead it is easy to see why control is imperfect. For conventional British development plans (i.e. those prepared under the Acts of 1947 and 1962) are pale shadowy images of the variety of the real world of people, homes, factories, shops, journeys, transactions in land, subtle shifts in land use, density and flows with which the planner has to deal. That is why ad hoc control is invoked in which the planner's brain tries to provide the variety lost in the development plan.

But this huge feedback provided by ad hoc control—a continuous torrent of development decisions, appeal decisions, building inspectors' reports, Registrar-

Generals' mid-year estimates, Board of Trade returns, Ministry of Labor figures, county surveyors' annual traffic census returns, site inspections, letters from irate residents–usually overwhelms him. In its turn it requires armies of clerks, junior technicians, administrative assistants, and consideration of mechanized data-processing systems, punched cards, computers and so on. As Beer says of this form of control the "arrangements are typically so simple that they cannot go right . . . the system is trying exhaustively to enumerate the proliferating variety of the world situation, which it must do since it has allowed the necessary feedback to be supplied point by point" (Beer, 1966: 311-312).

The variety of the real world must be matched by at least equivalent variety in the control device. How is this to be achieved? There is no alternative to producing a model of the real world in which variety is reduced, but in such a way that it can be regenerated later on. This requires a flexible model design in which elements from two sets are allowed to combine freely; the first set of elements is called *structural* and sets out in non-quantified terms the relationships which are believed to persist in the real world–for example between population and employment, between trip-making and distance, between land values and density, between accessibility and population growth, etc. The second set of elements is called *parametric* and consists of actual numerical data which describe the real-world situation. In both sets of elements, structural and parametric, large reductions are made in variety compared with that of the real world, but when allowed by the model designer and operator to combine in different ways, paired elements from these two sets can generate the requisite variety because both structural and parametric elements have been based on careful study of the real world; the structural parts of the model express what are believed to be enduring relationships between human activities and communications in the spatial sense, while the parametric elements have set down (following conventional statistical analyses) the probabilities that each relationship will take up certain positions on a range of numerical values. For example, the structural element of the modelling may state that population will be disposed around employment nodes according to some inverse function of travel time; the parametric element will then embody a statistical statement about the range of values of parameters of the time/distance measure.

Conventional development plans, i.e. normative models of the real, are crude and unreal. For in them "relations exist which have no quantity, and numbers exist that stand in no relation to each other" (Beer, 1966: 319). The flexible approach to model design suggested here follows the important cybernetic principle, found in many controls for complex systems, of constructing a high-variety device by the free combination of low-variety components.

The model of the real world can now be used to obtain predictions or system trajectories as explained in Chapters 8 and 9. Consider the situation when, for the first time, it is possible to compare the model's prediction with that of the real world–i.e. between the first "state" set out in the development plan and the actual state of the city or region. It is unlikely that a very good fit will be found but in this comparison lies the key to successful control. For if the relationship between real world and the model are analyzed and the results *fed back* to the model's structural and parametric design elements, *its predictive powers are being amplified by a learning process.* The diagram (Figure 1) might make clearer much of the preceding discussion.

The control operation is shown as C1 and C2 implementing the plan's sequence of intended states M2 and M3. (The diagram can be imagined as continuing indefinitely towards the right with the passage of time.) Control at C1 must operate in ad hoc fashion in trying to regulate the disturbances (i.e. development proposals) which are operating on the real world represented by the surveys S1. As time advances the crude predictions produced by the model at M2 may be compared with the real world revealed at S2 (e.g. in a census year or otherwise) in the process of comparative analysis CP2.[3] Two outputs from CP2 are used: one to amplify the model's predictive power—as shown by the double arrow leading to the forecast or plan M3, and the other to amplify the sensitivity of the control device at C2 making it a better regulator of the disturbances impinging on the real world between S2 and S3.

In practical terms, the M-sequence is the result of the process of forecasting, modelling and selecting described in Chapters 8, 9 and 10.* The S-sequence represents the continuing process of surveys described in Chapter 7.* It is clear that the speed at which the "learning" process of system modelling and control can proceed is governed by the frequency with which the comparative operations (CP) can occur; ideally these processes co-exist at all times although in practice this ideal may not be reached.

*Not included herein.—Ed.

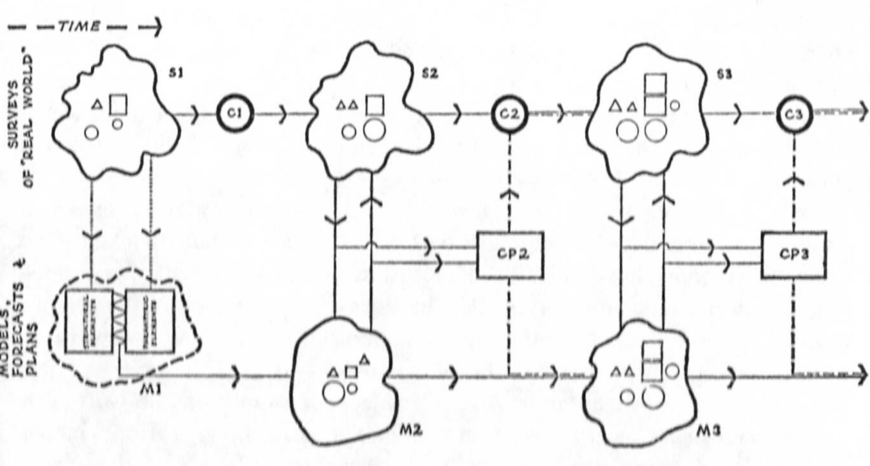

Figure 1: CONTROL PROCESS

One essential point is that the technical and administrative channels of communication should be firmly established and continually nourished by supplies of information. The other is that the operations called plan-making, control, implementation and review are integrated within a cybernetic framework; also, *planning may be regarded as a servo-system by which society seeks to amplify its powers of controlling the evolution of cities and regions.*

A good practical example of a plan which reflects some essentials of cybernetic control and implementation discussed above is the final report of the Tees-side Survey and Plan (1968). Mentioning the need to keep developments under constant observation, the report states that the monitoring services should consist of (a) regular collection of statistics, (b) improved forecasting methods, and (c) local planning experience. The authors go on to list in detail the kinds of statistics which should be collected. The main headings are demographic indices, economic indices, housing indices, statistics of income, expenditure and retailing, and finally those concerned with transportation. The section concludes by reminding us how "it is important the future data are in a form that is compatible with the data collected by Tees-side Survey and Plan. This applies to definitions, particularly the zoning systems" (i.e. areas to which the data relate).

In the context of planning of urban and regional systems as set out in this chapter, reviews of the plan are quite simply longer, harder, more fundamental periodic examinations of the relationships between intentions and actions. All the essential work is already being done from day to day by the control operations; there is no need therefore to mount a "one-off" job consuming precious resources of skill and time as so often happens in British planning today; review becomes simply a longer beat in the rhythm of the whole process of implementation. There are two main outcomes possible if reviews show that the system is significantly "off-course." The first is to use all the aids at the planner's command (including the models of the system developed to prepare and test plans) to indicate what actions are needed to put the system back on course and what the various advantages and disadvantages of such activities are. The other possible outcome is to consider the desirability of the deviant course in its own right and this involves thinking afresh about the major objectives of the plan and whether or not the time has come to recast them by deletion, addition or modification. In this case, as the Tees-side report states, "the decision to change the objectives would be a vital political decision whose implications should be closely investigated before any action is taken. Once made, the new planning objective could make necessary substantial changes to the recommended planning proposals." In other words, the cycle of the planning process comes full circle, returning from implementation and review to the re-examination and re-statement of goals and objectives.

Finally, the implementation of a plan depends wholly on the *will* of the planners and their "clients" to do so. We have stressed the logical and practical frameworks of the planning office in this chapter; truly they are *necessary* conditions but not *sufficient.* Irreducible requirements include a clear definition of the roles of central and local governments and other public bodies as these affect the plan; the relationships between the public bodies and private citizens, indicating their rights and responsibilities under statute law and administrative procedures; the duties of preparing, executing, controlling and reviewing the plan and how these devolve upon the bodies concerned, paying particular attention to responsibilities for public investment in buildings, plant, roads and so on. The "hardware" of the plan must be properly mated with the "software" of the appropriate human organization and relationships both within and between the various political and professional groups concerned (Cherns, 1967).

NOTES

1. References not included herein.–Ed.

2. The paragraphs which follow owe a great deal to the work of Beer (1966: ch. 13). The reader who would like to pursue the fundamentals of control is strongly advised to read the whole of Beer's book.

3. In Beer's original treatment the comparators CP2, CP3, etc., are "Black Boxes"–one of the important concepts of cybernetics. A full theoretical discussion of the Black Box is not necessary here but the interested reader is referred to Ashby (1956: ch. 6) and Beer (1959: ch. VI and 1966: 293-298) for full accounts.

Chapter 17

CONTINUOUS MASTER CITY PLANNING

Melville C. Branch

What must gradually replace the grand master plan delusion and the after-the-fact type of city plan is continuous master planning, in which certain elements of the city are projected far into the future, others for the middle range, some short-range, and a few not at all. The master or general city plan is not a document which emerges from some mammoth crash program of total effort, revelation, and resolution to be sporadically altered until another productive spasm can be afforded years later. It is always up-to-date as necessary. No pretense is made that it is an intellectually or analytically complete statement at any given moment. Rather, it is the continuously changing representation of what the city can and intends to carry out with respect to its future. Specific plans and programs are formulated for those municipal functions, elements, or projects which are of such nature or are sufficiently circumscribed that they can be analyzed with the necessary precision and reliability. Different municipal utilities illustrate functional systems which can be planned separately with precision, but less exactly as they are combined into larger subsystems of the total system constituting the city as a whole. Tax policies or new technologies cannot be forecast and planned as reliably as the physical system or facilities they may vitally affect. Thus, public education is financially threatened because of its dépendence on the real property tax, and a municipal water supply or mass transportation system may require revision or warrant replacement as the recycling of waste water is made technically feasible in the first instance, and new types of vehicles become practical in the second.

City planning must incorporate analytically current information, conditions, and decisions to a much greater extent than is now the case. Longer-range plans must represent the outcome of a succession of actions and anticipations rooted in the past but beginning or continuing in the present. To formulate longer-range plans without working out their derivation from the present through the intermediate future, is analytically invalid as well as indefensible in practice. On the other hand, city planning certainly cannot assume the operating functions of municipal departments such as finance, building and safety, traffic, public works, or social welfare. Day-to-day management and long-range planning for each such vital function constitute a full-time task. City planning is the central mechanism for synthesizing the operations, budgets, and plans of separate municipal departments with relation to the total city system and its projected future. In this particular respect, the master city plan and the corporate business plan serve the same purpose of coordinating the plans of different groups, divisions, or departments in the organization (see Branch, 1962: 37-55).

Master planning must encompass the spectrum from the past, to the present, toward the distant future: obligations and commitments from the past, immediate needs and long-range objectives, tactics and strategy, certainties and uncertainties. Some elements, such as freeway and primary water-supply lines, are projected fifty and more years into the future. Some, such as land use in certain areas, may not be planned more than five years ahead. Others, such as changes in restrictions on outdoor advertising, in the policies of private lending institutions investing in urban land and real property, or the forms of government subsidy and incentive, may at times be difficult or impossible to forecast.

The city plan must incorporate information and projections for each principal urban element separately, and portray their synthesis into a combined pattern of actions and objectives over time for the best benefit of the city as a whole. It must be maintained and displayed in such form that it can be revised regularly, and completely and quickly changed when need be. Above all, it must always be sufficiently up-to-date to serve as the basic analytical simulation of the municipality and the official reference for discussing and deciding many different matters. It is "ahead of the game" rather than "running to catch up." To function in these ways, the master city plan cannot be so restricted by legislation requiring needless and prolonged formalities that the necessary combination of fixed objectives and flexibility is impossible. It will probably include budgets for one or two years, operating plans for two to three years, and longer-range projections, policies, and plans for various periods in the future. Rather than the booklet or brochure which has been the accepted way in the past of expressing and using a master city plan, it must in the future be a far more flexible and versatile simulative device, similar to the "planning rooms" of many large corporations and—on a larger scale and more as an operational than advance planning mechanism—to the NASA spaceflight center familiar to millions of television viewers. Eventually, simulation for city planning purposes may be handled entirely on output-display devices connected with electronic computers and videotape storage, but this will be some time in coming (see Mecklin, 1967; Southern California Association of Governments, 1970; Harmon & Knowlton, 1969; Sutherland, 1970).

MECHANISM OF CONTINUOUS CITY PLANNING

Figures 1, 2, and 3 illustrate the new form of city planning which must develop if the endeavor is to be effective. Both the form and content of this continuous master city planning are very different from present practices. Figure 1 portrays the central mechanism of analysis, display, and decision. In the main part of the installation, discussants, participants, or audience are surrounded on almost three sides by sliding wall panels containing the core information and analysis most essential to planning the city. The recommending or decision-making body and staff are on a slightly raised dais at the end of the room opposite the projection room and the doorways on each side of it. Two portions of the analysis-display wall which encompasses this slightly raised space on three sides, can be swung out as shown for easier viewing by those seated in the fixed seats and by those on the platform also. The fixed seats are wide enough or swivel to allow the occupant to turn partly to either side and view the side panel walls more directly. The side aisles are wider than usual to allow small discussion groups to stand comfortably in front of analysis-display panels placed in the side walls.

Next to this auditorium type of room and connected by the door at the rear of the dais, is space for staff meetings, analysis, and maintenance of the master plan. Here, staff groups can meet at the same time the main room adjacent is in use, or people can gather less formally and in somewhat larger numbers around the table for working sessions of many sorts. Connected with this staff space is the third room for master plan maintenance. Here, desks and files are arranged to facilitate work directly on the analysis-display panels as they stand in the wall space built to contain them. By creating and maintaining the displays directly on the panels in this upright position, inflexible and costly drafting and redrafting are avoided, as well as the delays of continually transporting the panels to and from another location where more formal drafting is possible.

It will have been noted in examining Figure 1 that provision for analysis-display panels is made in most walls throughout the installation. These walls contain track with rollers at intervals making it easy to slide the panels back and forth. Since there can be as many as six of these tracks, transparent or overlay-type panels can be slid in front of an opaque "base" or reference panel behind. Or a number of panels of any sort can be placed side by side in the same or adjacent tracks. Many superpositions or groupings of the analysis-display panels are possible without moving them to different tracks, but the wall recesses are designed so they can be shifted readily from one track to another.

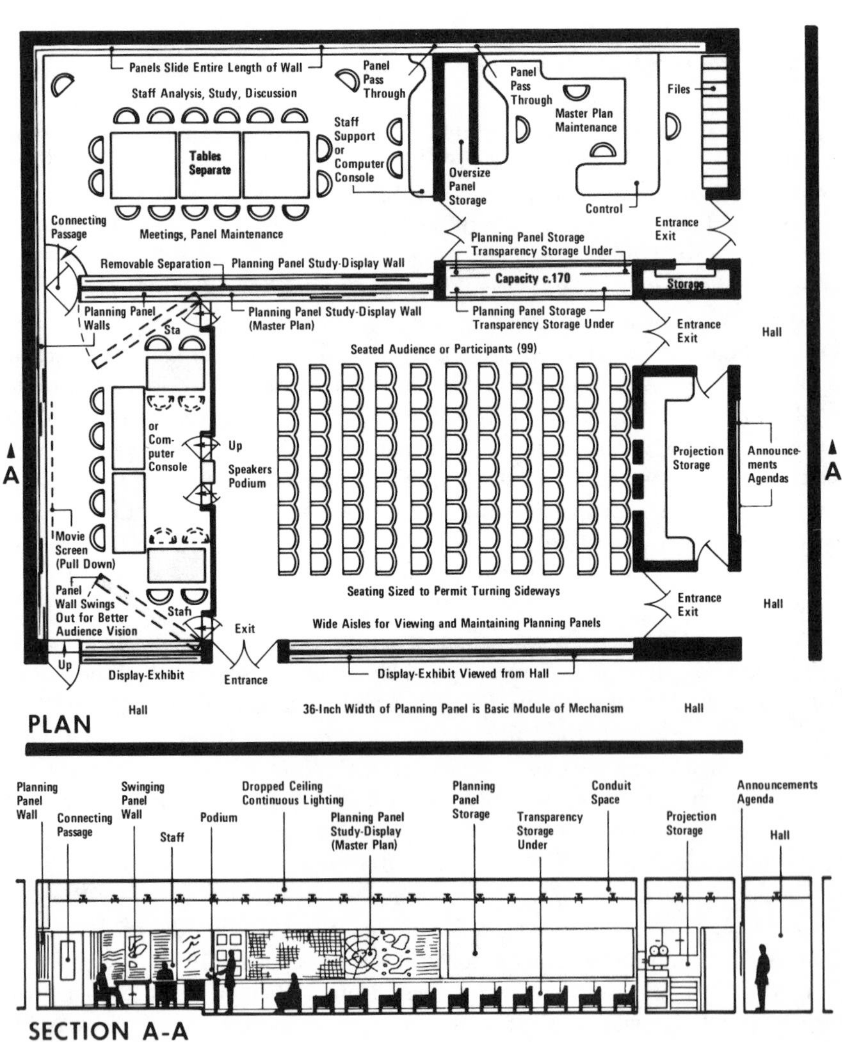

Figure 1: MECHANISM OF CONTINUOUS MASTER CITY PLANNING

The walls of both sides of the main auditorium room are designed so that panels may be placed and moved from either side of the wall. Thus, staff can manipulate panels facing the fixed seating, from the staff space on the other side of the separating wall; or they can reach through, remove, and reverse panels which have been used in the main room, for reference and study from the staff side. In similar fashion, panels can be shifted in the wall between the main auditorium room and the side corridor so they can be seen from either side. In this way, certain analysis-display panels can be used to provide advance information to people in the corridor outside, or comprise changing "exhibits" drawn from the master plan. Between the main and the master plan maintenance rooms is wall storage for standard-size panels which are not kept in the display wall recesses. Another storage space in the master plan maintenance room, so labeled in Figure 1, is for oversized panels twice as wide as the standard module of three feet; these are more convenient for the presentation of some statistical data. At least 300 standard-size panels can be displayed in the space shown in Figure 1. If ease of rearrangement were sacrificed by filling the wall-recess tracks leaving little unoccupied space, over twice this number could be maintained. As discussed below and shown in Figure 3, 200 panels would probably be the maximum needed or feasible for a continuous master plan for a city such as Los Angeles.

Locations are designated for computer consoles in both main auditorium and staff study rooms. As more information can be absorbed and utilized in the process of analysis and decision-making, computer consoles can be used for data retrieval, display, and manipulation. The information could be shown on movie-size screens so that it can be seen by everyone in each room. In time, the entire mechanism described in Figure 1 might be replaced by highspeed electronic analysis and display, but not before decision-makers can absorb and use it, because otherwise it is largely wasted.

The panels in the rooms comprise the official master city plan. When part of this needs to be issued so that it can be kept and used elsewhere—for example, proposed district plans for local review and reaction—the panels with this material are photographed and reproduced as a brochure. The size of the panels, 36 by 52 inches, is selected so they can be carried by one person and transported behind the front seat of the average-size automobile. City councilmen, other officials, and private groups or persons may not wish or be able to come to the planning center, but be willing to receive material if it is brought to them.

The panels are of two types: opaque and transparent. The latter, of course, are slid in front of other panels to permit direct comparison of information by this superposition. If the information shown on one transparent panel does not prevent seeing through it to the next panel behind, as many as four superposed panels may be correlated. Opaque panels can be hard-surfaced to receive "stick-on" graphical materials which can be changed over and over again, or grease pencils and wick pens which can be erased easily. Panels can be surfaced with metal so that materials with magnets attached to the back may be moved

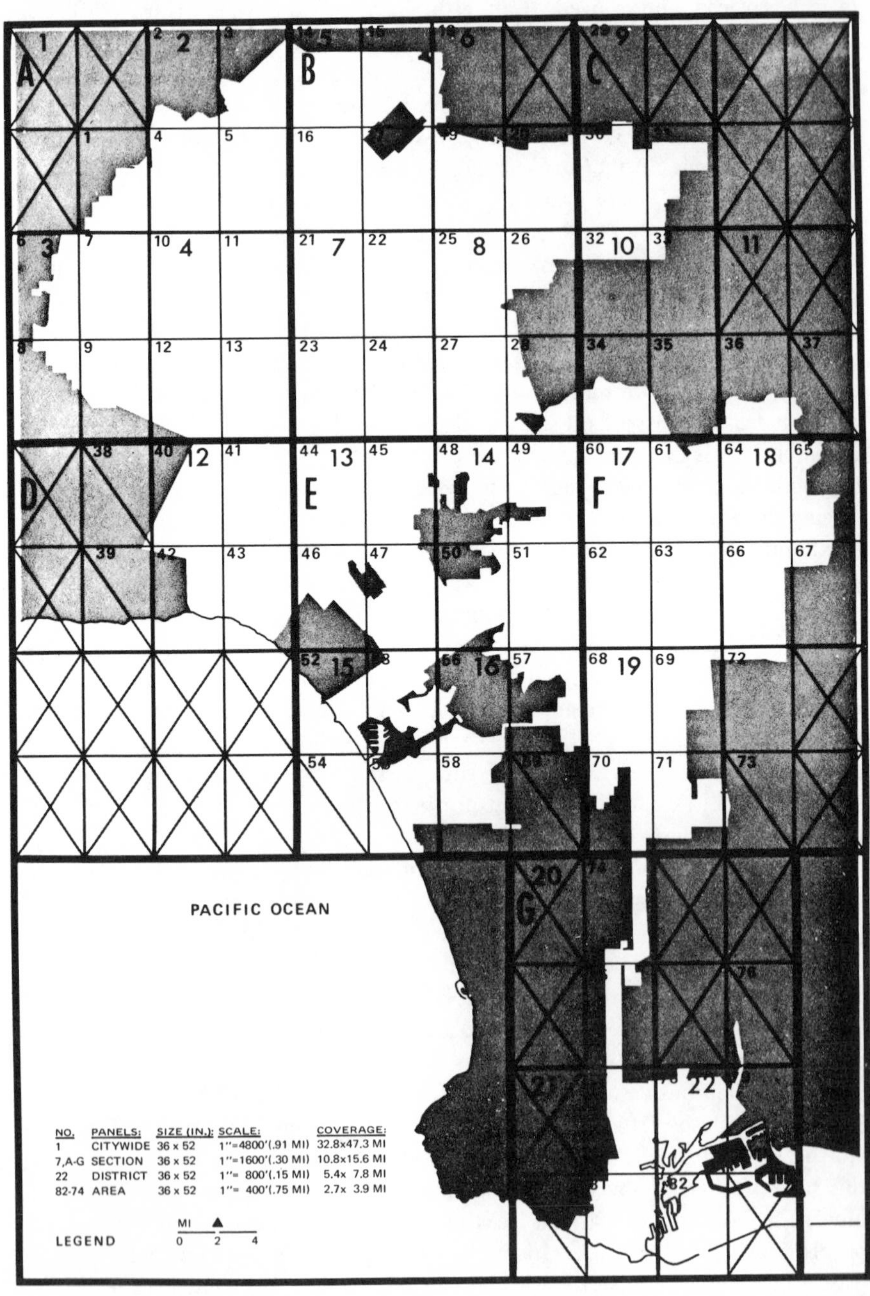

Figure 2: DIVISION OF LARGE CITY INTO ANALYSIS-DISPLAY AREAS

about on the vertical surface almost as easily as on a horizontal surface. When maximum ease of rearrangement or tentative placement assist the analysis, magnetic panels are helpful. "Menu" boards are another kind of opaque panel, particularly suited to statistical arrays of many types. With reusable plastic letters and numbers, numerical material can be quickly set up and maintained. As has long been recognized, panels with a blackboard or greenboard surface for chalk crayons are uniquely suited to "chalk talk" or the instantaneous expression or notation which is so important when exploratory analysis is under way. In some planning rooms, an entire wall surface is made available for use as a blackboard, providing the very large surface which is indispensable at times for the uninterrupted formulation of an idea or working out a complicated program or procedure.

The way in which a city can be subdivided for its representation on analysis-display panels is shown in Figure 2 for Los Angeles. Since Los Angeles covers one of the largest municipal areas of any city in the world—465 square miles—it is a rigorous test of the practicality of continuous master planning as envisioned here. Each rectangle in Figure 2, without diagonal line(s), is a portion of the city portrayed on a panel, 36 by 52 inches. The smallest rectangles are enlarged the most to fill the surface of a display panel, and are therefore at a larger scale than the rectangles encompassing larger areas of the city on the ground, which must be at a smaller scale to fit on the panels. The following table taken from Figure 2 indicates the number of panels required to depict Los Angeles cartographically at four different scales and ground-area coverage.

No.	Panels:	Size (in.):	Scale:	Coverage:
1	Citywide	36 x 52	1"= 4800′(.91 Mi)	32.8 x 47.3 Mi
7,A-G	Section	36 x 52	1"= 1600′(.30 Mi)	10.8 x 15.6 Mi
22	District	36 x 52	1"= 800′(.15 Mi)	5.4 x 7.8 Mi
82-74	Area	36 x 52	1"= 400′(.75 Mi)	2.7 x 3.9 Mi

Naturally, as the scale increases the number of panels needed to cover the entire city increases also. Thus, at the largest scale suggested above of 1 inch = 400 feet, between 74 and 82 analysis-display panels are required to portray the entire city. Whether it is the smaller or larger of these two numbers which is needed depends on whether small areas of the city "left over" from an adjacent panel are shown as an "insert" or supplement on this adjacent panel, or another entire panel is used to display the very small area. In Figure 2, places where this choice exists are indicated by a single diagonal line in the rectangle, for example numbers 38, 39, 54, and 73. The rectangles with two crossed diagonal lines are not part of the master plan because they are beyond the city limits, but they are part of the surrounding metropolitan background.

Citywide panels would naturally be used to analyze and view the city and its elements as a whole: transportation, utility, and facility networks; land use pattern; centers of activity and growth; metropolitan-regional developments

CATEGORIES OF INFORMATION	CONCEPTUALIZATION-DISPLAY-ANALYS[IS]

Supplementary Notes:

(1) Size of all panels = 36" x 52" (3' x 4'4")
(2) Scale: 1" = 4800' (.909 mile); single panel includes city
(3) Scale: 1" = 1600' (.303 mile); 7 panels cover city
(4) Scale: 1" = 400' (.076 mile); 79 panels cover city
(5) Interval when information is revised or renewed
(6) Overlay at same scale as: C (Citywide), S (Section), or A (Area) panels
(7) Information is maintained for: C (Citywide), S (Section), and/or A (Area) level(s)
(8) ● = Transparent Panel superposed on Base Panel; ◆ = different information of one category on 1 Transparent Panel (shown on same horizontal line); ✦ = different information in different categories on 1 Transparent Panel (shown in same vertical column); ↕ identifies the categories of information shown on this Transparent Overlay, which are not listed consecutively in the chart. Transparent Overlays are attached to Panels and stored in drawers
(9) ◇ Identifies statistical-type display panels which are not transparent

Information Category No.	Category	Opaque Base Panels (1)(8): Map: Citywide (2)	Photo: Section (Semi-Controlled Mosaic) (3)	Photo: Area (Semi-Controlled Mosaic) (4)	Recycle Time (Years, Months, Weeks) (5)	Transparent Panels and Overlays (1)(8): Present: Base Panel as Background (6)	Present: Spatial Unit for Information (7)	Projection: Short Range (Year 1)	Projection: Medium Range (Year 5)	Projection: Long Range (Year 20)	Past: Historical (Past Years as Shown)	Other Panels: Statistical Array (9)	Other Panels: Trend Line, Bar Chart, Other (9)	Correlation[s]: Correlations achieved by: 30–Superposition of Transparent Panels and/or Overlays at the same scale; 15–Comparing different Panels and/or Overlays of different scale side by side; 3–Observation of Statistical Arrays, Tables, Charts, etc. 3 or 4 Transparencies		
	POPULATION, HOUSING															
1	Population Distribution: –18, 18-60, 60+; Major Ethnic Groups (8)	◆	●	X	2	S	A	X	◆	20	5	X	X	4/12	13/14	18/
2	Population Distribution: Income	◆	X	X	2	C	C	X	◆	20	5	X	X	4/		
3	Population: Growth, Decline	◆	X	X	2	A	A	X	◆	20	5	◇	X	4/20		
4	Residential Housing: Supply, Characteristics, Distribution	X	◆	X	6M	S	A	X	◆	20	5	◇	◇	1/2	3/8	16/
	LAND USE, TRANSPORTATION															
5	Land Use: Residences, Industry, Commerce, Institutions, Recreation, Transportation Routes	✦	X	↕	W	C/A	C/A	X	◆	20	5	◇	X	6/7	15/16	18/21
6	Ground Transportation: Freeways, Major and Secondary, Highways; Rail	✦	X	↕	W	C/A	C/A	◆	◆	20	X	X	X	5/7	18/	
7	Air Transportation: Airports, Helistops, Airways	✦	X	↕	W	C/A	C/A	◆	◆	20	X	X	X	5/6	18/	
	UTILITIES															
8	Water Supply: Main Lines, Secondary System, Reservoirs, Pumping Stations	✦	X	X	1	C	C	◆	◆	20	X	X	X	4/		
9	Storm Drainage and Sewerage: Main Lines, Secondary System, Collectors, Plants	●	◆	X	1	C/S	C/S	◆	◆	X	X	X	X	4/		
10	Solid Waste Disposal: Systems, Disposal Sites	◆	X	X	1	C	C	◆	◆	X	X	X	X			
11	Power-Electric, Gas, Other: Main and Secondary Lines, Plants, Stations	✦	X	X	1	C	C	◆	◆	X	X	X	X	18/		
	FACILITIES, SERVICES															
12	Education: Universities, Colleges, Schools	✦	X	↕	1	C/A	C/A	X	◆	X	X	◇	X	1/		
13	Health: Hospitals, Clinics, Sanitariums, Other	✦	X	↕	1	C/A	C/A	X	◆	X	X	◇	X	1/		
14	Governmental: Police, Fire, Parks and Playgrounds, Other; Administrative Centers	✦	X	↕	1	C/A	C/A	X	◆	X	X	◇	X	1/		
	ENVIRONMENTAL: POLLUTION, DETERIORATION															
15	Physically Blighted Areas: Smog, Noise, Neighborhood Deterioration, Other	X	◆	X	M	S	A	X	◆	X	5	X	X	5/		
16	Socially Blighted Areas: Crime, Delinquency, Drug Addiction	X	◆	X	M	S	A	X	◆	X	5	◇	X	4/5		
	EMPLOYMENT															
17	Distribution: Unemployment, Welfare by Age and Ethnic Groups	X	◆	X	M	S	A	◆	◆	X	5	◇	X	2/4	6/15	16/18
18	Major Employment Centers and Sites: Areas, Plants, Places	●	◆	X	M	S	A	X	◆	X	5	◇	X	5/6	7/11	
	ECONOMIC, FINANCIAL															
19	Source and Application of Funds: Municipal, County, State, Federal	X	X	X	Y	X	X	X	X	X	X	◇	X			
20	Economic Condition: Employment; $ Volume: Manufacture, Retail Sales, Construction, Other	X	X	X	Y	X	X	X	X	X	X	◇	X	3/4		
	EFFECTUATION															
21	Zoning: Residences (Multiple and Single Family), Industry, Commerce, Institutions, Recreation	X	X	◆	W	A	A	X	◆	X	5	◇	X	5/		
22	Capital Works Programs: Municipal, County, State, Federal	X	◆	X	Y	S	A	◆	◆	X	X	◇	X	5/		

Base Panels are kept up to date: Citywide map panels by cartographic revision, photo-mosaic Section and Area panels by new photography at least once a year. Further information is not applied to the surfaces of Base Panels, except temporarily to display a particular situation. Transparent Panels may have information applied directly to their surfaces. Transparent Overlays – displaying various information and storable in map drawers – may be attached to the Transparent Panels by corner pins. Other Panels are for statistical type information: plain surface with stick-on materials, menu-board, magnetic, etc.

TOTALS					
14	8	7	Categories of Information	13	1
X	X	158	Transparent Overlays	4	
1	7	79	Opaque Base Panels	X	X
8	56	5	Transparent Overlay Panels	X	X
9	63	84	TOTAL NO. OF PANELS	4	

Figure 3: ILLUSTRATIVE INFORMATION TO COMMENCE CONTINUOUS MASTER CITY PLANNING

affecting the city; and the like. Panels showing the city in seven sections permit the greater detail possible at a scale three times as large, and still include enough ground area (168 square miles) for various subsystems to be shown and studied. Area panels provide the largest scale and the level of detail needed for zoning and other decisions involving individual properties of small size. Since each of these panels displays only 10½ square miles, so many of them are required to cover the entire city that it is not feasible to maintain more than one such set of between 74 and 82 panels—not only because they must be brought up to date regularly but because of cost, storage space requirements, and the importance of quick accessibility. When scale and coverage intermediate between those of the section and area panels are needed, the city can be shown additionally by 22 district subdivisions. Most cities will require far fewer analysis-display panels than Los Angeles.

Figure 3 illustrates categories of core information which might be maintained in continuous master city planning. It indicates whether this would be displayed on opaque or transparent panels, and at what scale and coverage. For the most part, it is suggested that opaque panels comprise the background for transparent overlay panels containing most of the information which is revised regularly. In the illustration, district panels are not used. Recycle times vary from every week to yearly, depending on the need for closely up-to-date information, its availability, and cost. Also indicated in Figure 3 are the areal or spatial units at which information is maintained, and projections into the future and historical data concerning the past are also shown. Some panels carry statistical arrays and other graphical expressions such as trend lines, bar charts, and the like. Finally, the correlations between different categories of core information which might be the most useful in observing, analyzing, and planning the city are identified. Some of these would be shown by observing one or more transparencies superposed one on top of another or in front of an opaque base panel. Others would be maintained by statistical comparison, ratio analysis, mathematical models, and other methods. The core information selected for Figure 3 is illustrative or suggestive only; some cities might choose quite different information for their continuous master city planning. What is shown in Figure 3 requires 81 opaque panels, 158 transparent panels, and 4 for statistical arrays—a total of 162. The master planning mechanism depicted in Figure 1 (see Branch, 1962) is designed to handle many more than this number.

There is a limit, of course, to the core information and analysis which can be processed, maintained, and conceptualized for regular reference and decision-making. How this is organized and carried out is clearly crucial to successful city planning, for decisions are only as sound as the information and analysis on which they are founded. Undoubtedly, the specific information maintained and the particular ways of handling it will vary considerably among different cities, but there are basic requirements which must be met by all mechanisms for continuous city planning. Only that data is incorporated which has the requisite reliability, can be updated as frequently as needed, is critical to the most important decisions to be made, and is understood and absorbed by those directly involved. Most important of all, information and analysis are introduced into the mechanism of continuous master city planning only as fast as they can be formulated and interrelated with the data and analysis already incorporated. At all times, the total construct of material must be meaningfully interrelated analytically, and presented clearly enough for decision-makers to make conscious use of it all together as their main means of evaluation and conclusion. Any device of collection, storage, processing-manipulation, analysis, or display can be employed which contributes to meeting these basic requirements (the substantive and intellectual scope of city planning as conceived today is represented in Branch, 1970).

Obviously, some form of representation on simulation of a city is absolutely essential in city planning. The city must be portrayed or described in ways which are sufficiently representative of its reality to permit meaningful study and valid conclusion. This is done, of course, in many different ways. A map shows ground features of the city in proper scale and spatial interrelationships. A statistical tabulation depicts population characteristics, costs, retail sales, or some other fact or trend numerically descriptive of the city. Instruments measure urban air, water, noise, and other kinds of pollution or unhealthy conditions. Descriptive writing may be the best way of expressing certain urban features and developments. In each case, an aspect of the city is being simulated by the most appropriate form of representation.

Drawing and photography or remote sensing are not only the sole substitutes for direct human viewing, but they are the only way of picturing a large city. Even were the city planning analyst or decision-maker able to visit all parts of the city and store a complete picture of what he saw in his mind, it would very likely require a drawing or photograph to trigger to consciousness many of these visual memories.

> "All matters which an individual reviews and decides upon are referred to his mind and memory–what might be called his personal internalized simulation, the product of accumulated observations, experience, formal knowledge, and thought. . . . The accomplished decision maker in city planning visualizes a plan picture of the metropolitan region as a whole, as it would appear from an aircraft high above. This internalized view is derived from direct observation on the ground or from the air, from maps and photographs" [Branch, 1966: 149].

Aerial photography provides the visualization of the three-dimensional reality of the city which cannot be acquired in any other way–except possibly in very small communities–and which is essential for urban analysis and most city planning decisions. Even when a person examines a city in perspective from a tall building or nearby hilltop, most of the street pattern and many other features are hidden from his view by intervening structures or terrain. Much less of the whole city can be seen, of course, standing on the ground at one point within the community. The closest approximation to a total view of the city is provided by vertical aerial photography. Certainly, there are features which are not shown even in this picturization from overhead, because they are beneath an intervening structure or vegetation, too small to be detected at the photo scale, or for another reason. Nevertheless, aerial photography provides the most complete and useful visual simulation of a city. Besides the information which it presents in itself, it acts as a trigger to recall to view within the conscious mind of each individual various pictures of parts of the city stored in his memory. In a large municipality, with many decisions to be made relating to places all over the city and frequently within legal or other time limits, only those in a position to know are aware of how often the person in the planning department making a recommendation has not examined the site or area involved beforehand. Aerial photography can serve as a close substitute for the visit to the site involved in each decision which is clearly desirable but frequently simply impossible or impractical. If new aerial photography is taken every six months or every year, this most important visual simulation is kept closely up-to-date, and an historical record is accumulated for comparative planning purposes and general urban studies. In Figure 2, the area panels comprise this photographic view of the city from above, at a scale large enough (1 inch = 400 feet) to identify single parcels of land, see a great deal of detail, and generally visualize the entire municipal area as it is actually.

REFERENCES

Branch, Melville C. "Comprehensive Urban Planning: A Selective Annotated Bibliography with Related Materials" (Beverly Hills, Calif.: Sage Publications, 1970).

---. *Planning: Aspects and Applications* (New York: John Wiley & Sons, 1966).

---. *The Corporate Planning Process* (New York: American Management Association, 1962).

Harmon, Leon D and Kenneth C. Knowlton. "Picture Processing by Computer," Science, Vol. 164, No. 3875 (April 4, 1969), pp. 19-29.

Mecklin, John. "Jim Webb's Earthy Management of Space," Fortune, Vol. LXXVI, No. 2 (August 1967), pp. 82-87 ff.

Southern California Association of Governments. "Southern California Regional Information Study," Computer Graphics, SCRIS Report No. 1, Los Angeles, California (January 1970).

Sutherland, Ivan E. "Computer Displays," Scientific American, Vol. 222, No. 6 (June 1970), pp. 56-60 ff.

PART TWO

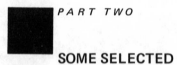

SOME SELECTED CASE STUDIES

INTRODUCTORY NOTE

To illustrate the applicability of the five-step rational planning process, or parts of it, and the specific new methods appropriate to each step in the processes that were discussed in Part One, Part Two includes selections and excerpts describing four case studies. The four case studies selected cover a variety of planning situations or problems to which the planning process, or parts of it, and some of the specific new planning methods, can be applied. They include the federally assisted Model Cities Program, the purpose of which is to assist selected cities to develop and implement a coordinated program to rebuild neighborhoods suffering from physical blight and to meet the social and economic problems of their inhabitants; the federally assisted Community Renewal Program, which was adopted in 1959, whose purpose is to provide federal grants to assist localities in the preparation of long-range renewal programs; a regional land use and transportation study and plan; and a mathematical simulation model used to assist in formulating alternative policies and programs for an urban sub-system, housing and/or residential renewal.

The selections included to illustrate each of these case studies were taken from reports prepared by federal, regional, and local agencies describing the results of and recommendations regarding their investigations.

The specific case studies selected to illustrate the four planning situations or problems are not only acknowledged to be representative, but also each approached its problem in a somewhat unique way. The Chicago Model Cities Program is generally recognized as one of the best; the Philadelphia CRP was one of the earliest efforts to try to integrate program budgeting techniques with urban planning; the Southeastern Wisconsin Land Use and Transportation Study and Plan is considered one of the most comprehensive and sophisticated studies of its kind; and the San Francisco Community Renewal Simulation Model not only broke new ground in the use of this new method, but also is one of the few models of this kind that has actually become operational.

Each example illustrates, of course, only one among many possible ways to approach that particular planning situation or problem more objectively. Other cities and metropolitan areas might be expected to develop their own unique variation of the planning process and of the specific methods used. These case studies are intended only to illustrate how one particular planning agency or community did, indeed, approach or analyze a basic local planning function.

None of the four case studies deals with all of the five steps in the planning process completely. Each concentrates on certain steps. The Chicago Model Cities Program concentrates on the identification of objectives and programs, is only beginning to pay attention to the prediction and evaluation phases, and is strong with respect to programming for implementation. By way of contrast, the Philadelphia CRP stresses the identification of a hierarchy of goals, objectives, and programs, with the identification of alternative programs only preliminary, and the remaining three steps not completed or contemplated at all. In Southeastern Wisconsin, the identification of objectives and prediction of consequences and effectiveness emphasized quantitative methods of analysis, while the identification of programs was generalized and the evaluation of alternatives subjective.

The fourth case study, the San Francisco Community Renewal Simulation Model, was selected to illustrate the use of simulation methods in the plan-formulation stage of the planning process, specifically, as an aid in designing alternative housing and residential renewal policies and programs and predicting the consequences and effectiveness of each alternative. However, this is not to say that all of the other steps in the process were completely ignored. Beyond the broad goal of an adequate and suitable supply of housing, the specific objectives for San Francisco's housing sub-system are not explicitly identified and explored; their actual formulation is more or less left to the third step, evaluation of alternatives, which itself, was left relatively unstructured. The alternative programs and policies affecting the housing sub-system are consequently not identified directly in terms of objectives, but rather in terms of those basic characteristics of housing supply which the objectives will eventually address–type, condition, quantity, and cost. Alternative governmental policies and actions aimed at these different housing characteristics could be tested through the operation of the model, each new combination of specific policies and proposed actions calling for a new run of the model. The programming-implementation step is basic to the concept underlying the San Francisco Community Renewal Program, for which the model was developed, for the output of the test runs and evaluation stage by local decision-makers and planners is a time-phased and staged program of action covering both public and private activities.

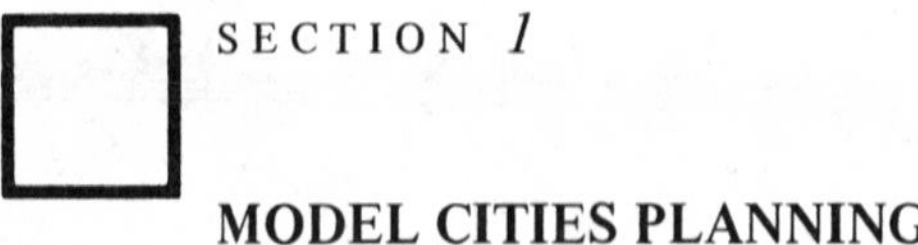

SECTION *1*

MODEL CITIES PLANNING

Chapter 18

PLANNING REQUIREMENTS FOR MODEL CITIES PROGRAM

Model Cities Administration, Department of Housing and Urban Development

1. MODEL CITIES PLANNING REQUIREMENTS

INTRODUCTION

1. Basic Instructions[1]

The Comprehensive Demonstration Program consists principally of three parts. They are:

i. Problem Analysis, Goals and Program Approaches and Strategy,
ii. The Five-Year Forecast, and
iii. The One-Year Action Program.

a. The first part should be submitted in draft from about two-thirds the way through the planning year or as soon as the city is satisfied that it is properly completed. This draft submission will take the place of the mid-period planning statement called for on page 4 of CDA Letter No. 1.

b. The Federal Government will review the draft and discuss it with the city. This discussion, and any local review of the draft which the city undertakes, may suggest revisions of the draft.

Reprinted from *Measures of Living Quality in Model Neighborhoods: A HUD Handbook* (Technical Assistance Bulletin No. 2, July 1968), Chapters 2-5, 7, and from *Comprehensive Program Submission Requirements: A HUD Handbook* (CDA letter No. 4, July 1968), pp. 1-7, 9-11, 13-16, Appendix 2 - p. 1, Appendix 3 - pp. 1-2, 8-13; both prepared by the Model Cities Administration, Department of Housing and Urban Development.

c. The revised draft of Part One and Parts Two and Three should be submitted to the Department of Housing and Urban Development near the end of the planning year. Together, these will constitute the city's application for first-year action funds.

d. The format outlined in this Letter need not be followed rigidly. Cities may wish to rearrange or add sections, attach appendices, or elaborate on material covered in the body of the draft. Such changes should be discussed with the city's Model Cities representatives as they develop.

2. Relationship Among the Three Parts

a. Part One, "Problem Analysis, Goals and Program Approaches, and Strategy," sets forth the problems of the model neighborhood and its residents, the long-range goals and program approaches of the comprehensive program, and the strategy to be used in pursuing those goals. It does not deal with fixed time periods or specific projects.

b. Part Two, "Five-Year Forecast," derives logically from the needs and lines of action described in Part One. It deals with a fixed period of time–five years–and projects more specific objectives to be reached in this period and estimates costs to reach those objectives.

c. Part Three, "One-Year Action Program," specifies how the city intends to take the first-year steps towards achieving the objectives of the Five-Year Forecast by making the best possible use of available resources and by beginning the work of changing those existing practices and institutions that need to be changed to better solve the problems and achieve the goals set forth in Part One.

As the city and the neighborhood make progress in the program, they will continue the process of analysis, thought and decision-making. HUD assumes that this process will identify new problems to be dealt with, develop new information and understanding about problems already identified, and develop new possibilities for change and new opportunities for solutions.

All of this will have its impact on the Comprehensive Demonstration Program. Each year, the changes created by these developments may be reflected in revisions of the problem analysis, goals and program approaches and strategy. They will be reflected in revisions of the Five-Year Forecast, and in the successive One-Year Action Programs. . . .

PROBLEM ANALYSIS, GOALS AND PROGRAM APPROACHES, AND STRATEGY
(Part I of the Comprehensive Program)

SECTION 1. PROBLEM ANALYSIS

5. Introduction

This section should describe the problems and conditions of the model neighborhood and its residents, what caused them and what sustains them. The problem analysis should cover all significant problems but the depth of analysis can vary according to the significance of the problem and data available. High priority problems should receive the most attention the first year. Future planning should direct attention to those significant problems not adequately covered during this first year of planning. Although this section and its contents will vary according to local conditions and according to local understanding of problems, it should not avoid significant and historical causes of deprivation and inequality.

6. Problem Analysis

The problem analysis should be done in two parts:

a. Initial Conditions. To the extent possible, describe in measurable terms the conditions in the model neighborhood and in the lives of its residents. These will be the same measures by which the city marks its progress toward meeting goals.

b. Causes. For each initial condition which describes an important problem, analyze its causes in terms of:

(1) Basic Causes. The underlying causes of initial conditions should be analyzed here. Because conditions vary from community to community and because each community sees its problems differently, this section should be considered as the place to demonstrate how fully those problems are understood by the people who took part in the problem analysis. This section might well include analysis of factors such as the following illustrative examples:

the attitude of people in the city as a whole towards the model neighborhood and its residents;

the attitude of neighborhood residents towards themselves and their neighborhood and the city;

the rate and type of economic development in the model neighborhood, city and the metropolitan area;

migration in and out of the model neighborhoods.

(2) Deficiencies in existing public and private services to the model neighborhood and its residents and in the administration of those services. All kinds of services should be considered: schools, hospitals, employment, police and fire, real estate, commercial, welfare, transportation and many others, though cities may have time to analyze deeply only those services found most inadequate by neighborhood residents. This analysis should consider questions such as those suggested by the following purely illustrative examples.

What is the purpose of the service?

Is the service relevant to the problem and does the service reach the people whom it is supposed to serve?

Are those people involved, in any way, in determining what services are to be provided and how?

Are those people involved, in any way, in providing the services?

If there are deficiencies in any such service systems, the causes of the deficiencies and how they operate to maintain or worsen initial conditions should be analyzed.

If a service appears to be performing well, the city should analyze the reasons for the quality of that service in order to aid in development of other programs and to assist in showing by contrast what deficiencies exist in other services. . . .

SECTION 2. GOALS AND PROGRAM APPROACHES

9. Goals

The long-range goals of the city should provide for improving the initial conditions listed in Section 1 so that conditions for residents in the model neighborhood are comparable to conditions in a wider community. It is towards achievement of these goals that the program approaches and changes listed in this Section are aimed. (See the discussion of goals and program approaches in Appendix 1.*) This does not mean that there need be a separate goal for each initial condition. Indeed, it is likely that, because problems are interrelated in the model neighborhood and the lives of its residents, cities may well want to define relatively few goals, each of which reflects its solution of several interrelated problems. But each city's goals and strategy must be sufficiently comprehensive to deal effectively with all of the problem areas and conditions covered by Section 103 of the Act. This section will be one place to demonstrate understanding of the interrelationships among problems and the need for linking action to solve them.

While long-range goals will be broadly stated, most of them can and should be broken down into measurable components.

10. Program Approaches

Usually, more than one program approach must be used to achieve a goal or even part of a goal. For example, the program approaches of rehabilitation, new construction, and improved access to occupancy of existing standard housing may all be used to achieve a broad goal in the field of housing.

Alternative program approaches considered, but not planned for implementation, should be noted. In some cases, it will be neither possible nor desirable to specify which program approaches in each goal area will be selected ultimately for implementation. In such cases, it is entirely appropriate (and desirable) to list the alternative program approaches under consideration. However, there should not be so many decisions postponed that the city cannot develop its strategy and arrive at a statement of it.

11. Changes Unrelated to Program Approaches

There are things to be done which the city may not choose to define as a program approach but which are important changes the city wants to make.

a. Changes may well be needed in areas such as the structure of local government; racial and ethnic attitudes and relationships; policies, laws and administrative regulations and practices which govern the operation of building codes, civil service, etc.

*Not included herein.–Ed.

b. Such changes could, however, relate to local conditions which limit the amount of State, Federal, local or private money that can be invested effectively in programs and the rate at which programs can be carried out. These conditions will affect the five-year forecasting described in Chapter 3 [Part II of the Comprehensive Program]. For example, adherence to outmoded personnel selection regulations can make it impossible to staff a program regardless of how much money is available for staff salaries. Or, a cumbersome, unresponsive contracting procedure within local government could limit the rate at which money available for urgently needed contract services could be spent. Or, the undeveloped state of the local construction industry could limit the rate at which new housing could be built. Such constraints should be identified and discussed here.

12. Additional Elements

a. The city, after stating program approaches for each goal, should also discuss those other changes which it has identified as needed to achieve that particular goal but which are not discussed under any particular program approach.

b. If a program approach or change is relevant to more than one goal, it should be listed under all appropriate goals and referred back to the goal where it is described.

c. Not all changes identified above, nor all program approaches, need be completely implemented in five years. But they should be started. The Five-Year Objectives Tables explained in Chapter 3 will show how much progress the city expects to make towards its long-range goals by the end of five years. . . .

SECTION 3. STRATEGY

15. Purpose

This section should describe and explain the order, priority, and relative emphasis among actions necessary to achieve the city's goals.

16. Strategy Levels

There are two levels of strategy cities should explain. The first is strategy among goals. The second is strategy among the program approaches and changes within a goal.

a. A purely illustrative (and oversimplified) example of strategy among goals:

> A city attaches greatest importance to goal A. It decides that, in order to fully achieve this high-priority goal, it must first make considerable progress toward goal B while doing the best it can with existing programs in goal A. However, before it can achieve goal B, the city feels it must achieve certain other objectives as a pre-condition. Having achieved these objectives, the city sees its way clear to making the big push in goal A. This strategy will help determine how and when and in what order the city allocates resources among its goals over the five years.

b. A city's explanation of its strategy within a goal would involve the reasoning for the amount, timing and sequencing of program approaches to achieve that goal in a manner similar to the type of reasoning illustrated above. It would also explain the order in which the changes discussed earlier are recommended (if the changes are sequentially related). . . .

FIVE-YEAR FORECAST
(Part II of the Comprehensive Program)

19. Introduction

The Five-Year Forecast described:

a. the progress the city expects to make in five years toward achieving its long-range goals;

b. what existing or new projects it wants to carry on during the first two years;

c. what program approaches it plans to work towards in future years;

d. how much those projects and program approaches will cost;

e. where the funds are expected to come from.

20. Limiting Factors

Although cities should do their five-year forecasting without assuming any particular limit on Federal funding after the first year, there are other factors which limit the amount of money and the rate at which programs can be carried out. Illustrative examples of such factors could be constraints on the amount of land available, dependence of one project on completion of another, and the tax base of the city. The city's forecast should reflect these other limiting factors, which will have been discussed earlier [Part I of the Comprehensive Program].

21. Initial Cost Data

Information about costs should be presented in as much detail as possible. Much of the data presented will have to be estimated. Where estimates are made, state the basis of the estimates.

22. Cost Data Refinement

In each successive year, as the city continues to plan and to evaluate what it has done, it will be expected to develop more precise data about ongoing activities and better techniques for projecting what it will need to do in the future. This increased capability should be reflected in annual revisions of the Five-Year Forecast and in each successive One-Year Action Program.

23. Required Tables

For each goal listed in Section 2, above, provide two tables.

a. The first table (Five-Year Fiscal Needs Table, see Appendix 3) describes *all* existing efforts (both changed and unchanged) and new efforts affecting the model neighborhood and shows how much such efforts will cost each year and over five years. Because the first year of the Five-Year Forecast reflects the first One-Year Action Program, sources of funds for this first year should be as detailed as possible. Unless definitely and specifically known, only the general sources should be specified for the second year of the forecast. The third through the fifth year should be summarized in one cost figure for each program approach.

(1) Where a goal calls for continuation of an existing basic service (such as the public school system or trash collection), the tables should reflect the gross cost of the portion of such basic services applicable to the model neighborhood as well as its total citywide costs. Such comparison will show the extent of concentration of resources in the model neighborhood. When a significant change is to be made in any such basic service, and separate project description and costing is possible, the changed part of the basic program should be shown separately. All other existing or new program approaches or projects in any goal area should be given descriptive labels and costed separately.

(2) The fiscal year periods of some cities may be different than the fiscal years of states, schools, or other systems operating in the model neighborhood area. The beginning of the Model Cities action will rarely coincide with a city's funding cycle. In presenting information in its forecast, each city may select whatever fiscal or funding year is most convenient and helps it most in its planning effort. The city should indicate when its fiscal year begins.

(3) The table should label and cost all projects that are being carried on for the benefit of the model neighborhood during the 12 months that precede the first action year. This 12-month period is referred to as the initial condition year. The initial condition year will be the base on which the Five-Year Forecast will build and against which it can be compared. In some cases, HUD may require a city to present this information for a period that goes back more than 12 months prior to the first action year. For the first action year, programs (other than continuing basic services) should be described at the project level and the descriptions grouped by program approaches. For the second action year, programs should be described at the project level wherever planning is definite enough to make such detail meaningful. Otherwise, description and costing at the level of program approaches is adequate. For the last three years, programs should be described at the program approach level and should not be broken down year by year. Costs should be estimated and tabulated for the three-year period as a whole.

(4) Projects should be grouped as logically as possible under program approaches. In some cases, a project may be logically related to more than one program approach. In such cases, a city should choose the program approach most related to the project.

b. The second table for each goal (Five-Year Objectives Table, see Appendix 3) should show how much progress the city expects to make toward achieving its goals over the five-year period. Such progress defines five-year and one-year objectives. Under each goal, list the program apprɔaches shown in the Five-Year Fiscal Needs Table. Show how each will contibute to the five-year and one-year objectives.

(1) Yearly progress toward some goals (education, for instance) may be slow and the results of program approaches may be difficult to measure in the same terms used to measure objectives. Increased levels of academic achievement might be an example of an objective which the city will be slow to reach. It might be hard to trace the contribution of individual education program approaches toward an academic achievement goal. In such cases, the contribution of the program approach should be stated and measured in the most meaningful terms feasible. These statements can be made in the table or in narrative following the appropriate table.

24. Required Narrative

Following the Five-Year Fiscal Needs and Objectives Tables for each goal, the city should provide narrative which covers the following three areas:

a. How is the strategy outlined in Section 3, above, reflected in the allocation of resources shown in these tables?

b. What proportion of city resources are allocated to the model neighborhood? To what extent will resources be concentrated more in the model neighborhood?

c. In those cases where the program approach cannot be measured in the same terms as the objective, provide narrative showing how the program approach is expected to help achieve the objective. For the educational area, for example, the program approach might be to increase the number and quality of teachers, even though the five-year objective is actually measured in terms of academic achievement. In this case, the city would explain how the program approach is expected to improve academic achievement. . . .

ONE-YEAR ACTION PROGRAM
(Part III of the Comprehensive Program)

27. Supplemental Grant Statement

This submission should describe the strategy for the use of supplemental funds. For each goal in which supplemental funds are proposed to be used, describe how and why supplemental funds are proposed to be used in the following categories: new and innovative activities; redirection of existing resources to better use; mobilization of additional resources. If a city foresees problems or special opportunities in the use of supplemental funds in the first and succeeding years, it should state them.

Using the information and format provided by the city in the first-year portion of the Five-Year Fiscal Needs Table, the city should show the following information for each goal: the expected results at the end of the first year; total first-year cost of project; amount of supplemental funds used in that project;

proportion of supplemental funds to total project cost; amount and source of other project funds, if any; total amount of supplemental funds for that goal and for each program approach.

28. Project Description

a. Projects on which no Model Cities Supplemental Funds are to be used.

(1) The submission must include a description, not expected to exceed two pages, of each project which is to be undertaken or continued as part of the first One-Year Action Program. All new projects as well as expansion of existing projects and continuation of presently operating projects should be included. Only the non-Federal contributions to projects included in this statement will be included in the calculation of the city's base for supplemental funds.

(2) Each project description should begin on a new page and should be appropriately identified by goal and program approach. The description for all projects not funded by supplemental funds should include all information called for in CDA 1, Section 5.3. The description should also indicate whether the project is new, substantially changed, or unchanged. If it is substantially changed, then the description should state how and why it is to be changed. If it is unchanged, the description should state its significance to the program.

b. Projects Funded in Whole or in Part by Model Cities Supplemental Funds.

(1) Each project that will be funded in whole or in part by supplemental funds must include a work program and a budget (in lieu of the information required in Section 5.3 of CDA 1). The purpose of the work program is to provide a description of the activities that will be conducted during the project. This description should be sufficiently clear and detailed so that:

(a) There is an adequate basis for MCA review.
(b) There is sufficient justification for the proposed budget.
(c) The work program can provide a guide to the subsequent work of the applicant in carrying out the component project. However, it is not expected that the work program for any project will exceed three pages.

(2) Each work program (except for the Administration Work Program) must provide an answer to the questions listed under the following headings:

(a) *Purpose and beneficiaries.* What is the component project intended to achieve and who will benefit from it? What basis is there for anticipating that the project will actually achieve the intended results? If it involves the expansion of activities already underway in the community, what have been the results accomplished to date?
(b) *Scope and content.* What action will be undertaken during the course of the component project?
(c) *Timetable.* What will be the sequence of activities to be undertaken? How do they relate to one another in time and how can the entire project be initiated and completed in the estimated time?
(d) *Administration and organization.* What is the name of the operating entity? What are the qualifications of the entity to undertake and complete the project? What staff and other resources that will be necessary? How will the CDA supervise and coordinate the projects with other components of the program?
(e) *Evaluation.* How will the accomplishments of the project be measured?
(f) *Citizen participation.* What opportunity will the residents of the areas and members of the groups be served have to obtain employment in and otherwise participate in the conduct and administration of the project?

29. Budget

Budget requirements and forms for MCA-funded projects will be set forth in a forthcoming CDA Letter on Program Budgets.

30. Administrative Structure, Continuing Planning and Evaluation

The Model Cities Program is intended to be an instrument of coordination and change. Coordination and change will not occur without a strong and well designed administrative structure, a process for continuing planning, a procedure for extensive evaluation of results of local Model Cities programs and use of this evaluation in program revision.

a. Statement of Administrative Structure. Section 7 of CDA 1 describes the statement of administrative structure. These instructions supplement CDA 1.

(1) The statement of administrative structure should reflect the basic function of the CDA as a planning and policy coordination vehicle. Program operation will normally remain the responsibility of operating agencies. The local program must work with the full support and commitment of the elected governmental structure. The CDA cannot be a separate agency such as an independent housing authority or renewal agency and be effective.

(2) In addition to reflecting these fundamental relationships, the statement of administrative structure should consider the relationships with the elements of the structure of government responsible for the ordinary municipal services such as trash and garbage collection, police and fire protection and code enforcement, as well as the more obvious services like renewal, education, housing, manpower, and health and welfare. The statement should also clearly reflect the CDA's relationship with those responsible for the many services in the model neighborhood which are not controlled directly by the local unit of government—the independent school boards, state and county highway and welfare departments, community health and welfare councils, chambers of commerce, central labor councils and the private sector generally.

b. Continuing Planning and Evaluation. Section 6.2 of CDA 1 describes the Planning and Evaluation Program Statement. In addition, that statement should indicate what parts of the administrative budget and project budgets reflect the cost of continuing planning and evaluation.

(1) Evaluation is an area that is traditionally neglected by all levels of government. Cities are not necessarily expected to present a complete evaluation plan in the first submission. Each city should recognize the importance of beginning an evaluation process. Every city is encouraged to try new and innovative ideas in this area.

(2) Additional information on continuing planning and evaluation will be provided in a forthcoming Technical Assistance Bulletin. Budget requirements and forms will be set forth in a forthcoming CDA Letter on program budgets.

31. Statement of Non-Federal Contribution

The non-Federal contributions required to be made to all projects assisted by Federal grant-in-aid programs which are carried out in connection with the

Comprehensive City Demonstration Program must be specifically enumerated in this section. These projects must be closely related to the physical and social problems of the area and be reasonably expected to have a noticeable effect upon such problems. Forthcoming material will give (1) information as to the projects within the city which may be enumerated, (2) the format in which to present this information, and (3) the rules which HUD will use in calculating the amount of the non-Federal contribution which may be included.

32. Relocation

The submission must include a Comprehensive Relocation Plan and a Relocation Program. Detailed requirements will be set forth in a forthcoming CDA Letter on relocation.

33. Statutory Checklist

The submission must include a completed Statutory Checklist (Appendix 4*). For each requirement, note the page or pages in the Five-Year Forecast and/or One-Year Action Program which show how the Comprehensive Demonstration Program meets the requirement.

*Not included herein.–Ed.

APPENDIX 2

Relation Among Goals, Program Approaches and Projects

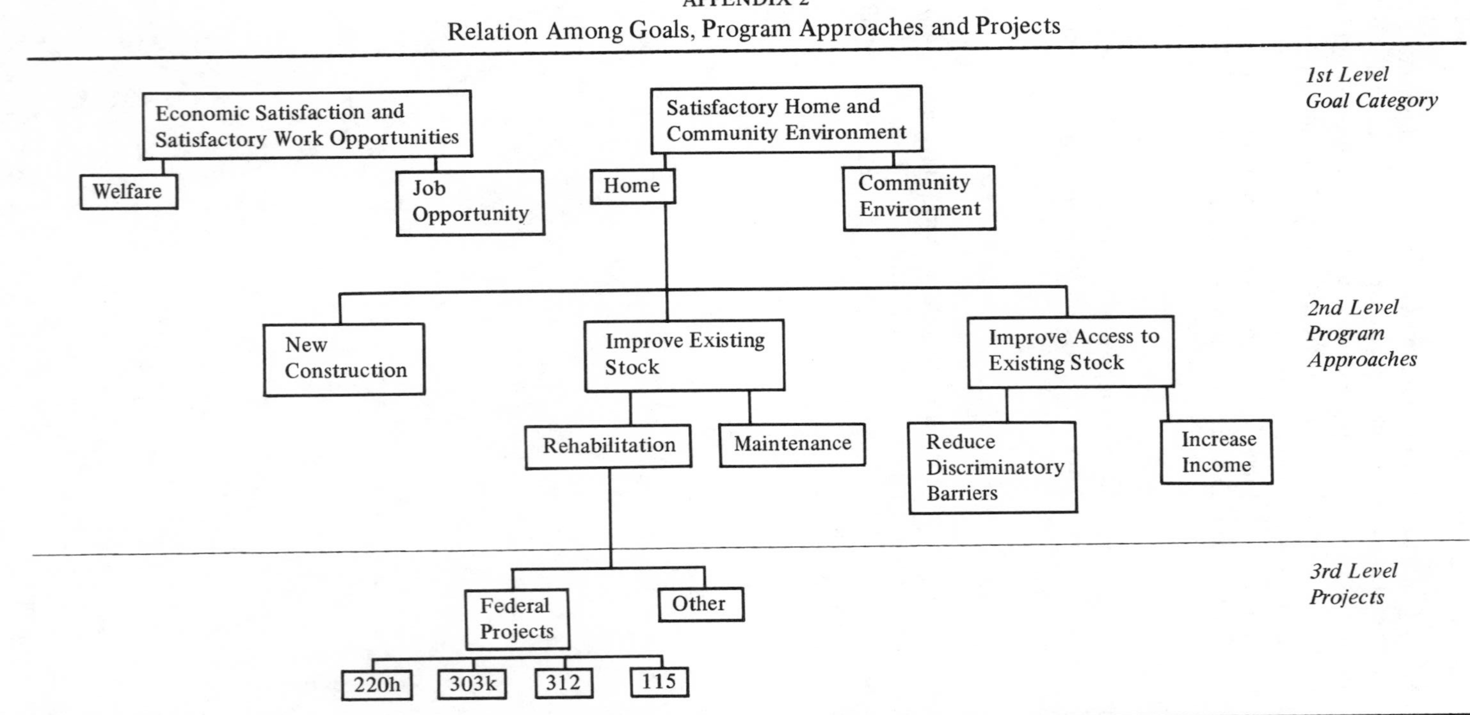

Cities may subdivide each level to the extent deemed desirable. Some entry should appear, however, at each level for each goal. The categories specified at the first level, abbreviated here, should be stated in terms of measurable goals.

APPENDIX 3. FIVE-YEAR FISCAL NEEDS AND OBJECTIVES STATEMENTS

1. Format

This appendix suggests a format for the statements of Five-Year Fiscal Needs and Five-Year Objectives. The tables presented here illustrate some of the alternatives cities have in thinking about and presenting data. They are not intended to suggest the substance of goals, objectives, program approaches or projects. Nor do they serve as exclusive models of how data must be presented by cities, though tabular form is preferred. However, cities are required to meet the following criteria in presenting their data:

a. Objectives, program approaches and projects which logically relate to each other should be shown together.

b. The program approaches used in the statements should be the same program approaches discussed in the strategy chapter of Part One. The data in the statements should be consistent with the discussion of strategy.

c. Total city-wide expenditures and model neighborhood expenditures for each goal should be shown adjacent to one another.

d. The main body of the statement should be as simple and comprehensible as possible. The method of presentation should facilitate ready reference from one part to another. Explanatory material or material the city wants to incorporate in its presentation (e.g., a cost-benefit analysis) should be presented in footnotes or technical appendices. Footnotes should appear on the same page as the material to which they are related.

2. Illustrations Chosen

Housing and education data* were chosen to illustrate the tables in this appendix because they require two different types of presentation. In housing, for the most part, the results of projects and program approaches are directly related to objectives. For example, Project X produces 25 units toward achieving an objective of 100 units. In education, on the other hand, the outputs of projects and program approaches cannot always be directly related to the achievement of an objective. One cannot be certain, for example, that success in the program approach of raising teacher quality increases grade-level performance, the objective, by a specified amount. But he can test that hypothesis in succeeding years.

*Not included herein.–Ed.

APPENDIX 3–TABLE 1

Five Year Fiscal Needs (thousands of dollars)

Goal II: Housing	*Initial Condition 4/68-3/69*	*Year I 4/69-3/70*	*Year II 4/70-3/71*	*Year III-V 4/71-3/74*	*Total*
Total expenditure–city	$2,900	$4,270	$7,500	$32,700	
Total expenditure–MN	90	920	2,510	10,500	
Objective 1: To increase the percentage of MN families living in standard units to 75%					
Objective 2: To reduce the gap between the percentage of families living in overcrowded conditions in the MN to the percentage of families in similar conditions in the rest of the city by 50%					
Program Approach					
A. Improvement, existing housing supply	90	755	2,100	7,300	$10,245
Unchanged					
Urban renewal A-27, Stone-Hyde[a]	(see project IIIB5, Community Environment Goal; see project IIA1, IIB1)				
1. Code enforcement Stone-Hyde	20 local, 40 HUD	30 local, 60 HUD			
Changed					
Urban renewal A-31, Barn Area	(see project IIIB6, Community Environment Goal; see project VA2, Manpower & Employment Goal)				
2. Code enforcement Barn Area	10 local, 20 HUD	80 local, 160 HUD			
New					
3. Housing improvement grants, low income residents		50 local, 150 HUD	100 local, 300 HUD		
4. Rent Supplement		100 HUD			
5. NFP Housing Cooperative Finance Corporation		125 MC			
B. New construction	0	110	300	2,500	2,910
Unchanged					
Changed					
1. Moderate income, senior citizens Stone-Hyde Area[b]	See narrative, non-financial change	25,50 local, HUD	100 local		
New					
2. Rent Supplement		5 MC	200[c] HUD		

Objective 3: To increase the number of families presently living in the MN who own their own homes to 10%					
A. Increasing ability of low income resident to become homeowners	0	55	110	700	865
Unchanged					
Changed					
New					
1. Housing Information Service		5, 20 local, MC			
		(see also project VIC1)			
2. Family Financial Counseling		30 MCA			
TOTALS (for three objectives)	$ 90	$ 920	$2,510	$10,500	$14,020

a. Urban renewal project A-27, Stone-Hyde Area. This project is entered under Program Approach A even though its costs are shown elsewhere because of its strong secondary effect on this program approach and goal. The number of "see" references for this entry gives an indication of its strategic importance in the Comprehensive Demonstration Program.

b. Moderate income, senior citizens, Stone-Hyde Area. This project has been changed even though there is no entry for expenditures during the year of initial condition. The change, therefore, did not involve any money. The exact change would be described in the narrative part of the One Year Action Program.

c. 200 HUD. In this project, the city feels that Year II is the first year in which large expenditures will be made. The project description should contain information explaining the expenditure pattern.

APPENDIX 3–TABLE 2
Five Year Objectives

Goal II–Housing	*Initial Conditions* 4/68-3/69	*Year I* 4/69-3/70	*Year II* 4/70-3/71	*Year III-V* 4/71-3/74	*Totals*
Objective 1[a]: To increase the percentage of MN families living in standard housing units to 75%					
(see explanatory table on next page for relationship between	1,500 families[b] in st. units, 33%	1,600 families in st. units, 35%	1,900 families in st. units, 40%	4,000 families in st. units, 75%	2,500 additional living in st. units
Objective 2: To reduce the gap between the percentage of families living in overcrowded conditions in the MN to the proportion of families in similar conditions in the rest of the city by 50%					
	2,250 families overcrowded, 50%	2,250 families overcrowded, 48%	2,125 families overcrowded, 45%	1,250 families overcrowded, 25%	1,000 families moved from overcrowded units
Program Approach[c]					
A. Improvement of existing housing	35 additional families living in st. units	75 additional families living in st. units	200 additional families living in st. units	1,700 additional families living in st. units	1,975 additional families living in st. units
B. New construction	10 additional families living in st. units	25 additional families living in st. units	100 additional families living in st. units	400 additional families living in st. units	525 additional families living in st. units
Objective 3: To increase the number of families presently living in the MN who own their own home to 10%					
	45 families homeowners, 1%	70 families homeowners, 1½%	118 families homeowners, 2½%	535 families homeowners, 10%	
Program Approach					
a. Increasing ability of low-income residents to become homeowners	No families assisted	50 families assisted successfully	100 families assisted successfully	300 families assisted successfully	450 families assisted successfully

Explanatory table showing relation between Objectives 1 and 2[d]

	Initial Conditions 4/68-3/69			Year I 4/69-3/70			Year II 4/70-3/71			Year V 3/74		
	Families in st. units	Families in ss. units										
Families in over-crowding	1,000	1,250	2,250 (50%)	1,000	1,250	2,250 (48%)	975	1,150	2,125 (45%)	500	750	1,250 (25%)
Families not in overcrowding	500	1,750	2,250 (50%)	600	1,750	2,350 (52%)	925	1,675		3,500	1,000	4,500 (75%)
	1,500 (33%)	3,000 (66%)		1,600 (35%)	3,000 (65%)		1,900 (40%)	2,825 (60%)		4,000 (75%)	1,250 (25%)	
			4,500 (total families)			4,600 (total families)			4,725 (total famliies)			5,250 (total families)

a. Objective 1. Objectives 1 and 2 are shown together because, in the view of the city, they are closely related to each other. Whenever a forecast table places two objectives together, the objectives tables should do likewise.

b. 1,500 families. Both numbers of families and percentage are included in the statement of objectives to present a more understandable table.

c. Program Approach. Listed under the set of objectives are those program approaches the city feels are programmatically most related to the objectives. The results (output) of the program approaches is stated in the table. In the case of these particular program approaches, the results translate directly into a measure (families moved into standard units) which is comparable to the statement of objectives.

d. (Explanatory Table.) Because the two measures are so closely related, the city has decided to show how they relate to each other. In order to keep the body of the table simple, a table which appears at the bottom of the page is referenced. A special technical appendix would also have served the purpose.

In detailed planning to meet housing objectives, it may be necessary to consider cost and number of rooms as well as condition. In this case, more elaborate analysis and tables showing housing units by cost, condition, size and occupancy would be attached in technical appendices.

3. Footnotes

The tables presented here are heavily footnoted so that CDA staff and all those involved in local model cities planning can understand the different types of data shown.

NOTE

1. City Demonstration Agency Letter No. 1 (CDA) promised cities a supplement which would describe the format of the Comprehensive Demonstration Program which cities are required to submit. This Letter does that. CDA 1 and the Demonstration Cities and Metropolitan Development Act of 1966 should be read again for fuller understanding of this CDA Letter.

To make this Letter as clear as possible, we are including a glossary of the terms used in it, a graphic illustration of the basic planning concept of this paper and illustrative tables for the presentation of necessary data. They are found at the end of this Letter as Appendices A, B and C [not included herein.–Ed.].

2. MEASURES OF LIVING QUALITY

INTRODUCTION

This Bulletin is designed to provide assistance to cities in carrying out the Model Cities planning and programming process. It does not contain new requirements.

CDA Letter No. 1 (Model Cities Planning Requirements) and the Program Guide[1] set forth the following basic requirements:

> Cities need to measure and describe the extent and severity of problems affecting the living quality of residents in the model neighborhoods, particularly those to which statutory requirements are addressed. The problems should be measured in terms which relate to the city's program goals and objectives.
>
> Cities need to establish long-range goals which are comprehensive enough to meet or exceed achievement standards in statutory areas of concern. (See Program Guide, Chapter 1, Part 4.) The program goals, while broadly stated, should be broken down as much as possible into objectives which relate directly to the problem analysis and measurement.
>
> Cities need to establish, to the extent possible, quantified five and one-year objectives which are measurable in the same terms as their long-range goals and existing problems.

In order to meet these requirements, cities have to select and utilize various measures relating to living quality. This Technical Bulletin illustrates the types of measures[2] which are needed. It does not specify which ones should be used. It provides guidance on formulating initial conditions, program goals, and objectives.

The succeeding pages discuss various aspects of measures and their uses in the planning process. [They] illustrate the type of goals which would be appropriate for a Model Cities plan, indicate the kinds of data that would be appropriate to obtain in assessing the problems to which statutory requirements are addressed, and gives examples of quantified five-year and one-year objectives.

Not all cities will carry out the work which the Bulletin implies during the initial planning period. While cities should attempt to do as much as they can during this period, the Model Cities program is a continuous process of planning and programming. It may be difficult to obtain the types of data implied by the examples in this Bulletin, particularly during the initial planning period. It may be necessary at the outset to make estimates or to employ data that are not current. Cities must plan to develop better data in the future as part of their required continuing planning and evaluation process.

DEMONSTRATION PURPOSES AND MEASUREMENT NEEDS

A basic purpose of the Model Cities program is to improve the quality of life for people living in model neighborhoods. This means that gross differentials or gaps between their living conditions and the living conditions of residents living in a wider community must be reduced. Therefore, the illustrative examples of goals and objectives have been framed in terms of reducing gaps.

For many goal categories, and in different cities, it may not be appropriate to provide the same type of service to the model neighborhood as to the rest of the city. For example, model neighborhoods may need a different type of public transportation service with respect to accessibility or frequency or time of service. The same type of difference may be true with respect to other goal categories. However, for the sake of simplicity in these examples, and because the closing of gaps is meaningful in many cases, the goals and objectives have all been framed in terms of gaps. Goals and objectives must be suited to local circumstance and should not be framed in terms of gaps which are not meaningful to the goal being described.

In changing the quality of life for model neighborhood residents, cities will be demonstrating what combination of programs, projects, and other activities over a five-year period can effectively and efficiently improve life quality and close gaps. A major purpose of the program, then, is to know what was successful and why it was successful.

1. Planning Decisions

During the life of the program, cities will decide what to undertake and when. They will have to allocate and coordinate available resources so that the greatest improvement in living quality for model neighborhood residents will be achieved. These resources include funds available for existing Federal grant-in-aid programs, Model Cities supplemental grant program funds, and funds from State and local governments and private sources.

Because resources are not unlimited, each additional unit of resource in one use means less resources available for other possible uses. Choices have to be made between alternative projects and program approaches. Choices also have to be made regarding the scale and rate at which each project and program approach should be implemented.

In order to make such choices, cities should try to relate program efforts (or inputs) to desired program results (or outputs) in quantifiable terms. They should attempt to estimate how much more improvement in living quality would result from one project or program approach as opposed to another, and what increase in results would result from *more* effort in a given project or program approach.

2. Need for Evaluation

Each local Model Cities program is part of a national demonstration designed to benefit all cities in the country. Each local program must be evaluated on the basis of the results which are obtained in order to gain knowledge from diverse program efforts and make available to other cities the lessons learned.

In order to determine what works and what does not work, cities must be able to evaluate actual progress towards objectives and the type and amount of program inputs which made that progress possible.

3. Need for Measures

In order to make planning decisions and evaluate program results, yardsticks or measures are needed for measuring program inputs and program outputs.

The measures will help cities make more rational planning decisions as well as provide the basis by which cities and the Department of Housing and Urban Development (HUD) will be able to monitor the progress of local programs toward attaining goals. In addition, they will provide an empirical base for the development of cost/benefit analyses encouraged under the law.

4. Focus on Performance Measures (Output)

The focus of this Bulletin is on output measures or measures of performance.[3] Inputs are readily and fairly easily quantified in terms of per-unit dollar costs. Program outputs, the impact or effect on problems, are not readily or meaningfully translated into dollar terms. It is difficult to assign dollar values to desired program outputs such as improved housing conditions, reduced severity and incidence of poverty, and improved health. Such outputs reflect social as well as monetary values.

OUTPUT MEASURES

Output (or performance) measures are required in Model Cities planning to:

(1) describe initial conditions in the model neighborhood (identify problem conditions and assess their extent and severity);

(2) set forth, to the extent possible, quantifiable program goals and establish quantitative objectives for the five-year plan and the annual one-year action program (establish the level of performance that program inputs must produce);

(3) evaluate goal achievement (determine periodically the degree of improvement which has been achieved.

1. Relationship of Measures to Program Goals

Measures define and isolate the specific things which are examined in describing and evaluating quality of life. Therefore, they should relate to those characteristics which must reflect the quality of life in the goal areas. For example, in the area of housing such characteristics as the physical conditions of the unit, the cost of the unit relative to household income and the number of people living in the unit in relation to its size would be appropriate. Housing quality expressed and measured in these terms can indicate the effect housing has on the lives of the occupants and can provide the basis for making objective comparisons between various geographical areas and over periods of time.

Goals are an expression of values. Measures are used to approximate the values and allow us to relate projects and program approaches to the values. There are no perfect measures which comprehensively express all the facets of living quality and which take into account the particular conditions and circumstances of all the people described by the measure. Every measure has some limitation. Cities must attempt, though, to define measures or combinations of measures which relate as closely as possible to their goals and values.

2. Goal Statements

The goals, and consequently the measures, should relate to ends and not to specific means which may be necessary to achieve the goals. For example, the goal should be to eliminate educational disadvantage and not to provide new textbooks. Providing new textbooks may be one of the means to eliminate educational disadvantage, but it is not an end in itself.

The local program should aim not only at improving living conditions, but also at insuring that the improved status can be maintained. In the area of housing, for example, the goal should not only be to provide residents with physically standard, uncrowded units within their financial means. Achievement of the goal should also insure the residents of being able to maintain standard housing conditions over time. This means that output measures should be defined which relate to the ongoing ability of the residents to obtain the resources or services appropriate to maintaining the goals, not merely to overcoming conditions that exist at the outset.

3. Objectives and Program Approaches

Objectives are the levels of performance, quantified where possible, which measure the progress of the city towards achieving its goals. The measures used in the objectives serve the dual purpose of establishing levels of performance and allowing for the evaluation of goal achievement by specifying what is to be evaluated.

Cities will use resources in different ways to reach objectives. These different basic ways to use resources are called program approaches. For example, achievement of an educational objective could involve using resources to increase teaching quality, developing a better curriculum, using existing facilities more efficiently, building new facilities or improving existing plant, and establishing better school-community relationships. Each of these uses would be a program approach.

Sometimes the output of a program approach can be measured the same way that objectives are measured. For example, program approaches for a housing objective might be rehabilitation, new construction, and temporary housing. The results of these program approaches can be easily expressed in housing units or families moved into housing units. However, the program approaches cited above in education cannot be directly translated into an education objective of academic achievement. The city would have to hypothesize what effect each program had on achieving the objective. In future years, then, the evaluation program would be designed to find out whether the hypothesis was valid or whether resources should be diverted to another program approach.

The results of program approaches sometimes cannot be easily described in the same measures used for Five and One-Year Objectives, but the city can state what might be termed intermediate results. Improving teacher quality, for example, could be indirectly measured by training, experience levels, etc. The problem still remains, though, of relating these measures to achievement of the objective. This must be done by evaluation over the life of the program.

4. Citizen Participation

Since the measures are used to evaluate the quality of residents' lives, the residents should be involved in selecting them. Residents are best able to indicate the specific aspects of life which are most important to them, even though technicians may be more professionally equipped to define the specific terms which could be used for the measures. Therefore, residents' judgments should be reflected in the goal statements and in the measures selected to approximate the goals.

5. Data Needs

Cities should analyze their goals to decide what measures are necessary to reflect the values in each goal statement. To the extent that resources permit, the complete set of measures should be used to described initial conditions, specify goals, and evaluate the program and how it affects the quality of life. In some cases, the inability to obtain requisite data for a measure may suggest a reformulation of the long-range goal statement. In some instances, the data needed to measure initial conditions will not be regularly collected by public bodies. In other cases where critical data are not available and cannot be collected within the time and money available, informed judgments should be used and plans established for collecting the requisite data as soon as possible. At a minimum, cities should seek to obtain a good first approximation of initial conditions as a baseline against which progress toward goals can be measured over time. Cities will be expected to identify clearly any gaps in information. The planning and evaluation program should show how the data gaps will be filled.

At the same time, specific improvements that must be made in urban data sytems at the local, State and Federal levels should be planned. As rapidly as possible, improvements should be made in these data systems so that increased precision and sensitivity can be introduced into the measurement and analysis. In particular, it is desirable over the long run that data series be modified to develop greater sensitivity to the output objective that is being measured. Where possible, data series should be standardized to permit aggregation and comparisons.

USE OF OUTPUT MEASURES IN THE PLANNING PROCESS

The output (or performance) measures should be applied to the model neighborhood as a whole[4] and, as appropriate, to the rest of the city or a wider community. The discrepancy or gap between the two measures defines the "relative deprivation" of the target population and the inequalities between population groups living within the city. Comparisons over time between the absolute values of the measures will reveal both the severity of the deprivation gap and how fast the gap is being narrowed.

1. Quantifying Long-Range Goals

Cities should seek, at a minimum, to close the gap between the living conditions of the residents in the model neighborhood and the living conditions for the rest of the population in the city (or metropolitan area).[5] For purposes of simplification, comparison will hereafter be made only to the rest of the city. The amount of improvement is defined, therefore, by the discrepancy in the performance level of the model neighborhood and the performance level of the rest of the city.

In some cases, the amount of improvement which the long-range goals might reflect could be greater than the existing discrepancy in performance because conditions elsewhere in the city provide too low a standard. In other cases, city-wide goals might dictate higher levels of performance for plan development than presently achieved by the rest of the city. For example, the goal of a decent, safe and sanitary home within a standard environment for all families has been adopted by some cities as a city goal against which all programs are to be developed. Long-range goals for the model neighborhood should reflect and be consistent with such city-wide goals and standards.

In still other cases, anticipated and significant increases in levels of performance for the rest of the city would require more improvement for the model neighborhood than the gap defined by existing discrepancies.

2. Measuring Extent and Severity of Problems (Assessing Initial Conditions)

Comparison between conditions in the model neighborhood and the rest of the city will help define what conditions are problems. However, quantitative differences do not necessarily define the relative importance of the problems. Which problems will get most attention depends on the priority of goals, the problem analysis, and the interrelationships recognized between the various problems and the goals having priority. For example, discrepancy between the performance of the model neighborhood and the rest of the city with respect to a housing measure may be greater than the measured discrepancy with respect to employment measures. There might be 50% substandard housing in the model neighborhood as against 10% in the rest of the city and 15% unemployment in the model neighborhood as against 4% in the rest of the city. Yet given the interrelationship between employment and one's ability to secure standard housing, eliminating the employment discrepancy could be given greater priority by the city.

3. Quantifying Five-Year Objectives

Five-year objectives should define how much impact on initial conditions the city will be able to attain by the end of five years. In many cases, it should be possible within that time period to make necessary institutional and legal changes at the State and local level and to initiate projects and activities which, when carried to completion, will achieve the long-range goals.

The quantitative amounts associated with the five-year objectives should not be defined without an evaluation of the problems, their priorities, and the relative effectiveness of alternative resource allocations. Continuing planning and evaluation may cause a city to reformulate its goals and objectives in future years.

Cities will have to make choices about the relative weight and importance given to different goals. Should additional resources be added to reduce unemployment or increase educational achievement? Should programs be expanded or added to achieve $100 per family more of income per year, or should infant mortality be reduced by an additional 5%?

4. Quantifying One-Year Objectives

One-year objectives should specify the level of performance which is to be realized at the end of a year's time. In cases where only administrative or legal changes are required to effect performance levels, significant changes in performancy levels can be achieved within the first one-year period. In other cases, however, it may take longer than a year for an action program to result in measurable changes in the output or performance measures. The plan would, however, include project and program approach inputs necessary to achieve desired outputs even though no measurable changes would be anticipated during the first year.

ILLUSTRATIVE EXAMPLES* OF LONG-RANGE GOALS, OUTPUT MEASURES, INITIAL CONDITIONS AND FIVE- AND ONE-YEAR OBJECTIVES

The examples which follow are illustrative of the type of goals and objectives which a city might formulate for its Model Cities plan. They encompass the range of legislative concerns. The actual format of presentation in this TAB is, of course, in no way tied to the way cities may choose to present such material in their plans. The definition of goal categories, similarly, is at the option of the city and the definition presented here is only one way of specifying goals. Cities may choose to combine some goal areas or define others differently. Further, the characteristics of most concern to model residents in different cities will vary, even in the same goal category. Measures of significance would vary accordingly. Cities should be aware, therefore, that the material presented [here] is only suggestive.

The measures in the illustrations have not been specifically defined. To avoid ambiguity or misinterpretation, each measure should be defined as clearly and as precisely as possible. For example, cities should define specifically what is meant by such terms as "family," "housing unit," etc., as used in any of the measures. Such definitions could be included in technical appendices to the plan or in footnotes to tables.

Many model neighborhoods have significantly different population groupings, in terms of race, income status, family type, or ethnic background. Also, certain measures are appropriate to specific groups defined by sex, age, etc. The examples in the next section do not consider these distinctions. As appropriate and in accordance with resources and priorities, cities should make these distinctions in defining and using output (performance) measures.

For purposes of simplifying the examples, comparison in the goals and measures is made only to the rest of the city. Other bases of comparison should be used as appropriate. (See note 6.)

EDUCATION

Statutory Provision. The local program should be designed to make marked progress in reducing educational disadvantage and to provide educational services necessary to serve the poor and disadvantaged in the area.

Long-Range Goals

1. To bring the educational performance of the school-age population in the model neighborhood up to the educational performance of the school-age population in the rest of the city.

*Only the examples of Education and Housing are included herein; the original also includes a discussion of Income Maintenance and Social Services, Recreational and Cultural Opportunities, Transportation, Physical Environment, Health, Crime and Delinquency, and Employment.–Ed.

Measure. Test scores on reading and arithmetic achievement tests of school-age population.

Initial Conditions. Number and proportion of school population in model neighborhood achieving test scores at grade level; number and proportion of population in the rest of the city achieving test scores at grade level.

Five-Year Objective. To reduce the differential between proportion of model neighborhood children achieving test scores at grade level and proportion of children achieving such test scores in the rest of the city by (specify) amount.

One-Year Objectives. In many cases discernible changes in the measures can be achieved within a one-year period; here one-year objectives would parallel the five-year objective statement, varying only in the degree of reduction to be achieved. In other cases there may not be discernible changes within the first year, but essential steps which are prerequisites to making discernible changes in future periods may have been taken. These steps would be reported in the plan.

2. To increase the proportion of area residents obtaining higher levels of education equal to the proportion of residents obtaining higher levels of education in the rest of the city.

Measures

a. Enrollment in school.

b. Secondary school dropout rates.

c. Enrollment in college and post secondary schools.

Initial Conditions

a. Number and proportion of model neighborhood school-age population enrolled in school by age categories; number and proportion of school-age population in the rest of the city enrolled in school by age categories.

b. Number and proportion of high school freshmen (9th graders) graduating from high school in the model neighborhood; number and proportion of high school freshmen in the rest of the city graduating from high school.

c. Number and proportion of model neighborhood high school graduates annually enrolling in colleges and other post-secondary schools; number and proportion of high school graduates in the rest of the city annually enrolling in college and other secondary schools.

Five-Year Objectives

a. To reduce the differential by (specify amount) between the proportion of school-age children in the model neighborhood enrolled in school and the proportion of school-age children in the rest of the city enrolled in school by age categories.

b. To reduce the differential between the proportion of high school freshmen graduating from high school in the model neighborhood and the proportion of high school freshmen in the rest of the city schools graduating by (specify amount).

One-Year Objectives (see statement on One-Year Objectives, above).

3. To increase the level of educational services available to residents of the model neighborhood (children and adults) up to the quality of education available to residents elsewhere in the city.

Measures

a. Per pupil expenditure.

b. Educational background and educational status of professional staff.

c. Type of educational programs available and type of curriculum.

Initial Conditions

a. Expenditures per pupil in the public schools in the model neighborhood (elementary, secondary); expenditures per pupil in the rest of the city.

b. Number and proportion of teachers in the public schools in the model neighborhood with education beyond a B.S. degree; number and proportion of teachers in the public schools in the rest of the city with education beyond a B.S. degree. Number and proportion of teachers in public schools in the model neighborhood who have tenure (as opposed to substitute teachers); number and proportion of teachers in public schools in the rest of the city who have tenure.

c. Appraisal of the educational programs (i.e., academic, vocational, adult education, pre-school training, etc.) available in the model neighborhood relative to educational programs available elsewhere in the city, by type, scope, capacity, hours available, etc.

Five-Year Objectives

a. Per pupil expenditure of $ (specify) in public schools in the model neighborhood.

b. To increase the proportion of teachers in model neighborhood schools with degrees beyond a B.S. to (specify); to increase the proportion of teachers in model schools who have tenure to (specify).

c. To increase the type of educational programs which are available to the model neighborhood in (specify ways) and to (specify) degrees; e.g.:

(1) To increase the capacity of adult education classes in the model neighborhood to (specify) students.

(2) To increase the capacity of pre-school training program to (specify) students, etc.

(Because educational programs should be geared to the needs of the population they are to serve, a city-wide standard should be considered only a minimum level to be achieved for these objectives. In many instances, the amount of achievement specified for these objectives should exceed city-wide levels. In particular, the qualification of the teachers and the type of programs should reflect what the particular model neighborhood population requires in order to achieve higher educational performance levels as measured by goal 1, above.)

One-Year Objectives (see statement on One-Year Objectives, above).

4. To obtain and recognize as much involvement of parents in policy making and in the development and administration of the school program in the model neighborhood as is true for school programs in the rest of the city.[6]

Measures

a. Existence of and extent of participation in parent participation groups.

b. Channels of communication between the school administration and parents, and procedures for handling parent complaints or expressed concerns.

HOUSING

Statutory Provision. The local program should be designed to contribute to a well-balanced city with a substantial increase in the supply of standard housing of low and moderate cost, with maximum opportunities in the choice of housing accommodations for all citizens of all income levels.

Long-Range Goals

1. To provide as high a proportion of model neighborhood families with standard housing adequate to their family needs and within their financial ability as the proportion of families with such housing living elsewhere in the city.

Measures

a. Physical condition of housing units.

b. Rent/income ratio.

c. Number of persons/rooms.

d. Number of families/housing unit.

Initial Conditions

a. Number and proportion of families in the model neighborhood by physical condition of housing unit (as defined in terms of "standard" and "not standard"); number and proportion of families in the rest of the city by physical condition of housing unit.

b. Number and proportion of families in the model neighborhood by amount of rent paid for housing relative to amount of family income; number and proportion of families in the rest of the city by amount of rent paid relative to amount of family income.

c. Number and proportion of families in the model neighborhood by number of persons living in the housing unit relative to number of rooms in unit; number and proportion of families in the rest of the city by number of persons living in the housing unit.

(Because the goal of the model city program is to affect the living conditions of model neighborhood families, the data needed for describing initial conditions are indicated here in terms of number of families living in housing of given characteristics. Much housing data (e.g., census data) are reported in terms of number of housing units of given characteristics within specified geographic locations and not number of families living in housing units of specified characteristics. Where existing data are to be used, therefore, interpolations and adjustments would have to be made.)

Five-Year Objectives

a. To increase the proportion of model neighborhood families living in standard housing units—without decreasing the proportion of families living in standard housing units in the rest of the city by (specify amount).

b. To reduce the proportion of model neighborhood families in the model neighborhood paying more than the income-rent ratio holding for the rest of the city by (specify amount).

c. To reduce the proportion of model neighborhood families living in housing units in the model neighborhood having higher number of persons per room than the person per room ratio for the city as a whole by (specify amount).

d. To reduce the proportion of model neighborhood families living more than one family to a housing unit to the proportion of families living doubled up elsewhere in the city.

One-Year Objectives. In many cases discernible changes in the measures can be achieved within a one-year period; here one-year objectives would parallel the five-year objective statement, varying only in the degree of reduction to be achieved. In other cases there may not be discernible changes within the first year, but essential steps which are prerequisites to making discernible changes in future periods may not have been taken. These steps would be reported in the plan.

2. To increase the supply of standard low and moderate-cost housing in the city and metropolitan area at large to meet existing and projected future demands for such housing.

Measures

a. Rental charges of existing housing supply (excluding substandard units).
b. Sales prices of existing housing supply (excluding substandard housing).
c. Rate and cost of new construction, by unit size.
d. Rate and cost of rehabilitation of substandard units, by unit size.

Initial Conditions

a. Number and proportion of housing units (excluding substandard units) in the city (and/or metropolitan area) by amount of rent charged, in comparison with number and proportion of families renting homes by income categories (using a specified income/rent ratio as basis for comparison).

b. Number and proportion of sales housing in the city (and/or metropolitan area, excluding substandard units) by sales price in comparison with number and proportion of housing owners by income categories (using a specified income/sales price ratio as basis for comparison).

c. Number of new dwelling units started a year (by type, rental, sales price) in the city (and/or metropolitan area).

d. Number of units of substandard housing rehabilitated a year (by type, rental, sales price) in the city (and/or metropolitan area).

Five-Year Objectives

a. To reduce the deficiency between the existing supply of low and moderate-cost rental housing and the existing demand for such housing by (specify).

b. To increase the supply of low and moderate-cost sales housing by (specify).

c. To increase the rate of new construction a year by type of low and moderate-cost housing to (specify).

d. To increase the rate of rehabilitation per year by type of low and moderate-cost housing to (specify).

One-Year Objectives (see statement on One-Year Objectives, above).

3. To provide to all households in the city equal accessibility to all housing in the city and/or metropolitan area with access based solely upon ability to pay.

Measures

a. Tenure (rent or own), by income level.

b. Geographic distribution of Negro and other minority populations, by income level.

c. Availability of existing housing supply to various ethnic, racial or religious groups, by income level.

Initial Conditions

a. Number and proportion of families in the model neighborhood by tenure of housing unit (rent, own); number and proportion of families in the rest of the city by tenure.

b. Number and proportion of Negro and other minority populations by geographic designations (i.e., census tracts) throughout the city (and/or the metropolitan area).

c. Proportion of the housing stock, by price or rental ranges, which is unavailable to various groups on ethnic, racial or religious grounds.

Five-Year Objectives

a. To reduce the differential between the proportion of model neighborhood families owning their own homes and the proportion of families owning their own homes in the rest of the city by (specify).

b. To reduce the proportion of the city (or metropolitan area) in which no Negro and/or other minority family lives by (specify). (Proportion of the city described in terms of the geographic unit used in describing initial conditions).

c. To reduce the proportion of the existing housing stock which is unavailable to model neighborhood families on ethnic, racial or religious grounds by (specify) percent. (Specify for various price and rental ranges and various ethnic, racial and religious groups.)

One-Year Objectives (see statement on One-Year Objectives, above).

NOTES

1. *Improving the Quality of Urban Life: A Program Guide to Model Neighborhoods in Demonstration Cities,* HUD, pp. 6-47, December 1967.

2. This bulletin does not cover the myriad technical issues involved in selecting and utilizing measures, nor does it discuss how the measures relate to each other and how changes in one measure will influence other measures. This Bulletin attempts to provide a common framework for measurement activities. Cities should refer to the bibliography [not included herein–Ed.] for further discussion on measures and their use in the planning process.

3. Output or performance measures are variously referred to as "criteria," "social indicators," or "descriptors," in the literature.

4. Appropriate proposals for problem solution may vary according to the population to be affected. Therefore, where significantly different population groups (defined in terms of race, income, and family status) reside within the model neighborhood, the measures should be applied to both the model neighborhood as a whole and to the different population groupings. This will enable cities to identify the distribution and concentration of the various problems within the model neighborhood; i.e., differences in severity of problems as they affect the different racial groupings, the young as against the elderly, the poor as against the more affluent, etc.

5. The appropriate basis of comparison will depend on the circumstances of the specific city. If the model neighborhood embraces most of the poverty, unemployment, physical blight, etc., of the community, then comparison to more advantaged portions of the city would be appropriate with respect to a number of goals; with respect to other goals, such as housing, comparisons to the metropolitan area might be more appropriate. If the model neighborhood contains only a portion of such problems so that the levels of the rest of the city are themselves quite low, comparison to the metropolitan or regional area–which would include the more advantaged suburbs–would be more appropriate. In small cities in which all or most of the population is included within the model neighborhood, comparison to the county, greater metropolitan area, or even State could be appropriate.

6. This objective illustrates clearly how the concept of gap may or may not be acceptable, depending on local circumstances. Some cities may have programs where there is already more involvement of parents in the model neighborhood, or in some of the schools. Or cities might feel that the involvement of model neighborhood parents cannot be comparable. However, this example has been presented in this form for two reasons: (a) to make it comparable in style to the other examples; (b) to show that even though an objective may be difficult to measure, it should still be stated by the city.

Chapter 19

CHICAGO MODEL CITIES PROGRAM: FIVE-YEAR FORECAST

Office of the Mayor, Chicago Model Cities Program

INTRODUCTION

The goal for the Model Cities Housing Program reflects in broad terms the policies and objectives of the city's general plan. The Comprehensive Plan of Chicago prepared by the Department of Development and Planning identifies seven basic objectives for the city's residential areas. These are:

(1) To improve the environmental quality, facilities and services and the housing quality of all existing residential areas
(2) To meet the housing needs of moderate and low income families and to develop additional financial sources for the purchase and rehabilitation of older property
(3) To change patterns of massive racial transition and to achieve equal housing opportunity
(4) To increase the amount of land devoted to housing and expand the total housing supply within the city
(5) To provide more diversity in choices of housing type within the city
(6) To develop residential density patterns which are related to natural and man-made assets of the city and which encourage more residential diversity in many parts of the city
(7) To distribute and design public facilities so that they provide maximum service to residential areas and encourage participation in community activities

The housing program presented here represents a response to the goals, objectives and program approaches which have been enunciated by the Model Area Planning Councils, the objectives of the Comprehensive Plan and the technical analysis of existing conditions and trends by the Model Cities staff.

Reprinted from *Model Cities Program, II: Five-Year Forecast,* by the Office of the Mayor, Chicago Model Cities Program, 1964, pp. 124-147, 158.

Program objectives have been defined so as to be readily subject to measurable achievement. Program approaches have been broadened so as to include the greatest possible range of project activities as well as to simplify program organization.

Each of the program suggestions and ideas for the housing system generated by the Model Area Planning Councils is encompassed by this framework of objectives and approaches. Program content has also been drawn from suggestions and ideas of public agencies, as well as community groups both city-wide and in the target areas. Of particular note are the contributions made by The Woodlawn Organization, the Kenwood-Oakland Community Organization, and the Lawndale Peoples Planning and Action Committee.

Relation of Goals, Objectives, and Program Approaches

The housing programs which have been developed for the Model Cities target areas are inextricably related to city-wide and metropolitan programs of housing improvement. Improvement of housing conditions in the target areas without corollary improvement in the rest of the city might very well, in the long run, work to the disadvantage of the present residents of the target areas. Further, certain program elements can only be effective if directed toward the larger community of which the Model Cities area is a part. For this reason, the Chicago Model Cities housing program includes certain city-wide objectives and program commitment which will support the improvement effort in each of the four target areas. The following goal and objectives have been established for city-wide housing programs:

GOAL: To insure adequate housing for every family and individual and to develop an environment that will fully support the life style goals of the community.

This will call for the city to:

(1) Develop 50,000 new low and moderate income housing units of which 30,000 are suitable to the needs of large families.
(2) Rehabilitate 150,000 substandard or deficient housing units.
(3) Increase areas of choice for minority groups.

While specific project activity proposed in each of the target areas will vary depending upon the particular needs of the area, target area objectives are identical in form, differing in quantitative measure according to target area needs. Target area objectives seek to:

(1) Increase the proportion of sound, standard housing units to 80%. In 1960, 77.4% of all housing units in the city were in sound condition and contained all plumbing facilities. This percentage has undoubtedly risen somewhat since that date, and therefore a proportion of 80% has been established as an objective for the Model Cities Target Areas.

(2) Remove substandard housing units. While it will probably not be possible to remove every substandard unit in each target area through rehabilitation or clearance, a sufficient number in each area should be removed to reduce the proportion to the city-wide average or less. In 1960, 14% of all housing units were substandard.

(3) Develop new housing with primary emphasis on units for large families with limited incomes. To the extent vacant land can be made available, new housing will be constructed in the target areas which will be compatible with sound planning for the community.

(4) Reduce the proportion of overcrowded units to 10%. Through rehabilitation and redevelopment, it is anticipated that it will be possible to reduce the number of overcrowded units housing more than one person per room to below the 1960 city-wide percentage of 11.7%.

(5) Increase the proportion of owner-occupancy to 30%. As the 1960 proportion of owner-occupancy for the city was 32.7%, the objective for each Model Cities Target Area will be to approximate this city-wide level.

(6) Reduce the proportion of families paying in excess of 25% of income for rent to 30%, which is commensurate to the city percentage for white families.

The project activities which will contribute to the achievement of these objectives fall within three broad program approaches.

A. Improve the existing supply of housing. Through the expansion of renewal programs on a city-wide level it is expected, that over the next five years, an estimated 65,000 residential housing units will be improved to contemporary standards of living through rehabilitation of older structures. Expansion and intensification of the city's systematic code enforcement and Title I programs, along with the implementation of the Neighborhood Development Program, should contribute greatly to the realization of this five year goal. These federally assisted programs will stimulate more private rehabilitation and thus supplement already ongoing activities.

B. Develop new housing resources. The Department of Urban Renewal, the Chicago Housing Authority, and the Chicago Dwellings Association, further assisted by the Neighborhood Development Program and private development, expect to construct, within the next five years, at least 50,000 new residential housing units. This five year goal is within reach because of federal funding available through FHA Section 221 (d) (3) and with the addition of Section 235 and 236 by the Housing Act of 1968. In addition, city agencies are currently making studies in an effort to find tracts of land of sufficient size to make possible the realization of economies in construction. To date one such plausible site has been found (New Town In-Town) and plans are now being formulated for its development with moderate income housing.

C. Increase the housing of individual families. It is the policy of the City of Chicago to assure full and equal opportunity of all residents of the city to obtain fair and adequate housing for themselves and their families in the city without discrimination because of race, color, religion, national origin or ancestry. In keeping with this policy the city is working to develop programs that will reduce the cost of housing purchase and rehabilitation and that will make decent, safe, and sanitary housing available to all income groups. This involves the availability of money from private lending institutions, as well as public programs of community improvement and housing construction. The city will use its housing program capabilities to encourage banks and savings and loan associations to make mortgage loans more readily available in indigent communities. Working with local community groups, city policy-makers are continually searching for direct actions available to the city which will improve minority group housing and eliminate discrimination.

A fourth program approach is applicable to city-wide research and study projects.

D. Research and Development. Developing a program for action which meets with community consensus is no easy task. Such a program must take into account strategic objectives as well as improvement targets. It must be based on adequate factual information, professional judgment, and policy review to assure realism and significance. The action program also needs refinement and detailing which come through analysis and review by both policy-makers and citizens, improved cost-benefit and social analysis techniques, and improved social and physical programming procedures. Only through such research and development can Chicago expect to provide adequate solutions to its existing housing problems.

Strategies and Priorities

Perhaps the single most serious aspect of housing problems in the city is the shortage of standard housing units for large families of low and moderate incomes. An estimated 21,000 families of seven or more persons have inadequate housing. Though these large families comprise only 10% of the total number of families in need of housing assistance, their situation is most acute since the private market provides virtually no resources to meet their need. Therefore, the thrust of public programs must be primarily directed toward increasing the supply of adequate housing for large families of modest means. Until their needs are met, neighborhood renewal and development programs will encounter understandable, popular objection.

The single greatest fear of Model Area residents in respect to housing is the fear of being displaced by renewal and rehousing activity. The Model Cities housing program will aim at improved housing with minimum displacement of present residents. In the first year, primary emphasis has been given to projects which will make use of existing vacant land, staged rehabilitation with minimum displacement, and increasing the capability of Target Area residents to compete effectively in the metropolitan housing market. While planning of redevelopment projects requiring displacement will be undertaken in the first year, implementation of these projects will be scheduled in subsequent years to provide time for the development of maximum possible relocation resources for families, individuals and businesses displaced. This strategy clearly reflects the order of priority established in the MAPC discussions of program strategy.

In the first year, therefore, special efforts will be undertaken to coordinate and improve various conservation and code enforcement programs to upgrade the present supply of housing. To meet the immediate and pressing need for substantially improved property and environmental maintenance throughout

Model Area, Neighborhood Maintenance Corporations will be established as part of the first year strategy. These corporations will perform emergency repairs, train residents in property management and maintenance, make physical improvements to buildings, and conduct workshops for tenants and landlords. The long range objective will be to expand home ownership and to ensure that the property measures up to all code requirements. This will not be accomplished unless special assistance is given to potential or present owners.

Similarly, the Chicago Dwellings Association will continue its efforts to attract private sponsors for rehabilitation, and to secure vacant sites for the immediate construction of modular housing. Experimental techniques of rehabilitation and new construction will be encouraged. Also, various private, not-for-profit sponsors of moderate income housing, which have been attempting to get feasible projects off the ground, will be given special aid and attention.

The housing objectives outlined here will require a monumental increase in the capacity of the public and private sectors to build housing for moderate income families. New construction will have to be increased at an unprecedented rate.

Relationship of Housing Program With Other Components

The Model Cities Housing Program proposed in this submission as the First Year Action Program is necessarily related with several other program components for education and leisure time, but also will be influenced by the success of employment, environment, and transportation programs.

Specifically, school construction and rehabilitation, proposed as part of the Education Component, depend greatly on the amount of housing proposed, the types of units, and the location of new construction which will be undertaken as part of the housing program in each of the model neighborhoods.

Similarly, new housing construction and rehabilitation of the existing housing supply in the model areas must be closely coordinated with the provision of additional play space and other recreational facilities. The proposed program for redesign of street patterns and parkway beautification will greatly enhance all programs of rehabilitation and new construction.

Programs in the Child and Family Services component, which would amend public aid regulations and supplement allotments to families on a demonstration basis, will begin to ease the hardships suffered by low income families and could expand the housing choices available to these families through expanded utilization of the existing leasing program of the Chicago Housing Authority.

The Neighborhood Maintenance Corporation proposal confronts problems identified in housing and in employment. This project proposes the development of community corporations to contract for maintenance services and management of real estate. As part of the project, neighborhood residents would be instructed in management and maintenance skills and provision of emergency repairs.

The Economic Development component includes two proposals which would exert a definite impact on the housing program as it develops over the next five years. Of immediate importance to homeowners and business is an information project which explains the newly developed State Guaranteed Insurance Program for homeowners and business people in areas which have traditionally suffered from standard underwriting procedures. The development of shipping centers and possible improvement of existing business districts will also have a mutually beneficial impact on housing programs in each model area. The equity fund proposed in the first year will make interim financing available to minority contractors and developers.

Programs proposed in the Manpower Component, in the long run, should generate the most significant impact on the proposed housing programs. Specific projects such as the New Careers Program, the Concentrated Employment Program and The Cooperative Area Manpower Planning System will broaden the range of housing possibilities available to model neighborhood residents. The degree of success achieved by such employment programs will constitute the best solution to the existing critical shortage of low income housing in the Chicago Metropolitan Area by raising income levels and the ability to purchase in a broader market.

Constraints

The specific constraints which may impede the achievement of objectives in the housing program fall into three general categories: fiscal constraints, limitations of physical capacity and methods of production. Fiscal constraints include the availability of grant reservations for renewal programs, unit allocations for public housing and FHA BMIR programs, and availability of mortgage money both public and private. Also included would be factors which affect the economic feasibility of private development such as the market interest rate or availability of fire insurance.

In order to achieve the housing objectives, it is essential that there be an adequate and consistent flow of mortgage funds into the low and moderate income market. It is necessary to secure this segment sufficiently to attract prospective investors. Further, financial incentives for private rehabilitation in designated areas should be made available to encourage rehabilitation of dwellings for the low-moderate income group. New sources for mortgage funds must be sought; these new sources depend upon government guarantees and a marketable obligation. Achievement of objectives in housing assumes the availability of funds and a reasonably stable economy.

The limitations of physical capacity would include the availability of vacant land for new development, the administrative capacity of public and private agencies to undertake and effectively implement programs and the ability of communities to develop consensus on plans and programs.

Because of the scarcity of land in the built-up areas of the center city and because of the change in political jurisdiction between these areas and the less built-up suburbs, availability of land for development depends to a great extent on clearance. This process creates an increased number of relocatees, as does rehabilitation involving deconversion. Systems for utilizing scattered, vacant lots should be studied, as should land fill and air-rights projects. Also, arbitrary administrative and code restrictions on density should be analyzed to allow an efficient utilization of land. A substantial net increase in standard units depends to a great extent on technical developments and growth in the rehabilitation and construction industries. Although the strain placed on administrative capacity would be substantial, the availability of adequate numbers of skilled workers may also be critical.

Also necessary are techniques for developing community consensus. This should involve expediting community discussion; training community leaders, and improving communications. Caution must be exercised, however, to train the leadership strata without eliminating spontaneous response and suggestion.

Constraints within the methods of production include the need for technological improvement in the housing industry, tight statutory restrictions and administrative regulations, and an inflexible labor market and standards.

For a variety of reasons, technological advances have not been absorbed into the housing industry. Although some studies and projects to date have concerned themselves with cost reduction in the basic structural shell, the same type of studies must be applied to mechanicals and equipment and labor costs. Failures thus far in attempts at reducing cost through mass production indicate a need for careful cost analysis and market research. Savings achieved in this manner have often been offset by unexpected new costs such as the transportation and storage of prefabricated units.

Many public agencies have been inflexible in the administration of statutory regulations, and have made no allowances for alternative solutions. Among these are the trade codes such as building, plumbing and electrical which have remained unresponsive to possible advancements. Zoning ordinances have often placed arbitrarily high and rigid restrictions on medium density residential areas. Administrative restrictions on rental limitations and architectural and site designs, and the evaluation techniques employed severely limit effective use of federal programs for new construction and rehabilitation.

One of the most serious problems requiring attention of the construction industry is the labor market, its practices and standards. The fluctuations and uncertainty of seasonal work and the adherence to traditional construction patterns and techniques have hampered efficient production. Studies for increasing efficiency are needed. Without the adoption of one or more modernizing techniques, there will be an inadequate number of skilled workers available to dramatically increase production to a level necessary to achieve the housing goals both locally and nationally.

TABLE 1

Objectives and Program Approaches for Housing: Chicago Model Cities Program, North Model Neighborhood

Objective	*Achievement Measure*	*Five-Year Achievement Target*	*Program Approach*	*Programs Included**	*Expected Five-Year Impact*
1. Increase the proportion of sound housing units	% of total	80%	A. Improve the existing housing supply	1. DUR–Conservation 2. Neighborhood Service Program	6,500 deficient units rehabilitated 7,000 sound units renovated
2. Replace substandard housing units	Number	8,000 units		3. Chicago Dwellings Association 4. Building Department	8,000 substandard units removed
3. Develop new housing units	Number	6,000 units	B. Develop new housing resources	1. DUR–Redevelopment 2. CHA–Public Housing 3. CDA–Conventional and Modular	1,000 public housing units
4. Reduce the proportion of overcrowded units	% of total	10%		4. Private development 5. New Town In-Town	5,000 moderate-income units
5. Increase the proportion of owner-occupied units	% of total	30%	C. Increase housing opportunities for individual residents	1. Additional homeowners 2. Renters assisted	5,500 families 4,000 families
6. Reduce the proportion of families paying in excess of 25% of income for rent					

*NOTE: For a description of these programs and the responsible agencies, see text herein, pp. 467.

A survey by the staff of the President's Committee on Urban Housing reports that there are 23 major public and private participants in the housing production process and that there are 17 major public and private sources of laws, rules, and practices, which restrict the process. Some of these restrictions are easily overcome; others involve intensive research and analysis. The Model Cities housing program recognized these needs. It is expected that the program will encourage modifications in these areas and substantially reduce impediments to the achievement of the housing goals.

HOUSING PROGRAMS

Program Descriptions

The city-wide housing program is comprised of the improvement and expansion of existing public and private agencies. It is designed to develop inner city communities in general and the Model Cities target areas in particular. The nature and content of these program elements are described below for each participating agency or special project activity.

Department of Urban Renewal

The Chicago Department of Urban Renewal has primary responsibility for carrying out the city's federally assisted Urban Renewal Programs. In the course of little or more than two decades, better than a billion dollars in private and public funds have been invested in Chicago's effort to improve the quality of urban life through programs of slum clearance, redevelopment and neighborhood conservation.

Urban Renewal activities are currently being executed in project areas totaling over 2,250 acres. Completed programs were responsible for the redevelopment of over 500 acres of land in Chicago.

Thus far, approximately 7,000 new homes and apartments have been completed on renewal sites and another 10,000 are presently committed.

The cumulative total valuation of rehabilitation in the existing conservation projects including code enforcement is estimated at $55,043,826 covering more than 35,000 dwelling units.

The City's first four completed industrial renewal projects have an assessed valuation of $17,151,000 as compared to $5,046,000 before redevelopment, while some eight-one buildings have been completed or are in varying phases of construction, providing employment for an estimated 6,900 persons, an increase of 3,089 jobs over the previous employment figure of 3,811.

Approximately 32% of the total land area in all renewal projects thus far has been designated for public and institutional reuse. Almost 18% of the land area after redevelopment has been allocated for commercial and industrial reuse, and 26% has been devoted to residential redevelopment.

On June 14, 1966, the voters of Chicago approved at referendum six general obligation bond issues totaling $195,000,000. One of these six bond issues was

$50,000,000 for community improvement programs to be undertaken by the Department of Urban Renewal. Since approval of the bond issue, the staff of the Department of Urban Renewal has developed specific program recommendations for the city's renewal program. Twenty separate areas of the city have been identified for a variety of urban renewal programs which will involve an estimated total cost of approximately $180,000,000. The federal capital grants which will be required are estimated at $120,000,000.

Following passage of the 1968 Housing Act, the Department of Urban Renewal has prepared and submitted to the Department of Housing and Urban Development an application for funding the city's first Neighborhood Development Program. The Neighborhood Development Program contemplates both planning and implementation activities in twenty-seven areas of the city including previously approved projects which would not be brought to completion within a one-year period and community areas where planning has been proceeding in consultation with local community organizations. In addition, Chicago's renewal program includes the completion of on-going activities in existing Title I projects and the implementation of additional programs in the Model Cities target areas.

Through the expansion of renewal programs on a city-wide level, it is expected that at least 20,000 new residential units will be constructed on sites made available for redevelopment and an estimated 65,000 units will be improved to contemporary standards of living through the rehabilitation and renovation of older structures over the next five years. Approximately 100 acres of land will be made available for much needed open space in the city's residential communities for additions to school sites, playgrounds and neighborhood parks. The public and semi-public community facilities which serve vital functions in these residential communities will be improved and enlarged through the provision of additional space totaling an estimated 150 acres. The pattern of retail shopping will be improved through the elimination of obsolete strip commercial areas and its consolidation into compact areas; it is estimated that 75 acres of land will be available for new shopping centers designed to better serve residential areas.

Altogether the program will encompass a total land area of nearly 10,000 acres. It is anticipated that the activities to be undertaken will involve the clearance and redevelopment of approximately 2,000 acres of land; 8,000 acres will be the subject of a concentrated program of building, rehabilitation and conservation.

Neighborhood Service Program

The city's Neighborhood Service Program is a concentrated code enforcement and rehabilitation service program being carried out in ten areas of the city. The program receives federal financial assistance under Section 117 of the 1965 Housing Act.

During 1967, nine service centers were opened in Austin, East Garfield Park, West Garfield Park, Lakeview, Lower West Side, South Shore, Uptown, West Lawndale, and West Woodlawn.

The specific areas covered by the program comprise 10% of the city's population and about 11% of its housing, with a substantial proportion of these units being substandard. In all, these areas cover approximately 6,000 acres, containing about 33,000 buildings and 139,000 dwelling units.

The Neighborhood Service Centers are staffed by specialist personnel to carry out the code enforcement and rehabilitation program. Housing inspectors conduct systematic surveys of the area and also respond to complaints. Rehabilitation and financial advisors help landlords and tenants to eliminate code violations and upgrade housing in the most efficient and economical way, and assist in obtaining necessary financing.

Community Relations representatives maintain close contact with community organizations, property owners and tenants to increase communication and understanding of the program. Relocation advisors provide necessary services where families may be displaced. Tenant education specialists advise tenants of their rights and duties, and furnish information on housekeeping, safety, and sound health practices.

As of June, 1968, a total of 80,000 units had been inspected in the nine service areas. The inspections revealed that 61,000 units contained code violations, of which 36,000 have subsequently been brought up to code. The remaining 55,000 units in the nine existing areas will be inspected and deficient units will be brought to code compliance within the next two years. It is expected that portions of the four Model Cities Target Areas would be added to the workload of the Neighborhood Service Program. Based on current and anticipated workload, it is expected that 80,000 units would be brought up at least to code standards during the next five years.

Department of Buildings

The Department of Buildings' comprehensive program for code compliance includes annual fee inspections, inspections based on complaints and referrals, the program to eliminate dangerous and hazardous buildings, and the systematic community and neighborhood survey and enforcement program, including participation in rodent control and service center activities.

During 1967, the Department of Buildings made a total of 602,024 inspections of all types, including a record total of 158,252 housing code inspections. The results of these enforcement activities are reflected in the permits issues in 1967 for the correction of code violations. Nearly 2,700 permits were obtained for the repair and rehabilitation of residential, commercial, industrial and institutional structures. These permits represented a record estimated investment of nearly $2.5 million.

Permits were issued in 1967 to build 11,680 new dwelling units, compared with 10,446 in 1966. While permits for new apartment construction increased significantly during 1967, other types of construction declined. During the year the total dollar volume of permits issued for buildings and repairs was $299,354,275, compared with the 1966 record total of $506,826,336. The Lakeview, Uptown, Rogers Park, and Douglas community areas were among the highest in new building construction as indicated in the Department of Buildings' community area report for 1967.

In 1967, the city's program for the demolition of open, abandoned dangerous and hazardous buildings established an all-time record by removing 1,340 buildings containing 3,725 substandard dwelling units. This represented an increase of 20% over the previous record of 1,111 structures removed in 1966. The 1,340 buildings removed in 1967 included 140 single family homes, 586 apartment buildings, 207 mixed-use apartment buildings, and 407 non-residential buildings.

Of the total number of buildings demolished, 811 were removed through court action, such proceedings being undertaken only after every effort had been made to have the owner repair the building. As a result of notices from the Department of Buildings, 529 buildings were removed by the owners themselves. Under this program the city spent $1,204,004 for building demolition in 1967. To recover some of these funds, liens are placed against the remaining property.

For the past two years, the city's demolition program has been aided by a federal matching grant under the provisions of Section 116 of the 1965 Housing Act. This grant has assisted in financing an intensified demolition program in three areas covering about 65% of the city. During 1966 and 1967, a total of 1,792 buildings were demolished in these three demolition grant areas.

An appropriation of $750,000 has been allocated in the city's 1968 corporate budget for the demolition program, an amount almost double the $400,000 allocated in 1967. It is estimated that some 1,400 structures will be demolished in 1968, about 65% of these being removed by the city.

As a result of these continuing efforts, significant progress has been made in processing the removal of dangerous, dilapidated and abandoned buildings. As a rule, within 30 days of a first inspection, a case is filed to secure a court order authorizing demolition of the structure unless permits are secured to rehabilitate the building.

Another significant aspect of the code enforcement program is the growing use of Certificates of Inspection which are issued at the request of the owner or agent as a record of any major building or zoning violations which may exist on the property at the time of inspection. In 1967, the Department of Buildings issued 1,075 certificates, a 34.9% increase over the 667 issued in 1966. Since the program began in 1965, the department has issued 2,231 certificates. It is anticipated that this program will be greatly expanded in the coming year, as financial and real estate institutions are becoming increasingly aware of its purpose, and the Federal Housing Administration has made it a prerequisite for loan approval.

In 1967, the Department of Buildings instituted a new procedure in which a "Notice of Violation" is formally transmitted to the Office of the County

Recorder when the city has filed a law suit against a property. This notice is made a part of the individual property record and is designed to reduce the transfer of defective properties.

In 1967, the Department of Law filed 4,815 suits to compel building owners to bring their buildings up to code standards or to remove them as hazards. A total of 1,059 demolition suits were filed and 1,525 suits were filed for injunctions, receiverships and vacations. With the transfer of emphasis to code-violation cases before the Chancery Division of the Circuit Court, the legal enforcement procedure is being expedited. Suits are now filed seeking direct injunctions or vacation and demolition orders, instead of the initial imposition of fines with further prosecution necessary to secure more definitive compliance action.

Over the five year period of the Model Cities Program, it is expected that augmented code enforcement efforts will result in initial inspections of 85,000 structures each year, and that, as a result of compliance action, a total of at least 75,000 structures will be brought into compliance with city codes.

Building permits issued for code work throughout the city can be expected to reach a total of 300,000 over five years. The number of violation notices issued are expected to average about 70,000 per year and satisfaction of violations eliminated should total 150,000 cases over the next five years. The total number of buildings demolished as a result of code enforcement efforts by the Building Department is expected to reach 5,000 structures in the next 5 years, with the greater proportion of these buildings being eliminated during 1969 and 1970. At least 25,000 suits to compel building owners to meet code standards or to remove hazardous structures can be expected to be filed by the Department of Law through the life of the Model Cities effort.

Chicago Housing Authority

The Chicago Housing Authority, a municipal not-for-profit corporation, was created by State law in 1937 to clear slums and to build and operate decent, safe and sanitary housing for the city's low-income families. To carry out its responsibilities the Authority is empowered to enter into contracts with, and to obtain financial assistance from, private sources or the Federal, State or local governments. The Authority is governed by a five-man Board of Commissioners who serve without pay. They are appointed by the Mayor of Chicago, subject to approval by the State Housing Board.

By the end of 1968, the Authority had cleared more than 920 acres of slums and blight and replaced them with 34,500 standard housing units for 29,200 families and 5,500 elderly in 74 housing developments. An additional 1,500 low-income elderly persons and families were housed under the Authority's Section 23 leasing program, whereby the Authority leases dwellings in private housing and subleases them to low-income families, the difference in rent being subsidized by the federal government. Total number of dwellings in operation at the end of 1968 was 36,011.

The Authority's operating expense for 1968, including extraordinary maintenance, betterments and additions, is estimated at $30,500,000. To enable the Authority to keep rents within the budgets of low-income families, the federal government will contribute approximately $26,800,000, which will be used to pay interest and principal on 40-year bonds sold to finance building construction.

During 1968, the Authority continued to expand its housing for Chicago's low-income population. Some 887 elderly units were completed in five high-rise elevator buildings, including 233 units at Sheridan and Leland, 188 at Lincoln and Sheffield, 125 at 69th and South Chicago, 165 at 64th and University, and 174 at 49th and Langley. All the buildings were fully occupied at the end of 1968.

At the end of 1968 there were 1,632 family units and 2,492 elderly units under construction or in various stages of land acquisition or design. Among the family housing developments to be completed in 1969 or 1970 are 187 units at 12th and Washtenaw, 109 at Adams and Woods, 151 at 42nd and Drexel, 256 on scattered sites, and 98 at 43rd and Princeton. Also to be completed were 453 at 39th and Cottage, 6 at Sedgwick and Wisconsin, 12 at Hudson and Sedgwick, 169 at 31st and Prairie, 186 on Lawndale scattered sites, and 6 at 75th and Eggleston.

Also in progress at the end of 1968 were 122 dwellings in Lawndale being rehabilitated by the Authority for low-income families. Among the elderly housing developments under construction are 339 units at 43rd and Princeton, 194 at 31st and Wentworth, 138 at Dickens and Burling, 100 at Clark and Webster, and 194 at Clark and Irving. Also, 218 units at Chestnut and Noble, 121 at Wicker Park, 203 at 43rd and Evans, 206 at Lincoln and Sheffield, and 450 at Sheridan and Devon. Under design are 224 at 64th and Yale and 105 at Larrabee and Wisconsin.

During 1968, the Authority approved the sale of Racine Courts, a 120-unit City-State financed low-income housing development at 110th and Racine, as a private cooperative, with preference being given to present occupants who wish to buy their own dwellings. By the end of the year, several residents had already signed purchase agreements and others were ready to close deals.

Also, during the year the Authority purchased and installed 30 mobile homes to provide interim or "instant" housing for low and moderate-income families living in Lawndale buildings being rehabilitated. The mobile homes, now all occupied, are located in the vicinity of the buildings being rehabilitated. Locating the mobile units nearby allows the families to stay in the neighborhoods and the children in the same school during the short period of rehabilitation.

As a pilot project, the Authority is acquiring from the Federal Savings and Loan Corporation 37 repossessed buildings containing approximately 120 dwellings. They will be rehabilitated and sold at cost to moderate-income families.

In December, 1968, the Authority approved plans to apply to the federal government for a program reservation of an additional 10,000 units. It is the intent of the Authority to locate these units throughout the city, with 1,500 allocated to the leasing program (in addition to 1,000 units recently applied for under the program) and the balance of 8,500 for construction of new family and elderly units. Family units will be mainly rowhouses, duplexes and single-family dwellings. Elderly buildings will consist mainly of high-rises, which are preferred by senior citizens.

There is a need for an additional allocation of low-income housing for Chicago. It is the intent of the Authority to request an additional allocation of 5,000 units for 1969 and 5,000 units for 1970, subject to the availability of these units by the government. This would increase to approximately 24,300, the number of additional units to be added to the City's housing for low-income families. By the end of 1973, the Authority expects to be operating some 60,300 units, of which 39,200 will be for families, 16,400 for elderly, and 4,700 for families and elderly in the leasing program.

Chicago Dwellings Association

The Chicago Dwellings Association was created as a non-profit corporation to use public funds as equity for FHA insured and conventional mortgages in the construction and rehabilitation of moderate income housing. It is governed by a Board of Directors whose members serve without pay and are appointed by the Mayor. This Board consists of the five commissioners of the Chicago Housing Authority, plus five members who are solely Association members.

The Association was established in 1948 to broaden the city's housing efforts, especially for those families whose incomes are just above the public housing eligibility ceiling and too low to obtain adequate quarters in the private housing market. From 1948 to 1965, the Association constructed a total of 900 dwelling units for moderate income families, consisting of 112 single family houses and 728 apartment units in three buildings. All the single-family units have been sold but CDA has retained ownership of and manages the apartment units. By the end of 1967, an additional 166 dwelling units in 44 structures were under construction.

In 1965, the Board of Directors approved an augmented receivership program, whereby the courts may appoint the Dwellings Association as receiver for deteriorating buildings. As appointed receiver, the Association recommends to the court either rehabilitation of the structure, or, if that is economically infeasible, demolition. This procedure has assisted the city's Building Department and Department of Law in accelerating action on problem buildings. Through 1967, the CDA has been appointed receiver for 321 buildings containing 3,035 dwelling units.

The initial phase of the Chicago Dwellings Association's city-wide rehabilitation program is underway in four communities: Uptown, Lawndale, South Shore and Lakeview. In May of 1966, the Federal Housing Administration agreed to earmark $3,000,000 for the Association to carry out a rehabilitation program of approximately 500 apartments under the FHA 221 (d) (3) insured mortgage program of 100% acquisition and rehabilitation costs, three percent interest, and 40 years amortization. This program, known as the "Chicago Plan," permits a number of buildings to be packaged together under one mortgage. As of December 1967, a total of 567 dwelling units were being rehabilitated through the "Chicago Plan" and an additional 28 dwelling units had been rehabilitated through normal procedures.

During 1968, the Chicago Dwellings Association initiated an "instant housing" program utilizing prefabricated units which can be combined to provide two and four story townhouses designed for moderate income families. A factory for the production of these units is to be developed in Chicago. Anticipated production is expected to reach 2,000 units per year.

Participation by the Dwellings Association in the housing field over the next five years is expected to provide 10,000 housing units for moderate income families on a city-wide basis. This would include approximately 5,000 new units of conventional or modular construction, and 5,000 rehabilitation units in the existing housing stock.

In response to the low and moderate income housing shortage in Chicago, the Dwellings Association has proposed the development of a consulting service designed particularly to assist potential non-profit sponsors of 221 (d) (3) housing. A service of this type would be particularly valuable in encouraging non-profit groups, which typically have only limited knowledge of the housing field, to invest available resources in expanding the housing supply in this critical area.

Private Development

Increasingly, in recent years private developers have made use of FHA Section 221 (d) (3) BMIR, Mortgage Insurance in new housing developments in the city of Chicago. For example, in 1967, of the FHA insurance commitments for 6,336 new housing units, approximately two-thirds or 4,140 were for developments to be built under this vehicle. Approximately 800 of these (d) (3) units committed in 1967 were for developments within urban renewal projects and over 3,300 for units proposed for construction on sites privately acquired throughout the city. While 1967 very nearly doubled the number of units committed in previous four years combined, applications in 1968 would tend to demonstrate a continuing high level of interest by private developers in construction under this program on privately acquired sites. With the addition of Section 235 and 236 by the Housing Act of 1968, there is every reason to believe that the experience of the last two years will be reflected in continued developer-interest in moderate income housing construction. Therefore, in looking to the achievement of city-wide objectives set for the Chicago Model Cities Program, it is anticipated that private development of moderate income housing will continue at a rate of at least 3,000 units per year.

New Town in-Town

One of the major constraints to the development of moderate cost housing has been the unavailability of tracts of land of sufficient size to make possible the realization of economies of construction. With the exception of the urban renewal program and two not-for-profit developments on the far south side, development of moderate income housing in the city has been largely in elevator buildings containing predominantly smaller units. However, redevelopment through slum clearance typically does not make an appreciable net addition to the housing inventory and also creates the additional burden of relocation. Therefore, to achieve a significant addition to the housing supply without the concomitant loss of existing housing units and to provide additional relocation resources, particularly for families with children, the city will undertake to make available for private development, a tract of undeveloped land of approximately 500 acres.

Chicago Mortgage Bankers Association

The CMBA has proposed to undertake two programs which will serve to stimulate private development in inner city areas and broaden the housing opportunities of residents. The first program will be to establish an advisory committee enlisting the aid of other professional groups to provide counsel and assistance to local not-for-profit groups interested in undertaking housing development.

The second program will be to establish a referral service to assure that inquiries regarding FHA financing receive attention by a member of the Association. This referral service will be an integral part of the CMBA objective of arranging FHA insured loans, on terms comparable to the most favorable available in the Chicago Metropolitan areas, for the following purposes:

(1) Owner-occupant, inner city properties containing up to four dwelling units.
(2) Financing a home elsewhere in the Chicago Metropolitan Area for present residents of inner city areas.

Loans under this program are to be initiated and serviced by members of the Chicago Mortgage Bankers Association.

Funds for the program will be made available by leading Chicago financial institutions, supplemented by funds from the "billion dollar program" of life insurance companies.

It is anticipated that this referral service and lending program will be of benefit to the Model Cities Program of the city of Chicago.

The ability of CMBA to implement this program depends heavily upon action in 1969 by the Illinois State Legislature to exempt FHA (and Veterans Administration) loans from the usury statute. Present laws have sufficient ambiguity to have caused a number of members of the Association to withdraw from any FHA lending program until legislative action is taken.

Chicago Commission of Human Relations

Established in 1947, the Commission on Human Relations was the first such city agency in the United States to concern itself with assuring fair and equal treatment to all people, regardless of race, religion or nationality.

Fifteen civic leaders are appointed by the Mayor to serve as unpaid Commissioners. They establish policy and have the basic responsibility for the Commission's work. A great number of other dedicated people are involved in the important work of the Commission. Hundreds of private citizens serve on advisory committees and dozens of organizations and agencies cooperate to establish equality of opportunity throughout the city.

Responsibility for enforcement of the Chicago Fair Housing Ordinance is among the major responsibilities of the Human Relations Commission. Commission staff is responsible for the collection of all facts pertinent to complaints filed against owners and managers of housing accommodations. Reports summarizing individual investigations are reviewed by the Commission on Human Relations and a finding is made. The Commission then decides whether there is probable cause that the ordinance has been violated. If the Commission determines no probable cause, it dismisses the complaint. If the Commission determines that probable cause exists, the respondent is summoned to a Conciliation Conference in an effort to settle the matter.

The Conciliation Conference is conducted with the parties to the complaint and is presided over by a Commission Conciliator. The conference is held within five days after mailing of the notice of the Conciliation Conference. All parties to the complaint must attend the conference in order to settle the matter in a positive way. The only reason for non-attendance that is accepted is one of genuine emergency.

If the Conciliation Conference fails to produce an agreement which is satisfactory to both the parties and to the Commission, the law requires that a public hearing be called. The public hearing is conducted to ascertain if a violation of the Fair Housing Ordinance has or has not occurred. In the case of a real estate broker, if it is found that the Fair Housing Ordinance has been violated, the Commission shall recommend to the Mayor that the broker's license be suspended or revoked. In the case of any other person charged, if a violation of the Fair Housing Ordinance is found, the Commission shall recommend to the Corporation Counsel that he initiate an ordinance violation action in the Circuit Court. The maximum fine that can be assessed is $500.00

New Town Out-of-Town

To meet the future needs of the people of Chicago and to assure orderly development, the city through feasiblity studies will search for land which could lend itself to construction of a "new town." A new town development would be related to the Model Neighborhoods, to transportation, employment and centers of culture. New Town Out-of-Town, a study being implemented by the Department of Development and Planning, is an example of the comprehensive steps being taken by the city to affect its present and future growth. This represents an allocation of resources specifically directed to meet critical housing needs. Success will have a great impact upon the housing situation of the entire city and particularly the Model Neighborhoods.

Affirmative Action Program (Community Renewal Program–Leadership Council)

As an integral part of the Community Renewal Program for the city of Chicago, the Leadership Council will develop an affirmative program for a 5 to 10 year period setting forth specific objectives and programs to meet these objectives. The explicit purpose of the affirmative action program is to expand housing opportunities available to minority groups in the city through increases in the quantity and improvements in the quality of available housing, and the elimination of discriminatory barriers obstructing open access to housing.

The program will be expressed in terms of specific quantified action targets to be met in improving the quality of housing available to minority groups. It will survey, analyze, and program full use of all public means and other direct actions available to the city to improve minority group housing and eliminate discrimination. Consideration will be given to local laws, administrative organization, citizen participation, employment, education and housing of low-income and minority populations. The Leadership Council will develop this comprehensive program through consultation with key persons in each of the following major functional and occupational groups within the Chicago Metropolitan Area:

(1) Government (Town, City, County, State and Federal)
(2) Industry
(3) Labor
(4) Developers
(5) Education (Public and Private)
(6) Realtors
(7) Financial Institutions
(8) Religious Institutions
(9) Hospitals and Welfare Agencies
(10) Community and civic Groups

Project Threshold

The Chicago Housing Authority has proposed a program which provides a broad range of assistance to families living in CHA units who are about to reach the maximum income limitations for public housing eligibility. Purpose of this endeavor will be to minimize the hardships typically experienced by such families when they enter the private housing market. The Authority now permits over-income families to pay an economic rent and remain indefinitely in public housing if they are unable to find adequate housing in the private market. Also, the Authority grants preference to over-income families in purchasing City-State financed housing developments sold as private cooperatives. Such preference is also given over-income public housing families by the Chicago Dwellings

Association in buying duplexes and single family dwellings built by the Association on scattered sites.

Cook County Department of Public Aid Housing Program

In a program directed against substandard living conditions CCDPA is withholding rent from landlords offering such housing to Public Aid clients. In addition, CCDPA has joined with a number of community organizations to support the tenants who have filed suits against owners who fail to improve their properties.

The Cook County Department of Public Aid and the Department of Urban Renewal of the city of Chicago have worked out a cooperative arrangement for relocating public assistance families and individuals displaced as a result of public activity such as urban renewal projects, building code enforcement expressway construction, etc. where the Department of Urban Renewal is responsible for relocation. Public Assistance recipients frequently are affected by the renewal program and need assistance in securing new housing as well as providing some financial assistance if needed. The Cook County Department of Public Aid–Public Assistance Division assists in interpreting to applicants and recipients the urban renewal program and the services provided by the Department of Urban Renewal.

In line with the above cooperative arrangement the Cook County Department of Public Aid–Public Assistance Division follows established procedure in providing allowances for needed furniture, emergency assistance to meet the new rental and, if necessary, approval for rental payments in excess of agency standards. The Public Assistance Division caseworker assists the Department of Urban Renewal by providing information such as size and composition of family or physical handicaps that will assist the Department in relocating a public assistance family.

Development of New Land Resources

In order to more effectively mobilize the resources of the city in attacking the shortage of standard housing for families of low and moderate income, the Department of Development and Planning will undertake a research program to seek out and determine the feasibility of utilizing land presently devoted to other purposes for residential development. This study program will explore, among other possibilities, the following:

(1) The possibility of converting existing, but under-used, park land to either temporary or permanent residential use with subsequent replacement at more suitable locations through the urban renewal program
(2) The feasibility of constructing air rights over the city's expressways
(3) The use of air rights over the CTA Rapid Transit terminals and yards
(4) The utilization of vacant or marginally used property along the Chicago River
(5) Potential development of the railway yard south of the Loop as railroad terminal consolidation proceeds.

Centralized Property Data System

Development of a centralized property data system, utilizing the most recent achievements in the field of computer science will be undertaken in order to facilitate the compilation and use of the latest property data by a wide range of public and private agencies.

Study of Ways to Improve Amenities of Public Housing

A coordinated study by the Chicago Housing Authority and the Department of Development and Planning to identify a broad range of alternative ways in which existing public housing developments could be improved. Major emphasis would be given to reducing the institutional atmosphere which exists in some projects and to meeting the particular needs of low income families.

During 1968 the Authority conducted a survey of all its residents to find out what physical improvements should be made at each housing development to improve the quality of life. On the basis of their responses, the Authority applied to the federal government for a $27 million modernization grant. The Authority's proposal was approved and an initial sum of $10 million made available to begin on the priority improvements. During the next five years the Authority plans to make other surveys and seek federal funds that may become available to improve amenities in its public housing developments.

Study of Tax Structure Relationship to Maintenance of Older Residential Structures

The Planning Department will undertake to identify ways in which the present tax structure could be modified in order to encourage regular maintenance and rehabilitation by the property-owners of the significant stock of existing residential structures.

New Construction and Rehabilitation Techniques

Because the solutions of existing housing problems in the Chicago area are dependent on the development of new techniques for rehabilitation and new construction, it has been proposed that the major agencies which are responsible for housing in the city initiate a demonstration program to test and improve such innovation techniques. Such techniques could then be applied on a massive city-wide scale in order to effectively deal with the present housing situation.

In order to facilitate this study, the city of Chicago will immediately apply to the U.S. Department of Housing and Urban Development to be included in the 20-story "in-city" experiment using new technology to produce large scale multi-family housing. The city of Chicago will also apply to the Department of Housing and Urban Development for participation in the experimentation authorized by Congress in Section 108 of the 1968 Housing Act, which permits HUD to sponsor the production of 1,000 housing units per year for five years in each of five years in each of five technologies. By participating in this pioneering venture, Chicago can have a key role in developing what has long been needed—a sophisticated mass housing industry.

Neighborhood Introductions

A. North

Residential properties in the Uptown Area consist mainly of large structures containing relatively small rental apartments. There were 30,246 housing units in the Target Area in 1960, of which only about four percent were owner-occupied, while in the rest of the city nearly one-third the housing units were tenanted by their owners. Over four-fifths of the housing units were in 10-or-more unit structures, but in the rest of the city three-fourths the residential structures contained less than ten housing units.

Although the buildings were large, the individual apartments were small. Over one-third of the units had only one room, and another 23% had only two rooms. Comparable figures for the city as a whole were 9% and 8% respectively. About one-half the families had lived in the housing unit they occupied in 1960 for less than two years. Over 14% of the units in the Target Area were vacant, compared with a city-wide vacancy rate of less than 5%.

The median rent in the area was $80 per month. This was $8.00 per month lower than the median rent for the city. But since so many of the apartments in the area had two rooms or less, and in view of the general condition of these apartments, it is quite probable that area residents were paying higher rents for the size and quality of the accommodations they received than were residents of most of the other areas in the city. At the time of the 1960 Census, 12.3% of the units in the area were overcrowded (containing more than one person per room). The overall percentage for the city was less than 2%.

Practically all residential structures that existed in the area in 1960 were built before 1929, with only 405 units being built in 1930s and 303 between 1940 and 1960. While only 202 units were built between 1950 and 1960, the Census of Housing for 1950 and 1960 shows an increase of 5,075 units during the decade. Part of this increase can be explained by the change in the Census definitions from "dwelling units" in 1950 to "housing units" in 1960. For the most part, however, this increase indicates a very substantial amount of conversion of bigger units to a larger number of small units.

Of the 30,246 units in the area in 1960, a total of 10,714 were substandard (lacking all essential plumbing and/or dilapidated). In the rest of the city less than 14% of the units were substandard.

The socio-economic character of the area does not seem to have changed much since 1960. However, a building boom has developed recently. Approximately 125 units were built between 1960 and 1963, and no units were built in 1964 and 1965. In 1966, however, permits were issued for the construction of 668 units; in 1967, for 357 units; and for the first 10 months of 1968, for 1,035 units. Practically all of these units for which permits were issued in 1966-68 were, however, built with some form of assistance. Of the permits for 668 units issued in 1966, a total of 436 were for Chicago Housing Authority housing for the elderly. Most of the remaining permits were issued to limited-dividend developers operating with 221 (d) (3) funds. In all, FHA mortgage commitments were approved for 1,374 new 221 (d) (3) units in the area. The number could have been much larger but for the lack of 221 (d) (3) funds.

In all, close to 2,300 new units were constructed in the area since 1960. At the same time about 750 units were demolished, for a net gain of over 1,500 units.

A substantial portion of the North Target Area is now included in either a federally assisted urban renewal project or code enforcement project. Program priority should therefore be directed toward effective completion of these programs already begun and the initiation of appropriate action in that portion of the target area not yet scheduled for treatment.

To date, public housing developed in the North Target Area has been primarily designed for elderly persons. As there is an expressed need for low-income family housing, priority should also be given to the development of public housing units for large families.

As the most serious constraint in the Uptown Area is the availability of land with which to meet all of the diverse community needs, effort must be made to maximize the use of that which is available. For example, perhaps greater emphasis here should be placed on leasing programs for low income families so as not to require the use of land solely for public housing.

The North Model Cities Target Area contains within its boundaries the greater portion of the Uptown Conservation Area. This includes the Uptown Neighborhood Development Area, which is coterminous with the conservation area, and Uptown Project I, the first urban renewal conservation program for the area.

The 460 acre Conservation-Neighborhood Development Program area is bounded by Argyle Street on the north, West Montrose Avenue on the south, Marine Drive on the east and North Clark Street on the west. Of this area, some 65 acres or 14% of the total lie outside the Model Cities target area.

The first phase of the Neighborhood Development Program for the Uptown Area is Project I. The gross area of Project I is 144 acres, containing residential, commercial and institutional land uses. The project is generally bounded by Argyle Street on the north, Marine Drive on the east, West Montrose Avenue on the south, and North Sheridan Road on the west.

The program for this project is one of rehabilitation, building as much as possible on the basic community strengths already present, in conformance with the goals and objectives established in the Uptown Conservation Area Plan. Thus, a major objective is the restoration of the area as a prime residential section of the Uptown community.

According to the Plan, 16 sites will be redeveloped in low density residential use, restricted to 20 dwelling units per acre; one site will be medium density at a maximum 60 units per acre; and one site will be high density at a maximum 200 units per acre. This will result in the construction of approximately 635 new dwelling units. Of these, 600 will be constructed within the Model Cities target area.

Four sites have been designated for public uses which will provide land for expansion of the McCutcheon School site, new school-park sites at Hazel and

North Target Area

Goal: Housing	Initial Conditions 1/68-12/68	Year I 1/69-12/69	Year II 1/70-12/70	Year III-V 1/71-12/73	Total
Objective 1: Increase the proportion of sound housing units to 80%					
	18,052 units 60%	22,785 units 77%	25,403 units 85%	25,552 units 90%	7,500 additional sound units
Objective 2: Replace 8,000 substandard housing units					
	10,714 units 35%	9,714 units 33%	7,714 units 26%	2,714 units 10%	8,000 substandard units replaced
Objective 3: Develop 6,000 new housing units					
		500 units	1,750 units	3,750 units	6,000 new units constructed
Objective 4: Reduce the proportion of overcrowded units to 10%					
	3,735 units 12%	3,000 units 10%	2,000 units 7%	1,812 units 6%	1,923 overcrowded units removed
Program Approach					
A. Improve existing housing supply					
1. Deficient units rehabilitated		500 units	500 units	500 units	1,500 units
2. Sound units renovated		500 units	1,500 units	5,000 units	7,000 units
3. Substandard units removed or rehabilitated		1,000 units	2,000 units	5,000 units	8,000 units
B. Develop new housing resources					
1. Public housing		0	250 units	750 units	1,000 units
2. Moderate income housing		500 units	1,500 units	3,000 units	5,000 units
Objective 5: Increase the proportion of owner-occupied units to 30%					
	1,076 units 4%	1,350 units 5%	2,100 units 7%	6,100 units 22%	6,100 units 22%
Objective 6: Reduce the proportion of families paying in excess of 25% of income for rent to 30%					
	50%+ (estimated)	48%	41%	30%	30%
C. Increase housing opportunities for individual residents					
1. Additional homeowners		250 families	750 families	4,000 families	5,000 families
2. Renters assisted		500 families	1,000 families	2,500 families	4,000 families

Wilson Avenues, and a small park or tot-lot on Ainslie Street. Three sites have been identified for additional hospital facilities in the vicinity of Weiss Memorial Hospital and the Fox River Pavilion.

The project plan provides for the acquisiton of 121 parcels of property and the relocation of an estimated 1,400 families, 400 individuals, and 45 business establishments. Approximately 70% of these activities will take place within the Model Cities target area.

Future renewal programs in the Uptown Area will focus upon the rehabilitation of existing sound residential neighborhoods, the reorganization of the regional commercial complex, and the expansion of institutional facilities.

The Lawrence-Broadway-Wilson Area of Uptown is a regional shopping center of historical significance. One of the objectives in the conservation program is the reorganization and redevelopment of the shopping area to meet contemporary shopping requirements. The presently conceived approach to achieve this end utilizes the major existing stores as the nucleus for future expansion. Redevelopment of the area should result in a more compact center with fewer stores, larger variety of shopper's goods, interior pedestrianways free of vehicular traffic, and sufficient off-street parking.

Chicago City College is planning the construction of a new junior college in the area bounded by Wilson, Montrose, Racine and the CTA right-of-way. The campus will cover approximately 15 acres of land and will accommodate 10,000 students, half of whom will be in full-time attendance. The development cost is expected to be between $23 and $25 million.

The Uptown Neighborhood Development Program area encompasses a substantial portion of the Model City Target Area. Only that part of the target area south of Montrose Avenue will not be a part of a federally assisted rehabilitation program. Therefore, it is recommended that the existing Neighborhood Development Program be extended to the southern portion of the target area. Implementation of an additional rehabilitation program in this relatively small area would cost an estimated $300 thousand of which $100 thousand would be local and $200 thousand would be the federal grant requirements.

The Chicago Housing Authority is now operating three buildings for senior citizens in the Uptown Area: 163 units at 3930 N. Clark, 235 at 4645 Sheridan Road, and 201 at 4945 Sheridan. Operating expenditures for 1968 were approximately $287,520. Because of the difficulty of securing vacant sites, the Authority has not previously constructed any family housing in the Uptown Area.

The Authority has, however, leased more than 310 dwellings in standard private housing in Uptown and subleased these units to low-income families. Under the 20,000-unit program reservation for which the Authority will seek federal approval, it is expected that an additional 1,000 units in private housing will be leased and 500 new family units and 500 new units for the elderly will be constructed by 1973.

In Uptown, the Chicago Dwellings Association expects to rehabilitate 1,250 existing units and construct 620 new units through conventional methods and 380 modular homes within the next 5 years.

In every target area programs of city-wide relevance designed to increase the housing opportunities of inner city residents will be brought to bear with particular emphasis. These programs are described in the city-wide housing program. . . .

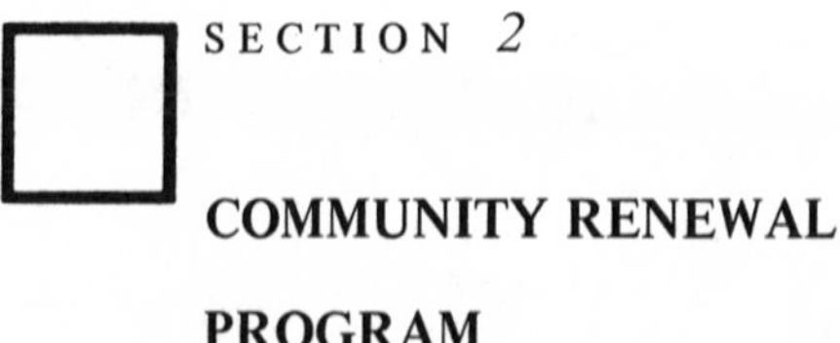

SECTION *2*

COMMUNITY RENEWAL PROGRAM

Chapter 20

APPLICATION OF PROGRAMMING APPROACH TO DEVELOPMENT PLANNING

Philadelphia Community Renewal Program, City Planning Commission

PROGRAMMING CONCEPT IN THE CRP STUDY

In 1968 you may receive a copy of the *Annual Development Program for Philadelphia.* Its Table of Contents may read:

A. Foreword: A brief written review of highlights in program performance for the previous year.

B. Annual Review of Conditions: A brief description of basic trends (economic, social, land use) observed during the prior year and how these influence the City's development assumptions and forecasts and objectives.

C. Statements of Objectives: A summary in charts and text of the City's goals and the broad implementing objectives which underlie its development investments for the next five years.

D. Program Reports: For each program, a description of its objectives, agency responsible for its execution, interrelationships with other agencies and programs, method of evaluation, foreseeable performance targets, and costs by year over the next five years.

E. Financing the Program:

(1) Charts of available governmental resources Federal, State, and Local
(2) Chart of present financial commitments
(3) Private investment required
(4) Summary of programs by sources of funds and by total costs, operating and capital requirements per program.

Reprinted from *Community Renewal Programming* (Technical Report No. 4, December 1962), pp. 6-14, Program Plan Format, and Footnotes, and from *Development Programming as Applied to West Philadelphia* (February 1964), i-vii, Appendix B pp. B-1–B-8; both prepared by the Philadelphia Community Renewal Program, City Planning Commission.

The CRP study staff is working toward the construction of such an *Annual Development Program.* Although a final product embodying *all* aspects of development activity may not be in hand by the end of the study period, each of the necessary preliminary studies will have been framed in this overall context, and each will lead to the eventual production of such a document.

The Annual Development Program places heavy emphasis on the statement of objectives and the listing of programs. It implies the involvement of non-pulbic agencies and private citizens. It also suggests that important elements of the present Capital Program will have been absorbed into it as well as many aspects of the Operating Budget.

Definition of a Program

A properly descriptive program statement would suggest a mobilization of resources toward definable objectives. It would convey a picture of what an organization, in this case a community, wants to accomplish as distinguished from the material it purchases, buildings it constructs, people it hires, contracts it lets, or land it acquires. A program statement would mix these ingredients and describe their purpose.

The Defense Department has allocated its resources on a program basis since 1949. The B-70 Bomber Program controversy in the summer of 1962 illustrates the concept of programming in action. The discussion in Congress and in thypress centered on what this bomber could contribute to our national defense which alternative missile programs could not. The money, engineering, hardware, manpower and contracts involved were subordinated to the basic *choice* between competing weapons programs and their projected performance.

The CRP staff sees great advantage in employing a comparable approach to Philadelphia's municipal development. The staff recognizes on the one hand, the implications of such a suggestion but, on the other, it notes a current trend already in this direction within the City administration. For instance, each operating budget request which calls for an increase of funds, a proposed expansion in program or a proposed new program must now be justified by a program statement and by a statement of how the new funds will be spent by object class and by the recurring or non-recurring nature of the expenditure. In recent years, also, four year projections of funds for all new programs have been called for by the Director of Finance.

The following advantages may accrue from extending the approach:

1. By making our program objectives explicit, policy makers and citizens alike can be presented with a manageable array of alternatives. From this list they can select and combine, emphasize or defer programs according to their own preferences. They can be aware of what is foregone in their decisions as well as what is adopted.

Few people can now intelligently and rationally make these decisions in the light of any true measure of their relative significance and impact. Within the program framework these choices would be clarified. For some it may simply mean sharpening the choice between money to be expended to improve living conditions versus money to improve employment opportunity. To others the choice will demand a much closer inspection of the alternatives. Nevertheless the program framework provides a common language for citizen and official alike, and therefore permits a joint pattern of decision-making.

2. Programs also provide a common means for relating physical development accomplishment with accomplishment in other realms of activity. For example, it may prove possible to evaluate the relative effectiveness of additional expenditures for clearance of substandard houses as compared to the same expenditure for human relations assistance in neighborhoods of less dilapidated structures. More important than any precise measurement, these alternative uses of resources would be posed in relation to one another under a program approach which would clarify the possible choices.

3. Budget analysis of a program makes possible the use of new analytical techniques to describe how variation of the amounts of money assigned to a program will affect the accomplishments of the program. Prediction of changes in results of a program by changes in investment gives the decision-maker a much better knowledge of the likely consequences of his budgetary acts. Ideally budget analysis of programs would also include cost comparisons of alternative means to the same level of accomplishment.

APPLICATION OF A PROGRAM APPROACH TO PHILADELPHIA DEVELOPMENT PLANNING

A full cataloguing of Philadelphia's existing programs related to community renewal is a first step already completed in the direction of a development program. The staff has chosen to illustrate, through selection of the most familiar program categories, how an inventory of programs might be structured for all aspects of development. Even this partial list includes over 100 different, definable programs and subordinate activities, each mobilizing limited community resources in a distinct manner, each aimed at some special need, and each with its own administrative structure, its own fiscal and administrative ties to higher levels of government and its own practical limitations.

The Statement of Needs

Concurrent with the initial inventory of programs, therefore, CRP has to inventory needs and to do it in such a way that the resulting picture can be continually updated. This work is concurrently in process and involves a complex job of data collection, classification and analysis. The CRP study has begun several work elements designed to determine needs fully and sharply. Studies of property conditions, social resources, land use and community facilities including schools, public and private economic factors and physical design are in process.

The relation between the CRP determination of needs and the program inventories cannot be sufficiently emphasized. The staff does not intend to list what the City can do and then set in motion a process of finding places to do it. Rather the staff wants to discover what has to be done and then to call upon the existing inventory of programs to supply whatever contribution it can towards the objectives.

Land use and community facilities needs have, of course, been embodied in the *Comprehensive Plan.* The *Comprehensive Plan* has, however, certain limitations for development programming. The first of these is the acknowledged fact that the present Plan omits certain critical elements of physical development such as schools, utilities and private institutions, all land-demanding uses which require a share of the City's limited resources. Second, the Plan deals primarily with a desired future distribution of land uses and community facilities, physical by-products of future decisions based on objectives, some of which will bear no direct relation to the physical environment. Without a systematic presentation of the various interim objectives which may have to be met before the called for distribution results, the Plan serves more as a backdrop for decisions than as a primary target for accomplishment. Third, the Plan is concerned more with future land use relationships resulting from public and private activity than with designing a course of action to be followed during the extended period of time required to attain these relationships. In this sense the Plan provides an inadequate basis for the staging of activities.

For these reasons, the Comprehensive Plan can only be considered a part of the framework for actions under the CRP. It must be further enriched, tested and amended; it must be used to maximum advantage but not to the exclusion of the broad range of the City's non-physical renewal problems and programs designed for their solution.

Setting the Objectives

A comprehensive analysis of needs takes on meaning when compared against sets of aims or goals which tie together the various objectives of all the programs and activities contributing to the total development process. As has been demonstrated in the discussion of the *Comprehensive Plan,* the goals range beyond the traditional sphere of the physical planner. Consequently, to meet the requirement of these goal statements the CRP will rely heavily upon the City administration for contributions by the professionals responsible for these separate programs.

To illustrate the concepts presented heretofore, the staff has drafted for discussion purposes a description of this difficult material concerned with multiple goals.

The CRP staff sees the total scope of present City investments broken down into six major functional categories each with a predominant goal to which each of the individual program objectives grouped under it bears a substantial relation:

> Investment in People; Investment in Property; Investment in Housing and the Physical Environment; Investment in Transportation; Investment in Economic Growth; Investment in General Support.

Investment in People. All programs listed under this major category have in common a product or service having a direct benefit to the general pubic as separate individuals or families.

> Health; Shelter and Care; Recreation; Human Relations; Reading and Research; Guidance; Law Enforcement/Crime Prevention; Confinement and Rehabilitation; Education and Vocational Training; Financial Assistance; Fire Protection.

Investment in Property. The programs listed below have in common the objective of providing the necessary public services for the development and service of property, public and private.

> Streets; Street Lighting; Utilities; Refuse Disposal; Traffic Devices.

Investment in Housing and the Physical Environment. Programs under this heading are those which either act on or have as a primary aim improvement in housing or the environment for people.

Goals	*Implementing Objectives for Housing and Physical Environment (1st level)*
Investment in People	*New Construction and Conversion* To assure that the City has an adequate supply of dwellings to accommodate families and individuals with reasonable housing wants who want to live in Philadelphia
Investment in Property	*Acquisition of Dwelling Accommodations* To assure that families and individuals with reasonable housing wants are able to acquire dwelling accommodations satisfactory to them
Investment in Housing and the Physical Environment To assure that every family and individual who wants to live in Philadelphia has an opportunity to satisfy reasonable housing wants in a good physical environment	*Maintenance and Improvement* To assure that owners and occupants of existing dwellings have an opportunity to satisfy reasonable housing wants in terms of maintenance and improvements in their dwellings and immediate surroundings
Investment in Transportation	
Investment in Economic Growth	*Controls and Regulations* To assure that adequate controls are maintained over changes to structures or the remainder of the environment, which safeguard all persons
Investment in General Support	

Implementing Objectives

Goals	*1st Level*	*2nd Level*	*3rd Level*	*4th Level*
People			*Credit Assistance*	207 FHA Mortgage Ins. 213 FHA Mortgage Ins. 220 FHA Mortgage Ins. 221 FHA Mortgage Ins. 231 FHA Mortgage Ins. Nursing Home FHA Mortgage Ins.
			Direct Loans	FHA Insured Home Improvement Loans
	New Construction and Conversion	*Financing Aids* To reduce the monthly cash outlay for rent (price) of new real estate to its market level	*Land Write Down*	Title I Non-Title I
Property	Acquisition of Dwelling Accommodations		*Tax Subsidy*	Redevelopment Authority dwellings Housing Authority dwellings
			Direct Construction	State subsidy to construction of low rent homes
Housing and the Physical Environment		*Construction Agents* To make possible the necessary instruments for low rent/price housing	*Limited Dividend Housing Corp.* *Redevelopment Authority* *Housing Authority*	
	Maintenance and Improvement	*Land Assembly, Improvements Disposition* To guide contrucstion to certain locations	*Title I* *Non-Title I* *Limited Dividend Co.* (condemnation with approval of State) *Land Utilization* (tax delinquent properties)	
Transportation	Controls and Regulations	*Technical Assistance* To smooth out financing process and to guide location	*Promotion, Brokerage and Expediting Services*	ODC Private Non-Profit Corporations, WPC
Economic Growth		*Research & Development* To raise profit margins and stimulate construction at various price levels	*Building Products* *Housing Needs*	
General Support				

Goals	1st Level	2nd Level	3rd Level	4th Level
People			*Credit Assistance*	203 FHA Mortgage Ins. 207 FGA Mortgage Ins. 213 FHA Mortgage Ins. 220 FHA Mortgage Ins. 221 FHA Mortgage Ins. 231 FHA Mortgage Ins. Nursing Home FHA Mortgage Ins.
Property	New Construction and Conversion	*Financing Aids* To reduce the rent (price) of real estate to its market level	*Direct Grants*	Rent Certificates Relocation
			Direct Loans	Loans by the Pa. Housing Agency P.L. 1688 ($450,000 appropriated; agency members not appointed)
Housing and the Physical Environment	*Acquisition of Dwelling Accommodations*	*Law Enforcement* To eliminate discrimination in the housing market and prevent tension and violence	*Human Relations Services* Commission on Human Relations *Human Relations Unit* Police Department	
Transportation	Maintenance and Improvements			
Economic Growth	Controls and Regulations	*Technical Assistance* To provide brokerage services and to guide location	*Relocation Guidance Services*	Central Relocation Bureau Services
			Human Relations Guidance Sercices	
General Support			*Promotion, Brokerage Expediting Services*	Non-Profit Corps such as West Phila. Corp.

Goals	*1st Level*	*2nd Level*	*3rd Level*		*4th Level*
People	New Construction and Conversion	*Maintenance Level* To keep record current of condition of structures and to obtain reasonable efforts to compliance with minimum acceptable standards of safety and sanitation	*Measurement and Control*	*Code Inspections Compliance*	Area Code Inspections Complaints Licensed Multiple Dwellings Redevelopment Surveys
				Public Remedy	Building interior repair Nuisance abatement on lots and in vacant buildings Dilapidated building demolition
Property			*Education*		*Community Relations (L % I)* *Tenant Education Programs*
	Acquisition of Dwelling Accommodations	*Property Rehabilitation* To stimulate the reinvestment of time and funds into existing property	*Financing Aids* *Construction Agents* *Land Assembly*		similar to those for *New Construction* similar to those for *New Construction* similar to those for *New Construction*
Housing and the Physical Environment			*Technical Assistance*		*Promotion Brokerage* *Friends Self-Help* *Leadership* *Neighborhood Improvement (L & I)* *West Phila. Corp. Demonstration*
			Research & Development		similar to those for *New Construction*

Transportation

Economic Growth

General Support

- *Maintenance and Improvements*
  - *Area Improvements* — To stimulate the reinvestment of time and funds into the existing neighborhood
    - *Public Improvements and Services*
      - *Schools*
      - *Recreation*
      - *Parking (residential)*
      - *Streets and Lighting*
      - *Welfare*
      - *Health*
      - *Refuse Collection*
      - *Police Protection*
      - *Air Pollution Control*
    - *Clearance*
      - *Title I*
      - *Non-Title I*
      - *Amortization (zoning)*
    - *Technical Assistance*
      - *Community Organization Planning and Execution*
        - Clean blocks
        - Rat control
        - Garden blocks
        - 4H Club gardens, playlots
        - Neighborhood Renewal Corps
      - *Notification*
        - Zoning Advisory Service
        - Liquor License Advisory service
      - *Counsel*
        - Neighborhood zoning counsel
  - *Area Reconstruction* — To replan and reconstruct portions or all of neighborhoods when its capacity for satisfaction of any reasonable housing wants has been exhausted
    - *Survey and Planning*
    - *Acquisition and Relocation*
    - *Demolition*
- Controls and Regulations

Goals	*1st Level*	*2nd Level*	*3rd Level*	*4th Level*
People				
Property				
Housing and the Physical Environment	New Construction and Conversion			
	Acquisition of Dwelling			
	Maintenance and Improvements			
	Controls and Regulations	*Safety in Construction* To prevent harm to person or property caused by faulty construction	*Building Code, Plumbing and Electrical Ordinance Review*	Plan Examination Site Inspection
			Construction Permits Issuance	
			Construction Follow-up Complaints Inspections	
			Electrical Plan Examinations and Inspections	Plan Examination Inspections
			Plumbing Permits Issuance	
			Water and Sewer Construction Permits Issuance	
			Street Use Permits Issuance	
			Commercial and Industrial Compliance	Plan Examinations Permits Issuance for oil burners and Air Pollution control Inspections
		Control of Nuisances To regulate the activities of potential nuisances	*Circuses* *Overhead Wires and Poles* *Outdoor Advertising* *Signs* *Others*	
		Control of Land Subdivision and Development To prevent unhealthy arrangements of houses in relation to each other and to public services	*Design* *Improvements* *Administration*	
		Control of Land and Structure Use and Bulk of Structures To prevent unhealthy and uneconomic changes in land use and structures	*Land Use Planning and Control* *Zoning Administration*	
Transportation				
Economic Growth				
General Support				

Investment in Transportation. The programs listed below are keyed by the objective of providing major transportation facilities, rail transit, highways, parking, water, air.

> Major Intra-City Transportation; Commuter Transportation; Major Inter-Regional Transportation; Parking for Major Traffic Centers.

Investment in Economic Growth. The City now has a battery of activities and programs that are primarily motivated by a desire to keep the City prosperous.

> Promotion; Industrial Aid; Commercial Aid; Major Special Facilities; Economic Research.

Investment in General Support. Without the programs listed below the City Government could not function.

> Administration (Planning, Records, Management, Property, Law); Elections; Justice/Prosecution; Personnel.

Of the six major categories of current investment the one dealing with "Investment in housing and the physical environment" is closest to the present concept of urban renewal and to the core of CRP's concern. It is with this in mind that a draft of an integrated system of objectives has been set out in detail to illustrate the principles of the array of programs represented in this category.

The system of objectives so framed shows the directions toward which the programs aim. Once the analysis of existing conditions produces actual dimensions of needs which must be met, then the objectives can be converted into work or program targets for the short-range period covered in the Development Program. The charts represent at this stage a proposed system for future decision-making. Alternative measures can be tested within the system for contribution through the various steps toward the accomplishment of the goal. In this way a total picture of accomplishment can be built up through intervening steps.

The origin and defense of this approach come from two present sources in the Federal Government. As indicated earlier, a primary source of actual experience comes from the Defense Department which has divided its operations into nine major programs, sufficiently packaged into sub-programs to permit analysis and choice. The nine programs serve as the basis of an extensive planning and control system of Defense Department program elements and resources required.[1]

A second source derives from a paper written by Raymond E. Kitchell, Director, Office of Management and Organization, Bureau of the Budget.[2] On the subject of objectives Kitchell says meaningful objectives can provide management with (1) coordinated planning, (2) a basis for decentralization, (3) a method of control and (4) a system of indoctrination, training and motivation. He goes on to say:

> "It is often *useful to break down long-range goals* into short and intermediate range objectives or targets which represent steps toward the accomplishment of the long-range goal. The creation of interim objectives has several advantages:

1. Objectives can be made more meaningful, precise and tangible.
2. They can provide a more workable time span in the establishment of realistic target dates.
3. They can provide benchmarks for the measurement of progress in the achievement of long range goals.
4. Interim objectives can provide a bridge between the known and the unknown, or the realistic and the unrealistic.
5. And finally, interim objectives, because they can be made more specific, are more useful to management for programming coordination and control purposes."[3]

Program Plan Reporting

As a first draft the system of objectives must be examined for completeness and consistency. For this examination to be meaningful, uniform reporting of all programs contributing to the implementation objectives is required. The reporting must go deeper than mere project listings. A Program Plan format such as shown on the following pages would recast a program statement into terms which would provide these advantages.

1. Program objectives could be compared with the tentative implementation objectives appearing on the charts. For example, one secondary implementation objective under "New construction" is "Financing aids. To reduce the monthly cash outlay for rent (price) of new real estate to its market levels." Five different types of means are available as shown on the chart headed "New construction and conversion." For each of these types and for each of the programs listed under them there should be statements of objectives. Thus, Section 220 of the U.S. Housing Act provides mortgage insurance on new construction or conversion projects for different types of dwellings. The insurance reduces the carrying charges on a project of this sort. Therefore, there is a substantial tie-in of objectives between the secondary and lower levels of implementation objectives. The tie-in between the primary and secondary levels depends upon the impact of this insurance program on the actual production of additional dwellings. For this information we have to turn to measures of performance.

2. The second advantage of the Program Plan is that it forces the program reporter to judge his program in terms of performance. If the program's impact bears no substantial relation to the objective, then the system will break down. In the case of 220 insurance, the performance must be measured in terms of the housing produced at a certain price level which would not have been produced without this financial aid.

3. The other advantages of the Program Plan are directed at assistance in top level policy-making. The program's characteristics, the types of conditions which warrant and lead to the successful application of the program, its reliance on other programs and other agencies, its method of evaluation and the costs, are all essential parts of the decision-maker's knowledge before he can rationally approve application of the program to any given area.

NEXT STEPS TOWARD COMMUNITY RENEWAL PROGRAMMING

This report has described the commitment of the CRP staff to community renewal programming as a first step in the creation of an annual process for program and budget analysis of all city activities. Although the concept embodies all city activities, the CRP staff believes there would be limited utility

Suggested Program Plan Format:
Philadelphia Community Renewal Program

Program No. *Date:* *Agency:*	
Public ( ) *Private* ( ) *Existing Program* ( ) *New Program* ( ) *Modified Program* ( )	*Permanent* ( ) *Temporary* ( ) *Research* ( ) *Pilot* ( ) *Demonstration* ( )
Program Title:	
Program Objectives:	Indicate the primary and secondary goals to which this program applies. Identify more specific objectives and sub-objectives. Identify specific agency objectives for this program.
Program Description:	Itemize program components, subprograms, or major activities. Describe agency criteria for applying the program. Describe phasing of activities as necessary.
Basis for Involvement:	State specific statutory or other authority for conducting the program.
Preconditions for Effectiveness:	Describe the particular needs, problems, conditions, or services which this program is designed to meet, remedy, or provide.
Program Relationships:	Describe the administrative organization for this program, including its tie-in with other agencies, public and private.
Specific Targets for Accomplishment:	For each objective stated earlier, define a target for accomplishment expressed (a) in numerical units, (b) over a period of years reasonable for this program, and (c) in cumulative as well as annual terms.
Program Evaluation Methods:	Identify methods for charting, reporting, controlling, or appraising progress toward each target expressed above.
Resources Required:	Show in tabular form the dollars spent on this program by source, capital or operating fund, annual and five-year past experience, annual and five-year projection, and expenditure category.
Alternative Programs Considered:	Describe possible alternatives for meeting the same general objectives and why these alternatives were rejected.
Problems or Difficulties:	Describe problems foreseen and possible remedies for the successful operation of the program.

in the detailed exposition at this time of a plan for all City operations based on the concept. Such a plan could only be overly presumptive and beyond the scope of the City's contract with the Federal Government. If the first steps towards community renewal programming prove successful, then an orderly extension of programming to other activities of the City may be occasioned.

At the outset the CRP staff has to satisfy the contract requirements of recommending alternative programs for improvement in the physical environment, especially in the areas of housing and economic growth. These are the traditional responsibilities of the Office of Development Coordinator, Planning Commission, Department of Licenses and Inspections, Redevelopment Authority and Housing Authority, all of which are represented on the CRP Committee and the Interagency Committee on Housing. In the process of meeting these contract requirements the CRP staff will be relying heavily on existing methods for stating objectives, measuring of need and analyzing programs which have been used in the Comprehensive Plan, housing inspection scoring systems, and the Capital Program. The staff wants to foster the continued evolution and refinement of these methods.

If there is a further principle under which the CRP staff is operating, it is that program planning and evaluation must be an integral part of each agency's operations. The CRP can assist in the creation of a uniform reporting system, but cannot usurp in any way the responsibility of existing agencies. Nonetheless, there will be short and long range ramifications of the program approach on the administrative organization of the City government. A special work element will be devoted to this subject later on in the CRP study. The work element will have to answer some of the following questions implicit in this report. How will agreement be reached within the City administration on the analysis of existing conditions and the setting of objectives, initially for community renewal activities, eventually for all City activities? How can citizen representation be improved in the formulative stages of program planning? Who will be responsible for new program research and analysis of program interrelationships?

The immediate task for the CRP staff is to design a work outline and schedule which will provide answers along two lines. One is the intensive question of whether or not workable measures of program accomplishment can be uncovered for each of the programs making a contribution to community renewal objectives. The other is the extensive question of whether or not program targets of accomplishment can be set for a section of the City over a stated period of time and how much relation one type of target bears to another, in physical accomplishment, in use of manpower, in use of public funds, in relocation of the population, in amount of community organization participation and in amount of private investment required among others.

Part of both the intensive job of analyzing programs and the extensive one of tentatively assigning and relating programs will be the search for new activities, new programs which might improve the City's community renewal operations. Sources for new ideas may evolve from discussions with the executives or staffs of the operating departments, from people living with problems on a day to day basis in neighborhoods, from newspaper accounts and published reports from other cities. The CRP staff will continually search for these ideas.

The end product of these two parallel study elements will be a statement of community renewal objectives and preliminary sets of alternative programs for each planning district of the City. Initial results will be delivered to the Planning Commission's District Planning Division for incorporation into the West Philadelphia District Plan and Program.* In the logic of work schedule for the CRP study this delivery will have to take place well before the June 1963 deadline for presentation of the draft of a West Philadelphia District Plan and Program.

However, before community renewal objectives for West Philadelphia can be stated even preliminarily, and this applies as well to each of the successive planning districts, there has to be a summary of current need in the district. The CRP staff is preparing a work outline for bringing together the necessary information to summarize needs in West Philadelphia in terms of community renewal activities. The information will include:

(1) Public plans for the district evidenced in the Comprehensive Plan, the School Construction Program and the backlog of capital projects in each operatg agency.
(2) Private plans for areas within the district evidenced by major educational and health institutions, by developers, by business groups, by industrialists and by neighborhood groups.
(3) Surveys within the CRP study such as the property data analysis, spcoal profile and field reconnaissance of the physical planning team.
(4) Interviews and meetings with elected officials, representatives of the administration, technicians in the field, resident groups and service organizations.
(5) Reading of reports of hearings, files of complaints, files of new construction and zoning appeals and newspapers.

Only after a synthesis has been made of this material can an ordered set of objectives be drafted and alternative sets of programs be aligned to meet these objectives.

For the detailed program information to be useful beyond its incorporation into the tentative program for West Philadelphia, the CRP will maintain a program plan book. The book will grow out of the explicit statements of the actual program administrators, which will be solicited by CRP staff members using the program outline shown in the test of this report. The staff members will make themselves available to the agencies involved for purposes of data collection and review, even employing additional professional assistance on a consulting basis as necessary to come up with instructive measures of cost and accomplishment. Because the success of the CRP as an on-going instrument of decision-making depends upon the degree of involvement of each agency in program planning, the staff cannot substitute itself for the agency's staff. Furthermore, successful financing of the City's share of the CRP study depends upon generous donations of staff services by City agencies.

*See the following Section.–Ed.

Initially the book of program plans will be descriptive of the types of community renewal activities which the city has conducted or could possibly conduct. Once an annual process for revising these plans has been instituted the plans will begin to reflect what the agency plans to do in the future.

The initial inventory of programs has been framed with the system of objectives leading to the goal of "Housing and the physical environment" in mind. As soon as a goal and system of objectives has been drawn for "Economic growth," a further list of programs will emerge. The important point is that the overall system recognizes the multiplicity of objectives in some programs and provides a means for comparison of secondary impact on a number of goal structures outside the primary purpose of the program. Rat control for instance contributes not only to environmental health, but also to neighborhood pride and upkeep.

The following programs, which at first glance seem to make a contribution to the goal of "Housing and the physical environment" as stated previously, comprise the initial inventory for which the CRP staff will attempt to obtain program statements. The list is by no means complete and will be supplemented by new programs as they are devised and by additional programs which may be peculiar to districts other than West Philadelphia which has received early emphasis.

Initial Program Inventory

Redevelopment Authority

Title I Renewal
Non-Title I Renewal
Construction/Rehabilitation of Dwellings
Community Organization Service
Relocation Service
Housekeeping Self-help Service
Others

Housing Authority

Construction/Rehabilitation of Dwellings
Homemaking Consultant Service
Social Services
Others

Office of Development Coordinator

Financing Aids (FHA 203, 207, 213, 220, 221, 231, Nursing; Home Mortgage Insurance, Insured; Home Improvement Loans, Penna. Housing Agency; Loans, State subsidy to construction of low rent homes.)
Open Space (Title 7 Open Space)
Promotion, Brokerage, Expediting Service
Others

Department of Licenses and Inspections

Land Utilization of Tax Delinquent Properties
Code Compliance
Redevelopment Area Code Survey

Neighborhood Improvement
Zoning Administration
Licensing and Permits
Others

City Planning Commission

Land Planning and Control (Zoning Changes)
Control of Land Subdivision
Others

Department of Streets, Sanitation Division

Sanitation
Street Lighting
Street Grading and Paving
Snow Removal
Others

Department of Public Health

Vector Control (Rats)
Air Pollution Control
Others

Department of Recreation

A program plan for each type of facility on which recreation activities are based.
Others

Department of Public Property

Residential Parking
Others

Police Department, Juvenile Aid Division

Gang Control
Human Relations
Others

Department of Public Welfare, Youth Conservation Service

Field Operations Counseling Service
Community Leadership
Youth Conservation Corps
Referral (with Police Department Juvenile Aid)
Area Youth Work (with Crime Prevention Associations)
Others

Commission on Human Relations

Public Law and Employment
Housing
Community Relations

Board of Education

Community Extension Centers
Child Care Centers
Homemaking Consulting Service
A program plan for each type of facility in which education activities are based
Others

West Philadelphia Corporation

Promotion, Brokerage, Expediting Service
Demonstration Rehabilitation Clinics
Community Commons
Others

Neighborhood Garden Association

Garden Blocks
4-H Clubs
Special Gardens and playlots
Others

Neighborhood Renewal Corps

Self-help Parks and Playgrounds
Others

Citizens' Council on City Planning

Zoning Advisory Service
Liquor License Advisory Service
Neighborhood Zoning Counsel Service
Public Policy Review and Recommendation
Others

Philadelphia Housing Association

Public Policy Review and Recommendation
Others

NOTES

1. See Study Report "Programming System for the Office of the Secretary of Defense." OASD(C) Programming, Directorate for Systems Programming, Washington, D.C. 1962.

2. Raymond E. Kitchell, "A Summary of Current Planning Concepts" Office of Management and Organization, Bureau of the Budget, U.S. Government, 1962. (An unpublished paper for internal use by the executive branch.)

3. Ibid. p. 10. Kitchell talks of the hierarchy of management objectives as "means-end chains" quoting from William N. Newman and Charles E. Sumner Jr. *The Process of Management Concepts, Behavior and Practice,* Prentice-Hall, New Jersey, 1961. Kitchell says (p. 9) "The broad overall goal or objective is broken into sub-objectives which in turn become the means, when accomplished, for achieving the overall objective. In turn, the sub-objectives themselves may be broken down into more detailed ends whose accomplishment, when realized, would lead to the successful attainment of sub-objectives. Such means-end chains fit into the hierarchic structure of complex organizations, and correspond frequently to the various levels. From the standpoint of higher authority, a particular objective may be looked upon as one of the means for accomplishing its major goal; for the subordinate officials this sub-objective is looked upon as the major goal for their activity rather than the means. This difference in viewpoint depending upon the decision-maker's place in the organization, is one of the major causes for the confusion that exists in the definition of terms."

DEVELOPMENT PROGRAMMING AS APPLIED TO WEST PHILADELPHIA

This report, "Development Programming as Applied to West Philadelphia," is intended to be read with the District Plan for West Philadelphia. While the Plan presents a series of firm policy recommendations and planning proposals, this report is illustrative and not a statement of policy. It is intended to serve the following purposes:

(1) To explain the concept of programming and to apply it to West Philadelphia.
(2) To consider questions of staging and timing in carrying out proposals of the District Plan.
(3) To determine what existing programs are available and how they might best be arranged to carry out the objectives of the Plan.
(4) To disclose areas where available programs fall short of meeting Plan objectives and where, as a consequence, there is a need for modified or new approaches.

This report is an early product of the City's Community Renewal Program which seeks to develop a logical and sensitive framework for making development policy. It marks a first and experimental step illustrated for a major City district toward preparing a Development Program in accord with the planning system illustrated in Chart A and explained in detail in the District Plan itself.

The broad objectives of the District Plan itself may be summarized as follows:

Assurance of a Safe and Secure Environment for Living
Development of an Environment of Quality
Opportunity for Mobility and Freedom of Location
Expansion of Employment Opportunity
Provision for Educational Opportunity
Respect for Variety and Individuality

In setting forth programs furthering these objectives, it should be clearly understood that the present report is based upon *existing programs, available information,* and *current resources.* The CRP staff is now examining new programs to meet existing gaps; it is constantly improving information about the District; and it is assessing the resource requirements of City development. The following report will need to be revised in the light of changes stemming from these further studies. The requirements of the City's other districts will also affect the content of this report and the make-up of a first City-wide Development Program. Then, and only then, will the kind of program proposals

COMPREHENSIVE PLAN

SCALE · CITY WIDE
CONTENT · GOALS FOR PHYSICAL DEVELOPMENT
TIME · 20 TO 40 YEARS

COMMUNITY RENEV L PROGRAM

SCALE · CITY WIDE
CONTENT · RESOURCES FOR CARRYING OUT DEVELOPMENT PLAN
TIME · 20 TO 40 YEARS

DISTRICT PLANS

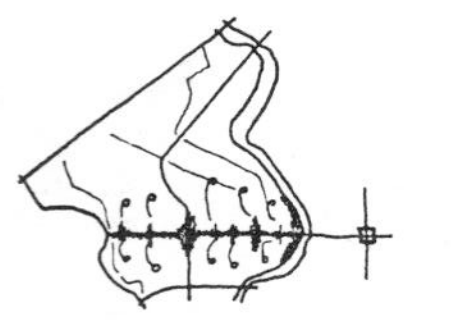

SCALE · DISTRICT
CONTENT · DISTRICT OBJECTIVES AND OPPORTUNITIES FOR SOCIAL AND PHYSICAL DEVELOPMENT
TIME · 20 TO 40 YEARS

ANNUAL DEVELOPMENT PROGRAM

SCALE · CITY WIDE
CONTENT · PROGRAMMING OF CAPITAL PROJECTS AND OPERATING PROGRAMS TO MEET NEEDS AND GOALS ESTABLISHED IN PLANS
SCOPE · 1 TO 6 YEAR PROGRAMS

OPERATING PROGRAMS | RENEWAL PLANS AND PROJECTS | CAPITAL PROGRAMS made in this report become program recommendations to be reflected in the City's capital and operating budgets.

SUMMARY OF REPORT

1. Development Commitments

A. Redevelopment Authority Programs

West Philadelphia is today the scene of extensive and varied urban renewal action. Projects encompassing 856 acres are now either in execution or in planning (see Map 1). Included are clearance projects (University Units 3 and 5) which will permit the expansion of educational and employment opportunity in the core of University City; two large residential conservation projects (Haddington and West Mill Creek) which are designed to preserve essentially sound residential areas and to create safe and secure environments for living; and a small area, the Mount Olivet Project, which will permit the expansion of a vital community institution together with housing units for the elderly.

Other Authority commitments in West Philadelphia include the Powelton Village certification for FHA financing and, more recently, a similar program for the Cedar Park neighborhood which is still pending Federal approval.

All told, more than $25 millions have been invested in these programs in the District, with an additional 41 millions presently scheduled in the City's Capital Program for the years 1964-1969 and after 1969 for selected areas of the District.

This pattern of renewal projects reflects past and current strategy governing the City's overall renewal program. The earlier projects, dating to 1949 in the University Area, involved acquisition of blighted properties for major universities; partly by Title I projects to the extent federal and local funds could be allocated, partly by non-Title I projects for which the institution involved paid all costs in order to proceed with expansion more rapidly than available Title I funds allowed. The conservation projects further westward in the district, reflect the change in policy that occurred in 1957 when the emphasis was also given to the conservation of basically sound residential neighborhoods showing initial signs of deterioration.

Additional urban renewal actions of all types are made possible by the recent certification of a major portion of the West Philadelphia district for Redevelopment purposes under State Law. (Certification of an area enables the Redevelopment Authority to operate a program within that area. The Act of Certification does not, however, constitute a commitment to undertake renewal action. The purpose of certification is to make available Title I and other renewal activities, as well as other City programs, as possible courses of action that might be taken in that area of the City.) This action, taken by the City Planning Commission in August, 1963, consolidated all earlier certified areas and

Map 1: SUMMARY OF COMMITMENTS

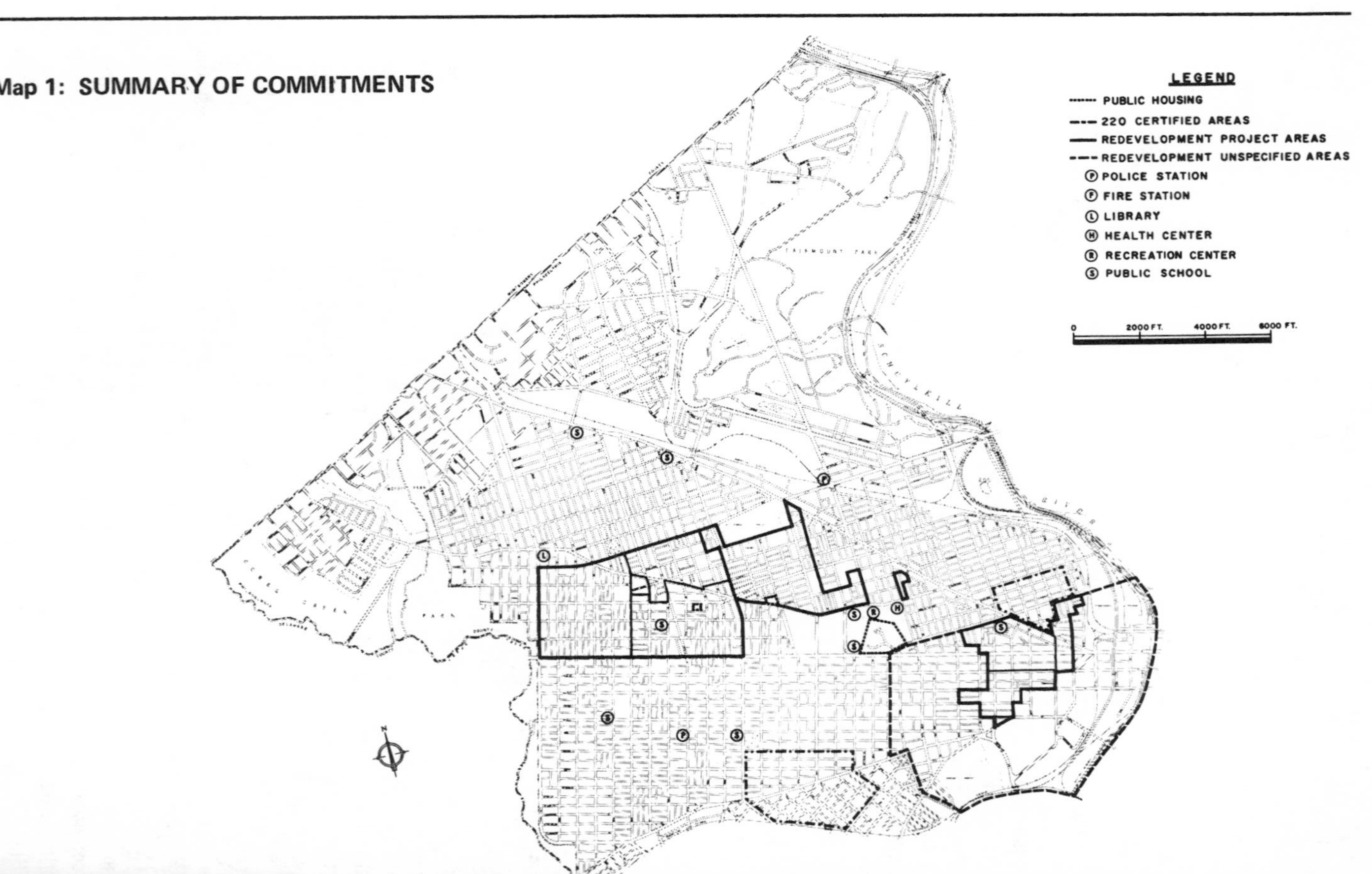

extended this certification to other portions of the district. This action itself indicates a major commitment to continue renewal activities that are appropriate to the needs of the District's several sub-areas.

(If the 1957 policy in allocating Title I funds were applied to this large certified area mentioned above, new projects west and north of the existing University and Powelton projects would be initiated in sequence, expanding out from the renewed central core. At the same time, new conservation projects would be initiated in sequence adjacent to stable outer residential areas or to conservation projects already in the program, and moving in toward the central core. In addition, small institutional projects would be undertaken in intermediate blighted areas where strengthening community institutions would help to stabilize the area pending full area treatment some years in the future.)

B. Other City Programs

Redevelopment Authority operations are being complemented by many other investments in the housing and physical environment of West Philadelphia. Map 1 also indicates a wide group of capital facilities, such as recreation areas, fire stations, and health centers, that have been or are now scheduled for construction in the District. An effort is made each year to dovetail many of these investments with renewal project actions, thus contributing non-cash credits to the City's development investment. The combined cost of all capital facilities programmed in the District exceeds $50 millions for the years 1964-1969.

Public housing new construction and rehabilitation programs are both represented in the present pattern of commitment. These represent a total contemplated investment of $13,000,000 and will provide 770 public housing units.

Difficult to present in terms of geographic areas are a multitude of other City service operations that support and complement the basic development programs. These include the various programs of the Department of Licenses and Inspections, the Commission on Human Relations, and the Health Department, to mention only a few that are directly involved in maintaining the physical environment of West Philadelphia. Time and staff limitations have prevented a full portrayal of all of these activities that go on without fanfare but which provide a strong base upon which the total development program rests.

C. Board of Public Education Programs

In addition to City investments, the construction program of the School District of Philadelphia greatly assists the renewal of West Philadelphia. Noted in the report are 8 construction projects for which sites have been acquired and commitments made. These programs represent an investment of $11,000,000. Many other school facilities to meet educational needs are now being scheduled and will be soon added to this roster of investment.

Map 2: SUMMARY OF DISTRICT PLAN PROPOSALS

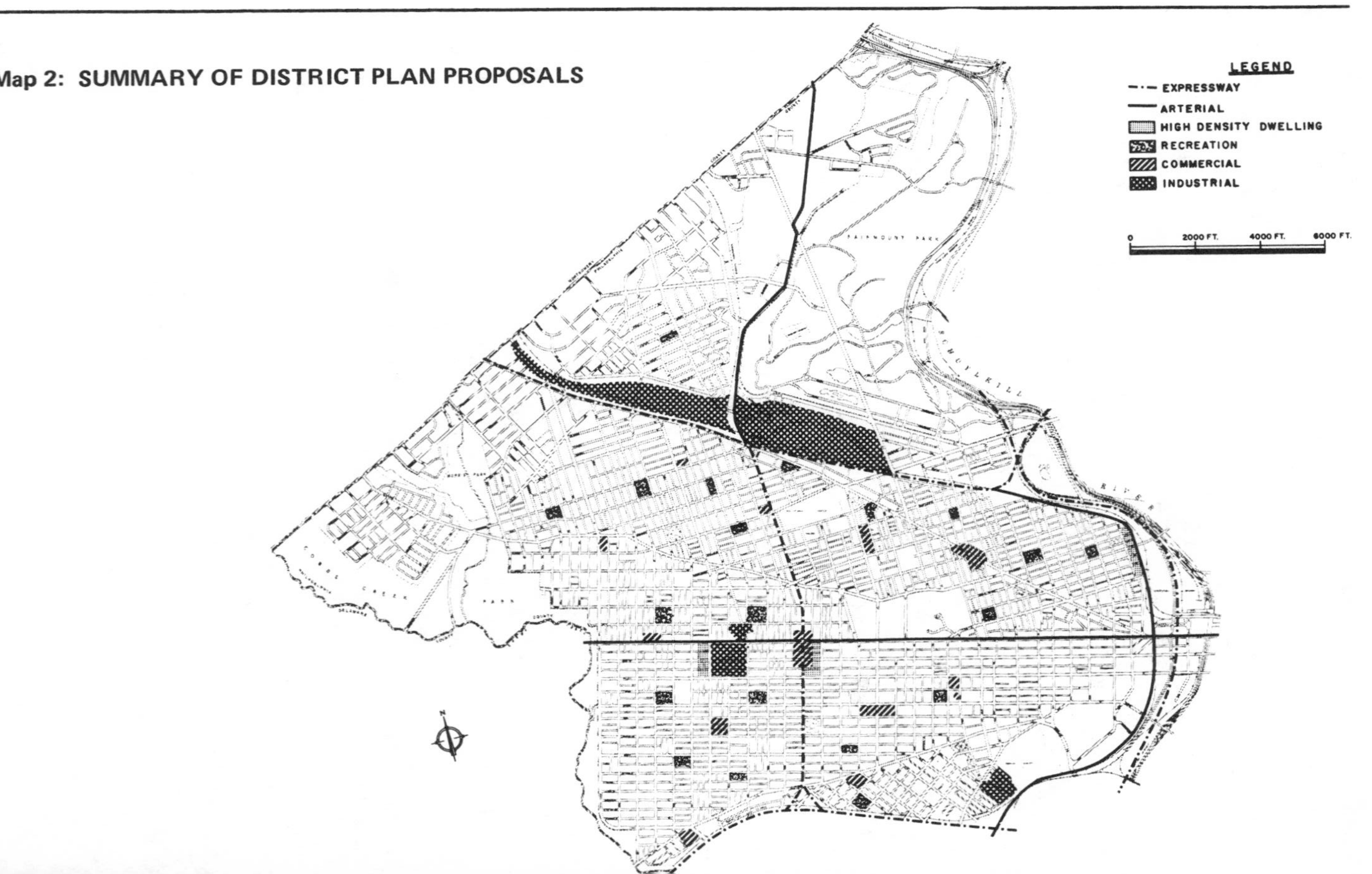

2. District Planning Proposals

The District Plan for West Philadelphia presents a refinement and modification of the City's Comprehensive Plan (see Map 2). The proposals contained in the Plan supersede those of the Comprehensive Plan and contribute to a broad arnge of objectives. Land use proposals include the provision of needed recreation areas and broad-scale treatments for residential sections of West Philadelphia (see Map 3). Perhaps the most significant changes would result from the proposed system of major expressways and arterial roads. Still another set of proposals stem from a District-wide physical design statement which contributes to the goal of an environment of quality.

For each subdistrict in West Philadelphia, the report summarizes major proposals, together with a preliminary estimate of cost. This listing is in contrast to the presentation by function in the Plan itself. The proposals cross-referenced in this manner are those most critical to the Plan and are expected to be achieved over a period of 30 to 40 years.

3. Proposed Programs and Scheduling

Proposed programs and a time sequence for their implementation are also listed for each sub-district. In composite form, these are the programs that are now available to meet requirements set forth in the District Plan. They are not intended to achieve all the Plan's land use or other objectives, but are intended for use in the plannable future of 6 to 10 years. In other words, the programs noted are programs that can work where assigned.

At this point in the preparation of the CRP, the combination of programs does not comprise a new total strategy or development policy. Rather, they are the building blocks from which a strategy for the district will be built when the Community Renewal Program is completed for the City as a whole.

The programs listed have been designated on the basis of descriptions summarized in Appendix A* of this report. They are largely programs that address the objectives of building a safe and secure environment, and an environment of quality.

The residential programs support the general treatments noted in the District Plan. They re consistent, for example, with the Plan's position that total clearance, as a single treatment, is not to be considered for even the most deteriorated areas of West Philadelphia. In such areas, the report suggests a program "mix" involving a variety of actions calculated to effect land use changes over time but accompanied by other programs that meet the requirements of the residents of such areas. An appropriate program "mix" might include for example economic, educational, and relocation programs. Work in detailing such a careful sequencing of programs is now underway with respect to the Mantua area.

*Not included herein.–Ed.

Map 3: RESIDENTIAL TREATMENT

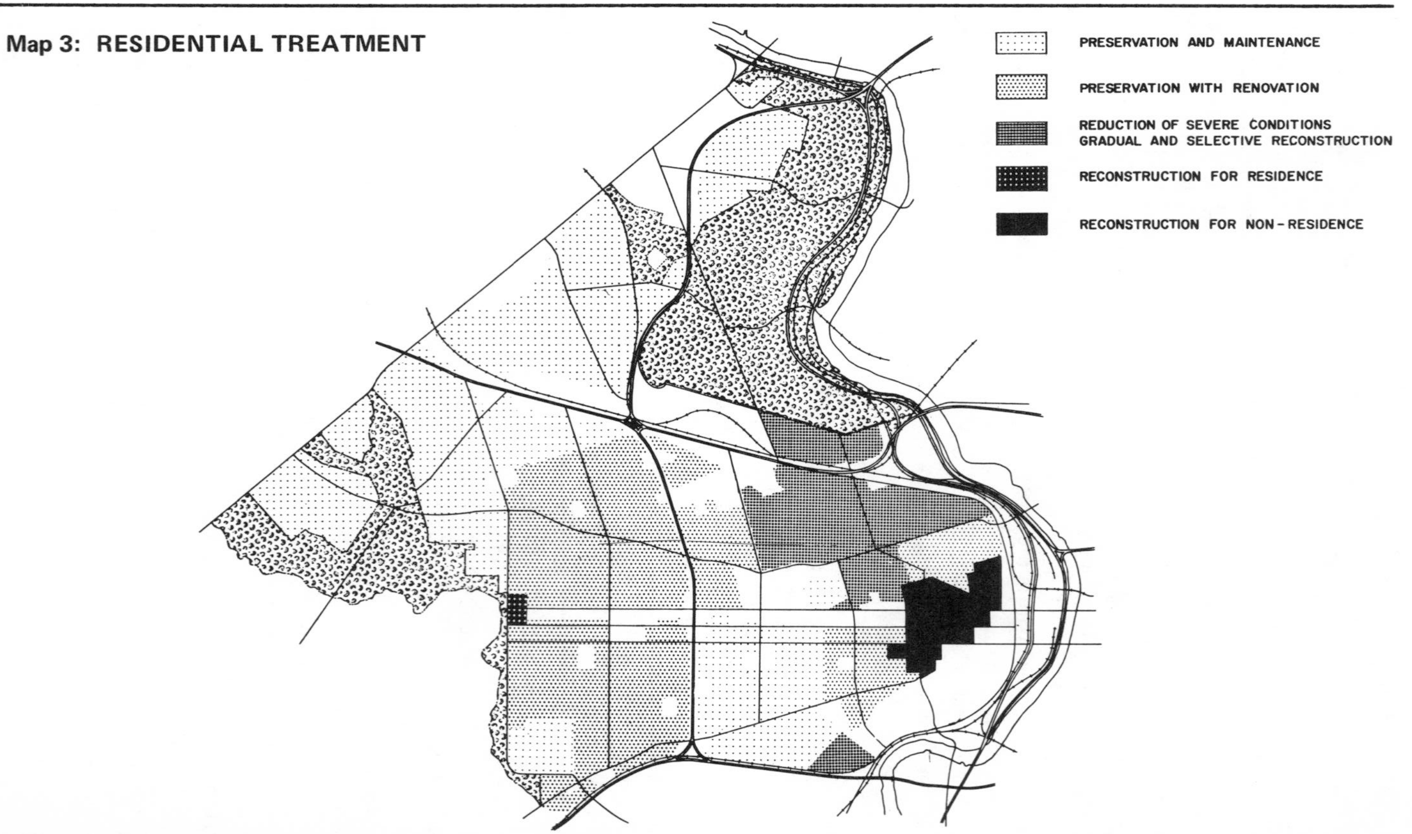

Mantua, however, is only one example of where the report sheds light upon gaps in available techniques for meeting District requirements. In terms of physical programs alone, it is demonstrated that there is a need to provide:

(1) A variety of middle and low income housing, both new and rehabilitated.
(2) Ways of introducing community facilities into neighborhoods where structures are sound but where the population requires schools, recreation areas, parking facilities and other supporting facilities.
(3) Effective means of consolidating many outworn strip commercial areas.

In a sense, the report is useful because it does focus upon such problems that stand clearly in the path of Plan achievement.

No part of West Philadelphia has been excluded from the report. West Philadelphia is viewed as one development area, requiring vastly different kinds of attention and investment. The report differs in this respect from the CURA study of 1957 which concentrated only on the central parts of the district and which spoke solely of general renewal treatments.

The report illustrates the importance of inter-meshing the programs of City agencies funded by both operating and capital budgets. It stresses the steps preparatory to major redevelopment actions and the critical role of staging these actions.

Finally, the report begins to set the District Plan in action and to place its time dimension in realistic terms. It thus gives perspective to planning proposals and provides a new vehicle for discussion of development policy.

APPENDIX B. SAMPLE PROGRAM PLAN

P.H.A. No. 2 DATE: August 12, 1963
AGENCY: Philadelphia Housing Authority

Public	(X)	Permanent	(X)
Private	( )	Temporary	( )
		Research	( )
Existing Program	(X)	Pilot	( )
New Program	( )	Demonstration	( )
Modified Program	( )		

PROGRAM TITLE: Housing For The Elderly

Program Objectives

The Housing for the Elderly Program contributes to the goal of "Housing and the physical environment." The immediate objectives of the program are:

Map 4: SUMMARY OF PROPOSED PROGRAM

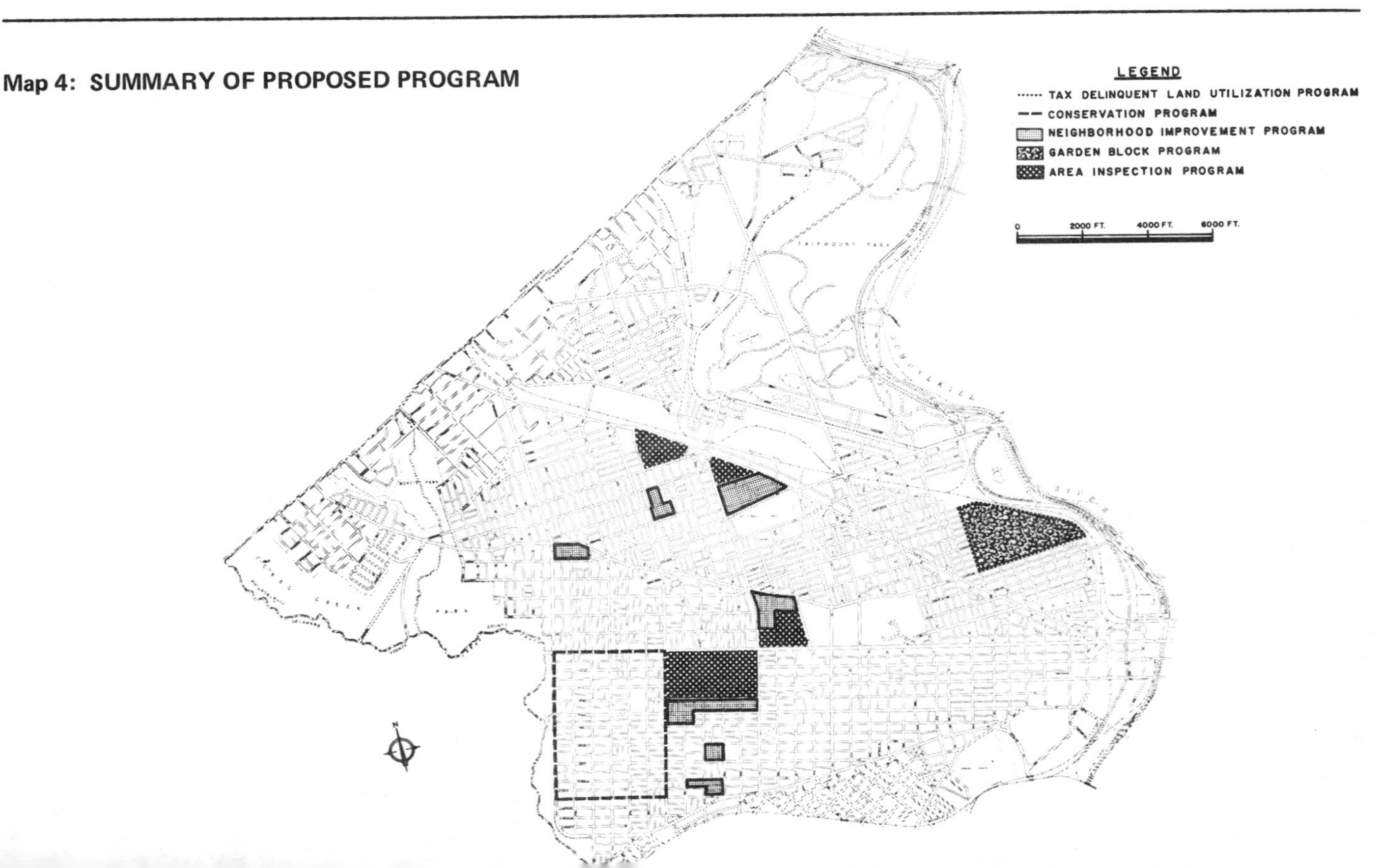

(1) To provide public housing accommodations for the elderly persons who are unable to secure adequate private housing because of their limited resources.

(2) To construct such housing, in groups not exceeding 100 units, on sites located in blight-free areas, which are convenient to transportation and community facilities.

(3) To provide housing for the elderly, in as many locations throughout the City as possible, including those communities which normally object to the construction of public housing under other programs.

This Program contributes to the goal of "Housing and the physical environment" through implementation of the general objective of "New construction and conversion" by expanding the City's supply of new dwelling accommodations to help meet the needs of the elderly.

Program Description

The program is carried out as follows:

(A) Site Selection and Approval Phase:

(1) Information on potential sites is gathered by the Planning and Development Division of the Authority, from the Inter-Agency Sub-Committee on Housing, the Philadelphia Housing Authority staff, the Office of the Development Co-ordinator, realtors, and other public and private agencies.

(2) The Executive Director of the Philadelphia Housing Authority, Authority Board Members, the Director of Development and Planning, and some staff members examine, in the field, the potential sites, and recommend selected sites for processing.

(3) The Regional Office of the Public Housing Administration gives tentative site approval.

(4) The Office of the Development Co-ordinator investigates the site location and approves or disapproves.

(5) The City Planning Commission approves site location, feasibility and area density.

(6) The Redevelopment Authority approves the site location, if the proposed site is within a redevelopment area.

(7) The Philadelphia Housing Association's Committee on Public Housing Development Policy provides advice, comment, and either approval or disapproval of the site proposal.

(B) Development Program and Annual Contributions Contract Phase:

(1) The Planning and Development Division of the Authority prepares a detailed Development Program for the site.

(2) The Development Program is submitted to the Regional Office of the Public Housing Administration for review and approval.

(3) The Annual Contributions Contract is then negotiated between the Public Housing Administration and the Philadelphia Housing Authority. This contract is prepared on the basis of information submitted in the

Development Program. The Annual Contributions Contract commits the Federal Government to loan the Authority funds sufficient to meet the development costs.

(C) Site Acquisition and Demolition Phase:

(1) Private appraisers are employed by the Authority to estimate the costs of acquiring the parcels of land within the site area.

(2) Real Estate negotiators are appointed by the Authority to negotiate acquisitions.

(3) Final Settlement is conducted directly by the Authority with the individual owners.

(4) Bids are received for the demolition contract and demolition begins after 70-80% of the site has been acquired.

(5) Where necessary, the Authority will use its power of eminent domain in order to complete site acquisition.

(D) Contract and Construction Phase:

(1) Private architects, selected on the basis of proven ability, are engaged by the Authority to prepare complete plans and specifications for the selected Housing Development so that construction bids may be taken.

(2) The Authority awards the construction contracts to the lowest bidders. The contracts are then forwarded to the Regional Office of the Public Housing Administration for approval, after which a proceed order is given.

(3) The architects and the Authority cooperate in furnishing inspection personnel as the Housing Development is being built. After completion and acceptance by the architects and the Authority, the Housing Development is turned over to the Management Division for occupancy.

Basis for Involvement

(1) The U.S. Housing Act of 1937, as amended.

(2) The Housing Authority Act, Pa., P.L. 935, as amended.

(3) Consolidated Financial Assistance Contract between the Housing Authority and the Public Housing Administration, dated April 1, 1959.

(4) Cooperation Agreement, 1950, between the City of Philadelphia, the Housing Authority, and the Board of Education.

Preconditions for Effectiveness:

(1) Site Criteria: The proposed site should be located in a blight-free area, convenient to all essential facilities.

(2) Construction Criteria: The proposed site should accommodate a maximum of 100 units; the height of each dwelling unit should not exceed 2 stories; and the square footage per unit should be the maximum according to government regulations.

(3) Recreation facilities should be included in the project itself, or conveniently located nearby.

(4) Special safety devices (e.g. ramps, hand rails, etc.) should be included in all units for the elderly.

(5) Where units for the elderly are included in a high-rise multiple-occupancy project, these units should have the previously mentioned facilities and conveniences.

Program Relationships

The program of the Housing for the Elderly has immediate relationships with the following programs or agencies:

(1) The Office of the Development Co-ordinator performs an intelligence and liaison function between the Authority and various City agencies and assists in recommending sites for development.

(2) The Department of Licenses and Inspections provides housing inspection data for areas of potential site locations, as well as areas contiguous to present Housing Developments.

(3) The Regional Office of the Public Housing Administration approves site selections, Development Program, and construction contracts and grants the Annual Contribution Contract to meet development costs.

(4) The City Planning Commission approves site, location, density and site plans. It also supports zoning ordinances, zoning variances and street vacation ordinances.

(5) The Philadelphia Art Commission approves the development design, as indicated by the preliminary plans.

(6) The Philadelphia Housing Association's Committee on Public Housing Development gives advice and comment on site selection and project development.

(7) A centralized Relocation Bureau provides technical and financial assistance for persons displaced by government action.

Method for Evaluating Program's Ability to Achieve Objectives

Evaluation of the Program may be conducted by an analysis of the following:

(1) Number of units constructed:
- (a) Number in projects exclusively planned for the elderly.
- (b) Number in all other projects.

(2) Demand and needs for the Elderly for this type of housing:
- (a) Present and projected needs and demand.
- (b) Number of applications received; number accommodated.
- (c) The number of elderly presently living in these units.
- (d) Rate of occupancy turn-over; average occupancy duration.

Resources Required

Estimated development costs for 162 dwelling units in three projects[a] planned primarily or exclusively for the Elderly and due for completion in 1965:

(e) Planning	$ 173,041
(b) Site Acquisition	425,598
(c) Administration	42,703
(d) Interest	49,005
(e) Construction and equipment	1,804,864
(f) Contingency Fund	124,963
(g) Initial Operating Deficit	4,050
Total Development Costs	$2,624,224[b]
Average Unit Cost	$ 16,198

a. These projects are:

Collegeview	(Robert Morris)	= 54 units
Fairmount	(50th & Haverford)	= 41 units
Point Breeze		= 67 units

Development costs are not available for the Welsh Elderly Project planned for completion in 1965.

b. Included within this total are the costs for completion of nine dwelling units for large families in the Fairmount Project.

Specific Targets for Accomplishment

(1) New dwelling units:	1960-1961	1962	1963	1964	1965 a
(a) In-projects built primarily for the elderly	22[a]				228[c]
(b) High rise buildings	Eff. 93 1 br 32[b]	Eff. 34 1 br 11	Eff. 154 1 br 52	Eff. 40 1 br 39	
(c) All others			Eff. 8 1 br 10[b]	Eff. 60 1 br 31	
Annual totals	147	45	224	170	228[a]
(2) Cumulative total for period 1960-1965	814				
Number of dwelling units accommodating the elderly built prior to 1960	731				
Total	1,545				

a. In-projects built primarily for the elderly the dwelling unit distribution is approximately the following: 25% eff; 5% 2 br, and 70% 1 br.

b. In order to properly reflect the scope of the program, one-half of all projected and existing one bedroom units have been included as units for the elderly.

c. This total is subject to minor variations until the final approval is forthcoming.

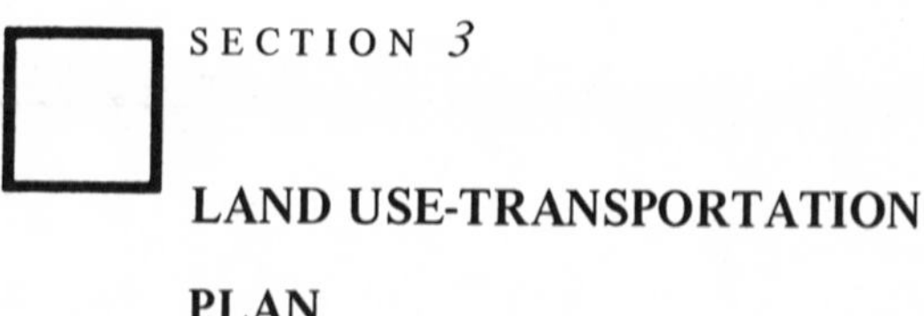

SECTION *3*

LAND USE-TRANSPORTATION PLAN

Chapter 21

THE SOUTHEASTERN WISCONSIN LAND USE-TRANSPORTATION PLAN

Southeastern Wisconsin Regional Planning Commission

SECTION 1. INTRODUCTION

This report is the second in a series of three volumes, which together present the major findings and recommendations of the SEWRPC Regional Land Use-Transportation Study. The first volume, published in May 1965, set forth the basic principles and concepts underlying the study and presented in summary form the basic facts which together describe the existing state of the systems being planned and are, therefore, pertinent to long-range land use and transportation planning in southeastern Wisconsin.

This, the second volume, is concerned with the formulation of regional development objectives, principles, and standards; the forecast of future growth and change in the Region; and the presentation and evaluation of alternative land use-transportation plans designed to meet the anticipated growth and change. This report is intended to provide the basis for the selection of the final regional land use-transportation plan from among the alternative development plans proposed.

The third and final volume of the series will detail the land use-transportation plan finally selected and recommended for implementation. It will propose a staging for land use and transportation system development and will set forth detailed plans for certain selected corridors of transportation movement.

Reprinted from "Land Use-Transportation Study, Forecasts and Alternative Plans 1990," Planning Report No. 7, 2 (1966), pp. 1-5, 7-11, Table 1, 155-158 (top), 189-190, 190-195, 196 (bottom), 198-201 (top), 206-208.

THE LAND USE-TRANSPORTATION PLANNING PROCESS–A BRIEF REVIEW

The nature of the land use-transportation planning problem, the basic principles and concepts underlying the land use-transportation planning process, and the process itself were all described in the first volume of this series; and reference should be made to that volume of this series; and reference should be made to that volume for a more detailed discussion of the need for, purposes of, and methods of planning for regional land use and transportation system development.

It is important to note in review, however, that the generalized alternative land use-transportation plans presented in this volume have been developed through a seven-step planning process by which the Region and its principal functional relationships can be accurately described, both graphically and numerically; the complex movement of people and vehicles over highway and transit facilities simulated; and the effects of different courses of action with respect to regional land use and transportation system development evaluated. The seven steps involved in this planning process are: (1) study design; (2) formulation of objectives, principles, and standards; (3) inventory; (4) analysis and forecast; (5) plan design; (6) plan test and evaluation; and (7) plan selection and adoption. Plan implementation, although necessarily a step beyond the foregoing planning process, must be considered throughout the process if the plans are to be realized. In fact, one of the primary objectives of the critical plan test and evaluation step is to test plan proposals for feasibility of implementation.

The first of these seven steps in the planning process–study design–has been described and its results set forth in the original study prospectus, in the detailed study design, and in the procedural manuals governing the study.[1] The third step–inventory–has been described and its findings set forth in Volume 1 of this report services.[2] This important step provided the necessary information base for step four–analysis and forecast; step five–plan design; and step six–plan test and evaluation. This volume will describe and present the results of these three steps in the planning process, together with the formulation of objectives and standards. A brief examination of each of these steps is included here in order to clarify their function in the planning sequence. The seventh step in the planning process–plan selection and adoption–together with its results, will be the subject of Volume 3 in this report series.

Formulation of Objectives and Standards

Since planning is a rational process for formulating and meeting objectives, the formation of objectives is an essential task which must be undertaken before plans can be prepared. The objectives chosen guide the preparation of alternative plans and, when converted to standards, provide the criteria for evaluating and selecting from among the alternatives. Since objectives provide the logical basis for plan synthesis, the formulation of sound objectives is a crucial step in the planning process. Yet, the process of formulating objectives has received relatively little attention in most planning operations. The lack of a comprehensive and tested approach to the problem of formulating objectives, however, provides no valid excuse for neglecting this fundamental task.

It is important to recognize that, because the formulation of objectives involves a formal definition of a desirable physical system by listing, in effect, the broad needs which the system aims to satisfy, the objectives implicitly reflect an underlying value system. Thus, every physical development plan is accompanied by its own unique value system. The diverse nature of value systems in a complex urban society complicates the process of goal formulation and makes it one of the most difficult tasks of the planning process. This difficulty relates in part to the lack of a clear-cut basis for a choice between value systems and in part to the reluctance of public officials to make an explicit choice of ultimate goals. Yet, it is much more important to choose the "right" objectives than the "right" plan. To choose the wrong objectives is to solve the wrong problem; to choose the wrong plan is merely to choose a less efficient physical system. While, because of differing value systems, there may be no single argument to support a given choice of objectives, it is possible to state certain planning principles which provide at least some support for the choice; and this has been done herein.

Objectives cannot be intelligently chosen without knowledge of the causal relationships existing between objectives and means. This suggests that the formulation of objectives is best done by people with prior knowledge of the social, economic, and technical means of achieving the objectives, as well as of the underlying value systems. Even so, it must be recognized that the objectives may change as a selection is attempted from among alternative means or plans. In the process of evaluating alternative plans, the various alternative plan proposals are ranked according to ability to meet objectives. If the best plan so identified nevertheless falls short of the chosen objectives, either a better plan must be synthesized or the objectives must be compromised. The plan evaluation provides the basis for deciding which objectives to compromise. The compromises may take three forms: certain objectives may be dropped because their satisfaction has been proven unrealistic; new objectives may be suggested; or conflicts between inconsistent objectives may be balanced out. Thus, formulation of objectives must proceed hand in hand with plan design and plan implementation as a part of a continuing planning process.

Concern for objectives cannot end with a mere listing of desired goals. The goals must be related in a demonstrable and, wherever possible, quantifiable manner to physical development proposals. Only through such a relationship can alternative development proposals be properly evaluated. This relationship is accomplished through a set of supporting standards for each chosen objective.

Forecasting–The Determination of Future Needs

Although the preparation of forecasts is not planning, the preparation of all plans must begin with some kind of forecast. In any planning effort, forecasts are required of all future events and conditions which are outside the scope of the plan but which will affect plan design or implementation. For example, the future demand for land transportation, and natural resources will depend primarily upon the size of the future population and the nature of future economic activity within the Region. Control of changes in population and economic activity levels lies largely outside the scope of governmental activity at the regional and local levels, outside the scope of the physical planning process, and certainly outside the scope of a land use-transportation plan. Future population and economic activity levels must, therefore, be forecast. These levels, in turn, determine the aggregate future land use demand. This is not to say, however, that governmental policies at the regional and local levels cannot influence the course of economic development and consequently of population growth. For example, the provision of efficient regional transporation and utility systems can contribute to favorable industrial location decisions even though the provision of such systems cannot directly generate economic growth.

The preparation of a transportation plan by itself, as has been the practice in some metropolitan areas, requires that the spatial distribution of future land use, too, be considered outside the scope of the plan and, therefore, an element to be forecast. In the SEWRPC regional land use-transportation planning program, however, the spatial distribution of future land use is within the scope of the plan and, therefore, becomes a design rather than a forecast problem. Indeed the preparation of a forecast of the spatial distribution of land use would be a contradiction of the basic principles and concepts underlying the regional land use-transportation study.

It should be noted, however, that it is necessary to forecast the future gross regional requirements for each of the major land use categories even though it is not necessary to forecast the spatial distribution of these land uses. This is necessary since the land use plans to be prepared must meet these regional needs. These forecasts of gross land use requirements, along with the forecasts of future levels of population and employment on which they are based, and forecasts of income, automobile and truck availability, and public revenues are presented herein.

Two important considerations involved in the preparation of necessary forecasts are the forecast target date and the forecast accuracy requirements. Both the land use pattern and the transportation system must be planned for anticipated demand at some future point in time. In the planning of transportation systems, this "design year" is usually established by the expected life of the first facilities to be contructed in implementation of the plan. This also permits associated forecasts to be more readily tempered by predictable changes in technology. Although it may be argued that the design year for land use development should be extended further into the future than that for transportation facilities because of the basic irreversibility of many land development decisions, practical considerations dictate that the land use planning design year be scaled to the facility design year requirement.

Forecast accuracy requirements depend on the use to be made of the forecasts; and, as applied to land use and transportation planning, the critical question relates to the effect of any forecast inaccuracies on the basic structure of the plans to be produced. It is important to keep the forecast tolerances within that range wherein only the timing and not the basic structure of the plans will be affected.

Plan Design

Plan synthesis or design forms the heart of the planning process. The most well-conceived objectives; the most sophisticated data collection, processing, and analysis operations; and the most accurate forecasts are of little value if they do not ultimately result in sound plans to meet the objectives in light of forecast needs. The outputs of each of the three planning operations–formulation of objectives and standards, inventory, and forecast–become inputs to the design problem of plan synthesis.

The land use plan design problem consists essentially of determining the allocation of a scarce resource–land–between competing and often conflicting demands. This allocation must be accomplished so as to satisfy the aggregate needs for each land use and comply with the design standards derived from the plan objectives, all at a feasible cost. The transportation plan design problem requires a similar reconciliation between travel demand derived from the land use plan adopted, transportation design standards, existing facilities, and new facility costs.

The task of designing two of the major components of an environment for over two million people is a most complex and difficult problem. Not only is each component in itself a major problem in terms of the sheer size of the system to be designed, but the pattern of interaction between the components is exceedingly complex and constantly changing. The land use pattern must enable people to live in close cooperation and yet freely pursue an enormous variety of interests. It must minimize conflicts between population growth and limited land and water resources; maintain an ecological balance of human, animal, and plant life; and avoid gross public health and welfare problems. The transportation system must not only serve and promote a desirable land use pattern but do so without creating a demand which aggravates its own congestion. The combined land use-transportation system must be organized so that its construction and reconstruction does not constantly disrupt its performance.

The magnitude of such a design problem approaches an almost insoluble level of complexity; yet, no substitute for intuition in plan design has so far been found, much less developed to a practical level. Means do exist, however for reducing the gap between the necessary intuitive and integrative grasp of the problem and its growing magnitude; and these have been fully applied in the regional land use-transportation study. They center primarily on the application of systems engineering techniques to the quantitative test of both the land use and transportation system plans, as described below under the plan test and evaluation phase. Yet, the quantitative tests involved in these techniques, while powerful aids to the determination of the adequacy of the plan design, are of strictly limited usefulness in actual plan synthesis. Consequently, it is still necessary to develop both the land use and transportation plan by traditional graphic and analytical "cut and try" methods, then to quantitatively test the resulting design by application of simulation model techniques, and then make necessary adjustments in the design until a workable plan has been evolved.

Yet the same mathematical techniques which make quantitative plan test possible may eventually make a more logical and efficient plan synthesis possible. Indeed, such application has been explored by the Commission with promising results for land use plan design application.[3] These techniques are not yet sufficiently developed, however, to be applied practically; and no efforts have been made to apply these techniques to regional land use or transportation plan synthesis.

In order to overcome the limitations of individual intuitive grasp of the design problem, maximum resort was made to team effort in the actual plan synthesis; the knowledge and experience of those state and local planners and engineers most familiar with selected geographic and functional areas was applied to the plan synthesis process through careful committee review and, where necessary, interchange of staff. Finally and most importantly, it should be noted that in both land use and transportation plan synthesis the Commission had at its disposal far more definitive information bearing on the problem than has ever before been available; and this fact alone made the traditional plan synthesis techniques applied far more powerful.

Plan Test and Evaluation

If the plans developed in the design stage of the planning process are to be practical and workable and thereby realized in terms of actual land use and transportation system development, some measures must be applied as quantitative tests of the feasibility of alternative plans during plan synthesis and in advance of plan adoption and implementation. Traffic simulation models have been developed over the past decade for application in transportation planning that make it possible to determine the existing and potential travel demand on any proposed transportation network.

Using these simulation models, it is possible to test and verify the workability and efficiency of any proposed transportation system network. The quantitative assignment of traffic to the network will reveal areas of over or under capacity and provide the basis for network modification during plan design, ultimately resulting in a practical and efficient transportation system plan for which development costs can be calculated. Such assignment also permits the calculation of user benefits for benefit-cost analyses. Finally, such assignment provides a more precise basis for the application of standards so that the degree to which each alternative transportation plan meets the chosen objectives can be better determined.

While the validity and usefulness of this transportation simulation technique has been proven in other urban transportation studies, similar model techniques suitable for testing the feasibility of proposed land use plans have not yet been successfully applied. Conventional land use planning techniques normally involve quantitative test only to the degree that the aggregate areas allocated to the various land uses in the alternative plans are scaled against the various land use demands. Test and evaluation beyond such scaling of supply versus demand normally involve qualitative evaluation of the degree to which each alternative land use plan meets development objectives and standards and of the legal feasibility of the alternatives. These conventional techniques have all been applied in the land use-transportation study; and, in addition, the effects of each alternative land use plan on the natural resource base have been both qualitatively and quantitatively evaluated and the financial feasibility of each alternative land use plan established.

Many private decisions by individual land developers, builders, and households, as well as public decisions by units and agencies of government, interact to determine the regional land use pattern. A need, therefore, exists to test the feasibility of any regional land use plan proposals beyond the gross demand tests provided by the expanded conventional land use planning techniques. In the regional land use-transportation study, an experimental land use simulation model capable of representing the decision processes of households and business firms influential in land development has been developed to meet this need. The basic problem of land use plan test using simulation model techniques may be stated as: given a target plan, determine whether this plan can be attained considering behavioral patterns of land developers, builders, and households; public land use controls; and public works programs. Using a land use simulation model, a number of experimental simulation runs can be performed with differing land use control policies and the practicality of the plan determined.

Plan Selection and Adoption

In the land use-transportation study, not one but a number of alternative land use plans were developed, each with its supporting transportation system plan. These are presented herein in summary form. The general approach contemplated for the selection of one plan from among these alternatives is to proceed through the use of the advisory committee structure and hearings to a final decision and plan adoption by the Commission, in accordance with the provisions of the state enabling legislation. Since plan selection and adoption necessarily involve both technical and nontechnical policy determinations, they must be founded in the active involvement throughout the entire planning process of the various governmental bodies, technical agencies, and private interest groups concerned with regional development. Such involvement is particularly important in light of the advisory role of the Commission in shaping regional development. The use of advisory committees and both formal and informal hearings appears to be the most practical and effective procedure available for involving public officials, technicians, and citizens in the planning process and of openly arriving at a agreement among the affected governmental bodies and agencies on objectives and on plans which can be jointly implemented.

SECTION 2. OBJECTIVES, PRINCIPLES, AND STANDARDS

As previously noted, planning is a rational process for formulating and meeting objectives; and the formulation of objectives is, therefore, an essential task which must be undertaken before plans can be prepared. The formulation of objectives for organizations whose functions are directed primarily at a single purpose or interest and, therefore, are direct and clear cut is a relatively easy task. The seven-county Southeastern Wisconsin Planning Region is, however, composed of many diverse and often divergent interests; consequently, the formulation of objectives for the preparation of advisory comprehensive regional development plans is a very difficult task.

Soundly conceived regional development objectives should incorporate the combined knowledge of many people who are informed about the Region and should be established by duly elected or appointed representatives legally assigned this task, rather than by planning technicians. This is particularly important because of the value system implications inherent in any set of development objectives. Active participation by duly elected or appointed public officials and by citizen leaders in the regional planning program is implicit in the structure and organization of the Southeastern Wisconsin Regional Planning Commission itself. Moreover, the Commission very early in its existence recognized that the task of guiding the broad spectrum of related public and private development programs which would influence, and be influenced by, a comprehensive regional planning program would require an even broader opportunity for the active participation of public officials and private interest groups in the regional planning process. In light of this recognition, the Commission provided for the establishment of advisory committees to assist the Commission and its staff in the conduct of the regional planning program.

The advisory committee structure created by the Commission for the regional land-use transportation study has been described in Volume 1 of this report. The use of these advisory committees appears to be the most practical and effective procedure available for involving officials, technicians, and citizens in the regional planning process and of openly arriving at decisions and action programs which can shape the future physical development of the Region. Only by combining the accumulated knowledge and experience which the various advisory committee members possess about the Region can a meaningful expression of the desired direction, magnitude, and quality of future regional development be obtained. One of the major tasks of these committees, therefore, is to assist in the formulation of regional development objectives, supporting planning principles, and planning standards. This chapter sets forth the regional land use-transportation planning objectives, principles, and standards which have been adopted by the Commission after careful review and recommendation by the advisory committees concerned.

BASIC CONCEPTS AND DEFINITIONS

The term "objective" is subject to a wide range of interpretation and application and is closely linked to other terms often used in planning work which are equally subject to a wide range of interpretation and application. The following definitions have, therefore, been adopted in order to provide a common frame of reference:

(1) Objective: a goal or end toward the attainment of which plans and policies are directed.
(2) Principle: a fundamental, primary, or generally accepted tenet used to support objectives and prepare standards and plans.
(3) Standard: a criterion used as a basis of comparison to determine the adequacy of plan proposals to attain objectives.
(4) Plan: a design which seeks to achieve agreed upon objectives.
(5) Policy: a rule or course of action used to ensure plan implementation.
(6) Program: a coordinated series of policies and actions to carry out a plan.

Although this chapter deals only with the first three of these terms, an understanding of the interrelationship between the foregoing definitions and the basic concepts which they represent is essential to the following discussion of objectives, principles, and standards.

OBJECTIVES

Objectives, in order to be useful in the regional land use-transportation planning process, must be sound logically and related in a demonstrable and measurable way to alternative physical development proposals. This is necessary because it is the legal duty and function of the Commission to prepare a comprehensive plan for the physical development of the Region and, more particularly, because it is the purpose of the regional land use-transportation study to prepare two of the key elements of such a plan: a land use plan and a transportation plan. Only if the objectives are clearly relatable to physical development and only if they are subject to objective test can an intelligent choice be made from among alternative plans in order to select the one plan or combination of plans which best meets the agreed upon objectives.

Recognizing that (1) various public and private interest groups within a region as large and diverse as southeastern Wisconsin may have varying and at times conflicting objectives; (2) many of these objectives are of a qualitative nature and, therefore, difficult to quantify; and (3) many objectives which may be held to be important by the various interest groups within the Region may not be related in a demonstrable manner to physical development plans, the Commission has identified two basic types of objectives. These are: general development objectives, which are by their very nature either qualitative or difficult to relate directly to development plans, and specific development objectives, which can be directly related to physical development plans and at least crudely quantified.

General Objectives

The following general development objectives have been adopted by the Commission after careful review and recommendation by the Technical Coordinating and Advisory Committee and the Intergovernmental Coordinating Committee on Regional Land Use-Transportation Planning:

(1) Economic growth at a maximum rate, consistent with regional resources, and primary dependence on free enterprise in order to provide maximum employment opportunities for the expanding labor force of the Region.
(2) A wide range of employment opportunities through a broad, diversified economic base.
(3) Conservation and protection of desirable existing residential, commercial, industrial, and agricultural development in order to maintain desirable social and economic values; renewal of obsolete and deteriorating residential, commercial, and industrial areas in the rural as well as in the urban areas of the Region; and prevention of slums and blight.
(4) A broad range of choice among housing designs, types, and costs, recognizing changing trends in age group composition, income, and family living habits.
(5) An adequate and balanced level of community services and facilities.
(6) An efficient and equitable allocation of fiscal resources within the public sector of the economy.
(7) An attractive and healthful physical and social environment with ample opportunities for education, cultural activities, and outdoor recreation.
(8) Protection, wide use, and sound development of the natural resource base.
(9) Development of communities having distinctive individual character, based on physical conditions, historical factors, and local desires.

The foregoing general development objectives are proposed as goals which public policy within the Region should promote. They are all necessarily general but, nevertheless, provide the broad framework within which regional planning can take place and the more specific goals of the various functional elements and component parts of the Region stated and pursued. The statement of these objectives is concerned entirely with ends and not with means, and the principal emphasis of these general objectives is on those aspects of regional development which relate either to the expenditure of public funds or to the effects of government actions and regulations. With respect to these general development objectives, it will be deemed sufficient to arrive at a consensus among the advisory committees and the Commission itself that the plan proposals do not conflict with the objectives. Such a consensus represents the most practical evaluation of the ability of the alternative plan proposals to meet the general development objectives.

Specific Development Objectives

Within the framework established by the general development objectives, a secondary set of more specific objectives can be postulated which will be directly relatable to physical development plans and an be at least crudely quantified. The quantification is facilitated by complementing each specific objective with a set of quantifiable planning standards which are, in turn, directly relatable to a planning principle which supports the chosen objective. The planning principles thus augment each specific objective by asserting its inherent validity as an objective.

The specific objectives which have been adopted by the Commission after careful review and recommendation by the advisory committees are herein listed separately for land use and transportation planning purposes. It should be emphasized, however, that land use and transportation are inextricably linked; and, therefore, land use planning objectives cannot be separated from transportation planning objectives. The separate listing of the specific objectives herein is only for convenience of organization and presentation.

Land Use Development Objectives

The specific objectives adopted for the regional land use plan are largely self-descriptive. They are concerned primarily with spatial allocation to, and distribution of, the various land uses, land use compatibility, resource protection, and accessibility. The following specific land use development objectives have been adopted by the Commission after careful review and recommendation by the Technical Coordinating and Advisory Committee and the Intergovernmental Coordinating Committee on Regional Land Use-Transportation Planning:

(1) A balanced allocation of space to the various land use categories which meets the social, physical, and economic needs of the regional population.
(2) A spatial distribution of the various land uses which will result in a compatible arrangement of land uses.
(3) A spatial distribution of the various land uses which will result in the protection, wise use, and development of the natural resources of the Region: soils, inland lakes and streams, wetlands, woodlands, and wildlife.
(4) A spatial distribution of the various land uses which is properly related to the supporting transportation, utility, and public facility systems in order to assure the economical provision of transportation, utility, and public facility services.
(5) The development and conservation of residential areas within a physical environment that is healthy, safe, convenient, and attractive.
(6) The preservation and provision of a variety of suitable industrial and commercial sites both in terms of physical characteristics and location.
(7) The preservation and provision of open space to enhance the total quality of the regional environment, maximize essential natural resource availability, give form

and structure to urban development, and facilitate the ultimate attainment of a balanced year-round outdoor recreational program providing a full range of facilities for all age groups.

(8) The preservation of land areas for agricultural uses to provide for certain special types of agriculture, provide a reserve for future needs, and ensure the preservation of those rural areas which provide wildlife habitat and which are essential to shape and order urban development.

Transportation System Development Objectives

The specific objectives adopted for the regional transportation plan are concerned primarily with a balanced transportation system, alleviating traffic congestion, reducing travel times and accident exposure, and minimizing costs and disruptive effects upon communities and natural resources. The following specific transportation development objectives have been adopted by the Commission after careful review and recommendation by the Technical Coordinating and Advisory Committee and the Intergovernmental Coordinating Committee on Regional Land Use-Transportation Planning:

(1) An integrated transportation system which will effectively serve the existing regional land use pattern and promote the implementation of the regional land use plan, meeting the anticipated travel demand generated by the existing and proposed land uses.

(2) A balanced transportation system providing the appropriate types of transportation service needed by the various subareas of the Region at an adequate level of service.

(3) The alleviation of traffic congestion and the reduction of travel time between component parts of the Region.

(4) The reduction of accident exposure and provision of increased travel safety.

(5) A transportation system which is both economical and efficient, meeting all other objectives at the lowest cost possible.

(6) The minimization of disruption of desirable existing neighborhood and community development and of deterioration or destruction of the natural resource base.

(7) A high aesthetic quality in the transportation system with proper visual relation of the major transportation facilities to the land and cityscape.

PRINCIPLES AND STANDARDS

Complementing each of the foregoing specific land use and transportation development objectives is a planning principle and a set of planning standards. These are set forth in Table 1. Each set of standards is directly relatable to the planning principle, as well as to the objective, and serves to facilitate quantitative application of the objectives in plan design, test, and evaluation. The planning principle, moreover, supports each specific objective by asserting its validity. In the preparation of the necessary planning principles, a careful search of the planning literature failed to reveal a documented set of comprehensive principles which were universally accepted as tenets basic to the physical planning process.

It was necessary, therefore, to adapt such principles as could be found to the regional planning effort and then to draw upon the collective experience of the practitioners of the many technical disciplines represented on the Technical Coordinating and Advisory Committee to formulate additional principles to augment those adapted from the literature. Thus, through the combined knowledge of experienced technicians, a set of comprehensive planning principles was formulated which can be used as guidelines in the planning process. While it is probable that the rapidly developing technology of planning will ultimately modify the principles so prepared and will require and suggest additional principles, it is hoped that those herein adopted will form a sound initial basis for future improvement and expansion.

TABLE 1
Land Use Planning Objectives, Principles, and Standards: Southeastern Wisconsin Regional Planning Commission

Objective No. 5

The development and conservation of residential areas within a physical environment that is healthy, safe, convenient, and attractive.

Principle

Residential areas developed in designed planning units can assist in stabilizing community property values, preserving residential amenities, and promoting efficiency in the provision of public and community service facilities; can best provide a desirable environment for family life; and can provide the population with improved levels of safety and convenience.

Standards

1. Residential planning units should be physically self-contained within clearly defined and relatively permanent isolating boundaries, such as arterial streets and highways, major park and open-space reservations, or significant natural features, such as rivers, streams, or hills.

2. Residential planning units should contain enough area to provide: housing for the population served by one elementary school and one neighborhood park; an internal street system which discourages penetration of the unit by through traffic; and all of the community and commercial facilities necessary to meet the day-to-day living requirements of the family within the immediate vicinity of its dwelling unit. To meet these requirements at varied residential densities, the following specific standards should be met:

Land Use	*Low-Density Development (2 mi. sq.) % of Area*	*Medium-Density Development (1 mi. sq.) % of Area*	*High-Density Development (½ mi. sq.) % of Area*
Residential	80.0	71.0	66.0
Streets & utilities	16.5	23.0	25.0
Parks & playgrounds	1.5	2.5	3.5
Public elementary school	0.5	1.5	2.5
Other governmental & institutional	1.0	1.0	1.5
Commercial	0.5	1.0	1.5
Total	100.0	100.0	100.0

3. Each residential planning unit should be designed to include a wide range of housing types, designs, and costs.

TABLE 1 (continued)

Objective No. 7

The preservation and provision of open space to enhance the total quality of the regional environment, maximize essential natural resource availability, give form and structure to urban development, and facilitate the ultimate attainment of a balanced year-round outdoor recreational program providing a full range of facilities for all age groups.

Principle

Open space is the fundamental element required for the preservation, wise use, and development of such natural resources as soil, water, woodlands, wetlands, and wildlife; it provides the opportunity to add to the physical, intellectual, and spiritual growth of the population; it enhances the economic and aesthetic value of certain types of development and is essential to outdoor recreational pursuits.

Standards

1. Local park and recreation open spaces should be provided within a maximum service radius of one-half mile of every dwelling unit in an urban area, and each site should be of sufficient size to accommodate the maximum tributary service area population at a use intensity of 675 persons per acre.
2. Regional park and recreation open spaces should be provided within an approximately one-hour travel time of every dwelling unit in the Region and should have a minimum site area of 250 acres.
3. Areas having unique scientific, cultural, scenic, or educational value should not be allocated to any urban or agricultural land uses; and adjacent surrounding areas should be retained in open-space use, such as agriculture or limited recreation.

The planning standards herein adopted fall into two groups: comparative and absolute. The comparative standards, because of their very nature, can be applied only through a comparison of alternative plan proposals. An example of such a standard is minimizing the total vehicle miles of travel within the Region. No desirable value can be realistically assigned to this standard. Its application, therefore, must be a comparative one in which the alternative plan resulting in the lowest vehicle miles of travel is deemed to best meet this standard. Absolute standards can be applied individually to each alternate plan proposal since they are expressed in terms of maximum, minimum, or desirable values. An example of such a standard is the desirable maximum walking distance of one-half mile from any home to a local park.

The standards set forth herein should serve not only as aids in the development, test, and evaluation of regional land use and transportation plans but also in the development, test, and evaluation of local land use and transportation plans and in the development of plan implementation policies and programs as well.

OVERRIDING CONSIDERATIONS

In the application of the planning standards and in the preparation of the regional land use-transportation plans, several overriding considerations must be recognized. First, it must be recognized that each proposed transportation plan must constitute an integrated system. It is not possible from an application of the standards alone, however, to assure such a system since they cannot be used to determine the effect of individual facilities on each other or on the system as a whole. This requires the application of traffic simulation models to quantitatively test the proposed system; thereby permitting adjustment of the spatial distribution and capacities of the system to the existing and future travel demand as derived from the land use plan. Second, it must be recognized that an overall evaluation of each transportation plan must be made on the basis of cost. Such an analysis may show that the attainment of one or more of the standards is beyond the economic capability of the Region and, therefore, that the standards cannot be met practically and must be either reduced or eliminated. Third, it must be recognized that it is unlikely that any one plan proposal will meet all of the standards completely; and the extent to which each standard is met, exceeded, or violated must serve as a measure of the ability of each alternative plan proposal to achieve the specific objectives which the given standard complements. Fourth, it must be recognized that certain objectives and standards may be in conflict, requiring resolution through compromise, and that meaningful plan evaluation can only take place through a comprehensive assessment of each of the alternative plans against all of the standards. Finally, it must be recognized that the standards must be very judiciously applied to areas or facilities which are already partially or fully developed since such application may require extensive renewal or reconstruction programs. Particularly, in this respect, it should also be noted that the land use standards which are concerned with natural resource protection use, or development relate primarily to those areas of the Region where the resource base has not as yet been significantly deteriorated, depleted, or destroyed. In areas where such deterioration, depletion, or destruction has already occurred, application of the standards may make it necessary to inaugurate programs which would restore the resource base to a higher level of quality, as well as quantity. [4] . . .

SECTION 6. ALTERNATIVE PLAN COMPARISON AND EVALUATION

After alternative plans have been designed, these plans must be evaluated in order to determine the degree to which they meet the established regional development objectives and standards formulated to serve as the criteria for plan selection. Presently, the techniques available for transportation system plan evaluation are more highly developed than those available for land use plan evaluation. Not only have traffic simulation models been developed for the quantitative test of the engineering feasibility of transportation plans, but also the transportation system development objectives and standards are more readily quantifiable than are the land use development objectives and standards. Moreover, the benefit–cost analysis method of evaluating investment in public works is more readily applicable to the evaluation of transportation facility plans than to land use plans.

Although a benefit-cost approach may be theoretically applicable to land use plan evaluation, the method loses much of its effectiveness in such application because of the following limitations:

(1) It is impractical to assign a monetary value to the many intangible benefits and costs that relate to the most important land use development objectives, and it is extremely difficult to assign monetary values to even the direct benefits and costs associated with a given land use plan.
(2) Because of the relatively greater uncertainty associated with land use plan implmentation than with transportation system plan implementation, there can be no assurance that the potential benefits will ever be realized, even though many of the costs associated with the development of a given land use plan may, nevertheless, be incurred through public facility and utility construction.
(3) Finally, a complete benefit-cost analysis of a land use plan would require the development of benefits and costs associated with the construction of the complete public facility and utility systems associated with the given land use plan, a task beyond the budgetary limitations and capabilities of public planning operations today.

To provide an alternative to the overriding criteria of system integration and benefit-cost analyses applied in the evaluation of the transportation system plan, as well as to provide a method for quantitatively evaluating the ability of both the land use and transportation system plans to achieve stated development objectives, the alternative plans were scaled against the standards supporting each regional development objective, and the results evaluated by the Technical Coordinating and Advisory and the Intergovernmental Coordinating Committees on Regional Land Use-Transportation Planning and by the Regional Planning Commission itself. In addition, the foregoing plan evaluation through Committee and Commission review was supplemented by application of a method of plan evaluation which seeks to assign a value to each alternative plan. The method chosen overcomes, to a considerable extent, the difficulties inherent in the application of system integration and benefit-cost analyses to land use plan evaluation and is an adaptation of the rank-based expected value method [5] used in corporate and military decision-making. This method avoids the difficulty associated with the assignment of monetary values to the benefits and costs associated with alternative land use plans by limiting the plan evaluation problem to one of rank ordering each alternative under each of the stated development objectives, since it is usually much easier to quantitatively rank the effectiveness of a given plan in achieving a given development objective than it is to attempt to assign a monetary value to the benefits accruing to the attainment of the same objective.

The difficult problems associated with uncertainty of plan implementation are also recognized in the rank-based expected value method of plan evaluation through the medium of probability estimation. Some alternative plans, while theoretically more desirable, may have a low probability of implementation; and, in the application of the method, such plans are assigned a lower value for probability of implementation. Other plans, while theoretically less desirable on the basis of their ability to attain development objectives, may have a higher actual value because of a greater likelihood of implementation. This concept of considering the uncertainty of plan implementation in plan evaluation is particularly important in relation to regional land use plans prepared as a basis for the planning and design of public works. Construction of the latter may require a high investment of public funds, and such an investment cannot be made on the sole basis of a land use plan which cannot be practically implemented.

In plan evaluation, then, the application of the rank-based expected value method involves the following sequence of activities:

(1) All specific development objectives, n in number, are ranked in order of importance to the general development objectives and assigned values of n, n minus 1, n minus 2 . . . to n minus (n−1) in descending rank order.

(2) The alternative plans, m in number, are ranked under each of the specific land use development objectives and assigned a value of m, m minus 1, m minus 2 . . . to m minus (m−1) in descending rank order.

(3) TA probability, p, of implementation is assigned to each of the plans being ranked.

(4) The value, V, of each alternative plan is then determined by summing the products of n times m times p for each of the specific development objectives.

$$V = p\,\Sigma\,(n_1m_1 + n_2m_2 + \ldots + n_nm_n)$$

The matrix table shown below illustrates a simple theoretical application of the method for three specific development objectives.

TABLE 2

Plan	Specified Development Objective: *Balanced Allocation of Land* — *Rank Order Value of Objective n = 2* — *Rank Order Value of Plan, m*	*Natural Resource Conservation* — *Rank Order Value of Objective n = 3* — *Rank Order Value of Plan, m*	*Facility Costs* — *Rank Order Value of Objective n = 1* — *Rank Order Value of Plan, m*	*Plan Value, V* — $V = p\,\Sigma\,(n_1m_1+n_2m_2+n_3m_3)$
1. Probability of implementation p = 0.6	3	1	3	0.6[(2x3)+(3x1)+(1x3)] = 7.2
2. Probability of implementation p = 0.5	2	2	1	0.5[(2x2)+(3x2)+(1x1)] = 5.5
3. Probability of implementation p = 0.9	1	3	2	0.9[(2x1)+(3x3)+(1x2)] = 11.7

In the hypothetical plan evaluation shown in the table, Plan No. 3 would be selected as that plan which best meets the development objectives.

In Chapter II of this volume, specific regional land use and transportation system development objectives were expanded into a set of supporting standards which could be used to evaluate the ability of an alternative plan to achieve a given specific development objective. Any ranking of an alternative plan for a given specific development objective must, therefore, be consistent with the ability of the plan to achieve the standards formulated for that objective. To achieve this consistency, it is first necessary to compute a value for each of the alternative plans according to the standards formulated for each specific development objective before arriving at an overall value for each plan in relation to the development objectives. This subsidiary evaluation can utilize a series of matrix tables similar to that given in the preceding example, except that the development standards replace the development objectives in the matrix table and that it is usually not necessary to assign a probability estimate for the standard evaluation.

HIERARCHICAL STRUCTURE OF OBJECTIVES AND STANDARDS

In plan evaluation it is important to recognize that the development objectives and standards formulated possess an implicit hierarchy; that is, a multi-level structure relating to differing stages and levels of detail in the land use-transportation planning process, as well as to differing levels of implementation. An example of an objective with its related standards that ranks at the highest level of the hierarchical structure is regional land use development objective No. 1, which calls for the provision of a supply of land for each use corresponding to the anticipated demand for that use. Such a design requirement can be complied with only at the regional level of plan design since it is only at this level that total land use allocation is ever known.

Other objectives and standards stand lower in the hierarchy and may directly affect plan design only at the neighborhood unit level. Examples of these kinds of standards occur under regional land use development objective No. 5, which specifies design standards for residential areas. Most of the standards supporting this objective can be finally met only through the detailed design of neighborhood unit development plans, even though a regional plan might provide the framework for such detailed design. In this connection it should be noted that the existence of a hierarchy of development objectives and standards should not create the false impression that higher levels in the hierarchy do not affect lower levels. It is quite possible that a feature of a regional plan could prevent or seriously interfere with the attainment of a neighborhood level development objective. For example, the standard requiring a diversity of housing types, designs, and costs could be defeated by the concentration of a certain class of housing in a few areas at the regional level. The hierarchical structure of the regional land use and transportation system development objectives is illustrated in Table 3 and 4.

Since regional planning is primarily concerned with land use activities and public works facilities of the kind that have areawide implications, it is apparent that the regional land use-transportation plan may not directly affect the attainment of all of the development objectives and standards. Lower level objectives and standards not directly influenced by the regional plan are, nevertheless, required to provide guidelines for planning at the community and neighborhood levels. Regionally, it is important only that compliance with lower level standards not be in conflict with the regional plan.

The following section presents in summary form a comparison of the three alternative regional land use and transportation system plans and an evaluation of these alternatives in terms of the recommended regional development objectives and standards.*

Plan Evaluation—Satisfaction of Objectives

The tabulations of the relative ability of the alternative land use and transportation plans to meet the development standards were carefully evaluated by the Technical Coordinating and Advisory and the Intergovernmental Coordinating Committees on Regional Land Use-Transportation Planning and by the Regional Planning Commission itself. Through these committee and Commission evaluations, it was concluded that the degree to which the alternative plans met the development standards, and therefore the development objectives, did not vary sufficiently to justify recommending a radical departure from historic develoment trends, thereby disregarding the heavy commitment of capital to public utilities and facilities by certain units and agencies of government within the Region in anticipation of development. This conclusion was substantiated by an independent staff evaluation of the alternative plans utilizing the rank-based expected value method. Application of this method permitted determination of the extent to which each land use and transportation plan met each specific regional land use and transportation system development objective. Application of this method required the following steps:

(1) The land use and transportation standards were ranked under each objective in order of importance.

(2) Each standard was assigned a numerical value based upon the extent to which it was met under each alternative land use and transportation plan. A numerical value of 3, 2, or 1 was assigned to each standard in one of two ways: if the standard was expressed in numerical terms, the three values were assigned to the three alternative plans on the basis of the rank order of the quantified criteria; if each alternative plan met the standard to the same degree, as determined by

*Not included herein except for Tables 5 and 6.

TABLE 3

Hierarchy of Land Use Planning Objectives and Standards for the Region

	Objective 1 Standards	*Objective 2 Standards*	*Objective 3 Standards*	*Objective 4 Standards*	*Objective 5*	*Objective 6 Standards*	*Objective 7 Standards*	*Objective 8 Standards*
Regional Level	1,2a,3, 4,5a	2,3	A-1,A-2,A-3, B-1,B-2,B-3, B-5,B-6,C-1, D-1,D-3,E-1	2,5, 6,7		1,3	2	1,2
	Standards	*Standard*	*Standards*	*Standards*	*Standard*	*Standard*	*Standard*	
Community Level	2b,5b	1	B-4,D-2	1,3,4	1	2	1	
						Standards		
Neighborhood Level						2,3		

NOTE: Objective and standard numbers are the same as those assigned in Section 2, Table 1.

TABLE 4

Hierarchy of Transportation Planning Objectives and Standards for the Region

	Objective 1 Standards	*Objective 2 Standards*	*Objective 3 Standards*	*Objective 4 Standards*	*Objective 5 Standards*	*Objective 6 Standards*	*Objective 7 Standards*
Regional Level	1,2	1,7,8 9,10,11	1,2,3	1,2	1,2,3	1,2,3 4,5,6,7	1,2
		Standards					
Community Level		2,3,4,5, 6,12,13					
Neighborhood Level							

NOTE: Objective and standard numbers are the same as those assigned in Section 2, Table 2 [not included herein.–Ed.].

numerical criteria, or if the standard was expressed in qualitative terms, a value was assigned on the basis of whether the standard was fully met (3), partially met (2), or could be met (1) through community, neighborhood, or private planning efforts.

Once each plan had been assigned a value under each standard, a plan value was computed for each specific regional development objective by multiplying the value of the plan under each supporting standard by the rank order of the standard under each objective, and summing these products for each plan. The resulting plan values were then assigned rank order values on the basis of the results of the procedure. The computations are shown in matrix form in Appendix Tables A-29 and A-30,* and the results were summarized for Tables 7 and 8.

Plan Evaluation–Plan Selection

The final selection of a recommended land use and transportation plan from among the alternatives, as indicated earlier, is predicated on the total ability of each of the alternative plans to meet the specific land use and transportation system development objectives. Since some of the objectives pertain to similar functional areas and since the satisfaction of the various objectives have varying importance, the land use and transportation system development objectives were each grouped into three major categories in order to facilitate total plan evaluation. These groups were then, in accordance with the first steps of the rank based expected value method, ranked in order of importance. It should be noted, however, that this ranking of the grouped objectives is necessarily conditioned by present environmental conditions within the Region and the present state of planning at the regional level. As time passes and certain areawide development objectives are fulfilled, others may grow in relative importance. Thus, plan evaluation must also be a part of the continuing land use-transportation planning process. The grouped objectives are shown in Appendix Table A-31 and Appendix Table A-32.*

The next step in the rank based expected value method of plan evaluation and selection requires that each alternative plan be assigned a value under each group of ranked development objectives in descending rank order. A plan implementation probability value is then selected for each alternative plan, and the value of each alternative plan computed.

Plan implementation probability values of 0.6, 0.3, and 0.1 were assigned to the controlled existing trend, corridor, and satellite city plan alternatives, respectively. The Controlled Existing Trend Plan was assigned the highest probability of implementation because of its heavy reliance on the continued effect of the urban land market in determining the location, intensity, and character of future development within the Region and its conformance to logical utility service areas and local development plans. Thus, historic

*Not included herein.–Ed.

TABLE 5
Comparison of Relative Ability of the Proposed Alternative Land Use Plans to Meet Land Use Development Standards

Objective	*Controlled Existing Trend Plan*	*Corridor Plan*	*Satellite City Plan*
Objective No. 1			
Standard			
1. Residential land allocation			
a. Low-density–250 acres/1,000 persons[a]	Met	Met	Met
b. Medium-density–70 acres/1,000 persons[a]	Met	Met	Met
c. High-density–25 acres/1,000 persons[a]	Met	Met	Met
2. Governmental and institutional land allocation[b]			
a. Local–6 acres/1,000 added population	Partially met	Partially met	Partially met
b. Regional–3 acres/1,000 added population	Partially met	Partially met	Partially met
3. Park and recreation land allocation			
a. Local–10 acres/1,000 added population[b]	2.80 ac/1,000	2.57 ac./1,000	2.78 ac./1,000
b. Regional–4 acres/1,000 added population	5.10 ac./1,000	5.10 ac./1,000	5.10 ac./1,000
4. Commercial land allocation[b]			
a. 5 acres/100 added employees	3.37 ac./100	3.20 ac./100	3.43 ac./100
5. Industrial land allocation[b]			
a. 7 acres/100 added employees	6.34 ac./100	6.21 ac./100	7.04 ac./100
Objective No. 2			
Standard			
1. Residential planning units[c]	Could be met	Could be met	Could be met
2. Regional commercial land location[a]	Met	Met	Met
3. Major industrial land location[a]	Met	Met	Met
Objective No. 3			
Standard			
1. Soils			
a. Urban uses[a]	Met	Met	Met
b. Rural uses[a]	Met	Met	Met
c. Sanitary sewer service areas[a]	Met	Met	Met
2. Inland lakes and streams			
a. Large inland lakes–over 50 acres			
(1) 25% of shore in natural state	Met for 55 of 99 lakes	Met for 55 of 99 lakes	Met for 55 of 99 lakes
(2) 10% of shore in public use	Met for 17 of 99 lakes	Met for 17 of 99 lakes	Met for 17 of 99 lakes
(3) 50% of shore in nonurban uses	Met for 62 of 99 lakes	Met for 62 of 99 lakes	Met for 62 of 99 lakes
b. Small inland lakes–under 50 acres			
(1) 25% of shore in natural state[c]	Could be met	Could be met	Could be met
c. Perennial streams			
(1) 25% of shore in natural state[b]	Met for 121 of 129 streams	Met for 121 of 129 streams	Met for 121 of 129 streams
(2) 50% of shore in nonurban uses[b]	Met for 121 of 129 streams	Met for 121 of 129 streams	Met for 121 of 129 streams
(3) Restrict urban uses in flood plains[a]	Met	Met	Met

TABLE 5 (continued)

(4) Restrict development in channels and floodways[a]	Met	Met	Met
3. Wetlands			
a. Protect wetlands over 50 acres and those with high resource value[a]	Met	Met	Met
4. Woodlands			
a. 10% of watershed[b]	Partially met	Partially met	Partially met
b. 40 acres each of 4 forest types[c]	Could be met	Could be met	Could be met
c. 5 acres/1,000 population[d]	23 ac./1,000	23 ac./1,000	23 ac./1,000
5. Wildlife[b]			
a. Maintain a wholesome habitat	Met	Met	Met
Objective No. 4			
Standard			
1. Major transportation routes penetrating residential planning units[b]	Could be met	Could be met	Could be met
2. Major transportation routes penetrating resource areas[b]	Partially met	Partially met	Partially met
3. Transportation service to appropriate areas[c]	Could be met	Could be met	Could be met
4. Transportation terminal areas[c]	Could be met	Could be met	Could be met
5. Sewer service to residential areas	100% served	95% served	87% served
6. Water supply to residential areas	100% served	95% served	87% served
7. Maximize use of existing transportation and utility facilities[a]	Met	Met	Met
Objective No. 5			
Standard			
1. Physical self-containment of residential planning units[c]	Could be met	Could be met	Could be met
2. Appropriate land uses within residential planning units[c]	Could be met	Could be met	Could be met
3. Variety of housing within residential planning units[c]	Could be met	Could be met	Could be met
Objective No. 6			
Standard			
1. Major industrial site requirements[a]	Met	Met	Met
2. Local commercial site requirements[c]	Could be met	Could be met	Could be met
3. Major commercial site requirements[a]	Met	Met	Met
Objective No. 7			
Standard			
1. Local park spatial location[c]	Could be met	Could be met	Could be met
2. Regional park spatial location[a]	Met	Met	Met
Objective No. 8			
Standard			
1. Preserve prime agricultural areas	95% preserved	96% preserved	97% preserved
2. Preserve other appropriate agricultural areas	35,000 ac. lost	18,000 ac. lost	25,000 ac. lost

SOURCE: SEWRPC.

a. This standard has been met under each of the alternative land use plans because it served as an input to the plan design process.

b. This standard is explained briefly in the accompanying text.

c. This standard could be met only by local community action.

d. Only that woodland cover contained within the primary environmental corridor was assumed to be preserved.

TABLE 6

Comparison of Relative Ability of the Proposed Transportation System to Meet the Transportation System Development Standards Under Each Land Use Plan Alternative

Objective	*Controlled Existing Trend Plan*	*Corridor Plan*	*Satellite City Plan*
Objective No. 1			
Standard			
1. Adequate accessibility[a]	Met	Met	Met
2. Volume-to-capacity ratio equal to or less than 1.0[a]	93.1% of arterial streets and highways; 100% of transit route mileage	93.1% of arterial streets and highways; 100% of transit route mileage	94.0% of arterial streets and highways; 100% of transit route mileage
Objective No. 2			
Standard			
1. Transit warrants[b]	Met	Met	Met
2. Local transit service[c]	Could be met	Could be met	Could be met
3. Transit headways[c]	Could be met	Could be met	Could be met
4. Transit stop spacing[c]	Could be met	Could be met	Could be met
5. Transit loading factors[c]	Could be met	Could be met	Could be met
6. Transit route alignment[c]	Could be met	Could be met	Could be met
7. Percentage transit to CBD[a]			
Milwaukee	22.8%	24.0%	21.8%
Racine	4.3%	4.1%	3.8%
Kenosha	3.6%	3.5%	3.6%
8. Provision of transit peak hours[b]	Met	Met	Met
9. Parking at park-and-ride stations[c]	Could be met	Could be met	Could be met
10. Freeway warrants[b]	Met	Met	Met
11. Arterial warrants[b]	Met	Met	Met
12. Walking distance for short-term parkers[c]	Could be met	Could be met	Could be met
13. Parking spaces in CBD's[c]	Could be met	Could be met	Could be met
Objective No. 3			
Standard			
1. Minimize vehicle hours of travel	928,000 hrs/day	930,000 hrs/day	931,000 hrs/day
2. Overall speeds			
Freeways	42 mph	42 mph	42 mph
Standard arterials	30 mph	30 mph	31 mph
3. Maximize proportion of vehicle miles on freeways	42.6%	42.9%	42.4%
Maximize percentage rapid and modified rapid transit utilization	38.2%	42.5%	37.6%
Objective No. 4			
Standard			
1. Volume-to-capacity equal to or less than 0.9	88.0% of arterial streets and highways	87.7% of arterial streets and highways	89.6% of arterial streets and highways
2. Maximize proportion of vehicle miles on freeways	42.6%	42.9%	42.4%
Maximize percentage transit utilization	5.9%	6.3%	5.6%

TABLE 6 (continued)

Objective No. 5			
Standard			
1. Minimize operating costs[d]	\$22.06 billion	\$22.11 billion	\$22.21 billion
Minimize capital investment[e]	\$ 2.06 billion	\$ 2.05 billion	\$ 2.09 billion
Minimize total costs	\$24.12 billion[f]	\$24.16 billion[f]	\$24.30 billion[f]
2. Minimize vehicle miles of travel	31,822,000 mi/day	31,912,000 mi/day	32,331,000 mi/day
3. Use of existing and committed transportation system[b]	Met	Met	Met
Objective No. 6			
Standard			
1. Minimize penetration of neighborhoods[c]	Could be met	Could be met	Could be met
2. Minimize dislocation[c]	Could be met	Could be met	Could be met
3. Minimize penetration of environmental corridors[c]	Could be met	Could be met	Could be met
4. Advance reservation of right-of-way[a]	Partially met	Partially met	Partially met
5. Minimize destruction of cultural sites[c]	Could be met	Could be met	Could be met
6. Minimize use of land for transportation system	65.99 sq. mi.	61.25 sq. mi.	66.34 sq. mi.
Objective No. 7			
Standard			
1. Minimize disruption of visual axes[c]	Could be met	Could be met	Could be met
2. Design standards[c]	Could be met	Could be met	Could be met

SOURCE: SEWRPC.

a. This standard is explained briefly in the accompanying text.

b. This standard has been met under each of the alternative land use plans because it served as an input to the plan design process.

c. This standard could be met only by local community or private action.

d. Only includes travel on SEWRPC net (interzonal travel only).

e. Includes maintenance (includes off-net facilities).

f. Does not include cost of rapid transit proposals estimated at \$20,575,000 under the Controlled Existing Trend and Satellite City plans, or \$36,145,000 under the Corridor Plan.

TABLE 7

Comparison of Relative Ability of the Alternative Land Use Plans to Meet the Specific Development Objectives

	Plan Value Under Land Use Plan (V)		
Objective	*Controlled Existing Trend Plan*	*Corridor Plan*	*Satellite City Plan*
1	2	1	3
2	2	2	2
3	2	2	2
4	3	2	1
5	1	1	1
6	2	2	2
7	2	2	2
8	1	2	3

SOURCE: SEWRPC.

TABLE 8

Comparison of Relative Ability of the Planned Transportation System to Meet the Transportation Objectives Under the Alternative Land Use Plans

	Plan Value Under Land Use Plan (V)		
Objective	*Controlled Existing Trend Plan*	*Corridor Plan*	*Satellite City Plan*
1	2	1	3
2	3	2	1
3	3	2	1
4	2	3	1
5	3	2	1
6	2	3	1
7	1	1	1

SOURCE: SEWRPC.

TABLE 9

Land Use Plan Selection Criteria

Plan	*Major Group Objective*	*Provide for a Balanced Allocation of Land*[a]	*Provide for an Appropriate Spatial Distribution of Land Uses*[a]	*Meet the Design Requirements of the Major Land Uses*[a]	
		Rank Order of Group Objective = 3	*Rank Order of Group Objective = 2*	*Rank Order of Group Objective = 1*	
		Rank Order Value of Plan[b]	*Rank Order Value of Plan*[b]	*Rank Order Value of Plan*[b]	*Plan Value*
Controlled existing trend	Probability of implementation = 0.6	2	3	1	7.8
Corridor	Probability of implementation = 0.3	1	2	2	2.7
Satellite city	Probability of implementation = 0.1	3	1	3	1.4

SOURCE: SEWRPC.

a. Includes the objectives listed under this group in Appendix Table A-31.

b. Based on the rank order value as shown in Appendix Table A-29.

TABLE 10
Transportation Plan Selection Criteria

Plan	*Major Group Objective*	*Serve Land Use Pattern and Meet Travel Demand*[a]	*Provide Appropriate Transportation at an Adequate Service Level*[a]	*Provide for an Economical Transportation System*[a]	
		Rank Order of Group Objective = 3	*Rank Order of Group Objective = 2*	*Rank Order of Group Objective = 1*	
Plan		*Rank Order Value of Plan*[b]	*Rank Order Value of Plan*[b]	*Rank Order Value of Plan*[b]	*Plan Value*
Controlled existing trend	Probability of implementation = 0.6	2	3	3	9.0
Corridor	Probability of implementation =0.3	3	2	2	4.5
Satellite city	Probability of implementation =0.1	3	1	1	1.2

SOURCE: SEWRPC.

a. Includes the objectives listed under this group in Appendix Table A-32.

b. Based on the rank order value as shown in Appendix Table A-30.

development trends would be altered only slightly under the Controlled Existing Trend Plan, as required to meet regional development objectives. The Corridor Plan was assigned an intermediate probability of implementation value because, while it represents a more radical departure from historic development trends, it does recognize the continued effect of major transportation routes upon the location, intensity, and character of future development. Historic development trends would have to be more severely altered than under the Controlled Existing Trend Plan and development restricted in certain areas already committed to development through utility service extensions. The Satellite City Plan was assigned the lowest probability of implementation value because it represents the most radical departure from historic development trends. It not only ignores local development plans to a considerable extent but would require severe development restrictions to be imposed on areas presently committed to development.

The final results of the plan evaluation and selection procedure are shown in matrix form for the alternative land use plans in Table 9 and for the alternative land use-transportation system plan combinations in Table 10. These results indicate that the Controlled Existing Trend Plan best meets the regional land use and transportation system development objectives.

OVERRIDING CONSIDERATIONS

Earlier in this report, it was emphasized that full evaluation of the alternative plans could not be achieved through application of the development objectives and standards alone but that five overriding considerations would have to be recognized in the full plan evaluation process.

First, it was indicated that each proposed transportation plan must constitute an integrated system. Each alternative land use and transportation plan proposed herein meets this requirement since the plan design methodology applied dealt with the transportation elements solely as an integrated system and incorporated the application of traffic simulation models for quantitative plan test.

Second, it was indicated that, in addition to application of the development standards, an evaluation of each transportation system plan must be made on the basis of cost. Total construction and maintenance cost estimates were, therefore, prepared for the transportation element of each alternative land use and transportation plan; and these are summarized in a following section of this report.

Third, it was indicated that it was unlikely that any one plan proposal would meet all of the development standards completely and that the extent to which each standard was met, exceeded, or violated must serve as a measure of the ability of each alternative plan proposal to achieve the specific objectives which the given standard complements. An evaluation procedure was developed to accommodate this consideration and thereby facilitate the plan evaluation and selection process. This procedure consists of an adaptation of the rank-based expected value method of evaluation applied in corporate decision-making, and the results were described in the preceding section of this report.

Fourth, it was indicated that certain objectives and standards may be in conflict and require resolution through compromise and that meaningful plan evaluation can take place only through a comprehensive assessment of each of the alternative plans against all of the objectives and standards.

Application of the rank-based expected value method of plan evaluation utilized herein assists in achieving the necessary comprehensive assessment, and any compromises necessary to resolve conflicts are accommodated in the ranking of development standards and objectives.

Finally, it was indicated that the standards must be very judiciously applied to areas or facilities which are already partially or fully developed, since strict application might indicate the requirement of extensive renewal or reconstruction programs. Accommodation of this consideration was achieved for the land use plans through evaluation of the plans against the development standards on the basis of the incremental land use proposals rather than on the basis of the ultimate land use pattern proposed. For the transportation system plans, hoever, the evaluation was based upon the full ultimate system; and careful consideration was given to the need for facility reconstruction.

TRANSPORTATION SYSTEM COST ANALYSIS

In order to facilitate full plan evaluation, estimates of the overall cost of implementing the proposed transportation plan under each of the alternative land use plans were prepared. These estimates were prepared by applying unit improvement costs to the estimated mileage of proposed future improvements, including construction of new facilities and reconstruction of certain existing facilities, which would be required to provide adequate arterial street and highway system capacity by 1990; by applying unit improvement costs to the estimated mileage of new collector and local or minor streets necessary to serve new urban development; and by preparing special estimates of the cost of constructing the proposed bus rapid transit facilities. In addition, the costs of maintaining the proposed and existing arterial street and highway systems and the proposed and existing collector and minor street systems were separately estimated.*

SUMMARY

This section has presented a description, comparison, and evaluation of three alternative land use and transportation plans designed to meet anticipated growth and change within the Region while attaining stated regional development objectives. The most important elements of these two sections [Section 5, not included herein.—Ed.] are summarized below.

1. Three alternative regional development plans were prepared and evaluated under the regional land use-transportation study: a Controlled Existing Trend, a Corridor, and a Satellite City Plan. Each represents an attempt to meet the regional development objectives with a basically different land use arrangement. While many variations of these three basic development patterns are possible, it is believed that the three patterns selected represent the basic choices with respect to future development patterns practically available to the Region.

2. The Controlled Existing Trend Plan represents a conscious continuation of historic development trends with urban development occurring in concentric rings along the full periphery of, and outward from, the existing major urban centers within the Region. This plan places heavy reliance on the effect of the urban land market in determining the location, intensity, and character of future development. It does, however, propose to regulate in the public interest the effect of this market on development in order to provide for a more orderly and economic regional development pattern and avoid intensification of areawide development and environmental problems. Under this plan the historic growth trends would be altered by guiding intensive urban development into those areas of the Region having both soils suitable for such development and gravity

*The remainder of this section, detailing the costs and benefits of the alternative transportation systems, is not included herein.—Ed.

drainage sanitary sewer service readily available. In addition, the floodways and flood plains; the best remaining woodlands, wetlands, and fish and game habitat areas; and the best remaining potential park and related open-space sites would be protected from urban development and would form the basic framework for an integrated system of park and open-space areas within the Region. The allocation of future land use within each county of the Region under this plan would be such as to approximate the forecast population levels within each county and, to the extent possible, the proposals contained in existing community development plans and zoning documents. The plan would add approximately 200 square miles of new urban development within the Region by 1990.

3. The Corridor Plan represents an attempt to concentrate new urban development within the Region in radial corridors centered on major transportation routes emanating from the existing major urban centers within the Region. Higher densities of development than under the Controlled Existing Trend Plan would be emphasized, and the radial corridors of urban development would be alternated with wedges of agricultural and other open-space uses. The plan would add approximately 170 square miles of new urban development within the Region by 1990.

4. The Satellite City Plan represents an attempt to concentrate new urban development within the Region in five outlying communities of the Region, relatively independent of commerical and industrial development in the larger central cities and separated from these cities by large areas of open space. The plan would add 180 square miles of new urban development within the Region by 1990.

5. The Controlled Existing Trend Plan would convert more prime agricultural land from rural to urban use than the other two alternatives and proposes the greatest increase in low-density residential development. The Satellite City Plan proposes the greatest increase in medium-density residential development. The Corridor Plan proposes the greatest increase in high-density residential development and would convert the least amount of prime agricultural land from rural to urban use.

6. The Satellite City Plan proposes eight new major industrial areas, while each of the other two alternatives propose only six new major industrial areas within the Region by 1990. Each of the alternative plans proposes 10 new major commercial areas, but under the Satellite City Plan two of these areas would be located in outlying communities instead of in the vicinity of the older central cities within the Region.

7. The Controlled Existing Trend Plan would permit the highest proportion of the urbanized area and the highest proportion of the population to be served by public sanitary sewer and water facilities.

8. The total future travel demand generated by the three alternative land use patterns would not be significantly different. Total person trips generated within the Region would be expected to increase from the 1963 level of 3.6 million

person trips per average weekday to a 1990 level of 6.1 million under the Controlled Existing Trend Plan, 6.0 million under the Corridor Plan, and 6.1 million under the Satellite City Plan. Vehicle trips would similarly be expected to increase from the 1963 level of 2.9 million vehicle trips per average weekday to a 1990 level of 5.1 million under the Controlled Existing Trend Plan, 4.9 million under the Corridor Plan, and 5.0 million under the Satellite City Plan.

9. Somewhat greater differences were found between the three alternative land use plans with respect to transit trip generation and utilization. The Region in 1963 generated a total of 384,000 transit trips per average weekday. This is expected to increase by 1990 to 488,000 under the Controlled Existing Trend Plan, to 508,000 under the Corridor Plan, and to 471,000 under the Satellite City Plan. Although the total number of transit trips within the Region is expected to increase during the period 1963 to 1990, a reversal of historic trends, the proportion of transit utilization is expected to decrease under each of the three alternative plans from about 9 percent of the total person trips per average weekday in 1963 to about 6 percent by 1990.

10. Total vehicle miles of travel within the Region are expected to remain essentially the same under each of the three alternative land use plans, increasing from the 1963 level of about 13.2 million vehicle miles per average weekday to 31.8 million vehicle miles by 1990 under the Controlled Existing Trend Plan, 31.9 million vehicle miles under the Corridor Plan, and 32.3 million vehicle miles under the Satellite City Plan.

11. Automobile availability within the Region is expected to be highest under the Satellite City Plan, increasing from the 1963 level of 527,000 automobiles to 1,056,000 by 1990. Automobile ownership would be expected to increase to 1,042,000 by 1990 under the Controlled Existing Trend Plan and to 1,002,000 under the Corridor Plan.

12. Essentially the same system of freeways would be required to serve the Region under each of the alternative plans, although the required capacity of the standard arterial street and highway system would differ, with the Satellite City Plan requiring the greatest investment for additional highway capacity by 1990. Eight new freeways proposed under each of the alternative plans total approximately 256 miles in length.

13. In addition to and complementing the proposed freeway system, an expanded modified rapid transit system is recommended, which would provide the most heavily urbanized portions of the Region with an efficient and economical as well as a high level of transit service. Under the Corridor Plan, the construction of two fully grade-separated bus rapid transit lines would be justified, totaling about 12 miles in length, while under the Controlled Existing Trend and Satellite City plans only one such bus rapid transit line, totaling about 7 miles in length, would be justified.

14. The total improvement costs involved in the implementation of the highway transportation plan elements would be about $932 million under the Controlled Existing Trend Plan, $931 million under the Satellite City Plan.

These costs would be incurred over the 1967-1990 plan implementation period and are well within the financial ability of the Region, as indicated by public revenue forecasts for highway construction purposes. Benefit-cost analyses indicate, moreover, that the expenditure for highway improvements would represent a sound investment of public funds, with the benefit-cost ratio varying from 1.4 under the Satellite City Plan to 1.7 under the Corridor Plan. The cost of implementing the proposed rapid transit plan recommendations would be $36,145,000 under the Corridor Plan and $20,575,000 under the Controlled Existing Trend and Satellite City plans.

15. The controlled existing trend land use plan appears to satisfy more of the land use development standards than either of the other two alternatives. Plan evaluation, utilizing the rank-based expected value method, further indicates that the Controlled Existing Trend Plan best meets the stated regional development objectives.

NOTES

1. See SEWRPC Regional Planning Program Prospectus, April 1962; SEWRPC *Regional Land use-Transportation Study Design,* August 1963; SEWRPC Procedural Manual No. 1, *Organization Charts and Position Descriptions,* July 1963; SEWRPC Procedural Manual No. 2, *Home Interview Survey,* December 1963; SEWRPC Procedural Manual No. 3, *Truck and Taxi Survey,* May 1964; SEWRPC Procedural Manual No. 4, *External Survey,* August 1963; SEWRPC Procedural Manual No. 5, *Land Use Survey,* May 1963; SEWRPC Procedural Manual No. 6, *Coding,* May 1964.

2. SEWRPC Planning Report No. 7, Volume 1, *Inventory Findings–1963,* May 1965.

3. SEWRPC Technical Report No. 3, "A Mathematical Approach to Urban Design," January 1966.

4. For a detailed analysis of stream water quality conditions and an evaluation of water quality standards, see SEWRPC Technical Report No. 4, "'Water Quality and Flow of Streams in Southeastern Wisconsin."

5. See H. Igor Ansoff, *Corporate Strategy,* McGraw-Hill, New York, 1965.

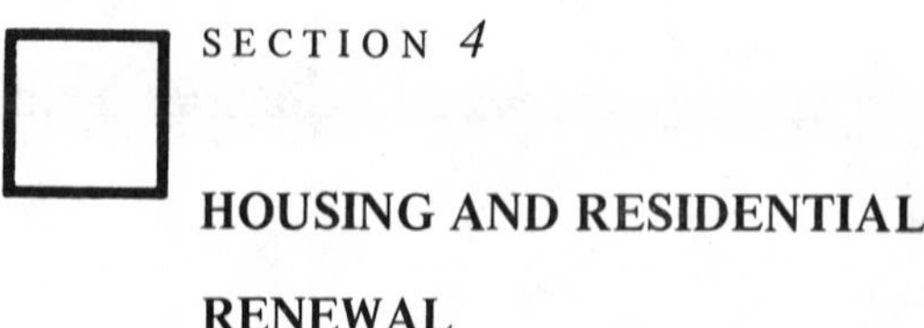

SECTION *4*

HOUSING AND RESIDENTIAL RENEWAL

Chapter 22

THE SAN FRANCISCO COMMUNITY RENEWAL SIMULATION MODEL

San Francisco Department of City Planning

I. BACKGROUND

A. Model Building for the Community Renewal Program

The goal of a Community Renewal Program is to bring together those individual projects and actions aimed at improving the living environment of a city and coordinate them in such a way that the maximum benefits may be realized by unified and mutually consistent programs.

A central issue that must be dealt with is the extent to which each of the individual actions affect the community as they interact upon the environment. An intelligent and coordinated policy can only be developed when the combined effects of separate policies are understood. But such understanding cannot be achieved unless the "whole" of the problem is conceived, a conception that permits the construction of a framework into which the individual parts logically fit. The idea of constructing such a framework was fundamental in selecting the simulation model approach as a way of understanding the behavior of the housing market. As the consultants noted in an early progress report to the Department of City Planning,

> "The fundamental objective of the CRP is its programming function; that is, the establishment of a schedule of actions, both private and public, on a time phase basis. Such programming requires an overall view of the system being programmed–that is, the City and its interrelated elements–so that the renewal planners can have

Reprinted from "Status of the San Francisco Simulation Model" by the Department of City Planning, City and County of San Francisco (September 1968), 27 pp. Reprinted by permission of the Director of Planning of the Department.

> reference at all times to the state of the system and to the changes in that state which will be occasioned by individual program actions. The systems concept, utilizing a mathematical model adapted to electronic computers, offers the most promising method of dealing with the complexities involved" [San Francisco Community Renewal Program, 1963: 21].

Early in the program, there was consideration of a very ambitious model building program which would comprehend the entire spectrum of city processes. However, following the preliminary discussions, the decision was made to concentrate effort on the development of a model of the housing market.

In particular, the purpose of this housing model would be to test the effects of various public policy programs upon the supply of housing in the city–quantity, quality, general location, rents, prices, etc.–in relation to the demand for that housing. Implicit in the construction and use of the housing model was the "statement" that if the city had certain housing objectives or needs–how much housing of what sizes, for whom, where and at what prices–the model could project what the consequences of public policies and public and private actions would be in relation to those objectives or needs.

This decision to construct a model of the housing market was influenced by a number of factors. Housing was a principal issue for the Community Renewal Program to study. The structure of the housing market was felt to be sufficiently well understood so that it could be cast into the explicit framework required for model building. Finally, the Census of 1960 had made available a considerable amount of data that would be necessary if the model were to be made operational. Work commenced on the design of the model in early 1964. By March 1965, a number of pilot runs had been made, and in June 1965, the final runs of the first version of the model were completed as a part of the Community Renewal Program.

B. Systems Analysis, Simulation Models and the Computer

The systems analysis approach to problem solving–in this case, problems related to housing–requires first that the problem be well defined; second, that the individual elements of the problem be clearly identified; and third, that the relationship of the elements, both to the general problem of which they are a part and to each other, be specified. The value of the method depends upon the precision with which each of these steps are accomplished. The end product of successful application of systems analysis is a statement of the problem in which the whole and its parts are clearly distinguished and their inter-relationships clearly established.

Simulation modeling requires the same steps to understanding as are found in systems analysis. Once having achieved these steps, the model builder creates a simpler framework which contains all of the significant parts in their appropriate relationships to the whole and to each other. The object of building a model is to recreate the more complex phenomena of the real world in a form that can be easily grasped and manipulated. The usefulness of the model is to be found in the ease with which it can be used to represent differing circumstances. A well constructed model, capable of manipulation, may have the property of providing information about the real world that is either not available, or is available at such cost that experiment is not feasible.

For instance, suppose that a supplier of automobile parts has to cover the needs of a number of dealers. He cannot carry a sufficient inventory of parts to assure that every unanticipated order can be filled. Yet he must be able to have enough stock to supply most of the orders or he will lose his customers. One course of action he can follow is to guess the needs of his customers, based on experience. For a small business, dealing in a familiar area, this is often sufficient. However, as the size of the area and the demand for a variety of stock increases, the ability to guess correctly diminishes and the danger of an incorrect guess increases. For intuition, he may want to substitute a more precise method of anticipating his inventory needs. Given knowledge of the various elements of his market, of the relationship between supply and demand, and the constraints under which his business must operate, it is possible that a model may be constructed which accurately represents his situation. Using the model, he may experiment with different inventory compositions and eventually settle on one which will offer the best solution to his problem, i.e., maintaining an inventory that will satisfy most of his customers' demand and one which will not be beyond his capacity. If he had to carry out his experiments directly, the chances are that he could not afford the price of a single experimental failure. However, the use of a model permits him to examine alternative solutions to his problem before he makes a major investment of capital. At the very least, it reduces the probability of failure and, at an optimum, provides for a reasonable expectation of success. This particular application of the modeling concept is very common in business and has proven its worth during the past decade numerous times.

The electronic computer makes many models possible simply because it can manage enormous amounts of information. It is not a magic device and in order to use it effectively the requirements of systems analysis and model building outlined above must be rigorously observed. Computers must be told precisely what to do, what to do with it, when to do it, and how to make the information available to the user. Inadequate systems analysis and poorly contrived models do not affect the operation of the computer. Like any desk calculator, it will do an effective job of processing with bad data and it will ask no questions about the validity or the use of the data. However, the results produced in these adverse circumstances will be worthless, and may even be dangerously misleading. The computer is a useful, even necessary tool, as is the hammer to the carpenter. To be used well, it must be handled skillfully, and in the instance of systems analysis and model building, it must now be apparent that all of these components are complementary: without adequate systems analysis, a good model cannot be constructed; without a good model, the information handling capacity of the computer is useless.

II. THE SIMULATION MODEL OF THE HOUSING MARKET

A. The Purpose and Use of the Model

The model is intended to be a means by which the effects of housing policies and programs can be measured. The subject of the measurement is the supply of housing, its kind, condition, quantity and cost to the consumer. The span of time for which the measurement is made, eighteen years, corresponds to that span of time for which effective housing policy can be formulated, programs carried out, and the effects of these programs felt in the housing market. The use of the model is to help the policy maker have a quantitative basis for choosing the best possible combination of programs that will enable the goal of an adequate and suitable supply of housing to be realized.

The effective use of the model depends upon the existence of alternative policies between which policy makers must choose when they are considering the programs that are aimed at achieving the goal of a well-balanced housing supply. The model is operated using the same basic information for each alternative set of housing policies and their implementing programs. The outcome of each operation corresponding to a different housing policy is then compared, and the quantitative measurements, noted above, provide clues to which one of the alternatives proved the most effective in reaching the goals set by the policy maker. This permits the elimination of those alternatives which show themselves to be grossly ineffective. Policies appearing to have a greater chance for success may then be tested further, perhaps recombined, and ultimately, the combination having the greatest promise is selected. At all times in this process, the policy maker may intervene, either to change the basic information with which the model operates, or to modify the housing policies. It is this quality of dynamic interaction which makes the model a useful tool. The results provided by the model are always relative, both to the basic information about the housing market and the policy alternatives considered. Results of the model are therefore comparative measurements which depend upon the comparison of the outcomes of model operations, either by varying the conditions of the basic information or the policy alternatives under consideration. The following diagram (Figure No. 1) shows the manner in which the model would normally be employed. Housing policy alternatives are prepared independently of the model. Each is then given a separate computer operation, and the outcomes of each of the operations (runs) are then compared and evaluated by the policy makers. After comparisons, the alternative which promises the most effective achievement of the goal is then proposed as the desirable policy for the community to pursue. The model may also be used to test the effects of a single policy under differing basic conditions. In this case, the policy would remain constant for the separate runs of the model, and the basic information would be altered. An example of this would be the testing of a

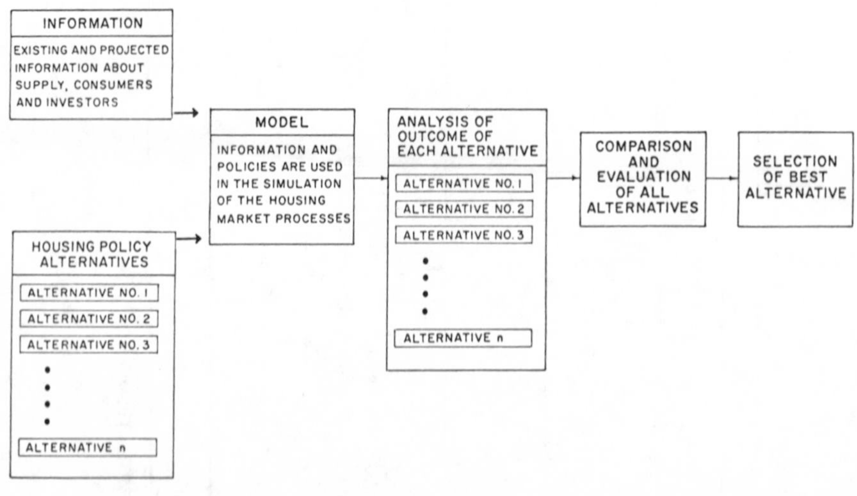

Figure 1: OPERATION AND USE OF HOUSING MODEL

particular housing policy given differing population projections, as reflected in the number and composition of the households consuming housing.

B. Operation of the Simulation Model

In what follows, a general and non-technical description of the operation of the simulation model is provided. In order to do so effectively, the operation of the model is considered in two phases: (1) the complete operation, or "run"; and (2) the operation of a single period of the model.

1. *Description of Complete Run*

The present version of the model considers the period 1960-1978, an eighteen-year span. This span is divided into nine two-year periods and in each of these periods the operation of the model is the same, though particular items of information may differ for each period.

At the commencement of model operations, 1960 housing stock information, as compiled by the Bureau of the Census, was used with respect to the number of units in terms of type, condition, location and average rent. During each successive period, the housing stock is modified by the operation of the model, and the new stock becomes the state of the stock for the following period. At the end of nine periods, the stock that was initially used in the model has undergone nine successive modifications, corresponding to the nine periods in the eighteen-year span. The final state of the stock in 1978 is, therefore, the

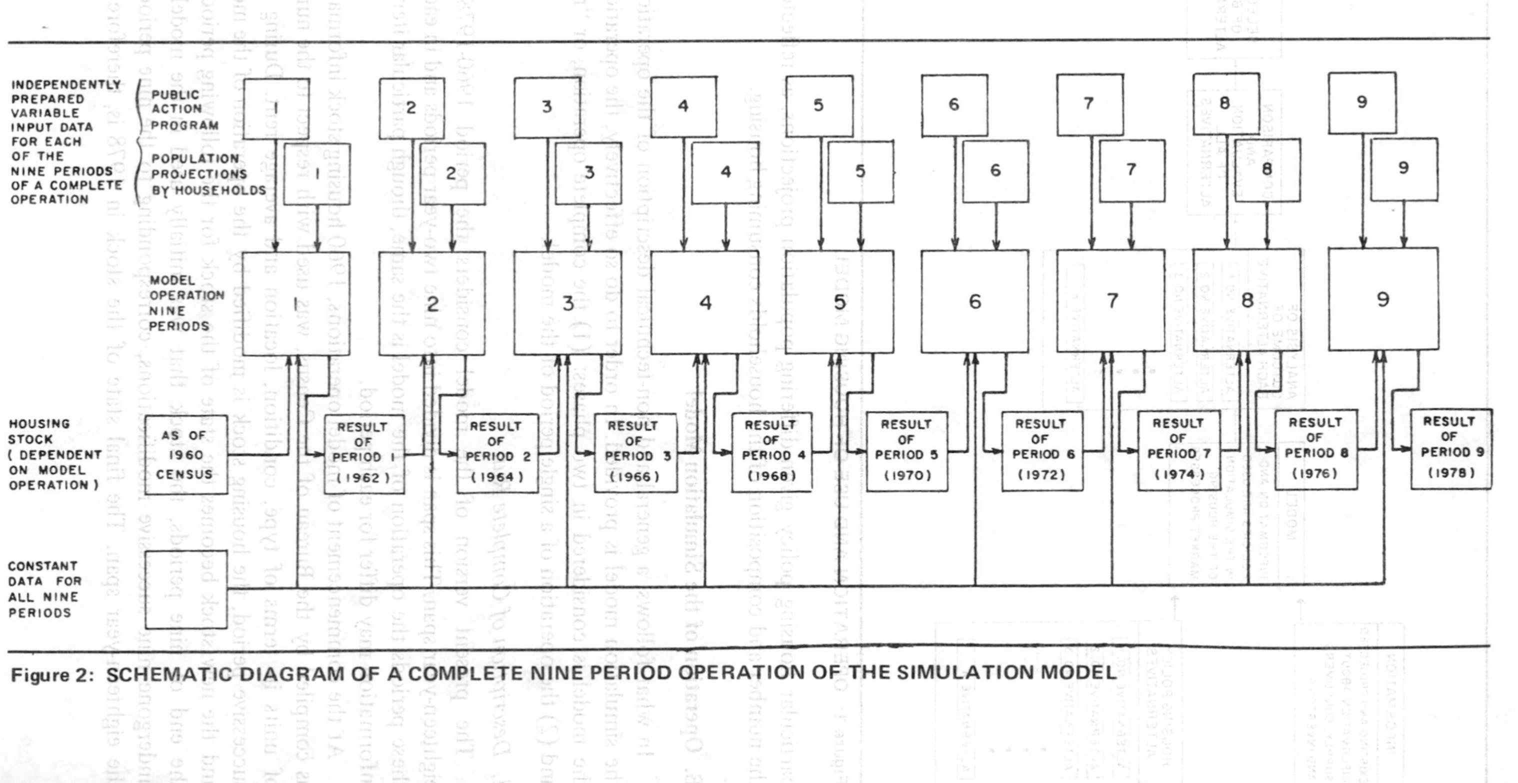

Figure 2: SCHEMATIC DIAGRAM OF A COMPLETE NINE PERIOD OPERATION OF THE SIMULATION MODEL

outcome of the action of various factors which have affected stock during the entire span of time (Figure No. 2).

The model is based upon the process by which housing is consumed and produced in the market place. The housing stock used in the model represents the supply in the market at any given time. The families seeking housing represent the consumers of that supply, or demand, actual and potential. The model matches supply and demand. If the supply is entirely adequate to match the demand, the state is said to be in equilibrium, or balanced. If, on the other hand, the supply and demand are not in balance, the resulting *dis*-equilibrium causes opportunities for changes in the stock. In the model, these opportunities are evaluated in terms of: (1) their profitability; and (2) whether or not they would be permitted by the zoning ordinance. Demand for uneconomic or forbidden choices is ignored and the stock is changed only in the direction of those choices which are both profitable and permissible. The model then modifies the housing supply accordingly for the period and the altered stock becomes the beginning state of the next period. The household population (families) consumes the supply and its demand for housing is recorded in the computer. The demand is evaluated using criteria of profitableness to the private investor and likely housing development is noted. These are then screened by the computer to determine whether or not they conform to the permissible housing density established by the zoning ordinance and, if they do, they become a list from which the most profitable projects are selected and executed. The housing stock is changed accordingly and the inventory at the end of the first period, 1961-1962, becomes the housing supply for the second period, 1963-1964. This process is repeated eight more times for a full nine-period operation of the model.

The evaluation of the results of the nine-period run in terms of the inventory of housing, number, type, condition and rent are based on the output from this final period of operation. When this is considered in the context of the goals set for program achievement and factors such as the nature of the population projection used for the period, a comparison is made with alternative policies using the same basic information. The analyst can then draw conclusions regarding the relative effectiveness of the program being tested. If, for instance, the housing stock resulting from the program being considered falls far short of the goals it is intended to achieve, and an alternative approach produces a more satisfactory balance, clearly the latter alternative would be desirable. Decisions regarding the best alternative to follow are not automatically given by the computer; they are arrived at through careful scrutiny of the results provided by the model and consideration of aspects which may not be quantifiable but nonetheless may be principal determinants in the selection of housing policy.

2. *Description of a Single Period*

A complete run of the model consists of nine repetitive units, referred to as "periods." An understanding of how the model works can be gained from an examination of a single period, the building block of the complete run. With the minor exception of the elimination of the "aging" process in the first period, all periods are identical with respect to operation. The heart of each period consists of two cycles of market operation, each of them identical. (Although the period corresponds to a two-year span in the "real world," the use of two cycles is purely a matter of choice. In early versions of the model, three cycles were used.)

The cycle, which corresponds to the operation of demand and supply to the housing market, consists of the following steps:

- Households seek, bid for, and consume housing stock according to their ability to pay;
- Unsatisfied effective demand for housing stock is computed, rents (prices) of housing are altered in response to demand;
- The profitableness (for the private investor) of satisfying the effective demand for each desired housing type is evaluated (in terms of the amount of demand for that type, the cost of change, and the minimum yield such an investment would have to provide the investor);
- The most profitable changes in the stock, and those permitted by the zoning ordinance are made;
- The housing inventory is accordingly modified.

The modified housing inventory produced by the first cycle of the model becomes the basic stock for the second cycle. Finally, the housing inventory as it has been modified by the two cycles becomes the state of the stock at the completion of the period.

The principal elements of the simulation model are named in the description of the cycle and their relationships to each other are identified. These elements may be identified as:

(a) Households, the consumers of housing;
(b) Investors, the private market suppliers of housing;
(c) Government, whose actions affect the process of the private market directly or indirectly;
(d) Housing Stock, the supply of housing.

Each of these elements is represented in the model by information that describes their characteristics. It is upon this information that the model, utilizing the computer program, operates. The information used in the model is briefly described to provide an understanding of its scope and origin.

a. Households. The basic consuming unit in the model is the household. The population of the city is partitioned into households by the number of persons, their relationship to the head of the household, the household income range, age of the head, and race. The resulting partition provides eighty-four different groups. For each period of the run, a separate population forecast by households is prepared and distributed among the eighty-four groups. Each household group has associated with it a list of up to fifty housing preferences and a range of rental paying ability. These are used in the process of bidding for and consuming housing. The data used for the differentiation of household groups and for the establishment of their housing preferences and rent paying ability has been derived from a special cross tabulation of the 1960 Census of Population and Housing of San Francisco prepared especially for this study. Any and all of these characteristics, including the basic partition of the population into households, may be altered during the run. In the development phase of the model, the practice has been to keep all factors constant except for changes in the population of household groups by period. Assumptions about the future housing consumption patterns of the city have been varied by this means alone.

b. Investors. In the model, the element that makes the decision to satisfy demand is termed the investor. This embraces all of the diverse collection of occupations and organizations which, in the real world, create the supply of housing. There is no attempt, in this model, to reflect the diversity or the operation of these highly variegated institutions. Rather, emphasis is placed on the profitability of the investment itself in terms of whether or not the change will result in a return equal to or greater than a minimum yield the investor would have to make on that investment. In making this decision, the rents obtainable from the existing use, those from the proposed use, and the cost of making the change are computed to provide a yield figure. This figure is compared to a figure representing the minimum yield which a rational investor would have to realize from an investment in a housing type. If the ratio is equal to or greater than 1, the project has a chance of being executed; if not, the project is discarded, regardless of the demand for it.

The information used in this operation consists of the costs of building anew, the minimum yield expected for such a return, and the rents returned from the various housing types. The first two items were determined by special studies carried out by the consultant. The last item is based on the data provided by the special cross tabulation of housing mentioned in the Household element, and is modified by the demand generated in each cycle of the model's operation. If there is demand, the rents are raised, if there is no demand they are lowered, and if the supply is in balance, they are not altered. While costs and minimum yields may be altered in the course of model operation, they have not been in current practice.

c. Government. Governmental agencies are represented in the model by various actions, executed either directly or indirectly, which affect the supply of housing through intervention in the normal market process. An explicit action, zoning, has already been mentioned in the explanation of the operation of the individual cycle. Other actions directly or explicitly affecting the housing supply now used in the operation of the model consist of: code enforcement, removal of units for a public purpose, redevelopment of areas for new housing, and provision of public housing. Although it has not yet been attempted, other and more indirect actions by government which affect the yields on investments (e.g., changes in the rates of property assessment), could be simulated. The restriction of governmental actions to relatively few explicit actions is the result of our limited operational experience with the simulation model.

Governmental actions are prepared for each period of the operation of the model, and the actions enter the program during the operation of the model, as do the alterations in the population projection. A public action, such as clearance and redevelopment, may require more than one period for its completion. This is reflected in the model by scheduling the different phases, beginning with acquisition of the site, then clearance, and finally rebuilding and marketing by a continuing series of actions covering several periods of operation. From this example, it may be seen that public actions may be experimented with from a scheduling standpoint. Thus a particular redevelopment project might be varied in terms of the number of years required for its completion, a factor that might bear importantly on its market impact. This information is based on programs and policies prepared by those responsible for such policy and translated into the special vocabulary of the model by the systems analyst. Their effect is determined, as noted above, by the impact of the set of policies upon the housing stock and the comparison of this effect with the impact of alternative policies.

d. The Housing Stock. The product of the interaction of the elements described above is the supply of housing. In the model, the housing supply is described in the following terms:

Single Family, Rooms: 1-4; 5-6; 7 or More
Two to Four-Unit Structures, Rooms: 1-4; 5 or More
Five or More Unit Structures, Rooms: 1; 2; 3-4; 5 or More

Each of these nine basic housing types are further described in terms of four conditions of housing, corresponding to defintions used by the Bureau of the Census. These are:

Condition 1 – Sound, All Facilities
Condition 2 – Needing Minor Repair
Condition 3 – Deteriorating
Condition 4 – Dilapidated

Finally, the nine types are grouped according to one of eight areas of the city in which they are located. These areas have been defined in terms of the predominant housing type of the area, and the rental range, as reported in the 1960 Census, of the area. The eight "locational" categories, as they are called, are as follows:

Location Category	*Dominant Housing Type*	*Monthly Rental Range*
1	Single Family	0–$140
2	" "	$140–$275
3	" "	$275 or More
4	2–4 Unit Structures	0–$ 75
5	" " "	$ 75 or More
6	5 or More Unit Structures	0–$ 75
7	" " "	$ 75–$150
8	" " "	$150 or More

These categories are employed in the current version of the simulation model.

The eight areas of the city are shown in the accompanying map.* The housing stock of the city is represented in the model by up to 288 separate types, the product of the three partitions mentioned above. This permits a very high degree of differentiation of the stock.

Associated with each housing type is a factor used in a model process that "ages" the housing according to its "normal usage." The process is based on a special study of the housing stock of the city which traced the condition of housing from the Real Property Survey of the late 1930's and correlated that work with subsequent reports of the city's housing condition by the Census of Housing. The average rent paid for housing by type was computed by an analysis of rents paid for housing in 1960. The basic rental information is modified by each cycle of the model operation and the price of housing (the rents asked) varies from period to period and is a function of demand and supply.

The interaction of consumer, supplier, and government affect the supply of housing. Thus, the medium for the measurement of the efffect of programs is analysis of the supply of housing at the end of the run with respect to its quantity and quality.

The single period is the module of the nine-period run, and within it, the two-cycle operation is the basic element. As noted, some of the information with which the model operates is invariable for the length of the run (though there are exceptions to this) while other information, especially the population and public or governmental actions, is varied from period to period. While the actual operation of the model is a complicated process, the above description approximates it. Throughout this section, the use of the model as a device to assist policymakers has been emphasized. We now turn to its state of development at the termination of the Community Renewal Program in 1965.

III. FURTHER DEVELOPMENT OF THE SIMULATION MODEL

A. Development of the Model Since June 1965

In 1965, the Community Renewal Program Study came to an end, and formal effort by the consultant on the simulation model was halted. The model, consisting of its program and data, the various runs that had been executed, and much technical information was turned over to the Department of City Planning. During the development phase, a member of the Department's staff had worked closely with the consulting firm on model operations, and had been especially involved in the analysis of the results produced by the computer. This participation was important to the city, for it assured that there was a staff member familiar with the technical operation of the simulation model, and a continuity between consultant and client was thus established.

*Not included herein.–Ed.

The model developed during the Community Renewal Program had undergone a number of changes and modifications, especially in final months of work. Two full nine-period runs were made—one incorporating the public actions recommended by the Community Renewal Program, and one omitting these actions. Both used the same population projection, the so-called "target" population developed for the Community Renewal Program which generally posited maintaining the same population characteristics found in the 1960 population of San Francisco. With qualifications, certain conclusions were drawn concerning the relative effectiveness of the Community Renewal Program in achieving its housing goals. These conclusions were tentative simply because there had not been sufficient time to review the results of the operations.

As the consultants indicated in their report:

> "Interpretation of the model results is even more demanding than its use. The outputs are of a form requiring skill to disaggregate and develop suitable tables, and the interpretation thereafter must be done by people who are not only acquainted with details of the model but who are also thoroughly experienced with the City of San Francisco and with the characteristics of its housing and construction activities" [San Francisco Community Renewal Program, 1966: 5].

The performance of the model had been sufficiently promising to provide an incentive for its further development. The Department of City Planning decided to develop the model further in order that it could be brought to a more fully operational status. It was recognized that although the model had produced an output, there were a number of changes that could be made to simplify it, to incorporate features that appeared desirable, and to make changes in some of the data used for its operation.

A year passed before staff and appropriations could be made available for the further development of the model. In August 1966, with the assistance of the firms of Arthur D. Little, Inc., and Information Management, Inc., a program for work on the model began.

The budget for making changes to the model was limited; it was therefore concluded that no basic changes in the structure of the model would be possible. Priorities for improvement were given to simplifying the detail of the model, shortening the operating time, making the data imput operation simpler, and changing the basic neighborhood unit. One circumstance, unanticipated in 1965, was the elimination of the computer system on which the model had originally been operated. Fortunately, much of the model's program had been written in a generally used computer language, FORTRAN IV. However, because a significant number of computer routines depended upon the particular configuration of the now eliminated computer system, provision had to be made to seek another machine system and to rewrite those parts of the program which were dependent upon the by now unavailable system. Freeing the model from that particular system brought with it the advantage of operating the model on larger and more flexible equipment, and so ultimately reducing the operating time from over two hours to substantially less than one hour. Furthermore, the new machine would permit the elimination of a number of troublesome routines and thus simplify the complicated model program. In Fall 1966, with these objectives and constraints in mind, the team set about making the modifications. By Spring 1968, the model was finally tested with a single full operation. The changes described below, the analysis of the operation of the model, and the evaluation of its capabilities are based on that run which occurred in April 1968.

B. Changes Made in the Simulation Model

As a result of the development program, five major categories of change have been made in the simulation model. Two of these were directed to the computer operation of the model; the other three concern the housing, population and neighborhood elements of the model.

1. COMPUTER OPERATIONS

a. Change of Computer Facility. Elimination of the original system made a search necessary for a new facility on which to operate the model. In selecting a facility for the operation of the model, its requirements for large, readily accessible information storage and table generation had to be kept in mind. No local machines with the desired capacity and processing characteristics were available at the time the development commenced. The City of San Francisco was just beginning its program of acquiring large capacity machines, and it was determined that these would not be available during the development phase of the program. The choice of a machine was narrowed to a General Electric 625/35 Computer operated by MATRIX Corporation in Los Angeles. It had the capability of taking the entire load of input information in "core," the central and immediately accessible memory storage of a computer, and generating the very large tables needed for the operation without resorting to the complicated operations used to fit the model into the original machine. The effect of this would be to simplify the computer program, eliminate machine links that were time consuming (and always added to the possibility of error), and thus reduce the running time of the program and increase its reliability. The opportunity to rewrite the program using larger amounts of FORTRAN IV would benefit users of the model since it would make the model available to a wider range of computers than had been the case with the original version.

In the course of adapting the program for the new facility, a number of the routines which had been designed for the original program, some of which had not been used, were eliminated. The resulting simplification, combined with the greater power of the new facility, has resulted in a considerable reduction of the operating time of the model.

b. Development of New Input/Output Routines. In the original operation of the model, the data used were contained in keypunch card form. The cards were read by the computer and the internal storage established. Because of the quantity of information used, it had been recognized that this was both cumbersome and subjected the data to error through the possibility of the loss or inadvertent misfiling of cards. Further, the data were difficult to verify since the print-out was not conveniently formatted and, except to the specialist, almost impossible to read. Finally, when it was necessary to change any unit of information, the card deck had laboriously to be searched and the card altered manually or replaced with another card. To remedy this situation, an "input" program was devised. This program incorporated the desirable feature of taking a card input, converting it to either a deck of cards or to magnetic tape and producing a legible output whose figures could be conveniently reviewed by non-technical personnel. Even more useful was the fact that through the inclusion of a special "up-dating" feature, the information on the tape could be modified by the use of a relatively simple coding operation. This eliminated recourse to the manual review of hundreds of punched cards and assured the operator that the information was safely stored in the correct location. Furthermore, this entire operation reduced the model program from up to ten boxes or files of punched cards to a single, mailable, magnetic tape. This program also has the virtue of being able to run on a smaller and less expensive computer, generally more available than those which must be used for the operation of the model itself.

At the other end of the model operation, output, the need for a summary had long been apparent. The original model output had contained two printing formats. One of these had been designed for policymakers; the other for technicians concerned with internal review of model processes. The latter was voluminous, detailed, highly useful, and very time consuming to analyze. It was determined that a summary of some of the information it contained would assist the operational analysis of the model, and a relatively simple auxiliary output routine was produced. The output which had been designed for use by the policymaker (i.e., non technician) was shelved during the latest development phase. If the model is to be used at some future time, it should be reviewed and reactivated.

2. CHANGES IN THE HOUSING AND POPULATION ELEMENTS OF THE MODEL

a. Housing Elements. The typology of housing currently used in the model has been discussed above, in the section describing the operation of a single period of the model. Twenty-two housing types, by structure and room size, had been differentiated in the original version of the model. Fourteen locational categories had been employed. In reviewing these, the development team came to the conclusion that the information produced by the model was not sufficiently accurate to warrant this differentiation into such a large number of categories. The situation is analogous to the use of ten decimal places in the solution of a problem when the reliability of the figures merits four at most.

Thus the decision to reduce the typology to nine types of housing for the private market and three for public housing was made. Similarly, the use of eight location categories instead of fourteen was determined. The decisions were reached by a review of the extant information used to operate the model, and usefulness of the results. Since the model is more reliable in the large than the small, and in the sum than the parts, the loss of useful information was deemed negligible.

In making the change, all of the associated factors, such as costs of new construction and rehabilitation, aging coefficients, minimum yields, and average rents had to be reexamined and many recomputed. To some extent, the passage of time since the original work on this phase of the development of the model had produced new insight and information which improved the quality of some of these factors.

b. Population Element. A review of the number of types of population groups and the quantity of households contained in each of them led the team to the conclusion that, given the grossness of the model, the bidding of groups that contained fewer than one percent of the total household population would not effectively be registered in the demand pattern. In fact, in the original version of the model, some groups contained as few as twenty households, and the effective information obtained was impossible to evaluate. It was determined, therefore, to combine certain categories of household types in a manner that would be logically consistent, yet permit a more effective participation in the bidding process. This has been accomplished; of the 114 groups used in the original version of the model, 84 remain. The reduction has also resulted in some saving in the running time of the model.

The new combinations also made possible a reconsideration of the system of housing preference selection. The introduction of several new criteria for selecting the fifty housing preferences given each consumer group is a conceptual improvement over the previous system. Rent paying abilities for each group were also recomputed, based on the Census of 1960, and modified in view of the newly formed groups. Changes in the manner in which the population of consumers bid for stock were made to improve the simulation of the market processes. The effectiveness of these changes will be discussed in the analysis and evaluation of the results of the last major run of the model.

3. CHANGE IN THE NEIGHBORHOOD UNIT

In the original version of the model, a special neighborhood unit was developed, often referred to as a Community Renewal Program Neighborhood. This neighborhood was composed of several of the enumeration districts used in the Census of 1960. The neighborhoods created imposed a completely new pattern for the city, one which did not correspond to any in common use by the Department of City Planning or other departments. The rationale for such a creation was that these neighborhood units would provide a finer discrimination of information than possible on a more conventional basis, such as the Census Tract. Upon review, several difficulties with this concept have become apparent. First, the information provided does not necessarily provide for finer discrimination of characteristics by area, since, in many cases the Community Renewal Program Neighborhoods resulting from the combination of enumeration districts (a requirement, incidentally, imposed by the Bureau of Census to protect the confidence of its interview information) are often as large, or larger than Census Tracts. Secondly, the boundaries of the neighborhoods are as arbitrary as those of the Census Tract. Third, enumeration district boundaries may change from census to census and continuity of information is thus endangered. Finally, and perhaps most seriously, it became evident that these units, because they are not in use or readily translated to the boundaries of other, more commonly shared units, are of limited usefulness and make the model less useful.

With these considerations in mind, the decision was made to change the basic neighborhood unit to the generally used Census Tract. The accomplishment of this change was integrated with changes in the housing elements mentioned above, especially with respect to the consolidation of location categories.

IV. ANALYSIS AND EVALUATION OF THE CURRENT MODEL OPERATION

In the evaluation of the performance of the current version of the simulation model, three stages may be distinguished. The first stage is confined to the analysis of the computer operation and is concerned with whether or not the machine operations appear to be in order. The second stage is concerned with the results produced by the model as a simulation of the subject, the housing market, and is a measurement of the reliability of the model. The third stage has to do with whether or not the model can be used in an effective operational sense to perform the function for which it was designed. Each of these steps follow from the other. If the mechanical operation of the model is grossly defective, it is impossible to expect reliable results. If it is operative in the narrow sense but produces results that are not credible, it cannot be used for its purpose. Finally, even if it is mechanically sound and demonstrably reliable, its use may involve difficulty of a scale that prevents its employment for testing programs. Each of these stages will be considered in turn.

A. Computer Operation

Testing the current version of the model which incorporates the changes in its program, operation on the new computer facility, and modifications of the elements of the model commenced in the Fall of 1967. At this time, the completely revised information became available, permitting full-scale operation for the first time since 1965. Until the time of the full nine-period run in April of this year, some fifteen partial runs were made, each yielding new information that led to changes or modifications in the program of the model to enable it to run. The process of finding errors, retracing them through the program, correcting them and testing the effect of the changes, is time consuming. Often, the discovery of one error laid bare another, and the process of correction had to be undertaken again. The interrelationships between the parts of the model and its program are sufficiently complex so that several trials were often necessary before the difficulties could be resolved. This kind of effort must be expected when so complex a system is operated. One of the major uses of the final run was to attempt to determine whether or not the model, in this restricted sense, is free enough from program errors to be pronounced operational.

From all of the evidence that the results of the final run have produced, the model IS operational in this sense: it can be run without discernible difficulties. Even now, caution is necessary, because without a series of additional test runs varying the data extensively, it is not possible to detect sources of error that would not otherwise appear. Again, from all of the available evidence, the changes in the computer program appear to have been accomplished and the model can be run and run sufficiently well to permit the next stage of evaluation to be made. However, it is important to understand that no matter how effective or error free the computer program may be, the product of a computer operation is only as reliable as the information used for its input. This is especially true of this model which relies upon a considerable amount of material, some of which, like that based on the Bureau of Census surveys, is of known reliability while others, such as the minimum yield information, is open to question. The next section deals with the reliability of the model as a simulation of the market and factors affecting the reliability of the model are further discussed.

B. Reliability

The question of reliability and its measurement is central to the evaluation of the effectiveness of simulation models. Perfect correspondence between the simulation and the real world, is, of course, the ideal and desired end of a simulation. In practice, that condition, except for very general and uncomplicated models, is virtually impossible to achieve. The effective compromise usually reached by model builders is that the simulation approximates the real world situation in some degree. The following discussion of the reliability of the San Francisco simulation model can better be understood if this context is kept in mind. To further clarify this context, these points need to be made.

First, even if the model were an ideal simulation, that degree of precision may not be necessary for the purposes of evaluating policies and programs. It may well be sufficient that the policymaker be given a good qualitative estimate of the impact that proposed policies may have on the market for housing, and a quantitative estimate that varies within about ten percent of what may be expected to occur. In most simulation modeling, that is considered excellent performance.

Second, from what is known of the various data used for the simulation process, even the most reliable, that of the Bureau of Census, will not be completely accurate, and within that information there will be variation in the quality of the data reported from item to item. This is especially true of housing condition as reported by the Census. Therefore, the information base is not such that it will reflect the housing market with complete accuracy. Other items of information may be subject to variation that is difficult to measure and hence a standard of reliability hard to provide. It is also important to note that any forecast of the future is largely a matter of conjecture, and that it is impossible to make predictions of such things as population trends with absolute assurance that they will occur. The reliability of the simulation must, therefore, be based only on known or historic information.

Third, simulation models are usually built because the processes with which they deal are not fully understood. If they were, another kind of model, namely a deterministic one in which no probabilistic relationships occur, would be appropriate. There are few situations in the real world in which deterministic models can be built, but the conditions are approached in fairly straightforward circumstances such as mechanical engineering where the nature of the materials and the design criteria are well understood theoretically and the information used is measurable within known limits of accuracy. This is not the case with the housing market, where neither its theoretical structure nor all of the implications that maybe drawn from it are clearly specified and the information available is both difficult to obtain and to measure. The best the simulation modeler can do, in these difficult circumstances, is to abstract clearly the elements that he can identify in the situation, establish their relationships, and build his model. The model is, therefore, a set of hypotheses, and these are modified as the model is operated. The process of "tuning" the model, in which the results of the simulation and the real world are matched and elements of the model adjusted accordingly to provide for a better approximation, is really the process of improving the understanding of the subject being modeled. Simulation must be understood in the light that it not only is designed to produce results that approximate the behavior, in this case, of the housing market, but that it also provides a framework within which a better understanding of the subject is achieved, and the model is improved. Repeated operation of a simulation model is the only real guarantee of its successful representation of the subject, since each new operation brings the modeler closer to an understanding of the structure of the subject and of the influence of conditions upon the structure.

With the apparent success of the computer operation of the model, the next stage of evaluation is concerned with the credibility or reliability of the model as a representation of the processes of the housing market. The reliability of the model is determined by comparing the results produced by its operation with data from the real world for the period of the simulation. If the results which the model produces correspond with those that appear in the market place for the same period of time, the model is judged reliable and faith may be placed in the results for those periods.

The problem of verification is made difficult because the data available for that purpose are extremely limited. Except for the decennial Census of Housing and Population, no information concerning the quality of housing (condition), the average rents paid for it, its occupancy, etc., is available on a comprehensive basis. The only information which now can be used for this evaluation has to do with the number of new dwelling units produced in the city. Since 1966, the Department of City Planning has kept an inventory of units completed and available for occupancy. This inventory has served as the basis for two reports on the state of the housing inventory in the city in terms of the number of units added to and taken from the stock. It is kept by type of structure (i.e., the number of units in a building) and by area (i.e., Census Tract). The existence of this information, itself an outgrowth both of the needs of the model and of recommendations contained in the Community Renewal Program report, has enabled review of current model operations in finer detail than was possible previously.

Evaluation of the performance of the model is also contingent upon the information used in the operation of the model. In order to produce a simulation of the market, the information used must correspond as closely as possible to the conditions that actually occurred if a historical comparison is to be made. Therefore, to evaluate the performance of the model, it is important first to describe the information used in the model in terms of the four elements of the model: households, investors, government, and housing stock. The description of the information used is confined to the time span for which data for verification are available, the years 1961-1966 or periods 1-3 of model operation. After describing the information used to operate the model during this period, the results of the operation will be compared with data on housing units added to the stock provided by the housing inventory studies conducted by the Department. On this basis, the evaluation of its reliability will be made.

1. General Description of Information and Assumptions, 1960-1966

The description of information and assumptions used in the period 1960-1966, or periods 1-3 of model operation, will be treated in summary form for each of the elements separately. The aim of the simulation during this period was to reproduce as closely as possible the conditions of the real world. Projections of population had to be employed, since there was no regularly maintained source of information on numbers of households. Governmental programs were reviewed and their actual execution was approximated as closely as possible. Where insufficient knowledge of conditions made impossible accurate revisions of information, the basic data derived for the model input year, 1960, were employed. The development team decided that it was safer to posit little or no change in these factors than to attempt, especially within limited resources available, their revision.

a. Households. During the period, 1960 to 1966, the projected total number of households declined from 291,000 to 288,000 or about 1%. Within this decline, however, the composition of the households changed significantly. White households declined from nearly 250,000 in 1960 to about 235,000 in 1966. At the same time, a sharp increase, 29%, of non-white households from

41,000 in 1960 to 53,000 in 1966 occurred. White households with children increased from about 65,000 to 71,000 during the period. The maintenance of a constant proportion of children in the population coupled with a slightly declining average household size is responsible for this increase. Even more dramatic, however, is the 43% rise of non-white households with children from about 20,000 in 1960 to slightly more than 28,000 in 1966. In households of adults without children, white households dropped from 185,000 to 164,000, a decline of 11%, and non-white households increased from nearly 22,000 to 25,000 or about 14%. These figures are based on the Departmental projection published in the document "Population Projections for San Francisco, 1960-1990." They differ markedly from the population projections used in the earlier version of the model, and for that reason, the performance of the earlier and later version of the model cannot really be compared.

For the period, the relative age distribution has been kept constant, as has the income distribution of the various household groups. These distributions are based on the information obtained from the Census of 1960 and, given the constraints mentioned above, seemed reasonable assumptions to make for the relatively short time span of six years. Further, the housing preferences of the households are also based on information obtained from the 1960 Census, an even more tenable assumption given the short span of time, inflexibility of the housing stock, and the fact that realistic housing preferences depend to a large extent on current offerings in the marketplace.

b. Investors. The principal data with which the investor element of the model is concerned are the yields which various kinds of housing proposals must produce before they become eligible for consideration as a feasible project (minimum yields) and costs of the transition from one form of use to the other (new construction and rehabilitation costs). Studies of minimum yield by housing type were carried out during the Community Renewal Program Studies, and these were preserved in the present version of the model, with few exceptions. It is apparent that this coefficient plays a vital role in the model and deserves detailed study. However, without a new study of yields available, the decision to keep the original figures provided the most reasonable alternative. Costs for transitions, either to entirely new units or bringing existing units up to standard, were revised slightly for this version of the model.

c. Government. The actions of government have an impact on the housing market in a number of ways. Some of these are obvious and direct, others indirect and subtle though no less influential. While it is possible to incorporate some of the latter in the simulation model, e.g., a change in interest rates occasioned by action of the Federal Reserve Bank, the state of the art has precluded this at the present time. In the simulation of the years 1960-1966, only the most directly influential actions occurring in those years have been incorporated in the model. They consist of clearance and redevelopment, conservation area code enforcement, clearance for a freeway project, additions to public housing, and a radical change in zoning density. These have been based upon programs in the execution phase. Each will be explained in turn.

Clearance and Redevelopment. This process consists of the removal from the market of existing housing units in a specified project area and their eventual replacement with other uses which may include housing. Between 1960 and 1966, three specific projects have been under way and are incorporated in the model program. A map is provided for reference to each project area.

Western Addition Project A-1. This project had been underway since the late 1950's. To simulate the end of the acquisition of units, 275 units were removed from the housing market in the first period (1960-1962). (Note: The numbers of units in an action do not always exactly correspond to the number in the actual project. This is due to the necessity for using a special density figure for housing types by location in order to "fit" the information into the computer's storage capability.)

In the second period, 1963-1964, over 900 units became available for occupancy through the redevelopment program. No marked release occurred in the third period, 1965-1966.

Golden Gateway Project. The land acquired by the Redevelopment Agency for this project consisted largely of commercial development and the few housing units taken had been removed from the housing stock before the period of simulation. The first major release of housing units from this project occurs in the third period (1965-1966) and consists of 1,196 apartment units and 58 townhouse units.

Diamond Heights Project. The Diamond Heights project utilizied largely undeveloped land and resulted in few displacements. In the third period, 1965-1966, 180 single-family units and 160 apartment units came into the market.

Code Enforcement by Conservation Area. In 1960, the City instituted a program of systematic building inspection by area designed to bring structures into conformity with city codes. This program has been incorporated in the model for the period 1960-1966. The model treats the program simplistically, automatically bringing from substandard conditions (Conditions 3 and 4 of the model's housing stock) a designated proportion of the housing stock of any selected neighborhood (Census Tract) to standard condition (Condition 1). Thus, any housing in a conservation area not changed by regular market action will be "forced" into standard condition using the code enforcement mechanism. The programs, either completed, or under way during this period of time (see map for location) were the following:

Pacific Heights Conservation Area partially completed
West Nob Hill Conservation Area partially completed
Visitacion Valley Conservation Area partially completed
Buena Vista Heights Conservation Area commenced in Period 3 (1965-1966)

The amount of compliance effected during this time, together with the percentage of structures affected were worked out by examination of the reports on progress in the various areas.

Clearance for the Southern Freeway Extension. During the period 1960-1966, approximately 150 single-family homes were demolished in Census Tracts in the right of way adjacent to the route of the Southern Freeway Extension. The action occurred in the first period of simulation, 1960-1962.

Public Housing. This is represented in the model by special housing types which are made available to the preference lists of households eligible for them. Special provision for their incorporation in the stock must be made. Within the period of simulation, six projects were completed, but owing to an input error, only four of

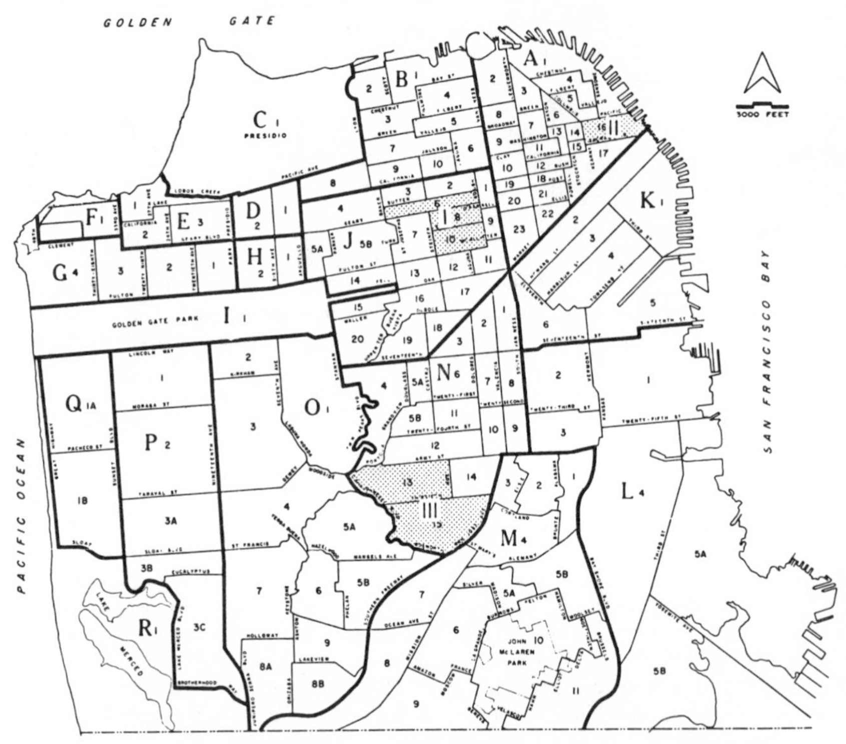

ACTIONS BY GOVERNMENT: CLEARANCE AND REDEVELOPMENT, 1960 - 1966

1960 CENSUS TRACTS

I. WESTERN ADDITION A-I

II. GOLDEN GATEWAY PROJECT

III. DIAMOND HEIGHTS PROJECT

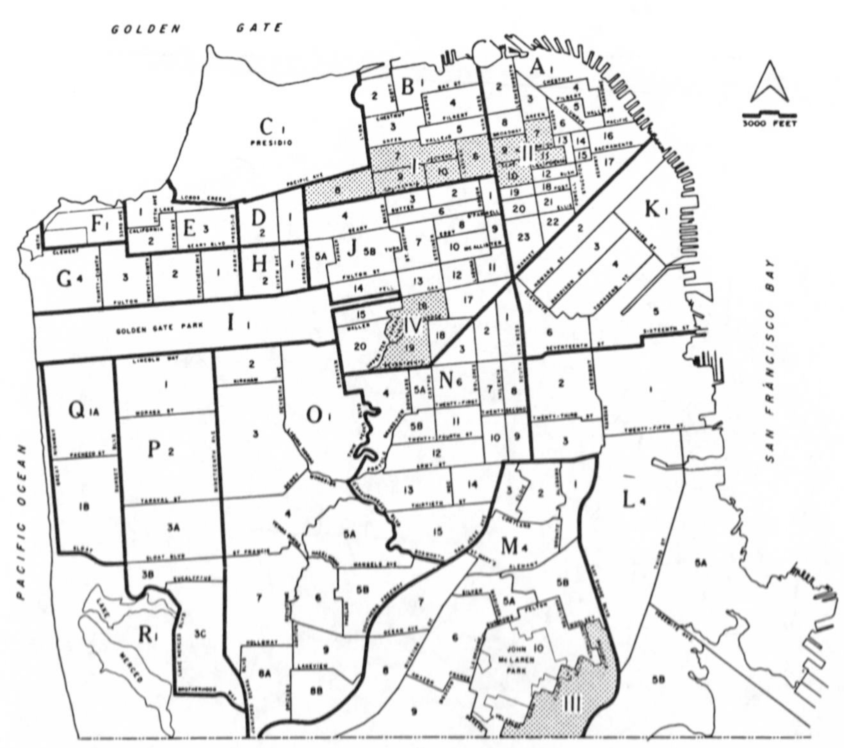

ACTIONS BY GOVERNMENT: CODE ENFORCEMENT BY CONSERVATION AREA

1960 CENSUS TRACTS

I. PACIFIC HEIGHTS CONSERVATION AREA
II. WEST NOB HILL CONSERVATION AREA
III. VISITACION VALLEY CONSERVATION AREA
IV. BUENA VISTA HEIGHTS CONSERVATION AREA

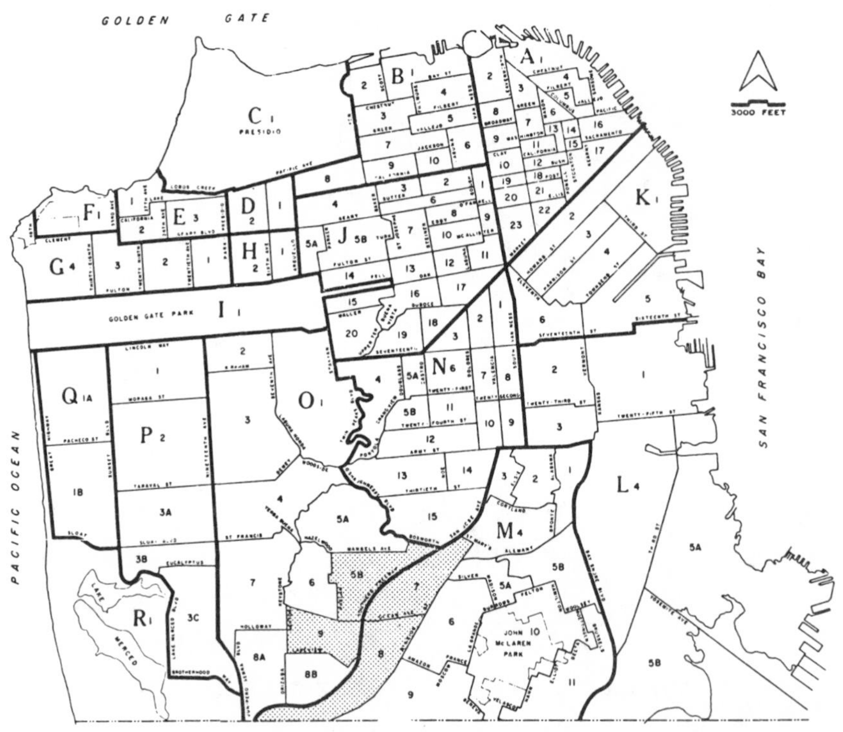

ACTIONS BY GOVERNMENT: CLEARANCE FOR SOUTHERN FREEWAY EXTENSION

1960 CENSUS TRACTS

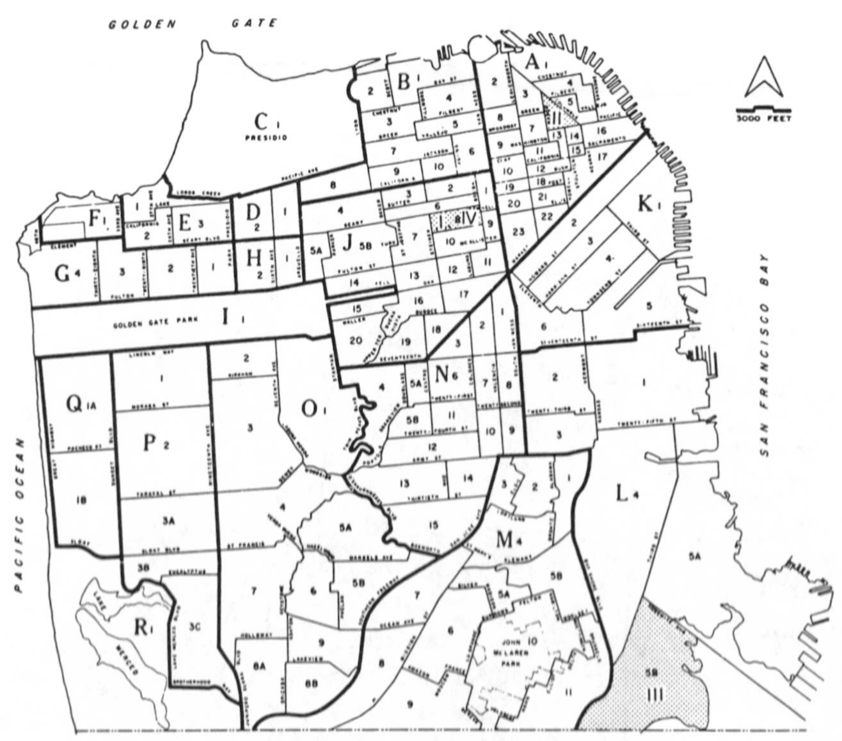

ACTIONS BY GOVERNMENT: PUBLIC HOUSING

1960 CENSUS TRACTS

I. YERBA BUENA PLAZA ANNEX
II. PING YUEN NORTH
III. ALICE GRIFFITH GARDEN HOMES
IV. HAYES VALLEY APARTMENTS

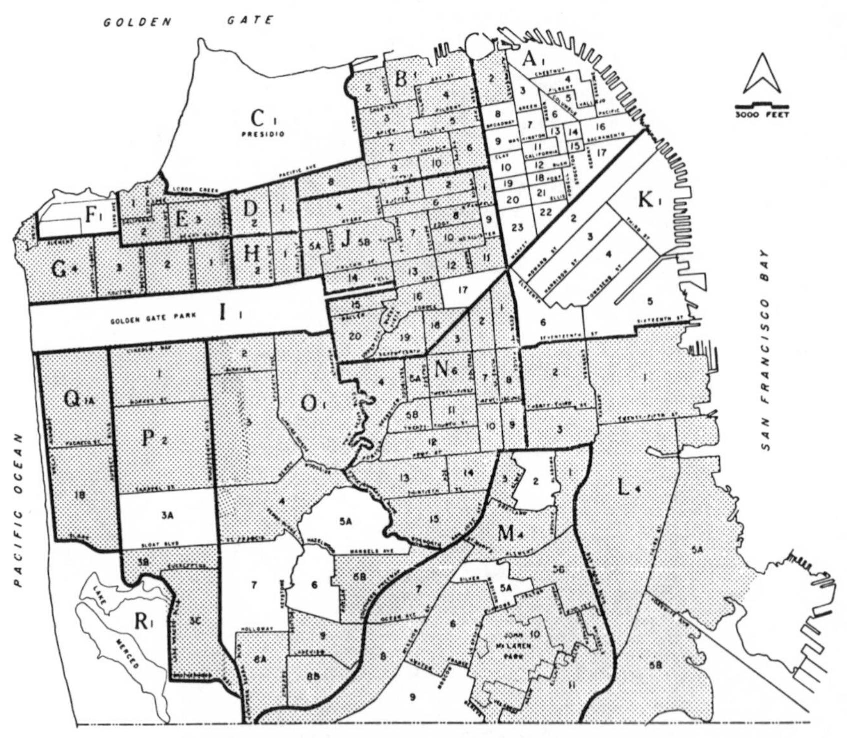

ACTIONS BY GOVERNMENT: MODIFICATION OF THE R-3 DENSITY STANDARD OF THE PLANNING CODE

1960 CENSUS TRACTS

these were actually provided for in the simulation operation. These four projects are:

Yerba Buena Plaza Annex	211 units
Ping Yuen North	194 units
Alice Griffith Garden Home	354 units
Hayes Valley Apartments	328 units

Inadvertently omitted were:

John F. Kennedy Towers	98 units
Mission Dolores	92 units

The latter projects were designed for housing elderly citizens.

Modification of the R-3 Density Standard of the Planning Code. The simulation model is currently equipped to deal with the density standards of the Planning Code (zoning ordinance) by limiting the amount of development in categories of structure. There are three such categories: single-family structures, two to four unit structures, and five or more unit structures. Thus, three categories of density of development are represented in the model, given that each structure, in general, occupies a single lot. The R-3 (low-density apartment house district) section of the Planning Code, as passed in 1960, made possible the development of five or more unit structures on a lot. Subsequent review resulted in the revision of this section of the ordinance which restricted the density of the development to the two to four unit category. To reflect this change, which came into effect in 1965, the portions of each Census Tract designated in R-3 zoning were computed and the intensity of development of the five or more unit category decreased and the two to four unit category correspondingly increased.

d. Housing Stock. The city's housing stock has been described above. As an initial input to the simulation, the stock is used as it was reported by the Census of Housing in 1960 in terms of quantity by type, condition, location and average rent paid. Associated with each housing type is a factor used in the model to "age" the housing stock. This information was developed by the consultants as part of a special study, reported in their Technical Paper No. 2, *Models for Condition Aging,* and has been retained for use in the present version of the model.

2. *Comparison of Results of Model Operation with Market Information*

Whether or not the model is an effective simulation of the housing market can only be determined by reference to data provided by the market operation for that period of time corresponding to the simulation. The simulation commences with the housing stock of 1960 and is completed by 1978. Data available for confirming or disconfirming the results occupy the period 1960-1966, or periods one through three of the simulation process. As noted, the only source of interim data available for comparison consists of that information developed by the Department of City Planning in its regular housing inventory studies, and the emphasis is given to the number and kind of units added to the market during the period 1960-1966. These data were developed subsequent to the operation of the original version of the model and in its detail and specificity far surpasses the information that was available in 1965 used to assess the original version. Our analysis of model operations will be confined to its first three periods of operation, corresponding to the "real world" time span of 1960-1966. It is important to bear in mind the fact that for this period, the information used to "drive" the model was made to correspond as closely as possible to conditions that were current, as we have explained in the previous section.

While it has already been pointed out that a direct comparison of results of this latest model operation are not comparable with the previous model's results, it is worth reiterating those results to indicate why it was considered worthwhile to pursue the further development of the model. At that time, comparison of model results with market operations was limited to the first two periods, 1960-1964, of simulation. Further, the data used were based on citywide building permit information as reported to the Bureau of Census, and breakdowns by location categories and by types within location categories were not possible. Finally, these data are based on applications for permits, rather than upon the completion and readiness of the units for occupancy. Table 7 from the report, "Model of the San Francisco Housing Market," is reproduced:

TABLE 7
Comparison of New Units Constructed

	San Francisco Actual			
	Single Family	*2-4 Units*	*5+ Units*	*Total*
Period 1 (1961-1962)	1,415	756	5,891	8,062
Period 2 (1963-1964)	855	790	8,240	9,885
Total	2,270	1,546	14,131	17,947
	Simulation Runs			
Period 1 (1961-1962)	428	828	6,886	8,142
Period 2 (1963-1964)	798	560	7,830	9,188
Total	1,226	1,388	14,716	17,330

The following table shows the percentage by which model varied from the market information.

1965 Version of the Simulation Model (in percentages)

	Percentage Variation of Simulation Results from Market Data			
	Single Family	*2-4 Units*	*5+ Units*	*Total*
Period 1 (1961-1962)	−70	10	17	1
Period 2 (1963-1964)	−7	−29	−5	−7
Total	−46	−10	4	−3

The encouragement for continuing the development of the model rested on the figures for the gross total units (a 3% variation) and in the 4% figure for the five or more category. It was recognized that compensating errors may have accounted for the closer approximation in the total. Nevertheless, from the modeler's standpoint the figures gave support to the view that the model could be made to work and produce significantly more reliable results, especially since the somewhat anomalous behavior of the market for single-family homes could be explained and accounted for in subsequent development of the model.

The evaluation of the current version of the model can be made in much greater detail because of the data supplied by the housing studies. For this reason, the effectiveness of the model may be more accurately judged.

A brief explanation of the importance of the "density factor" and its role in affecting the results of the simulation model when compared to the real world is necessary before attempting the evaluation of current performance. When the model was originally conceived, it was hoped that representation could be given to the individual housing unit. However, the fact that some 300,000 units exist in San Francisco quickly made this detailed representation an impossibility, given the limits of the computer's capacity for storing detail. It was determined that housing types would have to be grouped in such a way that an average density could be used to represent them. As it evolved, this concept of an average density for representation was based on the three basic structural types: single family, 2 - 4 units and 5 or more unit buildings. Analysis of the city revealed that densities for these types varied with the area of the city considered, and therefore the density measurements, that is, the number of housing units of a particular type divided by one-half the net acreage occupied by the housing type, were further categorized in terms of the location categories. The differentiation provided a total of 24 individual density factors, shown on the accompanying table, which correspond to the three basic structural types and the eight location categories. The use of this factor carries with it the problem of "rounding" fractions of units. Thus, if the number of density units, obtained by dividing the total number of housing units by the density factor for the particular structural type and location category, amounts to a whole number and a fraction, the number will be rounded up in the machine if the fraction is half or more of a whole unit, and remain unchanged if it is less. The implication is that even under the most favorable of circumstances, the simulation model will not exactly approximate the behavior of the market in quantitative terms. Taking this into consideration, the accompanying tables display the actual market data, and the best possible simulation that could have resulted. The differences between the market data for the period 1960 to 1966 and the operation of the model if it were operating ideally have been calculated and the percentages of variation between market data and model results taken. In the following table, utilizing the same format employed above, an idea of possible accuracy of the results are shown.

Density of Housing Units Per Two-Acre Unit of Area by Structure Type and Location Category

	Structure Type		
L Category	*Single Family Density*	*2-4 Units Density*	*5+ Units Density*
1	36	80	160
2	30	67	160
3	24	60	160
4	48	90	196
5	34	78	216
6	56	118	275
7	48	85	250
8	32	64	156

Again, it is interesting to note the role of compensating error. Within periods and structure categories, the variation is wider than for the period as a total number of units and for statistical categories as a sum of the three periods. The next table, again employing the same format, is an analysis of the results obtained from the actual model run shown in the accompanying table.

A comparison of the results of the actual operation with the best possible operation indicates that the model, except for the grand total of units, is far from approaching a truly reliable operational standard. The fact that the variation is not systematic leads to the conclusion that the problem is not simple, such as might be produced by a serious miscarriage of the computer operations, but lies within the model.

The existence of the housing inventory data by location categories, as well as by structure types, permits further evaluation of the model's capability to simulate market activity within broad neighborhood groupings, a comparison that could not previously have been made. The importance of this comparison lies in the fact that unless the model is capable of reasonably accurate simulation within these broad categories, its reliability could further be called into question.

Present Version of the Model (in percentages)

	Percentage Variation of Best Possible Simulation Results from Market Data			
	Single Family	*2-4 Units*	*5+ Units*	*Total*
Period 1 (1960-1962)	–1	5	–4	–2
Period 2 (1963-1964)	0.0	12	0.0	1
Period 3 (1965-1966)	–12	–16	–2	–4
Total	–3	0.0	–2	–2

New Construction Actual Market Performance 1960-1966

	Structure Type			
	Single Family	*2-4 Units*	*5+ Units*	*Total Units*
Period 1				
L 1	755	336	962	2,053
2	170	115	544	829
3	17	0	20	37
4	16	73	229	318
5	127	87	734	948
6	13	76	812	901
7	3	17	673	693
8	2	2	60	64
Total	1,103	706	4,034	5,843
Period 2				
L 1	782	379	1,033	2,194
2	176	124	857	1,157
3	14	2	0	16
4	8	56	319	383
5	90	76	1,119	1,285
6	27	84	2,020	2,131
7	2	8	880	890
8	2	3	116	121
Total	1,101	732	6,344	8,177
Period 3				
L 1	485	361	1,472	2,318
2	134	127	328	589
3	11	0	6	17
4	9	33	354	396
5	9	93	535	637
6	18	128	2,193	2,339
7	4	24	840	868
8	2	9	80	91
Total	672	775	5,808	7,255
Grand total	2,876	2,213	16,186	21,275

Summarizing the results of these tables in convenient form and only with respect to the total number of units within each location category, the following comparison of performance can be made.

In the best possible simulation, 15 out of 22 instances fall within 10% or less variation from the data supplied by the market. None of the variations is higher than the 71 to 80% category. However, in the actual model operation only one case falls in the less than 10% variation category and three show variation of over 100% from the market data. The accompanying tables show the percentage of variation within each structure type by location category and the conclusions drawn from the above summaries may further be confirmed by the information tabulated; i.e., that the model falls far short of performing satisfactorily within the broad groupings of neighborhoods and further, that the closer agreement of

New Construction Best Possible Simulation Results

	Structure Type			
	Single Family	*2-4 Units*	*5+ Units*	*Total Units*
Period 1				
L 1	756	320	960	2,036
2	180	134	480	794
3	24	–	–	24
4	–	90	196	286
5	136	78	648	862
6	–	118	825	943
7	–	–	750	750
8	–	–	–	–
Total	1,096	740	3,859	5,695
Period 2				
L 1	792	400	960	2,152
2	180	134	800	1,114
3	24	–	–	24
4	–	90	392	482
5	102	78	1,080	1,260
6	–	118	1,925	2,043
7	–	–	1,000	1,000
8	–	–	156	156
Total	1,098	820	6,313	8,231
Period 3				
L 1	468	320	1,440	2,228
2	120	134	320	574
3	–	–	–	–
4	–	–	392	392
5	–	78	432	510
6	–	118	2,200	2,318
7	–	–	750	750
8	–	–	156	156
Total	588	650	5,690	6,928
Grand total	2,782	2,210	15,862	20,854

gross totals depends largely on a series of compensating errors. A table has also been included to show the percentage of variation by each location category and structure type of the actual simulation run from the best possible simulation and this information indicates that the model is not performing at an acceptable standard by comparison with the benchmark of the best simulation.

Finally, it will be noted that there are instances where simulation would have occurred under best possible conditions and where it would not, owing to the influence of the density factor. These results may be summarized as follows:

(1) Instances in which best possible simulation could not have occurred and would not have reflected market activity

Single Family	14
2-4	8
5 or More	3
Total	25

New Construction Model Simulation Results 1-3, 1960-1966

	Structure Type				*% Deviation Total Units Model from Market*
	Single Family	*2-4 Units*	*5+ Units*	*Total Units*	
Period 1					
L 1	684	800	320	1,804	−12
2	0	0	640	640	−23
3	0	0	0	0	–
4	0	450	0	450	+42
5	0	468	864	1,332	+40
6	56	0	1,650	1,706	+89
7	0	0	500	500	−28
8	0	0	1,092	1,092	+1,600
Total	740	1,718	5,066	7,524	+29
Period 2					
L 1	684	720	960	2,364	+8
2	180	0	800	980	−15
3	48	0	0	48	+200
4	0	0	0	0	–
5	0	312	0	312	−76
6	0	0	3,025	3,025	+42
7	0	0	0	0	–
8	0	0	1,872	1,872	+1,447
Total	912	1,032	6,657	8,601	+5
Period 3					
L 1	1,080	0	160	1,240	−46
2	240	0	0	240	−59
3	96	0	0	96	–
4	0	0	0	0	–
5	136	0	216	352	−45
6	0	1,062	0	1,062	−55
7	0	0	500	500	−42
8	0	0	0	0	–
Total	1,552	1,062	876	3,490	−52
Grand total	3,204	3,812	12,599	20,615	−3

(2) Instances where actual operation of model did not stimulate activity that could have been represented in best possible simulation

Single Family	4
2-4	8
5 or More	8
Total	20

(3) Instances where actual operation simulated activity that would not have occurred in best possible simulation

Single Family	3
2-4	0
5 or More	1
Total	4

What this says, in effect, is that in the 69 instances, by location category and structure type where market activity occurred during the three periods of

Present Version of the Model (in percentages)

	Percentage Variation of Actual Model Results from Market Data			
	Single Family	*2-4 Units*	*5+ Units*	*Total*
Period 1 (1960-1962)	−33	143	26	29
Period 2 (1963-1964)	−17	41	5	4
Period 3 (1965-1966)	131	37	−85	−50
Total	11	72	−22	−1

Percentage of Variation of Model from Housing Inventory Data in Best Possible Simulation 1960-1966 (in percentages)

	Structure Type			
	Single Family	*2-4 Units*	*5+ Units*	*Total Units*
Period 1				
L 1	0	−5	0	−1
2	+6	+17	−12	−4
3	+41	–	–	−35
4	–	+23	−14	−10
5	+7	−10	−12	−9
6	–	+55	+2	+5
7	–	–	+11	+8
8	–	–	–	–
Total	−1	+5	−4	−2
Period 2				
L 1	+1	+6	−7	−2
2	+2	+8	−7	−4
3	+71	–	–	+50
4	–	+61	+23	+26
5	+13	+3	−3	−2
6	–	+40	−5	−4
7	–	–	+14	+12
8	–	–	−34	−29
Total	0	+12	0	+1
Period 3				
L 1	−4	−11	−2	−4
2	−10	+6	−2	−2
3	–	–	–	–
4	–	–	+11	−1
5	–	−16	−19	−20
6	–	−8	0	−1
7	–	–	−11	−3
8	–	–	+95	+71
Total	−12	−16	−2	−4
Grand total	−3	0	−2	−2

Number of Instances of Variation in Total Units by Location Category for Three Periods of Operation 1960-1966

Percentage of Variation	Best Possible from Market	Actual Operation from Market
0- 10	15	1
11- 20	2	2
21- 30	2	2
31- 40	1	1
41- 50	1	5
51- 60	–	2
61- 70	–	–
71- 80	1	1
81- 90	1	1
91-100	–	–
Over 100	0	3
Total	22	18

Actual Run of the Simulation Model (in percentages)

	Percentage of Variation from Housing Inventory Data by Structure Type and Location Category 1960-1966		
	Structure Type		
	Single Family	*2-4 Units*	*5+ Units*
Period 1			
L 1	–9	+138	–67
2	–	–	+18
3	–	–	–
4	–	+516	–
5	–	+438	+18
6	+330	–	+103
7	–	–	–26
8	–	–	+1,720
Period 2			
L 1	–12	+90	–7
2	+2	–	–7
3	+243	–	–
4	–	–	–
5	–	+310	–
6	–	–	+50
7	–	–	–
8	–	–	+1,513
Period 3			
L 1	+122	–	–89
2	+79	–	–
3	+85	–	–
4	–	–	–
5	+1,411	–	–60
6	–	+730	–
7	–	–	–40
8	–	–	–

Percentage of Variation of Actual Model Run from Best Possible Simulation 1960-1966 (in percentages)

	Structure Type			
	Single Family	*2-4 Units*	*5+ Units*	*Total Units*
Period 1				
L 1	−10	+150	−66	−11
2	–	–	+33	−19
3	–	–	–	–
4	–	+400	–	+57
5	–	+500	+33	+54
6	–	–	+100	+81
7	–	–	−33	−33
8	–	–	–	–
Total	−32	+132	+31	+32
Period 2				
L 1	−14	+80	0	+10
2	0	–	0	−12
3	–	–	–	–
4	–	–	–	–
5	–	+300	–	−75
6	–	–	+57	+48
7	–	–	–	–
8	–	–	+1,100	+1,100
Total	−17	+26	+31	+4
Period 3				
L 1	+131	–	−88	−44
2	+100	–	–	−58
3	–	–	–	–
4	–	–	–	–
5	–	–	−50	−57
6	–	+800	–	−54
7	–	–	−33	−33
8	–	–	–	–
Total	+164	+63	−85	−50
Grand total	+15	+72	−21	−1

simulation, the best possible simulation would have failed to reflect 25 of these because of the influence of the density factor. In the actual operation of the model, this total is increased by another 24 instances, either because the model failed to stimulate activity that it might have been expected to, or it simulated activity that did not take place.

Given the above analysis, our evaluation of the model is that it is not, at present, a reliable device for simulation of the market. The range of variation between it and the best possible simulation which could have occurred under the influence of the density factor is simply too great to warrant faith in its long-term results. For that reason, it would be unwise to draw conclusions from the full operation of the model regarding the possible impact of public policies upon the housing market.

What are the reasons for this rather bleak picture of the model's unreliability following the period of intensive development of the previous two years? First, of course, is the fact that the data now used to evaluate the performance of the model are considerably more detailed and accurate than that used previously. This alone is an important factor since it permits the analyst to pinpoint the problems of the model's output and seek answers to the questions posed by the anomalous results. Second, and more fundamental, a review of the operation of the model has led the team to conclude that the fundamental structure and the computer operation have not been discredited by the findings. During preliminary operations, the influence of a number of factors has been examined, especially with respect to the problems posed by manipulation of the minimum yield factor in respect to the building of projects. A primary reason for the model's deficiency as a reliable simulation lies in its data. The quantity and quality of information used are simply not sufficient for the operation of a model of this size and complexity. Finally, a model as ambitious as this one has not been adequately tried under a number of conditions to test our hypotheses. A single nine-period run cannot be expected to do much more than test the operating system of the model, and lacking the kind of information about the housing market which is required by a simulation of this magnitude and detail, little can be done to correct data which may play an influential role in the performance of the model.

C. Usefulness

Although the model did not measure up in the second stage of evaluation, comments on the third stage are in order. Even had the model proven a completely reliable simulation and had it been possible to draw inferences about the impact of present policies and assumed population projections upon the housing stock of the future, serious difficulties in the employment of the model would remain to impede its effective use. Since it is possible that the model may undergo development to make it more reliable as a simulation, several observations should be made concerning factors that may limit its usefulness.

1. Understanding of the Use and Operation of the Model is Limited. At the present time, a very small core of professional staff have knowledge of the use to which the model may be put and the manner in which it is used and operated. Of the core group only one is connected with a public agency. The limits of time and money have sharply proscribed widespread involvement in the operation of the model, and it is also difficult to recruit personnel for involvement in the project given the heavy workload of this Department. There have not been sufficient funds to prepare a detailed flowchart and documentation of the computer program which would make examination and modification of it a relatively straightforward matter. There is no general "systems manual" which explains, beyond the computer program, how materials are prepared for model use, how the various parts of the model fit together in operation, who is responsible for developing public actions and other governmental aspects of the model, nor how the results should be interpreted. A number of conflicting statements about the operational capabilities of the model have been made, many on relatively scant evidence. These limitations have complicated circumstances for potential users of the model and have deferred the real promise of this device. In order for the simulation model to become an effective instrument for policy testing, its purpose and use must become much better understood by a larger segment, especially in the governmental sector. Such an understanding would be materially increased by the preparation of the computer program flowchart, a systems manual, and direct participation in the operation of the simulation model. Until that occurs, the usefulness of the model will remain limited.

2. Analysis of the Results Produced by the Model is Cumbersome. If the model is going to be used effectively, the present mode of manual analysis must be supplanted by computer routines which simplify, tabulate, and distribute the results produced by the computer into easily read tables and charts in which the implications of the figures are clear to those having relatively little time and expertise. Present operations on the output of the model involve inordinate amounts of time to reach relatively simple conclusions. Exhaustive analysis of the results, desirable in the event the model displays greater reliability than it presently does, would require the expenditure of many hours of manual computation. If, in the future, the model is used, time and money should be spent to determine the kinds of tables a computer could prepare from the output of the model. This would provide a straightforward examination of the results and would permit rapid interpretation, both of which are especially critical during simultaneous examination of several alternative programs of public actions. In conjunction with this program of output analysis, it may prove desirable to simplify further certain categories of the model, providing there is not a drastic loss of information.

3. Informational Support for the Model is Inadequate. It has been noted often in the preceding pages how dependent the model is on information that is either out of date or of questionable quality. The failure of the model to simulate the market accurately between the years 1960 and 1966, insofar as it has been investigated, seems to point more directly to the information with which the model must operate than to the basic structure of the model itself. The model's requirements for information, as it is presently designed, are enormous. For example, each population group (household type) has associated with it the following items of information: (1) rental range (high and low figure); (2) 50 housing choices; (3) actual or estimated population by period (nine figures). The items of information for each group amount to 61 and when this is multiplied by the 84 population groups currently used, there are over 5,000 units of information, each of which has some empirical basis or close approximation necessary if the model is to behave with accuracy. In both the earlier and the current version of the model, it has been necessary to depend upon the Census of Housing and Population for much of this material, simply because that appears to be the only comprehensive source of such data. Yet it is known that census data, while comprehensive, are not always accurate, particularly on the neighborhood scale. Furthermore, local data needs are not always reflected in the Census, and often there are changes in definition which render accurate comparison of results between Census periods difficult and occasionally impossible (e.g., the changing definition of dwelling units from 1930 on). Finally, data supplied by the census are rarely made current, if at all, in the ten-year period between Censuses. If the model is going to be a useful device, changing conditions of the housing market should be reflected in the information used to operate the model. A necessary adjunct to model operation is a comprehensive information system dealing with consumers, investors and housing stock. This system should be contained in local government so that it is independent and responsive.

4. *The Model is Still, Relatively Speaking, Machine Dependent.* While the model has been largely reprogrammed in FORTRAN IV, it remains relatively dependent on its present installation for technical reasons. These reasons are not insuperable, but if further work on the model is contemplated, one of the first steps should be to render it as versatile as possible by making it even more generally operational. It is recognized that a certain amount of adaptation to specific machines is always necessary, but the effort required for such adaptation should be further reduced.

5. *To Become Effective, the Model Must Be Used.* The final point may seem paradoxical, for it can be asked, "If the model is not now operational, in the effective sense, what is the point of continuing to use it?" The answer is that only through use can the various aspects of the model be tested and proven out. Testing the effect of the data upon the results, testing the structure of the model for inconsistencies, testing the computer program to determine mechanical sources of error, these can only be accomplished through repeated trials of the model. However, this process is expensive and time consuming. To attempt to accomplish it as a subsidiary activity, given the foregoing problems, is unrealistic. Only an ability to commit both considerable amounts of time and money will accomplish the goal of making it an effective operational device.

V. CONCLUSIONS AND RECOMMENDATIONS

Conclusions. The foregoing evaluation of the performance of the current version of the simulation model of the housing market has lead the staff of the Department of City Planning, responsible for its further development, to the conclusion that the model is still beyond our means for effective employment. It has not yet proven a reliable simulation, although there remains the prospect that its program can be refined. However, at this point it remains cumbersome to use, its function is not yet well understood by a sufficiently broad representation of agencies, and it has not yet received the kind of testing necessary to establish its full range of strength and weakness.

To undertake the improvement of the simulation model, in order to make it an effective device involves the following tasks, some of which may be costed:

(1) Flowcharting and documentation of the program, variously estimated to cost between $5,000 and $15,000;
(2) Preparation of a detailed systems manual to describe its operation and specific employment, especially for program testing by the Department;
(3) Establishment of an independent information system to supply data is badly needed by the model in the course of its operation. This item has been of concern to the Department, and not only in respect to the model. The Housing Inventory Studies represent the first stage of the system and have already proven useful in evaluation of current model results and programs of a number of other related departments. At the present time, a feasibility study to determine the establishment of a system on an interdepartmental basis is under way. However, the Department is aware that the undertaking of such a system is beyond its present capability to effect;
(4) Simplification of the detail and formalization of the analysis of results is essential if the model is to be effectively used;
(5) Repeated use of the model must occur before it is completely understood and full reliance placed upon its results.

It is important to emphasize that the development of the model, as a conception of the housing market, has provided an orientation and a training ground for the staff involved in it with respect to the operation of the market. It has paved the way for a systematic examination of the kinds of information that are necessary to understand the market, particularly with respect to the impact of public policies upon it. The development of the model by the Department has provided a valuable "in house" acquaintance with systems analysis on a first-hand basis and with both the opportunities and limitations of the applications of the computer to planning. The structure it has provided, necessarily precise and specific, has been a valuable orientation. Further, the willingness to the Department to work on the model to the limits of its capabilities is a demonstration of its good faith to the Federal Government in assuming the responsibilities of the Community Renewal Program. In undertaking this work, the experience of this Department may be shared with other jurisdictions, and may save unnecessary repetition of the less fruitful avenues of research.

Recommendations. It is clear that neither existing funds, nor the staff available to pursue further development of this model, are adequate to the scope of the task of bringing it to operational effectiveness. The current workload of the Department makes further development unfeasible, and one which cannot be accomplished without considerable funding. Furthermore, one of the most basic components of the model, current and accurate information about its various elements, is simply not available at this time. The cost of bringing the model to the desired operational state has been variously estimated at between $250,000 and $500,000. These estimates recognize the magnitude of the task and indicate the impossibility of realizing it within the budget constraints of local government, given higher and more immediate priorities. In order to accomplish this development, it is clear that the funding would have to come from sources outside local government who have an interest in the development of the simulation model.

It is recommended therefore:

(1) That further operations with the simulation model be terminated at this time in the interest of other work programs of the Department.
(2) That the money originally appropriated for the simulation model operation be used in upcoming surveys of the housing market to provide the information about the housing stock and its users which may, in the long run, serve the end of an improved information system that will permit improvement of the model;
(3) That sources of funds outside the City be sought as quickly as possible to flowchart and document the computer program and to prepare a detailed systems manual that will describe the operation and use of the model;
(4) That sources of funds outside the City be sought for the establishment of the independent information system required for effective operation of the simulation model;
(5) That sources of funds be sought to bring information about the housing stock of the City and the various demands that will be made upon it in the future up to date.

REFERENCES

San Francisco Community Renewal Program. "Model of San Francisco Housing Market," Technical Paper Number 8 (Arthur D. Little, January 1966).

--- San Francisco Community Renewal Program. "Purpose, Scope and Method," A Progress Report to the San Francisco Department of City Planning (Arthur D. Little, August 1963).

SELECTED BIBLIOGRAPHY

Emerging New Approaches and Methods: An Overview

Banfield, Edward C. "Ends and Means in Planning," UNESCO International Social Science Journal, Vol. 11, No. 3 (1959), pp. 361-368.

Bolan, Richard S. "Emerging Views of Planning," Journal of the American Institute of Planners, Vol. 33, No. 4 (July 1967), pp. 233-245.

Branch, Melville C. "Delusions and Diffusions of City Planning in the United States," Management Science, Vol. 16, No. 12 (August 1970), pp. B714-B732.

Duke, Richard. "Urban Planning and Metropolitan Development–The Role of Technology." *Applying Technology to Unmet Needs.* The Report of the National Commission on Technology, Automation, and Economic Progress, Appendix, Vol. V (February 1966), pp. V7-V11.

Dyckman, John W. "The Scientific World of the City Planners," American Behavioral Scientist, Vol. 6, No. 5 (January 1963), pp. 46-50.

Erber, Ernest (ed.) *Urban Planning in Transaction* (New York: Grossman Publisher, 1970).

Fagin, Henry. "The Evolving Philosophy of Urban Planning," in Leo F. Schnore and Henry Fagin (eds.) *Urban Research and Policy Planning* (Beverly Hills: Sage Publications, 1967), pp. 309-328.

Foley, Donald L. "Implications for Metropolitan Planning," in Melvin M. Webber, et al. (eds.) in *Explorations Into Urban Structure* (Philadelphia: University of Pennsylvania Press, 1964), pp. 56, 78.

Gans, Herbert J. "The Need for Planners Trained in Policy Formulation," in Ernest Erber (ed.) *Urban Planning in Transaction* (New York: Grossman Publishers, 1970), pp. 239-245.

Goodman, William I. and Jerome L. Kaufman *City Planning in the Sixties: A Restatement of Principles and Techniques* (Urbana, Illinois: Bureau of Community Planning, University of Illinois, 1955).

Harris, Britton, "The New Technology and Urban Planning," Urban Affairs Quarterly, Vol. 3, No. 2 (December 1967), pp. 14-40.

Lindblom, Charles E. "The Science of Muddling Through," Public Administrative Review, Vol. 19, No. 2 (Spring 1959), pp. 79-88.

Mitchell, Robert B. "The New Frontier in Metropolitan Planning," Journal of the American Institute of Planners, Vol. 27, No. 3 (August 1961), pp. 169-175.

Perin, Constance. "A Noiseless Secession From the Comprehensive Plan," Journal of the American Institute of Planners, September 1967, pp. 336-347.

Rothblatt, Donald N. "Rational Planning Reexamined," Journal of the American Institute of Planners, January 1971, pp. 26-37.

Webber, Melvin M. "The Roles of Intelligence Systems in Urban-Systems Planning," Journal of the American Institute of Planners, Vol. 31, No. 4 (November 1965), pp. 189-196.

——— "Comprehensive Planning and Social Responsibility," Journal of the American Institute of Planners, Vol. 29, No. 4 (November 1963), pp. 232-241.

Wheaton, William L. C. "Operations Research for Metropolitan Planning," Journal of the American Institute of Planners, Vol. 29 No. 4 (November 1963), pp. 250-259.

Systems Analysis: Theory and Concepts

Churchman, E. West, Russell L. Ackoff, and Leonard E. Arnoff. *Introduction to Operations Research* (New York: John Wiley & Sons, 1957).

Fisher, Gene H. "The Role of Cost-Utility Analysis in Program Budgeting," in David Novick (ed.) *Program Budgeting* (Washington, D.C.: U.S. Government Printing Office, 1965), Ch. 3, pp. 61-78.

Fox, Peter D. "A Theory of Cost-Effectiveness for Military Systems Analysis," Operations Research, 13 (March-April 1965), pp. 191-201.

Hall, Arthur D. *A Methodology for Systems Engineering* (New York: Van Nostrand, 1962).

Maass, Arthur, and Maynard Huffchmidt, et al. *Design of Water-Resource Systems* (Cambridge, Mass.: Harvard University Press, 1962).

McKean, Rowland N. *Efficiency in Government Through Systems Analysis* (New York: John Wiley & Sons, 1958).

McLoughlin, J. Brian. *Urban and Regional Planning: A Systems Approach* (New York: Frederick A. Praeger, 1969).

Optner, Stanford L. *Systems Analysis for Business and Industrial Problem-Solving* (Englewood Cliffs, N.J.: Prentice-Hall, 1965).

Quade, Edward S. (ed.) *Analysis for Military Decisions* (Amsterdam: North Holland Publishing, distributed by Rand McNally, 1964), pp. 370.

——— and W. I. Boucher. *Systems Analysis and Policy Planning: Applications in Defense* (New York: American Elsevier Publishing, 1968).

Schick, Allen. "Systems Politics and Systems Budgeting," Public Administration Review, Vol. 29, No. 2 (March-April 1969), pp. 137-151.

Wildavsky, Aaron. "The Political Economy of Efficiency: Cost-Benefit Analysis, Systems Analysis, and Program Budgeting," Public Administration Review, Vol. 26 (December 1966), pp. 292-310.

Traditional Approaches and Methods

Bartholomew, Harland. "The Plan–Its Preparation, Composition, and Form," *American Planning and Civic Annual, 1951* (Washington, D.C. 1951), pp. 97-102.

Bassett, Edward M. *The Master Plan* (New York: Russell Sage Foundation, 1928).

——— Frank B. Williams, Alfred Bettman, and Robert Whitten. *Model Laws for Planning Cities, Counties, and States Including Zoning, Subdivision Regulation, and Protection of Official Map.* (Cambridge, Mass.: Harvard University Press, 1935.)

Berkeley City Planning Commission. *Berkeley Master Plan* (Berkeley, Calif., 1955).

Bettman, Alfred. "City Planning Legislation," in John Nolen (ed.) *City Planning: A Series of Papers Presenting the Essential Elements of a City Plan* (New York: D. Appleton, 1929), pp. 431-471.

——— "The Relationship of the Functions and Powers of the City Planning Commission to the Legislative, Executive, and Administrative Departments of City Government," *Planning Problems of Town, City, and Region: Papers and Discussions at the Twentieth National Conference on City Planning, Held at Dallas and Fort Worth,* Texas, May 7-10, 1928. (Philadelphia: William F. Fill, 1928), pp. 142-159.

Black, Alan. "The Comprehensive Plan," in William I. Goodman and Eric C. Freund (eds.) *Principles and Practice of Urban Planning* (Washington, D.C.: International City Manager's Association, 1968), pp. 349-378.

California Assembly. Interim Committee on Conservation, Planning and Public Works. *Planning for Growth: A Report on the Status of City and Regional Planning in California.* (Sacramento: Legislative Bill Room, 1955).

Chamber of Commerce of the United States. Construction and Civic Development Department. *City Planning and Urban Development* (Washington, D.C., 1952).

Chapin, F. Stuart, Jr. *Urban Land Use Planning,* Second Edition (Urbana: University of Illinois Press, 1968).

Cincinnati (Ohio) City Planning Commission. *The Cincinnati Metropolitan Master Plan and the Official City Plan of the City of Cincinnati,* adopted November 22, 1948 (Cincinnati, Ohio, 1948).

Cleveland City Planning Commission. *The General Plan of Cleveland* (Cleveland, 1950).

Detroit City Plan Commission. *Detroit Master Plan; the Official Comprehensive Plan for the Development and Improvement of Detroit* (Detroit: The Commission, 1951).

Haar, Charles M. "The Content of the Master Plan: A Glance at History," Journal of the American Institute of Planners, Vol. 21, No. 23 (Spring-Summer, 1955), pp. 66-70.

Jones, Holway R. "A Bibliographic Essay on the Urban General Plan," in Thomas J. Kent (ed.) *The Urban General Plan* (San Francisco: Chandler Publishing), pp. 189-210.

Kent, Thomas J. (ed.) *The Urban General Plan* (San Francisco: Chandler Publishing, 1964).

Lovelace, Eldridge. "1. You Can't Have Planning Without a Plan. 2. Needed: One-Dimensional City Plans. 3. The Flexible City Plan is No City Plan at All," *Journal of the American Institute of Planners,* Vol. 24, No. 1 (1958), pp. 7-10.

Oakland City Planning Commission. *Oakland General Plan.* (Oakland, Calif.: The Commission, 1959).

Olmsted, Frederick Law, Jr. "Introduction," in John Nolen (ed.) *City Planning: A Series of Papers Presenting the Essential Elements of a City Plan* (New York: D. Appleton, Second Edition, 1929), pp. 1-18.

Philadelphia City Planning Commission. *Comprehensive Plan: The Physical Development Plan for the City of Philadelphia* (Philadelphia, 1960).

U.S. Department of Commerce. Advisory Committee on City Planning and Zoning. *A Standard City Planning Enabling Act* (Washington, D.C.: Government Printing Office, 1928).

Goal-Setting

Alesch, D. J. "Improving Decision-Making About Priorities in State Government" (Santa Monica: RAND Corporation, September 1969) RAND Paper P-4187.

Altshuler, Alan. "The Goals of Comprehensive Planning," Journal of the American Institute of Planners, Vol. 31, No. 3 (August 1965), pp. 186-197.

Beal, Franklin H. "Defining Development Objectives" in William I. Goodman and Eric C. Freund (eds.) *Principles and Practice of Urban Planning* (Washington, D.C.: International City Manager's Association, 1968), pp. 327-359.

Blackman, Allan. "The Meaning and Use of Standards," in Henrik Blum (ed.) *Notes on Comprehensive Planning for Health* (Berkeley: School of Public Health, University of California, 1968), pp. 4.32-4.41.

Branch, Melville C. and Ira M. Robinson. "Goals and Objectives in Civil Comprehensive Planning," The Town Planning Review, Vol. 38, No. 4 (January 1968), pp. 261-274.

Chapin, F. Stuart, Jr. "Foundations of Urban Planning," in Werner Z. Hirsch (ed.) *Urban LIfe and Form* (New York: Holt, Rinehart & Winston, 1963), pp. 217-248.

City of Chicago. "The Policies Plan," *The Comprehensive Plan of Chicago* (December 1966), pp. 30-74.

Coleman, James S. "The Possibility of a Social Welfare Function," American Economic Review, Vol. 56, No. 5 (December 1966), pp. 1107-1122.

Community Goals Committee. *Tucson-Community Goals* (Tucson: Office of City Manager, May 1966).

Dubbink, Mollie. "Unique Goals for Dallas Program Systematically Involves Thousands of Citizens," AIP Newsletter (December 1969), pp. 5-7.

Environmental Goals Committee, Los Angeles Region Goals Project. *Environmental Goals for the Los Angeles Region* (Los Angeles: City of Los Angeles, July 1967).

Graduate Research Center of the Southwest, *Goals for Dallas* (Dallas: Southern Methodist University, 1966).

Granger, Charles H. "The Hierarchy of Objectives," Harvard Business Review, Vol. 42 (May-June 1964), pp. 63-74.

Kreditor, Alan and Lyle Sachs. "A Framework for Dynamic Ends," Planning Commentary, Vol. 1, No. 1 (Philadelphia: University of Pennsylvania, Department of City Planning, 1962), pp. 17-28.

Kristof, Frank S. "Housing Policy Goals and the Turnover of Housing," Journal of the American Institute of Planners, Vol. 31 (August 1965), pp. 232-244.

Lamanna, Richard A. "Value Consensus Among Urban Residents," Journal of the American Institute of Planners, Vol. 30, No. 4 (November 1964), pp. 317-322.

Leven,Charles L. "Establishing Goals for Regional Economic Development," Journal of the American Institute of Planners, Vol. 30 (May 1964), pp. 100-110.

Lynch, Kevin. *The Image of the City* (Cambridge: Technology Press and Harvard University Press, 1960).

Michelson, William. "Urban Sociology as an Aid to Urban Physical Development: Some Research Strategies," Journal of the American Institute of Planners, Vol. 34, No. 2 (March 1968), pp. 105-108.

Minneapolis Planning Commission. *Goals for Central Minneapolis* (Minneapolis: The Commission, 1959).

Mitchell, Robert B. (special editor) "Urban Revival: Goals and Standards," Annals of the American Academy of Political and Social Science, Vol. 352 (March 1964), pp. 1-151.

National Capital Planning Commission and National Capital Regional Planning Council. *The Nation's Capital: Policies Plan for the Year 2000* (Washington, D.C.: The Commission, 1961).

President's Commission on National Goals. *Goals for Americans* (New York: Prentice-Hall, 1960).

Tullock, Gordon. "The General Irrelevance of the General Impossibility Theorem," Quarterly Journal of Economics, Vol. 81, No. 2 (May 1967), pp. 256-270.

Tulsa Metropolitan Area Planning Commission. *Comprehensive Plan* (Tulsa, Okla.: The Commission, 1960).

Wilson, Robert L. "Livability of the City: Attitudes and Urban Development," in F. Stuart Chapin, Jr. and Shirley Weiss (eds.) *Urban Growth Dynamics* (New York: John Wiley & Sons, 1966), pp. 359-399.

Young, Robert C. "Goals and Goal-Setting," Journal of the American Institute of Planners, Vol. 32, No. 2 (March 1966), pp. 76-85.

Urban Indicators, Social Indicators and Social Accounts

Agocs, C. "Social Indicators: Selected Readings," in Bertram M. Gross and Michael Springer (special editors) "Political Intelligence for America's Future," Annals of the American Academy of Political and Social Science, Vol. 338 (March 1970), pp. 127-132.

Bauer, Raymond A. (ed.) *Social Indicators* (Cambridge, Mass.: MIT, 1966).

Department of Health, Education and Welfare. *Health Education and Welfare Trends* (annual) and Health, Education and Welfare Indicators (monthly).

Federal Bureau of Investigation, *Uniform Crime Reports for the United States,* published annually by the FBI (Washington, D.C.: Government Printing Office).

Fein, Rashi. "The Economic and Social Profile of the Negro American," Daedalus, Vol. 94 (1965), pp. 815-846.

Fisher, Joseph L. "The Natural Environment," in Bertram M. Gross (special editor), The Annals of the American Academy of Political and Social Science, Vol. 371 (May 1967), Vol. 1: *Social Goals and Indicators for American Society,* pp. 127-140.

Gross, Bertram M. "The New Systems Budgeting," Public Administration Review, Vol. 29, No. 2 (March-April 1969), pp. 113-151.

---. "The City of Man: A Social Systems Reckoning," in William R. Ewald, Jr. (ed.) *Environment for Man* (Bloomington, Ind.: Indiana University Press, 1967), pp. 136-156.

---. (Special editor) "Social Goals and Indicators for American Society," Vol. 1 of two volumes of special issue of The Annals of the American Academy of Political and Social Science, Vol. 371 (May 1967).

--- and Michael Springer. "A New Orientation in American Government," in Bertram M. Gross (special editor) The Annals of the American Academy of Political and Social Science, Vol. 1: *Social Goals and Indicators for American Society,* pp. 1-19.

Hamilton, Calvin S. "Monitor System for Urban Planning," in Clark D. Rogers (ed.) *Urban Information for Policy Decisions.* Selected Papers from the Second Annual Conference on Urban Planning Information Systems and Programs, September 24, 1966 (Pittsburgh: Institute of American Government, Graduate School of International and Public Affairs, 1966), pp. 23-41.

Hoos, I. R. "Information Systems and Public Planning," Working Paper 112 (Berkeley: Space Sciences Laboratory, University of California, January 1970).

Kneese, Allen V. "How Much is Air Pollution Costing Us in the United States?" Paper prepared for the National Conference on Air Pollution (U.S. Public Health Service, Division of Air Pollution, December 13, 1966).

Linder, Forrest E. "The Health of the American People," Scientific American (June 1966).

Moynihan, Daniel P. "Urban Conditions–General," in Bertram M. Gross (special editor) The Annals of the American Academy of Political and Social Science, Vol. 371 (May 1967) Vol. 1: *Social Goals and Indicators for American Society,* pp. 159-177.

Niskanen, William A. "The Use of Intrametropolitan Data," in Werner Z. Hirsch (ed.) *Elements of Regional Accounts* (Baltimore: Johns Hopkins Press, 1964), pp. 131-141.

Perle, Eugene D. (special editor) "Urban Indicators," Urban Affairs Quarterly, Vol. 6 No. 2 (December 1970), pp. 133-250.

Perloff, Harvey S. and Charles L. Leven. "Toward an Integrated System of Regional Accounts: Stocks, Flows, and the Analysis of the Public Sector," in Werner Z. Hirsch (ed.) *Elements of Regional Accounts* (Baltimore: Johns Hopkins Press, 1964), pp. 175-210.

President Herbert Hoover's Research Committee on Social Trends. *Recent Social Trends in the United States* (1943).

Rice, Dorothy P. "Estimating the Cost of Illness," Public Health Service Publication, No. 947-6 (Washington, D.C.: Government Printing Office, May 1966).

Rokeach, M. and S. Parker. "Values as Social Indicators of Poverty and Race Relations in America," in Bertram M. Gross and Michael Springer (special editors) "Political Intelligence for America's Future," Annals of the American Academy of Political and Social Science, Vol. 388 (1970), pp. 97-111.

Schelling, T. C. "The Life You Save May be Your Own," paper prepared for the Second Conference on Government Expenditures, September 15-16, 1966 (Washington, D.C.: To be published by the Brookings Institution).

Sheldon, E. B. and H. E. Freeman. "Notes on Social Indicators: Promises and Potential," Policy Sciences Vol. I, No. 1 (Spring 1970), pp. 97-111.

Siegel, Paul M. "On the Cost of Being a Negro," Sociological Inquiry, Vol. 35, No. 1 (Winter 1965), pp. 41-57.

Springer, M. "Social Indicators, Reports, and Accounts: Toward the Management of Society," in Bertram M. Gross and Michael Springer (sepecial editors) "Political Intelligence for America's Future," Annals of the American Academy of Political and Social Science, Vol. 388 (March 1970), pp. 1-14.

Stagner, R. "Perceptions, Aspirations, Frustrations, and Satisfactions: An Approach to Urban Indicators," in Bertram M. Gross and Michael Springer (special editors) "Political Intelligence for America's Future," Annals of the American Academy of Political and Social Science, Vol. 388 (1970), pp. 59-68.

Thompson, Wilbur R. "Urban Economic Development," in Werner Z. Hirsch (ed.) *Regional Accounts for Policy Decisions* (Baltimore: Johns Hopkins Press, 1966), pp. 81-91, 110-121.

Wilson, John O. "Regional Differences in Social Welfare," Department of Economics (New Haven, Conn.: Yale University, 1968), pp. 1-28.

Wingo, Lowdon, Jr. "Urban Renewal: A Strategy for Information and Analysis." Journal of the American Institute of Planners, Vol. 32, No. 3 (May 1966), pp. 143-154.

New Plan-Formulation Methods, Including Mathematical Models

Boyce, David, Norman D. Day and Chris McDonald. *Metropolitan Plan-Making: An Analysis of Experience with the Preparation and Evaluation of Alternative Land Use and Transportation Plans.* Monograph Series Number Four (Philadelphia, Penn.: Regional Science Research Institute, 1970), pp. 29-49.

Carrothers, Gerald A. P. "An Historical Review of the Quality and Potential Concepts of Human Interaction," Journal of the American Institute of Planners, Vol. 22, No. 2 (Spring 1956), pp. 94-102.

Dyckman, John W. "Transporation in Cities," *Cities: A Scientific American Book* (New York: Alfred A. Knopf, 1965), pp. 133-155.

Fleisher, Aaron. "On Prediction and Urban Traffic," Papers and Proceedings of the Regional Science Association, Vol. 7 (1961), pp. 43-50.

Hansen, Walter G. "How Accessibility Shapes Land Use," Journal of the American Institute of Planners, Vol. 25, Number 2 (May 1959), pp. 73-76.

Harris, Britton. "Conference Summary and Recommendations," *Urban Development Models.* Special Report No. 97. (Washington, D.C.: Highway Research Board, 1968) pp. 3-17.

———. "The City of the Future: The Problem of Optimal Design," Papers, Regional Science Association, Vol. 19 (1967), pp. 185-195.

———. "New Tools for Planning," Journal of the American Institute of Planners," Vol. 31 No. 2 (May 1965), pp. 90-95.

———. "Plan or Projection," Journal of the American Institute of Planners, Vol. 26, No. 4 (November 1960), pp. 265-272.

Hill, Donald M. "A Growth Allocation Model for the Boston Region," Journal of the American Institute of Planners, Vol. 31, No. 2 (May 1965), pp. 111-120.

Kilbridge, Morris D., Robert P. O'Black and Paul V. Teplitz. "A Conceptual Framework for Urban Planning Models." Management Science, Vol. 15, No. 6 (February 1969), pp. 246-266.

Lamb, Donald D. *Research of Existing Land Use Models,* No. 1045 (Pittsburgh: Southwestern Pennsylvania Regional Planning Commission, March 1967).

Lathrop, George T. and John R. Hamburg. "An Opportunity-Accessibility Model for Allocating Regional Growth," Journal of the American Institute of Planners, Vol. 31, No. 2 (May 1965), pp. 95-103.

Lowry, Ira S. "A Short Course in Model Design," Journal of the American Institute of Planners, Vol. 31, No. 2 (May 1965), pp. 158-166.

———. *A Model of Metropolis,* Memorandum RM-4035-RC (Santa Monica, Calif.: RAND Corporation, 1964).

Schlager, Kenneth J. "A Land Use Plan Design Model," Journal of the American Institute of Planners, Vol. 31, No. 2 (May 1965), pp. 103-111.

Seidman, D. R. *The Construction of an Urban Growth Model,* DVRPC Plan Report No. 1, Technical Supplement, Vol. A (Philadelphia: Delaware Valley Regional Planning Commission, 1969).

Voorhees, Alan M. "The Nature and Uses of Models in City Planning," Journal of the American Institute of Planners, Vol. 25, No. 2 (May 1959), pp. 57-60.

Futures Planning and Technological Forecasting

Architectural Design, 2000+, special issue (London, February 1967).

Ayres, Robert U. *Technological Forecasting and Long-Range Planning* (New York: McGraw-Hill, 1969).

Bell, Daniel. "Twelve Modes of Prediction-a Preliminary Sorting of Approaches in the Social Sciences," Daedalus (Summer 1964), pp. 865.

Bright, James R. *Technological Forecasting for Industry and Government* (Englewood Cliffs, N.J.: Prentice-Hall, 1968).

Brown, Harrison, James Bonner and John Weir. *The Next Hundred Years* (New York: Viking Press, 1957).

Calder, Nigel. *The Environment Game* (London: Secker & Warburg, 1967).

Cheaney, E. S. *Technical Forecasting as a Basis for Planning,* with an appendix "A Technique for Forecasting the Attainability of Technical Concepts" by R. J. McCrory, ASME Paper 66-MD-67, presented at the Design Engineering Conference, (Chicago, Ill., May 9-12, 1966) ASME (American Society of Mechanical Engineers), New York.

Clark, Charles H. *Brainstorming–the Dynamic New Way to Create Successful Ideas* (Garden City, N.Y.: Doubleday, 1958).

de Jouvenel, Bertrand. *The Art of Conjecture* (New York: Basic Books, 1967).

Fuller, R. Buckminster and John McHale. *World Design Science Decade, 1965-1975* (Carbondale, Ill.: Published by the World Resources Inventory, Southern Illinois University, 1963 to 1965).

Gabor, Dennis. *Inventing the Future* (London: Secker & Warburg, 1963, Pelican, Book A 663, Penguin Books, Harmondsworth, Middlesex, 1964).

Gordon, Theodore J. *The Future* (New York: St. Martin's Press, 1965).

——— and Olaf Helmer. *Report on a Long-Range Forecasting Study,* Report P-2982 (Santa Monica, Calif.: RAND Corporation, September 1964).

Harris, Britton. *Inventing the Future Metropolis* (Philadelphia: Institute for Environmental Studies, University of Pennsylvania, 1966).

Helmer, Olaf. *Social Technology* (New York and London: Basic Books, 1966).

Jantsch, Erich. "From Forecasting and Planning to Policy Sciences," Policy Sciences, Vol. 1 (1970), pp. 31-47.

———. *Technological Forecasting in Perspective* (Paris, France: Organization for Economic Cooperation and Development, 1967).

Jestice, Aaron L. *Project PATTERN–Planning Assistance Through Technical Evaluation of Relevance Numbers,* paper presented to the Joint National

Meeting Operations Research Society of American and The Institute of Management Sciences, Minneapolis, Minn., October 7-9, 1964 (Washington, D.C.: Pamphlet, Honeywell).

Kahn, Herman. *On Alternative World Futures: Issues and Themes,* Report HI-525-D for the Martin Company (New York: Hudson Institute, Harmon-on-Hudson, May 20, 1965).

––– and Anthony J. Wiener. *The Year 2000* (New York: Macmillan Company, 1967).

Magee, John F. "Decision Trees for Decision Making,"Harvard Business Review, Vol. 42 (July-August 1964), pp. 126-138.

Michael, Donald N. *The Unprepared Society* (New York: Basic Books, 1968).

Ozbekhan, Hasan. *Technology and Man's Future,* Report SP-2494 (Santa Monica: System Development Corporation, May 27, 1966).

–––. *The Idea of a "Look-Out" Institution* (Santa Monica: System Development Corporation, March 1965).

Paine, Thomas O. "The City as an Information Network," address delivered at IEEE International Convention and Exhibition, on March 22, 1966, in New York; Paper 66-TMP-32, TEMPO Center for Advanced Studies. (Santa Barbara: General Electric, 1966).

Prehoda, Robert. *Designing the Future, The Role of Technological Forecasting* (Philadelphia: Chilton, June 1967).

Schon, Donald A. "Forecasting and Technological Forecasting," Daedalus, Vol. 96, No. 3 (Summer 1967), pp. 759-770.

Siegel, Irving H. "Technological Change and Long Run Forecasting," The Journal of Business, Vol. 26, No. 3 (July 1953), pp. 141-156.

Sigford, J. V., and R. H. Parvin. *Project PATTERN: A Methodology for Determining Relevance in Complex Decision-Making,* IEEE Transactions on Engineering Management, Vol. EM-12, No. 1 (March 1965), pp. 9-13.

U.S. National Aeronautics and Space Administration, *Conference on Space, Science and Urban life,* Conference held at the Dunsmuir House, Oakland, California March 28-30, 1963 (Washington, D.C.: NASA, NASA Report SP-37, 1963).

Waskow, Arthur I. "Looking Forward: 1999," New University Thought, Vol. 6, No. 3 (May-June 1968), pp. 35-55.

Zwicky, Fritz. *Morphology of Propulsive Power,* Monographs on Morphological Research No. 1 (Pasadena: Society for Morphological Research, 1962).

Plan-Evaluation

Boyce, David, Norman D. Day and Chris McDonald. *Metropolitan Plan-Making: An Analysis of Experience with the Preparation and Evaluation of Alternative Land Use and Transportation Plans.* Monograph Series Number Four (Philadelphia: Regional Science Research Institute, 1970), pp. 49-81.

Bruck, H. W., Stephen H. Putman and Wilbur A. Steger. "Evaluation of Alternative Transportation Proposals: The Northeast Corridor," Journal of the American Institute of Planners, Vol. 32, No. 6 (November 1966), pp. 322-333.

Clawson, Marion. *Methods of Measuring the Demands for and Value of Outdoor Recreation* (Washington, D.C.: Resources for the Future, 1959).

Eckstein, O. *Water Resources Development: The Economics of Project Evaluation.* (Cambridge, Mass.: Harvard University Press, 1958).

Falk, Edward L. "Measurement of Community Values: The Spokane Experiment," Highway Research Record," No. 229 (Washington, D.C.: Highway Research Board, 1968), pp. 53-64.

Feldstein, M. S. "Cost-Benefit Analysis and Investment in the Public Sector," Public Administration, Vol. 42 (Winter 1964), pp. 351-372.

Gerwin, Donald. "A Proposed Model to Aid in Urban Renewal Choices." Unpublished paper prepared for the Pittsburgh Community Renewal Program Study (Consad Research Corporation, October 1964).

Hill, Morris. "A Method for Evaluating Alternative Plans: The Goals Achievement Matrix Applied to Transportation Plans." Ph.D. dissertation (University of Pennsylvania, 1966).

Kozlowski, J. and J. T. Hughes. "Urban Threshold Theory and Analysis," Journal of the Town Planning Institute, Vol. 53, No. 1 (January 1969), pp. 55-66.

Krutilla, John V. "Welfare Aspects of Benefit-Cost Analysis," Journal of Political Economy, Vol. 69, No. 3 (1961) pp. 226-255.

Lichfield, Nathaniel. "Cost Benefit Analysis in Urban Expansion: A Case Study of Peterborough," Regional Studies, Vol. 3, No. 2 (September 1969), pp. 123-155.

---. "Cost-Benefit Analysis in Urban Redevelopment: A Case Study–Swanley," Urban Studies, Vol. 3 (November 1966), pp. 215-249.

---. "Spatial Externalities in Urban Public Expenditures," in Julius Margolis (ed.), *The Public Economy of Urban Communities* (Washington, D.C.: Resources for the Future, 1965), pp. 107-250.

---. "Cost-Benefit Analysis in Plan Evaluation," The Town Planning Review, Vol. 35 (July 1964), pp. 159-169.

---. *Cost Benefit Analysis in Urban Redevelopment,* Research Report 20, Real Estate Research Program, (Berkeley: University of California, Institute of Business & Economic Research, 1962).

---. "Cost Benefit Analysis in City Planning," Journal of the American Institute of Planners, Vol. 26, No. 4 (November 1960), pp. 273-279.

---. *Economics of Planned Development* (London: Estates Gazette, 1956), pp. 253-280.

--- and H. Chapman. "Cost Benefit Analysis and Road Proposals in a Shopping Centre: A Case Study of Edgemore," Journal of Transport Economics and Policy, Vol. 2 (1968), pp. 280-320.

Lichfield, Nathaniel and Julius Margolis. "Benefit-Cost Analysis as a Tool in Urban Government Decision Making," in Howard G. Schaller (ed.) *Public Expenditure Decisions in the Urban Community* (Washington, D.C.: Resources for the Future, 1963), pp. 118-146.

Loubal, Peter S. "The Evaluation of Alternative Transportation Networks," in Philip M. Morse (ed.) assisted by Laura W. Bacon, *Operations Research for Public Systems* (Cambridge: MIT Press, 1967), pp. 95-126.

Maass, A. "Benefit-Cost Analysis: Its Relevance to Public Investment Decision," Quarterly Journal of Economics, Vol. 80 (May 1966), pp. 208-26.

Marglin, S. *Public Investment Criteria* (Cambridge, Mass.: MIT Press, 1967).

Prest, A. R. and R. Turvey. "Cost-Benefit Analysis: A Survey," The Economic Journal, Vol. 75 (December 1965), pp. 683-735.

Schlager, Kenneth. "The Rank-Based Expected Value Method of Plan Evaluation," Highway Research Record, No. 238 (Washington, D.C.: Highway Research Board, 1967), pp. 153-158.

Steger, Wilbur A. and T. R. Lakshmanan. "Plan Evaluation Methodologies: Some Aspects of Decision Requirements and Analytical Response," in *Urban Development Models,* Special Report No. 97 (Washington, D.C.: Highway Research Board, 1968), pp. 33-72.

Teitz, M. B. "Cost Effectiveness: A Systems Approach to Analysis of Urban Services," Journal of the American Institute of Planners, Vol. 34, No. 5 (September 1968), pp. 303-311.

Thomas, E. N. and J. L. Schofer. *Strategies for the Evaluation of Alternative Transportation Plans,* National Cooperative Highway Research Program Report (Washington, D.C.: Highway Research Board, 1970).

U.S. Federal InterAgency Committee on Water Resources, Sub-Committee on Evaluation Standards. *Proposed Practices for Economic Analysis of River Basin Projects* (Washington, D.C.: Government Printing Office, 1958).

Wilson, G. et al. *The Impact of Highway Investment on Development* (Washington, D.C.: Brookings Institution, 1966).

Wingo, Lowdon, Jr. and Harvey S. Perloff. "The Washington Transportation Plan: Technics or Politics?" in Gerald A. P. Carrothers (ed.) *Papers and Proceedings of the Regional Science Association,* Vol. 7 (1961), PP. 249-262.

Plan-Implementation

American Institute of Planners. *Report of the Planning-Policy Committee on Financing the Plan* (Washington: The Institute, February 1963).

American Society of Planning Officials. Planning Advisory Service Information Report No. 151: *Capital Improvement Programming* (Chicago: The Society, October 1961).

American Society of Planning Officials. Planning Advisory Service Information, Report No. 160: *New Techniques for Shaping Urban Expansion* (Chicago: The Society, July 1952).

Bacon, Edmund N. "Capital Programming and Public Policy," Journal of the American Institute of Planners, Vol. 22 (Winter 1956), pp. 35-38.

Blair, Lachlan F. "Programming Community Development," in William I. Goodman and Eric C. Freund (eds.) *Principles and Practices of Urban Planning* (Washington, D.C.: International City Managers' Association, 1968), Ch. 14, pp. 379-400.

Brown, W. H., and C. E. Gilbert. *Planning Municipal Investment: A Case Study of Philadelphia* (Philadelphia: University of Pennsylvania Press, 1961).

Burns, Leland. "A Programming Model for Urban Development," Papers and Proceedings of the Regional Science Association, Vol. 11 (1963), pp. 195-210.

City of Chicago. "The Improvement Plan," *The Comprehensive Plan of Chicago* (December 1966), pp. 75-106.

Committee for Economic Development. *Budgeting for National Objectives* (New York: Committee for Economic Development, 1966).

Coughlin, Robert E. "The Capital Programming Problem," Journal of the American Institute of Planners, Vol. 26, No. 1 (February 1960), pp. 39-48.

Coughlin, Robert E. and Charles A. Pitts. "The Capital Programming Process," Journal of the American Institute of Planners, Vol. 26 (August 1960), pp. 236-241.

Coughlin, Robert E. and Benjamin H. Stevens. "Public Facility Programming and the Achievement of Development Goals," Unpublished paper presented for the Seminar on Land Use Models (Pennsylvania: Institute for Urban Studies, University of Pennsylvania, October 1964).

Crane, David A. "The City Symbolic," *Journal of the American Institute of Planners, Vol. 26, No. 4 (November 1960), pp. 280-292.*

Doggett, Rosalyn P. "The Development Sector Approach to Regional Planning," Journal of the American Institute of Planners, Vol. 35, No. 3 (May 1969), pp. 169-177.

Downs, Anthony. "PPBS and the Evolution of Planning," in *Planning 1967* (Chicago: American Society of Planning Officials, 1967), pp. 91-99.

Grossman, David A. "The Community Renewal Program," Journal of the American Institute of Planners, Vol. 29, No. 4 (November 1963), pp. 259-269.

Haar, Charles M. "Budgeting for Metropolitan Development: A Step Toward Creative Federalism," Journal of the American Institute of Planners, Vol. 34, No. 2 (March 1968), pp. 102-104.

Herman, Robert S. "Two Aspects of Budgeting: I. The Budget Functions in Modern Government. II. Some Uses and Limitations of Performance Budgeting," Indian Journal of Public Administration, Vol. 8, No. 3 (July-September 1962), pp. 317-331.

Hovey, Harold A. *The Planning-Programming-Budgeting Approach to Government Decision-Making* (New York: Frederick A. Praeger, 1968).

Johnson, L. B. "Introduction of New Government-Wide Planning and Budgeting Systems." Statement to a Cabinet Meeting (August 25, 1965).

Kreditor, Alan. "Capital Design: A Tool for Effectuation" (an unpublished paper prepared for a course in City Planning, University of Pennsylvania, May 1961).

Lombardi, Frank. "The Planning Agency and Capital Improvement Programs," Journal of the American Institute of Planners, Vol. 20 (Spring 1954), pp. 95-101.

Lyden, Fremont J. and Ernest G. Miller (eds.) *Planning Programming Budgeting: A Systems Approach to Management* (Chicago: Markham Publishing, 1967).

Mann, Lawrence D. "Research for National Urban Development Planning," in H. Wentworth Eldridge (ed.) *Taming Megalopolis, Vol. 2: How to Manage an Urbanized World* (Garden City, N.Y.: Anchor Books, Doubleday, 1967), pp. 1042-1067.

Meyerson, Martin. "Building the Middle-Range Bridge for Comprehensive Planning," Journal of the American Institute of Planners, Vol. 22, No. 2 (Spring 1956), pp. 58-64.

Millward, Robert E. "PPBS: Problems of Implementation," Journal of the American Institute of Planners, Vol. 34, No. 2 (March 1968), pp. 88-94.

National Resources Planning Board. *Long-Range Programming of Municipal Public Works* (Washington, D.C.: Government Printing Office, June 1941).

New York State, Division of the Budget and the Office of Planning Coordination. *Guidelines for Integrated Planning, Programming, Budgeting* (Albany, 1965-66).

Novick, David (ed.) *Program Budgeting: Program Analysis and the Federal Budget* (Washington, D.C.: Government Printing Office, 1965).

Orange County Planning Development. *Orange County General Planning Program: Program Overview–Part II.* (Orange County, Calif.: Orange County Planning Department, June 3, 1969).

Page, David. "The Federal Planning-Programming-Budgeting System," Journal of the American Institute of Planners, Vol. 33, No. 4, (July 1967), pp. 256-259.

Planning-Programming-Budgeting System Reexamined: Development, Analysis, and Criticism (Symposium). Public Administration Review, Vol. 29 (March-April 1969), pp. 111-202.

Providence Community Renewal Program, Section Four. *Design for a Decade: A Ten Year Improvement Program* (City of East Providence, R.I.: Department of Planning and Urban Development, 1968).

Reps, John W. "Requiem for Zoning," *Planning 1964* (Chicago: American Society of Planning Officials, November 1964), pp. 56-67.

Robinson, Ira M. "Beyond the Middle-Range Planning Bridge," Journal of the American Institute of Planners, Vol. 31, No. 4 (November 1965), pp. 304-312.

Ross, William B. "Some Perspective on Federal PPBS," *Planning 1967* (Chicago: American Society of Planning Officials, 1967), pp. 87-91.

Segoe, Ladislas. Local Planning Administration (Chicago: The International City Managers' Association, 1941), First Edition, Ch. 14.

State-Local Finances Project. *PPB Pilot Project Reports from the Participating 5 States, 5 Counties and 5 Cities* (Washington, D.C.: George Washington University, 1969).

Taylor, Graeme M. *PPB in New York City,* ICH13C22 (Cambridge, Mass.: Intercollegiate Case Clearinghouse, Howard University Business School, 1968).

U.S. Bureau of the Budget. "Planning-Programming-Budgeting," Bulleton No. 66-3 (Washington, D.C.: Bureau of the Budget, October 12, 1965).

Walker, Robert A. The Planning Function in Urban Government *(Chicago: University of Chicago Press, 1941), First Edition.*

Plan-Review and Feedback

Deutsch, K. W. *The Nerves of Government* (New York: Free Press, 1966).

Forrester, J. W. *Industrial Dynamics* (Cambridge, Mass.: MIT Press, 1961).

Savas, E. S. "Cybernetics in City Hall," Science, Vol. 168, No. 3935 (March 29, 1970), pp. 1066-1071.

Wiener, N. *Cybernetics* (Cambridge, Mass.: MIT Press, 1948).

CASE STUDIES

Community Renewal Program

Blair Associates. *Providence Community Renewal Program,* 1963-1970 (Providence, R.I.: Blair Associates–Planners, December 1963).

Chicago Community Renewal Program. *Community Renewal Program Report: Proposals for Discussion* (Chicago: Community Renewal Program, March 1964).

---. *Housing and Urban Renewal Progress Report* (Chicago: Community Renewal Program, December 31, 1963).

Little, Arthur D., Inc. *Community Renewal Programming.* A San Francisco Case Study (New York: Frederick A. Praeger, 1966), pp. 53-63.

---. *San Francisco Community Renewal Program (CRP).* Final Report to City Planning Commission, City and County of San Francisco, California (San Francisco: Arthur D. Little, October 1965).

---. *San Francisco Community Renewal Program (CRP): Purpose, Scope and Methodology.* A progress report to the San Francisco Department of City Planning (San Francisco: Arthur D. Little, August 1963).

National Association of Housing and Redevelopment Officials. *Community Renewal Program Experience in Ten Cities.* Report on a workshop sponsored by NAHRO and the Urban Renewal Administration, March 9-10, 1964,

Washington, D.C. (Washington, D.C.: National Association of Housing and Redevelopment Officials, August 1964).

New York Community Renewal Program. *New York City's Renewal Strategy, 1965* (New York: Community Renewal Program, December 1965).

Pittsburgh Department of City Planning. *General Progress Report.* Community Renewal Program Progress Report No. 7 (Pittsburgh: Department of City Planning, January 1964).

Land Use-Transportation Studies and Plans

Baltimore Regional Planning Council. *Futures for the Baltimore Region: Alternative Plans and Projectives* (Baltimore, Md.: Baltimore Regional Planning Council, September 1965).

Boyce, David, Norman D. Day and Chris McDonald. *Metropolitan Plan-Making:* An Analysis of Experience with the Preparation and Evaluation of Alternative Land Use and Transportation Plans. Monograph Series Number Four (Philadelphia: Regional Science Research Institute, 1970), Appendix: Seven Study Summaries, pp. 136-426.

Brand, Daniel, Brian Barber and Michael Jacobs. "A Systematic Technique for Relating Transportation Improvements and Urban Development Patterns," 46th Annual Meeting of Highway Research Board (January 1967).

Campbell, E. W. "An Evaluation of Alternative Land Use and Transportation Systems in the Chicago Area," Highway Research Record, No. 238 (Washington, D.C.: Highway Research Board (1968).

Chicago Area Transportation Study, Vol. III. *Transportation Plan, Final Report* (Chicago, Ill.: Chicago Area Transportation Study, April 1962).

Hamburg, John R. and Roger L. Creighton. "Predicting Chicago's Land Use Pattern," Journal of the American Institute of Planners, Vol. 25, No. 2 (May 1959), pp. 67-72.

Hill, Donald M. et al. "Prototype Development of a Statistical Land Use Prediction Model for the Greater Boston Region," Highway Research Record, Vol. 114 (1965), pp. 51-70.

Inter-Agency Land Use and Transportation Planning Program (Joint Program), *Selecting Policies for Metropolitan Growth,* Report No. 4 (Minneapolis, Minn.: Inter-Agency Land Use and Transportation Planning Program, January 1967).

Inter-Agency Land Use and Transportation Planning Program (Joint Program), *Twin Cities Area Metropolitan Development Guide,* Report No. 5 (Minneapolis: Inter-Agency Land Use and Transportation Planning Program, April 1968).

Metropolitan Area Planning Council. *The Empiric Model and Land Use Forecasting* (Boston: Metropolitan Area Planning Council, October 1967).

Northeastern Illinois Planning Commission. *The Plan Study: Summary of Methodology* (Chicago: Northeastern Illinois Planning Commission, November 1967).

Southeastern Wisconsin Regional Planning Commission. *A Land Use Plan Design Model, Vol. 1–Model Development,* Technical Report No. 8 (Milwaukee, January 1968).

———. *Land Use-Transportation Study, Vol. III, Recommended Regional Land Use and Transportation Plans–1990,* Planning Report No. 7 (Milwaukee, November 1967).

———. *Land Use-Transportation Study, Vol. II, Forecasts and Alternative Plans–1990,* Planning Report No. 7 (Milwaukee, June 1966).

Transportation and Land Use Study. *Some Aspects of Plan Evaluation Methodology* (Detroit: Detroit Regional Transportation and Land Use Study, March 1968).

Housing-Residential Mathematical Models

Chapin, F. Stuart, Jr. "A Model for Simulating Residential Development," Journal of the American Institute of Planners, Vol. 31, No. 2 (May 1965), pp. 120-125.

——— et al. *A Probabilistic Model for Residential Growth* (Chapel Hill: Institute for Research in Social Sciences, University of North Carolina, 1964).

Crecine, John P. *A Dynamic Model Of Urban Structure,* RAND Report No. P-3803 (Santa Monica: RAND Corporation, March 1968).

Donnelly, Thomas G., F. Stuart Chapin, Jr. and Shirley F. Weiss. *A Probabilistic Model for Residential Growth* (Chapel Hill, N.C.: Institute for Research in Social Science, May 1964).

Harris, Britton. *Basic Assumptions for a Simulation of the Urban Residential Land Market* (Philadelphia: Institute for Environment Studies, University of Pennsylvania, 1966).

Herbert, John D. and Benjamin H. Stevens. "A Model for the Distribution of Residential Activity in Urban Areas," Journal of Regional Science, Vol. 2, No. 2 (1960), pp. 21-36.

Little, Arthur D., Inc. *Model of the San Francisco Housing Market,* Technical Paper No. 8 (San Francisco: San Francisco Community Renewal Program, Department of City Planning, 1966).

Lowry, Ira A. *A Model of Metropolis,* RM-4035-RC. (Santa Monica: RAND Corporation, August 1964).

Pittsburgh Department of City Planning. *Simulation Model,* Community Renewal Program, Program Report No. 5 (Pittsburgh: Department of City Planning, January 1964).

Robinson, Ira M., Harry B. Wolfe and Robert L. Barringer. "A Simulation Model for Renewal Programming," Journal of the American Institute of Planners, Vol. 31, No. 2 (May 1965), pp. 126-134.

Steger, Wilbur A. "The Pittsburgh Urban Renewal Simulation Model," Journal of the American Institute of Planners, Vol. 31, No. 2 (May 1965), pp. 144-150.

——— and T. R. Lakshmannan. "Review of Analytic Techniques for the CRP," Journal of the American Institute of Planners, Vol. 25, No. 2 (May 1959), pp. 166-172.

Stegman, Michael A. "Accessibility Models and Residential Location," Journal of the American Institute of Planners, Vol. 35, No. 1 (January 1969), pp. 22-29.

Wolfe, Harry B. and Martin L. Ernst. "Simulation Models and Urban Planning," in Philip M. Morse (ed.) assisted by Laura W. Bacon, *Operations Research for Public Systems* (Cambridge, Mass.: MIT Press, 1967).

INDEX

Abt Associates, computer models by, 174
ACHIEVEMENT GOALS
crisis-related origins of, 86-87
defined, 36, 40, 44
and economic growth rates, 90
Ackoff, Russell L., 201, 206, 259, 264, 265
Action sets, alternative, value of, 299-303
Aerial photography, in plan-review, 394, 418-419
Aerojet, morphological research by, 172
Air Force
applied uses of relevant tree schemes, 173
Symposium on Long Range Forecasting, 154
Alexander, Christopher, 142-143, 150, 259
Allocation model, conceptual formulation of, 255-256
Alonso, William, 120, 136, 137
Altshuler, Alan, 35, 43, 46, 49-50, 57, 58, 59
Amenity Budget, described, 315, 327-339
American Academy of Arts and Sciences, Year 2000 Program, 174
American Assembly, 54
American Institute of Planners, constitution of, cited, 49
American Management Association, long-range planning courses of, 154
Ansoff, H. Igor, 552
Appleyard, Donald, 198, 206
Arrow, Kenneth J., 52, 58
Arthur D. Little, Inc.
forecast reports by, 170
and San Francisco Simulation Model, 99
Ashby, Lowell D., 403, 407
ASPIRATION GOALS
defined, 40, 90-91
estimating dollar costs of, 91-94
Attitude sampling techniques, value of forced choices, 38, 58
Ayres, Robert U., 171, 175

Bacon, Laura W., 375
Baker, M. R., 160, 171, 175
Banfield, E. C., 27, 46, 205
Barringer, Robert L., 375
Bassett, Edward, 95
Battelle Memorial Institute, 154, 170, 173-174
Battersby, A., 310
Bauer, Raymond A., 39
Baumol, William J., 205
Beer, Stafford, 403, 404, 407
Bellman, Richard, 149, 150
Bellon, J. L., 380, 390
Berry, Brian J. L., 137
Boeing, decision matrices used by, 173
Bosman, A., 380, 390
Boston, transit link alternatives for, 345, 355
Boyce, David E., 39, 62, 68, 69, 81, 84, 97, 98
Brainstorming, and forecasting techniques, 169-174 *passim*
Branch, Melville, 22, 41, 394, 409, 410, 417, 418, 419
Brand, Daniel, 259, 375
Brandenburg, Richard G., 160, 171, 176
Brennan, Maribeth, 174
Bright, James R., 154, 155, 176
BRITAIN
Coventry research project, 182-183
financing of public development projects in, 284-286
as fruitful source of new planning methodology, 22
local government system in, 274
Tee-side Survey and Plan, described, 406
Brown, H., 315
Brown, W. H., Jr., 46
Brussee, C. Roger, 259, 375
Budget Advisory Council (Citizen), suggested, 45
BUDGET PROCESS
Amenity Budget, described, 315, 327-339
diagramming, 327-329
and planning process, linked, 313-318, 327, 329, 340-342
programming function of, 45
as reconciliation mechanism, 93
urban capital budget, suggested, 45
See also Cost-benefit analysis; Planning-programming-budgeting systems (PPBS)
Burkhead, Jesse, 209
Burns, L. S., 316
Business models, and forecasting techniques, 152

Capital budget and amenity budget, compared, 327
Carroll, J. Douglas, Jr., 98
Carrothers, Gerald A. P., 98, 185
Chadwick, G. F., 114
Chapin, F. Stuart, Jr., 29, 34, 108, 137, 375
Chapman, J., 179
Charnes, Abraham, 259
CHICAGO
agencies involved in planning for, 467-478

Area Transportation Study (CATS), 98
community participation in plan-making, 53-57 *passim*, 58*n*
Community Renewal Program of, 477
comprehensive plan of (1966), 312
Model Cities Program in, 423-424, 459-484
new construction and rehabilitation programs in, 479-484
private housing development in, 474-475
Christenson, C., 379, 390
Churchman, C. W., 259, 264, 265
CITIES
capital budget and development map of, suggested, 45
comparative studies of, as counterproductive, 121
growth crisis of, 9-10
as self-regulating systems, 403-404
as socio-economic systems, 35-36, 44, 96
"State of the City" report, suggested, 45
subsystems and components of, listed, 68-69
Citizen Budget Advisory Council, suggested, 45
Citizen participation. *See* Community participation in planning
City planning. *See* Planning
Cloghaneely (Ireland), optional tourism budgets for, 331-339
Coleman, James S., 38, 53, 58
Colm, Gerhard, 40
Combs, M., 160
Comes, G., 380, 390
Community decision criteria
formulation of, 242-244
listed, 261-262
Community Development Programming, key elements of, 312-313
COMMUNITY PARTICIPATION IN PLANNING
bargaining as essence of, 51-53
in Chicago, 53-57 *passim*, 58*n*
Citizen Budget Advisory Council, suggested, 45
in Dallas, 54-57 *passim*
and goal-setting, 36-38, 49-58
as instrument of social action, 13, 96-97
in Los Angeles, 54-57 *passim*
in New York City, 57
obstacles to, 57-58
in Philadelphia, 57
in plan-evaluation, 180-182, 202, 227-228, 242-244
planner as "coordinator" of, critiqued, 34-37, 43-44, 49-50
and political leaders, attitudes of, 58
in "quality of life" measurement, 449
voting models for, 51-53
COMMUNITY RENEWAL PROGRAM
of Chicago, 477
District Plan, case study of, 505-518
model building for, 555-557
of Philadelphia, 316, 423-424, 487-518
program approach, defined, 487-489
purpose of, 423
sample program plan, 513-518
San Francisco Simulation Model for, 99, 423-424, 555-595
as short- and middle-range plans, 312
and simulation models, evolution of, 99
COMPUTERS IN PLANNING
as "designer" of alternative plans, 99
domestication of technology, advocated, 13
evolving uses of, described, 97-100
limitations of, 134-135, 148, 557
linear programming examples, displayed, 355-369
and Model Cities Program alternatives, evaluation of, 316-317
plan-evaluation benefits of, 183, 256-257
plan-formulation benefits of, 100, 135, 316
programming techniques, in land use design models, 145-146, 148-149
and technological forecasting, 153
See also Mathematical models
Content analysis, of performance characteristic statements, 70-79
Contexual mapping, in forecasting, 172-174
Cooper, Leon, 136
COST-BENEFIT ANALYSIS
"balance sheet of development" approach, assessed, 188-191
in local government planning strategies, 290-294, 333-339
and monetary criteria, complexity of, 225-226
and planning-programming-budgeting systems (PPBS), compared, 212-213
traditional concepts of, critiqued, 180, 185-188
See also Economic theory and planning; Goals-achievement matrix; Plan-evaluation; Planning-programming-budgeting systems (PPBS)
Cost-estimating techniques
and goal-setting, 39-40
in land use design model, 147
Cotton, Joseph F., 209, 237
Coughlin, Robert E., 185, 203, 207, 315-316, 345, 375
Council of Urban Development Advisors, suggested and described, 45
Coventry (U.K.), local government research project in, 182-183
CRITERIA SELECTION
and citizen-government relations, 227-228
cultural bias in, 237*n*
definition and expression of, 221-223
general properties sought, 214-216
and government objectives, 217-218
illustrative list of, 230-236
and intangibles, 228-229
levels of, 218-219
and long-range estimates, 223-224
monetary impact, 224-226
need for, 214
and program area, 219-221
political considerations, 228
and target groups, distinction between, 221

weighting techniques, 262-268
See also Plan-evaluation; Standards
Criterion statement
defined, 65-66
See also Indicators, Urban; Performance characteristic statement; Standards
Critical path analysis, in local government planning strategies, 279
Culhane, J. H., 378, 390
Cybernetic controls, in plan-review, 393, 402-406

Daland, Robert T., 46
Dallas, community participation in goal-setting for, 54-57 *passim*, 59*n*
Dansereau, H. Kirk, 259
Dantzig, George B., 257, 259
Data resources, and simulation modeling, 106
Davidoff, Paul, 22, 59, 204-205
Day, N. D., 68, 81, 84
Dean, Burton V., 259
Decision criteria. *See* Criteria selection; Plan-evaluation
Decision-making studies, and comprehensive goal-setting, 35-36
Delphi technique of forecasting, 157-174 *passim*
Democratic decision processes, 52-53. *See also* Community participation in planning
Denver, metropolitan plan for (1963), critiqued, 179
Design, Urban, Office of, suggested, 45-46
Donegal County (Ireland), tourism planning for, 320-328
Donnelly, Thomas G., 137
Downs, Anthony, 24
Dreyfus, Stuart E., 150
Drucker, P. F., 378, 390
Dunham, Alison, 49, 58
Dynamic programming. *See* Computers in planning

Eckenrode, Robert T., 259, 262
Economic growth
and national goals, relationship outlined, 87
target rates of, modeled, 89-91
ECONOMIC THEORY AND PLANNING
"added future earnings" concept, disputed, 238*n*
and forecasting techniques, 152, 169-174 *passim*
"discounting" dollar flows, 226
disparate approaches of, 118-119
market as distributor of public goods, 50-51, 88-89, 186-187
optimizing and equilibrium concepts, critiqued, 125-127
partial equilibrium analysis, problems in, 122-123
profit-maximizing (business) firm *versus* public sector, 186
supply and demand models, need for refinement of, 121
Eddison, R. T., 390
EDUCATION
alternative model solutions for, 336-367
criteria of evaluation, listed, 233-235
linear programming model for, 360-363
Model Cities Program goals for, illustrated, 452-454
performance objectives, in model neighborhood, 346
Effectiveness matrix technique, in plan-evaluation, 182, 244-255 passim
"Effect units," typology of, 182-183, 284-287
Eisenhower (President). *See* President's Commission on National Goals
Employment Act of 1946, as symbol of goal consciousness, 86
EMPLOYMENT GOAL-SETTING
alternative model solutions for, 336-367
community participation in, 56
linear programming model for, 360-363
performance objectives, in model neighborhood, 346
Environment, performance objectives for, 346
Erber, Ernest, 21, 23, 49
Estimation. *See* Forecasting methodology
Evaluation. *See* Plan-evaluation

Fagin, Henry, 21, 22, 292
Falk, Edward L., 374
Family decision process, as paradigm of group choice, 52
Farbey, M., 114
Farhi, Al, 62, 68, 69, 81, 84
Federal Highway Act, impact on transportation planning process, 98
Feedback. *See* Plan-review and feedback
Fire prevention and firefighting, criteria for evaluation of, 231
Fishburn, Peter C., 259, 262
Fisher, Walter D., 343
Fluxton (fictional town). *See* Local government planning strategies
Forbartha, An Foras, 314, 319
FORECASTING METHODOLOGY
applications, outlined and exemplified, 169-174
cost-effectiveness of, assessed, 170-171
diffusion of ideas about, 153-155
evolution of formal techniques, reviewed, 151-155
exploratory *versus* normative techniques, 155-161
feedback systems in, 160-161, 167
improvised models, uses of, 63
"insight" argument for, 170
levels of technology transfer, listed, 162
morphological research in, 158-159, 166, 172-174
outlined, 101-102
and performance characteristic statements, 66-67
ranking procedures, 171
relevant tree concepts in, 160, 166, 169-174 *passim*

shortcomings of, 171
state of the art, 168-169, 174-175
symposia on, 154-155
See also Futures planning
Freund, Eric C., 375
Friedmann, John, 35-36, 39, 57, 59
Friedrich, Carl J., 46, 136
Friend, J. K., 182, 269, 318
FUTURES PLANNING
characteristics of, 101
defined, 100-101
as element of current planning models, 139
and systems analytic view of future, 102
See also Forecasting methodology

Galbraith, John Kenneth, 205
Gaming techniques
in business forecasting, 172
semi-projective, described, 38
Gans, Herbert, 21, 22
General Electric
Atomic Power Department, network techniques of, 173
See also TEMPO Center
Gilbert, B., 315
Gilbert, C. E., 46
Goal-achievement. *See* Performance goals; Plan-evaluation
GOALS-ACHIEVEMENT MATRIX
appraised, 203-204
costs and benefits of, 194-195
defined, 180, 191-192, 344
goals-achievement account, described, 198-199
limitations of, 203, 204
procedure, 192-194
quantitative *versus* qualitative objectives, 195-198
relative weights in, 202-203
transformation functions, 201
weighted index approach, described, 199-201
GOAL-SETTING
bargaining as essence of, 51-53
categories of, distinguished, 33-34
community participation in, 36-38, 180
and community problems, 33-34
comprehensiveness as tenet of, 34-36, 43-44, 49-50
and cost-estimating techniques, 39-40
"feasible priority combinations," defined, 91
government *versus* private sector roles in, 88-89
human resources as "ends" and "means" in, 88
methodological issues involved in, 34
in Model Cities Program, 430-431
and plan-formulation, relationship explained, 104-105
and statistical indicators, value of, 38-41
traditional procedures, described, 36-37
voting models for, 51-53
See also Achievement goals; Aspiration goals; Performance goals; President's Commission on National Goals
Goals-achievement matrix, defined, 180
GOALS RESEARCH
approaches to, 87-89
basic concepts of, 89-91
evolution of national goals consciousness, 86-87
functions of, suggested, 94
purpose of, 85-86
quantifying costs in, 91-92
and reconciling aspirations with resources, 93
ultimate *versus* proximate values in, 91
Goldman, Alan J., 209
Goodman, William L., 375
Gordon, R., 174
Government program analysis. *See* Plan-evaluation
Grecco, W. L., 181, 375
Greenberger, Martin, 137, 138
Greeson, Gary, 46
Gross, Bertram, 39
Gupta, Shiv, 317

Hadley, G., 257, 259
Hansen, Willard B., 132, 375
Harmon, Leon D., 411, 419
Harris, Britton, 23, 27, 98, 99, 100, 136, 137, 183
Harvard Economic Project, 173
Hatry, Harry P., 181, 237
Hay, George A., 259
Health care. *See* Public health
Helmer, Olaf, 174
Hemmens, George C., 259
Herbert, John, 132, 137, 374
Herman, Robert, 313
Hertz, D. B., 378, 390
Hespos, R. F., 378, 390
Hightower, Henry C., 27
Highways. *See* Federal Highway Act; Transportation
Hill, Morris, 112, 133, 180, 207, 259, 316, 344-345, 374
Hirsch, Werner Z., 46-47
Hitch, C. J., 255, 259
Hodge, Gerald, 206
Homeostasis. *See* Cybernetic controls in plan-review
Honeywell (U.S.), PATTERN technique, 153, 158, 160, 166-174 *passim*
Hoover Commission recommendations, 210
Hoover, E., 120
HOUSING
alternative model solutions for, 364-365, 369
community participatin in goal-setting for, 55-56
in Chicago, Model Cities Program for, 459-484
constraints on plan-achievement in, 464-467
criteria for evaluation of, listed, 235-236
density law, as descriptive postulate, 120
deteriorating, described, 270-273
five-year objectives statements, exemplified, 439-443
linear programming model for, 358-359

Model Cities Program goals for, illustrated, 454-457
and other program components, related, 463-464
performance objectives, in model neighborhood, 346
programs-effectiveness matrix for, displayed, 356
simulation model of, 558-593
and shopping, construction of joint effect tables on, 304-306
Housing and Urban Development (HUD), Department of, planning requirements for Model Cities Program, 427-444
Hudson Institute, and scenario-writing, 174
Hufschmidt, Maynard, 185, 206
HUMAN RESOURCES
and dollar costs of aspiration goals, 93-94
as "means" and "ends," in goal-setting, 88
Humphrey, Hubert, 159
Hurter, Arthur P., 343

Implementation. *See* Plan-implementation
"Impossibility theorem" of majority rule, 52-53
INDICATORS, URBAN
defined, 41*n*
and lack of urban macro-theory, 62
and land use planning, 61
parameters for analysis of, listed, 68-69
and performance characteristic statements, compared, 66, 67, 79
value of, explained, 38-41, 44-45, 57, 61-62, 393
See also Criterion statement; Performance characteristic statements; Standards
Industrial revolution, and urban crisis, 10
Industrial siting, 271
Information technology
Presidential Advisory Staff on Scientific Information Management, recommended, 159
and technological forecasting, 153
See also Computers in planning
Institute of Management Sciences, and technological forecasting, 154
INVESTMENT DECISIONS, SEQUENTIAL
limitations on planning flexibility, 378-379
optimality *versus* robustness, 389-390
plant location, as case study in, 381-389
risk analysis in, 378
"robustness" as measure of flexibility, 318, 379-381
stable initial decisions, defined, 387
and uncertainty of future conditions, 377-379
Ireland, tourism planning process in, 314-315, 319-342
Irwin, Neil A., 259

Jahoda, M., 206
Jamieson, M., 114
Jantsch, Erich, 101-102, 151
Jessiman, William, 259, 375
Jessop, W. N., 182, 269, 318
Johnson, D., 395, 402
Johnson, Lyndon B., and PPBS in the federal bureaucracy, 314
Joint effect tables
construction of, 304-306
significance of, 306-308
Judgment rate of economic growth, defined, 90

Kahn, Herman, 174
Kaplan, Abraham, 196, 206
Kast, Fremont E., 395, 402
Kiefer, M., 171, 176
Kitchell, Raymond E., 497, 504
Klein, Burton, 259
Knowlton, Kenneth C., 411, 419
Korbel, John, 137, 138
Krutilla, John V., 205

Lakshmanan, T. R., 132
Lamanna, Richard A., 38, 58, 59, 207
LAND USE
design process for, outlined, 142-144
design standards for, 63
input data for model application, 147-148
locational analysis, factors affecting, 120-122, 134
and metropolitan growth model, 107-108
plan design model for, 139-149, 344
planners as experts for evaluating, 49
planning indicators for, 61
planning variables, listed, 143
plant location, as case study in investment planning, 381-389
simulation model for plan design of, 99, 139-149 *Passim*
See also Open space; Wisconsin, Southeastern, Land Use-Transportation Plan
Land Use Planning, Office of, suggested, 46
Latchford, M., 114
Law enforcement, criteria for evaluation of, listed, 230-231
Law of Requisite Variety, explained, 403
Lecht, Leonard A., 40, 85
Lesourne, Jacques, 259
Lichfield, Nathaniel, 179, 188-190, 205-206
Linear programming. *See* Computers in planning
Little, John D. C., 375
LOCAL GOVERNMENT PLANNING STRATEGIES
assumptions, questioning of, 303-304, 309-310
alternative action sets, value of, 299-303
versus central government obligation, 294
cost-benefit balancing, 290-294
"crash" strategy, defined, 278
critical path analysis, 279
decision problems, location of, 275
design choices and timing options, 272, 273-275
"effect units," typology of, 182-183, 284-287
expansion strategy, defined, 278
joint effect tables, construction of, 304-306

measurement of (potential) effects, 284-287, 308-309
option graphing, 275-278, 280-282
policy-makers *versus* planners in, 269, 274
sequential network charting, 278-279
solutions, narrowing choice of, 282-283, 287-290, 294-295
trade-off rates, 293-298, 309-310
uncertainties in priority-setting, 298-299
Los Angeles
analysis-display panels for, 415-417
Regional Goals Project, cited, 37, 54-58 *passim*
Louisville (Kentucky)
community decision criteria, establishment of, 242-244
Metropolitan Comprehensive Transportation and Development Program, 181-182, 253
Lowry, Ira S., 124, 132, 133, 137, 375, 401
Lynch, Kevin, 198, 206

Maass, Arthur, 206
Manpower. *See* Employment; Human resources
March, J. G., 380, 390
Margolis, Julius, 179, 205
Market distribution of public goods, 50-51, 88-89
Martin, Roscoe C., 46
MATHEMATICAL MODELS
alternative model solutions, displayed, 357, 364-369
coefficients of determination, and model reliability, 131-132
common interest in, by decision-makers and social scientists, 115, 122
conditions for use of, 143
cost parameters, usefulness of, 350-351
defining characteristics of, 117, 344, 368-369
effectiveness predictions in, 352-353
evolving uses of, 97-100
guidelines for continuing research, suggested, 373-374
information requirements for, 345, 347, 352
interdenpendencies and linearities of, 353-355
for land use plan designs, 143-149
linear programming examples, displayed, 355-369
"optimal" solutions, nonexistence of, 357, 368-369
past modeling efforts, reviewed, 344-347
and planning process, 23
and programs-objectives matrix, development of, 343-344, 351-352
revising solutions in, 371-372
sensitivity analyses of, 369-371
McDonald, C., 62, 68, 69, 81, 84
McEachron, W. D., 377, 390
McKay, Mary E., 114
McKean, Roland N., 205
McLoughlin, J. Brian, 96, 97, 103, 393, 395
Measures for determining goals. *See* Criteria selection; Indicators, urban
Mecklin, John, 411, 419
Meckling, William, 259
Metropolitan growth model, uses of, 107-108
Meyer, J. R., 198, 206
Meyerson, Martin, 27, 46, 205, 311-312, 391-392
Milliman, J. W., 204, 207
Millward, Robert E., 313
Mitchell, Robert, 33, 107, 392
MODEL CITIES PROGRAM
basic instructions for, issued by HUD, 427-428
of Chicago, 423-424, 459-484
cost parameters, predicted, 348-351
five-year objectives statements, preparation of, 439-444, 451
goals and program approaches, 430-431, 448-449, 460-462, 466
illustrative examples of, 451-457
mathematical programming techniques in, 316-317
measures of living quality, need for, 445-447
objectives of, 346, 347-350, 423
output measures, uses of, 447-451
one-year action program, outlined, 434-438, 451
problem analysis, 428-430
program components, related, 463-464
strategies for, recommended, 431-434, 462-463
MODELS
accuracy and utility of, assessed, 132-134
advantages of specificity in, 121-122
applied dimensions of, 130-132
descriptive *versus* analytic, 119-122
future of, 134-136
macro- *versus* micro-, 123-125
in the policy-making context, 117-118, 122, 133-134
probabilistic, 128-129
simultaneous *versus* sequential, 129-130
and spatial distribution of social problems, 134
static *versus* dynamic, 125-127, 133
structural *versus* parametric elements in, 404
and theories, compared, 116-117
See also Mathematical models; Simulation Models
Mol, J., 380, 390
Morlok, Edward K., 259
Morphological approach to exploratory forecasting, 158, 159, 166, 172-174
Morse, Philip M., 375
Moynihan, Daniel P., 39
Mueller, Dennis C., 53, 58
Murchland, M., 114
Muth, Richard F., 120, 136, 138

NASA, applied use of PATTERN technique, 173
National Capitol Planning Commission, 105
National goals
evolving consciousness of, 86-87
See also Goal-setting; Goals research; Pres-

ident's Commission on National Goals
National Security Industrial Association, symposium on forecasting, 155
National Planning Association, Center for Priority Analysis, 88, 92-94
Navy, applied uses of relevant tree schemes, 173
Network charting, sequential, 278-279
Network models, in forcasting, 160, 173-174
Newman, William N., 504
New York City Community Renewal Program Report, 38, 57
Nishry, Meir J., 259
North American Aviation, decision matrices used by, 173

Open space
  performance statements regarding, 78-80, 81 (table)
  See also Land use
Operations research, and technological forecasting, 153, 169-174 *passim*
Opinion polls. *See* Attitude sampling techniques; Community participation in planning
Optimal solutions, nonexistence of, 357, 368-369
Option capacity diagramming, 325-327
Option graphing, in local government planning strategies, 275-278, 280-282
Orcutt, Guy, 128-129, 137, 138
Organizational performance, criteria for evaluation of, 227, 238

Parsons, Talcott, 205
Penn-Jersey Transportation Study (PJ), impact of, 98
Pennsylvania, Southwestern, Regional Planning Commission, 47
PERFORMANCE CHARACTERISTIC STATEMENTS
  adopting values for, 83
  content analysis of, 68-79
  and criterion statements, compared, 65-66, 67
  defined, 63-67 *passim*
  and forecasts, compared, 66-67
  frequency count of, exemplified, 69-70
  and indicators, compared, 66, 67, 79
  in plan-making, uses of, 79, 81-83
  and problem-solving, related, 62-63
  and standards, compared, 65, 67
  threshold value of, 65
PERFORMANCE GOALS
  crisis-related origins of, 86
  defined, 36, 44
  for hypothetical model neighborhood, 346
Perle, Eugene, 39
Perloff, Harvey S., 115
Pessemier, Edgar A., 259
Peterson, George L., 343, 345, 375
PHILADELPHIA COMMUNITY RENEWAL PROGRAM
  agencies involved in, 507-509
  cited, 38, 423-424
  community participation in, 57
  plan format, suggested, 498-504
  PPBS used in, 316
  program approach, applied, 489-498
  programming concept, defined, 487-489
  sample program plan, 513-518
  West Philadelphia, District Plan for, 505-518
Pitts, Charles A., 315
PLAN-EVALUATION
  allocation model for, 255-256
  "balance sheet of development," assessed, 179, 188-191
  community decision criteria in, 242-244, 261-262
  community participation in, 180, 181-182, 202, 227-228, 242-244
  and computers, benefits of using, 183
  cost-benefit analysis in, critiqued, 180, 185-188
  criteria weighting techniques, 262-268
  defining decision variables in, 255
  effectiveness matrix technique, 182, 244-255 *passim*
  "effect unit," defined and applied, 182-183, 284-287
  evolving search for useful criteria in, 177-179
  linear programming approach to, 256-257
  measurement of (potential) effects, 284-287, 308-309
  "output measure," defined, 237*n*
  parametric programming approach, 257
  requirements for useful techniques in, 180
  scales of measurement for, 180, 196
  scoring model for, 246-248
  tangibles *versus* intangibles in, 180, 187, 228-229
  See also Criteria selection; Goals-achievement matrix
PLAN-FORMULATION
  alternative plans, benefits of, 97-98, 103, 112
  and computers, advantages in using, 100
  design model for, 139-149
  general procedures for, described, 106-108
  and goal-setting, relationship explained, 104-105
  mathematical models in, 97-100
  systems view of: form and content of plans, 108-113; land use design model, based on, 139-149; methodology, 96; simulated trajectories, 103-106
  traditional approach, described, 95-96
  See also Futures planning; Planning process
PLAN-IMPLEMENTATION
  Amenity Budget, described, 315, 327-339
  capacity diagramming of options, 325-327
  choice of options, 320-322
  client projections, 322-325
  and Community Development Programming, 312, 313
  comprehensive plan allocation profile, 315-316
  and cost parameters, usefulness of, 350-351

effectiveness predictions, 352-353
flexibility *versus* early commitment, 317-318
guidelines for continuing research, suggested, 373-374
and Model Cities Program, recommended strategy for, 431-434
need for strategy in, 311-312, 317
"optimal" solutions, nonexistence of, 357, 368-369
performance objectives for hypothetical neighborhood, 346
plan-budget process, suggested, 340-342
programs-objectives matrix, 343-344, 351-352
revising solutions, 371-372
"robustness," as measure of flexibility, 318, 379-381
sample questions for, listed, 396-397
sensitivity analyses in, 369, 371
statment of options, 319-320
uncertainty, in sequential plan decisions, 377-379

PLANNERS
action orientation of, 21-22, 314
activities of, listed, 43-44
architectural origins of, 97
education of, 27
new roles for, 21-22, 25
philosophical divisions among, 9
professional evolution of, 11-12, 21-24
and public administrators, compared, 12
resistance to new methods, explained, 24-25
search for new identity, 12-13
and selective borrowing from other disciplines, 23-24
self-image of, 43
social class biases of, 51
welfare goals of, 51

PLANNING
as anticipatory decision-making, 10-11
as coordination of "the public interest," disputed, 34-37, 43-44, 49-50
defined, 43
and policy-making, distinguished, 44
search for new methodology, described, 22-26
and social revolution, 11, 12
and social science, inadequacies of, 13-14
as synthetic field, 22-24
and systems engineering, relationship between, 12

Planning commissions, traditional role of, 36-37
Planning methodology, lack of literature on, 26-27

PLANNING PROCESS
and budgetary process, linked, 313-318, 327, 329, 340-342
and continuous master planning, 409-411
defined, 21-22, 33
deisgn/evaluation as single problem in, 63
functional relationships in, 140-142
and longer-term perspective, need for, 13
output measures in, 450-452
paradigm of, evaluated, 9, 27-28, 81-82, 95-96, 311-312, 391
proposed revision of, outlined, 82-83
public access to, 13, 49-58, 96-97
rationality criterion, defined, 185
as a servo-system, 406
as three-stage operation, 117-118
See also Community participation in planning; Goal-setting; Local government planning strategies

PLANNING-PROGRAMMING-BUDGETING SYSTEMS (PPBS)
advantages and disadvantages of using, 213
basic purpose of, 210
and budget process, contrasted, 211
characteristics of, 210-213
and cost-benefit analyses, compared, 212-213
criteria-defining function of, 181
origins of, 313-314
and program budgeting, contrasted, 211
and urban planners, influence on, 12, 24
See also Budget process; Cost-benefit analysis

PLAN-REVIEW AND FEEDBACK
actual *versus* intended system states, 395-396
aerial photography in, 394, 418-419
analysis-display mechanisms for, 411-419
continuous master planning, need for, 409-411
"control," defined, 395
cybernetic controls in, 393, 402-406
intelligence centers for monitoring, 393-394
Law of Requisite Variety, explained, 403
need for, 391-392
"program" *versus* "systems" performance standards, 392-393
public *versus* private developments, control principles for, 399-400
strategic *versus* tactical conformity, 398-399
techniques for, in forecasting, 160-161, 167, 174
variables used in, 401-402

Police. *See* Law enforcement
Political considerations in criteria selection, 228
Political definition of public interest, 51-53
Political leaders, and community participation in planning, 58
Polling. *See* Attitude sampling technique
Pound, W. H., 160, 171, 175
Prediction. *See* Forecasting methodology
President's Commission on National Goals (1960)
cost estimates for, 40, 87-88
and urban development, 33
PPB. *See* Planning-programming-budgeting systems (PPBS)
Prest, A. R., 206
Program budgeting *versus* PPB, 211
Programs-objectives matrix, 343-344, 351-352
Public administrators, and urban planners, compared, 12

PUBLIC HEALTH
performance objectives, in model neighborhood, 346
criteria for evaluation of, listed, 231-233
Public interest in planning. *See* Community participation in planning
Pushkarev, Boris, 198, 206

Quality of life, measures of, 445-458 *passim*
Quantum Science Corporation, forecasting applications by, 173

Rabinowitz, F. F., 46
RAND Corporation, 149, 153, 173, 174
Réalités, Symposium on the Future (1966), 154
Regional Economic Simulation Model, 141
Reiner, Thomas A., 22, 205
Relevant tree concepts in forecasting, 160, 166, 169-174 *passim*
Revolutionary approach to urban crisis, assessed, 12
Ridley, T. M., 260
Rivlin, Alice M., 137, 138
Robinson, Ira M., 41, 312, 375
Ronaldson, A. M., 378, 390
Rosenhead, Jonathan, 317
Rosenzweig, James E., 395, 402
Ross, Robert S., 313
Rothenberg, Jerome, 52, 58

SAN FRANCISCO COMMUNITY RENEWAL SIMULATION MODEL
cited, 99, 423-424
computer operation of, evaluated, 570-571
data and assumptions used in, 573-581
and market data, compared, 581-591
operation of, 559-565
purpose of, 558-559
recent development of, 565-570
recommendations regarding, 595
reliability of, assessed, 571-573
usefulness of, 591-595
San Francisco Mint, "cost-benefit" analysis of, 190
Scenario-writing, as forecasting technique, 169-174 *passim*
Schaller, Howard G., 205
Schimpeler, Charles G., 181, 375
Schlager, Kenneth J., 99, 150, 344, 355, 374
Schofer, Joseph L., 260
Scoring model, in plan-evaluation, 246-248
Scott, S., 51
Segoe, Ladislas, 314
Seidman, David R., 136, 138
Sensitivity analyses, in mathematical programming, 369-371
SHOPPING CENTERS
and housing, construction of joint effect tables on, 304-306
siting of, 273
Siegel, Irving H., 151, 176
Silvers, A. L., 375
Simon, Herbert A., 205, 380, 390

SIMULATION MODELS
accuracy and utility of, 100
evolving uses of, 97-100
factors affecting choice of, in plan-formulation, 105-106
value of, explained, 40-41, 556-557
See also San Francisco Community Renewal Simulation Model
Size, of plan area, and simulation modeling, 106
Sloan, A. K., 375
Social change
and longer-term perspective, need for, 13
and urban crisis, 9-11
Social cost-benefit analysis, need for, 186-188
Social sciences, inadequacies of, 13-14, 58
Social indicators. *See* Indicators, urban
Sonenblum, Sidney, 36, 46
Southwest Center for Advanced Studies, cited, 37, 54
Springer, Clifford H., 39
STANDARDS
as binary function, defined, 65
traditional application of, critiqued, 81-82
See also Criteria selection; indicators, urban; Performance characteristic statements
Stanford Research Institute, forecasting reports by, 170
Statistical indicators. *See* Indicators, urban
Steger, Wilbur A., 375
Stern, Louis, 36, 46
Stevens, Benjamin H., 132, 137, 185, 203, 207, 316, 374, 375
Stigler, G., 380, 390
Strassman, P. A., 378, 390
Stuart, Darwin G., 316-317, 376
Sumner, Charles E., Jr., 504
Sutherland, Ivan E., 411-419
Sweezy, Eldon E., 160, 176
System Development Corporation, 160, 173, 174
SYSTEMS ANALYTIC APPROACH
attitude of planners toward, 12
and goal-setting, 36
and plan-formulation, methodology of, 103-114
requirements for, 556-557
and technological forecasting, 153, 160, 169-174 *passim*

Tabibian, Jivan, 102
Target rate of economic growth, defined, 89
Technology and planning, domestication of computer science, advocated, 13
Technology transfer scheme, in forecasting, 155-157
TEMPO Center, systems analysis approach of, 160, 173, 174
Terleckyj, Nestor, 209
Thomas, Edwin N., 260
Threshold value, as time-dependent, 65
Tourism planning, 314-315
Town planning. *See* Local government planning strategies

Trade-off rates, in ranking feasible solutions, 293-298, 309-310
TRANSPORTATION
for Boston, link alternatives weighed, 345, 355
community decision criteria for, 181-182
content analysis of performance statements about, 70-77
design standards for problem-solving, 63
and evolution of new planning methods, 98
land use effects on, simulated, 142
measurable objectives of new routes, listed, 197-198
plan-evaluation of, 241-242, 345
traffic assignment model, suggested, 107, 108, 114*n*
yardsticks for deterimining effectiveness values, listed, 249-253
See also Wisconsin, Southeastern, Land Use-Transportation Plan
TRW Systems, 172
Tullock, Gordon, 38, 52-53, 58
Tumminia, Alfred, 259, 375
Tunnard, Christopher, 198, 206
Turvey, R., 206

Unilever (U.K.), forecasting applications by, 172
United Kingdom, *See* Britain
Urban capital budget, suggested, 45
URBAN CRISIS
and goal-setting by planners, 33-34
as growth crisis, 9-11
new urgency about resolving, 11-12
Urban Design Office, suggested, 45-46
Urban Development Advisors (Council of), suggested and described, 45
Urban indicators. *See* Indicators, urban
Urban planning. *See* Planning process
Urban renewal. *See* Community Renewal Program

Values, proximate *versus* ultimate, in goals research, 91
Vogt, Robert S., 246, 260
Vorhees, Alan M., 98
Voting models, compared, 52-53

Walker, Robert A., 314
Washington, D.C., metropolitan plan for (1963), critiqued, 179
Water supply, criteria for evaluation of, listed, 236
Webber, Melvin, 37, 393
Weber, Alfred, 136
Weisbrod, Burton A., 207
Weiss, Shirley F., 137
Wheaton, Margaret, 37-38
Wheaton, William L. C., 37-38, 179
Wilson, Robert, 38
Wingo, Lowdon, Jr., 115, 120, 136, 138
WISCONSIN, SOUTHEASTERN, LAND USE-TRANSPORTATION PLAN
basic concepts, 529
cited, 141, 147, 423-425, 521
forecasting future needs, 524-525
objectives and standards, 522-523, 528-534, 538-539
overriding considerations, 534-535, 548-549
plan design, 525-526
plan evaluation and selection, 526-528, 535-547
summary, 549
Wisconsin, Southeastern, Regional Planning Commission, 98, 99, 141
Wolfe, Harry B., 375
Worrall, R. D., 260
Wurster, Catherine Bauer, 33

Xerox Corporation, computer models, by, 172

Zimmerman, R. M., 378, 390
Zwicky, M., 152

CONTRIBUTORS

DAVID E. BOYCE is Associate Professor of Regional Science and Transportation at the University of Pennsylvania. Dr. Boyce holds a B.S. degree in Civil Engineering, the Master of City Planning degree, and a Ph.D. in Regional Science. During the past several years, he has been intensively engaged in research on metropolitan land use and transportation planning.

MELVILLE C. BRANCH is Professor of Planning in the Graduate Program of Urban and Regional Planning at the University of Southern California. He holds Bachelor of Arts and Master of Fine Arts degrees from Princeton University, and his Ph.D. in Regional Planning from Howard University is one of the first advanced graduate degrees awarded in the field of planning in the U.S. Dr. Branch has had an unusually varied experience in different forms and applications of planning. His activities have included being a member of the Los Angeles Planning Commission for nine years, a planning consultant and staff member for various private corporations, and a teacher (at U.C.L.A. and the University of Chicago). Dr. Branch is the author of numerous professional papers and books on various aspects of planning, his latest being *City Planning and Aerial Information* (1971), from which the paper included in this volume was taken.

GERHARD COLM, prior to his death several years ago, was Chief Economist for the National Planning Association in Washington, D.C. Prior to coming to NPA, Dr. Colm served as an economist for the President's Council of Economic Advisers; he has also taught at the New School for Social Research, the George Washington University, and at several universities in Germany, where he was born. Dr. Colm has written extensively in the fields of public finance, fiscal policy, and national planning.

JOHN FRIEDMANN is Professor and Head of the Urban Planning Program in the School of Architecture and Urban Planning at the University of California (Los Angeles). Dr. Friedmann has been a member of the Division of Regional Studies of the Tennessee Valley Authority, an adviser on regional planning in Brazil, Chief of the Development Branch for the U.S. Aid Program in Korea, a consultant to the Guayana Program in Venezuela, and Director of the Ford Foundation Program in Urban and Regional Development in Chile. Dr. Friedmann previously was on the faculty at MIT and obtained his Ph.D. in planning from the University of Chicago. He has written extensively on the problems of regional planning and the theory of planning.

JOHN K. FRIEND joined the British Institute for Operational Research (which functions as an independent research unit within the wider framework of the Tavistock Institute of Human Relations located in London, England) a few months after its founding in 1963. He was resident in the City of Coventry on a full-time basis throughout the duration of the research, which formed the basis for the book he and W. N. Jessop co-authored, *Local Government and Strategic Choice.* His previous experience included eight years in the application of operational research to management problems in British Overseas Airways Corporation and in the plastics industry where he was responsible for initiating a new OR activity for a group of associated companies. Friend is currently Chairman of the Institute's local government program and is involved in continuing work in the field of public planning, with particular reference to regional development and to decision processes where several different organizations are involved.

WILLIAM L. GRECCO is Associate Professor of Civil Engineering at Purdue University. He received his B.S. from the University of Pittsburgh, M.S. and Ph.D. (in Transportation) from Michigan State University. Dr. Grecco served on the Information System Storage and Retrieval Committee of the Highway Research Board, is a member of the American Society of Civil Engineers, the American Society for Engineering Education and the Institute of Traffic Engineers, and is the former Editor of the Journal of Urban Planning and Development Division of ASCB. His current research interests include urban traffic forecasting by systems engineering, recreational travel, and synthetic travel patterns.

SHIV K. GUPTA is Professor of Statistics and Operations Research and a senior staff member of the Management and Behavioral Science Center at the Wharton School of Finance and Commerce, University of Pennsylvania. He received his B.A. and M.A. in Mathematics from Delhi University in India, and Ph.D. in Operations Research from Case Institute of Technology. Dr. Gupta has had extensive consulting experience on industrial and government research projects in the United States and was in charge of a number of industrial and government research projects in India. His current research interests include long-range planning, production and inventory control, replacement and maintenance logistics, and operations research in education.

BRITTON HARRIS is Professor of City and Regional Planning and newly-appointed Chairman of the Department of City and Regional Planning at the University of Pennsylvania. He is also a member of the staff of that university's Institute for Environmental Studies. He previously worked for the Penn-Jersey Transportation Study and the Chicago Housing Authority. Mr. Harris also has served as a planning consultant to the Economic Development Administration of the Government of Puerto Rico; the Ford Foundation Team for the Metropolitan Plan for Delhi, India; the Philadelphia City Planning Commission; the Pittsburgh, New York, and San Francisco CRP Studies; the California State Office of Planning; the United Nations Planning Program of the Government of Singapore; and many others. He has done extensive research and writing on the mathematical simulation of urban phenomena. He obtained his B.A. (in Mathematics) from Wesleyan University and an M.A. (in Planning) from the University of Chicago.

HARRY P. HATRY was formerly Deputy Director of the State-Local Finances Project at George Washington University during which time he prepared several studies on various aspects of PPBS, from one of which the paper included in this volume was taken. Mr. Hatry is currently with The Urban Institute in Washington, D.C., where he is Director of the State-Local Government Research Program. This program is working with state and local governments to develop and test new techniques to strengthen the ability of states and local governments to more effectively use their scarce resources.

MORRIS HILL is Chairman of the Graduate Committee on Urban and Regional Studies in the Faculty of Architecture and Town Planning at the Technion University, Haifa, Israel; he is also Senior Lecturer at the Hebrew University in Jerusalem. He has served as Visiting Associate Professor in the Department of City and Regional Planning, University of North Carolina. His paper included in this volume is based on his doctoral dissertation, "A Method for Evaluating Alternative Plans: The Goals-Achievement Matrix Applied to Transportation Plans," University of Pennsylvania, 1966, in which a fuller discussion of some of the concepts explored in this paper may be found.

W. NEIL JESSOP, who died in 1969, was a prime mover in the foundation of the Institute for Operational Research and was subsequently appointed as its first Director. He personally initiated and directed the research in the City of Coventry of which his (and Dr. Friend's) book is the outcome. Prior to joining the Institute, Mr. Jessop served for sixteen years as an operational research worker and Manager in the steel and textile industries, and also played an active role on the councils of the Operational Research Society and the Royal Statistical Society.

ERICH JANTSCH is currently Visiting Lecturer in the Department of City and Regional Planning and Research Planner in the Institute of International Studies, University of California (Berkeley). Previously he was Richard Merton Professor at the Technical University, Hanover (Federal Republic of Germany) and Research Associate at the Alfred P. Sloan School of Management at the Massachusetts Institute of Technology. Dr. Jantsch is presently co-editor of the new international journal, *Technological Forecasting.* He is the author of several papers and books concerned with forecasting and its relationship to planning and the policy sciences, including the study he undertook for the Organization for Economic Co-Operation and Development, *Technological Forecasting in Perspective,* from which the paper included in this volume was taken.

J. BRIAN McLOUGHLIN is on the faculty of the Department of Town and Country Planning at the University of Manchester. He received a degree in Planning from the University of Durham. He has worked in local planning offices in Tyneside, Caernarvonshine (Wales) and Leicestershire, where he was director of the Leicester and Leicestershire Sub-Regional Planning Study. His current research focuses on urban and regional systems.

IRA M. ROBINSON is Professor of City and Regional Planning in the Graduate Program of Urban and Regional Planning at the University of Southern California in Los Angeles. He was formerly Chairman and Director of that Program. He received his Bachelor's degree from Wesleyan University and his M.A. and Ph.D. in Planning from the University of Chicago. He is a member of various professional organizations and advisory committees, including the American Institute of Planners, the Regional Science Association, and the National Advisory Committee on American-Yugoslav Studies in Urban and Regional Planning; he is also a Fellow of the Royal Society of Health. Currently, he is Principal Investigator for a major research project, sponsored by the U.S. Public Health Service, concerned with the identification of environmental preferences of selected groups of residents as a basis for developing performance criteria to be used in planning the residential environment. Dr. Robinson was previously a senior staff member with the firm of Arthur D. Little, Inc., during which time he was in charge of the study which led to the development of the San Francisco Community Renewal Program. He has taught at the University of British Columbia and the University of California (Berkeley and Davis campuses). He has had practical planning experience in Chicago, San Francisco, and Vancouver (Canada); served as a consultant to local, regional and national bodies in the U.S., Canada, and Europe; and has assisted in training planners in Yugoslavia. During 1971-1972, while on sabbatical leave, Dr. Robinson was Visiting Professor of Town Planning at The Technion, the Hebrew University, and the University of Haifa–in Israel; Visiting Senior Scientist with the Norwegian Institute of Urban and Regional Research in Oslo, Norway; consultant to the Institute of Social Studies in The Hague; and participated in a Summer Workshop in Advanced Urban and Regional Planning in Ljubljana, Yugoslavia. Dr. Robinson is the author of numerous articles and reports on planning and programming methods, housing and urban renewal, regional planning and development, urban amenities, and new towns.

JONATHAN V. ROSENHEAD is Lecturer in Operational Research at the London School of Economics and Political Science. He received a B.A. and M.A. from Cambridge University and an M.Sc. in Statistics from University College, London. After five years working in industry, he spent a year at the Management Science Center, University of Pennsylvania, during which period the work reported in this volume was carried out with Dr. Gupta. His current major research areas deal with the simulation of a market and decision criteria model for long-range planning and with the development of methods for handling uncertainty in urban and other planning situations.

CHARLES C. SCHIMPELER is a co-partner in the firm of Schimpeler-Schuette Associates, Engineering and Urban Planning Consultants, based in Louisville, Kentucky. The paper Dr. Schimpeler co-authored with Dr. Grecco (included in this volume) is based on his experience as Director of the Louisville Metropolitan Comprehensive Transportation Development Program. He obtained a B.S. and M.S. in civil engineering from the University of Kentucky, and a Ph.D. in urban planning and engineering from Purdue University. He currently serves as Adjunct Associate Professor in the Urban Studies Center at the University of Kentucky, and previously taught at Bellarmine College in Louisville. Dr. Schimpeler holds membership in various professional societies, including the American Society of Civil Engineers, the Operations Research Society of America, and the American Institute of Planners; and is the author of many papers, reports, and articles concerned with transportation planning, land use models, plan-evaluation, and airport planning.

KENNETH J. SCHLAGER, at the time he wrote the paper included in this volume, was Chief Systems Engineer for the Southeastern Wisconsin Regional Planning Commission and a member of the faculties at Marquette University and the University of Wisconsin in management science and systems analysis. His undergraduate education was obtained at the United States Naval Academy, and he holds masters degrees from the University of Wisconsin (electrical engineering) and MIT (industrial management).

DARWIN G. STUART is a Research Associate with Barton-Aschman Associates, Chicago Planning and Engineering Consultants, and Visiting Assistant Professor of Urban Planning at the University of Illinois at Urbana-Champaign. His article is based upon research conducted for the Chicago Department of Development and Planning, and for his Ph.D. dissertation in civil engineering at Northwestern University. Dr. Stuart's research and planning interests lie in the areas of systems analysis applied to urban problems and urban transportation/land use coordination.

MARGARET FRYE WHEATON is currently a Ph.D. candidate in City and Regional Planning at the University of California (Berkeley). She served on the staffs of the National Capital Planning Commission and Alan M. Voorhees and Associates, Inc. and is currently analyzing statistical data and report systems of the California Division of Highways for the Legislative Analyst Office. Mrs. Wheaton obtained degrees in Architecture from Radcliffe College and Ecole des Beaux Arts, and a masters degree in City Planning from the University of Pennsylvania.

WILLIAM L.C. WHEATON is Dean of the College of Environmental Design and formerly Director of the Institute of Urban and Regional Development at the University of California (Berkeley). He was U.S. representative to the U.N. Committee on Housing, Building and Planning and is the current chairman of the Intergovernmental Council on Urban Growth for California. Dr. Wheaton has served as consultant to the U.S. State Department, the Department of Housing and Urban Development, the Agency for International Development, and Urban America, Inc. to the cities of Boston, Worcester, Philadelphia, and Baltimore, and to the states of New York, Massachusetts, and California. He received his B.A. from Princeton University and a Ph.D. (in Political Science) from the University of Chicago.

KURT C. SCHLICHTING

TERMINAL

Railroads, Engineering, and Architecture in New York City

THE JOHNS HOPKINS UNIVERSITY PRESS | BALTIMORE AND LONDON

This book has been brought to publication with the generous assistance of the Alfred P. Sloan Foundation.

Printed in the United States of America on acid-free paper
9 8 7 6 5 4 3 2 1

The Johns Hopkins University Press
2715 North Charles Street
Baltimore, Maryland 21218-4363
www.press.jhu.edu

Library of Congress Cataloging-in-Publication Data

Schlichting, Kurt C.
Grand central terminal : railroads, engineering, and architecture in New York City / Kurt C. Schlichting.
p. cm.
Includes bibliographical references and index.
ISBN 0-8018-6510-7 (hardcover)
1. Grand Central Terminal (New York, N.Y.)—History. 2. Railroad terminals—New York (State)—New York—History. 3. Railroad terminals—Conservation and restoration—New York (State)—New York. I. Title.
TF302.N7 S35 2001
385.3′14′097471—dc21 00-008641

A catalog record for this book is available from the British Library.

Frontispiece: Grand Central Terminal from 42nd Street.
Endpapers: Architect Whitney Warren's annotated drawing of the front facade in his design for Grand Central Terminal.

TO

George C. Schlichting
Bernice O'Connell Schlichting Dunn
William Dunn

John Q. Murphy
Kathleen Gray Murphy

Kerry Murphy Schlichting
Kara Murphy Schlichting

CONTENTS

Preface ix
Acknowledgments xi

Prologue 1

One | *The Commodore's Grand Central* 8

Two | *The Engineer's Grand Central* 55

Three | *The Architect's Grand Central* 115

Four | *New York's Grand Central* 155

Epilogue 194

Notes 223
A Note on Sources 233
Illustration Credits 235
Index 237

PREFACE

The story of my connection to Grand Central Terminal in New York begins at a very tender age, with fond memories of train trips to New York with a grandmother who worked as a clerk for the New York, New Haven, and Hartford Railroad. Naturally, the trip to New York ended majestically at Grand Central. Holding hands, we ventured across the floor of the Grand Concourse, engulfed by the hurry of New York. I clutched her hand tighter for fear of becoming parted and being carried away by the dashing crowd. When I became a little older, highlights of each summer in the mid-1950s were trips with my grandfather to Grand Central and then on to the Lexington Avenue subway to the Bronx and the Mecca for all ten-year-old boys—Yankee Stadium. My grandfather and I always stopped for lunch at Volks, a German restaurant close to Grand Central; the restaurant is long gone, a victim of the relentless development pressures in the area around 42nd Street.

For young people growing up in Fairfield County, a rite of passage became a trip alone, not with grandparents or parents but with friends, to "the city," as everyone referred to New York. Viewing ourselves as quite sophisticated, we sauntered through Grand Central and then out onto the magical streets of New York. We might venture to a museum or, as we got older, to McSorely's to test our "proof," but as the day wore on we returned to Grand Central and the embrace of our commuter train for the trip home.

My true coming-of-age occurred when I moved to New York for

graduate school at NYU. Grand Central remained the nexus for visits home or to friends who still lived in the distant suburbs. My first teaching position, at Queens College, involved the subway to Grand Central and then down to the Flushing line for the trip to Flushing in Queens and the bus to the campus.

This book began with research for a scholarly paper on social change in New York City at the turn of the century, including the construction of the "new" Grand Central Terminal, opened in 1913. A number of my sources cited the papers of William J. Wilgus in the manuscript collection of the New York Public Library. Examining the Wilgus papers, I realized what a treasure they represented. Wilgus, the chief engineer of the New York Central Railroad at the turn of the century, was a meticulous documenter. The papers recording his ideas for and work on Grand Central fill carton after carton. Here, in great detail, was the record of the creation of the magnificent terminal complex on 42nd Street. Several journal articles followed, but I also realized that the story of the construction of the Grand Central complex that we see today waited to be recounted. Wilgus's notes and private records detail the complex engineering involved and also the human drama behind the creation of one of New York's masterpieces. The Wilgus papers led me to the New York Public Library's vast collection of the records of the New York Central Railroad and its brief successor, the ill-fated Penn Central. Two other pioneering electrical engineers, Frank Sprague and Bion Arnold, also left substantial collections of materials to the library, and these resources proved invaluable as well.

The story of the creation of Grand Central brings together a number of important themes of New York's history: the forces for urban change, powerful individuals, brilliant engineers, and the dynamic influence of technology on history. Without the successful introduction of electricity to power the trains to 42nd Street, the building of the new terminal and an accompanying two-story underground train yard stretching many city blocks to the north would have been impossible. Grand Central, more than any other building complex in New York, captures the vibrant energy of the city and represents American drive and genius at its best.

ACKNOWLEDGMENTS

The effort to write this book involved the assistance of many people and institutions. Only with their help and encouragement was I able to complete the project.

The papers of William J. Wilgus, part of the manuscript collection of the New York Public Library, served as a major resource. Melanie Yules, senior archivist at the library, provided priceless support. Despite repeated requests for just one more box from the collection, she always maintained a smile, even as closing time approached. At the end of a long afternoon, as I prepared to leave the Manuscript Room, she asked in passing, "Have you looked at the 'secret file' about the Woodlawn wreck, in box 7?" This led to Wilgus's private records concerning a disastrous wreck in the Bronx which occurred just as the new electric engines entered service. Ms. Yules also assisted with the New York Central Railroad materials as well as with the Frank Sprague and Bion Arnold archives. I owe the New York Public Library gratitude for its unceasing efforts to maintain its superb resources. The recent restoration of the main reading room makes a day at the libary that much more rewarding.

The librarians and staff at the Fairfield University library also deserve my thanks. They patiently processed scores of interlibrary loan requests for journal articles from the turn of the century and before. No matter the number of requests, the staff always worked diligently to track down each journal or newspaper reference.

A number of research trips included visits to the Schenectady Museum

in Schenectady, New York, which has a valuable collection of historical materials from the General Electric Company, which played a major role in the Grand Central electrification. John Anderson's assistance made my time there productive, and he helped select photos from the museum's collection. The librarians at the Pierpont Morgan Library in New York guided me through the syndicate books of J. P. Morgan and Company, who financed construction of the terminal.

The curators in the Library of Congress Prints and Photographs Division facilitated my locating photographs from the library's extensive collection recording the passage of American history. Mary Ison responded patiently to questions regarding permission to publish from the library's collection, and Kathryn Engstrom of the Geography and Map Division assisted in selecting the historic Sanborn insurance maps of the Grand Central area. Holly Hinmus at the New-York Historical Society served as a key resource in obtaining copies of the society's recently acquired photos of Grand Central's construction.

George Walker, superintendent of the Metro-North Commuter Railroad, and Dave Treasure graciously conducted a tour of the underground train yard, including a descent into the labyrinth of tunnels under the terminal. Mr. Walker's insights into the challenges Metro-North faced with the Grand Central renovations were valuable in filling out the story of the terminal's rebirth. Frank English, Metro-North's talented photographer, helped select the photos from the railroad's collection which grace the text. Mr. English took most of those photographs.

The Alfred P. Sloan Foundation of New York provided financial support for completion of the book. Doron Weber, senior officer, maintained a steadfast belief in the project. A grant from the Sloan Foundation allowed me to take a sabbatical leave to complete the manuscript. The grant also paid for reproduction of the photographs in the book, which come from the collections of the Avery Architectural Library, Columbia University, the New-York Historical Society, the Library of Congress, the New York Public Library, the Museum of the City of New York, and the Schenectady Museum. Many of the photographs have never been published before.

Bob Brugger, my editor at the Johns Hopkins University Press, worked with me from my initial contact through to the completion of the book.

His patience and strong sense of the shape of the story proved invaluable. Anne Whitmore's conscientious manuscript editing contributed enormously. Melody Herr and Martha Farlow, the art director at the press, kept track of hundreds of details. Any errors or omissions in this book are solely mine.

On a personal level, I have many others to thank. During my education I encountered a number of wonderful teachers. In particular, Arthur Anderson and Leo Fay from my undergraduate days at Fairfield University and Richard Maisel at New York Universty made indelible impressions on me. It is difficult to find the proper words to thank my most loyal supporter and most insightful critic, my wife, Mary. She read every word of every version of the manuscript and her counsel proved always to be wise. I know at many stages I tried her patience. Mary's most difficult task was to occupy our daughters, Kerry and Kara, who never could understand why I had to spend so much time at the computer or days at the library in New York. Mary's own experience served her well. Completing her Ph.D. in English at New York University, she wrote her dissertation after the birth of our daughters and earned a special distinction—Ph.D. with twins. Finally, I owe a debt of immense gratitude to my wife's parents and especially to my parents, who conveyed to me the gift of imagination. I hope that this book reflects that imagination.

GRAND CENTRAL TERMINAL

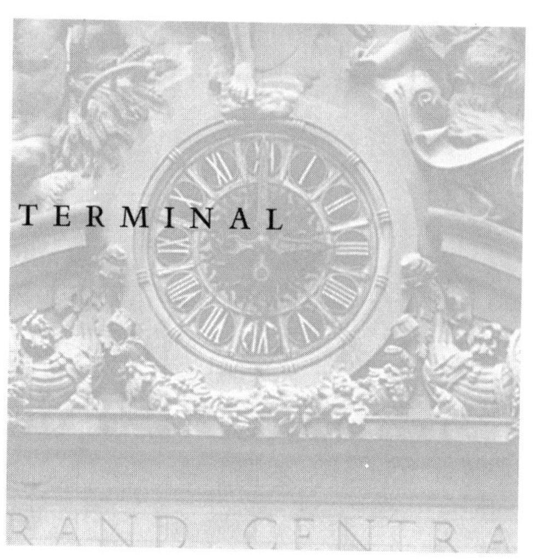

Prologue

Few buildings capture the public imagination as does Grand Central Terminal, the very mention of whose name brings to mind Beaux-Arts magnificence on 42nd Street in New York City. Standing in the heart of midtown Manhattan, the terminal serves as an urban crossroads. Thousands pass through the Grand Concourse every day. Commuters hurry by. Visitors pause in the city's great public square. For millions, even for those who have never visited the terminal, Grand Central remains a symbol of New York and its power, instantly recognizable for what it is and nearly as familiar as the soaring skyline of Manhattan Island.

Not surprisingly, a great many New Yorkers gathered on October 1, 1998, to celebrate and rededicate the newly refurbished Grand Central. "Once threatened with demolition, gnawed by decades of urban grime, obscured by ungainly advertising, corroded by roof leaks and just plain unloved by the 500,000 people who sprint through its cavernous halls each day on the way to somewhere else," observed the *New York Times,* Grand Central reopened as an illustrious place—"a destination in its own right." With sunlight piercing its windows and skylights and matching marble staircases gracefully drawing attention to a platform of notables on the east side of the main concourse, the eighty-five-year-old structure was "once again so imposing that it dwarfed those who came to praise it during the spirited rededication ceremony."[1] Cynical New Yorkers

A statue of Mercury tops the 42nd Street facade of Grand Central Terminal, the gateway to the greatest city in the world

remarked that the Metropolitan Transportation Authority (M.T.A.), the public agency responsible for Grand Central's rebirth, might have saved the money it spent that day on a laser light show and the Big Apple Circus; at one point a trapeze artist dangled from the ceiling of the concourse, more than one hundred feet above the floor, as the sounds of Gershwin's *Rhapsody in Blue* echoed through the building.

Yet voices of approval reigned. One speaker on the platform, Virgil Conway, chairman of the M.T.A., declared, "We put the *grand* back into Grand Central," and no one disputed him. "We have not just brought back the historic grandeur," added the governor of New York, George Pataki; "We have prepared it for the twenty-first century."[2] John F. Kennedy Jr. accepted a plaque honoring the role his mother, Jacqueline Kennedy Onassis, had played in saving Grand Central from destruction. "If the city could be characterized by one building, it would be Grand Central," reflected a leading paper in nearby Connecticut. "Gleam on, Grand Central. You look like the grand dame of American landmarks."[3] The architecture firm of Beyer Blinder Belle was responsible for the overall restoration, earning the role based on its success with earlier his-

The Grand Concourse, New York's civic cathedral, ca. 1925

One of the constellations in the restored ceiling of the Grand Concourse

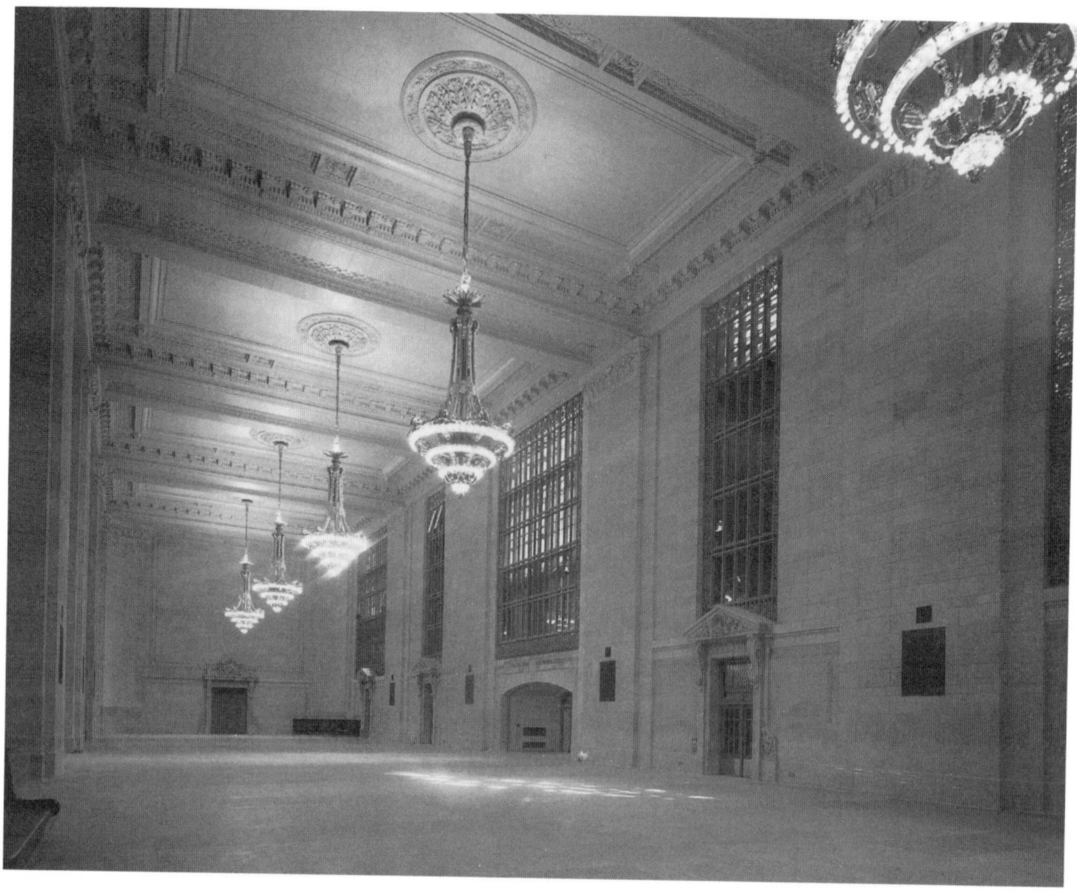

The waiting room, Vanderbilt Hall, restored

toric preservation projects that included the renovation of Ellis Island and the South Street Seaport Museum in New York. Speaking for the firm, John Belle summed up the reaction of many visitors: "I can't tell you what it does to an old architect's heart to stand in the main concourse and see how much people are enjoying that space and responding to it. This classic building is New York for New Yorkers." He judged Grand Central among the greatest buildings in the United States.[4]

No praise seemed adequate to capture Grand Central's rebirth. Perhaps the exuberance stemmed from the realization that, except for a fortuitous chain of events in the late 1960s and early 1970s, the terminal's glory could have vanished. Just a little south and west, on 34th Street, Madison Square Garden stands where once one could find New York's other monument to rail travel, Pennsylvania Station. Penn Station's destruction in 1965 registered a singular failure of public imagination, the weakness of

public support for the cause of preserving New York's architectural heritage. "Now," commented Fred Koetter, former dean of the Yale School of Architecture, "they are recognizing the value of a place like Grand Central. This means that public consciousness of the city has come a long way."[5]

Always more than a mere railroad terminal, Grand Central represents a triumph of imagination and daring. In 1903, when construction began, only thirty-eight years had passed since the end of the Civil War, and yet the country had experienced vast changes. Technology had transformed daily life for many Americans, who had witnessed extraordinary demographic change, as well. In 1890 the Census Bureau reported the closing of the American frontier; ten years later, almost as many Americans lived in cities as on farms. Supplying a good example of urban American confidence and exuberance, Grand Central marked the emergence in America of a distinctive building art—a combination of imaginative architectural design and innovative engineering. To some of the people living through these changes, their impact seemed ominous. Henry Adams, a Harvard professor and the grandson and great-grandson of presidents,

Eagles from the 1898 Grand Central being moved to the new Lexington Avenue entrance

had traveled to Chicago in 1893 to visit the Columbian Exposition, where no one could doubt America's coming-of-age. "One lingered among the dynamos," Adams later wrote, "for they were new, and they gave history a new phase." It was being declared that this new age required new men, and to Adams no one better exemplified these "new men" than the professional engineers and managers who had built and were building the country's far-flung railroads, and no place better demonstrated the physical effects of such change than New York. Returning in 1905 after a long absence, he compared the city with the New York he remembered from 1868: "The outline of the city became frantic in its efforts to explain something that defied meaning. Power seemed to have outgrown its servitude and to have asserted its freedom. The cylinder had exploded, and thrown great masses of stone and steam against the sky."[6]

Along with Edison's practical electricity, Bell's telephone, the first skyscrapers, the city subway system, and the Brooklyn Bridge, Grand Central symbolized the era that historian and critic Howard Mumford Jones called simply the "Age of Energy."

CHAPTER ONE

The Commodore's Grand Central

During the first half of the nineteenth century, New York grew at a frenzied pace, with residential and commercial development continuing a relentless march up the island of Manhattan. New Yorkers once considered Canal Street the city's northern border; later Houston Street and then 14th Street came to be regarded as the northern limit. A new form of transportation appeared in the teeming city when, on November 26, 1832, the Harlem River Railroad began rail service in lower Manhattan. It ran at grade level in the middle of the street. First horse-drawn cars and later steam-powered trains thundered up and down Fourth Avenue, and as New York grew at a breakneck pace, the public increasingly objected to the disruption caused by the Harlem's trains traveling on city streets. Once the railroad switched to steam power, public criticism only magnified. While steam engines seem now to evoke a sense of romance and nostalgia, in reality they generated clouds of steam, soot, and gases, which the public, in a crowded city like New York, objected to in the strongest terms.

The Harlem's original charter prohibited the railroad from operating steam locomotives south of 14th Street. As the Harlem's traffic grew, the company needed an additional station, so, working within the limitation placed upon it, in 1845 the railroad built a station at 26th Street on Fourth (now Park) Avenue (later the site of the first Madison Square Garden).

The station consisted of two parallel wings separated by a covered platform area. Because the steam trains could not proceed below 14th Street, they waited at 26th Street for the horse-drawn cars coming up Fourth Avenue from the south. Passengers then transferred to the steam-powered train for the rest of the run northward to Harlem, the Bronx, or eventually into Westchester County.

As the city grew northward, the area around the Harlem's 26th Street station developed. As more people and businesses moved to the immediate area, public objections to steam operations at 26th Street followed. In 1859, the City of New York placed further limits on the Harlem and required the railroad to move its steam operations farther north. This time the city prohibited the operation of steam trains on the city's streets below 42nd Street. Bowing to public pressure, the Harlem relocated its rail facilities to property it owned on 42nd Street. Soon, a domineering figure entered the affairs of the Harlem River Railroad; as Cornelius Vanderbilt assembled his railroad empire, he set in motion the forces that led to the building of Grand Central Terminal on the Harlem's property at 42nd Street.

Cornelius Vanderbilt, "The Commodore"

Cornelius Vanderbilt's life began inauspiciously. Born to Jacob and Phoebe Van der Bilt, as the family then spelled their name, in May of 1794, Cornelius spent his childhood on the family farm on Staten Island. Apparently he finished an indifferent schooling at the age of eleven; for the rest of his life he remained an atrocious speller and read little but the daily newspapers. Vanderbilt began his working career operating a sail-driven ferry between Staten Island and Manhattan. Ever ambitious, he acquired larger and larger boats and eventually expanded to carrying freight along the Atlantic Coast and Long Island Sound.

Vanderbilt's fortunes grew dramatically during the gold rush to California in 1849, when he successfully organized a combined sea and land route from New York down to Central America, across Nicaragua, and then up the California coast to San Francisco and the gold fields beyond. Early in 1853, Vanderbilt boasted to a friend that his fortune exceeded $11,000,000. Even greater triumphs followed during the Civil War, when

Cornelius Vanderbilt, "The Commodore"

the Union navy contracted to lease Vanderbilt's growing fleet of ships to supply Union forces blockading the South. Vanderbilt earned handsome fees for leasing his ships to the Northern cause, and after the war President Grant awarded him a medal for his contributions to the Union victory. Vanderbilt also enjoyed great success with his Hudson River steamboats, which operated between New York and Albany carrying the lucrative passenger and freight trade moving over the Erie Canal to the Midwest.

Vanderbilt's fortune placed him among the wealthiest individuals in the country by the time he reached his late sixties. At an age when many would have considered a leisurely retirement, he began a new career—railroading. With his characteristic drive and ruthlessness, in a stunningly brief period of time, Vanderbilt assembled an extensive railroad empire and in the process became the wealthiest man in the United States—some

claimed the wealthiest in the world. Vanderbilt's railroad empire started modestly when he began to increase his holdings in the Harlem Railroad in 1862.

The New York and Harlem Railroad

Although the New York and Harlem Railroad's main line tracks never extended more than 132 miles from New York City, the Harlem possessed one asset of immense value: the right of direct rail access to the east side of Manhattan Island. In 1831, the company received a franchise to build a railroad from lower Manhattan to the village of Harlem on the northern tip of the island. Legislation passed by New York State on April 25, 1831, gave the Harlem broad discretion as to the location of the rail line, giving it "power to construct a single or double railroad or way from any point on the north bounds of Twenty-third Street to any point on the Harlem River between the east bounds of Third Avenue and the west bounds of the Eighth Avenue with a branch to the Hudson River between One Hundred and Twenty-fourth Street and the north bounds of One Hundred and Twenty-ninth Street, to transport, take and carry property and persons upon the same by the power and force of steam, or animals or any other mechanical or other power, or any combination of them which the said company may choose to employ."[1]

The Harlem chose to construct its rail line, linking Harlem to lower Manhattan, down Fourth Avenue, later to become the world-famous Park Avenue. At first the tracks consisted of strips of wood with iron strapping nailed on top; passengers rode in open carriages pulled by teams of horses. With less than a mile of track, the first section of the Harlem, from Prince Street on the Lower East Side to Union Square at 14th Street, opened on November 26, 1832, with a one-way fare of one cent. It took an additional two years for the Harlem to reach Yorkville, the neighborhood at 86th Street, four and a half miles north of Prince Street. Finally, in October of 1837, the Harlem Railroad's track arrived at the village of Harlem, long delayed by the hard rock of Observation Hill, near 96th Street, which required the blasting of a tunnel at great expense. Harlem, a farming community first settled by the Dutch, served as a location for the estates of prosperous New Yorkers who retreated there

during the sweltering summer months. Before the arrival of the railroad, a stagecoach line on Third Avenue and a ferry from 125th Street provided transportation to and from the city.

After successfully petitioning the state legislature to extend its rails north into the Bronx and Westchester County, the Harlem opened service to White Plains on June 1, 1844, and further north to Dover Plains in December of 1848. Tracks finally reached Chatham, in Columbia County, in January of 1852. At Chatham, 132 miles from Manhattan, the Harlem Railroad connected with the Boston and Albany Railroad. Now a traveler could leave lower Manhattan, ride the Harlem to Chatham, switch trains, and continue on to Albany or Boston.

By the 1850s the Harlem operated three types of service: intracity travel for passengers traveling from lower Manhattan to Yorkville or Harlem, suburban commuter service to White Plains and the eastern portion of Westchester County, and through service to Chatham with connections to Albany and Boston. In addition, the Harlem signed an agreement with the New York and New Haven Railroad in 1848 allowing the New Haven joint use of its tracks and terminal facilities from Woodlawn in the Bronx to lower Manhattan. Since the agreement with the New Haven extended for four hundred years, this second railroad played a role in Grand Central's history.

The Harlem deliberately chose an inland route from the Hudson River, so as not to antagonize the powerful Hudson River steamboat companies. Before the Civil War, steamboat lines, including Commodore Vanderbilt's, dominated travel between New York and Albany, providing fast, efficient, and inexpensive service. The Harlem Railroad wisely chose not to compete with the Hudson River steamboats and built its line to serve the inland portion of Westchester, Putnam, Dutchess, and Columbia counties, which were rural and agricultural. Little industry ever developed there, and to this day the area remains pastoral, populated by wealthy suburbanites and a few dairy and apple farms. Even as late as the 1890s, the Harlem ran only three passenger trains and one freight train each day between New York and Chatham. Service to rural Pawling, Millerton, or Boston Corners hardly made for a great railroad empire.

When the Harlem introduced steam locomotives to New York in 1837, it had required a facility in Manhattan to service the steam engines.

The company chose 42nd Street as the location for a maintenance barn and fuel lot. The earliest accounts of the Harlem Railroad record a number of property transactions, totaling $56,262, for the land between 42nd and 43rd streets on the west side of Fourth Avenue. As the Harlem's steam operations in New York expanded, the railroad acquired additional land around its original 42nd Street property, purchased during the 1830s and 1840s. In 1859, it bought the land between 42nd and 43rd streets east of Park where Grand Central Terminal now stands. In May of 1860, the Harlem paid $5,957 for an "engine house, filling up lots, laying tracks etc." on the site. Later expenses involved construction of a new facility to service wood-burning steam locomotives and cars as they replaced horse-drawn rail cars. The Harlem's books showed the value of the real estate where Grand Central now stands as $2,379,414.95. Ultimately the railroad bought eleven parcels of land in the area from 42nd to 48th streets between Lexington and Madison avenues. This land comprised the Harlem's second precious asset: property in midtown Manhattan that eventually became among the most valuable real estate in the world.[2]

The Harlem Railroad's rapid expansion up Manhattan Island into the Bronx and beyond to Westchester County and north Chatham required significant expenditure and the company's debts mounted. While passenger traffic in Manhattan grew substantially, the railroad's freight business north of the city languished; the Hudson River steamboats continued to transport the bulk of the freight traffic between New York and Albany. In 1863, the Harlem could not afford to pay any dividends and its stock declined to a low of $9 a share before recovering somewhat as summer approached. Quietly, Vanderbilt began to purchase more Harlem stock, acquiring 55,000 shares in 1862, and he hatched a complicated plan to improve the fortunes of the railroad and make himself a substantial gain. With Vanderbilt's guidance, the Harlem petitioned the Common Council of the City of New York for a franchise for a streetcar line up Broadway. With the franchise in hand, the company's money problems would disappear, he thought.

Vanderbilt did not account for the deviousness of the members of the Common Council and his numerous enemies, who included Daniel Drew. An illiterate former cattleman, Drew had held a deep-seated animosity toward Vanderbilt from the time he started his own Hudson River

steamboat line in 1834 in direct competition to Vanderbilt's steamboats. Their relationship worsened after Drew became a director of the Erie Railroad in 1857. As the vote of the Common Council on the Harlem's street franchise neared, in the hot summer of 1863, Drew and his allies planned to sell their Harlem stock short as the stock rose in anticipation of the new franchise. With the Common Council suitably bribed, Drew eagerly awaited a sharp drop in Harlem stock once the council voted to deny the railroad its franchise for a street railway on Broadway.

Just as Drew planned, on June 25, the Common Council denied the Harlem Railroad the new franchise and its stock dropped from $110 to $72. However, Drew and the corrupt politicians on the council underestimated Vanderbilt. The Commodore, along with family, friends, and stockbrokers, continued to buy Harlem stock and, as Drew and the astounded councilmen looked on, Harlem stock leveled off and then began, slowly, to rise. Vanderbilt committed a major part of his fortune to the Harlem, and soon the price moved past par and quickly spurted to $125 and then $150, to the dismay of the short sellers who had guaranteed to deliver—at $110. Vanderbilt held the stock in his safe and demanded a king's ransom—$180 per share. Drew and his greedy friends on the council lost $70 on each share they sold short. Vanderbilt made yet another fortune from the "Harlem corner," and he gained control of his first railroad. As the Commodore's first biographer, William Croffut, observed in 1886, this was the venture that would lead him to the greatest fortune in the world.[3]

The Hudson River Railroad

The Hudson River Railroad formed the second piece of Vanderbilt's rail empire. As with many railroads, the Hudson began with the dreams of a group of local businessmen and boosters in a small city, Poughkeepsie, New York, located on the east bank of the Hudson River fifty miles north of New York City. The Hudson River steamboat lines made stops at Poughkeepsie but provided limited service, preferring to concentrate their energies on the much more lucrative traffic between New York City and the state capital, Albany; and during the winter months the steamboats suspended service, virtually cutting off the city. Poughkeep-

sie's leaders reasoned that if a rail line linked Poughkeepsie to New York their city would prosper.

In 1846, the New York State legislature passed a law incorporating the Hudson River Railroad and granting it a franchise to construct a rail line along the east bank of the Hudson River, entering Manhattan at Spuyten Duyvil, at the northern tip of the island, and then running along the west side to lower Manhattan. Offering direct rail access into Manhattan, the Hudson River Railroad's franchise represented as valuable an asset as the Harlem's. However, the Hudson's franchise restricted it to the west side of Manhattan, while the city's residential growth remained concentrated on the east side. As New York's population expanded up the island, fashionable residential development characterized the east side while the west side evolved as more industrial, especially with the shipping businesses along the piers lining the Hudson River. The Hudson Railroad's freight business proved to be very lucrative; a major share of the country's international trade crossed the piers lining the Hudson River, served by the tracks of the railroad.

The original backers of the Hudson River Railroad encountered much higher construction costs than they anticipated when building the line from Poughkeepsie to New York City, and the tracks did not reach Canal Street, in lower Manhattan, until 1847. Despite the fact that traffic remained below projections, the Hudson River Railroad kept extending its line, north of Poughkeepsie, until in 1851 it reached East Albany, directly across the Hudson River from Albany. With the expansion to the Albany area, the railroad ran for 155 miles along the east side of the Hudson River, from Chambers Street in lower Manhattan to East Albany. By that time, construction costs had consumed all of the original capital and the railroad slid into debt. Despite the income from its freight business, during the 1850s the company fell into poor financial condition, ripe for a takeover.

At the same time that Vanderbilt gained control of the Harlem Railroad, he turned his eyes on the Hudson and quietly began to acquire its stock as well. He used profits made from leasing his steamships to the Union navy during the Civil War to buy additional shares of the Hudson; by the winter of 1863 he controlled the railroad. The Commodore stood poised to dominate rail service to New York; his Harlem road held the

exclusive right to the east side of the city and the Hudson to the west side. Competing railroads, the Pennsylvania and the Erie among them, operated at a severe disadvantage. Their tracks approached New York City but reached only as far as the New Jersey side of the Hudson River; they lacked the all-important direct rail access to Manhattan. Passengers and freight arriving in Jersey City or Hoboken had to be loaded onto ferries for the remaining part of the journey to New York. Vanderbilt, although approaching his seventieth birthday, had shrewdly pulled off a great triumph: he alone controlled direct rail service to the preeminent city in the land.

To increase efficiency, Vanderbilt planned to merge the Hudson with the Harlem. For this he needed enabling legislation from New York State, and the Commodore again found himself enmeshed in politics and embattled with Daniel Drew. Vanderbilt traveled to Albany in 1864, with plenty of money to secure the necessary votes from the politicians in the legislature. Drew, seeking revenge for the "Harlem corner," decided to bribe the politicians himself, prevent the merger bill from passing, and sell Harlem stock short for a second time.

Once again Vanderbilt faced ruin at the hands of Drew and a group of corrupt politicians. Persuaded by Drew's money, the legislators, sure that Vanderbilt was in no position to fight back, sold Harlem stock short, risking as much as each dared. Then they voted down the consolidation bill. The price of Harlem stock had risen to $150 in anticipation that the merger would lead to increased earnings. After the legislative defeat, it dropped to $90.

Just as in the Harlem corner, the Commodore fought back tenaciously, eventually acquiring every share of Harlem stock available on Wall Street. Left with no stock of their own, the short-sellers came to Vanderbilt and asked what price he wanted for his shares. Without hesitation, he demanded $1,000 per share, sending a shudder through Wall Street; many speculators faced utter ruin. In the end, Vanderbilt agreed to sell Harlem shares for $285, saving a number of Wall Street brokerage houses. But many corrupt legislators in Albany who, along with Daniel Drew, had sold Harlem short, suffered heavy losses. Vanderbilt's profit totaled $25,000,000.

Although the Commodore won the second Harlem corner, he failed

to obtain the necessary legislation to merge his two railroads. Unfazed, he decided to operate them as if they constituted a single line, and he set out to improve both railroads. At this time, William Henry Vanderbilt, the Commodore's oldest son, entered the management of the expanding railroad empire, becoming president of the Hudson River Railroad.

Fresh from his two victories over Daniel Drew and the politicians in New York City and Albany, Vanderbilt sought to expand his railroad holdings further. He turned his attention to the New York Central Railroad in upstate New York. If he gained control of the Central, his railroad empire would extend from New York City to Buffalo. From there he could look westward to the great city rising on Lake Michigan—Chicago—the goal for all major eastern railroads.

The New York Central

The mighty New York Central Railroad started life quite modestly, in the middle of the nineteenth century, as a series of small railroads in upstate New York linking Albany and Buffalo. These small railroads, their names long forgotten by most people, followed the route of the famous Erie Canal, built by the State of New York and completed in 1825.

Between Albany on the Hudson River and Buffalo on Lake Erie lies a geographical feature significant to the entire North American continent. From Alabama north to Newfoundland stretch the Appalachian Mountains, separating the East Coast from the rest of the country. Only one location offers a wide, water-level gap in the Appalachian Mountain chain—upstate New York.[4] The passageway follows the Hudson River north from New York City to Albany, then west up the Mohawk River Valley to Syracuse, and finally over gently rolling countryside to Rochester and Buffalo. Providing the easiest route between the middle and northern Atlantic states and the Midwest, this gap, known as the "water level" route, played a prominent role in the early settlement of the territory beyond the original colonies, in Ohio, and beyond to Chicago and St. Louis.

After the United States completed the Louisiana Purchase in 1803, debate ensued over the question of "internal improvements" to provide communication between the thirteen original states and the vast new

territory beyond the Appalachian Mountains added by the Purchase. At the beginning of the nineteenth century, "internal improvements" meant roads and canals. In 1808, Albert Gallatin, Thomas Jefferson's secretary of the treasury, published "Report on Roads and Canals," in which he urged the federal government to take the lead in financing national roads and canals to link the East with the new territory. A fierce debate ensued over whether the federal government had the power to finance these internal improvements or whether they must be left to private enterprise or the individual states. No clear consensus emerged on the national level regarding federal financing of roads and canals, so private enterprise and the states seized the initiative and created the much-needed communication links with the far-flung regions of the country.

New York, under the farsighted leadership of Governor DeWitt Clinton, undertook the greatest internal improvement of the age, a canal from Albany to Buffalo using the water level route along the Mohawk River Valley west to Lake Erie. In the spring of 1817, the State of New York appropriated the first funds and, after a prodigious effort, the canal opened in 1825. At the time the longest canal in the world, stretching for more than 363 miles, it proved an immediate success. Transportation costs from the Midwest to New York City declined dramatically, and the volume of goods shipped over the canal exceeded all expectations. Once the canal opened, the cost of shipping a barrel of flour from Ohio to New York declined from $12 to $1. By 1840, New York handled more of the nation's grain than did New Orleans, at the mouth of the Mississippi River. Making superb use of the Appalachian Mountain gap, the Erie Canal ensured the emergence of New York City as the greatest port in the country. In the space of a few years, the Erie Canal succeeded beyond the dreams of even its most ardent backers and solidified New York state and city's leading role in the economic life of the country.

Despite its success, the Erie Canal suffered from a number of limitations. In the first place a canal could not operate year-round. In the winter months, all transportation on the canal ceased. Although the canal was never intended to be primarily a means of transporting people, the passengers it did carry found the trip slow and uncomfortable. Erie Canal barges became notorious for their filth and the slovenliness of their bargemen.

Almost as soon as the Erie Canal opened, the development of the first

practical steam locomotives inspired businessmen in upstate New York, led by George Featherstonhaugh from Duanesburg, New York, near Albany, to dream of a railroad paralleling the route of the canal. A railroad would provide year-round service and promise passengers a quicker and more comfortable form of transportation. Featherstonhaugh, aware of the rapid progress of steam railroads in England, secured the backing of Stephen Van Rensselaer, a powerful figure in New York State politics; and together they planned to build a railroad between Albany and Schenectady, a distance of only sixteen miles. The mighty New York Central, eventually the cornerstone of the Vanderbilt railroad empire, began with Featherstonhaugh and Van Rensselaer's modest rail line, the first in the series of railroads along the water level route from Albany to Buffalo.

On December 19, 1825, Featherstonhaugh and Rensselaer petitioned the state legislature for a charter to incorporate the Mohawk and Hudson Rail Company to construct a rail link between Albany and Schenectady. Five years later, the first passenger trip drawn by a steam locomotive in New York State, appropriately named the "DeWitt Clinton," took place, on August 9, 1831. By 1834 the Mohawk and Hudson advertised five departures daily from Albany, at 9:00 and 11:00 A.M., and 3:00, 5:00, and 9:00 P.M.; with three return departures from Schenectady, at 12:00, 3:00, and 8:30 P.M. Passengers paid a one-way fare of fifty cents.

The next link in the chain to Buffalo covered a substantially longer distance than the Mohawk and Hudson's sixteen miles. On August 29, 1833, the Utica and Schenectady Railroad secured a charter to provide passenger service between those two cities, a distance of seventy-eight miles. However, the power of the Erie Canal interests remained vigilant, and the state legislature prohibited the new railroads from carrying "property of any description except the ordinary baggage of passengers."[5] Not until 1844 did the railroads finally obtain permission to carry freight, and then only when the canal closed down for the winter.

The Utica and Schenectady carried its first passengers on August 1, 1836. A line between Syracuse and Utica opened in 1839, as did the Auburn and Syracuse Railroad further to the west toward Buffalo. The next line west, the Auburn and Rochester, chartered in 1836, began service in 1841. Four other small railroads followed, completing the links to Buffalo in 1843; it now became possible to travel the entire distance

from Albany to Buffalo by rail. The trip took thirty hours over seven separate railroads, required changing cars more than six times, and carried a one-way fare of between eight and ten dollars. Despite the inconvenience of changing railroads, passenger traffic between Albany and Buffalo grew phenomenally, because even thirty hours with six changes represented a vast improvement over the ten or more days aboard a foul-smelling barge on the Erie Canal.

Both management and investors in the new railroads recognized the logic of consolidation. Increased traffic would follow if a single railroad provided direct service; ticketing, billing, and convenience for the traveling public would improve significantly. At a meeting in Albany in February of 1851, representatives of all the railroads gathered to discuss a merger. After some tough bargaining, they agreed to petition the New York State legislature for enabling legislation to merge the separate lines into a single railroad between Albany and Buffalo. The New York legislature authorized consolidation on April 2, 1853.

Acting swiftly, the railroads met again on April 12th, to work out the details. Attending were representatives of ten separate railroads: Albany and Schenectady, Schenectady and Troy, Utica and Schenectady, Mohawk Valley, Syracuse and Utica, Syracuse and Utica Direct, Rochester and Syracuse, Buffalo and Rochester, Buffalo and Lockport, and the Rochester, Lockport, and Niagara Falls.[6] Formal incorporation of this conglomerate, the New York Central system, took place on July 6, 1853, after some hard bargaining among the ten railroads over the number of New York Central shares each would receive in exchange for their own shares. A number of the railroads, well built and quite profitable, demanded a premium in the exchange of stock.

Erastus Corning, the former mayor of Albany and president of the Utica and Schenectady Railroad, provided the driving force behind the consolidation and became the New York Central's first president. Corning, a long-time power in New York Democratic politics, maintained varied business interests, including the Albany Iron Works, which manufactured wheels and rails for the railroads he controlled. Like Commodore Vanderbilt, Corning never built railroads: he played the role of organizer and financier and left the difficult construction problems and day-to-day management to others.

Map of the Water Level Route from Albany to Buffalo, showing the Erie Canal and railroads that merged in 1853 to form the New York Central

The New York Central dominated railroading in upstate New York, but it faced competition for its market. One major competitor proved to be the Erie Railroad, whose name was synonymous with every kind of shady railroad dealing of the age. Its officers included Daniel Drew and two other of the most notorious of Wall Street manipulators, Jay Gould and Jim Fisk. Begun in 1832 as an alternative link between New York City and Lake Erie, the Erie Railroad lacked access to Manhattan or, initially, even to the Jersey side of the Hudson River. The Erie's tracks ran through the hilly regions of northern New Jersey and the less populated southern part of New York State. Because its first eastern terminus was in tiny Piermont, on the west bank of the Hudson, some ten miles north of New York City, passengers and freight were transferred to a ferry to complete the trip down the Hudson River to the city. For the western end of its line, the railroad selected Dunkirk, New York, on Lake Erie south of Buffalo. Dunkirk proved to be a poor choice, given that the Erie Canal had already established Buffalo as the major eastern terminus for Great Lakes shipping. The Erie eventually bought track rights into Buffalo but remained the weakest of the trunk lines between the East Coast and the Midwest. Drew, Fisk, Gould, and other Erie investors focused their energy on stock manipulation and raids on the railroad's treasury rather than on the more mundane day-to-day world of railroading. They readily initiated rate wars to win a greater share of the lucrative through traffic, even at the cost of further weakening the Erie by diverting revenue

Currier and Ives cartoon of Commodore Vanderbilt racing Jim Fisk of the Erie Railroad, 1870

from needed improvements. The line remained in precarious financial shape, even after creeping closer to Manhattan by securing track rights to Jersey City, but that did not stop Drew and company from further fiscal machinations. Despite its lesser status, the Erie created problems for the New York Central for decades.

As business prospered in the 1850s, the Central's management faced a crucial decision: whether or not to expand westward to capture a share of the lucrative Great Lakes traffic between Chicago and Buffalo. While the managers were pondering this, the Central's chief rival, the Pennsylvania, led by a true railroad builder and innovator, J. Edgar Thomson, continued track construction past Pittsburgh toward Chicago and elsewhere in the Midwest. For the eastern railroads, expansion to the Midwest proved crucial to financial survival. Chicago, by 1850 the fastest-growing city on the face of the earth, emerged as the great metropolis of the American heartland. The railroad that established the most efficient rail link to Chicago and the other major cities beyond the Appalachians stood to prosper. All four major trunk lines, the Central, the Pennsylvania, the

Baltimore and Ohio, and the Erie, sought to dominate this major transportation market.

Despite the growing competition from the dynamic Pennsylvania, Corning and New York Central moved cautiously. Tentatively, the railroad began to purchase some stock in railroads to the west, including the Great Western Railroad, which ran from the Central's bridge over the Niagara River at the falls, across the southern tip of the Province of Ontario, to Detroit. The railroad also purchased stock in the Michigan Central Railroad, building across Michigan from Detroit toward Chicago. Even given these cautious expansion moves, under Corning's leadership the New York Central remained very much an upstate New York railroad. Further, the Central still did not offer service into New York City. At Albany, passengers and freight transferred to the Hudson River steamboat lines for the ninety-mile trip down the river to New York. The New York Central would have to wait for the leadership of Cornelius Vanderbilt and his son William Henry Vanderbilt before it would possess the energy and imagination to go head to head with the Pennsylvania to dominate the rich Midwest market.

The Commodore Gains Control

Cornelius Vanderbilt played no role in the earliest years of the New York Central Railroad. He began to buy New York Central stock in 1865, in the midst of the second Harlem corner and, by 1866, owned more than $2,500,000 worth of Central stock. Vanderbilt's interest stemmed from his frustration as he watched Corning's New York Central send a growing volume of passengers and freight down the Hudson River by steamboat while the trains of his Hudson River Railroad stood waiting just across the river. Only in the winter, when the Hudson froze, did the Central use the Hudson River Railroad to get its passengers and freight to New York City. To increase Vanderbilt's anger further, the Central favored the steamships of the People's Line, owned by his archrival Daniel Drew. If, instead, the Central were to construct a bridge across the Hudson to connect with Vanderbilt's line, his Hudson River Railroad would enjoy a dramatic increase in year-round traffic.

The Commodore's competitive nature demanded action, and with his purchase of a major share of the Central's stock, he expected a seat on the board of directors. Corning and the other upstate businessmen who dominated the board refused; they remained determined not to let Vanderbilt gain a foothold in their railroad. In time, a number of the directors of the Central expressed strong dissatisfaction with Corning's timid leadership, and in 1863 a group of Central shareholders, led by Thomas Olcott of Albany, mounted a challenge to Corning, with Vanderbilt's tacit support. Corning realized that he lacked the support to keep Vanderbilt at bay and decided instead to cooperate. He agreed to step down from the presidency of the Central but remained on the board of directors. Dean Richmond of Buffalo became president and immediately obtained board approval to build a bridge over the Hudson, establishing a direct rail link with Vanderbilt's Hudson River Railroad. With the completion of the bridge, the volume of traffic over the Hudson River Railroad increased dramatically.

Not satisfied, Commodore Vanderbilt and William Henry Vanderbilt, who by now had become a full partner in his father's railroad interests, began discussions with the Central toward a formal merger with their Hudson River Railroad. As talk of the merger spread, the stock of both companies rose. All seemed to be moving smoothly ahead when, once again, Daniel Drew entered the picture. Drew's steamboat line stood to lose a great deal of business if the merger of the two railroads proceeded, and he itched to get back at the Commodore for outfoxing him in the two Harlem corners.

Daniel Drew and William Fargo, a founder of Wells, Fargo and Company and a board member and major stockholder in the Central, decided to mount another short-selling raid, this time against the stock of the Central. Two other legendary Wall Street manipulators, LeGrand Lockwood and Henry (The Silent) Keep joined Drew and Fargo in the scheme. Lockwood and Keep, like Drew, held longstanding grudges against Vanderbilt from earlier railroad deals in which the crafty Commodore had gotten the best of them.

The conspirators hatched a simple plan. Fargo would use his power on the Central board to kill the merger with the Hudson River Railroad. Before the news became public Fargo, Keep, Lockwood, and Drew would

sell Central stock short and garner a fortune as the stock declined. Once again, Vanderbilt learned of the scheme and plotted a countermove.

First, the Commodore quickly sold 60,000 shares of his Central stock before the price went down. His next move required the assistance of weather. January 15, 1867, dawned cold and blustery; the frozen Hudson River prevented any shipments from Albany to New York City via the river. Drew's steamboats could offer no further assistance to the Central until the river thawed in the spring. Vanderbilt placed advertisements in the major Albany and New York City newspapers announcing that the Hudson River Railroad would no longer accept transfer passengers or freight from the New York Central. The advertisement closed with the statement: "By the above notice passengers will observe that the ERIE RAILWAY is the only route by which they can reach NEW YORK from Buffalo without CHANGE of coaches or RECHECKING of baggage."[7]

Desperately, the Central attempted to organize another route for its traffic to New York via the Boston and Albany, Stockbridge, Housatonic, and New Haven railroads. For three days passengers and freight piled up at Albany; the alternative route proved much too complicated. In the state legislature calls rang out for action to force Vanderbilt to reopen the link between the two railroads. The stock of the Central plummeted before Drew, Fargo, Keep, and Lockwood could sell, and they all lost a great deal of money. As soon as the stock bottomed out, Vanderbilt bought back the original 60,000 shares he had sold earlier.

Public outcry, as well as pressure from the Central's own stockholders, forced the directors of the Central to deal with Vanderbilt. The Commodore agreed to restore the free flow of traffic between the Central and the Hudson railroads, Central stock shot back up, and Vanderbilt collected yet another fortune. By 1867, he completed his conquest of the Central by assuming the office of president. Fargo, Keep, and their supporters departed, replaced on the board of directors by Vanderbilt family members and close associates. William H., the Commodore's heir apparent, became vice president.

Once Vanderbilt gained control of the New York Central he proceeded toward a formal merger of the Hudson River and Central railroads. Merging the two lines would smooth the flow of traffic from Buffalo, through Albany, to New York City. In 1869, the railroads were

combined under the name New York Central and Hudson River Railroad. With track stretching from New York City to Buffalo, it became the second largest railroad in the country; only the Pennsylvania rivaled the Central.

An immensely complicated business emerged. Suddenly freight volume and ticket sales in Buffalo became crucial pieces of information to the railroad's senior management in New York City, hundreds of miles away. Elaborate schedules demanded standardized track maintenance so that a train dispatched from New York arrived on time in Buffalo.

If a manufacturer in the Midwest shipped goods by train to Manhattan via the Central for loading onto a ship bound for Europe, the railroad needed proper paperwork to bill the manufacturer and, simultaneously, ensure that the goods reached the wharfs lining the Hudson River. A new system for managing routine activities like billing and routing guaranteed that they occurred regularly—not just at the station of origin, but at every station—not just once, but every day. Such a system demanded not just the efforts of one or two trained individuals but of thousands. All of this routine repeated each day, each week, each year. The world of modern business arrived with the consolidation of Vanderbilt's railroads.

In the space of six brief years, beginning with the purchase of the Harlem Railroad in 1863 and concluding with the merger of the Central and Hudson in 1869, Vanderbilt assembled a sprawling railroad empire. With this stunning achievement, he became one of the most powerful figures in American railroading. His personal fortune reached a stupendous level, and all of this wealth and power had been accumulated by a man approaching seventy-five years of age.

To Chicago

As Cornelius Vanderbilt neared the end of his life, the expansion of his railroad system to Chicago and the rest of the Midwest continued and involved the acquisition of the Michigan Central Railroad and the Lake Shore and Michigan Southern Railroad. William H. was assuming a greater role in the management of the family railroad empire, and he executed an agreement that expanded the Central westward. In 1870, he established a "community of interest" with the Michigan Central Rail-

road and with the Great Western Railroad, which ran across Ontario, Canada, north of Lake Erie, connecting Detroit directly with Buffalo. By this "community of interest" agreement, the Michigan Central shipped all of its through traffic to New York via the Great Western and the New York Central, guaranteeing the Central substantial traffic from the Midwest. In turn, the Central pledged to use the Michigan Central and the Great Western for its traffic to Detroit and beyond to Chicago.

With this extension of rail service came innovations in passenger travel. Modern rail passenger service began in 1870 when William H. forged the agreement with the Michigan Central. For the first time, one railroad offered through service from the East Coast to the Midwest. With comfortable sleeping cars, a passenger could ride on the "Vanderbilt System" the nine hundred miles from Manhattan to downtown Chicago, quickly and in relative comfort, without changing trains.

A formal merger of the Michigan Central and the New York Central never took place. In the meantime, the Vanderbilts moved to acquire another railroad that would strengthen ties to the Midwest. The Lake Shore and Michigan Southern Railroad, built along the southern shore of Lake Erie, provided an alternative link between Buffalo and Detroit. Serving the booming industrial cities of northern Ohio, the Lake Shore, well built and crossing the flat land of Ohio and Indiana, could be a money-making machine. Eventually extending to Chicago, the rails literally followed a water-level route; and with no serious grades to overcome, its speedy trains carried passengers and freight at low rates and yet generated strong profits. The Lake Shore would add immeasurably to the Vanderbilt system, especially since the Pennsylvania Railroad's trunk line, already past Pittsburgh, was marching on toward Chicago.

Cornelius Vanderbilt's old enemies from the New York Central merger, LeGrand Lockwood and William Keep, controlled the Lake Shore and refused to consider any accommodation with the Vanderbilts. William H., backed by his father's fortune, set about buying shares in the Lake Shore in early 1869 and awaited an opportunity to strike. That opportunity arose on "Black Friday" in September of 1869, when Jim Fisk and Jay Gould attempted to corner the gold market and failed, ruining many speculators, including LeGrand Lockwood. Desperate to raise money, Lockwood, the principal shareholder, agreed to sell his shares in the Lake

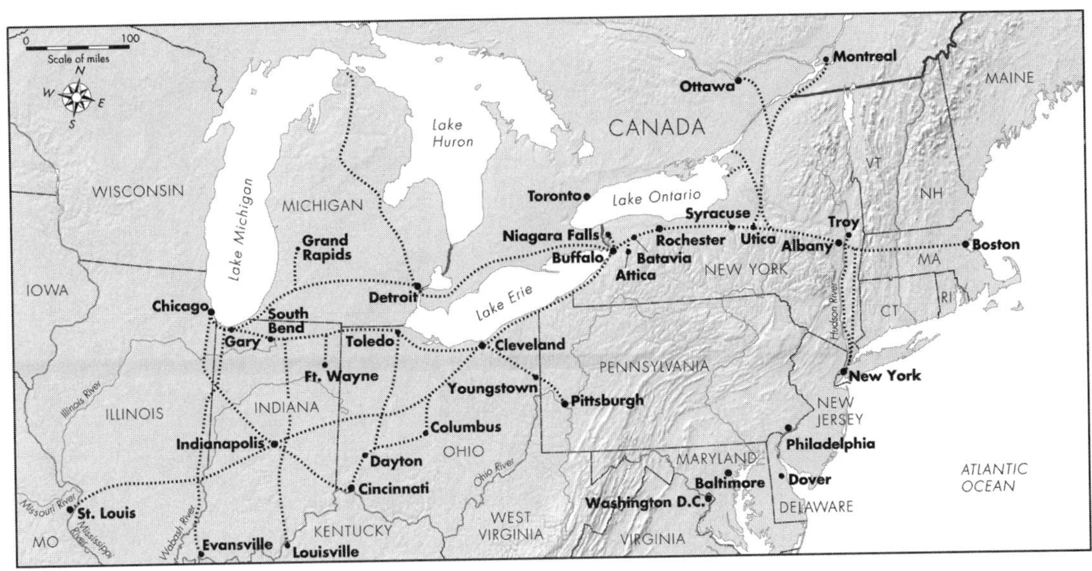

The Vanderbilt System, stretching from New York to Chicago, Cincinnati, and St. Louis

Shore for the bargain price of $10 million. With the acquisition of the Lake Shore, the Vanderbilts completed their trunk line system to Chicago and other critical points in the Midwest.

As expansion of the Vanderbilt system continued over the next thirty years, New York Central's organizational chart became increasingly complicated. The Central expanded by leasing railroads, as in the case of the Boston and Albany, or through majority stock ownership, as with the Lake Shore. All of the newly acquired railroads remained independent corporate entities with separate management. The Vanderbilts and their allies controlled these railroads through their positions on the boards of directors and through their choice of senior managers. On a day-to-day basis, the individual railroads did not coordinate operational efforts. Each railroad in the Vanderbilt system managed its own operations and kept separate books. Contributions to the overall finances of the Central came through remission of revenue and payment of stock dividends. Revenue generated by the leased or controlled lines, recorded as nonoperating revenue, formed an important component of the Central's overall financial resources.

An alternative would have been to absorb the new railroads directly into the New York Central and operate them as additional divisions. The Pennsylvania Railroad proceeded in this fashion. As the Pennsylvania

acquired new lines, they became part and parcel of the overall system under direct control of central management in Philadelphia.

Failure to consolidate remained a serious problem into the next century. At a meeting of the executive committee of the board of directors in December of 1903, William K. Vanderbilt, grandson of the Commodore, complained, "The New York Central has a large interest in Lake Shore, Michigan Central, Cleveland, Cincinnati, Chicago and St. Louis. . . . as matters now stand these companies are managed, both in relation to their finances and operation, in many aspects as if the New York Central was without interest in them. . . . the New York Central finds itself unable to formulate a comprehensive plan for the operation of all lines in its system." He suggested that a committee of the board of directors be formed "with a view of formulating a plan for the closer relations of the companies forming the New York Central System."[8]

The task before the committee was a daunting one; the Vanderbilt system formed a complex and unruly monster. Moody's railroad manual, a contemporary guide to the industry, detailed the complexity: The parent New York Central leased twenty-five lines including the Boston and Albany, Mohawk and Malone, Harlem River, Rome, Watertown and Ogdensburg, West Shore, and Lake Shore, to name a few. In turn the Lake Shore and Michigan Southern Railway leased or controlled eight additional railroads, among them the Cincinnati, Indiana and Southern Railroad. Next on the list, the Cleveland, Cincinnati, Chicago and St. Louis Railroad, nicknamed The Big Four, ran extensive operations in the Midwest. In total, Moody's credited the Vanderbilt system with 12,300 miles of track and a gross business of $240,000,000 in 1907.[9] Yet the New York Central itself and the lines it directly controlled accounted for only 3,484 miles of track, less than one-third of the system's total, by virtue of legal intricacies. For example, the Harlem Railroad retained a separate corporate identity after the New York Central leased the railroad, for a period of 401 years, in 1873. The Vanderbilts completely controlled the Harlem and operated it as an integral part of the Central's operations in New York. By the time the Grand Central project commenced, the railroad referred to the New York and Harlem Railroad as simply "the Harlem Division."

The Commodore's Grand Central

While assembling his great railroad empire, Commodore Vanderbilt decided that the Vanderbilt system, among the largest business enterprises in the country, needed an appropriate passenger terminal in the heart of New York. He envisioned a terminal with style and panache, proclaiming to all New York the power and might of his vast rail empire.

Vanderbilt chose to unify the passenger operations of his railroads in the city at the Harlem Railroad's property on 42nd Street. Even Vanderbilt's supporters cautioned him that the 42nd Street area "was still well outside the city"; in the 1870s, 42nd Street lay north of the city's main commercial and residential areas. Also, at the time, the spot did not seem the proper environment for a passenger station. On one side of 42nd Street the engine house, where the Harlem serviced its steam engines, sent up a pall of smoke; on the other, gangs of horses worked in treadmills cutting wood for hungry fire boxes. Historian Edward Hungerford described the reaction to the Commodore's plans: "People would never come up to Forty-second Street . . . they all told Commodore Vanderbilt that."[10] Vanderbilt ignored the warnings and, in his typical fashion, pushed forward. He realized that his Hudson River Railroad's passenger terminal on the west side of lower Manhattan at St. John's Park occupied the wrong location. The west side of Manhattan had evolved as a more commercial than residential area and the Hudson's tracks on the west side primarily served the growing volume of freight carried to the businesses and piers lining the Hudson River.

Since the Hudson River Railroad's tracks crossed the Harlem River onto the west side of Manhattan at Spuyten Duyvil, Vanderbilt needed a link from Spuyten Duyvil to the Harlem line at Mott Haven. In 1869, he incorporated the Spuyten Duyvil and Port Morris Railroad and constructed a rail line along the north bank of the Harlem River to Mott Haven, where the Port Morris tracks joined the Harlem's. Once Vanderbilt completed the new line, passenger trains of the New York Central and Hudson River Railroad could switch at Spuyten Duyvil, travel the five miles to Mott Haven, and then continue down the tracks of the Harlem to Midtown.

The new passenger terminal at 42nd Street would serve three railroads: the New York Central and Hudson River, the Harlem, and the New York, New Haven and Hartford. The New Haven provided commuter service to lower Fairfield County in Connecticut and long-distance trains to New England. In 1845, before Vanderbilt entered the picture, the Harlem had signed a four-hundred-year lease with the New Haven allowing joint use of the Harlem's Fourth Avenue tracks and guaranteeing the New Haven's passenger trains joint use of its station facilities in Manhattan.

Commodore Vanderbilt's intentions for a new passenger terminal at 42nd Street ran to the palatial; he commissioned architect John Snook and engineer Isaac Buckhout to design a structure to celebrate his triumphs in assembling a railroad empire. The design they produced set out to awe the traveler and the casual visitor with the power and glory of the Vanderbilt railroad empire. Formally called Grand Central Depot, the structure included an imposing station building at the front and an arched train shed in the rear. When completed in 1871, Grand Central Depot was the largest rail facility in the world, larger even than London's St. Pancras Station. Like the present Grand Central, it served as more than a terminal; it symbolized the power of Vanderbilt's railroads and the role they played in the life of New York City, the state, and the country.

During the Age of Energy, architects and the powerful clients they served sought an architectural style to express the power and might of the new business enterprises, railroads foremost among them, that were reshaping American society. Vanderbilt's vision for the first Grand Central station began an association with the French Classical style which continued with the second Grand Central. Lewis Mumford, the famed social critic, referred to the building sarcastically as an "Imperial Facade."[11]

Forming an L shape, the classical terminal building, bearing a striking resemblance to the Louvre in Paris, ran along 42nd Street for 370 feet, and then turned up Vanderbilt Avenue on the west side of the Harlem's property for a depth of almost 700 feet. The three railroads using the facility occupied separate sections of the building, each with its own ticket, baggage, and waiting rooms. Railroad offices occupied the second and third stories.

In the rear, the train shed comprised the most impressive part of the

The first Grand Central, from Vanderbilt Place and 42nd Street, 1871

new terminal, concealed from view along 42nd Street by the L-shaped station building. Inspired by London's Crystal Palace, the train shed consisted of an immense arched structure constructed of iron trusses, imported from England, more than 200 feet in width, creating the largest interior space in America. The arched roof rose to a height of 100 feet above the tracks and the entire shed ran over 600 feet in length. A lattice work of iron with glass panels, the roof enclosed seventeen tracks, twelve for outgoing trains and five for incoming trains.

Using the width of the train shed as a measure, the next largest train station in the country was the second La Salle Street Station in Chicago (built 1868–72), which spanned 186 feet; Park Square Station in Boston (1872–74) had a train shed measuring 128 feet across.[12] Not until 1888 did the Pennsylvania Railroad's massive station in Jersey City eclipse Grand Central in size and scale, spanning 252 feet.

With an iron and glass train shed and classical station building, Grand Central Depot represented a tension inherent in the use of the classical style for railroad stations during the Age of Energy. Railroads embodied the modern, the mechanical, and the application of the newest technology to solve transportation problems. Fabricated in England, the soaring iron arches supporting the train shed constituted the largest arches erected in the United States to date. By contrast, the station building, with its stone and brick ornamentation and the mansard roof with five domes, mirrored the classical tradition, particularly the classicism of the Second Empire of Napoleon III. The juxtaposition of the classical and the machine age created a stark contrast. Approaching Grand Central Depot, the traveler confronted a classical building, in this case a building modeled after the Louvre in Paris, which provided no hint of the function hidden behind its "Imperial Facade," to use Mumford's term. Passing through the waiting room to the train shed, the traveler entered a great space created without a trace of the classical. Inside it, the new machine age, filled with

The first Grand Central, from Park Avenue and 42nd Street, with streetcar tracks in foreground, ca. 1884

the sights and sounds of the railroad, ushered in the change from the ancient to the modern. This juxtaposition remains in the present Grand Central, but in order to view it one must descend to the platforms and peer into the darkness of the underground tracks and train yard supported by a massive steel structure enclosed in concrete. By contrast the Grand Concourse remains firmly anchored in the classical.

In Europe, where train travel remains a major mode of transportation, a number of terminals retain the flavor that was found in Grand Central Depot. St. Pancras in London, and the Gare du Nord and the Gare de Lyon in Paris, all combine classical terminal buildings with iron and glass train sheds in the rear. Approaching these stations, the visitor views a classical building with a facade similar to a museum or government office building. Behind the facade stands the great train shed covering the platforms. At the Gare du Nord the train shed soars overhead in a great arch as did the shed at Grand Central Depot. Today electric and diesel engines operate where steam engines once ruled, but the space, with cast-iron columns and soaring arches, still conveys a sense of the beginning of the machine age.

The train shed in rear of the terminal building, looking south from 44th Street and Lexington Avenue

Interior of train shed, looking north from second-floor balcony

Grand Central Depot was a terminal, referred to as a "head house," as opposed to a side station or through station where platforms lined the tracks and trains stopped briefly to discharge or board passengers. The tracks literally ended there. Grand Central marked the end of the line, the final destination. Once a train reached a head house terminal, train crews shunted the engine and cars to make up outgoing trains. This switching necessitated a great deal of moving cars and engines back and forth, and a head house terminal required a large train yard for the servicing engines and cars and the assembling of outgoing trains. Beyond the train shed, the railroad built a vast rail yard, running north to 58th Street and stretching from Lexington almost to Madison Avenue, creating an impenetrable barrier in midtown Manhattan for almost twenty blocks.

All of this activity contributed to making major terminals and train yards such as Grand Central immensely complicated to design and manage. Busy train yards needed numerous storage tracks, switches, and signals to control incoming and outgoing trains and switching operations,

Interior of train shed, looking north from concourse

as shuttle engines moved back and forth to assemble new trains. Signaling and control became a major science for the American railroads, and the New York Central established a separate division for the planning, construction, and operation of its signaling system at 42nd Street and throughout its entire system.

Massive new railroad facilities like Grand Central demanded precision, routine, and rigid operating procedures. Employees who worked the trains, signal, and switching systems found themselves part of an elaborate machine the work of which was governed by a strict set of rules and regulations. Individual initiative found little place in this new system of work. Adherence to the established procedures remained an absolute necessity, for reasons of safety and efficiency. With the railroads came the modern industrial world of work where the individual performed routine tasks day in and day out. In the case of the railroads, without strict procedures to control train operations, chaos would ensue. Such a complicated system could only have been the product of the modern world,

with its notions of systematization, clearly spelled-out rules and regulations, and a work force accustomed to the machine and the system.

At Grand Central the "flying switch" provides an example of the precision of the signal and control system. Before development of the flying switch, trains arrived at the platforms in a head house terminal like Grand Central with their engines in the front of the train, a railroad worker uncoupled the emptied passenger cars, and a yard engine hauled them away. Then the engine backed away to a turntable in preparation for departure. All of this activity required numerous shunting movements and contributed to the overall complexity of a busy train yard.

To minimize the number of train movements, the railroads using Grand Central perfected the flying switch. As a train emerged from the Park Avenue tunnel at 56th Street, approaching Grand Central, it accelerated; and the brakeman, perched precariously over the coupler linking the engine to the first passenger car, tripped the coupler and freed the engine, which continued to accelerate. In the control tower, the switchman pulled the proper lever to send the engine onto a siding and then immediately threw the switch back so that the passenger cars continued on toward the

Train yard during the days of steam, looking south toward Grand Central from 48th Street

train shed. As the passenger cars moved under the train shed and alongside the platforms, now traveling on their own momentum, the brakemen scrambled to the hand brakes and, turning the brake wheels furiously, brought the passenger cars to a halt in their proper position next to the platform so that passengers could exit the train. The flying switch saved a great deal of time and switching. Obviously, it required split-second timing and great skill on the part of the railroad employees, but the railroads used this procedure until work on the new Grand Central began, without a single mishap, a testimony to the elaborate system of signaling and control perfected by the railroad.

A Symbol of the Age

Vanderbilt's new 42nd Street terminal became a major tourist attraction, primarily because of the train shed; many New Yorkers could not understand how the arched structure stood, seemingly without support. "New York opened its eyes and gasped," the *New York Times* later recalled. "Nothing like it had ever before been seen. It had fifteen tracks in its train shed. Some folks said that Commodore Vanderbilt was in his dotage. Others explained the great depot by saying that the Commodore was simply building a terminal that would last for all time."[13]

On October 7, 1871, the first train departed from the new terminal and the facility proved to be an immediate success. During the first year of operation, the three railroads ran an average of 88 scheduled trains a day and more than 4,000,000 passengers passed through its gates.

Grand Central Depot heralded a new era in train travel to and from New York City. The new terminal consolidated, in one location, the passenger operations of the railroads serving New York. In addition to extensive commuter service to Westchester and Fairfield counties, the lines provided long-distance service to New England, upstate New York, Cleveland, Detroit, Chicago, St. Louis, and to thousands of points in between. As soon as the new depot opened, the New York Central's timetable for through service highlighted the fact that the establishment of the Vanderbilt system eliminated the necessity to transfer trains at Buffalo. A bold headline read: "No More Transfer at Buffalo!" In 1872, the timetable listed six daily trains that provided service to upstate New

York and on to Midwest cities: Cleveland, Toledo, Detroit, Columbus, Cincinnati, Indianapolis, Louisville, St. Louis, and Chicago.

A trip from New York to Rochester, in upstate New York, took twelve hours, while the daily train to Chicago left New York at 10:30 A.M. and arrived in Chicago the following day at 8:00 P.M. In subsequent decades, the Central reduced the travel time to Chicago significantly, especially after the introduction of its world-famous Twentieth Century Limited. Thirty-three and a half hours may seem an eternity today, but in the 1870s to travel such a distance in so short a period of time seemed miraculous.

The New York Central's schedule reminded the traveling public of the prime advantage the railroad offered—direct rail access to midtown Manhattan: "This is the only line landing passengers in the city of New York within ten minutes of the principal hotels and is not impeded by Ferry transfers." All of the Central's competitors terminated at points across the Hudson in New Jersey. To complete the journey to Manhattan, their passengers had to board a ferry to cross the Hudson River. For good measure, the Central advertised that the absence of a ferry ride combined with the railroad's luxury sleeping cars: "renders a journey upon it a pleasant pastime rather than a distasteful necessity."[14]

Vanderbilt intended his new Grand Central Depot as a fitting stage for a journey to Rochester, Buffalo, Cleveland, Detroit, and Chicago. Since the New Haven Railroad shared facilities at the 42nd Street terminal, trains also served Boston, the rest of New England, and Canada. Grand Central followed logically from the growth of Vanderbilt's huge railroad empire. Even at a cost of $3 million for the building and train shed and an additional $3 million for the expanded train yard, the Commodore raised no objections; the depot provided the monument he wanted.

The great rail terminals of the era stood literally at the end of the "metropolitan corridor," the end of the journey between rural and urban America. An article published in *Century Magazine* portrayed the great urban terminal as the port of entry to the city: "The gate-way of the city marks the beginning and end of many things. Here the traditional young man from the country is confronted by a confused view of the city he has come to conquer. . . . Here again, after conquering, or being conquered he slowly retraces his youthful steps, to retire upon his farm—or the

county's."[15] A powerful image in American letters depicts a youth moving from a rural farm or small town to the big city, seeking fame or fortune or just a change from the boredom and sheer hard work of life on the farm. This journey of adventure, or perhaps desperation, ends in the great terminal in the heart of the metropolis. As the train arrives, the protagonist confronts the energy and chaos of the new urban society. In the end, the journey results in either great triumph or great tragedy, as the author of the *Century* article suggests. Great railroad terminals like Grand Central provided the stage for this unfolding drama, as a rural, agrarian society urbanized. In 1897, as a new century dawned, the editor of the *Commercial and Financial Chronicle* summed it up: "The fact is the railroad revolutionized everything."[16] No aspect of American life remained unaffected by the railroads in the period after the Civil War; the railroad ushered in America's modern age.

William H. Vanderbilt Assumes Control

Soon after Grand Central Depot opened and as his son and heir apparent, William Henry, continued to expand the Vanderbilt system to Chicago and St. Louis, the Commodore entered the twilight of life. His health deteriorated and his behavior at times seemed bizarre. His first wife, Sophia, died in 1868, in the midst of the battles for his railroad empire. After his wife's death, the old man became obsessed with the occult and consorted with a number of "mediums" in attempts to contact Sophia and his long-dead mother and father. In his dealings with the occult he crossed paths with Victoria Woodhull and her sister, Tennessee Claflin, two mediums with questionable reputations and unlimited ambition, who set out to ensnare the Commodore and his fortune.

Woodhull and Claflin remain larger-than-life characters in the drama of the Gilded Age. Born in Tennessee to a drunkard and wastrel father, they survived and even flourished on their beauty, wit, and charm. Woodhull, in addition to a career as a medium, became the first woman to address a joint session of Congress, served as the editor of her own weekly newspaper, *Woodhull and Claflin's Weekly*, which championed women's rights, free love, and the suffragette movement, and, with Vanderbilt's help, opened a stock brokerage company. Woodhull ran for pres-

ident of the United States against Ulysses S. Grant and Horace Greeley and became involved in one of the most notorious scandals of the time—Henry Ward Beecher's affair with Elizabeth Tilton. Finally, after a number of tumultuous years in New York, Victoria and Tennessee decamped to England, where they married into the British nobility and retired to the English countryside, rich and somewhat infamous.

As Vanderbilt's relationship with the sisters deepened, his family became alarmed. Victoria and Tennessee became part of the Commodore's household; he called Tennessee "my little sparrow." Sordid details of his relationship with Tennessee later emerged, during the bitter contest over Vanderbilt's will. Just a few short months after his wife's death, he had announced to his stunned family that his "little sparrow" would soon become his new wife. This William Henry and the Commodore's daughters refused to accept. In late fall of 1868 they arranged for Vanderbilt to meet a much more suitable candidate, Miss Frank Crawford of Mobile, Alabama, a distant cousin. With the family's approval, the two began a whirlwind courtship. Frank Crawford, twenty-nine years old, married the seventy-four-year-old Vanderbilt a year later and remained with him for the last seven years of his life.

Commodore Vanderbilt died on January 4, 1877, after a long illness. At the time of his death, many assumed Vanderbilt to be the richest man in the country, and intense speculation swirled through society about his will and the division of the fortune between his two living sons, William Henry and Cornelius Jeremiah. His remaining children, all daughters, in an age when women were still excluded from business, could not expect to inherit the Commodore's railroad empire.

Vanderbilt left almost his entire fortune to William. Inheriting over $90 million, including all of the Commodore's railroad stock, William Henry found himself rich beyond imagination and in sole control of the New York Central Railroad, the centerpiece of the Vanderbilt empire, and of the Commodore's magnificent terminal on 42nd Street. The elder Vanderbilt had believed in only one way to preserve his railroad empire: leave it all to his most promising heir. Cornelius, the other surviving son, had proved a great disappointment to his father. A gambler and wastrel, he had been exiled to a farm outside of Hartford, Connecticut, where the Commodore hoped he would reform. When Cornelius continued to

drink and gamble, his father left him out of the major portion of the fortune, providing Cornelius with only the income from a trust fund of $200,000 administered by his brother.

A bitter battle ensued over the will. Cornelius joined his sisters in a lawsuit to overturn the will; the Commodore had left each daughter just $250,000. Obviously the daughters expected much, much more. The future of the Vanderbilt railroad empire stood in the balance. If Cornelius and his sisters won the lawsuit and the millions of dollars they demanded, William would have no recourse but to sell his controlling interest in the New York Central. William faced two choices: win the lawsuit or make a deal with Cornelius and his sisters.

In November of 1877, the trial began; it lasted for a year and a half. William sat in court and listened as the sordid details of his father's last years became public. Newspaper sales soared as the press detailed the Commodore's relationship with Tennessee Claflin. After eighteen months, William decided to end the lawsuit rather than wait for the court's decision: he gave Cornelius an extra $200,000 in cash and a trust fund of $400,000 in addition to the income from the $200,000 trust fund he had received under the will. William gave each of his sisters the same settlement. Compared to the fortune of $90 million he had inherited, these sums pale. William Henry preserved the Commodore's railroad empire. He retained 87 percent of the shares of the New York Central Railroad, the parent company of the Vanderbilt system, and emerged from the battle with his siblings the richest man in the United States.

Sadly, Cornelius J. Vanderbilt's life did not improve, even with the additional money the settlement provided. On April 2, 1882, after a night of gambling, Cornelius returned to his hotel in New York City and killed himself with a pistol.

William H. Vanderbilt continued his active interest in the affairs of the New York Central and its subsidiary lines. Less flamboyant than his father, still he moved quickly when he perceived a threat to the Vanderbilt system. In October of 1882, he purchased the Nickel Plate Railroad, built by a group of speculators to parallel the Lake Shore from Buffalo to Chicago. Cheaply built, the railroad served the speculators as a means to threaten the Central with a ruinous rate war and to force William H. to buy the line to protect the Vanderbilt interests. Less than a year after he

bought the line it went bankrupt; he considered the purchase the worst business decision of his life.

William H. found the running of the railroad empire a demanding affair. One day in October of 1882, during a period of deep involvement in the Nickel Plate negotiations, two reporters interviewed him as he rested in his private railway car in Chicago. The reporters questioned Vanderbilt about the Nickel Plate battle and plans to drop a fast mail train the Central ran between New York and Chicago. The *New York Times* reported, in detail, the Vanderbilt interview:

Q: Does your limited express pay?
A: No; not a bit of it. We only run it because we are forced to do so by the action of the Pennsylvania Road.
Q: But don't you run it for the public benefit?
A: *The public be damned.* What does the public care for the railroads except to get as much out of them for as small a consideration as possible?[17]

When the public learned of Vanderbilt's exclamation, "the public be damned," outraged reaction came fast and furious. Flashed over the telegraph, his words found the front page of newspapers all over the country, and condemnation of William H. followed. America was finding the accumulation of great wealth deeply troubling and feared the emergence of gigantic corporate entities such as the New York Central which seemed to hold so much power over the lives and livelihoods of average citizens. "The public be damned" became a rallying cry for the populists and politicians, who demanded that the government curb the powers of the new corporate giants, especially the railroads. Ironically, William H. Vanderbilt, the richest man in the country, the man who controlled the New York Central, had uttered the words that brought success to the forces seeking to regulate the railroads. Eventually government regulation of the railroads, in the name of the public, almost destroyed them.

Social critics attacked the giant corporations, the trusts, and the railroads for their misdeeds. Henry D. Lloyd's *Wealth against Commonwealth* (1894), Ida M. Tarbell's *History of the Standard Oil Company* (1904), Upton Sinclar's *The Jungle* (1906), and Theodore Dreiser's trilogy: *The Financier* (1912), *The Titan* (1914), and *The Genius* (1915), all chronicled the transgressions of the giant businesses that emerged after the Civil War. Both

the companies and the men who ran them, and amassed such prodigious fortunes, came under harsh criticism.

Because the railroads constituted the largest and most powerful businesses of the time, they served as touchstones for criticism and discontent. Thomas Nast's cartoons portrayed the Vanderbilts and the New York Central as exercising a stranglehold on the commerce of New York City and State. The American labor movement began with efforts to organize railroad workers and, in 1894, just a year after the Columbian Exposition in Chicago opened, the American Railway Union, led by Eugene Debs, organized the first major strike in the nation's history, against the railroads. In Pittsburgh, violence broke out and the governor of Pennsylvania finally called for federal troops to restore order after millions of dollars of Pennsylvania Railroad property went up in smoke. Railroad service across the East shut down.

The Vanderbilts and the Gilded Age

Both the Commodore and his wealthy son lived comparatively frugally, given their enormous wealth. William Henry's yearly income averaged $10,000,000 but his expenses ran less than $200,000. Over the remaining years of his life his fortune doubled. As Commodore Vanderbilt quipped: "Any fool can make a fortune. It takes a man of brains to hold on to it after it is made." By 1883, William Henry's wealth had reached the staggering total of $194 million.

Unlike his father, William H. Vanderbilt spent at least some of his fortune, becoming the first Vanderbilt to build a mansion on Fifth Avenue in New York, the fashionable address favored by the millionaires of the Gilded Age, the Age of Energy. His second son, William K., and his ambitious wife, Alva, persuaded him that as the richest man in the world he needed a home befitting his stature. Issac Buckhout, who had collaborated in the plans for the first Grand Central, designed the mansion at 640 Fifth Avenue, which occupied the entire block between 51st and 52nd streets.

At one point, six hundred workmen and sixty sculptors were working on the mansion, which was completed in December of 1881. Critics poked fun at William Henry's new home. One critic called it a "gloomy

Mansion of William H. Vanderbilt (first two facades at left), *on Fifth Avenue looking north from 51st Street*

waste of rubbed sandstone" and added, "The baroque interior of the home of the head of the House of Vanderbilt was a tasteless hodgepodge, ostentatiously crammed with riches. . . . It was a stylistic mess that cost a fortune."[18]

The mansion, perhaps a "stylistic mess," started a family tradition that in the end bankrupted the family fortune. The millions spent on 640 Fifth Avenue represented just the start. William Henry's sons, William K. and Cornelius II, lavished millions more on their homes on Fifth Avenue and in Newport, Rhode Island. In Asheville, North Carolina, his third son, George, constructed the largest private home ever built in this country—Biltmore—set amidst 146,000 acres of countryside. The next generation of Vanderbilts followed their parents' example, spending millions more on their homes, summer estates, and "camps" in the Adirondacks—all constructed not for comfort but for grandeur, to celebrate and glorify the House of Vanderbilt.

William H. Vanderbilt retired from active railroad affairs in 1883, retaining only his directorship in the New York Central. He devoted much

Interior of the William H. Vanderbilt mansion at Fifth Avenue and 51st Street, 1883

of his time to horses and his art collection and prepared to turn over the Vanderbilt fortune to his sons. A gigantic fortune indeed. "I am the richest man in the world. I am worth one hundred ninety-four million dollars," William Henry boasted to a friend one day. Apparently he was. His only rival, England's Duke of Westminster, held a fortune worth somewhere around $200,000,000, but it was almost all in land. Henry Clews, a legendary Wall Street operator and social gadfly, in his memoirs commented on Vanderbilt's fortune: "The ordinary human mind fails to grasp the idea of such a vast amount of wealth. If converted into gold it

would take five hundred strong horses to draw it from Grand Central Depot to the Sub-Treasury in Wall Street."[19] Wealth of this magnitude appears staggering today, and William H. enjoyed his wealth before the federal income tax became permanent.

On December 7, 1885, William Henry met with Robert Garrett, the president of the Baltimore and Ohio Railroad, in Vanderbilt's mansion on Fifth Avenue. Garrett arrived without an appointment to discuss the B&O's desperate need for access to New York harbor via the Jersey side of the Hudson. The B&O faced bankruptcy unless it could deliver freight and passengers directly to New York City, the key advantage enjoyed by Vanderbilt's rail lines. At around 2:00 P.M., William suddenly grabbed at his throat and fell to the floor dead. He had outlived the Commodore by only eight years. Now, the responsibility fell to William Henry's sons to oversee the fortunes of the Vanderbilt railroad empire and of its crown jewel, Grand Central.

The Grandsons of the Commodore

William Henry's death, like his father's, sparked intense interest in the division of his fortune among his heirs. William H. Vanderbilt had four sons—Cornelius II, William Kissam, Frederick, and George—and four daughters. His two eldest sons served as officers in the railroad business, as their father and grandfather had demanded. While they both learned the railroad business thoroughly, their temperaments differed. Cornelius II was a serious man. Friends and acquaintances reported that they never saw him smile. He taught Sunday school at St. Bartholomew's Church, where he met his future wife, Alice Claypoole Gwynne. William K., on the other hand, appears to have been dedicated to pleasure and his social life, as well as to the railroad business.

When William H. died, he left $10 million to his sons Frederick and George and the same amount to each of his daughters. The remainder of the fortune he left equally to Cornelius II and William K.; each inherited $65 million. William H. dared to do what the Commodore had cautioned him never to do. He divided the bulk of his estate between his two eldest sons, leaving neither as the clear head of the House of Vanderbilt, further weakening the Vanderbilt grip on the New York Central.

The Commodore had been a little rough around the edges; he had not been raised in luxury. William H. had spent years on a farm on Staten Island raising hogs and vegetables. By contrast the grandsons of the Commodore received the finest educations money could buy in Europe and America and, by the time of William's death, had achieved a degree of social respectability, a fortune of $200 million being hard for the social arbiters to ignore. Still the old Knickerbocker elite of New York City withheld their acceptance of Cornelius II and William K., but their wives set out to change that.

William K.'s formidable wife, Alva, took the lead. Armed with the Vanderbilt millions, Alva Smith Vanderbilt, counseled by the social dandy Ward McAllister, plotted to conquer New York society. McAllister, who coined the term the "Four Hundred" to describe New York's social elite, chose the term because that was the number of people who could fit comfortably into the ballroom of Mrs. Caroline Schermerhorn Astor, *the* Mrs. Astor. For years Mrs. Astor dominated the social elite of New York and refused to recognize the Vanderbilts. Alva simply would not be deterred and, with McAllister's assistance, finally triumphed, with a fancy dress ball held on March 26, 1883, at her new mansion at 660 Fifth Avenue. The ball reportedly cost $75,000, and even Mrs. Astor attended. Guests came dressed as knights and fairy tale characters: Cornelius II appeared as King Louis XVI and Alva dressed as a Venetian princess. William H., accompanied by Ulysses S. Grant, attended in black tie.

Here New Yorkers witnessed spending beyond avarice. Flowers for the ball cost $11,000, some guests' costumes ran as high as a $1,000. Henry Clews, with a strong sense of irony, compared the Vanderbilt ball favorably to the antics at Versailles and the entertainments of the Roman emperors.[20]

Not more than four blocks to the east, next to the New York Central train yard at 42nd Street, stood squalid tenements filled with Irish, German, and Jewish immigrants who considered $1 a day a good wage. Nothing so clearly illustrates the contrasts of the Gilded Age more than this juxtaposition of the Vanderbilt ball and the lives of the millions of ordinary Americans struggling for a decent life and unable to comprehend the wealth amassed by the Commodore and his son, wealth that funded a fancy dress ball so that Alva Vanderbilt could have her social triumph.

The mansion of Cornelius Vanderbilt II, at Fifth Avenue and 57th Street, replaced by the Bonwit Teller department store

The ball represented only the beginning. New mansions followed in New York and lavish "summer cottages" in Newport, Rhode Island: the Breakers for Cornelius and the even more expensive Marble House for William K. and Alva, both designed by Richard Morris Hunt.

When Cornelius Vanderbilt II completed the Breakers in 1895, the reputed cost of the building alone totaled $2 million, with an additional $9 million spent on furnishings. Newport endures as a place where the excesses of the Gilded Age remain on view. Armies of servants catered to every whim of the newly created class of self-styled aristocrats. For sumptuous balls, the wives and daughters spent thousands on gowns, while at the same time the laborers working at Grand Central received $1 a day for ten hours of work.

On September 29, 1904, the board of directors of the New York Central awarded pensions to three long-time employees. John W. Horan, aged seventy, had worked for the railroad for forty-four years as a clerk, and the board set his pension as $20 a month. Richard Hennessey, sixty-eight, had labored for fifty-one years as a section hand, while James Cleary, eighty-two, had served as a baggageman for fifty-six years. Both

Hennessey and Cleary, "unable to work" any longer, received pensions of $15 a month.[21] Did Cornelius II and William K., sitting on the board with J. P. Morgan and William Rockefeller, brother of John D., think about the vast gulf between a pension of $15 a month and the millions they spent?

Succeeding generations of Vanderbilts continued to spend until the fortune ran out. In the space of four generations, a major part of the largest fortune in American history simply disappeared. As the riot of spending continued unabated, direct involvement of the Vanderbilt family in the New York Central Railroad, the cornerstone of the Vanderbilt fortune, declined. At the time of Cornelius's death in 1899, William K. was living abroad for long periods of time. Day-to-day management of the Central rested in the capable hands of its professional managers; the Vanderbilts eventually came to play the role of minor stockholders. A congressional investigation in 1931 determined that the entire stock holdings of the various Vanderbilt descendants totaled less than 5 percent of the stock of the New York Central Railroad.

"The Gilded Age," an expression coined by Mark Twain to characterize the extravagance, waste, and frivolity of the period after the Civil War, coincides exactly with Howard Mumford Jones's "Age of Energy." Those years saw great achievements in American material progress and the unleashing of the industrial age. Yet, parallel to this constructive energy stands the conspicuous display of personal wealth.

The End of the Commodore's Grand Central

When first opened in 1871, the Grand Central Depot generated awe. However, by the time of William Henry Vanderbilt's death in 1885, the steady growth in traffic for the railroads using the terminal had generated enormous problems. With only fifteen tracks, the arched train shed became inadequate as long-haul and commuter traffic grew at a rate far exceeding all projections. Envisioned to serve the needs of the railroads for twenty-five to thirty-five years, the terminal reached capacity much more quickly. In 1886, just fourteen years after Grand Central first opened its doors for business, an annex with seven additional tracks was added on the east side of the train shed, along Depew Place. Even these addi-

Grand Central in 1898, from 42nd Street, with cable cars on 42nd Street and showing the station for the Third Avenue El at right

tional tracks provided only short-term relief as passenger volume increased relentlessly.

In 1898, the railroads once again improved Grand Central, with a three-story addition to the terminal building and a major reconfiguration of the waiting rooms. The most important change involved the construction of an enlarged concourse across the head of the tracks in the train shed. Prior to this alteration, each railroad had provided a separate waiting room and access to the train platforms. A passenger arriving on a New York Central train and departing on a New Haven train had to walk through the New York Central waiting room, out onto the street, proceed to the entrance of the New Haven waiting room, and walk through it to board the New Haven train. The new concourse cost $2,500,000, but it dramatically improved the flow of people through the station and

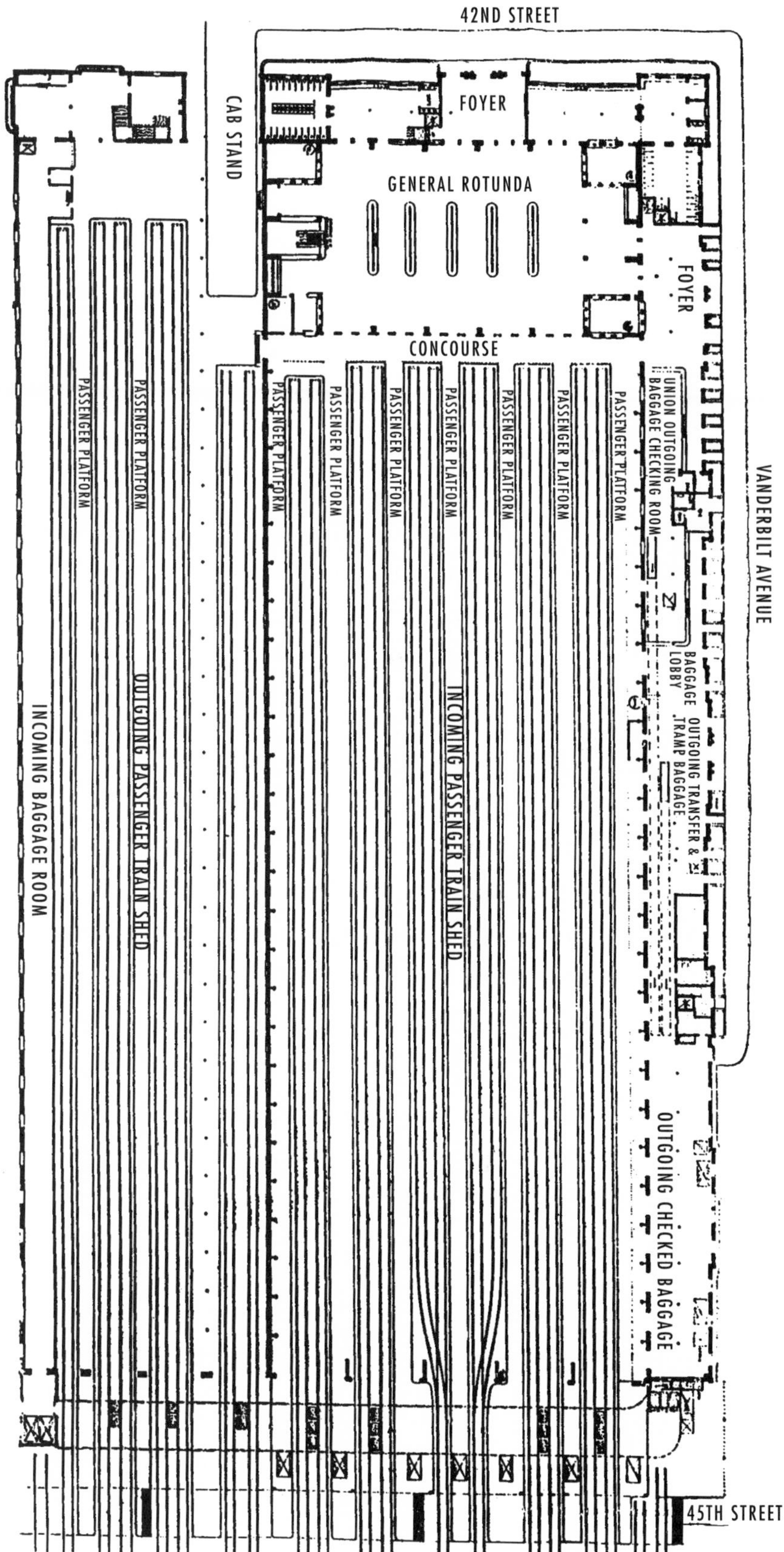

Plan for 1898 renovations of the train shed

among the three railroads' platforms. However, it failed to solve the underlying problem: too few platforms to serve the growing volume of passenger traffic.

As the century drew to a close, critics labeled Grand Central the worst rail facility in the country and New Yorkers increasingly complained about the crowded terminal and open train yard to the north. A *New York Times* editorial condemned Grand Central for aesthetic reasons and as a health hazard: "It is known to travelers as one of the most inconvenient and unpleasant railroad stations in the whole country. The statement errs on the side of moderation. When our pretentiously named station was new it aroused a considerable amount of local pride . . . but that day passed long ago and for many a humiliating year the ugly structure has been a cruel disgrace to the metropolis and its inhabitants. At present the odors that permeate its waiting rooms . . . reach every would-be passenger, disgust him with plain hints of gross uncleanliness, and threaten him with typhoid and diphtheria."[22] The last part of the editorial is a thinly veiled reference to the flood of immigrants using Grand Central to travel to other parts of the country after being processed at Ellis Island. In the remodeled Grand Central an "immigrant waiting room," in the basement, served recently arrived immigrants waiting to board special trains the railroad ran to the Midwest.

To many New Yorkers, Grand Central no longer conveyed a sense of grandeur for a city that prided itself on its preeminent place in American life. Newspapers criticized both the building and New York Central for not providing a more fitting terminal:

> Nothing pertaining to New York City except its government has been so discreditable to it as its principal railroad station. Wretchedly cramped in space, stingy of the many accommodations demanded by arriving and departing travelers, ill-arranged, dark and repelling, this utterly inadequate structure has been considered by its owners to be good enough for New York. . . . The privilege conferred upon these railroads of possessing the only terminal station on Manhattan Island is one of immense value. . . . the Grand Central Station furnishes terminal accommodations which would be considered adequate in Sandusky, Ohio. . . . It is a long standing affront to the

> people of New York, an evidence of disgraceful ingratitude and indifference on the part of the railroad companies.[23]

Here the editors touched on a key point concerning Grand Central and the New York Central Railroad—its monopoly on direct rail access to Manhattan, the cornerstone of the entire Vanderbilt system. The company remained vulnerable to the charge that it provided inadequate service and accommodations in exchange for a monopoly on direct rail access to New York, an asset of immense value.

Commodore Vanderbilt's cramped and overburdened terminal provided a concrete, everyday focus for the criticism of all of the vast changes taking place in the lives of the people of New York and the entire country. One of the country's largest and most powerful railroads, the New York Central stood accused of ignoring the needs of the traveling public and of being more concerned with profits than with providing decent service. Even the conservative *Scientific American,* not known as a muckraking publication, recognized the seriousness of the congestion at Grand Central and called for large-scale changes: "Grand Central Station at Forty-second Street will continue to be the only great terminal in New York. . . . radical change must be made in this terminal or the traffic within the next few years will be thrown into a condition approaching deadlock."[24]

Only one real solution remained: replace Grand Central Depot with a completely new facility, a new terminal with vastly increased capacity. This is precisely what the New York Central Railroad set out to do.

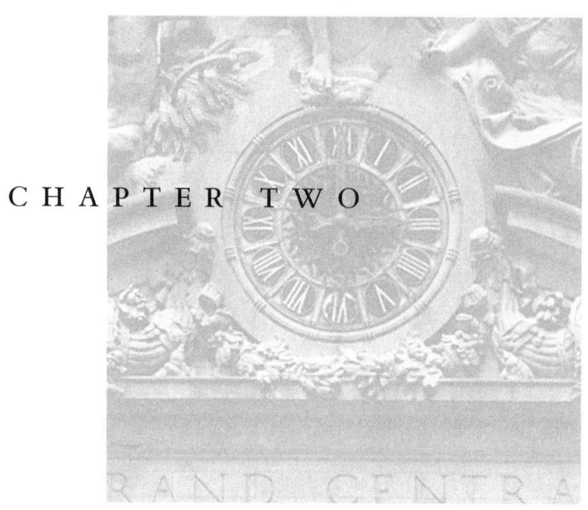

CHAPTER TWO

The Engineer's Grand Central

On January 8, 1902, the 8:17 commuter train from Danbury, Connecticut, paused in the Park Avenue tunnel at 58th Street, awaiting a signal to proceed. Smoke and steam choked the tunnel. Despite warning lights and signals, a train from White Plains, New York, crashed into the rear of the Danbury train, killing fifteen passengers and injuring scores more. Screams filled the splintered cars at the rear of the Danbury train. Coals from the stoves used to heat the passenger cars spilled out, and the danger of fire spread. New York City firemen quickly arrived on the scene; Battalion Chief Thomas Freel heroically climbed down into the tunnel and crawled through the cars, amidst the dead, in a frantic search for survivors. Upon hearing the alarm, William K. Vanderbilt, then a board member of the New York Central and Hudson River Railroad, rushed to the scene from his Fifth Avenue mansion. Unable to offer any assistance, he went to the railroad's headquarters at Grand Central to await further news.[1]

Reaction to the tragedy, indignant and impassioned, pressured New York's district attorney to indict the operator of the White Plains train, Charles Wisker, for manslaughter. An inflamed press demanded the indictment of the officers and directors of the New York Central for the operation of a public health hazard, the Park Avenue tunnel. In May of 1903, in response to the tragedy, New York City and the State of New York outlawed the operation of steam locomotives south of the Harlem

River (in effect, all of Manhattan Island), including the Park Avenue tunnel, after July 1, 1908. The New York Central desperately needed to solve the tunnel problem. They also needed to deal with their antiquated passenger facilities at Grand Central Depot or relocate passenger operations from 42nd Street, an unthinkable alternative.

William J. Wilgus, the Chief Engineer

One of the officials of the New York Central who recognized the serious problems the railroad faced with its outdated facilities at 42nd Street was William J. Wilgus. Born in Buffalo, New York, in 1865, he never attended college but his brilliance propelled him to a distinguished career as a self-taught railway engineer. In 1883, after completing high school, Wilgus began his railroad career working with the Minnesota and Northwestern Railroad and the Duluth and Winnipeg Railroad. He joined the New York Central in 1893 and, in less than a decade, rose to the position of chief engineer. During the First World War, Wilgus served with the American Expeditionary Force under General Pershing. In France, he ran the railroads for the Military Railroad Commission with such distinction that the French government awarded him a medal; thereafter Wilgus proudly used the title *Colonel.* A final triumph came during the Great Depression when President Franklin Roosevelt appointed Wilgus director of the Emergency Relief Bureau for New York City, an agency charged with the awesome responsibility of alleviating the ravages of the Depression in the nation's largest metropolis. In his later years, he established a lucrative practice as a consulting engineer and eventually retired to his farm in Claremont, New Hampshire, where he died peacefully, at the age of eighty-three, in 1949. After Grand Central Terminal, Wilgus's most important work involved serving as a consulting engineer on construction of the Holland Tunnel, completed in 1927, which linked lower Manhattan to Jersey City.

In 1902, Wilgus had recently been promoted to the position of fifth vice president and placed in charge of all engineering for the New York Central. He knew that another remodeling of Grand Central Depot simply would not suffice.

The officials of the New York Central never considered relocating its

William J. Wilgus, chief engineer of the New York Central Railroad and the genius behind the plans for the new Grand Central

terminal facilities; they knew the superb advantages afforded by the 42nd Street location. At the turn of the century, as New York spread steadily up Manhattan Island, 42nd Street became the heart of Midtown. The Harlem Railroad's original choice of Fourth Avenue (Park Avenue) as its north-south route and the emergence of Fifth Avenue as the city's premier address channeled high-class residential and commercial development of the city toward the east side of the island. As the city expanded northward, Grand Central emerged as the transportation hub for fashionable Midtown: numerous streetcar lines converged at 42nd Street, and the IRT (Interborough Rapid Transit), the city's subway, built a major station underground adjacent to the terminal. Adding to the transportation mix, the Third Avenue elevated railway's spur above 42nd Street stopped at Grand Central's front door.

The depot covered three city blocks, but the prohibitively high price of the surrounding land kept the New York Central from acquiring additional property to expand the terminal horizontally. In a stroke of genius, Wilgus envisioned expanding not horizontally but vertically, and not up but down—building two terminals, one over the other. A two-

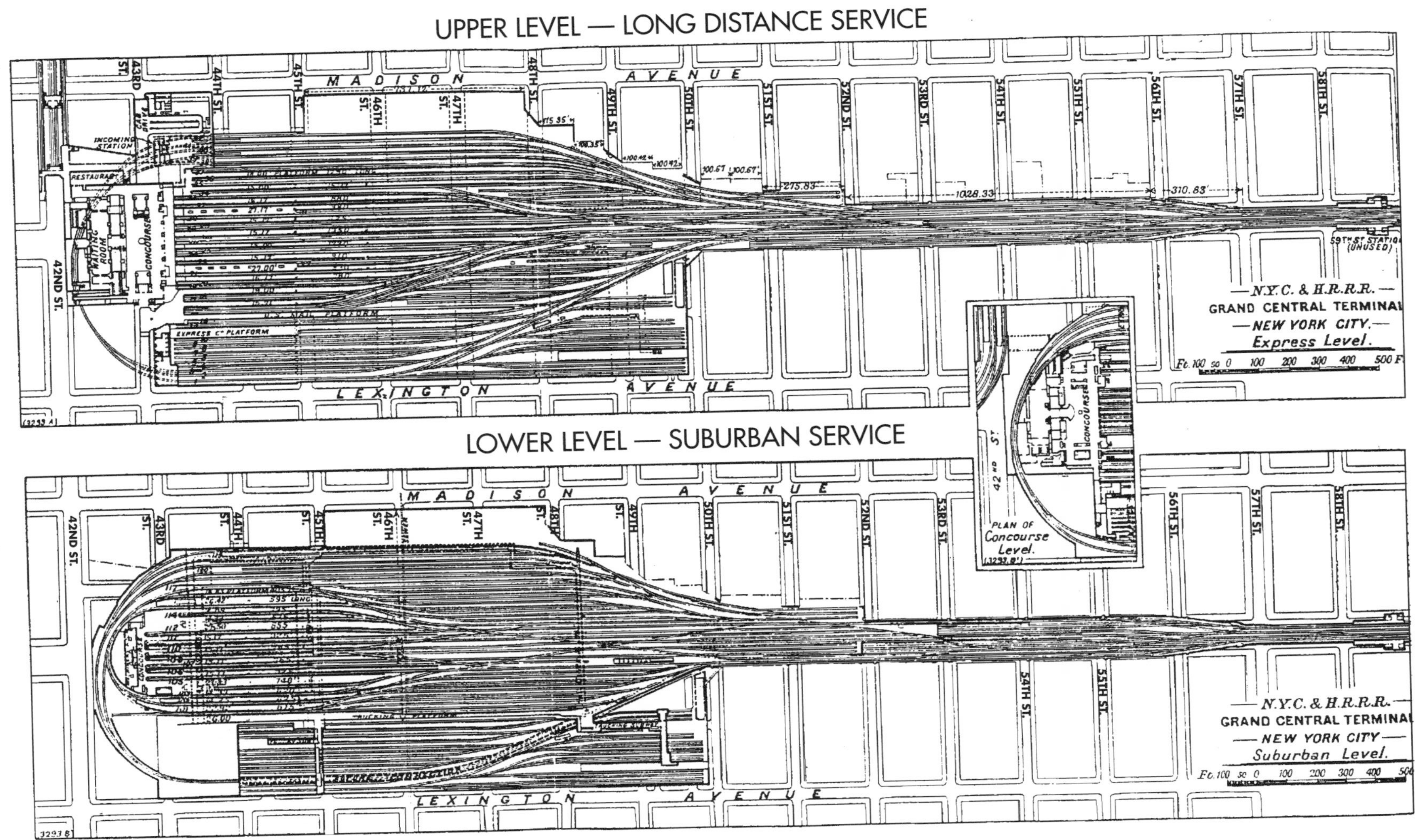

William Wilgus's plan for two-level underground terminal and train yard

story underground facility, with one set of tracks over the other, would provide vastly increased capacity to serve the ever-increasing volume of long-distance and commuter passengers.

Another obstacle remained: if the New York Central continued to use steam engines for motive power, then the problems associated with the Park Avenue tunnel—smoke, soot, and heat—remained. In addition, the legal mandate that resulted from the tunnel accident required the complete elimination of steam operations below the Harlem River by 1908. To Wilgus the solution demanded a change from steam to electric power. Switching to electric power would eliminate both the dangerous conditions in the Park Avenue tunnel and allow for the construction of an underground two-story train yard.

Wilgus, not a modest man, took full credit for the new Grand Central Terminal and the complex of buildings around 42nd Street, later hailed as "Terminal City," that resulted from this plan. In a lengthy article published in *Transactions,* the journal of the American Society of Civil Engineers, in 1940, he explained his "Concept of an Entirely New Terminal Utilizing Air Rights." He described how, dissatisfied with the other proposals for expansion, he had wondered if the best solution might not be to "tear down the old building and train shed and in their place, and in the yard on the north, create a double-level, under-surface terminal on which to superimpose office quarters and revenue producing structures made possible by the intended use of electric power."[2]

Wilgus touched on two key elements of the new Grand Central station. Without doubt, any solution would involve enormous costs. How would the railroad finance these enormously expensive improvements? Wilgus proposed to use the "air rights" above the new underground terminal to construct revenue-producing buildings with income sufficient to finance the changes. He stated somewhat dramatically: "Thus from the air would be taken wealth with which to finance obligatory vast changes otherwise nonproductive. Obviously it was the right thing to do."[3] In a letter to New York Central's president, William H. Newman, he proposed a fifteen-story office building over the 200,000 square feet of surface area then occupied by the old terminal building and train shed. Wilgus projected rental income of $1,350,000 a year, representing a 3.5 percent return on "all of the Grand Central Station terminal changes,

including those for depression of the tracks, yard improvements, etc.," including electrification.[4] Wilgus's ideas proved extremely attractive to Newman and the board of directors, who approved the vast undertaking with no dissenting voices.

A Multifunctional Plan

Wilgus followed his letter of December 22, 1902, to President Newman with another, in March of 1903, in which he laid out, in detail, all the component parts of the immensely complicated project. Remarkably, nearly one hundred years later, the Grand Central Terminal complex embodies almost all of the elements Wilgus proposed in 1903:

1. a double level, underground terminal with a loop track at the suburban (lower) level
2. an elevated driveway around the twelve-story building connecting Park Avenue north and south of the new terminal
3. the elevated driveway carried on an arch bridge over 42nd Street connecting with Park Avenue south to the street
4. north of the terminal from 45th to 48th streets, over the underground train yard, provision made for a "grand court or park" over the train yard and for future development of revenue producing buildings
5. a new hotel on Madison Avenue between 43rd and 44th streets to be "run on first class lines, similar to the Waldorf-Astoria"
6. a waiting room eighty feet in width extending across the entire station
7. the main concourse, sixty feet in width, with direct connections to Vanderbilt Avenue on the west and Depew Place on the east
8. from the concourse, ramps leading down to the long-haul train platforms
9. ramps from the concourse, along with stairs and elevators, to the lower concourse, where ramps would lead to the suburban train platforms
10. a direct connection with the IRT subway at the suburban level
11. north of the station between 45th and 48th streets, construction of a separate baggage facility connected to the tracks below by elevators and "endless belts"

12. changing from steam to electric power which would make possible "all of these improvements, which otherwise would be impracticable owing to smoke, cinders and gas"

13. separation of the suburban from the through service

Wilgus predicted that, with the improvements enumerated above, the railroad's commuter traffic to New York's northern suburbs would triple or even quadruple. He added that a new terminal of "monumental appearance" would have a positive impact on public opinion: "the entire project will probably make it the most attractive locality in New York and gain for us the approval of the general public and the municipal authorities."[5] After the disastrous train wreck in the Park Avenue tunnel, the Central certainly needed to generate favorable public opinion.

Busy railroad terminals, especially a major facility like Grand Central, bustled with activity: Trains arrived and departed, passengers hurried back and forth along the platforms, baggage moved to and from the trains, while suburban riders rushed to their jobs or appointments in the city. With the addition of mail and express service, railroad terminals constituted the busiest and most congested of buildings, filled with the energy of people traveling near and far.

Planning railroad facilities, especially a head terminal such as Grand Central, proved challenging and few designs succeeded. Early head terminals, including the first Grand Central, included a concourse running at a right angle to the platforms and tracks. The second La Salle Street Station in Chicago (1868–72), Park Square Station in Boston (1872–74), and the Central Railroad of New Jersey Station in Jersey City (1887–88) all shared the same basic head house design with its inherent limitations. Platforms simultaneously served incoming and departing trains, long-haul and commuter service, baggage and freight. Departing passengers intermingled with incoming passengers while railroad employees unloaded baggage, mail, and freight. Waiting areas and restaurants, located in the concourse at the end of the train platforms, only added to the congestion.

Wilgus's design brought order to the inherent chaos by separating activities. He planned the lower level of the two-story underground facility exclusively for commuter service and reserved the upper level

concourse for *departing* long-distance trains. For the heart of Grand Central Terminal he envisioned a central concourse providing an appropriate stage for New York Central's famous passenger trains, which had colorful names like the Twentieth Century Limited, the Empire State Express, and the Wolverine. Departing passengers, descending via ramps to a concourse, would purchase tickets and proceed to the gate to board their train. No dashing commuters or piles of baggage would interfere. Departing from Grand Central eventually evolved into a grand adventure, a lavish procession through New York's most magnificent public space.

Since the lower level served only suburban trains, the twice daily commuter rush hours no longer interfered with the railroad's more glamorous long-distance trains. With ramps connected directly to the city streets and to the IRT subway, commuters could complete their journey to work without crossing the concourse on the upper level. On the west side of the upper level, Wilgus set aside a number of platforms to serve all incoming, long-distance trains. Arriving passengers exited their trains and proceeded up ramps to a large reception area. At this "Incoming Station" they met friends and relatives or proceeded up a flight of stairs to an enclosed cab stand and street exit. Elevators provided direct access to the lobby of the Biltmore Hotel, built over the Incoming Station. Wilgus planned the Incoming Station, completely separate from the main concourse, for passengers arriving from upstate New York, the Midwest, and New England, on the long-distance trains of the New York Central and the New Haven railroads.

Wilgus devised an ingenious way to handle baggage. As part of the project the Central constructed a detached baggage facility between 43rd and 44th streets, reached by means of an elevated roadway. Taxis and freight wagons dropped off and picked up baggage far from the train platforms. Elevators moved the baggage to and from the train platforms, eliminating any need to cross the concourse. Spaced along the platforms, ten elevators served the outgoing trains and nine the incoming. Departing passengers proceeded to the platforms while their baggage descended from the baggage building to the trains waiting below. At the Incoming Station, baggage moved directly from the trains to the baggage building above. For arriving passengers staying at the Biltmore Hotel, baggage went by elevator directly to their rooms.

When Grand Central Terminal opened, the *Railway Age Gazette* pointed out that Wilgus's clever plan for baggage handling solved a problem other terminal designs failed to deal with effectively: "In this way all conflict in the handling of baggage is eliminated and interference with passengers is reduced to a minimum."[6] In 1964, as long-distance train travel continued the inexorable decline it began in the 1930s, the Pan American office building replaced the baggage building. However, the elevators remain part of the fabric of Grand Central. Commuters now use both the upper and lower levels and pass around the old baggage elevators as they hurry to and from their trains, without a thought to a time when long-distance train travel from Grand Central represented the height of luxury and sophistication.

Wilgus's plans included provisions for U.S. mail carriage and express freight service, two other important railroad functions. Along with the other major railroad systems, the New York Central carried mail under contract to the U.S. Post Office. When railroading first began, mail contracts provided the fledgling railroads with an important source of revenue and promoted an efficient and inexpensive mail service that knitted the country together. On the east side of the upper level of the new Grand Central, Wilgus reserved a number of tracks and platforms for mail and freight service. In 1907, the railroad built a new post office building on the corner of Lexington Avenue and 45th Street and leased the facility to the U.S. Post Office for $51,981 a year.[7] Elevators connected the post office with the platforms below, allowing arriving mail to move directly to the sorting room above.

In partnership with the American and Adams express companies, the Central provided freight service at 42nd Street. The express companies shipped high-value freight in the Central's long-distance trains and split the fees fifty-fifty with the railroad. As Grand Central Terminal neared completion, the railroad constructed a new building for Adams Express at Lexington Avenue and 48th Street, on the future site of the Waldorf-Astoria Hotel. For the American Express Company, the railroad built a new building on Lexington Avenue between 43rd and 44th streets adjacent to the post office. At both express facilities elevators moved freight from the train platforms below ground to the warehouses above.

Wilgus's plan provided for all of the different functions and services

needed at the 42nd Street terminal and succeeded beyond all expectations. Grand Central remains, to this day, the most complex of urban forms and stands as the centerpiece of a thriving transportation and commercial nexus in the heart of New York City. Almost one hundred years after Wilgus first described his bold ideas to the president of the New York Central Railroad, his innovative concept still functions superbly.

A Massive Construction Project

For many New Yorkers and people throughout the country, the image of Grand Central remains the building's world-famous facade on 42nd Street. Behind it stands the Grand Concourse, surrounded by stately columns rising to the vaulted ceiling over which the Milky Way is spread. Forgotten now are the less showy elements of the epic effort undertaken by the New York Central Railroad at the turn of the century; for the new Grand Central complex involved much more than just the famous terminal building on 42nd Street.

To begin, the vast two-story underground train yard, which stretched to 56th Street, required the excavation of more than three million cubic yards of dirt and rock. Plans to convert from steam to electric power necessitated the building of electric power generating plants and an elaborate distribution system through the areas to be electrified in Manhattan, the Bronx, and Westchester. Finally, a massive real estate development of the air rights over the railroad's property in midtown Manhattan followed the completion of the underground facilities and the switch to electric power. Such a complicated construction effort had never before been attempted in any American city.

To complete such a complicated construction effort required superb organizational skills. William Wilgus, in charge of all construction and electrification, divided the work into eight separate projects:

1. Grand Central Yard
   Excavation of the train yard, construction of the two-story underground terminal
2. Grand Central Station
   Construction of the new station building

3. Electrification
   Hudson Division—from Grand Central to Croton-on-Hudson
   Harlem Division—from Grand Central to North White Plains
   New Haven Railroad—supply electric power to New Haven from Woodbridge to Grand Central
4. Port Morris Branch Depression
   Lower tracks from Mott Haven to Port Morris in the Bronx
5. Marble Hill Cut-Off
   Build tunnels in Bronx under Marble Hill just over Harlem River to shorten and straighten tracks between Hudson River and Mott Haven
6. High Bridge, Morris Heights and Fordham Heights
   Eliminate grade crossings on Harlem Division between Mott Haven and Woodlawn in Bronx
7. Hudson Division
   Four tracking of line from Mott Haven to Croton-on-Hudson
8. Harlem Division
   Four tracking of line from Mott Haven to North White Plains.[8]

He appointed competent subordinates to manage each project, but retained overall control and responsibility. Since each part of the project affected all the others, Wilgus's brilliant leadership ensured overall coordination.

Construction began in the summer of 1903 and would continue until the summer of 1912. Yearly, Wilgus provided Newman and the board of directors with a detailed summary of progress on each of the eight separate projects, accompanied by updated cost estimates. Wilgus's first report, in 1904, estimated the total cost of all planned work at $40,746,350, an immense sum even given the wealth of the New York Central. To put the project in perspective, for the 1902–3 fiscal year, total revenue of the New York Central slightly exceeded $82 million. The New York Central faced the daunting challenges of managing the most complicated building project in New York's history and securing the staggering sums needed to fund it and run a profitable enterprise at the same time.

To complicate matters further, costs escalated almost from the first day work got under way in 1903. Just one year into the undertaking, the original estimate of $40.7 million rose to $59.9 million and in 1906 to

$71.8 million.[9] Wilgus struggled to justify the project's increased expenditures, which doubled in two short years. Despite the rapidly escalating costs, the railroad remained committed to building the largest railroad complex in the world and to accomplishing the task with style and grace, regardless of the ultimate expenditure.

This construction project illustrates the confidence that drove large businesses and the leading engineers and builders during the Age of Energy. In 1898, the entire outstanding indebtedness of the New York Central Railroad, second in size only to the Pennsylvania Railroad, totaled only $64 million. Three years later, the Central decided to proceed with the Grand Central project, at a cost equivalent to billions of dollars in today's terms. Faced with capital demands on this scale, a business proceeds only if it harbors superb faith in its own future. During the Age of Energy the transformation of American society succeeded because company after company, and the individuals who led them, exhibited unbounded faith in the future and in their own abilities.

Despite the criticism of the conspicuous consumption of the Gilded Age and the extravagance of the Fifth Avenue and Newport mansions, the fact remains that American business in the period after the Civil War created the largest industrial system in the world. Engineers and builders met any challenge, whether it involved a bridge across the East River or a canal across Panama. Grand Central Terminal serves as a conspicuous example of the imagination and daring that characterized a remarkable age. If the New York Central's executives had been timid, or even just more cautious, one of the great glories of New York might never have been created.

Excavation

One challenge dominated all others: to build a completely new terminal while not interrupting scheduled service at the 42nd Street terminal. Each day hundreds of trains arrived and departed and thousands of long-distance passengers as well as an army of commuters hurried through the terminal. How could the gigantic construction effort be carried out without disrupting an already crowded schedule? Throughout the nine long years it required to complete the project, the operating division, responsible for maintaining scheduled service, waged a constant struggle

with Wilgus and other railroad officials in charge of the new construction. To complicate matters further, throughout the entire construction period, passenger volume steadily increased.

Maps of the Grand Central area from 1898 illustrate the magnitude of the undertaking. The original Grand Central building and train shed stretched from 42nd to 45th streets between Depew Place and Vanderbilt Avenue. An open train yard reached to Madison Avenue on the west, while turntables and an engine house filled the yard to the east, next to the American and Adams express company warehouses along Lexington Avenue. Narrowing to four tracks at 49th Street, the rails ran in an open cut until entering the Park Avenue tunnel at 56th Street.

Wilgus devised a plan to manage the excavation and construction in stages by dividing the old terminal building, train shed, and train yard into a series of bites and having construction proceed one bite at a time. In each bite, work began by demolishing all structures within the bite and removing the existing railroad tracks. Once cleared, work crews excavated to a depth of between 50 and 60 feet. With excavation completed, construction began on the two-story underground structure. As soon as work crews completed the new platforms and tracks, the operating division assumed control and the excavation and construction workers moved on to the next bite.

Railway Age Gazette described the complicated nature of the construction process: "It has been possible to withdraw only a small section of area of the old terminal from service at any one time, and it has been necessary to complete work on a corresponding section and put it into service before another portion is disturbed. In this way the old terminal has been gradually replaced by the new until the last tracks in the old station were taken out of service on June 21, 1912."[10]

Wilgus mapped out a total of twelve longitudinal bites, starting with the east side of the train shed and yard along Depew Place. The schedule called for the completion of the first bite and release to the operating department by December of 1905. The final bites, on the west side, were to be completed between December of 1907 and January of 1908. Wilgus's ambitious schedule included dates for the start of concrete work and erection of the steel framework in each bite.

After receiving bids from thirteen companies and comparing them

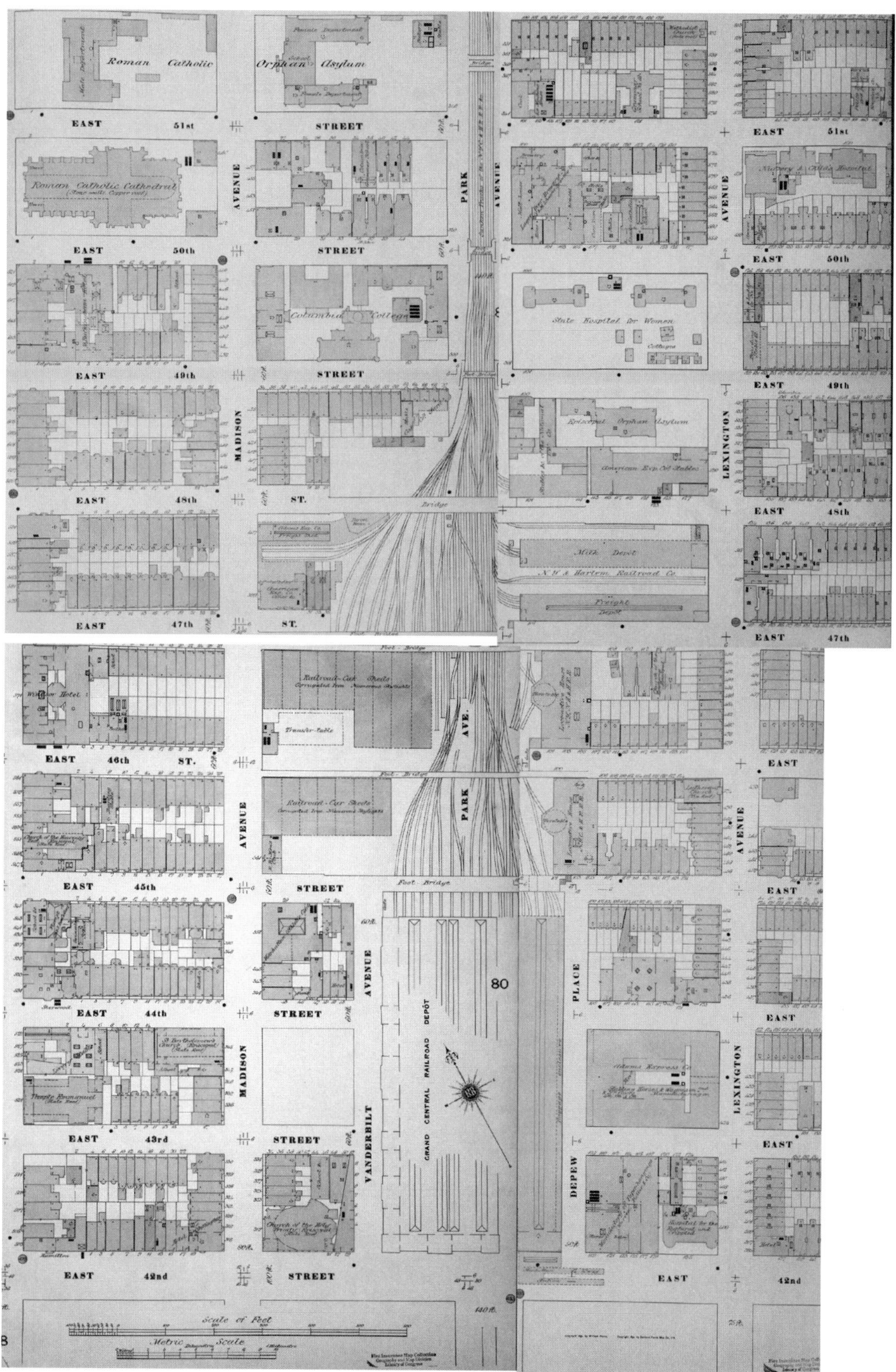

The area surrounding Grand Central Depot in 1890, before electrification and construction of the new terminal

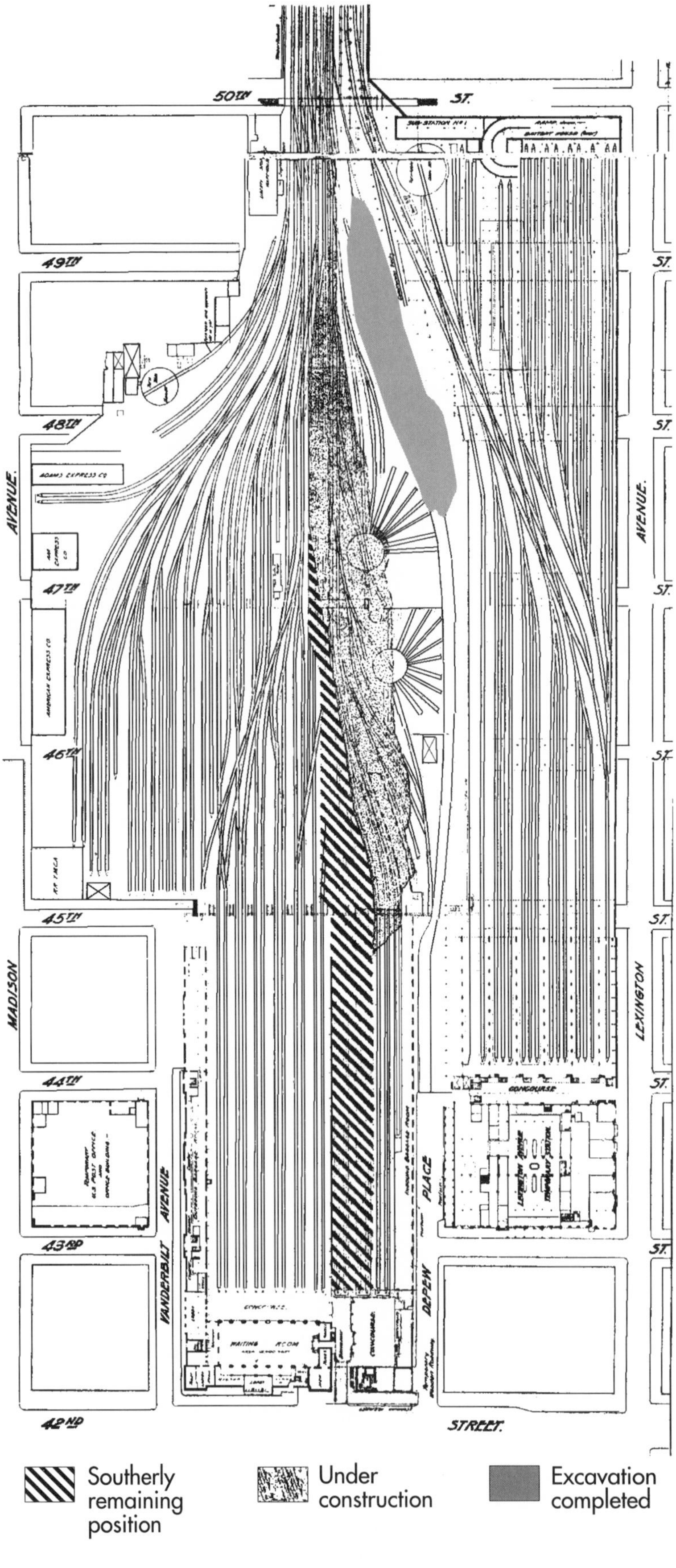

Wilgus's excavation plan for Bite no. 2

Southerly remaining position

Under construction

Excavation completed

carefully, the railroad signed a contract on August 7, 1903, with the O'Rourke Construction Company of New York for the excavation of the train yard. O'Rourke's contract specified the completion of all excavation work south of 57th Street for $8,555,000. Excavating more than 3,000,000 cubic yards of material required a great deal of blasting, since the hard Manhattan schist lay only a few feet below the surface.

O'Rourke's most difficult problem was how to haul away the tremendous amount of earth and rock they excavated without creating massive traffic jams in Midtown. In 1903, the horse-drawn wagons used on most construction sites had extremely limited capacity—three or four cubic yards filled a wagon. At that rate, the Grand Central excavation would generate more than one million wagonloads. O'Rourke and the railroad needed an alternative hauling system.

The Panama Canal, the most massive excavation project of the age, provided a model for a solution. When the French, led by the hero of the Suez Canal, Ferdinand de Lasseps, had tried to build a canal across the Isthmus of Panama, they had failed because they never devised an adequate system for removing the excavated material. When John Stevens arrived in Panama in 1905 to lead the American effort, he recognized the key to building the canal: organizing an efficient system for hauling away the tremendous amount of earth his steam shovels dug each day.[11] To do this, he built an elaborate railroad system. Steam shovels filled one railroad car after another, as they waited on tracks laid alongside the excavation site. Once the cars were filled, steam engines pulled them to dump sites, the largest of which formed the Pacific terminus of the canal at Colon. As the shovels dug deeper into the cuts, the railroad advanced with them. To keep the excavation going required careful scheduling, continuous relocation of tracks, and a never-ending supply of cars. Stevens' railroad system proved to be the crucial component of the American success in Panama.

The Panama Canal involved excavation on a scale that vastly exceeded the efforts at Grand Central, but Stevens and the engineers in Panama were working where nothing had been built before, the opposite of the problem confronting engineers at 42nd Street. At Grand Central, construction crews faced limited space, adjacent property owners, numerous surrounding buildings, and a tremendous amount of outside traffic. For example, on Park Avenue at 49th Street, the F. and M. Schaefer Brewery

Excavation along Park Avenue between 49th and 50th streets, looking north, 1906

filled an entire block. Because excavation would be proceeding right next to the brewery's foundation, the railroad erected costly shoring to reinforce the brewery walls. Despite these efforts, the brewery sued the railroad for substantial damages to their property caused, in their view, by the excavation for the underground train yard.

At Grand Central, Wilgus and his fellow engineers set up a railroad system to remove the earth and stone from the 42nd Street site in the exact same manner as in Panama. The Central provided the O'Rourke Construction Company with hopper cars. Once filled, the railroad cars carried the rock and earth through the Park Avenue Tunnel, out of the city, and dumped some of the rock and earth along the Hudson River north of New York City, to widen the right of way along the river bank. With the remaining material, the railroad created a giant landfill at Croton-on-Hudson, for a new train yard, where long-distance trains could switch from steam to electric engines for the run to Grand Central. As the O'Rourke steam shovels moved deeper into each bite, crews relocated the tracks to keep pace with the excavation.

Excavation of southern portion of Bite no. 2, 1907

Carting away the excavated material posed a major scheduling problem. In addition to the thousands of train movements needed each day to maintain scheduled passenger service, the operating department struggled to manage the trains moving back and forth to the dumping sites in Westchester County. Later, when construction began, trains also transported iron, steel, cement, and other construction materials to 42nd Street from the Central's storage yard at Mott Haven in the Bronx.

Scheduling difficulties notwithstanding, this imaginative use of the Central's existing rail network greatly facilitated both the excavation and the construction efforts. Subsequent large-scale construction projects in Manhattan have not had access to the rail system used so effectively for this massive building effort at the turn of the century. The congestion around major construction sites, so frustrating to generations of New Yorkers, serves as testimony to the efficiency of using a railroad solution for the most complex construction project in the city's history.

To oversee the excavation and construction phase of the project, Wilgus set up the Construction Committee, consisting of New York Central

engineers, including himself, and representatives from the O'Rourke Construction Company. The committee carefully monitored the progress of the excavation in hopes of maintaining Wilgus's tight schedule; any delay jeopardized meeting the city's deadline for eliminating all steam operations in Manhattan. As importantly, delays cost the railroad money.

When the O'Rourke Construction Company began work at 42nd Street, the *New York Times* reported that the company planned to complete the entire excavation in just two and a half years and to employ 3,000 men in the effort. Confidently, John O'Rourke, president of O'Rourke Construction Company, told a reporter from the *New York Daily Tribune* that he foresaw "no danger of the work being delayed." When pressed about the contract deadline, O'Rourke added, "I'll beat the life out of it."[12]

To begin, more than two hundred buildings awaited demolition before any excavation could start in Bite 1, including eighty-six buildings between 45th Street and 50th Street along Lexington Avenue. On the block bounded by 44th and 45th streets from Depew Place to Lexington Avenue stood twenty-five buildings, including a large storage warehouse on 44th Street. Eight five-story apartment buildings lined Lexington Avenue, and a number of two- and three-story residential buildings would have to be removed from 45th Street. In 1900, 875 people lived on the block between 44th and 45th streets, but they had to move as the railroad acquired the property and began demolition.

From the very start of excavation work, O'Rourke simply could not keep up with the schedule. At the beginning of 1905, the company informed the Construction Committee that the deadline for completion of the excavation of Bite 1, July 1, 1906, could not possibly be met.[13] At meeting after meeting, O'Rourke's representatives blamed the operating division for refusing to release tracks in a timely fashion to enable excavation to proceed on schedule.

Problems with the schedule continued into the following year. At one meeting O'Rourke promised to add Sunday shifts. However, the following month, the railroad again complained about the slow pace of excavation and pointed to the "lack of sufficient forces" on the Sunday shift. O'Rourke admitted that the company had failed in efforts to recruit a Sunday labor force. They had attempted to hire seventy carpenters

N. Y. C. & H. R. R. R.
Leased and Operated Lines
GRAND CENTRAL YARD IMPROVEMENTS:
New York City:
East 44th St. to East 45th St.
Buildings To Be Demolished
1905

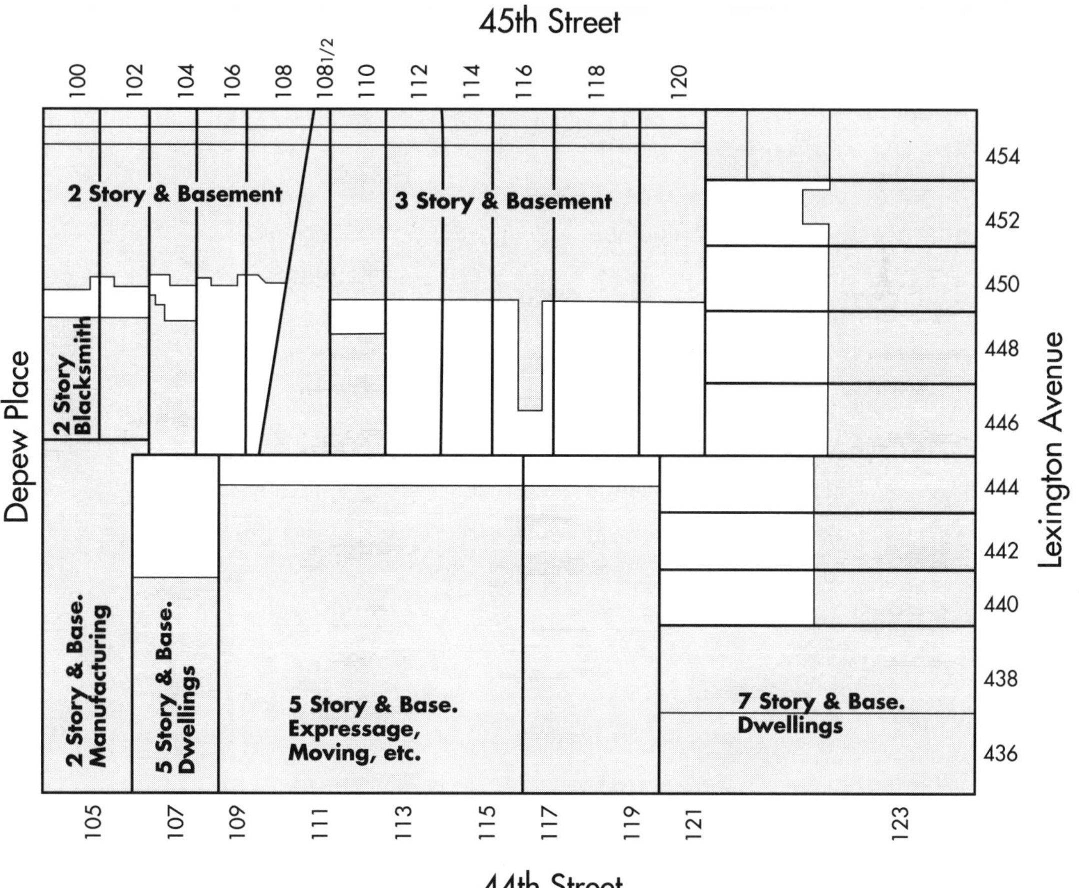

Buildings to be demolished

Area cleared

Scale: 1 inch = 50 feet

A demolition plan from William J. Wilgus's papers

Excavation of southern portion of Bite no. 2, from Depew Place looking south with the old Grand Central Depot on the right

and five hundred laborers to work on Sunday, but on the most recent Sunday only twenty-four carpenters and one hundred ninety laborers had reported for work. Wilgus countered that the problem resulted from O'Rourke's pay scale and insisted that the O'Rourke Company "pay the market price for such labor."[14] A standoff continued; the railroad demanded that O'Rourke meet the schedule spelled out in their contract, even if it required paying higher wages. On the other hand, O'Rourke wanted to keep costs as low as possible to ensure handsome profits.

Charles Knowlton, one of the New York Central engineers, reported that, in one eleven-day period, the excavation rate dropped from 9,000 cubic yards every six days to only 6,000 cubic yards in eleven days.[15] At the rate of 545 cubic yards a day, Knowlton calculated, the excavation would require 5,504 days to complete. Clearly, the Central found the pace of excavation unacceptable. O'Rourke countered that the railroad,

Excavation for the underground train yard, looking west toward St. Patrick's Cathedral, 1908

late in the delivery of plans, continually failed to provide the one hundred railroad cars needed each day to haul away excavated material.

Finally, in May of 1907, the board of directors reached the limits of its patience and decided to cancel O'Rourke's contract and complete the excavation with its own work force. Wilgus agreed but reminded the board that the O'Rourke Company still had outstanding invoices to the Central totaling $1,220,000 and that, in his judgment, the Central owed O'Rourke at least $664,624 for work completed. To settle matters as quickly as possible, the board ordered the contract canceled and negotiated a final payment to O'Rourke of $750,000.[16]

Wilgus, writing privately in December of 1906 to W. C. Brown, a senior vice president of the New York Central, admitted that some of the responsibility for the delays did in fact rest with the railroad, and he identified the railroad's operating division as the culprit in the process. Wilgus

pointed to the reluctance of the operating division to relinquish any space for the new construction: "my experience in the past two years has shown the hesitancy of those charged with the responsibility of operating the terminal of giving up any space that is turned over to them." Referring to his original timetable for the first three bites and the ever-growing volume of passenger service using Grand Central, Wilgus warned that all construction might grind to halt: "If the constantly growing traffic of the company demands the entire use of three bites . . . we will be facing not only a practical cessation of the work enlarging the terminal or at least lengthening of the time of construction."[17] The problem seemed to be intractable, yet throughout the decade-long construction, the volume of passenger traffic increased steadily while construction continued.

The Underground Train Yard

Construction of the underground platforms and tracks followed as soon as excavation allowed. Because each bite constituted a small part of the planned underground train yard, construction in one bite added only a portion of the underground facility. Work in each bite involved multiple stages: excavation; building foundations; erecting the steel frame to support the two levels of the train yard and the streets above; pouring the concrete floor, walls, and ceiling; building platforms; installing all necessary utilities; laying tracks and third rails (which carried the electrical current); and finally installing switches and signaling systems. With the next bite, the construction crews repeated the process all over again. Each bite constituted an independent construction project; only at the very end of the long and complicated effort would the separate bites be joined to complete the underground complex. This sectional construction allowed parts of the new underground facility to open as soon as work crews finished laying tracks and signals. At the same time, excavation and construction in the next bite proceeded at a fevered pace.

No model for this kind of engineering challenge existed. *Engineering News* described the complexity: "numerous complications and variations arise. . . . this resulted in very heavy concentrated loads. . . . it required many columns to be supported on girders, since the columns in the suburban story had to be located between the suburban tracks, while those in

Construction of upper and lower tracks and platforms in the underground train yard, looking south from 48th Street, 1911

the express story had to be set between express tracks, the track layouts of the two yards being quite different. . . . remarkably heavy girder construction results."[18] The design of the underground train yard consisted of a giant concrete and steel box with the city streets carried overhead, from east to west, by viaducts. Complete roofing over of the upper level did not occur until the development of the air rights over the terminal north of 44th Street after the new Grand Central opened in 1913.

One of the unprecedented engineering tasks was designing two completely different track layouts on the upper and lower levels, with tracks and platforms on the upper level not directly over those on the lower level. Supporting columns on the lower level needed sufficient strength to carry not only the weight of the concrete floor and platforms above, but also the tremendous weight of trains moving through the upper level and stopping alongside the passenger platforms. The columns on the lower level would need to carry loads of 3,000,000 foot-pounds and in

some cases more than 7,000,000 foot-pounds, while on the upper level columns would carry both the cross streets and eventually the air rights buildings above. The design of the upper level formed a massive railroad bridge, its steel girders in many places being seven feet in depth and in some places ten feet, calling for the most sophisticated engineering available. A two-story station designed to have trains arriving and departing on one level with a second set of trains arriving and departing on another, never attempted before, challenged all of the skills of the engineers and builders involved.

The generations of long-distance travelers in the past and the commuters who pass through the terminal today hardly give a second thought to the complexity of the massive structure. Platform lighting in the underground train yard casts shadows over the supporting structures, and concrete covers the massive steel columns and cross girders. Beyond the platforms, the train yard looms as a dark, mysterious cavern through which trains glide, the structure hidden from view. An absence of any

Construction of 48th Street viaduct over upper and lower tracks in Bite no. 2, 1908

clear view of the massive steel frame masks the innovative engineering employed at Grand Central. By contrast, the engineering of the Brooklyn Bridge, visible for all to see, contributes to an appreciation of the bridge as an engineering marvel as well as an aesthetic achievement of American building. Truly a triumph of engineering, the underground train yard remains overshadowed by the famous palatial building on 42nd Street and its world-famous Grand Concourse. With the possible exception of Roebling's work on the Brooklyn Bridge, the engineers of the Age of Energy toiled in relative obscurity. McKim, Mead and White, Richard Morris Hunt, Carrère and Hastings, Cass Gilbert, and other gifted architects of the era remain celebrated, while engineers like William Wilgus, who engineered and supervised the construction of the magnificent structures the architects designed, receive far less attention. Certainly as much as the architects of the age, they deserve attention for creating these great achievements in American building art.

Loop Tracks

As construction of Grand Central moved forward, planning turned to the loop tracks, an integral part of Wilgus's original concept. Loop tracks solved one of the most vexing design problems head terminals such as Grand Central faced. In all head terminals, arriving trains stopped and discharged passengers. Train crews then backed the train away from the platform, separated the engine from the passenger cars, turned the engine around, and reorganized cars and engines to make up departing trains. All of this activity necessitated a significant number of train movements, and the flying switch would be far too dangerous in an underground train yard. Wilgus's plan for loop tracks eliminated these problems. Arriving trains would stop briefly at the Incoming Station to discharge passengers and then proceed around the loop to the other side of the train yard for servicing and preparations for departure. By pointing the engine in the right direction for departure, the loop tracks eliminated numerous switching and shunting movements.

Loop tracks required a substantial radius, and at Grand Central the needed space extended beyond the perimeter of the new terminal building on both the upper and lower levels. On the west side, the loops

Construction of loop tracks at corner of 42nd Street and Lexington Avenue, 1912

extended under Vanderbilt Avenue to the next block west, while on the east side the loops reached to Lexington Avenue.

A major obstacle stood in the way. To the east, the New York Central did not own the property at 42nd Street and Lexington Avenue. On the corner stood the Hospital for the Ruptured and Crippled; a row of commercial buildings that included the Warner Fuller Wall Paper Company and Brandess Brothers grocery filled the rest of the block. To complete the loop tracks, the railroad needed to purchase the entire block from 42nd to 43rd streets between Lexington Avenue and Depew Place. Not until construction of the terminal building neared completion in 1910 did the railroad finally obtain the property, purchasing it for $1,350,000.[19] Whitney Warren, at that time chief architect of the terminal, opposed the loop tracks, and his opposition delayed construction of the loop tracks considerably.[20] Despite Warren's opposition, the operating and engineering departments, who clearly saw the advantages of the loop tracks,

mounted a campaign to include the loop tracks, and ultimately their arguments prevailed. Work on the loop tracks began in January of 1913.

When Grand Central opened, the *New York Times* predicted that the new terminal, with its loop tracks on both the upper and lower levels, would "permit the passing through its gateway of 100,000,000 persons every year." The editors rhetorically asked what accommodations would be necessary when volume exceeded even that figure: "When the traffic exceeded that who knows? It has been suggested that by that time the growth of New York and the swelling of the tide of traffic will force the station to some new position beyond the Harlem River."[21] The number of passengers never approached 100,000,000 people a year; traffic peaked in 1947, when 65,000,000 passengers passed through the terminal. Long-distance passenger traffic soon declined dramatically, as airline and automobile travel, heavily subsidized by the federal government, lured long-distance travelers from the nation's trains. Even before the advent of the airline and automobile age, Grand Central's capacity went underutilized; but at the turn of the century, the future for the railroads appeared limitless and a facility as large as Grand Central seemed more than justified.

Technology at Grand Central: The Advent of the Electric Age

While excavation and construction of the underground train yard moved forward, Wilgus turned his attention to the task of electrifying the railroad's operations in Manhattan, the Bronx, and Westchester. Electric technology made the entire Grand Central project possible. Wilgus premised his plan on the successful switch from steam to electric power—a leap into the unknown. Until then, no American railroad had electrified its main line service for any considerable distance.

Eliminating the steam locomotive provided the key to solving the interrelated problems faced at the 42nd Street facility. Switching to electric power allowed for the radical new terminal design and the resulting dramatic increase in capacity. Eventually, the new underground train yard covered a total of seventy-nine acres on the two levels, more than three times the area of the old facility. In the Commodore's train shed, even with the addition of an annex built along Depew Place, only nineteen tracks ran next to passenger platforms. By comparison, the new two-

story underground facility included seventeen platform tracks on the suburban level and thirty-three on the upper level, an increase in capacity of more than 150 percent. Electricity also solved the pollution problem in the Park Avenue tunnel and allowed the railroad to develop its "air rights" in Midtown, eventually creating Terminal City. The *New York Times* noted electricity's crucial role in the new station's design: "Here we reach the keynote of the whole great project, for without electrically hauled trains the improvement could not have been developed along the proud and original lines that mark it."[22] Grand Central represents not just a triumph of American building art, but also a triumph of technology.

Wilgus proceeded in his usual systematic manner. First he established the Electric Traction Commission, separate from the Construction Committee, to oversee all aspects of the planning and installation of the electric system. He suggested to company president Newman that the commission include Wilgus, George Gibbs, who was another New York Central engineer, and two outside consultants, Bion Arnold and Frank Sprague, well-known figures in railroad electrification in America. Sprague's fame rested on the successful completion of the country's first electric street railway in Richmond, Virginia. Wilgus proposed yearly consulting fees of between $7,500 and $10,000 for both Sprague and Arnold. Newman quickly endorsed the idea.

For its initial agenda, the Electric Traction Commission carefully considered a number of crucial questions: the geographical size of the "electric zone," the type of current to use (direct versus alternating), whether to transmit the current via overhead wires or to use a third rail, and the number of power plants to build.[23] The work of the Electric Traction Commission reflected the professional thoroughness with which planning of the Grand Central effort proceeded. Wilgus and the railroad left little to chance. With the leading experts in the field as consultants, the commission carefully reviewed the latest electrical research, worked out the design and specifications for all the new equipment, selected the manufacturers to build the new engines and other equipment, set up an exhaustive testing program, and carefully monitored all installations within the electric zone. When the first electric engines entered service in 1907, the New York Central anticipated no major problems. This confidence rested in no small measure on the work of the Electric Trac-

tion Commission, whose deliberations serve as a testament to careful, rigorous technological innovation.

Electric Power Needs

As the Electric Traction Commission considered the myriad questions entailed in the conversion from steam to electric traction, a spirited discussion of the comparative advantages of electric versus steam power arose among professional railroad engineers. John Droege, a noted railroad professional, succinctly set out the advantages and disadvantages of electric service for any railroad contemplating switching to electric.

> The benefits of electric operation as compared with steam, or claimed by the electrical engineers and other supporters of electrification, may be divided into four classes: (1) freedom from smoke; (2) greater engine efficiency; (3) elimination of coaling, watering etc.; (4) reduced operating costs.
>
> The disadvantages claimed by opponents of electrification may be divided into four groups: (1) the heavy capital outlay required; (2) the additional danger due to high voltage lines; (3) additional opportunities for delay to trains; (4) higher operating costs.[24]

Bion Arnold, one of Wilgus's consultants, published an article in the *Railroad Gazette* in 1902, in which he examined the advantages of electric power based on his research conducted for the Electric Traction Commission. Arnold set out to determine the number of kilowatts needed to power the 600 train movements at Grand Central on an average day. He used a dynamometer car attached behind a steam engine to measure the drawbar pull that steam engines exerted when accelerating from a dead stop to normal running speed. He measured the drawbar pull for different sizes of trains and computed the average drawbar pull for each class of service (determined by factors like number of cars, weight). Arnold then converted the drawbar pull to horsepower and calculated the number of kilowatts per hour necessary to supply the needed horsepower. He estimated the electric generation capacity needed at 1,800 kilowatts per hour, if all trains to and from Grand Central ran on electric power. In a typical year, he projected, total electric consumption would

be 15,768,000 kilowatt hours for 205,285,710 ton-miles of service, an average of 63 watts per ton-mile.[25] A ton-mile served as the standard measure by which the railroads calculated the cost of transporting passengers or freight.

At this point, the disadvantages of electric traction that Droege had pointed out became apparent. To build a power plant capable of generating a minimum of 1,800 kilowatts required a very substantial investment, and the cost of a transmission system would need to be added to it. Arnold, Wilgus, and the other engineers realized that electric traction for heavy railroad service would require a substantial initial capital investment. Electric street railways, which the newspaper editorialists pointed to as models for solving the Central's problems, provided no real comparisons. Ton-miles for an electric powered streetcar system paled next to the requirements for hauling heavy, long-distance trains. A typical train weighed in excess of 800 tons; even a string of streetcars fully loaded, weighed far less and demanded much less power. Sprague's electric engines for the Richmond street railway developed 15 horsepower; Arnold estimated that the new electric engines for use at Grand Central would require 2,500 horsepower. The system would demand power on a scale far exceeding that of any street railway in the country.

Even with the large initial capital investment, Arnold estimated the overall long-term cost of electric operations to be about the same as steam service. Steam engines required much more maintenance; when an engine had completed a scheduled run, a railroad pulled it out of service to add water and fuel and to remove ashes. In addition, steam acted as a powerful corrosive agent, and engines periodically needed major overhauls to clean boilers and keep their complicated machinery in working order. Electric engines, much simpler in design with far fewer parts, operated for longer periods between scheduled maintenance.

Arnold's research compared steam and electric operating costs on a locomotive mile basis; his calculations showed that operating costs for steam engines averaged 23.05 cents per mile versus only 15.8 cents for the electric engine. However, fixed charges for the electric engines, to cover the initial investment for generating plants and transmission lines, stood at 7.8 cents a mile versus 1.1 cents for steam locomotives. Arnold estimated total costs for the new electric engines at 23.6 cents a mile, only slightly

Turbine room in the Port Morris power plant, serving the electric zone, using equipment manufactured by the General Electric Company, 1906

lower than for steam, 24.2 cents a mile. He concluded that the "savings in operational expenses by the electric system would be sufficient to offset the increased charges due to the additional investment made necessary by its adoption."[26]

In the final analysis, the Central's decision to convert to electric traction did not rest solely on a cost-benefit basis but on a legal one. New York City and State, backed by strong public opinion, had demanded the elimination of steam at Grand Central and especially in the Park Avenue tunnel. Though pressured to switch, Wilgus and the Electric Traction Commission remained confident that operating savings would offset the initial capital costs, once the new the electric equipment replaced the railroad's steam operations in the New York metropolitan region. In addition, the railroad planned to supply electricity from its generating plant at 49th Street and Park Avenue to the new buildings constructed over the underground train yard.

The Electric Zone

A key issue the Electric Traction Commission considered at its early meetings in 1903 was how far north from Manhattan to extend the new electric service. The legislation passed by the city and state required eliminating steam power only from Manhattan Island. Early discussions focused on switching from steam to electric engines at Mott Haven just over the Harlem River in the Bronx. In a farsighted move, Wilgus pressed to extend the electric zone farther north, through the Bronx and into Westchester County.

Wilgus proposed electric service as far as Croton-on-Hudson, thirty-three miles from Grand Central, on the Hudson Division and to North White Plains, twenty-three miles to the north, on the Harlem Division. The topography of the New York Central's rights of way in the Bronx and Westchester County, having no severe grade changes, posed no special difficulty for electric engines. In addition, switching from steam to electric engines at two separate locations, one each for the Hudson and Harlem divisions, rather than only at Mott Haven in the Bronx, promised considerable time savings.

Wilgus's most persuasive argument involved the railroad's commuter service to the growing suburbs north of New York. By the turn of the century, the Central was generating substantial revenue by providing daily service for people living outside of the urban core who commuted back and forth each day to work. In 1904, Wilgus reported to board member William K. Vanderbilt that in 1899 the Harlem and Hudson divisions had carried 4,146,239 suburban passengers and that in 1903 suburban volume had grown to 6,239,399 passengers, an increase of more than 50 percent in four years.[27]

Steam-powered locomotives had proved ill-suited for short-haul commuter service, which made frequent stops covering short distances between stations. Slow to accelerate, steam engines took a considerable amount of time to reach running speed. The stop-and-go service of a commuter train required an engine capable of reaching full speed rapidly and then, a short distance later, stopping quickly. Wilgus, confident that the new electric equipment would meet these requirements perfectly, predicted a significant increase in the railroad's commuter business.

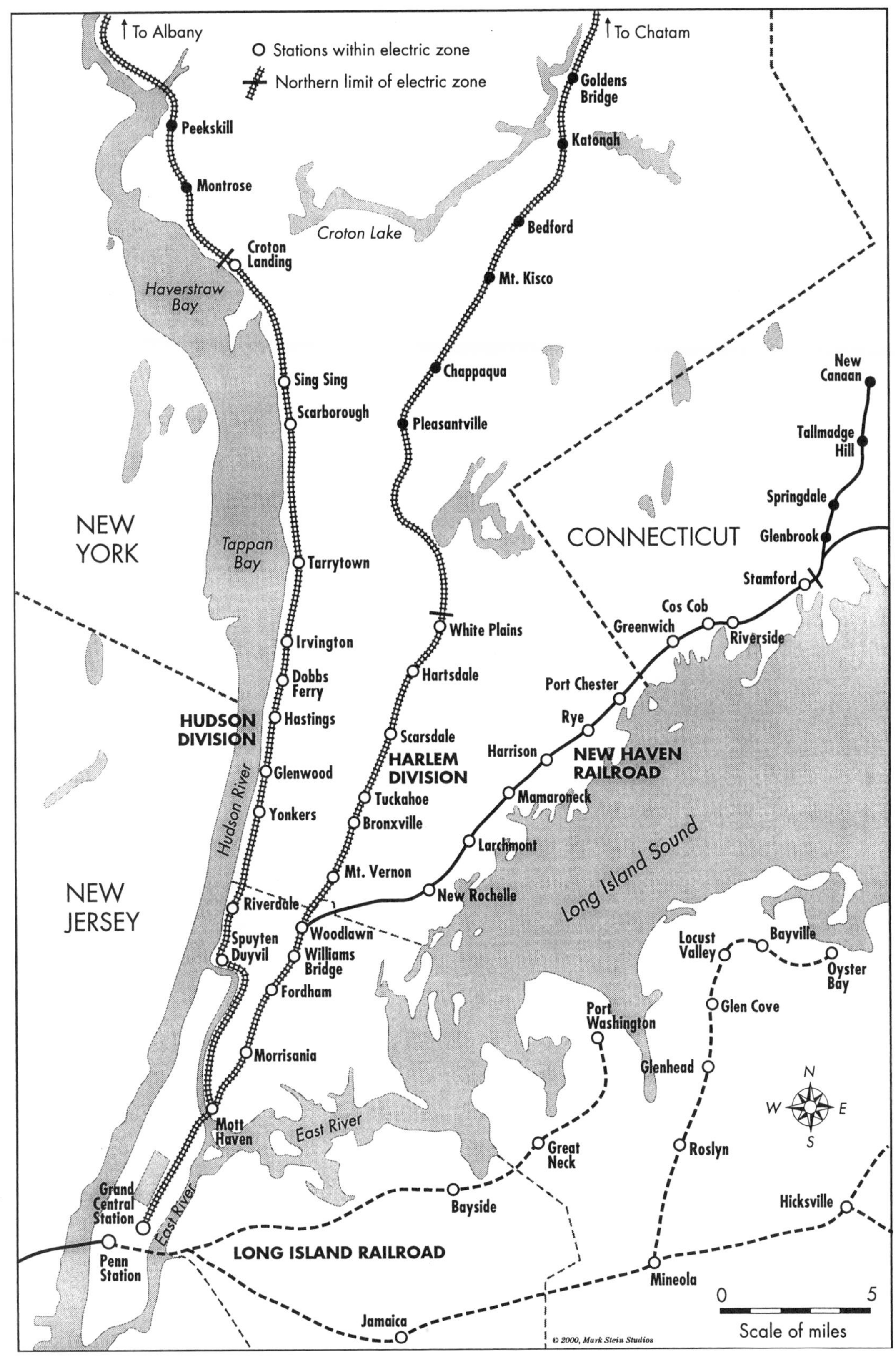

The electric zone, encompassing the Harlem and Hudson divisions of the New York Central Railroad and the New Haven Railroad

At first, the Electric Traction Commission resisted the idea of expanding the electric zone. In late October of 1903, the plan for an expanded electric zone passed by a vote of only three to two, with Wilgus casting the deciding ballot. However, at a meeting in November, after a very persuasive presentation by Wilgus, the commission voted unanimously to recommend extending the electric power system through the Bronx and into Westchester County.

Direct versus Alternating Current

A second decision to be made by the Electric Traction Commission was the choice between direct and alternating current; this debate, over the most suitable type of current, involved not just the engineering profession. The sometimes-public "battle of the currents" also engaged two emerging corporate giants, each fighting to dominate the electricity business. Westinghouse Electric, led by the domineering George Westinghouse, already world renowned for developing his Westinghouse airbrake for the railroads, emerged as the leading corporate proponent of alternating current. General Electric Company, more experienced with direct current applications for transportation, pushed for its adoption.

While the Electric Traction Commission prudently considered both types of power, from the beginning they leaned toward direct current. Edison's first electric generating plant on Pearl Street in lower Manhattan, Sprague's first electric street railway in Richmond, the IRT subway, and the first electric elevators in New York's skyscrapers all used direct current. In February of 1902, Sprague submitted a detailed feasibility study for the Central's electrification in which he carefully reviewed all uses of electric traction by railroads to date. He listed fourteen examples of direct current installations, including the Central London Underground, the Orleans Railway running from the Gare d'Austerlitz to the new Gare D'Orsay in Paris, the elevated railways in Chicago, and the Baltimore and Ohio tunnel (through which a small electric engine pulled steam-powered trains). Sprague included three alternating current railways; all were small rail lines in Switzerland. With more direct current systems already in place, he said, he could legitimately "confine my recommendations to the Direct Current Motor System which has demonstrated its ability to fully meet the conditions imposed by your service as far as

motive power is concerned."[28] Despite Sprague's careful analysis, the "battle over the currents" for the Grand Central electrification intensified and soon reached a very public stage.

Bion Arnold, the Central's other outside expert on the Electric Traction Commission, also favored direct current for the Central's purposes, however, he believed alternating current to be more suitable for long-haul service, because of the efficiency associated with the transmission of alternating current over long distances. On the other hand, given the demands of suburban commuter service, he favored direct current for the Grand Central electrification: "I believe that the alternating current railroad motor will yet prove to be most efficient for long distance railways . . . however, it has not demonstrated its ability to start under load as efficiently or to accelerate a train as rapidly as the direct current motor."[29] With two of the five members of the commission leading proponents of direct current, without surprise, the commission officially recommended direct current.

Westinghouse Electric and George Westinghouse, bitterly disappointed, continued to argue in public for alternating current and strongly criticized the Central's decision in favor of direct current. In December of 1905, Westinghouse wrote an open letter to President Newman of the New York Central in the *Railroad Gazette*, bluntly recommending, "Change your plans providing for the use of the continuous current, third-rail equipment, to those employing the alternating current, single-phase, overhead system." Westinghouse claimed the installation cost of alternating current, with an overhead distribution system, to be $15,350 per mile, substantially less than the cost per mile for a direct current system. Westinghouse followed up his letter to Newman with an open letter attacking Frank Sprague suggesting that the real reason behind the Central's decision to use direct current was the General Electric Company. Despite Sprague's international reputation as a giant in electrical engineering and electric traction, Westinghouse accused Sprague of a conflict of interest. The alleged conflict arose because the General Electric Company used Sprague's multiple control system in its electric engines; G.E. had acquired the rights to Sprague's patents when it absorbed the Sprague General Electric Company in 1903. Sprague, according to Westinghouse, stood to gain financially and had used his position to influence the Central to select General Electric's direct current equipment.

Sprague answered immediately with an open letter of his own. He expressed outrage at Westinghouse's charge: "This contract, under present conditions, confers upon the officials of the General Electric Company no authority whatsoever, so far as I am concerned, and no man knows better than yourself that I would brook no interference by individual or corporation with my professional opinion."[30] Sprague then listed the "facts" presented in Westinghouse's open letter to Newman and challenged each. Sprague reminded Westinghouse that his inventions had served as stepping stones to Westinghouse's own fortune and ended the letter by reiterating his commitment to the highest standards of the engineering profession: "My engineering convictions and conclusions are my own. They are dictated by no man or corporation."[31] Like Wilgus, he considered himself, above all else, a professional engineer dedicated to the highest scientific standards. In Sprague's view, all his work, and that of the other professionals serving on the Electric Traction Commission, rested on sound scientific evidence and careful deliberation. Westinghouse's public attacks on Sprague and, by inference, on the Electric Traction Commission accomplished little; the Central continued its plan to use direct current in the electric zone.

In addition to advocating alternating current motors, Westinghouse argued for the use of overhead transmission lines to distribute electric power. Developed for the country's street railways, overhead transmission equipment formed an important part of Westinghouse's business. Wilgus and the Electric Traction Commission decided on a third rail distribution system, in which each engine was equipped with contact shoes extending from the side of the engine's frame to draw electric power from the third rail. The IRT subway adopted a third rail system, which proved to be quite successful.

Westinghouse charged that a third rail system, expensive to build, posed a hazard to railway workers, especially in crowded railway yards. In addition, heavy snow could potentially disrupt a third rail system; by contrast an overhead wire transmission system remained immune to the effects of the weather.

Wilgus countered by pointing to European rail systems' successes with third rails. As part of the Paris Exposition of 1900, the Paris and Orleans Railroad constructed a two-mile extension, in a tunnel along the left

bank of the Seine, from the Gare d'Austerlitz to a new station near the exposition site. Service on the Quai d'Orsay extension employed direct current transmitted via a third rail. Completed in 1900, the Gare d'Orsay represented an important development in the evolution of electric railway traction because of the use of the third rail. The new Paris station revolutionized rail terminal design. With electric power, trains arrived, one story below ground level, directly into the main concourse of the station. In addition the use of a third rail proved hardly noticeable; overhead wires would have been much more intrusive.

Wilgus carefully considered the problems and hazards a third rail transmission system entailed and, with the ever-inventive Frank Sprague, designed a solution. In 1905, Wilgus and Sprague patented a third rail electric transmission system with the rail enclosed on three sides by a wooden cover. Wilgus and Sprague's patented cover protected the electrified third rail from the top and the two sides; only the bottom of the third rail remained exposed. Shoes, extending from the sides of the new electric engines, remained in contact with the underside of the rail by means of upward pressure exerted by springs. With the third rail covered on top and both sides, a railway worker could not accidentally touch the

Electric engines manufactured by General Electric in Schenectady, N.Y., for the Paris-Orleans Railway

An early electrified station, Gare d'Orsay (now Museum d'Orsay) in Paris, 1902

third rail, unless he made contact with the exposed bottom of the rail. With this simple, elegant technical solution, Wilgus and Sprague eliminated the objection that a third rail distribution system posed a danger to railroad workers. In addition, the cover protected the third rail from rain and snow, no small consideration given the often heavy winter snows.

To avoid the appearance of a conflict of interest in their patent, Wilgus and Sprague refused royalties from the New York Central for its use of their third rail system in the railroad's electric zone. Nevertheless, they actively pursued licensing their design to other railroads switching from steam to electric power.

The New Electric Engines

By May of 1903, the Electric Traction Commission had completed detailed specifications for the new electric engines, and they invited ten firms to submit bids, including only two American companies, General Electric and Westinghouse Electric. The remaining eight companies, all

European, reflected the more extensive development of electric traction in Europe at the time. Specifications required the new electric engines to be capable of completing a round trip from Grand Central to Harmon, New York, a distance of thirty-four miles each way, in one hour with a 550-ton train in tow.

After considering all bids, in November of 1903 the commission recommended to the board of directors that the railroad accept the proposal presented by the General Electric Company. Winning the contract represented an important victory over G.E.'s archrival, the Westinghouse Electric Company. G.E. believed electric power to be the wave of the future for the railroads and put its reputation on the line to build the new engines within the allotted time frame and to meet all specifications.

The New York Central drove a hard bargain. Wilgus had informed the General Electric Company that the railroad judged its initial price unacceptable: "We do not believe the prices named in your original proposal are entirely satisfactory to us and therefore we make to you the proposition that your company furnish us the electric locomotives as follows: thirty engines at $30,526.31 each, for a total contract cost of $915,789.30." He further stipulated, "This proposal is also conditioned upon the manufacture by the G.E. Co. of the first locomotive within a short period of time, say eight (8) months, and the thorough testing of said locomotive under the actual severe conditions recited in the specifications on an elemental stretch of track not less than five miles in length."[32] General Electric, with little hesitation, agreed to the Central's terms.

General Electric's stock rose sharply following the announcement of the contract to build engines for the Central's massive electrification project in New York. As soon as the news became public, G.E. stock went up six points.[33] A nearly million-dollar contract was important to a company whose revenue in the previous year had totaled $22 million. G.E. manufactured the electric motors and the control mechanism, while the American Locomotive Company, like G.E. located in Schenectady, New York, built the chassis and wheel trucks for the new electric engines, under subcontract to General Electric.

With a deadline of less than eight months, G.E. assigned its best engineers and workmen to the project. In late 1904, Wilgus informed the Electric Traction Commission of G.E's successful test of the electric en-

gine, on October 27. The electric engine had hauled eight passenger cars on a ten-mile test track equipped with a third rail. The engine had achieved a top speed of 55 miles per hour. Crucially, the new electric engine had accelerated from a dead stop to a speed of 30 miles an hour in one minute, exactly the type of performance needed for the Central's commuter service.

An article published in 1904 in the *Railroad Gazette* pointed to these first tests as a historic milestone in the evolution of transportation technology: "The occasion marks a new era in the development of transportation facilities in this country. . . . the New York Central's electrification scheme is the first radical change on the part of an existing steam road to electric operation for comparatively long distances."[34] The *Gazette* mentioned that two or more of the new electric engines could be operated together for especially heavy trains, because they came equipped with the Sprague–General Electric system of multiple unit control.

To make the first tests more dramatic, G.E. and the Central staged a race between two trains on the test tracks; each train consisted of eight passenger cars, one powered by the new electric engine, the other by a steam engine. The new electric engine won handily; it accelerated more rapidly and beat the steam engine over a four-mile distance by more than half a mile. G.E. made no special changes to strengthen the test track *except* to add special clips, bolted to the ties, to each rail "to prevent any possibility of the rails spreading," called "nosing," in which the weight and driving force spread the tracks.[35] Ominously, the tendency for the new electric engines to spread the track eventually came back to haunt Wilgus and everyone involved in the electrification effort.

Officials of the New York Central and G.E. basked in the success of the first tests. A *New York Herald* headline read "Electric Engine Beats All Rivals," and the article pointed out that railroad officials from all over the country had attended the test, an indication of the importance of this new technological development.[36] Wilgus, in an interview with the *New York Times*, emphasized that the tests proved that the new electric engine performed "better than the builders thought possible and that questions of electric traction for high speed trains [had been] solved for all times." He pointed to the significance of the successful test for one of the major problems the Grand Central project needed to solve—the Park Avenue tunnel.

The new electric service would "relieve New York of all trials and tribulations that travel through the tunnels has forced upon them for years past."[37] Since electricity provided the key to solving a number of interrelated challenges faced at 42nd Street, the successful tests of the first electric engine marked a crucial step forward. Wilgus reported to the Electric Traction Commission that General Electric had performed "marvelously."

Not satisfied with a single series of tests, the engineers wanted to be sure the design would hold up under the demands of heavy use. On the test track near Schenectady, the new electric engine ran continuously with careful monitoring and, as problems emerged, G.E. and American Locomotive undertook any needed modifications. Over the following months, the engine ran a total of 45,000 miles, operating eight hours a day for 112 days at an average speed of 50 miles an hour with numerous starts and stops. The test program, a model of technical rigor, ensured the New York Central that its innovative electric service did not depend on unproven technology. Once introduced, the new electric service had to perform flawlessly. If not, the railroad ran the real risk of missing the legal deadline for eliminating steam operations in Manhattan.

Prior to the electrification of Grand Central, no railroad had used electric traction to power heavy trains at high speeds for long distances. Street railway systems operated light trolley cars at low speeds. Previous electric traction projects with heavier trains had involved only short distances and slow speeds. In Baltimore, the B&O's electrified Howard Street tunnel ran for only 1.5 miles and the electric engines usually operated at a speed of 15 miles an hour or less. *Leslie's Weekly* commented that the Central's new engine represented "the most powerful electric engine in the world, capable of pulling nine heavy Pullman cars at up to ninety miles an hour—an unheard of speed—over long distance."[38]

If anything went wrong with this project, the credibility of the engineers and the companies involved, both the New York Central and General Electric, stood to be seriously compromised; and if electric traction failed, the state and city legislatures might impose draconian limitations on the Central's all-important franchise to operate trains to midtown Manhattan. With so much riding on the successful introduction of electric traction, Wilgus and the other engineers on the Electric Traction Commission believed the extensive testing program worth the time and

The first electric train to Grand Central ready to leave the terminal, September 30, 1906, with William J. Wilgus at the controls

expense it entailed. Above all else, the Central needed the new electric engines to be both reliable and safe.

On September 30, 1906, the new electric engine completed a first run into Grand Central from Woodlawn in the Bronx. William Wilgus manned the controls, joined by officials from the New York Central and the General Electric Company; riding along were observers from other railroads. Wilgus confronted one problem on the run. There was a one thousand–foot gap in the third rail beginning at 56th Street. Upon leaving the Park Avenue tunnel, he simply accelerated and let momentum carry the electric engine and cars smoothly across the gap. Officials of the New York Central expressed deep satisfaction with the progress to date and Wilgus added that "the trip was thoroughly successful."[39] A reporter for the *Railroad Gazette* summed up the significance of the first run to Grand Central: "There is no more interesting or vital question to be settled regarding the future of railroad operation in this country than the success of electric operation in regular service." The *Gazette* praised the New

TABLE 2.1

	Steam	Electric	Total	% Electric
Scheduled N.Y. Central	0	240	240	100%
Shop trains to/f Mott Haven	15	99	114	87%
Subtotal N.Y. Central	15	339	354	96%
Scheduled New Haven	122	30	152	20%
TOTAL	137	369	506	73%

SOURCE: Quoted from William J. Wilgus, "The Grand Central Terminal in Perspective," *Transactions of the American Society of Civil Engineers* 106, Oct. 1940, p. 1013.

York Central and its new electric equipment as "remarkably successful, particularly for an undertaking which is so much of an experiment."[40]

Just as Wilgus had predicted, the advent of electric service generated a great deal of favorable publicity. A headline in the *World* read: "First Electric Train Enters New York City, Thousands of Spectators Cheer."[41] The *New York Times,* in an editorial published the day of the first run to Grand Central, stated the popular view: "No announcement could be better adapted to cheer the northward commuter in particular, and the traveling public in general, than that now made that an electric train will actually run today through the Harlem tunnel to the Grand Central Station."[42]

The Central appeared to be in a position to beat, by over a year, the deadline of July 1, 1908, imposed by the city and state legislatures to end steam operations in Manhattan. Scheduled train service with the new electric engines began on December 11, 1906, and as fast as G.E. delivered the new equipment, the railroad replaced its steam engines with electric ones. By July of the following year electricity powered almost all of the New York Central's trains. Wilgus provided the board of directors a summary of the electric traction situation at Grand Central as of July 1, 1907 (see Table 2.1). By comparison, the New Haven's electrification efforts lagged far behind, although they labored under the same deadline to switch from steam to electric service above 42nd Street.

Even George Westinghouse's attacks could not diminish the accomplishments of Wilgus and the Electric Traction Commission. In only four years, they planned, tested, and put into service a totally innovative electric traction system. Where once only noisy steam engines spewing smoke and soot had operated, clean and quiet electric engines now powered trains in and out of midtown Manhattan. One of Wilgus's fellow engineers, Arthur M. Waitt of the American Society of Civil Engineers, whose opinion mattered greatly to Wilgus, summarized the achieve-

ment: "The change from steam to electric power at the New York terminal of the New York Central and Hudson River Railroad—the most congested terminal in the world—with but little derangement of the train service, is but little short of a miracle; and up to the present time, it may be properly rated as one of the most difficult and complicated engineering problems which has been undertaken and successfully carried through."[43] Wilgus could be justifiably proud.

The Woodlawn Wreck

Wilgus's intensive efforts overseeing the entire Grand Central project took a physical toll on him, and at the end of 1906, the incessant work and responsibility had left him drained. In January 1907, Wilgus requested a one-month leave of absence for health reasons, and the executive committee of the board of directors immediately approved. In recognition of his outstanding work, the committee increased his salary by $5,000 to $40,000 a year—a very substantial salary in 1907. John Stevens, while directing the massive effort to build the Panama Canal, had received only $30,000 a year. Wilgus left for the southwestern United States for a much needed rest, as the Central steadily and rapidly added electric service.

On February 15, 1907, the New York Central proudly introduced a new electric train on the Harlem Division, an express to White Plains departing each evening at 6:15 P.M. Newspaper accounts reported that the commuters riding the first trip "were delighted except for the one objection voiced by many passengers after the first trip—that the train went at too great a speed." The next evening, the train left Grand Central a little late; at Woodlawn in the Bronx, the train rounded a curve at 205th Street and flew off the tracks. At least twenty people died instantly and more than 150 more received injuries, many serious. Rescue workers desperately searched for survivors as hundreds of onlookers gathered to stare at the wreckage, which stretched along the tracks for over a mile.[44]

For the second time in less than a decade, a terrible train wreck threw the New York Central and the public into turmoil. All the favorable public opinion the railroad garnered for its introduction of electric service and the removal of steam engines from the Park Avenue tunnel disappeared in a moment. Public condemnation escalated; the district

attorney's office in New York called for the indictment of the railroad officials who were responsible, just as it had done in 1902 when the deadly wreck occurred in the Park Avenue tunnel.

First reports from the crash site described the train as traveling at an excessive speed. However, by midnight the railroad's investigation attributed the wreck to the spreading apart of the tracks, and Superintendent Ira McCormick reported: "As nearly as I can make out, by the dim light of lanterns, the accident was caused by the spreading of rails, but whether or not this was due to the heavy weight of the motor cars or to a broken fishplate I am unable to state. There is, however, a broken fishplate between 204th and 205th streets."[45] A fishplate was a forged metal plate on which the rails rested inside a flange. Spikes, driven through holes in the fishplate, secured the plate and the rail to the wooden tie. McCormick admitted that the train had departed behind schedule and taken the curve at a high rate of speed, but he added that the curve's banked construction met all standards for high-speed use.

Coverage of the wreck dominated the city's newspapers for the next few days, and sensational headlines fanned the flames of public indignation. In the *New York Herald,* the story filled the front page under the banner: "Twenty-Five Killed and Seventy-Five Injured as an Electric Train on the New York Central is Wrecked on a Curve: Victims Burned to Death After Cars Set on Fire by the 'Electrified Rail.' "[46] The press portrayed the New York Central as a callous corporate giant operating in a manner that endangered the lives of its passengers. The *New York Times* traced the Central's history of accidents in a long story titled: "Previous Central Wrecks: Several Serious Ones in Recent Years on the Road"[47] and reminded readers of the Park Avenue tunnel crash.

More devastating to the interests of Wilgus and the Electric Traction Commission, an editorial in the *New York Journal* linked the accident directly to the design of the new engines: "The theory of Assistant District Attorney Smith, that the [electric engines] are too heavy for the rails, is worthy of investigation. One of these motors weighs as much as a locomotive and tender. Because of the compact build of the motor, the strain on the rail is much greater than under the locomotive. . . . If the Assistant District Attorney's theory is correct, the wreck was preventable."[48]

If negligence caused the wreck, then someone bore direct respon-

sibility and Assistant District Attorney Smyth already had a suspect—William J. Wilgus. The following week, the *New York World* identified Wilgus publicly: "Asks Indictment of Wilgus for Central Wreck: Assistant District Attorney Smyth Wants Him and Others Tried for Manslaughter" and reported Smyth's opening remarks to the coroner's jury, where he placed the blame squarely on Wilgus's shoulders. To make matters worse, William Newman, president of the New York Central, and vice president and general manager A. H. Smith, appearing before the State Railroad Commission the very next day after District Attorney Smyth's damning statement, both placed blame on Wilgus. Distraught and angry, Wilgus was determined to defend his honor and his professional reputation.

Wilgus hurriedly returned to New York. His entire professional career and the years of careful, meticulous work on the electrification of the Central's service in New York now stood in jeopardy. If the official investigations found Wilgus negligent, his reputation in the eyes of his fellow professional engineers, extremely important to him, faced ruin. Despite his years of distinguished service to railroading and the New York Central, he might be remembered only as the Central officer responsible for the deaths of more than twenty people one horrible night in the Bronx.

Wilgus finally testified before the coroner's jury and mounted a vigorous defense. In his testimony Wilgus defended the design of the new electric engines and the exhaustive testing that had been undertaken by the railroad and the manufacturer before the first electric engines entered service: "There had never been a feature of the system installed that had not been approved by every member of the commission and every outside authority consulted on it."[49] He remained determined to protect his professional reputation despite the effect this defense might have on his relationship with the New York Central. Wilgus's defense of his work and that of the Electric Traction Commission proved successful; suspicion shifted to other possible causes for the wreck.

A bitter battle continued within the ranks of the senior management of the New York Central over the real cause of the wreck and who bore ultimate responsibility. Almost thirty years after the Woodlawn wreck, Wilgus assembled an exhaustive file of material (more than five hundred typed pages) concerning the accident and the ensuing conflict among the rail-

Original design for the first electric engine: four driving wheels, two guide wheels in front and back, with the weight of the engine concentrated in the center over the driving wheels

road's executives. He placed the file among his papers, given to the New York Public Library, and left instructions that, until his death, no one could examine the file without his permission. A five-page introduction signed and dated by Wilgus on July 6, 1936, began the secret file: "Much ill feeling within the ranks of the railroad company [New York Central] resulted from inquiries that followed the accident."[50] Wilgus then explained the stunning events that compelled him to assemble the file: on April 4, 1907, the senior vice president of the company, Mr. W. C. Brown, stated to Wilgus his belief that responsibility for the accident rested on the flawed design of the new electric engines. Despite what the officers of the Central said publicly or under oath to the coroner's jury, grand jury, or the New York State Railroad Commission, at least Brown believed the design of the new engines to be the cause of the Woodlawn wreck.

Wilgus had been stunned by Brown's accusation and responded by writing him a ten-page letter, with numerous exhibits attached, five days later, on April 9. In the letter, Wilgus presented a detailed defense of the design of the new electric engines and discussed, at some length, the attention given to the "nosing" problem. Nosing presented an obvious potential for derailment, exactly what happened at Woodlawn on the fateful night of February 16, 1907.

General Electric knew of the nosing problem. William B. Potter, chief engineer of G.E.'s Electric Railway Department, who had played a key

Modified design for the first electric engine: four wheel ponies added to front and back to spread the weight of the engine away from the center

role in the development of the Central's new electric engines, in his reminiscences, written in 1930, commented on the tests of the first engine: "this locomotive ran well for about 20,000 miles and then, as the track alignments and joints were worn by the many repeated passages, the locomotive developed a tendency toward horizontal alignment, or nosing."[51] At the insistence of the Electric Traction Commission, G.E. and American Locomotive added two-axle guiding trucks to the front of the test engine to solve the problem. After more tests, the changes seemed to eliminate the problem, and on August 7, 1906, G.E. and American Locomotive certified "that in their judgment no detrimental nosing would occur in the New York District."[52]

Whether Wilgus realized it or not, his letter to Brown represented a time bomb for the New York Central. Wilgus, in his usual painstaking detail, provided a record of two and a half years of efforts to deal with the nosing problem. He may have been satisfied, but how might the district attorney, the Railroad Commission, or the public react if they learned that the Central knew of the potential for the new electric engines to nose? Barely two months after the new engines entered service, the disastrous wreck occurred precisely because the tracks spread apart on the Woodlawn curve.

Brown never responded to Wilgus's letter, but on April 12, 1907, just three days later, Ira A. Place, vice president and chief legal counsel of the New York Central, visited Wilgus. Place described the potentially devas-

tating consequences to the railroad if Wilgus's letter became public and demanded that Wilgus burn the letter along with all copies. With his career hanging in the balance, Wilgus agreed.

A cover-up at the highest corporate levels of the New York Central Railroad ensued. The chief legal office of the company went to two of the Central's vice presidents and demanded that they destroy materials—potentially of great interest in the ongoing investigations of the Woodlawn accident. Wilgus and Brown both agreed to the cover-up and destroyed their copies of the letter. Despite a promise Place made to Wilgus to keep him informed of any additional action on the part of the Central to redesign the electric engines, the railroad proceeded to do just that—undertake significant modifications—without Wilgus's knowledge or involvement.

When he learned of the modifications, Wilgus felt he had been double-crossed, and on April 26 he wrote a threatening letter to Place. To protect himself, he informed Place, he had re-created the letter sent to Brown. A handwritten note appears on the document indicating that Wilgus never sent it to Place, but rather informed him verbally of its content.

Wilgus's reconstruction of his letter to Brown served as a form of blackmail, his motive—to forestall continuation of the Central's internal investigation of the design of the electric engines. The Central's moving forward with major modifications would represent an explicit condemnation of the original design, calling into question the professional work of Wilgus and the rest of the Electric Traction Commission. Wilgus

Redesigned electric engine developed after the Woodlawn wreck

simply could not abide this challenge to his professional competence.

Despite his threat, the railroad pushed ahead with a redesign. J. F. Deems, superintendent of motive power, ordered the American Locomotive Company to replace the pony trucks under each end of the electric engines with four wheel trucks. The wheel modifications represented an implicit admission that the original design of the electric engines, with all weight concentrated over the driving wheels, might have been the real cause of the Woodlawn wreck.

Wilgus mounted a vigorous opposition to the proposed changes. In June, he wrote to Newman protesting Deems's plan to modify the new electric engines. Wilgus pointed out that the electric engines had already been run for a total 271,681 miles with only one mishap. He added, "No indications have developed of nosing action of electrical equipment on tracks."[53] This last statement seems disingenuous; William Potter of G.E., for one, knew of the nosing problem and, in reference to the Woodlawn accident, stated bluntly, "It is no doubt the running qualities would have been much improved by lengthening the locomotive, increasing the distance between truck centers and wheel base of the guiding trucks."[54]

On July 11, 1907, William J. Wilgus submitted his resignation to the president and directors of the New York Central Railroad, to take effect on September 30, 1907. A proud individual at the height of his professional career, Wilgus could not stay on after the challenge to his professional competence and authority as an engineer. Rather than continuing to work for the New York Central and have his integrity questioned further, he resigned.

Eventually, the railroad significantly modified the design of the electric engines, adding four wheel bogies to the front and back of its engines. These modifications spread the weight of the engine from the center driving wheels and eliminated completely the danger of nosing. Neither the public, the district attorney, nor the State Railroad Commission drew a connection between the modified design and the Woodlawn accident. All official inquiries placed the blame for the wreck on excessive operating speed.

Despite the Woodlawn wreck and Wilgus's enduring bitterness, he deserves credit for a splendid achievement. In the annals of engineering at

the turn of the nineteenth century, the New York Central electrification stands as one of the most important accomplishments in the history of technological innovation.

The End of the Commodore's Grand Central

Amid the horror of the Woodlawn accident and the scandal surrounding the ensuing investigations, the railroad continued with the excavation and construction of the underground train yard. As soon as work crews finished the new tracks and train platforms in Bites 1 and 2 on the east side of the train yard, the railroad opened a temporary passenger station at Lexington and 43rd Street, using the first floor of Grand Central Palace, an exhibition hall for trade shows and conventions built by the Harlem Railroad. All three railroad lines, the Central, Harlem, and the New Haven, first shifted their commuter service from the old Grand Central to the temporary station; long-haul service continued from the old depot. As construction progressed, the railroads gradually switched long-distance trains to the temporary facility.

On June 5, 1910, the last trains left from the old Grand Central. At 9:44 P.M. the New York Central's Pacific Express, to Buffalo, departed, followed at the stroke of midnight by the Owl, the New Haven's overnight train for Boston; silence fell. Commodore Vanderbilt's depot, so proudly opened in 1871, had reached the end of its useful life and now awaited the wrecker's ball.

Dismantling the iron and glass train shed, the most striking part of the old Grand Central, began even before all service had shifted to the temporary station. Wilgus and the Central engineers devised an ingenious method for removing the arched train shed while continuing to use the tracks below. They constructed a giant wooden scaffold, spanning the entire width of the train shed and resting on train wheels. The lowest level of the scaffold was high enough for trains to pass under, and the top level reached to the shed roof, almost one hundred feet above. Workmen climbed to the top of the scaffold to dismantle the roof of the train shed from the inside out. Demolition began at the rear section of the train shed and as each section came down, workmen positioned the scaffold under the next section. The traveling platform functioned flawlessly. During

Demolition of a segment of the train shed, looking south toward 42nd Street, 1908

the entire time it took to dismantle the old train shed, scheduled service continued without interruption and not a single injury befell a passenger or workman. Newspaper accounts pointed out how difficult a challenge removing the old shed represented. One reporter went so far as to call the project "one of the most daring in the history of building."[55] The ingenuity of the demolition platform captures the simple elegance and brilliant application of engineering principles to everyday problems that allowed scheduled service to continue uninterrupted in the midst of the massive construction project.

The New Terminal Building on 42nd Street

As the end of 1911 approached, work on the terminal building on 42nd Street, the new Grand Central, began. Construction followed the sectional technique that had been used for the underground train yard. As

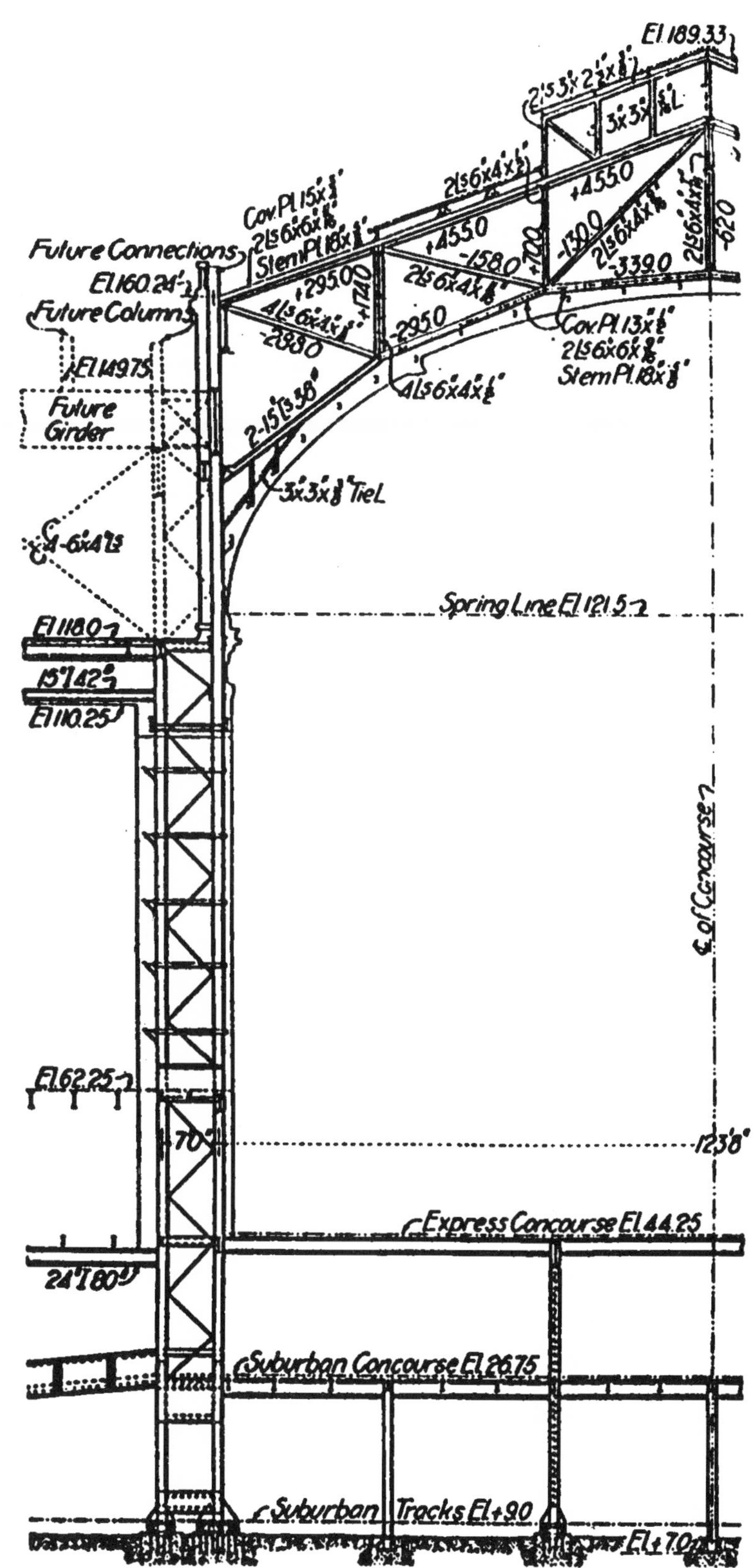

PART SECTION THROUGH CONCOURSE

ABOVE AND FACING PAGE: *Plans for steel work in Grand Concourse and ceiling*

LONGITUDINAL AND TRANSVERSE SECTIONS OF CONCOURSE CEILING

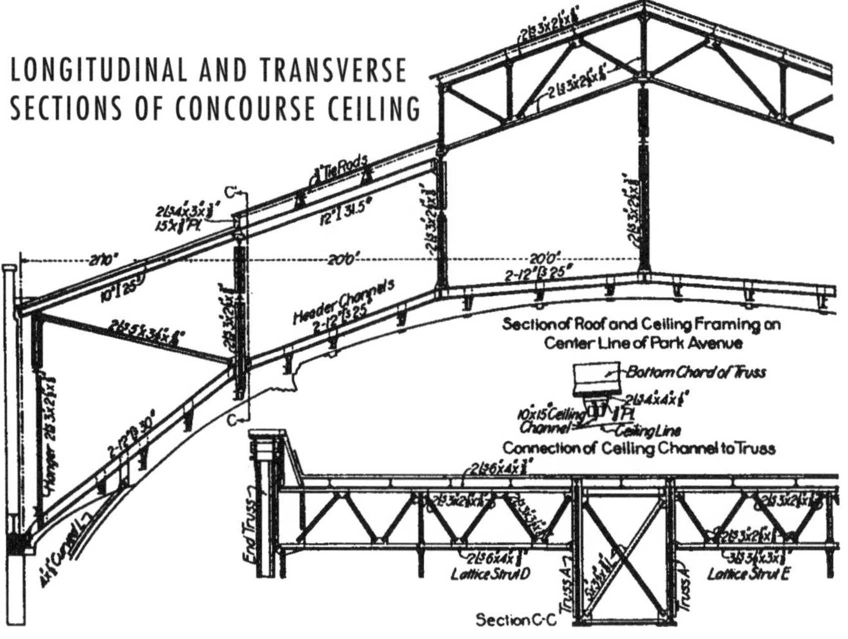

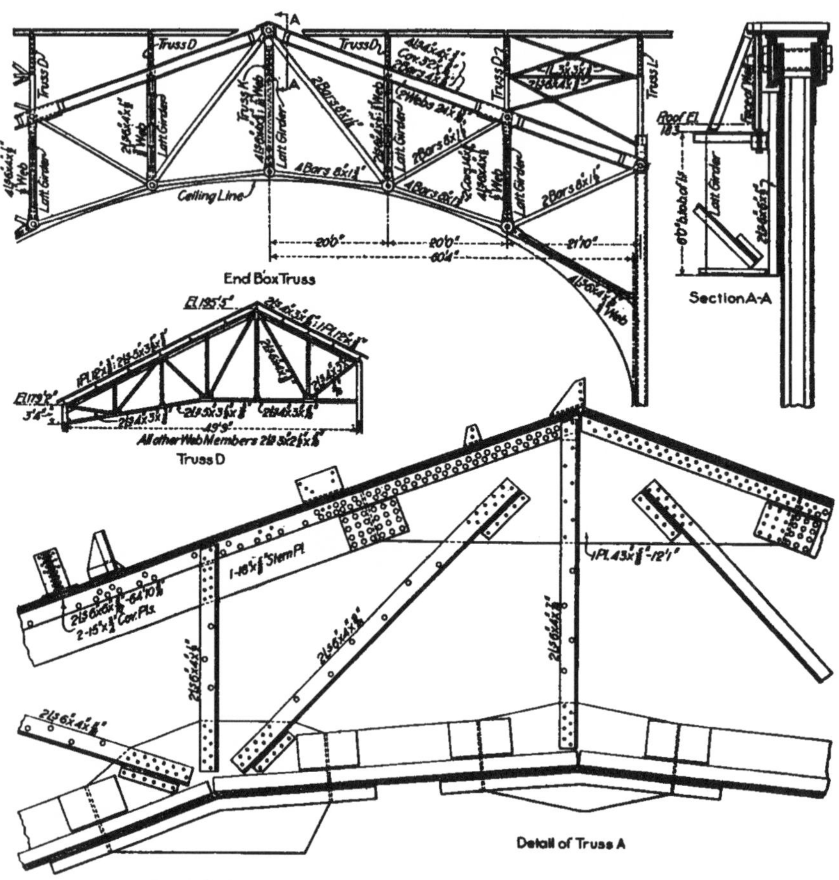

DETAILS OF RIVETED AND PIN-CONNECTED ROOF TRUSSES

Engineering Record reported, the building, "entirely of steel frame construction," rose as a series of "separate longitudinal, full-length zones reaching from 42nd Street north to column line 20"; the article added, "the work has been difficult, complicated and dangerous."[56] Construction of each zone or section proceeded from the base up to the concourse roof, with the first section on the east side erected between May and September of 1911 using 4,831 tons of steel. Work proceeded on each additional section, moving from east to west.

Erection of steel for ceiling of Grand Concourse, looking east toward Lexington Avenue, ca. 1911

Construction of terminal building, from Lexington Avenue, January 1912

Roof trusses spanned the entire width of the Grand Concourse, and from them hung the vaulted ceiling. Two large derricks lifted the roof trusses, assembled on the floor of the concourse and riveted together, and held them in place while workers riveted the trusses to the cross beams. Grand Central, by no means the first steel frame building, demanded exacting construction techniques because of the size of the steel members used in the construction and the widths to be spanned.

Even as construction of the terminal building commenced, the final configuration of the interior remained undecided. A heated debate was going on over whether to use ramps or stairs. Wilgus's original concept included the use of ramps wherever possible instead of stairs, to facilitate the movement of large numbers of people efficiently throughout the station. With the Grand Concourse below street level and the express and suburban tracks further underground, he argued, ramps and gravity

Construction of terminal building two months later, from 42nd Street

would draw passengers from the street down to the concourse and suburban levels and from there down to the waiting trains. As he did with many of the key features of the original plan, Whitney Warren, the architect who assumed design control in 1907, opposed the use of ramps and insisted on replacing them with stairs. Wilgus, as long as he remained with the New York Central, argued for retaining the ramps.

Wilgus and the other advocates of a stairless station prevailed. The use of ramps in Grand Central remains one of its most innovative features. Press descriptions of the new facility pointed out that travelers could "go from the point where the red cross-town car dropped them at Forty-second Street straight to their waiting berth in the Pullman, one level below the street, without finding a single step to descend."[57] Like many of the essential elements of the plan Wilgus presented to the New York Central in 1903, the ramps proved an ingredient in the success of Grand Central. Today, thousands pass through each day, hurrying to trains or simply crossing the concourse as they travel through the midtown business district. Without ramps, the Grand Concourse, one story below street level, could not function as smoothly as the crossroads of New York and as one of the city's great public spaces.

Completion of the Terminal

After Wilgus's abrupt departure from New York Central, construction of the terminal continued for another six years. Creating Terminal City, the associated collection of hotels, apartments, and office buildings which transformed Midtown, continued into the 1920s.

While construction proceeded, the Central's board of directors struggled with the ever-increasing costs. As of December 31, 1907, the cost of all completed work totaled $29,484,620, including more than $12 million for electrification, $5.5 million for the excavation and building of the underground train yard, $7 million for four-tracking of the Harlem and Hudson divisions, and $2.4 million for the construction of the new Grand Central building. Such an enormous financial gamble could only succeed if passenger volume increased and, as importantly, earnings from the railroad's freight business expanded as well. Without continued growth, the railroad could not hope to service the huge amounts of capital it had committed to Grand Central. In the final analysis, the Central's bold leap into the future failed. Yet, as the new century began, the future for the railroad's flagship station appeared limitless.

In November of 1911, news of the opening of Pennsylvania Station overshadowed the progress at Grand Central. The New York Central's archrival, the Pennsylvania Railroad, beat the Central by a decisive margin in the race to construct a new passenger facility to serve Manhattan. Press reports lavished praise on McKim, Mead and White's Pennsylvania Station, with its classical Beaux-Arts design. The Pennsylvania and Long Island railroads immediately saw heavy traffic flowing through their magnificent new station on 33rd Street.[58]

The Opening of Grand Central

Finally, in February of 1913, after almost a decade of construction and the expenditure of millions of dollars, the New York Central proudly announced the completion of the new terminal and underground train yard. Reaction to the new facility seemed nothing short of ecstatic. The usually reserved *New York Times* called the new Grand Central the "great-

est railway terminal in the world." John Droege praised the new Grand Central as a great civic center: "The Grand Central Terminal is not only a station; it is a monument, a civic center or, if one will, a city. Without exception, that part of it which is the station is not only the greatest head station in the United States but the greatest station of any type not only on this continent but in the world."[59] An article in the popular journal *Munsey's Magazine* also recognized the new Grand Central as the "The Greatest Railroad Terminal in the World." The article described, in detail, the complicated construction process: "No similar enterprise was ever undertaken on so gigantic a scale, or in the face of such conditions . . . on the site of the old terminal, which could not be abandoned." *Munsey's* concluded by pointing to the significance of Grand Central in terms of American building art: "[Grand Central] promises to be the most successful combination of the esthetic and the practical in city building yet planned in America. . . . you will find that it is much more than a railroad station. It will be a new city center; a vast theater of great events; another triumph of constructive American achievement."[60]

During the Age of Energy—an era which witnessed the construction of the transcontinental railroad, the Brooklyn Bridge, the Panama Canal, Pennsylvania Station, the New York subway, and the first skyscrapers—Grand Central Terminal stood as yet another stirring triumph of American building art. The United States emerged as the most powerful nation in the world, and the country's engineers, architects, and builders overcame every challenge they faced. Yet just over the horizon loomed the automobile and truck, destined to challenge the railroads and drive them to the brink of disaster. In that process, Grand Central itself faced destruction. Amidst the celebration, no one imagined the threats that lay ahead.

CHAPTER THREE

The Architect's Grand Central

As a new century began, the completion of Grand Central marked the emergence of a distinctive building art in the United States, a style that combined imaginative architectural design, innovative engineering, and daring construction. The term *American Renaissance* captures the period beginning with the completion of the Brooklyn Bridge in 1883.[1] The longest bridge in the world at the time, the Brooklyn Bridge represented a triumph of engineering and aesthetics and brought the Roeblings, father and son engineers, national and international acclaim.

New York saw a transformation of its built environment; there the American Renaissance produced its greatest achievements, including the largest subway system in the world, the Brooklyn Bridge, the tallest buildings in the world, and two stunning railroad facilities, Pennsylvania Station and Grand Central. "Skyscrapers" rose in lower Manhattan—the Singer Building (1907–8) on lower Broadway, Louis Sullivan's Bayard Building (1897–98) on Bleecker Street, and Daniel Burnham's Flatiron Building (1901–2) at the corner of Broadway and Fifth Avenue at 23rd Street. Made possible by invention of the elevator and iron and steel frame construction, the skyscraper allowed the city to move upward and served as an expression of the ingenuity and exuberance of American society as the nineteenth century came to a close and the twentieth century began.

William Morris Hunt, Daniel Burnham, Cass Gilbert, and Charles

McKim, among the most famous architects of the Age of Energy, represented the ascendence of Beaux-Arts design, named after the Ecole des Beaux-Arts in Paris, where many of America's leading architects trained. The Beaux-Arts school focused on the classical forms of ancient Greece and Rome and married this aesthetic form with iron and steel construction. In New York, in addition to Grand Central, the U.S. Customs House (1901–7) on Bowling Green designed by Cass Gilbert, the New York Public Library (1902–11) by Carrère and Hastings, and the Pennsylvania Station (1901–11), McKim, Mead and White's masterpiece, all reflected a striving for the ideals of classical form.

Grand Central also reflects the fledgling efforts of Americans to organize a systematic response to the conditions of the swelling American city, to beautify and bring order out of chaotic growth. After the Civil War, American cities grew at a rate never before experienced in history and became crowded, dirty, congested, and filled with millions of immigrants struggling to gain a foothold in American life. In 1890, Jacob Riis, a Danish immigrant and crusading journalist, published his famous pictorial essay on the lives of the poor, *How the Other Half Lives*. Riis captured the harsh reality of the urban poor in New York. Over a century later, the photographs of people sleeping in cellars, or the drunks in all-night saloons swilling cheap whiskey, or the homeless children huddled together sleeping in a doorway still tug at the reader's emotions. Riis described the conditions of Jewish immigrants on the Lower East Side of New York just before the turn of the century, when the first Vanderbilt mansions were rising on Fifth Avenue to the north: "It is said that nowhere in the world are so many people crowded together on a square mile as here. The average five-story tenement adds a story or two to its stature in Ludlow Street and an extra building on the rear lot. . . . The sanitary policeman whose beat this is will tell you that it contains thirty-six families. . . . In Essex Street two small rooms in a six-story tenement were made to hold a 'family' of father and mother, twelve children and six boarders."[2] Riis's work inspired a legion of reformers dedicated to ameliorating the worst conditions of urban life.

Efforts to deal with the appalling conditions in American cities took a number of forms. Protestant churches organized missionary activities to bring moral uplift to the immigrant masses: the Young Men's Chris-

tian Association built residential and recreation facilities in the cities; Y.M.C.A.s provided places where young men could find clean and decent housing in a religious atmosphere. Jane Addams, a disciple of the American philosopher William James, sought to duplicate the ties of the small town and rural village within the confines of the teeming urban ghettos by founding Hull House in Chicago in 1889. Addams intended to re-create a sense of community amidst the alienation and disorganization of an emergent urban society. Although few in number, settlement houses represent the first secular attempts to alleviate the appalling social conditions created by industrialization and rapid urban growth.

Settlement houses focused on assisting people living in slum neighborhoods; another group of social activists argued that efforts had to be undertaken to alter the physical makeup of the American city and, in the process, to do away with slum neighborhoods. Cities needed an overall plan for their physical development; the shaping of the built environment could not be left to the haphazard forces of private development. Advocates of planned development believed that having a city plan would bring a modicum of order to the chaos of the exploding cities. Calls for systematic planning in the American city led to the emergence of the City Beautiful movement, which not only advocated large-scale urban planning but also sought to beautify the city.

Grand Central Terminal exemplifies both the Beaux-Arts style and the City Beautiful movement. Whitney Warren, the architect of the terminal building on 42nd Street, trained at the Ecole des Beaux-Arts, and his design reflected all of the elements the Beaux-Arts sought to achieve. Grand Central also embodied the goals of the City Beautiful—systematic planning and building on a grand scale with a conscious effort to beautify as well as to provide the most modern railroad terminal in the world. How the terminal complex achieved these lofty goals involves a complicated story with a fascinating cast of characters.

The Architectural Competition

In early 1903, the board of the New York Central approved Wilgus's dramatic plan and announced an architectural competition for the new terminal building on 42nd Street, inviting four firms to submit prelimi-

nary plans and drawings. Two of the firms, D. H. Burnham and Company of Chicago and McKim, Mead and White of New York, among the most prominent in the country, seemed logical choices. Samuel Huckel Jr. of Philadelphia, the third firm, had designed a number of stations for the Pennsylvania Railroad. The remaining firm to be invited was Reed and Stem of St. Paul, Minnesota, far removed from New York, whose previous commissions included a number of local stations for the Central and its subsidiaries.

Burnham and McKim, Mead and White were at the forefront of American architecture at the turn of the century. Daniel Burnham had risen to national prominence as director of planning for the World's Columbian Exposition, held in Chicago in 1893. Burnham's most famous buildings included the Marshall Field department store in Chicago (1893), the Flatiron Building in New York (1903), and the magnificent Union Station in Washington, D.C. (1903–8). McKim, Mead and White, with offices in New York, played as prominent a role in American architecture as Daniel Burnham. Charles Follen McKim trained at the Ecole des Beaux-Arts, and his firm served as architects to the American aristocracy of the Gilded Age, designing numerous homes in New York and "cottages" in Newport for their wealthy clients. Stanford White learned his trade as an apprentice and traveled extensively in France and Italy, where he absorbed the classical architectural models. White, a prominent socialite as well as a brilliant architect, led a scandalous life, cutting an imposing figure in the night life of New York until driven to bankruptcy by high living. White's life ended tragically in an infamous scandal in 1906, when the irate husband of his lover, the beautiful Evelyn Nesbit, shot him dead in the restaurant atop Madison Square Garden, one of his most notable designs. Just before White's death, the Pennsylvania Railroad had chosen McKim, Mead and White to design the company's new terminal at 33rd Street. Pennsylvania Station came to be celebrated, along with Grand Central, as among the most beautiful buildings ever constructed in the United States. When in 1968 the new Madison Square Garden sports and entertainment complex replaced McKim, Mead and White's building, forcing Pennsylvania Station into the basement of the new building, one prominent critic called the demolition the worst act of urban vandalism in American history.

Reed and Stem's plan for a Grand Central Terminal topped with twelve stories of rental space and ringed by an elevated roadway with a bridge over 42nd Street connecting it to Park Avenue

Reed and Stem, of St. Paul, were not in the same league as Burnham or McKim, Mead and White, but they enjoyed a good regional reputation. William Wilgus influenced their inclusion in the design competition. He had been favorably impressed with their work, and happened to be married to Charles Reed's sister. Charles Reed and William Wilgus discussed ideas for the new terminal at some length before Reed and Stem's formal submission. Wilgus's letter to New York Central president Newman in March of 1903, where he first laid out his ideas for a new terminal, had included a number of the key elements of the plan Reed

Reed and Stem's plan for a Court of Honor, lining Park Avenue north of the new terminal

and Stem submitted to the competition. Wilgus included an elevated roadway around the terminal, with an arched bridge over 42nd Street to link Park Avenue north and south of the terminal, restoring Park Avenue as a north-south artery in the city. Most crucially, Wilgus premised his entire conception of the project on the construction of a revenue-producing building over the new underground station and train yard. In turn, Reed and Stem's submission featured a twelve-story office building rising from 42nd Street, just as Wilgus had proposed to Newman.

McKim, Mead and White's proposal, bold in concept, included a sixty-five-story tower atop a fourteen-story office building, which would have been the tallest building in the world at the time. Their plan included a fixed white beam atop the tower illuminated from below with red lights. Modeled after the palaces of Florence, the design reflected the classical themes emphasized by the Beaux-Arts and featured a dramatic arched passageway through the building, connecting north and south Park Avenue, with space to drop off and pick up passengers.

Reed and Stem's plan, not without its classical elements, incorporated a "Court of Honor" north of the terminal, facing up Park Avenue, and included plans for two classical buildings facing across Park, one for the Metropolitan Opera and the other for the New York Academy of Design. Befitting a Beaux-Arts plan, the buildings provided a classical terminus for Park Avenue, destined to become Manhattan's grand boulevard.

Reed and Stem's design won the competition. Wilgus stated, some-

what disingenuously, that the selection of Reed and Stem's plan rested on their idea for an elevated roadway around the terminal building and a bridge over 42nd Street connecting Park Avenue north and south of the new terminal. While the elevated roadway provided an important element of the plan, it seemed rather a thin reason for choosing Reed and Stem's plan over the other submissions. Wilgus's family ties to Charles Reed obviously played a major role. Family ties continued to play a major role in the design of Grand Central, but in a manner which William Wilgus eventually found quite unpleasant.

Whitney Warren

Architect Whitney Warren attended the Ecole des Beaux-Arts from 1888 to 1891, following in the footsteps of the renowned Richard Morris Hunt, Louis Sullivan, and Charles McKim. Warren returned from Paris in 1892 to form the architectural firm of Warren and Wetmore. Warren's most important commission to date, the New York Yacht Club, on West 43rd Street, opened to widespread praise in 1901. Warren was also a distant cousin and social acquaintance of William K. Vanderbilt, who in 1903 played a prominent role on the board of directors of the New York Central and Hudson River Railroad, simultaneously serving on the board's powerful Executive Committee.

Warren recognized the importance of the new Grand Central, destined to be among the most important set of buildings ever constructed in New York City, and desperately wanted the commission. Fame and fortune awaited the architect who designed the new Grand Central. Warren privately prevailed upon William K. Vanderbilt to include his firm and, in turn, Vanderbilt set out to use his considerable influence with the board. Wilgus rather cryptically remarked later, "In the latter part of 1903, Warren and Wetmore of New York proposed themselves in connection with the Grand Central Terminal design."[3]

In spite of the outcome of the formal competition, Vanderbilt insisted that Reed and Stem join forces with Warren and Wetmore in the design of the entire project. The reaction of Reed and Stem can only be imagined: their elation after being selected over both Burnham and McKim, Mead and White and their outrage at being forced to share the design

work for the new terminal complex with Warren and Wetmore. Reed and Stem recognized the formidable forces they faced and reluctantly agreed to the proposed arrangement. On February 8, 1904, they signed a contract with the New York Central Railroad and officially became partners in Associated Architects.

The February 9, 1904, minutes of the Executive Committee include a copy of the contract with Associated Architects. The motion approving the contract allowed the Central to cancel the contract at will: "The Company reserves the right to cancel at any time." A note penciled next to the sixth clause, signed by the secretary, notes: "Ordered added, upon being read at meeting of February 19, 1904." Oddly, the minutes of February 19 do not include any reference to the contract with Associated Architects.[4] This added clause, allowing the Central to cancel the contract with Associated Architects at any time, took on great importance when the railroad abruptly canceled the contract with Associated Architects after the untimely death of Charles Reed in December of 1911.

Upon Reed's death, and without wasting a moment, the Central immediately entered into a new contract, with Warren and Wetmore solely, to complete all design work. Charles Wetmore, Warren's partner, engineered the underhanded deal with President Newman as they returned to New York in Newman's private railroad car after attending Reed's funeral in Scarsdale, New York. Warren and Wetmore, with Reed hardly cold in his grave, conspired with the railroad to take over all design work for the Grand Central project.

Outraged, Allen Stem and Reed's estate sued Warren and Wetmore for breach of contract. The firm stood accused not only of seeking to defraud Reed and Stem of money owed for work completed at the time of Reed's death but also of seeking to secure all credit for the new Grand Central. During the protracted legal proceedings, Wilgus vigorously supported Reed's claims, but the New York Central avoided being dragged into the lawsuit because of the cancellation clause in its contract with Associated Architects. Without that clause, Charles Reed's estate would certainly have also sued the New York Central Railroad for breach of contract. After a bitter legal battle that dragged on for almost a decade, in January of 1920, New York's highest court found Warren and Wetmore guilty and ordered them to pay Reed and Stem $223,981 for the firm's share of the

design work completed or in progress at the time of Reed's death.[5] Not only did they pay substantial damages, but they also suffered public humiliation. The American Institute of Architects, the most prestigious professional organization in the field of architecture, expelled Warren for breaching its code of professional conduct. Ironically, despite the lawsuit and professional censure, Whitney Warren remains to this day the architect most associated with the design of Grand Central.

Controversy

Controversy over credit for the design of Grand Central continued for years. William Wilgus took credit for the idea of a two-story underground terminal powered by electricity and for using the air rights to pay for the vast changes planned for the 42nd Street station. He never claimed any credit for the architectural design of the terminal building itself; a brilliant engineer, Wilgus had no training or expertise as an architect. In turn, Wilgus attributed to Reed and Stem the idea for the elevated roadway around the building and the arched bridge carrying Park Avenue over 42nd Street.

Warren and Wetmore's major contributions included replacing the twelve-story revenue building, proposed by Wilgus and Reed and Stem, with a lower but more monumental structure devoted to railroad functions with limited commercial space. Warren and Wetmore's design proclaimed the glory and might of the New York Central Railroad by adopting the language of the Beaux-Arts in a classical, low-rise building with arches and portals crowned by ornamental statues and detailing. Warren focused on the monumental aspect, rather than the mundane world of square footage and rental income. In addition, Warren's building did not include the elevated driveways of Reed and Stem's design. Wilgus, angered at the decision to abandon both the revenue-producing building and the elevated roadways, maintained that Warren's design involved only the exterior treatment of the station and did not alter the essential circulation and separation of functions he had originally proposed to Newman in 1903. Wilgus summarized the changes from his perspective: "The Company, however, while not approving the change from the fundamental features of the original inception, contrary to the

views of its Vice President [Wilgus], concluded that the exterior treatment of the station proper, consisting of a low monumental effect without the elevated driveway and 42nd Street bridge, was preferable to the revenue producing type with the Reed and Stem driveways."[6] To the end of his life, Wilgus remained embittered at William K. Vanderbilt's intrusion into the design of Grand Central and his insistence that Whitney Warren play a pivotal role.

But more than just personal connections had led to Warren's inclusion. Vanderbilt, enamored of the Beaux-Arts, in the 1890s commissioned Richard Morris Hunt to design his New York mansion on Fifth Avenue at 52nd Street and the Marble House, his summer home in Newport, Rhode Island. Marble House presents the classical model so favored by the Beaux-Arts, drawing heavily on Jacques-Ange Gabriel's Petit Trianon at Versailles for inspiration. Facing Newport's fashionable Bellevue Avenue, the Marble House's front facade includes four huge Corinthian columns dividing the exterior into a series of classical, symmetrical bays. Over the front entrance Hunt included the head of Apollo. Today, as guides for the Newport Preservation Society escort tourists through the Marble House, they point out William K. Vanderbilt's initials carved into the sculpture. The Vanderbilts, never reticent, felt comfortable with Hunt's use of the ancient gods to adorn their summer pleasure palaces.

If Vanderbilt chose Versailles as a model for his Marble House, it remains no wonder that Warren persuaded him to adopt a monumental, Beaux-Arts design for Grand Central, the crown jewel of the New York Central Railroad, the "Vanderbilt System." Warren's design for the facade of Grand Central, facing south down Park Avenue, mirrored the symmetry of the Marble House. Instead of the four bays of Hunt's Beaux-Arts design, Warren incorporated three bays, each with arched windows, and ten Corinthian columns. Just as the Marble House evoked the grandeur of Versailles and Louis XIV, Warren's design for the Grand Central terminal building drew on the classical grandeur of Greece and Rome for its inspiration. Warren crowned the facade of Grand Central, not with Apollo, whom Hunt had selected for the doors of the Marble House, but with Mercury, Minerva, and Hercules.

Warren's plans dramatically changed Reed and Stem's design for the interior of the terminal building. Reed and Stem's plan provided for a

large amount of retail space along 42nd Street and Vanderbilt Avenue and for a narrow concourse running across the full width of the interior from Depew Place to Vanderbilt Avenue. Warren's interior, monumental in nature and mirroring his exterior, revolved around a much more spacious central concourse, with an arched ceiling high overhead and viewing galleries at the upper level. Entering the terminal via 42nd Street, departing passengers would pass through an elaborate waiting room, purchase tickets, and proceed majestically through the Grand Concourse before descending to the underground platforms and the waiting express trains. Warren's interior embodied the Beaux-Arts precept of designing a public building around its central space, in this case the Grand Concourse, from which other rooms should radiate. Warren wanted to remove the experience of train travel from the ordinary and utilitarian and to evoke the romance of travel, especially on the Central's glamorous long-distance trains. To accomplish this end, Warren devoted a substantial share of Grand Central's total interior volume to the Grand Concourse at the heart of the terminal. Entering Warren's concourse, both traveler and the pedestrian knew, without doubt, that they had arrived in a special place. In the final analysis, Warren deserves the major credit for the appearance of the interior of Grand Central and particularly the Grand Concourse, which came to be hailed as New York's forum, its Piazza San Marco.

Whitney Warren also deserves full credit for the exterior treatment of the building. His daughter, in 1941, gave the Cooper-Hewitt Museum, in New York, Warren's signed original sketch of the south-facing facade of Grand Central. Sketched are three triumphal arches facing down Park Avenue, adorned by Corinthian columns with a heroic sculpture centering the cornice. A more finely detailed drawing of the south facade, with a number of notes in Warren's hand, is held by the New-York Historical Society.

As the design controversy simmered, construction of the two-story underground train yard, begun in 1904, moved forward. Since construction of the new terminal building on 42nd Street was to follow the completion of the underground train yard and creation of the electric zone, arguments over the final design of the terminal building dragged on until December of 1909.

To complicate matters further, the New Haven Railroad entered the

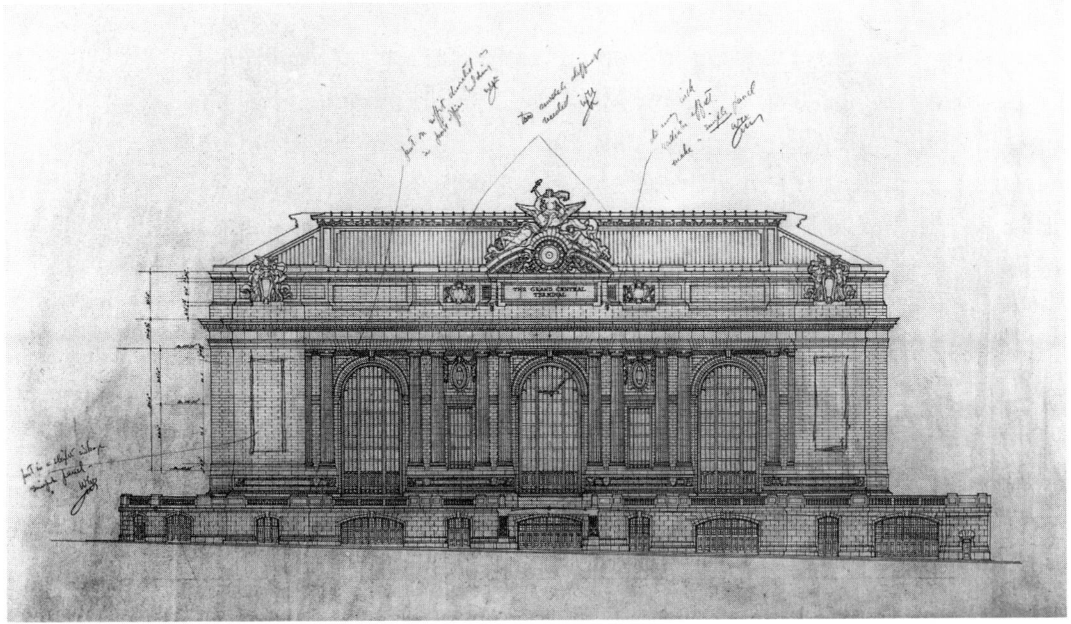

Whitney Warren's drawing of the front facade of Grand Central, with his annotations

fray. The New York Central's long-term agreement with the New Haven allowed for joint use of the Park Avenue tracks and of the Central's terminal facilities in Manhattan. Further, the agreement required the New Haven to pay a fee to the Central for each passenger hauled between Woodlawn in the Bronx, where the New Haven tracks joined the Central's, and Manhattan and to pay one-third of the cost of any improvements to the railroad's terminal facilities in Manhattan.

Since the New Haven shared the costs for any improvements, it insisted on the right to approve any plans for changes to the 42nd Street facilities. The two railroads formed a joint committee in May of 1906 to ensure the New Haven's involvement in the planning process. At the very first meeting of the joint committee the New Haven asserted its right, not only to be consulted, but also to approve the final design: "the New Haven Company believes that it should be consulted and its consent obtained before any permanent change in the present Grand Central Station is adopted by either the Central Company or the Harlem Company."[7]

Minutes of the May meeting of the joint committee indicate that the New Haven knew quite well the cost implications of Warren's plan for a low monumental building instead of Wilgus's and Reed and Stem's original concept for a twelve-story building with ten floors devoted to rental

space. The New Haven officials raised serious objections: "The second plan [Warren's] provides for no office space over the Railroad Terminal south of 43rd Street. . . . such a building as contemplated by the first plan [Reed and Stem's] is more suitable as a piece of architecture, is as well adapted to electrical operation, is just as efficient as [the second] and more economical." New Haven officials continued their objections in the most forceful of terms: they refused to pay their one-third of the cost of the monumental building proposed by Warren and supported by William K. Vanderbilt: "The New Haven is willing to bear one-third of the charges on the cost of the first plan. . . . it is not willing to bear such proportions of the charges on the cost of the second plan."[8] Unlike the Central and Vanderbilt, the New Haven resisted helping to fund a monument to the grandeur of the New York Central Railroad and the Vanderbilts.

The lower cost of Wilgus's and Reed and Stem's design was one of its appeals to the New Haven Railroad. The joint committee estimated that, with its twelve-story revenue-generating building, it would cost $36,194,000, leaving the New Haven's share of the financing at $281,170 per year. By comparison, Warren's monumental building, estimated to cost $42,000,000 to build, would require the New Haven to contribute $382,042 a year. Warren's plan increased the New Haven's share by $100,000 a year, an increase of 36 percent over the Reed and Stem plan.

With the joint committee unable to reach a consensus, a showdown came in December of 1909, when the boards of directors of the two railroads entered the controversy and assumed direct responsibility. The two boards formed a second "joint" committee, whose composition is revealing. William K. Vanderbilt, William H. Newman, and three other board members represented the Central, while the New Haven members included J. P. Morgan, William Rockefeller, Lewis Cass Ledyard, William Skinner, and the president of the New Haven, Charles Mellen. Not coincidentally, J. P. Morgan, William Rockefeller, and Lewis Cass Ledyard also served on the board of directors of the New York Central.

How could the interests of the New Haven be independently represented by men who at the same time served as directors of the Central? To modern judgment, a conflict of interest appears obvious, but to the turn-of-the-century corporate world, such interlocking relationships were all too common.

Two days before Christmas in 1909, the new committee presented its recommendation to the directors of the New York Central. Newman explained the committee's discussions regarding the pros and cons of the Reed and Stem building versus the Warren building. After Newman's presentation, William Rockefeller moved that the board approve Warren's plans for the building; the minutes report simply that Rockefeller's motion carried with no recorded vote.[9] Still, the board added one crucial change. Rockefeller's motion required that the Warren plan incorporate the foundations for a high-rise revenue building, to be constructed sometime in the future; this proved to be a very significant addition. After World War II, when the Central, desperate for additional revenue, sought to develop the air rights directly over Grand Central, the strengthened foundation, required by Rockefeller's motion, encouraged the railroad's efforts.

After Rockefeller's motion passed, Lewis Ledyard moved that the elevated roadway carrying Park Avenue around the terminal building which had been proposed by Reed and Stem, also be included. Ledyard's motion carried. Wilgus later claimed that the inclusion of Reed and Stem's elevated roadway, a key feature of their plan, had been a principal reason for the selection of Reed and Stem in the original architectural competition. Wilgus, writing in 1913, argued that the decisions made by the board of directors in 1909 vindicated his original ideas as well as those of Reed and Stem. He wrote that the board "reverted to the original Reed and Stem plan" and explained further, "Subsequent to the writer's severance of connection with the improvements, the elevated driveways and 42nd Street bridge crossings, which had been omitted contrary to his recommendations, were restored, the steel work in the main building north of 43rd St. has been designed and built for future additional revenue-producing stories." Wilgus concluded with a note of triumph, "Thus has the improvement been completed to accord with the fundamental features proposed in the original inception of 1902, and with an exterior treatment of the station building that displays the architectural ideas of Warren and Wetmore combined with the novel elevated driveway features of the Reed and Stem plan."[10]

While the board did restore the elevated roadway, a significant contribution from Reed and Stem's original design submission, the final design of the terminal building itself, the masterpiece on 42nd Street most famil-

iar to the public reflects Whitney Warren's hand. The low-rise, classical Beaux-Arts exterior and the monumental interior concourse resulted from Warren's concept of Grand Central as a fitting gateway to the greatest city in the country.

At that meeting on December 23, 1909, the Central's board dealt with another important issue. Lewis Ledyard proposed to have the New Haven Railroad share with the New York Central the cost of any real estate projects the Central planned for the 42nd Street area not specifically earmarked for railroad purposes. The New York Central Railroad intended to enter the real estate development business and wanted the New Haven as a partner. Jointly the two railroads agreed to advance the initial capital needed to develop the air rights over the underground train yard and to share in rental or lease income. In 1912, the directors of the two railroads reorganized the New York State Terminal Realty Company, which became the two railroads' real estate development subsidiary. Eventually the railroads agreed to advance the necessary capital on a fifty-fifty basis and to share net revenue on the same basis.

In retrospect, the decisions made at the December 1909 meeting of the boards of directors proved to be crucial ones. After years of bitter debate, the board finally decided in favor of the low monumental building first proposed by Whitney Warren to William K. Vanderbilt in 1904.

William Wilgus argued vigorously, for the rest of his life, that he deserved credit for the original concept for the overall Grand Central project. When the new Grand Central opened in 1913, articles filled the leading magazines and New York newspapers. A number of stories gave a prominent place to the role played by Wilgus in the overall concept of the project as well as offering some credit to Reed and Stem. By contrast, the New York Central Railroad was far less generous. To coincide with the opening, the company published an elaborate brochure that included a number of colored drawings depicting the new terminal and the entire "Terminal City" development. In his papers, Wilgus included one of these brochures with extensive annotations. His notes reflect his bitterness at the omission of mention of himself and Reed and Stem from the Central's official publication. In his later years, Wilgus wrote poignant letters to editors and authors of articles on Grand Central whenever they failed to give him the credit he believed he so richly deserved.

Any serious study of Grand Central leads to the conclusion that the genius of William J. Wilgus stands behind the project. While Wilgus played only an indirect role in the design of the terminal building itself, that was just one component of an immensely complicated effort. He deserves recognition for the scope of his imagination: he looked at the Commodore's Grand Central Depot with its open train yard to the north and envisioned a project that transformed the entire thirty-block area into one of the most vibrant urban concentrations in the world. Grand Central still resonates with the life and vitality of the city and functions efficiently almost one hundred years after Wilgus first wrote to the president of the New York Central and presented his revolutionary plans.

The Beaux-Arts

During the period after the Civil War, as America emerged as the most powerful nation in the world and as the country's businesses prospered, American building art searched for an appropriate style to express the country's new position. While critics like Lewis Mumford have referred to the Beaux-Arts derisively as "imperial," in city after city civil and business leaders chose the Beaux-Arts for important public and private buildings. Grand Central Terminal and Pennsylvania Station, two of the major buildings constructed in New York around the turn of the century, both epitomize the influence of this style. As gateways to the most important city in the country, these terminals combined monumental scale with the capacity to handle a large flow of people daily and their architecture provided the perfect solution to the challenge at hand.

The history of American architecture involves "the search for a usable past."[11] Whitney Warren wrote, "Architecture being a seasoned art, for any specific purpose there should be precedent and tradition."[12] In each major time period in the country's history, architects and builders sought a vocabulary with which to express the American experience. The lack of a long collective history created a vacuum but also offered opportunity. Absent an established style, in a country which glorifies the self-made man, the possibility for reinvention abounds. In the period after the Civil War, the rise of big business and the creation of stupendous personal fortunes offered a unique opportunity to create a new built en-

vironment. In cities across the country, but especially in New York, strong-willed clients—governments as well as private businesses and individuals—sought an architectural style that would proclaim their preeminence and wealth. Commodore Vanderbilt, his son William H., and his grandson William K., all forceful and impassioned men, imagined their terminals in New York to stand for all time as monuments to their wealth and power. They needed a "usable past" and the Beaux-Arts fitted their desires perfectly.

Just after the Civil War, when the Age of Energy commenced, anyone could call himself an architect and open a practice, regardless of formal study. Only one school in the country offered a formal program of study in architecture; architectural training came by way of an apprentice system, whereby an aspiring architect worked for a period of time in the office of a practicing architect or draftsman before setting out on his own. Thomas Jefferson, celebrated as a great American architect for the design of his home, Monticello, the campus of the University of Virginia, and the Virginia State Capitol in Richmond, was completely self-trained. He absorbed the classical style from careful reading and study of Andrea Palladio's *Four Books of Architecture,* first published in 1570. The Massachusetts Institute of Technology established the first academic architectural training program in the United States in 1865, followed by the School of Architecture at Cornell University in 1871 and the University of Illinois and Syracuse University in 1873. As an alternative, Americans interested in architecture could study abroad, especially in Paris at the most famous school of architecture in the world.

The Beaux-Arts style takes its name from the Ecole des Beaux-Arts in Paris. At the end of the nineteenth century and well into the beginning of the twentieth, the Ecole's influence reigned supreme in American architecture. The impact the Beaux-Arts school exerted on American architects, including the architect most responsible for the design of the exterior of Grand Central and the Grand Concourse, cannot be overestimated. This influence came in a most direct way. Aspiring American architects left the United States, went to France, and enrolled in the famous academy on the Rue Bonaparte. There, they followed a course of study that had been in place for more than a hundred years.

Nothing in the young United States compared with the glory of the

monumental architecture of Paris and Versailles and the attraction of Paris itself, the City of Light. At a time when few American cities boasted a population approaching one hundred thousand, Paris's population already numbered over a million. The city's streets and boulevards included the greatest concentration of classically inspired buildings and monuments in the world. With the rebuilding of Paris from 1853 to 1870 under Napoleon III by the prefect of the Seine, Baron Georges Eugène Haussmann, the monumental and awe-inspiring nature of the French capital only increased.

The Ecole traced its origins to the reign of Louis XIV and the establishment of the Académie Royale d'Architecture by Colbert in 1671, with a commission to provide architecture for the royal crown. Louis, with Colbert's guidance, named a group of architects to meet periodically to advise the crown on the design of royal buildings, with the implicit purpose of increasing the glory of Louis's reign. To ensure that young architects of the realm might benefit from its studies, the Académie established a school of architecture. During the eighteenth century, the Académie developed a full course of study, including a series of design competitions which became central to the architectural training provided by the Académie and later by the Ecole des Beaux-Arts.

After the French Revolution, the revolutionary forces suppressed all royal academies, and a bitter struggle followed for control over the training of artists and architects. With the restoration of the monarchy, in December of 1816 Louis XVIII ordered that the former Convent des Petits-Augustins on the Quais Malaquais and the Rue Bonaparte, on the left bank of the Seine, be assigned to the Ecole Royale et Speciale des Beaux-Arts. A royal order in 1819 united the special schools of architecture, painting, and sculpture into the Ecole Royale des Beaux-Arts. By 1819 the architecture program established a separate curriculum from those in painting and sculpture.[13]

The 1819 curriculum remained in place for over a century and a half; the course of study proceeded in a hierarchical fashion. A student first found a master, an architect with an established reputation, who oversaw an atelier, a studio, near the Ecole, where students spent most of their time working together. Once admitted to an atelier, the student formally applied as an "aspirant" to the Ecole and prepared for the entrance exam-

inations. A French citizen had only to be between the ages of fifteen and thirty; a foreign student required a letter of introduction from his ambassador. Study at the Ecole was free to any student, French or foreign, capable of passing the entrance examinations, which tested students in mathematics, geometry, history, drawing, and architecture. A difficulty for American students proved to be mastering the French language sufficiently to pass the entrance examinations. American aspirants often took the examinations a number of times before gaining admission to the Ecole. Once admitted, a student entered the "second class," the first stage in the curriculum.

Faculty offered formal lectures on architectural history, ornamentation, and other subjects but did not require students to attend. The heart of the curriculum consisted of a series of formal competitions in which students first prepared sketches at the Ecole in solution of a design problem. With a twelve-hour time limit, these preliminary drawings demanded an ability to respond quickly to a complex design problem. After completing their sketches, the students returned to their ateliers to complete formal plans and elevations within two months for judgment by the faculty.

Work on plans and elevations proceeded at a feverish pace, and active encouragement and critique were provided by fellow students. Weekly visits from the *patron* of the atelier offered an opportunity for review of the work in progress, often accompanied by stinging critiques and suggestions for improvements. It was in these cramped, dirty, drafty, and cold studios that the real architectural training occurred. Students remained with an atelier for years; the atmosphere, decidedly bohemian, contributed to the sense of adventure and romance surrounding study at the Ecole, especially for the American students. Louis Sullivan described his atelier in a letter home in 1874: "It is the dammedest pigsty I ever got into. First it's cold, and when you light the fire it smokes so that it nearly puts your eyes out, and you have to open the windows, which makes a devil of a draft, which is not recommended for people with a cold."[14] Students in an atelier did not pay their *patron*; rather, he received a salary from the Ecole and earned additional fees from private practice.

Students vied for admission to the ateliers of the most famous of the French architects. Victor Laloux, who designed the Gare d'Orsay, an

important precursor to Grand Central, served as a *patron* at the turn of the century. A description by one of Laloux's students captures the atmosphere of a *patron* in his atelier: "Followed by his pupils, he went from table to table, giving his criticism to each student in turn; having made the rounds, he would bow, put on his silk hat and quietly leave the room, but no sooner was the door shut than pandemonium would break loose and a noisy discussion of what he said follow."[15]

To move from the second to the first class at the Ecole required a student to pass a number of *concours*, or competitions, including four in construction employing stone, wood, and iron. Each competition required numerous drawings, showing the central elements of a projected building with stone, iron, and wood detailing, and mathematical calculations demonstrating the structural integrity of the building. Including the proper engineering details provided the hardest challenge for first-year students. This training, with its emphasis on all aspects of building design, proved invaluable to the American students when they returned to a country engaged in a building frenzy. Back in the United States, Ecole-trained architects and their partners easily won one major architectural competition after another.

The curriculum of the first class placed even greater emphasis on the *concours*. Design problems focused on plans for major public buildings—museums, hotels, train stations. Study at the Ecole culminated in the competition for the Grand Prix de Rome, open only to French students and judged by members of the French Academy. The press followed the competition closely. At the ateliers, first class students competing for the Grand Prix received a great deal of attention from the *patron*; winning the Grand Prix brought great prestige not only to the student but to his atelier and his *patron*. The winner of the Grand Prix went to Rome to study, at government expense, for four or five years. Upon returning to Paris, many winners of the Grand Prix went on to brilliant architectural careers.

Not all students who attended the Ecole passed from the second to the first class. In fact, many students, especially the American students, merely studied at the Ecole for a number of years and then left to establish an architectural practice. The American Institute of Architects, founded in 1857, required an apprenticeship or attendance at either the Ecole des

Beaux-Arts or the Royal Academy of Design in London before application for membership. The A.I.A. viewed study at the Ecole or the Royal Academy as evidence of sufficient training in the field of architecture for membership in the country's most influential architectural organization. In 1863, the French government introduced a *diplome* to those who completed the curriculum at the Ecole, and by the turn of the century obtaining the *diplome* had become the goal of American students at the Ecole.

Until the First World War the Ecole flourished and continued to attract a large number of American students. In 1968, after the student uprising in Paris, the French government distributed architecture studies from the Ecole to a number of other institutes of higher education. On the Rue Bonaparte and Quai Malaquais, the buildings of the Ecole, visibly suffering the ravages of time, now serve as a fine arts school run by the French Ministry of Education. Just off the Rue Bonaparte stands the Palais des Etudes with its covered courtyard, the famous Salles des Etudes Antique, once the heart of the Ecole. Formerly filled with models of ancient Roman and Greek statues, the Salles des Etudes Antiques now stands empty and forlorn. On the second floor, the library, dusty and dark, is crammed with architectural drawings growing brittle with age. Only echoes of the vitality and energy of the architectural glory of the Ecole at the turn of the century remain.

The Beaux-Arts and American Architecture

Training provided at the Ecole, firmly rooted in the classical past, provided the United States with precisely the right architecture for the Age of Energy. With its foundations in the classical beauty of Greece and Rome and the glory of the *ancien régime* in France, the Ecole training provided a means of architectural expression which communicated the confidence and exuberance of a young nation destined to dominate the world stage. Whether for city governments striving to bring order and dignity to the exploding American city, powerful companies seeking a monumental building to symbolize corporate strength, or newly minted millionaires desiring a grand town house or summer home, the architecture taught at the Ecole provided a suitable "usable past."

Richard Morris Hunt, the first American to attend the Ecole des Beaux-Arts, enrolled in 1846 and remained in Paris for eight years. After completing his studies, he returned to the United States and embarked upon a distinguished architectural career; ultimately Hunt's work became synonymous with the age. He first served as an assistant on the construction of the Capitol in Washington and thereafter proceeded from one major commission to another. His last major design, the magnificent Fifth Avenue entrance to the Metropolitan Museum of Art, was completed by his son Richard Holland Hunt, after the senior Hunt's death in 1895. Richard Morris Hunt served as court architect to the Vanderbilts: he designed the Marble House and the Breakers in Newport for William K. and Cornelius II, respectively, and for George the famous Biltmore in Asheville, North Carolina, the largest private home ever built in America.

H. H. Richardson followed Hunt to the Ecole in 1862 and stayed through the Civil War years. Richardson, a southerner born on a plantation in St. James Parish, Louisiana, in 1838 and raised in New Orleans, went north in 1854 to study engineering at Harvard University. After returning from Paris, Richardson won the competition for his most famous design, Trinity Church and Rectory on Copley Square in Boston.

Soon other Americans followed in the footsteps of Hunt and Richardson, eight students in 1888, twenty-two by 1895. Whitney Warren completed the first-class examination in 1890.[16] Until the outbreak of the First World War, the number of Americans enrolled at the Ecole averaged about twenty each year. A roster of American graduates of the Ecole comprises a veritable who's who of American architecture at the turn of the century, including Sullivan, McKim, Carrère, Warren, Pope, Kahn, and Van Alen. Not only did many of the most famous American architects of the era attend the Ecole, they went on to found architectural firms where they shared their training with like-minded colleagues, further reinforcing the dominance of the Beaux-Arts style. Certainly the most famous of these firms was McKim, Mead and White. Charles McKim, an Ecole graduate, teamed up with the brilliant Stanford White to design a number of the most famous buildings ever built in this country, including Grand Central's rival, Pennsylvania Station.

In city after city, America was demanding architects with imagination,

to establish a new form of architectural expression to capture the age. Ecole graduates, with their experience of numerous design competitions while in Paris, were superbly prepared for the architectural competitions by which the designs for state capitols, public buildings, great libraries, railroad stations, and the like were chosen. For example, between 1886 and 1926 twenty-four new state capitols were designed and built and almost all involved a formal design competition. Ecole-trained architects' well-developed presentation skills won almost every major architectural commission.

An early triumph of Beaux-Arts design on the American shore came with the World's Columbian Exposition in 1893. The Exposition included construction of the White City, a series of Beaux-Arts buildings which served as exhibition halls to display the new products of the American industrial revolution. Millions of Americans journeyed to Chicago to visit the White City and gaze upon the wondrous products of American

The Beaux-Arts on display in America: the central lagoon at the World Columbian Exposition, Chicago, 1893

genius, energy, and imagination. Daniel Burnham of Chicago, chief architect of the Exposition and a graduate of the Ecole, assembled a distinguished group of American architects and artists to design the buildings, grounds, fountains, and statues for the fair. Included among the Exposition's architects were a number of illustrious graduates of the Ecole: Richard Morris Hunt, H. H. Richardson, Louis Sullivan, and Charles McKim.

The Columbian Exposition's White City drew its inspiration directly from the Paris Universal Exposition of 1889, where Ecole architects designed the major buildings, including the Petit Palais by Girault and the Grand Palais by Deglane. Both the Petit Palais and the Grand Palais remain, as does the most famous structure built for the Paris Exposition, the Eiffel Tower. Chicago's White City of 1893 perfectly mirrored the buildings constructed in Paris four years earlier. Daniel Burnham's central role ensured the dominance of the Beaux-Arts and confirmed the Beaux-Arts as the most forceful means for architectural expression at the turn of the century.

The Grand Court at the Columbian Exposition, illuminated by electricity

America's Beaux-Arts buildings did not merely copy buildings of Paris

The Beaux-Arts in New York: McKim, Mead and White's Pennsylvania Station at 33rd Street

or Rome; rather, they expressed a particular American interpretation of the lessons of the Ecole. Their sheer energy and vitality distinguished them from their European predecessors. Even Le Corbusier, the acerbic architectural theorist and polemicist for modern architecture, soon to replace Beaux-Arts, recognized the uniqueness and originality of the Beaux-Arts in the United States: "In New York then, I learn to appreciate the Italian Renaissance. It is so well done that you could believe it to be genuine. It even has a strange, new firmness which is not Italian, but American!"[17] Vincent Scully, renowned architectural and art historian, simply and eloquently characterized the achievements of the Beaux-Arts in America at the turn of the century: "The Beaux-Arts tended to build better monuments and urban spaces than the later period, at least in America, has been able to do."[18]

Grand Central and Beaux-Arts Design

Graduates of the Ecole found great success in New York. The list of important public and private buildings designed by graduates of the

Drawing of the interior of Grand Central, detailing the complexity of the new, multilevel facility

Ecole includes the Customs Building, the Municipal Building across from City Hall, the Post Office at 34th Street, the Flatiron Building, Pennsylvania Station, the New York Public Library, and the Chrysler Building. Grand Central Terminal embodies all of the essential elements the training at the Ecole des Beaux-Arts sought to impart. Above all else, Grand Central's design allows for the steady flow of thousands of people each day to and from the heart of the metropolis. The arrangement of interior spaces composes a clearly laid out pattern of circulation so that passengers move from the street to their trains smoothly and without confusion. At the Ecole, design problems often involved the planning of large public buildings, and the arrangement of the interior was of paramount importance. Interior rooms, regardless of size, had to lead logically from the entrance to the "main element." At the heart of a Beaux-Arts building, the central space, where the primary function of the building took place, provided the focal point for the entire design.

The New York Public Library, on Fifth Avenue at 42nd Street, two blocks from Grand Central, provides a perfect example of this principle. Constructed at the same time as the terminal and designed by John M. Carrère and Thomas Hastings, both of whom studied at the Ecole, the

library includes a clearly defined path leading from the entrance on Fifth Avenue to the central space, the main reading room. The main reading room sits at the top of the building, three stories above the primary entrance. Beaux-Arts design requires a clear path, and at the library this is provided by a series of grand stairways that lead through a series of galleries and corridors. Anticipation builds as the visitor climbs to the third floor to the McGraw Rotunda, with carved-wood walls and a painted ceiling, and then through the catalogue room to the climactic space. Recently, the restoration of the main reading room of the library returned this magnificent space to its turn-of-the-century glory.

As soon as Whitney Warren became involved with the design of Grand Central, his attention turned to the "main element," the space at the heart of the terminal. Reed and Stem's plans included a central concourse with

Final floor plan of the new Grand Central

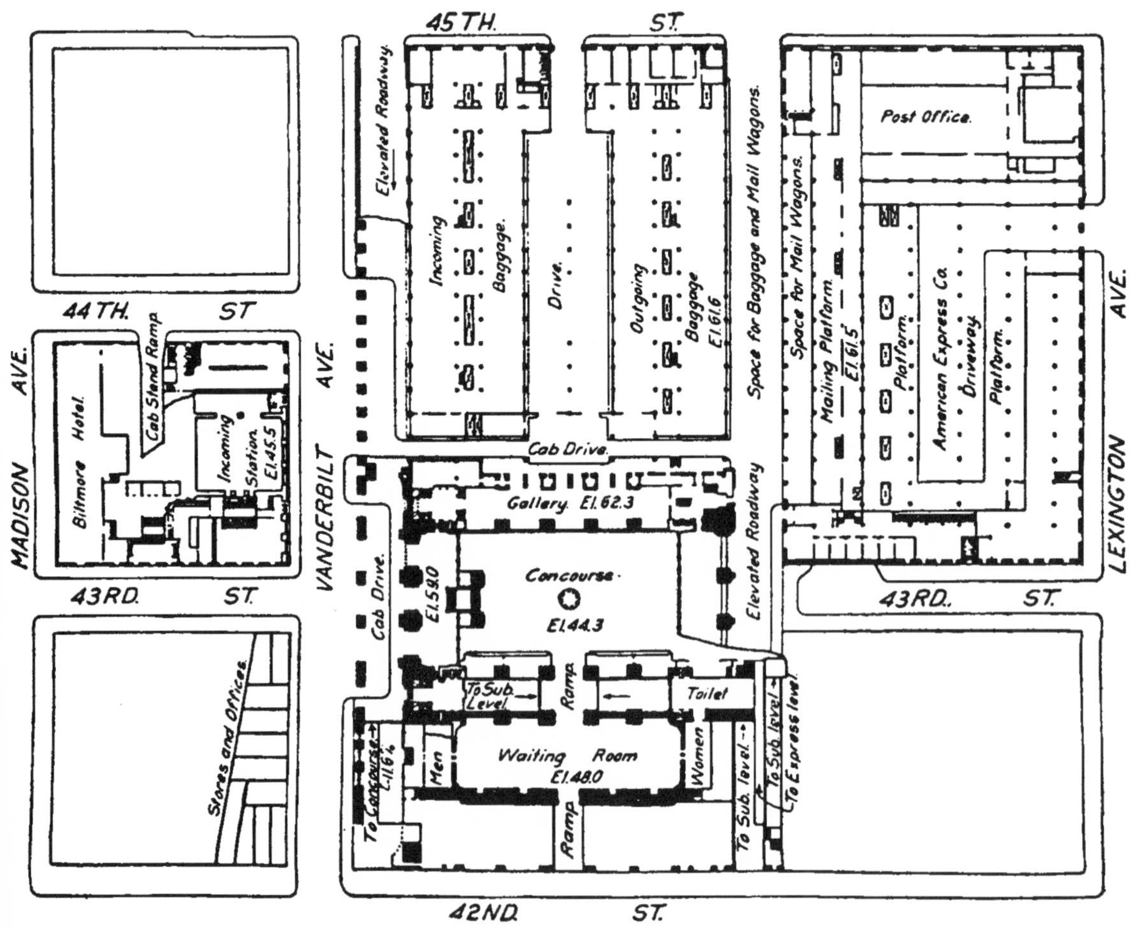

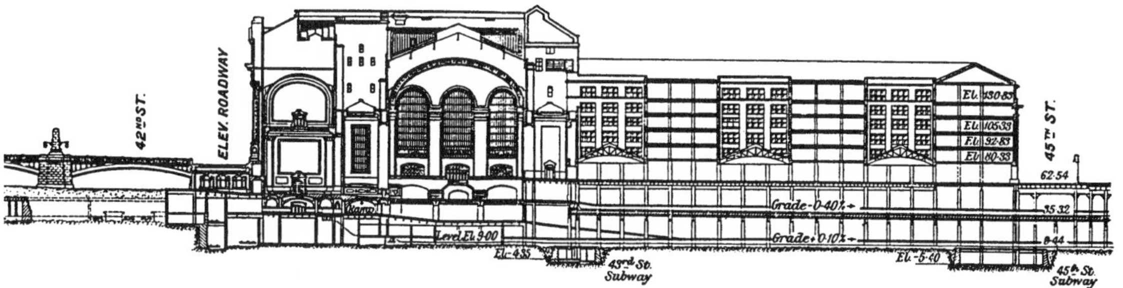

SECTION THROUGH LEXINGTON AVENUE LOOKING WEST

Cross-sectional drawing showing elevations of each level of Whitney Warren's design

access to the train tracks, but their concourse was relatively small in scale. Warren dramatically altered the nature of the concourse and made it the central focus of the plan, so that the entire terminal revolved around a much larger central space. Soaring higher than five stories, with second-floor galleries overlooking the first floor, Warren's Grand Concourse clearly reflects his training at the Ecole des Beaux-Arts. On a somewhat smaller scale, Warren repeated this scheme on the lower, suburban level, which has its own concourse providing access to the train platforms. On both the through and suburban levels, Warren's design used an axial arrangement of space and succession of spaces to move passengers to their trains with clarity and without confusion.

The building's central public spaces for handling incoming and departing passengers provide a model of coherence and clarity. From the main entrance on 42nd Street, the path leads downward, by ramp, through the waiting room, to the Grand Concourse. From the cab stand on Vanderbilt Avenue, the path leads to a balcony overlooking the central space of the building and then down a processional staircase, modeled after Garnier's staircase in the Paris Opera, to the floor of the Grand Concourse. Other spaces radiate outward. Ramps continue the march to the lower level concourse; the path remains clear and unequivocal.

An essential element of Beaux-Arts design is that the outside of a building reveals what is within. According to Garnier, this was "a great first principle, a principle of reason and truth. It is the requisite: the exterior mass, the composition of the outside, indicate the interior plane, the composition of the inside."[19] The classical exteriors of both the New York Public Library and Grand Central signify the important functions within. Not intended to house ordinary commercial activities, the New

York Public Library and Grand Central Terminal serve knowledge on the one hand and travel on the other. One cannot mistake these Beaux-Arts buildings for anything else; their exterior language speaks clearly.

Warren insisted on a low-rise, monumental exterior for Grand Central instead of the high-rise office building of the original Reed and Stem design. He realized that a high-rise office building with the railroad terminal occupying the first three or four stories would simply be another office building in a city filling with such structures. By contrast, his monumental treatment, with its triumphal arches facing south down Park Avenue, created the triumphal entryway that, he wrote, every great city deserved. Whitney Warren's original elevation for Grand Central includes three grand arches flanked by paired columns, suggesting the arched gateways to the city of Paris, topped by a large sculpture consisting of figures from the ancient myths. Exterior ornamentation, not for mere show or decoration, set the scale of the building and reflected the importance of the activity to take place within. Exterior ornamentation followed the interior plan, and the classical ornamentation of the Beaux-

The Grand Concourse at the opening of the terminal in 1913, from the balcony, looking east

Arts style served to complement the rationality of the interior plan, not to overwhelm it. At Grand Central, the elaborate exterior clearly conveyed a sense of exuberant wealth and power. Warren's patrons, the New York Central and the Vanderbilts, expected nothing less.

Warren crowned the south facade with a pure Beaux-Arts sculpture. No building of a monumental nature could be considered complete without ancient gods to adorn it. The sculptor chosen to execute the statues for the south facade, Jules Alexis Coulan of Paris, held the coveted position of professor at the Ecole des Beaux-Arts. Whitney Warren had studied with Coulan while in Paris. William K. Vanderbilt played a role in selecting Mercury as the personage to crown the building's south facade. He knew his mythology; after all, he had directed Richard Morris Hunt to adorn the doors of his Newport mansion with Apollo. The *New York Times* described the theme of the sculpture as "an attempt to offer a

The waiting room, Vanderbilt Hall, 1914

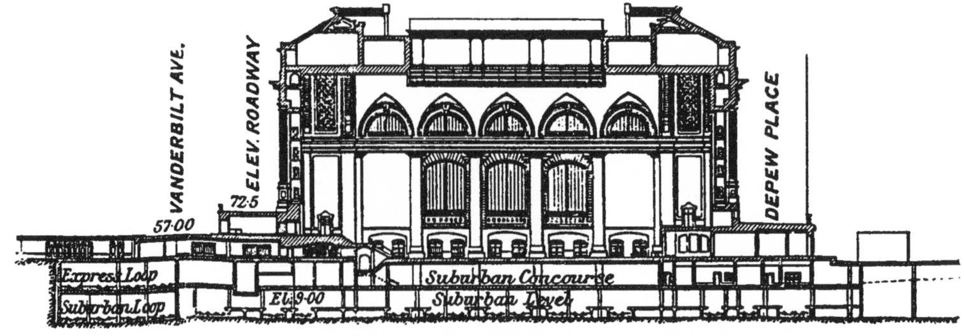

SECTION THROUGH CONCOURSE

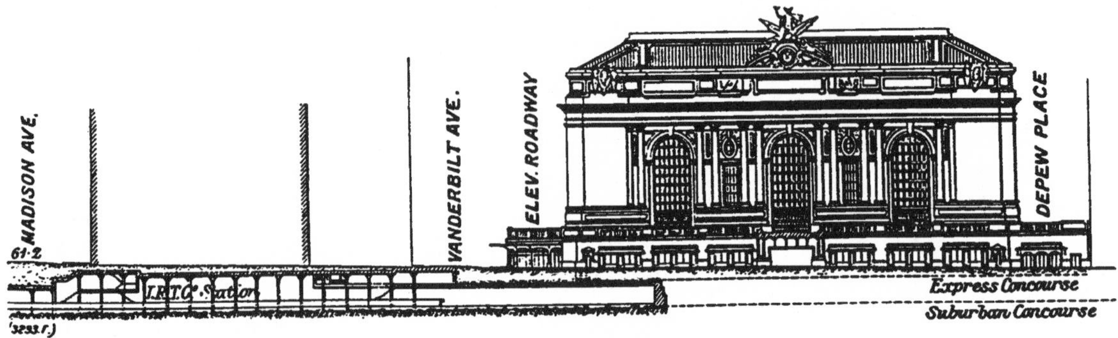

42ND STREET ELEVATION

Facade and sectional views of the 42nd Street side of Warren's building

tribute to the glory of commerce as exemplified by [the New York Central] . . . the whole to stand as a monument to the glory of commerce as typified by Mercury, supported by moral and mental energy—Hercules and Minerva. All to attest that this great enterprise has grown and exists, not merely from the wealth expended, nor by the revenue derived, but by the brain and brawn constantly concentrated upon its development for nearly a century."[20] If William K. Vanderbilt had a god bedecking his monument to himself in Newport, then his railroad needed at least three gods to adorn its monument in New York. The Central envisioned the new terminal's lasting through the ages in the heart of the greatest city in the world. Three triumphal arches facing down Park Avenue, with the gods soaring overhead, reminded all New York of the important role played by the New York Central Railroad, the heart of the Vanderbilt system.

An early architectural evaluation of Grand Central argued that New Yorkers would soon come to regard the Beaux-Arts exterior of the new terminal as a work of great beauty: "It is expected that the exterior shall

The Beaux-Arts at Grand Central: erection of Jules Coulan's sculpture of Mercury, Minerva, and Hercules at top of the 42nd Street facade, 1914

appeal to the average citizen, that in its shape and in the composition of lights and shadows which give it its character—lights and shadows formed by cornices and pilasters, not to mention windows and doors—there shall be something that will have that quality which the public understands as architectural beauty."[21] Indeed, Grand Central, although constructed by a private company, serves as a public building in the broadest sense of the word. The Grand Concourse, the central element of the building, provides a secular cathedral to the spirit of commerce and the exuberance of travel. It continues to serve as both a gateway to the city and as a magnificent public building that lifts the spirits of all who pass through it.

Grand Central and the City Beautiful

During the 1900s, New York's population grew at a frenzied pace. Social and physical disorganization prevailed. Even on Fifth Avenue, where fashionable stores catered to the affluent, no symmetry or similarity of

style characterized the architecture. New York did not pass its first zoning law until 1916, only then dividing the city into districts for residential and commercial use and limiting tenement density, to ensure adequate light and air for the city's poor. Reformers led by George McAneny called for the city to organize a citizen's advisory committee to draft the first master plan for New York, to beautify the city streets, build parks and recreation areas for the poor, and recommend laws to regulate building height and tenement construction.

New York's tentative steps represented the influence of the City Beautiful movement, which at the turn of the century sought to bring beauty and harmony to the chaos of the American city. With an emphasis on aesthetics as well as systematic planning, the movement proposed to improve the environment in the country's teeming urban centers by constructing magnificent public and private buildings, civic centers, boulevards, and parks. Proponents argued that more beautiful and dignified physical surroundings would influence city residents and lead to a more harmonious life for all residents, from the humblest tenement dweller to the richest resident in the most exclusive neighborhood.[22] In the United States, the origins of the City Beautiful concept began with the evolution of the profession of landscape architecture and in particular with the work of Frederick Law Olmsted, who, with his partner Calvert Vaux, designed and oversaw the construction of Central Park.[23] Central Park remains the crowning achievement of the landscape architecture movement in the mid-nineteenth century. Olmsted intended the park to beautify the city as well as to bring a sense of order and decorum to the urban scene. Central Park further stimulated the movement of New York's population up Manhattan Island, especially after the city paved Fifth Avenue from 14th Street to 58th Street, the southern entrance to the park. With the opening of Central Park, Fifth Avenue north of 42nd Street emerged as the most fashionable address in the city, home to the Vanderbilts and other titans of the Gilded Age. A resounding success, Central Park prospers today, one of the great urban parks in the world.

In Europe, the transformation of Paris by Baron Haussmann during the Second Empire directly influenced the idea of the City Beautiful in the United States. Haussmann reconstructed large parts of Paris, building the grand boulevards that lend so much to the beauty and grandeur of

that city. These boulevards created great urban vistas terminating at the sites of Paris's monumental buildings, which had been designed by architects trained at the Ecole des Beaux-Arts. City Beautiful plans in this country usually included both grand boulevards and monumental civic buildings, to provide the American city with the broad vistas and soaring civic complexes Haussmann so successfully introduced into the Parisian landscape.

The Columbian Exposition's White City epitomized the City Beautiful's commitment to comprehensive planning, for its monumental buildings and exhibition halls were constructed around a central lagoon. Neoclassical in design, all of the main buildings reflected the Beaux-Arts style and the influence of chief architect Daniel Burnham. Visitors to the White City drew the obvious contrast between the order, harmony, and sheer beauty of the Exposition and the ugliness and squalor of America's cities. If the White City could be beautiful and harmonious, why couldn't New York or Chicago or Cleveland also be?

Burnham himself grasped the essential issue and wrote that, at the Exposition's White City, "a great truth, set forth by artists, was taught to our people. The truth is the supreme one of the need of design and plan for whole cities."[24] To implement the City Beautiful, to construct a White City in an American city required a comprehensive master plan. Not surprisingly, calls for master plans by City Beautiful advocates immediately encountered resistance from property interests in cities, who objected to having limitations placed upon the use of their private property.

This battle between private property rights and a desire for public planning to regulate the use of private property to promote the "common good" echoes to the present day. When the City of New York passed its Landmarks Preservation Law in 1965, the law saved Grand Central from destruction. In turn, the New York Central Railroad argued that Grand Central's landmark designation deprived the company of the rights inherent in its private property. Eventually the legal battle reached the U.S. Supreme Court. Advocates of landmarks preservation argued that buildings like Grand Central and the New York Public Library are not merely utilitarian structures but also serve to beautify and inspire and that New York had an obligation to see to their active preservation, or all traces of the best of the city's architectural heritage would disappear.

In New York, the City Beautiful movement led to the first master plan for the City of New York, prepared in 1907 by the New York Public Improvement Committee. Great fanfare greeted publication of the plan. However, the plan achieved limited success because it ignored the underlying economic forces shaping the city and proved unable to reconcile private property rights with the need for government regulation to order the built environment.

At the very time the Public Improvement Committee published its ambitious plan, the New York Central's new terminal complex was moving forward at a frenzied pace. When completed, the project had transformed a sprawling section of midtown Manhattan into a harmonious complex of hotels, offices, and apartments, the kind of planned urban environment the City Beautiful envisioned; at 42nd Street rose New York's version of the White City. An early evaluation of the impact of Grand Central on the area around the terminal praised the new buildings as "most harmonious and better balanced than any group of buildings in any other American city."[25] Newspaper and magazine accounts placed the new rail facility and the accompanying "Terminal City" development squarely in the context of efforts to beautify the American city. In 1910, before the new terminal opened, a *New York Herald* article entitled "More Millions to be Spent in Beautifying the New Grand Central Terminal" commented on the likely impact of the sums being spent by the New York Central. According to the paper, the railroad's effort had evolved "with a view to making its Forty-second Street terminal one of the beauty spots of the city."[26] Robert Pope, writing in one of the first issues of *Town Planning Review,* the official journal of the new profession of urban planning, added: "When all the buildings that cover the surface of this huge terminal are completed they will form one of the most wonderfully beautiful groups of structures in the world. . . . In this section of New York, at least, there will be a level sky line, like that which is so much admired in the cities of Europe."[27] In his view, Grand Central stood among the most beautiful buildings in the world and the New York Central's planned collection of buildings around Grand Central, all of a uniform height and design, compared favorably with the best of Paris.

A review in the *New York Times* made reference to the original Reed and Stem plan for a "Court of Honor," which the writer expected to be

constructed along the newly restored Park Avenue, north of the terminal and, according to the newspaper, soon to be the new home of the Metropolitan Opera: "The possibility was immediately presented [the directors of the Metropolitan Opera House], of having Park Avenue open into a great plaza with a stately new opera house set in the center, rivaling the beauty of the Place de l'Opera in Paris."[28] While the 1907 master plan for New York never materialized, Grand Central achieved a greater impact on the urban fabric of New York than any other building project in the first half of the twentieth century, until construction began on Rockefeller Center.

Charles Mumford Robinson, a leading advocate of comprehensive planning at the turn of the century, identified three goals of the City Beautiful: "a bettering of those circulatory problems that have been created by congested traffic, the improvement of social conditions in many directions, and increasing the visible beauty and splendor of cities."[29] The Grand Central project more than met all three of Robinson's goals.

Grand Central represented systematic planning and construction on a grand scale; the railroad took an open train yard that ran from 42nd to 54th streets between Lexington and Madison avenues and placed it underground. In the air, over the two-story underground railroad yard and terminal, the railroad constructed a new terminal, followed by hotels, offices, and apartment buildings. The railroad deliberately set out, as the *Times* described it, "to fashion anew that entire section of the city where the old station stood, to build or cause to be built thirty blocks of buildings in Manhattan, all guided by one hand that would supervise their purpose and direct the general harmony of architecture."[30]

Advocates for the City Beautiful, Robinson and Pope among them, realized that for the turn-of-the-century city to function properly, improved transportation was vital. In New York, a step in this direction came with the construction of the city's first subway, the Interborough Rapid Transit, to run under Fourth (Park) Avenue to Grand Central, turn to the west under 42nd Street to Broadway at Times Square, and then continue uptown. From the first, plans for Grand Central included links to the city's new subway system. William Wilgus envisioned the New York Central's tracks connecting directly with the subway "so that

certain portions of the trains can pass under 42nd Street and thence to the Battery."[31] Wilgus's plan for a direct connection with the IRT was never realized. Even without it, Grand Central remains the preeminent example of the type of transportation hub Robinson and the City Beautiful advocates espoused.

A central goal of the City Beautiful movement involved improvement of social conditions in the American city. The first Grand Central's open train yard hardly benefited social conditions in the neighborhood to the north and east of the station. By comparison, the new Grand Central served as a catalyst for the transformation of the east side of Manhattan in the vicinity of 42nd Street. Wilgus wrote that the open train yard from 45th to 49th streets had acted as a "veritable 'Chinese Wall' to separate the city into two parts for fourteen blocks—nearly three quarters of a mile—between 42nd Street and 56th Street, and forced the discontinuance of a leading north and south thoroughfare, then known as Fourth Avenue."[32] Crossing these obstacles to normal urban traffic were the footbridges and viaducts that spanned the train yard, but the noise, steam, and dirt had discouraged all but the hardiest travelers from crossing.

Commercial activity had intermingled with residential buildings around the old Grand Central. Both the Adams Express and American Express companies operated freight buildings on 48th and Lexington Avenue adjacent to the train yard and the American Express Company's stables occupied a building on 42nd Street between Second and Third avenues. The F. and M. Schaeffer Brewery filled the block from 49th to 50th streets, the present site of the Waldorf-Astoria Hotel, and further north the Steinway Piano factory stood on the corner of Park and 52nd Street. Slaughterhouses and meat-packing plants, such as United Dressed Beef at 43rd and the Sulzberger Slaughter House at 44th, lined the East River.

After construction of the new Grand Central, apartments and the most fashionable hotels in New York rose over the underground rail yard as part of Terminal City: the Ambassador, Biltmore, Commodore, and eventually the Waldorf-Astoria, in 1932. Office buildings followed: the Graybar Building on Lexington between 42nd and 43rd and the New York Central Building on 54th Street; later the Chrysler Building (1930)

at 42nd and Lexington and the Daily News Building (1930) at 42nd and Second Avenue. Grand Central Terminal stimulated the development of the entire district around 42nd Street. This accomplishment fulfilled hopes that the City Beautiful would serve as a catalyst for urban change.

The comprehensively designed project converted Grand Central from an obstacle to urban development into a dynamic catalyst for change, transforming Park Avenue north of 45th Street into Manhattan's only grand boulevard. A Park Avenue association soon formed and provided the funds to landscape the center median as a park with walkways, flowers, and benches, mirroring the boulevards of Paris. Park Avenue flourished as the most prestigious residential district in New York and in the entire country, precisely the goal of the City Beautiful—the transformation of the crowded, decayed, and ugly into the harmonious and beautiful.

The boulevard provided the perfect setting for the Beaux-Arts buildings that followed. Warren's New York Central Building, built in 1929, further enhanced the beauty of Park Avenue and fit perfectly with the series of apartment buildings constructed over the New York Central's underground train yard. These first air rights buildings, of uniform design and height, with matching cornices, created a sense of continuity as they flowed northward from the New York Central Building. Given the width of the new Park Avenue, these grand buildings did not overpower the street below.

Since the City Beautiful movement sought to increase the beauty and splendor of the city, to magnify a sense of grandeur, the Beaux-Arts neoclassical style provided the perfect architectural vocabulary. Whitney Warren compared Grand Central to the triumphal gates of ancient cities: "This portal was usually decorated and elaborated into an Arch of Triumph, erected to some naval or military victory or the glory of some personage. The city of today has no surrounding wall that may serve, by elaboration, as a pretext to such glorification, but none the less, the gateway must exist, and in the case of New York and other cities, it is through a tunnel which discharges the human flow in the very center of the town. Such is the Grand Central terminal and the motive of the facade is an attempt to offer a tribute to the glory of commerce as exemplified by that institution."[33] Warren's comments apply to the interior

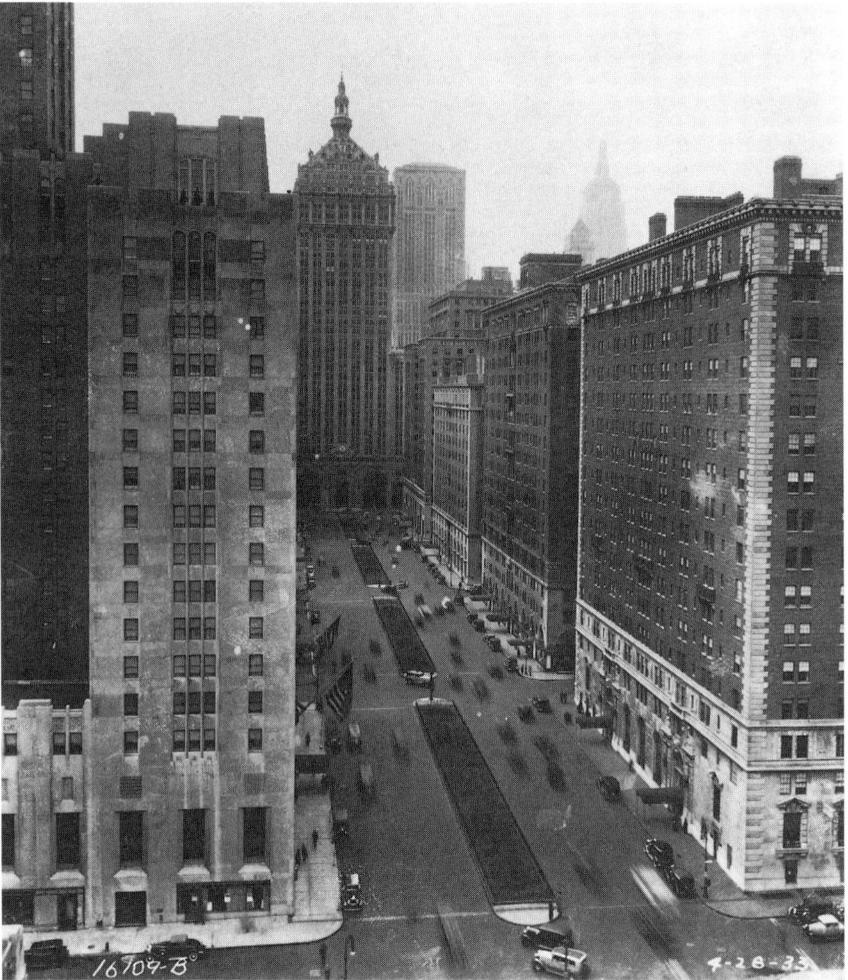

Original air rights buildings along Park Avenue north of Grand Central, looking south from 49th Street toward the New York Central Building, 1933

of Grand Central as well. The Grand Concourse became New York's most famous interior space and provided New York with a secular cathedral larger than the nave of Notre Dame in Paris.

Certainly Grand Central's architecture inspired hymns, but at what cost? An article in *Railway Age Gazette* in 1913 pointed to the extraordinary capital costs of both Grand Central and Pennsylvania Station: "The new passenger terminal facilities of the New York Central in New York City will probably cost $200,000,000 when completed. This sum would build 2,000 miles of double track road at $100,000 a mile. The fixed charges, taxes and depreciation will amount to nearly $20,000,000 per annum."[34] Operating expenses and maintenance for the two facilities

added $3,000,000 in expenses. For Grand Central, yearly costs equaled 80 percent of the New York Central and New Haven railroads' combined gross from passenger revenue to and from New York. Building and operating these monumental terminals strained even the wealth of the mighty Central and Pennsylvania systems.

In an ironic comment, the author of the *Railroad Age Gazette* article chastised the railroads for spending such profligate sums on passenger terminals when their freight business provided a more important source of both revenue and profit: "vast sums are, or have been, expended in providing elaborate passenger terminals and only insignificant appropriations made for handling the more important freight traffic."[35] The comment proved prophetic: soon enough the railroads entered a period of slow, steady decline, losing the battle for passenger travel to the automobile and airplane and the battle for freight traffic to the truck. When the decline set in, passenger service became unprofitable first. Maintenance costs for palatial railroad terminals on the scale of Grand Central and Pennsylvania Station contributed significantly to overall losses. In the early 1900s, railroad executives could not have imagined the competitive forces just over the horizon.

CHAPTER FOUR

New York's Grand Central

As the new Grand Central took shape at 42nd Street, the social transformation of New York continued. Waves of immigrants from southern and eastern Europe changed the complex mix of people crowded onto Manhattan Island. The population of the outer boroughs grew as the city's first subway lines allowed the more affluent to move. As suburban rail lines stretched into Westchester and Fairfield counties to the north and Nassau County to the east, the wealthy, and soon New York's expanding middle class, could contemplate moving farther from the city's urban core.

New York was a place of extraordinary contrast, where the lives of the rich and the poor and the various ethnic enclaves stood in stark contrast with one another. The city's expanding rapid transit system offered the opportunity to glimpse the juxtaposition. William Dean Howells, in his novel *A Hazard of New Fortune,* captures this contrast as his middle-class character March travels downtown on the Third Avenue El: "He went over to Third Avenue and took the elevated down to Chatham Square. He found the variety of people in the car as unfailingly entertaining as ever. . . . Now and then he found himself in a car mostly filled with Neapolitans from the construction far up the line, where he had read that they are worked and fed and housed like beasts. . . . March never entered a car without encountering some interesting shape of shabby adversity, which was always adversity of foreign birth. . . . The small eyes, the high

cheeks, the broad noses, the puff lips, the bare, cue-filiated skulls, of Russians, Poles, Czechs, Chinese; the furtive glitter of Italians, the blond dullness of Germans; the cold quiet of Scandinavians—fire under ice."[1]

In this remarkable passage Howells distilled all of the prejudice and fear that the immigrant city evoked in the mind of the native born. A clash seems obvious; the newcomer remains foreign, different. Howells muses whether these immigrants will ever be assimilated into the American commonwealth. Just three or four blocks to the west, where the new Grand Central rose, and along Madison and Fifth avenues, lay another America, into which few Russians, Neapolitans, Germans, or Scandinavians ventured unless they worked as servants for the self-styled American aristocracy—the Vanderbilts, Morgans, and Astors.

The Grand Central complex exerted a greater influence on the social, residential, and commercial structure of Manhattan Island and New York City than any other building project in the city's history. With perhaps the exception of Pierre L'Enfant's and later James McMillan's plans for the nation's capital, no other building project ever produced as great an effect on an American city.

At the dawn of the twentieth century, the New York Central set out not only to build a magnificent new terminal but also to develop its extensive real estate holdings in Midtown, with new office buildings, hotels, and apartments over the new underground terminal and train yard to the north. Whether intentionally or not, the ownership of the railroad became the major real estate developer in midtown Manhattan while remaining the proprietors of the second largest railroad system in the country.

Air Rights

William Wilgus premised his entire plan for the new Grand Central on the development of the "air rights" over the new station and the electrification of the train yard. Wilgus believed that "the use of electricity dispenses with the necessity for the old style trainsheds. . . . there is no reason why we should not utilize all of the valuable 'air' rights now covered by trainsheds, aggregating over 200,000 square feet of surface area."[2] Wilgus had first suggested developing the air rights directly above the arched train

shed of the old Grand Central. These rights alone, according to Wilgus's calculations, would pay for the construction of the new Grand Central and the depression and electrification of the entire train yard. As the Grand Central projected unfolded, it became obvious to Wilgus, President William Newman, and the other officers of the Central that the opportunity existed to develop not just the air rights over the terminal area, but also over all of the railroad's extensive holdings in midtown Manhattan.

The railroad's property stretched north from 42nd Street to 54th Street, between Madison and Lexington avenues. Acquired over time, first by the Harlem Railroad and later by the New York Central, the property had initially served as only a train yard for the railroad's operations in Manhattan. When the Harlem first purchased property at 42nd Street in the mid-1800s, the location stood well north of the city's developed area, which was concentrated on the southern end of Manhattan Island. The Harlem did not acquire the land because of any farsighted plan to develop the real estate; rather, the railroad bought the property for a train yard precisely because the location was far removed from the city proper. As a result, the railroad encountered little opposition as it steadily expanded its facilities at 42nd Street.

As time passed, the neighborhood around 42nd Street emerged as a thriving midtown business, commercial, and residential area. By the time the New York Central began planning for the new Grand Central, the railroad's property at 42nd Street had become extremely valuable, not as a rail yard, but as real estate. Wilgus pointed out to the railroad that his proposed twelve-story office building, with 2,300,000 square feet of rental space, would generate net revenue of $1,350,000 per year.[3] If a single office building could generate in excess of one million dollars in profit per year, what would be the potential financial gain to the Central if it built office buildings, hotels, and apartments over all of the railroad's property in Midtown? For the 1901–2 fiscal year, revenue of the New York Central, from all its vast railroad operations stretching from New York to Chicago and St. Louis, totaled $61 million. By developing just a small portion of the railroad's acreage in the city, the railroad stood to gain almost $1.3 million in additional *profit*. Potentially, the New York Central's property at 42nd Street represented a tremendous asset, once the air rights development got under way.

The term *air rights* embodied a new concept in property ownership. An article in *Railway Age* observed that the Grand Central project "introduced in our system of railroad economics the conception of a new value of railroad property; namely, that of air rights over railroad tracks and new facilities."[4] Hugh Thompson, writing in *Munsey's Magazine*, defined precisely what air rights involved and explained their potential value: "Air rights simply mean the right to build over ground you own. Most people do not stop to consider that ordinarily there are three rights in the ownership of property—the ground right, giving possession of the surface; the lower right, giving power to excavate or mine; and the upper right or air right. . . . the air rights will doubtless prove immensely valuable."[5] Thompson could not have foreseen just how valuable the New York Central's air rights would prove to be. Today, the air rights over the underground terminal remain the most valuable real estate in the world.

Taking advantage of air rights would allow railroads to become significantly involved in real estate development. However, Joshua D'Esposito, in the *Railway Age* article on air rights, advised that real estate development should remain a sideline for railroads: "It is important to keep in mind one cardinal principle: that the railroad needs are always paramount, and the air rights incidentals. After all, the principal duty of a railroad is to manufacture and sell transportation, and every other activity should be subordinated to this primary requirement."[6] Irony abounds in these remarks. In 1970 the Penn Central, successor to the New York Central, declared bankruptcy—the largest corporation to that date in American history to do so. Yet the railroad's real estate holdings in midtown New York continued to be immensely valuable. The railroad's painful decline had reversed Pope's dictum; the Penn Central's air rights development, no mere "incidentals," composed the company's major assets, but its efforts to sell transportation had led to bankruptcy.

A Civic Center in Midtown

Recognizing the potential financial gains, the railroad set out to construct a "terminal city" utilizing all of the company's air rights from 42nd Street to 56th Street. When completed, the result was a vast real estate empire. Wilgus, writing in 1940, summarized the development of the

Painting of Terminal City which appeared on the cover of New York Central's brochure celebrating the opening of Grand Central in February 1913

Central's real estate in Midtown and called the cluster of buildings a "Superimposed Civic Center": "It will be recalled with the coming of electricity as motive power, and the opportunity thereby presented for the enjoyment of air rights which until then necessarily had lain fallow, it was proposed that buildings should be erected over the terminal that would produce revenue. In fact, steel columns beneath had been designed sufficiently strong for that purpose. Gradually, in time, primarily under the guidance of Mr. Newman, this has been brought about to a degree that has far exceeded the fond expectations of the writer." Over the underground tracks rose world-class hotels—the Biltmore, the Commodore, the Roosevelt—and office buildings—the Graybar and the New York Central building. In addition the air rights included special-purpose buildings—Grand Central Palace, the Yale Club, and the U.S. Post Office—and stately rows of apartment buildings of the highest class along Park and Lexington avenues as far north as 50th Street and along Madison Avenue and Vanderbilt Avenue as far north as 48th Street and 49th Street, respectively. Wilgus concluded, "The Grand Central Zone has become a self-contained city clearly evident to the casual onlooker who little

knows that beneath it are the terminal yards of two great railroad systems."[7] Wilgus's description applies to many of the hundreds of thousands who work and stroll through the Grand Central zone today.

Plans for Terminal City moved beyond the size and scope of any other building project ever undertaken in New York or in any American city. In the first place, a single entity, the New York Central Railroad, directed the entire effort. In a thirty-block area of Manhattan, a single company built a complex of buildings all linked to a central core, Grand Central. Tunnels and underground passages allowed people to move from the terminal to hotels and office buildings without venturing onto the city streets. Most importantly, the overall control exercised by the railroad ensured a harmonious blend of architectural style and elevation. Just as Haussmann had imposed a uniformity of design and elevation along the boulevards of Paris, the Central planned a harmony of design for its Terminal City, earning the applause of urban planners in the City Beautiful movement, such as Robert Pope.[8]

Bemoaning the lack of consistency amidst the building frenzy in America's cities, city planners and advocates of the City Beautiful pointed out that no zoning regulations or building codes shaped the type of structures that could be constructed right next to each other. No powerful monarchy as in Europe controlled the architecture of cities by decree or used the resources of the state to construct harmonious buildings infused with a sense of monumental glory. In the United States, by contrast, a strong tradition of privacy of property meant that one owner could build totally at odds with his neighbors. However, because the New York Central owned so much property around Grand Central, the company could impose harmony of design and detail. As the *New York Times* wrote when Grand Central opened in 1913: "They undertook to fashion anew that entire section of the city where the old station stood, to build or cause to be built thirty blocks of buildings in Manhattan, all guided by one hand that would supervise their purposes and direct the general harmony of architecture. The result is a real estate development of monumental proportions."[9] With the exception of Rockefeller Center and the urban renewal projects after the Second World War, no other development in New York's history covered such an extensive area of the city with a harmonious blend of buildings.

City Beautiful advocates urged property owners when building to be guided by the comprehensive plans fashioned by the new planning professionals. In almost all cases, the plans fell by the wayside as each property owner built as he pleased. With Terminal City around Grand Central, the New York Central ensured harmony. Writing even before the railroad completed the first phase of the project, historian Edward Hungerford grasped the significance of the plans for Terminal City and recognized that they exemplified the push for civic planning at the turn of the century: "in midtown has begun to rise the most important single development that New York has ever known. . . . And the city of New York gets at a fell swoop a civic center such as is the aim and hope of every progressive American town of today."[10]

A second reason for Terminal City's success lay in the size of the railroad company's financial resources. Through its investment bankers, J. P. Morgan and Company, New York Central tapped the financial market for the capital necessary to build the new Grand Central and the electrified underground train yard, as well as to develop the air rights over all of its midtown property.

New York State Terminal Realty Company

The New York Central decided to form a real estate company to oversee the development of Terminal City. At a meeting of the executive committee of the board of directors held on December 15, 1903, the directors voted to establish the New York State Terminal Realty Company, whose purpose would be "to construct, acquire, own and manage buildings and structures of all kinds of property including depots, offices, stores, hotels and apartments." The board voted to issue a thousand shares of stock at $100 par. William K. Vanderbilt subscribed to 950, William Rockefeller 10, J. P. Morgan 10, and the remaining shares were purchased by other directors.[11] The stock distribution ensured that the new company would remain under the control of the railroad.

The new company separated the Central's real estate development around Grand Central from its railroad operations. Later the Central added a partner to its efforts at 42nd Street—the New York, New Haven and Hartford Railroad. The tripartite lease with the New Haven and the

Harlem required the Central to share its terminal facilities and to include the New Haven in any real estate projects undertaken in Midtown. Each railroad contributed capital to the realty company, which in turn managed the real estate development projects. Terminal Realty paid the parent companies interest on their investment and eventually returned the initial capital they had advanced. Having a separate real estate company simplified bookkeeping for both the Central and the New Haven.

Terminal Realty proceeded to develop the Central's real estate around the station, either by constructing buildings which it then rented out or by leasing air rights to private developers. For example, it constructed a new U.S. Post Office building, on the corner of Lexington Avenue and 43rd Street, at a cost of $931,000 and rented it to the U.S. Post Office for $18,620 a year. For the Biltmore Hotel, the real estate company entered into a lease with the United Hotels Corporation, which erected the thirteen-story hotel boasting one thousand rooms. United Hotels would contribute $3,000,000 toward the projected total cost of $6,200,000; Terminal Realty provided the balance. United Hotels' lease ran for twenty-one years at a minimum rent of $280,000 a year to Terminal Realty.[12] The Biltmore represented an excellent investment: lease payments from United Hotels represented a return of over 7 percent on the capital the railroads planned to commit toward the construction of the Biltmore.

In the spring of 1912, the board of directors of the New York Central established a "sinking fund" to account for both the capital advanced to Terminal Realty and the payments received in return. Payments went directly to an account at Guaranty Trust of New York where the money was invested in railroad bonds. Guaranty Trust kept a separate account for each real estate project and, when the account totaled the amount of capital the Central and New Haven had originally contributed, transferred the funds to the two railroads—a very conservative form of financial management. Neither railroad recorded the income on their books until the capital initially advanced for each building had been fully returned with interest.

The Building of Terminal City

Terminal City proceeded in three phases; the first involved the construction of the buildings directly around the new Grand Central. As the

new terminal neared completion, construction commenced on the hotels and office buildings immediately adjacent: the Biltmore and Commodore hotels, the Post Office building, and the Adams Express building on Lexington Avenue. The second phase, beginning several years after Grand Central opened, involved apartments and office buildings on Park Avenue north of the new terminal buildings. Development along Park Avenue, directly over the new underground train yard, continued through the 1920s and into the 1930s. The Waldorf-Astoria Hotel at Park and 49th Street was completed in 1931. During the Depression years of the 1930s, only one additional building rose, 330 Park Avenue, in 1938. A final phase commenced after World War II.

William Wilgus, preparing his history of the Grand Central project, compiled a list of twelve buildings completed in Phase 1 and estimated their replacement cost as of 1939–1940 (see Table 4.1).

Preparation for the first air rights development along Park Avenue, looking south from 50th Street with Biltmore Hotel construction to the right of Grand Central, 1913

Beginning in 1908, just after the completion of the electric zone, and continuing till 1918, these twelve new buildings rose skyward. By 1918, Terminal City already included almost twenty million dollars' worth of new construction and was far from complete. Since Terminal Realty Company's lease payments averaged a 6 percent return on capital, the first phase generated at least a million dollars of revenue a year. In addition, the New York Central received revenue from the heat and electricity it sold to the lessors and tenants of the buildings from its new power plant located on Park Avenue at 49th Street.

With the completion of the first of the air rights buildings around 42nd Street, the immediate area around Grand Central quickly emerged as a fashionable hotel and business district. Soon, the old train yard disappeared, replaced by a collection of the most harmonious and stylish buildings in the city. Even the usually staid *Engineering News-Record* lavishly praised the first phase of the development of the Central's air rights: "The term 'Grand Central' no longer designates a mere railroad station, but a large and impressive civic center. The story of its development in the last twenty years is a romance. . . . The terminal area itself, because of its

Air rights development under way on Park Avenue, looking south from 49th Street, 1918

TABLE 4.1
Terminal City - Phase 1

Building	Address	Year Built	Cost*
U.S. Post Office	Lexington Av. 44–45th	1908	$1,800,000
Grand Central Palace	Lexington Av. 46–47th	1910	$825,000
Adams Express	Lexington Av. 45–46th	1914	$282,000
American Express	Lexington Av. 43–44th	1914	$394,000
United Cigar Building	Vanderbilt Av. 42–43rd	1914	$278,000
Biltmore Hotel	Vanderbilt Av. 43–44th	1914	$4,600,000
Yale Club	Vanderbilt Av. 43rd	1914	$725,000
Vanderbilt-Concourse	Vanderbilt Av. 44th	1914	$850,000
350 Park Av.	Park Av. 51–52nd	1915	$675,000
Marguery Hotel	Park Av. 47–48th	1917	$3,170,000
Chatham Hotel	Park Av. 49–50th	1917	$950,000
Commodore Hotel	Lexington Av. 42–43rd	1918	$5,500,000
TOTAL			$19,224,000

SOURCE: William J. Wilgus Papers, New York Public Library, box 6.
*Wilgus compiled the table in 1938–39 and estimated the buildings' value as 1939 replacement cost.

attractiveness, has become the heart of still greater development, radiating from it in every direction. In fact the whole surrounding neighborhood now goes by the name of the Grand Central District, and is one of the chief business centers of the metropolis."[13]

The description of Terminal City as "radiating" outward proved appropriate. At the center stood Grand Central, the hub of the entire development. With its superb transportation facilities, Grand Central provided smooth entry and exit to the new midtown district arising around 42nd Street. No other business or residential area in New York boasted such a superb transportation network at its core, a prime goal of the City Beautiful.

Commenting on the first phase of the air rights building, the *Engineering News-Record* added a note of praise for the management of the Central: "As a civic as well as a railroad-terminal development, it is unique and stands as a monument to the foresight and ability of the New York Central's officers."[14] After being vilified in the press for years for its failure to build new facilities at 42nd Street, the Central now garnered praise from many quarters with the completion of Grand Central and the first phase of Terminal City. Not only did New York have a magnificent new rail terminal, but the air rights property around Grand Central became decidedly upscale with high-rent office buildings, fashionable hotels, and the Yale Club, where the city's elite could meet in sedate comfort to plan the future.

The second phase of the air rights development carried through the

TABLE 4.2
Terminal City - Phase 2

Building	Address		Year Built	Cost*
460 Lexington Av.	Lexington Av.	45–46th	1920	$3,800,000
290 Park Av.	Park Av.	48–49th	1921	$2,325,000
300 Park Av.	Park Av.	49–50th	1921	$2,425,000
Knapp Building	Park Av.	46–47th	1922	$1,325,000
Knapp Building #2	Park Av.	46–47th	1922	$1,325,000
Park-Lex. Building	Park Av.	46–47th	1923	$1,850,000
Roosevelt Hotel	Vanderbilt Av.	45–46th	1924	$4,400,000
Postum Building	Vanderbilt Av.	46–47th	1924	$3,350,000
277 Park Av.	Park Av.	47–48th	1924	$3,400,000
Park Lane Hotel	Park Av.	48–49th	1924	$2,100,000
Vanderbilt Building	Vanderbilt Av.	42–43rd	1925	$750,000
Barclay Hotel	Lexington Av.	48–49th	1927	$2,800,000
Graybar Building	Lexington Av.	43–44th	1927	$8,500,000
New York Central Bld.	Park Av.	45–46th	1929	$10,550,000
Waldorf-Astoria Hotel	Park Av.	49–50th	1931	$16,200,000
TOTAL				$65,100,000

SOURCE: William J. Wilgus Papers, New York Public Library, box 6.

*Wilgus compiled the table in 1938–39 and estimated the buildings' value as 1939 replacement cost.

decade of the 1920s with construction shifting to Park Avenue north of Grand Central, soon to be regarded as the most beautiful and fashionable avenue in America (see Table 4.2).

Development of the air rights along Park Avenue north of the new terminal provided a number of engineering challenges. Support columns for the new buildings reached down to the bedrock at the lower level of the two-story underground train yard, in some places seventy feet below the surface. The engineers, concerned that the heavy trains passing below would vibrate and transfer the vibrations to the buildings above, isolated the support columns. Wherever a support column passed through the underground structure, the engineers left a clearance space around the column to prevent train vibrations from affecting the buildings above—a costly but absolutely necessary step.

Another challenge involved providing for the necessary utilities. In conventional construction, the heating and water systems occupied the basement, which the air rights buildings lacked; trains, platforms, and tracks filled the area directly below ground. As part of the overall project, the railroad constructed a coal-fired power plant on Park Avenue between 49th and 50th streets, the future home of the Waldorf-Astoria, to provide steam and hot water to the new Grand Central and all of the air rights buildings at the same time, solving the missing-basement problem.

Power plant at Park Avenue and 49th Street, future site of the Waldorf-Astoria Hotel, 1914

The railroad sold steam and hot water to the buildings composing Terminal City, earning a steady profit while offsetting the cost of the power plant. At one time, the power plant provided for twenty-eight air rights buildings running from 42nd to 50th streets between Lexington and Madison avenues.

As construction of additional air rights buildings continued, the power plant at 49th Street reached capacity, and in 1918 the railroad built a second power plant one hundred feet underground at 43rd Street and Lexington between the Commodore Hotel and the Graybar office building. Ingeniously, the designers concealed the smokestack of the second power plant in the northwest corner of the Commodore Hotel, constructed at the same time. In 1929, the railroad contracted with Consolidated Edison to provide power to Grand Central and dismantled the power plants, the facility at 49th making way for the Waldorf-Astoria Hotel.

Together, the total investment in the first two phases of the air rights

Waldorf-Astoria Hotel, at Park Avenue and 49th Street, constructed in 1931

development around Grand Central reached nearly eighty-five million dollars. Never before in the history of New York had a single development led to the investment of such enormous sums in such a brief period of time, representing a massive commitment to the future of the midtown business and residential district.

As early as 1906, before the air rights development got under way, the *New York Times* pointed out that the two new terminals being built in New York, Grand Central and Pennsylvania Station, increased property values in their proximity as opposed to depressing property values, as

TABLE 4.3
Assessed Value, in Millions of Dollars

	1904	1930	Increase $	Increase %
New York City	5,015	19,717	14,702	293
Borough of Manhattan	3,677	10,102	6,425	175
Section 5				
Within the Grand Central zone[a]	700	2,427	1,727	247
Beyond the Grand Central zone[b]	432	1,150	727	168
The Grand Central Zone and Beyond[c]				
Actual	268	1,268	1,000	374
Computed at same rate of increase as Manhattan (174.7%)	268	735	467	175
Increase attributable to the [Grand Central] Transformation	0	533	533	

SOURCE: Quoted from William J. Wilgus, "The Grand Central Terminal in Perspective," *Transactions of the American Society of Civil Engineers* 106, Oct. 1940, p. 1021. (Footnotes in original.)

[a] Between 40th and 96th streets from East River to Sixth Avenue as far north as 59th Street then to 5th Avenue as far north as 96th Street.

[b] Exterior to the Grand Central zone and beyond, to 96th Street.

[c] Between 42nd Street and 96th Street and between Madison Avenue and Lexington Avenue.

open train yards and steam operations had done: "Proximity to a railroad station in many cases has been a rather doubtful recommendation for a property, but at the back, front, and both sides of New York's great transportation center there is apparently no question as to the increased value and utility of every square foot of ground."[15] Wilgus, methodical as ever, developed a detailed analysis of the impact of Grand Central on property values. Wilgus's research focused on the increase in assessed value of property in the Grand Central Zone, defined as the area from 42nd to 96th streets between Lexington and Madison avenues. For comparative purposes he included data for the City of New York, the entire Borough of Manhattan, and Section 5—designated by the City of New York's Tax Assessment office as most of upper Manhattan on the east side (see Table 4.3).

Wilgus argued that if Grand Central had not been built and the open train yard had remained between 42nd and 56th streets, the value of the property in the Grand Central zone would have increased at a rate no greater than that for the Borough of Manhattan in general, which between 1904 and 1930 was 175 percent. In fact, with the construction of Grand Central and Terminal City, the value of property in the Grand Central Zone increased by 374 percent, from $268,000,000 in 1904 to $1.2 billion in 1930. If the property had only increased at the same rate as

Aerial view, ca. 1920, illustrating Grand Central's role as a catalyst for development

all property in Manhattan, its value in 1930 would have been $735,000,000 or $533 million less. Wilgus calculated the impact on the city's tax revenue to be over $14 million a year.

This rapid growth in the value of real estate brought great benefits to the City of New York and to the Central Railroad. As the midtown business district grew, the value of New York Central's own real estate increased; however, the railroad was less concerned with its assessed value than with the value the property commanded on the rental market.

Catalyst to Development

The Commodore's Grand Central Depot, built at ground level, blocked the north-south flow of the city's traffic on the east side at 42nd Street, interrupting the pattern of development in midtown Manhattan

that the city's grid pattern encouraged. The open train yard, stretching north to 56th Street, effectively blocked the development of high-class commercial and residential property to the north and east of the terminal. This separation continued up the east side, because steam, smoke, soot, and noise bellowed up from the tracks, which ran under Park Avenue in the roofed tunnel all the way to 96th Street.

To the west of Park Avenue, especially along Fifth Avenue, the area evolved as the most fashionable residential and commercial district in New York. By contrast, to the east of Park Avenue, the Upper East Side remained a tenement district, home to vast numbers of the city's poor. Factories, breweries, and slaughterhouses intermingled with four- and five-story cold-water tenements.

New York's first subway line started from the Battery, at the southern tip of the island, and traveled north on the east side of Manhattan, where the city's population and commerce were concentrated. The IRT continued north under Park Avenue until it reached the impenetrable barrier

The open train yard that ran from 42nd to 56th streets, spreading soot and noise, 1899

of Grand Central: As part of the planning for Grand Central, the railroad had obtained the underground rights to its property at 42nd Street. This blocked development under Park Avenue north of 42nd Street for ten city blocks and left the subway builders no choice but to turn the subway west toward Times Square before resuming its journey to the northern tip of Manhattan.

In addition to increasing property values, Grand Central strongly influenced a number of crucial changes in the social geography of midtown Manhattan. With the placement under ground of the train yard that had inhibited the growth of midtown Manhattan along the axis of Park Avenue, Wilgus's "Chinese wall" separating the upper east side of Manhattan into two separate and distinct districts moved east. Grand Central became a catalyst rather than a hindrance for urban development. Private developers constructed hundreds of buildings to accompany the railroad's air rights development. Terminal City spread to encompass an even wider area around the new rail facility, many blocks in all directions.

The Chrysler Building provides a clear example of Grand Central's stimulus. Designed by William Van Alen, a graduate of the Ecole des Beaux-Arts and built on the east side of Lexington Avenue at 42nd Street directly across from Grand Central, the Chrysler Building stood as the tallest building in the world until the completion of the Empire State Building in 1931. The Chrysler Building dramatically increased the commercial space available at 42nd Street and added thousands of jobs, and commuters, to the Grand Central district. The increased flow of people

The open train yard in a 1906 photograph contrasted with a drawing predicting vast improvement after the yard's electrification

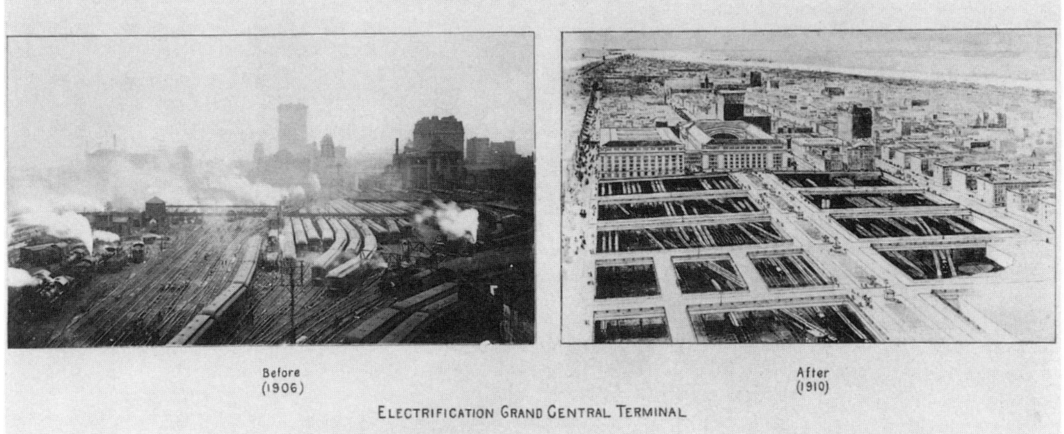

to the Chrysler Building and the other commercial buildings in the area could easily be accommodated by the superb transportation facilities provided by Grand Central.

Other new buildings followed the lead of the Chrysler Building as the axis of development on Manhattan shifted to the east. Third Avenue now marked the line separating the wealthy and poor on New York's east side above Midtown. Until the removal of the Third Avenue El in the early 1950s, the area from Third Avenue to the East River remained a tenement and mixed industrial area, while the area from Lexington to Fifth Avenue increased in prestige, especially Park Avenue to the north of the new terminal.

Gateway to New York

By the turn of the century, most New Yorkers regarded the Commodore's old Grand Central Depot as a totally inadequate entry port to the greatest city in the country. A traveler arrived at the old terminal after enduring the Park Avenue tunnel, choked with steam and smoke, which spoiled the keen anticipation of New York. Today, landing from abroad at Kennedy Airport's International Arrival Building provides a parallel experience; the traveler plunges into a series of narrow, crowded corridors, with low ceilings and all the architectural charm of a laundromat.

By contrast, the new Grand Central completely transformed the experience of entering New York. A traveler who arrived at the Incoming Station and the Grand Concourse entered a secular cathedral; passengers knew, without any doubt, that they had arrived in a special place. The Grand Concourse enclosed the largest interior space in the country and served as the focal point of the railroad's magnificent contribution to the newly vitalized midtown business district. The daily commuters from the city's northern suburbs enjoyed their own concourse on the suburban level. While not as monumental as the space directly above, the suburban concourse provided a vast improvement over the facilities it replaced.

With Grand Central's connections to the growing city subway system, the elevated railroads, and the street railways, it emerged as the most important transportation hub in the city, serving as an easy link to the city's circulatory system. As a direct result, the midtown business district

around the terminal prospered. Robert Pope, writing in 1911, predicted the role Grand Central would come to play in the city's transportation system: "This Grand Central point will be perhaps the greatest traffic center in the world."[16] The ground-level and underground transit system of which Grand Central was the hub continued vertically, as people rode elevators directly from the station to a number of high-rise buildings, including the Biltmore and Commodore hotels and the Graybar Building. Until the building of Rockefeller Center in the 1930s, no other place in New York, or in any other city in America, included a transportation center with both horizontal and vertical dimensions. Construction of the Pan American building in 1963 added another type of vertical transportation to Grand Central: escalators carried people directly from the Grand Concourse one flight up to the building's elevators.

That this unique combination of the horizontal with the vertical occurred first in New York, where the skyscraper flourished, is logical. Manhattan's geography, offering limited space, forced real estate developers and builders to consider taller and taller buildings. During the Age of Energy, the application of the steel frame construction techniques freed the architect and builder from the height limitations imposed by masonry construction, in which thick walls on the lower floors supported the weight of the floors above. With the steel frame to carry the weight of the structure and the use of electric elevators to reach the upper floors quickly, skyscrapers replaced a city of four- and five-story masonry buildings. Daniel Burnham's Flatiron Building (1902) on Madison Square and Henry Flagg's Singer Building (1908) in lower Manhattan served as the forerunners of the skyscrapers soon to dominate the Manhattan skyline and give New York its singular visual image. Grand Central, linking the skyscraper directly to the city's underground and surface transportation system, allowed people to travel both horizontally and vertically between home and office, a uniquely American innovation.

Park Avenue

Grand Central's greatest localized impact came on Park Avenue north of 45th Street. When Grand Central Depot and the open train yard were in place, Park Avenue from 42nd to 49th streets simply did not exist.

North of the train yard, Park Avenue ran on both sides of the four-track open cut and tunnel that carried the Central's tracks north toward the tip of Manhattan Island. Park Avenue, formerly known by its more utilitarian designation, Fourth Avenue, remained decidedly unfashionable. Four- and five-story walk-up apartments, loft buildings, and factories lined the street: at 50th Street the Schaefer Brewery occupied the entire block between 50th and 51st streets; the Steinway Piano factory stood on the corner of 52nd Street. From 45th to 49th, the open train yard stretched between Depew Place and Madison Avenue, and only pedestrian footbridges at 45th, 46th, and 47th streets allowed people to cross.

A first step in removing the barrier separating the upper east side of Manhattan into two sections involved restoring the north-south flow of Park Avenue. The first plans envisioned by Wilgus and by Reed and Stem carried Park Avenue around the new Grand Central on an elevated roadway and then north over the underground train yard. Reed and Stem added a bridge to carry Park Avenue over 42nd Street to link Park Avenue north and south of the terminal. Wilgus noted that after Whitney Warren entered the design process, the Central abandoned the elevated roadway. As the architectural battles continued, the fate of the elevated roadway and bridge over 42nd Street remained in doubt. At the insistence of the New Haven Railroad and a number of key Central officers, final plans included the elevated roadway carrying Park Avenue around the new station. Wilgus noted with satisfaction, "Subsequent to the writer's severance of connection with the improvements, the elevated driveways and 42nd Street bridge crossings, which had been omitted contrary to his recommendations, were restored."[17] Wilgus viewed the Park Avenue elevated roadway around the terminal as one of the key features of the entire Grand Central project. The *New York Times* echoed Wilgus's view of the importance of the elevated roadway to the city: "A handsome bridge crossing Forty-second Street will give the city another main artery of travel from the top of the Bowery to the Harlem River. . . . Where Fourth Avenue changes its name to Park northward to the end of the tunnel [96th Street] the street will be one of the finest in the borough. Real estate values will be greatly increased, and the city will benefit by the increased tax yield."[18]

Park Avenue north of Grand Central, already the widest north-south

New York's "Grand Boulevard," Park Avenue, in the 1920s, looking north from 50th Street with St. Bartholomew's Episcopal Church at right

avenue in Manhattan, became the city's showcase. Its increased width exceeded 140 feet. By comparison, Madison Avenue averaged 55 feet in width and Lexington Avenue only 42 feet in the Grand Central area. Over the new underground train yard, Park Avenue included a landscaped median, enhancing the sense of width and space and stretching north for forty City Beautiful blocks. When the plans were announced, an article in the *Times* caught the drama these changes would introduce into the otherwise crowded confines of Manhattan: "It is proposed to continue Park Avenue at about its present width to the north end of the new terminal, beautifying it with small parks in the center to divide the two roadways."[19] To this day, Park remains the only major avenue in the city without public bus service and the Park Avenue Association carefully tends the gardens on the median dividing the two roadways. With its dramatic width, Park Avenue provides one of the grand vistas in the city.

Standing at 69th Street and looking south offers one of New York's most inspiring views; the skyward sweep of buildings does not dwarf the wide expanse of the avenue. Dramatically, the vista ends at Whitney Warren's New York Central Building, now the Helmsley Building, with two wings curving out as if to touch the buildings on either side of the avenue.

The New York Central carefully reviewed design of the buildings constructed along both sides of Park Avenue north of the terminal during Phase 2. Many of the buildings constructed by private developers leasing air rights from the New York State Terminal Realty Company were designed by Whitney Warren to harmonize with the terminal building. Warren's designs ensured that all the buildings shared the same Beaux-Art architectural style; their uniformity of design and scale proved unique in New York, where buildings often had little or no architectural or aesthetic relationship to their neighbors. Until Rockefeller Center went up,

Park Avenue immediately north of Grand Central and the New York Central Building in 1936, showing uniformity of design in the original air rights buildings

these buildings along Park Avenue formed the most harmonious group of structures in the entire city.

Once the electrification of the Park Avenue tunnel eliminated escaping smoke and steam, new buildings rose all the way to 96th Street. Elegant apartment buildings replaced block after block of four-story apartments, low-rise commercial buildings, and factories. This fine architecture has endured. In fact, the stretch of Park Avenue from 69th to 96th Street closely resembles what it looked like in the 1910s and 1920s.

The new hotels became the most fashionable in the city; the Park Lane, Marguery, and the Waldorf-Astoria acquired connotations of glamour, power, and wealth. The famous and the infamous stayed at the Waldorf, including diplomats, heads of state, and European royalty. When President Franklin Roosevelt stayed at the Waldorf, his train would stop on the upper level of the underground train yard directly under the hotel. This enabled the president's aides to carry the paralyzed Roosevelt through a special door and then by elevator directly to his room, avoiding the public altogether. Park Avenue became the street where the most successful, talented, and hard-driving citizens of New York came to reside.

The International Style

After World War I and with the onset of the Great Depression, the Beaux-Arts movement lost momentum. World War I killed the flower of an entire generation of men on the bloody fields of Flanders and Verdun and destroyed Europe's primacy as a source of inspiration for American architects and planners. Critics of the use of Beaux-Arts design in the United States became more vocal in their condemnation of an architectural style that they judged to be too imitative of the bankrupt aristocratic style of Europe and too fixated on the classical past.

In the 1930s a new architectural style emerged and swept the Beaux-Arts aside. This new form came to be called the International Style, and after World War II, it completely dominated the architecture of New York. With origins at the Bauhaus School in Weimar, Germany, founded by Walter Gropius in 1919, the International Style attempted to break completely with the past, to fashion a new aesthetic that was simple and "pure," lacked any references to classical antiquity, and was completely

devoid of ornamentation. The International Style diametrically opposed the architecture inspired by the Ecole des Beaux-Arts.

In 1932, the newly formed Museum of Modern Art in New York mounted a show of architectural drawings and models to introduce Bauhaus design and its leading light, Walter Gropius, to America. The show's catalogue, written by Henry-Russell Hitchcock and the young director of the museum's architectural division, Philip Johnson, provided a ringing manifesto for the new style and dismissed the architecture of the nineteenth century and early twentieth century: "The nineteenth century failed to create a style of architecture because it was unable to achieve a general discipline of structure and design in terms of the day. The revived 'styles' were but a decorative garment to architecture, not the interior principles according to which it lived and grew. . . . Today the strict issue of reviving the styles of the distant past is no longer one of serious consequences."[20] No longer would the aspiring American architect journey to Paris to study monuments from Classical Greece and Rome or France's *ancien régime*; these new principles had no foundation in the classical past. With the evolution of the steel frame structure in the United States, architects could break from strict adherence to the Beaux-Arts principles of plan, section, and elevation.

According to Hitchcock and Johnson, the fundamental principles of the modern style included architecture as volume, the proper surfacing material, regularity, and the avoidance of allied decoration. The first principle, a focus on volume, reflected the freedom the evolution of the steel frame allowed. As the catalogue authors noted, "the effect of mass, of static solidity, hitherto the prime quality of architecture, has all but disappeared; in its place there is an effect of volume, or more accurately, of plane surfaces bounding a volume. The prime architectural symbol is no longer the dense brick but the open box. Indeed, the great majority of buildings are in reality, as well in effect, mere planes surrounding a volume. With skeleton construction enveloped only by a protective screen, the architect can hardly avoid achieving this effect of surface of volume."[21] A glass-walled building without any surface ornamentation perfectly reflected the new principles. Beaux-Arts buildings such as Grand Central, Pennsylvania Station, and the New York Public Library represented the antithesis of the type of buildings the International Style demanded.

The Museum of Modern Art's exhibition of the International Style exerted enormous influence, and the movement gained further momentum when Walter Gropius, Mies van der Rohe, and other luminaries from the Bauhaus came to reside in the United States in the late 1930s as refugees fleeing Nazi Germany. Gropius became head of the Architecture Department at Harvard University. Van der Rohe went to the Amour Institute in Illinois, where he designed an entirely new campus in Chicago which became the Illinois Institute of Technology. Philip Johnson left the Museum of Modern Art to study architecture under Gropius at Harvard.

The triumph of the International Style had to await the end of the Great Depression and World War II. The Beaux-Arts style did not simply disappear from the architectural horizon. The New York Beaux-Arts Society, founded in 1916, continued to sponsor the Beaux-Arts Institute of Design in New York, modeled after the Ecole des Beaux-Arts and offering classical training to aspiring architects. Each year the institute held the Paris Prize Competition for architectural students with a first prize of admission to the first class at the Ecole des Beaux-Arts without examination and with sufficient funds for two years of study in Paris. Every year, the society held a yearly Beaux-Arts ball to raise money for the institute. In 1925, Whitney Warren, acting director of the institute, and his wife served as official patrons of that year's ball. Beaux-Arts balls continued into the 1930s, and in 1935 the society's gala, held in the newly completed Waldorf-Astoria, chose as its theme "George III Regrets." In recognition of the hard times the Depression was causing for architects in New York, some of the money raised at the ball went to a fund for destitute architects.[22]

Once the Second World War ended and American society began to prosper, the real estate market in New York, ravaged by the Depression and dormant during the war, revived and the demand for office space increased dramatically, nowhere more strongly than in Midtown. The original air rights buildings along Park Avenue, from 45th to 52nd, stood only eight or nine stories. Postwar zoning laws allowed for the construction of taller buildings with more interior volume, and the Central quickly realized that the construction of new, taller buildings would generate significant additional revenue. Raw business logic proved in-

escapable: the "old" must be replaced with the new. If the railroad's real estate could add increased income, then any aesthetic considerations would be ignored. In the space of two decades, the 1950s and 1960s, new construction replaced almost all of the Beaux-Arts buildings constructed as part of the first two phases of Terminal City. All of the office towers built over New York Central's air rights reflected the International Style. Modern glass-curtain skyscrapers replaced the classical Beaux-Arts buildings whose facades displayed a harmony of design and uniform height. An air of inevitability accompanied the change, which encountered only modest public opposition, from architectural traditionalists and preservationsts and from those alarmed by the heedless pace of the change.

North of the Central's air rights, the triumph of International Style over the Beaux-Arts continued, as developers constructed more glass-curtain buildings farther up Park Avenue. In 1952, the firm of Skidmore, Owings, and Merrill designed one of the most famous of the new glass towers, Lever House, at Park and 53rd Street, as headquarters for the Lever Brothers soap company. Lever House, celebrated as one of the best examples of the new style, was completely devoid of external ornamentation; the exterior walls consisted of glass plates that revealed the stark simplicity of the interior structure. All exterior planes were unbroken, as the modern style demanded.

Six years after Lever House's completion came the most famous of the International Style buildings: the Seagram Building, the epitome of the modern. Designed by Mies van der Rohe with Philip Johnson as his assistant, the building stands back from the streetscape, its bronze-clad frame visible for all to see. In stark contrast, straight across the street from the Seagram Building, McKim, Mead and White's New York Racquet Club retains its Beaux-Arts facade. Perhaps nowhere else in New York can the public appraise the old and the new styles so directly. Separated by Park Avenue, the ornamentation and lushness of the Racquet Club's stone facade can be seen reflected in the sleek glass of the Seagram Building across the way. The Racquet Club itself barely survived the relentless development pressure. With the exception of the New York Central Building and the Waldorf-Astoria, the new modernist style heavily influenced the design of all the corporate skyscrapers built during Terminal City's last phase (see Table 4.4).

TABLE 4.4
Terminal City - Phase 3

Air Rights Building	Address	Replacement	Year Completed
Hotel Marguery	Park Ave. 47–48th Sts.	Union Carbide Building	1960
290 Park Avenue	Park Ave. 48–49th Sts.	Bankers Trust Building	1962
300 Park Avenue	Park Ave. 49–50th Sts.	Colgate-Palmolive Building	1956
Knapp Building	Park Ave. 46–47th Sts.	Postum Building	ca. 1952
Park-Lexington Building	Park Ave. 46–47th Sts.	American Brands Building	1968
277 Park Avenue	Park Ave. 47–48th Sts.	Chemical Bank	1964
Park Lane Hotel	Park Ave. 48–49th St.	West Vaco Building	1967
Biltmore Hotel	Vanderbilt Ave. 43–44th Sts.	Bank of America Building	1981
Commodore Hotel	Lexington Ave. & 42nd St.	Grand Hyatt Hotel	1976
New York Central Building	Park Ave. 45–46th Sts.		
Waldorf-Astoria Hotel	Park Ave. 49–50th Sts.		

SOURCE: Compiled from data in William J. Wilgus Papers, New York Public Library.

In the course of the third phase of the air rights development around Grand Central, the character of Park Avenue just north of 45th Street changed from residential to commercial. A number of commercial buildings had been constructed as part of Terminal City, but on Park Avenue from 45th to 51st streets, the original air rights buildings consisted largely of hotels and apartments.

In the 1980s, development pressure even threatened St. Bartholomew's Church, on Park and 50th Street, just north of the Waldorf-Astoria. Developers proposed dramatic changes for the church's property. Realizing that a storm of criticism would greet any effort to demolish the church building itself, the builders planned for a high-rise office building on the site of the church's community house, just off Park Avenue on 50th Street. A bruising battle ensued, dividing the St. Bartholomew's congregation and triggering the firestorm the developers had hoped to avoid. In the end, the New York City Landmarks Commission refused to approve any alteration to either of St. Bartholomew's buildings, and plans for the high-rise have been dropped—for the time being.

Pressure to utilize the property along Park Avenue to its maximum continues, and every angle is being worked to accomplish this. Just across the street from St. Bartholomew's Church stands 320 Park Avenue, a high-rise office building constructed in 1961, just before passage of Midtown zoning laws that would have prohibited construction of a building of its volume. Mutual of America Life Insurance Company bought the building from the ailing Olympic and York real estate conglomerate in 1992 for $130 million. Mutual plans to renovate rather than rebuild,

thereby circumventing the limitations in the zoning law. The existing building has 620,000 square feet of space, but under current zoning a new building on the same lot could have only 441,000 square feet. Mutual of America gains 179,000 square feet more rental space than it would have if it were to tear down the older building and construct a new office tower. Richard Hayden, the architect for the building, characterizes the project as "zoning calculations with the skin strapped on." The project rests not on esthetic considerations but on exploiting the zoning law. New York City officials seemed pleased with Mutual's plans; the company's alternative, to relocate to Long Island, would result in major job losses.[23]

Grand Central, since its conception, has served as a catalyst, transforming a key area of Midtown into the planned, integrated, harmonious urban development envisioned by the City Beautiful at the turn of the century. Unfortunately for New York and other American cities, few other projects have been as comprehensive and imaginative as Grand Central. Too often New York's relentless growth has consisted of a hodgepodge of isolated developments, one next to the other, with no overall coordination or architectural integration. They lack an essential ingredient, the driving force of a single corporate entity as powerful as the New York Central Railroad.

The Commuter Railroad

With its new electric service to the Bronx and beyond into Westchester and Fairfield counties, Grand Central also stimulated growth of the city's outlying boroughs and the suburban communities to the north, as did New York's growing subway system. The process of suburbanization has continued unabated throughout the twentieth century, forever altering the character of New York City and the entire metropolitan region. Steadily, persistently, population has spread outward from the city's original urban core on Manhattan Island. At the end of the twentieth century, New York stands in the center of a vast metropolitan complex stretching from Suffolk County on Long Island north through Fairfield County, Connecticut, and west across northern New Jersey to the Pennsylvania border. It is home to some twenty million residents. While William Wilgus predicted that the Grand Central project and the electrification of

the railroad's service to the Bronx and Westchester County would increase the company's suburban commuter business, he could not have foreseen the consequences that unbridled suburbanization would have for New York and the region beyond the city.

In 1831, when the New York and Harlem Railroad incorporated and received the all-important franchise to operate down the east side of Manhattan, the railroad planned to link the southern tip of the island, where the bulk of the city's population resided, with the "village" of Harlem, 6.5 miles to the north. The railroad finally extended to Harlem in 1837; in 1849 the railroad effected a connection with the New Haven Railroad at Woodlawn junction in the Bronx; and then it continued construction north into Westchester County and beyond, reaching Chatham, New York, 131 miles from New York City in 1852. Almost all of the Harlem's early traffic moved between Manhattan, the Bronx, and the embryonic suburbs north in Westchester County. Long-distance passenger traffic proved negligible; the railroad's core business remained its commuter service to Manhattan, the Bronx, and Westchester.

At first, the construction of the Harlem Railroad stimulated the growth of Manhattan Island and the Bronx, and to a lesser extent the eastern part of Westchester County. Rather than providing a link between New York and other major cities, as the longer trunk railroads did, the Harlem, from its first days, functioned as a commuter railroad within the city and its immediate suburbs, allowing the population of Manhattan to continue to spread up the island, into the Bronx, and then on into Westchester. Soon Harlem lost its identity as a separate community and became just another neighborhood in New York, although certainly a famous one.

In fact, the Harlem Railroad, soon joined by the Hudson River and New Haven commuter railroads, served a far narrower portion of the population than did the omnibuses, elevated railways, streetcars, or New York's first subway lines. Commuter rail lines provided a relatively expensive form of transportation. A ride from City Hall to Harlem in 1839 cost twenty-five cents at a time when many people survived on a dollar a day or less. When the IRT subway opened in 1904, a passenger could ride from lower Manhattan to the Bronx for a one-cent fare. Commuter railroads like the Harlem served the more affluent citizens; the opening of

the Harlem gave birth to the suburban commuter, the middle-class executive whose workplace remained in Manhattan but who could now live in a more bucolic setting removed from the bustle and congestion in the city's core. As New York's commuter lines extended farther into Westchester, Fairfield, and Nassau counties, the affluent commuter had more choices of a place to reside in suburban comfort. In 1903, when the plans for Grand Central became public, the *New York Times* foresaw the impact the improved commuter service would have on the residential patterns of the area: "The country lying between the Sound and the Hudson in Westchester County will be brought into such a close touch with the business part of the city that it will attract a tremendous influx of people who now live in the heart of the city."[24] In truth, the people moving from the heart of the city formed a very selective segment of the city's diverse population.

Soon the communities in Westchester and in Fairfield served by the new "electric zone" became synonymous with affluence and exclusivity. *Century Magazine* in 1907 identified Grand Central as the best place to view this new species of rail traveler: "At the Grand Central Station, in New York, the 'substantial banker' is likely to show 'Greenwich' on his monthly ticket, whereas the man behind, who is like him, but with less substance, will probably go on to Stamford. Similarly the horsiest and yachtiest commuters are apt to live in Larchmont, while the not quite so pronounced get off in New Rochelle."[25] The "Neapolitans, Russians, and dull Germans" observed by William Dean Howells's character March while riding the Third Avenue El did not follow him to Grand Central to board trains for Greenwich, Larchmont, or Scarsdale.

Commuter railroads contributed to the forces of decentralization, but in a selective manner. With the introduction of fast, efficient electric service on the Harlem and Hudson divisions of the New York Central and the provision of a separate suburban concourse and tracks at the new Grand Central, the affluent and the middle class could move far from the teeming masses in the city. For the "Neapolitans" or "Chinese" whom Howells described riding the El, little choice existed except living in crowded tenements on the Lower East Side or Upper East Side of New York. They could not afford the cost of a daily ride on the Harlem to Scarsdale, nor could they afford the housing there. An article in the real

estate section of the *New York Times* in 1910, after completion of the electric zone, spoke of the "charms of Bronxville" and identified this Westchester County community as the "ideal suburban community," where "a tract of sixty acres of high wooded land has been purchased by L.D. Garrett, who will develop it as a restricted residential district."[26] The *Times* did not explain exactly what a "restricted residential district" was, but L.D. Garrett didn't plan housing for the "huddled masses yearning to breathe free" on his sixty acres in Bronxville.

Most histories of the American railroads have focused primarily on the building of the trunk lines linking the country's cities and the truly heroic tale of the completion of the transcontinental rail lines. Yet, the intra-urban and early suburban services deserve as much attention. Even major railroads like the New York Central and Pennsylvania, with their sprawling systems stretching from the East to the Midwest, also operated extensive suburban commuter service. In fact, from the very first day they opened, both the new Grand Central and Pennsylvania Station served more commuter passengers than people traveling on the glamorous trains to Boston, Chicago, and St. Louis. The Long Island railroad, in the first year of operation to the new Pennsylvania station at 33rd Street, carried over six million commuter passengers. By 1893, each workday, the New York Central operated more than forty trains each way between New York and Peekskill on the Hudson Division and twenty-five to White Plains on the Harlem Division.

The Central railroad actively promoted the growth of the suburban areas in the vicinity of its stations in the Bronx and Westchester counties. Under the innovative leadership of George H. Daniels, general passenger agent in New York, the railroad began publication of informational pamphlets, the "Four-Track Series," in 1890 to promote its suburban business. One of the early publications in the Four-Track Series, entitled "Suburban Homes North of the Harlem," listed each of the stations and communities served by the Harlem and Hudson divisions and provided a brief description of each. The promotional piece included detailed maps of Manhattan, the Bronx, and the area from Westchester County north to Albany along the east side of the Hudson River served by the railroad.

Each entry listed the distance from New York, the number of daily trains each way, the commuting times, regular fares, monthly commuta-

tion, and family trip ticket costs. Listings included prosaic descriptions of the delights of each town. For example, on the Hudson Division:

> *Irvington,* named in honor of Washington Irving, whose gifted pen immortalized many of the neighboring localities, among them the far-famed "Sleepy Hollow" and "Wolfert Roost," is 23 miles from New York. Twenty-one trains each way; on Sundays 13 trains from New York, 12 trains to New York; time about 45 minutes. Regular fare 44 cents; monthly commutation 10½ cents per ride; 50 trip family tickets 28½ cents per ride.
>
> *Tarrytown,* delightfully situated on an elevated plateau overlooking the wide expanse of the Tappan Zee and the surrounding country for many miles, is 25 miles from New York. Twenty-seven trains each way; on Sundays 16 trains from New York, 15 to New York; time about 45 minutes. Regular fare 50 cents; monthly commutation 11 cents per ride; 50 trip family tickets 30½ cents per ride.
>
> *Sing Sing,* a handsome little city of 10,000 inhabitants . . .[27]

The entry for Tarrytown included a picture of Washington Irving's home, Sunnyside, at Irvington-on-Hudson.

A later edition in the Four-Track Series, published in 1904 under Daniels's supervision, "Real Rapid Transit: to Ninety Suburban Towns located in the Commutation District," included an opening page bearing the rhetorical question "Where to go, what to see, and where to find a near-by home in the country?" The updated descriptions of the towns and districts served included lot and home prices, along with rental costs, and the pamphlet directed the reader seeking further housing information to real estate agents either in New York or in the local community. The Central railroad formed a series of marketing arrangements with local real estate agencies to promote housing sales and new construction.

On the Harlem Division, the entry for the Melrose section of the Bronx listed lots for sale between $800 and $10,000, houses selling for between $3,000 and $25,000, and house rentals from $300 to $1,000 per year. All houses were described as "equipped with modern improvements. Water, sewer, gas, electric lights, electric cars, asphalt and macadam streets and flag sidewalks." The entry listed two real estate agents: "T.S. Barnes, opposite New York Central Station, Melrose, N.Y., or D.L.

Woodall, Morrisania, N.Y."[28] Further on into Westchester County, the promotional brochure listed lots in Scarsdale selling for between $200 and $500, with houses running from $2,500 to $12,000. To the modern eye these prices seem absurdly low, but at the time such costs remained beyond the reach of all but the most affluent. Laborers working on construction of the new Grand Central earned between a dollar and a dollar and a half for a day's labor—ten long and hard hours. Even skilled craftsmen, carpenters and masons, received less than three dollars a day, a yearly income of far less than a thousand dollars. A home in Scarsdale, in an era before the advent of long-term, low-interest mortgages, remained a distant dream for most of New York's working population.

Wilgus, in a 1904 report to William K. Vanderbilt, detailed the growth of the railroad's commuter service to the Bronx and Westchester County: In 1899, the Harlem and Hudson suburban trains had carried a total of 4,146,239 passengers, and by 1903 the total had risen to 6,239,399, an increase of 50 percent in just four years.[29] Despite continued criticism of the railroad's antiquated facilities at 42nd Street and the more heated condemnation of conditions in the Park Avenue tunnel, in 1906 the railroad carried nearly ten million suburban passengers. Commuter traffic on the Central's Harlem and Hudson divisions came to exceed through passengers by a substantial margin.[30] Between 1913, when the new Grand Central opened and the electric zone came into full operation, and 1920, commuter passengers increased by another 127 percent—a phenomenal increase in just seven years.

While the city's society pages breathlessly reported the arrival and departure of important long-distance travelers on the Central's famous trains like the world-renowned Twentieth Century Limited, a more important development unfolded on the suburban concourse. Grand Central now provided the crucial transportation link that allowed for the rapid growth of the affluent suburbs to the north and northwest. Not only did the Central's suburban traffic grow exponentially, but the New Haven's service to Westchester and lower Fairfield County expanded as well. The New Haven carried three million suburban commuters in 1903, and that number increased to over eight million in 1920.[31] Wilgus's prediction in 1903, that the new electrified service would lead to a substantial increase in the railroad's suburban commuter traffic proved to be

more than accurate; in fact, growth exceeded even his most optimistic projections. But Wilgus did not foresee all the consequences of the railroad's increased commuter business. Soon, the relentless growth of the suburbs came to threaten New York City's very survival as the core of an ever-expanding metropolitan region.

The Rise of New York's Suburbs

With the coming of the commuter railroad, residential development spread farther from the urban core on Manhattan Island than the omnibus, elevated railway, street railway, or even the subway had allowed. Once the Harlem Railroad reached White Plains, New York, in 1844, it became possible for the affluent commuter to move to any of the small towns along the Harlem's path from Grand Central to White Plains, or later on the Hudson Division to Croton-on-Hudson. A trip from White Plains or Croton to New York took less than an hour and transformed once rural farming communities in Westchester and Fairfield counties into nascent suburban retreats where family life flourished far removed from the industrial and commercial world of the city. By 1900 New York had more suburbs within a twenty-five-mile radius of its center than any other city in the world, and more than 118,000 suburban commuters rode to Grand Central each day.[32]

The opening of Central and New Haven's electric zone to the north of New York exerted a dramatic impact on the population of the Bronx, Westchester, and lower Fairfield County. In the Bronx, population exploded. At the turn of the century the entire borough included only 200,507 residents and it remained a place of small farms and woodlands. In the space of a single decade, the population doubled to over four hundred thousand and then almost doubled again in the next decade, reaching 732,016 in 1920.[33]

Westchester County also grew at a phenomenal pace as soon as the railroads improved their suburban service and made commuting from the county to Manhattan a reasonable daily journey. From a population of less than 185,000 in 1900, the number of residents reached 283,055 in 1910, an increase of more than 50 percent for the decade; the population increased by another 87 percent in the next ten years.[34]

In order to assess the impact of the Grand Central project on Westchester County, Wilgus again analyzed the growth in property values. He proceeded from the premise that without Grand Central and the new all-electric commuter service to the county, property values in Westchester would not have grown as dramatically as they had. Wilgus estimated the proportion of the increase in assessed value of property in Westchester County attributable to the changes at Grand Central at almost one billion dollars for the period from 1906 through 1930.[35]

In this early stage of metropolitan development, the suburbs remained strongly tied to the urban core. New York thrived as the place to which the commuter traveled each day to work; wealthy shoppers traveled to the city to browse in the fashionable stores on Broadway and Fifth Avenue. Without employment in Manhattan and efficient commuter rail service, the affluent suburbs could not have grown so dramatically. The vitality of the entire metropolitan area depended on the commercial and industrial life of New York City.

Across the Hudson River, the growth of the Jersey Central Railroad enabled New York's suburbanization to spread westward to the counties in northern New Jersey. To the east, on Long Island beyond Brooklyn and Queens, lie Nassau County and then Suffolk County, which extends another eighty miles to Montauk Point. With the opening of the new Pennsylvania Station in 1911, the Long Island Railroad, with extensive service to 33rd Street, evolved into the busiest commuter railroad in the country. As the Long Island Railroad extended its electrified lines into Nassau County, suburban growth exploded in the communities strung out along the Long Island's right of way. Port Washington and Manhasset on the North Shore and Valley Stream and Garden City in the center of the county became as fashionable suburban addresses as Scarsdale, New York, and Greenwich, Connecticut.

At Grand Central's opening in 1913, stories in the press pointed out the significant movement of commuters to and from New York City each day: "More than a million commuters come into New York every morning from points within a radius of twenty-five miles, and a considerable part of this human stream pours through Grand Central. It must be handled without interfering with the through business. . . . This present work began with a study of possible improvement in managing this near-

by traffic."[36] William Wilgus realized the importance of this revolution in transportation: "The electrification of the passenger traffic of two of the most important steam railroads in the world [the New York Central and the Harlem], for the distance of from 25 to 35 miles, radiating from a terminus in the greatest city in the Western hemisphere, may well be termed the marking of the commencement of a new epoch in the history of transportation."[37]

It would not be long before the suburbs lost their dependence on the city they surrounded. The coming of the automobile and truck and the building of an extensive highway system in New York's metropolitan region combined to lessen the ties between New York and its suburban ring. Once the link broke, residents of the suburbs could both live and work outside the city; their energy and vitality strengthened the communities where they lived and worked at the direct expense of the city. As the suburbs continued to grow, they accounted for an ever-increasing share of the region's people, economic activity, and taxable wealth. For New York, the long-term consequences proved to be disastrous.

In the period after World War II, businesses and the middle class followed the affluent to the promised land of the suburbs. Fashionable stores opened branches or relocated to suburban shopping malls in Westchester, Nassau, and Bergen counties, leaving many retail districts in New York in shambles. Millions of square feet of new office space arose on campuslike settings miles distant from the downtown and midtown business districts. Even manufacturing enterprises, once tied to New York's waterfront and railroads, relocated to the suburbs, where trucks, traveling on the new highway system, delivered raw materials and hauled away finished products.

By 1970, the process of suburbanization seemed complete. In that year the census reported that, across the country, more Americans lived in the suburbs than in the country's once vital and flourishing core cities. For New York City, the times could not have been worse. The decline became painfully obvious throughout the city, from the graffiti-filled subways, to the city parks filled with drug addicts, to a city treasury lurching toward bankruptcy, to neighborhood after neighborhood once again crowded with the poor and downtrodden, to the abandoned tenements in the Bronx burning through the long nights. Wilgus's electrifica-

tion scheme had succeeded in dramatically increasing the railroad's commuter business, but at the same time it had contributed to the forces propelling the vitality of the region out of the city and pushing New York towards collapse.

New York City increasingly provided home to the very rich and the very poor, while the affluent middle class stayed in the suburbs. Theodore Dreiser observed at the turn of the twentieth century that "the drama of the city is at its extremes,"[38] and New York became the exemplar of that drama. Fifth Avenue and Park Avenue remain among the premier addresses in America, boasting the most expensive apartments in the city. But beyond the glitter of Fifth Avenue, Park Avenue, Museum Row, and the Upper East Side lies another New York, a New York at the other extreme. The two New Yorks today are the New York of the rich and that of the poor, the New York of an affluent white population and that of a poor African-American and Hispanic one that has absorbed a million immigrants from the developing world. Tom Wolfe, in his acerbic novel *Bonfire of the Vanities,* creates a fictional clash of the two extremes to illustrate the drama that fascinated Dreiser a hundred years earlier: The mayor of New York, attempting to hold a town meeting in Harlem, leaves the stage, forced off by the anger of the people without wealth, without resources, who increasingly make up a major portion of the city's population. As a TV crew films the confrontation, the narrator exults: "It'll be on TV. The whole city will see it. They'll love it. Harlem rises ups! . . . He's only mayor of some of the people! He's the mayor of white New York. Set fire to the Mutt! The Italians will watch this on TV, and they'll love it. And the Irish. Even the Wasps. They won't know what they're looking at. They'll sit in their co-ops on Park and Fifth and East Seventy-second Street and Sutton Place, and they'll shiver with the violence of it and enjoy the show. . . . Open your eyes! The greatest city of the twentieth century! Do you think money will keep it yours?"[39] Wolfe's central character, Sherman McCoy, lives in a luxurious co-op on Park Avenue, the very boulevard created by Grand Central's electrification. His friend Rawlie Thorpe reminds him that the only way to survive in New York is to "insulate, insulate, insulate" from the teeming hordes passing below on the city's streets.[40] McCoy, a Wall Street bond trader and "Master of the Universe" seems unaware of the vast social changes

under way in New York. However, for Sherman McCoy and the truly wealthy of New York, an alternative remains—a trip to Grand Central and then a commuter train to Bronxville or Chappaqua in Westchester County or Darien in Connecticut. Wilgus, Vanderbilt, Reed and Stem, and Whitney Warren planned Grand Central as the gateway to a great city, not as an avenue of escape from the city.

Epilogue

At the turn of the twentieth century, as the New York Central Railroad began planning for the new Grand Central Terminal, the railroads reigned supreme. Railroad companies, including the New York Central and its rival the Pennsylvania Railroad, ranked among the largest business enterprises in the country. In 1900, the railroads operated 192,556 miles of main line track, 37,633 locomotives, 34,713 passenger cars, and 1,365,531 freight cars. They transported 576,831,000 passengers a total of 16,038,000,000 miles and generated revenue of $323,716,000.[1] Four major trunk lines, the Baltimore and Ohio, the Erie, the Pennsylvania, and the New York Central, offered through rail service from the East Coast to Chicago and the Midwest. Both the Central and the Pennsylvania invested heavily in passenger service between New York and Chicago; their all-reserved trains, the Twentieth Century Limited and the Broadway Limited, embodied speed, efficiency, and luxury.

Over the next fifty years, the railroads declined precipitously. Revenue steadily fell; costs, especially labor, increased year after year. Across the country, highways filled with passenger cars and trucks captured a major share of the transportation business once provided solely by the railroads. In New York, Grand Central and Pennsylvania Station entered a period of slow, steady deterioration as both railroads cut back on essential maintenance and capital improvements. The crisis reached a peak in

A streamlined steam locomotive from the 1930s

1965, when the Pennsylvania Railroad tore down Pennsylvania Station to build a new Madison Square Garden. Long-distance Pennsylvania passengers and commuters now shuffled through second-rate facilities tucked below the Garden; all sense of glamour and majesty disappeared as travelers moved through narrow, dirty passageways to and from their trains. Across town, a similar fate awaited Grand Central; the New York Central, as starved for revenue as the Pennsylvania, considered demolition and redevelopment.

How did the seemingly all-powerful railroads of 1900 arrive at such desperate straits a few decades after a time when they dominated the transportation landscape?

Regulation, Competition, Decline

Although they represented a triumph of technology and enterprise, the railroads from their inception generated public suspicion, if not hostility. Social critics branded the railroads "monopolies," and the railroads came to symbolize the profound change that characterized the Age of Energy. Reformers demanded that the political system curb the monopoly power of the railroads and regulate their activities in the public interest.

Certainly, the railroads engaged in practices that inspired public outrage; most notoriously, the railroads covertly provided rebates to their largest customers, ensuring them a decided advantage in the marketplace. John D. Rockefeller's Standard Oil received secret discounts from both the New York Central and the Pennsylvania railroads.[2] With clandestine rebates secretly in hand, Rockefeller sold his oil and kerosene at a cheaper price and drove his competitors out of business. By 1900, the Standard Oil Company had formed a classic monopoly, aided by these arrangements, which the railroads exchanged for the company's shipping business.

With the passage of the Interstate Commerce Act, in 1887, Congress outlawed rebates and "pooling" arrangements whereby railroads divided a given transportation market into fixed shares for each participating railroad, thus avoiding fare wars. In 1906, Congress passed the Hepburn Act, permitting the Interstate Commerce Commission to set maximum rates for freight and passenger service and prohibiting the railroads from appealing the I.C.C. rate decisions to the courts. "Maximum" rates became the base rates charged by all the railroads, and in effect the federal government, through the I.C.C., controlled the rates the railroads charged.

Strong government regulation set the stage for the decline of the country's railroads. The I.C.C. rarely granted the railroads' repeated requests for rate increases. Between 1900 and 1915, the general level of prices in the country increased by 35.1 percent, railroad wages by 50 percent, and the taxes paid by the railroads by 200 percent. During the

entire time period, the I.C.C. granted only one freight rate increase—5 percent in 1913. Locked in a web of regulation that prevented them from raising prices, the railroads proved incapable of meeting rising costs, let alone generating surpluses for reinvestment in their infrastructure. Progressive regulation that had been designed to bridle the power of the railroads eventually strangled them.

Not only did the railroads face fierce demands from the reformers for ever-increasing government regulation, but, as ominously, competition from the automobile and truck loomed on the horizon.

In the syndication books of J. P. Morgan and Company, in an entry following the details of the New York Central's massive $100 million bond issue of 1897, appears a much smaller bond issue—only $2 million. Morgan raised the two million for the fledgling Dodge Brothers Manufacturing Company of Detroit, Michigan, among the pioneers in still another transportation revolution, one just getting under way at the turn of the century.[3]

Although the internal combustion engine had first powered a horseless carriage decades earlier, the development of a reliable automobile required a considerable period of time. In 1900, American companies manufactured 4,100 vehicles and registration of motor vehicles totaled only 8,000 for the entire country.[4] With limited production, the American automobile industry hardly represented a mortal threat to the railroads, who in that same year transported nearly six hundred million passengers more than sixteen billion passenger miles!

This new transportation revolution found a powerful ally in federal, state, and local governments. Government, at all levels, spent billions of dollars to subsidize the rise of the auto and the truck—at the direct expense of the railroads. Eventually, a massive road and highway system crisscrossed the country, extending into the most rural byways. Between 1917 and 1921, the country built a total of 12,919 miles of highway; and by 1941, just before World War II, the federal highway system totaled 316,432, miles, exceeding the main line track of all the nations' railroads combined (244,263 miles).[5]

Even the Great Depression did not seem to slow the onslaught of the automobile. *Railway Age* reported that in 1935 the railroads transported

The advent of the highway age: George Washington Bridge crossing the Hudson River from Manhattan Island, with tracks of the New York Central in foreground, 1932

2,443,532 fewer passengers to and from New York City than in the previous year, while traffic on the newly completed George Washington Bridge increased by 3.9 percent and in the Holland Tunnel by 5.6 percent from 1934 to 1935.[6] The competition from automobiles, fostered by federal aid to the country's highway system, accelerated after the Second World War with the decision, in 1956, to construct the Interstate Highway System. In partnership with the states, the federal government financed the construction of more than 40,000 miles of limited-access, high-speed thruways linking all the major cities in the country. By the 1960s, federal highway construction averaged more than four billion dollars a year and provided the railroads with subsidized competition they simply could not hope to beat.

The loss of traffic to the automobile and truck severely affected the New York Central, as it did all highly capitalized railroads, because of their desperate need for a steady cash flow to service their enormous debt. In 1911, the par value of the Central's stock had stood at $222 million and its bonded debt at $299 million. Just three years later, as the new Grand Central opened, the debt of the railroad rose to $377 million, reflecting the enormous sums required to complete the station and train yard and to begin construction of Terminal City.[7]

In 1932, as the impact of the Great Depression accelerated, the Central reached a crisis point. First the railroad tried to float a new bond issue to meet expenses and to pay off maturing bonds. Wall Street investors proved unwilling to purchase the company's securities: the bond issue failed miserably. With no recourse left, the Central suspended payment of dividends for 1932. The once powerful New York Central, a symbol of the proud American railroad industry, stood humiliated. Long castigated for its arrogance and power, the railroad assembled by the Commodore and expanded dramatically by his son William Henry could not afford to pay a dividend to its stockholders.

World War II provided a brief reprieve for the Central and other railroads. The country mobilized for war, and demand for passenger and freight service increased dramatically as American industry recovered from the Depression years and proceeded to turn the country into the "Arsenal of Democracy." But the Second World War afforded only a brief hiatus from the underlying problems the nation's railroads faced. As soon

as the war ended, the shift of transportation from the railroads to the highways resumed and the airline industry began to offer additional competition for the long-distance passenger.

For the New York Central Railroad, competition from the newly completed New York State Thruway proved disastrous. When planning for New York's portion of the Interstate Highway System, engineers had examined the topography of New York State and recognized the most logical route for the thruway to follow—along the Hudson River north to Albany, up the Mohawk River Valley, and then across the flat plains of upstate New York through Utica, Syracuse, and Rochester to Buffalo. In other words, the New York State Thruway followed the exact route of the Erie Canal and the New York Central Railroad across the state. In numerous places in upstate New York, it is possible to view, in one scene, the Erie Canal (now the New York State Barge Canal), the former main line of the New York Central Railroad, and the thruway, all built along the "water level route," the flattest and most efficient route from the East to the American Midwest.

Merger and Bankruptcy

From their very beginnings, the Pennsylvania and New York Central railroads competed vigorously and built and operated more passenger and freight capacity than necessary. Both railroads rejected talk of a merger before World War II and resisted any serious discussions of their shared problems into the mid-1950s. Proud companies, once among the most profitable in America, they remained fierce rivals; but competition from the truck and automobile only increased.

With tortuous twists and turns, the two railroads moved inexorably toward a merger and in 1968 finally agreed to join forces, forming the Penn Central Transportation Company, the largest transportation company in the country. Of course, the New York Central's valuable real estate empire in midtown Manhattan, including Grand Central, constituted a prize asset of the new company.

Unfortunately, the times proved inauspicious for the new railroad company. Between 1967 and 1970 the economy grew at a modest 2.7 percent, putting severe pressure on the revenue of all railroads, including

the new Penn Central. Two years after the merger, which had been greeted with great fanfare by the press, politicians, and the public, Penn Central filed for bankruptcy protection, on June 22, 1970—the largest bankruptcy in American corporate history. In the final days before the bankruptcy, officers of the railroad hurried to Washington to argue for federal loan guarantees, without which the banks refused to lend Penn Central any more money.

Congress expressed outrage at the state of affairs and called for an investigation into the collapse of the railroad. All of the federal and state investigations could not alter a fundamental fact: private railroad transportation simply could not survive the combined effect of onerous government regulation and a publicly financed highway system. Only one viable alternative, not long in coming, remained—to replace the private railroads in New York and the Northeast with a public railroad system.

Grand Central at Risk

As the fortunes of the New York Central plummeted, the railroad turned a cold eye to its flagship terminal on 42nd Street; maintenance declined precipitously, the roof leaked, the underground train tracks accumulated piles of garbage, the destitute of New York found their way into the terminal's labyrinth of tunnels. Architectural disfigurement invaded the Grand Concourse: a massive Kodak display filled the east balcony, blocking the natural light from the concourse's soaring windows facing Lexington Avenue; and Merrill Lynch opened a glass-enclosed office steps away from the famous information booth in the heart of Whitney Warren's Beaux-Arts temple.

Threats to Grand Central had unfolded even before the disastrous merger of the New York Central and the Pennsylvania railroads. In 1958, the railroad entered negotiations with the developer Erwin Wolfson to demolish the railroad's baggage building just north of the terminal and erect the fifty-nine-story Pan American building. Ironically, the building housed the headquarters of Pan American Airways, whose planes carried the long-distance passengers once served by Grand Central. Still desperate for revenue, the railroad explored the possibility of constructing another office tower on 42nd Street to mirror the Pan Am building. In

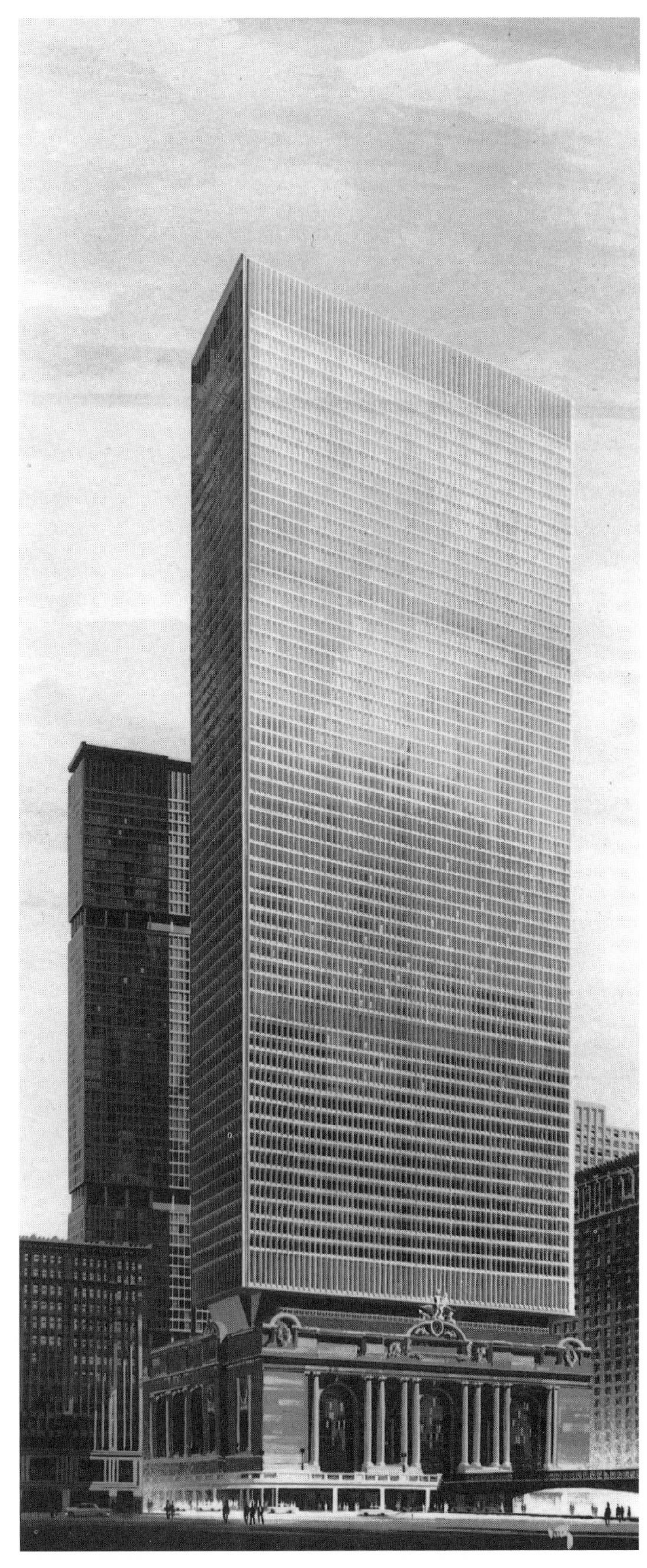

Marcel Breuer–designed building proposed for construction on top of Grand Central in 1968

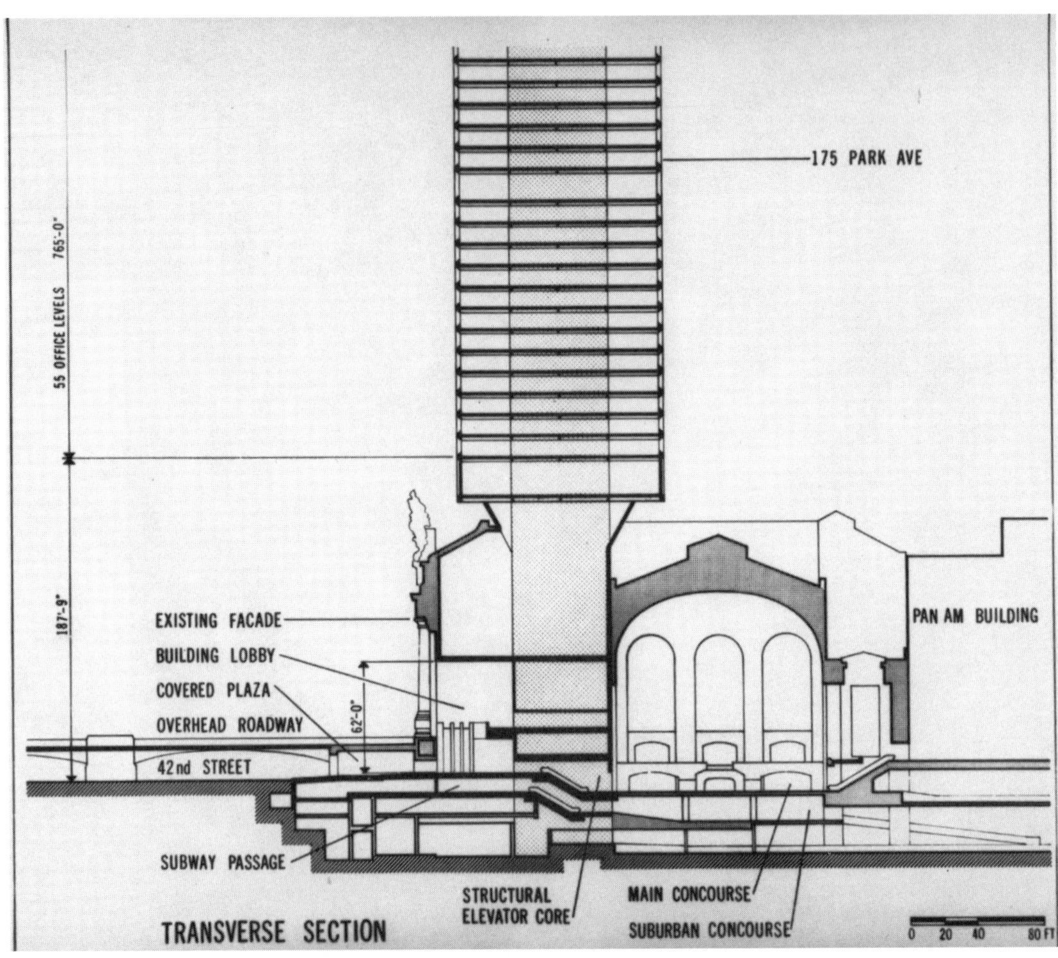

Transverse section of building in Breuer proposal

March of 1969, Penn Central and the developer Morris Saady announced plans for a Marcel Breuer–designed fifty-five-story office building on top of Grand Central. The ruin of the world-renowned building seemed but days away. Before the company could proceed, formidable opposition arose.

Efforts in New York to preserve the city's historic past, being led by Jacqueline Kennedy Onassis, Brendan Gill, and other prominent New Yorkers, galvanized. In 1965, New York City had passed its Landmarks Preservation Law, spurred by the destruction of Pennsylvania Station. The law, designed to foster "civic pride in the beauty and noble accomplishments of the past" and to promote "the use of historic districts, landmarks, interior landmarks and scenic landmarks for the education, pleasure and

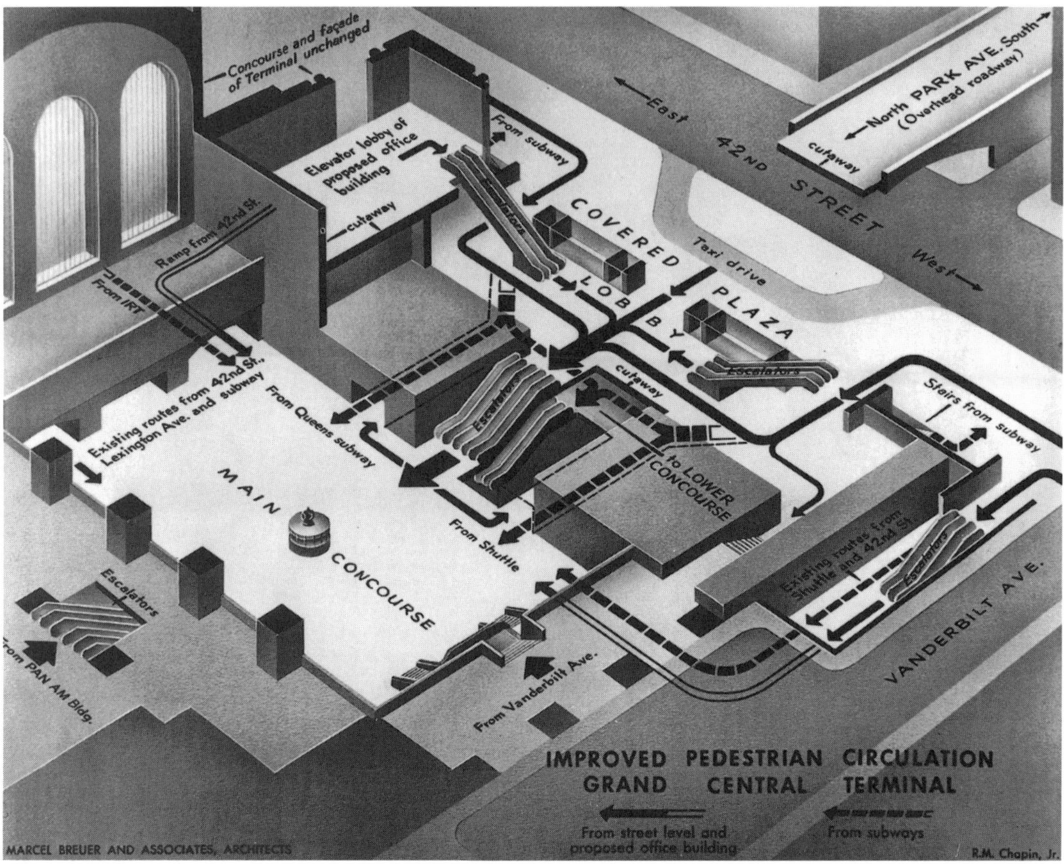

Revision of pedestrian traffic flow in Breuer proposal, which would have destroyed the elegant engineering of traffic patterns in Grand Central

welfare of the people of the city," established the Landmarks Preservation Commission to designate buildings as landmarks.[8] After a building's designation as a landmark, the law required the building's owner to keep the exterior in "good repair" and empowered the commission to approve any plans to alter the exterior of the building or to make any other substantive alterations. On August 2, 1969, with great fanfare, the commission designated Grand Central Terminal a landmark.

Penn Central, by 1967 sliding toward bankruptcy, refused to abandon efforts to destroy Grand Central and appealed to the courts. After a decade of litigation, the case reached the Supreme Court, and in October of 1978 the Court issued a truly historic decision. With Justice William Brennan writing for the majority, the Court first noted: "The Terminal, which is owned by the Penn Central Transportation Co. and its affiliates (Penn Central), is one of New York City's most famous buildings.

Opened in 1913, it is regarded not only as providing an ingenious solution to the problems presented by urban railroad stations, but is also a magnificent example of the French beaux arts style."[9]

The Supreme Court carefully weighed the Penn Central's argument that the application of the Landmark Preservation Law to Grand Central represented a taking of their property. Above all, the company argued that if the City of New York wanted to preserve Grand Central as it was, the city would have to pay the company "just compensation." Of course, in the view of Penn Central, the compensation should be based on the value of its property on 42nd Street with the planned 55-story tower above. The Court rejected this argument.

In the final analysis, the Court's decision represented a turning point; in the future, citizens and their governments might preserve the urban environment and not have to yield to commercial pressure. With the Supreme Court's ruling, it became possible to strike a balance between the forces of change and the desire to preserve great buildings that provide grace and style to the American city. No finer representative existed than Grand Central and it seems fitting that the Supreme Court's historic ruling involved this masterpiece.

For the moment, the Supreme Court had saved Grand Central, but monumental challenges remained. Penn Central, mired in bankruptcy, stopped spending money even for the most pressing needs. Years of neglect lay ahead: the leaking roof worsened, cracks appeared in the marble walls, and the star-studded ceiling of the Grand Concourse began to fall in places. While the Supreme Court ruling had upheld Grand Central's landmark status, the ruling did not magically produce the money needed to prevent this magnificent building from continued deterioration.

The Public to the Rescue

Efforts to rescue the railroads proceeded on multiple fronts. In 1971, Congress passed legislation establishing the National Railroad Passenger Corporation, Amtrak, to take over Penn Central's long-distance passenger operations and eventually the long-distance passenger service of all railroads across the country. Penn Central reorganized, concentrating on freight operations; but losses mounted, forcing Congress, in 1976, to

establish a second public-private rail organization, Conrail, to deal with freight and operate the commuter service of the bankrupt railroads in the Northeast, including the Penn Central.

Conrail concentrated its energy on improving freight operations in the Northeast, devoting little effort to commuter operations in the New York metropolitan region. Conditions on the commuter trains became deplorable. Trains were filthy, broken windows went unrepaired, lavatories were never cleaned, and conductors became more surly as service declined. These conditions forced action. With some reluctance, the political leadership of New York City and State recognized their responsibility. If private railroads could no longer provide commuter trains to New York's flourishing suburbs, this vital rail service must become a public responsibility.

On January 1, 1983, the State of New York, in partnership with Connecticut, created the Metro-North Commuter Railroad, as a subsidiary of the Metropolitan Transportation Authority. Metro-North absorbed the lines in the Bronx, Westchester, and Fairfield counties originally established by the Harlem, Hudson River, and New Haven railroads over a century before. The new commuter rail line's assets included more than three hundred miles of track in New York and Connecticut and 118 passenger stations. The queen of train terminals, Grand Central, also became Metro-North's operational responsibility. One crucial problem remained: ownership of Grand Central and the railroad's real estate empire in midtown Manhattan remained in the hands of Penn Central. Like the proverbial phoenix rising from the ashes, the Penn Central Transportation Company, after emerging from bankruptcy, metamorphosed into a real estate development, entertainment, and oil pipeline company, relocating its corporate offices to Cincinnati, Ohio. Later Penn Central became a part of American Premier Underwriters, Inc., primarily an insurance company, who retain ownership of Grand Central. Metro-North's lease includes an option to buy.

Metro-North Commuter Railroad recognized the daunting challenge Grand Central represented: the terminal's decline continued. George Walker, general manager of Metro-North, recalled that when Metro-North had taken custodianship of Grand Central in 1983 they had hardly

grasped the extent of the deterioration. Equipment from the turn of the century was literally falling apart and replacement parts proved impossible to obtain. Every part of the terminal, from mechanical systems to the leaking roof over the Grand Concourse, demanded immediate attention.[10] Metro-North had to arrest the rot and decay before any thought could be given to restoring the terminal to its former glory.

A major challenge confronted Metro-North. Revenue from commuter service did not cover operating costs; commuter service remained a money-losing operation. With no alternative, the railroad turned to the New York State legislature for needed capital. After a number of bruising battles in Albany, the state began to provide much-needed funds for capital improvements. Between 1983 and 1993 Metro-North undertook thirty million dollars' worth of repairs to Grand Central's basic infrastructure.

No one can accuse Metro-North of lacking imagination and ambition for Grand Central. In 1988 the railroad commissioned Beyer Blinder Belle, architects, and the engineering firm of STV/Seeyle Stevenson Value and Knecht of New York to undertake a detailed study of the work needed to restore Grand Central. Jessica Stern, writing in *Railway Age*, reported the estimated cost of complete renovation to be $400 million.[11] Even the most ardent supporters of the restoration stood aghast—four hundred million dollars! As generous as New York's politicians might be, there was little chance of the New York legislature ever appropriating $400 million for Grand Central. Metro-North did not even own the building, and the old Penn Central Company kept making noises about not receiving fair value from its real estate on 42nd Street. Plans would have to be scaled back and creative financing secured if even a portion of the ambitious agenda stood a chance of completion.

Beyer Blinder Belle completed its meticulous inspection of every square inch of Grand Central in 1992. Its report included a detailed historical analysis of the building's past, which involved examining the original architectural and construction drawings, housed at the Smithsonian Institution in Washington. By 1994, an alternative scheme emerged, one that stood a real chance of receiving approval from the M.T.A. and the state legislature. First, Beyer Blinder Belle, in consultation with Metro-North, scaled back restoration plans to a more realistic $200 mil-

lion cost. After years of hard bargaining Metro-North reached a long-term lease arrangement with the Penn Central Company. In 1994 the M.T.A., Metro-North's parent organization, signed a 110-year lease for Grand Central with the right to buy the terminal outright in twenty-five years. As part of the deal, Penn Central finally relinquished rights to develop the air rights above the building.

While negotiations with Penn Central dragged on, Metro-North and the M.T.A. developed an innovative plan to finance a major portion of the renovation by redeveloping all the retail space in the terminal. For a model, Metro-North turned to the widely heralded restoration of Union Station in Washington, D.C., and its transformation into a major upscale retail and commercial venue. Union Station had suffered the same slow, painful decline as Grand Central and Pennsylvania Station. As the railroads using the station in the heart of the nation's capital had gone into slow, steady death spirals, Daniel Burnham's classic Beaux-Arts station, a short walk from the Capitol building, had suffered. An ill-fated attempt in the 1960s to turn the once-magnificent station into a National Visitors Center failed miserably. Salvation came via the combined efforts of LaSalle Partners of Chicago and Williams Jackson Ewing of Baltimore, who conceived of financing the restoration of Union Station by generating higher lease revenue. Filled with trendy restaurants and smart shops, Union Station now serves as both a busy rail facility and as one of Washington's most popular attractions.

In March of 1994, the M.T.A. approved an agreement with LaSalle Partners and Williams Jackson Ewing to begin a $100 million retail development program, hoping that the partnership could replicate the magic of Washington's Union Station at 42nd Street in New York. In turn, the M.T.A. planned to issue $84 million in bonds backed by the anticipated revenue from the renovated and expanded retail space, with the remaining costs for the renovation work coming from the M.T.A.'s capital budget. Plans involved increasing retail space from 105,000 square feet to more than 150,000, with one-third devoted to restaurants and cafés. LaSalle Partners projected rental income rising from the $7 million it was earning to $13 million a year, after leasing of all commercial space. This would provide more than enough funds to service the M.T.A's bonds.[12]

Restoration

Any restoration of Grand Central's interior had to await completion of repairs to the roof. The building's deterioration included numerous leaks in its 81,000-square-foot roof, which was covered with over an acre of copper sheeting. Water dripped down the massive columns surrounding the Grand Concourse, leaving visible stains. In August of 1986 Metro-North engaged the firm of Simpson, Gumpertz and Heger of Arlington, Massachusetts, to complete a $4.5-million reconstruction of the roof. A series of sloppy repairs that had been made over the years complicated the work. In the end, the most economical plan involved replacing all fifty tons of the original copper sheeting, even as copper prices rose to 84 cents a pound.[13]

Along the edge of the roof, an ornamental frieze surrounds the top of the building. To accomplish its restoration, the contractor located a number of craftsmen who had worked on the original construction. Because replacement of the original frieze would be too costly, repairs began to the stamped copper original. First workers cleaned the frieze; then they removed it in six-foot sections, to install a waterproof membrane underneath it. The cleaned frieze and the new copper roof will together acquire a rich patina and look the same age, as though installed together. This painstaking attention to detail in restoring the roof may be lost on the thousands of people passing far below each day, but it signified Metro-North's commitment to restoring Grand Central to its former glory. When Beyer Blinder Belle performed their detailed evaluation, they praised the work of the roofers.[14]

At the front edge of the roof, Jules Alexis Coulan's magnificent sculpture of Mercury, Minerva, and Hercules surrounded an ornate clock. The sculpture group stands fifty feet tall, spans almost sixty feet, and weighs fifteen hundred pounds. Coulan had constructed the sculpture by crafting individual stone blocks twenty inches in depth and assembling them in courses connected by copper clamps. Over the years, water had seeped into the joints between the courses and eroded a number of the clamps holding the sculpture together. Metro-North commissioned skilled stone

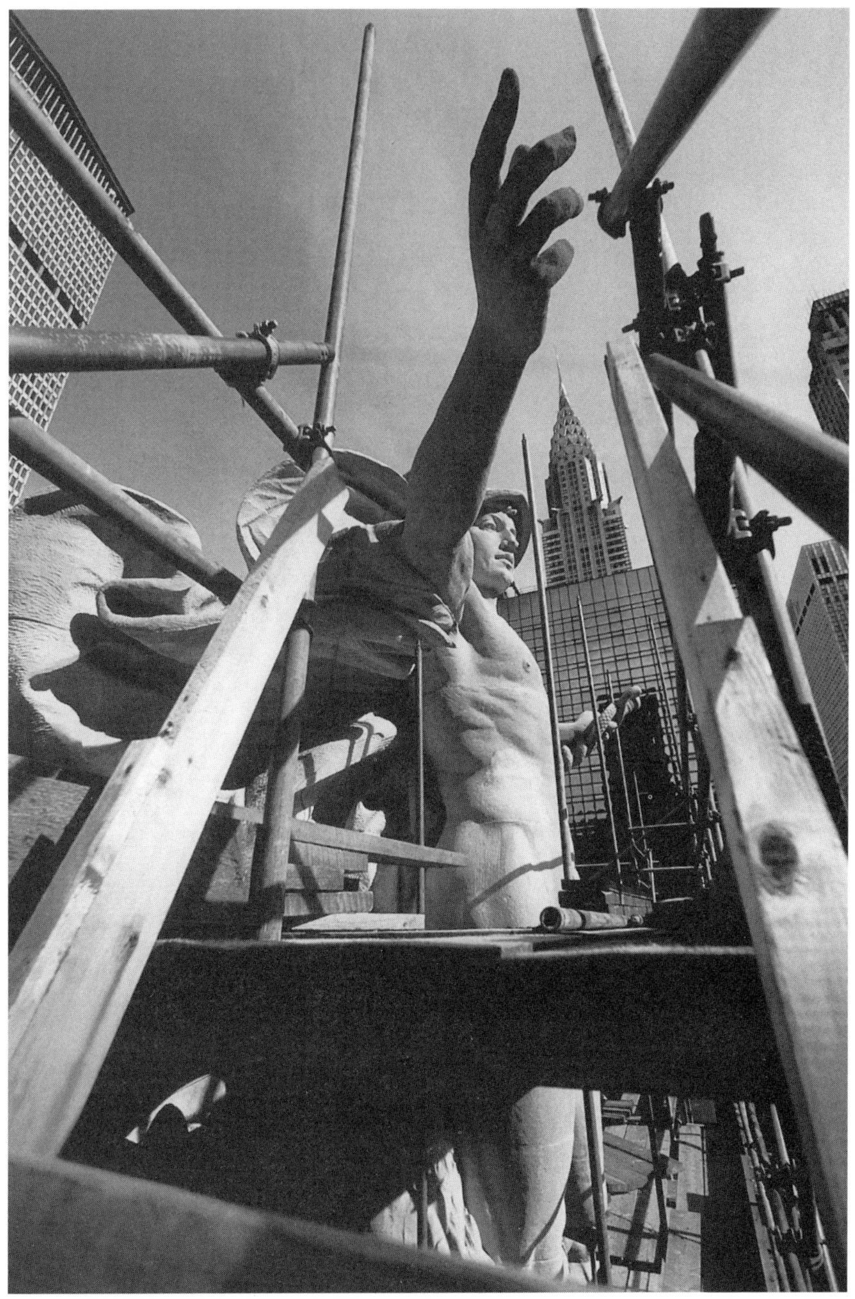

Restoration of Jules Coulan's statue of Mercury atop the 42nd Street facade, with the Grand Hyatt Hotel and spire of the Chrysler Building in background

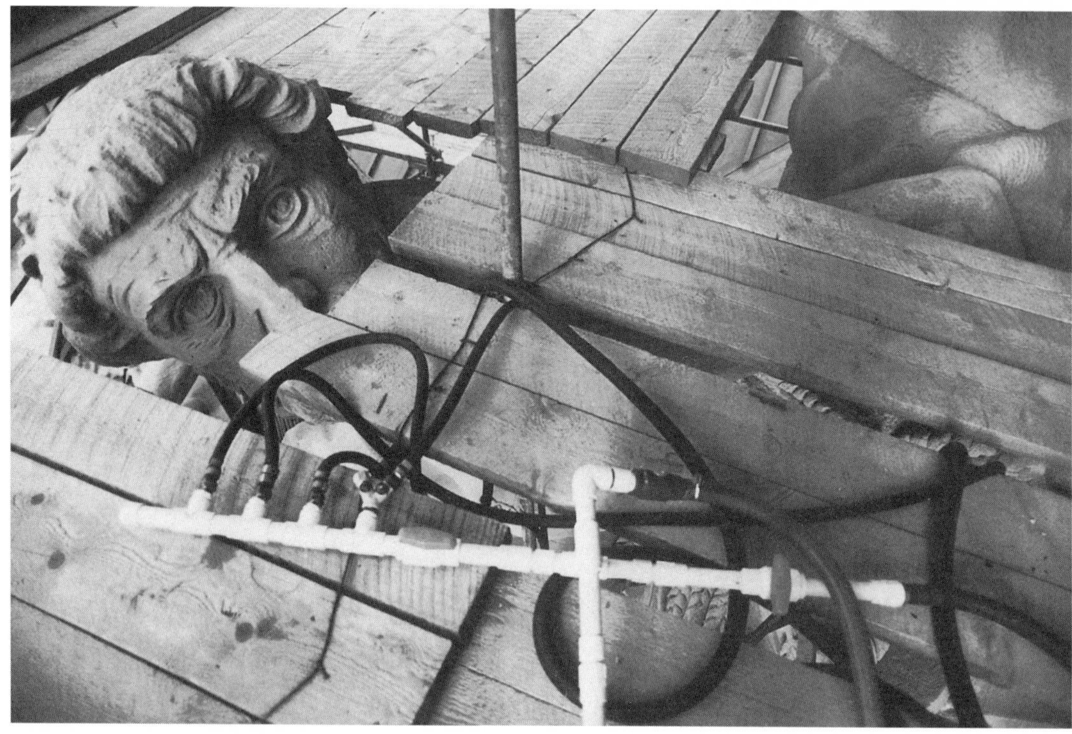

Restoration of sculpture on the 42nd Street facade

masons to repair all of the clamps and thoroughly clean the statues. Today, the restored gods of ancient Rome, adorning the top of Grand Central, catch the eye of all who travel up Park Avenue toward 42nd Street, just as Whitney Warren and Jules Coulan intended.

Metro-North proceeded with major changes to the Grand Central's pedestrian circulation system. First, in the terminal building itself, major repairs to the 42nd Street entrance ramps on the east and west ends were undertaken. The east passage from 42nd Street adjacent to the Grand Hyatt required the most extensive changes, including a dramatic widening of the cramped, narrow width and reopening of the ramp to the lower-level concourse, which had been blocked off for many years. Just off the Grand Concourse, on the both the east and west sides, the railroad installed escalators between the upper level and the suburban concourse on the lower level.

Whitney Warren's original plan for the Grand Concourse included dramatic stairways, modeled after the main stairway in the Paris Opera, on both sides, sweeping up to the second-floor balconies. On the Vanderbilt Avenue side, the west side, the stairs led to the covered entrance-

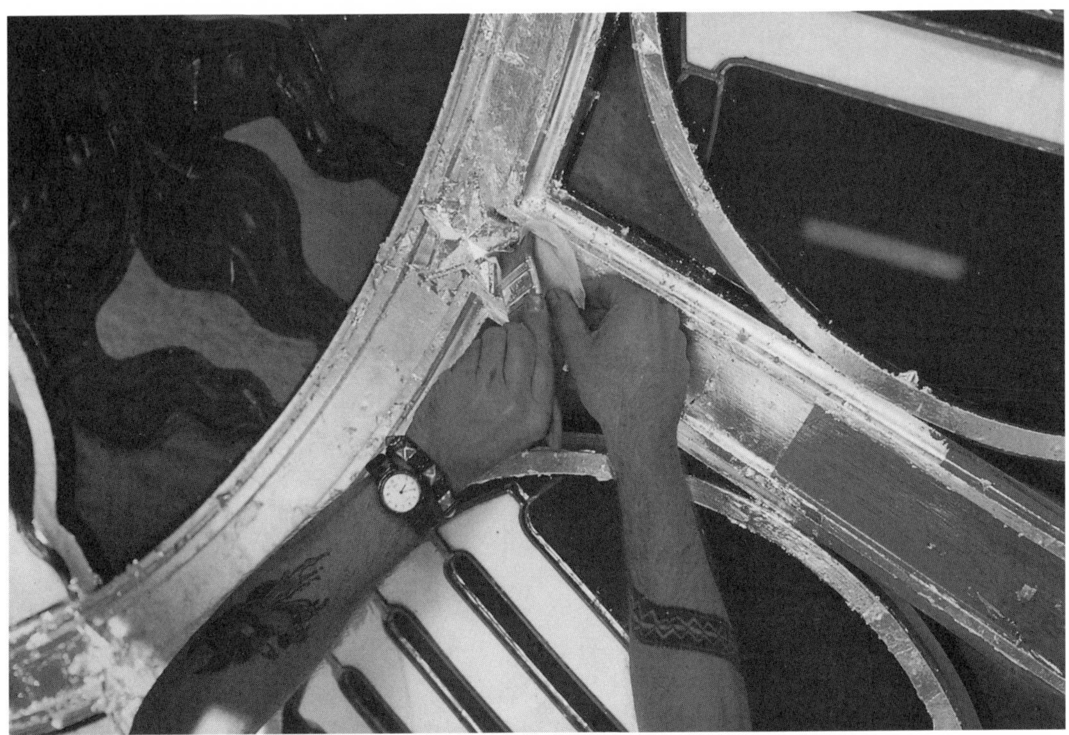

Regilding of the clock on the 42nd Street facade

way and taxi stand. For some reason, the New York Central had never completed the stairway on the east side of the concourse. After some diligent detective work, Metro-North located the quarry that had provided the marble for the west stairway and commissioned artisans to duplicate Warren's design on the east side of the Grand Concourse, adding another element of Beaux-Arts symmetry.

By far, the most dramatic changes to the terminal's circulatory system came in September of 1999, with the opening of completely new entrances directly to the underground train yard and platforms from the north, along Park. At 48th Street and Park Avenue and 47th Street and Madison, street-level vestibules now lead to stairs descending to a new cross-passage, under 47th over the upper-level platforms. Stairs lead further downward to the train platforms. Two long passageways connect the new uptown entrances to the Grand Concourse farther south. Additional entrances link with the new passageways in the Helmsley Building at 45th Street and Park Avenue.

The new entrances and passageways required sophisticated engineer-

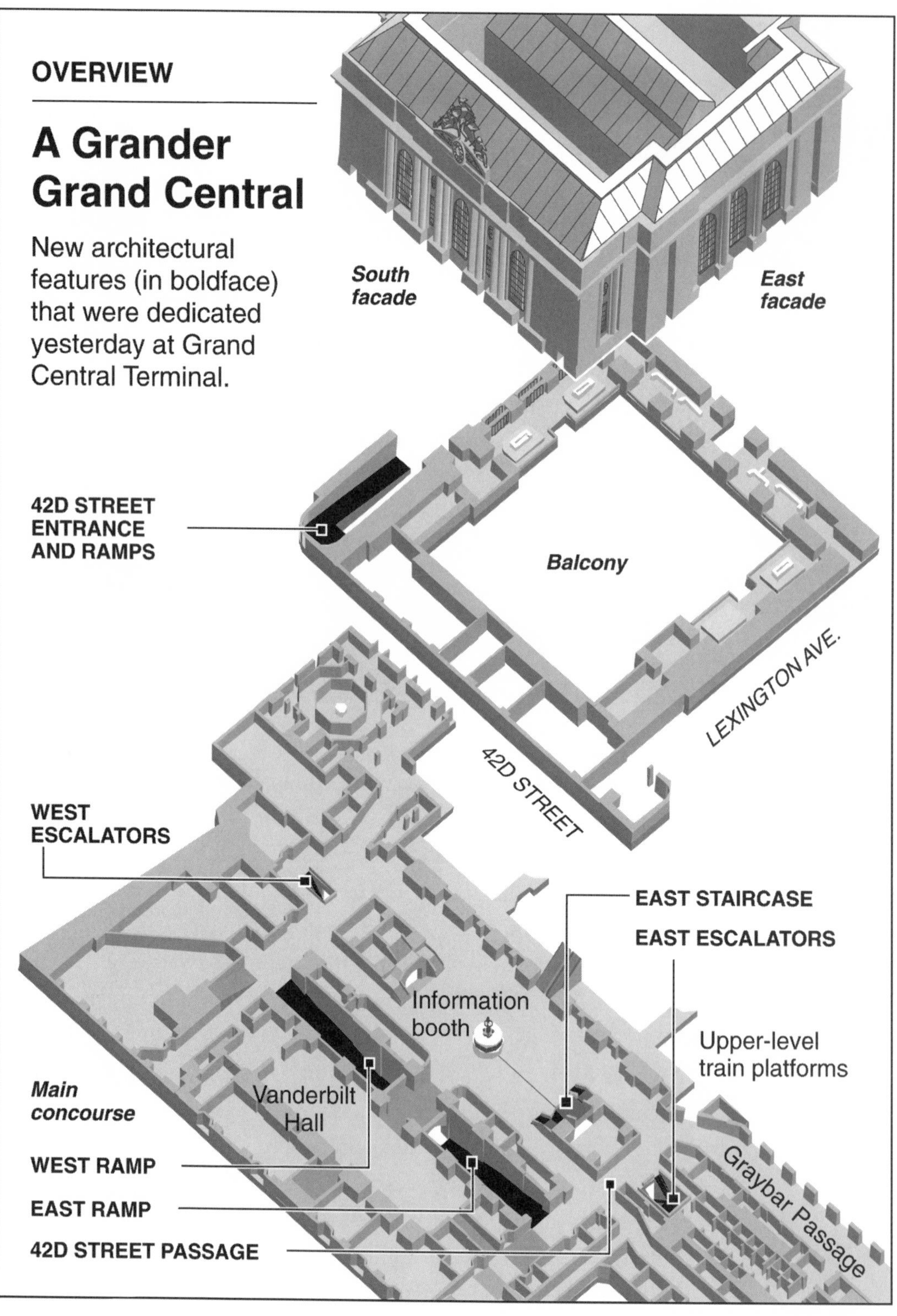

Alterations made by Metro-North to Grand Central's pedestrian circulation system, published in the New York Times *on October 2, 1998*

Restoration work on the east balcony

ing to fit within the existing structure, and first estimates placed their cost at over $70 million dollars.[15] Metro-North calculated that forty thousand of the daily commuters using the terminal work at destinations to the north of the terminal; the new entrances would save them fifteen minutes of time each day. Now they would be able to enter Grand Central and walk directly to the train platforms without the long walk down to Grand Central and then through the track gates on either the upper or lower level.

Metro-North faced another daunting challenge when they turned their attention to Grand Central's structural and mechanical systems, installed at the turn of the century and, in some cases, little altered. While the public sees the soaring spaces of the Grand Concourse and the marble and sandstone interior of the Vanderbilt waiting room on 42nd Street, hidden from sight, often far underground, are the building's essential mechanical systems.

Water proved to be the source of almost all structural problems uncovered in the building itself and in the underground train yard. Over

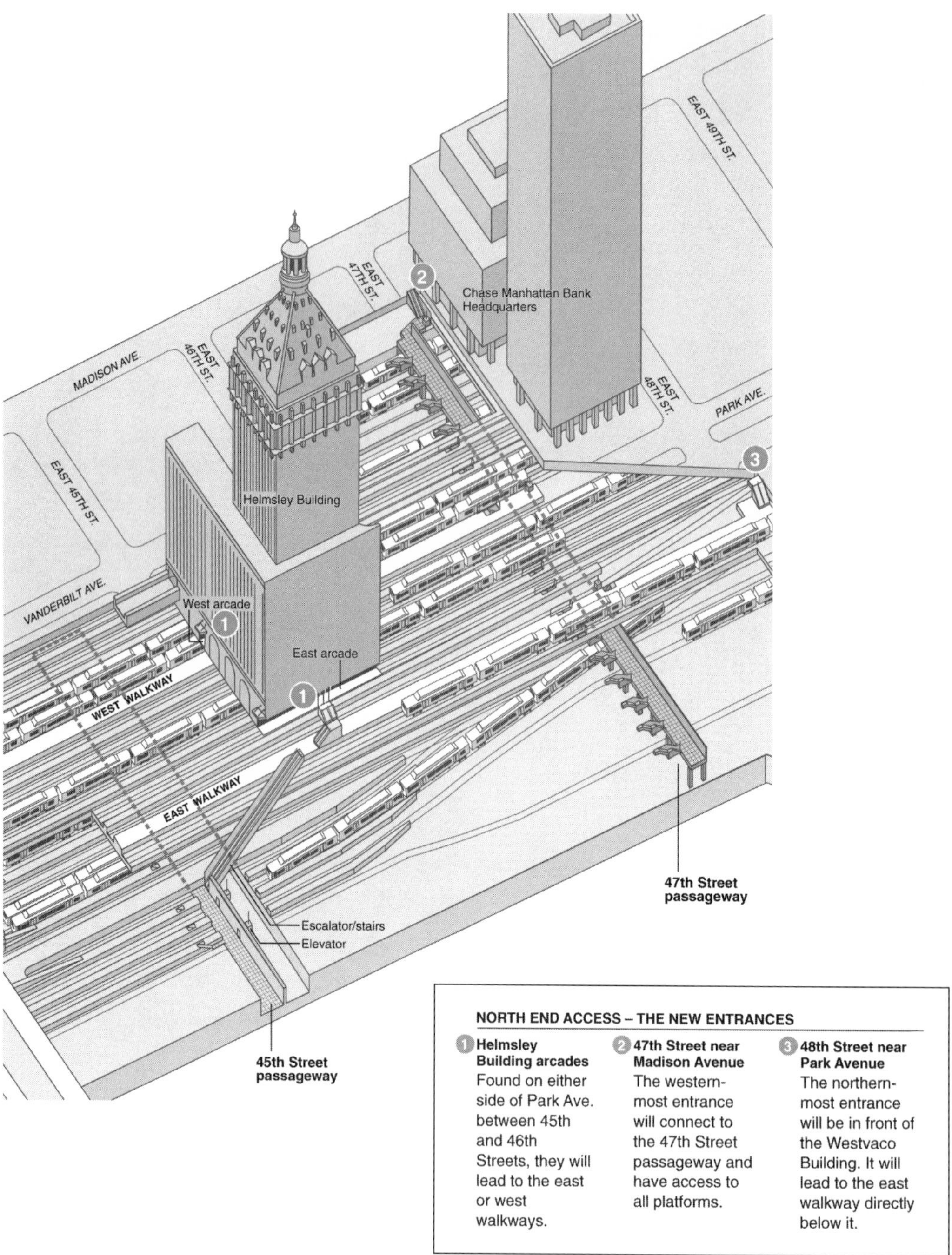
EAST 49TH ST.
EAST 47TH ST.
Chase Manhattan Bank Headquarters
MADISON AVE.
EAST 46TH ST.
EAST 48TH ST.
PARK AVE.
EAST 45TH ST.
Helmsley Building
VANDERBILT AVE.
West arcade
East arcade
WEST WALKWAY
EAST WALKWAY
47th Street passageway
Escalator/stairs
Elevator
45th Street passageway
NORTH END ACCESS – THE NEW ENTRANCES
1 Helmsley Building arcades
Found on either side of Park Ave. between 45th and 46th Streets, they will lead to the east or west walkways.
2 47th Street near Madison Avenue
The western-most entrance will connect to the 47th Street passageway and have access to all platforms.
3 48th Street near Park Avenue
The northern-most entrance will be in front of the Westvaco Building. It will lead to the east walkway directly below it.

New entrances to the station and the underground train platforms at 47th and 48th Streets and through the Helmsley Building, formerly the New York Central Building

time, neglect of the roof had exerted a high cost. Beyer Blinder Belle found rusting structural members throughout the facility and recommended that when the full restoration began, serious effort be devoted to repairing the damages to the structure.[16] Of course, the repairs to the roof would halt the water infiltration at its source.

The study of the terminal published in 1992 concluded: "Some systems are operational, but are beyond normal life expectancy. Some systems are no longer functional. None of the systems comply with current performance or safety codes."[17] A truly complicated task confronted Metro-North—replacing or extensively upgrading all of the terminal's mechanical systems. Initial estimates placed the cost of this work at almost $20 million dollars. When official New York and the public celebrated Grand Central's rebirth, few dignitaries descended 100 feet below ground, under the new food court off Lexington Avenue, to inspect the original rotary convertors manufactured by General Electric more than eighty years earlier and now replaced by a state-of-the-art electric system. Nor did they view the terminal's brand new heating and air-conditioning system. Without Metro-North's commitment of significant resources to upgrading the building's essential infrastructure, the celebration would have been a hollow one.

In the restoration of the interior spaces of Grand Central, Metro-North faced not only physical and structural repairs but a disheartening human problem. As work began on the waiting room, the railroad and public officials confronted another symbol of Grand Central's decline; homeless New Yorkers wandered throughout the terminal, loitered in the waiting room, and had taken up residence in the labyrinth of tunnels formerly used to move baggage.

New York City tried to address the problem in myriad ways—increasing the number of beds available in the city's shelters and moving aggressively to pass antiloitering laws, so that the homeless could be arrested for sleeping in public transportation facilities unless they provided a "satisfactory explanation" for their presence. Advocates for the homeless challenged the constitutionality of the antiloitering law in the courts. In February of 1988, New York's Court of Appeals ruled the law, banning loitering in public transportation facilities, to be unconstitutional. Much controversy greeted the court's decision and Metro-North police chief

The G.E. rotary convertors, which changed alternating current to direct current, have been left in place deep under 43rd Street between the Grand Hyatt Hotel and the Graybar office building

John Esposito vowed to continue to eject homeless persons from Grand Central.[18] During the 1990s, sympathy for the homeless and the poor in general seemed to wane, and, with the combination of increased social services and aggressive policing, the homeless have departed from Grand Central—at least for the present.

Metro-North selected the firm of George Campbell Construction to undertake the $5.9 million restoration of the waiting room. One especially troublesome task involved cleaning the surfaces of the walls. The usual cleaning agents just soaked into the limestone walls, carrying the dirt with them. Eventually the preservation architects and conservators hit on the right formula, employing a mixture of ammoniated latex. Left on the surface to dry for four hours, the mixture peeled off the dirt and grime.[19]

By far, the most impressive piece of the restoration is the vaulted ceiling soaring 125 feet above the Tennessee marble floor of the Grand Concourse. Based on a design by the French painter Paul Helleu, the original ceiling included the constellations of the Milky Way, formed by

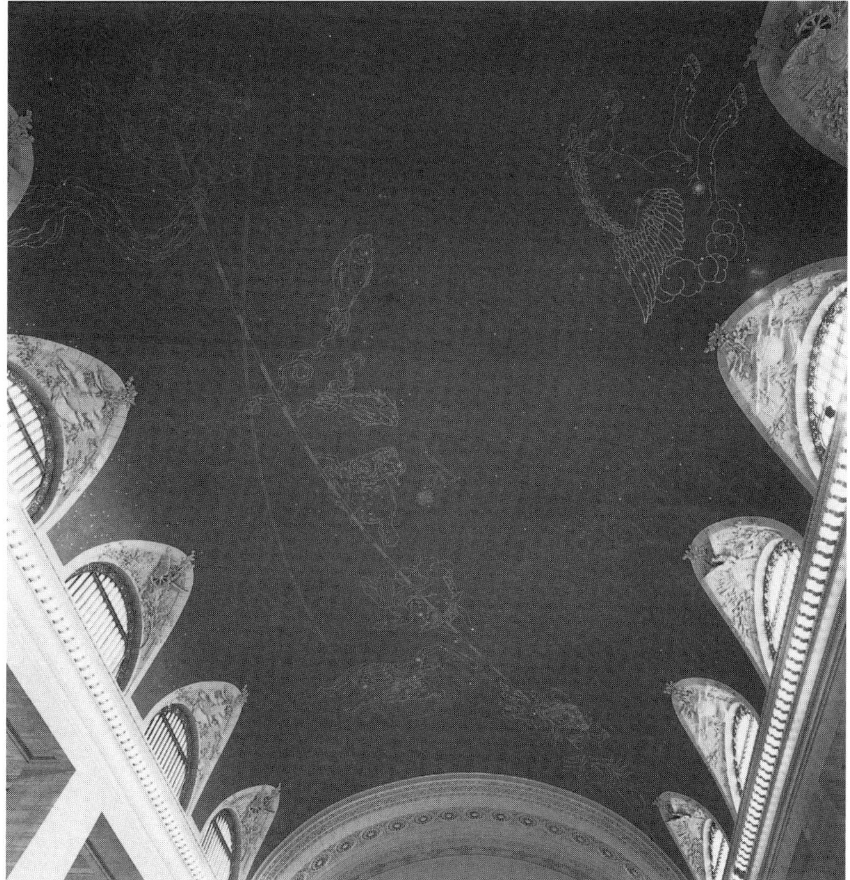

The restored ceiling of the Grand Concourse with the Milky Way visible again from the floor

more than 2,500 gold-leaf stars; 59 light bulbs lit the major stars. Water damage in 1945 led to the replacement of the original mural with painted panels glued to the ceiling. The concourse's stars generated controversy; astronomers pointed out that the constellations were displayed backward. Grand Central's defenders countered that Helleu intended the ceiling to represent the view of the Milky Way from outside of the solar system.

Craftsmen from the firm of John Canning and Company, based in Connecticut, meticulously cleaned the 25,000-square-foot ceiling. Sixty years of grime befouled the mural; the stars barely shone. When comparisons to the restoration of the Sistine Chapel appeared in the press, John Canning pointed out that Michelangelo had painted on fresco in the Vatican chapel whereas the artisans at Grand Central had used oil paint, but that his firm was employing similar cleaning agents, a mixture of sodium bicarbonate and citric acid in water, to remove years of grime.

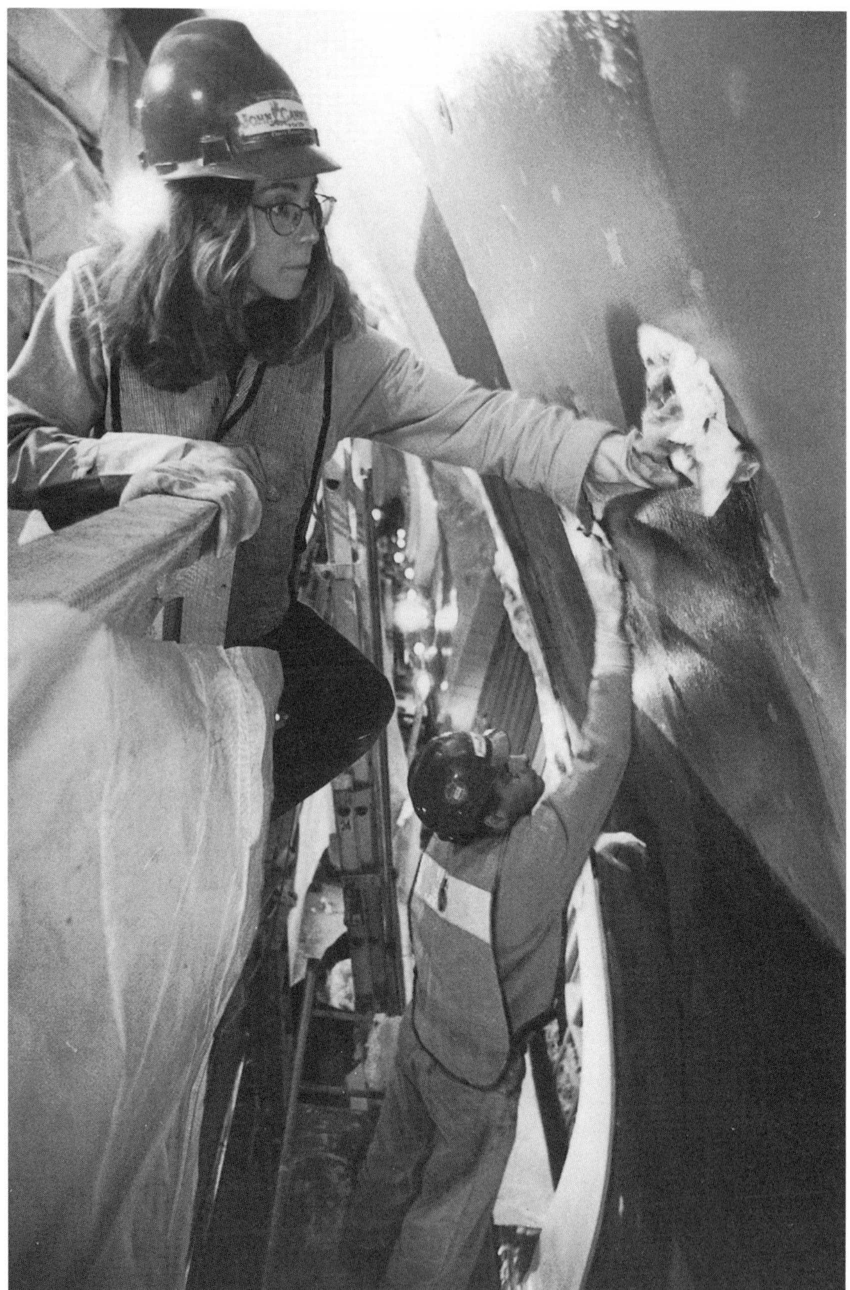

Cleaning the ceiling of the Grand Concourse

Restored chandeliers in the north balcony of the Grand Concourse

The heart of Grand Central, the Grand Concourse, restored

Once the ceiling was cleaned, judicious applications of blue acrylic paint and 23-karat gold leaf restored the brilliance of the stars soaring overhead. Canning commented: "We are totally respecting the original work with minimum intervention."[20] This portion of the total restoration project, the refurbishment of the ceiling of the Grand Concourse, reminds even the most blasé New Yorker of the splendor of the city's civic cathedral.

The ten enormous brass chandeliers that hang high above the balconies surrounding the concourse also received meticulous attention. Work crews carefully removed the massive lighting fixtures, weighing

1,600 pounds each, and shipped them to Utah (the location of the lowest bidder) for a complete overhaul. Patrons dining at Michael Jordan's steakhouse, located on the north balcony, now sit under dazzling chandeliers restored to their turn-of-the-century brilliance.

When the terminal was rededicated, with great fanfare, in October of 1998, the final configuration of the waiting room remained undecided. Plans for the restored great space include restaurants and other vendors. Currently the waiting room serves as a space for temporary exhibits and for catered parties. Rail passengers using Grand Central today have less use for a waiting room. Little long-distance train travel remains in the United States, despite the valiant efforts of Amtrak, and all Amtrak service in New York City operates out of Pennsylvania Station.

Built to serve railroading's glamorous long-distance trains, Grand Central is now, ironically, the focal point of the commuter service to New York's northern suburbs. People no longer leave from Gate 29 on the Twentieth Century Limited, the all first-class luxury train to Chicago; rather they depart to more immediate destinations on the 5:22 to Scarsdale or the 6:25 to New Canaan, Connecticut. Built by private enterprise as a monument to commerce, Grand Central Terminal has always functioned as a magnificent civic structure. It has been saved by a collaboration of private and public efforts, and the public of New York City continues to rush through its tunnels, ramps, and corridors and to mingle on its Grand Concourse. Built in the Age of Energy, Grand Central, all movement and blur, continues to exude the enormous energy and vitality of New York City.

NOTES

Prologue

1. Sarah Sachs, "From Gritty Depot, A Glittery Destination; Refurbished Grand Central Depot, Worthy of Its Name Is Reopened," *New York Times,* Oct. 2, 1998, sec. B, p. 1, col. 4.

2. "Grander Than Ever," *Daily News,* Oct. 2, 1998, p. 20.

3. "Grand Gateway to Gotham," *Hartford Courant,* Oct. 4, 1998, sec. C, p. 2.

4. Michael O. Allen, "Grand New Age for Central Landmark," *Daily News,* Sept. 27, 1998, p. 32.

5. Ibid.

6. Henry Adams, *The Education of Henry Adams* (New York: Time, Book Division, 1964), vol. 2, pp. 120, 296.

CHAPTER ONE | *The Commodore's Grand Central*

1. *State of New York, Laws of 1831,* chap. 263, p. 323.

2. Data from New York and Harlem Railroad Co., "Detail of Real Estate in the City as of December 31, 1934," New York Central and Hudson River Railroad Papers, Manuscripts and Archives Division, New York Public Library, Astor, Lenox and Tilden Foundations (hereafter cited as NYCP), box 74.

3. William Croffut, *The Vanderbilts and the Story of Their Fortune* (London: Griffith, Farran, Okeden, & Welsh, 1886), p. 159.

4. Albro Martin, in his study of American railroads, assigns great importance to this gap, describing it as "the most important geographic feature of our planet." Martin, *Railroads Triumphant* (New York: Oxford University Press, 1992), p. 7.

5. Edward Hungerford, *Men and Iron: The History of the New York Central* (New York: Thomas C. Crowell Co., 1938), p. 24.

6. Aaron E. Klein, *New York Central* (New York: Bonanza Books, 1985), p. 23.

7. Robert Sobel, *Fallen Colossus* (New York: Weybright and Tally, 1977), p. 55.

8. Minutes of the Executive Committee, Board of Directors, New York Central and Hudson River Railroad, Dec. 8, 1903, NYCP, box 94.

9. *Moody's Analysis of Railroad Investments, 1907* (New York: Analyses Publishing, 1909), p. 383.

10. Edward Hungerford, "The Greatest Railway Terminal in the World," *Outlook* 102, Dec. 28, 1912, p. 904.

11. Lewis Mumford, *Sticks and Stones: A Study of American Architecture and Civilization* (New York: Dover, 1955), p. 123.

12. Carol Meeks, *The Railroad Station: An Architectural History* (New Haven: Yale Universtiy Press, 1956), pp. 170–71.

13. "City's Growth Epitomized in Terminal Changes," *New York Times,* Feb. 2, 1913, sec. 9, p. 3, col. 6.

14. "New York Central and Hudson River Railroad," timetable, Apr. 1, 1885, National Railroad Association Library, Washington, D.C.

15. Jesse Lynch Williams, "The Gates of the City," *Century Magazine* 74, no. 4, Aug. 1907, p. 488.

16. Quoted in Martin, *Railroads Triumphant,* p. 32.

17. "Vanderbilt in the West: The Railroad Millionaire Expresses Himself Freely," *New York Times*, Oct. 9, 1882, p. 1, col. 3.

18. Arthur Vanderbilt, *Fortune's Children: The Fall of the House of Vanderbilt* (New York: Morrow, 1989), p. 133.

19. Henry Clews, *Fifty Years in Wall Street* (New York: Irving Publishing, 1908), p. 388.

20. Ibid., p. 371.

21. Minutes of the Board of Directors of the New York Central and Hudson River Railroad, Sept. 29, 1904, NYCP, box 94.

22. Editorial, *New York Times,* Sept. 20, 1899, p. 6, col. 5.

23. Editorial, *New York Times,* Mar. 26, 1899, p. 18, col. 6.

24. "Congestion of the Traffic at the Grand Central Station," *Scientific American* 83, Dec. 1, 1900, p. 338.

CHAPTER TWO | *The Engineer's Grand Central*

1. "Fifteen Killed in Rear End Collision," *New York Times,* Jan. 9, 1902, p. 1, col. 5.

2. William J. Wilgus, "The Grand Central Terminal in Perspective," *Transactions of the American Society of Civil Engineers* 106, Oct. 1940, p. 1003.

3. Ibid.

4. William J. Wilgus to William H. Newman, Dec. 22, 1902, William J. Wilgus Papers, Manuscripts and Archives Division, New York Public Library, Astor, Lenox and Tilden Foundations (hereafter cited as WWP), box 1.

5. Wilgus to Newman, Mar. 19, 1903, WWP, box 1.

6. "The Grand Central Terminal in New York," *Railway Age Gazette* 54, no. 7, Feb. 14, 1913, p. 284.

7. Minutes of the Board of Directors of the New York Central and Hudson River Railroad, Nov. 20, 1907, NYCP, box 95.

8. William J. Wilgus, "Inception of Grand Central," WWP, box 2. *Hudson Division* and *Harlem Division* refer to the suburban areas in Westchester County and the Bronx, respectively, served by the track of the original Hudson River and New York and Harlem railroads.

9. Wilgus to Newman, Sept. 4, 1906, WWP, box 6.

10. "Progress on the Grand Central Terminal," *Railway Age Gazette* 53, no. 21, Nov. 22, 1912, p. 982.

11. See David McCullough, *The Path between the Seas* (New York: Simon & Schuster, 1977).

12. "New York Central Contract Signed," *New York Daily Tribune,* Aug. 12, 1903, p. 1.

13. Minutes of the Construction Committee of the New York Central and Hudson River Railroad, Feb. 2, 1906, WWP, box 6.

14. Ibid., May 22, 1906.

15. Ibid., Mar. 3, 1907.

16. Minutes of the Board of Directors of the New York Central and Hudson River Railroad, May 15, 1907, NYCP, box 95.

17. William J. Wilgus to W. C. Brown, Dec. 11, 1906, WWP, box 6.

18. "The New Grand Central Terminal Station in New York City: An Underground Double-Deck Terminal," *Engineering News* 69, no. 18, May 1, 1913, p. 891.

19. Minutes of the Board of Directors of the New York Central and Hudson River Railroad, Dec. 7, 1910, NYCP, box 94.

20. "Terminal Trains Run by Loop System," *New York Times,* Feb. 2, 1913, sec. 9, p. 6, col. 1.

21. Ibid.

22. "New Grand Central Opens Its Doors," *New York Times,* Feb. 2, 1913, sec. 9, p. 1, col. 2.

23. Wilgus to Newman, Dec. 15, 1902, WWP, box 9.

24. John A. Droege, *Passenger Terminals and Trains* (New York: McGraw-Hill, 1916), p. 307.

25. Bion Arnold, "A Comparative Study of Steam and Electric Power for Heavy Railroad Service," *Railroad Gazette* 34, no. 26, June 27, 1902, p. 498.

26. Ibid., p. 499.

27. William J. Wilgus to William K. Vanderbilt, Sept. 6, 1904, WWP, box 4.

28. Frank J. Sprague to William J. Wilgus, *General Report,* Feb. 4, 1902, WWP, box 4.

29. Bion Arnold, "Report of Bion Arnold to William J. Wilgus Upon the Proposed Electric Equipment of the Hudson Division of the New York Central Railroad," Bion T. Arnold Papers, Manuscripts and Archives Division, New York Public Library, box 6.

30. Frank J. Sprague, "An Open Letter to Mr. Westinghouse," *Railroad Gazette* 40, no. 1, Jan. 5, 1906, p. 8.

31. Ibid., p. 9.

32. Regular Meeting of the Executive Committee of the New York Central and Hudson River Railroad, Nov. 15, 1903, NYCP, box 94.

33. "Electricity for the New York Central," *New York Times,* Nov. 21, 1903, p. 3, col. 2.

34. "Test of the New York Central Electric Locomotive," *Railroad Gazette* 37, no. 23, Nov. 18, 1904, p. 552.

35. Ibid., p. 554.

36. "Electric Engine Beats All Rivals," *New York Herald,* Nov. 13, 1904. p. 4.

37. "Electric Locomotive Perfect, Test Proves," *New York Times,* Nov. 13, 1904, p. 3, col. 1.

38. "A Big Railroad Trying Electric Power," *Leslie's Weekly,* Dec. 1, 1904, p. 12.

39. "First Electric Train at Grand Central," *New York Times,* Oct. 1, 1906, p. 16, col. 4.

40. "The New York Central's Electrification in New York," *Railroad Gazette* 41, no. 14, Oct. 5, 1906, p. 297.

41. "First Electric Engine Enters New York City," *World,* Oct. 1, 1906, p. 5, col. 1.

42. Editorial, *New York Times,* Sept. 30, 1906, p. 8, col. 5.

43. William Wilgus, "The Electrification of the Suburban Zone of the New York Central and Hudson River Railroad in the Vicinity of New York City," *Transactions of the American Society of Civil Engineers* 61, Dec. 1908, p. 111.

44. "Only Second Trip of Doomed Train," *New York Times,* Feb. 17, 1907, sec. 1, p. 3, col. 1. (The various accounts of the accident differ as to the numbers of dead and injured.)

45. "Wreck News at Grand Central," ibid., p. 4, col. 1.

46. "Twenty-Five Killed and Seventy-Five Injured," *New York Herald,* Feb. 17, 1907, p. 1.

47. "Previous Central Wrecks," *New York Times,* Feb. 17, 1907, sec. 1, p. 4, col. 2.

48. "Twenty-Five Killed," *New York Journal,* Feb. 19, 1907, p. 1.

49. "Wilgus Shifts Blame for Wreck," *New York Times,* Feb. 28, 1907, p. 11, col. 3.

50. William Wilgus, "Woodlawn Wreck," WWP, box 7, p. v.

51. William Potter, "Recollections of William B. Potter," General Electric Historical File, Hammond Historical Files, Schenectady Museum, vol. J, p. 836.

52. Wilgus, "Woodlawn Wreck," p. 5.

53. Wilgus to Newman, June 25, 1907, WWP, box 6.

54. Potter, "Recollections," p. 836.

55. "New Grand Central Opens Its Doors," *New York Times,* Feb. 2, 1913, sec. 9, p. 1, col. 7.

56. "Erecting the Grand Central Terminal," *Engineering Record* 66, no. 8, Aug. 24, 1912, p. 222.

57. "First Great Stairless Railway Station," *New York Times,* Feb. 2, 1913, sec. 9, p. 5, col. 1.

58. "Year of Traffic in Pennsylvania Station," *New York Times,* Nov. 27, 1912, p. 8, col. 4.

59. Droege, *Passenger Terminals and Trains,* p. 159.

60. Hugh Thompson, "The Greatest Railroad Terminal in the World," *Munsey's Magazine* 45, Apr. 1911, pp. 27, 38, 40.

CHAPTER THREE | *The Architect's Grand Central*

1. Brooklyn Museum, *American Renaissance: 1876–1917* (Brooklyn, N.Y.: Brooklyn Museum, 1979).

2. Jacob A. Riis, *How the Other Half Lives: Studies among the Tenements of New York,* Bedford Series in History and Culture, David Leviatin, ed. (New York: Bedford Books, St. Martin's Press, 1996), p. 129.

3. William Wilgus, "Record of the Inception and Creation of the Grand Central Improvement 1902–1913," WWP, box 1, p. 31.

4. Executive Committee of the Board of Directors of the New York Central and Hudson River Railroad, Feb. 9, 1904, NYCP, box 94.

5. *Allen H. Stem v. Whitney Warren et al.*, Court of Appeals of New York (1920), 227 N.Y. 538; 125 N.E. 811, p. 6.

6. Wilgus, "Record of the Inception," p. 31.

7. Meeting of the Joint Committee of the New York Central and the New York, New Haven, and Hartford in Regard to Grand Central Terminal, Mar. 3, 1906, WWP, box 8, p. 1.

8. Ibid., May 23, 1906, p. 3.

9. Minutes of the Board of Directors of the New York Central and Hudson River Railroad, Dec. 23, 1909, NYCP, box 94.

10. Wilgus, "Record of the Inception," p. 77.

11. For a thorough discussion of American architecture, see Robert A. M. Stern, *Pride of Place: Building An American Dream* (Boston: Houghton Mifflin, 1986).

12. "Monumental Gateway to a Great City," *Scientific American* 107, no. 23, Dec. 7, 1912, p. 484.

13. Richard Chaffee, "The Teaching of Architecture at the Ecole des Beaux-Arts," in *The Architecture of the Ecole des Beaux Arts,* ed. Richard Drexler (New York: Museum of Modern Art, 1977), p. 61.

14. Louis Sullivan to William Sullivan, Dec. 7, 1874, quoted in Drexler, *Architecture of the Ecole,* p. 90.

15. Quoted in Drexler, *Architecture of the Ecole,* p. 94.

16. "Application of Whitney Warren," Feb. 21, 1907, Archives of the American Institute of Architects, Washington, D.C.

17. Quoted in Brooklyn Museum, *American Renaissance,* p. 109.

18. Vincent Scully, *American Architecture and Urbanism* (New York: Henry Holt and Co., 1969), p. 140.

19. Quoted in Drexler, *Architecture of the Ecole,* p. 118.

20. "Facade of the Terminal the Keynote to the Structure," *New York Times,* Feb. 2, 1913, sec. 9, p. 2, col. 3.

21. Theodore Starrett, "The Grand Central Terminal Station," *Architecture and Building* 45, no. 4, Apr. 1913, p. 129.

22. For a comprehensive history of the City Beautiful movement, see William H. Wilson, *The City Beautiful Movement* (Baltimore: Johns Hopkins University Press, 1989).

23. For a detailed history of Central Park and its role in the life of New York, see Roy Rosenzweig and Elizabeth Blackmar, *The Park and the People: A History of Central Park* (Ithaca: Cornell University Press, 1992).

24. Daniel H. Burnham, "White City and Capital City," *Century* 63, Feb., 1902, p. 619.

25. Joshua D'Esposito, "Some Fundamental Principles of Air Rights," *Railway Age* 83, no. 17, Oct. 22, 1927, p. 757.

26. "More Millions to be Spent in Beautifying the New Grand Central Terminal," *New York Herald,* Mar. 4, 1910, p. 4.

27. Robert Pope, "Grand Central Terminal Station in New York," *Town Planning Review* 2, Apr. 1911, p. 61.

28. "New Grand Central Terminal Opens Its Doors," *New York Times,* Feb. 2, 1913, sec. 9, p. 1, col. 5.

29. Charles M. Robinson, "The Replanning of Cities," *Charities and Commons* 19, no. 1, Feb. 1908, p. 1489.

30. "New Grand Central Terminal Opens Its Doors," p. 1, col. 2.

31. Wilgus to W. H. Newman, Mar. 19, 1903, WWP, box 1.

32. William J. Wilgus, "The Grand Central Terminal in Perspective," *Transactions of the American Society of Civil Engineers* 106, Oct. 1940, p. 997.

33. Whitney Warren, "Monumental Gateway to a Great City," *Scientific American* 107, no. 23, Dec. 7, 1912, p. 484.

34. L. C. Fritch, "Railway Terminals," *Railway Age Gazette* 54, no. 3, Feb. 17, 1913, p. 109.

35. Ibid.

CHAPTER FOUR | *New York's Grand Central*

1. William Dean Howells, *A Hazard of New Fortune,* (New York: New American Library, 1965), pp. 158–59.

2. William Wilgus to William Newman, Dec. 22, 1902, WWP, box 1.

3. Ibid.

4. Joshua D'Esposito, "Some of the Fundamental Principles of Air Rights," *Railway Age* 83, no. 17, Oct. 22, 1927, p. 759.

5. Hugh Thompson, "The Greatest Railroad Terminal in the World," *Munsey's Magazine* 45, Apr., 1911, p. 39.

6. D'Esposito, "Some Fundamental Principles of Air Rights," p. 758.

7. William Wilgus, "The Grand Central Terminal in Perspective," *Transactions of the American Society of Civil Engineers* 106, Oct. 1940, p. 1018.

8. Robert Pope, "Grand Central Terminal Station in New York," *Town Planning Review* 2, Apr. 1911, p. 61.

9. "New Grand Central Opens its Doors," *New York Times,* Feb. 2, 1913, sec. 9, p. 1, col. 1.

10. Edward Hungerford, "The Greatest Railway Terminal in the World," *Outlook* 102, Dec. 28, 1912, pp. 905, 906.

11. Executive Committee of the Board of Directors of the New York Central and Hudson River Railroad, Dec. 15, 1903, NYCP, box 94.

12. Ibid., June 14, 1922, box 52.

13. "The Grand Central Terminal: A Great Civic Improvement," *Engineering News-Record* 85, no. 11, Sept. 9, 1920, p. 484.

14. Ibid.

15. "Values Higher in All Directions Around Proposed Railroad Stations," *New York Times,* Mar. 25, 1906, sec. 5, p. 5, col. 2.

16. Pope, "Grand Central Terminal Station in New York," p. 56.

17. William Wilgus, "Record of the Inception and Creation of the Grand Central Improvement 1902–1913," WWP, box 2, p. 77.

18. "The Park Avenue Plaza," *New York Times,* Mar. 5, 1910, p. 8, col. 3.

19. "More Millions to be Spent in Beautifying the New Grand Central Terminal," *New York Times,* Mar. 4, 1910, p. 1, col. 4.

20. Henry-Russell Hitchcock and Philip Johnson, *The International Style* (New York: W. W. Norton, 1966), pp. 18–19.

21. Ibid., p. 41.

22. Whitney Warren File, American Institute of Architects archives, Washington, D.C.

23. "Building's New Look Shaped by Old Zoning," *New York Times,* Nov., 14, 1993, sec. 10, p. 10.

24. "Details of Central's Electric Road Plans," *New York Times,* Nov. 22, 1903, p. 13, col. 1.

25. Jesse Lynch Williams, "The Gates of the City," *Century Magazine* 74, no. 4, Aug., 1907, p. 490.

26. "The Running of Electric Trains to White Plains Means the Opening of a New Era for the Entire Territory," *New York Times,* Mar. 13, 1910, pt. 8, p. 6.

27. "Suburban Homes North of the Harlem," Four-Track Series, no. 4 (New York: New York Central & Hudson River Railroad, 1894), Warshaw Collection, Smithsonian Institution.

28. "Real Rapid Transit to Ninety Suburban Towns Located in the Commutation District," Four-Track Series, no. 23 (New York: New York Central & Hudson River Railroad, 1904), Warshaw Collection, Smithsonian Institution.

29. William Wilgus to William K. Vanderbilt, Sept. 6, 1904, WWP, box 11.

30. William Wilgus, "Passengers In and Out of New York Metropolitan Terminals," WWP, box 4.

31. Ibid.

32. *The Encylcopedia of New York City,* ed. Kenneth Jackson (New Haven: Yale University Press, 1995), p. 1135.

33. Ibid., p. 921.

34. U. S. Bureau of the Census, *Abstract of the Fourteenth Census of the United States: 1920* (Washington, D.C., 1923), table 9, p. 23.

35. Wilgus, "Grand Central in Perspective," p. 1021.

36. "City's Growth Epitomized in Terminal Changes," *New York Times,* Feb. 2, 1913, sec. 9, p. 2, col. 7.

37. Wilgus, "Record of the Inception," p. 94.

38. Theodore Dreiser, *The Color of a Great City* (New York: Boni and Liveright, 1923), p. 123.

39. Tom Wolfe, *Bonfire of the Vanities* (New York: Farrar, Straus, Giroux, 1987), pp. 6–7.

40. Ibid., p. 55.

Epilogue

1. U.S. Bureau of the Census, *Historical Statistics of the United States, Colonial Times to 1970,* pt. 2, ser. Q 284–312 (Washington, D.C., 1975), pp. 729–30.

2. See Ron Chernow, *Titan: The Life of John D. Rockefeller, Sr.,* (New York: Random House, 1998).

3. J. P. Morgan and Co., *Syndication Book 1,* J. P. Morgan Library, New York, pp. 113–14.

4. Bureau of the Census, *Historical Statistics,* ser. Q 148–62, p. 716.

5. Ibid., pp. 711, 728.

6. "New York Passenger Traffic," *Railway Age* 100, no. 18, May 2, 1936, p. 738.

7. *Moody's Analysis of Railroad Investments, 1917* (New York: Analyses Publishing, 1919), p. 448.

8. *Landmark Preservation Law,* New York City Administrative Code 1965, ch 8-A, 205–1.0(b).

9. *Penn Central Transportation Company et al. v. City of New York,* (1978) 438 US 104, 57 L Ed 2d 631, p. 642.

10. George Walker, general manager, M.T.A. Metro-North Commuter Railroad, interview by author, New York City, Oct. 12, 1998.

11. Jessica Stern, "Grand Central, Grand Plan; Metro-North Commuter Railroad Plans Renovation of New York's Grand Central Terminal," *Railway Age* 191, no. 6, June 1990, p. 52.

12. Shawn Kennedy, "Bringing Symmetry and Logic Back to 'New York's Living Room,' " *New York Times,* Nov. 26, 1995, sec. 1, p. 41, col. 1.

13. Heather A. Hatfield, "A Grand Old Roof Shines Again: Renovation Covers a New York City Landmark in Copper," *Engineering News-Record*, Sept. 24, 1987, p. 22.

14. Beyer Blinder Belle et al., *Grand Central Terminal: Historic Structure Report, Vol. 11* (New York, 1992), IIIF.3.

15. David Dunlap, "Grand Central Gets Northern Exposure," *New York Times,* Feb. 25, 1998, sec. B, p. 1, col. 2.

16. Beyer Blinder Belle et al., *Grand Central Terminal*, IIIG.7.

17. Ibid., IIIG.14.

18. Kevin Flynn, "Decision's Effect on Loitering Law is Still Unclear," *Newsday*, Feb. 29, 1988, p. 19, col. 3.

19. Joan Kelly Bernard, "A Tale of Two Terminals: At Grand Central, Elegance Restored; at Penn Station, More Space on the Way," *Newsday*, Nov. 19, 1992, p. 82, col. 3.

20. Scott Hartley, "Reaching for the Stars: The Restoration of Grand Central Terminal," *Trains Magazine* 57, no. 6, June 1997, p. 57.

A NOTE ON SOURCES

The primary archival material for the history of Grand Central Terminal resides in the collections of the Manuscripts and Archives Division of the New York Public Library, Astor, Lenox and Tilden Foundations. First and foremost are the papers of William J. Wilgus, vice president and chief engineer of the New York Central and Hudson River Railroad. Frank J. Sprague, a leading electrical inventor and entrepreneur, served as a consulting engineer for the Grand Central electrification. His papers and those of electrical engineer and consultant Bion T. Arnold are also part of the New York Public Library's manuscript collections.

Following the bankruptcy of the Penn Central Corporation, the New York Public Library acquired the corporate records of the New York Central Railroad and its subsidiary lines, including the Harlem River Railroad. The Manuscripts Division has commenced the challenging task of cataloguing this material.

The Schenectady Museum, in Schenectady, New York, houses an important collection of General Electric Company records in the Hammond Historical Files. In Washington, D.C., the Smithsonian Institution's Warshaw Collection contains New York Central memorabilia and advertising material, and the archives of the American Institute of Architects include details of Whitney Warren's censure.

ILLUSTRATION CREDITS

The illustrations in this volume, indicated below by page numbers, are reproduced courtesy of, and where necessary by permission of, the following sources:

Agence Photographique Roger-Viollet, Paris: 92
Avery Architectural and Fine Arts Library, Columbia University: 81, 112, 140, 146, 163, 167
Engineering, Gillard Welch Ltd, Knowle, England: 58, 141, 142, 145
Engineering News-Record, McGraw-Hill: 108, 109
Library of Congress: 3, 10, 22, 32, 45, 46, 49, 51, 66, 74, 137, 138, 139, 143, 144, 159, 170, 195, 198
Mark Stein Studios, Middle Village, N.Y.: 21, 28, 88
MTA Metro-North Railroad: 210, 212, 220, 221; (Dan Cornish, photographer): 5; (Frank English, photographer): ii–iii, 2, 4, 6, 211, 214, 217, 218, 219
Museum of the City of New York: 33, 36, 37, 110, 164, 168, 202, 203, 204
New-York Historical Society: 35, 71, 75, 77, 79, 106, 111, 126, 171, 176, 177
New York Public Library (William Wilgus Papers, Manuscripts Division, Astor, Lenox and Tilden Foundations): 34, 68, 70, 73, 85, 97, 119, 120, 153, 172
New York Times (John Papasian, NYT Graphics): 213, 215
Railway Age, Simons-Boardman Rail Group: 52
Schenectady Museum Archives: 91, 102, 103, 104
Technical World Magazine: 57

INDEX

Page numbers in italics refer to tables and figures.

Académie Royale d'Architecture, 132
Adams, Henry, 6–7
Adams, Express Company, 63, 67, 151, 163, *165*
Addams, Jane, 117
Age of Energy: civil engineering in, 79–80, 114; confidence in, 66; symbols of, 196; use of term, 7; wealthy lifestyles in, 44–50. *See also* Beaux-Arts design
airbrake, 89
airline industry, 173, 200, 201
air rights: concept of, 156–158; development of, 158–161, 164–170
Albany and Schenectady Railroad, 20
Albany Iron Works, 20
Ambassador Hotel, 151
American Express Company, 63, 67, 151, *165*
American Institute of Architects, 123, 134–135
American Locomotive Company, 94, 96, 103, 105
American Premier Underwriters, 206
American Railway Union, 44
American Renaissance, 115–117
American Society of Civil Engineers, 59
Amtrak (National Railroad Passenger Corporation), 205–208, 222
architecture: American traditions in, 6–7, 115–117; blended development in, 160–161; classical and technological juxtaposed in, 33–34; controversy over, 124–130; design competition in, 117–121; skyscrapers as, 115, 174; as symbol of power, 31, 130–132, 146, 152–153, 178; training in, 131–135, 136, 140, 178. *See also* Beaux-Arts design; City Beautiful movement; International Style
Arnold, Bion, x, 83, 84–86, 90
Associated Architects, 122–123
Astor, Caroline Schermerhorn, 48
Auburn and Rochester Railroad, 19
Auburn and Syracuse Railroad, 19
automobiles, 191, 194, 197–200

baggage handling, 62–63
Baltimore and Ohio Railroad, 23, 47, 89, 96, 194
Barclay Hotel, *166*
Bauhaus School (Germany), 178–180
Bayard Building, 115
Beaux-Arts design: City Beautiful movement and, 146–154; demise of, 178–181; description of, 130–135; Grand Central as, 120–121, 139–146; United States influenced by, 115–116, 124, 135–139, 177–178
Beaux-Arts Institute of Design (N.Y.C.), 180
Belle, John, 5
Beyer Blinder Belle (architectural firm), 2, 5, 207–208, 209, 216
Biltmore Estate (N.C.), 45, 136
Biltmore Hotel, 62, 151, 159, 162, 163, *165*, 174, *182*
Boston and Albany Railroad, 12, 28, 29
Brandess Brothers grocery, 81
Breakers (house), 49, 136
Brennan, William, 204–205
Breuer, Marcel, *202*, 203, *204*
Breuer building, *202*, 203, *204*
bridges, 23–24, 79, 115, *198*, 199
Broadway Limited, 194
Brooklyn Bridge, 80, 115

Index

Brown, W. C., 76, 102–104
Buckhout, Isaac, 31, 44, *45*, *46*
Buffalo and Lockport Railroad, 20
Burnham, Daniel, 115–116, 118, 138, 148, 174, 208

canals, 17, 18–19, 20, *21*, 200
Canning, John, 218, *219*, 221
Carrère, John Merven, 80, 116, 136, 140–143
Central Park, 147
Central Railroad of New Jersey Station, 61
Chatham Hotel, *165*
Chicago: department store in, 118; electric traction in, 89; rail access to, 22–23; railway stations in, 32, 61; settlement house in, 117; world's exposition in, 7, 118, 137–138, *137*, *138*, 148
Chrysler Building, 140, 151–152, 172–173, *210*
Cincinnati Railroad, 29
City Beautiful movement, 117, 146–154, 160–161
Claflin, Tennessee, 40–41, 42
Cleveland, Cincinnati, Chicago and St. Louis Railroad ("Big Four"), 29
Clews, Henry, 46–47, 48
Clinton, DeWitt, 18
Colbert, Jean-Baptiste, 132
Commodore Hotel, 151, 159, 163, *165*, 167, 174, *182*
Common Council (N.Y.C.), 13–14
commuter lines, 183–193, 206, 222
Connecticut, railroad established by, 206
Conrail, 205–208
Consolidated Edison, 167
construction: costs of, 65–66; demolition in, 73, *74*, 106–107; design controversy in, 124–130; electrification in, 82–84; excavation in, 67–76; of loop tracks, 80–81, *81*; organization of, 64–65; of terminal building, 107–113; of underground train yard, 77–80. *See also* Terminal City, construction of
Conway, Virgil, 2
Cooper-Hewitt Museum, 125
Cornell University, 131
Corning, Erastus, 20, 23, 24
Coulan, Jules Alexis, 144–145, *146*, 209–211
Court of Honor, proposed, 120, 149–150
crashes, 55–56, 59, 99–105
Crawford, Miss Frank, 41
Croffut, William, 14

D. H. Burnham and Company, 118, 119
Daily News Building, 152
Daniels, George H., 186–187
Debs, Eugene, 44
Deems, J. F., 105
Deglane, Henri, 138
D'Esposito, Joshua, 158
Dodge Brothers Manufacturing Company, 197
Dreiser, Theodore, 43, 192
Drew, Daniel: Erie Railroad and, 21–22; steamboat line of, 23, 24–25; Vanderbilt versus, 13–14, 16, 17
Droege, John, 84, 85, 114
Duluth and Winnipeg Railroad, 56

Ecole des Beaux-Arts (Paris), 144, 148; training at, 131–135, 140; United States influenced by, 135–139, 180. *See also* Beaux-Arts design
Edison, Thomas, 89
Eiffel Tower, 138
electricity: development of, 82–84; direct versus alternating current, 89–93, *217;* importance of, x, 156, 178
electric locomotives: compared to steam locomotives, 84–86, *172;* conversion to, 59, 64, 87, 98–99; design of, 91–98, *97*, *102*, *103*, *104;* success of, 97–99, 188–192; wreck linked to, 100–105; zone for, 87–89, *88*, 185
Electric Traction Commission: conversion and, 83–84, 98–99; on direct versus alternating current, 89–90, 90–91; on electric zone, 87–89, *88;* engine design and, 93–97, *97;* Woodlawn wreck and, 101–105
Emergency Relief Bureau (N.Y.C.), 56
Empire State Building, 172
L'Enfant, Pierre, 156
Erie Canal, 17, 18–19, 20, *21*, 200
Erie Railroad, 14, 16, 21–22, 23, 194
Esposito, John, 217
Europe: architectural influence of, 118; electric traction in, 89, 91–92; engine design in, 93–94; passenger terminals in, 34. *See also* London (U.K.); Paris (France)
Ewing, Williams Jackson, 208

F. and M. Schaefer Brewery, 70–71, 151, 175
fares/rates, 11, 19, 20, 184, 196–197
Fargo, William, 24–25
Featherstonhaugh, George, 19
Fisk, Jim, 21–22, *22*, 27
Flagg, Henry, 174
Flatiron Building, 115, 118, 140, 174
flying switch, 37–38, 80
42nd Street facility, 13, 30–34. *See also* Grand Central Depot
"Four Hundred," 48
Fourth Avenue. *See* Park Avenue
Four-Track Series, 186–187
Freel, Thomas, 55
freight, 63, 206; profits from, 30, 154; rate limits on, 196–197; right to carry, 19

Gabriel, Jacques-Ange, 124
Gallatin, Albert, 18
Gare d'Orsay (Paris), 92, *93*, 133–134
Garnier, Charles, 142
Garrett, L. D., 186
Garrett, Robert, 47
General Electric Company: in debate over direct versus alternating current, 89–90, 90–91; engine design and, 93–97, *97*, *102*, *103*, 105; equipment from, *86*, *92*, 216, *217;* nosing problem and, 103
George Campbell Construction Company, 217

George Washington Bridge, *198*, 199
Gibbs, George, 83
Gilbert, Cass, 80, 115–116
Gilded Age. *See* Age of Energy
Gill, Brendan, 203
Girault, Charles, 138
Gould, Jay, 21–22, 27
Grand Central Depot: advantages of, 56–57; cost of, 39; criticism of, 53–56; description of, 31–35; end of, 106–107; during excavation, *75;* expansion of, 50–53, 57–60; management of, 35–38; plan of, 67, *68*; symbolism of, 38–40
Grand Central Palace, 106, 159, *165*
Grand Central Terminal: costs of, 13, 113, 127, 153–154; decline of, 194–195, 201–208; design and style of, 117–121, 124–135, 139–146; electricity's advent at, 82–84; opening of, 113–114, *159;* ownership of, 206; passenger capacity of, 80–81; plans for, 60–64, *141, 142, 145;* property values of, 168–170; as public building, 146; ramps in, 111–112, 142; rededication of, 1–7, 222; schedules and, 66–67, 72, 77; symbolism of, 115–117, 173–174. *See also* air rights; construction; Grand Concourse; real estate development; restoration; sculpture; Terminal City; Vanderbilt Hall
Grand Central zone, 159–160, 169–170
Grand Concourse: concept of, 125, 173; constellations on ceiling of, *4*, 64, 205, 217–218, *218, 219;* construction of, *108–109, 110,* 111; decline of, 201, 205, 207, 209; ramps and stairs in, 111–112, 142, 211–212; restoration of, 217–222; style of, *3*, 34, 142, *143*, 153
Grand Hyatt Hotel, *210*, 211
Grand Prix de Rome, 134
Grant, Ulysses S., 10, 41, 48
Graybar Building, 151, 159, *166*, 167, 174
Great Western Railroad, 23, 26–27
Greeley, Horace, 41
Gropius, Walter, 178–180
Guaranty Trust of New York, 162

Harlem Railroad (New York and Harlem Railroad): electrification and, *88*, 99; expansion of, 11–13; leasing of, 29; merger of, 16–17, 184; original charter of, 8–9; as passenger carrier, 87, 184–186, 187–189; real estate development and, 157, 161–162; schedules of, 38; terminal for, 31, 57; Vanderbilt's holdings of, 13–14
Hastings, Thomas, 80, 116, 140–143
Haussmann, Georges Eugène, 132, 147–148, 160
Hayden, Richard, 183
head house, 35, 61, 80
Helleu, Paul, 217–218
Helmsley Building. *See* New York Central Building
Hepburn Act (1906), 196
highways, development of, 191, 194, 197–200
Hitchcock, Henry-Russell, 179
Holland Tunnel, 56
Hospital for the Ruptured and Crippled, 81
Howells, William Dean, 155–156, 185
Huckel, Samuel, Jr., 118
Hudson River Railroad: competition for, 23–24; electric zone of, *88;* franchise for, 14–15; as freight carrier, 30; merger of, 16–17, 25–26; as passenger carrier, 87, 186–189. *See also* New York Central and Hudson River Railroad
Hungerford, Edward, 30, 161
Hunt, Richard Holland (son), 136
Hunt, Richard Morris (father), 49, 80, 115–116, 124, 136, 138, 144
Illinois Institute of Technology, 180
immigrants, 5, 48, 53, 116–117, 155–156, 192
Incoming Station, 62, 80
Indiana and Southern Railroad, 29
"internal improvements" debate, 17–18
International Style, 178–183
Interstate Commerce Act (1887), 196–197
Interstate Commerce Commission, 196–197
IRT (Interborough Rapid Transit), 57, 89, 91, 150–151, 171–172, 184

J. P. Morgan and Company, 161, 197
Jersey Central Railroad, 190
John Canning and Company, 218, *219*, 221
Johnson, Philip, 179, 180, 181
Jones, Howard Mumford, 7, 50

Kahn, Louis, 136
Keep, Henry (The Silent), 24–25, 27–28
Kennedy, John F., Jr., 2
Knapp buildings, *166, 182*
Knowlton, Charles, 75
Kodak Company, 201
Koetter, Fred, 6

labor movement, 44
Lake Shore and Michigan Southern Railroad, 26–29
Laloux, Victor, 133–134
Landmarks Preservation Commission (N.Y.C.), 182, 203–204
Landmarks Preservation Law (N.Y.C., 1965), 148, 203–205
LaSalle Partners, 208
Lasseps, Ferdinand de, 69
Le Corbusier, 139
Ledyard, Lewis Cass, 127–129
legislation: on Harlem and Hudson railroads, 11, 12, 15, 16; on Mohawk and Hudson Rail Company, 19; on preservation, 148, 203–205; on railroad consolidation, 20; on rebates and

legislation (*cont.*)
pooling, 196–197; on steam power, 55–56, 73, 87, 98; to support railroads, 205–208; on Utica and Schenectady Railroad, 19
Lever House, 181
Lloyd, Henry D., 43
Lockwood, LeGrand, 24–25, 27–28
locomotives. *See* electric locomotives; steam locomotives
London (U.K.): Crystal Palace in, 32; electric traction in, 89; railway station in, 31, 34; training in, 135; underground in, 89
Long Island Railroad, 113, 186, 190

Madison Square Garden, 5, 8, 118, 195
Marble House, 49, 124, 136
Marguery Hotel, *165*, 178, *182*
Massachusetts Institute of Technology, 131
McAllister, Ward, 48
McAneny, George, 147
McCormick, Ira, 100
McKim, Charles Follen, 80, 113, 115–116, 118, 136, 138
McKim, Mead and White: style of, 136, 181; terminal design and, 118, 119, 120. *See also* Pennsylvania Station
McMillan, James, 156
Mead, William R., 80, 113. *See also* McKim, Mead and White
Mellen, Charles, 127
Merrill Lynch, 201
Metro-North Commuter Railroad, 206–217
Metropolitan Museum of Art, 136
Metropolitan Opera House, 120, 150
Metropolitan Transportation Authority (M.T.A.), 2, 206, 207–208
Michigan Central Railroad, 23, 26–27
Michigan Southern Railway, 29
Midtown. *See* Terminal City
Mies van der Rohe, Ludwig, 180, 181
Military Railroad Commission (France), 56
Minnesota and Northwestern Railroad, 56
Mohawk and Hudson Rail Company, 19
Mohawk and Malone Railroad, 29
Mohawk Valley Railroad, 20
monopolies, criticism of, 43–44, 54, 196
Morgan, J. P., 127, 161, 197
M.T.A. (Metropolitan Transportation Authority), 2, 206, 207–208
Mumford, Lewis, 31, 33, 130
Municipal Building, 140
Museum of Modern Art, 179–180
Mutual of America Life Insurance Company, 182–183

Nast, Thomas, 44
Nesbit, Evelyn, 118
New Haven Railroad (New York, New Haven, and Hartford Railroad): electrification of, 98; Harlem's agreement with, 12, 184; passenger terminal for, 31; real estate development and, 161–162; schedules of, 38–39; terminal design and, 125–129. *See also* New York State Terminal Realty Company
Newman, William H.: electrification and, 83, 90; expansion plan and, 59–60; real estate development and, 157, 159; terminal design and, 119–120, 122, 127–128; Woodlawn wreck and, 101, 104
Newport Preservation Society, 124
New York Academy of Design, 120
New York and Harlem Railroad. *See* Harlem Railroad
New York Beaux-Arts Society, 180
New York Central and Hudson River Railroad: control of, 41–42, 47, 50, 104; crashes, 99–106; criticism of, 53–54, 99–101; electric zone of, 87–89, *88*, 185; expanded sphere of, 26–28; financial crisis of, 199–201; high point for, 194; management of, 28–29, 38–39; operating division of, 73, 75–77. *See also* electric locomotives; Grand Central Depot; Grand Central Terminal; real estate development
New York Central Building: construction of, 151, 152, 159, *182;* cost of, *166;* terminal renovation and, 212, *215;* views of, *153,* 177
New York Central Railroad: beginning of, 17–20; expansion of, 21–23; Vanderbilt's role in, 23–26. *See also* New York Central and Hudson River Railroad
New York City: Beaux-Arts style in, 139–140; Grand Central as gateway to, 173–174; growth of, 8–9, 146–147, 169–170; homeless in, 216–217; rail access to, 11, 15–16, 39; social structure in, 155–156, 185, 192–193; suburbanization and, 183–193
New-York Historical Society, 125
New York Public Library, 102, 116, 140–143, 233
New York Racquet Club, 181
New York State, railroad established by, 206
New York State Railroad Commission, 101, 103, 105
New York State Terminal Realty Company: construction by, 162–170; development controlled by, 177–178; establishment of, 129, 161–162
New York Yacht Club, 121
Nickel Plate Railroad, 42–43

Olcott, Thomas, 24
Olmsted, Frederick Law, 147
Olympic and York (real estate conglomerate), 182

Onassis, Jacqueline Kennedy, 2, 203
O'Rourke, John, 73, 75
O'Rourke Construction Company, 69–76
Owl (train), 106

Pacific (train), 106
Panama Canal, 69–70, 99
Pan American building, 174, 201
Paris (France): electric traction in, 89, 91–92; expositions in, 91, 138; Louvre in, 31, 33; railway stations in, 34, 92, 133–134; reconstruction of, 147–148, 160; United States influenced by, 116, 118, 124, 132. *See also* Ecole des Beaux-Arts
Paris and Orleans Railroad, 89, 91–92
Paris Opera House, 142
Paris Prize Competition, 180
Park Avenue: development of, 174–178, 182–183; landscaping of, 152, 176
Park Avenue Association, 176
Park Avenue tunnel: crash in, 55–56, 59; electrification and, 83, 86, 95–96, 178; in overall plan, 67
Park Lane Hotel, *166*, 178
Park-Lexington Building, *166*, 182
Park Square Station (Boston), 32, 61
passenger service: for commuters, 183–193, 206, 222; decline of, 197, 199; increase in, 82; innovations in, 27; public rescue of, 205–206. *See also specific railroads*
Pataki, George, 2
Penn Central Railroad: bankruptcy of, 158, 201; expansion of, 22–23, 27, 28–29; merger of, 200; size of, 16, 26, 194; station for, 32, 113
Penn Central Transportation Company, 200–201, 204–208
Pennsylvania Station: costs of, 153–154; demise of, 5–6, 194–195, 203; design of, 116, 118, 130, 136, *139*, 140; opening of, 113, 115
pensions, New York Central, 49–50
People's Line (steamboats), 23
Place, Ira A., 103–104
Pope, John Russell, 136
Pope, Robert, 149, 150, 158, 160, 174
Port Morris power plant, *86*
Postum Building, *166*
Potter, William B., 102–103, 105
power plants, *86*, 166–167
property rights: discourse on, 148, 160–161; preservation versus, 204–205; transportation and value of, 168–170. *See also* air rights
Public Improvement Committee (N.Y.C.), 149

railroads: airbrake for, 89; competition among, 21–22; conflict of interest in, 127–128; consolidation and mergers of, 16–17, 20, 25–26, 184, 200; decline of, 154, 194–196, 200–201; fortunes made in, 10–11, 194; impact of, 7, 8, 40; management of, 26, 28, 36–39; planning of facilities for, 60–64; regulations on, 43, 196–197; "water level" route for, 17–19, *21*. *See also* baggage handling; freight; passenger service; tracks; train sheds and yards
rates/fares, 11, 19, 20, 184, 196–197
real estate development: air rights in, 156–158; beginning of, 129; catalyst to, 170–173; construction in, 162–170; funding of, 161; on Park Avenue, 174–178, 182–183; post-Depression revival of, 180–181; suburbanization and, 183–193. *See also* Terminal City
Reed, Charles, 119, 121, 122
Reed and Stem: contract with, 121–123; contributions of, 123, 141–142; design controversy and, 124–130; Park Avenue development and, 175; terminal design and, 118, 119–121
restoration: funding for, 207–208; of Grand Concourse, 217–222; interest in, 203–205; public efforts in, 203–207; roof repairs in, 209–211; of stairways and entrances, 211–214, *215*; of structural and mechanical systems, 214–216, *217*
Richardson, H. H., 136, 138
Richmond, Dean, 24
Riis, Jacob, 116
Robinson, Charles Mumford, 150, 151
Rochester, Lockport, and Niagara Falls Railroad, 20
Rochester and Syracuse Railroad, 20
Rockefeller, John D., 196
Rockefeller, William, 127–128, 161
Rockefeller Center, 160, 174
Roebling, J. A., 80, 115
Roebling, W. A., 80, 115
Rome Railroad, 29
Roosevelt, Franklin D., 56, 178
Roosevelt Hotel, 159, *166*

Saady, Morris, 203
St. Bartholomew's Episcopal Church, *176*, 182
Schenectady and Troy Railroad, 20
Scully, Vincent, 139
sculpture, *2*, *6*, 124, 144–145, *146*; restoration of, 209–211
Seagram Building, 181
signaling systems, 36–38
Simpson, Gumpertz and Heger, 209
Sinclair, Upton, 43
Singer Building, 115, 174
Skidmore, Owings and Merrill, 181
Skinner, William, 127
Smith, A. H., 101
Smyth (district attorney), 101, 103
Snook, John, 31
social problems: City Beautiful movement and, 151; expansion of, 116–117, 155–156; renovation and, 216–217

Sprague, Frank, x, 83, 85, 89–91, 92–93
Spuyten Duyvil and Port Morris Railroad, 30
Standard Oil Company, 196
steamboat and shipping business, 9–10, 12–15, 23. *See also* canals
steam locomotives: banned in city, 55–56, 73, 87, 98; development of, 19; difficulties with, 8–9, 87; electric locomotives compared to, 59, 84–86, 95–96; maintenance of, 12–13; streamlined, *195*
Steinway Piano Company, 151, 175
Stem, Allen, 121–123. *See also* Reed and Stem
Stern, Jessica, 207
Stevens, John, 69–70, 99
streetcar lines, 57, 85, 89
STV/Seeyle Stevenson Value and Knecht, 207
suburbs: commuter trains' impact on, 183–189; emergence of, 189–193
subway. *See* IRT (Interborough Rapid Transit)
Sullivan, Louis, 115, 133, 136, 138
Sulzberger Slaughter House, 151
Switzerland, electric traction in, 89
Syracuse and Utica Railroad, 20

Tarbell, Ida M., 43
technology: railroad as, 33; steel and, 110, *108–109*, 115–116, 174, 179; systematization and, 36–37; transformation via, 6–7. *See also* electricity
Terminal City: brochure on, 129; City Beautiful movement and, 149; construction of, 113, 162–170; development of, 151–52, 158–161; expansion of, 172–173. *See also* Beaux-Arts design; International Style
Terminal Realty. *See* New York State Terminal Realty Company
Thompson, Hugh, 158
Thomson, J. Edgar, 22
tracks: costs of, 15; design of, 11, 78–79, 91–93; loop, 80–82, *81;* maintenance of, 26; "nosing" of, 95, 100, 102–105
train sheds and yards: construction of, 77–80; description of, 32–34, *35*, 50–54, 106–107; excavation of, 64, 67–77; head house in, 35, 61, 80–82; management of, 36–38; as obstacle to development, 170–171, *172*, 175; size of, 35, *37*, 82–83; social impact of, 151
trucking, 191, 197, 199. *See also* automobiles
Twentieth Century Limited, 39, 188, 194, 222
26th Street station, 8–9

Union Station (Washington, D.C.), 118, 208
United Cigar Building, *165*
United Dressed Beef, 151
United Hotels Corporation, 162
U.S. Customs House, 116, 140
U.S. Post Office building, 63, 140, 159, 162, 163, *165*
U.S. Supreme Court, 148, 204–205
urban planning: emergence of, 148–151; terminal's influence on, 151–153, *154*. *See also* real estate development
Utica and Schenectady Railroad, 19–20

Van Alen, William, 136, 172–173
Vanderbilt, Alice Claypoole Gwynne, 47
Vanderbilt, Alva Smith, 44, 48, 49
Vanderbilt, Cornelius, II, 45, 47–50, 136
Vanderbilt, Cornelius Jeremiah, 41–42
Vanderbilt, Cornelius "The Commodore": background of, 9–11, 44, 48; images of, *10, 22;* last years of, 40–42; railroad dealings of, 13–17, 23–26; terminal envisioned by, 30–38, 39
Vanderbilt, Frederick, 47
Vanderbilt, George, 45, 47, 136
Van der Bilt, Jacob, 9
Van der Bilt, Phoebe, 9
Vanderbilt, Sophia, 40
Vanderbilt, William Henry: lifestyle of, 44–47, 48; railroad dealings of, 17, 24–28, 41–43
Vanderbilt, William Kissam: homes of, 44, 45, 49, 124, 136; lifestyle of, 47–50; railroad dealings of, 29, 55, 121, 127, 144–145; real estate development and, 161
Vanderbilt Building, *166*
Vanderbilt Hall, *5*, *144*, *165*, 217, 222
Vanderbilt system. *See* New York Central and Hudson River Railroad
Van Rensselaer, Stephen, 19
Vaux, Calvert, 147
Virginia State Capitol, 131

waiting rooms, *5*, 51, 53, *144*, *165*, 217, 222
Waitt, Arthur M., 98–99
Waldorf-Astoria Hotel, 151, 163, 166–167, *168*, 178, 180, *182*
Walker, George, 206
Warner Fuller Wall Paper Company, 81
Warren, Whitney: architectural style and, 117, 130, 180; on loop tracks, 81; Park Avenue development and, 175, 177–178; on ramps versus stairs, 112; training of, 136
Warren and Wetmore: contract with, 121–123; contributions of, 123–125, *126;* design controversy and, 124–130; style of, 141–146, 152–153
Watertown and Ogdensburg Railroad, 29
Westinghouse, George, 89, 90–91, 98
Westinghouse Electric Company, 89, 90–91, 93–94
West Shore Railroad, 29

Wetmore, Charles, 121–122. *See also* Warren and Wetmore
White, Stanford, 80, 113, 118, 136. *See also* McKim, Mead and White
Wilgus, William J.: accusations against, 101–105; background of, x, 56, *57*, 79–80, 98–99; commuter service and, 188–189, 190, 191–192; construction costs and, 65–66; construction organized by, 64–65; demolition plans of, 73, *74*, 106–107; electrification and, 82–84, 87–89, 91–93, 98–99, 183–184; engine design and, 93–97, *97;* excavation and, 67–73, 75–77; loop tracks and, 80–82, *81;* real estate development and, 156–160, 163, *165,* 169–170, 175; subway plans and, 150–151; terminal design and, 57–64, 107, 111–113, 119–124, 128–130
Wisker, Charles, 55
Wolfe, Tom, 192–193
Wolfson, Erwin, 201
Woodhull, Victoria, 40–41
Woodlawn wreck, 99–106
working class, wages of, 48, 49–50, 75, 188, 196–197
World's Columbian Exposition (1893), 7, 118, 137–138, 148
World War II, railroads and, 199–200
wrecks, 55–56, 59, 99–106

Yale Club, 159, 165
Young Men's Christian Association (Y.M.C.A.), 116–117

zoning laws, 147, 160, 180, 182–183

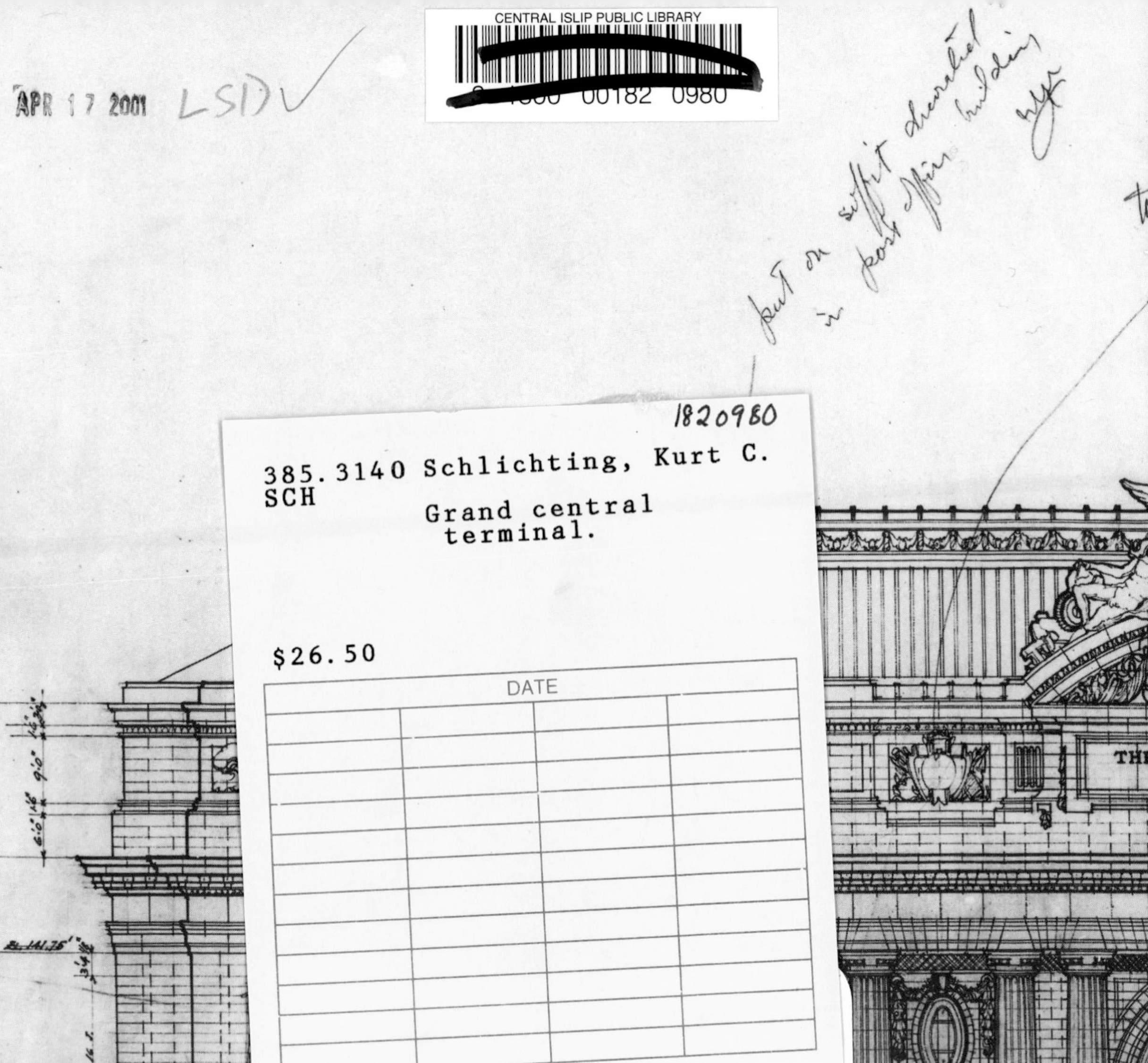
put on soffit decorated in post office building

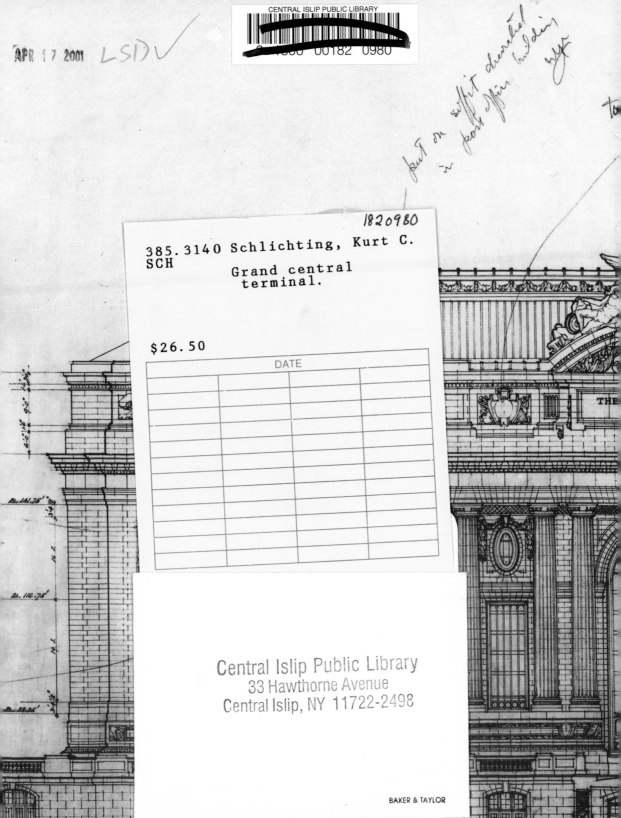